CengageNOW™
Just What You Need to Know and Do NOW!

CengageNOW is a completely online product that includes a personalized learning path, ebook, and other learning resources. Each student who purchases CengageNOW with a new text also automatically receives access to the Business and Company Resource Center (BCRC) database. For more information, visit **www.cengage.com/now.**

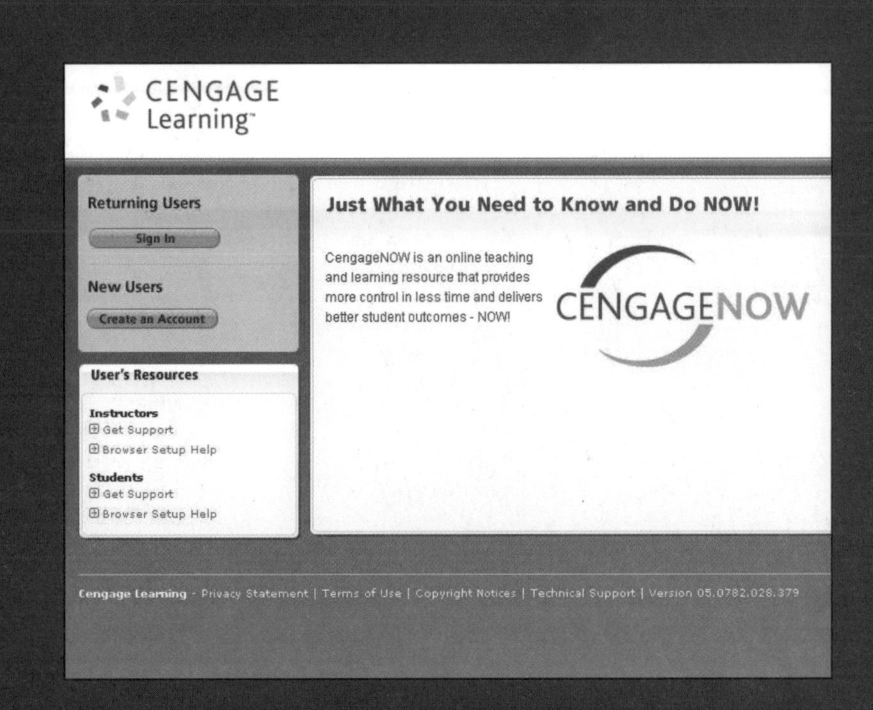

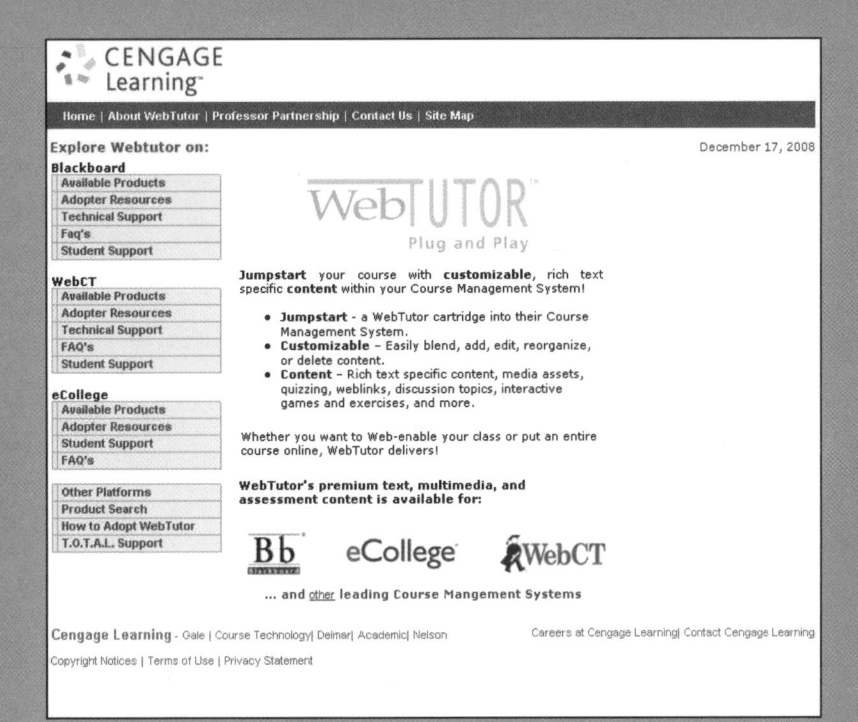

WebTutor™

WebTUTOR™

This content-rich, web-based teaching and learning aid reinforces chapter concepts and acts as an electronic student study guide. WebTutor provides you with interactive chapter review quizzes, writing improvement exercises, and flash cards of glossary terms. WebTutor also provides PowerPoint® review slides, links to videos, and threaded discussions. WebTutor can be used with both WebCT® and Blackboard®.

Business

10th Edition

William M. Pride
Texas A&M University

Robert J. Hughes
Richland College, Dallas County Community Colleges

Jack R. Kapoor
College of DuPage

Australia • Brazil • Japan • Korea • Mexico • Singapore • Spain • United Kingdom • United States

Business, 10e
William M. Pride, Robert J. Hughes, and Jack R. Kapoor

Vice President of Editorial, Business: Jack W. Calhoun

Vice President/Editor-in-Chief: Melissa Acuña

Senior Acquisitions Editor: Erin Joyner

Senior Developmental Editor: Joanne Dauksewicz

Executive Marketing Manager: Kimberly Kanakes

Senior Content Project Manager: Colleen A. Farmer

Marketing Communications Manager: Sarah Greber

Media Editor: Kristen Meere

First Print Buyer: Miranda Klapper

Production Services: LEAP Publishing Services, Inc., and Macmillan Publishing Solutions

Senior Art Director: Stacy Shirley

Internal Designer: Craig Ramsdell

Cover Designer: Craig Ramsdell

Photo Manager: Jennifer Meyer Dare

Photo Researcher: Susan G. Holtz

Cover Images: © Getty Images/Stone

Senior Rights Acquisition Account Manager: Katie Huha

Library of Congress Control Number: 2008944239

ISBN-13: 978-0-324-82955-6
ISBN-10: 0-324-82955-8
Loose-leaf version ISBN 13: 978-1-4390-3763-8
Loose-leaf version ISBN 10: 1-4390-3763-9
Instructor's Edition ISBN 13: 978-1-4390-3739-3
Instructor's Edition ISBN 10: 1-4390-3739-6

South-Western Cengage Learning
5191 Natorp Boulevard
Mason, OH 45040
USA

Cengage Learning products are represented in Canada by Nelson Education, Ltd.

For your course and learning solutions, visit **academic.cengage.com**

Purchase any of our products at your local college store or at our preferred online store **www.ichapters.com**

Printed in the United States of America
1 2 3 4 5 6 7 14 13 12 11 10

Brief Contents

Contents

Chapter 5: Small Business, Entrepreneurship, and Franchises 135

Part 3: Management and Organization 165

Chapter 6: Understanding the Management Process 166

Chapter 7: Creating a Flexible Organization 189

Chapter 8: Producing Quality Goods and Services 215

About the Authors

William M. Pride

Texas A&M University

William M. Pride is Professor of Marketing, Mays Business School at Texas A&M University. He received his Ph.D. from Louisiana State University. He is the author of Cengage Learning's *Marketing,* 15th edition, a market leader. Dr. Pride's research interests are in advertising, promotion, and distribution channels. Dr. Pride's research articles have appeared in major journals in the fields of advertising and marketing such as *Journal of Marketing, Journal of Marketing Research, Journal of the Academy of Marketing Science,* and the *Journal of Advertising.* Dr. Pride is a member of the American Marketing Association, Academy of Marketing Science, Association of Collegiate Marketing Educators, Society for Marketing Advances, and the Marketing Management Association. Dr. Pride has taught principles of marketing and other marketing courses for more than 30 years at both the undergraduate and graduate levels.

Robert J. Hughes

Richland College, Dallas County Community Colleges

Robert J. Hughes (Ph.D., University of North Texas) specializes in business administration and college instruction. Currently, he teaches Introduction to Business and Personal Finance both on campus and online for Richland College—one of seven campuses that are part of the Dallas County Community College District. In addition to *Business* and *Foundations of Business*, published by Cengage Learning, he has authored college textbooks in personal finance and business mathematics, served as a content consultant for two popular national television series, *It's Strictly Business* and *Dollars & Sense: Personal Finance for the 21st Century*, and is the lead author for a business math project utilizing computer-assisted instruction funded by the ALEKS Corporation. He is also active in many academic and professional organizations and has served as a consultant and investment advisor to individuals, businesses, and charitable organizations. Dr. Hughes is the recipient of three different Teaching in Excellence Awards at Richland College. According to Dr. Hughes, after 30 years of teaching Introduction to Business, the course is still exciting: "There's nothing quite like the thrill of seeing students succeed, especially in a course like Introduction to Business, which provides the foundation for not only academic courses, but also life in the real world."

Jack R. Kapoor

College of DuPage

Jack R. Kapoor (EdD, Northern Illinois University) is Professor of Business and Economics in the Business and Services Division at the College of DuPage, where he has taught since 1969. He previously taught at Illinois Institute of Technology's Stuart School of Management, San Francisco State University's School of World Business, and other colleges. Professor Kapoor was awarded the Business and Services Division's Outstanding Professor Award for 1999–2000. He served as an Assistant National Bank Examiner for the U.S. Treasury Department and as an international trade consultant to Bolting Manufacturing Co., Ltd., Mumbai, India.

Dr. Kapoor is known internationally as a coauthor of several textbooks and has served as a content consultant for the popular national television series *The Business File: An Introduction to Business* and developed two full-length audio courses in business and personal finance. He has been quoted in many national newspapers and magazines, including *USA Today, U.S. News & World Report,* the *Chicago Sun-Times, Crain's Small Business*, the *Chicago Tribune*, and other publications.

Dr. Kapoor has traveled around the world and has studied business practices in capitalist, socialist, and communist countries.

Dear Business Students,

Welcome to the new, tenth edition of *Business* where the ***sky's the limit*** for your success—inside the classroom and in the workplace!

Business will provide you with the rock-solid foundation you need to succeed in today's competitive business world.

Much has changed since the last edition. It's a different business world and the fully updated tenth edition of *Business* covers all the bases. We have completely redesigned the entire textbook package to highlight its strengths as the most accessible, up-to-date, and student-friendly instructional package available. Powerful new online resources maximize your success and mastery through premium web-based study content including practice tests, flashcards, MP3 audio chapter summaries and quizzes, interactive games, and Career Snapshots.

In addition, the text is packed with cutting-edge content, offering insightful, detailed coverage that helps you make sense of the 2008 economic crisis and its impact on many areas of business as well as your world. We even offer suggestions on how to manage personal financial planning in the midst of economic ups and downs.

Concise new eye-catching boxed features capture and maintain interest with themes including Entrepreneurial Challenge, Jump-Starting Your Career, Ethics Matters, The Business of Green, and Going Global. Each chapter also includes a special Sustaining the Planet insert as well as Spotlight features presenting data in a vividly illustrated, easy-to-understand format—making the text even more visually appealing and relevant to real-world business.

Living up to its reputation for complete coverage, the new edition continues to deliver a current, thorough overview of the functional areas of business—management, marketing, accounting, finance, and information technology—while highlighting such core topics as ethics and social responsibility, forms of business ownership, small business concerns, and international issues. This edition also offers a wealth of resources for instructors as well as complete coverage and innovative learning tools for you.

We invite you to examine the visual guide that follows to see how Pride/Hughes/Kapoor can help invite you into business and develop a successful business career. With the new, tenth edition of *Business,* we think you will find that the sky truly is the limit for success in business!

Sincerely,

WMP, RJH, JRK

The Sky's the Limit with *Business, 10e's* New Features!

With **Business, *10e's*** student-focused features, *the sky's the limit* on comprehension. Exciting, practical, and in tune with real-world practice, these insightful features give you an up-close, insider's look at business in practice—as well as hands-on experience grappling with the ethical, green, global, entrepreneurial, and career issues of real business.

inside business

JPMorgan Chase Banks on Wall Street and Main Street

When Aaron Burr founded the Bank of the Manhattan Company in 1799 to finance waterworks for New York City, he could not have foreseen how large and powerful his fledgling bank would become. Over the next 200 years, the bank was renamed numerous times as it merged with or acquired hundreds of financial institutions in New York and beyond, widening its scope and expanding its reach worldwide. It has been associated with some of the most famous names in finance, including David Rockefeller and J. Pierpont Morgan. Some of the banks in its past helped fund the Erie Canal and the Brooklyn Bridge, among many other major projects.

The bank that Burr founded has changed dramatically since the 1990s, when it absorbed two big rivals, Chemical Bank and Manufacturers Hanover Bank, in its quest for growth. In 2000, it joined with the global investment bank JP Morgan to form JPMorgan Chase. By merging with Bank One in 2004, the bank expanded its branch system nationwide and brought millions of additional bank and credit accounts under its corporate umbrella.

The economic turmoil of 2008 led to new opportunities—and new risks. Bear Stearns, then one of the nation's leading investment banks, faced a credit crunch so severe that it was on the verge of collapse. With the blessing of the Federal Reserve Bank, JPMorgan Chase quickly stepped in to buy the company at a steep discount. This move not only reassured the financial markets, but it also added to JPMorgan Chase's strength on Wall Street.

Months later, the U.S. government asked JPMorgan Chase to make another last-minute acquisition. This time, it took over Washington Mutual Savings and Loan (WaMu), which had failed under the weight of bad mortgage loans. JPMorgan Chase had thought about buying WaMu for some time but now it was able to complete the deal at a bargain price, gain entrance to new markets, and introduce itself to millions of new customers.[1]

JPMorgan Chase's purchase of WaMu during the 2008 economic turmoil enabled it to make the deal at a bargain price, gain entrance to new markets, and introduce itself to millions of new customers.

The Banking Crisis! Those three words say a lot about the recent downturn in the nation's economy. Those same three words also don't tell the entire story because the banking crisis caused a ripple effect through the entire economy. In fact, the economic problems caused by the banking crisis affected everyone in the United States in some way. For example,

- Many individuals lost their homes because they obtained loans they couldn't afford.
- The nation experienced record numbers of unemployed workers.
- Many people watched helplessly as their retirement accounts and investments decreased in value.

In reality, most Americans were frightened by an economic crisis that some experts described as the worst the nation had seen since the Great Depression.

To help solve the problems, the Federal Reserve Bank became heavily involved in an effort to inject cash in to the nation's banking system. The government also protected bank customers by merging "troubled" banks with financially stable banks. The merger between JPMorgan Chase and Washington Mutual (WaMu) described in this chapter's Inside Business opening case is one example of the government's efforts to protect bank customers. While Washington Mutual had been struggling with bad mortgage debt and nonperforming loans and for a time looked like

Chapter 18: Understanding Money, Banking, and Credit 527

Global Economic Crisis Coverage

New! Hot-off-the-press coverage of the 2008 financial crisis is included throughout the text. The authors discuss how recent economic events have impacted almost every aspect of business in the United States and throughout the world. They also include advice on how to manage personal financial planning in the midst of economic ups and downs.

New Boxed Features

New! The all-new feature boxes in this edition have been re-designed to capture and maintain your interest. Themes in the tenth edition include: Entrepreneurial Challenge, Jump-Starting Your Career, Ethics Matters, The Business of Green, and Going Global.

Jump-Starting Your Career

Life After Acquisition

What will happen to you if your employer acquires a company or your employer is acquired by another firm? Although mergers and acquisitions often result in job losses, don't automatically assume that your job will go away. In fact, experts say this is a good opportunity to show how well you adapt to change and how valuable you can be to the new organization.

Be patient, be positive, be proactive, and above all, be a problem solver. Complete your assignments and meet your deadlines, but also look for ways to get involved during the transition. Answer questions, anticipate problems, and volunteer possible solutions. Keep up your current contacts and get to know your new colleagues and managers. Meanwhile, update your résumé with your latest skills and accomplishments. You may need to reapply for your current job or try for a different job in the new organization—or elsewhere.

Sources: Scott Moeller, "Trade Secrets: Surviving a Merger," *Personnel Today*, October 8, 2007, **www.personneltoday.com**; Kelley Holland, "Life After a Merger: Learning on Both Sides," *New York Times*, June 24, 2007, p. BU21; Rob Garretson, "How to Survive a Corporate Integration," *Network World*, January 25, 2007, **www.networkworld.com/careers.**

may take specific actions sometimes referred to as "poison pills," "shark repellents," or "porcupine provisions" to maintain control of the firm and avoid the hostile takeover. Whether mergers are friendly or hostile, they are generally classified as *horizontal, vertical,* or *conglomerate* (see Figure 4.5).

and South America, such as Argentina, Colombia, Peru, Venezuela, and Brazil. Growth in the region was projected at 4.4 percent in 2008 and 3.6 percent in 2009.

Japan Japan's economy is regaining momentum. Stronger consumer demand and business investment make Japan less reliant on exports for growth. The IMF estimated the growth for Japan at 1.4 percent in 2008 and 1.5 percent in 2009.

Asia The economic growth in Asia remained strong in 2007. Growth was led by China, where its economy expanded by 11.4 percent in the second half of 2007, but it was estimated at 9.3 percent in 2008. Growth in India slowed modestly to 8.5 percent in 2007 and 7.9 percent in 2008. A strong consumer demand supported economic growth in Indonesia, Malaysia, Hong Kong, the Philippines, and Singapore. The growth in emerging Asia remained at 7.5 percent in 2008 and 7.8 percent in 2009.

Ethics Matters

Where There's Smoke . . .

Limit smoking and tobacco advertising—that's the World Health Organization's formula for saving a billion lives during the 21st century. Despite on-pack warnings and advertising restrictions, smoking is on the rise in developing nations. For example, China is home to 30 percent of the world's smokers. In fact, its smoking population of 350 million people is larger than the entire U.S. population.

The Chinese government owns the country's largest tobacco companies, and a package of cigarettes is far cheaper in China than anywhere else in the world, two factors that complicate efforts to curb smoking. Still, China recently began requiring prominent health warnings on cigarette packs

In addition, each chapter now includes a special insert entitled **Sustaining the Planet,** as well as two Spotlight features that present factual data in an easy to understand, illustrated format. All of these features make the text even more visually appealing and relevant to real-world activities.

Sustaining the Planet

More companies are doing more to save the planet—and, like UPS, telling the world in yearly sustainability reports that highlight energy efficiency, water conservation, recycling, and more. UPS's annual reports show how it is progressing toward long-term sustainability targets such as minimizing waste and reducing emissions from the company's trucks and aircraft.
www.ups.com

The Challenges Ahead

There it is—the American business system in brief. When it works well, it provides jobs for those who are willing to work, a standard of living that few countries can match, and many opportunities for personal advancement. However, like every other system devised by humans, it is not perfect. Our business system may give us prosperity, but it also gave us the Great Depression of the 1930s and the economic problems of the 1970s, the late 1980s, and the first part of the twenty-first century.

Obviously, the system can be improved. Certainly, there are plenty of people who are willing to tell us exactly what *they* think the American economy needs. But these people provide us only with conflicting opinions. Who is right and who is wrong? Even the experts cannot agree.

The experts do agree, however, that several key issues will challenge our economic system (and our nation) over the next decade. Some of the questions to be resolved include:

- How can we encourage Iraq and Afghanistan to establish a democratic and

The Business of Green

Best Foot Forward for Timberland

Socially responsible Timberland, based in Stratham, New Hampshire, is putting its best foot forward to label its shoe products to show their environmental impact. Just as foods carry nutrition labels and major appliances carry energy efficiency labels, Timberland's shoes carry "green index tags" rating each product in terms of greenhouse gas emissions, use of chemicals, and use of organic, renewable, or recycled materials. The lower the score, the more earth friendly the product.

According to Timberland's CEO, the idea is to help consumers "make value judgments at the point of sale." However, the labeling project has been challenging because the company had to "go back to the cow" to assess the environmental effects of raw materials provided by suppliers as well as the effect of manufacturing, transportation, and store activities.

As more shoe companies add such labeling, "it will become automatic for shoppers to compare green tags among brands, just like they compare price and color," the CEO adds. "When that happens, we'll all be fighting to have the best tag . . . no shoe company will want to be known for the least environmentally friendly shoes."

Sources: Mark Borden and Anya Kamenetz, "The Prophet CEO," *Fast Company*, September 2008, **http://www.fastcompany.com/magazine/128/the-prophet-ceo.html**; Claudia H. Deutsch, "Seeking a Joint Effort for Greener Athletic Shoes," *New York Times*, September 29, 2007, p. C2; Amy Cortese, "Friend of Nature? Let's See Those Shoes," *New York Times*, March 7, 2007, p. H5.

Streamlined Content

New! The chapters on e-Business and Management Information Systems have been combined into a more streamlined chapter, bringing the text to 20 chapters.

New End-of-Chapter Materials

within a half-day's drive of the distribution center in Brighton, Massachusetts. Because Newbury Comics owns six trucks, it can resupply every store at least three times a week. Many competitors are far bigger, but no competitor knows its customers and its products better than the team at Newbury Comics.[22]

For more information about this company, go to **www.newburycomics.com.**

3. Newbury Comics was started without a formal business plan. If you were writing its plan today, what critical risks and assumptions would you examine—and why?

CASE 5.1 Tumbleweed Tiny House Company

The average American home is between 2000 and 2500 square feet in size. Jay Shafer's hand-crafted 89-square-foot house on wheels is so small he can almost parallel-park it.

Ecological concerns have merged with an uncertain real estate market to give a big boost to the small-house movement, which promotes simple living in tiny spaces. A growing number of people are happily living in houses ranging from just 70 to 800 square feet, small enough to fit on a flatbed truck and pull into a field or farmstead.

One of the pioneer builders of such tiny homes is the Tumbleweed Tiny House Company, the brain child of Shafer, a 40-something professor-turned-designer who has lived in three of his own creations over the last several years. His young do-it-yourself company, which was a one-person operation until just a year ago, builds and provides plans for several different models and sizes of tiny houses, with fully equipped but scaled-down kitchens and baths, windowed sleeping lofts under peaked roofs, front porches, and lots of ingenious storage space. The houses are designed to hook up to public water and waste lines; many buyers use them as primary homes, but they can also serve as studios,

his website; plans cost about $1,000 a set and the houses cost from $20,000 to $90,000 to build (the services of a professional contractor are recommended). Shafer also conducts workshops on tiny-house living, sometimes travels around the country with his house, and maintains a blog and active discussion board on his website. He has big plans for Tumbleweed, but rapid expansion doesn't fit his very personal business philosophy. "We are still in our infancy and still building our foundation for growth," he explains on his website. "We have a business plan that we are adhering to. Everything in due time." Among his future dreams are finding partners to represent Tumbleweed homes (real estate license required), partners to build them (licensed contractors only need apply), and makers of products like solar panels and lumber for incorporation into his homes (but nothing that would require redesigning any Tumbleweed products).

In the long term, Shafer would even like to see a whole village of Tumbleweed homes, "even if it's just 3 houses." For now, though, like its products, Tumbleweed remains a small and very carefully built affair.[23]

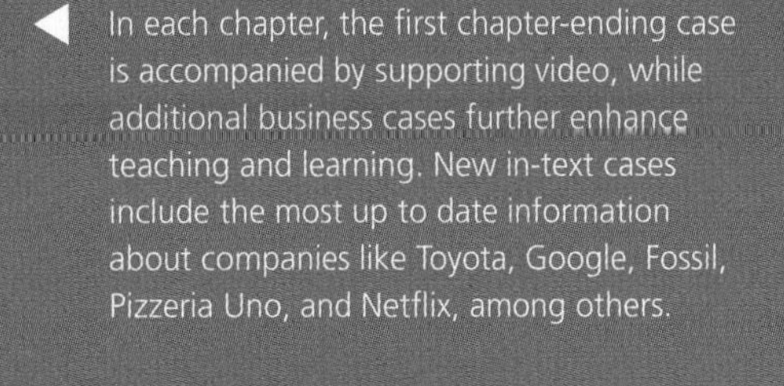

In each chapter, the first chapter-ending case is accompanied by supporting video, while additional business cases further enhance teaching and learning. New in-text cases include the most up to date information about companies like Toyota, Google, Fossil, Pizzeria Uno, and Netflix, among others.

An ongoing video case featured at the end of each Part provides you with an insider's perspective on Finagle A Bagel, a bagel bakery/café. This firsthand look into one business's day-to-day operations allows you to gain a better understanding of the real challenges business owners face. You can also apply what you learn by analyzing problems, solutions, and actions taken at the company.

Running a Business Part 2

Finagle A Bagel: A Fast-Growing Small Business

Finagle A Bagel, a fast-growing small business co-owned by Alan Litchman and Laura Trust, is at the forefront of one of the freshest concepts in the food-service business: fresh food. Each of the twenty stores bakes a new batch of bagels every hour, and each receives new deliveries of cheeses, vegetables, fruits, and other ingredients every day. Rather than prepackage menu items, store employees make everything to order so that they can satisfy the specific needs of each guest (Finagle A Bagel's term for a customer). As a result, customers get fresh food prepared to their exact preferences—whether it's extra cheese on a bagel pizza or no onions in a salad—along with prompt, friendly service.

"Every sandwich, every salad is built to order, so there's a lot of communication between the customers and the cashiers, the customers and the sandwich makers, the customers and the managers," explains Trust. This allows Finagle A Bagel's store employees ample opportunity to build customer relationships and encourage repeat business. Many, like Mirna Hernandez of the Tremont Street store in downtown Boston, are so familiar with what certain customers order that they spring into action when regulars enter the store. "We know what they want, and we just ring it in and take care of them," she says. Some employees even know their customers by name and make conversation as they create a sandwich or fill a coffee container.

'What kind of croutons do you want? What kind of dressing? What kind of mustard?' When we're ready to go in that direction, it is going to be a fairly sizable technology venture for us to undertake."

Finagle A Bagel occasionally receives Web or phone orders from customers hundreds or thousands of miles away. Still, the copresidents have no immediate plans to expand outside the Boston metropolitan area. Pointing to regional food-service firms that have profited by opening more stores in a wider geographic domain, Trust says, "We see that the most successful companies have really dominated their area first. Cheesecake Factory is an example of a company that's wildly successful right now, but they were a concept in California for decades before they moved beyond that area. In-and-Out Burger is an outstanding example of a food-service company in the west that's done what we're trying to do. They had seventeen stores at one time, and now they have hundreds of stores. They're very successful, but they never left their backyard. That's kind of why we're staying where we are."

FINANCING A SMALL BUSINESS

Some small businesses achieve rapid growth through franchising. The entrepreneurs running Finagle A Bagel resisted franchising for a long time. "When you franchise, you gain a large influx of capital," says Trust, "but you begin to lose control over the people, the

neurial team enjoys applying their educational background and business experience to build a company that satisfies thousands of customers every day.

you license the Finagle A Bagel brand? Why or why not?

Building a Business Plan Part 1

A *business plan* is a carefully constructed guide for a person starting a business. The purpose of a well-prepared business plan is to show how practical and attainable the entrepreneur's goals are. It also serves as a concise document that potential investors can examine to see if they would like to invest or assist in financing a new venture. A business plan should include the following twelve components:

- Introduction
- Executive summary
- Benefits to the community
- Company and industry
- Management team
- Manufacturing and operations plan
- Labor force
- Marketing plan
- Financial plan
- Exit strategy
- Critical risks and assumptions
- Appendix

A brief description of each of these sections is provided in Chapter 5 (see also Table 5.4 on page 145).

This is the first of seven exercises that appear at the ends of each of the seven major parts in this textbook. The goal of these exercises is to help you work through the preceding components to create your own business plan. For example, in the exercise for this part, you will make decisions and complete the research that

bonus, you are more likely to develop a quality business plan if you really want to open this type of business.

Now that you have decided on a specific type of business, it is time to begin the planning process. The goal for this part is to complete the introduction and benefits-to-the-community components of your business plan.

Before you begin, it is important to note that the business plan is not a document that is written and then set aside. It is a living document that an entrepreneur should refer to continuously in order to ensure that plans are being carried through appropriately. As the entrepreneur begins to execute the plan, he or she should monitor the business environment continuously and make changes to the plan to address any challenges or opportunities that were not foreseen originally.

Throughout this course, you will, of course, be building your knowledge about business. Therefore, it will be appropriate for you to continually revisit parts of the plan that you have already written in order to refine them based on your more comprehensive knowledge. You will find that writing your plan is not a simple matter of starting at the beginning and moving chronologically through to the end. Instead, you probably will find yourself jumping around the various components, making refinements as you go. In fact, the second component—the executive summary—should be written last, but because of its comprehensive nature and its importance to potential investors, it appears after the introduction in the final business plan. By the end of this course, you should be

The end-of-part Building a Business Plan project walks you step-by-step through the preparation of a real Business Plan. This feature also coordinates with the Online Business Plan Builder available.

The Sky's the Limit with Technology for *Business, 10e!*

With ***Business, 10e's*** exciting new technology options, "the sky's the limit" for hands-on learning. **CengageNOW™** delivers an ebook, access to an online database of company information, and a personalized learning path, all in one, completely online product. **WebTutor™** offers comprehensive, content-rich, electronic study materials. And the **Business Plan Builder** walks you step-by-step through the creation of a solid business plan that you can immediately put into action. With ***Business, 10e's*** technology tools, "the sky's the limit" to what you can accomplish—in class and out!

South-Western's Global Economic Crisis (GEC) Resource Center

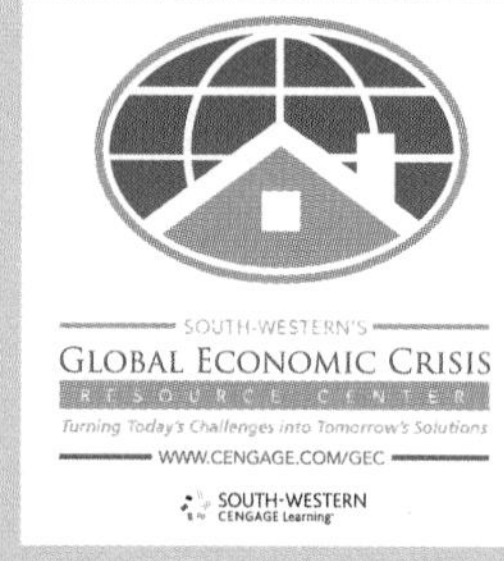

Your source for turning today's challenges into tomorrow's solutions

Today's economy leaves a lot of questions... and South-Western delivers answers! The current global economic crisis presents one of the most memorable moments of the century. South-Western helps you make the most of it!

Our new online web portal features the solutions you want in an easy-to-use format, including:

- A global issues database
- A thorough overview and timeline of events leading up to the global economic crisis
- Links to the latest news and resources

For more information on how you can access this resource, please visit **www.cengage.com/gec.**

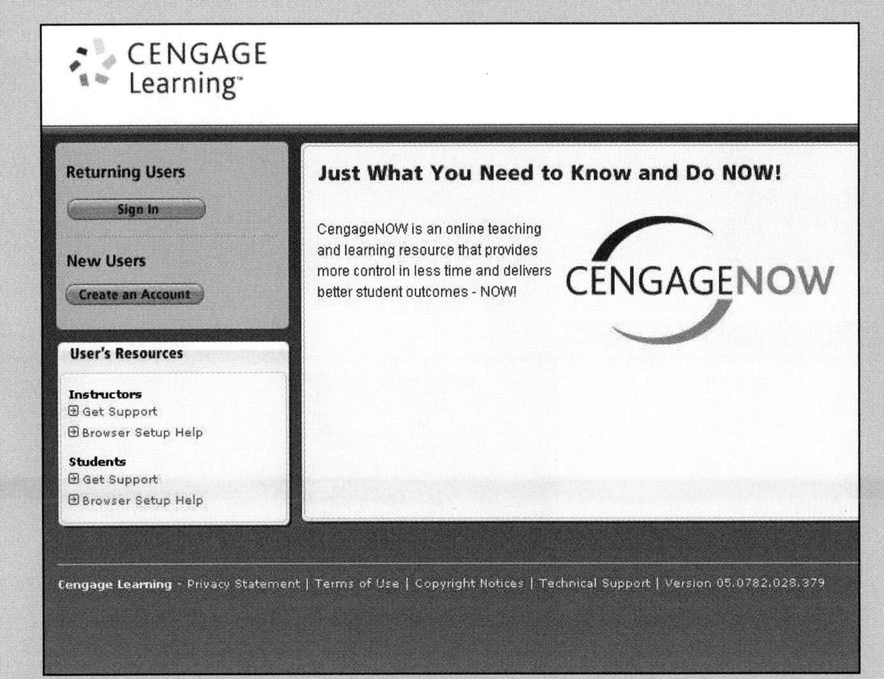

CengageNOW™

Just What You Need to Know and Do NOW!
CengageNOW is an online product that includes pre-populated homework assessments with a personalized learning path, an (ebook), and much more! Each student who purchases CengageNOW with a new text also automatically receives access to the Business and Company Resource Center (BCRC) database. For more information, visit **www.cengage.com/now.**

CENGAGENOW

More Benefits | Try it Out! | Success Stories | Talk to Us!

Learn more about CengageNOW!

Just what you need to know and do NOW!

CengageNOW is an **Online Teaching and Learning Resource**
CengageNOW offers all of your teaching and learning resources in one intuitive program organized around the essential activities you perform for class - lecturing, creating assignments, grading, quizzing, and tracking student progress and performance. CengageNOW, in most cases, provides students access to an integrated eBook, interactive tutorials, videos, animations, games and other multimedia tools to help them get the most out of your course.

CengageNOW provides **More Control In Less Time**
CengageNOW's flexible assignment and grade book options provides you more control while saving you valuable time in planning and managing your course assignments. With CengageNOW, you can automatically grade all assignments, weigh grades, choose points or percentages and set the number of attempts and due dates per problem to best suit your overall course plan.

CengageNOW **Delivers Results**
CengageNOW Personalized Study; a diagnostic tool (featuring a chapter specific Pre-test, Study Plan, and Post-test) empowers students to master concepts, prepare for exams, and be more involved in class. It's easy to assign and have results automatically post to your grade book. Results to Personalized Study provide immediate and ongoing feedback regarding what students are mastering and why they're not - to both you and the student.

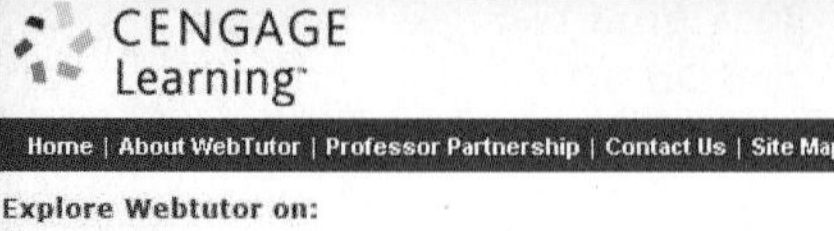

WebTutor™

WebTutor is an epack that can be used with both WebCT® and Blackboard®. This content-rich, web-based teaching and learning aid reinforces chapter concepts and acts as an electronic student study guide. WebTutor provides you with interactive chapter review quizzes, writing improvement exercises, and flash cards of glossary terms. WebTutor also provides PowerPoint® review slides, links to videos, and threaded discussions.

Business Plan Builder

This powerful, interactive online tool walks you step-by-step through the process of building a business plan—a skill that will benefit you throughout your career. The system provides informational modules about each part of the business plan and then prompts you to fill in the templates with information supporting your own business plan. Step-by-step, the program literally "builds" the business plan from the ground up for future entrepreneurs and business leaders.

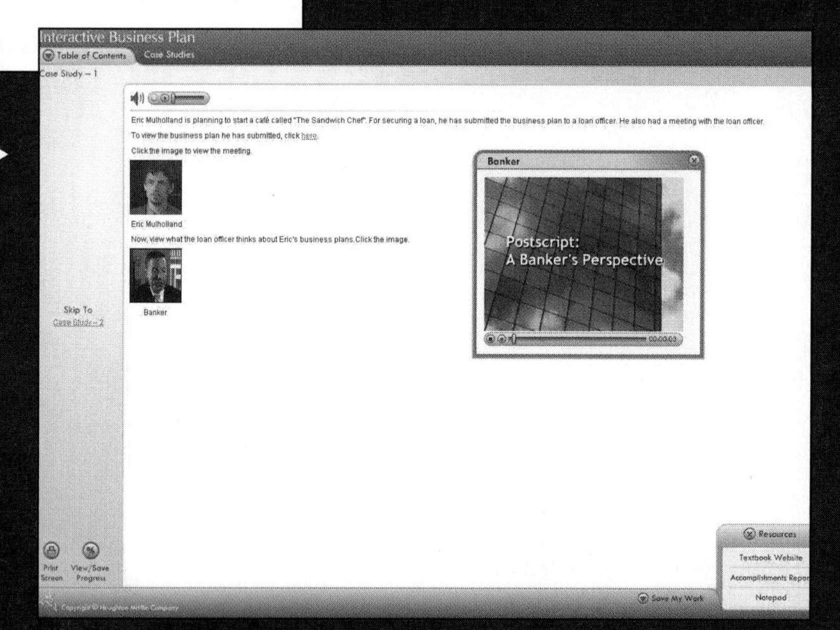

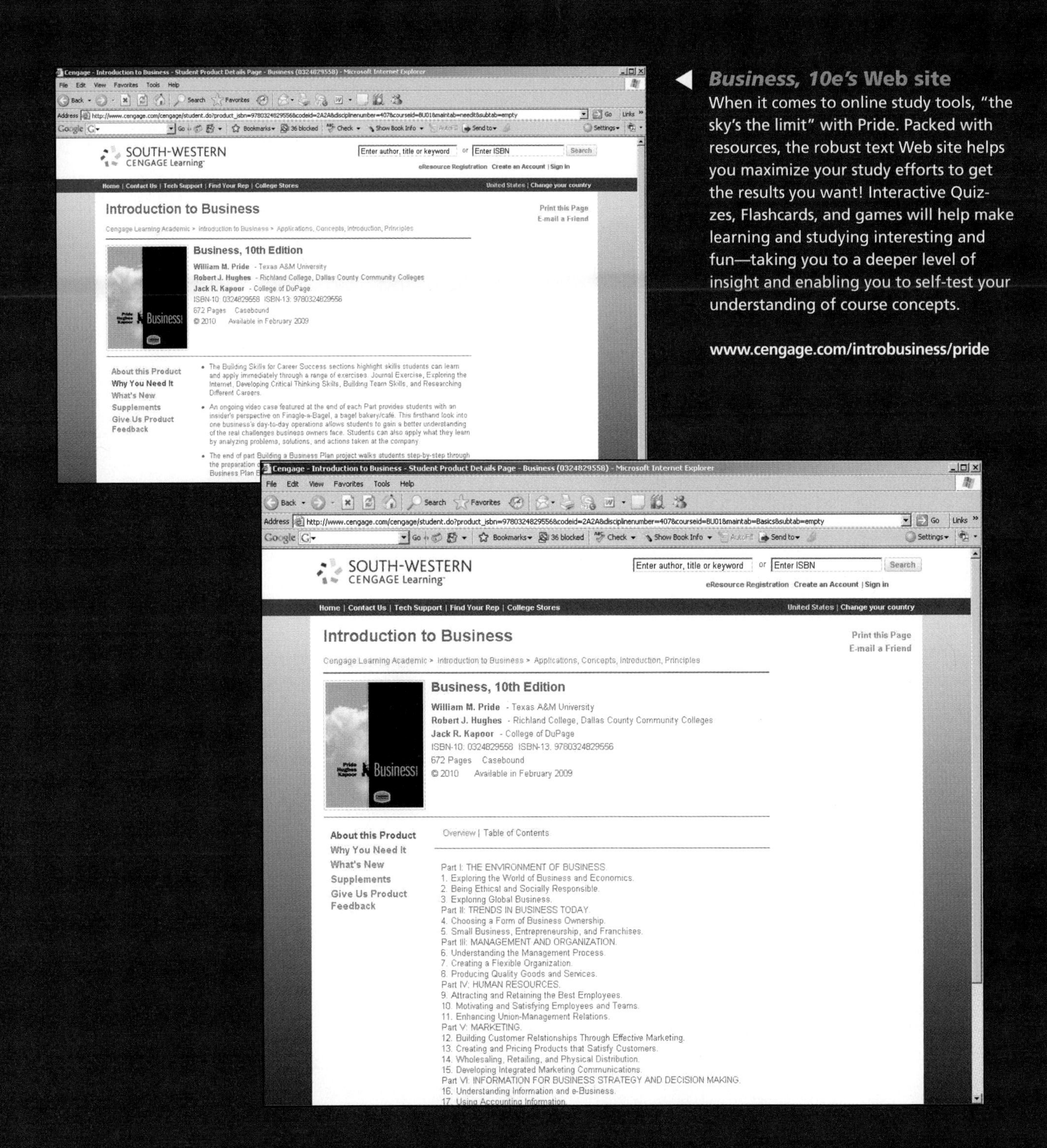

Business, 10e's Web site

When it comes to online study tools, "the sky's the limit" with Pride. Packed with resources, the robust text Web site helps you maximize your study efforts to get the results you want! Interactive Quizzes, Flashcards, and games will help make learning and studying interesting and fun—taking you to a deeper level of insight and enabling you to self-test your understanding of course concepts.

www.cengage.com/introbusiness/pride

Business 10e's Finagle A Bagel Video Case

An ongoing video case featured at the end of each Part provides you with an insider's perspective on Finagle A Bagel, a bagel bakery/café. This firsthand look into one business's day-to-day operations allows you to gain a better understanding of the real challenges business owners face. You can also apply what you learn by analyzing problems, solutions, and actions taken at the company.

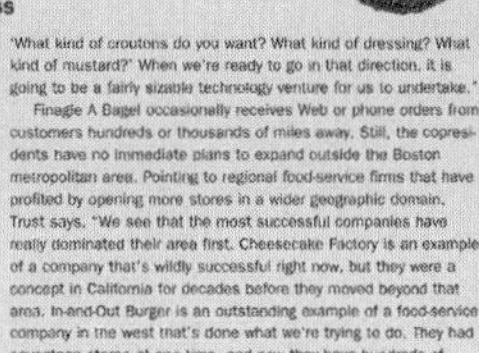

Running a Business Part 2

Finagle A Bagel: A Fast-Growing Small Business

Finagle A Bagel, a fast-growing small business co-owned by Alan Litchman and Laura Trust, is at the forefront of one of the freshest concepts in the food-service business: fresh food. Each of the twenty stores bakes a new batch of bagels every hour, and each receives new deliveries of cheeses, vegetables, fruits, and other ingredients every day. Rather than prepackage menu items, store employees make everything to order so that they can satisfy the specific needs of each *guest* (Finagle A Bagel's term for a customer). As a result, customers get fresh food prepared to their exact preferences—whether it's extra cheese on a bagel pizza or no onions in a salad—along with prompt, friendly service.

"Every sandwich, every salad is built to order, so there's a lot of communication between the customers and the cashiers, the customers and the sandwich makers, the customers and the managers," explains Trust. This allows Finagle A Bagel's store employees ample opportunity to build customer relationships and encourage repeat business. Many, like Mirna Hernandez of the Tremont Street store in downtown Boston, are so familiar with what certain customers order that they spring into action when regulars enter the store. "We know what they want, and we just ring it in and take care of them," she says. Some employees even know their customers by name and make conversation as they create a sandwich or fill a coffee container.

BUYING AND BUILDING THE BUSINESS AND BRAND

The combination of a strong local following and favorable brand image is what attracted the entrepreneurs to Finagle A Bagel. Looking back, Litchman says that he and his wife recognized that

'What kind of croutons do you want? What kind of dressing? What kind of mustard?' When we're ready to go in that direction, it is going to be a fairly sizable technology venture for us to undertake."

Finagle A Bagel occasionally receives Web or phone orders from customers hundreds or thousands of miles away. Still, the copresidents have no immediate plans to expand outside the Boston metropolitan area. Pointing to regional food-service firms that have profited by opening more stores in a wider geographic domain, Trust says, "We see that the most successful companies have really dominated their area first. Cheesecake Factory is an example of a company that's wildly successful right now, but they were a concept in California for decades before they moved beyond that area. In-and-Out Burger is an outstanding example of a food-service company in the west that's done what we're trying to do. They had seventeen stores at one time, and now they have hundreds of stores. They're very successful, but they never left their backyard. That's kind of why we're staying where we are."

FINANCING A SMALL BUSINESS

Some small businesses achieve rapid growth through franchising. The entrepreneurs running Finagle A Bagel resisted franchising for a long time. "When you franchise, you gain a large influx of capital," says Trust, "but you begin to lose control over the people, the place, and the product." Since the beginning, the owners and their senior managers routinely popped into different Finagle A Bagel stores every day to check quality and service. Now the company says that it will begin granting franchises in the near future and institute a stringent quality-control regimen to maintain the highest standards wherever the brand name appears.

Videos for *Business,* 10e

No.	Title
Part I	The Rise of Finagle A Bagel
Part II	Finagle A Bagel: A Fast-Growing Small Business
Part III	Finagle A Bagel's Management, Organization, and Production Finesse
Part IV	Inside the People Business at Finagle A Bagel
Part V	Finagle A Bagel's Approach to Marketing
Part VI	Information Systems and Accounting at Finagle A Bagel
Part VII	Managing Money at Finagle A Bagel
1a	Overview of Chapter 1: Exploring the World of Business and Economics
1b	Definition of Business (Minyard Food Stores)
1c	Business Cycle
1d	Peet's Coffee and Tea: Building a Community
2a	Overview of Chapter 2: Being Ethical and Socially Responsible
2b	Serving Economically Depressed Areas (Minyard Food Stores)
2c	Recycling (Kodak)
2d	At New Belgium Brewing, Greater Efficiency Is Blowing in the Wind
3a	Overview of Chapter 3: Exploring Global Business
3b	Importing (Pier 1)
3c	Global Business Fundamentals
3d	Fossil: Keeping Watch on a Global Business
4a	Overview of Chapter 4: Choosing a Form of Business Ownership
4b	Sole Proprietorship (Teddy Bear Shoe Care Company)
4c	Partnership (Studios at Las Colinas)
4d	Having Fun Is Serious Business at Jordan's Furniture
5a	Overview of Chapter 5: Small Business, Entrepreneurship, and Franchises
5b	Developing a Business Plan (Alford Media Services)
5c	Franchising
5d	No Funny Business at Newbury Comics
6a	Overview of Chapter 6: Understanding the Management Process
6b	Top Management (Southwest Airlines)
6c	Middle Management (Southwest Airlines)
6d	Student Advantage Helps College Students Stay Organized
7a	Overview of Chapter 7: Creating a Flexible Organization
7b	Methods of Organizing
7c	Departmentalization by Product (General Mills)
7d	Organizing for Success at Green Mountain Coffee Roasters
8a	Overview of Chapter 8: Producing Quality Goods and Services
8b	The Importance of Services (Ritz Carlton)
8c	Planning and Control (Gulfstream Aircraft Company)
8d	Washburn Guitars: Signature Model Quality
9a	Overview of Chapter 9: Attracting and Retaining the Best Employees
9b	Cultural Diversity (Texas Instruments)
9c	Recruitment and Selection (Southwest Airlines)
9d	The New England Aquarium Casts A Wide Recruitment Net
10a	Overview of Chapter 10: Motivating and Satisfying Employees and Teams
10b	Employee Satisfaction
10c	Self Motivation
10d	American Flatbread Fires Up Employees
11a	Overview of Chapter 11: Enhancing Union-Management Relations
11b	Tools Used by Unions and Management
11c	Unions in Other Countries
11d	Boston Ballet/Boston Musicians Association
12a	Overview of Chapter 12: Building Customer Relationships Through Effective Marketing
12b	Marketing Strategy (Coca-Cola)
12c	Environmental Forces (Sprint)
12d	Harley-Davidson: More Than Just a Motorcycle
13a	Overview of Chapter 13: Creating and Pricing Products that Satisfy Customers
13b	Product Successes and Failures (New Products Learning Center)
13c	Pricing (Vector Aeromotive)
13d	The Smart Car: Tiny with a Price Tag to Match
14a	Overview of Chapter 14: Wholesaling, Retailing, and Physical Distribution
14b	Types of Retailing
14c	Types of Transportation Modes
14d	Netflix Gains Competitive Advantage Through a Unique Distribution System
15a	Overview of Chapter 15: Developing Integrated Marketing Communications
15b	Sales Promotion (Church's Chicken)
15c	Public Relations (Church's Chicken)
15d	The Toledo Mud Hens Make Marketing Fun
16a	Overview of Chapter 16: Understanding Information and e-Business
16b	Information Organization
16c	Managers' Information Requirements (Information Resources)
16d	Travelocity Takes e-Business a Long Way
17a	Overview of Chapter 17: Using Accounting Information
17b	Why Accounting Is Important
17c	Balance Sheet, Income Statement, and Cash Flow Statement
17d	The Ethics of "Making the Numbers"
18a	Overview of Chapter 18: Understanding Money, Banking, and Credit
18b	Money
18c	The Federal Reserve
18d	First Bank Corporation
19a	Overview of Chapter 19: Mastering Financial Management
19b	Sources of Short-Term Financing
19c	Sources of Equity and Debt Financing
19d	Pizzeria Uno
20a	Overview of Chapter 20: Understanding Personal Finances and Investments
20b	Developing an Investment Plan
20c	How Securities Are Bought and Sold
20d	Is a Bull or Bear Market Ahead for Build-A-Bear Workshop?

Acknowledgments

We thank Jack and Carmen Powers of Monroe Community College for their help with the Instructor's Manual and Catharine Curran of the University of Massachusetts, Dartmouth, for her help with the Test Bank. We also thank Kathryn Hegar of Mountain View College for developing many of the online study elements. We thank the R. Jan LeCroy Center for Educational Telecommunications of the Dallas County Community College District for the Telecourse partnership and providing the related student and instructor materials. Finally, we thank the following people for technical assistance: Malvine Litten, Ruth Beasley, Susan Kahn, Clarissa Means, Megan O'Leary, Marian Wood, Theresa Kapoor, Dave Kapoor, David Pierce, Karen Guessford, Kathryn Thumme, Margaret Hill, Nathan Heller, and Karen Tucker.

For the generous gift of their time and for their thoughtful and useful comments and suggestions, we are indebted to the following reviewers of this and previous editions. Their suggestions have helped us improve and refine the text as well as the whole instructional package.

David V. Aiken
Hocking College
Phyllis C. Alderdice
Jefferson Community College
Marilyn Amaker
Orangeburg-Calhoun Technical College
Harold Amsbaugh
North Central Technical College
Carole Anderson
Clarion University
Lydia E. Anderson
Fresno City College
Maria Aria
Camden County College
James O. Armstrong, II
John Tyler Community College
Ed Atzenhoefer
Clark State Community College
Harold C. Babson
Columbus State Community College
Xenia P. Balabkins
Middlesex County College
Gloria Bemben
Finger Lakes Community College
Charles Bennett
Tyler Junior College
Patricia Bernson
County College of Morris
Robert W. Bitter
Southwest Missouri State University
Angela Blackwood
Belmont Abbey College
Wayne Blue
Allegany College of Maryland
Mary Jo Boehms
Jackson State Community College
Stewart Bonem
Cincinnati Technical College
James Boyle
Glendale Community College
Steve Bradley
Austin Community College
Lyle V. Brenna
Pikes Peak Community College
Tom Brinkman
Cincinnati Technical College
Robert Brinkmeyer
University of Cincinnati
Harvey S. Bronstein
Oakland Community College
Edward Brown
Franklin University
Joseph Brum
Fayetteville Technical Institute
Janice Bryan
Jacksonville College
Howard R. Budner
Manhattan Community College
Clara Buitenbos
Pan American University
C. Alan Burns
Lee College
Frank Busch
Louisiana Technical University
Paul Callahan
Cincinnati State University
Joseph E. Cantrell
DeAnza College
Brahm Canzer
John Abbot College
Don Cappa
Chabot College
Robert Carrel
Vincennes University
Richard M. Chamberlain
Lorain County Community College
Bruce H. Charnov
Hofstra University
Lawrence Chase
Tompkins Cortland Community College
Felipe Chia
Harrisburg Area Community College
Michael Cicero
Highline Community College
William Clarey
Bradley University
Robert Coiro
LaGuardia Community College
Don Coppa
Chabot College
Robert J. Cox
Salt Lake Community College
Susan Cremins
Westchester Community College
Bruce Cudney
Middlesex Community College
Andrew Curran
Antonelli Institute of Art and Photography
Gary Cutler
Dyersburg State Community College
Rex R. Cutshall
Vincennes University
John Daily
St. Edward's University

Brian Davis
Weber State University
Gregory Davis
Georgia Southwestern State University
Helen M. Davis
Jefferson Community College
Peter Dawson
Collin County Community College
Harris D. Dean
Lansing Community College
Wayne H. Decker
Memphis State University
Sharon Dexter
Southeast Community College
William M. Dickson
Green River Community College
M. Dougherty
Madison Area Technical College
Michael Drafke
College of DuPage
Richard Dugger
Kilgore College
Sam Dunbar
Delgado Community College
Robert Elk
Seminole Community College
Pat Ellebracht
Northeastern Missouri State University
Pat Ellsberg
Lower Columbia College
John H. Espey
Cecil Community College
Carleton S. Everett
Des Moines Area Community College
Frank M. Falcetta
Middlesex County College
Thomas Falcone
Indiana University of Pennsylvania
Janice Feldbauer
Austin Community College
Coe Fields
Tarrant County Junior College
Carol Fischer
University of Wisconsin—Waukesha
Larry A. Flick
Three Rivers Community College
Gregory F. Fox
Erie Community College
Michael Fritz
Portland Community College at Rock Creek
Fred Fry
Bradley University
Eduardo F. Garcia
Laredo Junior College
Arlen Gastineau
Valencia Community College
Richard Ghidella
Citrus College
Carmine Paul Gibaldi
St. John's University
Edwin Giermak
College of DuPage
Debbie Gilliard
Metropolitan State College
R. Gillingham
Vincennes University
Robert Googins
Shasta College
Karen Gore
Ivy Technical State College
W. Michael Gough
DeAnza College
Cheryl Davisson Gracie
Washtenaw Community College
Joseph Gray
Nassau Community College
Michael Griffin
University of Massachusetts—Dartmouth
Ricky W. Griffin
Texas A & M University
Stephen W. Griffin
Tarrant County Junior College
Roy Grundy
College of DuPage
John Gubbay
Moraine Valley Community College
Rick Guidicessi
Des Moines Area Community College
Ronald Hadley
St. Petersburg Junior College
Carnella Hardin
Glendale Community College
Aristotle Haretos
Flagler College
Keith Harman
National-Louis University
Richard Hartley
Solano Community College
Richard Haskey
University of Wisconsin
Carolyn Hatton
Cincinnati State University
Linda Hefferin
Elgin Community College
Sanford Helman
Middlesex County College
Victor B. Heltzer
Middlesex County College
Ronald L. Hensell
Mendocino College
Leonard Herzstein
Skyline College
Donald Hiebert
Northern Oklahoma College
Nathan Himelstein
Essex County College
L. Duke Hobbs
Texas A & M University
Charles Hobson
Indiana University Northwest
Marie R. Hodge
Bowling Green State University
Gerald Hollier
University of Texas—Brownsville
Jay S. Hollowell
Commonwealth College
Townsend Hopper
Joseph Hrebenak
Community College of Allegheny County—Allegheny
John Humphreys
Eastern New Mexico University
James L. Hyek
Los Angeles Valley College
James V. Isherwood
Community College of Rhode Island
Charleen S. Jaeb
Cuyahoga Community College
Sally Jefferson
Western Illinois University
Jenna Johannpeter
Belleville Area College
Gene E. A. Johnson
Clark College
Carol A. Jones
Cuyahoga Community College
Pat Jones
Eastern New Mexico University
Robert Kegel
Cypress College
Isaac W. J. Keim, III
Delta College
George Kelley
Erie Community College
Marshall Keyser
Moorpark College
Betty Ann Kirk
Tallahassee Community College
Edward Kirk
Vincennes University
Judith Kizzie
Clinton Community College
Karl Kleiner
Ocean County College
Clyde Kobberdahl
Cincinnati Technical College
Connie Koehler
McHenry County College
Robert Kreitner
Arizona State University

David Kroeker
Tabor College
Patrick Kroll
University of Minnesota, General College
Bruce Kusch
Brigham Young University
Kenneth Lacho
University of New Orleans
John Lathrop
New Mexico Junior College
R. Michael Lebda
DeVry Institute of Technology
Martin Lecker
SUNY Rockland Community College
George Leonard
St. Petersburg Junior College
Marvin Levine
Orange County Community College
Chad Lewis
Everett Community College
Jianwen Liao
Robert Morris College
Ronnie Liggett
University of Texas at Arlington
William M. Lindsay
Northern Kentucky University
Carl H. Lippold
Embry-Riddle Aeronautical University
Thomas Lloyd
Westmoreland County Community College
J. B. Locke
University of Mobile
Paul James Londrigan
Mott Community College
Kathleen Lorencz
Oakland Community College
Fritz Lotz
Southwestern College
Robert C. Lowery
Brookdale Community College
Anthony Lucas
Community College of Allegheny County—Allegheny
Monty Lynn
Abilene Christian University
Sheldon A. Mador
Los Angeles Trade and Technical College
Joan Mansfield
Central Missouri State University
Gayle J. Marco
Robert Morris College
John Martin
Mt. San Antonio Community College
Irving Mason
Herkimer County Community College
Douglas McCabe
Georgetown University
Barry McCarthy
Irvine Valley College
John F. McDonough
Menlo College
Catherine McElroy
Bucks County Community College
L. J. McGlamory
North Harris County College
Charles Meiser
Lake Superior State University
Ina Midkiff-Kennedy
Austin Community College—Northridge
Tony Mifsud
Rowan Cabarrus Community College
Edwin Miner
Phoenix College
Nancy Ray-Mitchaell
McLennan Community College
Jim Moes
Johnson County Community College
Dominic Montileone
Delaware Valley College
Linda Morable
Dallas County Community Colleges
Charles Morrow
Cuyahoga Community College
T. Mouzopoulos
American College of Greece
Gary Mrozinski
Broome Community College
W. Gale Mueller
Spokane Community College
C. Mullery
Humboldt State University
Robert J. Mullin
Orange County Community College
Patricia Murray
Virginia Union University
Robert Nay
Stark Technical College
James Nead
Vincennes University
Jerry Novak
Alaska Pacific University
Grantley Nurse
Raritan Valley Community College
Gerald O'Bryan
Danville Area Community College
Larry Olanrewaju
Virginia Union University
David G. Oliver
Edison Community College
John R. Pappalardo
Keene State College
Dennis Pappas
Columbus Technical Institute
Roberta F. Passenant
Berkshire Community College
Clarissa M. H. Patterson
Bryant College
Kenneth Peissig
College of Menominee Nation
Jeffrey D. Penley
Catawba Valley Community College
Constantine Petrides
Manhattan Community College
Donald Pettit
Suffolk County Community College
Norman Petty
Central Piedmont Community College
Joseph Platts
Miami-Dade Community College
Gloria D. Poplawsky
University Of Toledo
Greg Powell
Southern Utah University
Fred D. Pragasam
SUNY at Cobleskill
Peter Quinn
Commonwealth College
Kimberly Ray
North Carolina A & T State University
Robert Reinke
University of South Dakota
William Ritchie
Florida Gulf Coast University
Kenneth Robinson
Wesley College
John Roisch
Clark County Community College
Rick Rowray
Ball State University
Jill Russell
Camden County College
Karl C. Rutkowski
Pierce Junior College
Martin S. St. John
Westmoreland County Community College
Ben Sackmary
Buffalo State College
Eddie Sanders, Jr.
Chicago State University
P. L. Sandlin
East Los Angeles College

Nicholas Sarantakes
Austin Community College
Wallace Satchell
St. Philip's College
Warren Schlesinger
Ithaca College
Marilyn Schwartz
College of Marin
Jon E. Seely
Tulsa Junior College
John E. Seitz
Oakton Community College
J. Gregory Service
Broward Community College—North Campus
Lynne M. Severance
Eastern Washington University
Dennis Shannon
Southwestern Illinois College
Richard Shapiro
Cuyahoga Community College
Raymond Shea
Monroe Community College
Lynette Shishido
Santa Monica College
Cindy Simerly
Lakeland Community College
Anthony Slone
Elizabeth Community & Technical College
Anne Smevog
Cleveland Technical College
James Smith
Rocky Mountain College
David Sollars
Auburn University Montgomery
Carl Sonntag
Pikes Peak Community College
Russell W. Southhall
Laney College
Raymond Sparks
Pima College
John Spence
University of Southwestern Louisiana
Rieann Spence-Gale
Northern Virginia Community College
Nancy Z. Spillman
President, Economic Education Enterprises
Richard J. Stanish
Tulsa Junior College
Jeffrey Stauffer
Ventura College
Jim Steele
Chattanooga State Technical Community College
William A. Steiden
Jefferson Community College
E. George Stook
Anne Arundel Community College
W. Sidney Sugg
Lakeland Community College
Lynn Suksdorf
Salt Lake Community College
Richard L. Sutton
University of Nevada—Las Vegas
Robert E. Swindle
Glendale Community College
William A. Syvertsen
Fresno City College
Lynette Teal
Ivy Technical State College
Raymond D. Tewell
American River College
George Thomas
Johnston Technical College
Judy Thompson
Briar Cliff College
Paula Thompson
Florida Institute of Technology
William C. Thompson
Foothill Community College
Karen Thomas
St. Cloud University
James B. Thurman
George Washington University
Patric S. Tillman
Grayson County College
Frank Titlow
St. Petersburg College
Charles E. Tychsen
Northern Virginia Community College—Annandale
Ted Valvoda
Lakeland Community College
Robert H. Vaughn
Lakeland Community College
Frederick A. Viohl
Troy State University
C. Thomas Vogt
Allan Hancock College
Loren K. Waldman
Franklin University
Stephen R. Walsh
Providence College
Elizabeth Wark
Springfield College
John Warner
The University of New Mexico—Albuquerque
Randy Waterman
Dallas County Community Colleges
W. J. Waters, Jr.
Central Piedmont Community College
Philip A. Weatherford
Embry-Riddle Aeronautical University
Martin Welc
Saddleback College
Kenneth Wendeln
Indiana University
Jerry E. Wheat
Indiana University, Southeast Campus
Elizabeth White
Orange County Community College
Benjamin Wieder
Queensborough Community College
Ralph Wilcox
Kirkwood Community College
Charlotte Williams
Jones County Junior College
Larry Williams
Palomar College
Paul Williams
Mott Community College
Steven Winter
Orange County Community College
Wallace Wirth
South Suburban College
Amy Wojciechowski
West Shore Community College
Nathaniel Woods
Columbus State Community College
Gregory J. Worosz
Schoolcraft College
Marilyn Young
Tulsa Junior College

Many talented professionals at Cengage Learning have contributed to the development of *Business*, Tenth Edition. We are especially grateful to Jack Calhoun, Melissa Acuña, Erin Joyner, Kimberly Kanakas, Joanne Dauksewicz, Colleen Farmer, Sarah Greber, Kristen Meere, Renee Yocum, Jana Lewis, and Shanna Shelton. Their inspiration, patience, support, and friendship are invaluable.

PART 1 The Environment of Business

In Part I of *Business*, first, we begin with an examination of the world of business. Next, we discuss ethical and social responsibility issues that affect business firms and our society. Then we explore the increasing importance of international business.

Tom Bonaventure/The Image Bank/Getty Images

1 Exploring the World of Business and Economics

LEARNING OBJECTIVES
What you will be able to do once you complete this chapter:

1. Discuss your future in the world of business.
2. Define *business* and identify potential risks and rewards.
3. Define *economics* and describe the two types of economic systems: capitalism and command economy.
4. Identify the ways to measure economic performance.
5. Outline the four types of competition.
6. Summarize the factors that affect the business environment and the challenges that American businesses will encounter in the future.

Imaginechina via AP Images

inside business

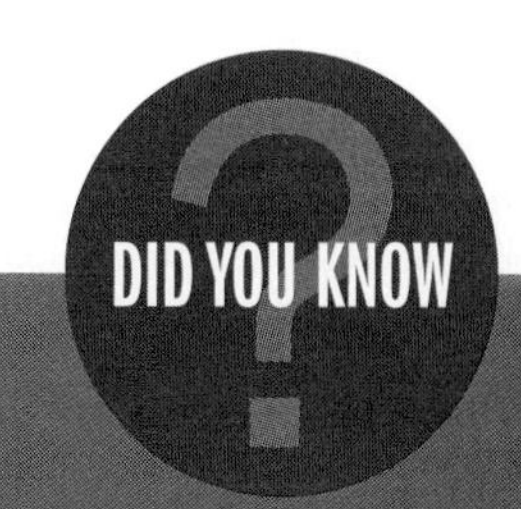

To stay ahead of competitors such as Microsoft and Motorola, Apple constantly adds new features, improves its technology, and updates its products' design.

Getting to the Core of Apple's Business Success

Does the *i* in iPod, iPhone, iMac, and iTunes stand for innovative design, information technology, or international competitiveness? All three *i* phrases are at the core of Apple's business success. A pioneer in the personal computer industry, Apple now employs 32,000 people and annually rings up $32 billion in global sales. It works closely with partners and suppliers around the world to create, manufacture, and market an ever-expanding array of electronic products and online services.

Thanks to Apple's careful attention to innovative design and its expertise in information technology, its Macintosh and iMac personal computers are both stylish and easy to use. Despite the intense competition from Dell and other computer companies, Apple's computers have become even more popular in recent years because of the company's success with other products.

Apple didn't invent the digital music player or the cell phone, yet it has made its name worldwide by reinventing both products through stylish design and cutting-edge technology. To stay ahead of competitors such as Microsoft and Motorola, Apple constantly adds new features, improves its technology, and updates its products' design. Over time, iPods and iPhones have become slimmer, more colorful, more convenient, and more powerful—a winning combination for the company and its customers. This is why Apple sells tens of millions of iPod entertainment players and iPhone cell phones every year, all over the planet.

High-tech services are another Apple specialty. The company didn't invent the online entertainment store, yet its iTunes Store has been extremely successful, attracting millions of customers and selling more than 5 billion songs and movies in its first five years. The App Store, an online-only service pioneered by Apple, sells software application downloads such as games that have been designed especially for the iPhone. And every retail Apple Store has a Genius Bar, where experts answer customers' questions and provide technical support for everything Apple sells.

More than 30 years after Apple took its first bite out of business, the company continues to polish its profits by focusing on innovative design, information technology, and international competitiveness.[1]

Wow! What a challenging world we live in. Just for a moment, think about the challenges that both individuals and businesses have experienced since the beginning of the twenty-first century. We have experienced

- The tragic events of September 11 and fought wars on terrorism in Iraq and Afghanistan.
- An escalation of tensions in the Middle East and other parts of the world.
- A large number of business failures and high unemployment rates.
- An awakening of the need to protect our environment and conserve natural resources.
- A financial crisis that threatens the home mortgage industry, homebuilders, and individual homebuyers.
- A staggering economy that has many economists, business owners, and politicians debating whether we are in a recession or even the beginning of a depression.

At the time of publication, perhaps the biggest threats to the nation's economy and the American way of life were the problems associated with the depressed housing, banking, and financial industries. With record home foreclosures, troubled banks on the verge of failure, and stock values dropping on Wall Street, Congress passed and the president signed the Economic Stabilization Act—commonly referred to as the banking rescue bill or simply the bailout plan. The **Economic Stabilization Act** was a $700 billion bailout plan created to stabilize the nation's economy and restore confidence in the banking and financial industries. While the politicians, the president, economists, business leaders, and the general public still debate the merits of a federal rescue plan, one factor became very apparent. Something had to be done to correct what some experts described as the nation's worst economic problems since the Great Depression. Despite all of the problems described above, make no mistake about it, our economic system will survive. In fact, our economy continues to adapt and change to meet the challenges of an ever-changing world.

Economic Stabilization Act a $700 billion bailout plan created to stabilize the nation's economy and restore confidence in the banking and financial industries

Our economic system provides an amazing amount of freedom that allows businesses that range in size from the small corner grocer to Apple to adapt to changing business environments. Within certain limits, imposed mainly to ensure public safety, the owners of a business can produce any legal good or service they choose and attempt to sell it at the price they set. This system of business, in which individuals decide what to produce, how to produce it, and at what price to sell it, is called **free enterprise**. Our free-enterprise system ensures, for example, that Dell Computer can buy parts from Intel and software from Microsoft and manufacture its own computers. Our system gives Dell's owners and stockholders the right to make a profit from the company's success. It gives Dell's management the right to compete with Hewlett-Packard, Sony, and Apple. And it gives computer buyers the right to choose.

free enterprise the system of business in which individuals are free to decide what to produce, how to produce it, and at what price to sell it

In this chapter, we look briefly at what business is and how it got that way. First, we discuss your future in business and explore some important reasons for studying business. Then we define *business*, noting how business organizations satisfy needs and earn profits. Next, we examine how capitalism and command economies answer four basic economic questions. Then our focus shifts to how the nations of the world measure economic performance and the four types of competitive situations. Next, we look at the events that helped shape today's business system, the current business environment, and the challenges that businesses face.

Your Future in the Changing World of Business

1

Learning Objective: Discuss your future in the world of business.

The key word in this heading is *changing*. When faced with both economic problems and increasing competition not only from firms in the United States but also from international firms located in other parts of the world, employees and managers now began to ask the question: What do we do now? Although this is a fair question, it is difficult to answer. Certainly, for a college student taking business courses or a beginning employee just starting a career, the question is even more difficult to answer. And yet there are still opportunities out there for people who are willing to work hard, continue to learn, and possess the ability to adapt to change. Let's begin our discussion in this section with three basic concepts.

- What do you want?
- Why do you want it?
- Write it down!

During a segment on the Oprah Winfrey television show, Joe Dudley, one of the world's most successful black business owners, gave the preceding advice to anyone who wants to succeed in business. And his advice is an excellent way to begin our discussion of what free enterprise is all about. What is so amazing about Dudley's success is that he started a manufacturing business in his own kitchen, with his wife and children serving as the new firm's only employees. He went on to develop his own line of hair-care products and to open a chain of beauty schools and beauty supply stores. Today, Mr. Dudley has built a multimillion-dollar empire and is president of Dudley Products, Inc.—one of the most successful minority-owned companies in the nation. Not only a successful business owner, he is also a winner of the Horatio Alger Award—an award given to outstanding individuals who have succeeded in the face of adversity.[2] While many people would say that Joe Dudley was just lucky or happened to be in the right place at the right time, the truth is that he became a success because he had a dream and worked hard to turn his dream into a reality. Today, Dudley's vision is to see people succeed—to realize "The American Dream." He would be the first to tell you that you have the same opportunities that he had. According to Mr. Dudley, "Success is a journey, not just a destination."[3]

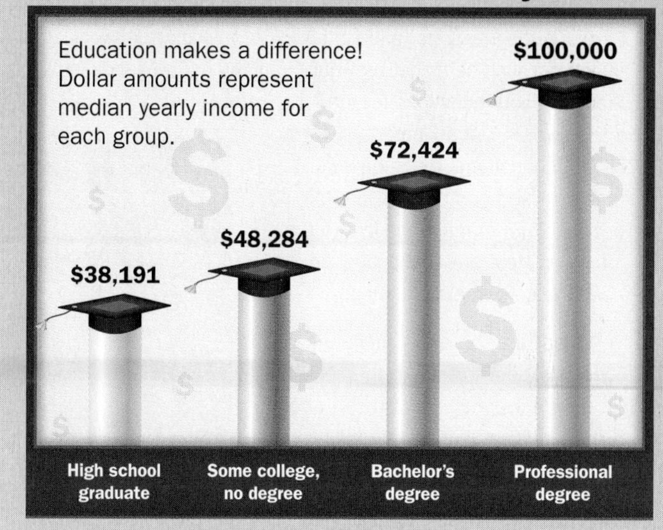

Source: *2008 Statistical Abstract of the United States.*

Whether you want to obtain part-time employment to pay college and living expenses, begin your career as a full-time employee, or start a business, you must *bring something to the table* that makes you different from the next person. Employers and our capitalistic economic system are more demanding than ever before. Ask yourself: What can I do that will make employers want to pay me a salary? What skills do I have that employers need? With these two questions in mind, we begin the next section with another basic question: Why study business?

Why Study Business?

The potential benefits of higher education are enormous. To begin with, there are economic benefits. Over their lifetimes, college graduates on average earn much more than high school graduates. And while lifetime earnings are substantially higher for college graduates, so are annual income amounts—see the above Spotlight feature.

The nice feature of education and knowledge is that once you have it, no one can take it away. It is yours to use for a lifetime. In this section, we explore what you may expect to get out of this business course and text. You will find at least four quite compelling reasons for studying business.

For Help in Choosing a Career What do you want to do with the rest of your life? Someplace, sometime, someone probably has asked you this same question. And like many people, you may find it a difficult question to answer. This business course will introduce you to a wide array of employment opportunities. In private enterprise, these range from small, local businesses owned by one individual to large companies such as American Express and Marriott International that are owned by thousands of stockholders. There are also employment opportunities with federal, state, county, and local governments and with not-for-profit organizations such as the Red Cross and Save the Children. For help in deciding what career might be right for you, read Appendix A: Careers in Business, which appears on the text website. To view this information:

1. Make an Internet connection and go to **www.cengage.com/introbusiness/pride/**.
2. Click on the link for Appendix A.

In addition to career information in Appendix A on the text website, a number of additional websites provide information about career development. For more information, visit the following sites:

- Career Builder at **www.careerbuilder.com**
- Career One Stop at **www.careeronestop.org**

Jump-Starting Your Career

Questions, Questions, Questions

Part of getting ready for a job interview is practicing answers to questions such as "What are your strengths and weaknesses?" Practicing your questions for the interviewer is just as important. If you have no questions, the interviewer may think you don't care about the job or haven't given much thought to the interview. Here are a few questions to keep the conversation flowing:

- "What are the main challenges I can expect to face in this job?" (Learn as much as you can about potential problems upfront.)
- "What skills and training are especially critical to success in this job?" (See whether your qualifications fit the job.)
- "What are the company's goals and how would an effective employee in this job help achieve those goals?" (Find out where the company is headed and how this job contributes to its success.)
- "Why is this job open at this time?" (Learn whether the last person in this job was promoted, transferred, or let go.)
- "How will you measure success in this job?" (Understand how job performance will be assessed.)

Corbis RF

One final question to ask, tactfully: "When do you expect to make a decision about hiring for this position?" See the online career appendix for more information.

Sources: Maureen Moriarty, "Workplace Coach: What Not to Do During the Job Interview," *Seattle Post-Intelligencer,* August 10, 2008, **http://seattlepi.nwsource.com/business/374357_workcoach11.html;** Marshall Krantz, Nine Things to Ask Your Future Boss, the CEO," *CFO.com,* September 4, 2008, **www.cfo.com.**

- Monster at **www.monster.com**
- Yahoo! Hot Jobs at **http://hotjobs.yahoo.com**

One thing to remember as you think about what your ideal career might be is that a person's choice of a career ultimately is just a reflection of what he or she values and holds most important. What will give one individual personal satisfaction may not satisfy another. For example, one person may dream of a career as a corporate executive and becoming a millionaire before the age of thirty. Another may choose a career that has more modest monetary rewards but that provides the opportunity to help others. One person may be willing to work long hours and seek additional responsibility in order to get promotions and pay raises. Someone else may prefer a less demanding job with little stress and more free time. What you choose to do with your life will be based on what you feel is most important. And the *you* is a very important part of that decision.

To Be a Successful Employee Deciding on the type of career you want is only a first step. To get a job in your chosen field and to be successful at it, you will have to develop a plan, or road map, that ensures that you have the skills and knowledge the job requires. You will be expected to have both the technical skills needed to accomplish a specific task and the ability to work well with many types of people in a culturally diverse work force. **Cultural (or workplace) diversity** refers to the differences among people in a work force owing to race, ethnicity, and gender. These skills, together with a working knowledge of the American business system and an appreciation for a culturally diverse workplace, can give you an inside edge when you are interviewing with a prospective employer.

cultural (or workplace) diversity differences among people in a work force owing to race, ethnicity, and gender

This course, your instructor, and all the resources available at your college or university can help you to acquire the skills and knowledge you will need for a successful career. But don't underestimate your part in making your dream a reality. It will take hard work, dedication, perseverance, and time management to achieve your goals. Communication skills are also important. Today, most employers are looking for employees who can compose a business letter and get it in mailable form. They also want employees who can talk with customers and use e-mail to communicate with people within and outside the organization. Employers also will be interested in any work experience you may have had in cooperative work/school programs, during summer vacations, or in part-time jobs during the school year. These things can make a difference when it is time to apply for the job you really want.

Meet Sharon Cote. *Back in 2000, Ms. Cote became an entrepreneur when she decided to risk her time, effort, and money and open a small business. Today her company, SBH Services, is successful (and profitable) because it provides construction contracting and trucking services to commercial and residential customers in Anchorage, Alaska.*

AP Photo/Alaska Journal of Commerce, Claire Chandler

To Start Your Own Business Some people prefer to work for themselves, and they open their own businesses. To be successful, business owners must possess many of the same skills that successful employees have. And they must be willing to work hard and put in long hours.

It also helps if your small business can provide a product or service that customers want. For example, Mark Cuban started a small Internet company called Broadcast.com that provided hundreds of live and on-demand audio and video programs ranging from rap music to sporting events to business events over the Internet. And because Cuban's company met the needs of his customers, Broadcast.com was very successful. When Cuban sold Broadcast.com to Yahoo! Inc., he became a billionaire.[4]

Unfortunately, many small-business firms fail; 70 percent of them fail within the first five years. Typical reasons for business failures include undercapitalization (not enough money), poor business location, poor customer service, unqualified or untrained employees, fraud, lack of a proper business plan, and failure to seek outside professional help. The material in Chapter 6 and selected topics and examples throughout this text will help you to decide whether you want to open your own business. This material also will help you to overcome many of these problems.

To Become a Better Informed Consumer and Investor The world of business surrounds us. You cannot buy a home, a new Solstice convertible from the local Pontiac dealer, a Black & Decker sander at an ACE Hardware store, a pair of jeans at Gap Inc., or a hot dog from a street vendor without entering a business transaction. Because you no doubt will engage in business transactions almost every day of your life, one very good reason for studying business is to become a more fully informed consumer. Many people also rely on a basic understanding of business to help them to invest for the future. According to Julie Stav, Hispanic stockbroker-turned-author/radio personality, "Take $25, add to it drive plus determination and then watch it multiply into an empire."[5] The author of *Get Your Share,* a *New York Times* best-seller, believes that it is important to learn the basics about the economy and business, stocks, mutual funds, and other alternatives before investing your money. And while this is an obvious conclusion, just dreaming of being rich doesn't make it happen. In fact, like many facets of life, it takes planning and determination to establish the type of investment program that will help you to accomplish your financial goals.

Special Note to Students

It is important to begin reading this text with one thing in mind: *This business course does not have to be difficult.* In fact, *learning about business and how you can be involved as an employee, business owner, consumer, or investor can be fun!*

We have done everything possible to eliminate the problems that students encounter in a typical class. All the features in each chapter have been evaluated and recommended by instructors with years of teaching experience. In addition, business students were asked to critique each chapter component. Based on this feedback, the text includes the following features:

- *Learning objectives* appear at the beginning of each chapter.
- *Inside Business* is a chapter-opening case that highlights how successful companies do business on a day-to-day basis.

- *Margin notes* are used throughout the text to reinforce both learning objectives and key terms.
- *Boxed features* highlight environmental issues, career information, starting a business, ethical behavior, and global issues.
- *Spotlight* features highlight interesting facts about business and society and often provide a real-world example of an important concept within a chapter.
- *Sustainability features* provide information about companies working to protect the environment.
- *End-of-chapter materials* provide questions about the opening case, a chapter summary, a list of key terms, review and discussion questions, and two cases. The last section of every chapter is entitled Building Skills for Career Success and includes exercises devoted to building communication skills with a journal exercise, exploring the Internet, developing critical-thinking skills, building team skills, and researching different careers.
- *End-of-part materials* provide a continuing video case about the Finagle A Bagel company that operates a chain of retail outlets in the northeastern section of the United States. Also at the end of each major part is an exercise designed to help you to develop the components that are included in a typical business plan.

In addition to the text, a number of student supplements will help you to explore the world of business. We are especially proud of the website that accompanies this edition. There, you will find online study aids, including interactive study tools, practice tests, audio reviews for each chapter, flashcards, and other resources. If you want to take a look at the Internet support materials available for this edition of *Business,*

1. Make an Internet connection and go to **www.cengage.com/introbusiness/pride/**.
2. Click on the Book Companion Site link and choose Book Resources.

As authors, we want you to be successful. We know that your time is valuable and that your schedule is crowded with many different activities. We also appreciate the fact that textbooks are expensive. Therefore, we want you to use this text and get the most out of your investment. In order to help you get off to a good start, a number of suggestions for developing effective study skills and using this text are provided in Table 1.1. Why not take a look at these suggestions and use them to

Table 1.1: Seven Ways to Use This Text and Its Resources

1. Prepare before you go to class.	Early preparation is the key to success in many of life's activities. Certainly, early preparation can help you to participate in class, ask questions, and improve your performance on exams.
2. Read the chapter.	Although it may seem like an obvious suggestion, many students never take the time to really read the material. Find a quiet space where there are no distractions, and invest enough time to become a "content expert."
3. Underline or highlight important concepts.	Make this text yours. Don't be afraid to write on the pages of your text. It is much easier to review material if you have identified important concepts.
4. Take notes.	While reading, take the time to jot down important points and summarize concepts in your own words. Also, take notes in class.
5. Apply the concepts.	Learning is always easier if you can apply the content to your real-life situation. Think about how you could use the material either now or in the future.
6. Practice critical thinking.	Test the material in the text. Do the concepts make sense? To build critical-thinking skills, answer the questions that accompany the cases at the end of each chapter. Also, many of the exercises in the Building Skills for Career Success require critical thinking.
7. Prepare for exams.	Allow enough time to review the material before exams. Check out the summary and review questions at the end of the chapter. Then use the resources on the text website.

help you succeed in this course and earn a higher grade. Remember what Joe Dudley said, "Success is a journey, not a destination."

Since a text always should be evaluated by the students and instructors who use it, we would welcome and sincerely appreciate your comments and suggestions. Please feel free to contact us by using one of the following e-mail addresses:

Bill Pride: **w-pride@tamu.edu**
Bob Hughes: **bhughes@dcccd.edu**
Jack Kapoor: **kapoorj@cdnet.cod.edu**

Business: A Definition

2 **Learning Objective: Define *business* and identify potential risks and rewards.**

business the organized effort of individuals to produce and sell, for a profit, the products and services that satisfy society's needs

Business is the organized effort of individuals to produce and sell, for a profit, the goods and services that satisfy society's needs. The general term *business* refers to all such efforts within a society (as in "American business") or within an industry (as in "the steel business"). However, *a business* is a particular organization, such as Kraft Foods, Inc., or Cracker Barrel Old Country Stores. To be successful, a business must perform three activities. It must be organized. It must satisfy needs. And it must earn a profit.

The Organized Effort of Individuals

For a business to be organized, it must combine four kinds of resources: material, human, financial, and informational. *Material* resources include the raw materials used in manufacturing processes, as well as buildings and machinery. For example, Sara Lee Corporation needs flour, sugar, butter, eggs, and other raw materials to produce the food products it sells worldwide. In addition, this Illinois-based company needs human, financial, and informational resources. *Human* resources are the people who furnish their labor to the business in return for wages. The *financial* resource is the money required to pay employees, purchase materials, and generally keep the business operating. And *information* is the resource that tells the managers of the business how effectively the other resources are being combined and used (see Figure 1.1).

Today, businesses usually are organized as one of three specific types. *Manufacturing businesses* process various materials into tangible goods, such as delivery trucks or towels. Intel, for example, produces computer chips that, in turn, are sold to

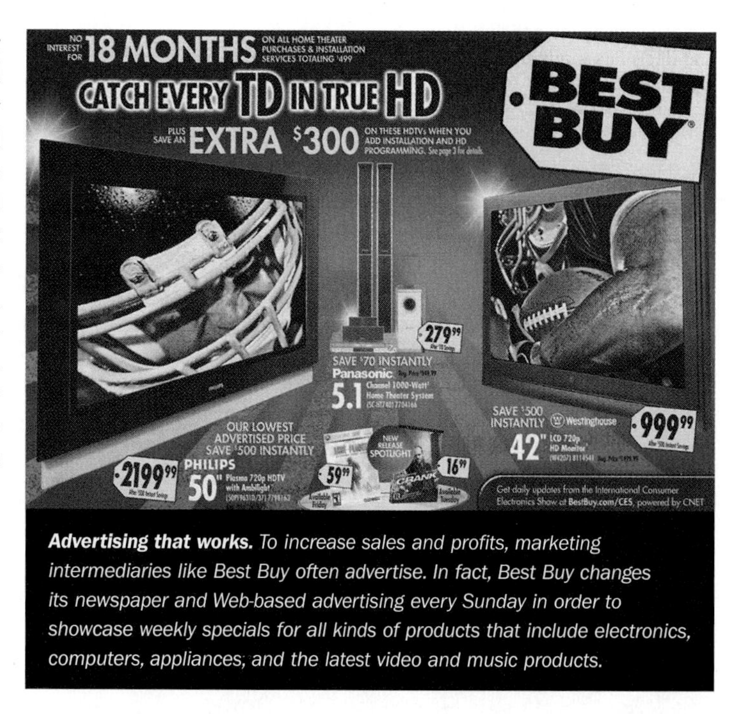

Advertising that works. *To increase sales and profits, marketing intermediaries like Best Buy often advertise. In fact, Best Buy changes its newspaper and Web-based advertising every Sunday in order to showcase weekly specials for all kinds of products that include electronics, computers, appliances, and the latest video and music products.*

Courtesy Best Buy

Figure 1.1: Combining Resources

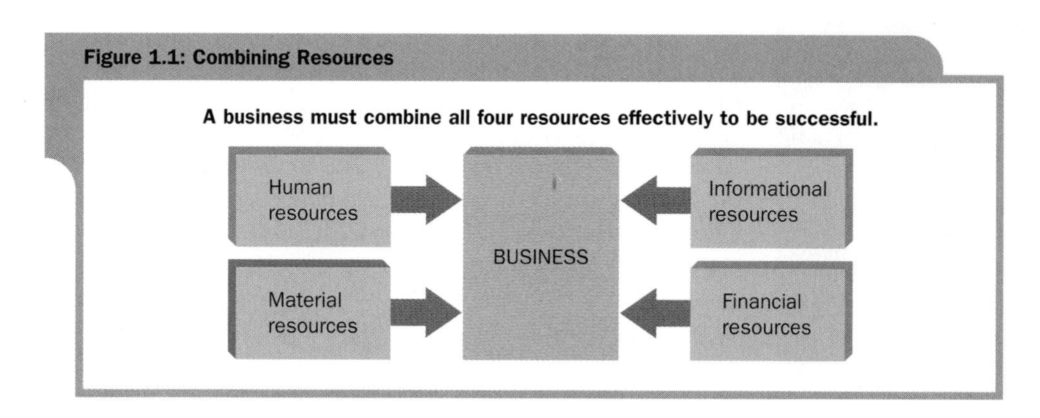

companies that manufacture computers. *Service businesses* produce services, such as haircuts, legal advice, or tax preparation. And some firms called *marketing intermediaries* buy products from manufacturers and then resell them. Sony Corporation is a manufacturer that produces stereo equipment, among other things. These products may be sold to a marketing intermediary such as Best Buy or Circuit City, which then resells the manufactured goods to consumers in their retail stores.

Satisfying Needs

The ultimate objective of every firm must be to satisfy the needs of its customers. People generally do not buy goods and services simply to own them; they buy products and services to satisfy particular needs. Some of us may feel that the need for transportation is best satisfied by an air-conditioned BMW with stereo compact-disc player, automatic transmission, power seats and windows, and remote-control side mirrors. Others may believe that a Ford Focus with a stick shift will do just fine. Both products are available to those who want them, along with a wide variety of other products that satisfy the need for transportation.

When firms lose sight of their customers' needs, they are likely to find the going rough. However, when businesses understand their customers' needs and work to satisfy those needs, they are usually successful. Back in 1962, Sam Walton opened his first discount store in Rogers, Arkansas. Although the original store was quite different from the Wal-Mart Superstores you see today, the basic ideas of providing customer service and offering goods that satisfied needs at low prices are part of the reason why this firm has grown to become the largest retailer in the world. Although Wal-Mart has almost 3,500 retail stores in the United States and over 3,200 retail stores in thirteen different countries, this highly successful discount-store organization continues to open new stores to meet the needs of its customers around the globe.[6]

profit what remains after all business expenses have been deducted from sales revenue

stakeholders all the different people or groups of people who are affected by the policies and decisions made by an organization

Oil or wind power? *To protect the environment as well as to reduce our dependence on foreign nations, many utility companies are developing alternative energy sources such as "wind power." Once developed, these new energy sources may actually be cheaper than using foreign oil. For business firms, reduced energy costs can increase profits. For consumers, reduced energy costs can mean there is more money for spending or investing.*

morguefile.com

Business Profit

A business receives money (sales revenue) from its customers in exchange for goods or services. It also must pay out money to cover the expenses involved in doing business. If the firm's sales revenues are greater than its expenses, it has earned a profit. More specifically, as shown in Figure 1.2, **profit** is what remains after all business expenses have been deducted from sales revenue. A negative profit, which results when a firm's expenses are greater than its sales revenue, is called a *loss*. A business cannot continue to operate at a loss for an indefinite period of time. Management and employees must find some way to increase sales revenues and/or reduce expenses in order to return to profitability. If some specific actions aren't taken to eliminate losses, a firm may be forced to file for bankruptcy protection. In some cases, the pursuit of profits is so important that some corporate executives, including those from such corporations as Enron, WorldCom, and mortgage-lender Fannie Mae have fudged their profit figures to avoid disappointing shareholders, directors, Wall Street analysts, lenders, and other stakeholders. The term **stakeholders** is used to describe all the different people or groups of people who are affected by the policies, decisions, and activities made by an organization.

The profit earned by a business becomes the property of its owners. Thus, in one sense, profit is the reward business owners receive for producing goods and services that consumers want. Profit is also the payment that business owners

Figure 1.2: The Relationship Between Sales Revenue and Profit

Profit is what remains after all business expenses have been deducted from sales revenue.

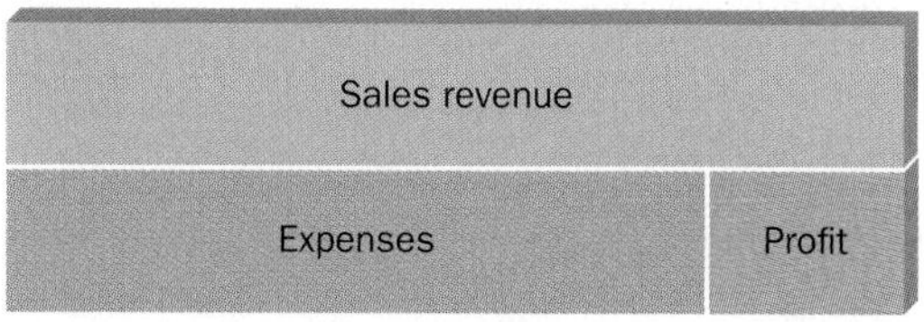

Sales revenue	
Expenses	Profit

receive for assuming the considerable risks of ownership. One of these is the risk of not being paid. Everyone else—employees, suppliers, and lenders—must be paid before the owners.

A second risk that owners undertake is the risk of losing whatever they have invested into the business. A business that cannot earn a profit is very likely to fail, in which case the owners lose whatever money, effort, and time they have invested.

To satisfy society's needs and make a profit, a business must operate within the parameters of a nation's economic system. In the next section, we define economics and describe two different types of economic systems.

Types of Economic Systems

3

Learning Objective: Define economics and describe the two types of economic systems: capitalism and command economy.

Economics is the study of how wealth is created and distributed. By *wealth*, we mean "anything of value," including the products produced and sold by business. *How wealth is distributed* simply means "who gets what." Experts often use economics to explain the choices we make and how those choices change as we cope with the demands of everyday life. In simple terms, individuals, businesses, governments, and society must make decisions that reflect what is important to each group at a particular time. For example, you want to take a weekend trip to some exotic vacation spot, and you also want to begin an investment program. Because of your financial resources, though, you cannot do both. You must decide what is most important. Business firms, governments, and to some extent society face the same types of decisions. And each group must deal with scarcity when making important decisions. In this case, *scarcity* means "lack of resources"—money, time, natural resources, etc.—that are needed to satisfy a want or need.

economics the study of how wealth is created and distributed

Today, experts often study economic problems from two different perspectives: microeconomics and macroeconomics. **Microeconomics** is the study of the decisions made by individuals and businesses. Microeconomics, for example, examines how the prices of homes affect the number of homes built and sold. On the other hand, **macroeconomics** is the study of the national economy and the global economy. Macroeconomics examines the economic effect of taxes, government spending, interest rates, and similar factors on a nation and society.

microeconomics the study of the decisions made by individuals and businesses

macroeconomics the study of the national economy and the global economy

The decisions that individuals, business firms, government, and society make and the way in which people deal with the creation and distribution of wealth determine the kind of economic system, or **economy**, that a nation has.

economy the way in which people deal with the creation and distribution of wealth

Over the years, the economic systems of the world have differed in essentially two ways: (1) the ownership of the factors of production and (2) how they answer four basic economic questions that direct a nation's economic activity. **Factors of production** are the resources used to produce goods and services. There are four such factors:

factors of production resources used to produce goods and services

- *Land and natural resources*—elements that can be used in the production process to make appliances, automobiles, and other products. Typical examples include crude oil, forests, minerals, land, water, and even air.

Land and natural resources can be beautiful. *Business firms that operate in any type of economic system must use land and natural resources in order to be successful. And yet, today's business owners and managers are very much aware of the concept of sustainability and protecting our planet.*

- *Labor*—the time and effort that we use to produce goods and services. It includes human resources such as managers and employees.
- *Capital*—the facilities, equipment, and machines used in the operation of organizations. While most people think of capital as just money, it also can be the manufacturing equipment on a Ford automobile assembly line or a computer used in the corporate offices of McDonald's.
- *Entrepreneurship*—the resources that organize land, labor, and capital. It is the willingness to take risks and the knowledge and ability to use the other factors of production efficiently. An **entrepreneur** is a person who risks his or her time, effort, and money to start and operate a business.

entrepreneur a person who risks time, effort, and money to start and operate a busines

A nation's economic system significantly affects all the economic activities of its citizens and organizations. This far-reaching impact becomes more apparent when we consider that a country's economic system determines how the factors of production are used to meet the needs of society. Today, two different economic systems exist: capitalism and command economies. The way each system answers the four basic economic questions below determines a nation's economy.

1. What goods and services—and how much of each—will be produced?
2. How will these goods and services be produced?
3. For whom will these goods and services be produced?
4. Who owns and who controls the major factors of production?

Capitalism

capitalism an economic system in which individuals own and operate the majority of businesses that provide goods and services

Capitalism is an economic system in which individuals own and operate the majority of businesses that provide goods and services. Capitalism stems from the theories of the eighteenth-century Scottish economist Adam Smith. In his book *Wealth of Nations,* published in 1776, Smith argued that a society's interests are best served when the individuals within that society are allowed to pursue their own self-interest. In other words, people will work hard and invest long hours to produce goods and services only if they can reap the rewards of their labor—more pay or profits in the case of a business owner. According to Smith, when an individual is acting to improve his or her own fortunes, he or she indirectly promotes the good of his or her community and the people in that community. Smith went on to call this concept the "invisible hand." The **invisible hand** is a term created by Adam Smith to describe how an individual's own personal gain benefits others and a nation's economy. For example, the only way a small-business owner who produces shoes can increase personal wealth is to sell shoes to customers. To become even more prosperous, the small-business owner must hire workers to produce even more shoes. According to the invisible hand, people in the small-business owner's community not only would have shoes, but some workers also would have jobs working for the shoemaker. Thus, the success of people in the community and, to some extent, the nation's economy is tied indirectly to the success of the small-business owner.

invisible hand a term created by Adam Smith to describe how an individual's own personal gain benefits others and a nation's economy

Figure 1.3: Basic Assumptions for Adam Smith's Laissez-Faire Capitalism

Laissez-faire capitalism

- Right to create wealth
- Right to own private property and resources
- Right to economic freedom and freedom to compete
- Right to limited government intervention

Adam Smith's capitalism is based on four fundamental issues illustrated in Figure 1.3. First, Smith argued that the creation of wealth is properly the concern of private individuals, not government. Second, private individuals must own the resources used to create wealth. Smith argued that the owners of resources should be free to determine how their resources are used. They also should be free to enjoy the income, profits, and other benefits they might derive from the ownership of these resources. Third, Smith contended that economic freedom ensures the existence of competitive markets that allow both sellers and buyers to enter and exit as they choose. This freedom to enter or leave a market at will has given rise to the term *market economy*. A **market economy** (sometimes referred to as a *free-market economy*) is an economic system in which businesses and individuals decide what to produce and buy, and the market determines quantities sold and prices. Finally, in Smith's view, the role of government should be limited to providing defense against foreign enemies, ensuring internal order, and furnishing public works and education. With regard to the economy, government should act only as rule maker and umpire. The French term *laissez-faire* describes Smith's capitalistic system and implies that there should be no government interference in the economy. Loosely translated, this term means "let them do" (as they see fit).

market economy an economic system in which businesses and individuals decide what to produce and buy, and the market determines quantities sold and prices

Capitalism in the United States

Our economic system is rooted in the laissez-faire capitalism of Adam Smith. However, our real-world economy is not as laissez-faire as Smith would have liked because government participates as more than umpire and rule maker. Our economy is, in fact, a **mixed economy**, one that exhibits elements of both capitalism and socialism.

mixed economy an economy that exhibits elements of both capitalism and socialism

In a mixed economy, the four basic economic questions discussed at the beginning of this section (what, how, for whom, and who) are answered through the interaction of households, businesses, and governments. The interactions among these three groups are shown in Figure 1.4.

Households Households, made up of individuals, are the consumers of goods and services, as well as owners of some of the factors of production. As *resource owners*, the members of households provide businesses with labor, capital, and other resources. In return, businesses pay wages, rent, and dividends and interest, which households receive as income.

As *consumers*, household members use their income to purchase the goods and services produced by business. Today,

The problem with SUVs: Gas Prices! *When the price of gas increased to $4 a gallon, many salespeople like AutoNation's Al Johnson realized that consumers were reluctant to use household income to purchase new automobiles. As a result, lower demand for large SUVs and trucks meant fewer sales.*

AP Photo/Pat Caster

Figure 1.4: The Circular Flow in Our Mixed Economy

Our economic system is guided by the interaction of buyers and sellers, with the role of government being taken into account.

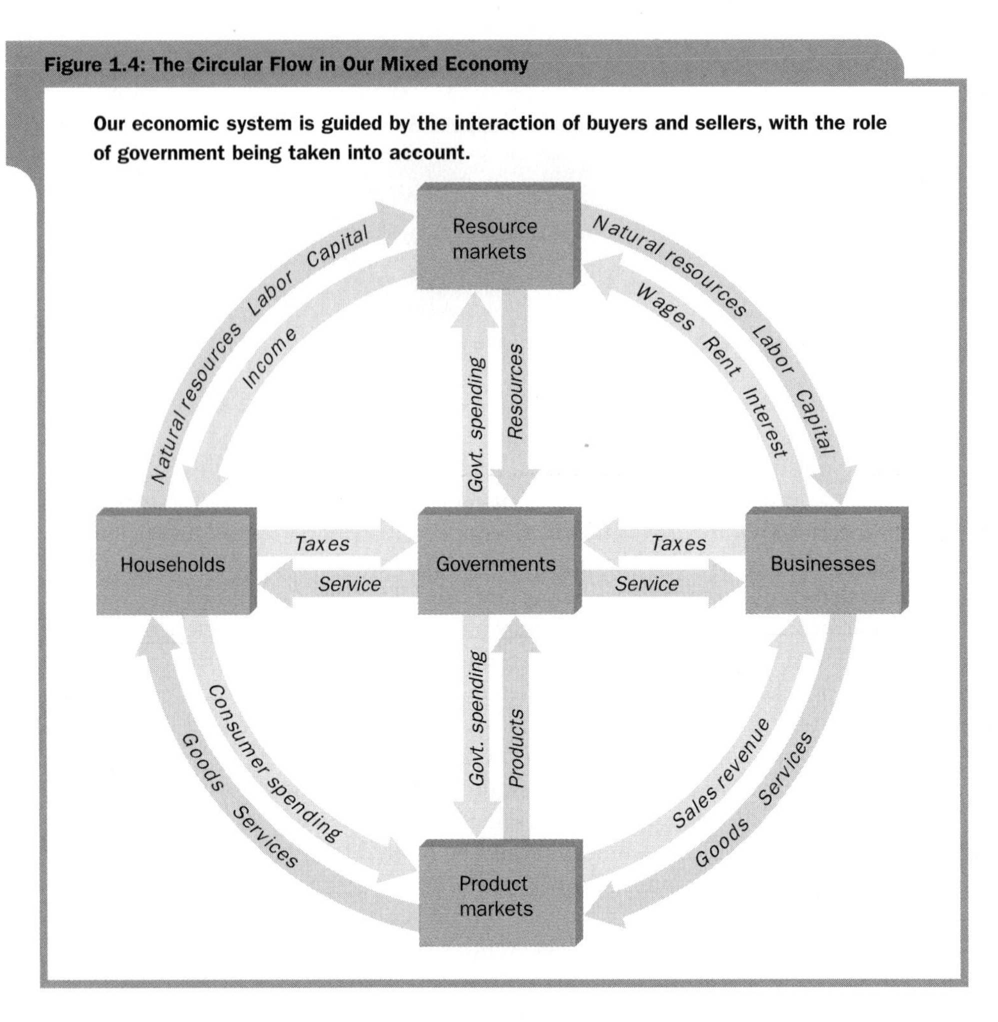

consumer products goods and services purchased by individuals for personal consumption

approximately 70 percent of our nation's total production consists of **consumer products**—goods and services purchased by individuals for personal consumption.[7] This means that consumers, as a group, are the biggest customers of American business.

Businesses Like households, businesses are engaged in two different exchanges. They exchange money for natural resources, labor, and capital and use those resources to produce goods and services. Then they exchange their goods and services for sales revenue. This sales revenue, in turn, is exchanged for additional resources, which are used to produce and sell more goods and services. Thus, the circular flow of Figure 1.4 is continuous.

Along the way, of course, business owners would like to remove something from the circular flow in the form of profits. And households try to retain some income as savings. But are profits and savings really removed from the flow? Usually not! When the economy is running smoothly, households are willing to invest their savings in businesses. They can do so directly by buying stocks in businesses, by purchasing shares in mutual funds that purchase stocks in businesses, or by lending money to businesses. They also can invest indirectly by placing their savings in bank accounts. Banks and other financial institutions then invest these savings as part of their normal business operations.

When business profits are distributed to business owners, these profits become household income. (Business owners are, after all, members of households.) And, as we saw, household income is retained in the circular flow as either consumer spending or invested savings. Thus, business profits, too, are retained in the business system, and the circular flow is complete. How, then, does government fit in?

Governments The framers of our Constitution desired as little government interference with business as possible. At the same time, the Preamble to the Constitution sets forth the responsibility of government to protect and promote the public welfare. Local, state, and federal governments discharge this responsibility through regulation and the provision of services. The numerous government services are important but either (1) would not be produced by private business firms or (2) would be produced only for those who could afford them. Typical services include national defense, police and fire protection, education, and construction of roads and highways. To pay for all these services, governments collect a variety of taxes from households (such as personal income taxes and sales taxes) and from businesses (corporate income taxes).

Figure 1.4 shows this exchange of taxes for government services. It also shows government spending of tax dollars for resources and products required to provide those services.

Actually, with government included, our circular flow looks more like a combination of several flows. In reality, it is. The important point is that together the various flows make up a single unit—a complete economic system that effectively provides answers to the basic economic questions. Simply put, the system works.

Command Economies

Before we discuss how to measure a nation's economic performance, we look quickly at another economic system called a *command economy*. A **command economy** is an economic system in which the government decides what goods and services will be produced, how they will be produced, for whom available goods and services will be produced, and who owns and controls the major factors of production. The answers to all four basic economic questions are determined, at least to some degree, through centralized government planning. Today, two types of economic systems—*socialism and communism*—serve as examples of command economies.

command economy an economic system in which the government decides what goods and services will be produced, how they will be produced, for whom available goods and services will be produced, and who owns and controls the major factors of production

Socialism In a socialist economy, the key industries are owned and controlled by the government. Such industries usually include transportation, utilities, communications, banking, and industries producing important materials such as steel. Land, buildings, and raw materials also may be the property of the state in a socialist economy. Depending on the country, private ownership of smaller businesses is permitted to varying degrees. People usually may choose their own occupations, but many work in state-owned industries.

What to produce and how to produce it are determined in accordance with national goals, which are based on projected needs and the availability of resources. The distribution of goods and services—who gets what—is also controlled by the state to the extent that it controls taxes, rents, and wages. Among the professed aims of socialist countries are the equitable distribution of income, the elimination of poverty, the distribution of social services (such as medical care) to all who need them, and the elimination of the economic waste that supposedly accompanies capitalistic competition. The disadvantages of socialism include increased taxation and loss of incentive and motivation for both individuals and business owners.

Today, many of the nations that traditionally have been labeled as socialist nations, including France, Sweden, and India, are transitioning to a free-market economy. And currently, many countries that once were thought of as communist countries are now often referred to as socialist countries. Examples of former communist countries often referred to as socialists (or even capitalist) include most of the nations that were formerly part of the Union of Soviet Socialist Republics (USSR), China, and Vietnam. Other, more authoritarian countries actually may have socialist economies; however, we tend to think of them as communist because of their almost total lack of freedom.

Communism If Adam Smith was the father of capitalism, Karl Marx was the father of communism. In his writings during the mid-nineteenth century, Marx advocated a classless society whose citizens together owned all economic resources.

All workers then would contribute to this *communist* society according to their ability and would receive benefits according to their need.

Since the breakup of the Soviet Union and economic reforms in China and most of the Eastern European countries, the best remaining examples of communism are North Korea and Cuba. Today these so-called communist economies seem to practice a strictly controlled kind of socialism. The government owns almost all economic resources. The basic economic questions are answered through centralized state planning, which sets prices and wages as well. Emphasis is placed on the production of goods the government needs rather than on the products that consumers might want, so there are frequent shortages of consumer goods. Workers have little choice of jobs, but special skills or talents seem to be rewarded with special privileges. Various groups of professionals (bureaucrats, university professors, and athletes, for example) fare much better than, say, factory workers.

Measuring Economic Performance

4

Learning Objective: Identify the ways to measure economic performance.

Today, it is hard to turn on the radio, watch the news on television, or read the newspaper without hearing or seeing something about the economy. Consider for just a moment the following questions:

- Are U.S. workers as productive as workers in other countries?
- Is the gross domestic product for the United States increasing or decreasing?
- What is the current balance of trade for our country?
- Why is the unemployment rate important?

The information needed to answer these questions, along with the answers to other similar questions, is easily obtainable from many sources. More important, the answers to these and other questions can be used to gauge the economic health of a nation.

The Importance of Productivity in the Global Marketplace

productivity the average level of output per worker per hour

One way to measure a nation's economic performance is to assess its productivity. **Productivity** is the average level of output per worker per hour. An increase in productivity results in economic growth because a larger number of goods and services are produced by a given labor force. Productivity growth in the United States has increased dramatically over the last several years. For example, overall productivity growth averaged 3.9 percent for the period from 1979 through 2006.[8] (*Note:* At the time of publication, 2006 was the last year that complete statistics were available.) This is an extraordinary statistic when compared against historical standards. And yet, before you think that all the nation's economic problems are over, consider the following questions:

Productivity matters. *For Gabriela Rodriguez, an employee at the Joseph Abboud garment manufacturing plant in New Bedford, Massachusetts, increasing productivity helps the company known for stylish clothing and home furnishings reduce costs and increase profits.*

AP Photo/Michael Dwyer

Question: *How does productivity growth affect the economy?*

Answer: Because of productivity growth, it now takes just 90 workers to produce what 100 workers produced in 2001.[9] As a result, employers have reduced costs, earned more profits, and/or sold their products for less. Finally, productivity growth helps American business to compete more effectively with other nations in a competitive world.

Question: *How does a nation improve productivity?*

Answer: Reducing costs and enabling employees to work more efficiently are at the core of all attempts to improve productivity. For example, productivity in the United States is expected to improve dramatically as more economic activity is transferred onto the Internet, reducing costs for servicing customers and handling routine ordering functions between businesses. Other methods that can be used to increase productivity are discussed in detail in Chapter 8.

Question: *Is productivity growth always good?*

Answer: While economists always point to increased efficiency and the ability to produce goods and services for lower costs as a positive factor, fewer workers producing more goods and services can lead to higher unemployment rates. In this case, increased productivity is good for employers but not good for unemployed workers seeking jobs in a very competitive work environment.

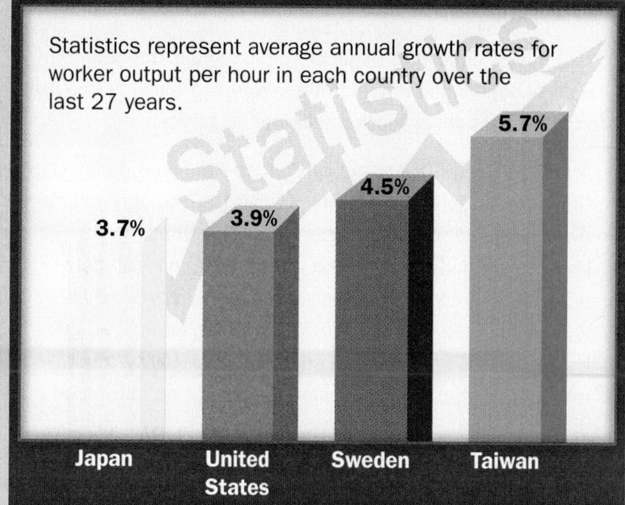

Source: The Bureau of Labor Statistics website at **www.bls.gov**, September 12, 2008.

Employers in Japan, China, Korea, Taiwan, Germany, and other countries throughout the world are also concerned about productivity. For example, consider the economic growth of China. About 200 years ago, Napoleon returned from China and said, "That is a sleeping dragon. Let him sleep! If he wakes up he will shake the world."[10] Today, China is awake and is shaking the world. Increased productivity has enabled the Chinese to manufacture products that range from trinkets to sophisticated electronic and computer products. And China is just one country. There are many other countries that understand the economic benefits of increased productivity.

Important Economic Indicators That Measure a Nation's Economy

In addition to productivity, a measure called *gross domestic product* can be used to measure the economic well-being of a nation. **Gross domestic product (GDP)** is the total dollar value of all goods and services produced by all people within the boundaries of a country during a one-year period. For example, the value of automobiles produced by employees in both an American-owned General Motors plant and a Japanese-owned Toyota plant *in the United States* are both included in the GDP for the United States. The U.S. GDP was $13.8 trillion in 2007.[11]

gross domestic product (GDP) the total dollar value of all goods and services produced by all people within the boundaries of a country during a one-year period

The GDP figure facilitates comparisons between the United States and other countries because it is the standard used in international guidelines for economic accounting. It is also possible to compare the GDP for one nation over several different time periods. This comparison allows observers to determine the extent to which a nation is experiencing economic growth. For example, government experts project that GDP will grow to $22.6 trillion by the year 2016.[12]

To make accurate comparisons of the GDP for different years, we must adjust the dollar amounts for inflation. **Inflation** is a general rise in the level of prices. (The opposite of inflation is deflation.) **Deflation** is a general decrease in the level of prices. By using inflation-adjusted figures, we are able to measure the *real* GDP for a nation. In effect, it is now possible to compare the products and services produced by a nation in constant dollars—dollars that will purchase the same amount of goods and services. Figure 1.5 depicts the GDP of the United States in current dollars and the *real* GDP in inflation-adjusted dollars. Note that between 1985 and 2007, America's *real* GDP grew from $6.1 trillion to $11.5 trillion.[13]

inflation a general rise in the level of prices

deflation a general decrease in the level of prices

Entrepreneurial Challenge

Surviving a Tough Economy

When the going gets tough, the tough get going: How entrepreneurs cope with rising costs and sluggish demand in a tough economy can make all the difference between survival and failure. Tips from successful small businesses:

- *Think creatively.* The owner of Charles Chocolates in California boosts business by reaching out to customers in every possible way. In addition to selling through retailers like Whole Foods Market and on the Web, the company offers factory tours to attract chocolate lovers of all ages.
- *Price with the customer in mind.* How high can prices go? Henry Molded Products in Pennsylvania is paying much more for energy and raw materials, but it has not raised its prices very much because, the owner says, "We will lose customers if we try to pass along these huge amounts."
- *Go back to basics.* Simple changes can mean keep costs down—for everyone. After Wiley Office Furniture in Springfield, Illinois, revamped its delivery schedule, it found customers didn't mind waiting a little longer for purchases to arrive if they could save a little money too.

Sources: Gene Marks, "How to Get the Most Out of Your Assets," *Forbes*, September 5, 2008, **www.forbes.com;** Jeremy Quittner, "Price Increases Hurt Entrepreneurs," *BusinessWeek Small Business Frontline*, August 22, 2008, **www.businessweek.com;** Mickey Meece, "Small Businesses Feel Sting of Inflation," *New York Times*, May 22, 2008, p. C1.

In addition to GDP and *real* GDP, other economic measures exist that can be used to evaluate a nation's economy. The **consumer price index (CPI)** is a monthly index that measures the changes in prices of a fixed basket of goods purchased by a typical consumer in an urban area. Goods listed in the CPI include food and beverages, transportation, housing, clothing, medical care, recreation, education and communication, and other goods and services. Economists often use the CPI to determine the effect of inflation on not only the nation's economy but also individual consumers. Another monthly index is the producer's price index. The **producer price index (PPI)** measures prices at the wholesale level. Since changes in the PPI reflect price increases or decreases at the wholesale level, the PPI is an accurate predictor of both changes in the CPI and prices that consumers will pay for many everyday necessities. Some additional terms are described in Table 1.2. Like the measures for GDP, these measures can be used to compare one economic statistic over different periods of time.

The Business Cycle All industrialized nations of the world seek economic growth, full employment, and price stability. However, a nation's economy fluctuates rather than grows at a steady pace every year. In fact, if you were to graph the economic growth rate for a country such as the United States, it would resemble a roller coaster ride with peaks (high points) and troughs (low points). These fluctuations generally are referred to as the **business cycle**, that is, the recurrence of periods of growth and recession in a nation's economic activity. At the time of publication, many experts believe the U.S. economy is in a recession caused by a depressed housing market and related problems in the banking and financial industries. Unemployment rates were high,

consumer price index (CPI) a monthly index that measures the changes in prices of a fixed basket of goods purchased by a typical consumer in an urban area

producer price index (PPI) an index that measures prices at the wholesale level

business cycle the recurrence of periods of growth and recession in a nation's economic activity

Figure 1.5: GDP in Current Dollars and in Inflation-Adjusted Dollars

The changes in GDP and *real* GDP for the United States from one year to another year can be used to measure economic growth.

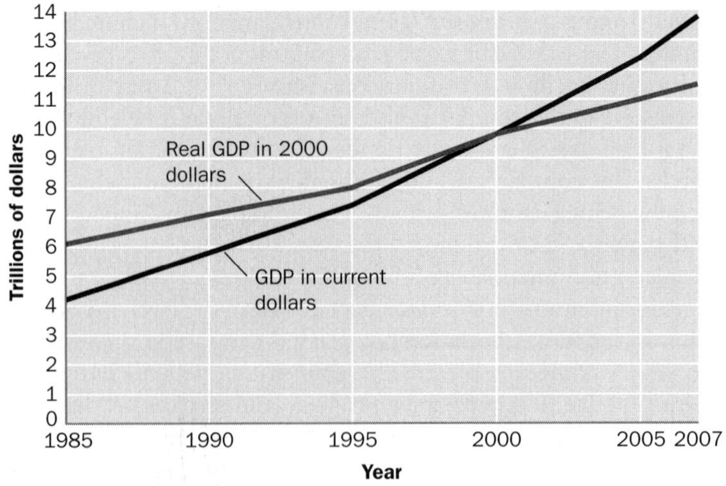

Source: U.S. Bureau of Economic Analysis website at **www.bea.gov,** accessed September 14, 2008.

Table 1.2: Common Measures Used to Evaluate a Nation's Economic Health

Economic Measure	Description
1. Balance of trade	The total value of a nation's exports minus the total value of its imports over a specific period of time.
2. Bank credit	A statistic that measures the lending activity of commercial financial institutions.
3. Corporate profits	The total amount of profits made by corporations over selected time periods.
4. Inflation rate	An economic statistic that tracks the increase in prices of goods and services over a period of time. This measure usually is calculated on a monthly or an annual basis.
5. National income	The total income earned by various segments of the population, including employees, self-employed individuals, corporations, and other types of income.
6. New housing starts	The total number of new homes started during a specific time period.
7. Prime interest rate	The lowest interest rate that banks charge their most creditworthy customers.
8. Unemployment rate	The percentage of a nation's labor force that is unemployed at any time.

and people were frightened by the prospects of a prolonged down turn in the economy. To help restore confidence in the economy, the Economic Stabilization Act was passed by Congress and signed by the president. This $700 billion bailout plan was designed to aid the nation's troubled banks and Wall Street firms and restore confidence in the nation's economy. The bill also contained provisions to help individuals weather the economic storm. It was the hope that this economic stimulus package would help the nation turn the corner from recession to recovery.

The changes that result from either growth or recession affect the amount of products and services that consumers are willing to purchase and, as a result, the amount of products and services produced by business firms. Generally, the business cycle consists of four states: the peak (sometimes called prosperity), recession, the trough, and recovery (sometimes called *expansion*).

recession two or more consecutive three-month periods of decline in a country's GDP

During the *peak period,* unemployment is low, and total income is relatively high. As long as the economic outlook remains prosperous, consumers are willing to buy products and services. In fact, businesses often expand and offer new products and services during the peak period in order to take advantage of consumers' increased buying power.

Economists define a **recession** as two or more consecutive three-month periods of decline in a country's GDP. Because unemployment rises during a recession, total buying power declines. The pessimism that accompanies a recession often stifles both consumer and business spending. As buying power decreases, consumers tend to become more value conscious and reluctant to purchase frivolous items. In response to a recession, many businesses focus on

AP Photo/Mark Lenihan

A job search can be frustrating. *Often a nation's unemployment rate is a key indicator that can gauge a nation's economy. In this photo, eager job applicants wait in line to interview with New York utility company Con Edison.*

depression a severe recession that lasts longer than a recession

monetary policies Federal Reserve decisions that determine the size of the supply of money in the nation and the level of interest rates

fiscal policy government influence on the amount of savings and expenditures; accomplished by altering the tax structure and by changing the levels of government spending

federal deficit a shortfall created when the federal government spends more in a fiscal year than it receives

national debt the total of all federal deficits

the products and services that provide the most value to their customers. Economists define a **depression** as a severe recession that lasts longer than a recession. A depression is characterized by extremely high unemployment rates, low wages, reduced purchasing power, lack of confidence in the economy, and a general decrease in business activity.

Economists refer to the third phase of the business cycle as the *trough*. The trough of a recession or depression is the turning point when a nation's output and employment bottom out and reach their lowest levels. To offset the effects of recession and depression, the federal government uses both monetary and fiscal policies. **Monetary policies** are the Federal Reserve's decisions that determine the size of the supply of money in the nation and the level of interest rates. Through **fiscal policy**, the government can influence the amount of savings and expenditures by altering the tax structure and changing the levels of government spending.

Although the federal government collects approximately $2.5 trillion in annual revenues, the government often spends more than it receives, resulting in a **federal deficit**. For example, the government had a federal deficit for each year between 2002 and 2007. The total of all federal deficits is called the **national debt**. Today, the U.S. national debt is $9.6 trillion, or approximately $32,000 for every man, woman, and child in the United States.[14]

Some experts believe that effective use of monetary and fiscal policies can speed up recovery and reduce the amount of time the economy is in recession. *Recovery* (or *expansion*) is movement of the economy from recession or depression to prosperity. High unemployment rates decline, income increases, and both the ability and the willingness to buy rise.

Since World War II, business cycles have lasted from three to five years from one peak period to the next peak period. During the same time period, the average length of recessions has been eleven months.[15] At the time of publication, many business leaders and politicians are debating whether the U.S. economy is in recession, in the trough, or beginning recovery. While the Federal Reserve has used monetary policy to reduce the effects of a sagging economy and the federal government has implemented an economic stimulus program to increase consumer spending, the nation is still experiencing economic problems.

Types of Competition

5

Learning Objective: Outline the four types of competition.

competition rivalry among businesses for sales to potential customers

Our capitalist system ensures that individuals and businesses make the decisions about what to produce, how to produce it, and what price to charge for the product. Mattel, Inc., for example, can introduce new versions of its famous Barbie doll, license the Barbie name, change the doll's price and method of distribution, and attempt to produce and market Barbie in other countries or over the Internet at **www.mattel.com.** Our system also allows customers the right to choose between Mattel's products and those produced by competitors.

Competition like that between Mattel and other toy manufacturers is a necessary and extremely important by-product of capitalism. Business **competition** is essentially a rivalry among businesses for sales to potential customers. In a capitalistic economy, competition also ensures that a firm will survive only if it serves its customers well by providing products and services that meet needs. Economists recognize four different degrees of competition ranging from ideal, complete competition to no competition at all. These are perfect competition, monopolistic competition, oligopoly, and monopoly. For a quick overview of the different types of competition, including numbers of firms and examples for each type, look at Table 1.3.

perfect (or pure) competition the market situation in which there are many buyers and sellers of a product, and no single buyer or seller is powerful enough to affect the price of that product

Perfect Competition

Perfect (or pure) competition is the market situation in which there are many buyers and sellers of a product, and no single buyer or seller is powerful enough to affect the price of that product. Note that this definition includes several important ideas. First, we are discussing the market for a single product, say, bushels of wheat. Second, all

Table 1.3: Four Different Types Of Competition

The number of firms determines the degree of competition within an industry.

Type of Competition	Number of Business Firms or Suppliers	Real-World Examples
1. Perfect	Many	Corn, wheat, peanuts
2. Monopolistic	Many	Clothing, shoes
3. Oligopoly	Few	Automobiles, cereals
4. Monopoly	One	Software protected by copyright, local public utilities

sellers offer essentially the same product for sale. Third, all buyers and sellers know everything there is to know about the market (including, in our example, the prices that all sellers are asking for their wheat). And fourth, the overall market is not affected by the actions of any one buyer or seller.

When perfect competition exists, every seller should ask the same price that every other seller is asking. Why? Because if one seller wanted 50 cents more per bushel of wheat than all the others, that seller would not be able to sell a single bushel. Buyers could—and would—do better by purchasing wheat from the competition. On the other hand, a firm willing to sell below the going price would sell all its wheat quickly. But that seller would lose sales revenue (and profit) because buyers actually are willing to pay more.

In perfect competition, then, sellers—and buyers as well—must accept the going price. The price of each product is determined by the actions of *all buyers and all sellers together* through the forces of supply and demand.

When stores compete, consumers can buy products for less. *Wal-Mart is now the world's largest retailer because it is known for its low prices. The items in this photo—all priced for $10—are just one reason why many Americans shop in one of the discounter's 3,500 U.S. retail stores.*

AP Photo/Ric Francis

The Basics of Supply and Demand

The **supply** of a particular product is the quantity of the product that producers are willing to sell at each of various prices. Producers are rational people, so we would expect them to offer more of a product for sale at higher prices and to offer less of the product at lower prices, as illustrated by the supply curve in Figure 1.6.

supply the quantity of a product that producers are willing to sell at each of various prices

The **demand** for a particular product is the quantity that buyers are willing to purchase at each of various prices. Buyers, too, are usually rational, so we would expect them—as a group—to buy more of a product when its price is low and to buy less of the product when its price is high, as depicted by the demand curve in Figure 1.6.

demand the quantity of a product that buyers are willing to purchase at each of various prices

The Equilibrium, or Market, Price

There is always one certain price at which the demanded quantity of a product is exactly equal to the quantity of that product produced. Suppose that producers are willing to *supply* 2 million bushels of wheat at a price of $8 per bushel and that buyers are willing to *purchase* 2 million bushels at a price of $8 per bushel. In other words, supply and demand are in balance, or in equilibrium, at the price of $8. Economists call this price the *market price*. The **market price** of any product is the price at which the quantity demanded is exactly

market price the price at which the quantity demanded is exactly equal to the quantity supplied

Figure 1.6: Supply Curve and Demand Curve

The intersection of a supply curve and a demand curve is called the *equilibrium*, or *market, price*. This intersection indicates a single price and quantity at which suppliers will sell products and buyers will purchase them.

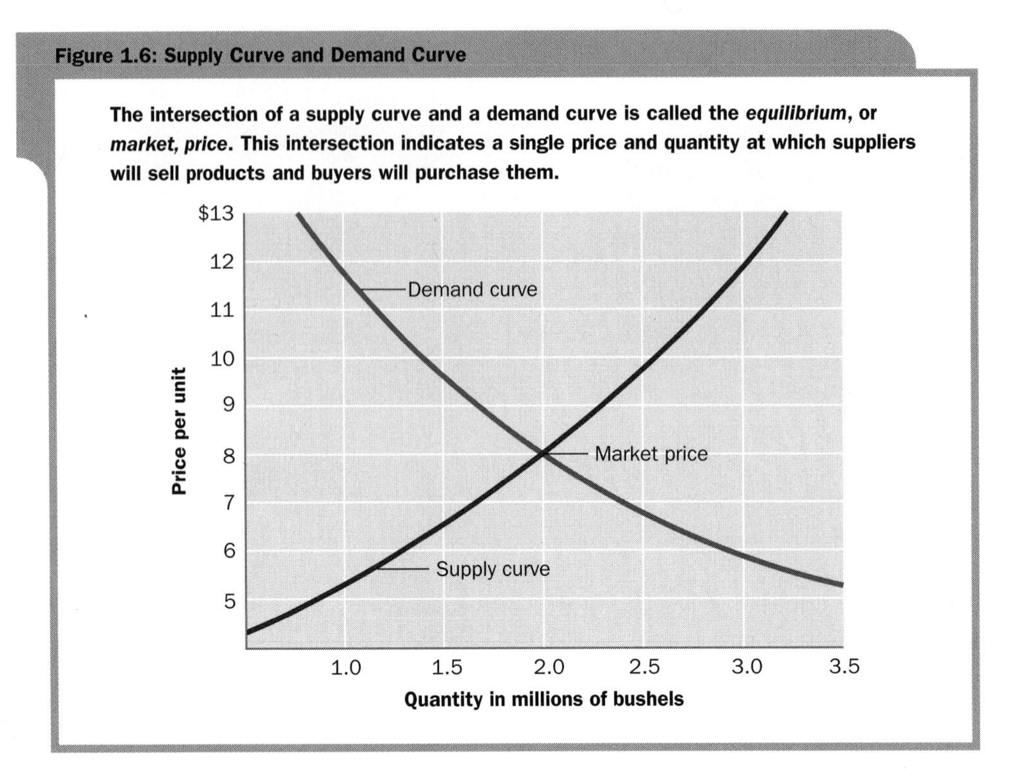

equal to the quantity supplied. If suppliers produce 2 million bushels, then no one who is willing to pay $8 per bushel will have to go without wheat, and no producer who is willing to sell at $8 per bushel will be stuck with unsold wheat.

In theory and in the real world, market prices are affected by anything that affects supply and demand. The *demand* for wheat, for example, might change if researchers suddenly discovered that it offered a previously unknown health benefit. Then buyers would demand more wheat at every price. Or the *supply* of wheat might change if new technology permitted the production of greater quantities of wheat from the same amount of acreage. Other changes that can affect competitive prices are shifts in buyer tastes, the development of new products, fluctuations in income owing to inflation or recession, or even changes in the weather that affect the production of wheat.

Perfect competition is quite rare in today's world. Many real markets, however, are examples of monopolistic competition.

Monopolistic Competition

monopolistic competition a market situation in which there are many buyers along with a relatively large number of sellers who differentiate their products from the products of competitors

Monopolistic competition is a market situation in which there are many buyers along with a relatively large number of sellers. The various products available in a monopolistically competitive market are very similar in nature, and they are all intended to satisfy the same need. However, each seller attempts to make its product different from the others by providing unique product features, an attention-getting brand name, unique packaging, or services such as free delivery or a "lifetime" warranty.

product differentiation the process of developing and promoting differences between one's products and all similar products

Product differentiation is the process of developing and promoting differences between one's products and all similar products. It is a fact of life for the producers of many consumer goods, from soaps to clothing to furniture to shoes. A furniture manufacturer such as Thomasville sees what looks like a mob of competitors, all trying to chip away at its market. By differentiating each of its products from all similar products produced by competitors, Thomasville obtains some limited control over the market price of its product.

Oligopoly

oligopoly a market (or industry) in which there are few sellers

An **oligopoly** is a market (or industry) situation in which there are few sellers. Generally, these sellers are quite large, and sizable investments are required to enter into their market. Examples of oligopolies are the automobile, airlines, car rental, cereal, and farm implement industries.

Because there are few sellers in an oligopoly, the market actions of each seller can have a strong effect on competitors' sales and prices. If General Motors, for example, reduces its automobile prices, Ford, Chrysler, Toyota, and Nissan usually do the same to retain their market shares. In the absence of much price competition, product differentiation becomes the major competitive weapon; this is very evident in the advertising of the major auto manufacturers. For instance, when General Motors began offering employee-discount pricing, Ford and Chrysler also launched competitive financing deals.

Monopoly

A **monopoly** is a market (or industry) with only one seller. In a monopoly, there is no close substitute for the product or service. Because only one firm is the supplier of a product, it would seem that it has complete control over price. However, no firm can set its price at some astronomical figure just because there is no competition; the firm soon would find that it had no customers or sales revenue either. Instead, the firm in a monopoly position must consider the demand for its product and set the price at the most profitable level.

monopoly a market (or industry) with only one seller

Classic examples of monopolies in the United States are public utilities. Each utility firm operates in a **natural monopoly**, an industry that requires a huge investment in capital and within which any duplication of facilities would be wasteful. Natural monopolies are permitted to exist because the public interest is best served by their existence, but they operate under the scrutiny and control of various state and federal agencies. While many public utilities are still classified as natural monopolies, there is increased competition in many industries. For example, there have been increased demands for consumer choice when selecting a company that provides electrical service to both homes and businesses.

natural monopoly an industry requiring huge investments in capital and within which any duplication of facilities would be wasteful and thus not in the public interest

A legal monopoly—sometimes referred to as a *limited monopoly*—is created when the federal government issues a copyright, patent, or trademark. Each of these exists for a specific period of time and can be used to protect the owners of written materials, ideas, or product brands from unauthorized use by competitors that have not shared in the time, effort, and expense required for their development. Because Microsoft owns the copyright on its popular Windows software, it enjoys a limited-monopoly position. Except for natural monopolies and monopolies created by copyrights, patents, and trademarks, federal antitrust laws prohibit both monopolies and attempts to form monopolies.

American Business Today

6

Learning Objective: Summarize the factors that affect the business environment and the challenges American businesses will encounter in the future.

While our economic system is far from perfect, it provides Americans with a high standard of living compared with people in other countries throughout the world. **Standard of living** is a loose, subjective measure of how well off an individual or a society is mainly in terms of want satisfaction through goods and services. Also, our economic system offers solutions to many of the problems that plague society and provides opportunity for people who are willing to work and to continue learning.

To understand the current business environment and the challenges ahead, it helps to understand how business developed.

Early Business Development

standard of living a loose, subjective measure of how well off an individual or a society is mainly in terms of want satisfaction through goods and services

Our American business system has its roots in the knowledge, skills, and values that the earliest settlers brought to this country. Refer to Figure 1.7 for an overall view of our nation's history, the development of our business system, and some major inventions that influenced the nation and our business system.

The first settlers in the New World were concerned mainly with providing themselves with basic necessities—food, clothing, and shelter. Almost all families lived on farms, and the entire family worked at the business of surviving. They used their surplus for trading, mainly by barter, among themselves and with the English trading ships that called at the colonies. **Barter** is a system of exchange in which goods or services

barter a system of exchange in which goods or services are traded directly for other goods and/or services without using money

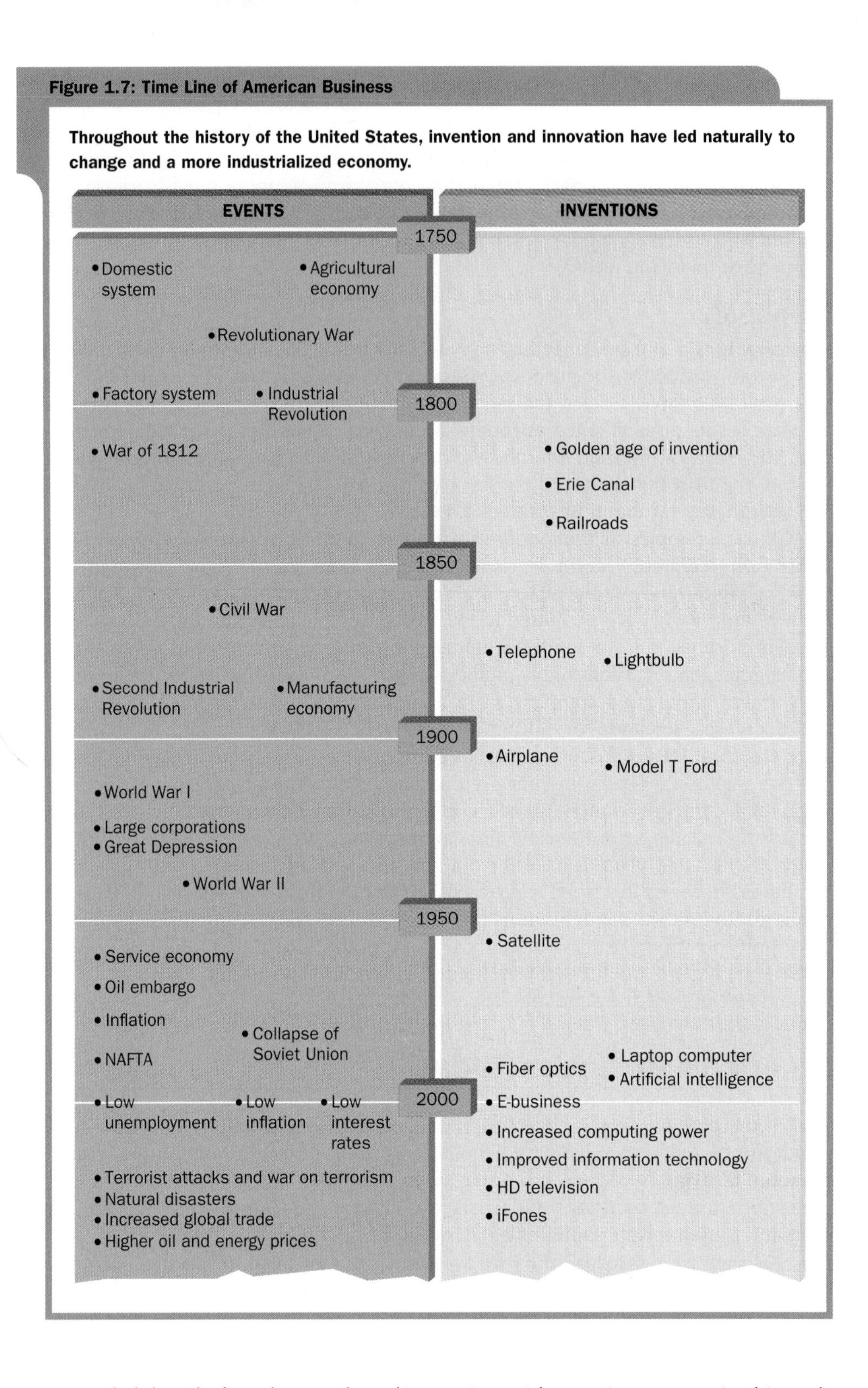

are traded directly for other goods and/or services without using money. As this trade increased, small-scale business enterprises began to appear. Some settlers were able to use their skills and their excess time to work under the domestic system of production. The **domestic system** was a method of manufacturing in which an entrepreneur distributed raw materials to various homes, where families would process them into finished goods. The merchant entrepreneur then offered the goods for sale.

domestic system a method of manufacturing in which an entrepreneur distributes raw materials to various homes, where families process them into finished goods to be offered for sale by the merchant entrepreneur

Then, in 1789, a young English apprentice mechanic named Samuel Slater decided to sail to America. At this time, British law forbade the export of machinery, technology, and skilled workers. To get around the law, Slater painstakingly memorized the plans for Richard Arkwright's water-powered spinning machine, which had revolutionized the British textile industry, and left England disguised as a farmer. A year later, he set up a textile factory in Pawtucket, Rhode Island, to spin raw cotton into thread. Slater's ingenuity resulted in America's first use of the **factory system** of manufacturing, in which all the materials, machinery, and workers required to manufacture a product are assembled in one place. The Industrial Revolution in America was born. A manufacturing technique called *specialization* was used to improve productivity. **Specialization** is the separation of a manufacturing process into distinct tasks and the assignment of the different tasks to different individuals.

factory system a system of manufacturing in which all the materials, machinery, and workers required to manufacture a product are assembled in one place

specialization the separation of a manufacturing process into distinct tasks and the assignment of the different tasks to different individuals

The years from 1820 to 1900 were the golden age of invention and innovation in machinery. Elias Howe's sewing machine became available to convert materials into clothing. The agricultural machinery of John Deere and Cyrus McCormick revolutionized farm production. At the same time, new means of transportation greatly expanded the domestic markets for American products. Many business historians view the period from 1870 to 1900 as the second Industrial Revolution. Certainly, many characteristics of our modern business system took form during this time period.

The Twentieth Century

Industrial growth and prosperity continued well into the twentieth century. Henry Ford's moving automotive assembly line, which brought the work to the worker, refined the concept of specialization and helped spur on the mass production of consumer goods. Fundamental changes occurred in business ownership and management as well. No longer were the largest businesses owned by one individual; instead, ownership was in the hands of thousands of corporate shareholders who were willing to invest in—but not to operate—a business.

The Roaring Twenties ended with the sudden crash of the stock market in 1929 and the near collapse of the economy. The Great Depression that followed in the 1930s was a time of misery and human suffering. People lost their faith in business and its ability to satisfy the needs of society without government involvement. After Franklin D. Roosevelt became president in 1933, the federal government devised a number of programs to get the economy moving again. In implementing these programs, the government got deeply involved in business for the first time.

The economy was on the road to recovery when World War II broke out in Europe in 1939. The need for vast quantities of war materials spurred business activity and technological development. This rapid economic pace continued after the war, and the 1950s and 1960s witnessed both increasing production and a rising standard of living.

In the mid-1970s, however, a shortage of crude oil led to a new set of problems for business. As the cost of petroleum products increased, a corresponding price increase took place in the cost of energy and the cost of goods and services. The result was inflation at a rate well over 10 percent per year during the early 1980s. Interest rates also increased dramatically, so both businesses and consumers reduced their borrowing. Business profits fell as the purchasing power of consumers was eroded by inflation and high interest rates.

A peaceful (and prosperous) time in our economy. *After World War II, the United States became the most productive nation in the world. Sustained economic growth during the 1950s and 1960s made it possible for an American family to purchase homes, automobiles, and other consumer goods that made the American standard of living the envy of the world.*

By the early 1990s, unemployment numbers, inflation, and interest—all factors that affect business—were now at record lows. In turn, business took advantage of this economic prosperity to invest in information technology, cut costs, and increase flexibility and efficiency. The Internet became a major force in the economy, with computer hardware, software, and Internet service providers taking advantage of the increased need for information. e-Business—a topic we will continue to explore throughout this text—became an accepted method of conducting business. **e-Business** is the organized effort of individuals to produce and sell *through the Internet*, for a profit, the products and services that satisfy society's needs. As further evidence of the financial health of the new economy, the stock market enjoyed the longest period of sustained economic growth in our history. Unfortunately, by the last part of the twentieth century, a larger number of business failures and declining stock values were initial signs that larger economic problems were on the way.

e-business the organized effort of individuals to produce and sell *through the Internet*, for a profit, the products and services that satisfy society's needs

A New Century: 2000 and Beyond

According to many economic experts, the first few years of the twenty-first century might be characterized as the best of times and the worst of times rolled into one package. On the plus side, technology became available at an affordable price. Both individuals and businesses now could access information with the click of a button. They also could buy and sell merchandise online.

In addition to information technology, the growth of service businesses and increasing opportunities for global trade also changed the way American firms do business in the twenty-first century. Because they employ over 80 percent of the American work force, service businesses are a very important component of our economy.[16] As a result, service businesses must find ways to improve productivity and cut costs while at the same time providing jobs for an even larger portion of the work force.

On the negative side, it is hard to watch television, surf the Web, listen to the radio, or read the newspaper without hearing some news about the economy. Because many of the economic indicators described in Table 1.2 on page 19 indicate troubling economic problems, there is still a certain amount of pessimism surrounding the economy.

The Current Business Environment

Before reading on, answer the following question:

In today's competitive business world, which of the following environments affects business?

a. The competitive environment
b. The global environment
c. The technological environment
d. The economic environment
e. All of the above

The correct answer is "e." All of the environments listed affect business today. For example, businesses operate in a *competitive environment*. As noted earlier in this chapter, competition is a basic component of capitalism. Every day, business owners must figure out what makes their businesses successful and how their businesses are different from the competition. Often, the answer is contained in the basic definition of business on page 9. Just for a moment, review the definition:

Business is the organized effort of individuals to produce and sell, for a profit, the goods and services that satisfy society's needs.

Note the phrase *satisfy society's needs*. Those three words say a lot about how well a successful firm competes with competitors. If you meet customer needs, then you have a better chance at success.

Related to the competitive environment is the *global environment*. Not only do American businesses have to compete with other American businesses, but they also must compete with businesses from all over the globe. According to

The Business of Green

Green Goes Global

Green has a double meaning in today's business environment. It means profit—and it also means addressing environmental issues wherever companies do business around the world. Here's what three companies are doing to follow independently recognized guidelines for going green globally.

The Accor Hotel chain, based in France, follows "Plant for the Planet" guidelines to protect local plants when it builds new hotels. It has also stepped up recycling and other earth-friendly activities at its hotels worldwide. Fujitsu, which is headquartered in Japan, designs at least 20 percent of its electronics products to be "Super Green"—environmentally safe. And its technology centers meet "Green Grid" guidelines for highly efficient energy use.

U.S.-based McDonald's follows the World Wildlife Federation's guidelines for buying eco-friendly paper and packaging products internationally. In addition, it recycles some used cooking oil as fuel and buys coffee from growers that follow Rainforest Alliance guidelines for protecting the rainforest.

Sources: Sarah Barrell, "The Rise of the Urban Eco-hotel," *The Independent (U.K.)*, September 7, 2008, **www.independent.co.uk**; "Fujitsu Extends Environmental Initiative with Membership in U.S. EPA SmartWay Transport Partnership," *MarketWatch*, September 8, 2008, **http://www.marketwatch.com/news; apps.mcdonalds.com/bestofgreen/**.

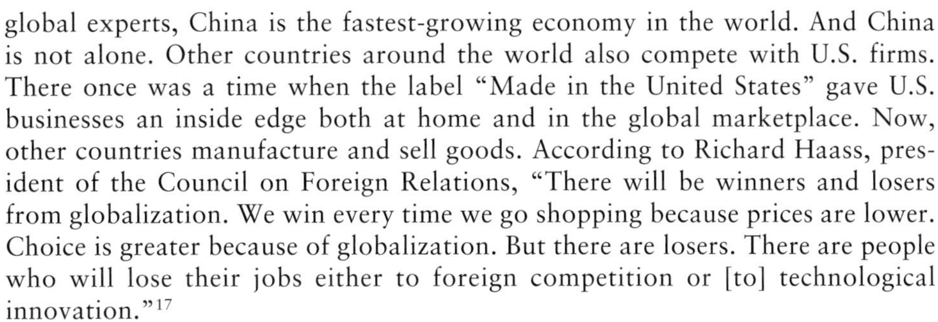

global experts, China is the fastest-growing economy in the world. And China is not alone. Other countries around the world also compete with U.S. firms. There once was a time when the label "Made in the United States" gave U.S. businesses an inside edge both at home and in the global marketplace. Now, other countries manufacture and sell goods. According to Richard Haass, president of the Council on Foreign Relations, "There will be winners and losers from globalization. We win every time we go shopping because prices are lower. Choice is greater because of globalization. But there are losers. There are people who will lose their jobs either to foreign competition or [to] technological innovation."[17]

While both foreign competition and technological innovation have changed the way we do business, the *technology environment* for U.S. businesses has never been more challenging. While many of us take technological change for granted, it does change the way we do business. Changes in manufacturing equipment, communication with customers, and distribution of products are all examples of how technology has changed everyday business practices. And the technology will continue to change. New technology will require businesses to spend additional money to keep abreast of an ever-changing technology environment.

In addition to the competitive, global, and technology environments, the *economic environment* always must be considered when making business decisions. While many people believe that business has unlimited resources, the truth is that managers and business owners realize that there is never enough money to fund all the activities a business might want to fund. This fact is especially important when the nation's economy takes a nosedive or an individual firm's sales revenue and profits are declining. For example, both small and large business firms reduced both spending and hiring new employees over the last two to three years because of economic concerns related to the depressed housing, banking, and financial industries.

In addition to economic pressures, today's socially responsible managers and business owners must be concerned about the concept of sustainability. According to the U.S. Environmental Protection Agency, **sustainability** means meeting the needs of the present without compromising the ability of future generations to meet their own needs.[18] A combination of forces including economic factors, growth in population, increased energy use, and concerns for the environment are changing the way individuals live and businesses operate.

sustainability meeting the needs of the present without compromising the ability of future generations to meet their own needs

When you look back at the original question we asked at the beginning of this section, clearly, each different type of environment affects the way a business does *business*. As a result, there are always opportunities for improvement and challenges that must be considered.

Sustaining the Planet

More companies are doing more to save the planet—and, like UPS, telling the world in yearly sustainability reports that highlight energy efficiency, water conservation, recycling, and more. UPS's annual reports show how it is progressing toward long-term sustainability targets such as minimizing waste and reducing emissions from the company's trucks and aircraft.
www.ups.com

The Challenges Ahead

There it is—the American business system in brief. When it works well, it provides jobs for those who are willing to work, a standard of living that few countries can match, and many opportunities for personal advancement. However, like every other system devised by humans, it is not perfect. Our business system may give us prosperity, but it also gave us the Great Depression of the 1930s and the economic problems of the 1970s, the late 1980s, and the first part of the twenty-first century.

Obviously, the system can be improved. Certainly, there are plenty of people who are willing to tell us exactly what *they* think the American economy needs. But these people provide us only with conflicting opinions. Who is right and who is wrong? Even the experts cannot agree.

The experts do agree, however, that several key issues will challenge our economic system (and our nation) over the next decade. Some of the questions to be resolved include:

- How can we encourage Iraq and Afghanistan to establish a democratic and free society and resolve possible conflict with North Korea and other countries throughout the world?
- How can we create a more stable economy and create new jobs?
- How can we meet the challenges of managing culturally diverse work forces to address the needs of a culturally diverse marketplace?
- How can we make American manufacturers more productive and more competitive with foreign producers who have lower labor costs?
- How can we preserve the benefits of competition and small businesses in our American economic system?
- How can we encourage economic growth and at the same time continue to conserve natural resources and sustain our environment?
- How can we best market American-made products in foreign nations?
- How can we meet the needs of two-income families, single parents, older Americans, and the less fortunate who need health care and social programs to exist?
- How can we restore the public's confidence in the banking and financial industries?
- How can we regulate banks, savings and loan associations, credit unions, and other financial institutions to prevent the type of abuses that led to a banking crisis?

The answers to these questions are anything but simple. In the past, Americans always have been able to solve their economic problems through ingenuity and creativity. Now, as we continue the journey through the twenty-first century, we need that same ingenuity and creativity not only to solve our current problems but also to compete in the global marketplace.

According to economic experts, if we as a nation can become more competitive, we may solve many of our current domestic problems. As an added bonus, increased competitiveness also will enable us to meet the economic challenges posed by other industrialized nations of the world. The way we solve these problems will affect our own future, our children's future, and that of our nation. Within the American economic and political system, the answers are ours to provide.

The American business system is not perfect by any means, but it does work reasonably well. We discuss some of its problems in Chapter 2 as we examine the topics of social responsibility and business ethics.

return to inside business

Apple

Apple never stops reinventing both design and technology to remain competitive around the world. Its iPod has become an icon, holding an impressive 70 percent share of the U.S. market for digital entertainment players. Every time Apple introduces a new version of its sleek iPhone, tens of thousands of buyers crowd into Apple Stores. Its Macintosh computers are not yet as popular as PCs made by Hewlett-Packard, Dell, Lenovo, and its many other rivals, but Apple is steadily gaining a loyal following among consumers and business customers alike.

Now Apple's plans for growth include aggressive expansion in China. Today, the iPod's market share in China is less than 8 percent and the Mac's market share is less than 1 percent. Can Apple translate its recipe for success yet again to build sales and profits in China?

Questions

1. Why must Apple pay attention to the business cycle when planning to sell more products in China?
2. Is Apple operating under conditions of perfect competition, monopolistic competition, oligopoly, or monopoly? How do you know?

Summary

Discuss your future in the world of business.

For many years, people in business—both employees and managers—assumed that prosperity would continue. When faced with both economic problems and increased competition, a large number of these same people then began to ask the question: What do we do now? Although this is a fair question, it is difficult to answer. Certainly, for a college student taking business courses or a beginning employee just starting a career, the question is even more difficult to answer. And yet there are still opportunities out there for people who are willing to work hard, continue to learn, and possess the ability to adapt to change. To be sure, employers and our capitalistic economic system are more demanding than ever before. As you begin this course, ask yourself: What can I do that will make employers want to pay me a salary? What skills do I have that employers need? The kind of career you choose ultimately will depend on your own values and what you feel is most important in life. But deciding on the kind of career you want is only a first step. To get a job in your chosen field and to be successful at it, you will have to develop a plan, or road map, that ensures that you have the necessary skills and the knowledge the job requires to become a better employee. By studying business, you also may decide to start your own business and become a better consumer and investor.

2 Define *business* and identify potential risks and rewards.

Business is the organized effort of individuals to produce and sell, for a profit, the goods and services that satisfy society's needs. Four kinds of resources—material, human, financial, and informational—must be combined to start and operate a business. The three general types of businesses are manufacturers, service businesses, and marketing intermediaries. Profit is what remains after all business expenses are deducted from sales revenue. It is the payment that owners receive for assuming the risks of business—primarily the risks of not receiving payment and of losing whatever has been invested in the firm.

Define *economics* and describe the two types of economic systems: capitalism and command economy.

Economics is the study of how wealth is created and distributed. An economic system must answer four questions: What goods and services will be produced? How will they be produced? For whom will they be produced? Who owns and who controls the major factors of production? Capitalism (on which our economic system is based) is an economic system in which individuals own and operate the majority of businesses that provide goods and services. Capitalism stems from the theories of Adam Smith. Smith's pure laissez-faire capitalism is an economic system in which the factors of production are owned by private entities, and all individuals are free to use their resources as they see fit; prices are determined by the workings of supply and demand in competitive markets; and the economic role of government is limited to rule maker and umpire.

Our economic system today is a mixed economy. In the circular flow that characterizes our business system (see Figure 1.4), households and businesses exchange resources for goods and services, using money as the medium of exchange. In a similar manner, government collects taxes from businesses and households and purchases products and resources with which to provide services.

In a command economy, government, rather than individuals, owns the factors of production and provides the answers to the three other economic questions. Socialist and communist economies are—at least in theory—command economies. In the real world, however, communists seem to practice a strictly controlled kind of socialism.

4 Identify the ways to measure economic performance.

One way to evaluate the performance of an economic system is to assess changes in productivity, which is the average level of output per worker per hour. Gross domestic product (GDP) also can be used to measure a nation's economic well-being and is the total dollar value of all goods and services produced by all people within the boundaries of a country during a one-year period. This figure facilitates comparisons between the United States and other countries because it is the standard used in international guidelines for economic accounting. It is also possible to adjust GDP for inflation and thus to measure *real* GDP. In addition to GDP, other economic indicators include a nation's balance of trade, bank credit, corporate profits, consumer price index (CPI), inflation rate, national income, new housing starts, prime interest rate, producer price index (PPI), and unemployment rate.

A nation's economy fluctuates rather than grows at a steady pace every year. These fluctuations generally are referred to as the business cycle. Generally, the business cycle consists of four states: the peak (sometimes referred to as prosperity), recession, the trough, and recovery. Some experts believe that effective use of monetary policy (the Federal Reserve's decisions that determine the size of the supply of money and the level of interest rates) and fiscal policies (the government's influence on the amount of savings and expenditures) can speed up recovery and even eliminate depressions for the business cycle.

Outline the four types of competition.

Competition is essentially a rivalry among businesses for sales to potential customers. In a capitalist economy, competition works to ensure the efficient and effective operation of business. Competition also ensures that a firm will survive only if it serves its customers well. Economists recognize four degrees of competition. Ranging from most to least competitive, the four degrees are perfect competition, monopolistic competition, oligopoly, and monopoly. The factors of supply and demand generally influence the price that consumers pay producers for goods and services.

Summarize the factors that affect the business environment and the challenges that American businesses will encounter in the future.

From this beginning, through the Industrial Revolution of the early nineteenth century, and to the phenomenal expansion of American industry in the nineteenth and early twentieth centuries, our government maintained an essentially laissez-faire attitude toward business. However, during the Great Depression of the 1930s, the federal government began to provide a number of social services to its citizens. Government's role in business has expanded considerably since that time.

During the 1970s, a shortage of crude oil led to higher prices and inflation. In the 1980s, business profits fell as the consumers' purchasing power was eroded by inflation and high interest rates. By the early 1990s, the U.S. economy began to show signs of improvement and economic growth. Unemployment numbers, inflation, and interest—all factors that affect business—were now at record lows. Fueled by investment in information technology, the stock market enjoyed the longest period of sustained economic growth in our history. Increased use of the Internet and e-business now is changing the way that firms do business. Other factors that affect the way firms do business include the increasing importance of services and global trade. Unfortunately, by the last part of the 1990s, a larger number of business failures and declining stock values were initial signs that more economic problems were on the way as we entered the twenty-first century.

Now more than ever before, the way a business operates is affected by the competitive environment, global environment, technological environment, and economic environment. As a result, business has a number of opportunities for improvement and challenges for the future.

Key Terms

You should now be able to define and give an example relevant to each of the following terms.

Economic Stabilization Act (4)
free enterprise (4)
cultural (or workplace) diversity (6)
business (9)
profit (10)
stakeholders (10)
economics (11)
microeconomics (11)
macroeconomics (11)
economy (11)
factors of production (11)
entrepreneur (12)
capitalism (12)
invisible hand (12)
market economy (13)

mixed economy (13)
consumer products (14)
command economy (15)
productivity (16)
gross domestic product (GDP) (17)
inflation (17)
deflation (17)
consumer price index (CPI) (18)
producer price index (PPI) (18)
business cycle (18)
recession (19)
depression (20)
monetary policies (20)
fiscal policy (20)
federal deficit (20)
national debt (20)
competition (20)
perfect (or pure) competition (20)
supply (21)
demand (21)
market price (21)
monopolistic competition (22)
product differentiation (22)
oligopoly (22)
monopoly (23)
natural monopoly (23)
standard of living (23)
barter (23)
domestic system (24)
factory system (25)
specialization (25)
e-business (26)
sustainability (27)

Review Questions

1. What reasons would you give if you were advising someone to study business?
2. What factors affect a person's choice of careers?
3. Describe the four resources that must be combined to organize and operate a business. How do they differ from the economist's factors of production?
4. Describe the relationship among profit, business risk, and the satisfaction of customers' needs.
5. What are the four basic economic questions? How are they answered in a capitalist economy?
6. Explain the invisible hand of capitalism.
7. Describe the four basic assumptions required for a laissez-faire capitalist economy.
8. Why is the American economy called a mixed economy?
9. Based on Figure 1.4, outline the economic interactions between business and households in our business system.
10. How does capitalism differ from socialism and communism?
11. Define gross domestic product. Why is this economic measure significant?
12. How is the producer price index related to the consumer price index?
13. What are the four steps in a typical business cycle? How are monetary and fiscal policy related to the business cycle?
14. Choose three of the economic measures described in Table 1.2 and describe why these indicators are important when measuring a nation's economy.
15. Identify and compare the four forms of competition.
16. Explain how the equilibrium, or market, price of a product is determined.
17. Four different environments that affect business were described in Chapter 1. Choose one of the environments and explain how it affects a small electronics manufacturer located in Oregon.
18. What do you consider the most important challenges that will face people in the United States in the years ahead?

Discussion Questions

1. In what ways have the economic problems caused by the recent crisis in the banking and financial industries affected business firms? In what ways have these problems affected employees and individuals?
2. What factors caused American business to develop into a mixed economic system rather than some other type of economic system?
3. Does an individual consumer really have a voice in answering the basic economic questions?
4. Is gross domestic product a reliable indicator of a nation's economic health? What might be a better indicator?
5. Discuss this statement: "Business competition encourages efficiency of production and leads to improved product quality."
6. In our business system, how is government involved in answering the four basic economic questions? Does government participate in the system or interfere with it?
7. Choose one of the challenges listed on page 28 and describe possible ways that business and society could help to solve or eliminate the problem in the future.

Video Case 1.1

Peet's Coffee & Tea: Building a Community

In 1966, Alfred Peet opened a shop selling coffee beans and loose tea—and unknowingly started the gourmet coffee movement in America. Peet's family had been in the coffee business in Holland; so Peet decided he would roast the coffee beans in his Berkeley, California, shop just as they did in the old country. Customers would come into the shop, and Peet would offer them a cup of coffee while they waited for their beans to be roasted. The community atmosphere in the shop became contagious, with customers enjoying and talking about coffee. Peet's Coffee & Tea now has more than 120 neighborhood stores selling a variety of coffee and tea products that are consumed on and off the premises.

Throughout its history, Peet's stores have been the hub of the business. This is where most people discover Peet's unique coffee and tea products for the first time. Store personnel are constantly introducing new coffees to customers. In fact, there are pots of new flavors for visitors to sample in each of its stores. Peet's employees are enthusiastic about coffee and tea, and they share their enthusiasm with store visitors. Educating customers as to what makes Peet's different is an important part of their responsibilities.

Peet's also sells coffee and tea through home delivery which over time has become a significant part of its business. Customers from all over the world can now order Peet's products through their call center or website. Because Peet's is able to roast its coffee, pack it, and ship it the same day, it can ensure the freshest possible product reaches those customers that don't live near a Peet's store. In 2003, Peet's introduced its Peetniks Program. This automatic replenishment program allows customers to have one or more products shipped to them on a regular basis. Over time, Peet's expanded this replenishment service to a true loyalty program. The program is completely flexible in that customers can spend as much or little as they want and still be a member. Peetniks members experience a sense of community similar to that in the stores. Members have a special phone number to call in their orders and a special place on the website for managing their deliveries. Also Peetniks are sent special offerings that are only available to members which give them a strong sense of belonging. When the company sends out surveys, it gets a tremendous amount of feedback from members who say they love being a Peetnik. The name Peetnik is what Peet's calls its employees. By extending the name to the members of the Peetniks Program, it is making them part of the Peet's family. In addition to this sense of community, Peetniks receive the convenience of a constant supply of great tasting coffee, a 15 percent discount off shipping and special merchandise. For example, members of the program were recently sent a free Peetnik embroidered baseball cap which was very well received.

Peet's informs its customers about new coffee and tea products in a number of ways. In addition to in-store sampling, it trains its call center employees to fully engage customers when they place an order. Telephone personnel look at what customers have been ordering, ask them what flavors and qualities in coffee they like, and recommend new coffees. Peetniks Program members also receive e-mails announcing new products, describing their flavor and origin and discussing what makes them special. Peet's discovered that one of the most effective ways to get customers to try new products is through coffee samplers. These are promoted through its stores, call center, and the Peetniks Program and online.

Over the years, Peet's has built a strong relationship with its customers through education and information. Peet's has successfully bridged the gap between its past and the future. By staying true to its traditions such as hand roasting and by constantly creating a sense of community with its users, it has developed a loyal international group of satisfied customers.[19]

For more information about this company, go to **www.peets.com.**

Questions

1. Is Peet's market monopolistic or an oligopoly?
2. What are some ways that Peet's Coffee & Tea tries to differentiate its product offering?
3. What consumer needs is Peet's satisfying?

Case 1.2 Wipro Vies to Bring Business to Bangalore

As global demand rises for technology and engineering services, Wipro, Ltd., wants to bring much of the business to Bangalore. The Indian company—which has offices across Europe, Asia, and the United States—writes software, handles back-office operations, and designs high-tech products for some of the world's largest corporations. When Fiat wanted a satellite navigation system for its Alfa Romeo sports cars, it hired Wipro. Nokia, Morgan Stanley, Cisco, Honeywell, and General Motors are among the 420 other companies that have drawn on Wipro's expertise.

Wipro is prospering from the trend toward outsourcing, in which companies reduce their costs by sending projects or jobs to countries where labor costs are lower. Skilled technology professionals in India are paid far less than their counterparts in Western Europe and the United States. Although Wipro raises salaries regularly and offers employees stock and other benefits, "the cost advantage is still in India's favor," observes the chief marketing officer. This is why some companies hire Wipro or its main Indian competitors, Tata Consultancy Services and Infosys Technologies, to perform functions such as providing technical support to customers.

In only six years, Wipro's annual sales have soared from $150 million to nearly $2 billion. To keep up with this explosive growth, the company hires three new employees every hour of every business day. In 2002, 14,000 people were on the payroll; today, nearly 42,000 are on the payroll, including several thousand who work on assignment for months at a time at customers' offices in the United States, Japan, or Europe.

By hiring Wipro to deal with operational nuts and bolts such as processing paperwork, business customers can focus on the tasks that make a difference to *their* customers. Florida's E-OPS, for example, is a start-up company that markets mortgage-processing services to banks. Instead of having their own employees fill out forms, make multiple copies, and send documents to different departments and organizations, banks seeking to cut costs and save time can hire E-OPS. Wipro does the actual processing, whereas E-OPS concentrates on signing new customers and meeting their needs. "It's amazing that you can run a national company with just a handful of employees, and Wipro does the rest," says the CEO of E-OPS.

As Wipro expands its menu of services, it faces tough competition not only from Indian firms but also from IBM, Accenture, and other corporations with decades of experience in working with a global customer base. Profits are healthy, and customers are satisfied, yet Wipro is constantly on the lookout for ways to improve. Not long ago, Wipro managers toured a nearby Toyota factory and came away with ideas for reconfiguring workspaces, boosting employee involvement, and more—ideas that took quality to a new level and hiked efficiency by more than 40 percent.

Wipro is also investing in new facilities for specialized services, both in India and in other countries. One of the newest is a software-development center in Beijing's high-tech district. A senior Wipro manager points out that China is best known as the world's factory, but in the future, "there will be a shift toward the knowledge or services sector." By opening a development center now, the company will have the time to study the foreign companies that plan to do business in China and figure out how to profit from tomorrow's opportunities. Around the world and around the clock, Wipro is pushing hard to bring more business to Bangalore.[20]

For more information about this company, go to **www.wipro.com.**

Questions

1. How is Wipro using the factors of production to fuel global growth?
2. What are the advantages and disadvantages of using a manufacturer like Toyota as a role model for a service business like Wipro?
3. What effect might the trend toward outsourcing have on the economy of India? What effect might this trend have on the economy of the United States?

Building Skills for Career Success

1. JOURNALING FOR SUCCESS

Much of the information in Chapter 1 was designed to get you to think about what it takes to be a successful employee in the competitive business world.

Assignment

Assume that you are now age 25 and are interviewing for a position as a management trainee in a large corporation. Also assume that this position pays $45,000 a year.

1. Describe what steps you would take to prepare for this interview.
2. Assuming that you get the management trainee position, describe the personal traits or skills that you have that will help you to become successful.
3. Describe the one personal skill or trait that you feel needs improvement. How would you go about improving your weakness?

2. EXPLORING THE INTERNET

The Internet is a global network of computers that can be accessed by anyone in the world. For example, your school or firm most likely is connected to the Web. You probably have access through a commercial service provider such as AT&T Yahoo! or a host of other smaller Internet service providers.

To familiarize yourself with the wealth of information available through the Internet and its usefulness to business students, this exercise focuses on information services available from a few popular "search engines" used to explore the Web.

To use one of these search engines, enter its *Internet address* in your Web browser. The addresses of some popular search engines are

www.ask.com
www.google.com
www.msn.com
www.yahoo.com

Visit the text website for updates to this exercise.

Assignment

1. Examine the ways in which two search engines present categories of information on their opening screens. Which search engine was better to use in your opinion? Why?
2. Think of a business topic that you would like to know more about, for example, careers, gross domestic product, or another concept introduced in this chapter. Using your preferred search engine, explore a few articles and reports provided on your topic. Briefly summarize your findings.

3. DEVELOPING CRITICAL-THINKING SKILLS

Under capitalism, competition is a driving force that allows the market economy to work, affecting the supply of goods and services in the marketplace and the prices consumers pay for those goods and services. Let's see how competition works by pretending that you want to buy a new car.

Assignment

1. Brainstorm the following questions:
   a. Where would you go to get information about new cars?
   b. How will you decide on the make and model of car you want to buy, where to buy the car, and how to finance it?
   c. How is competition at work in this scenario?
   d. What are the pros and cons of competition as it affects the buyer?
2. Record your ideas.
3. Write a summary of the key points you learned about how competition works in the marketplace.

4. BUILDING TEAM SKILLS

Over the past few years, employees have been expected to function as productive team members instead of working alone. People often believe that they can work effectively in teams, but many people find working with a group of people to be a challenge. Being an effective team member requires skills that encourage other members to participate in the team endeavor.

College classes that function as teams are more interesting and more fun to attend, and students generally learn more about the topics in the course. If your class is to function as a team, it is important to begin building the team early in the semester. One way to begin creating a team is to learn something about each student in the class. This helps team members to feel comfortable with each other and fosters a sense of trust.

Assignment

1. Find a partner, preferably someone you do not know.
2. Each partner has two to three minutes to answer the following questions:
   a. What is your name, and where do you work?
   b. What interesting or unusual thing have you done in your life? (Do not talk about work or college; rather, focus on such things as hobbies, travel, family, and sports.)
   c. Why are you taking this course, and what do you expect to learn? (Satisfying a degree requirement is not an acceptable answer.)
3. Introduce your partner to the class. Use one to two minutes, depending on the size of the class.

5. RESEARCHING DIFFERENT CAREERS

In this chapter, *entrepreneurship* is defined as the willingness to take risks and the knowledge and ability to use the other factors of production efficiently. An *entrepreneur* is a person who risks his or her time, effort, and money to start and operate a business. Often, people believe that these terms apply only to small business operations, but recently, employees with entrepreneurial attitudes have advanced more rapidly in large companies.

Assignment

1. Go to the local library or use the Internet to research how large firms, especially corporations, are rewarding employees who have entrepreneurial skills.
2. Find answers to the following questions:
   a. Why is an entrepreneurial attitude important in corporations today?
   b. What makes an entrepreneurial employee different from other employees?
   c. How are these employees being rewarded, and are the rewards worth the effort?
3. Write a two-page report that summarizes your findings.

2 Being Ethical and Socially Responsible

LEARNING OBJECTIVES

What you will be able to do once you complete this chapter:

1. Understand what is meant by *business ethics*.
2. Identify the types of ethical concerns that arise in the business world.
3. Discuss the factors that affect the level of ethical behavior in organizations.
4. Explain how ethical decision making can be encouraged.
5. Describe how our current views on the social responsibility of business have evolved.
6. Explain the two views on the social responsibility of business and understand the arguments for and against increased social responsibility.
7. Discuss the factors that led to the consumer movement and list some of its results.
8. Analyze how present employment practices are being used to counteract past abuses.
9. Describe the major types of pollution, their causes, and their cures.
10. Identify the steps a business must take to implement a program of social responsibility.

PRNewswire/Habitat for Humanity

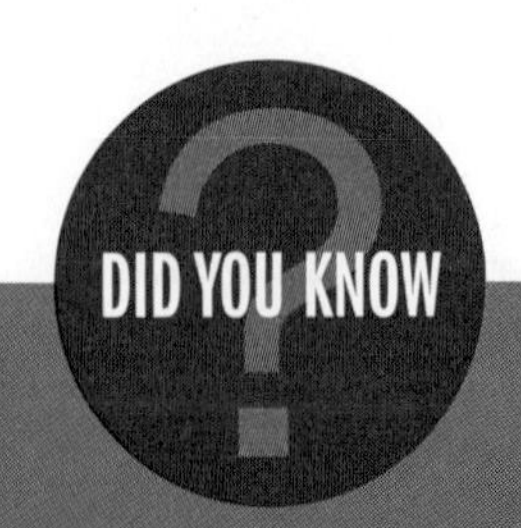

inside business

Dancing Deer donates 35 percent of the price of its Sweet Home Project cookies and gingerbread house kits to One Family, a nonprofit organization that helps homeless families.

Values Are Baked into Dancing Deer

Boston-based Dancing Deer began as a tiny start-up bakery and is now a thriving $11 million business with social responsibility baked into every product. Founded in 1994, Dancing Deer gained national recognition a few years later, when its Molasses Clove Cookie received a prestigious food industry award. Although the cookie was originally intended as a limited-time holiday item, it quickly turned into Dancing Deer's most popular year-round product.

The company makes all of its cookies, cakes, brownies, cake kits, and pancake mixes without preservatives and chemicals. It wraps its all-natural gourmet goodies in environmentally friendly packaging. And it's deeply committed to supporting the inner-city neighborhoods of Boston. "We've created a brand with important values," says CEO Patricia Karter, a co-founder whose official title is "Chief Deer, Floor Sweeper."

Dancing Deer puts its social responsibility to work in Boston in two ways. First, it provides badly needed jobs by hiring locally. Its workforce of 100 full-time and 65 seasonal employees (known internally as "deer") includes many recent immigrants. No rigid hierarchy here: Employees and managers work as colleagues to get things done.

Although the company is small, its workforce enjoys many benefits, such as profit sharing, health insurance, free lunch, public transit subsidies, and—of course—cookie-tasting privileges. Not surprisingly, its employees are extremely loyal, and turnover is very low. In fact, when the company outgrew its facility in a former brewery in the Roxbury section, the CEO never considered looking outside the city limits because she knew her employees relied on public transportation to get to work.

Second, Dancing Deer is committed to supporting local community groups. It also donates boxes of cookies for nonprofit groups to sell during fundraising events. The CEO says: "Whether it's the Sweet Home Project or helping an individual walk in to Dancing Deer with no skills and walk out the door with a career, we're helping people who need it."[1]

Obviously, organizations like Dancing Deer want to be recognized as responsible corporate citizens. Such companies recognize the need to harmonize their operations with environmental demands and other vital social concerns. Not all firms, however, have taken steps to encourage a consideration of social responsibility and ethics in their decisions and day-to-day activities. Some managers still regard such business practices as a poor investment, in which the cost is not worth the return. Other managers—indeed, most managers—view the cost of these practices as a necessary business expense, similar to wages or rent.

Most managers today, like those at Dancing Deer, are finding ways to balance a growing agenda of socially responsible activities with the drive to generate profits. This also happens to be a good way for a company to demonstrate its values and to attract like-minded employees, customers, and stockholders. In a highly competitive business environment, an increasing number of companies are, like Dancing Deer, seeking to set themselves apart by developing a reputation for ethical and socially responsible behavior.

We begin this chapter by defining *business ethics* and examining ethical issues. Next, we look at the standards of behavior in organizations and how ethical behavior can be encouraged. We then turn to the topic of social responsibility. We compare and contrast two present-day models of social responsibility and present arguments for and against increasing the social responsibility of business. After that, we examine the major elements of the consumer movement. We discuss how social responsibility in business has affected employment practices and environmental concerns. Finally, we consider the commitment, planning, and funding that go into a firm's program of social responsibility.

Business Ethics Defined

Learning Objective: Understand what is meant by *business ethics.*

ethics the study of right and wrong and of the morality of the choices individuals make

business ethics the application of moral standards to business situations

Ethics is the study of right and wrong and of the morality of the choices individuals make. An ethical decision or action is one that is "right" according to some standard of behavior. **Business ethics** is the application of moral standards to business situations. Recent court cases involving unethical behavior have helped to make business ethics a matter of public concern. In one such case, Copley Pharmaceutical, Inc., pled guilty to federal criminal charges (and paid a $10.65 million fine) for falsifying drug manufacturers' reports to the Food and Drug Administration. In another much-publicized case, lawsuits against tobacco companies have led to $246 billion in settlements, although there has been only one class-action lawsuit filed on behalf of all smokers. That case, *Engle* v. *R. J. Reynolds* could cost tobacco companies an estimated $500 billion. In yet another case, Adelphia Communications Corp., the nation's fifth-largest cable television company agreed to pay $715 million to settle federal investigations stemming from rampant earnings manipulation by its founder John J. Rigas and his son, Timothy J. Rigas. Prosecutors and government regulators charged that the Rigases had misappropriated Adelphia funds for their own use and had failed to pay the corporation for securities they controlled.[2]

Ethical Issues

Learning Objective: Identify the types of ethical concerns that arise in the business world.

Ethical issues often arise out of a business's relationship with investors, customers, employees, creditors, or competitors. Each of these groups has specific concerns and usually exerts pressure on the organization's managers. For example, investors want management to make sensible financial decisions that will boost sales, profits, and returns on their investments. Customers expect a firm's products to be safe, reliable,

Meet Lehman Brothers Holding Inc.'s chief executive Richard S. Fuld Jr., who earned more than $40 million in 2007. *Here, Mr. Fuld is hassled by protesters as he leaves Capitol Hill after testifying before the House Oversight and Government Reform Committee. Just days from becoming the largest bankruptcy in U.S. history, Lehman Brothers gave millions to departing executives even while pleading for a federal bailout plan.*

AP Photo/Susan Walsh

Ethics Matters

Says Who?

When consumers don't know who is behind a business communication, is it mysterious or is it misleading? Knowing that customers may tune out traditional advertising, some companies try to reach out in less conventional ways. However, communications that are meant to intrigue may actually backfire instead:

- Sony and Wal-Mart both faced criticism when they set up promotional blogs that appeared to have been written by ordinary people rather than being company sponsored.
- Questions were raised when one of AT&T's ad agencies had "Bobby Choice"—not his real name—talk up the company's U-verse television service in person and on a special website, arguing for choices beyond cable television.

Although anonymous marketing activities are largely outlawed in the United Kingdom, companies are not always required to disclose their sponsorship of business communications in the United States. In fact, some companies hire specialized agencies to create a buzz by having "brand ambassadors" start conversations about their products. To avoid misunderstandings, the Word of Mouth Marketing Association has established a three-point ethics code for such situations. Brand ambassadors should: (1) say who they're speaking for, (2) say what they believe, and (3) not obscure their identities.

Sources: "Sowing the Seeds of Change," *Marketing Week*, May 29, 2008, p. 18; Jonathan Lucas, "Stealth Marketing Hits SoNo Scene," *Stamford Advocate (Stamford, CT)*, June 17, 2007, n.p.; Angelo Fernando, "Transparency Under Attack," *Communication World*, March-April 2007, pp. 9+; **womma.org.**

and reasonably priced. Employees demand to be treated fairly in hiring, promotion, and compensation decisions. Creditors require accounts to be paid on time and the accounting information furnished by the firm to be accurate. Competitors expect the firm's competitive practices to be fair and honest. Consider TAP Pharmaceutical Products, Inc., whose sales representatives offered every urologist in the United States a big-screen TV, computers, fax machines, and golf vacations if the doctors prescribed TAP's new prostate cancer drug Lupron. Moreover, the sales representatives sold Lupron at cut-rate prices or gratis while defrauding Medicare. Recently, the federal government won an $875 million judgment against TAP.[3]

In late 2006, Hewlett-Packard Co.'s chairman, Patricia Dunn, and general counsel, Ann Baskins, resigned amid allegations that the company used intrusive tactics in observing the personal lives of journalists and company's directors, thus tarnishing Hewlett-Packard's reputation for integrity. According to Congressman John Dingell of Michigan, "We have before us witnesses from Hewlett-Packard to discuss a plunderers' operation that would make (former president) Richard Nixon blush were he still alive."

Businesspeople face ethical issues every day, and some of these issues can be difficult to assess. Although some types of issues arise infrequently, others occur regularly. Let's take a closer look at several ethical issues.

Fairness and Honesty

Fairness and honesty in business are two important ethical concerns. Besides obeying all laws and regulations, businesspeople are expected to refrain from knowingly deceiving, misrepresenting, or intimidating others. The consequences of failing to do so can be expensive. Recently, for example, Keith E. Anderson and Wayne Anderson, the leaders of an international tax shelter scheme known as Anderson's Ark and Associates, were sentenced to as many as twenty years in prison. The Andersons, among their associates, were ordered to pay over $200 million in fines and restitution.[4] In yet another case, the accounting firm PricewaterhouseCoopers LLP agreed to pay the U.S. government $42 million to resolve allegations that it made false claims in connection with travel reimbursements it collected for several federal agencies.[5]

Deere & Company requires each employee to deal fairly with its customers, suppliers, competitors, and employees. "No employee should take unfair advantage of anyone through manipulation, concealment, abuse of privileged information, misrepresentation of material facts or any other unfair dealing practice."[6]

Personal data security breaches have become a major threat to personal privacy in the new millennium. Can businesses keep your personal data secure?

Organizational Relationships

A businessperson may be tempted to place his or her personal welfare above the welfare of others or the welfare of the organization. For example, in late 2002, former CEO of Tyco International, Ltd., Leo Dennis Kozlowski was indicted for misappropriating $43 million in corporate funds to make philanthropic contributions in his own name, including $5 million to Seton Hall University, which named its new business-school building Kozlowski Hall. Furthermore, according to Tyco, the former CEO took $61.7 million in interest-free relocation loans without the board's permission. He allegedly used the money to finance many personal luxuries, including a $15 million yacht and a $3.9 million Renoir painting, and to throw a $2 million party for his wife's birthday.[7] Relationships with customers and coworkers often create ethical problems. Unethical behavior in these areas includes taking credit for others' ideas or work, not meeting one's commitments in a mutual agreement, and pressuring others to behave unethically.

Conflict of Interest

Conflict of interest results when a businessperson takes advantage of a situation for his or her own personal interest rather than for the employer's interest. Such conflict may occur when payments and gifts make their way into business deals. A wise rule to remember is that anything given to a person that might unfairly influence that person's business decision is a bribe, and all bribes are unethical.

For example, Nortel Networks Corporation does not permit its employees, officers, and directors to accept any gifts or to serve as directors or officers of any organization that might supply goods or services to Nortel Networks. However, Nortel employees may work part time with firms that are not competitors, suppliers, or customers. At AT&T, employees are instructed to discuss with their supervisors any investments that may seem improper. Verizon Communications forbids its employees and executives from holding a "significant" financial stake in vendors, suppliers, or customers.

At Procter & Gamble Company (P&G), all employees are obligated to act at all times solely in the best interests of the company. A conflict of interest arises when an employee has a personal relationship or financial or other interest that could interfere with this obligation or when an employee uses his or her position with the company for personal gain. P&G requires employees to disclose all potential conflicts of interest and to take prompt actions to eliminate a conflict when the company asks them to do so. Receiving gifts, entertainment, or other gratuities from people with whom P&G does business generally is not acceptable because doing so could imply an obligation on the part of the company and potentially pose a conflict of interest.

Communications

Business communications, especially advertising, can present ethical questions. False and misleading advertising is illegal and unethical, and it can infuriate customers. Sponsors of advertisements aimed at children must be especially careful to avoid misleading messages. Advertisers of health-related products also must take precautions to guard against deception when using such descriptive terms as *low fat, fat free,* and *light.* In fact, the Federal Trade Commission has issued guidelines on the use of these labels.

Factors Affecting Ethical Behavior

3 Learning Objective: Discuss the factors that affect the level of ethical behavior in organizations.

Is it possible for an individual with strong moral values to make ethically questionable decisions in a business setting? What factors affect a person's inclination to make either ethical or unethical decisions in a business organization? Although the answers to these questions are not entirely clear, three general sets of factors do appear to influence the standards of behavior in an organization. As shown in Figure 2.1, the sets consist of individual factors, social factors, and opportunity.

Individual Factors Affecting Ethics

Several individual factors influence the level of ethical behavior in an organization.

- *Individual knowledge of an issue.* How much an individual knows about an issue is one factor. A decision maker with a greater amount of knowledge regarding a situation may take steps to avoid ethical problems, whereas a less-informed person may take action unknowingly that leads to an ethical quagmire.

Figure 2.1: Factors That Affect the Level of Ethical Behavior in an Organization

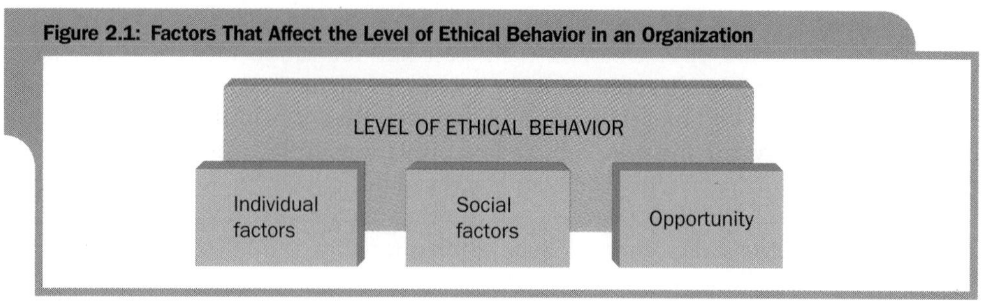

Source: Based on O. C. Ferrell and Larry Gresham, "A Contingency Framework for Understanding Ethical Decision Making in Marketing," *Journal of Marketing*, Summer 1985, p. 89.

- *Personal values.* An individual's moral values and central, value-related attitudes also clearly influence his or her business behavior. Most people join organizations to accomplish personal goals.
- *Personal goals.* The types of personal goals an individual aspires to and the manner in which these goals are pursued have a significant impact on that individual's behavior in an organization. The actions of specific individuals in scandal-plagued companies such as Adelphia, Arthur Anderson, Enron, Halliburton, Qwest, and WorldCom often raise questions about individuals' personal character and integrity.

Social Factors Affecting Ethics

- *Cultural norms.* A person's behavior in the workplace, to some degree, is determined by cultural norms, and these social factors vary from one culture to another. For example, in some countries it is acceptable and ethical for customs agents to receive gratuities for performing ordinary, legal tasks that are a part of their jobs, whereas in other countries these practices would be viewed as unethical and perhaps illegal.
- *Coworkers.* The actions and decisions of coworkers constitute another social factor believed to shape a person's sense of business ethics. For example, if your coworkers make long-distance telephone calls on company time and at company expense, you might view that behavior as acceptable and ethical because everyone does it.
- *Significant others.* The moral values and attitudes of "significant others"—spouses, friends, and relatives, for instance—also can affect an employee's perception of what is ethical and unethical behavior in the workplace.
- *Use of the Internet.* Even the Internet presents new challenges for firms whose employees enjoy easy access to sites through convenient high-speed connections at work. An employee's behavior online can be viewed as offensive to coworkers and possibly lead to lawsuits against the firm if employees engage in unethical behavior on controversial websites not related to their job. Interestingly, one recent survey of employees found that most workers assume that their use of technology at work will be monitored. A large majority of employees approved of most monitoring methods such as monitoring faxes and e-mail, tracking Web use, and even recording telephone calls.

"Opportunity" as a Factor Affecting Ethics

- *Presence of opportunity. Opportunity* refers to the amount of freedom an organization gives an employee to behave unethically if he or she makes that choice. In some organizations, certain company policies and procedures reduce the opportunity to be unethical. For example, at some fast-food restaurants, one employee takes your order and receives your payment, and another fills the order. This procedure reduces the opportunity to be unethical because the person handling the money is not dispensing the product, and the person giving out the product is not handling the money.

- *Ethical codes.* The existence of an ethical code and the importance management places on this code are other determinants of opportunity (codes of ethics are discussed in more detail in the next section).
- *Enforcement.* The degree of enforcement of company policies, procedures, and ethical codes is a major force affecting opportunity. When violations are dealt with consistently and firmly, the opportunity to be unethical is reduced.

Do you make personal telephone calls on company time? Many individuals do. Although most employees limit personal calls to a few minutes, some make personal calls in excess of thirty minutes. Whether or not you use company time and equipment to make personal calls is an example of a personal ethical decision.

Now that we have considered some of the factors believed to influence the level of ethical behavior in the workplace, let's explore what can be done to encourage ethical behavior and to discourage unethical behavior.

SPOTLIGHT

Items That Employees Pilfer in the Workplace

Source: "Top Item Employees Pilfer," The most popular items employees take from office-supply rooms for matters unrelated to the job. Vault's office survey of 1152 respondents. In Snapshots, *USA Today,* March 29, 2006, B1. Reprinted with permission.

Encouraging Ethical Behavior

4

Learning Objective: Explain how ethical decision making can be encouraged.

Most authorities agree that there is room for improvement in business ethics. A more problematic question is: Can business be made more ethical in the real world? The majority opinion on this issue suggests that government, trade associations, and individual firms indeed can establish acceptable levels of ethical behavior.

Government's Role in Encouraging Ethics

The government can encourage ethical behavior by legislating more stringent regulations. For example, the landmark **Sarbanes-Oxley Act of 2002** provides sweeping new legal protection for those who report corporate misconduct. At the signing ceremony, President George W. Bush stated, "The act adopts tough new provisions to deter and punish corporate and accounting fraud and corruption, ensure justice for wrongdoers, and protect the interests of workers and shareholders." Among other things, the law deals with corporate responsibility, conflicts of interest, and corporate accountability. However, rules require enforcement, and the unethical businessperson frequently seems to "slip something by" without getting caught. Increased regulation may help, but it surely cannot solve the entire ethics problem.

Sarbanes-Oxley Act of 2002 provides sweeping new legal protection for employees who report corporate misconduct

Trade Associations' Role in Encouraging Ethics

Trade associations can and often do provide ethical guidelines for their members. These organizations, which operate within particular industries, are in an excellent position to exert pressure on members who stoop to questionable business practices. For example, recently, a pharmaceutical trade group adopted a new set of guidelines to halt the extravagant dinners and other gifts sales representatives often give to physicians. However, enforcement and authority vary from association to association. And because trade associations exist for the benefit of their members, harsh measures may be self-defeating.

Individual Companies' Role in Encouraging Ethics

Codes of ethics that companies provide to their employees are perhaps the most effective way to encourage ethical behavior. A **code of ethics** is a written guide to

code of ethics a guide to acceptable and ethical behavior as defined by the organization

The year of the whistle-blower. *Meet Cynthia Cooper of WorldCom, Coleen Rowley of the FBI, and Sherron Watkins of Enron who couldn't take it any more. These employees with high personal ethics blew the whistle on unethical practices in their organizations. For their bold stands, which had profound effects, they were featured on the cover of* Time's *Persons of the Year.*

acceptable and ethical behavior as defined by an organization; it outlines uniform policies, standards, and punishments for violations. Because employees know what is expected of them and what will happen if they violate the rules, a code of ethics goes a long way toward encouraging ethical behavior. However, codes cannot possibly cover every situation. Companies also must create an environment in which employees recognize the importance of complying with the written code. Managers must provide direction by fostering communication, actively modeling and encouraging ethical decision making, and training employees to make ethical decisions.

During the 1980s, an increasing number of organizations created and implemented ethics codes. In a recent survey of *Fortune* 1000 firms, 93 percent of the companies that responded reported having a formal code of ethics. Some companies are now even taking steps to strengthen their codes. For example, to strengthen its accountability, the Healthcare Financial Management Association recently revised its code to designate contact persons who handle reports of ethics violations, to clarify how its board of directors should deal with violations of business ethics, and to guarantee a fair hearing process. S. C. Johnson & Son, makers of Pledge, Drano, Windex, and many other household products, is another firm that recognizes that it must behave in ways the public perceives as ethical; its code includes expectations for employees and its commitment to consumers, the community, and society in general. As shown in Figure 2.2, included in the ethics code of electronics giant Texas Instruments (TI) are issues relating to policies and procedures; laws and regulations; relationships with customers, suppliers, and competitors; conflicts of interest; handling of proprietary information; and code enforcement.

Assigning an ethics officer who coordinates ethical conduct gives employees someone to consult if they are not sure of the right thing to do. An ethics officer meets with employees and top management to provide ethical advice, establishes and maintains an anonymous confidential service to answer questions about ethical issues, and takes action on ethics code violations.

Sometimes even employees who want to act ethically may find it difficult to do so. Unethical practices can become ingrained in an organization. Employees with high personal ethics then may take a controversial step called *whistle-blowing*. **Whistle-blowing** is informing the press or government officials about unethical practices within one's organization.

whistle-blowing informing the press or government officials about unethical practices within one's organization

The year 2002 was labeled as the "Year of the Whistle-blower." Consider Joe Speaker, a 40-year-old acting chief financial officer (CFO) at Rite Aid Corp. in 1999. He discovered that inventories at Rite Aid had been overvalued and that millions in expenses had not been reported properly. Further digging into Rite Aid's books revealed that $541 million in earnings over the previous two years were really $1.6 billion in losses. Mr. Speaker was a main government witness when former Rite Aid Corp. Chairman and CEO Martin L. Grass went on trial. Mr. Speaker is among dozens of corporate managers who have blown the whistle. Enron's Sherron S. Watkins and WorldCom's Cynthia Cooper are now well-known whistle-blowers and *Time* magazine's persons of the year 2002. According to Linda Chatman Thomsen, deputy director for enforcement at the Securities and Exchange Commission, "Whistle-blowers give us an insider's perspective and have advanced our investigation immeasurably."

Whistle-blowing could have averted disaster and prevented needless deaths in the *Challenger* space shuttle disaster, for example. How could employees have known about life-threatening problems and let them pass? Whistle-blowing, on the other hand, can have serious repercussions for employees: Those who "blow whistles" sometimes lose their jobs. However, the Sarbanes-Oxley Act of 2002 protects whistle-blowers who report corporate misconduct. Any executive who

Figure 2.2: Defining Acceptable Behavior: Texas Instruments' Code of Ethics

Texas Instruments encourages ethical behavior through an extensive training program and a written code of ethics and shared values.

TEXAS INSTRUMENTS CODE OF ETHICS

"Integrity is the foundation on which TI is built. There is no other characteristic more essential to a TIer's makeup. It has to be present at all levels. Integrity is expected of managers and individuals when they make commitments. They are expected to stand by their commitments to the best of their ability.

One of TI's greatest strengths is its values and ethics. We had some early leaders who set those values as the standard for how they lived their lives. And it is important that TI grew that way. It's something that we don't want to lose. At the same time, we must move more rapidly. But we don't want to confuse that with the fact that we're ethical and we're moral. We're very responsible, and we live up to what we say."

Tom Engibous, President and CEO
Texas Instruments, 1997

We Respect and Value People By:

Treating others as we want to be treated.

- Exercising the basic virtues of respect, dignity, kindness, courtesy and manners in all work relationships.
- Recognizing and avoiding behaviors that others may find offensive, including the manner in which we speak and relate to one another and the materials we bring into the workplace, both printed and electronically.
- Respecting the right and obligation of every TIer to resolve concerns relating to ethics questions in the course of our duties without retribution and retaliation.
- Giving all TIers the same opportunity to have their questions, issues and situations fairly considered while understanding that being treated fairly does not always mean that we will all be treated the same.
- Trusting one another to use sound judgment in our use of TI business and information systems.
- Understanding that even though TI has the obligation to monitor its business information systems activity, we will respect privacy by prohibiting random searches of individual TIers' communications.
- Recognizing that conduct socially and professionally acceptable in one culture and country may be viewed differently in another.

We Are Honest By:

Representing ourselves and our intentions truthfully.

- Offering full disclosure and withdrawing ourselves from discussions and decisions when our business judgment appears to be in conflict with a personal interest.
- Respecting the rights and property of others, including their intellectual property. Accepting confidential or trade secret information only after we clearly understand our obligations as defined in a nondisclosure agreement.
- Competing fairly without collusion or collaboration with competitors to divide markets, set prices, restrict production, allocate customers or otherwise restrain competition.
- Assuring that no payments or favors are offered to influence others to do something wrong.
- Keeping records that are accurate and include all payments and receipts.
- Exercising good judgment in the exchange of business courtesies, meals and entertainment by avoiding activities that could create even the appearance that our decisions could be compromised.
- Refusing to speculate in TI stock through frequent buying and selling or through other forms of speculative trading.

Source: Courtesy of Texas Instruments, **www.ti.com/corp/docs/csr/corpgov/ethics/index.shtml**, accessed November 25, 2008.

retaliates against a whistle-blower can be held criminally liable and imprisoned for up to ten years.

Retaliations do occur, however. For example, in 2005, the U.S. Court of Appeals for the 8th Circuit unanimously upheld the right of Jane Turner, a twenty-five-year veteran FBI agent, to obtain monetary damages and a jury trial against the FBI. The court held that Ms. Turner presented sufficient facts to justify a trial by jury based on the FBI's retaliatory transfer of Ms. Turner from her investigatory position in Minot, North Dakota, to a demeaning desk job in Minneapolis. Kris Kolesnik, executive director of the National Whistle Blower Center, said, "Jane Turner is an American hero. She refused to be silent when her co-agents committed misconduct in a child rape case. She refused to be silent when her co-agents stole property from Ground Zero. She paid the price and lost her job. The 8th Circuit Court did the right thing and insured that justice will take place in her case."[8]

When firms set up anonymous hotlines to handle ethically questionable situations, employees actually may be more likely to engage in whistle-blowing. When firms instead create an environment that educates employees and nurtures ethical behavior, fewer ethical problems arise, and ultimately, the need for whistle-blowing is greatly reduced.

It is difficult for an organization to develop ethics codes, policies, and procedures to deal with all relationships and every situation. When no company policy or procedures exist or apply, a quick test to determine if a behavior is ethical is to see if others—coworkers, customers, and suppliers—approve of it. Ethical decisions always will withstand scrutiny. Openness and communication about choices often will build trust and strengthen business relationships. Table 2.1 provides some general guidelines for making ethical decisions.

Social Responsibility

social responsibility the recognition that business activities have an impact on society and the consideration of that impact in business decision making

Social responsibility is the recognition that business activities have an impact on society and the consideration of that impact in business decision making. In the first few days after Hurricane Katrina hit New Orleans, Wal-Mart delivered $20 million in cash (including $4 million to employees displaced by the storm), 100 truckloads of free merchandise, and food for 100,000 meals. The company also promised a job elsewhere for every one of its workers affected by the catastrophe. Obviously, social responsibility costs money. It is perhaps not so obvious—except in isolated cases—that social responsibility is also good business. Customers eventually find out which firms are acting responsibly and which are not. And just as easily as they cast their dollar votes for a product made by a company that is socially responsible, they can vote against the firm that is not.

Table 2.1: Guidelines for Making Ethical Decisions

1. Listen and learn.	Recognize the problem or decision-making opportunity that confronts your company, team, or unit. Don't argue, criticize, or defend yourself—keep listening and reviewing until you are sure that you understand others.
2. Identify the ethical issues.	Examine how coworkers and consumers are affected by the situation or decision at hand. Examine how you feel about the situation, and attempt to understand the viewpoint of those involved in the decision or in the consequences of the decision.
3. Create and analyze options.	Try to put aside strong feelings such as anger or a desire for power and prestige and come up with as many alternatives as possible before developing an analysis. Ask everyone involved for ideas about which options offer the best long-term results for you and the company. Then decide which option will increase your self-respect even if, in the long run, things don't work out the way you hope.
4. Identify the best option from your point of view.	Consider it and test it against some established criteria, such as respect, understanding, caring, fairness, honesty, and openness.
5. Explain your decision and resolve any differences that arise.	This may require neutral arbitration from a trusted manager or taking "time out" to reconsider, consult, or exchange written proposals before a decision is reached.

Source: Tom Rusk with D. Patrick Miller, "Doing the Right Thing," *Sky* (Delta Airlines), August 1993, pp. 18–22.

Jump-Starting Your Career

Volunteering for Experience

Can socially responsible volunteer work make a difference in your career? According to career counselors, employers, and job-seekers, volunteering can boost your career in several ways.

First, it can demonstrate your work ethic and your dedication to an important cause. The head of the Chicago recruiting firm Sklar and Associates emphasizes that volunteering "is a good way to show leadership and commitment to the community." Many companies, including General Electric and Home Depot, actively encourage employees and managers to volunteer locally as a way of giving back to the community. By listing your volunteer work on your résumé, you're telling potential employers that you share their values.

RF Corbis

Second, volunteering allows you to sharpen your communication skills, expand your personal and professional network, practice teamwork, and learn more about societal issues that directly or indirectly affect the business world. You'll also gain a broader perspective of your community and the wider world, which can be helpful in any job or career.

Finally, volunteering can help you explore a new career direction. Maybe you'll decide to work for a nonprofit organization; maybe you'll uncover an interest in public speaking or working with contributors. So go ahead and volunteer for the experience.

Sources: "Rachel, Help Me Write a Good Résumé," *Media Life*, August 28, 2008, **www.medialifemagazine.com;** Anjali Athavaley, "Home & Family: Students Craft Internships to Fit Interests," *Wall Street Journal*, March 6, 2008, p. D3; Jaclyne Badal, "On the Job: Teenagers, 'Responsible' Can Win You the Job."

Consider the following examples of organizations that are attempting to be socially responsible:

- Social responsibility can take many forms—including flying lessons. Through Young Eagles, underwritten by S. C. Johnson, Phillips Petroleum, Lockheed Martin, Jaguar, and other corporations, 22,000 volunteer pilots have taken a half million youngsters on free flights designed to teach flying basics and inspire excitement about flying careers. Young Eagles is just one of the growing number of education projects undertaken by businesses building solid records as good corporate citizens.
- The General Mills Foundation is one of the nation's largest company-sponsored foundations. Since the General Mills Foundation was created, it has awarded over $390 million to its communities. In fiscal 2007, the Foundation contributed over $20 million in grants in the communities it serves.

  In the Twin Cities, the foundation provides grants for youth nutrition and fitness, education, arts and culture, social services, and United Way. Beyond financial resources, the foundation also supports organizations with volunteers and mentors who share their expertise and talents. For example, General Mills plays a leadership role in supporting education, arts, and cultural organizations by matching employee and retiree contributions dollar for dollar. Foundation institutions matched contributions of nearly $1.8 million to eligible accredited educational and employee-supported arts and cultural organizations in 2007.[9]

Responding to the needs of communities. *Bechtel's commitment is to deliver quality and value to its customers. But its commitment also extends to improving the standard of living and quality of life of the communities where the company does business. Here, a Bechtel employee, James Beard, receives a thankful handshake from Hurricane Katrina victim John F. Smith.*

PRNewswire/Bechtel National Inc.

Corporate social responsibility may cost money, but it is also good business. *ConAgra Foods, one of North America's largest packaged food companies, is the national sponsor of Kids Cafes, which provide free meal service programs for children at-risk of hunger. Children who participate in Kids Cafe programs report earning better grades in school, having more energy, feeling less fatigued, and having improved concentration.*

Here, hungry children in Omaha, Nebraska, are enjoying an early Thanksgiving meal with turkeys donated by ConAgra Foods' Feeding Children Better Foundation and Butterball.

- As part of Dell's commitment to the community, the Dell Foundation contributes significantly to the quality of life in communities where Dell employees live and work. The foundation supports innovative and effective programs that provide fundamental prerequisites to equip youth to learn and excel in a world driven by the digital economy. The foundation supports a wide range of programs that benefit children from newborn to 18 years of age in Dell's principal U.S. locations and welcomes proposals from nonprofit organizations that address health and human services, education, and technology access for youth.

  Dell's global outreach programs include projects that bring technology to underserved communities around the world. For example, Dell Brazil launched the Digital Citizen Project in 2002 in conjunction with the State Government of Rio Grande do Sul to provide technical education to youth from low-income brackets through the creation of technology computing schools. In 2004, Dell partnered with Weyerhaeuser to deliver computers, keyboards, monitors, printers, and mouse pads to more than 100 schools in Uruguay where the technology is estimated to benefit more than 32,700 students. In addition, employees in Dell's Asia-Pacific Customer Center volunteered to create The Smart Village Project, a program to educate students in villages located near Penang, Malaysia. Dell is currently working with the Malaysian government to expand the program to more villages.[10]
- Improving public schools around the world continues to be IBM's top social priority. Its efforts are focused on preparing the next generation of leaders and workers. Through Reinventing Education and other strategic efforts, IBM is solving education's toughest problems with solutions that draw on advanced information technologies and the best minds IBM can apply. Its programs are paving the way for reforms in school systems around the world.

  To halt the spread of deadly infectious diseases threatening to reach epidemic proportions around the world, a research effort was launched by IBM,

The University of Texas Medical Branch, and the University of Chicago to discover drugs to treat and cure dengue fever, West Nile, encephalitis, hepatitis C, and other related diseases including yellow fever.[11]

IBM launched the World Community Grid in November 2004. It combines excess processing power from thousands of computers into a virtual supercomputer. This grid enables researchers to gather and analyze unprecedented quantities of data aimed at advancing research on genomic, diseases, and natural disasters. The first project, the Human Proteome Folding Project, assists in identifying cures for diseases such as malaria and tuberculosis and has registered 85,000 devices around the world to date.

- General Electric Company (GE) has a long history of supporting the communities where its employees work and live through GE's unique combination of resources, equipment, and employees' and retirees' hearts and souls. Today GE's responsibility extends to communities around the world.

  GE applies its long-standing spirit of innovation and unique set of capabilities to take on tough challenges in its communities. In 2007, GE dramatically expanded its signature programs, Developing Health Globally™ and Developing Futures™. Developing Health Globally is an initiative that began in 2004 with a $20-million product donation investment in rural African communities that has since expanded to a five-year, $30-million commitment that includes Latin America. The Developing Futures education program aims to raise standards and increase proficiency in math and science among U.S. students. To these ends, the GE Foundation has made a long-term, $100-million commitment to U.S. students beginning in five school districts (Louisville, Kentucky; Cincinnati, Ohio; Stamford, Connecticut; Erie, Pennsylvania; and Atlanta, Georgia) serving more than 215,000 students.[12]
- With the help of dedicated Schwab volunteers, Charles Schwab Foundation provides programs and funding to help individuals fill the information gap. For example, Schwab MoneyWise helps adults teach—and children learn—the basics of financial literacy. Interactive tools are available at **schwabmoneywise.com**, and local workshops cover topics such as getting kids started on a budget. In addition to these efforts, widely distributed publications and news columns by foundation President Carrie Schwab Pomerantz promote financial literacy on a wide range of topics—from savings for a child's education to bridging the health insurance gap for retirees.

  Most recently, Charles Schwab, founder and chairman of Charles Schwab Foundation, was named chairman of the newly formed President's Advisory Council on Financial Literacy. In this role, Mr. Schwab focuses national attention on the need for better financial education and helps find ways to improve financial literacy.[13]
- Improving basic literacy skills in the United States is among the Verizon Foundation's major priorities because of its enormous impact on education, health, and economic development. Here in the United States, more than 30 million American adults have basic or below average literacy skills. Thinkfinity.org is designed to improve education and literacy achievement. This comprehensive free website delivers online resources to advance student achievement. Thinkfinity delivers top-quality K-12 lesson plans, student materials, interactive tools, and connections to educational websites. It gives teachers, instructors, and parents the tools they need to increase student performance.

  In 2007, Verizon employees and retirees donated more than 485,000 hours of service and, with the Verizon Foundation, contributed $25 million in combined matching gift funds, making Verizon Volunteers one of the largest corporate volunteer incentive programs in the United States.

  Domestic violence is the greatest cause of injury to women between the ages of 15 and 44 in the United States—more than muggings, car accidents, and rapes combined. Furthermore, the Verizon Foundation supported domestic violence prevention organizations with $5.4 million in grants. In addition, Verizon

Grainger serves as National Founding Sponsor of the American Red Cross's **Ready When the Time Comes** ***program.*** *Since 2001, Grainger has partnered with the Red Cross to provide more than $4 million worth of financial support, essential products, and employee volunteer time. More than 400 of its employees have assembled care shelters for flood victims in Illinois, participated in a national bioterrorism response exercise, and staffed phone centers in Chicago and Denver following Hurricane Katrina.*

Wireless' HopeLine program, which puts wireless technology to work to help victims of domestic violence, collected more than 1 million no-longer-used phones, awarded more than $1.7 million in cash grants to domestic violence agencies, and distributed more than 20,000 phones—with the equivalent of 60 million minutes of service—to be used by victims of domestic violence.[14]

- ExxonMobil's commitment to education spans all levels of achievement. One of its corporate primary goals is to support basic education and literacy programs in the developing world. In areas of the world where basic education levels have been met, ExxonMobil supports education programs in science, technology, engineering, and mathematics.

  ExxonMobil recognizes the essential role that proficiency in math and science plays not only in the energy business, but also in fostering innovation and facilitating human progress. The company encourages new generations to pursue studies and careers in field involving math and science. Toward that goal, it supports programs focused on laying the foundation for long-term educational improvements, such as the National Math and Science Initiative and the Mickelson ExxonMobil Teachers Academy.

  Through its Educating Women and Girls initiative, ExxonMobil contributes to education projects in communities in which it operates around the world. Evidence shows that an educated population of women and girls fosters long-term improvements in health, greater economic growth, and increased education levels of the community as a whole. The Science Ambassador Program is one of many programs sponsored by ExxonMobil. More than 800 ExxonMobil employees and retirees serve as tutors, judge science fairs, and act as mentors and guest teachers. The program emphasizes science, math, and energy education to help encourage students to become the next generation of scientists and engineers.[15]
- AT&T has built a tradition of supporting education, health and human services, the environment, public policy, and the arts in the communities it serves

since Alexander Graham Bell founded the company over a century ago. Since 1984, AT&T has invested more than $600 million in support of education. Currently, more than half the company's contribution dollars, employee volunteer time, and community-service activities is directed toward education. In 1995, AT&T created the AT&T Learning Network, a $150 million corporate commitment to support the education of children in schools across the nation by providing the latest technology and cash grants to schools and communities. Since 1911, AT&T has been a sponsor to the Telephone Pioneers of America, the world's largest industry-based volunteer organization consisting of nearly 750,000 employees and retirees from the telecommunications industry. Each year, the Pioneers volunteer millions of hours and raise millions of dollars for health and human services and the environment. For example, through the AT&T Pioneers, nearly 350,000 AT&T employees and retirees contributed more than 10 million hours of volunteer time to community outreach activities nationwide in 2007. In schools and neighborhoods, the Pioneers strengthen connections and build communities.

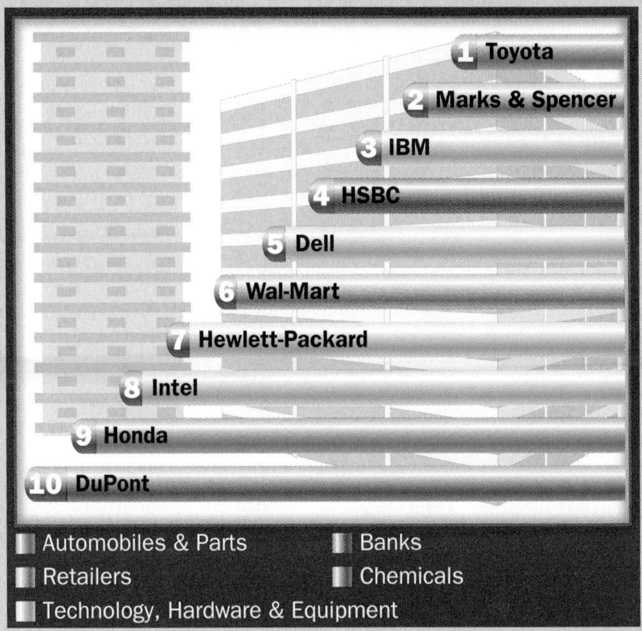

Source: Covalence Ethical Ranking 2007 Press Release 2 January 2008, © Covalence SA 2008 1, http://www.covalence.ch/docs/CovalenceEthicalRanking2007_PressRelease_02.01.2008.pdf.

In 2007, AT&T contributed more than $164 million to nonprofit organizations through corporate, employee, and AT&T Foundation-sponsored giving. AT&T's philanthropy is focused on education and workforce readiness. The AT&T Foundation, widely recognized as one of the more generous corporate foundations, provides more than 55 percent of its grants to underserved populations.

More than 20 percent of eligible voters in the 2008 presidential election were under 29, a demographic that includes some of the heaviest users of mobile phones and text messaging. That's why AT&T is working with Rock the Vote, a nonpartisan, nonprofit organization, to connect with these young citizens in their "own tongue," encouraging them to register to vote and receive news and reminders about the election by sending a text message. They can also download exclusive celebrity ringtones that promote the importance of voting.[16]

- At Merck & Co., Inc., the Patient Assistance Program makes the company's medicines available to low-income Americans and their families at no cost. When patients don't have health insurance or a prescription drug plan and are unable to afford the Merck medicines their doctors prescribe, they can work with their physicians to contact the Merck Patient Assistance Program. For nearly 50 years, Merck has provided its medicines completely free of charge to people in need through this program. Patients can get information through **www.merck.com** or by calling a toll-free number, 1-800-727-5400, or from their physician's office. For eligible patients, the medicines are shipped directly to their home or the prescribing physician's office. Each applicant may receive up to one year of medicines, and patients may reapply to the program if their need continues.

  Education programs often link social responsibility with corporate self-interest. For example, Bayer and Merck, two major pharmaceuticals firms, promote science education as a way to enlarge the pool of future employees. Students who visit the Bayer Science Forum in Elkhart, Indiana, work alongside scientists conducting a variety of experiments. And workshops created by the Merck Institute for Science Education show teachers how to put scientific principles into action through hands-on experiments.

These are just a few illustrations from the long list of companies big and small that attempt to behave in socially responsible ways. In general, people are more likely to want to work for and buy from such organizations.

The Evolution of Social Responsibility in Business

5

Learning Objective: Describe how our current views on the social responsibility of business have evolved.

Business is far from perfect in many respects, but its record of social responsibility today is much better than in past decades. In fact, present demands for social responsibility have their roots in outraged reactions to the abusive business practices of the early 1900s.

Historical Evolution of Business Social Responsibility

During the first quarter of the twentieth century, businesses were free to operate pretty much as they chose. Government protection of workers and consumers was minimal. As a result, people either accepted what business had to offer or they did without. Working conditions often were deplorable by today's standards. The average work week in most industries exceeded sixty hours, no minimum-wage law existed, and employee benefits were almost nonexistent. Work areas were crowded and unsafe, and industrial accidents were the rule rather than the exception. To improve working conditions, employees organized and joined labor unions. During the early 1900s, however, businesses—with the help of government—were able to use court orders, brute force, and even the few existing antitrust laws to defeat union attempts to improve working conditions.

caveat emptor a Latin phrase meaning "let the buyer beware"

Studies show that global warming is occurring and we are causing it by burning fossil fuels (coal, oil and natural gas) and cutting forests. *The U.S. National Academy of Sciences states, "It is vital that all nations identify cost-effective steps that they can take now, to contribute to substantial and long-term reduction in net global greenhouse gas emissions." Global warming is feared to cause the world's glaciers to melt and increase the frequency and intensity of many kinds of extreme weather, such as Hurricane Katrina.*

AP Photo/US Coast Guard, Petty Officer 2nd class Kyle Niemi

During this period, consumers generally were subject to the doctrine of **caveat emptor**, a Latin phrase meaning "let the buyer beware." In other words, "what you see is what you get," and if it is not what you expected, too bad. Although victims of unscrupulous business practices could take legal action, going to court was very expensive, and consumers rarely won their cases. Moreover, no consumer groups or government agencies existed to publicize their consumers' grievances or to hold sellers accountable for their actions.

Prior to the 1930s, most people believed that competition and the action of the marketplace would, in time, correct abuses. Government therefore became involved in day-to-day business activities only in cases of obvious abuse of the free-market system. Six of the more important business-related federal laws passed between 1887 and 1914 are described in Table 2.2. As you can see, these laws were aimed more at encouraging competition than at correcting abuses, although two of them did deal with the purity of food and drug products.

The collapse of the stock market on October 29, 1929, triggered the Great Depression and years of dire economic problems for the United States. Factory production fell by almost one-half, and up to 25 percent of the nation's workforce was unemployed. Before long, public pressure mounted for government to "do something" about the economy and about worsening social conditions.

Soon after Franklin D. Roosevelt was inaugurated as president in 1933, he instituted programs to restore the economy and improve social conditions. Laws were passed to correct what many viewed as the monopolistic abuses of big business, and various social services were provided for individuals. These massive federal programs became the

Table 2.2: Early Government Regulations That Affected American Business

Government Regulation	Major Provisions
Interstate Commerce Act (1887)	First federal act to regulate business practices; provided regulation of railroads and shipping rates
Sherman Antitrust Act (1890)	Prevented monopolies or mergers where competition was endangered
Pure Food and Drug Act (1906)	Established limited supervision of interstate sale of food and drugs
Meat Inspection Act (1906)	Provided for limited supervision of interstate sale of meat and meat products
Federal Trade Commission Act (1914)	Created the Federal Trade Commission to investigate illegal trade practices
Clayton Antitrust Act (1914)	Eliminated many forms of price discrimination that gave large businesses a competitive advantage over smaller firms

foundation for increased government involvement in the dealings between business and society.

As government involvement has increased, so has everyone's awareness of the social responsibility of business. Today's business owners are concerned about the return on their investment, but at the same time most of them demand ethical behavior from employees. In addition, employees demand better working conditions, and consumers want safe, reliable products. Various advocacy groups echo these concerns and also call for careful consideration of our earth's delicate ecological balance. Managers therefore must operate in a complex business environment—one in which they are just as responsible for their managerial actions as for their actions as individual citizens. Interestingly, today's high-tech and Internet-based firms fare relatively well when it comes to environmental issues, worker conditions, the representation of minorities and women in upper management, animal testing, and charitable donations.

Two Views of Social Responsibility

6

Learning Objective: Explain the two views on the social responsibility of business and understand the arguments for and against increased social responsibility.

Government regulation and public awareness are *external* forces that have increased the social responsibility of business. But business decisions are made *within* the firm—and there, social responsibility begins with the attitude of management. Two contrasting philosophies, or models, define the range of management attitudes toward social responsibility.

The Economic Model

According to the traditional concept of business, a firm exists to produce quality goods and services, earn a reasonable profit, and provide jobs. In line with this concept, the **economic model of social responsibility** holds that society will benefit most when business is left alone to produce and market profitable products that society needs. The economic model has its origins in the eighteenth century, when businesses were owned primarily by entrepreneurs or owner-managers. Competition was vigorous among small firms, and short-run profits and survival were the primary concerns.

economic model of social responsibility the view that society will benefit most when business is left alone to produce and market profitable products that society needs

To the manager who adopts this traditional attitude, social responsibility is someone else's job. After all, stockholders invest in a corporation to earn a return on their investment, not because the firm is socially responsible, and the firm is legally obligated to act in the economic interest of its stockholders. Moreover, profitable firms pay federal, state, and local taxes that are used to meet the needs of society. Thus, managers who concentrate on profit believe that they fulfill their social responsibility indirectly through the taxes paid by their firms. As a result, social responsibility becomes the problem of government, various environmental groups, charitable foundations, and similar organizations.

The Socioeconomic Model

In contrast, some managers believe that they have a responsibility not only to stockholders but also to customers, employees, suppliers, and the general public. This broader view is referred to as the **socioeconomic model of social responsibility**, which places emphasis not only on profits but also on the impact of business decisions on society.

socioeconomic model of social responsibility the concept that business should emphasize not only profits but also the impact of its decisions on society

Recently, increasing numbers of managers and firms have adopted the socioeconomic model, and they have done so for at least three reasons. First, business is dominated by the corporate form of ownership, and the corporation is a creation of society. If a corporation does not perform as a good citizen, society can and will demand changes. Second, many firms have begun to take pride in their social responsibility records, among them Starbucks Coffee, Hewlett-Packard, Colgate-Palmolive, and Coca-Cola. Each of these companies is a winner of a Corporate Conscience Award in the areas of environmental concern, responsiveness to employees, equal opportunity, and community involvement. And of course, many other corporations are much more socially responsible today than they were ten years ago. Third, many businesspeople believe that it is in their best interest to take the initiative in this area. The alternative may be legal action brought against the firm by some special-interest group; in such a situation, the firm may lose control of its activities.

The Pros and Cons of Social Responsibility

Business owners, managers, customers, and government officials have debated the pros and cons of the economic and socioeconomic models for years. Each side seems to have four major arguments to reinforce its viewpoint.

Arguments for Increased Social Responsibility Proponents of the socioeconomic model maintain that a business must do more than simply seek profits. To support their position, they offer the following arguments:

1. Because business is a part of our society, it cannot ignore social issues.
2. Business has the technical, financial, and managerial resources needed to tackle today's complex social issues.
3. By helping resolve social issues, business can create a more stable environment for long-term profitability.
4. Socially responsible decision making by firms can prevent increased government intervention, which would force businesses to do what they fail to do voluntarily.

These arguments are based on the assumption that a business has a responsibility not only to its stockholders but also to its customers, employees, suppliers, and the general public.

Arguments Against Increased Social Responsibility Opponents of the socioeconomic model argue that business should do what it does best: earn a profit by manufacturing and marketing products that people want. Those who support this position argue as follows:

1. Business managers are responsible primarily to stockholders, so management must be concerned with providing a return on owners' investments.
2. Corporate time, money, and talent should be used to maximize profits, not to solve society's problems.
3. Social problems affect society in general, so individual businesses should not be expected to solve these problems.
4. Social issues are the responsibility of government officials who are elected for that purpose and who are accountable to the voters for their decisions.

Table 2.3: A Comparison of the Economic and Socioeconomic Models of Social Responsibility as Implemented in Business

Economic Model Primary Emphasis		Socioeconomic Model Primary Emphasis
1. Production		1. Quality of life
2. Exploitation of natural resources		2. Conservation of natural resources
3. Internal, market-based decisions	Middle ground	3. Market-based decisions, with some community controls
4. Economic return (profit)		4. Balance of economic return and social return
5. Firm's or manager's interest		5. Firm's and community's interests
6. Minor role for government		6. Active government

Source: Adapted from Keith Davis, William C. Frederick, and Robert L. Blomstron, *Business and Society: Concepts and Policy Issues* (New York: McGraw-Hill, 1980), p. 9. Used by permission of McGraw-Hill Book Company.

These arguments obviously are based on the assumption that the primary objective of business is to earn profits and that government and social institutions should deal with social problems.

Table 2.3 compares the economic and socioeconomic viewpoints in terms of business emphasis. Today, few firms are either purely economic or purely socioeconomic in outlook; most have chosen some middle ground between the two extremes. However, our society generally seems to want—and even to expect—some degree of social responsibility from business. Thus, within this middle ground, businesses are leaning toward the socioeconomic view. In the next several sections, we look at some results of this movement in four specific areas: consumerism, employment practices, concern for the environment, and implementation of social responsibility programs.

Consumerism

7 Learning Objective: Discuss the factors that led to the consumer movement and list some of its results.

Consumerism consists of all activities undertaken to protect the rights of consumers. The fundamental issues pursued by the consumer movement fall into three categories: environmental protection, product performance and safety, and information disclosure. Although consumerism has been with us to some extent since the early nineteenth century, the consumer movement became stronger in the 1960s. It was then that President John F. Kennedy declared that the consumer was entitled to a new "bill of rights."

consumerism all activities undertaken to protect the rights of consumers

The Six Basic Rights of Consumers

President Kennedy's consumer bill of rights asserted that consumers have a right to safety, to be informed, to choose, and to be heard. Two additional rights added since 1975 are the right to consumer education and the right to courteous service. These six rights are the basis of much of the consumer-oriented legislation passed during the last forty years. These rights also provide an effective outline of the objectives and accomplishments of the consumer movement.

The Right to Safety The consumers' right to safety means that the products they purchase must be safe for their intended use, must include thorough and explicit directions for proper use, and must be tested by the manufacturer to ensure product quality and reliability. There are several reasons why American business firms must be concerned about product safety.

The Food Safety and Inspection Service, a public health regulating agency of the U.S. Department of Agriculture, protects consumers by ensuring that meat, poultry, and egg products are safe, wholesome, and accurately labeled. *Here, Agriculture Secretary, Ed Schafer, at the Cargill meat packing plant in Schuyler, Nebraska, expresses confidence in the nation's food safety system.*

Corrective Actions Can Be Expensive. Federal agencies such as the Food and Drug Administration and the Consumer Product Safety Commission have the power to force businesses that make or sell defective products to take corrective actions. Such actions include offering refunds, recalling defective products, issuing public warnings, and reimbursing consumers—all of which can be expensive.

Increasing Number of Lawsuits. Business firms also should be aware that consumers and the government have been winning an increasing number of product-liability lawsuits against sellers of defective products. Moreover, the amount of the awards in these suits has been increasing steadily. Fearing the outcome of numerous lawsuits filed around the nation, tobacco giants Philip Morris and R. J. Reynolds, which for decades had denied that cigarettes cause illness, began negotiating in 1997 with state attorneys general, plaintiffs' lawyers, and anti-smoking activists. The tobacco giants proposed sweeping curbs on their sales and advertising practices and the payment of hundreds of billions of dollars in compensation.

Consumer Demand. Yet another major reason for improving product safety is consumers' demand for safe products. People simply will stop buying a product they believe is unsafe or unreliable.

The Right to Be Informed The right to be informed means that consumers must have access to complete information about a product before they buy it. Detailed information about ingredients and nutrition must be provided on food containers, information about fabrics and laundering methods must be attached to clothing, and lenders must disclose the true cost of borrowing the money they make available to customers who purchase merchandise on credit.

In addition, manufacturers must inform consumers about the potential dangers of using their products. Manufacturers that fail to provide such information can be held responsible for personal injuries suffered because of their products. For example, Maytag provides customers with a lengthy booklet that describes how they should use an automatic clothes washer. Sometimes such warnings seem excessive, but they are necessary if user injuries (and resulting lawsuits) are to be avoided.

The Right to Choose The right to choose means that consumers must have a choice of products, offered by different manufacturers and sellers, to satisfy a particular need. The government has done its part by encouraging competition through antitrust legislation. The greater the competition, the greater is the choice available to consumers.

Competition and the resulting freedom of choice provide additional benefits for customers by reducing prices. For example, when personal computers were introduced, they cost over $5,000. Thanks to intense competition and technological advancements, personal computers today can be purchased for less than $500.

The Right to Be Heard This fourth right means that someone will listen and take appropriate action when customers complain. Actually, management began to listen to consumers after World War II, when competition between businesses that manufactured and sold consumer goods increased. One way that firms got a competitive edge was to listen to consumers and provide the products they said they wanted and needed. Today, businesses are listening even more attentively, and many larger firms have consumer relations departments that can be contacted easily via toll-free phone numbers. Other groups listen, too. Most large cities and some states have consumer affairs offices to act on citizens' complaints.

Additional Consumer Rights In 1975, President Gerald Ford added to the consumer bill of rights the right to consumer education, which entitles people to be fully informed about their rights as consumers. In 1994, President Bill Clinton added a sixth right, the right to service, which entitles consumers to convenience, courtesy, and responsiveness from manufacturers and sellers of consumer products.

Major Consumerism Forces

The major forces in consumerism are individual consumer advocates and organizations, consumer education programs, and consumer laws. Consumer advocates, such as Ralph Nader, take it on themselves to protect the rights of consumers. They band together into consumer organizations, either independently or under government sponsorship. Some organizations, such as the National Consumers' League and the Consumer Federation of America, operate nationally, whereas others are active at state and local levels. They inform and organize other consumers, raise issues, help businesses to develop consumer-oriented programs, and pressure lawmakers to enact consumer protection laws. Some consumer advocates and organizations encourage consumers to boycott products and businesses to which they have objections. Today, the consumer movement has adopted corporate-style marketing and addresses a broad range of issues. Current campaigns include efforts (1) to curtail the use of animals for testing purposes, (2) to reduce liquor and cigarette billboard advertising in low-income, inner-city neighborhoods, and (3) to encourage recycling.

Educating consumers to make wiser purchasing decisions is perhaps one of the most far-reaching aspects of consumerism. Increasingly, consumer education is becoming a part of high school and college curricula and adult-education programs. These programs cover many topics—for instance, what major factors should be considered when buying specific products, such as insurance, real estate, automobiles, appliances and furniture, clothes, and food; the provisions of certain consumer-protection laws; and the sources of information that can help individuals become knowledgeable consumers.

Table 2.4: Major Federal Legislation Protecting Consumers Since 1960

Legislation	Major Provisions
Federal Hazardous Substances Labeling Act (1960)	Required warning labels on household chemicals if they are highly toxic
Kefauver-Harris Drug Amendments (1962)	Established testing practices for drugs and required manufacturers to label drugs with generic names in addition to trade names
Cigarette Labeling Act (1965)	Required manufacturers to place standard warning labels on all cigarette packages and advertising
Fair Packaging and Labeling Act (1966)	Called for all products sold across state lines to be labeled with net weight, ingredients, and manufacturer's name and address
Motor Vehicle Safety Act (1966)	Established standards for safer cars
Wholesome Meat Act (1967)	Required states to inspect meat (but not poultry) sold within the state
Flammable Fabrics Act (1967)	Extended flammability standards for clothing to include children's sleepwear in sizes 0 to 6X
Truth in Lending Act (1968)	Required lenders and credit merchants to disclose the full cost of finance charges in both dollars and annual percentage rates
Child Protection and Toy Act (1969)	Banned toys with mechanical or electrical defects from interstate commerce
Credit Card Liability Act (1970)	Limited credit-card holder's liability to $50 per card and stopped credit-card companies from issuing unsolicited cards
Fair Credit Reporting Act (1971)	Required credit bureaus to provide credit reports to consumers regarding their own credit files; also provided for correction of incorrect information
Consumer Product Safety Commission Act (1972)	Established the Consumer Product Safety Commission
Trade Regulation Rule (1972)	Established a "cooling off" period of 72 hours for door-to-door sales
Fair Credit Billing Act (1974)	Amended the Truth in Lending Act to enable consumers to challenge billing errors
Equal Credit Opportunity Act (1974)	Provided equal credit opportunities for males and females and for married and single individuals
Magnuson-Moss Warranty-Federal Trade Commission Act (1975)	Provided for minimum disclosure standards for written consumer-product warranties for products that cost more than $15
Amendments to the Equal Credit Opportunity Act (1976, 1994)	Prevented discrimination based on race, creed, color, religion, age, and income when granting credit
Fair Debt Collection Practices Act (1977)	Outlawed abusive collection practices by third parties
Drug Price Competition and Patent Restoration Act (1984)	Established an abbreviated procedure for registering certain generic drugs
Orphan Drug Act (1985)	Amended the original 1983 Orphan Drug Act and extended tax incentives to encourage the development of drugs for rare diseases
Nutrition Labeling and Education Act (1990)	Required the Food and Drug Administration to review current food labeling and packaging focusing on nutrition label content, label format, ingredient labeling, food descriptors and standards, and health messages
Telephone Consumer Protection Act (1991)	Prohibited the use of automated dialing and prerecorded-voice calling equipment to make calls or deliver messages
Consumer Credit Reporting Reform Act (1997)	Placed more responsibility for accurate credit data on credit issuers; required creditors to verify that disputed data are accurate and to notify a consumer before reinstating the data
Children's Online Privacy Protection Act (2000)	Placed parents in control over what information is collected online from their children under age 13; required commercial website operators to maintain the confidentiality, security, and integrity of personal information collected from children
Do Not Call Implementation Act (2003)	Directed the FCC and the FTC to coordinate so that their rules are consistent regarding telemarketing call practices including the Do Not Call Registry and other lists, as well as call abandonment

Major advances in consumerism have come through federal legislation. Some laws enacted in the last forty-four years to protect your rights as a consumer are listed and described in Table 2.4. Most businesspeople now realize that they ignore consumer issues only at their own peril. Managers know that improper handling of consumer complaints can result in lost sales, bad publicity, and lawsuits.

Employment Practices

8 Learning Objective: Analyze how present employment practices are being used to counteract past abuses.

Managers who subscribe to the socioeconomic view of a business's social responsibility, together with significant government legislation enacted to protect the buying public, have broadened the rights of consumers. The last five decades have seen similar progress in affirming the rights of employees to equal treatment in the workplace.

Everyone should have the opportunity to land a job for which he or she is qualified and to be rewarded on the basis of ability and performance. This is an important issue for society, and it also makes good business sense. Yet, over the years, this opportunity has been denied to members of various minority groups. A **minority** is a racial, religious, political, national, or other group regarded as different from the larger group of which it is a part and that is often singled out for unfavorable treatment.

minority a racial, religious, political, national, or other group regarded as different from the larger group of which it is a part and that is often singled out for unfavorable treatment

The federal government responded to the outcry of minority groups during the 1960s and 1970s by passing a number of laws forbidding discrimination in the workplace. (These laws are discussed in Chapter 9 in the context of human resources management.) Now, forty-six years after passage of the first of these (the Civil Rights Act of 1964), abuses still exist. An example is the disparity in income levels for whites, blacks, Hispanics, and Asians, as illustrated in Figure 2.3. Lower incomes and higher unemployment rates also characterize Native Americans, handicapped persons, and women. Responsible managers have instituted a number of programs to counteract the results of discrimination.

Affirmative Action Programs

An **affirmative action program** is a plan designed to increase the number of minority employees at all levels within an organization. Employers with federal contracts of more than $50,000 per year must have written affirmative action plans. The objective of such programs is to ensure that minorities are represented within the organization

affirmative action program a plan designed to increase the number of minority employees at all levels within an organization

Figure 2.3: Comparative Income Levels

This chart shows the median household incomes of white, black, Hispanic, and Asian workers in 2007.

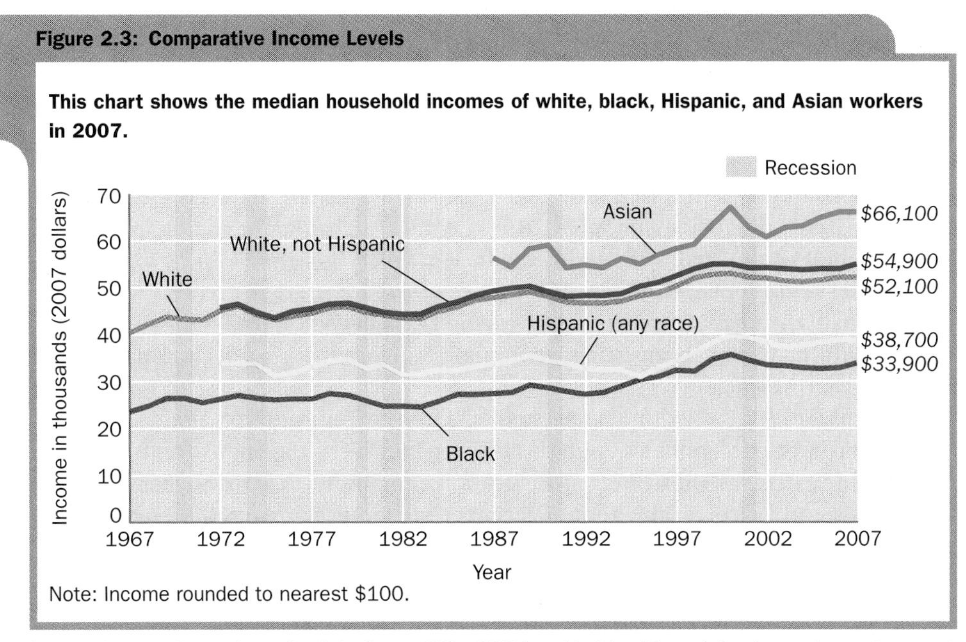

Note: Income rounded to nearest $100.

Source: U.S. Census Bureau, Current Population Survey, 1968 to 2008 Annual Social and Economic Supplements, *Income, Poverty, and Health Insurance Coverage in the United States: 2007,* issued August 2008, U.S. Census Bureau, U.S. Department of Commerce, p. 6.

Dean Duckett, a former NASCAR employee, has filed a complaint with the Equal Employment Opportunity Commission against his ex-employer. *Duckett, an African-American, stated, "During my employment I was subjected to different terms and conditions of employment and a hostile work environment because of my race and marital status and was wrongfully terminated."*

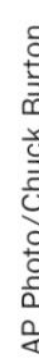

in approximately the same proportion as in the surrounding community. If 25 percent of the electricians in a geographic area in which a company is located are black, then approximately 25 percent of the electricians it employs also should be black. Affirmative action plans encompass all areas of human resources management: recruiting, hiring, training, promotion, and pay.

Unfortunately, affirmative action programs have been plagued by two problems. The first involves quotas. In the beginning, many firms pledged to recruit and hire a certain number of minority members by a specific date. To achieve this goal, they were forced to consider only minority applicants for job openings; if they hired nonminority workers, they would be defeating their own purpose. However, the courts have ruled that such quotas are unconstitutional even though their purpose is commendable. They are, in fact, a form of discrimination called *reverse discrimination.*

The second problem is that although most such programs have been reasonably successful, not all businesspeople are in favor of affirmative action programs. Managers not committed to these programs can "play the game" and still discriminate against workers. To help solve this problem, Congress created (and later strengthened) the **Equal Employment Opportunity Commission (EEOC)**, a government agency with the power to investigate complaints of employment discrimination and sue firms that practice it.

Equal Employment Opportunity Commission (EEOC) a government agency with power to investigate complaints of employment discrimination and power to sue firms that practice it

The threat of legal action has persuaded some corporations to amend their hiring and promotional policies, but the discrepancy between men's and women's salaries still exists, as illustrated in Figure 2.4. For more than fifty years, women have consistently earned only about 78 cents for each dollar earned by men.

Training Programs for the Hard-Core Unemployed

hard-core unemployed workers with little education or vocational training and a long history of unemployment

For some firms, social responsibility extends far beyond placing a help-wanted ad in the local newspaper. These firms have assumed the task of helping the **hard-core unemployed**, workers with little education or vocational training and a long history of

Figure 2.4: Relative Earnings of Male and Female Workers

The ratio of women's to men's annual full-time earnings was 78 percent in 2007, a new all-time high, up from 74 percent first reached in 1996.

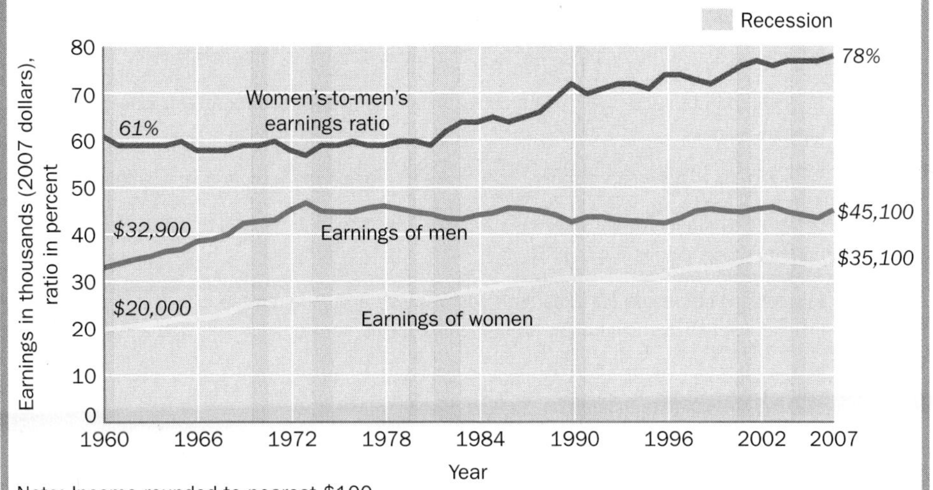

Note: Income rounded to nearest $100.

Source: U.S. Census Bureau, Current Population Survey, 1968 to 2008 Annual Social and Economic Supplements, *Income, Poverty, and Health Insurance Coverage in the United States: 2007,* issued August 2008, U.S. Census Bureau, U.S. Department of Commerce, p. 11.

unemployment. For example, a few years ago, General Mills helped establish Siyeza, a frozen soul-food processing plant in North Minneapolis. Through the years, Siyeza has provided stable, high-quality full-time jobs for a permanent core of eighty unemployed or underemployed minority inner-city residents. In addition, groups of up to a hundred temporary employees are called in when needed. In the past, such workers often were turned down routinely by personnel managers, even for the most menial jobs.

Obviously, such workers require training; just as obviously, this training can be expensive and time consuming. To share the costs, business and community leaders have joined together in a number of cooperative programs. One particularly successful partnership is the **National Alliance of Business (NAB)**, a joint business-government program to train the hard-core unemployed. The alliance's 5,000 members include companies of all sizes and industries, their CEOs and senior executives, as well as educators and community leaders. NAB, founded in 1968 by President Lyndon Johnson and Henry Ford II, is a major national business organization focusing on education and workforce issues.

National Alliance of Business (NAB) a joint business-government program to train the hard-core unemployed

Concern for the Environment

9 **Learning Objective: Describe the major types of pollution, their causes, and their cures.**

The social consciousness of responsible business managers, the encouragement of a concerned government, and an increasing concern on the part of the public have led to a major effort to reduce environmental pollution, conserve natural resources, and reverse some of the worst effects of past negligence in this area. **Pollution** is the contamination of water, air, or land through the actions of people in an industrialized society. For several decades, environmentalists have been warning us about the dangers of industrial pollution. Unfortunately, business and government leaders either ignored the problem or were not concerned about it until pollution became a threat to life and health in America. Today, Americans expect business and government leaders to take swift action to clean up our environment—and to keep it clean.

pollution the contamination of water, air, or land through the actions of people in an industrialized society

Effects of Environmental Legislation

As in other areas of concern to our society, legislation and regulations play a crucial role in pollution control. The laws outlined in Table 2.5 reflect the scope of current environmental legislation: laws to promote clean air, clean water, and even quiet work and living environments. Of major importance was the creation of the

Table 2.5: Summary of Major Environmental Laws

Legislation	Major Provisions
National Environmental Policy Act (1970)	Established the Environmental Protection Agency (EPA) to enforce federal laws that involve the environment
Clean Air Amendment (1970)	Provided stringent automotive, aircraft, and factory emission standards
Water Quality Improvement Act (1970)	Strengthened existing water pollution regulations and provided for large monetary fines against violators
Resource Recovery Act (1970)	Enlarged the solid-waste disposal program and provided for enforcement by the EPA
Water Pollution Control Act Amendment (1972)	Established standards for cleaning navigable streams and lakes and eliminating all harmful waste disposal by 1985
Noise Control Act (1972)	Established standards for major sources of noise and required the EPA to advise the Federal Aviation Administration on standards for airplanes
Clean Air Act Amendment (1977)	Established new deadlines for cleaning up polluted areas; also required review of existing air-quality standards
Resource Conservation and Recovery Act (1984)	Amended the original 1976 act and required federal regulation of potentially dangerous solid-waste disposal
Clean Air Act Amendment (1987)	Established a national air-quality standard for ozone
Oil Pollution Act (1990)	Expanded the nation's oil-spill prevention and response activities; also established the Oil Spill Liability Trust Fund
Clean Air Act Amendments (1990)	Required that motor vehicles be equipped with onboard systems to control about 90 percent of refueling vapors
Food Quality Protection Act (1996)	Amended the Federal Insecticide, Fungicide and Rodenticide Act and the Federal Food Drug and Cosmetic Act; the requirements included a new safety standard—reasonable certainty of no harm—that must be applied to all pesticides used on foods

Environmental Protection Agency (EPA), the federal agency charged with enforcing laws designed to protect the environment.

When they are aware of a pollution problem, many firms respond to it rather than wait to be cited by the EPA. Other owners and managers, however, take the position that environmental standards are too strict. (Loosely translated, this means that compliance with present standards is too expensive.) Consequently, it often has been necessary for the EPA to take legal action to force firms to install antipollution equipment and to clean up waste storage areas.

Experience has shown that the combination of environmental legislation, voluntary compliance, and EPA action can succeed in cleaning up the environment and keeping it clean. However, much still remains to be done.

Water Pollution The Clean Water Act has been credited with greatly improving the condition of the waters in the United States. This success comes largely from the control of pollutant discharges from industrial and wastewater treatment plants. Although the quality of our nation's rivers, lakes, and streams has improved significantly in recent years, many of these surface waters remain severely polluted. Currently, one of the most serious water-quality problems results from the high level of toxic pollutants found in these waters.

Among the serious threats to people posed by water pollutants are respiratory irritation, cancer, kidney and liver damage, anemia, and heart failure. Toxic pollutants also damage fish and other forms of wildlife. In fish, they cause tumors or reproductive problems; shellfish and wildlife living in or drinking from toxin-laden waters also have suffered genetic defects. Recently, the Pollution Control Board of Kerala in India ordered Coca-Cola to close its major bottling plant. For years,

The Business of Green

Best Foot Forward for Timberland

Socially responsible Timberland, based in Stratham, New Hampshire, is putting its best foot forward to label its shoe products to show their environmental impact. Just as foods carry nutrition labels and major appliances carry energy efficiency labels, Timberland's shoes carry "green index tags" rating each product in terms of greenhouse gas emissions, use of chemicals, and use of organic, renewable, or recycled materials. The lower the score, the more earth friendly the product.

According to Timberland's CEO, the idea is to help consumers "make value judgments at the point of sale." However, the labeling project has been challenging because the company had to "go back to the cow" to assess the environmental effects of raw materials provided by suppliers as well as the effect of manufacturing, transportation, and store activities.

As more shoe companies add such labeling, "it will become automatic for shoppers to compare green tags among brands, just like they compare price and color," the CEO adds. "When that happens, we'll all be fighting to have the best tag . . . no shoe company will want to be known for the least environmentally friendly shoes."

Sources: Mark Borden and Anya Kamenetz, "The Prophet CEO," *Fast Company,* September 2008, **http://www.fastcompany.com/magazine/128/the-prophet-ceo.html;** Claudia H. Deutsch, "Seeking a Joint Effort for Greener Athletic Shoes," *New York Times,* September 29, 2007, p. C2; Amy Cortese, "Friend of Nature? Let's See Those Shoes," *New York Times,* March 7, 2007, p. H5.

villagers in the nearby areas had accused Coke of depleting local groundwater and producing other local pollution. The village council president said, "We are happy that the government is finally giving justice to the people who are affected by the plant."

The task of water cleanup has proved to be extremely complicated and costly because of pollution runoff and toxic contamination. And yet improved water quality is not only necessary; it is also achievable. Consider Cleveland's Cuyahoga River. A few years ago, the river was so contaminated by industrial wastes that it burst into flames one hot summer day! Now, after a sustained community cleanup effort, the river is pure enough for fish to thrive in.

Another serious issue is acid rain, which is contributing significantly to the deterioration of coastal waters, lakes, and marine life in the eastern United States. Acid rain forms when sulfur emitted by smokestacks in industrialized areas combines with moisture in the atmosphere to form acids that are spread by winds. The acids eventually fall to the earth in rain, which finds its way into streams, rivers, and lakes. The acid-rain problem has spread rapidly in recent years, and experts fear that the situation will worsen if the nation begins to burn more coal to generate electricity. To solve the problem, investigators first must determine where the sulfur is being emitted. The costs of this vital investigation and cleanup are going to be high. The human costs of having ignored the problem so long may be higher still.

What does reducing waste mean? *When you avoid making garbage in the first place, you don't have to worry about disposing of waste or recycling it later. Changing your habits is the key–think about ways you can reduce your waste when you shop, work, and play. Americans throw away enough office paper each year to build a 12-foot high wall stretching from New York to San Francisco–that's 10,000 or so sheets per person.*

RF Getty Images

Air Pollution Aviation emissions are a potentially significant and growing percentage of greenhouse gases that contribute to global warming. Aircraft emissions are significant for several reasons. First, jet aircraft are the main source of human emissions deposited directly into the upper atmosphere, where they may have a greater warming effect than if they were released at the earth's surface. Second, carbon dioxide—the primary aircraft emission—is the main focus of international concern. For example, it survives in the atmosphere for nearly 100 years and contributes to global warming, according to the Intergovernmental Panel on Climate Change. The carbon dioxide emissions from worldwide aviation roughly equal those of some industrialized countries. Third, carbon dioxide emissions, combined with other gases and particles emitted by jet aircraft,

Sustainability Feature

Adidas is one of a growing number of companies that share sustainability ideas and practices through nonprofit groups such as Business for Social Responsibility. **www.bsr.org**

could have two to four times as great an effect on the atmosphere as carbon dioxide alone. Fourth, the Intergovernmental Panel recently concluded that the rise in aviation emissions owing to the growing demand for air travel would not be fully offset by reductions in emissions achieved solely through technological improvements.

Usually, two or three factors combine to form air pollution in any given location. The first factor is large amounts of carbon monoxide and hydrocarbons emitted by motor vehicles concentrated in a relatively small area. The second is the smoke and other pollutants emitted by manufacturing facilities. These two factors can be eliminated in part through pollution control devices on cars, trucks, and smokestacks.

A third factor that contributes to air pollution—one that cannot be changed—is the combination of weather and geography. The Los Angeles Basin, for example, combines just the right weather and geographic conditions for creating dense smog. Los Angeles has strict regulations regarding air pollution. Even so, Los Angeles still struggles with air pollution problems because of uncontrollable conditions.

How effective is air pollution control? The EPA estimates that the Clean Air Act and its amendments eventually will result in the removal of 56 billion pounds of pollution from the air each year, thus measurably reducing lung disease, cancer, and other serious health problems caused by air pollution. Other authorities note that we have already seen improvement in air quality. A number of cities have cleaner air today than they did thirty years ago. Even in southern California, bad air quality days have dropped to less than forty days a year, about 60 percent lower than just a decade ago. Numerous chemical companies have recognized that they must take responsibility for operating their plants in an environmentally safe manner; some now devote considerable capital to purchasing antipollution devices. For example, 3M's pioneering Pollution Prevention Pays (3P) program, designed to find ways to avoid the generation of pollutants, marked its thirtieth anniversary in 2005. Since 1975, more than 5,600 employee-driven 3P projects have prevented the generation of more than 2.2 billion pounds of pollutants and produced first-year savings of nearly $1 billion.

Land Pollution Air and water quality may be improving, but land pollution is still a serious problem in many areas. The fundamental issues are (1) how to restore damaged or contaminated land at a reasonable cost and (2) how to protect unpolluted land from future damage.

The land pollution problem has been worsening over the past few years because modern technology has continued to produce increasing amounts of chemical and radioactive waste. U.S. manufacturers produce an estimated 40 to 60 million tons of contaminated oil, solvents, acids, and sludges each year. Service businesses, utility companies, hospitals, and other industries also dump vast amounts of wastes into the environment.

Individuals in the United States contribute to the waste-disposal problem, too. A shortage of landfills, owing to stricter regulations, makes garbage disposal a serious problem in some areas. Incinerators help to solve the landfill-shortage problem, but they bring with them their own problems. They reduce the amount of garbage but also leave tons of ash to be buried—ash that often has a higher concentration of toxicity than the original garbage. Other causes of land pollution include strip-mining of coal, nonselective cutting of forests, and the development of agricultural land for housing and industry.

To help pay the enormous costs of cleaning up land polluted with chemicals and toxic wastes, Congress created a $1.6 billion Superfund in 1980. Originally, money was to flow into the Superfund from a tax paid by 800 oil and chemical companies that produce toxic waste. The EPA was to use the money in the Superfund to finance the cleanup of hazardous waste sites across the nation. To replenish the Superfund, the EPA had two options: It could sue companies guilty of dumping chemicals at specific waste sites, or it could negotiate with guilty companies and thus completely avoid the legal system. During the 1980s, officials at the EPA came under fire because they preferred negotiated settlements. Critics referred to these settlements as "sweetheart deals" with industry. They felt that the EPA should be much more aggressive in reducing land pollution. Of course, most corporate executives believe that cleanup efficiency and quality might be improved if companies were more involved in the process. Many firms, including Delphi Automotive Systems Corporation and 3M, have modified or halted the production and sale of products that have a negative impact on the environment. For example, after tests showed that ScotchGuard does not decompose in the environment, 3M announced a voluntary end to production of the forty-year-old product, which had generated $300 million in sales.

Noise Pollution Excessive noise caused by traffic, aircraft, and machinery can do physical harm to human beings. Research has shown that people who are exposed to loud noises for long periods of time can suffer permanent hearing loss. The Noise Control Act of 1972 established noise emission standards for aircraft and airports, railroads, and interstate motor carriers. The act also provided funding for noise research at state and local levels.

Noise levels can be reduced by two methods. The source of noise pollution can be isolated as much as possible. (Thus, many metropolitan airports are located outside the cities.) And engineers can modify machinery and equipment to reduce noise levels. If it is impossible to reduce industrial noise to acceptable levels, workers should be required to wear earplugs to guard against permanent hearing damage.

Who Should Pay for a Clean Environment?

Governments and businesses are spending billions of dollars annually to reduce pollution—over $45 billion to control air pollution, $33 billion to control water pollution, and $12 billion to treat hazardous wastes. To make matters worse, much of the money required to purify the environment is supposed to come from already depressed industries, such as the chemical industry. And a few firms have discovered that it is cheaper to pay a fine than to install expensive equipment for pollution control.

Who, then, will pay for the environmental cleanup? Many business leaders offer one answer—tax money should be used to clean up the environment and to keep it clean. They reason that business is not the only source of pollution, so business should not be forced to absorb the entire cost of the cleanup. Environmentalists disagree. They believe that the cost of proper treatment and disposal of industrial wastes is an expense of doing business. In either case, consumers probably will pay a large part of the cost—either as taxes or in the form of higher prices for goods and services.

Implementing a Program of Social Responsibility

10 Learning Objective: Identify the steps a business must take to implement a program of social responsibility.

A firm's decision to be socially responsible is a step in the right direction—but only the first step. The firm then must develop and implement a program to reach this goal. The program will be affected by the firm's size, financial resources, past record in the area of social responsibility, and competition. Above all, however, the program must have the firm's total commitment or it will fail.

Developing a Program of Social Responsibility

An effective program for social responsibility takes time, money, and organization. In most cases, developing and implementing such a program will require four steps:

securing the commitment of top executives, planning, appointing a director, and preparing a social audit.

Commitment of Top Executives Without the support of top executives, any program will soon falter and become ineffective. For example, the Boeing Company's Ethics and Business Conduct Committee is responsible for the ethics program. The committee is appointed by the Boeing board of directors, and its members include the company chairman and CEO, the president and chief operating officer, the presidents of the operating groups, and senior vice presidents. As evidence of their commitment to social responsibility, top managers should develop a policy statement that outlines key areas of concern. This statement sets a tone of positive support and later will serve as a guide for other employees as they become involved in the program.

Planning Next, a committee of managers should be appointed to plan the program. Whatever form their plan takes, it should deal with each of the issues described in the top managers' policy statement. If necessary, outside consultants can be hired to help develop the plan.

Appointment of a Director After the social responsibility plan is established, a top-level executive should be appointed to implement the organization's plan. This individual should be charged with recommending specific policies and helping individual departments to understand and live up to the social responsibilities the firm has assumed. Depending on the size of the firm, the director may require a staff to handle the program on a day-to-day basis. For example, at the Boeing Company, the director of ethics and business conduct administers the ethics and business conduct program.

social audit a comprehensive report of what an organization has done and is doing with regard to social issues that affect it

The Social Audit At specified intervals, the program director should prepare a social audit for the firm. A **social audit** is a comprehensive report of what an organization has done and is doing with regard to social issues that affect it. This document provides the information the firm needs to evaluate and revise its social responsibility program. Typical subject areas include human resources, community involvement, the quality and safety of products, business practices, and efforts to reduce pollution and improve the environment. The information included in a social audit should be as accurate and as quantitative as possible, and the audit should reveal both positive and negative aspects of the program.

Today, many companies listen to concerned individuals within and outside the company. For example, the Boeing Ethics Line listens to and acts on concerns expressed by employees and others about possible violations of company policies, laws, or regulations, such as improper or unethical business practices, as well as health, safety, and environmental issues. Employees are encouraged to communicate their concerns, as well as ask questions about ethical issues. The Ethics Line is available to all Boeing employees, including Boeing subsidiaries. It is also available to concerned individuals outside the company.

Funding the Program

We have noted that social responsibility costs money. Thus, just like any other corporate undertaking, a program to improve social responsibility must be funded. Funding can come from three sources:

1. Management can pass the cost on to consumers in the form of higher prices.
2. The corporation may be forced to absorb the cost of the program if, for example, the competitive situation does not permit a price increase. In this case, the cost is treated as a business expense, and profit is reduced.
3. The federal government may pay for all or part of the cost through tax reductions or other incentives.

return to inside business

Dancing Deer

Dancing Deer makes award-winning cakes, cookies, and brownies—and it also makes a difference in Boston's inner city by providing jobs, training, benefits, and charitable donations. The company is not only dedicated to helping people, it is dedicated to helping the environment. For example, its packaging uses recycled materials and its shipping containers are printed with earth-friendly soy ink.

Thanks to high-quality products and a loyal workforce, Dancing Deer has grown steadily over the past decade. Recently, it doubled its production capacity by opening a second inner-city bakery. More growth is ahead because "Dancing Deer is not big enough to make an impact, to be a social or economic force," the CEO says. "If I hit $50 million in sales, it can be."

Questions

1. Is it socially responsible or good business for Dancing Deer to help its employees pay for public transportation to and from work? Explain your answer.
2. Although Dancing Deer could probably cut costs by moving to the suburbs, it has chosen to remain in Boston. How do you think this affects the company's ability to fund social responsibility programs?

CHAPTER REVIEW

Summary

1 Understand what is meant by *business ethics.*

Ethics is the study of right and wrong and of the morality of choices. Business ethics is the application of moral standards to business situations.

2 Identify the types of ethical concerns that arise in the business world.

Ethical issues arise often in business situations out of relationships with investors, customers, employees, creditors, or competitors. Businesspeople should make every effort to be fair, to consider the welfare of customers and others within the firm, to avoid conflicts of interest, and to communicate honestly.

3 Discuss the factors that affect the level of ethical behavior in organizations.

Individual, social, and opportunity factors all affect the level of ethical behavior in an organization. Individual factors include knowledge level, moral values and attitudes, and personal goals. Social factors include cultural norms and the actions and values of coworkers and significant others. Opportunity factors refer to the amount of leeway that exists in an organization for employees to behave unethically if they so choose.

4 Explain how ethical decision making can be encouraged.

Governments, trade associations, and individual firms all can establish guidelines for defining ethical behavior. Governments can pass stricter regulations. Trade associations provide ethical guidelines for their members. Companies provide codes of ethics—written guides to acceptable and ethical behavior as defined by an organization—and create an atmosphere in which ethical behavior is encouraged. An ethical employee working in an unethical environment may resort to whistle-blowing to bring a questionable practice to light.

5 Describe how our current views on the social responsibility of business have evolved.

In a socially responsible business, management realizes that its activities have an impact on society and considers that impact in the decision-making process. Before the 1930s, workers, consumers, and government had very little influence on business activities; as a result, business leaders gave little thought to social responsibility. All this changed with the Great Depression. Government regulations, employee demands, and consumer awareness combined to create a demand that businesses act in socially responsible ways.

6 Explain the two views on the social responsibility of business and understand the arguments for and against increased social responsibility.

The basic premise of the economic model of social responsibility is that society benefits most when business is left alone to produce profitable goods and services. According to the socioeconomic model, business has as much responsibility to society as it has to its owners. Most managers adopt a viewpoint somewhere between these two extremes.

7 Discuss the factors that led to the consumer movement and list some of its results.

Consumerism consists of all activities undertaken to protect the rights of consumers. The consumer movement generally has demanded—and received—attention from business in the areas of product safety, product information, product choices through competition, and the resolution of complaints about products and business practices. Although concerns over consumer rights have been around to some extent since the early nineteenth century, the movement became more powerful in the 1960s when President John F. Kennedy initiated the consumer "bill of rights." The six basic rights of consumers include the right to safety, the right to be informed, the right to choose, the right to be heard, and the rights to consumer education and courteous service.

8 Analyze how present employment practices are being used to counteract past abuses.

Legislation and public demand have prompted some businesses to correct past abuses in employment practices—mainly with regard to minority groups. Affirmative action and training of the hard-core unemployed are two types of programs that have been used successfully.

9 Describe the major types of pollution, their causes, and their cures.

Industry has contributed to the noise pollution and the pollution of our land and water through the dumping of wastes and to air pollution through vehicle and smokestack emissions. This contamination can be cleaned up and controlled, but the big question is: Who will pay? Present cleanup efforts are funded partly by government tax revenues, partly by business, and in the long run by consumers.

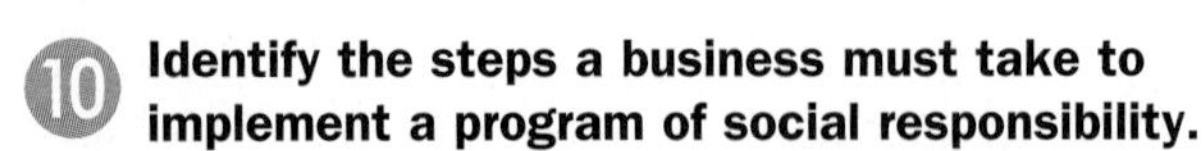

10 Identify the steps a business must take to implement a program of social responsibility.

A program to implement social responsibility in a business begins with total commitment by top management. The program should be planned carefully, and a capable director should be appointed to implement it. Social audits should be prepared periodically as a means of evaluating and revising the program. Programs may be funded through price increases, reduction of profit, or federal incentives.

Key Terms

You should now be able to define and give an example relevant to each of the following terms:

ethics (37)
business ethics (37)
Sarbanes-Oxley Act of 2002 (41)
code of ethics (41)
whistle-blowing (42)
social responsibility (44)
caveat emptor (50)
economic model of social responsibility (51)
socioeconomic model of social responsibility (52)
consumerism (53)
minority (57)
affirmative action program (57)
Equal Employment Opportunity Commission (EEOC) (58)
hard-core unemployed (58)
National Alliance of Business (NAB) (59)
pollution (59)
social audit (64)

Review Questions

1. Why might an individual with high ethical standards act less ethically in business than in his or her personal life?
2. How would an organizational code of ethics help to ensure ethical business behavior?
3. How and why did the American business environment change after the Great Depression?
4. What are the major differences between the economic model of social responsibility and the socioeconomic model?
5. What are the arguments for and against increasing the social responsibility of business?
6. Describe and give an example of each of the six basic rights of consumers.
7. There are more women than men in the United States. Why, then, are women considered a minority with regard to employment?
8. What is the goal of affirmative action programs? How is this goal achieved?
9. What is the primary function of the Equal Employment Opportunity Commission?
10. How do businesses contribute to each of the four forms of pollution? How can they avoid polluting the environment?
11. Our environment *can* be cleaned up and kept clean. Why haven't we simply done so?
12. Describe the steps involved in developing a social responsibility program within a large corporation.

Discussion Questions

1. When a company acts in an ethically questionable manner, what types of problems are caused for the organization and its customers?
2. How can an employee take an ethical stand regarding a business decision when his or her superior already has taken a different position?
3. Overall, would it be more profitable for a business to follow the economic model or the socioeconomic model of social responsibility?
4. Why should business take on the task of training the hard-core unemployed?
5. To what extent should the blame for vehicular air pollution be shared by manufacturers, consumers, and government?
6. Why is there so much government regulation involving social responsibility issues? Should there be less?

Video Case 2.1

At New Belgium Brewing, Greater Efficiency Is Blowing in the Wind

New Belgium Brewing (NBB), America's first wind-powered brewery, aims to make both a better beer and a better society. Founded by husband-and-wife entrepreneurs Jeff Lebesch and Kim Jordan, the company offers European-style beers under intriguing brands such as Fat Tire and Sunshine Wheat. Lebesch hatched the idea for brewing his own beers after sipping local beers while touring Belgium on bicycle. Returning home with a special yeast strain, Lebesch experimented in his basement and came up with a beer he dubbed Fat Tire Amber Ale in honor of his bicycle trip.

By 1991, he and his wife were bottling and delivering five Belgian-style beers to liquor stores and other retailers in and around their hometown of Fort Collins, Colorado. Within a few years, sales had grown so rapidly that NBB needed much more space. Lebesch and Jordan moved the operation into a former railroad depot and then moved again into a new state-of-the-art brewery.

Not only is the 80,000-square-foot facility highly automated for efficiency, but it is also designed with the environment in mind. For example, sun tubes bring daylight to areas that lack windows, which reduces the brewery's energy requirements. As another energy-saving example, the brewery's kettles have steam condensers to capture and reuse hot water again and again. The biggest energy-conservation measure is a special cooling device that reduces the need for air conditioning in warm weather. In the office section, NBB employees reuse and recycle paper and as many other supplies as possible.

Soon after opening the new brewery, the entire staff voted to convert it to wind power, which is kinder to the environment because it does not pollute or require scarce fossil fuels. In addition to saving energy and natural resources, NBB is actually transforming the methane from its waste stream into energy through the process of cogeneration. It also has found ways to cut carbon dioxide emissions and reuse brewing by-products as cattle feed. Going further, NBB donates $1 to charitable causes for every barrel of beer it sells—which translates into more than $200,000 per year. Moreover, it donates the proceeds of its annual Tour de Fat biking event to nonprofit bicycling organizations.

Employee involvement is a key element of NBB's success. Lebesch and Jordan have unleashed the entrepreneurial spirit of the workforce through employee ownership. Employees share in decisions, serve as taste testers, and receive detailed information about NBB's financial performance, including costs and profits. Being empowered as part owners not only motivates employees, but it also gives them a great sense of pride in their work. And reminiscent of the bicycle trip that prompted Lebesch to brew his own beers, all employees receive a cruising bicycle on their first anniversary of joining the company.

Still, customers are most concerned with the taste of NBB's beers, which have won numerous awards and have attracted a large, loyal customer base in twelve states. In the last five years, Fat Tire's annual sales have grown from 0.9 million cases to 2.6 million cases. Many people become customers after hearing about the beer from long-time fans, and as its popularity grows, the word spreads even further. NBB does some advertising, but its budget is tiny compared with deep-pocketed rivals such as Anheuser-Busch and Miller Brewing. Instead of glitzy commercials on national television, NBB uses a low-key approach to show customers that the company is comprised of "real people making real beer."

Today, the company employs 140 people and is the sixth largest company selling draft beer in America. Clearly, sales and profits are vital ingredients in NBB's long-term recipe, but they are not the only important elements. Jordan stresses that the company is not just about making beer—it is about creating what she calls "magic." Reflecting on her continued involvement in NBB, she says: "How do you support a community of people? How do you show up in the larger community? How do you strive to be a business role model? That's the part that keeps me really engaged here."

In fact, NBB has integrated social responsibility into its operations so successfully that it recently received an award from *Business Ethics* magazine. The award cited the company's "dedication to environmental excellence in every part of its innovative brewing process." Jordan, Lebesch, and all the NBB employee-owners can take pride in their efforts to build a better society as well as a better beer.[17]

For more information about this company, go to **www.newbelgium.com.**

Questions

1. What do you think Kim Jordan means when she talks about how New Belgium Brewing strives to be a "business role model," not just a beer maker?
2. Given New Belgium Brewing's emphasis on social responsibility, what would you suggest the company look at when preparing a social audit?
3. Should businesses charge more for products that are produced using more costly but environmentally friendly methods such as wind power? Should consumers pay more for products that are *not* produced using environmentally friendly methods because of the potential for costly environmental damage? Explain your answers.

Case 2.2 Belu Water

Many of us have been inspired to reduce our impact on the environment. Few, however, have gone as far as former reporter and documentary filmmaker Reed Paget. An American journalist covering the launch of the United Nation's Global Compact in 2001, Paget was deeply impressed by this environmental initiative's call to "use capitalism to change the world." What better mechanism is there for change, thought Paget, than business, with its wide financial and entrepreneurial resources and its risk-taking mindset?

Although he had no business experience, Paget determined to start a company that would be both socially responsible and environmentally friendly. When he learned from Al Gore's documentary "An Inconvenient Truth" that a quarter of the world's people have no access to clean water, he decided to create a bottled water company, both to alert the public to the global water crisis and to show that bottled water could be manufactured and marketed in an environmentally sustainable way. Finally, Paget determined that all his company's profits would be donated to clean-water projects around the world.

With start-up funding from the Idyll Foundation, a team of friends, and a stack of business how-to books, Paget sat down to develop a brand name, find a bottle design, work out a manufacturing deal, and find customers. Coming up with a name that wasn't already trademarked was a challenge, but the team settled on "Belu" (pronounced "belloo") to evoke the color of water and the idea of beauty. A deal with an upscale designer yielded an affordable glass bottle design, and after taste-test visits to more than seventy sources of water in the United Kingdom, Paget settled on a supplier of natural mineral water called Wenlock Water in the Shropshire hills. Not only was the water great; it was more ecologically friendly for a U.K. company than water shipped from the mountains of France, like that of competitors Evian and Highland Springs.

A marketing firm helped Belu land its first customer, the popular Waitrose supermarket chain. With additional funding to pay for the initial run of glass bottles, Belu delivered its first order in May 2004. A website, further funding, and marketing and sales growth, including the addition of the giant grocery chain Tesco, soon followed. Belu, the first bottled water that does not contribute to climate change, began to prove its appeal to consumers.

Another breakthrough came when the company found a manufacturer to produce corn-based bottles, which are completely stable on store shelves but biodegrade back to soil in just eight weeks under the right conditions of heat and humidity and with a little help from microorganisms.

Now that it has grown well over 550 percent from its founding in 2002, Belu Water reaches more than 500,000 consumers each month and, though a charity called WaterAid, has brought clean water, wells, and hand pumps to over 20,000 people in India and Mali, with expectations of helping at least 10 times that number in future years. It uses clean electricity and offsets its remaining carbon emissions and has won numerous awards, including Social Enterprise of the Year and Social Entrepreneur of the Year (in partnership with Schwab Foundation).

For more information about this company, go to **http://www.belu.org.**[18]

Questions

1. Belu Water gives all its profits away and bills its product as the first carbon-neutral bottled water and the first to come in corn bottles. Do you think its levels of eco-consciousness and social responsibility set a realistic model of environmental performance for other manufacturing companies? Why or why not?
2. Why does Belu Water produce a saleable product instead of just asking the public to donate money for clean-water projects?
3. Do you agree with Reed Paget that business is ideally suited to "change the world"? Why or why not?

Building Skills for Career Success

1. JOURNALING FOR SUCCESS

Discovery statement: This chapter was devoted mostly to business ethics, ethical concerns that arise in the business world, personal ethics, and social responsibility of business.

Assume that you are an accountant at ABC Corporation, where you question the company's accounting practices. What legal and managerial changes would you suggest to prevent the use of accounting tricks to manipulate corporate earnings?

Assignment

1. Assume that your manager refuses to incorporate any of your suggestions. Would you blow the whistle? Why or why not?
2. Suppose that you blow the whistle and get fired. Which law might protect your rights, and how would you proceed to protect yourself?

2. EXPLORING THE INTERNET

Socially responsible business behavior can be as simple as donating unneeded older computers to schools, mentoring interested learners in good business practices, or supplying public speakers to talk about career opportunities. Students, as part of the public at large, perceive a great deal of information about a company, its employees, and its owners by the positive social actions taken and perhaps even more by actions not taken. Microsoft donates millions of dollars of computers and software to educational institutions every year. Some people consider this level of corporate giving to be insufficient given the scale of the wealth of the corporation. Others believe that firms have no obligation to give back any more than they wish and that recipients should be grateful. Visit the text website for updates to this exercise.

Assignment

1. Select any firm involved in high technology and the Internet such as Microsoft or IBM. Examine its website and report its corporate position on social responsibility and giving as it has stated it. What activities is it involved in? What programs does it support, and how does it support them?
2. Search the Internet for commentary on business social responsibility, form your own opinions, and then evaluate the social effort demonstrated by the firm you have selected. What more could the firm have done?

3. DEVELOPING CRITICAL-THINKING SKILLS

Recently, an article entitled "Employees Coming to Terms with Moral Issues on the Job" appeared in a big-city newspaper. It posed the following situations:

You are asked to work on a project you find morally wrong.

Important tasks are left undone because a coworker spends more time planning a social event than working on a proposal.

Your company is knowingly selling defective merchandise to customers.

Unfortunately, many employees currently are struggling with such issues. The moral dilemmas that arise when employees find their own ethical values incompatible with the work they do every day are causing a lot of stress in the workplace, and furthermore, these dilemmas are not being discussed. There exists an ethics gap. You already may have faced a similar situation in your workplace.

Assignment

1. In small groups with your classmates, discuss your answers to the following questions:
   a. If you were faced with any of the preceding situations, what would you do?
   b. Would you complete work you found morally unacceptable, or would you leave it undone and say nothing?
   c. If you spoke up, what would happen to you or your career? What would be the risk?
   d. What are your options?
   e. If you were a manager rather than a lower-level employee, would you feel differently and take a different approach to the issue? Why?
2. In a written report, summarize what you learned from this discussion.

4. BUILDING TEAM SKILLS

A firm's code of ethics outlines the kinds of behaviors expected within the organization and serves as a guideline for encouraging ethical behavior in the workplace. It reflects the rights of the firm's workers, shareholders, and consumers.

Assignment

1. Working in a team of four, find a code of ethics for a business firm. Start the search by asking firms in your community for a copy of their codes, by visiting the library, or by searching and downloading information from the Internet.
2. Analyze the code of ethics you have chosen, and answer the following questions:
   a. What does the company's code of ethics say about the rights of its workers, shareholders, consumers, and suppliers? How does the code reflect the company's attitude toward competitors?
   b. How does this code of ethics resemble the information discussed in this chapter? How does it differ?
   c. As an employee of this company, how would you personally interpret the code of ethics? How might the code influence your behavior within the workplace? Give several examples.

5. RESEARCHING DIFFERENT CAREERS

Business ethics has been at the heart of many discussions over the years and continues to trouble employees and shareholders. Stories about dishonesty and wrongful behavior in the workplace appear on a regular basis in newspapers and on the national news.

Assignment

Prepare a written report on the following:

1. Why can it be so difficult for people to do what is right?
2. What is your personal code of ethics? Prepare a code outlining what you believe is morally right. The document should include guidelines for your personal behavior.
3. How will your code of ethics affect your decisions about:
   a. The types of questions you should ask in a job interview?
   b. Selecting a company in which to work?

3 Exploring Global Business

LEARNING OBJECTIVES

What you will be able to do once you complete this chapter:

1. **Explain** the economic basis for international business.
2. **Discuss** the restrictions nations place on international trade, the objectives of these restrictions, and their results.
3. **Outline** the extent of international trade and identify the organizations working to foster it.
4. **Define** the methods by which a firm can organize for and enter into international markets.
5. **Describe** the various sources of export assistance.
6. **Identify** the institutions that help firms and nations finance international business.

AP Photo/Peter Morgan

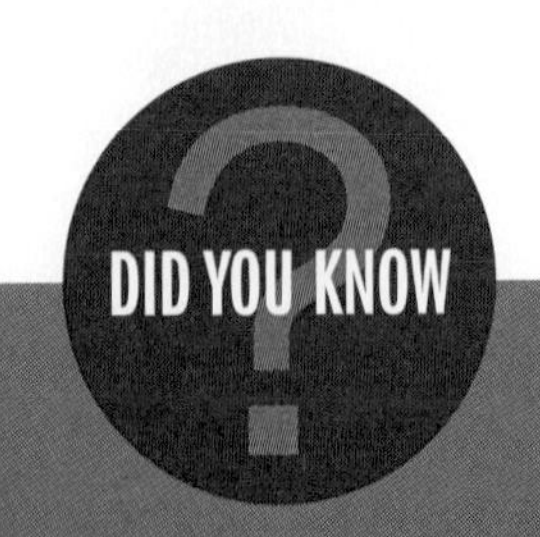

inside business

Shanghai GM, SAIC's $1.5 billion joint venture with Detroit's General Motors, annually sells more than 1 million cars in China, where rising incomes are pushing vehicle demand higher year after year.

SAIC Speeds Toward Higher Sales

One of China's oldest car makers, Shanghai Automobile Industry Corporation—SAIC for short—is racing to enter the ranks of the world's largest car companies within the next decade. Partly owned by the Shanghai government, SAIC has years of experience designing and building cars and trucks for the domestic Chinese market. In addition to successful joint ventures with both General Motors and Volkswagen, the company manufactures and markets its own Roewe sedan and recently brought the British MG sports car back to European roads.

Shanghai GM, SAIC's $1.5 billion joint venture with Detroit's General Motors, annually sells more than 1 million cars in China, where rising incomes are pushing vehicle demand higher year after year. This joint venture got a big boost from the special Pan-Asia Technical Automotive Center GM built to share automotive technology with its Chinese partner. Shanghai GM's first car was a mid-size Buick sedan, followed by a Buick station wagon. Next, the joint venture adapted the GM Brazilian car Opel Corsa for China, and later introduced new cars under GM's Chevrolet and Cadillac brands.

Shanghai VW, the joint venture with Germany's Volkswagen, has been manufacturing cars in China for more than 25 years. Santana, Polo, Passat, and Touran are among the joint venture's most popular models. These cars compete with cars made by Volkswagen's other joint venture in China, a partnership with First Automotive Works, one of SAIC's Chinese rivals.

Despite the potential for future growth and profits in China, the various joint ventures between local and global car manufacturers have added to the competitive pressure. Now SAIC is looking to make its mark outside its home country. Not long ago, it acquired a competitor that owned the rights to the MG name and to the British factory that once produced the sports car. SAIC took over the factory and went ahead with existing plans to launch the new MG in the United Kingdom. Down the road, can SAIC stay on course toward higher worldwide sales?[1]

Shanghai Automobile Industry Corporation is just one of a growing number of foreign companies, large and small, that are doing business with firms in other countries. Some companies, such as Coca-Cola, sell to firms in other countries; others, such as Pier 1 Imports, buy goods around the world to import into the United States. Whether they buy or sell products across national borders, these companies are all contributing to the volume of international trade that is fueling the global economy.

Theoretically, international trade is every bit as logical and worthwhile as interstate trade between, say, California and Washington. Yet nations tend to restrict the import of certain goods for a variety of reasons. For example, in the early 2000s, the United States restricted the import of Mexican fresh tomatoes because they were undercutting price levels of domestic fresh tomatoes.

Despite such restrictions, international trade has increased almost steadily since World War II. Many of the industrialized nations have signed trade agreements intended to eliminate problems in international business and to help less-developed nations participate in world trade. Individual firms around the world have seized the opportunity to compete in foreign markets by exporting products and increasing foreign production, as well as by other means.

Signing the Trade Act of 2002, President George W. Bush remarked, "Trade is an important source of good jobs for our workers and a source of higher growth for our economy. Free trade is also a proven strategy for building global prosperity and adding to the momentum of political freedom. Trade is an engine of economic growth. In our lifetime, trade has helped lift millions of people and whole nations out of poverty and put them on the path of prosperity.[2] In his national best-seller, *The World is Flat,*

Thomas L. Friedman states, "The flattening of the world has presented us with new opportunities, new challenges, new partners but, also, alas new dangers, particularly as Americans it is imperative that we be the best global citizens that we can be—because in a flat world, if you don't visit a bad neighborhood, it might visit you."

We describe international trade in this chapter in terms of modern specialization, whereby each country trades the surplus goods and services it produces most efficiently for products in short supply. We also explain the restrictions nations place on products and services from other countries and present some of the possible advantages and disadvantages of these restrictions. We then describe the extent of international trade and identify the organizations working to foster it. We describe several methods of entering international markets and the various sources of export assistance available from the federal government. Finally, we identify some of the institutions that provide the complex financing necessary for modern international trade.

The Basis for International Business

1 Learning Objective: Explain the economic basis for international business.

International business encompasses all business activities that involve exchanges across national boundaries. Thus, a firm is engaged in international business when it buys some portion of its input from or sells some portion of its output to an organization located in a foreign country. (A small retail store may sell goods produced in some other country. However, because it purchases these goods from American distributors, it is not engaged in international trade.)

international business all business activities that involve exchanges across national boundaries

Absolute and Comparative Advantage

Some countries are better equipped than others to produce particular goods or services. The reason may be a country's natural resources, its labor supply, or even customs or a historical accident. Such a country would be best off if it could *specialize* in the production of such products because it can produce them most efficiently. The country could use what it needed of these products and then trade the surplus for products it could not produce efficiently on its own.

AP Photo/Dennis Farrell

South Africa enjoys an absolute advantage in mining diamonds. *The nation's mining industry dates back to 1867 when diamonds were discovered in the Kimberley diamond fields. Later, in the early 20th century, it was discovered that diamonds could also be found on the seabed along the west coast of South Africa.*

SPOTLIGHT
The Growing Deficit

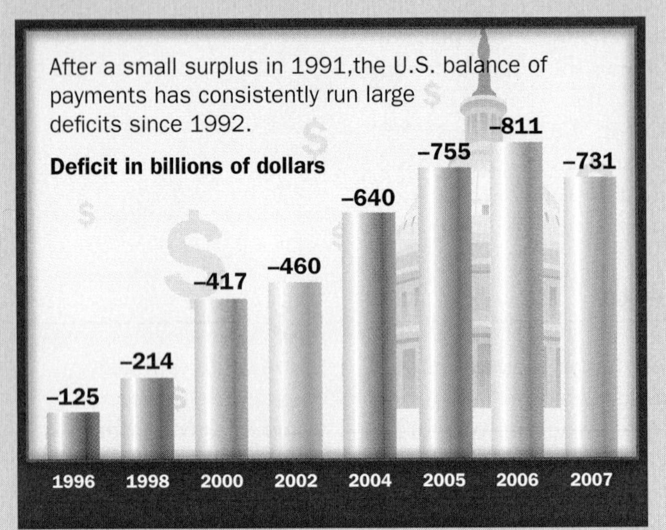

Source: U.S. Department of Commerce, Bureau of Economic Analysis, http://bea.gov/international/bp_web/simple.cfm?anon=78260&table_id=1&are_id=3, accessed September 19, 2008.

Saudi Arabia thus has specialized in the production of crude oil and petroleum products; South Africa, in diamonds; and Australia, in wool. Each of these countries is said to have an absolute advantage with regard to a particular product. An **absolute advantage** is the ability to produce a specific product more efficiently than any other nation.

One country may have an absolute advantage with regard to several products, whereas another country may have no absolute advantage at all. Yet it is still worthwhile for these two countries to specialize and trade with each other. To see why this is so, imagine that you are the president of a successful manufacturing firm and that you can accurately type ninety words per minute. Your assistant can type eighty words per minute but would run the business poorly. Thus, you have an absolute advantage over your assistant in both typing and managing. However, you cannot afford to type your own letters because your time is better spent in managing the business. That is, you have a **comparative advantage** in managing. A comparative advantage is the ability to produce a specific product more efficiently than any other product.

Your assistant, on the other hand, has a comparative advantage in typing because he or she can do that better than managing the business. Thus, you spend your time managing, and you leave the typing to your assistant. Overall, the business is run as efficiently as possible because you are each working in accordance with your own comparative advantage.

absolute advantage the ability to produce a specific product more efficiently than any other nation

comparative advantage the ability to produce a specific product more efficiently than any other product

The same is true for nations. Goods and services are produced more efficiently when each country specializes in the products for which it has a comparative advantage. Moreover, by definition, every country has a comparative advantage in *some* product. The United States has many comparative advantages—in research and development, high-technology industries, and identifying new markets, for instance.

Exporting and Importing

Suppose that the United States specializes in producing corn. It then will produce a surplus of corn, but perhaps it will have a shortage of wine. France, on the other hand, specializes in producing wine but experiences a shortage of corn. To satisfy both needs—for corn and for wine—the two countries should trade with each other. The United States should export corn and import wine. France should export wine and import corn.

exporting selling and shipping raw materials or products to other nations

Exporting is selling and shipping raw materials or products to other nations. The Boeing Company, for example, exports its airplanes to a number of countries for use by their airlines. Figure 3.1 shows the top ten merchandise-exporting states in this country.

importing purchasing raw materials or products in other nations and bringing them into one's own country

Importing is purchasing raw materials or products in other nations and bringing them into one's own country. Thus buyers for Macy's department stores may purchase rugs in India or raincoats in England and have them shipped back to the United States for resale.

balance of trade the total value of a nation's exports minus the total value of its imports over some period of time

Importing and exporting are the principal activities in international trade. They give rise to an important concept called the *balance of trade*. A nation's **balance of trade** is the total value of its exports *minus* the total value of its imports over some period of time. If a country imports more than it exports, its balance of trade is negative and is said to be *unfavorable*. (A negative balance of trade is unfavorable because the country must export money to pay for its excess imports.)

In 2007, the United States imported $2,346 billion worth of goods and services and exported $1,646 billion worth. It thus had a trade deficit of $700 billion. A **trade deficit** is a negative balance of trade (see Figure 3.2). However, the United States has consistently enjoyed a large and rapidly growing surplus in services. For example, in 2007, the United States imported $378 billion worth and exported $497 billion worth of services, thus creating a favorable balance of $119 billion.[3]

Question: Are trade deficits bad?
Answer: In testimony before the Senate Finance Committee, Daniel T. Griswold, associate director of the Center for Trade Policy at the Cato Institute, remarked, "The trade deficit is not a sign of economic distress, but of rising domestic demand and investment. Imposing new trade barriers will only make Americans worse off while leaving the **trade deficit** virtually unchanged."

On the other hand, when a country exports more than it imports, it is said to have a *favorable* balance of trade. This has consistently been the case for Japan over the last two decades or so.

trade deficit a negative balance of trade

A nation's **balance of payments** is the total flow of money into a country *minus* the total flow of money out of that country over some period of time. Balance of payments therefore is a much broader concept than balance of trade. It includes imports and exports, of course. But it also includes investments, money spent by foreign tourists, payments by foreign governments, aid to foreign governments, and all other receipts and payments.

balance of payments the total flow of money into a country minus the total flow of money out of that country over some period of time

A continual deficit in a nation's balance of payments (a negative balance) can cause other nations to lose confidence in that nation's economy. A continual surplus may indicate that the country encourages exports but limits imports by imposing trade restrictions.

Restrictions to International Business

2

Learning Objective: Discuss the restrictions nations place on international trade, the objectives of these restrictions, and their results.

Specialization and international trade can result in the efficient production of want-satisfying goods and services on a worldwide basis. As we have noted, international business generally is increasing. Yet the nations of the world continue to erect barriers to free trade. They do so for reasons ranging from internal political and economic

Figure 3.1: The Top Ten Merchandise-Exporting States

Texas and California accounted for over one-fourth of all 2005 U.S. merchandise exports.

Source: **http://www.ita.doc.gov/td/industry/otea/state/2005_year_end_dollar_value_05.html,** accessed September 15, 2008.

Figure 3.2: U.S. International Trade in Goods and Services

If a country imports more goods than it exports, the balance of trade is negative, as it was in the United States from 1987 to 2007.

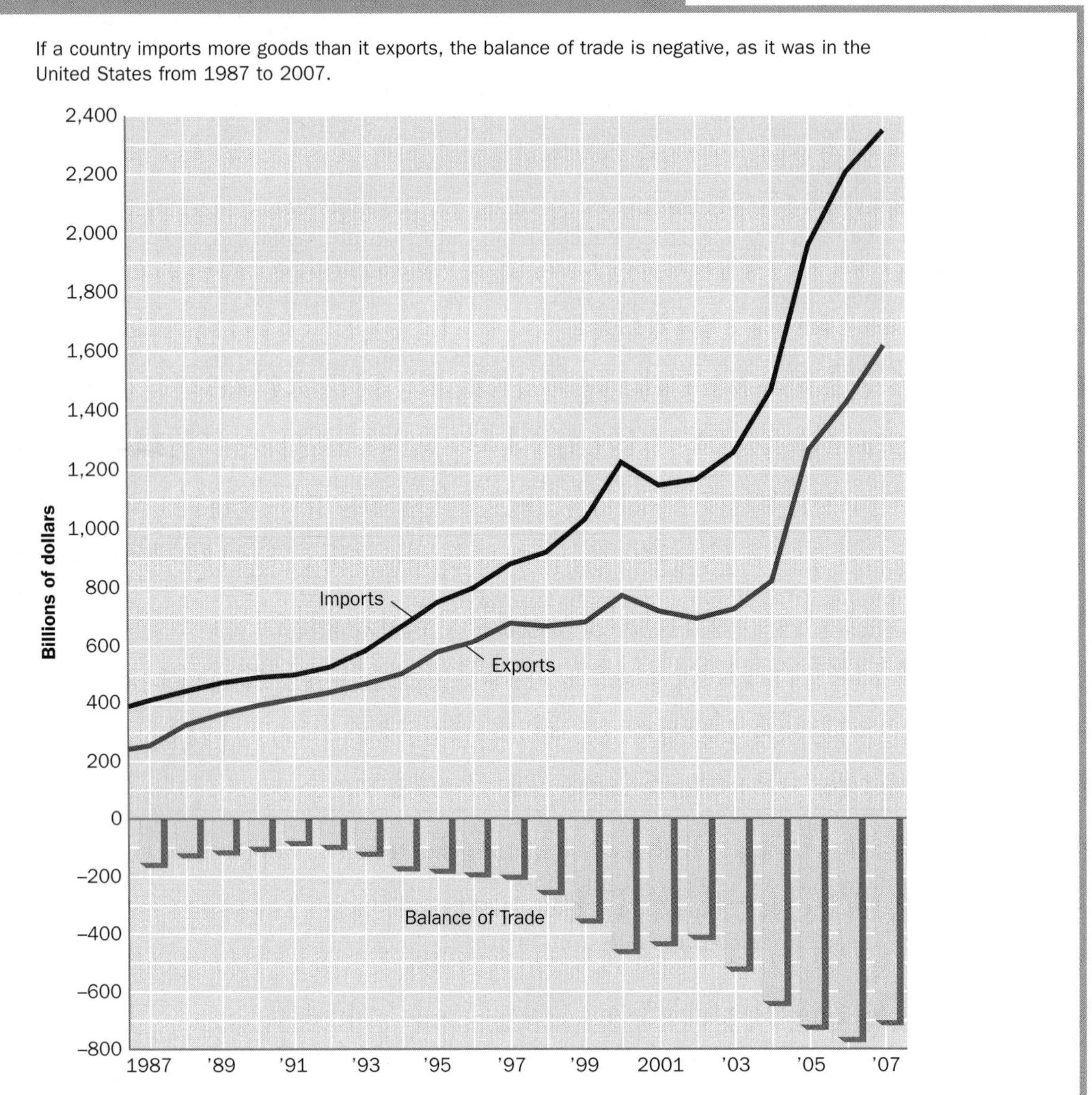

Source: U.S. Department of Commerce, International Trade Administration, U.S. Bureau of Economic Analysis, **http://bea.gov/international/bp_web/simple.cfm?anon=78260&table_id=1&area_id=3,** accessed September 18, 2008.

pressures to simple mistrust of other nations. We examine first the types of restrictions that are applied and then the arguments for and against trade restrictions.

Types of Trade Restrictions

Nations generally are eager to export their products. They want to provide markets for their industries and to develop a favorable balance of trade. Hence, most trade restrictions are applied to imports from other nations.

import duty (tariff) a tax levied on a particular foreign product entering a country

Tariffs Perhaps the most commonly applied trade restriction is the customs (or import) duty. An **import duty** (also called a **tariff**) is a tax levied on a particular foreign product entering a country. For example, the United States imposes a 2.2 percent import duty on fresh Chilean tomatoes, an 8.7 percent duty if tomatoes are dried and packaged, and nearly 12 percent if tomatoes are made into ketchup or salsa. The two types of tariffs are revenue tariffs and protective tariffs; both have the effect of raising the price of the product in the importing nations, but for different reasons. *Revenue tariffs* are imposed solely to generate income for the government. For example, the United States imposes a duty on Scotch whiskey solely for revenue purposes. *Protective* *tariffs,* on the other hand, are imposed to protect a domestic industry from competition by keeping the price of competing imports level with or higher than the price of similar domestic products. Because fewer units of the product will be sold at the increased price, fewer units will be imported. The French and Japanese agricultural sectors would both shrink drastically if their nations abolished the protective tariffs that keep the price of imported farm products high. Today, U.S. tariffs are the lowest in history, with average tariff rates on all imports of under 3 percent.

China's 1.3 billion consumers, with a growing middle class, can afford high-quality U.S. apples, but a 30 percent tariff imposed by the Chinese government limits the imports of Washington apples to China. *Here, the U.S. Agriculture Secretary Dan Glickman inspects a display of Washington apples in Beijing, China.*

Feature Photo Service/Washington AgriNews

Some countries rationalize their protectionist policies as a way of offsetting an international trade practice called *dumping.* **Dumping** is the exportation of large quantities of a product at a price lower than that of the same product in the home market.

Thus, dumping drives down the price of the domestic item. Recently, for example, the Pencil Makers Association, which represents eight U.S. pencil manufacturers, charged that low-priced pencils from Thailand and the People's Republic of China were being sold in the United States at less than fair value prices. Unable to compete with these inexpensive imports, several domestic manufacturers had to shut down. To protect themselves, domestic manufacturers can obtain an antidumping duty through the government to offset the advantage of the foreign product. In 2008, for example, the U.S. Department of Commerce imposed preliminary antidumping duties of up to 85.5 percent on a variety of steel products imported from China.

dumping exportation of large quantities of a product at a price lower than that of the same product in the home market

Nontariff Barriers A **nontariff barrier** is a nontax measure imposed by a government to favor domestic over foreign suppliers. Nontariff barriers create obstacles to the marketing of foreign goods in a country and increase costs for exporters. The following are a few examples of government-imposed nontariff barriers:

nontariff barrier a nontax measure imposed by a government to favor domestic over foreign suppliers

- An **import quota** is a limit on the amount of a particular good that may be imported into a country during a given period of time. The limit may be set in terms of either quantity (so many pounds of beef) or value (so many dollars' worth of shoes). Quotas also may be set on individual products imported from specific countries. Once an import quota has been reached, imports are halted until the specified time has elapsed.
- An **embargo** is a complete halt to trading with a particular nation or in a particular product. The embargo is used most often as a political weapon. At present, the United States has import embargoes against Iran and North Korea—both as a result of extremely poor political relations.
- A **foreign-exchange control** is a restriction on the amount of a particular foreign currency that can be purchased or sold. By limiting the amount of foreign currency importers can obtain, a government limits the amount of goods importers can purchase with that currency. This has the effect of limiting imports from the country whose foreign exchange is being controlled.
- A nation can increase or decrease the value of its money relative to the currency of other nations. **Currency devaluation** is the reduction of the value of a nation's currency relative to the currencies of other countries.

import quota a limit on the amount of a particular good that may be imported into a country during a given period of time

embargo a complete halt to trading with a particular nation or in a particular product

foreign-exchange control a restriction on the amount of a particular foreign currency that can be purchased or sold

currency devaluation the reduction of the value of a nation's currency relative to the currencies of other countries

Devaluation increases the cost of foreign goods while it decreases the cost of domestic goods to foreign firms. For example, suppose that the British pound is worth \$2. Then an American-made \$2,000 computer can be purchased for £1,000. However, if the United Kingdom devalues the pound so that it is worth only \$1, that

Many countries, including South Korea, banned imports of U.S. beef products in 2003, soon after one case of mad cow disease was found in the United States. *South Korea lifted the ban in 2008, and other Asian nations, such as Japan, Taiwan, and China may follow South Korea's lead. Here, in Seoul, South Korea, protestors march to the Presidential House during a protest against U.S. imported beef.*

same computer will cost £2,000. The increased cost, in pounds, will reduce the import of American computers—and all foreign goods—into England.

On the other hand, before devaluation, a £500 set of English bone china will cost an American $1,000. After the devaluation, the set of china will cost only $500. The decreased cost will make the china—and all English goods—much more attractive to U.S. purchasers. Bureaucratic red tape is more subtle than the other forms of nontariff barriers. Yet it can be the most frustrating trade barrier of all. A few examples are unnecessarily restrictive application of standards and complex requirements related to product testing, labeling, and certification.

Another type of nontariff barrier is related to cultural attitudes. Cultural barriers can impede acceptance of products in foreign countries. For example, illustrations of feet are regarded as despicable in Thailand. When customers are unfamiliar with particular products from another country, their general perceptions of the country itself affect their attitude toward the product and help to determine whether they will buy it. Because Mexican cars have not been viewed by the world as being quality products, Volkswagen, for example, may not want to advertise that some of its models sold in the United States are made in Mexico. Many retailers on the Internet have yet to come to grips with the task of designing an online shopping site that is attractive and functional for all global customers.

Reasons for Trade Restrictions

Various reasons are advanced for trade restrictions either on the import of specific products or on trade with particular countries. We have noted that political considerations usually are involved in trade embargoes. Other frequently cited reasons for restricting trade include the following:

- *To equalize a nation's balance of payments.* This may be considered necessary to restore confidence in the country's monetary system and in its ability to repay its debts.

- *To protect new or weak industries.* A new, or *infant,* industry may not be strong enough to withstand foreign competition. Temporary trade restrictions may be used to give it a chance to grow and become self-sufficient. The problem is that once an industry is protected from foreign competition, it may refuse to grow, and "temporary" trade restrictions will become permanent. For example, a recent report by the General Accounting Office (GAO), the congressional investigative agency, has accused the federal government of routinely imposing quotas on foreign textiles without "demonstrating the threat of serious damage" to U.S. industry. The GAO said that the Committee for the Implementation of Textile Agreements sometimes applies quotas even though it cannot prove the textile industry's claims that American companies have been hurt or jobs eliminated.
- *To protect national security.* Restrictions in this category generally apply to technological products that must be kept out of the hands of potential enemies. For example, strategic and defense-related goods cannot be exported to unfriendly nations.
- *To protect the health of citizens.* Products may be embargoed because they are dangerous or unhealthy (e.g., farm products contaminated with insecticides).
- *To retaliate for another nation's trade restrictions.* A country whose exports are taxed by another country may respond by imposing tariffs on imports from that country.
- *To protect domestic jobs.* By restricting imports, a nation can protect jobs in domestic industries. However, protecting these jobs can be expensive. For example, to protect 9,000 jobs in the U.S. carbon-steel industry costs $6.8 billion, or $750,000 per job. In addition, Gary Hufbauer and Ben Goodrich, economists at the Institute for International Economics, estimate that the tariffs could temporarily save 3,500 jobs in the steel industry, but at an annual cost to steel users of $2 billion, or $584,000 per job saved. Yet recently the United States imposed tariffs of up to 616 percent on steel pipes imported from China, South Korea, and Mexico. Similarly, it is estimated that we spent more than $100,000 for every job saved in the apparel manufacturing industry—jobs that seldom paid more than $15,000 a year.

Reasons Against Trade Restrictions

Trade restrictions have immediate and long-term economic consequences—both within the restricting nation and in world trade patterns. These include

- *Higher prices for consumers.* Higher prices may result from the imposition of tariffs or the elimination of foreign competition, as described earlier. For example, imposing quota restrictions and import protections adds $25 billion annually to U.S. consumers' apparel costs by directly increasing costs for imported apparel.
- *Restriction of consumers' choices.* Again, this is a direct result of the elimination of some foreign products from the marketplace and of the artificially high prices that importers must charge for products that still *are* imported.
- *Misallocation of international resources.* The protection of weak industries results in the inefficient use of limited resources. The economies of both the restricting nation and other nations eventually suffer because of this waste.
- *Loss of jobs.* The restriction of imports by one nation must lead to cutbacks—and the loss of jobs—in the export-oriented industries of other nations. Furthermore, trade protection has a significant effect on the composition of employment. U.S. trade restrictions—whether on textiles, apparel, steel, or automobiles—benefit only a few industries while harming many others. The gains in employment accrue to the protected industries and their primary suppliers, and the losses are spread across all other industries. A few states gain employment, but many other states lose employment.

3 The Extent of International Business

Learning Objective: Outline the extent of international trade and identify the organizations working to foster it.

Restrictions or not, international business is growing. Although the worldwide recessions of 1991, 2001–2002, and 2008 slowed the rate of growth, globalization is a reality of our time. In the United States, international trade now accounts for over one-fourth of GDP. As trade barriers decrease, new competitors enter the global marketplace, creating more choices for consumers and new opportunities for job seekers. International business will grow along with the expansion of commercial use of the Internet.

The World Economic Outlook for Trade

While the global economy continued to grow robustly in 2007 for the fourth consecutive year, economic performance has not been equal: growth in the advanced economies slowed, while emerging and developing economies continued to grow rapidly. Looking ahead, the International Monetary Fund (IMF), an international bank with 185 member nations, expected growth to decline in 2008 and 2009 in both advanced and emerging developing economies.[4]

U.S. beef processors and beef cattle ranchers lose billions of dollars in exports annually because of animal health and food safety restrictions in other countries. *Here, in a Tokyo supermarket, a salesperson arranges U.S. beef as Japan resumes sales. According to the U.S. International Trade Commission, animal health and food safety restrictions in importing countries reduced beef exports by $2.5 billion to $3.1 billion per year.*

AP Photo/Itsuo Inouye

While the U.S. economy has been growing steadily since 2000 and recorded the longest peacetime expansion in the nation's history, the worldwide recession has slowed the rate of growth. The IMF estimated that the U.S. economy grew by less than 2.2 percent in 2007 and, due to subprime mortgage lending and other financial problems, only 0.5 percent in 2008. International experts expected global economic growth of 3.7 percent in 2008 and 2009, despite the high oil prices. At this rate of growth, world production of goods and services will double by the year 2025.

Canada and Western Europe Our leading export partner, Canada, is projected to show the growth rate of 1.3 percent in 2008 and 1.9 percent in 2009. Economies in western Europe continued to expand gradually in 2007. The euro area grew by 1.5 percent in 2007, grew by 1.4 percent in 2008, and is expected to grow 1.2 percent in 2009. The United Kingdom enjoyed 2.5 percent economic growth in 2007 with the lowest level of unemployment in 25 years. Smaller European countries, such as Austria, the Netherlands, Sweden, and Switzerland, continued to grow.

Mexico and Latin America Our second largest export customer, Mexico, suffered its sharpest recession ever in 1995, but its growth rate in 2007 was just over 3 percent. In general, however, the Latin American economies grew 5.6 percent in 2007. Economic growth in the region grew by a robust 5.6 percent in 2007, the region's best four-year performance since the 1970s. Growth remained high in Central and South America, such as Argentina, Colombia, Peru, Venezuela, and Brazil. Growth in the region was projected at 4.4 percent in 2008 and 3.6 percent in 2009.

Japan Japan's economy is regaining momentum. Stronger consumer demand and business investment make Japan less reliant on exports for growth. The IMF estimated the growth for Japan at 1.4 percent in 2008 and 1.5 percent in 2009.

Asia The economic growth in Asia remained strong in 2007. Growth was led by China, where its economy expanded by 11.4 percent in the second half of 2007, but it was estimated at 9.3 percent in 2008. Growth in India slowed modestly to 8.5 percent in 2007 and 7.9 percent in 2008. A strong consumer demand supported economic growth in Indonesia, Malaysia, Hong Kong, the Philippines, and Singapore. The growth in emerging Asia remained at 7.5 percent in 2008 and 7.8 percent in 2009.

China's emergence as a global economic power has been among the most dramatic economic developments of recent decades. From 1980 to 2004, China's economy averaged a real GDB growth rate of 9.5 percent and became the world's sixth-largest economy. China's total share in world trade expanded from 1 percent in 1980 to almost 6 percent in 2003. By 2004, China had become the third-largest trading nation in dollar terms, behind the United States and Germany and just ahead of Japan.[5]

Emerging Europe Economic growth in this region was 5.8 percent in 2007. Hungary, Turkey, Estonia, and Latvia experienced a slower growth. Nonetheless, 2007 marked the sixth consecutive year during which emerging Europe grew much faster than western Europe. The 2008 growth for the region was expected to be 4.4 percent.

Ethics Matters

Where There's Smoke . . .

Limit smoking and tobacco advertising—that's the World Health Organization's formula for saving a billion lives during the 21st century. Despite on-pack warnings and advertising restrictions, smoking is on the rise in developing nations. For example, China is home to 30 percent of the world's smokers. In fact, its smoking population of 350 million people is larger than the entire U.S. population.

The Chinese government owns the country's largest tobacco companies, and a package of cigarettes is far cheaper in China than anywhere else in the world, two factors that complicate efforts to curb smoking. Still, China recently began requiring prominent health warnings on cigarette packs and banned smoking in Beijing's museums and other public buildings.

In India, the world's second-largest market for cigarettes, tobacco companies are not allowed to advertise their products. For years, they got around restrictions through "surrogate advertising," promoting different products with the same brand as their cigarettes. When India tightened regulation of surrogate advertising, many cigarette companies turned to sponsorship of sports and fashion events.

To save lives, the World Health Organization wants governments to ban all tobacco marketing and outlaw smoking in all workplaces. What's next for the global cigarette business?

Sources: "China Tobacco Merger to Form Industry Leader: Report," *Reuters*, August 26, 2008, **www.reuters.com**; Mark Magnier, "Smoke-Free Olympics," *Houston Chronicle*, May 11, 2008, p. 23; Niraj Sheth, "India Liquor, Tobacco Firms Shift Tack," *Wall Street Journal*, May 6, 2008, p. B8; Bill Marsh, "A Growing Cloud over the Planet," *New York Times*, February 24, 2008, p. WK-4; "How to Save a Billion Lives," *The Economist*, February 9, 2008, p. 66.

Commonwealth of Independent States The growth was expected to be 7 percent in 2008 and 6.5 percent in 2009. Strong growth was expected to continue in Azerbaijan and Armenia, while it will remain stable in Moldova, Tajikistan, and Uzbekistan.

After World War II, trade between the United States and the communist nations of central and Eastern Europe was minimal. The United States maintained high tariff barriers on imports from most of these countries and also restricted its exports. However, since the disintegration of the Soviet Union and the collapse of communism, trade between the United States and central and Eastern Europe has expanded substantially.

The countries that made the transition from communist to market economies quickly have recorded positive growth for several years—those that did not continue to struggle. Among the nations that have enjoyed several years of positive economic growth are the member countries of the Central European Free Trade Association (CEFTA): Hungary, the Czech Republic, Poland, Slovenia, and the Republic of Slovakia.

SPOTLIGHT

116 U.S. Cities Post Exports in Excess of $1 Billion

Source: **http://trade.gov/press/publications/newsletters/ita_0208/metrodata_0208.asp,** accessed November 26, 2008.

U.S. exports to central and Eastern Europe and Russia will increase, as will U.S. investment in these countries, as demand for capital goods and technology opens new markets for U.S. products. There already has been a substantial expansion in trade between the United States and the Czech Republic, the Republic of Slovakia, Hungary, and Poland. Table 3.1 shows the growth rates from 2006 to 2009 for most regions of the world.

Exports and the U.S. Economy Globalization represents a huge opportunity for all countries—rich or poor. The fifteen-fold increase in trade volume over the past fifty years has been one of the most important factors in the rise of living standards around the world. During this time, exports have become increasingly important to the U.S. economy. Exports as a percentage of U.S. GDP have increased steadily since 1985, except in the 2001 recession. And our exports to developing and newly industrialized countries are on the rise. Table 3.2 shows the value of U.S. merchandise exports to and imports from each of the nation's ten major trading partners. Note that Canada and Mexico are our best partners for our exports; China and Canada, for imports.

Table 3.1: Global Growth Remains Sluggish

Growth has been led by developing countries and emerging markets.

	2006	2007	Projected 2008	Projected 2009
	(annual percent change)			
World	5.0	4.9	3.7	3.9
United States	2.9	2.2	0.5	0.6
Euro area	2.8	2.6	1.4	1.2
United Kingdom	2.9	3.1	1.6	1.6
Japan	2.4	2.1	1.4	1.5
Canada	2.8	2.7	1.3	1.9
Other advanced economies	4.5	4.6	3.3	3.4
Newly industrialized Asian economies	5.6	5.6	4.0	4.4
Developing countries and emerging markets	7.8	7.9	6.7	6.6
Africa	5.9	6.2	6.3	6.4
Developing Asia	9.6	9.7	8.2	8.4
CIS	8.2	8.5	7.0	6.5
Middle East	5.8	5.8	6.1	6.1
Western Hemisphere	5.5	5.6	4.4	3.6

Source: *International Monetary Fund: World Economic Outlook* by International Monetary Fund. Copyright 2008 by International Monetary Fund. Reproduced with permission of International Monetary Fund via Copyright Clearance Center.

Table 3.2: Value of U.S. Merchandise Exports and Imports, 2007

Rank/Trading Partner	Exports ($ billions)	Rank/Trading Partner	Imports ($ billions)
1 Canada	248.9	1 China	321.4
2 Mexico	136.5	2 Canada	313.0
3 China	65.2	3 Mexico	210.8
4 Japan	62.7	4 Japan	145.5
5 United Kingdom	50.2	5 Germany	94.4
6 Germany	49.7	6 United Kingdom	56.9
7 South Korea	34.6	7 South Korea	47.6
8 Netherlands	33.0	8 France	41.6
9 France	27.4	9 Venezuela	39.9
10 Taiwan	26.3	10 Taiwan	38.3

Source: U.S. Department of Commerce, International Trade Administration, **http://www.census.gov/foreign-trade/statistics/highlights/top/top0712.html,** accessed September 22, 2008.

Figure 3.3 shows the U.S. goods export and import shares in 2007. Major U.S. exports and imports are manufactured goods, agricultural products, and mineral fuels.

International Trade Agreements

The General Agreement on Tariffs and Trade and the World Trade Organization

At the end of World War II, the United States and twenty-two other nations organized the body that came to be known as *GATT*. The **General Agreement on Tariffs and Trade (GATT)** was an international organization of 153 nations dedicated to

General Agreement on Tariffs and Trade (GATT) an international organization of 153 nations dedicated to reducing or eliminating tariffs and other barriers to world trade

Figure 3.3: U.S. Goods Export and Import Shares in 2007

About 39 percent of our exports and 43 percent of our imports in 2007 were from our leading trade partners Canada, Mexico, and China.

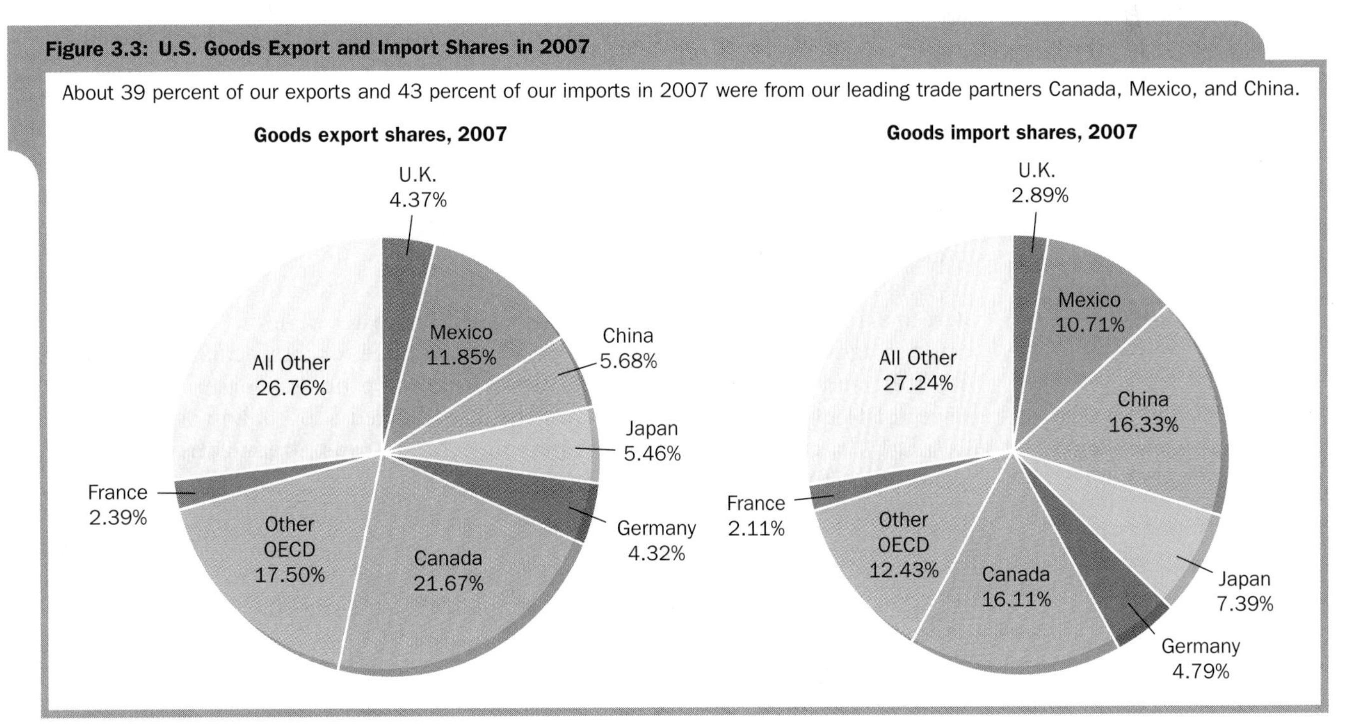

Source: Federal Reserve Bank of St. Louis, *National Economic Trends,* September 2008, p. 18.

In 2008, Ukraine became the WTO's 152nd member nation. *Here, Ukraine's President Victor Yushchenko, declared "Ukraine's membership to the WTO is truly an historic moment and is a decisive milestone in the development of our economy. We are convinced that our efforts will yield results and allow us to build closer economic ties worldwide."*

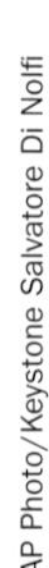

reducing or eliminating tariffs and other barriers to world trade. These 153 nations accounted for 90 percent of the world's merchandise trade. GATT, headquartered in Geneva, Switzerland, provided a forum for tariff negotiations and a means for settling international trade disputes and problems. *Most-favored-nation status* (MFN) was the famous principle of GATT. It meant that each GATT member nation was to be treated equally by all contracting nations. MFN therefore ensured that any tariff reductions or other trade concessions were extended automatically to all GATT members. From 1947 to 1994, the body sponsored eight rounds of negotiations to reduce trade restrictions. Three of the most fruitful were the Kennedy Round, the Tokyo Round, and the Uruguay Round.

The Kennedy Round (1964–1967) In 1962, the U.S. Congress passed the Trade Expansion Act. This law gave President John F. Kennedy the authority to negotiate reciprocal trade agreements that could reduce U.S. tariffs by as much as 50 percent. Armed with this authority, which was granted for a period of five years, President Kennedy called for a round of negotiations through GATT.

These negotiations, which began in 1964, have since become known as the *Kennedy Round.* They were aimed at reducing tariffs and other barriers to trade in both industrial and agricultural products. The participants succeeded in reducing tariffs on these products by an average of more than 35 percent. They were less successful in removing other types of trade barriers.

The Tokyo Round (1973–1979) In 1973, representatives of approximately one hundred nations gathered in Tokyo for another round of GATT negotiations. The *Tokyo Round* was completed in 1979. The participants negotiated tariff cuts of 30 to 35 percent, which were to be implemented over an eight-year period. In addition, they were able to remove or ease such nontariff barriers as import quotas, unrealistic quality standards for imports, and unnecessary red tape in customs procedures.

The Uruguay Round (1986–1993) In 1986, the *Uruguay Round* was launched to extend trade liberalization and widen the GATT treaty to include textiles, agricultural products, business services, and intellectual-property rights. This most ambitious and comprehensive global commercial agreement in history concluded overall negotiations on December 15, 1993, with delegations on hand from 109 nations. The agreement included provisions to lower tariffs by greater than one-third, to reform trade in agricultural goods, to write new rules of trade for intellectual property and services, and to strengthen the dispute-settlement process. These reforms were expected to expand the world economy by an estimated $200 billion annually.

World Trade Organization (WTO) powerful successor to GATT that incorporates trade in goods, services, and ideas

The Uruguay Round also created the **World Trade Organization (WTO)** on January 1, 1995. The WTO was established by GATT to oversee the provisions of the Uruguay Round and resolve any resulting trade disputes. Membership in the WTO obliges 148 member nations to observe GATT rules. The WTO has judicial powers to mediate among members disputing the new rules. It incorporates trade in goods, services, and ideas and exerts more binding authority than GATT.

The Doha Round (2001) On November 14, 2001, in Doha, Qatar, the WTO members agreed to further reduce trade barriers through multilateral trade negotiations over the next three years. This new round of negotiations focuses on industrial tariffs and nontariff barriers, agriculture, services, and easing trade rules. U.S. exporters of industrial and agricultural goods and services should have improved access to overseas markets. The Doha Round has set the stage for WTO members to take an important step toward significant new multilateral trade liberalization. It is a difficult task, but the rewards—lower tariffs, more choices for consumers, and further integration of developing countries into the world trading system—are sure to be worth the effort. Some experts suggest that U.S. exporters of industrial and agricultural goods and services should have improved access to overseas markets, whereas others disagree.

International Economic Organizations Working to Foster Trade

The primary objective of the WTO is to remove barriers to trade on a worldwide basis. On a smaller scale, an **economic community** is an organization of nations formed to promote the free movement of resources and products among its members and to create common economic policies. A number of economic communities now exist.

economic community an organization of nations formed to promote the free movement of resources and products among its members and to create common economic policies

- The *European Union* (EU), also known as the *European Economic Community* and the *Common Market,* was formed in 1957 by six countries—France, the Federal Republic of Germany, Italy, Belgium, the Netherlands, and Luxembourg. Its objective was freely conducted commerce among these nations and others that might later join. As shown in Figure 3.4, many more nations have joined the EU since then.
- On January 1, 2007, the twenty-five nations of the EU became the EU27 as Bulgaria and Romania became new members. The EU is now an economic force with a collective economy larger than much of the United States or Japan.

In celebrating the EU's fiftieth anniversary in 2007, the president of the European Commission, Jose Manuel Durao Baroso, declared, "Let us first recognize fifty years of achievement. Peace, liberty, and prosperity, beyond the dreams of even the most optimistic founding fathers of Europe. In 1957, fifteen of our twenty-seven members were either under dictatorship or were not allowed to exist as independent countries. Now we are all prospering democracies. The EU of today is around fifty times more prosperous and with three times the population of the EU of 1957."

Since January 2002, fifteen member nations of the EU are participating in the new common currency, the euro. The euro is the single currency of the European Monetary Union nations. But three EU members, Denmark, the United Kingdom, and Sweden, still keep their own currencies.

- A second community in Europe, the *European Economic Area* (EEA), became effective in January 1994. This pact consists of Iceland, Norway, Liechtenstein, and the twenty-seven member nations of the EU. The EEA, encompassing an area inhabited by more than 500 million people, allows for the free movement of goods throughout all thirty countries.
- The *North American Free Trade Agreement* (NAFTA) joined the United States with its first- and second-largest export trading partners, Canada and Mexico. Implementation of NAFTA on January 1, 1994, created a market of over 448 million people. This market consists of Canada (population 33 million), the United States (305 million), and Mexico (110 million). According to the Office of the U.S. Trade Representative, after 14 years,

AP Photo/Dennis Sarkic

From Tolars to Euros. *Slovenia got the green light to change Slovenia tolars to euros on January 1, 2007. A recent European Commission meeting gave Slovenia the charge to be the first Eastern European country with a euro currency. The Slovenians still pay with tolars but receive the return change in euros, causing calculation difficulties for the cashiers and customers.*

Figure 3.4: The Evolving European Union

The Evolving European Union: The European Union is now an economic force, with a collective economy larger than that of the United States or Japan.

Source: http://europa.eu/abc/european_countries/index_en.htm, accessed November 29, 2008.

NAFTA has achieved its core goals of expanding trade and investment between the United States, Canada, and Mexico. For example, from 1993 to 2007, trade among the NAFTA nations more than tripled, from $297 billion to $930 billion. Business investment in the Untied States has risen by 117 percent since 1993, compared to a 45 percent increase between 1979 and 1993. During the same period, the U.S. employment rose from 110.8 million people in 1993 to 137.6 million in 2007, an increase of 24 percent. The average unemployment rate was 5.1 percent in the period 1994–2007, compared to 7.1 percent during the period 1980–1993.[6]

NAFTA is built on the Canadian Free Trade Agreement (FTA), signed by the United States and Canada in 1989, and on the substantial trade and investment reforms undertaken by Mexico since the mid-1980s. Initiated by the Mexican government, formal negotiations on NAFTA began in June 1991 among the three governments. The support of NAFTA by President Bill Clinton, past U.S. Presidents Ronald Reagan and Jimmy Carter, and Nobel Prize–winning economists provided the impetus for U.S. congressional ratification of NAFTA in November 1993. NAFTA will gradually eliminate all tariffs on goods produced and traded among Canada, Mexico, and the United States to provide for a totally free-trade area by 2009. Chile is expected to become the fourth member of NAFTA, but political forces may delay its entry into the agreement for several years.

- The *Central American Free Trade Agreement* (CAFTA) was created in 2003 by the United States and four Central American countries—El Salvador, Guatemala, Honduras, and Nicaragua. The CAFTA became CAFTA-DR when the Dominican Republic joined the group in 2007. The volume of trade between the United States and its CAFTA partners has increased by 17 percent since 2005, rising from $27.9 billion in 2005 to $32.6 billion in 2007.[7]

- The *Association of Southeast Asian Nations* (ASEAN), with headquarters in Jakarta, Indonesia, was established in 1967 to promote political, economic, and social cooperation among its seven member countries: Indonesia, Malaysia, Philippines, Singapore, Thailand, Brunei, and Vietnam. With the three new members, Cambodia, Laos, and Myanmar, this region is already our fifth largest trading partner. The 10-member region, with a population of 580 million has $2.8 trillion in gross domestic product and accounts for over $169 million worth of trade with the United States.[8]
- The *Pacific Rim,* referring to countries and economies bordering the Pacific Ocean, is an informal, flexible term generally regarded as a reference to East Asia, Canada, and the United States. At a minimum, the Pacific Rim includes Canada, Japan, China, Taiwan, and the United States.
- The *Commonwealth of Independent States* (CIS) was established in December 1991 by the newly independent states (NIS) as an association of eleven republics of the former Soviet Union.
- The *Caribbean Basin Initiative* (CBI) is an inter-American program led by the United States to give economic assistance and trade preferences to Caribbean and Central American countries. CBI provides duty-free access to the U.S. market for most products from the region and promotes private-sector development in member nations.
- The *Common Market of the Southern Cone* (MERCOSUR) was established in 1991 under the Treaty of Asuncion to unite Argentina, Brazil, Paraguay, and Uruguay as a free-trade alliance; Colombia, Ecuador, Peru, Bolivia, and Chile joined later as associates. The alliance represents over 267 million consumers—67 percent of South America's population, making it the third-largest trading bloc behind NAFTA and the EU. Like NAFTA, MERCOSUR promotes "the free circulation of goods, services and production factors among the countries" and established a common external tariff and commercial policy.
- The *Organization of Petroleum Exporting Countries* (OPEC) was founded in 1960 in response to reductions in the prices that oil companies were willing to pay for crude oil. The organization was conceived as a collective-bargaining unit to provide oil-producing nations with some control over oil prices.
- The *Organization for Economic Cooperation and Development* (OECD) is a group of thirty industrialized market-economy countries of North America, Europe, the Far East, and the South Pacific. OECD, headquartered in Paris, was established in 1961 to promote economic development and international trade.

Methods of Entering International Business

Learning Objective: Define the methods by which a firm can organize for and enter into international markets.

A firm that has decided to enter international markets can do so in several ways. We will discuss several different methods. These different approaches require varying degrees of involvement in international business. Typically, a firm begins its international operations at the simplest level. Then, depending on its goals, it may progress to higher levels of involvement.

Licensing

licensing a contractual agreement in which one firm permits another to produce and market its product and use its brand name in return for a royalty or other compensation

Licensing is a contractual agreement in which one firm permits another to produce and market its product and use its brand name in return for a royalty or other compensation. For example, Yoplait yogurt is a French yogurt licensed for production in the United States. The Yoplait brand maintains an appealing French image, and in return, the U.S. producer pays the French firm a percentage of its income from sales of the product.

Licensing is especially advantageous for small manufacturers wanting to launch a well-known domestic brand internationally. For example, all Spalding sporting products are licensed worldwide. The licensor, the Questor Corporation, owns the Spalding name but produces no goods itself. Licensing thus provides a simple method for expanding into a foreign market with virtually no investment. On the other hand, if the licensee does not maintain the licensor's product standards, the product's image may be damaged. Another possible disadvantage is that a licensing arrangement may not provide the original producer with any foreign marketing experience.

Sony is set to export its 2 GB Memory Stick Entertainment Pack, loaded with one of the four movies: "Hitch," "S.W.A.T." "The Grudge" or "XXX: State of the Union." *Sony is also introducing tiny 2 GB and 4 GB Memory Stick Micro™ media cards for use with Sony Ericsson and other cellular phones.*

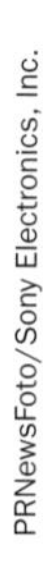
PRNewsFoto/Sony Electronics, Inc.

Exporting

A firm also may manufacture its products in its home country and export them for sale in foreign markets. As with licensing, exporting can be a relatively low-risk method of entering foreign markets. Unlike licensing, however, it is not a simple method; it opens up several levels of involvement to the exporting firm.

At the most basic level, the exporting firm may sell its products outright to an *export-import merchant,* which is essentially a merchant wholesaler. The merchant assumes all the risks of product ownership, distribution, and sale. It may even purchase the goods in the producer's home country and assume responsibility for exporting the goods. An important and practical issue for domestic firms dealing with foreign customers is securing payment. This is a two-sided issue that reflects the mutual concern rightly felt by both parties to the trade deal: The exporter would like to be paid before shipping the merchandise, whereas the importer obviously would prefer to know that it has received the shipment before releasing any funds. Neither side wants to take the risk of fulfilling its part of the deal only later to discover that the other side has not. The result would lead to legal costs and complex, lengthy dealings wasteful of everyone's resources. This mutual level of mistrust is in fact good business sense and has been around since the beginning of trade centuries ago. The solution then was as it still is today—for both parties to use a mutually trusted go-between who can ensure that the payment is held until the merchandise is in fact delivered according to the terms of the trade contract. The go-between representatives employed by the importer and exporter are still, as they were in the past, the local domestic banks involved in international business.

Here is a simplified version of how it works. After signing contracts detailing the merchandise sold and terms for its delivery, an importer will ask its local bank to issue a **letter of credit** for the amount of money needed to pay for the merchandise. The letter of credit is issued "in favor of the exporter," meaning that the funds are tied specifically to the trade contract involved. The importer's bank forwards the letter of credit to the exporter's bank, which also normally deals in international transactions. The exporter's bank then notifies the exporter that a letter of credit has been received in its name, and the exporter can go ahead with the shipment. The carrier transporting the merchandise provides the exporter with evidence of the shipment in a document called a **bill of lading**. The exporter signs over title to the merchandise (now in transit) to its bank by delivering signed copies of the bill of lading and the letter of credit.

letter of credit issued by a bank on request of an importer stating that the bank will pay an amount of money to a stated beneficiary

bill of lading document issued by a transport carrier to an exporter to prove that merchandise has been shipped

draft issued by the exporter's bank, ordering the importer's bank to pay for the merchandise, thus guaranteeing payment once accepted by the importer's bank

In exchange, the exporter issues a **draft** from the bank, which orders the importer's bank to pay for the merchandise. The draft, bill of lading, and letter of credit are sent from the exporter's bank to the importer's bank. Acceptance by the importer's bank leads to return of the draft and its sale by the exporter to its bank, meaning that the exporter receives cash and the bank assumes the risk of collecting the funds from the foreign bank. The importer is obliged to pay its bank on delivery of the merchandise, and the deal is complete.

In most cases, the letter of credit is part of a lending arrangement between the importer and its bank, and of course, both banks earn fees for issuing letters of credit and drafts and for handling the import-export services for their clients. Furthermore, the process incorporates the fact that both importer and exporter will have different local currencies and might even negotiate their trade in a third currency. The banks look after all the necessary exchanges. For example, the vast majority of international business is negotiated in U.S. dollars, even though the trade may be between countries other than the United States. Thus, although the importer may end up paying for the merchandise in its local currency and the exporter may receive payment in another local currency, the banks involved will exchange all necessary foreign funds in order to allow the deal to take place.

The exporting firm instead may ship its products to an *export-import agent,* which for a commission or fee arranges the sale of the products to foreign intermediaries. The agent is an independent firm—like other agents—that sells and may perform other marketing functions for the exporter. The exporter, however, retains title to the products during shipment and until they are sold.

An exporting firm also may establish its own *sales offices,* or *branches,* in foreign countries. These installations are international extensions of the firm's distribution system. They represent a deeper involvement in international business than the other exporting techniques we have discussed—and thus they carry a greater risk. The exporting firm maintains control over sales, and it gains both experience in and knowledge of foreign markets. Eventually, the firm also may develop its own sales force to operate in conjunction with foreign sales offices.

Joint Ventures

A *joint venture* is a partnership formed to achieve a specific goal or to operate for a specific period of time. A joint venture with an established firm in a foreign country provides immediate market knowledge and access, reduced risk, and control over product attributes. However, joint-venture agreements established across national borders can become extremely complex. As a result, joint-venture agreements generally require a very high level of commitment from all the parties involved.

A joint venture may be used to produce and market an existing product in a foreign nation or to develop an entirely new product. Recently, for example, Archer Daniels Midland Company (ADM), one of the world's leading food processors, entered into a joint venture with Gruma SA, Mexico's largest corn flour and tortilla company. Besides a 22 percent stake in Gruma, ADM also received stakes in other joint ventures operated by Gruma. One of them will combine both companies' U.S. corn flour operations, which account for about 25 percent of the U.S. market. ADM also has a 40 percent stake in a Mexican wheat flour mill. ADM's joint venture increased its participation in the growing Mexican economy, where ADM already produces corn syrup, fructose, starch, and wheat flour.

PRNewsFoto/Volkswagen of America

Venturing into a joint venture. *Archer Daniels Midland Company (ADM) and Volkswagen AG formed a joint research alliance to develop and use biodiesel fuels for the automotive industry. ADM is a world leader in renewable fuels. Volkswagen and ADM are now testing a blend of 20 percent biodiesel in order to provide ever-cleaner alternative and sustainable fuel choices.*

Totally Owned Facilities

At a still deeper level of involvement in international business, a firm may develop *totally owned facilities,* that is, its own

Going Global

It Takes Two

What does it take to make a joint venture work? First, both partners must see a real benefit in working together. When Sweden's Ericsson and the French-Italian firm STMicroelectronics formed a joint venture, one big benefit was that the new company instantly became the third-largest industry player in the global market for mobile phone chips. The joint venture also opened more opportunities for cost-savings and for selling to a larger customer base than either partner would have on its own.

Second, the partners must agree on how to manage the joint venture. When BP formed TNK-BP, a joint venture with Russian oil companies, it negotiated management for months. To get the joint venture going, BP eventually had to give up on its first pick for CEO and give up some control by allowing its partners additional board seats.

Finally, all partners must add value to the joint venture. When the e-commerce company Alibaba wanted to expand beyond China, it moved into Japan through a joint venture with a Tokyo-based firm and into India through a joint venture with a Mumbai-based firm. The joint ventures worked because Alibaba provided the e-commerce expertise and its partners provided their knowledge of local markets, needs, and customs.

Sources: Andrew E. Kramer, "BP Makes Deep Concessions in Agreement with Russian Partner," *New York Times*, September 5, 2008, **www.nytimes.com;** Richard Wray, "Telecoms: Ericsson Tosses Its Chips into European Joint Venture," *The Guardian (U.K.)*, August 21, 2008, **www.guardian.co.uk;** Bruce Einhorn, "China's Alibaba Expands to India, Japan," *BusinessWeek*, September 5, 2008, **www.businessweek.com.**

production and marketing facilities in one or more foreign nations. This *direct investment* provides complete control over operations, but it carries a greater risk than the joint venture. The firm is really establishing a subsidiary in a foreign country. Most firms do so only after they have acquired some knowledge of the host country's markets.

Direct investment may take either of two forms. In the first, the firm builds or purchases manufacturing and other facilities in the foreign country. It uses these facilities to produce its own established products and to market them in that country and perhaps in neighboring countries. Firms such as General Motors, Union Carbide, and Colgate-Palmolive are multinational companies with worldwide manufacturing facilities. Colgate-Palmolive factories are becoming *Eurofactories*, supplying neighboring countries as well as their own local markets.

A second form of direct investment in international business is the purchase of an existing firm in a foreign country under an arrangement that allows it to operate independently of the parent company. When Sony Corporation (a Japanese firm) decided to enter the motion-picture business in the United States, it chose to purchase Columbia Pictures Entertainment, Inc., rather than start a new motion-picture studio from scratch.

Strategic Alliances

strategic alliances a partnership formed to create competitive advantage on a worldwide basis

A **strategic alliance**, the newest form of international business structure, is a partnership formed to create competitive advantage on a worldwide basis. Strategic alliances are very similar to joint ventures. The number of strategic alliances is growing at an estimated rate of about 20 percent per year. In fact, in the automobile and computer industries, strategic alliances are becoming the predominant means of competing. International competition is so fierce and the costs of competing on a global basis are so high that few firms have all the resources needed to do it alone. Thus, individual firms that lack the internal resources essential for international success may seek to collaborate with other companies.

An example of such an alliance is the New United Motor Manufacturing, Inc. (NUMMI), formed by Toyota and General Motors to make automobiles of both firms. This enterprise united the quality engineering of Japanese cars with the marketing expertise and market access of General Motors.[9]

Trading Companies

trading company provides a link between buyers and sellers in different countries

A **trading company** provides a link between buyers and sellers in different countries. A trading company, as its name implies, is not involved in manufacturing or owning assets related to manufacturing. It buys products in one country at the lowest price consistent with quality and sells to buyers in another country. An important function of trading companies is taking title to products and performing all the activities necessary to move the products from the domestic country to a foreign country. For example, large grain-trading companies operating out of home offices both in the United States and overseas control a major portion of the world's trade in basic food commodities. These trading companies sell homogeneous agricultural commodities that can be stored and moved rapidly in response to market conditions.

Sustaining the Planet

Knowing that sustainability is a global business concern, the United Nations has set up a special division to focus on sustainable development. **www.un.org/esa/sustdev/**

Countertrade

In the early 1990s, many developing nations had major restrictions on converting domestic currency into foreign currency. Exporters therefore had to resort to barter agreements with importers. **Countertrade** is essentially an international barter transaction in which goods and services are exchanged for different goods and services. Examples include Saudi Arabia's purchase of ten 747 jets from Boeing with payment in crude oil and Philip Morris's sale of cigarettes to Russia in return for chemicals used to make fertilizers.

countertrade an international barter transaction

Multinational Firms

A **multinational enterprise** is a firm that operates on a worldwide scale without ties to any specific nation or region. The multinational firm represents the highest level of involvement in international business. It is equally "at home" in most countries of the world. In fact, as far as the operations of the multinational enterprise are concerned, national boundaries exist only on maps. It is, however, organized under the laws of its home country.

multinational enterprise a firm that operates on a worldwide scale without ties to any specific nation or region

Table 3.3 shows the ten largest foreign and U.S. public multinational companies; the ranking is based on a composite score reflecting each company's best three out of four rankings for sales, profits, assets, and market value. Table 3.4 describes steps in entering international markets.

According to the chairman of the board of Dow Chemical Company, a multinational firm of U.S. origin, "The emergence of a world economy and of the multinational corporation has been accomplished hand in hand." He sees multinational enterprises moving toward what he calls the "anational company," a firm that has

Table 3.3: The Ten Largest Foreign and U.S. Multinational Corporations

2007 Rank	Company	Business	Country	Revenue ($ millions)
1	Wal-Mart Stores	General merchandiser	United States	378,799
2	ExxonMobil	Energy	United States	372,824
3	Royal Dutch/ Shell Group	Energy	Netherlands/United Kingdom	355,782
4	BP	Energy	United Kingdom	291,438
5	Toyota Motor	Automobiles	Japan	230,201
6	Chevron	Energy	United States	210,783
7	ING Group	Financial services	Netherlands	201,516
8	Total	Energy	France	187,280
9	General Motors	Automobiles	United States	182,347
10	Conoco Phillips	Energy	United States	178,558

Source: Fortune Global 500, July 1, 2008, p. 165. Copyright © 2006 Time, Inc., **www.fortune.com**. All rights reserved.

Table 3.4: Steps in Entering International Markets

Step	Activity	Marketing Tasks
1	Identify exportable products	Identify key selling features Identify needs that they satisfy Identify the selling constraints that are imposed
2	Identify key foreign markets for the products	Determine who the customers are Pinpoint what and when they will buy Do market research Establish priority, or "target," countries
3	Analyze how to sell in each priority market (methods will be affected by product characteristics and unique features of country/ market)	Locate available government and private-sector resources Determine service and backup sales requirements
4	Set export prices and payment terms, methods, and techniques	Establish methods of export pricing Establish sales terms, quotations, invoices, and conditions of sale Determine methods of international payments, secured and unsecured
5	Estimate resource requirements and returns	Estimate financial requirements Estimate human resources requirements (full- or part-time export department or operation?) Estimate plant production capacity Determine necessary product adaptations
6	Establish overseas distribution network	Determine distribution agreement and other key marketing decisions (price, repair policies, returns, territory, performance, and termination) Know your customer (use U.S. Department of Commerce international marketing services)
7	Determine shipping, traffic, and documentation procedures and requirements	Determine methods of shipment (air or ocean freight, truck, rail) Finalize containerization Obtain validated export license Follow export-administration documentation procedures
8	Promote, sell, and be paid	Use international media, communications, advertising, trade shows, and exhibitions Determine the need for overseas travel (when, where, and how often?) Initiate customer follow-up procedures
9	Continuously analyze current marketing, economic, and political situations	Recognize changing factors influencing marketing strategies Constantly reevaluate

Source: U.S. Department of Commerce, International Trade Administration, Washington, D.C.

no nationality but belongs to all countries. In recognition of this movement, there already have been international conferences devoted to the question of how such enterprises would be controlled.

Sources of Export Assistance

5

Learning Objective: Describe the various sources of export assistance.

In September 1993, President Bill Clinton announced the *National Export Strategy* (NES) to revitalize U.S. exports. Under the NES, the *Trade Promotion Coordinating Committee* (TPCC) assists U.S. firms in developing export-promotion programs. The export services and programs of the nineteen TPCC agencies can help American firms to compete in foreign markets and create new jobs in the United States. Table 3.5 provides an overview of selected export assistance programs.

These and other sources of export information enhance the business opportunities of U.S. firms seeking to enter expanding foreign markets. Another vital energy factor is financing.

Table 3.5: U.S. Government Export Assistance Programs

1	U.S. Export Assistance Centers, **www.sba.gov/oit/export/useac.html**	Provides assistance in export marketing and trade finance.
2	International Trade Administration, **www.ita.doc.gov/**	Offers assistance and information to exporters through its domestic and overseas commercial officers.
3	U.S. and Foreign Commercial Services, **www.export.gov/**	Helps U.S. firms compete more effectively in the global marketplace and provides information on foreign markets.
4	Advocacy Center, **www.ita.doc.gov/advocacy**	Facilitates advocacy to assist U.S. firms competing for major projects and procurements worldwide.
5	Trade Information Center, **www.ita.doc.gov/td/tic/**	Provides U.S. companies information on federal programs and activities that support U.S. exports.
6	STAT-USA/Internet, **www.stat-usa.gov/**	Offers a comprehensive collection of business, economic, and trade information on the Web.
7	Small Business Administration, **www.sba.gov/oit/**	Publishes many helpful guides to assist small and medium-sized companies.
8	National Trade Data Bank, **www.stat-usa.gov/tradtest.nsf**	Provides international economic and export promotion information supplied by over twenty U.S. agencies.

Financing International Business

6

Learning Objective: Identify the institutions that help firms and nations finance international business.

International trade compounds the concerns of financial managers. Currency exchange rates, tariffs and foreign-exchange controls, and the tax structures of host nations all affect international operations and the flow of cash. In addition, financial managers must be concerned both with the financing of their international operations and with the means available to their customers to finance purchases.

Fortunately, along with business in general, a number of large banks have become international in scope. Many have established branches in major cities around the world. Thus, like firms in other industries, they are able to provide their services where and when they are needed. In addition, financial assistance is available from U.S. government and international sources.

Several of today's international financial organizations were founded many years ago to facilitate free trade and the exchange of currencies among nations. Some, such as the Inter-American Development Bank, are supported internationally and focus on developing countries. Others, such as the Export-Import Bank, are operated by one country but provide international financing.

The Export-Import Bank of the United States

The **Export-Import Bank of the United States**, created in 1934, is an independent agency of the U.S. government whose function it is to assist in financing the exports of American firms. *Eximbank*, as it is commonly called, extends and guarantees credit to overseas buyers of American goods and services and guarantees short-term financing for exports. It also cooperates with commercial banks in helping American exporters to offer credit to their overseas customers.

Export-Import Bank of the United States an independent agency of the U.S. government whose function it is to assist in financing the exports of American firms

Multilateral Development Banks

A **multilateral development bank (MDB)** is an internationally supported bank that provides loans to developing countries to help them grow. The most familiar is the World Bank, which operates worldwide. Four other MDBs operate primarily in Central and South America, Asia, Africa, and Eastern and Central Europe. All five are supported by the industrialized nations, including the United States.

multilateral development bank (MDB) an internationally supported bank that provides loans to developing countries to help them grow

Entrepreneurial Challenge

Ex-Pats Make a Market

Many entrepreneurs are building successful businesses by catering to the needs of expatriates, people who live and work far from their home countries. For example, specialty-food businesses in and around major cities import products to attract expatriates who crave a taste of home. When Oscar Espinosa teamed up with a partner to open De Mi Pueblo in Springfield, Virginia, they originally focused on cheeses from Central America. Today, they import hundreds of thousands of pounds of cheese, beans, crackers, and other foods every month from Nicaragua and surrounding nations.

Sonni Kohli opened Kohli's Indian Emporium in Pittsburgh to sell authentic ingredients such as atta flour and prepared foods such as rose, mango, and saffron-pistachio ice cream. In addition to serving expatriates, Kohli's also attracts local customers who are interested in Indian food.

Graciela and Inocente Hernandez started their first Mexican foods grocery store in Milwaukee in 2002. Sales were so strong that the couple decided to open a second store six years later. With the help of the Latino Entrepreneurial Network of southeastern Wisconsin, the Hernandezes created a solid business plan and found financing to set up their second store.

Sources: Tannette Johnson-Elie, "Network Pairs Hispanic Entrepreneurs with Resources," *Journal Sentinel Online (Milwaukee)*, September 16, 2008, **www.jsonline.com**; Marcela Sanchez, "Turning a Taste for Home into a Win-Win for Trade," *Washington Post.com*, September 5, 2008, **www.washingtonpost.com**; Cecilia Kang, "Ethnic Grocers Losing Their Niche," *Washington Post*, September 3, 2007, p. D1.

The *Inter-American Development Bank* (IDB), the oldest and largest regional bank, was created in 1959 by nineteen Latin American countries and the United States. The bank, which is headquartered in Washington, D.C., makes loans and provides technical advice and assistance to countries. Today, the IDB is owned by forty-seven member states.

With sixty-seven member nations, the *Asian Development Bank* (ADB), created in 1966 and headquartered in the Philippines, promotes economic and social progress in Asian and Pacific regions. The U.S. government is the second-largest contributor to the ADB's capital, after Japan.

The *African Development Bank* (AFDB), also known as *Banque Africaines de Development,* was established in 1964 with headquarters in Abidjan, Ivory Coast. Its members include fifty-three African and twenty-four non-African countries from the Americas, Europe, and Asia. The AFDB's goal is to foster the economic and social development of its African members. The bank pursues this goal through loans, research, technical assistance, and the development of trade programs.

Established in 1991 to encourage reconstruction and development in the Eastern and Central European countries, the London-based *European Bank for Reconstruction and Development* (EBRD) is owned by sixty-one countries and two intergovernmental institutions. Its loans are geared toward developing market-oriented economies and promoting private enterprise.

***Warwick Mills is a leader in the engineering of technical textiles for protective applications.** In 2008, Warwick Mills was awarded the Export Achievement Certificate by the U.S. Department of Commerce. In presenting the award, U.S. Commerce Deputy Assistant Secretary, Matt Priest said, "Warwick is a shining example of how exporting allows U.S. manufacturers to expand and thrive in the global economy."*

Courtesy Warwick Mills

The International Monetary Fund

The **International Monetary Fund (IMF)** is an international bank with 185 member nations that makes short-term loans to developing countries experiencing balance-of-payment deficits. This financing is contributed by member nations, and it must be repaid with interest. Loans are provided primarily to fund international trade.

International Monetary Fund (IMF) an international bank with 184 member nations that makes short-term loans to developing countries experiencing balance-of-payment deficits

return to inside business

SAIC

Through joint ventures with GM and VW, SAIC has gained access to new technology and to well-established car brands that appeal to buyers in China. Its automotive partners have benefited from SAIC's in-depth knowledge of local customers' needs and its years of local manufacturing experience.

These days, SAIC and its partners are experimenting with alternative fuel sources, advanced engineering, and other innovations to make their cars more efficient, more affordable, and more profitable. Even as SAIC continues to build on these strengths, it is accelerating into a highly competitive world market and must steer around profit-sapping economic potholes for ongoing growth.

Questions

1. Why would SAIC form joint ventures with both GM and VW? Why would both GM and VW want to partner with SAIC?
2. Do you agree with SAIC's decision to continue with the plan to launch a redesigned MG in Great Britain after acquiring the rival that had owned the MG name and factory? Explain your answer.

CHAPTER REVIEW

Summary

Explain the economic basis for international business.

International business encompasses all business activities that involve exchanges across national boundaries. International trade is based on specialization, whereby each country produces the goods and services that it can produce more efficiently than any other goods and services. A nation is said to have a comparative advantage relative to these goods. International trade develops when each nation trades its surplus products for those in short supply.

A nation's balance of trade is the difference between the value of its exports and the value of its imports. Its balance of payments is the difference between the flow of money into and out of the nation. Generally, a negative balance of trade is considered unfavorable.

Discuss the restrictions nations place on international trade, the objectives of these restrictions, and their results.

Despite the benefits of world trade, nations tend to use tariffs and nontariff barriers (import quotas, embargoes, and other restrictions) to limit trade. These restrictions typically are justified as being needed to protect a nation's economy, industries, citizens, or security. They can result in the loss of jobs, higher prices, fewer choices in the marketplace, and the misallocation of resources.

Outline the extent of international trade and identify the organizations working to foster it.

World trade is generally increasing. Trade between the United States and other nations is increasing in dollar value but decreasing in terms of our share of the world market. The General Agreement on Tariffs and Trade (GATT) was formed to dismantle trade barriers and provide an environment in which international business can grow. Today, the World Trade Organization (WTO) and various economic communities carry on that mission.

Define the methods by which a firm can organize for and enter into international markets.

A firm can enter international markets in several ways. It may license a foreign firm to produce and market its products. It may export its products and sell them through foreign intermediaries or its own sales organization abroad. Or it may sell its exports outright to an export-import merchant. It may enter into a joint venture with a foreign firm. It may establish its own foreign subsidiaries. Or it may develop into a multinational enterprise.

Generally, each of these methods represents an increasingly deeper level of involvement in international business, with licensing being the simplest and the development of a multinational corporation the most involved.

5 Describe the various sources of export assistance.

Many government and international agencies provide export assistance to U.S. and foreign firms. The export services and programs of the nineteen agencies of the U.S. Trade Promotion Coordinating Committee (TPCC) can help U.S. firms to compete in foreign markets and create new jobs in the United States. Sources of export assistance include U.S. Export Assistance Centers, the International Trade Administration, U.S. and Foreign Commercial Services, Export Legal Assistance Network, Advocacy Center, National Trade Data Bank, and other government and international agencies.

6 Identify the institutions that help firms and nations finance international business.

The financing of international trade is more complex than that of domestic trade. Institutions such as the Eximbank and the International Monetary Fund have been established to provide financing and ultimately to increase world trade for American and international firms.

Key Terms

You should now be able to define and give an example relevant to each of the following terms:

international business (73)
absolute advantage (74)
comparative advantage (74)
exporting (74)
importing (74)
balance of trade (74)
trade deficit (75)
balance of payments (75)
import duty (tariff) (76)
dumping (77)
nontariff barrier (77)
import quota (77)
embargo (77)
foreign-exchange control (77)
currency devaluation (77)
General Agreement on Tariffs and Trade (GATT) (83)
World Trade Organization (WTO) (84)
economic community (85)
licensing (87)
letter of credit (88)
bill of lading (88)
draft (88)
strategic alliance (90)
trading company (90)
countertrade (91)
multinational enterprise (91)
Export-Import Bank of the United States (93)
multilateral development bank (MDB) (93)
International Monetary Fund (IMF) (95)

Review Questions

1. Why do firms engage in international trade?
2. What is the difference between an absolute and a comparative advantage in international trade? How are both types of advantages related to the concept of specialization?
3. What is a favorable balance of trade? In what way is it "favorable"?
4. List and briefly describe the principal restrictions that may be applied to a nation's imports.
5. What reasons generally are given for imposing trade restrictions?
6. What are the general effects of import restrictions on trade?
7. Define and describe the major objectives of the World Trade Organization (WTO) and the international economic communities.
8. Which nations are the principal trading partners of the United States? What are the major U.S. imports and exports?
9. The methods of engaging in international business may be categorized as either direct or indirect. How would you classify each of the methods described in this chapter? Why?
10. In what ways is a multinational enterprise different from a large corporation that does business in several countries?
11. List some key sources of export assistance. How can these sources be useful to small business firms?
12. In what ways do Eximbank, multilateral development banks, and the IMF enhance international trade?

Discussion Questions

1. The United States restricts imports but, at the same time, supports the WTO and international banks whose objective is to enhance world trade. As a member of Congress, how would you justify this contradiction to your constituents?
2. What effects might the devaluation of a nation's currency have on its business firms? On its consumers? On the debts it owes to other nations?
3. Should imports to the United States be curtailed by, say, 20 percent to eliminate our trade deficit? What might happen if this were done?
4. When should a firm consider expanding from strictly domestic trade to international trade? When should it consider becoming further involved in international trade? What factors might affect the firm's decisions in each case?
5. How can a firm obtain the expertise needed to produce and market its products in, for example, the EU?

Video Case 3.1

Fossil: Keeping Watch on a Global Business

Since its founding in 1984, Fossil has grown into a global company and a world class brand in the fashion accessory industry. The core of the company is its watch division, which sells more than 500 styles in its line. They boast they have a watch for every wrist. Fossil also manufactures and markets sunglasses, belts, purses, and other related leather goods. The key to Fossil's success is its emphasis on fashion-forward design, creative packaging, and a distinctive marketing campaign that depicts the nostalgia of 1950s America. Every watch comes in a free collectible tin box reminiscent of that period. Its products are not retro, but their brand image is. This image is the heartbeat of the company, and Fossil believes its brand image gives it a differential advantage versus competitors such as Guess and Swatch.

Fossil has become the number one fashion watch line in almost every department store in the United States. The company has done this through value pricing, making it easy for customers to find their watches in stores, designing their products so they are easily identifiable, and by always being in the forefront of design and style. In short, Fossil tries to make the purchase of its products easy, quick, fun, and trendy.

Ten years ago, the company went international when it entered the German market. In the last five years, Fossil has concentrated on becoming a global company, and today its products are manufactured and sold in more than 70 countries around the world. The company's global expansion has been the result of a multifaceted strategic plan that consists of (1) working closely with international retailers to ensure that they have the right product for the market, (2) developing marketing programs that are uniform and cohesive worldwide, (3) ensuring they have the infrastructure to deliver their products and marketing programs to the proper channels, and (4) selecting the right partners to help them execute their plans. Partners include offshore manufacturers, distributors, sales representative companies, and of course, retailers. The company also has wholly owned subsidiaries in several countries.

Some of Fossil's strongest manufacturing and distribution partners are in Hong Kong. This is because the company believes that Hong Kong has the infrastructure and systems in place to manufacture and assemble products and deliver them in a timely manner, at an acceptable cost, anywhere in the world.

As a global company, Fossil keeps a watchful eye on an ever-changing worldwide political and economic environment. Currencies can literally devaluate 30 percent in one day and then bounce back 50 percent the next day. This kind of volatility can have a significant effect on the company's costs, revenues, and profitability. In order to deal with this changing environment, Fossil constantly monitors its business drivers. They talk to their distributors weekly, sometimes daily, to ensure they have enough product in the pipeline. Fossil's principals meet once a week to minimize the company's downside risk in the event a financial crisis occurs somewhere in the world. They do this by adjusting inventory, evaluating their purchasing needs, analyzing the sales of every watch style, and identifying business trends. This attention to detail has played an important role in the company's past success. With sales on the rise, new designs and products on the horizon, and a strong stable of international partners, Fossil is well on its way to achieving its number one goal: "To be the major fashion accessory brand in the world."[10]

Questions

1. What comparative advantage, if any, does Fossil have over its competitors?
2. If Brazil devaluated its currency by 50 percent, what effect would it have on Fossil?
3. Given that Fossil is not marketed in every country in the world, would you recommend that the company license its products to expand its presence in additional countries where it is not currently represented?

Case 3.2

Coca-Cola Pours into New Countries

Coca-Cola's red and white logo is a familiar sight all over the world, from Argentina to Zimbabwe. Battling rival PepsiCo as well as regional soft-drink manufacturers, the Atlanta-based beverage company has long viewed global markets as critical to its push for profits. It established operations in Canada and Central America before 1910, and today its products are available in more than 200 nations.

The company earns nearly three-quarters of its revenue outside the United States. However, growth in worldwide sales volume has slowed in recent years. As a result, Coca-Cola's senior managers are looking at ways to build sales in markets that previously seemed less promising because of low income levels, high inflation, currency fluctuations, volatile political conditions, supply and energy shortages, or other complications.

Few people in rural northern India, for example, can afford costly products such as kitchen appliances on the area's average monthly income of about $42. Even large-size soft drinks are out of reach for many. After losing millions of dollars as it gained first-hand knowledge of the market, however, Coca-Cola hit on the dual strategy of adjusting the bottle size—to make its sodas more affordable for buyers—and putting its products in as many outlets as possible.

Now Indians can buy a tiny 200-milliliter bottle of Coca-Cola for the equivalent of 12 cents at thousands of bus-stop stands, neighborhood grocery stores, and food stalls. The deputy president of Coca-Cola India explains the company's outlet-by-outlet drive for distribution: "Our hands are firmly in the dust here. It's the only way we can capture this market." And the drive has been successful: Coca-Cola has captured more than 50 percent of the market for carbonated soft drinks in India.

China is another fast-growing market where Coca-Cola is boosting sales by getting its beverages into as many stores and stands as possible. At one time, the company had to use pedicabs and other creative transportation methods to move beverages from bottling plants to outlets around Shanghai and other big cities. As the company built more bottling plants, it contracted with hundreds of thousands of distributors to get its beverages into local outlets. Thanks to this extensive distribution system, Coca-Cola sells nearly

$2 billion worth of soft drinks in China every year. China soon will overtake Brazil as the company's third-largest market (behind the United States and Mexico).

Coca-Cola's business in Brazil has been up and down as the country's economic situation has changed. After years of high inflation, the economy improved, and Brazilians began buying more soft drinks. Coca-Cola responded to stiff competition from low-priced local brands by cutting prices. However, the move hurt profitability and failed to spark a significant sales rally, so Coca-Cola changed tactics. As it did in India, the company started offering soft drinks in smaller bottles, each size carrying a correspondingly small price tag. Thinking small made all the difference: Coca-Cola's sales and profits are bubbling in Brazil.

Africa has proven to be a much bigger challenge. Runaway inflation, frequent power outages, and ongoing supply shortages have sapped Coca-Cola's profits in Zimbabwe and several other African nations. Despite the obstacles, the company is determined to continue doing business in those markets. It is moving ahead with plans to expand the number of stores that sell Coca-Cola beverages as a long-term foundation for future profitability. When and where consumers get thirsty, Coca-Cola will have its bottles and cans in a convenient outlet. "We want to be everywhere, and will be there forever," says Alex Cummings, president of Coca-Cola's Africa operations.[11]

For more information about this company, go to **www.cocacola.com.**

Questions

1. Why might a country in Latin America or Africa resist Coca-Cola's efforts to expand local sales?
2. Does the United States have a comparative advantage in soft drinks? Explain.
3. Knowing that smaller sizes have helped Coca-Cola increase sales and profits in India and China, do you think it should use the same approach in the United States? Why?

Building Skills for Career Success

1. JOURNALING FOR SUCCESS

Discovery statement: This chapter was designed to excite you about international business and how trade among nations affects our daily lives.

Assignment

1. Assume that your friend, who recently lost his job in the automobile industry, is critical of imported Toyotas, Hondas, and Volkswagens. How would you respond to his resentment of imported goods?
2. What specific reasons will you offer to your friend that international trade is beneficial to society as a whole.
3. Ask your friend what might be some consequences if the trade among nations was banned.

2. EXPLORING THE INTERNET

A popular question debated among firms actively involved on the Internet is whether or not there exists a truly global Internet-based customer, irrespective of any individual culture, linguistic, or nationality issues. Does this Internet-based universal customer see the Internet and products sold there in pretty much the same way? If so, then one model might fit all customers. For example, although Yahoo.com translates its Web pages so that they are understood around the world, the pages look pretty much the same regardless of which international site you use. Is this good strategy, or should the sites reflect local customers differently? Visit the text website for updates to this exercise.

Assignment

1. Examine a website such as Yahoo's (**www.yahoo.com**) and its various international versions that operate in other languages around the world. Compare their similarities and differences as best you can, even if you do not understand the individual languages.
2. After making your comparison, do you now agree that there are indeed universal Internet products and customers? Explain your decision.

3. DEVELOPING CRITICAL-THINKING SKILLS

Suppose that you own and operate an electronics firm that manufactures transistors and integrated circuits. As foreign competitors enter the market and undercut your prices, you realize that your high labor costs are hindering your ability to compete. You are concerned about what to do and are open for suggestions. Recently, you have been trying to decide whether to move your plant to Mexico, where labor is cheaper.

Assignment

1. Questions you should consider in making this decision include the following:
   a. Would you be better off to build a new plant in Mexico or to buy an existing building?
   b. If you could find a Mexican electronics firm similar to yours, would it be wiser to try to buy it than to start your own operation?
   c. What are the risks involved in directly investing in your own facility in a foreign country?
   d. If you did decide to move your plant to Mexico, how would you go about it? Are there any government agencies that might offer you advice?
2. Prepare a two-page summary of your answers to these questions.

4. BUILDING TEAM SKILLS

The North American Trade Agreement among the United States, Mexico, and Canada went into effect on January 1, 1994. It has made a difference in trade among the countries and has affected the lives of many people.

Assignment

1. Working in teams and using the resources of your library, investigate NAFTA. Answer the following questions:
   a. What are NAFTA's objectives?
   b. What are its benefits?
   c. What impact has NAFTA had on trade, jobs, and travel?

d. Some Americans were opposed to the implementation of NAFTA. What were their objections? Have any of these objections been justified?
e. Has NAFTA influenced your life? How?

2. Summarize your answers in a written report. Your team also should be prepared to give a class presentation.

5. RESEARCHING DIFFERENT CAREERS

Today, firms around the world need employees with special skills. In some countries, such employees are not always available, and firms then must search abroad for qualified applicants. One way they can do this is through global workforce databases. As business and trade operations continue to grow globally, you may one day find yourself working in a foreign country, perhaps for an American company doing business there or for a foreign company. In what foreign country would you like to work? What problems might you face?

Assignment

1. Choose a country in which you might like to work.
2. Research the country. The National Trade Data Bank (NTDA) is a good place to start. Find answers to the following questions:
   a. What language is spoken in this country? Are you proficient in it? What would you need to do if you are not proficient?
   b. What are the economic, social, and legal systems like in this nation?
   c. What is its history?
   d. What are its culture and social traditions like? How might they affect your work or your living arrangements?
3. Describe what you have found out about this country in a written report. Include an assessment of whether you would want to work there and the problems you might face if you did.

Running a Business Part 1

The Rise of Finagle A Bagel

Would bagels sell in Hong Kong? Laura Beth Trust and Alan Litchman planned to find out. Trust was in Hong Kong working in the garment manufacturing industry, and Litchman was in real estate, but they were eager to start their own business. They were particularly interested in running a business where they would have direct customer contact and be able to get first-hand feedback about their products and services. And no matter what kind of business they started, it would be a family undertaking: The two entrepreneurs recently had decided to get married.

Looking around Hong Kong, Litchman and Trust noticed numerous Western-style food chains such as McDonald's, Pizza Hut, KFC, and Starbucks but no bagel places. Yet they believed that Hong Kong's sophisticated, multicultural population would welcome authentic New York–style bagels. Although both the entrepreneurs had MBA degrees from the Sloan School of Management, neither had any restaurant experience or knew how to make a bagel. Still, because they sensed a profitable opportunity and possessed solid business skills, Trust and Litchman decided to move ahead. The two incorporated a company, found a partner, and then returned to the United States to investigate the bagel business. As part of their research, they approached two knowledgeable experts for advice.

One of the bagel experts was Larry Smith, who in 1982 had cofounded a tiny cheesecake store in Boston's historic Quincy Market. When business was slow, the store began selling bagels topped with leftover cream cheese. By the late 1980s, this sideline was doing so well that Smith and his partners changed their focus from cheesecakes to bagels and changed the store's name from Julian's Cheesecakes to Finagle A Bagel. They relocated the store from a cramped 63-square-foot storefront into a more spacious 922-square-foot space in the same busy market complex. Soon, so many customers were lining up for bagels that the owners began opening additional Finagle A Bagel stores around downtown Boston.

NEW OWNERSHIP, NEW GROWTH

By the time Trust and Litchman met Smith, he was operating six successful bagel stores, was ringing up $10 million in annual sales, and was looking for a source of capital to open more stores. Therefore, instead of helping the entrepreneurs launch a business in Hong Kong, Smith suggested that they stay and become involved in Finagle A Bagel. Because Litchman and Trust had roots in the Boston area, the opportunity to join a local bagel business was appealing both personally and professionally. Late in 1998, they bought a majority stake in Finagle A Bagel from Smith. The three owners agreed on how to divide management responsibilities and collaborated on plans for more aggressive expansion. Within a few years, Trust and Litchman completed a deal to buy the rest of the business and became the sole owners and copresidents.

The business has grown every year since the conversion to bagels. Today, Finagle A Bagel operates twenty stores in downtown Boston and the surrounding suburbs. Because Finagle A Bagel outgrew its original production facilities, the owners recently purchased a new corporate headquarters and production center in Newton, Massachusetts. This is where tens of thousands of bagels are prepared every day, along with enough cream cheese and cookies to supply a much larger network of stores.

BRANDING THE BAGEL

Over time, the owners have introduced a wide range of bagels, sandwiches, salads, and soups linked to the core bagel product. Bagels are baked fresh every day, and the stores receive daily deliveries of fresh salad fixings and other ingredients. Employees make each menu item to order while the customer watches. Some of the most popular offerings include a breakfast bagel pizza, salads with bagel-chip croutons, and BLT (bacon-lettuce-tomato) bagel sandwiches.

Finagle A Bagel is also boosting revenues by wholesaling its bagels to thousands of universities, hospitals, and corporate cafeterias. In addition, it sells several varieties of bagels under the Finagle A Bagel brand to the Shaw's Market grocery chain. Shaw's has been expanding in New England through mergers and acquisitions, opening new opportunities for its bagel supplier. "As they grow, we grow with them," comments Litchman. "More importantly, it gets our name into markets where we're not. And we can track the sales and see how we're doing." If a particular Shaw's supermarket registers unusually strong bagel sales, the copresidents will consider opening a store in or near that community.

THE BAGEL ECONOMY

Although Finagle A Bagel competes with other bagel chains in and around Boston, its competition goes well beyond restaurants in that category. "You compete with a person selling a cup of coffee; you compete with a grocery store selling a salad," Litchman notes. "People only have so many 'dining dollars' and you need to convince them to spend those dining dollars in your store." Finagle A Bagel's competitive advantages are high-quality, fresh products, courteous and competent employees, and clean, attractive, and inviting restaurants.

During a recent economic recession, Boston's tourist traffic slumped temporarily, and corporate customers cut back on catering orders from Finagle A Bagel. After the company's sales revenues remained flat for about a year, they began inching up as the economy moved toward recovery. Now the business sells more than $20 million worth of bagels, soups, sandwiches, and salads every year.

SOCIAL RESPONSIBILITY THROUGH BAGELS

Social responsibility is an integral part of Finagle A Bagel's operations. Rather than simply throw away unsold bagels at the end of the day, the owners donate the bagels to schools, shelters, and other nonprofit organizations. When local nonprofit groups hold fund-raising events, the copresidents contribute bagels to feed the volunteers. Over the years, Finagle A Bagel has provided bagels to bicyclists raising money for St. Jude Children's Research Hospital, to swimmers raising money for breast cancer research, and to people building community playgrounds. Also, the copresidents are strongly committed to being fair to their customers by offering good value and a good experience. "Something that we need to remember and instill in our people all the time," Trust emphasizes, "is that customers are coming in, and your responsibility is to give them the best that you can give them."

Even with 320-plus employees, the copresidents find that owning a business is a nonstop proposition. "Our typical day never ends," says Trust. They are constantly visiting stores, dealing with suppliers, reviewing financial results, and planning for the future. Despite all these responsibilities, this husband-and-wife entrepreneurial team enjoys applying their educational background and business experience to build a company that satisfies thousands of customers every day.

Questions

1. How has the business cycle affected Finagle A Bagel?
2. What is Finagle A Bagel doing to differentiate itself from competitors that want a share of customers' dining dollars?
3. Why would Finagle A Bagel donate bagels to local charities rather than give them away to customers or employees?
4. If you wanted to open a bagel restaurant in Hong Kong, would you license the Finagle A Bagel brand? Why or why not?

BUILDING A BUSINESS PLAN

Building a Business Plan Part 1

A *business plan* is a carefully constructed guide for a person starting a business. The purpose of a well-prepared business plan is to show how practical and attainable the entrepreneur's goals are. It also serves as a concise document that potential investors can examine to see if they would like to invest or assist in financing a new venture. A business plan should include the following twelve components:

- Introduction
- Executive summary
- Benefits to the community
- Company and industry
- Management team
- Manufacturing and operations plan
- Labor force
- Marketing plan
- Financial plan
- Exit strategy
- Critical risks and assumptions
- Appendix

A brief description of each of these sections is provided in Chapter 5 (see also Table 5.4 on page 147).

This is the first of seven exercises that appear at the ends of each of the seven major parts in this textbook. The goal of these exercises is to help you work through the preceding components to create your own business plan. For example, in the exercise for this part, you will make decisions and complete the research that will help you to develop the introduction for your business plan and the benefits to the community that your business will provide. In the exercises for Parts 2 through 7, you will add more components to your plan and eventually build a plan that actually could be used to start a business. The flowchart shown in Figure 3.5 gives an overview of the steps you will be taking to prepare your business plan.

THE FIRST STEP: CHOOSING YOUR BUSINESS

One of the first steps for starting your own business is to decide what type of business you want to start. Take some time to think about this decision. Before proceeding, answer the following questions:

- Why did you choose this type of business?
- Why do you think this business will be successful?
- Would you enjoy owning and operating this type of business?

Warning: Don't rush this step. This step often requires much thought, but it is well worth the time and effort. As an added bonus, you are more likely to develop a quality business plan if you really want to open this type of business.

Now that you have decided on a specific type of business, it is time to begin the planning process. The goal for this part is to complete the introduction and benefits-to-the-community components of your business plan.

Before you begin, it is important to note that the business plan is not a document that is written and then set aside. It is a living document that an entrepreneur should refer to continuously in order to ensure that plans are being carried through appropriately. As the entrepreneur begins to execute the plan, he or she should monitor the business environment continuously and make changes to the plan to address any challenges or opportunities that were not foreseen originally.

Throughout this course, you will, of course, be building your knowledge about business. Therefore, it will be appropriate for you to continually revisit parts of the plan that you have already written in order to refine them based on your more comprehensive knowledge. You will find that writing your plan is not a simple matter of starting at the beginning and moving chronologically through to the end. Instead, you probably will find yourself jumping around the various components, making refinements as you go. In fact, the second component—the executive summary—should be written last, but because of its comprehensive nature and its importance to potential investors, it appears after the introduction in the final business plan. By the end of this course, you should be able to put the finishing touches on your plan, making sure that all the parts create a comprehensive and sound whole so that you can present it for evaluation.

THE INTRODUCTION COMPONENT

1.1. Start with the cover page. Provide the business name, street address, telephone number, Web address (if any), name(s) of owner(s) of the business, and the date the plan is issued.

1.2. Next, provide background information on the company and include the general nature of the business: retailing, manufacturing, or service; what your product or service is; what is unique about it; and why you believe that your business will be successful.

1.3. Then include a summary statement of the business's financial needs, if any. You probably will need to revise your financial needs summary after you complete a detailed financial plan later in Part 6.

1.4. Finally, include a statement of confidentiality to keep important information away from potential competitors.

Figure 3.5: Business Plan

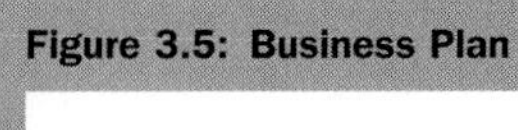

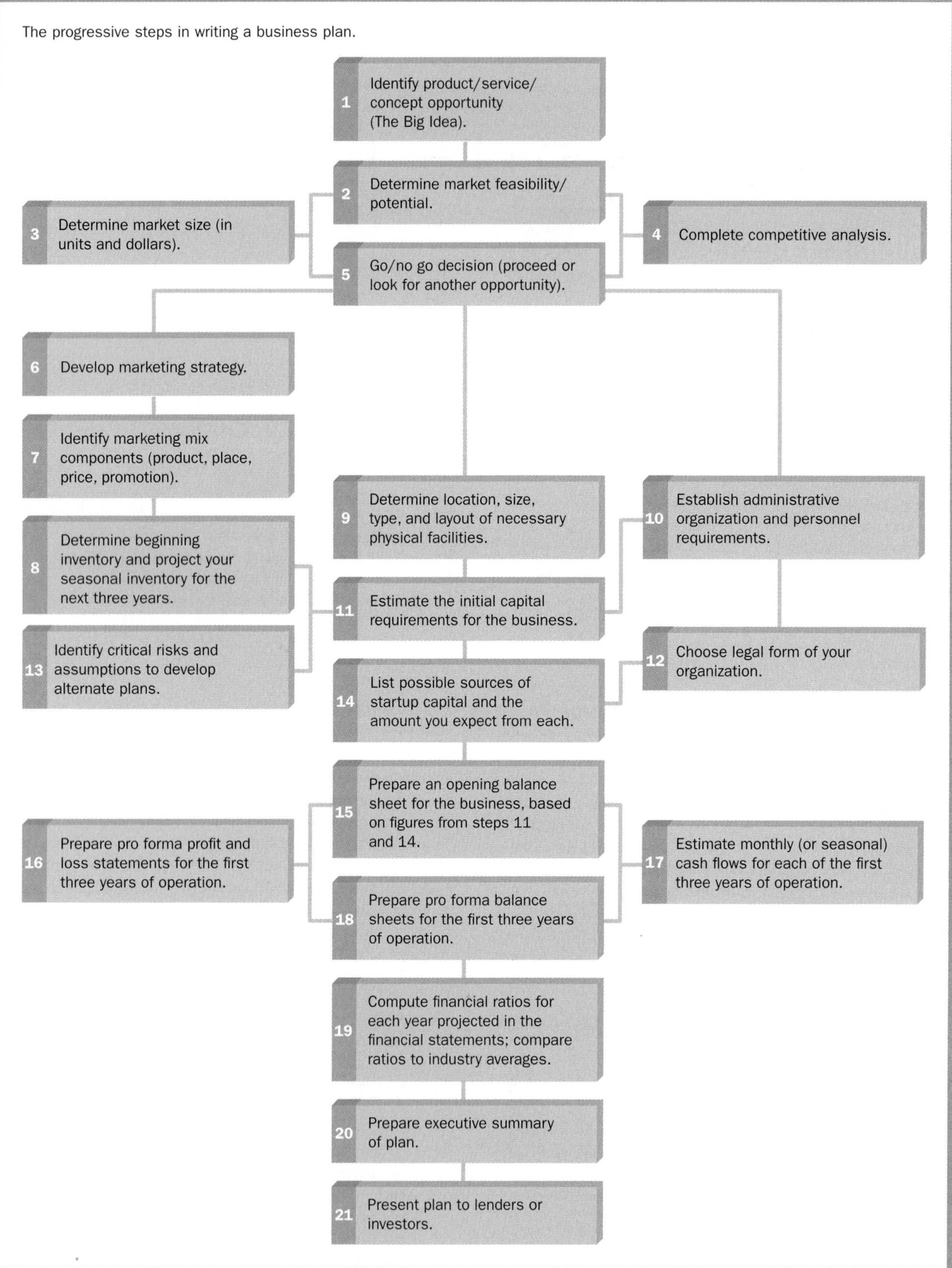

Source: Hatten, Timothy, *Small Business Management*, Fourth Edition. Copyright © 2009 by Houghton Mifflin Company. Reprinted with permission.

THE BENEFITS-TO-THE-COMMUNITY COMPONENT

In this section, describe the potential benefits to the community that your business could provide. Chapter 2 in your textbook, "Being Ethical and Socially Responsible," can help you in answering some of these questions. At the very least, address the following issues:

1.5. Describe the number of skilled and nonskilled jobs the business will create, and indicate how purchases of supplies and other materials can help local businesses.

1.6. Next, describe how providing needed goods or services will improve the community and its standard of living.

1.7. Finally, state how your business can develop new technical, management, or leadership skills; offer attractive wages; and provide other types of individual growth.

REVIEW OF BUSINESS PLAN ACTIVITIES

Read over the information that you have gathered. Because the Building a Business Plan exercises at the end of Parts 2 through 7 are built on the work you do in Part 1, make sure that any weaknesses or problem areas are resolved before continuing. Finally, write a brief statement that summarizes all the information for this part of the business plan.

The information contained in "Building a Business Plan" will also assist you in completing the online *Interactive Business Plan*.

PART 2

Trends in Business Today

In Part 2 of *Business* we look at a very practical aspect of business: How businesses are owned. Issues related to ownership are particularly interesting in today's world, where large global businesses coexist with small businesses. Also, because the majority of businesses are small, we look at specific issues related to small business.

AP Photo/Bill Haber

Choosing a Form of Business Ownership

4

LEARNING OBJECTIVES

What you will be able to do once you complete this chapter:

1. Describe the advantages and disadvantages of sole proprietorships.
2. Explain the different types of partners and the importance of partnership agreements.
3. Describe the advantages and disadvantages of partnerships.
4. Summarize how a corporation is formed.
5. Describe the advantages and disadvantages of a corporation.
6. Examine special types of corporations, including S-corporations, limited-liability companies, government-owned corporations, and not-for-profit corporations.
7. Discuss the purpose of a cooperative, joint venture, and syndicate.
8. Explain how growth from within and growth through mergers can enable a business to expand.

AP Photo/Kathy Willens

inside business

S.C. Johnson, a Family Company

In 1886, Samuel Curtis Johnson founded a small flooring business in Racine, Wisconsin, that has now expanded into a major global corporation, still owned and operated by the Johnson family. Originally, the company produced only parquet wood floors. When customers asked for a wax to protect their new floors, however, Johnson mixed up a paste wax that became an instant hit.

The business flourished as Johnson turned his attention to wax products. Twenty years later, Johnson's son joined as a partner, and the renamed S.C. Johnson & Son officially became a family company. Now, more than 120 years after the company was founded, the fifth generation of the Johnson family is leading the corporation beyond $8 billion in annual sales of well-known household brands such as Windex, Drano, Pledge, Glade, Ziploc, Raid, and Scrubbing Bubbles.

Over the years, S.C. Johnson's growth and profits have come from two sources: global expansion and new products, some developed internally and some acquired by purchasing other companies. S.C. Johnson began operating internationally in 1914, first in Great Britain, and then in Australia and Canada. Little by little, the company expanded into South America, across Europe, and into Africa, Asia, and the Middle East. Today, more than half of its sales are made outside the United States, and 70 percent of its 12,000 employees are based in other countries.

Many of S.C. Johnson's blockbuster brands came to the company via acquisitions made during the past thirty years. For example, when it acquired Drackett, S.C. Johnson became the owner of both Drano and Windex. When it acquired the DowBrands division of Dow Chemical, it took control of Ziploc, Saran, Fantastik, and Scrubbing Bubbles, among other well-established brands. S.C. Johnson has also grown from within by introducing a steady stream of new products under all its brands. What will this family-owned corporation do next to keep sales and profits growing?[1]

DID YOU KNOW ?

Today, more than half of S.C. Johnson's sales are made outside the United States, and 70 percent of its 12,000 employees are based in other countries.

While most of us think of S.C. Johnson as a corporation that manufactures products like Windex, Ziploc bags, or Scrubbing Bubbles, it is so much more. Consider three facts about this global company. First, it is a corporation. Although Samuel Curtis Johnson founded the original company as a sole proprietorship, it later became a corporation that employs 12,000 people in countries around the globe. Second, S.C. Johnson is successful. This global firm generates more than $8 billion in annual sales. While some would-be business owners think that if they incorporate, their business will automatically be successful, the fact is that there's more to increasing sales and earning profits than the type of ownership you choose. In today's competitive business world, any corporation, sole proprietorship, or partnership must produce products and services that customers want. Finally, S.C. Johnson is a good corporate citizen. This family-owned business places great emphasis on social responsibility and gives 5 percent of its profits to charities that make a difference in the communities in which it operates. In today's competitive environment, it's common to hear of profitable companies. It is less common to hear of profitable companies that are held in high regard because of their social responsibility programs.

Many people dream of opening a business, and one of the first decisions they must make is what form of ownership to choose. We begin this chapter by describing the three common forms of business ownership: sole proprietorships, partnerships, and corporations. We discuss how these types of businesses are formed and note the advantages and disadvantages of each. Next, we consider several types of business ownership usually chosen for special purposes, including S-corporations, limited-liability companies, government-owned corporations, not-for-profit corporations, cooperatives, joint ventures, and syndicates. We conclude the chapter with a discussion of how businesses can grow through internal expansion or through mergers with other companies.

Sole Proprietorships

1

Learning Objective: Describe the advantages and disadvantages of sole proprietorships.

sole proprietorship a business that is owned (and usually operated) by one person

A **sole proprietorship** is a business that is owned (and usually operated) by one person. Although a few sole proprietorships are large and have many employees, most are small. Sole proprietorship is the simplest form of business ownership and the easiest to start. In most instances, the owner (the *sole* proprietor) simply decides that he or she is in business and begins operations. Some of today's largest corporations, including Ford Motor Company, H.J. Heinz Company, and Procter & Gamble Company, started out as tiny—and in many cases, struggling—sole proprietorships.

As you can see in Figure 4.1, there are more than 20.6 million sole proprietorships in the United States. They account for 71.8 percent of the country's business firms. Although the most popular form of ownership when compared with partnerships and corporations, they rank last in total sales revenues. As shown in Figure 4.2, sole proprietorships account for just over $1 trillion, or about 4.2 percent, of total sales.

Sole proprietorships are most common in retailing, service, and agriculture. Thus, the clothing boutique, corner grocery, television-repair shop down the street, and small, independent farmers are likely to be sole proprietorships.

Advantages of Sole Proprietorships

Most of the advantages of sole proprietorships arise from the two main characteristics of this form of ownership: simplicity and individual control.

Ease of Start-Up and Closure Sole proprietorship is the simplest and cheapest way to start a business. Often, start-up requires no contracts, agreements, or other legal documents. Thus, a sole proprietorship can be, and most often is, established without the services of an attorney. The legal requirements often are limited to registering the name of the business and obtaining any necessary licenses or permits.

Figure 4.1: Relative Percentages of Sole Proprietorships, Partnerships, and Corporations in the United States

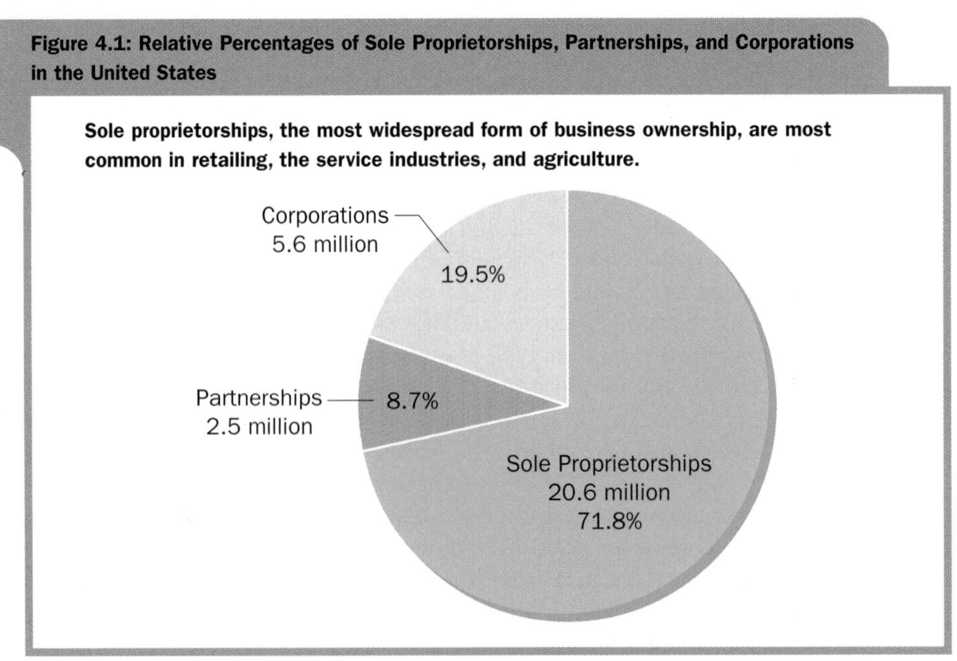

Source: U.S. Bureau of the Census, *Statistical Abstract of the United States,* Washington, D.C., 2008, p. 487 (**www.census.gov**).

If the enterprise does not succeed, the firm can be closed as easily as it was opened. Creditors must be paid, of course, but generally, the owner does not have to go through any legal procedure before hanging up an "Out of Business" sign.

Source: The U.S. Census Bureau, *Statistical Abstract of the United States: 2008*, p. 487.

Pride of Ownership A successful sole proprietor is often very proud of her or his accomplishments—and rightfully so. In almost every case, the owner deserves a great deal of credit for assuming the risks and solving the day-to-day problems associated with operating sole proprietorships. Unfortunately, the reverse is also true. When the business fails, it is often the sole proprietor who is to blame.

Retention of All Profits Because all profits become the personal earnings of the owner, the owner has a strong incentive to succeed. This direct financial reward attracts many entrepreneurs to the sole proprietorship form of business and, if the business succeeds, is a source of great satisfaction.

Flexibility of Being Your Own Boss A sole proprietor is completely free to make decisions about the firm's operations. Without asking or waiting for anyone's approval, a sole proprietor can switch from retailing to wholesaling, move a shop's location, open a new store, or close an old one. Suppose that the sole proprietor of an appliance store finds that many customers now prefer to shop on Sunday afternoons. He or she can make an immediate change in business hours to take advantage of this information (provided that state laws allow such stores to open on Sunday). The manager of a store in a large corporate chain such as Best Buy Company or Circuit City may have to seek the approval of numerous managers and company officials before making such a change.

Figure 4.2: Total Sales Receipts of American Businesses

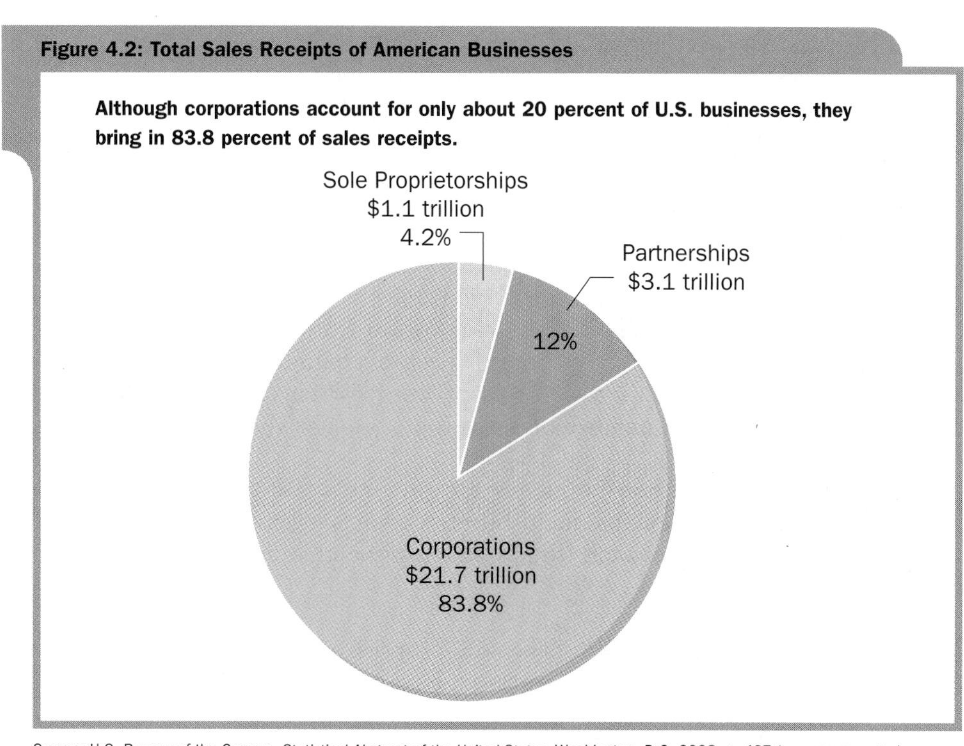

Source: U.S. Bureau of the Census, *Statistical Abstract of the United States*, Washington, D.C. 2008, p. 487 (**www.census.gov**).

One Happy Business Owner! *John Avila's smile could be because his company—Avila Retail Development and Management—has successful retail stores in Albuquerque, Denver, and Phoenix. Avila started his company in New Mexico—a state that leads the nation in the percentage of Hispanic-owned businesses according to the U.S. Commerce Department.*

No Special Taxes Profits earned by a sole proprietorship are taxed as the personal income of the owner. As a result, sole proprietors must report certain financial information on their personal income tax returns and make estimated quarterly tax payments to the federal government. Thus, a sole proprietorship does not pay the special state and federal income taxes that corporations pay.

Disadvantages of Sole Proprietorships

The disadvantages of a sole proprietorship stem from the fact that these businesses are owned by one person. Some capable sole proprietors experience no problems. Individuals who start out with few management skills and little money are most at risk for failure.

Unlimited Liability **Unlimited liability** is a legal concept that holds a business owner personally responsible for all the debts of the business. There is legally no difference between the debts of the business and the debts of the proprietor. If the business fails, or if the business is involved in a lawsuit and loses, the owner's personal property—including savings and other assets—can be seized (and sold if necessary) to pay creditors.

unlimited liability a legal concept that holds a business owner personally responsible for all the debts of the business

Unlimited liability is perhaps the major factor that tends to discourage would-be entrepreneurs with substantial personal wealth from using this form of business organization.

Lack of Continuity Legally, the sole proprietor *is* the business. If the owner retires, dies, or is declared legally incompetent, the business essentially ceases to exist. In many cases, however—especially when the business is a profitable enterprise—the owner's heirs take it over and either sell it or continue to operate it. The business also can suffer if the sole proprietor becomes ill and cannot work for an extended period of time. If the owner, for example, has a heart attack, there is often no one who can step in and manage the business. An illness can be devastating if the sole proprietor's personal skills are what determine if the business is a success or a failure.

Lack of Money Banks, suppliers, and other lenders usually are unwilling to lend large sums of money to sole proprietorships. Only one person—the sole proprietor—can be held responsible for repaying such loans, and the assets of most sole proprietors usually are limited. Moreover, these assets may have been used already as the basis for personal borrowing (a home mortgage or car loan) or for short-term credit from suppliers. Lenders also worry about the lack of continuity of sole proprietorships: Who will repay a loan if the sole proprietor dies? Finally, many lenders are concerned about the large number of sole proprietorships that fail—a topic discussed in Chapter 5.

The limited ability to borrow money can prevent a sole proprietorship from growing. It is the main reason that many business owners, when in need of relatively large amounts of capital, change from a sole proprietorship to a partnership or corporate form of ownership.

Limited Management Skills The sole proprietor is often the sole manager—in addition to being the only salesperson, buyer, accountant, and on occasion, janitor. Even the most experienced business owner is unlikely to have expertise in all these areas. Unless he or she obtains the necessary expertise by hiring employees,

assistants, or consultants, the business can suffer in the areas in which the owner is less knowledgeable. For the many sole proprietors who cannot hire the help they need, there just are not enough hours in the day to do everything that needs to be done.

Difficulty in Hiring Employees The sole proprietor may find it hard to attract and keep competent help. Potential employees may feel that there is no room for advancement in a firm whose owner assumes all managerial responsibilities. And when those who *are* hired are ready to take on added responsibility, they may find that the only way to do so is to quit the sole proprietorship and go to work for a larger firm or start up their own businesses. The lure of higher salaries and increased benefits (especially health insurance) also may cause existing employees to change jobs.

Beyond the Sole Proprietorship

Like many others, you may decide that the major disadvantage of a sole proprietorship is the limited amount that one person can do in a workday. One way to reduce the effect of this disadvantage (and retain many of the advantages) is to have more than one owner.

Partnerships

2

Learning Objective: Explain the different types of partners and the importance of partnership agreements.

A person who would not think of starting and running a business alone may enthusiastically seize the opportunity to enter into a business partnership. The U.S. Uniform Partnership Act defines a **partnership** as a voluntary association of two or more persons to act as co-owners of a business for profit. For example, in 1990, two young African-American entrepreneurs named Janet Smith and Gary Smith started Ivy Planning Group—a company that provides strategic planning and performance measurement for clients. Today, more than 15 years later, the company has evolved into a multimillion-dollar company that has hired a diverse staff of employees and provides cultural diversity training for *Fortune* 1000 firms, large not-for-profit organizations, and government agencies. In recognition of its efforts, Ivy Planning Group has been honored by DiversityBusiness.com as one of the top 50 minority-owned companies and by *Black Enterprise* and *Working Mother* magazines. And both Janet Smith and Gary Smith—Ivy Planning Group's founders—have been named "1 of 50 Most Influential Minorities in Business" by Minority Business and Professionals Network.[2]

partnership a voluntary association of two or more persons to act as co-owners of a business for profit

As shown in Figures 4.1 and 4.2, there are approximately 2.5 million partnerships in the United States, and this type of ownership accounts for about $3.1 trillion in sales receipts each year. Note, however, that this form of ownership is much less common than the sole proprietorship or the corporation. In fact, as Figure 4.1 shows, partnerships represent only about 9 percent of all American businesses. Although there is no legal maximum on the number of partners a partnership may have, most have only two. Large accounting, law, and advertising partnerships, however, are likely to have multiple partners. Regardless of the number of people involved, a partnership often represents a pooling of special managerial skills and talents; at other times, it is the result of a sole proprietor's taking on a partner for the purpose of obtaining more capital.

Types of Partners

All partners are not necessarily equal. Some may be active in running the business, whereas others may have a limited role.

General Partners A **general partner** is a person who assumes full or shared responsibility for operating a business. General partners are active in day-to-day business operations, and each partner can enter into contracts on behalf of the other partners. He or she also assumes unlimited liability for all debts, including debts incurred by any other general partner without his or her knowledge or consent. A **general partnership** is a business co-owned by two or more general partners who are liable for

general partner a person who assumes full or shared responsibility for operating a business

general partnership a business co-owned by two or more general partners who are liable for everything the business does

everything the business does. To avoid future liability, a general partner who withdraws from the partnership must give notice to creditors, customers, and suppliers.

limited partner a person who contributes capital to a business but has no management responsibility or liability for losses beyond the amount he or she invested in the partnership

limited partnership a business co-owned by one or more general partners who manage the business and limited partners who invest money in it

master limited partnership (MLP) a business partnership that is owned and managed like a corporation but often taxed like a partnership

Limited Partners A **limited partner** is a person who invests money in a business but who has no management responsibility or liability for losses beyond his or her investment in the partnership. A **limited partnership** is a business co-owned by one or more general partners who manage the business and limited partners who invest money in it. Limited partnerships may be formed to finance real estate, oil and gas, motion-picture, and other business ventures. Typically, the general partner or partners collect management fees and receive a percentage of profits. Limited partners receive a portion of profits and tax benefits.

Because of potential liability problems, special rules apply to limited partnerships. These rules are intended to protect customers and creditors who deal with limited partnerships. For example, prospective partners in a limited partnership must file a formal declaration, usually with the secretary of state or at their county courthouse, that describes the essential details of the partnership and the liability status of each partner involved in the business. At least one general partner must be responsible for the debts of the limited partnership. Also, some states prohibit the use of the limited partner's name in the partnership's name.

A special type of limited partnership is referred to as a *master limited partnership*. A **master limited partnership (MLP)** (sometimes referred to as a *publicly traded partnership*, or PTP) is a business partnership that is owned and managed like a corporation but often taxed like a partnership. This special ownership arrangement has a major advantage: Units of ownership in MLPs can be sold to investors to raise capital and often are traded on organized security exchanges. Because MLP units can be traded on an exchange, investors can sell their units of ownership at any time, hopefully for a profit. For more information on MLPs, visit the National Association of Publicly Traded Partnerships website at **www.naptp.org.**

Originally, there were tax advantages to forming an MLP because profits from this special type of partnership were reported as personal income. MLPs thus avoided the double taxation paid on corporate income. Today, the Internal Revenue Service

Two heads are better than one. *When Rachel Liu and Antoinette Giorgi began their organic clothing business, they made a decision to choose the partnership form of business ownership. For these two entrepreneurs, it was the right choice because their firm now produces and sells more than 300,000 organic garments each year.*

SIPA via AP Images

has limited many of the tax advantages of MLPs. While there are exceptions, most MLPs typically are in timber, energy, or real-estate-related businesses.[3]

The Partnership Agreement

Articles of partnership are an agreement listing and explaining the terms of the partnership. Although both oral and written partnership agreements are legal and can be enforced in the courts, a written agreement has an obvious advantage: It is not subject to lapses of memory.

Figure 4.3 shows a typical partnership agreement. The partnership agreement should state who will make the final decisions, what each partner's duties will be, and the investment each partner will make. The partnership agreement also should state how much profit or loss each partner receives or is responsible for. Finally, the partnership agreement should state what happens if a partner wants to dissolve the partnership or dies. Although the people involved in a partnership can draft their own agreement, most experts recommend consulting an attorney.

Figure 4.3: Articles of Partnership

Articles of partnership are a written or oral agreement that lists and explains the terms of a partnership.

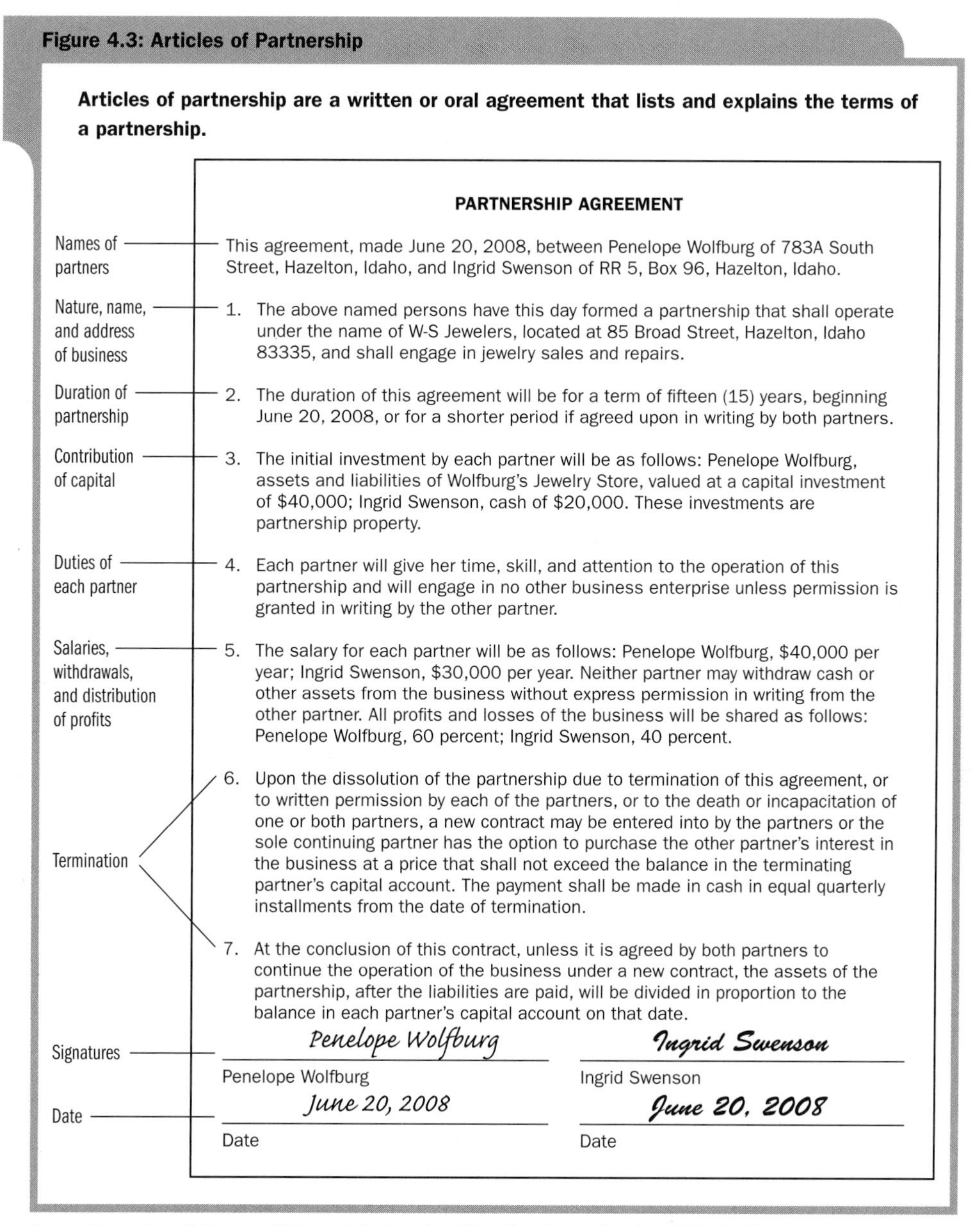

PARTNERSHIP AGREEMENT

Names of partners — This agreement, made June 20, 2008, between Penelope Wolfburg of 783A South Street, Hazelton, Idaho, and Ingrid Swenson of RR 5, Box 96, Hazelton, Idaho.

Nature, name, and address of business — 1. The above named persons have this day formed a partnership that shall operate under the name of W-S Jewelers, located at 85 Broad Street, Hazelton, Idaho 83335, and shall engage in jewelry sales and repairs.

Duration of partnership — 2. The duration of this agreement will be for a term of fifteen (15) years, beginning June 20, 2008, or for a shorter period if agreed upon in writing by both partners.

Contribution of capital — 3. The initial investment by each partner will be as follows: Penelope Wolfburg, assets and liabilities of Wolfburg's Jewelry Store, valued at a capital investment of $40,000; Ingrid Swenson, cash of $20,000. These investments are partnership property.

Duties of each partner — 4. Each partner will give her time, skill, and attention to the operation of this partnership and will engage in no other business enterprise unless permission is granted in writing by the other partner.

Salaries, withdrawals, and distribution of profits — 5. The salary for each partner will be as follows: Penelope Wolfburg, $40,000 per year; Ingrid Swenson, $30,000 per year. Neither partner may withdraw cash or other assets from the business without express permission in writing from the other partner. All profits and losses of the business will be shared as follows: Penelope Wolfburg, 60 percent; Ingrid Swenson, 40 percent.

Termination — 6. Upon the dissolution of the partnership due to termination of this agreement, or to written permission by each of the partners, or to the death or incapacitation of one or both partners, a new contract may be entered into by the partners or the sole continuing partner has the option to purchase the other partner's interest in the business at a price that shall not exceed the balance in the terminating partner's capital account. The payment shall be made in cash in equal quarterly installments from the date of termination.

7. At the conclusion of this contract, unless it is agreed by both partners to continue the operation of the business under a new contract, the assets of the partnership, after the liabilities are paid, will be divided in proportion to the balance in each partner's capital account on that date.

Signatures — *Penelope Wolfburg* / Penelope Wolfburg — *Ingrid Swenson* / Ingrid Swenson

Date — *June 20, 2008* / Date — *June 20, 2008* / Date

Source: Adapted from Goldman and Sigismond, *Business Law*, 7th edition. Boston: Houghton Mifflin, 2007. Copyright © 2007 by Cengage Learning Company. Reprinted with permission.

When entering into a partnership agreement, partners would be wise to let a neutral third party—a consultant, an accountant, a lawyer, or a mutual friend—assist with any disputes that might arise.

Advantages of Partnerships

Learning Objective: Describe the advantages and disadvantages of partnerships.

Partnerships have many advantages. The most important are described below.

Ease of Start-Up Partnerships are relatively easy to form. As with a sole proprietorship, the legal requirements often are limited to registering the name of the business and obtaining any necessary licenses or permits. It may not even be necessary to prepare written articles of partnership, although doing so is generally a good idea.

Sometimes it takes more than one business owner! *When an entrepreneur doesn't have what it takes to operate a successful business, many business owners opt to form a partnership. The ability to attract a partner(s) with the right combination of business skills, knowledge, and management expertise can increase the chances of success and reduce the risk of failure.*

PRNewswire/Black Enterprise

Availability of Capital and Credit Because partners can pool their funds, a partnership usually has more capital available than a sole proprietorship does. This additional capital, coupled with the general partners' unlimited liability, can form the basis for a better credit rating. Banks and suppliers may be more willing to extend credit or approve larger loans to such a partnership than to a sole proprietor. This does not mean that partnerships can borrow all the money they need. Many partnerships have found it hard to get long-term financing simply because lenders worry about the possibility of management disagreements and lack of continuity.

Personal Interest General partners are very concerned with the operation of the firm—perhaps even more so than sole proprietors. After all, they are responsible for the actions of all other general partners, as well as for their own. The pride of ownership from solving the day-to-day problems of operating a business—with the help of another person(s)—is a strong motivating force and often makes all the people involved in the partnership work harder to become more successful.

Combined Business Skills and Knowledge Partners often have complementary skills. The weakness of one partner—in manufacturing, for example—may be offset by another partner's strength in that area. Moreover, the ability to discuss important decisions with another concerned individual often relieves some pressure and leads to more effective decision making.

Retention of Profits As in a sole proprietorship, all profits belong to the owners of the partnership. The partners share directly in the financial rewards and therefore are highly motivated to do their best to make the firm succeed. As noted, the partnership agreement should state how much profit or loss each partner receives or is responsible for.

No Special Taxes Although a partnership pays no income tax, the Internal Revenue Service requires partnerships to file an annual information return that states the names and addresses of all partners involved in the business. The return also must provide information about income and expenses and distributions made to each partner. Then each partner is required to report his or her share of profit (or loss) from the partnership business on his or her individual tax return and is taxed on his or her share of the profit—in the same way a sole proprietor is taxed.

Disadvantages of Partnerships

Although partnerships have many advantages when compared with sole proprietorships and corporations, they also have some disadvantages, which anyone thinking of forming a partnership should consider.

Unlimited Liability As we have noted, each *general* partner has unlimited liability for all debts of the business. Each partner is legally and personally responsible for the debts and actions of any other partner conducting partnership business, even if that partner did not incur those debts or do anything wrong. General partners thus run the risk of having to use their personal assets to pay creditors. *Limited* partners, however, risk only their original investment.

Today, many states allow partners to form a *limited-liability partnership* (LLP), in which a partner may have limited-liability protection from legal action resulting from the malpractice or negligence of the other partners. Most states that allow LLPs restrict this type of ownership to certain types of professionals such as accountants, architects, attorneys, and similar professionals. (Note the difference between a limited partnership and a limited-liability partnership. A limited partnership must have at least one general partner that has unlimited liability. On the other hand, all partners in a limited-liability partnership may have limited liability *for the malpractice of the other partners.*)

Management Disagreements What happens to a partnership if one of the partners brings a spouse or a relative into the business? What happens if a partner wants to withdraw more money from the business? Notice that each of the preceding situations—and for that matter, most of the other problems that can develop in a partnership—involves one partner doing something that disturbs the other partner(s). This human factor is especially important because business partners—with egos, ambitions, and money on the line—are especially susceptible to friction. When partners begin to disagree about decisions, policies, or ethics, distrust may build and get worse as time passes—often to the point where it is impossible to operate the business successfully.

Lack of Continuity Partnerships are terminated if any one of the general partners dies, withdraws, or is declared legally incompetent. However, the remaining partners can purchase that partner's ownership share. For example, the partnership agreement may permit surviving partners to continue the business after buying a deceased partner's interest from his or her estate. However, if the partnership loses an owner whose specific management or technical skills cannot be replaced, it is not likely to survive.

Frozen Investment It is easy to invest money in a partnership, but it is sometimes quite difficult to get it out. This is the case, for example, when remaining partners are unwilling to buy the share of the business that belongs to a partner who retires or wants to relocate to another city. To avoid such difficulties, the partnership agreement should include some procedure for buying out a partner.

In some cases, a partner must find someone outside the firm to buy his or her share. How easy or difficult it is to find an outsider depends on how successful the business is and how willing existing partners are to accept a new partner.

Beyond the Partnership

The main advantages of a partnership over a sole proprietorship are the added capital and management expertise of the partners. However, some of the basic disadvantages of the sole proprietorship also plague the general partnership. One disadvantage in particular—unlimited liability—can cause problems. A third form of business ownership, the corporation, overcomes this disadvantage.

Corporations

4

Learning Objective: Summarize how a corporation is formed.

Back in 1837, William Procter and James Gamble—two sole proprietors—formed a partnership called Procter & Gamble and set out to compete with fourteen other soap and candle makers in Cincinnati, Ohio. Then, in 1890, Procter & Gamble incorporated to raise additional capital for expansion that eventually allowed the

Procter & Gamble's decision to incorporate. *William Procter and James Gamble—two separate sole proprietorships—decided to form a partnership and work together. Later, the two successful entrepreneurs made a decision to incorporate their business in order to raise needed capital for expansion. Today, Procter & Gamble Corporation is a global giant that sells many different consumer products.*

Courtesy Procter & Gamble

company to become a global giant. Today, 3 billion times a day, Procter & Gamble brands touch the lives of people in 80 countries around the globe.[4] While not all sole proprietorships and partnerships become corporations, there are reasons why business owners choose the corporate form of ownership. Let's begin with a definition of a corporation. Perhaps the best definition of a corporation was given by Chief Justice John Marshall in a famous Supreme Court decision in 1819. A corporation, he said, "is an artificial person, invisible, intangible, and existing only in contemplation of the law." In other words, a **corporation** (sometimes referred to as a *regular* or *C-corporation*) is an artificial person created by law, with most of the legal rights of a real person. These include the rights to start and operate a business, to buy or sell property, to borrow money, to sue or be sued, and to enter into binding contracts. Unlike a real person, however, a corporation exists only on paper.

There are 5.6 million corporations in the United States. They comprise only about 20 percent of all businesses, but they account for 83.8 percent of sales revenues (see Figures 4.1 and 4.2). Table 4.1 lists the seven largest U.S. industrial corporations, ranked according to sales.

corporation an artificial person created by law with most of the legal rights of a real person, including the rights to start and operate a business, to buy or sell property, to borrow money, to sue or be sued, and to enter into binding contracts

stock the shares of ownership of a corporation

stockholder a person who owns a corporation's stock

closed corporation a corporation whose stock is owned by relatively few people and is not sold to the general public

open corporation a corporation whose stock can be bought and sold by any individual

Corporate Ownership

The shares of ownership of a corporation are called **stock**. The people who own a corporation's stock—and thus own part of the corporation—are called **stockholders** or sometimes *shareholders*. Once a corporation has been formed, it may sell its stock to individuals or other companies that want to invest in the corporation. It also may issue stock as a reward to key employees in return for certain services or as a return to investors (in place of cash payments).

A **closed corporation** is a corporation whose stock is owned by relatively few people and is not sold to the general public. As an example, DeWitt and Lila Wallace owned virtually all the stock of Reader's Digest Association, making it one of the largest corporations of this kind. A person who wishes to sell the stock of a closed corporation generally arranges to sell it *privately* to another stockholder or a close acquaintance.

Although founded in 1922 as a closed corporation, the Reader's Digest Association became an open corporation when it sold stock to investors for the first time in 1990. An **open corporation** is one whose stock can be bought and sold by any individual. Examples of open corporations include General Motors, Microsoft, and Johnson & Johnson.

Table 4.1: The Seven Largest U.S. Industrial Corporations, Ranked by Sales Revenues

Rank 2008	Company	Revenues ($ millions)	Profits ($ millions)
1	Wal-Mart Stores	378,799.0	12,731.0
2	ExxonMobil	372,824.0	40,610.0
3	Chevron	210,783.0	18,688.0
4	GeneralMotors	182,347.0	–38,732.0
5	ConocoPhillips	178,558.0	11,891.0
6	General Electric	176,656.0	22,208.0
7	Ford Motor	172,468.0	–2,723.0

Source: *Fortune* website at **www.fortune.com**, accessed September 12, 2008.

Forming a Corporation

Although you may think that incorporating a business guarantees success, it does not. There is no special magic about placing the word *Incorporated* or the abbreviation *Inc.* after the name of a business. Unfortunately, like sole proprietorships or partnerships, incorporated businesses can go broke. The decision to incorporate a business therefore should be made only after carefully considering whether the corporate form of ownership suits your needs better than the sole proprietorship or partnership forms.

Sustaining the Planet

One way corporations such as J.C. Penney spread the word about their sustainability activities and achievements is through the Corporate Social Responsibility Newswire. **www.csrwire.com**

If you decide that the corporate form is the best form of organization for you, most experts recommend that you begin the incorporation process by consulting a lawyer to be sure that all legal requirements are met. While it may be possible to incorporate a business without legal help, it is well to keep in mind the old saying, "A man who acts as his own attorney has a fool for a client." Table 4.2 lists some aspects of starting and running a business that may require legal help.

Where to Incorporate A business is allowed to incorporate in any state that it chooses. The decision on where to incorporate usually is based on two factors: (1) the cost of incorporating in one state compared with the cost in another state and (2) the advantages and disadvantages of each state's corporate laws and tax structure. Most small and medium-sized businesses are incorporated in the state where they do the most business. The founders of larger corporations or of those that will do business nationwide often compare the benefits that various states provide to corporations. Some states are more hospitable than others, and some offer fewer restrictions, lower taxes, and other benefits to attract new firms. Delaware and Nevada are often chosen by corporations that do business in more than one state because of their corporation friendly laws.[5]

An incorporated business is called a **domestic corporation** in the state in which it is incorporated. In all other states where it does business, it is called a **foreign corporation**. Sears Holdings Corporation, the parent company of Sears and Kmart, is incorporated in Deleware, where it is a domestic corporation. In the remaining forty-nine states, Sears is a foreign corporation. Sears must register in all states where it does business and also pay taxes and annual fees to each state. A corporation chartered by a foreign government and conducting business in the United States is an **alien corporation**. Volkswagen AG, Sony Corporation, and the Royal Dutch/Shell Group are examples of alien corporations.

domestic corporation a corporation in the state in which it is incorporated

foreign corporation a corporation in any state in which it does business except the one in which it is incorporated

alien corporation a corporation chartered by a foreign government and conducting business in the United States

The Articles of Incorporation Once a home state has been chosen, the incorporator(s) submits *articles of incorporation* to the secretary of state. When the articles of incorporation are approved, they become a contract between a corporation and the state in which the state recognizes the formation of the artificial person

Table 4.2: Ten Aspects of Business That May Require Legal Help

1. Choosing either the sole proprietorship, partnership, or corporate form of ownership	6. Filing for licenses or permits at the local, state, and federal levels
2. Constructing a partnership agreement	7. Purchasing an existing business or real estate
3. Incorporating a business	8. Creating valid contracts
4. Registering a corporation's stock	9. Hiring employees and independent contractors
5. Obtaining a trademark, patent, or copyright	10. Extending credit and collecting debts

SPOTLIGHT
Corporate Profits

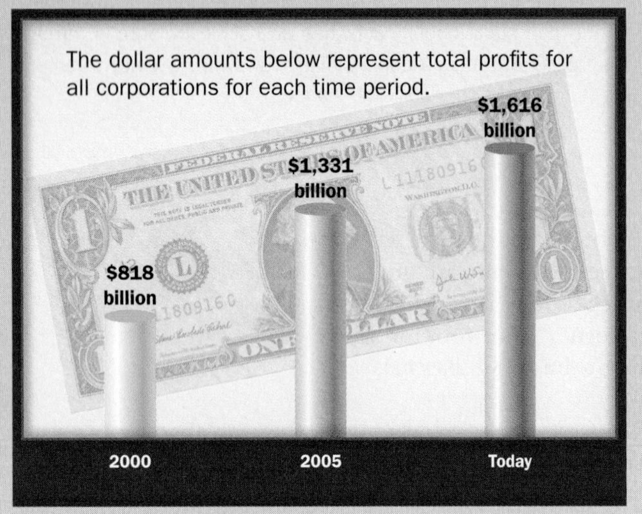

Source: The U.S. Census Bureau, *Statistical Abstract of the United States, 2008*, p. 514.

that is the corporation. Usually, the articles of incorporation include the following information:

- The firm's name and address
- The incorporators' names and addresses
- The purpose of the corporation
- The maximum amount of stock and types of stock to be issued
- The rights and privileges of stockholders
- The length of time the corporation is to exist

To help you to decide if the corporate form of organization is the right choice, you may want to review the material available on the Yahoo! Small Business website (**http://smallbusiness.yahoo.com**). Once at the site, click on News & Resources. In addition, before making a decision to organize your business as a corporation, you may want to consider two additional areas: stockholders' rights and the importance of the organizational meeting.

Stockholders' Rights There are two basic types of stock. Owners of **common stock** may vote on corporate matters. Generally, an owner of common stock has one vote for each share owned. However, any claims of common-stock owners on profits and assets of the corporation are subordinate to the claims of others. The owners of **preferred stock** usually have no voting rights, but their claims on dividends are paid before those of common-stock owners. While large corporations may issue both common and preferred stock, generally small corporations issue only common stock.

common stock stock owned by individuals or firms who may vote on corporate matters but whose claims on profit and assets are subordinate to the claims of others

preferred stock stock owned by individuals or firms who usually do not have voting rights but whose claims on dividends are paid before those of common-stock owners

Perhaps the most important right of owners of both common and preferred stock is to share in the profit earned by the corporation through the payment of dividends. A **dividend** is a distribution of earnings to the stockholders of a corporation. Other rights include receiving information about the corporation, voting on changes to the corporate charter, and attending the corporation's annual stockholders' meeting, where they may exercise their right to vote.

dividend a distribution of earnings to the stockholders of a corporation

Because common stockholders usually live all over the nation, very few actually may attend a corporation's annual meeting. Instead, they vote by proxy. A **proxy** is a legal form listing issues to be decided at a stockholders' meeting and enabling stockholders to transfer their voting rights to some other individual or individuals. The stockholder can register a vote and transfer voting rights simply by signing and returning the form. Today, most corporations also allow stockholders to exercise their right to vote by proxy by accessing the Internet or using a toll-free phone number.

proxy a legal form listing issues to be decided at a stockholders' meeting and enabling stockholders to transfer their voting rights to some other individual or individuals

Organizational Meeting As the last step in forming a corporation, the incorporators and original stockholders meet to adopt corporate by-laws and elect their first board of directors. (Later, directors will be elected or reelected at the corporation's annual meetings.) The board members are directly responsible to the stockholders for the way they operate the firm.

Corporate Structure

The organizational structure of most corporations is more complicated than that of a sole proprietorship or partnership. This is especially true as the corporation begins to grow and expand. In a corporation, both the board of directors and the corporate officers are involved in management.

board of directors the top governing body of a corporation, the members of which are elected by the stockholders

Board of Directors As an artificial person, a corporation can act only through its directors, who represent the corporation's stockholders. The **board of directors**

is the top governing body of a corporation and is elected by the stockholders. Board members can be chosen from within the corporation or from outside it. *Note:* For a small corporation, only one director is required in many states although you can choose to have more.

Directors who are elected from within the corporation are usually its top managers—the president and executive vice presidents, for example. Those elected from outside the corporation generally are experienced managers or entrepreneurs with proven leadership ability and/or specific talents the organization seems to need. In smaller corporations, majority stockholders usually serve as board members.

The major responsibilities of the board of directors are to set company goals and develop general plans (or strategies) for meeting those goals. The board also is responsible for the firm's overall operation.

Corporate Officers **Corporate officers** are appointed by the board of directors. The chairman of the board, president, executive vice presidents, corporate secretary, and treasurer are all corporate officers. They help the board to make plans, carry out strategies established by the board, hire employees, and manage day-to-day business activities. Periodically (usually each month), they report to the board of directors. And at the annual meeting, the directors report to the stockholders. In theory, then,

Entrepreneurial Challenge

Who's on Board?

Although many states don't require more than one director, a small business can really benefit from the background and experience of multiple board members. When the Santa Ana Business Bank opened in California, its outside directors included a lawyer who was also on a community college board; the head of the chamber of commerce; and two directors who had served on other banks' boards. What should you look for in a potential director?

- *Complementary skills and expertise.* Choose directors whose strengths complement yours, so you can learn from their feedback and advice.
- *Shared values.* Be sure your directors share the ethics and values on which your business is based.
- *Independent thinking.* Seek out directors who will carefully comb through your plans and ask probing questions, rather than simply rubber-stamping your decisions.
- *Commitment.* Expect your directors not only to attend board meetings but be available to give you advice and guidance via e-mail or phone when needed.

Sources: Jennifer Delson, "Santa Ana Bank Targets Locals," *Los Angeles Times,* December 3, 2007, p. B1; Jeff Wuorio, "Hiring a Board of Directors: 8 Tips," *Microsoft Small Business Center,* n.d., **http://www.microsoft.com/smallbusiness/resources/management/leadership-training/hiring-a-board-of-directors-8-tips.aspx#Hiringaboardofdirectorstips;** J. Robert Beyster, "Expert Q&A: Expectations for a Small Business Board of Directors," *American Small Business News,* February 20, 2008, **http://www.americanentrepreneurship.com/2008/02/20/expert-qa-expectations-for-a-small-business-board-of-directors.**

AP Photo/Thomas Kienzle

Who is the boss? *While Claus-Dietrich Lahrs is the new chief executive officer (CEO) of German fashion concern Hugo Boss, he was appointed by the board of directors. In a corporation, the stockholders elect the members of the board of directors. Then the board appoints the CEO, president, executive vice presidents, and other corporate officers.*

corporate officers the chairman of the board, president, executive vice presidents, corporate secretary, treasurer, and any other top executive appointed by the board of directors

Figure 4.4: Hierarchy of Corporate Structure

Stockholders exercise a great deal of influence through their right to elect the board of directors.

Stockholders (owners) → *Elect* → Board of directors → *Appoints* → Officers → *Hire* → Employees

limited liability a feature of corporate ownership that limits each owner's financial liability to the amount of money that he or she has paid for the corporation's stock

the stockholders are able to control the activities of the entire corporation through its directors because they are the group that elects the board of directors (see Figure 4.4).

5

Learning Objective: Describe the advantages and disadvantages of a corporation.

Advantages of Corporations

Back in October 2000, Manny Ruiz decided that it was time to start his own company. With the help of a team of media specialists, he founded Hispanic PR Wire. In a business where hype is the name of the game, Hispanic PR Wire is the real thing and has established itself as the nation's premier news distribution service reaching U.S. Hispanic media and opinion leaders. Today, the business continues to build on its early success.[6] Mr. Ruiz chose to incorporate this business because it provided a number of advantages that other forms of business ownership did not offer. Typical advantages include limited liability, ease of raising capital, ease of transfer of ownership, perpetual life, and specialized management.

Sometimes larger is not necessarily better. *According to Wayne St. John, one of three brothers who own the Fireside True Value store in Brattleboro, Vermont, business couldn't be better. Their competition across the street—a Home Depot store—closed because of low sales revenues.*

AP Photo/Jason R. Henske

Limited Liability One of the most attractive features of corporate ownership is **limited liability**. With few exceptions, each owner's financial liability is limited to the amount of money he or she has paid for the corporation's stock. This feature arises from the fact that the corporation is itself a legal person, separate from its owners. If a corporation fails, creditors have a claim only on the corporation's assets, not on the owners' (stockholders') personal assets. Because it overcomes the problem of unlimited liability connected with sole proprietorships and general partnerships, limited liability is one of the chief reasons why entrepreneurs often choose the corporate form of organization.

Ease of Raising Capital The corporation is by far the most effective form of business ownership for raising capital. Like sole proprietorships and partnerships, corporations can borrow from lending institutions. However, they also can raise additional sums of money by selling stock. Individuals are more willing to invest in corporations than in other forms of business because of limited liability, and they can sell their stock easily—hopefully for a profit.

Ease of Transfer of Ownership Accessing a brokerage firm website or a telephone call to a stockbroker is all that is required to put stock up for sale. Willing buyers are available for most stocks at the market price. Ownership is transferred when the sale is made, and practically no restrictions apply to the sale and purchase of stock issued by an open corporation.

Perpetual Life Since it is essentially a legal "person," a corporation exists independently of its owners and survives them. The withdrawal, death, or incompetence of a key executive or owner does not cause the corporation to be terminated. Sears, Roebuck incorporated in 1893 and is one of the nation's largest retailing corporations, even though its original owners, Richard Sears and Alvah Roebuck, have been dead for decades.

Specialized Management Typically, corporations are able to recruit more skilled, knowledgeable, and talented managers than proprietorships and partnerships. This is so because they pay bigger salaries, offer excellent fringe benefits, and are large enough to offer considerable opportunity for advancement. Within the corporate structure, administration, human resources, finance, marketing, and operations are placed in the charge of experts in these fields.

Disadvantages of Corporations

Like its advantages, many of a corporation's disadvantages stem from its legal definition as an artificial person or legal entity. The most serious disadvantages are described below. (See Table 4.3 for a comparison of some of the advantages and disadvantages of a sole proprietorship, general partnership, and corporation.)

Difficulty and Expense of Formation Forming a corporation can be a relatively complex and costly process. The use of an attorney usually is necessary to complete the legal forms that are submitted to the secretary of state. Application fees, attorney's fees, registration costs associated with selling stock, and other organizational costs can amount to thousands of dollars for even a medium-sized corporation. The costs of incorporating, in terms of both time and money, discourage many owners of smaller businesses from forming corporations.

Government Regulation and Increased Paperwork A corporation must meet various government standards before it can sell its stock to the public. Then it must file many reports on its business operations and finances with local, state, and federal governments. In addition, the corporation must make periodic reports to its stockholders about various aspects of the business. To prepare all the necessary reports, even small corporations often need the help of an attorney, certified public accountant, and other professionals on a regular basis. In addition, a corporation's activities are restricted by law to those spelled out in its charter.

Conflict Within the Corporation Because a large corporation may employ thousands of employees, some conflict is inevitable. For example, the pressure to increase sales revenue, reduce expenses, and increase profits often leads to increased stress and tension for both managers and employees. This is especially true when a

Table 4.3: Some Advantages and Disadvantages of a Sole Proprietorship, Partnership, and Corporation

	Sole Proprietorship	General Partnership	Regular (C) Corporation
Protecting against liability for debts	Difficult	Difficult	Easy
Raising money	Difficult	Difficult	Easy
Ownership transfer	Difficult	Difficult	Easy
Preserving continuity	Difficult	Difficult	Easy
Government regulations	Few	Few	Many
Formation	Easy	Easy	Difficult
Income taxation	Once	Once	Twice

corporation operates in a competitive industry, attempts to develop and market new products, or must downsize the workforce to reduce employee salary expense.

Double Taxation Corporations must pay a tax on their profits. In addition, stockholders must pay a personal income tax on profits received as dividends. Corporate profits thus are taxed twice—once as corporate income and a second time as the personal income of stockholders. *Note:* Both the S-corporation and the limited-liability company discussed in the next section are taxed like a partnership but still provide limited liability for the personal assets of the owners.

Lack of Secrecy Because open corporations are required to submit detailed reports to government agencies and to stockholders, they cannot keep their operations confidential. Competitors can study these corporate reports and then use the information to compete more effectively. In effect, every public corporation has to share some of its secrets with its competitors.

Special Types of Business Ownership

6

Learning Objective: Examine special types of corporations, including S-corporations, limited-liability companies, government-owned corporations, and not-for-profit corporations.

In addition to the sole proprietorship, partnership, and the regular corporate form of organization, some entrepreneurs choose other forms of organization that meet their special needs. Additional organizational options include S-corporations, limited-liability companies, government-owned corporations, and not-for-profit corporations.

S-Corporations

S-corporation a corporation that is taxed as though it were a partnership

If a corporation meets certain requirements, its directors may apply to the Internal Revenue Service for status as an S-corporation. An **S-corporation** is a corporation that is taxed as though it were a partnership. In other words, the corporation's income is taxed only as the personal income of its stockholders. Corporate profits or losses "pass through" the business and are reported on the owners' personal income tax returns.

Becoming an S-corporation can be an effective way to avoid double taxation while retaining the corporation's legal benefit of limited liability. To qualify for the special status of an S-corporation, a firm must meet the following criteria:[7]

1. No more than 100 stockholders are allowed.
2. Stockholders must be individuals, estates, or exempt organizations.
3. There can be only one class of outstanding stock.
4. The firm must be a domestic corporation eligible to file for S-corporation status.
5. There can be no nonresident-alien stockholders.
6. All stockholders must agree to the decision to form an S-corporation.

Limited-Liability Companies

limited-liability company (LLC) a form of business ownership that combines the benefits of a corporation and a partnership while avoiding some of the restrictions and disadvantages of those forms of ownership

A new form of ownership called a *limited-liability company* has been approved in all fifty states—although each state's laws may differ. A **limited-liability company (LLC)** is a form of business ownership that combines the benefits of a corporation and a partnership while avoiding some of the restrictions and disadvantages of those forms of ownership. Chief advantages of an LLC are as follows:

1. LLCs with at least two members are taxed like a partnership and thus avoid the double taxation imposed on most corporations. LLCs with just one member are taxed like a sole proprietorship.
2. Like a corporation, it provides limited-liability protection. An LLC thus extends the concept of personal-asset protection to small business owners.

An LLC doesn't have to be small. *Many people think that limited-liability companies are small, struggling enterprises. The truth is that even large companies often choose the LLC form of business ownership. In this photo, Madhu Vuppuluri, President and CEO of Essar Steel Minnesota, LLC breaks ground for a new $1.6 billion steel plant in Nashwauk, Minnesota.*

AP Photo/Mesabi Daily News, Mark Sauer

3. The LLC type of organization provides more management flexibility when compared with corporations. A corporation, for example, is required to hold annual meetings and record meeting minutes.

Although many experts believe that the LLC is nothing more than a variation of the S-corporation, there is a difference. An LLC is not restricted to 100 stockholders—a common drawback of the S-corporation. LLCs are also less restricted and have more flexibility than S-corporations in terms of who can become an owner. Although the owners of an LLC must file articles of organization with their state's secretary of state, they are not hampered by lots of Internal Revenue Service rules and government regulations that apply to corporations. As a result, experts are predicting that LLCs may become one of the most popular forms of business ownership available. For help in understanding the differences between a regular corporation, S-corporation, and limited-liability company, see Table 4.4.

Government-Owned Corporations

A **government-owned corporation** is owned and operated by a local, state, or federal government. The Tennessee Valley Authority (TVA), the National Railroad Passenger Corporation known as Amtrak, and the Federal Deposit Insurance Corporation (FDIC) are all government-owned corporations. They are operated by the U.S. government. In addition, most municipal bus lines and subways are run by city-owned corporations.

government-owned corporation a corporation owned and operated by a local, state, or federal government

SeaWorld & Busch Gardens Conservation Fund is all about service. *Each year, the SeaWorld & Busch Gardens Conservation Fund, a private charitable foundation, works with purpose and passion on behalf of wildlife and habitats worldwide, encouraging sustainable solutions through research, animal rescue and rehabilitation, and conservation education. To pay the bills, this not-for-profit conservation fund accepts contributions from the Busch Entertainment Corporation, other businesses, and individuals. For more information, go to* ***www.swbg-conservationfund.org.***

Table 4.4: Some Advantages and Disadvantages of a Regular Corporation, S-Corporation, and Limited-Liability Company

	Regular (C) Corporation	S-Corporation	Limited-Liability Company
Double taxation	Yes	No	No
Limited liability and personal-asset protection	Yes	Yes	Yes
Management and ownership flexibility	No	No	Yes
Restrictions on the number of owners/stockholders	No	Yes	No
Internal Revenue Service tax regulations	Many	Many	Fewer

A government corporation usually provides a service the business sector is reluctant or unable to offer. Profit is secondary in such corporations. In fact, they may continually operate at a loss, particularly if they are involved in public transportation. Their main objective is to ensure that a particular service is available.

Not-for-Profit Corporations

A **not-for-profit corporation** (sometimes referred to as *nonprofit*) is a corporation organized to provide a social, educational, religious, or other service rather than to earn a profit. Various charities, museums, private schools, and colleges are organized in this way, primarily to ensure limited liability. Habitat for Humanity is a not-for-profit corporation and was formed to provide homes for qualified low-income people who could not afford housing. Even though this corporation may receive more money than it spends, any surplus funds are "reinvested" in building activities to provide low-cost housing. It is a not-for-profit corporation because its primary purpose is to provide a social service. Other examples include the Public Broadcasting System (PBS), the Girl Scouts, and the Bill and Melinda Gates Foundation.

Cooperatives, Joint Ventures, and Syndicates

7

Learning Objective: Discuss the purpose of a cooperative, joint venture, and syndicate.

Today, three additional types of business organizations—cooperatives, joint ventures, and syndicates—are used for special purposes. Each of these forms of organization is unique when compared with more traditional forms of business ownership.

Cooperatives

A **cooperative** is an association of individuals or firms whose purpose is to perform some business function for its members. The cooperative can perform its function more effectively than any member could by acting alone. For example, cooperatives purchase goods in bulk and distribute them to members; thus the unit cost is lower than it would be if each member bought the goods in a much smaller quantity.

Although cooperatives are found in all segments of our economy, they are most prevalent in agriculture. Farmers use cooperatives to purchase supplies, to buy services such as trucking and storage, and to process and market their products. Ocean Spray Cranberries, Inc., for example, is a cooperative of some 650 cranberry growers and more than 100 citrus growers spread throughout the country.[8]

Joint Ventures

A **joint venture** is an agreement between two or more groups to form a business entity in order to achieve a specific goal or to operate for a specific period of time.

not-for-profit corporation a corporation organized to provide a social, educational, religious, or other service rather than to earn a profit

cooperative an association of individuals or firms whose purpose is to perform some business function for its members

joint venture an agreement between two or more groups to form a business entity in order to achieve a specific goal or to operate for a specific period of time

Both the scope of the joint venture and the liabilities of the people or businesses involved usually are limited to one project. Once the goal is reached, the period of time elapses, or the project is completed, the joint venture is dissolved.

Corporations, as well as individuals, may enter into joint ventures. Major oil producers often have formed a number of joint ventures to share the extremely high cost of exploring for offshore petroleum deposits. And many U.S. companies are forming joint ventures with foreign firms in order to enter new markets around the globe. For example, Wal-Mart has joined forces with India's Bharti Enterprises to begin selling merchandise and capture a share of India's $350 billion retail market. Together, the two firms will set up 15 wholesale cash-and-carry stores over the next seven years.[9] Finally, Japanese consumer electronics manufacturer Sony and Swedish telecom giant Ericsson have formed a joint venture to manufacture and market mobile communications equipment. Now, after more than seven years, the joint venture is profitable.[10]

Ethics Matters

Yogurt Responsibility

Can yogurt make the world a better place? Bangladesh's Grameen Bank and France's Danone think so. The two have teamed up in a joint venture called Grameen Danone Foods to fight malnutrition and raise the standard of living in northern Bangladesh.

Danone provided the start-up capital and designed the first factory, an environmentally friendly facility that runs partly on solar power. It also developed a recipe for specially fortified yogurt that could be sold for less than ten cents per biodegradable container. Grameen Bank lent local farmers money to buy cows and helped arrange centralized locations for milk collection. In addition, Grameen recruited "Grameen Ladies" who go door to door in and around the city of Bogra and earn about a penny for each cup of yogurt they sell.

Open since 2007, the factory now produces more than 10,000 cups of extra-nutritious, affordable yogurt every day. Counting the dairy farmers, factory workers, and Grameen Ladies, the joint venture provides much-needed income for more than 1,500 local residents. Just as important, the company is not a charity but will soon be self supporting. "The strength is that it is a business, and if it is a business, it is sustainable," says Danone's CEO.

Sources: Carol Matlack, "Danone Innovates to Help Feed the Poor," *BusinessWeek*, April 28, 2008, **www.businessweek.com**; Sheridan Prasso, "Saving the World with a Cup of Yogurt," *Fortune*, March 15, 2007, **http://money.cnn.com/magazines/fortune/fortune_archive/2007/02/05/8399198/index.htm**; **www.danonecommunities.com**.

Syndicates

A **syndicate** is a temporary association of individuals or firms organized to perform a specific task that requires a large amount of capital. The syndicate is formed because no one person or firm is willing to put up the entire amount required for the undertaking. Like a joint venture, a syndicate is dissolved as soon as its purpose has been accomplished.

Syndicates are used most commonly to underwrite large insurance policies, loans, and investments. To share the risk of default, banks have formed syndicates to provide loans to developing countries. Stock brokerage firms usually join together in the same way to market a new issue of stock. For example, Goldman Sachs, JP Morgan Chase, and other Wall Street firms formed a syndicate to sell shares of stock in MasterCard. The initial public offering (IPO) was one of the largest in U.S. history—too large for Goldman Sachs and JP Morgan Chase to handle without help from other Wall Street firms.[11] (An *initial public offering* is the term used to describe the first time a corporation sells stock to the general public.)

syndicate a temporary association of individuals or firms organized to perform a specific task that requires a large amount of capital

Corporate Growth

8

Learning Objective: Explain how growth from within and growth through mergers can enable a business to expand

Growth seems to be a basic characteristic of business. One reason for seeking growth has to do with profit: A larger firm generally has greater sales revenue and thus greater profit. Another reason is that in a growing economy, a business that does not grow is actually shrinking relative to the economy. A third reason is that business growth is a means by which some executives boost their power, prestige, and reputation.

Growth poses new problems and requires additional resources that first must be available and then must be used effectively. The main ingredient in growth is capital—and as we have noted, capital is most readily available to corporations. Thus, to a great extent, business growth means corporate growth.

PRNewsFoto/Wendy's International, Inc.

Northwest and Delta: It's a go! *Two flight attendants, Robyn Huser and Elizabeth Frankel, check out the newspaper headlines about the Northwest–Delta merger in a morning newspaper. Although many mergers are hostile, the merger between Northwest and Delta was a friendly, horizontal merger.*

Growth from Within

Most corporations grow by expanding their present operations. Some introduce and sell new but related products. Others expand the sale of present products to new geographic markets or to new groups of consumers in geographic markets already served. Currently, Wal-Mart has almost 3,500 stores in the United States and over 3,200 stores in thirteen different countries and has long-range plans for expanding into additional international markets.[12]

Growth from within, especially when carefully planned and controlled, can have relatively little adverse effect on a firm. For the most part, the firm continues to do what it has been doing, but on a larger scale. For instance, Larry Ellison, cofounder and CEO of Oracle Corporation of Redwood Shores, California, built the firm's annual revenues up from a mere $282 million in 1988 to approximately $22 billion today.[13] Much of this growth has taken place since 1994 as Oracle capitalized on its global leadership in information management software.

Growth Through Mergers and Acquisitions

merger the purchase of one corporation by another

hostile takeover a situation in which the management and board of directors of a firm targeted for acquisition disapprove of the merger

tender offer an offer to purchase the stock of a firm targeted for acquisition at a price just high enough to tempt stockholders to sell their shares

proxy fight a technique used to gather enough stockholder votes to control a targeted company

Another way a firm can grow is by purchasing another company. The purchase of one corporation by another is called a **merger.** An *acquisition* is essentially the same thing as a merger, but the term usually is used in reference to a large corporation's purchases of other corporations. Although most mergers and acquisitions are friendly, hostile takeovers also occur. A **hostile takeover** is a situation in which the management and board of directors of a firm targeted for acquisition disapprove of the merger.

When a merger or acquisition becomes hostile, a corporate raider—another company or a wealthy investor—may make a tender offer or start a proxy fight to gain control of the target company. A **tender offer** is an offer to purchase the stock of a firm targeted for acquisition at a price just high enough to tempt stockholders to sell their shares. Corporate raiders also may initiate a proxy fight. A **proxy fight** is a technique used to gather enough stockholder votes to control a targeted company.

If the corporate raider is successful and takes over the targeted company, existing management usually is replaced. Faced with this probability, existing management

Jump-Starting Your Career

Life After Acquisition

What will happen to *you* if your employer acquires a company or your employer is acquired by another firm? Although mergers and acquisitions often result in job losses, don't automatically assume that your job will go away. In fact, experts say this is a good opportunity to show how well you adapt to change and how valuable you can be to the new organization.

Be patient, be positive, be proactive, and above all, be a problem solver. Complete your assignments and meet your deadlines, but also look for ways to get involved during the transition. Answer questions, anticipate problems, and volunteer possible solutions. Keep up your current contacts and get to know your new colleagues and managers. Meanwhile, update your résumé with your latest skills and accomplishments. You may need to reapply for your current job or try for a different job in the new organization—or elsewhere.

Sources: Scott Moeller, "Trade Secrets: Surviving a Merger," *Personnel Today,* October 8, 2007, **www.personneltoday.com**; Kelley Holland, "Life After a Merger: Learning on Both Sides," *New York Times,* June 24, 2007, p. BU21; Rob Garretson, "How to Survive a Corporate Integration," *Network World,* January 25, 2007, **www.networkworld.com/careers.**

may take specific actions sometimes referred to as "poison pills," "shark repellents," or "porcupine provisions" to maintain control of the firm and avoid the hostile takeover. Whether mergers are friendly or hostile, they are generally classified as *horizontal, vertical,* or *conglomerate* (see Figure 4.5).

Horizontal Mergers A *horizontal merger* is a merger between firms that make and sell similar products or services in similar markets. The merger between Bank of America and Merrill Lynch is an example of a horizontal merger because both firms are in the financial services and banking industry. This type of merger tends to reduce the number of firms in an industry—and thus may reduce competition. While this merger was approved because of problems in the economy at the time of the merger, most mergers are reviewed carefully by federal agencies before they are approved.

Figure 4.5: Three Types of Growth by Merger

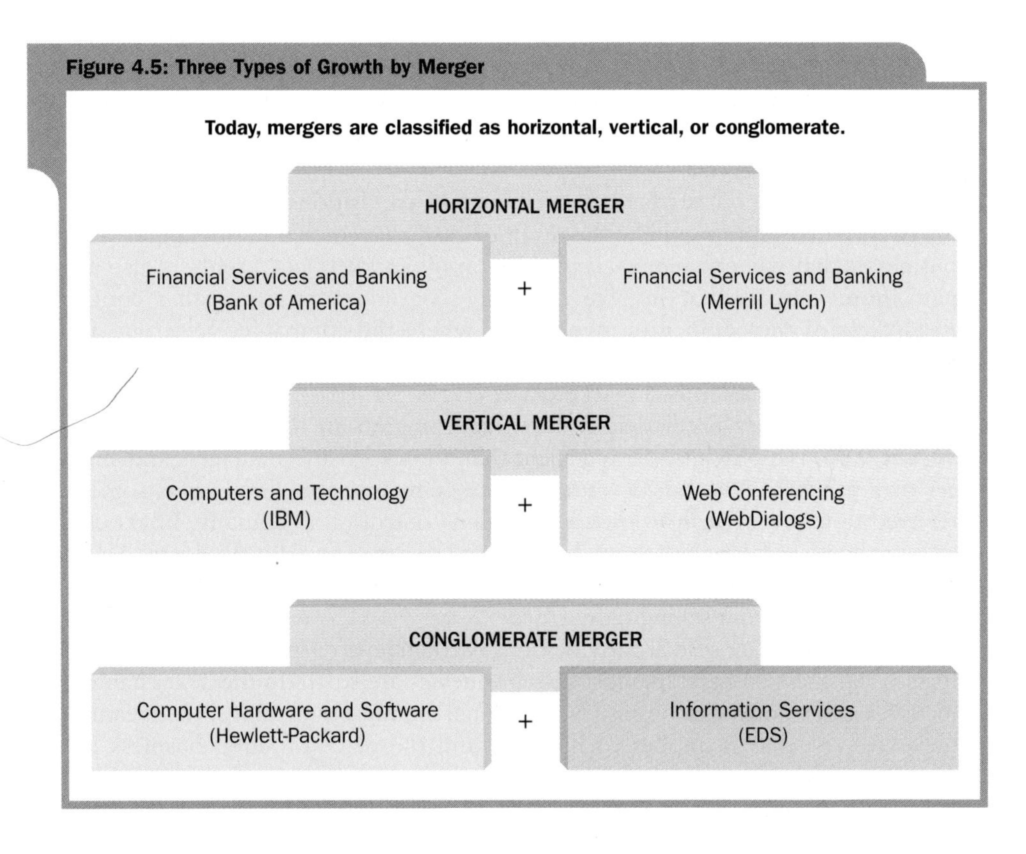

Vertical Mergers A *vertical merger* is a merger between firms that operate at different but related levels in the production and marketing of a product. Generally, one of the merging firms is either a supplier or a customer of the other. A vertical merger occurred when IBM acquired WebDialogs. At the time of the merger, WebDialogs, a privately held company, was a leading provider of Web conferencing services. At the same time, IBM needed this type of technology to enable companies of any size to use Web conferencing services. Rather than develop its own Web conferencing services, IBM simply purchased the WebDialogs company.[14]

Conglomerate Mergers A *conglomerate merger* takes place between firms in completely different industries. One of the largest conglomerate mergers in recent history occurred when Hewlett-Packard (computer hardware and software) merged with EDS (information services). While both companies were recognized as successful companies that have a history of increasing sales revenues and profits, they operate in different industries. The Hewlett-Packard–EDS merger was friendly because it was beneficial for both firms.

Current Merger Trends

Economists, financial analysts, corporate managers, and stockholders still hotly debate whether takeovers are good for the economy—or for individual companies—in the long run. One thing is clear, however: There are two sides to the takeover question. Takeover advocates argue that for companies that have been taken over, the purchasers have been able to make the company more profitable and productive by installing a new top-management team, by reducing expenses, and by forcing the company to concentrate on one main business.

Takeover opponents argue that takeovers do nothing to enhance corporate profitability or productivity. These critics argue that threats of takeovers have forced managers to devote valuable time to defending their companies from takeover, thus robbing time from new-product development and other vital business activities. This, they believe, is why U.S. companies may be less competitive with companies in such countries as Japan, Germany, and South Korea, where takeovers occur only rarely. Finally, the opposition argues that the only people who benefit from takeovers are investment bankers, brokerage firms, and takeover "artists," who receive financial rewards by manipulating U.S. corporations rather than by producing tangible products or services.

Most experts now predict that mergers and acquisitions during the first part of the twenty-first century will be the result of cash-rich companies looking to acquire businesses that will enhance their position in the marketplace. Analysts also anticipate more mergers that involve companies or investors from other countries. Regardless of the companies involved or where the companies are from, future mergers and acquisitions will be driven by solid business logic and the desire to compete in the international marketplace.

leveraged buyout (LBO) a purchase arrangement that allows a firm's managers and employees or a group of investors to purchase the company

Finally, experts predict more leveraged buyouts in the future. A **leveraged buyout (LBO)** is a purchase arrangement that allows a firm's managers and employees or a group of investors to purchase the company. (LBO activity is sometimes referred to as *taking a firm private.*) To gain control of a company, LBOs usually rely on borrowed money to purchase stock from existing stockholders. The borrowed money is later repaid through the company's earnings, sale of assets, or money obtained from selling more stock.

Whether they are sole proprietorships, partnerships, corporations, or some other form of business ownership, most U.S. businesses are small. In the next chapter, we focus on these small businesses. We examine, among other things, the meaning of the word *small* as it applies to business and the place of small business in the American economy.

return to inside business

S.C. Johnson

S.C. Johnson has not only retained the name of its founder throughout its long history, but it has also chosen to remain a family company, never going public to raise capital. Profits are very important, but they are not the only priority. S.C. Johnson puts great emphasis on social responsibility, donating 5 percent of its profits to charities and getting involved to improve local communities wherever it operates.

Now headed by Samuel Curtis Johnson's great-great-grandson, the company has been named one of *Fortune* magazine's "100 Best Companies to Work For" and one of *Working Mother* magazine's "100 Best Companies for Working Mothers." Such recognition reflects one of S.C. Johnson's guiding values: "We believe our fundamental strength lies in our people."

Questions

1. What are the advantages and disadvantages of keeping S.C. Johnson under family control rather than selling stock to the public?
2. Would you like to work for a corporation like S.C. Johnson? Why or why not?

Summary

1 Describe the advantages and disadvantages of sole proprietorships.

In a sole proprietorship, all business profits become the property of the owner, but the owner is also personally responsible for all business debts. A successful sole proprietorship can be a great source of pride for the owner. When comparing different types of business ownership, the sole proprietorship is the simplest form of business to enter, control, and leave. It also pays no special taxes. Perhaps for these reasons, 71.8 percent of all American business firms are sole proprietorships. Sole proprietorships nevertheless have disadvantages, such as unlimited liability and limits on one person's ability to borrow or to be an expert in all fields. As a result, this form of ownership accounts for only 4.2 percent of total revenues when compared with partnerships and corporations.

Explain the different types of partners and the importance of partnership agreements.

Like sole proprietors, general partners are responsible for running the business and for all business debts. Limited partners receive a share of the profit in return for investing in the business. However, they are not responsible for business debts beyond the amount they have invested. It is also possible to form a master limited partnership (MLP) and sell units of ownership to raise capital. Regardless of the type of partnership, it is always a good idea to have a written agreement (or articles of partnership) setting forth the terms of a partnership.

Describe the advantages and disadvantages of partnerships.

Although partnership eliminates some of the disadvantages of sole proprietorship, it is the least popular of the major forms of business ownership. The major advantages of a partnership include ease of start-up, availability of capital and credit, personal interest, combined skills and knowledge, retention of profits, and possible tax advantages. The effects of management disagreements are one of the major disadvantages of a partnership. Other disadvantages include unlimited liability (in a general partnership), lack of continuity, and frozen investment. By forming a limited partnership, the disadvantage of unlimited liability may be eliminated for the limited partner(s). This same disadvantage may be eliminated for partners that form a limited-liability partnership. Of course, special requirements must be met if partners form either the limited partnership or the limited-liability partnership.

Summarize how a corporation is formed.

A corporation is an artificial person created by law, with most of the legal rights of a real person, including the right to start and operate a business, to own property, to borrow money, to be sued or sue, and to enter into contracts. With the corporate form of ownership, stock can be sold to individuals to raise capital. The people who own a corporation's stock—and thus own part of the corporation—are called stockholders or sometimes shareholders. Generally, corporations are classified as closed corporations (few stockholders) or open corporations (many stockholders).

The process of forming a corporation is called incorporation. Most experts believe that the services of a lawyer are necessary when making decisions about where to incorporate and about obtaining a corporate charter, issuing stock, holding an organizational meeting, and all other legal details involved in incorporation. In theory, stockholders are able to control the activities of the corporation because they elect the board of directors who appoint the corporate officers.

5 Describe the advantages and disadvantages of a corporation.

Perhaps the major advantage of the corporate form is limited liability—stockholders are not liable for the corporation's debts beyond the amount they paid for its stock. Other important advantages include ease of raising capital, ease of transfer of ownership, perpetual life, and specialized management. A major disadvantage of a large corporation is double taxation: All profits are taxed once as corporate income and again as personal income because stockholders must pay a personal income tax on the profits they receive as dividends. Other disadvantages include difficulty and expense of formation, government regulation, conflict within the corporation, and lack of secrecy.

6 Examine special types of corporations, including S-corporations, limited-liability companies, government-owned corporations, and not-for-profit corporations.

S-corporations are corporations that are taxed as though they were partnerships but that enjoy the benefit of limited liability. To qualify as an S-corporation, a number of criteria must be met. A limited-liability company (LLC) is a form of business ownership that provides limited liability and has fewer government restrictions. LLCs with at least two members are taxed like a partnership and thus avoid the double taxation imposed on most corporations. LLCs with just one member are taxed like a sole proprietorship. When compared with a regular corporation or an S-corporation, an LLC is more flexible. Government-owned corporations provide particular services, such as public transportation, to citizens. Not-for-profit corporations are formed to provide social services rather than to earn profits.

7 Discuss the purpose of a cooperative, joint venture, and syndicate.

Three additional forms of business ownership—the cooperative, joint venture, and syndicate—are used by their owners to meet special needs, and each may be owned by either individuals or firms. A cooperative is an association of individuals or firms whose purpose is to perform some business function for its members. A joint venture is formed when two or more groups form a business entity in order to achieve a specific goal or to operate for a specific period of time. Once the goal is reached, the joint venture is dissolved. A syndicate is a temporary association of individuals or firms organized to perform a specific task that requires large amounts of capital. Like a joint venture, a syndicate is dissolved as soon as its purpose has been accomplished.

8 Explain how growth from within and growth through mergers can enable a business to expand.

A corporation may grow by expanding its present operations or through a merger or an acquisition. Although most mergers are friendly, hostile takeovers also occur. A hostile takeover is a situation in which the management and board of directors of a firm targeted for acquisition disapprove of the merger. Mergers generally are classified as horizontal, vertical, or conglomerate.

While economists, financial analysts, corporate managers, and stockholders debate the merits of mergers, some trends should be noted. First, experts predict that future mergers will be the result of cash-rich companies looking to acquire businesses that will enhance their position in the marketplace. Second, more mergers are likely to involve foreign companies or investors. Third, mergers will be driven by business logic and the desire to compete in the international marketplace. Finally, more leveraged buyouts are expected.

Key Terms

You should now be able to define and give an example relevant to each of the following terms:

sole proprietorship (108)
unlimited liability (110)
partnership (111)
general partner (111)
general partnership (111)
limited partner (112)
limited partnership (112)
master limited partnership (MLP) (112)
corporation (116)
stock (116)
stockholder (116)
closed corporation (116)
open corporation (116)
domestic corporation (117)
foreign corporation (117)
alien corporation (117)
common stock (118)
preferred stock (118)
dividend (118)
proxy (118)
board of directors (118)
corporate officers (119)
limited liability (120)
S-corporation (122)
limited-liability company (LLC) (122)
government-owned corporation (123)
not-for-profit corporation (124)
cooperative (124)
joint venture (124)
syndicate (125)
merger (126)
hostile takeover (126)
tender offer (126)
proxy fight (126)
leveraged buyout (LBO) (128)

Review Questions

1. What is a sole proprietorship? What are the major advantages and disadvantages of this form of business ownership?
2. How does a partnership differ from a sole proprietorship? Which disadvantages of sole proprietorship does the partnership tend to eliminate or reduce?
3. What is the difference between a general partner and a limited partner?
4. What issues should be included in a partnership agreement? Why?
5. Explain the difference between
   a. an open corporation and a closed corporation.
   b. a domestic corporation, a foreign corporation, and an alien corporation.
6. Outline the incorporation process, and describe the basic corporate structure.
7. What rights do stockholders have?
8. What are the primary duties of a corporation's board of directors? How are directors selected?
9. What are the major advantages and disadvantages associated with the corporate form of business ownership?
10. How do an S-corporation and a limited-liability company differ?
11. Explain the difference between a government-owned corporation and a not-for-profit corporation.
12. Why are cooperatives formed? Explain how they operate.
13. In what ways are joint ventures and syndicates alike? In what ways do they differ?
14. What is a hostile takeover? How is it related to a tender offer and a proxy fight?
15. Describe the three types of mergers

Discussion Questions

1. If you were to start a business, which ownership form would you choose? What factors might affect your choice?
2. Why might an investor choose to become a partner in a limited-liability partnership business instead of purchasing the stock of an open corporation?
3. Discuss the following statement: "Corporations are not really run by their owners."
4. What kinds of services do government-owned corporations provide? How might such services be provided without government involvement?
5. Is growth a good thing for all firms? How does management know when a firm is ready to grow?

Video Case 4.1

Having Fun Is Serious Business at Jordan's Furniture

Jordan's Furniture is a unique retail chain. In fact, every one of its stores in New England is unique—and highly profitable. And that's what caught the eye of Warren Buffett, the head of conglomerate Berkshire Hathaway, who is famous for his astute investments. Buffet bought Jordan's Furniture in 1999 and has left the founding family in charge to continue the retailer's winning ways.

The company's history stretches back to 1918, when Samuel Tatelman opened a small furniture store in Waltham, Massachusetts. His son Edward became involved in the family business during the 1930s. By the 1950s, Edward's children, Barry and Eliot, were learning about furniture retailing first-hand as they helped out during busy periods. In the early 1970s, the two brothers jointly assumed responsibility for running the store, which then had eight employees.

The brothers then made two key decisions that dramatically altered the future course of the business. First, they decided to gear their merchandise and store decor to 18- to-34-year-olds because people in this age group need furniture when they settle down and start families. Second, they resolved to make the business fun for themselves, their customers, and their employees by adding a large element of entertainment to the shopping experience.

For example, the 110,000-square-foot store in Natick, Massachusetts, evokes the spirit of Bourbon Street in New Orleans, complete with steamboat and Mardi Gras festivities. One section of the store holds a 262-seat IMAX 3D theater, popcorn and all. The Reading, Massachusetts, store is home to Beantown, a series of jelly-bean creations depicting Boston landmarks, such as the leftfield wall in Fenway Park, home of the Red Sox. Just as the Reading store is more than twice as large as the Natick store, its IMAX theater is also larger, roomy enough for an audience of 500 people.

The two-story Avon, Massachusetts, branch is home to the twenty-minute M.O.M., better known as the Motion Odyssey 3D Movie Ride, which draws children of all ages. Continuing the fun theme, visitors to the Nashua, New Hampshire, store are invited to munch on free fresh-baked chocolate chip cookies and sip coffee in the snack bar. And by the way, every one of the four stores also features a huge inventory of furniture for all tastes.

Ordinarily, customers shop for furniture only to fill a particular need. By making its stores exciting destinations for the entire family, Jordan's Furniture is out to change that behavior. When their children ask to visit the in-store IMAX theater, for instance, the parents may spot an entertainment unit or a chair they want to buy. "People come in here for fun," observes Eliot Tatelman. "They wind up having fun but also buying."

After Warren Buffett bought Jordan's Furniture, the brothers remained in charge to direct the chain's expansion. They also added a spiffy website and continued writing the funny television commercials for which the company was known throughout the Boston area. Eventually, they closed the original Waltham site to concentrate on the four stores built with entertainment in mind. By the time Barry left in 2006 to pursue a career as a Broadway producer, Eliot's two sons had followed family tradition and joined the company.

And that's how a small business founded as a sole proprietorship wound up as a corporation merged into a large conglomerate. Today, Jordan's Furniture is an established, profitable retail operation employing more than 1,200 people. It serves thousands of shoppers every day, and its sales average of $950 per square foot is considerably higher than that of the typical furniture store. But then, Jordan's Furniture is hardly a typical store, as its slogan suggests: "Not just a store, an experience!"[15]

For more information about this company, go to **www.jordans.com.**

Questions

1. Warren Buffett's Berkshire Hathaway owns three other furniture retailers in addition to Jordan's. Why do you think the conglomerate left the Tatelman family in charge of Jordan's after the merger?
2. What do you think Berkshire Hathaway and Jordan's have each gained from the merger?
3. How much influence are Berkshire Hathaway's stockholders likely to have (or want) over Jordan's management? Explain your answer.

Case 4.2

Stockholders Make Their Voices Heard at Disney

How much influence do stockholders wield over decisions made by and about the board of directors? Many stockholders of Walt Disney have been pushing for more say in key corporate governance issues such as how the board of directors is chosen and how corporate officers are supervised. Little by little, their voices have been heard. Disney has made a number of changes to the way directors are elected, reduced the size of its board, increased the number of independent members, and separated the role of chairman of the board from the role of chief executive officer.

Stockholders were looking forward to new leadership and new ideas when Michael Eisner was named CEO of Disney in the mid-1980s. The company's earnings were down, and its movies weren't drawing the huge audiences that management had hoped for. Eisner and his management team supercharged the theme park business, brought the company into the television industry by buying Cap Cities ABC, and put the magic back into Disney movies.

More than a decade into Eisner's revival of the Magic Kingdom's fortunes, however, some stockholders were grumbling. Disney had to write off millions that it had invested in its go.com Internet initiative as it changed its online strategy. Profits at the ABC Network were not up to par, and theme-park attendance was down following the terrorist attacks of 2001. Roy Disney, the last member of the Disney family to serve as a director, complained publicly about Eisner's management and the company's lagging share price. Eventually, he and another director resigned from the board and continued to push for management changes.

Eisner came under even more pressure when the cable company Comcast launched an unsolicited acquisition bid for Disney. As the company struggled against this unwanted takeover attempt—which it ultimately rebuffed—stockholders showed their displeasure with the CEO's performance. Eisner was running unopposed for reelection to the board, usually a routine event for a CEO who is also serving as chairman of the board. At this annual meeting, however, the CEO received a "withhold" vote from 45 percent of the shares.

Shareholders' voices were heard: The Disney board took the chairman's title away from Eisner that night, although he remained a director. No longer would the CEO be able to chair Disney's board of directors. Within months, Eisner announced he would soon retire. In preparation, the board scheduled a meeting with officials of major pension funds, which own sizable blocks of Disney stock, to hear their concerns about corporate governance and to discuss choosing Eisner's successor.

In the next few months, the board cut the total number of directors and added a new director considered to be independent of the company's management. It committed to rotating members among the board's committees to bring new viewpoints to such key areas of corporate governance as executive compensation. And most important, it changed the voting rules to require any director who receives a majority of "withhold" votes to submit a letter of resignation. George J. Mitchell, who replaced Eisner as chairman of the board, said in announcing the new voting rules: "Today's action is the latest in a series of steps we have taken to further strengthen Disney's corporate governance practices."

Meanwhile, capping months of debate over choosing a new CEO, the board finally named Robert A. Iger, who served as president under Eisner. More than two decades after taking the helm, Eisner stepped down as CEO and simultaneously resigned from the board. Iger quickly made peace with Roy Disney, who was named director emeritus and announced that he would support the new CEO. What will stockholders say as the new Disney era unfolds?[16]

For more information about this company, go to **www.disney.com.**

Questions

1. Generally, stockholders of a large corporation such as Disney are fairly complacent with existing management. And yet, these same stockholders eventually changed the way that Disney was managed. In this case, what actions provoked stockholders to become so vocal?
2. After Michael Eisner received such a high percentage of "withhold" votes, do you think the Disney board should have taken additional steps beyond taking away his chairmanship title?
3. Do you agree with the Disney board's decision to meet with the managers of large pension funds that own sizable blocks of Disney stock? Why or why not?
4. Why is it important for a board to have a certain number of directors who are not corporate officers and have no personal connection with corporate officers? What can board members who are outside the corporation contribute to the overall management of a large corporation?

Building Skills for Career Success

1. JOURNALING FOR SUCCESS

Today, many people work for a sole proprietorship, partnership, or corporation. Still others decide to become entrepreneurs and start their own business.

Assignment

1. Assume that you are now age 25 and have graduated from college. Would you prefer to work in someone else's business or one that you would start? Explain your answer.
2. Assuming that you have decided to start your own small business, what special skills and experience will you need to be successful? (*Note:* You may want to talk with someone who owns a business before answering this question.)
3. Now describe where and how you could obtain the skills and experience you need to be successful.

2. EXPLORING THE INTERNET

Arguments about mergers and acquisitions often come down to an evaluation of who benefits and by how much. Sometimes the benefits include access to new products, talented management, new customers, or new sources of capital. Often, the debate is complicated by the involvement of firms based in different countries.

The Internet is a fertile environment for information and discussion about mergers. The firms involved will provide their view about who will benefit and why it is either a good thing or not. Journalists will report facts and offer commentary as to how they see the future result of any merger, and of course, chat rooms located on the websites of many journals promote discussion about the issues. Visit the text website for updates to this exercise.

Assignment

1. Using an Internet search engine such as Google or Yahoo!, locate two or three sites providing information about a recent merger (use a keyword such as *merger*).
2. After examining these sites and reading journal articles, report information about the merger, such as the dollar value, the reasons behind the merger, and so forth.
3. Based on your assessment of the information you have read, do you think the merger is a good idea or not for the firms involved, the employees, the investors, the industry, and society as a whole? Explain your reasoning.

3. DEVELOPING CRITICAL-THINKING SKILLS

Suppose that you are a person who has always dreamed of owning a business but never had the money to open one. Since you were old enough to read a recipe, your mother allowed you to help in the kitchen. Most of all, you enjoyed baking and decorating cakes. You liked using your imagination to create cakes for special occasions. By the time you were in high school, you were baking and decorating wedding cakes for a fee. Also assume that after high school you started working full time as an adjuster for an insurance company. Your schedule now allows little time for baking and decorating cakes. Finally, assume that you inherited $250,000 and that changes at your job have created undue stress in your life. What should you do?

Assignment

1. Discuss the following points:
    a. What career options are available to you?
    b. If you decide to open your own business, what form of ownership would be best for your business?
    c. What advantages and disadvantages apply to your preferred form of business ownership?
2. Prepare a two-page report summarizing your findings.

4. BUILDING TEAM SKILLS

Using the scenario in Exercise 3, suppose that you have decided to quit your job as an insurance adjuster and open a bakery. Your business is now growing, and you have decided to add a full line of catering services. This means more work and responsibility. You will need someone to help you, but you are undecided about what to do. Should you hire an employee or find a partner? If you add a partner, what type of decisions should be made to create a partnership agreement?

Assignment

1. In a group, discuss the following questions:
    a. What are the advantages and disadvantages of adding a partner versus hiring an employee?
    b. Assume that you have decided to form a partnership. What articles should be included in a partnership agreement?
    c. How would you go about finding a partner?
2. Summarize your group's answers to these questions, and present them to your class.
3. As a group, prepare an articles-of-partnership agreement. Be prepared to discuss the pros and cons of your group's agreement with other groups from your class, as well as to examine their agreements.

5. RESEARCHING DIFFERENT CAREERS

Many people spend their entire lives working in jobs that they do not enjoy. Why is this so? Often, it is because they have taken the first job they were offered without giving it much thought. How can you avoid having this happen to you? First, you should determine your "personal profile" by identifying and analyzing your own strengths, weaknesses, things you enjoy, and things you dislike. Second, you should identify the types of jobs that fit your profile. Third, you should identify and research the companies that offer those jobs.

Assignment

1. Take two sheets of paper and draw a line down the middle of each sheet, forming two columns on each page. Label column 1 "Things I Enjoy or Like to Do," column 2 "Things I Do Not Like Doing," column 3 "My Strengths," and column 4 "My Weaknesses."
2. Record data in each column over a period of at least one week. You may find it helpful to have a relative or friend give you input.
3. Summarize the data, and write a profile of yourself.
4. Take your profile to a career counselor at your college or to the public library and ask for help in identifying jobs that fit your profile. Your college may offer testing to assess your skills and personality. The Strong-Campbell Interest Inventory and the Myers-Briggs Personality Inventory can help you to assess the kind of work you may enjoy. The Internet is another resource.
5. Research the companies that offer the types of jobs that fit your profile.
6. Write a report on your findings.

5 Small Business, Entrepreneurship, and Franchises

LEARNING OBJECTIVES
What you will be able to do once you complete this chapter:

1. Define what a small business is and recognize the fields in which small businesses are concentrated.
2. Identify the people who start small businesses and the reasons why some succeed and many fail.
3. Assess the contributions of small businesses to our economy.
4. Judge the advantages and disadvantages of operating a small business.
5. Explain how the Small Business Administration helps small businesses.
6. Appraise the concept and types of franchising.
7. Analyze the growth of franchising and franchising's advantages and disadvantages.

AP Photo/Lisa Poole

inside business

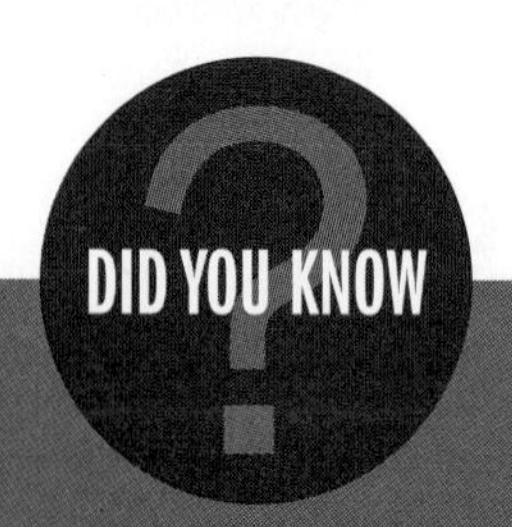

Today, The Chocolate Bar is open in Dubai and Qatar and is readying new cafés around the region.

The Chocolate Bar's Sweet Success

When Alison Nelson opened her first chocolate café in New York City, she thought she would eventually expand her business with additional cafés in the Midwest and on the West Coast. She never imagined that her growing chocolate empire would include two cafés in New York City, one in a New Jersey beach town, and three licensed locations in the Middle East.

Nelson's entrepreneurial journey into the world of luxury chocolate began in 2002, when she started The Chocolate Bar, a stylish, limited-menu restaurant for chocolate lovers who crave ultra-rich, top-quality chocolate desserts, drinks, and gelato. Knowing that customers' tastes were changing, she included both dark and milk chocolate treats. She also recruited Greenwich Village artists to design one-of-a-kind wrappers for her handmade chocolates.

That first café did so well that Nelson opened one inside the Henri Bendel store on New York's upscale Fifth Avenue. Although she added sandwiches, soups, and salads, chocolate was the main attraction. After opening a third location in New Jersey, Nelson took stock of the economic situation. With costs rising and consumers spending less freely in a slowing U.S. economy, she put her expansion plans on hold.

Then Nelson got a call from Mary Ghorbial in Dubai. Ghorbial wanted to open high-end chocolate cafés throughout the Middle East, where many special occasions are celebrated with deluxe chocolates. After months of negotiation, Ghorbial became a licensee of The Chocolate Bar. In addition to an upfront fee, Ghorbial agreed to pay Nelson a percentage of sales from the 30 cafés she planned to open in the coming decade. Guided by Ghorbial, Nelson reformulated her chocolates and redesigned the cafés to suit local tastes.

Today, The Chocolate Bar is open in Dubai and Qatar, and Ghorbial is readying new cafés around the region. If the U.S. economy hurts Nelson's cafés, she will still do well because of her deal with Ghorbial. "I think it'll be a great kind of American story—a little company that didn't make it big in America but made it in the global marketplace."[1]

Just as Alison Nelson's empire grew from one chocolate café in New York City, most businesses start small. Unlike Nelson's empire, most small businesses that survive usually stay small. They provide a solid foundation for our economy—as employers, as suppliers and purchasers of goods and services, and as taxpayers.

In this chapter, we do not take small businesses for granted. Instead, we look closely at this important business sector—beginning with a definition of small business, a description of industries that often attract small businesses, and a profile of some of the people who start small businesses. Next, we consider the importance of small businesses in our economy. We also present the advantages and disadvantages of smallness in business. We then describe services provided by the Small Business Administration, a government agency formed to assist owners and managers of small businesses. We conclude the chapter with a discussion of the pros and cons of franchising, an approach to small-business ownership that has become very popular in the last forty years.

small business one that is independently owned and operated for profit and is not dominant in its field

Small Business: A Profile

1

Learning Objective: Define what a small business is and recognize the fields in which small businesses are concentrated.

The Small Business Administration (SBA) defines a **small business** as "one which is independently owned and operated for profit and is not dominant in its field." How small must a firm be not to dominate its field? That depends on the particular industry it is in. The SBA has developed the following specific "smallness" guidelines for the various industries, as shown in Table 5.1.[2] The SBA periodically revises and simplifies its small-business size regulations.

Table 5.1: Industry Group-Size Standards

Small-business size standards are usually stated in number of employees or average annual sales. In the United States, 99.7 percent of all businesses are considered small.

Industry Group	Size Standard
Manufacturing	500 employees
Wholesale trade	100 employees
Agriculture	$750,000
Retail trade	$6.5 million
General & heavy construction (except dredging)	$31 million
Dredging	$18.5 million
Special trade contractors	$13 million
Travel agencies	$3.5 million (commissions & other income)
Business and personal services except	$6.5 million
• Architectural, engineering, surveying, and mapping services	$4.5 million
• Dry cleaning and carpet cleaning services	$4.5 million

Source: **http://www.sba.gov/services/contractingopportunities/sizestandardstopics/summarywhatis/**, accessed October 3, 2008.

Annual sales in the millions of dollars may not seem very small. However, for many firms, profit is only a small percentage of total sales. Thus, a firm may earn only $40,000 or $50,000 on yearly sales of $1 million—and that *is* small in comparison with the profits earned by most medium-sized and large firms. Moreover, most small firms have annual sales well below the maximum limits in the SBA guidelines.

The Small-Business Sector

In the United States, it typically takes four days and $210 to establish a business as a legal entity. The steps include registering the name of the business, applying for tax IDs, and setting up unemployment and workers' compensation insurance. In Japan, however, a typical entrepreneur spends more than $3,500 and thirty-one days to follow eleven different procedures (see Table 5.2).

A surprising number of Americans take advantage of their freedom to start a business. There are, in fact, about 27.2 million businesses in this country. Only just over 17,000 of these employ more than 500 workers—enough to be considered large.

Interest in owning or starting a small business has never been greater than it is today. During the last decade, the number of small businesses in the United States has increased 49 percent, and for the last few years, new-business formation in the United States has broken successive records, except during the 2001–2002 recession. Recently, nearly 637,000 new businesses were incorporated. Furthermore, part-time entrepreneurs have increased fivefold in recent years; they now account for one-third of all small businesses.[3]

According to a recent study, two-thirds of new businesses survive at least two years, 44 percent survive at least four years, and 31 percent survive at least seven years.[4] The primary reason for these failures is mismanagement resulting from a lack of business know-how. The makeup of the small-business sector thus is constantly changing. Despite the high failure rate, many small businesses succeed modestly. Some, like Apple Computer, Inc., are extremely successful—to the point where they can no longer be considered small. Taken together, small businesses are also responsible for providing a high percentage of the jobs in the United States. According to some estimates, the figure is well over 50 percent.

Table 5.2: Establishing a Business Around the World

The entrepreneurial spirit provides the spark that enriches the U.S. economy. The growth will continue if lawmakers resist the urge to overregulate entrepreneurs and provide policies that foster free enterprise.

	Number of Procedures	Time (days)	Cost (US$)	Minimum Capital (% per capita income)
Australia	2	2	402	0
Belgium	7	56	2,633	75.1
Canada	2	3	127	0
Denmark	4	4	0	52.3
France	10	53	663	32.1
Germany	9	45	1,341	103.8
Greece	16	45	8,115	145.3
Ireland	3	12	2,473	0
Italy	9	23	4,565	49.6
Japan	11	31	3,518	71.3
Netherlands	7	11	3,276	70.7
New Zealand	3	3	28	0
Norway	4	24	1,460	33.1
Portugal	11	95	1,360	43.4
Spain	11	115	2,366	19.6
Sweden	3	16	190	41.4
Switzerland	6	20	3,228	33.8
United Kingdom	6	18	264	0
United States	5	4	210	0

Sources: World Bank (2004); as found in *Inside the Vault,* Federal Reserve Bank of St. Louis, Fall 2004, p. 1.

Industries That Attract Small Businesses

Some industries, such as auto manufacturing, require huge investments in machinery and equipment. Businesses in such industries are big from the day they are started—if an entrepreneur or group of entrepreneurs can gather the capital required to start one.

By contrast, a number of other industries require only a low initial investment and some special skills or knowledge. It is these industries that tend to attract new businesses. Growing industries, such as outpatient-care facilities, are attractive because of their profit potential. However, knowledgeable entrepreneurs choose areas with which they are familiar, and these are most often the more established industries.

Small enterprise spans the gamut from corner newspaper vending to the development of optical fibers. The owners of small businesses sell gasoline, flowers, and coffee to go. They publish magazines, haul freight, teach languages, and program computers. They make wines, movies, and high-fashion clothes. They build new homes and restore old ones. They fix appliances, recycle metals, and sell used cars. They drive cabs and fly planes. They make us well when we are ill, and they sell us the products of corporate giants. In fact, 74 percent of real estate, rental, and leasing industries; 61 percent of the businesses in the leisure and hospitality services; and 86 percent of the construction industries are dominated by small businesses.[5] The

The Business of Green

Slow Food Builds Local Businesses

Fast food may be big business, but Slow Food is helping local businesses grow and prosper. The Slow Food movement began in Italy during the 1980s as a reaction to the rapid growth of giant fast-food restaurant chains. Not only does the movement promote the idea of savoring meals cooked slowly from scratch, it also encourages cooks to get fresh, quality ingredients from small farms and other local businesses.

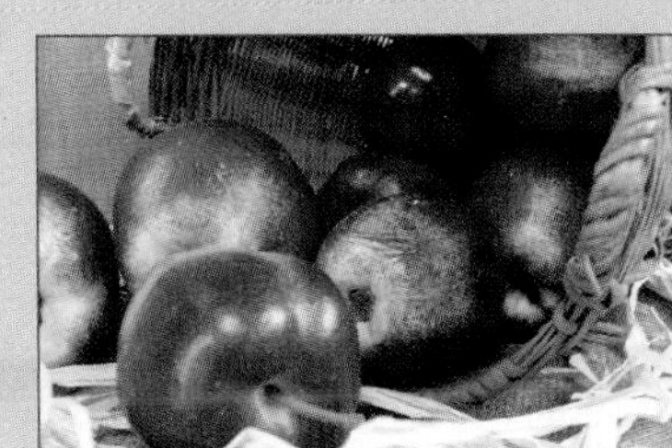

morguefile.com

Shipping fruits, vegetables, and other foods by train, plane, or truck to commercial kitchens thousands of miles away takes time and consumes a lot of energy. The Slow Food movement wants to reduce energy use and pollution by encouraging restaurants and other companies to buy fresh from local growers. Now big businesses are jumping on the Slow Food bandwagon. The food-services firm Sodexo buys produce from hundreds of small farmers in the communities where it does business. Chipotle Mexican Grill buys some of its produce from small growers near its 730 restaurants. And local honey producers, herb growers, and other small businesses are seeing sales go up as Slow Food catches on.

Sources: "Revolutionaries by the Bay," *The Economist*, September 11, 2008, **www.economist.com;** Bobby White, "The Challenges of Eating 'Slow,'" *Wall Street Journal*, September 2, 2008, **www.wsj.com**; Jane Black, "As Food Becomes a Cause, Meeting Puts Issues on the Table," *Washington Post*, August 30, 2008, p. A1.

various kinds of businesses generally fall into three broad categories of industry: distribution, service, and production.

Distribution Industries This category includes retailing, wholesaling, transportation, and communications—industries concerned with the movement of goods from producers to consumers. Distribution industries account for approximately 33 percent of all small businesses. Of these, almost three-quarters are involved in retailing, that is, the sale of goods directly to consumers. Clothing and jewelry stores, pet shops, bookstores, and grocery stores, for example, are all retailing firms. Slightly less than one-quarter of the small distribution firms are wholesalers. Wholesalers purchase products in quantity from manufacturers and then resell them to retailers.

Service Industries This category accounts for over 48 percent of all small businesses. Of these, about three-quarters provide such nonfinancial services as medical and dental care; watch, shoe, and TV repairs; haircutting and styling; restaurant meals; and dry cleaning. About 8 percent of the small service firms offer financial services, such as accounting, insurance, real estate, and investment counseling. An increasing number of self-employed Americans are running service businesses from home.

Production Industries This last category includes the construction, mining, and manufacturing industries. Only about 19 percent of all small businesses are in this group, mainly because these industries require relatively large initial investments. Small firms that do venture into production generally make parts and subassemblies for larger manufacturing firms or supply special skills to larger construction firms.

The People in Small Businesses: The Entrepreneurs

2 Learning Objective: Identify the people who start small businesses and the reasons why some succeed and many fail.

The entrepreneurial spirit is alive and well in the United States. A recent study revealed that the U.S. population is quite entrepreneurial when compared with those of other countries. More than 70 percent of Americans would prefer being an entrepreneur to working for someone else. This compares with 46 percent of adults in Western Europe and 58 percent of adults in Canada. Another study on entrepreneurial activity for 2002 found that of thirty-six countries studied, the United States was in the top third in entrepreneurial activity and was the leader when compared with Japan, Canada, and Western Europe.[6]

Small businesses typically are managed by the people who started and own them. Most of these people have held jobs with other firms and still could be so employed if they wanted. Yet owners of small businesses would rather take the risk of starting and operating their own firms, even if the money they make is less than the salaries they otherwise might earn.

Researchers have suggested a variety of personal factors as reasons why people go into business for themselves. These are discussed below.

Sweet smell of success. *Bill Gates, chairman and former CEO of Microsoft Corp., believes that the true measure of the company success is not just the power of its software, but the potential it unleashes in us all. With great ideas—and great software—our future has no limits. In the past 30 years, Microsoft has grown from a small start-up to a Fortune 500 success story. Here, Mr. Gates meets with Chicago-area eighth graders at the Museum of Science and Industry.*

Characteristics of Entrepreneurs

Entrepreneurial spirit is the desire to create a new business. For example, Nikki Olyai always knew that she wanted to create and develop her own business. Her father, a successful businessman in Iran, was her role model. She came to the United States at the age of seventeen and lived with a host family in Salem, Oregon, attending high school there. Undergraduate and graduate degrees in computer science led her to start Innovision Technologies while she held two other jobs to keep the business going and took care of her four-year-old son. Recently, Nikki Olyai's business was honored by the Women's Business Enterprise National Council's "Salute to Women's Business Enterprises" as one of eleven top successful firms. For three consecutive years, her firm was selected as a "Future 50 of Greater Detroit Company."

Other Personal Factors

Other personal factors in small-business success include

- Independence
- A desire to determine one's own destiny
- A willingness to find and accept a challenge
- Family background (In particular, researchers think that people whose families have been in business, successfully or not, are most apt to start and run their own businesses.)
- Age (Those who start their own businesses also tend to cluster around certain ages—more than 70 percent are between 24 and 44 years of age; see Figure 5.1.)

Motivation

There must be some motivation to start a business. A person may decide that he or she simply has "had enough" of working and earning a profit for someone else. Another may lose his or her job for some reason and decide to start the business he

Figure 5.1: How Old Is the Average Entrepreneur?

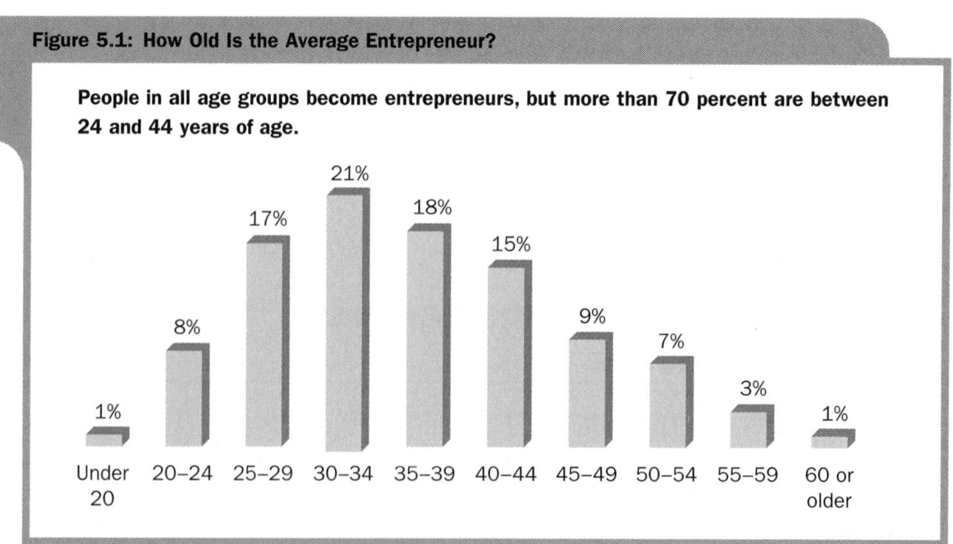

Source: Data developed and provided by the National Federation of Independent Business Foundation and sponsored by the American Express Travel Related Services Company, Inc.

Feature Photo Service/Microsoft Corp.

or she has always wanted rather than to seek another job. Still another person may have an idea for a new product or a new way to sell an existing product. Or the opportunity to go into business may arise suddenly, perhaps as a result of a hobby. For example, Cheryl Strand started baking and decorating cakes from her home while working full time as a word processor at Clemson University. Her cakes became so popular that she soon found herself working through her lunch breaks and late into the night to meet customer demand.

Women as Small-Business Owners

- Women are 51 percent of the U.S. population, and according to the SBA, they owned at least 50 percent of all small businesses in 2008.
- Women already own 66 percent of the home-based businesses in this country, and the number of men in home-based businesses is growing rapidly.
- According to the SBA, 10.4 million women-owned businesses in the United States provide almost 13 million jobs and generate $2 trillion in sales.
- Women-owned businesses in the United States have proven that they are more successful; over 40 percent have been in business for twelve years or more.
- According to Dun and Bradstreet, women-owned businesses are financially sound and creditworthy, and their risk of failure is lower than average.
- Compared to other working women, self-employed women are older, better educated, and have more managerial experience.
- Just over one-half of small businesses are home-based, and 91 percent have no employees. About 60 percent of home-based businesses are in service industries, 16 percent in construction, 14 percent in retail trade, and the rest in manufacturing, finance, transportation, communications, wholesaling, and other industries.[7]

Teenagers as Small-Business Owners

High-tech teen entrepreneurship is definitely exploding. "There's not a period in history where we've seen such a plethora of young entrepreneurs," comments Nancy F. Koehn, associate professor of business administration at Harvard Business School. Still, teen entrepreneurs face unique pressures in juggling their schoolwork, their social life, and their high-tech workload. Some ultimately quit school, whereas others quit or cut back on their business activities. Consider Brian Hendricks at Winston Churchill High School in Potomac, Maryland. He is the founder of StartUpPc and VB Solutions, Inc. StartUpPc, founded in 2001, sells custom-built computers and computer services for home users, home offices, small businesses, and students. Brian's services include design, installation of systems, training, networking, and on-site technical support. In October 2002, Brian founded VB Solutions, Inc., which develops and customizes websites and message boards. The firm sets up advertising contracts and counsels website owners on site improvements. The company has designed corporate ID kits, logos, and websites for clients from all over the world. Brian learned at a very young age that working for yourself is one of the best jobs available. According to Brian, a young entrepreneur must possess "the five P's of entrepreneurship"—planning, persistence, patience, people, and profit. Brian knows what it takes to be a successful entrepreneur. His accolades include Junior Achievement's "National Youth Entrepreneur of the Year" and SBA's 2005 "Young Entrepreneur of the Year" awards.[8]

In some people, the motivation to start a business develops slowly as they gain the knowledge and ability required for success as a business owner. Knowledge and ability—especially management ability—are probably the most important factors involved. A new firm is very much built around the entrepreneur. The owner must be able to manage the firm's finances, its personnel (if there are any employees), and its day-to-day operations. He or she must handle sales, advertising, purchasing, pricing, and a variety of other business functions. The knowledge and ability to do so are acquired most often through experience working for other firms in the same area of business.

Why Some Entrepreneurs and Small Businesses Fail

Small businesses are prone to failure. Capital, management, and planning are the key ingredients in the survival of a small business, as well as the most common reasons for failure. Businesses can experience a number of money-related problems. It may take several years before a business begins to show a profit. Entrepreneurs need to have not only the capital to open a business but also the money to operate it in its possibly lengthy start-up phase. One cash-flow obstacle often leads to others. And a series of cash-flow predicaments usually ends in a business failure. This scenario is played out all too often by small and not-so-small start-up Internet firms that fail to meet their financial backers' expectations and so are denied a second wave of investment dollars to continue their drive to establish a profitable online firm. According to Maureen Borzacchiello, co-owner of Creative Display Solutions, a trade show products company, "Big businesses such as Bear Stearns, Fannie Mae, Freddie Mac and AIG can get bailouts, but small-business owners are on their own when times are tough and credit is tight."

Many entrepreneurs lack the management skills required to run a business. Money, time, personnel, and inventory all need to be managed effectively if a small business is to succeed. Starting a small business requires much more than optimism and a good idea.

Success and expansion sometimes lead to problems. Frequently, entrepreneurs with successful small businesses make the mistake of overexpansion. Fast growth often results in dramatic changes in a business. Thus, the entrepreneur must plan carefully and adjust competently to new and potentially disruptive situations.

Every day, and in every part of the country, people open new businesses. For example, recently, 637,100 new businesses opened their doors, but at the same time, 560,300 businesses closed their business and 28,322 businesses declared bankruptcy. (See Table 5.3.)[9] Although many fail, others represent well-conceived ideas developed by entrepreneurs who have the expertise, resources, and determination to make their businesses succeed. As these well-prepared entrepreneurs pursue their individual goals, our society benefits in many ways from their work and creativity. Such billion-dollar companies as Apple Computer, McDonald's Corporation, and Procter & Gamble are all examples of small businesses that expanded into industry giants.

The Importance of Small Businesses in Our Economy

3

Learning Objective: Assess the contributions of small businesses to our economy.

This country's economic history abounds with stories of ambitious men and women who turned their ideas into business dynasties. The Ford Motor Company started as a one-man operation with an innovative method for industrial production. L.L.Bean, Inc., can trace its beginnings to a basement shop in Freeport, Maine. Both Xerox and Polaroid began as small firms with a better way to do a job.

Table 5.3: U.S. Business Start-ups, Closures, and Bankruptcies

	New	Closures	Bankruptcies
2007	637,100[e]	560,300[e]	28,322
2006	640,800[e]	587,800[e]	19,695
2005	644,122	565,745	39,201
2004	628,917	541,047	34,317
2003	612,296	540,658	35,037

e = Advocacy estimate. For a discussion of methodology, see Brian Headd, 2005 (**www.sba.gov/advo/research/rs258tot.pdf**).

Source: U.S. Department of Commerce, Bureau of the Census; Administrative Office of the U.S. Courts; U.S. Department of Labor, Employment and Training Administration, Small Business Administration, Office of Advocacy, *Frequently Asked Questions*, September 2008, **www.sba.gov/advo**, accessed October 4, 2008.

Providing Technical Innovation

Invention and innovation are part of the foundations of our economy. The increases in productivity that have characterized the past 200 years of our history are all rooted in one principal source: new ways to do a job with less effort for less money. Studies show that the incidence of innovation among small-business workers is significantly higher than among workers in large businesses. Small firms produce two and a half times as many innovations as large firms relative to the number of persons employed. In fact, small firms employ 40 percent of all high-tech workers such as scientists, engineers, and computer specialists. No wonder small firms produce thirteen to fourteen times more patents per employee than large patenting firms.[10]

According to the U.S. Office of Management and Budget, more than half the major technological advances of the twentieth century originated with individual inventors and small companies. Even just a sampling of those innovations is remarkable:

- Air conditioning
- Airplane
- Automatic transmission
- FM radio
- Heart valve
- Helicopter
- Instant camera
- Insulin
- Jet engine
- Penicillin
- Personal computer
- Power steering

Perhaps even more remarkable—and important—is that many of these inventions sparked major new U.S. industries or contributed to an established industry by adding some valuable service.

Lifetime Achievement Award. *Meet Al Gross, shown here with the world's first handheld walkie talkie he built in 1938. Gross invented other wireless devices such as the pager and the cordless telephone. He is the winner of the Lemelson-MIT Lifetime Achievement Award for Invention and Innovation. The award recognizes outstanding achievement in invention and innovation by living American inventors and innovators.*

AP Photo/Orbital Sciences Corporation

Providing Employment

Small firms traditionally have added more than their proportional share of new jobs to the economy. Recently, the U.S. economy created over 3 million new jobs. Seven out of the ten industries that added the most new jobs were small-business-dominated industries. Small businesses creating the most new jobs recently included business services, leisure and hospitality services, and special trade contractors. Small firms hire a larger proportion of employees who are younger workers, older workers, women, or workers who prefer to work part time. Furthermore, small businesses provide 67 percent of workers with their first jobs and initial on-the-job training in basic skills. According to the SBA, small businesses represent 99.7 percent of all employers, employ about 50 percent of the private workforce, and provide about two-thirds of the net new jobs added to our economy.[11] Small businesses thus contribute significantly to solving unemployment problems.

Providing Competition

Small businesses challenge larger, established firms in many ways, causing them to become more efficient and more responsive to consumer needs. A small business cannot, of course, compete with a large firm in all respects. But a number of small

Entrepreneurial Challenge

Artsy Etsy

Artists and craftspeople are clicking with customers at the online marketplace Etsy, "your place to buy and sell all things handmade." Founded in 2005, the website hosts more than 185,000 small businesses and lists nearly 2 million artsy items for sale at any one time. Because Etsy is as much an online community as a retail site, jewelry designers, furniture makers, glassblowers, quilters, potters, and other artisans can really connect with the people who buy their work. Just as important, these small businesspeople can sell to customers across the continent as easily as they can sell to customers across town.

Artisans pay nothing to set up an online Etsy "shop." They pay Etsy 20 cents per item for a four-month listing and, when the item sells, they pay Etsy a commission of 3.5 percent of the purchase price. Because buying and selling can be done with a few clicks, Artsy Etsy has become a hit with both customers and artisans. As one Etsy artisan says: "My favorite thing about Etsy is that I make a living at it."

Sources: Shara Tibken, "Beyond Fair Trade: The Web Has Given Artists an Easier Way to Pursue Their Passions," *Wall Street Journal*, June 16, 2008, p. R9; Thomas Pack, "Web Users Are Getting Crafty," *Information Today*, March 2008, pp. 36–37; Jim Cota, "At Etsy.com, Buyers Meet Their Creative Makers," *Indianapolis Business Journal*, July 7, 2008, p. 38A.

firms, each competing in its own particular area and its own particular way, together have the desired competitive effect. Thus, several small janitorial companies together add up to reasonable competition for the no-longer-small ServiceMaster.

Filling Needs of Society and Other Businesses

Small firms also provide a variety of goods and services to each other and to much larger firms. Sears, Roebuck purchases merchandise from approximately 12,000 suppliers—and most of them are small businesses. General Motors relies on more than 32,000 companies for parts and supplies and depends on more than 11,000 independent dealers to sell its automobiles and trucks. Large firms generally buy parts and assemblies from smaller firms for one very good reason: It is less expensive than manufacturing the parts in their own factories. This lower cost eventually is reflected in the price that consumers pay for their products.

It is clear that small businesses are a vital part of our economy and that, as consumers and as members of the labor force, we all benefit enormously from their existence. Now let us look at the situation from the viewpoint of the owners of small businesses.

The Pros and Cons of Smallness

4 Learning Objective: Judge the advantages and disadvantages of operating a small business.

Do most owners of small businesses dream that their firms will grow into giant corporations—managed by professionals—while they serve only on the board of directors? Or would they rather stay small, in a firm where they have the opportunity (and the responsibility) to do everything that needs to be done? The answers depend on the personal characteristics and motivations of the individual owners. For many, the advantages of remaining small far outweigh the disadvantages.

Advantages of Small Business

Small-business owners with limited resources often must struggle to enter competitive new markets. They also have to deal with increasing international competition. However, they enjoy several unique advantages.

Personal Relationships with Customers and Employees For those who like dealing with people, small business is the place to be. The owners of retail shops get to know many of their customers by name and deal with them on a personal basis. Through such relationships, small-business owners often become involved in the social, cultural, and political life of the community.

Relationships between owner-managers and employees also tend to be closer in smaller businesses. In many cases, the owner is a friend and counselor as well as the boss.

These personal relationships provide an important business advantage. The personal service small businesses offer to customers is a major competitive weapon—one that larger firms try to match but often cannot. In addition, close relationships with employees often help the small-business owner to keep effective workers who might earn more with a larger firm.

Ability to Adapt to Change Being his or her own boss, the owner-manager of a small business does not need anyone's permission to adapt to change. An owner may add or discontinue merchandise or services, change store hours, and experiment with various price strategies in response to changes in market conditions. And through personal relationships with customers, the owners of small businesses quickly become aware of changes in people's needs and interests, as well as in the activities of competing firms.

Sustaining the Planet

The Business Alliance for Local Living Economies seeks to strengthen local businesses and their communities by promoting key sustainability practices such as environmentally-friendly construction techniques. **www.livingeconomies.org**

Simplified Record Keeping Many small firms need only a simple set of records. Record keeping might consist of a checkbook, a cash-receipts journal in which to record all sales, and a cash-disbursements journal in which to record all amounts paid out. Obviously, enough records must be kept to allow for producing and filing accurate tax returns.

Independence Small-business owners do not have to punch in and out, bid for vacation times, take orders from superiors, or worry about being fired or laid off. They are the masters of their own destinies—at least with regard to employment. For many people, this is the prime advantage of owning a small business.

Other Advantages According to the SBA, the most profitable companies in the United States are small firms that have been in business for more than ten years and employ fewer than twenty people. Small-business owners also enjoy all the advantages of sole proprietorships, which were discussed in Chapter 4. These include being able to keep all profits, the ease and low cost of going into business and (if necessary) going out of business, and being able to keep business information secret.

Disadvantages of Small Business

Personal contacts with customers, closer relationships with employees, being one's own boss, less cumbersome record-keeping chores, and independence are the bright side of small business. In contrast, the dark side reflects problems unique to these firms.

AP Photo/Ng Han Guan

Getting personal. *For those who like dealing with people, small business is the place to be. Here, a salesperson demonstrates a mobile phone to a wheelchair-bound customer at a shop in Beijing, China.*

SPOTLIGHT

Small Business Bankruptcies

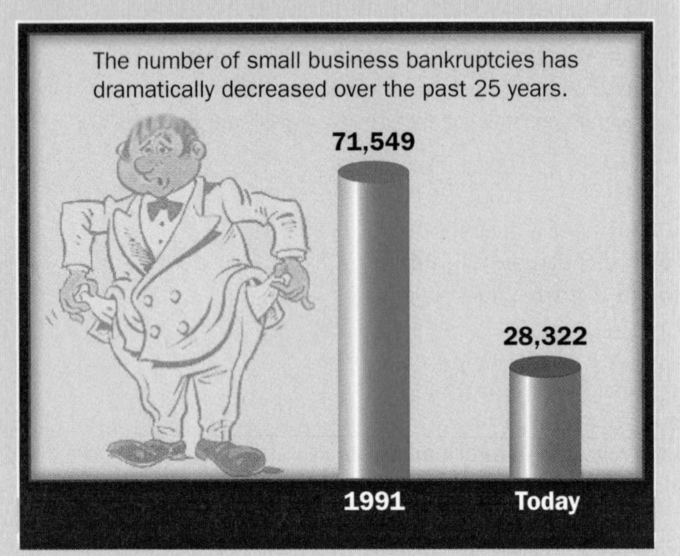

Source: U.S. Census Bureau, U.S. Department of Labor, Employment, and Training Administration, Administrative Office of the U.S. Courts, 2007; **www.sba.gov/advo/**, accessed October 4, 2008.

Risk of Failure As we have noted, small businesses (especially new ones) run a heavy risk of going out of business—about two out of three close their doors within the first six years. Older, well-established small firms can be hit hard by a business recession mainly because they do not have the financial resources to weather an extended difficult period.

Limited Potential Small businesses that survive do so with varying degrees of success. Many are simply the means of making a living for the owner and his or her family. The owner may have some technical skill—as a hair stylist or electrician, for example—and may have started a business to put this skill to work. Such a business is unlikely to grow into big business. Also, employees' potential for advancement is limited.

Limited Ability to Raise Capital Small businesses typically have a limited ability to obtain capital. Figure 5.2 shows that most small-business financing comes out of the owner's pocket. Personal loans from lending institutions provide only about one-fourth of the capital required by small businesses. About 50 percent of all new firms begin with less than $30,000 in total capital, according to Census Bureau and Federal Reserve surveys. In fact, almost 36 percent of new firms begin with less than $20,000, usually provided by the owner or family members and friends.[12]

Although every person who considers starting a small business should be aware of the hazards and pitfalls we have noted, a well-conceived business plan may help to avoid the risk of failure. The U.S. government is also dedicated to helping small businesses make it. It expresses this aim most actively through the SBA.

Figure 5.2: Sources of Capital for Entrepreneurs

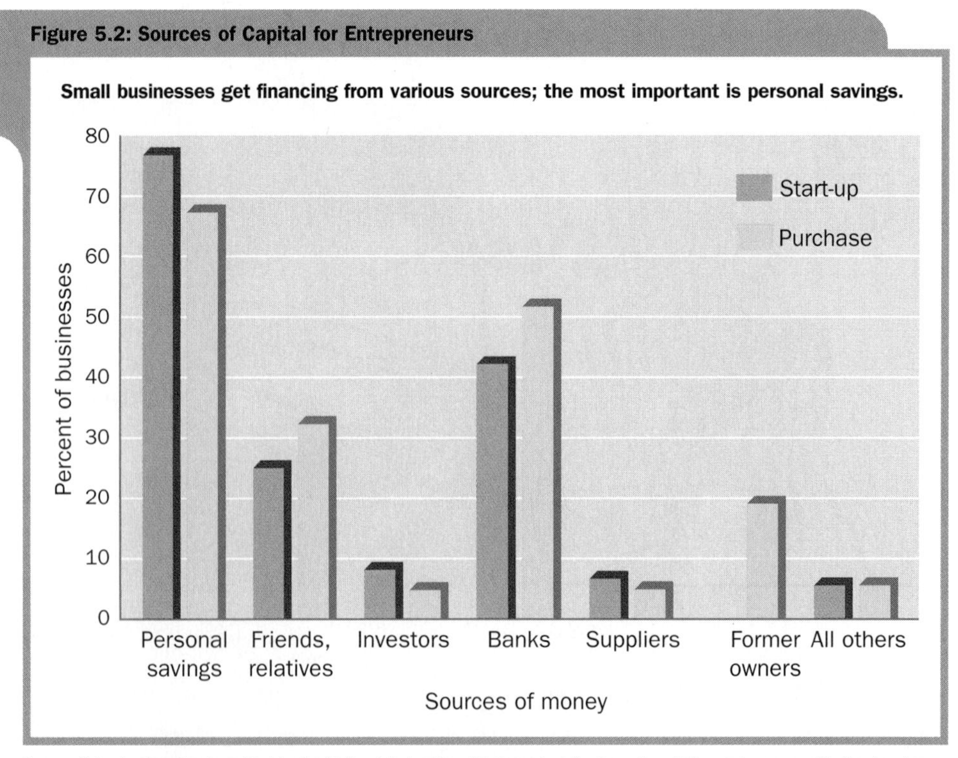

Source: Data developed and provided by the National Federation of Independent Business Foundation and sponsored by the American Express Travel Related Services Company, Inc.

Developing a Business Plan

Lack of planning can be as deadly as lack of money to a new small business. Planning is important to any business, large or small, and never should be overlooked or taken lightly. A **business plan** is a carefully constructed guide for the person starting a business. Consider it as a tool with three basic purposes: communication, management, and planning. As a communication tool, a business plan serves as a concise document that potential investors can examine to see if they would like to invest or assist in financing a new venture. It shows whether a business has the potential to make a profit. As a management tool, the business plan helps to track, monitor, and evaluate the progress. The business plan is a living document; it is modified as the entrepreneur gains knowledge and experience. It also serves to establish timelines and milestones and allows comparison of growth projections against actual accomplishments. Finally, as a planning tool, the business plan guides a businessperson through the various phases of business. For example, the plan helps to identify obstacles to avoid and to establish alternatives. According to Robert Krummer, Jr., chairman of First Business Bank in Los Angeles, "The business plan is a necessity. If the person who wants to start a small business can't put a business plan together, he or she is in trouble."

business plan a carefully constructed guide for the person starting a business

Components of a Business Plan

Table 5.4 shows the twelve sections that a business plan should include. Each section is further explained at the end of each of the seven major parts in the text. The goal of each end-of-the part exercise is to help a businessperson create his or her own business plan. When constructing a business plan, the businessperson should strive to keep it easy to read, uncluttered, and complete. Like other busy executives, officials of financial institutions do not have the time to wade through pages of

Table 5.4: Components of a Business Plan

1. *Introduction.* Basic information such as the name, address, and phone number of the business; the date the plan was issued; and a statement of confidentiality to keep important information away from potential competitors.
2. *Executive Summary.* A one- to two-page overview of the entire business plan, including a justification why the business will succeed.
3. *Benefits to the Community.* Information on how the business will have an impact on economic development, community development, and human development.
4. *Company and Industry.* The background of the company, choice of the legal business form, information on the products or services to be offered, and examination of the potential customers, current competitors, and the business's future.
5. *Management Team.* Discussion of skills, talents, and job descriptions of management team, managerial compensation, management training needs, and professional assistance requirements.
6. *Manufacturing and Operations Plan.* Discussion of facilities needed, space requirements, capital equipment, labor force, inventory control, and purchasing requirement.
7. *Labor Force.* Discussion of the quality of skilled workers available and the training, compensation, and motivation of workers.
8. *Marketing Plan.* Discussion of markets, market trends, competition, market share, pricing, promotion, distribution, and service policy.
9. *Financial Plan.* Summary of the investment needed, sales and cash-flow forecasts, breakeven analysis, and sources of funding.
10. *Exit Strategy.* Discussion of a succession plan or going public. Who will take over the business?
11. *Critical Risks and Assumptions.* Evaluation of the weaknesses of the business and how the company plans to deal with these and other business problems.
12. *Appendix.* Supplementary information crucial to the plan, such as résumés of owners and principal managers, advertising samples, organization chart, and any related information.

Source: Adapted from Timothy S. Hatten, *Small Business Management: Entrepreneurship and Beyond,* 4th ed. Copyright © 2009 by Houghton Mifflin Company, pp. 93–118. Reprinted with permission.

Table 5.5: Business Plan Checklist

1. Does the executive summary grab the reader's attention and highlight the major points of the business plan?
2. Does the business-concept section clearly describe the purpose of the business, the customers, the value proposition, and the distribution channel and convey a compelling story?
3. Do the industry and market analyses support acceptance and demand for the business concept in the marketplace and define a first customer in depth?
4. Does the management-team plan persuade the reader that the team could implement the business concept successfully? Does it assure the reader that an effective infrastructure is in place to facilitate the goals and operations of the company?
5. Does the product/service plan clearly provide details on the status of the product, the timeline for completion, and the intellectual property that will be acquired?
6. Does the operations plan prove that the product or service could be produced and distributed efficiently and effectively?
7. Does the marketing plan successfully demonstrate how the company will create customer awareness in the target market and deliver the benefit to the customer?
8. Does the financial plan convince the reader that the business model is sustainable—that it will provide a superior return on investment for the investor and sufficient cash flow to repay loans to potential lenders?
9. Does the growth plan convince the reader that the company has long-term growth potential and spin-off products and services?
10. Does the contingency and exit-strategy plan convince the reader that the risk associated with this venture can be mediated? Is there an exit strategy in place for investors?

Source: Kathleen R. Allen, *Launching New Ventures: An Entrepreneurial Approach,* 4th ed. Copyright © 2006 by Houghton Mifflin Company, p. 197. Reprinted with permission.

extraneous data. The business plan should answer the four questions banking officials and investors are most interested in: (1) What exactly is the nature and mission of the new venture? (2) Why is this new enterprise a good idea? (3) What are the businessperson's goals? (4) How much will the new venture cost?

The great amount of time and consideration that should go into creating a business plan probably will end up saving time later. For example, Sharon Burch, who was running a computer software business while earning a degree in business administration, had to write a business plan as part of one of her courses. Burch has said, "I wish I'd taken the class before I started my business. I see a lot of things I could have done differently. But it has helped me since because I've been using the business plan as a guide for my business." Table 5.5 provides a business plan checklist. Accuracy and realistic expectations are crucial to an effective business plan. It is unethical to deceive loan officers, and it is unwise to deceive yourself.

The Small Business Administration

5

Learning Objective: Explain how the Small Business Administration helps small businesses.

Small Business Administration (SBA) a governmental agency that assists, counsels, and protects the interests of small businesses in the United States

The **Small Business Administration (SBA)** created by Congress in 1953, is a governmental agency that assists, counsels, and protects the interests of small businesses in the United States. It helps people get into business and stay in business. The agency provides assistance to owners and managers of prospective, new, and established small businesses. Through more than 1,000 offices and resource centers throughout the nation, the SBA provides both financial assistance and management counseling. Recently, the SBA provided training, technical assistance, and education to over 3 million small businesses. It helps small firms to bid for and obtain government contracts, and it helps them to prepare to enter foreign markets.

SBA Management Assistance

Statistics show that most failures in small business are related to poor management. For this reason, the SBA places special emphasis on improving the management ability of the owners and managers of small businesses. The SBA's Management Assistance Program is extensive and diversified. It includes free individual counseling, courses, conferences, workshops, and a wide range of publications. Recently, the SBA provided management and technical assistance to nearly 1 million small businesses through its 1,100 Small Business Development Centers and 10,500 volunteers from the Service Corps of Retired Executives.[13]

Management Courses and Workshops The management courses offered by the SBA cover all the functions, duties, and roles of managers. Instructors may be teachers from local colleges and universities or other professionals, such as management consultants, bankers, lawyers, and accountants. Fees for these courses are quite low. The most popular such course is a general survey of eight to ten different areas of business management. In follow-up studies, businesspeople may concentrate in-depth on one or more of these areas depending on their particular strengths and weaknesses. The SBA occasionally offers one-day conferences. These conferences are aimed at keeping owner-managers up to date on new management developments, tax laws, and the like. The Small Business Training Network (SBTN) is an online training network consisting of eighty-three SBA-run courses, workshops, and resources. Recently, more than 240,000 small-business owners benefited from SBA's free online business courses.

SCORE The **Service Corps of Retired Executives (SCORE)** created in 1964, is a group of more than 10,500 retired businesspeople including over 2,000 women who volunteer their services to small businesses through the SBA. The collective experience of SCORE volunteers spans the full range of American enterprise. These volunteers have worked for such notable companies as Eastman Kodak, General Electric, IBM, and Procter & Gamble. Experts in areas of accounting, finance, marketing, engineering, and retailing provide counseling and mentoring to entrepreneurs.

Service Corps of Retired Executives (SCORE) a group of retired businesspeople who volunteer their services to small businesses through the SBA

A small-business owner who has a particular problem can request free counseling from SCORE. An assigned counselor visits the owner in his or her establishment and, through careful observation, analyzes the business situation and the problem. If the problem is complex, the counselor may call on other volunteer experts to assist. Finally, the counselor offers a plan for solving the problem and helping the owner through the critical period.

Consider the plight of Elizabeth Halvorsen, a mystery writer from Minneapolis. Her husband had built up the family advertising and graphic arts firm for seventeen years when he was called in 1991 to serve in the Persian Gulf War. The only one left behind who could run the business was Mrs. Halvorsen, who admittedly had no business experience. Enter SCORE. With a SCORE management expert at her side, she kept the business on track. In 2007, SCORE volunteers served 443,000 small-businesspeople like Mrs. Halvorsen.[14]

Nailing down a successful business. *Hanh Nguyen is one of a growing number of minority women who are small business owners. Hanh is an entrepreneur from Saigon, Vietnam, who wants her manicure business in Memphis, Tennessee, to succeed. She is determined to adjust to a new lifestyle in America and to learn a new language and the "American Way" of doing business. She even named her business "Kathy's Nails," after her newly adopted first name.*

Help for Minority-Owned Small Businesses Americans who are members of minority groups have had difficulty entering the nation's economic mainstream. Raising money is a nagging problem for minority business owners, who also may lack adequate training. Members of minority groups are, of course, eligible for all SBA programs, but the SBA makes a special effort to assist those who want to start small businesses or expand existing ones. For example, the Minority Business Development Agency awards grants to develop and increase business opportunities for members of racial and ethnic minorities.

Developing a tagline of success. *Since her college days, Celina Taganas Duffy ran her painting, graphic design, and greeting card business by the seat of her pants. Celina managed to achieve a measure of success—thanks to creative talent, hard work, and a unique line of patented envelope-free greeting cards. What is her best advice to someone starting a business? "Believe in your dreams, plan for your success and your business will flourish. Don't go it alone—seek business advice and counseling from SCORE."*

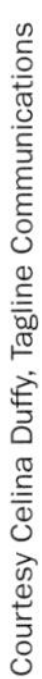

Helping women become entrepreneurs is also a special goal of the SBA. Emily Harrington, one of nine children, was born in Manila, the Philippines. She arrived in the United States in 1972 as a foreign-exchange student. Convinced that there was a market for hard-working, dedicated minorities and women, she launched Qualified Resources, Inc. *Inc.* magazine selected her firm as one of "America's Fastest Growing Private Companies" just six years later. Harrington credits the SBA with giving her the technical support that made her first loan possible. Finding a SCORE counselor who worked directly with her, she refined her business plan until she got a bank loan. Before contacting the SBA, Harrington was turned down for business loans "by all the banks I approached," even though she worked as a manager of loan credit and collection for a bank. Later, Emily Harrington was SBA's winner of the local, regional, and national Small Business Entrepreneurial Success Award for Rhode Island, the New England region, and the nation! For several years in a row, Qualified Resources, Inc., was named one of the fastest-growing private companies in Rhode Island. Now with over 100 Women's Business Centers, entrepreneurs like Harrington can receive training and technical assistance, access to credit and capital, federal contracts, and international markets. In fiscal 2007, Women's Business Centers counseled or trained more than 145,000 women.[15]

small-business institutes (SBIs) groups of senior and graduate students in business administration who provide management counseling to small businesses

Small-Business Institutes

Small-business institutes (SBIs) created in 1972, are groups of senior and graduate students in business administration who provide management counseling to small businesses. SBIs have been set up on over 520 college campuses as another way to help business owners. The students work in small groups guided by faculty advisers and SBA management-assistance experts. Like SCORE volunteers, they analyze and help solve the problems of small-business owners at their business establishments.

Small-Business Development Centers **Small-business development centers (SBDCs)** are university-based groups that provide individual counseling and practical training to owners of small businesses. SBDCs draw from the resources of local, state, and federal governments, private businesses, and universities. These groups can provide managerial and technical help, data from research studies, and other types of specialized assistance of value to small businesses. In 2008, there were over 1,100 SBDC locations, primarily at colleges and universities, assisting people such as Kathleen DuBois. After scribbling a list of her abilities and the names of potential clients on a napkin in a local restaurant, Kathleen DuBois decided to start her own marketing firm. Beth Thornton launched her engineering firm after a discussion with a colleague in the ladies room of the Marriott. When Richard Shell was laid off after twenty years of service with Nisource (Columbia Gas), he searched the Internet tirelessly before finding the right franchise option. Introduced by mutual friends, Jim Bostic and Denver McMillion quickly connected, built a high level of trust, and combined their diverse professional backgrounds to form a manufacturing company. Although these entrepreneurs took different routes in starting their new businesses in West Virginia, all of them turned to the West Virginia Small Business Development Center for the technical assistance to make their dreams become a reality. In Fiscal 2007, Small Business Development Centers served more than 600,000 entrepreneurs nationwide.[16]

small-business development centers (SBDCs) university-based groups that provide individual counseling and practical training to owners of small businesses

SBA Publications The SBA issues management, marketing, and technical publications dealing with hundreds of topics of interest to present and prospective managers of small firms. Most of these publications are available from the SBA free of charge. Others can be obtained for a small fee from the U.S. Government Printing Office.

SBA Financial Assistance

Small businesses seem to be constantly in need of money. An owner may have enough capital to start and operate the business. But then he or she may require more money to finance increased operations during peak selling seasons, to pay for required pollution control equipment, to finance an expansion, or to mop up after a natural disaster such as a flood or a terrorist attack. For example, the Supplemental Terrorist Activity Relief (STAR) program has made $3.7 billion in loans to 8,202 small businesses harmed or disrupted by the September 11 terrorist attacks. In October 2005, the SBA guaranteed loans of up to $150,000 to small businesses affected by Hurricanes Katrina and Rita. Since the 2005 hurricanes, SBA has made more than $4.9 billion in disaster loans to 102,903 homeowners and renters in the Gulf region. Businesses in the area received 16,828 business disaster loans with disbursements worth $1.5 billion.[17] The SBA offers special financial-assistance programs that cover all these situations. However, its primary financial function is to guarantee loans to eligible businesses.

Regular Business Loans Most of the SBA's business loans are actually made by private lenders such as banks, but repayment is partially guaranteed by the agency. That is, the SBA may guarantee that it will repay the lender up to 90 percent of the loan if the borrowing firm cannot repay it. Guaranteed loans approved on or after October 1, 2002, may be as large as $1.5 million (this loan limit may be increased in the future). The average size of an SBA-guaranteed business loan is about $300,000, and its average duration is about eight years.

Small-Business Investment Companies **Venture capital** is money that is invested in small (and sometimes struggling) firms that have the potential to become very successful. In many cases, only a lack of capital keeps these firms from rapid and solid growth. The people who invest in such firms expect that their investments will grow with the firms and become quite profitable.

venture capital money that is invested in small (and sometimes struggling) firms that have the potential to become very successful

The popularity of these investments has increased over the past thirty years, but most small firms still have difficulty obtaining venture capital. To help such

small-business investment companies (SBICs) privately owned firms that provide venture capital to small enterprises that meet their investment standards

businesses, the SBA licenses, regulates, and provides financial assistance to **small-business investment companies (SBICs)**.

An SBIC is a privately owned firm that provides venture capital to small enterprises that meet its investment standards. Such small firms as America Online, Apple Computer, Federal Express, Compaq Computer, Intel Corporation, Outback Steakhouse, and Staples, Inc., all were financed through SBICs during their initial growth period. SBICs are intended to be profit-making organizations. The aid the SBA offers allows them to invest in small businesses that otherwise would not attract venture capital. Since Congress created the program in 1958, SBICs have financed over 102,000 small businesses for a total of about $50.6 billion.[18]

We have discussed the importance of the small-business segment of our economy. We have weighed the advantages and drawbacks of operating a small business as compared with a large one. But is there a way to achieve the best of both worlds? Can one preserve one's independence as a business owner and still enjoy some of the benefits of "bigness"? Let's take a close look at franchising.

Franchising

6

Learning Objective: Appraise the concept and types of franchising.

franchise a license to operate an individually owned business as though it were part of a chain of outlets or stores

franchising the actual granting of a franchise

franchisor an individual or organization granting a franchise

franchisee a person or organization purchasing a franchise

A **franchise** is a license to operate an individually owned business as if it were part of a chain of outlets or stores. Often, the business itself is also called a *franchise*. Among the most familiar franchises are McDonald's, H & R Block, AAMCO Transmissions, GNC (General Nutrition Centers), and Dairy Queen. Many other franchises carry familiar names; this method of doing business has become very popular in the last thirty years or so. It is an attractive means of starting and operating a small business.

What Is Franchising?

Franchising is the actual granting of a franchise. A **franchisor** is an individual or organization granting a franchise. A **franchisee** is a person or organization purchasing a franchise. The franchisor supplies a known and advertised business name, management skills, the required training and materials, and a method of doing business. The franchisee supplies labor and capital, operates the franchised business, and

Maxing with RE/MAX. *Dave and Gail Liniger founded RE/MAX in Denver, Colorado, in 1973, prompted by their dissatisfaction with the way real estate business was conducted at the time. The most significant growth for RE/MAX in recent years has been from overseas, with expansion into Africa, Asia, Australia, the Caribbean, Central America, Europe, Mexico, New Zealand, and South America. RE/MAX is listed as No. 2 among Top Low-Cost Franchises and No. 7 among Fastest-Growing Franchises.*

AP Photo/Seth Perlman

Table 5.6: Basic Rights and Obligations Delineated in a Franchise Agreement

Franchisee rights include:	Franchisee obligations include:
1. use of trademarks, trade names and patents of the franchisor. 2. use of the brand image and the design and decor of the premises developed by the franchisor. 3. use of the franchisor's secret methods. 4. use of the franchisor's copyright materials. 5. use of recipes, formulae, specifications, processes, and methods of manufacture developed by the franchisor. 6. conducting the franchised business upon or from the agreed premises strictly in accordance with the franchisor's methods and subject to the franchisor's directions. 7. guidelines established by the franchisor regarding exclusive territorial rights. 8. rights to obtain suppliers from nominated suppliers at special prices.	1. to carry on the business franchised and no other business upon the approved and nominated premises. 2. to observe certain minimum operating hours. 3. to pay a franchise fee. 4. to follow the accounting system laid down by the franchisor. 5. not to advertise without prior approval of the advertisements by the franchisor. 6. to use and display such point of sale advertising materials as the franchisor stipulates. 7. to maintain the premises in good, clean and sanitary condition and to redecorate when required to do so by the franchisor. 8. to maintain the widest possible insurance coverage. 9. to permit the franchisor's staff to enter the premises to inspect and see if the franchisor's standards are being maintained. 10. to purchase goods or products from the franchisor or his designated suppliers. 11. to train your staff in the franchisor's methods to ensure that they are neatly and appropriately clothed. 12. not to assign the franchise contract without the franchisor's consent.

Source: Excerpted from the SBA's "Is Franchising for Me?" accessed on January 5, 2009 from **http://www.sba.gov.**

agrees to abide by the provisions of the franchise agreement. Table 5.6 lists the basic franchisee rights and obligations that would be covered in a typical franchise agreement.

Types of Franchising

Franchising arrangements fall into three general categories. In the first approach, a manufacturer authorizes a number of retail stores to sell a certain brand-name item. This type of franchising arrangement, one of the oldest, is prevalent in sales of passenger cars and trucks, farm equipment, shoes, paint, earth-moving equipment, and petroleum. About 90 percent of all gasoline is sold through franchised, independent retail service stations, and franchised dealers handle virtually all sales of new cars and trucks. In the second type of franchising arrangement, a producer licenses distributors to sell a given product to retailers. This arrangement is common in the soft-drink industry. Most national manufacturers of soft-drink syrups—The Coca-Cola Company, Dr. Pepper/Seven-Up Companies, PepsiCo, Royal Crown Companies, Inc.—franchise independent bottlers who then serve retailers. In a third form of franchising, a franchisor supplies brand names, techniques, or other services instead of a complete product. Although the franchisor may provide certain production and distribution services, its primary role is the careful development and control of marketing strategies. This approach to franchising, which is the most typical today, is used by Holiday Inns, Howard Johnson Company, AAMCO Transmissions, McDonald's, Dairy Queen, Avis, Hertz Corporation, KFC (Kentucky Fried Chicken), and SUBWAY, to name but a few.

The Growth of Franchising

7

Learning Objective: Analyze the growth of franchising and franchising's advantages and disadvantages.

Franchising, which began in the United States around the time of the Civil War, was used originally by large firms, such as the Singer Sewing Company, to distribute their products. Franchising has been increasing steadily in popularity since the early 1900s, primarily for filling stations and car dealerships; however, this retailing strategy has experienced enormous growth since the mid-1970s. The franchise proliferation

Going Global

Franchising Around the World

From hamburgers to hotels, real estate to retailing, franchising has gone international in a big way. Here are some familiar names in franchising that have spread around the world:

- *Fast food:* McDonald's franchisees operate thousands of restaurants on every continent. Other major fast-food chains with international franchisees include Domino's Pizza, KFC, Burger King, Dunkin' Donuts, and Papa John's.
- *Hotels:* Hilton, Wyndham, Westin, and Sheraton are just four of many hotel brands that have gone global through franchising.
- *Real estate:* Coldwell Banker, RE/MAX, Century 21, and other real estate firms franchise their brands and operational techniques to help franchisees sell homes and commercial properties in dozens of countries.
- *Retailing:* In the world of retail, 7-Eleven, ampm Mini Market, and the UPS Store are three major global franchisors.
- *Services:* Such diverse service businesses as SuperCuts hair salons, Merry Maid cleaning services, and Jazzercise exercise programs now franchise internationally.

Sources: Richard Gibson, "U.S. Restaurants Push Abroad," *Wall Street Journal*, June 18, 2008, **www.wsj.com**; Michael B. Baker, "Checking in: Loews Appoints First Vice President of Global Sales," *Business Travel News*, September 22, 2008, **www.btnmag.com**; "2008 Franchise 500," *Entrepreneur*, n.d., **www.entrepreneur.com**.

generally has paralleled the expansion of the fast-food industry. As Table 5.7 shows, seven of *Entrepreneur* magazine's top-rated franchises for 2008 were in this category.

Of course, franchising is not limited to fast foods. Hair salons, tanning parlors, and dentists and lawyers are expected to participate in franchising arrangements in growing numbers. Franchised health clubs, pest exterminators, and campgrounds

Table 5.7: Entrepreneur's Top Ten Franchises in 2008

Rank	Franchise	Total Investment	Franchise Fee	Royalty Fee	Net-Worth Requirement	Cash Requirement	Comments
1	7-Eleven	Varies	Varies	Varies	Varies	—	15-year renewable term
2	SUBWAY	$80,000–$310,000	$15,000	8%		$80,000–$310,000	20-year renewable term
3	Dunkin, Donuts	Varies	$40,000–$80,000	5.9%	$1,500,000	$750,000	
4	Pizza Hut Inc.	$1,100,000–$1,700,000	$25,000	6.5%	$1,000,000	$360,000	
5	McDonald's	$950,000–$1,800,000	$45,000	12.5%+		$250,000	20-year renewable. Renewal fee $4,900
6	Sonic Drive In Restaurants	$820,000–$2,300,000	$45,000	2–5%	$1,000,000	$500,000	20-year renewable. Renewable 10 years for $6,000
7	KFC	$1,100,000–$1,700,000	$45,000	4%	$1,000,000	$360,000	20-year renewable. Renewal fee $45,000
8	Inter-Continental Hotels Group	Varies	Varies	5%			10-year (average), renewable. Renewal fee varies
9	Domino's Pizza LLC	$118,500–$460,300	$25,000	5.5%		$75,000	10-year renewable
10	RE/MAX Int'l. Inc.	$35,000–$200,000	$12,000–$25,000	Varies	—	—	5-year renewable term, renewal fee varies

Source: **http://www.entrepreneur.com/franchises/toptenlists/index.html,** accessed October 6, 2008, with permission of Entrepreneur.com, Inc.

are already widespread, as are franchised tax preparers and travel agencies. The real estate industry also has experienced a rapid increase in franchising.

Also, franchising is attracting more women and minority business owners in the United States than ever before. One reason is that special outreach programs designed to encourage franchisee diversity have developed. Consider Angela Trammel, a young mother of two. She had been laid off from her job at the Marriott after 9/11. Since she was a member of a Curves Fitness Center and liked the concept of empowering women to become physically fit, she began researching the cost of purchasing a Curves franchise and ways to finance the business. "I was online looking for financing, and I linked to Enterprise Development Group in Washington, D.C. I knew that they had diverse clients." The cost for the franchise was $19,500, but it took $60,000 to open the doors to her fitness center. "Applying for a loan to start the business was much harder than buying a house," said Trammel. Just three years later, Angela and her husband, Ernest, own three Curves Fitness Centers with twelve employees. Recently, giving birth to her third child, she has found the financial freedom and flexibility needed to care for her busy family. In fact, within a three-year period, the Trammel's grew their annual household income from $80,000 to $250,000.[19] Franchisors such as Wendy's, McDonald's, Burger King, and Church's Chicken all have special corporate programs to attract minority and women franchisees. Just as important, successful women and minority franchisees are willing to get involved by offering advice and guidance to new franchisees.

Herman Petty, the first black McDonald's franchisee, remembers that the company provided a great deal of help while he worked to establish his first units. In turn, Petty traveled to help other black franchisees, and he invited new franchisees to gain hands-on experience in his Chicago restaurants before starting their own establishments. Petty also organized a support group, the National Black McDonald's Operators Association, to help black franchisees in other areas. Today, this support group has thirty-three local chapters and more than 330 members across the country. "We are really concentrating on helping our operators to be successful both operationally and financially," says Craig Welburn, the McDonald's franchisee who leads the group.

Dual-branded franchises, in which two franchisors offer their products together, are a new small-business trend. For example, in 1993, pleased with the success of its first cobranded restaurant with Texaco in Beebe, Arkansas, McDonald's now has over 400 cobranded restaurants in the United States. Also, an agreement between franchisors Doctor's Associates, Inc., and TCBY Enterprises, Inc., now allows franchisees to sell SUBWAY sandwiches and TCBY yogurt in the same establishment.

Are Franchises Successful?

Franchising is designed to provide a tested formula for success, along with ongoing advice and training. The success rate for businesses owned and operated by franchisees is significantly higher than the success rate for other independently owned small businesses. In a recent nationwide Gallup poll of 944 franchise owners, 94 percent of franchisees indicated that they were very or somewhat successful, only 5 percent believed that they were very unsuccessful or somewhat unsuccessful, and 1 percent did not know. Despite these impressive statistics, franchising is not a guarantee of success for either franchisees or franchisors. Too rapid expansion, inadequate capital or management skills, and a host of other problems can cause failure for both franchisee and franchisor. Thus, for example, the Dizzy Dean's Beef and Burger franchise is no longer in business. Timothy Bates, a Wayne State University economist, warns, "Despite the hype that franchising is the safest way to go when starting a new business, the research just doesn't bear that out." Just consider Boston Chicken, which once had more than 1,200 restaurants before declaring bankruptcy in 1998.

Brand marriage made in heaven. *According to Chuck Rawley, president and chief operating officer of Kentucky Fried Chicken, "KFC/A&W brands merge well. Both have a strong signature product: KFC's fried chicken and A&W's rootbeer floats. There are a lot of similarities with both established brands that are old yet contemporary."*

Susan Holz

Advantages of Franchising

Franchising plays a vital role in our economy and soon may become the dominant form of retailing. Why? Because franchising offers advantages to both the franchisor and the franchisee.

To the Franchisor The franchisor gains fast and well-controlled distribution of its products without incurring the high cost of constructing and operating its own outlets. The franchisor thus has more capital available to expand production and to use for advertising. At the same time, it can ensure, through the franchise agreement, that outlets are maintained and operated according to its own standards.

The franchisor also benefits from the fact that the franchisee—a sole proprietor in most cases—is likely to be very highly motivated to succeed. The success of the franchise means more sales, which translate into higher royalties for the franchisor.

To the Franchisee The franchisee gets the opportunity to start a business with limited capital and to make use of the business experience of others. Moreover, an outlet with a nationally advertised name, such as Radio Shack, McDonald's, or Century 21 Real Estate, has guaranteed customers as soon as it opens.

If business problems arise, the franchisor gives the franchisee guidance and advice. This counseling is primarily responsible for the very high degree of success enjoyed by franchises. In most cases, the franchisee does not pay for such help.

The franchisee also receives materials to use in local advertising and can take part in national promotional campaigns sponsored by the franchisor. McDonald's and its franchisees, for example, constitute one of the nation's top twenty purchasers of advertising. Finally, the franchisee may be able to minimize the cost of advertising, supplies, and various business necessities by purchasing them in cooperation with other franchisees.

Disadvantages of Franchising

The main disadvantage of franchising affects the franchisee, and it arises because the franchisor retains a great deal of control. The franchisor's contract can dictate every aspect of the business: decor, design of employee uniforms, types of signs, and all the details of business operations. All Burger King French fries taste the same because all Burger King franchisees have to make them the same way.

Contract disputes are the cause of many lawsuits. For example, Rekha Gabhawala, a Dunkin' Donuts franchisee in Milwaukee, alleged that the franchisor was forcing her out of business so that the company could profit by reselling the downtown franchise to someone else; the company, on the other hand, alleged that Gabhawala breached the contract by not running the business according to company standards. In another case, Dunkin' Donuts sued Chris Romanias, its franchisee in Pennsylvania, alleging that Romanias intentionally underreported gross sales to the company. Romanias, on the other hand, alleged that Dunkin' Donuts, Inc., breached the contract because it failed to provide assistance in operating the franchise. Other franchisees claim that contracts are unfairly tilted toward the franchisors. Yet others have charged that they lost their franchise and investment because their franchisor would not approve the sale of the business when they found a buyer.

To arbitrate disputes between franchisors and franchisees, the National Franchise Mediation Program was established in 1993 by thirty member firms, including Burger King Corporation, McDonald's Corporation, and Wendy's International, Inc. Negotiators have since resolved numerous cases through mediation. Recently, Carl's Jr. brought in one of its largest franchisees to help set its system straight, making most franchisees happy for the first time in years. The program also helped PepsiCo settle a long-term contract dispute and renegotiate its franchise agreements.

Because disagreements between franchisors and franchisees have increased in recent years, many franchisees have been demanding government regulation of franchising. In 1997, to avoid government regulation, some of the largest franchisors proposed a new self-policing plan to the Federal Trade Commission.

Franchise holders pay for their security, usually with a one-time franchise fee and continuing royalty and advertising fees, collected as a percentage of sales. As Table 5.6 shows, a McDonald's franchisee pays an initial franchise fee of $45,000, an annual fee of 4 percent of gross sales (for advertising), and a monthly fee of 4 percent of gross sales. In Table 5.7, you can see how much money a franchisee needs to start a new franchise for selected organizations. In some fields, franchise agreements are not uniform. One franchisee may pay more than another for the same services.

Even success can cause problems. Sometimes a franchise is so successful that the franchisor opens its own outlet nearby, in direct competition—although franchisees may fight back. For example, a court recently ruled that Burger King could not enter into direct competition with the franchisee because the contract was not specific on the issue. A spokesperson for one franchisor contends that the company "gives no geographical protection" to its franchise holders and thus is free to move in on them. Franchise operators work hard. They often put in ten- and twelve-hour days, six days a week. The International Franchise Association advises prospective franchise purchasers to investigate before investing and to approach buying a franchise cautiously. Franchises vary widely in approach as well as in products. Some, such as Dunkin' Donuts and Baskin-Robbins, demand long hours. Others, such as Great Clips hair salons and Albert's Family Restaurants, are more appropriate for those who do not want to spend many hours at their stores.

Global Perspectives in Small Business

For small American businesses, the world is becoming smaller. National and international economies are growing more and more interdependent as political leadership and national economic directions change and trade barriers diminish or disappear. Globalization and instant worldwide communications are rapidly shrinking distances at the same time that they are expanding business opportunities. According to a recent study, the Internet is increasingly important to small-business strategic thinking, with more than 50 percent of those surveyed indicating that the Internet represented their most favored strategy for growth. This was more than double the next-favored choice, strategic alliances reflecting the opportunity to reach both global

SPOTLIGHT

Subway's Foreign Franchising Around the World

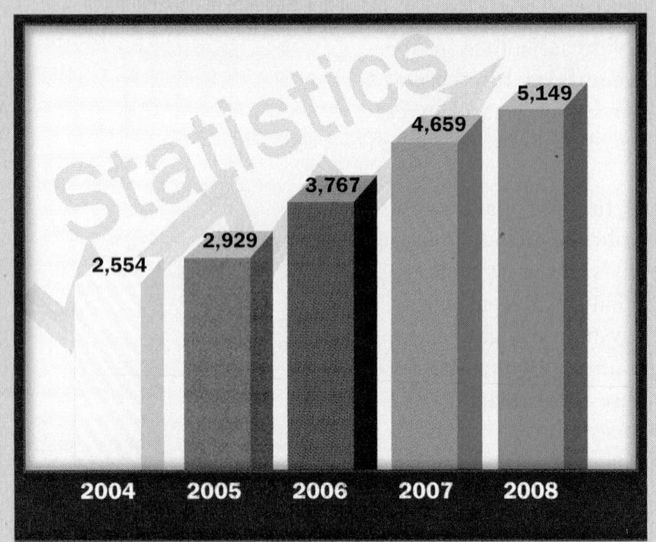

Source: http://www.entrepreneur.com/franchises/subway/282839-0.html, accessed December 1, 2008.

and domestic customers. The Internet and online payment systems enable even very small businesses to serve international customers. In fact, technology now gives small businesses the leverage and power to reach markets that were once limited solely to large corporations. No wonder the number of businesses exporting their goods and services has tripled since 1990, with two-thirds of that boom coming from companies with fewer than twenty employees.[20]

The SBA offers help to the nation's small-business owners who want to enter the world markets. The SBA's efforts include counseling small firms on how and where to market overseas, matching U.S. small-business executives with potential overseas customers, and helping exporters to secure financing. The agency brings small U.S. firms into direct contact with potential overseas buyers and partners. The SBA International Trade Loan program provides guarantees of up to $1.75 million in loans to small-business owners. These loans help small firms in expanding or developing new export markets. The U.S. Commercial Service, a Commerce Department division, aids small and medium-sized businesses in selling overseas. The division's global network includes over 108 offices in the United States and 151 others in eighty-three countries around the world.[21]

International trade will become more important to small-business owners as they face unique challenges in the new century. Small businesses, which are expected to remain the dominant form of organization in this country, must be prepared to adapt to significant demographic and economic changes in the world marketplace.

This chapter ends our discussion of American business today. From here on, we shall be looking closely at various aspects of business operations. We begin, in the next chapter, with a discussion of management—what management is, what managers do, and how they work to coordinate the basic economic resources within a business organization.

return to inside business

The Chocolate Bar

The Chocolate Bar has grown into an international business, thanks to founder Alison Nelson's deal with Dubai entrepreneur Mary Ghorbial. Nelson chose licensing instead of franchising because she had to adapt The Chocolate Bar's products and presentation to accommodate local needs and customs—changes not allowed under franchising. "It's not a franchise. It's the same brand, but with local touches," she explains.

Advised by Ghorbial, Nelson says she "got rid of things that were too American," including peanut butter ingredients, and added new flavors to suit local tastes. She also added fancy chandeliers and other opulent touches to the café's design. Even with these changes, chocolate remains the star of the menu—a treat in any language.

Questions

1. If you were working on a business plan for The Chocolate Bar in the United States, what potential risks would you mention? How would you suggest that the company deal with these risks?
2. Would you recommend that Alison Nelson franchise The Chocolate Bar within the United States? Explain your answer.

Summary

CHAPTER REVIEW

1 Define what a small business is and recognize the fields in which small businesses are concentrated.

A small business is one that is independently owned and operated for profit and is not dominant in its field. There are about 23 million businesses in this country, and more than 90 percent of them are small businesses. Small businesses employ more than half the nation's workforce, even though about 70 percent of new businesses can be expected to fail within five years. More than half of all small businesses are in retailing and services.

2 Identify the people who start small businesses and the reasons why some succeed and many fail.

Such personal characteristics as independence, desire to create a new enterprise, and willingness to accept a challenge may encourage individuals to start small businesses. Various external circumstances, such as special expertise or even the loss of a job, also can supply the motivation to strike out on one's own. Poor planning and lack of capital and management experience are the major causes of small-business failures.

3 Assess the contributions of small businesses to our economy.

Small businesses have been responsible for a wide variety of inventions and innovations, some of which have given rise to new industries. Historically, small businesses have created the bulk of the nation's new jobs. Further, they have mounted effective competition to larger firms. They provide things that society needs, act as suppliers to larger firms, and serve as customers of other businesses, both large and small.

Judge the advantages and disadvantages of operating a small business.

The advantages of smallness in business include the opportunity to establish personal relationships with customers and employees, the ability to adapt to changes quickly, independence, and simplified record keeping. The major disadvantages are the high risk of failure, the limited potential for growth, and the limited ability to raise capital.

5 Explain how the Small Business Administration helps small businesses.

The Small Business Administration (SBA) was created in 1953 to assist and counsel the nation's millions of small-business owners. The SBA offers management courses and workshops; managerial help, including one-to-one counseling through SCORE; various publications; and financial assistance through guaranteed loans and SBICs. It places special emphasis on aid to minority-owned businesses, including those owned by women.

Appraise the concept and types of franchising.

A franchise is a license to operate an individually owned business as though it were part of a chain. The franchisor provides a known business name, management skills, a method of doing business, and the training and required materials. The franchisee contributes labor and capital, operates the franchised business, and agrees to abide by the provisions of the franchise agreement. There are three major categories of franchise agreements.

Analyze the growth of franchising and franchising's advantages and disadvantages.

Franchising has grown tremendously since the mid-1970s. The franchisor's major advantage in franchising is fast and well-controlled distribution of products with minimal capital outlay. In return, the franchisee has the opportunity to open a business with limited capital, to make use of the business experience of others, and to sell to an existing clientele. For this, the franchisee usually must pay both an initial franchise fee and a continuing royalty based on sales. He or she also must follow the dictates of the franchise with regard to operation of the business.

Worldwide business opportunities are expanding for small businesses. The SBA assists small-business owners in penetrating foreign markets. The next century will present unique challenges and opportunities for small-business owners.

Key Terms

You should now be able to define and give an example relevant to each of the following terms:

small business (136)
business plan (147)
Small Business Administration (SBA) (148)
Service Corps of Retired Executives (SCORE) (149)
small-business institutes (SBIs) (150)
small-business development centers (SBDCs) (151)
venture capital (151)
small-business investment companies (SBICs) (152)
franchise (152)
franchising (152)
franchisor (152)
franchisee (152)

Review Questions

1. What information would you need to determine whether a particular business is small according to SBA guidelines?
2. Which two areas of business generally attract the most small businesses? Why are these areas attractive to small business?
3. Distinguish among service industries, distribution industries, and production industries.
4. What kinds of factors encourage certain people to start new businesses?
5. What are the major causes of small-business failure? Do these causes also apply to larger businesses?
6. Briefly describe four contributions of small business to the American economy.
7. What are the major advantages and disadvantages of smallness in business?
8. What are the major components of a business plan? Why should an individual develop a business plan?
9. Identify five ways in which the SBA provides management assistance to small businesses.
10. Identify two ways in which the SBA provides financial assistance to small businesses.
11. Why does the SBA concentrate on providing management and financial assistance to small businesses?
12. What is venture capital? How does the SBA help small businesses to obtain it?
13. Explain the relationships among a franchise, the franchisor, and the franchisee.
14. What does the franchisor receive in a franchising agreement? What does the franchisee receive? What does each provide?
15. Cite one major benefit of franchising for the franchisor. Cite one major benefit of franchising for the franchisee.

Discussion Questions

1. Most people who start small businesses are aware of the high failure rate and the reasons for it. Why, then, do some take no steps to protect their firms from failure? What steps should they take?
2. Are the so-called advantages of small business really advantages? Wouldn't every small-business owner like his or her business to grow into a large firm?
3. Do average citizens benefit from the activities of the SBA, or is the SBA just another way to spend our tax money?
4. Would you rather own your own business independently or become a franchisee? Why?

Video Case 5.1

No Funny Business at Newbury Comics

The two college students who started Newbury Comics have become serious business owners. Mike Dreese and John Brusger started Newbury Comics in 1978 with $2,000 and a valuable comic book collection. Their first store was actually a tiny apartment on Boston's popular Newbury Street, which they rented for $260 per month. Three decades later, the company operates twenty-six stores in Massachusetts, Maine, New Hampshire, and Rhode Island. It still does business on Newbury Street—in a spacious storefront that rents for $23,000 per month.

How did Newbury Comics grow into a multimillion-dollar business? First, the owners identified a need that they could fill. They understood what kind of comic books collectors were interested in buying, and they enjoyed dealing with these customers. They also realized that customer needs can change, which is why they have tested hundreds of new items over the years.

Second, Dreese and Brusger thought of their business as a business. As much as they liked comics, they recognized the profit potential of carrying other products. Over time, they started stocking music and added movies, novelty items, and clothing accessories. They were among the first U.S. stores to import recordings by European groups such as U2. Today, comic books account for only a fraction of Newbury Comics' revenue, whereas CDs and DVDs account for about 70 percent of the revenue.

Third, the entrepreneurs didn't do everything themselves—they knew when to delegate to others. As Newbury Comics expanded beyond comics and opened new stores, the owners hired professionals to negotiate leases, make buying decisions, and select the exact merchandise assortment for each store. They also hired technology experts to design systems for tracking what was in stock, what had been sold, how much the company was spending, and how much each store was contributing to total sales. Now, if a new CD or DVD is selling particularly well, the buyer will know within three minutes—in plenty of time to reorder and satisfy customer demand.

Fourth, Dreese and Brusger have paid close attention to Newbury Comics' financial situation. They're careful to pay suppliers on time, and in exchange, they can get fast-selling products even when supplies are limited. Consider what happened during the Pokemon fad. Newbury Comics originally ordered a small quantity of cards, which quickly sold out. Every time it placed another order, it sent the supplier a check by express delivery. By the height of the fad, when demand was so high that the supplier could not fill every retailer's order, Newbury Comics still got its shipment. By the time the fad faded, the company had sold $4 million worth of Pokemon cards and made more than $2 million in profits.

Newbury Comics remains profitable, although Dreese notes that sales growth has slowed during the past few years. As a result, he says, "We have all had to grow up a little" and improve the way

Newbury Comics operates. The company has formalized its store payroll budgets, assigned employees to check the quality of customer service at each store, and begun offering more products for sale online.

Despite the company's success, Dreese does not expect to expand beyond New England. A new superstore has opened in nearby Norwood, but he knows that a key strength is being able to restock quickly—and that means locating stores within a half-day's drive of the distribution center in Brighton, Massachusetts. Because Newbury Comics owns six trucks, it can resupply every store at least three times a week. Many competitors are far bigger, but no competitor knows its customers and its products better than the team at Newbury Comics.[22]

For more information about this company, go to **www.newburycomics.com.**

Questions

1. This chapter cites five advantages of small business. Which of these seems to apply to the owners' experience with Newbury Comics?
2. This chapter cites three disadvantages of small business. Based on what you know of Newbury Comics, which of these is likely to be the biggest problem in the coming years?
3. Newbury Comics was started without a formal business plan. If you were writing its plan today, what critical risks and assumptions would you examine—and why?

Case 5.2

Tumbleweed Tiny House Company

The average American home is between 2000 and 2500 square feet in size. Jay Shafer's hand-crafted 89-square-foot house on wheels is so small he can almost parallel-park it.

Ecological concerns have merged with an uncertain real estate market to give a big boost to the small-house movement, which promotes simple living in tiny spaces. A growing number of people are happily living in houses ranging from just 70 to 800 square feet, small enough to fit on a flatbed truck and pull into a field or farmstead.

One of the pioneer builders of such tiny homes is the Tumbleweed Tiny House Company, the brain child of Shafer, a 40-something professor-turned-designer who has lived in three of his own creations over the last several years. His young do-it-yourself company, which was a one-person operation until just a year ago, builds and provides plans for several different models and sizes of tiny houses, with fully equipped but scaled-down kitchens and baths, windowed sleeping lofts under peaked roofs, front porches, and lots of ingenious storage space. The houses are designed to hook up to public water and waste lines; many buyers use them as primary homes, but they can also serve as studios, guest rooms, weekend getaways, or home offices.

Shafer was inspired to found the company about a dozen years ago, while teaching drawing at the University of Iowa. "I was living in an average-sized apartment and I realized I just didn't need so much space," he says. After a false start living in an uninsulated Airstream trailer, he decided to build his own 100-square-foot house from scratch, parking it on a friend's farm because minimum-size housing standards prevented him from putting it on a city lot. Not long after, Gregory Paul Johnson, a friend who later founded the Small House Society, asked Shafer to build him a similar home, and Tumbleweed Tiny House Company was born.

Shafer and his company have been featured in *This Old House* magazine, *The New York Times, USA Today, Time, The Los Angeles Times, The Wall Street Journal,* numerous public radio programs, and the Oprah Winfrey show. He has sold more than a dozen homes and 50 sets of plans for the different models on view at his website; plans cost about $1,000 a set and the houses cost from $20,000 to $90,000 to build (the services of a professional contractor are recommended). Shafer also conducts workshops on tiny-house living, sometimes travels around the country with his house, and maintains a blog and active discussion board on his website. He has big plans for Tumbleweed, but rapid expansion doesn't fit his very personal business philosophy. "We are still in our infancy and still building our foundation for growth," he explains on his website. "We have a business plan that we are adhering to. Everything in due time." Among his future dreams are finding partners to represent Tumbleweed homes (real estate license required), partners to build them (licensed contractors only need apply), and makers of products like solar panels and lumber for incorporation into his homes (but nothing that would require redesigning any Tumbleweed products).

In the long term, Shafer would even like to see a whole village of Tumbleweed homes, "even if it's just 3 houses." For now, though, like its products, Tumbleweed remains a small and very carefully built affair.[23]

For more information about this company, go to **http://www.tumbleweedhouses.com.**

Questions

1. Do you think Shafer's plan to grow his business slowly is a good one? Why or why not?
2. What economic and social factors do you think have aided Tumbleweed's success so far? Which might be potential challenges for the firm that Shafer should consider?
3. Do you think a company like Tumbleweed could go global? Why or why not?

Building Skills for Career Success

CHAPTER REVIEW

1. JOURNALING FOR SUCCESS

Discovery statement: One of the objectives in this chapter was to make you aware of the advantages and disadvantages of owning a franchise.

Assignment

1. Assume that after evaluating your skills, experience, and financial situation, you have determined to purchase a franchise in your community. Identify and describe sources where you can obtain information on what the franchise package should contain.
2. List at least five reasons why you should choose franchising rather than starting a new, independent business.
3. Identify issues you need to be aware of as a franchisee.
4. Make a list of possible advantages and disadvantages of the franchise you are considering. What are your rights and your obligations as a franchisee?

2. EXPLORING THE INTERNET

Perhaps the most challenging difficulty for small businesses is operating with scarce resources, especially people and money. To provide information and point small-business operators in the right direction, many Internet sites offer helpful products and services. Although most are sponsored by advertising and may be free of charge, some charge a fee, and others are a combination of both. The SBA within the U.S. Department of Commerce provides a wide array of free information and resources. You can find your way to the SBA through **www.sbaonline.sba.gov** or **www.sba.gov.** Visit the text website for updates to this exercise.

Assignment

1. Describe the various services provided by the SBA site.
2. What sources of funding are there?
3. What service would you like to see improved? How?

3. DEVELOPING CRITICAL-THINKING SKILLS

Small businesses play a vital role in our economy. They not only contribute to technological innovation and to the creation of many new jobs, but they also ensure that customers have an alternative to the products and services offered by large firms. In addition, by making parts for large firms at a lower cost than the large firms could make the parts themselves, they help to keep the lid on consumer prices. Regardless of our need for them, many small businesses fail within their first five years. Why is this so?

Assignment

1. Identify several successful small businesses in your community.
2. Identify one small business that has failed.
3. Gather enough information about those businesses to answer the following questions:
   a. What role do small businesses play in your community?
   b. Why are they important?
   c. Why did the business fail?
   d. What was the most important reason for its failure?
   e. How might the business have survived?
4. Summarize what you have learned about the impact of small businesses on your community. Give the summary to your instructor.

4. BUILDING TEAM SKILLS

A business plan is a written statement that documents the nature of a business and how that business intends to achieve its goals. Although entrepreneurs should prepare a business plan *before* starting a business, the plan also serves as an effective guide later on. The plan should concisely describe the business's mission, the amount of capital it requires, its target market, competition, resources, production plan, marketing plan, organizational plan, assessment of risk, and financial plan.

Assignment

1. Working in a team of four students, identify a company in your community that would benefit from using a business plan, or create a scenario in which a hypothetical entrepreneur wants to start a business.
2. Using the resources of the library or the Internet and/or interviews with business owners, write a business plan incorporating the information in Table 5.4.
3. Present your business plan to the class.

5. RESEARCHING DIFFERENT CAREERS

Many people dream of opening and operating their own businesses. Are you one of them? To be successful, entrepreneurs must have certain characteristics; their profiles generally differ from those of people who work for someone else. Do you know which personal characteristics make some entrepreneurs succeed and others fail? Do you fit the successful entrepreneur's profile? What is your potential for opening and operating a successful small business?

Assignment

1. Use the resources of the library or the Internet to establish what a successful entrepreneur's profile is and to determine whether your personal characteristics fit that profile. Internet addresses that can help you are **www.smartbiz.com/sbs/arts/ieb1.html** and **www.sba.gov** (see "Start your Business" and "FAQ"). These sites have quizzes online that can help you to assess your personal characteristics. The SBA also has helpful brochures.
2. Interview several small-business owners. Ask them to describe the characteristics they think are necessary for being a successful entrepreneur.
3. Using your findings, write a report that includes the following:
   a. A profile of a successful small-business owner
   b. A comparison of your personal characteristics with the profile of the successful entrepreneur
   c. A discussion of your potential as a successful small-business owner

Running a Business Part 2

Finagle A Bagel: A Fast-Growing Small Business

Finagle A Bagel, a fast-growing small business co-owned by Alan Litchman and Laura Trust, is at the forefront of one of the freshest concepts in the food-service business: fresh food. Each of the twenty stores bakes a new batch of bagels every hour, and each receives new deliveries of cheeses, vegetables, fruits, and other ingredients every day. Rather than prepackage menu items, store employees make everything to order so that they can satisfy the specific needs of each *guest* (Finagle A Bagel's term for a customer). As a result, customers get fresh food prepared to their exact preferences—whether it's extra cheese on a bagel pizza or no onions in a salad—along with prompt, friendly service.

"Every sandwich, every salad is built to order, so there's a lot of communication between the customers and the cashiers, the customers and the sandwich makers, the customers and the managers," explains Trust. This allows Finagle A Bagel's store employees ample opportunity to build customer relationships and encourage repeat business. Many, like Mirna Hernandez of the Tremont Street store in downtown Boston, are so familiar with what certain customers order that they spring into action when regulars enter the store. "We know what they want, and we just ring it in and take care of them," she says. Some employees even know their customers by name and make conversation as they create a sandwich or fill a coffee container.

BUYING AND BUILDING THE BUSINESS AND BRAND

The combination of a strong local following and favorable brand image is what attracted the entrepreneurs to Finagle A Bagel. Looking back, Litchman says that he and his wife recognized that building a small business would require more than good business sense. "It has a lot to do with having a great brand and having great food and reinforcing the brand every day," he remembers. "That's one of the key things that we brought."

To further reinforce the brand and reward customer loyalty, Finagle A Bagel created the Frequent Finagler card. Cardholders receive one point for every dollar spent in a Finagle A Bagel store and can redeem accumulated points for coffee, juice, sandwiches, or other rewards. To join, customers visit the company's website (**www.finagleabagel.com**) and complete a registration form asking for name, address, and other demographics. Once the account is set up, says Litchman, "It's a web-based program where customers can log on, check their points, and receive free gifts by mail. The Frequent Finagler is our big push right now to use technology as a means of generating store traffic."

BAGELS ONLINE?

Soon Litchman plans to expand the website so that customers can order food and catering services directly online. Although some competitors already invite online orders, Finagle A Bagel has a more extensive menu, and its fresh-food concept is not as easily adapted to e-commerce. "In our stores, all the food is prepared fresh, and it is very customized," Litchman notes. "This entails a fair amount of interaction between employees and customers: 'What kind of croutons do you want? What kind of dressing? What kind of mustard?' When we're ready to go in that direction, it is going to be a fairly sizable technology venture for us to undertake."

Finagle A Bagel occasionally receives Web or phone orders from customers hundreds or thousands of miles away. Still, the copresidents have no immediate plans to expand outside the Boston metropolitan area. Pointing to regional food-service firms that have profited by opening more stores in a wider geographic domain, Trust says, "We see that the most successful companies have really dominated their area first. Cheesecake Factory is an example of a company that's wildly successful right now, but they were a concept in California for decades before they moved beyond that area. In-and-Out Burger is an outstanding example of a food-service company in the west that's done what we're trying to do. They had seventeen stores at one time, and now they have hundreds of stores. They're very successful, but they never left their backyard. That's kind of why we're staying where we are."

FINANCING A SMALL BUSINESS

Some small businesses achieve rapid growth through franchising. The entrepreneurs running Finagle A Bagel resisted franchising for a long time. "When you franchise, you gain a large influx of capital," says Trust, "but you begin to lose control over the people, the place, and the product." Since the beginning, the owners and their senior managers routinely popped into different Finagle A Bagel stores every day to check quality and service. Now the company says that it will begin granting franchises in the near future and institute a stringent quality-control regimen to maintain the highest standards wherever the brand name appears.

As a corporation, Finagle a Bagel could, as some other small businesses do, raise money for growth through an initial public offering (IPO) of corporate stock. The copresidents prefer not to transform their company into an open corporation at this time. "Going public is very tricky in the food-service business," Trust observes. "Some people have done it very successfully; others have not." The copresidents want to maintain total control over the pace and direction of growth rather than feeling pressured to meet the growth expectations of securities analysts and shareholders. Running a fast-growing small business is their major challenge for now.

Questions

1. Why would Finagle A Bagel maintain a business-to-customer (B2C) website even though it is not yet set up to process online orders from individuals?
2. Do you agree with Finagle A Bagel's plan to franchise its fresh-food concept and brand name? Support your answer.
3. Although opening new stores is costly, the copresidents have chosen not to raise money through an IPO. Do you agree with this decision? Discuss the advantages and disadvantages.
4. If you were writing the executive summary of Finagle A Bagel's business plan to show to lenders, what key points would you stress?

Building a Business Plan Part 2

BUILDING A BUSINESS PLAN

After reading Part 2, "Trends in Business Today," you should be ready to tackle the company and industry component of your business plan. In this section, you will provide information about the background of the company, choice of the legal business form, information on the product or services to be offered, and descriptions of potential customers, current competitors, and the business's future. Chapter 4 in your textbook, "Choosing a Form of Business Ownership," and Chapter 5, "Small Business, Entrepreneurship, and Franchises," can help you to answer some of the questions in this part of the business plan.

THE COMPANY AND INDUSTRY COMPONENT

The company and industry analysis should include the answers to at least the following questions:

2.1. What is the legal form of your business? Is your business a sole proprietorship, a partnership, or a corporation?
2.2. What licenses or permits will you need, if any?
2.3. Is your business a new independent business, a takeover, an expansion, or a franchise?
2.4. If you are dealing with an existing business, how did your company get to the point where it is today?
2.5. What does your business do, and how does it satisfy customers' needs?
2.6. How did you choose and develop the products or services to be sold, and how are they different from those currently on the market?
2.7. What industry do you operate in, and what are the industry-wide trends?
2.8. Who are the major competitors in your industry?
2.9. Have any businesses recently entered or exited? Why did they leave?
2.10. Why will your business be profitable, and what are your growth opportunities?
2.11. Does any part of your business involve e-business?

REVIEW OF BUSINESS PLAN ACTIVITIES

Make sure to check the information you have collected, make any changes, and correct any weaknesses before beginning Part 3. *Reminder:* Review the answers to questions in the preceding part to make sure that all your answers are consistent throughout the business plan. Finally, write a summary statement that incorporates all the information for this part of the business plan.

The information contained in "Building a Business Plan" will also assist you in completing the online *Interactive Business Plan.*

PART 3 Management and Organization

This part of the book deals with the organization—the "thing" that is a business. We begin with a discussion of the management functions involved in developing and operating a business. Next, we analyze the organization's elements and structure. Then we consider a firm's operations that are related to the production of goods and services.

The Canadian Press/Dave Chidley

6 Understanding the Management Process

LEARNING OBJECTIVES

What you will be able to do once you complete this chapter:

1. Define what management is.
2. Describe the four basic management functions: planning, organizing, leading and motivating, and controlling.
3. Distinguish among the various kinds of managers in terms of both level and area of management.
4. Identify the key management skills and the managerial roles.
5. Explain the different types of leadership.
6. Discuss the steps in the managerial decision-making process.
7. Describe how organizations benefit from total quality management.
8. Summarize what it takes to become a successful manager today.

© Construction Photos/Corbis

inside business

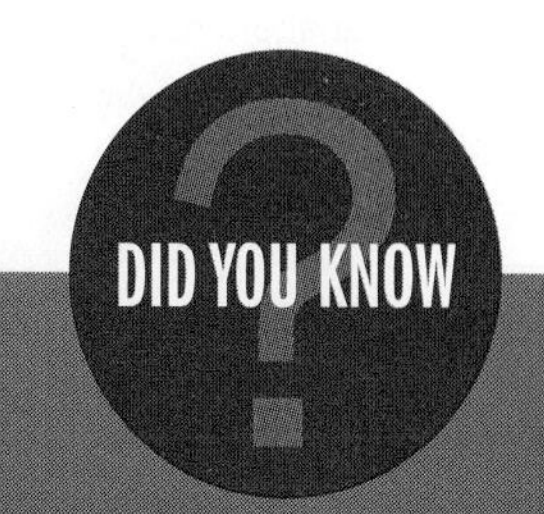

Through innovations, such as Gmail and Google Apps (Web-based software), plus the timely acquisition of hot companies such as YouTube, Google has become a global corporation with 11,000 employees and $16 billion in annual revenue.

Decisions at the Speed of Google

Co-founders Larry Page and Sergey Brin have kept management decisions clicking along at the speed of Google since their search engine went live in 1998. Google virtually dominates the Internet search business and is constantly looking for new ways to make searches faster, easier, and more accurate. Through innovations, such as Gmail and Google Apps (Web-based software), plus the timely acquisition of hot companies such as YouTube, it has become a global corporation with 11,000 employees and $16 billion in annual revenue.

To stay on top of technological changes and stay ahead of major competitors such as Microsoft, Google continues to emphasize speedy managerial decisions at all levels. "It's a think-out-loud culture," explains Google's head of human resources. "There is a constant flow of information about the business on a daily basis, so employees are immersed in the flow."

In fact, employees are allowed to attend nearly any meeting and offer their views as decisions are being made. And their views can make a real difference. For example, a newly hired engineer made a suggestion that was incorporated into an important management decision. "I joined fresh out of college and got to change the Google home page in my first week, a change that affected tens of millions of people," he says.

Corporate decisions are made by a cross-functional executive group consisting of the CEO, the two co-founders, and 11 top managers from operations, sales, finance, communications, engineering, product management, business operations, technology, legal, research, and human resources. These executives gather information and analyze it from every possible angle when considering a problem or an opportunity. According to the head of human resources, "All decisions are collaborative and made by consensus after we look at the data."

Not all Google decisions turn out as expected. Its Froogle shopping search was less popular than managers had hoped, so they renamed it Google Product Search and began testing new features. This points up another aspect of Google's decision making: Managers are ready and willing to make changes quickly if decisions don't lead where they want the company to go.[1]

The leadership employed at Google illustrates that management can be one of the most exciting and rewarding professions available today. Depending on its size, a firm may employ a number of specialized managers who are responsible for particular areas of management, such as marketing, finance, and operations. That same organization also includes managers at several levels within the firm. In this chapter, we define *management* and describe the four basic management functions of planning, organizing, leading and motivating, and controlling. Then we focus on the types of managers with respect to levels of responsibility and areas of expertise. Next, we focus on the skills of effective managers and the different roles managers must play. We examine several styles of leadership and explore the process by which managers make decisions. We also describe how total quality management can improve customer satisfaction. We conclude the chapter with a discussion of what it takes to be a successful manager today.

management the process of coordinating people and other resources to achieve the goals of an organization

What Is Management?

1 Learning Objective: Define what management is.

Management is the process of coordinating people and other resources to achieve the goals of an organization. As we saw in Chapter 1, most organizations make use of four kinds of resources: material, human, financial, and informational (see Figure 6.1).

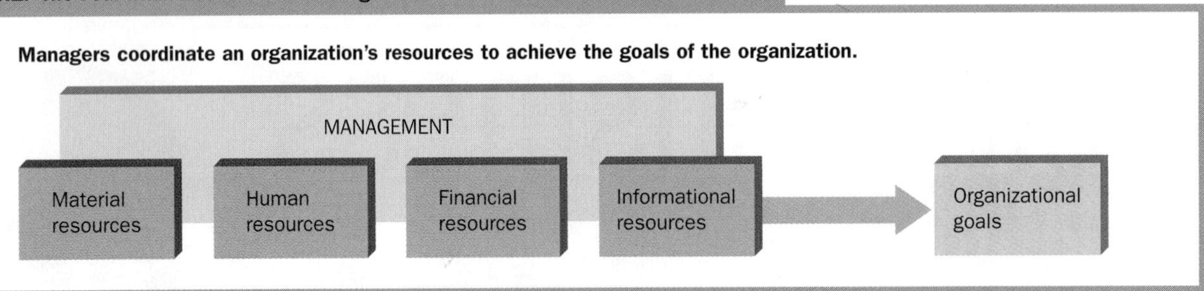

Material resources are the tangible, physical resources an organization uses. For example, General Motors uses steel, glass, and fiberglass to produce cars and trucks on complex machine-driven assembly lines. A college or university uses books, classroom buildings, desks, and computers to educate students. And the Mayo Clinic uses beds, operating room equipment, and diagnostic machines to provide health care.

Perhaps the most important resources of any organization are its *human resources*—people. In fact, some firms live by the philosophy that their employees are their most important assets. One such firm is Southwest Airlines. Southwest treats its employees with the same respect and attention it gives its passengers. Southwest selectively seeks employees with upbeat attitudes and promotes from within 80 percent of the time. In decision making, everyone who will be affected is encouraged to get involved in the process. In an industry in which deregulation, extreme price competition, and fluctuating fuel costs have eliminated several major competitors, Southwest keeps growing and making a profit because of its employees. Many experts would agree with Southwest's emphasis on employees. Some managers believe that the way employees are developed and managed may have more impact on an organization than other vital components such as marketing, sound financial decisions about large expenditures, production, or use of technology.

Financial resources are the funds an organization uses to meet its obligations to investors and creditors. A 7-Eleven convenience store obtains money from customers at the check-out counters and uses a portion of that money to pay its suppliers. Citicorp, a large New York bank, borrows and lends money. Your college obtains money in the form of tuition, income from its endowments, and state and federal grants. It uses the money to pay utility bills, insurance premiums, and professors' salaries.

Finally, many organizations increasingly find that they cannot afford to ignore *information*. External environmental conditions—including the economy, consumer markets, technology, politics, and cultural forces—are all changing so rapidly that a business that does not adapt probably will not survive. And to adapt to change, the business must know what is changing and how it is changing. Most companies gather information about their competitors to increase their knowledge about changes in their industry and to learn from other companies' failures and successes.

Human resources. *In most organizations, effective management of human resources is absolutely critical.*

PRNewswire/Giant Eagle Inc.

It is important to realize that the four types of resources described earlier are only general categories of resources. Within each category are hundreds or thousands of more specific resources. It is this complex mix of specific resources—and not simply "some of each" of the four general categories—that managers must coordinate to produce goods and services.

Another interesting way to look at management is in terms of the different functions managers perform. These functions have been identified as planning, organizing, leading and motivating employees, and controlling. We look at each of these management functions in the next section.

Basic Management Functions

2

Learning Objective: Describe the four basic management functions: planning, organizing, leading and motivating, and controlling.

Top managers at Kraft Foods decided to invest about $300 million on marketing, research and development, and other plans last year. This year, they have decided to increase the marketing budget again. In recent years, the maker of familiar brands, such as Kraft cheese, Oscar Mayer hot dogs, Maxwell House coffee, Oreo cookies, and Jell-O desserts, has closed factories, cut jobs, and sold brands to focus on cheese, snacks, and beverages. It has come up with four key strategies, including rewiring the organization for growth, making its categories more relevant to consumers, enhancing its sales capabilities, and driving down costs.[2]

Management functions such as those just described do not occur according to some rigid, preset timetable. Managers do not plan in January, organize in February, lead and motivate in March, and control in April. At any given time, managers may engage in a number of functions simultaneously. However, each function tends to lead naturally to others. Figure 6.2 provides a visual framework for a more detailed discussion of the four basic management functions. How well managers perform these key functions determines whether a business is successful.

Mission statement. *The mission statement of Microsoft is "We work to help people and businesses throughout the world realize their full potential."*

AP Photo/Ted S. Warren

Planning

Planning, in its simplest form, is establishing organizational goals and deciding how to accomplish them. It is often referred to as the "first" management function because all other management functions depend on planning. Organizations such as Nissan, Houston Community Colleges, and the U.S. Secret Service begin the planning process by developing a mission statement.

An organization's **mission** is a statement of the basic purpose that makes that organization different from others. Google's mission statement is "to organize the world's information and make it universally accessible and useful."[3] Houston Community College System's mission is to provide an education for local citizens. The mission of the Secret Service is to protect the life of the President. Once an organization's mission has been described in a mission statement, the next step is to develop organizational goals and objectives, usually through strategic planning. **Strategic planning** is the process of establishing an organization's major goals and objectives and allocating the resources to achieve them.

planning establishing organizational goals and deciding how to accomplish them

mission a statement of the basic purpose that makes an organization different from others

strategic planning the process of establishing an organization's major goals and objectives and allocating the resources to achieve them

Establishing Goals and Objectives A **goal** is an end result that an organization is expected to achieve over a one- to ten-year period. An **objective** is a specific statement detailing what the organization intends to accomplish over a shorter period of time.

goal an end result that an organization is expected to achieve over a one- to ten-year period

objective a specific statement detailing what an organization intends to accomplish over a shorter period of time

Figure 6.2: The Management Process

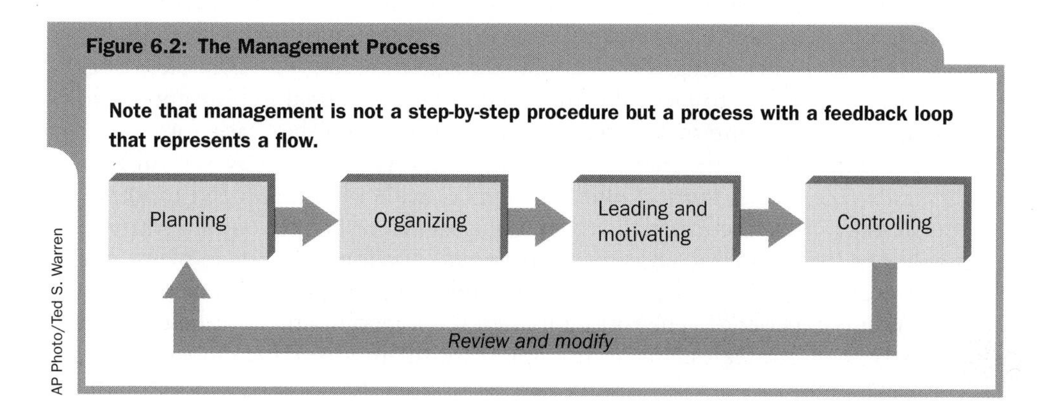

Goals and objectives can deal with a variety of factors, such as sales, company growth, costs, customer satisfaction, and employee morale. Whereas a small manufacturer may focus primarily on sales objectives for the next six months, a large firm may be more interested in goals for several years ahead. Under the leadership of CEO Will Manzer, Eastern Mountain Sports (EMS) has a goal to return to its roots as a hardcore sports gear provider. Over years of declining profits, EMS has blurred its image by shifting to "soft" merchandise that appeals to a broader market. The company's managers know that goals take time to achieve, and they are willing to invest to reach their goal of becoming the edgy outfitter they once were. They are taking action with objectives such as dropping all their "soft" merchandise, hiring hardcore sporting enthusiasts, and stocking gear for even the most fringe sports out there (e.g., kite skiing, ice climbing, and high-speed sledding).[4] Finally, goals are set at every level of an organization. Every member of an organization—the president of the company, the head of a department, and an operating employee at the lowest level—has a set of goals that he or she hopes to achieve.

The goals developed for these different levels must be consistent. However, it is likely that some conflict will arise. A production department, for example, may have a goal of minimizing costs. One way to do this is to produce only one type of product and offer "no frills." Marketing may have a goal of maximizing sales. One way to implement this goal is to offer customers a wide range of products and options. As part of goal setting, the manager who is responsible for *both* departments must achieve some sort of balance between conflicting goals. This balancing process is called *optimization.*

The optimization of conflicting goals requires insight and ability. Faced with the marketing-versus-production conflict just described, most managers probably would not adopt either viewpoint completely. Instead, they might decide on a reasonably diverse product line offering only the most widely sought-after options. Such a compromise would seem to be best for the whole organization.

plan an outline of the actions by which an organization intends to accomplish its goals and objectives

strategic plan an organization's broadest plan, developed as a guide for major policy setting and decision making

tactical plan a smaller-scale plan developed to implement a strategy

Establishing Plans to Accomplish Goals and Objectives Once goals and objectives have been set for the organization, managers must develop plans for achieving them. A **plan** is an outline of the actions by which an organization intends to accomplish its goals and objectives. Just as it has different goals and objectives, the organization also develops several types of plans, as shown in Figure 6.3.

Resulting from the strategic planning process, an organization's **strategic plan** is its broadest plan, developed as a guide for major policy setting and decision making. Strategic plans are set by the board of directors and top management and generally are designed to achieve the long-term goals of the organization. Thus, a firm's strategic plan defines what business the company is in or wants to be in and the kind of company it is or wants to be. When top management at one of the world's biggest consumer products companies, Procter & Gamble, decided to expand and to diversify its three main business units, they created separate executive teams for the global personal care products, global hair care products, and global prestige products. This long-term strategy has been adopted to more effectively compete globally and to better serve customers in numerous global markets.[5]

The Internet has challenged traditional strategic thinking. For example, reluctant to move from a face-to-face sales approach to a less personal website approach, Allstate has created an Internet presence to support its established sales force.

In addition to strategic plans, most organizations also employ several narrower kinds of plans. A **tactical plan** is a smaller-scale plan developed to implement a strategy. Most tactical plans cover a one- to three-year period. If a strategic plan will take five years to complete, the firm may develop five tactical plans, one covering each year. Tactical plans may be updated periodically as dictated by conditions and experience. Their more limited scope permits them to be changed more easily than strategies. In an attempt to fulfill its diversification strategy, Procter & Gamble purchased NIOXIN Research Laboratories, Inc., a leader in the

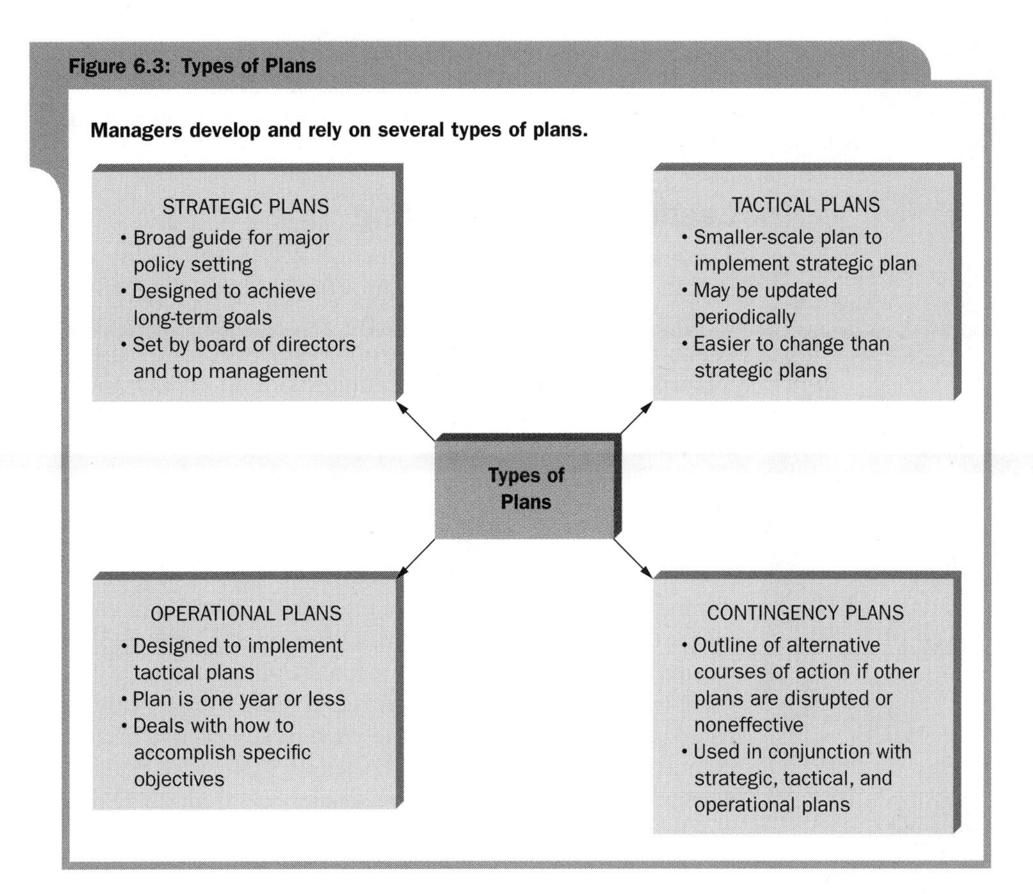

Figure 6.3: Types of Plans

scalp care part of the professional hair care product category. NIOXIN offers a range of innovative products that focus on problems associated with thinning hair and are distributed through salons and salon stores in more than 40 countries. This acquisition was in line with Procter & Gamble's strategy of focusing on faster growing, higher margin businesses and a tactical plan used for achieving its long-term goals.[6]

An **operational plan** is a type of plan designed to implement tactical plans. Operational plans usually are established for one year or less and deal with how to accomplish the organization's specific objectives. Procter & Gamble has adopted the *Go-to-Market plan* in order to speed up the availability of products to retailers and thus to consumers. The strategic and tactical plans have been kept in mind in order to achieve this plan. It includes making significant changes in the way that Procter & Gamble distributes its products.[7]

operational plan a type of plan designed to implement tactical plans

Regardless of how hard managers try, sometimes business activities do not go as planned. Today, most corporations also develop contingency plans along with strategies, tactical plans, and operational plans. A **contingency plan** is a plan that outlines alternative courses of action that may be taken if an organization's other plans are disrupted or become ineffective.

contingency plan a plan that outlines alternative courses of action that may be taken if an organization's other plans are disrupted or become ineffective

Organizing the Enterprise

After goal setting and planning, the second major function of the manager is organization. **Organizing** is the grouping of resources and activities to accomplish some end result in an efficient and effective manner. Consider the case of an inventor who creates a new product and goes into business to sell it. At first, the inventor will do everything on his or her own—purchase raw materials, make the product, advertise it, sell it, and keep business records. Eventually, as business grows, the inventor will need help. To begin with, he or she might hire a professional sales representative and a part-time bookkeeper. Later, it also might be necessary to hire sales staff, people to assist with production, and an accountant. As the inventor hires new personnel, he or she must decide what each person will do, to whom

organizing the grouping of resources and activities to accomplish some end result in an efficient and effective manner

Creating a satisfying work environment can be challenging. *Designers of the work environment at Google spent considerable time talking with approximately 350 employees regarding what they wanted in their offices and work areas.*

AP Photo/Keystone, Walter Bieri

each person will report, and how each person can best take part in the organization's activities. We discuss these and other facets of the organizing function in much more detail in Chapter 7.

Leading and Motivating

The leading and motivating function is concerned with the human resources within an organization. Specifically, **leading** is the process of influencing people to work toward a common goal. **Motivating** is the process of providing reasons for people to work in the best interests of an organization. Together, leading and motivating are often referred to as **directing**.

We have already noted the importance of an organization's human resources. Because of this importance, leading and motivating are critical activities. Obviously, different people do things for different reasons—that is, they have different *motivations*. Some are interested primarily in earning as much money as they can. Others may be spurred on by opportunities to get promoted. Part of a manager's job, then, is to determine what factors motivate workers and to try to provide those incentives to encourage effective performance. Jeffrey R. Immelt, GE's chairman and CEO has worked to transform GE into a leader in essential themes tied to world development, such as emerging markets, environmental solutions, demographics, and digital connections. He believes in giving freedom to his teams and wants them to come up with their own solutions. However, he does not hesitate to intervene if the situation demands. He believes that a leader's primary role is to teach, and he makes people feel that he is willing to share what he has learned. Mr. Immelt also laid the vision for GE's ambitious "ecomagination initiative" and has been named one of the "World's Best CEOs" three times by *Barron's*.[8]

leading the process of influencing people to work toward a common goal

motivating the process of providing reasons for people to work in the best interests of an organization

directing the combined processes of leading and motivating

controlling the process of evaluating and regulating ongoing activities to ensure that goals are achieved

A lot of research has been done on both motivation and leadership. As you will see in Chapter 10, research on motivation has yielded very useful information. Research on leadership has been less successful. Despite decades of study, no one has discovered a general set of personal traits or characteristics that makes a good leader. Later in this chapter, we discuss leadership in more detail.

Controlling Ongoing Activities

Controlling is the process of evaluating and regulating ongoing activities to ensure that goals are achieved. To see how controlling works, consider a rocket launched by NASA to place a satellite in orbit. Do NASA personnel simply fire the rocket and then check back in a few days to find out whether the satellite is in place? Of course not. The rocket is monitored constantly, and its course is regulated and adjusted as needed to get the satellite to its destination.

The control function includes three steps (see Figure 6.4). The first is *setting standards* with which performance can be compared. The second is *measuring actual performance* and comparing it with the standard. And the third is *taking corrective action* as necessary. Notice that the control function is circular in nature. The steps in the control function must be repeated periodically until the goal is achieved. For example, suppose that Southwest Airlines establishes a goal of increasing profits by 12 percent. To ensure that this goal is reached, Southwest's management might monitor its profit on a monthly basis. After three months, if profit has increased by 3 percent, management might be able to assume that plans are going according to schedule. Probably no action will be taken. However, if

The Business of Green

Technology Goes Green at Ford

Henry Ford revolutionized the car industry with his Model T. More than 100 years later, his great-grandson, William Clay Ford, Jr., is leading a green revolution inside the Ford Motor Company. When he was first named to the board of directors, he was told to "stop associating with any known or suspected environmentalists," he remembers. "And I said: 'No, of course I have no intention of stopping.'"

Now, as executive chairman, Ford has used his leadership position to move environmental initiatives into the fast lane at the company his family founded. For example, he led the $2 billion effort to revamp the firm's Rouge River factory in Dearborn, Michigan, into a model of green manufacturing. Much of the plant's power comes from renewable sources such as solar panels and fuel cells. The redesigned facility is cleaner and leaner, using less water and power. And the site is literally green with sustainable landscaping and wildlife habitats.

AP Photo/Carlos Osorio

Ford is also using his influence to encourage other business leaders to see green. "We need to do our part as an industry, but we are only one piece of a much bigger puzzle," he says.

Sources: "Ford Seeks Loan Guarantees for Green Tech," *Associated Press*, September 5, 2008, **www.cnnmoney.com**; Maria Bartiromo, "Bill Ford on Tipping Points and Thinking Small," *BusinessWeek*, August 11, 2008, p. 18; Jennette Smith, "Ford Calls for Greater R&D, Integrated Energy Policy," *Crain's Detroit Business*, June 4, 2007, p. M66; **www.ford.com.**

profit has increased by only 1 percent after three months, some corrective action would be needed to get the firm on track. The particular action that is required depends on the reason for the small increase in profit.

Figure 6.4: The Control Function

The control function includes three steps: setting standards, measuring actual performance, and taking corrective action.

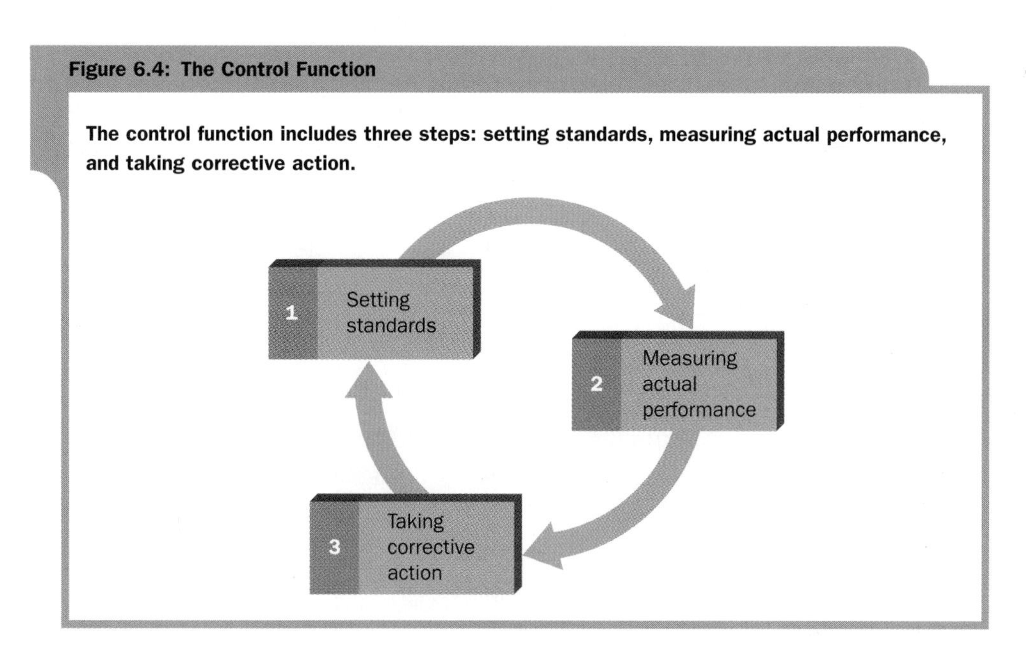

Kinds of Managers

Managers can be classified in two ways: according to their level within an organization and according to their area of management. In this section, we use both perspectives to explore the various types of managers.

3 Learning Objective: Distinguish among the various kinds of managers in terms of both level and area of management.

SPOTLIGHT

How Much Do Executives in Selected Business Areas Earn Yearly?

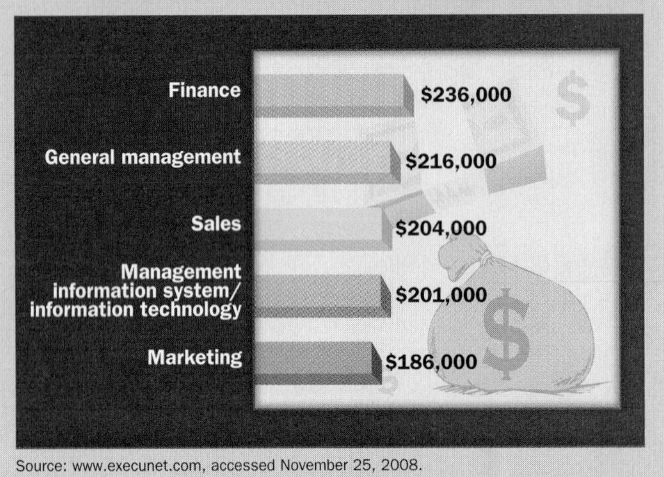

Source: www.execunet.com, accessed November 25, 2008.

Levels of Management

For the moment, think of an organization as a three-story structure (as illustrated in Figure 6.5). Each story corresponds to one of the three general levels of management: top managers, middle managers, and first-line managers.

Top Managers A **top manager** is an upper-level executive who guides and controls the overall fortunes of an organization. Top managers constitute a small group. In terms of planning, they are generally responsible for developing the organization's mission. They also determine the firm's strategy. It takes years of hard work, long hours, and perseverance, as well as talent and no small share of good luck, to reach the ranks of top management in large companies. Common job titles associated with top managers are president, vice president, chief executive officer (CEO), and chief operating officer (COO).

Middle Managers Middle managers probably make up the largest group of managers in most organizations. A **middle manager** is a manager who implements the strategy and major policies developed by top management. Middle managers develop tactical plans and operational plans, and they coordinate and supervise the activities of first-line managers. Titles at the middle-management level include division manager, department head, plant manager, and operations manager.

top manager an upper-level executive who guides and controls the overall fortunes of an organization

middle manager a manager who implements the strategy and major policies developed by top management

first-line manager a manager who coordinates and supervises the activities of operating employees

First-Line Managers A **first-line manager** is a manager who coordinates and supervises the activities of operating employees. First-line managers spend most of their time working with and motivating their employees, answering questions, and solving day-to-day problems. Most first-line managers are former operating employees who, owing to their hard work and potential, were promoted into management. Many of today's middle and top managers began their careers on this first management level. Common titles for first-line managers include office manager, supervisor, and foreman.

Figure 6.5: Management Levels Found in Most Companies

The coordinated effort of all three levels of managers is required to implement the goals of any company.

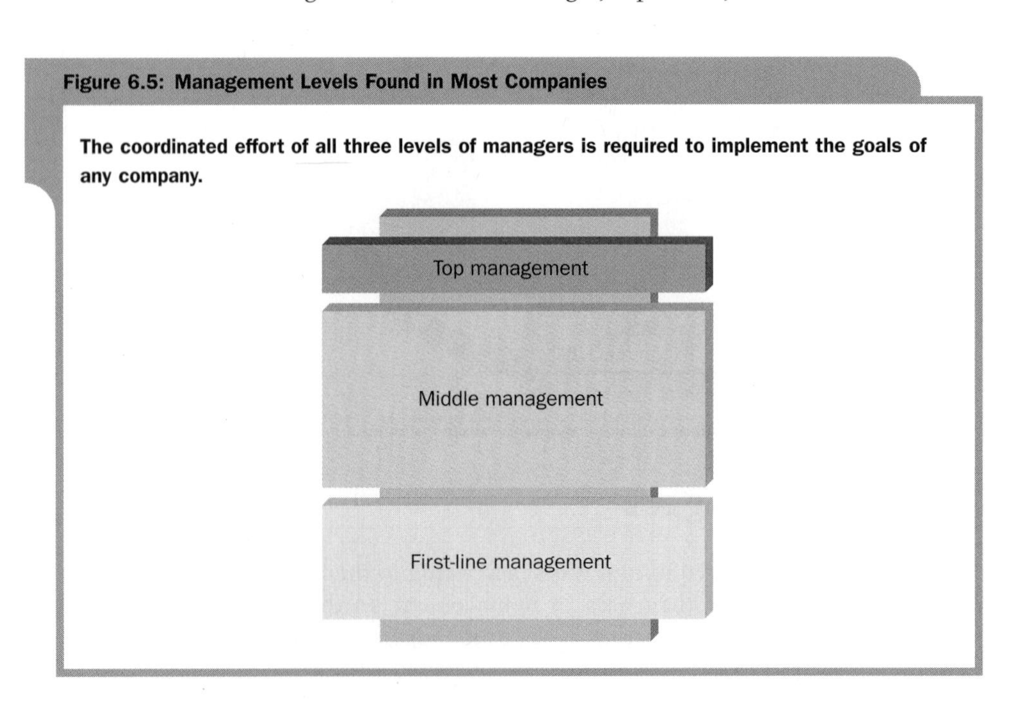

Jump-Starting Your Career

Promoted—Now What?

Congratulations on being promoted into the ranks of first-line management. Now you'll be supervising employees who just days ago were your peers. Some former peers may resent your promotion. Others may fear their friendly relationship with you will never be the same. You may feel awkward supervising people you once worked with as equals. What can you do to smooth your transition into management?

- *Start the conversation.* Meet with each member of your team to discuss individual goals and concerns. Also hold group meetings to discuss specific transition issues. Listen closely, express your expectations, invite new ideas, and emphasize the positive.
- *Champion your group.* Remind your employees that you can be a strong champion for the group because you are so familiar with its strengths and capabilities. You should also be a champion for change to improve your group's performance.
- *Be professional.* Any hint of favoritism will derail your transition. Use this opportunity to establish a professional, objective working relationship with all your employees.

Sources: Ron Brown, "Showing Them Who's Boss," *Condé Nast Portfolio,* September 23, 2008, **www.portfolio.com**; "Dear Jeremy: Problems at Work," *The Guardian (UK),* March 15, 2008, p. 4; Joanne Murray, "From Colleague to Boss: How to Navigate the Transition," *Monster Career Advice,* n.d., **career-advice.monster.com.**

Areas of Management Specialization

Organizational structure also can be divided into areas of management specialization (see Figure 6.6). The most common areas are finance, operations, marketing, human resources, and administration. Depending on its mission, goals, and objectives, an organization may include other areas as well—research and development (R&D), for example.

Financial Managers A **financial manager** is primarily responsible for an organization's financial resources. Accounting and investment are specialized areas within financial management. Because financing affects the operation of the entire firm, many of the CEOs and presidents of this country's largest companies are people who got their "basic training" as financial managers.

financial manager a manager who is primarily responsible for an organization's financial resources

Operations Managers An **operations manager** manages the systems that convert resources into goods and services. Traditionally, operations management has been equated with manufacturing—the production of goods. However, in recent years, many of the techniques and procedures of operations management have been applied to the production of services and to a variety of nonbusiness activities. As with financial management, operations management has produced a large percentage of today's company CEOs and presidents.

operations manager a manager who manages the systems that convert resources into goods and services

Marketing Managers A **marketing manager** is responsible for facilitating the exchange of products between an organization and its customers or clients. Specific areas within marketing are marketing research, product management, advertising, promotion, sales, and distribution. A sizable number of today's company presidents have risen from the ranks of marketing management.

marketing manager a manager who is responsible for facilitating the exchange of products between an organization and its customers or clients

Human Resources Managers A **human resources manager** is charged with managing an organization's human resources programs. He or she engages in human

human resources manager a person charged with managing an organization's human resources programs

Figure 6.6: Areas of Management Specialization

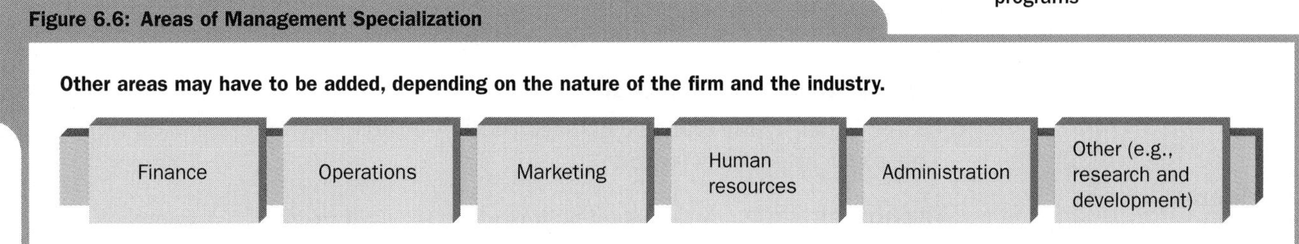

Managers work in teams. *Managers from various specializations work together in teams to generate favorable outcomes.*

resources planning; designs systems for hiring, training, and evaluating the performance of employees; and ensures that the organization follows government regulations concerning employment practices. Some human resources managers are making effective use of technology. For example, over 1 million job openings are posted on Monster.com, which attracts about 15 million visitors monthly.[9]

administrative manager a manager who is not associated with any specific functional area but who provides overall administrative guidance and leadership

Administrative Managers An **administrative manager** (also called a *general manager*) is not associated with any specific functional area but provides overall administrative guidance and leadership. A hospital administrator is an example of an administrative manager. He or she does not specialize in operations, finance, marketing, or human resources management but instead coordinates the activities of specialized managers in all these areas. In many respects, most top managers are really administrative managers.

Whatever their level in the organization and whatever area they specialize in, successful managers generally exhibit certain key skills and are able to play certain managerial roles. However, as we shall see, some skills are likely to be more critical at one level of management than at another.

What Makes Effective Managers?

4

Learning Objective: Identify the key management skills and the managerial roles.

In general, effective managers are those who (1) possess certain important skills and (2) are able to use those skills in a number of managerial roles. Probably no manager is called on to use any particular skill *constantly* or to play a particular role *all the time*. However, these skills and abilities must be available when they are needed.

Key Management Skills

The skills that typify effective managers fall into three general categories: technical, conceptual, and interpersonal.

technical skill a specific skill needed to accomplish a specialized activity

Technical Skills A **technical skill** is a specific skill needed to accomplish a specialized activity. For example, the skills engineers and machinists need to do their

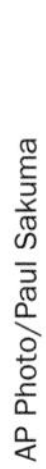
AP Photo/Paul Sakuma

jobs are technical skills. First-line managers (and, to a lesser extent, middle managers) need the technical skills relevant to the activities they manage. Although these managers may not perform the technical tasks themselves, they must be able to train subordinates, answer questions, and otherwise provide guidance and direction. A first-line manager in the accounting department of the Hyatt Corporation, for example, must be able to perform computerized accounting transactions and help employees complete the same accounting task. In general, top managers do not rely on technical skills as heavily as managers at other levels. Still, understanding the technical side of a business is an aid to effective management at every level.

SPOTLIGHT

When Working Remotely, Is the Quality of Your Work the Same?

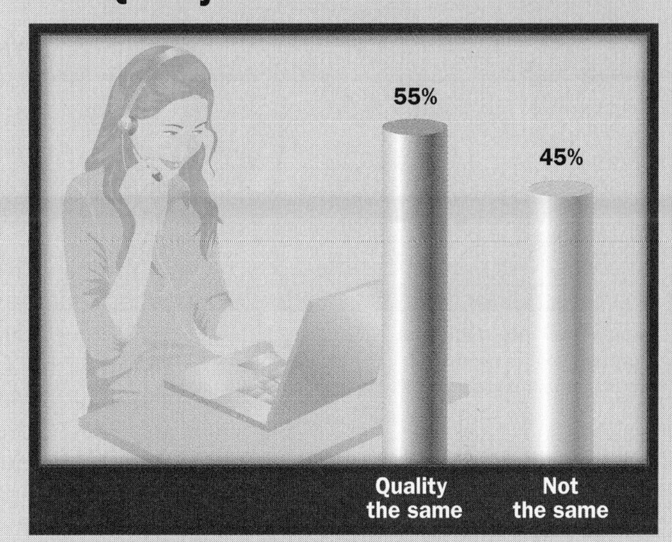

Source: hotjobs.yahoo.com, accessed November 25, 2008.

Conceptual Skills **Conceptual skill** is the ability to think in abstract terms. Conceptual skill allows a manager to see the "big picture" and understand how the various parts of an organization or idea can fit together. These skills are useful in a wide range of situations, including the optimization of goals described earlier. They are usually more useful for top managers than for middle or first-line managers.

Interpersonal Skills An **interpersonal skill** is the ability to deal effectively with other people, both inside and outside an organization. Examples of interpersonal skills are the ability to relate to people, understand their needs and motives, and show genuine compassion. One reason why Mary Kay Ash, founder of Mary Kay Cosmetics, has been so successful is her ability to motivate her employees and to inspire their loyalty to her vision for the firm. And although it is obvious that a CEO such as Mary Kay Ash must be able to work with employees throughout the organization, what is not so obvious is that middle and first-line managers also must possess interpersonal skills. For example, a

conceptual skill the ability to think in abstract terms

interpersonal skill the ability to deal effectively with other people

AP Photo/Beneto Matthews

Assistance for HR managers. *The Society for Human Resources Management indicates that Monster.com has highly useful tools for HR professionals.*

Top management. *J. W. Marriot, Jr., chairman and CEO of Marriot Hotels, participates in the re-opening of the company's hotel in downtown New Orleans.*

first-line manager on an assembly line at Procter & Gamble must rely on employees to manufacture Tide detergent. The better the manager's interpersonal skills, the more likely the manager will be able to lead and motivate those employees. When all other things are equal, the manager able to exhibit these skills will be more successful than the arrogant and brash manager who does not care about others.

Managerial Roles

Research suggests that managers must, from time to time, act in ten different roles if they are to be successful.[10] (By *role,* we mean a set of expectations that one must fulfill.) These ten roles can be grouped into three broad categories: decisional, interpersonal, and informational.

decisional role a role that involves various aspects of management decision making

Decisional Roles A **decisional role** involves various aspects of management decision making. The decisional role can be subdivided into four specific managerial roles. In the role of *entrepreneur,* the manager is the voluntary initiator of change. For example, the CEO of DuPont decided to put more financial resources into its Experimental Station, a large R&D center, to increase new products. This entrepreneurial emphasis on R&D led to the creation of Sorona, a synthetic fiber that could be used for clothing, car upholstery, and carpeting. DuPont hopes that these decisions will pay great dividends in the long run.[11] A second role is that of *disturbance handler.* A manager who settles a strike is handling a disturbance. Third, the manager also occasionally plays the role of *resource allocator.* In this role, the manager might have to decide which departmental budgets to cut and which expenditure requests to approve. The fourth role is that of *negotiator.* Being a negotiator might involve settling a dispute between a manager and a worker assigned to the manager's work group.

interpersonal role a role in which the manager deals with people

Interpersonal Roles Dealing with people is an integral part of the manager's job. An **interpersonal role** is a role in which the manager deals with people. Like the decisional role, the interpersonal role can be broken down according to three managerial functions. The manager may be called on to serve as a *figurehead,* perhaps by attending a ribbon-cutting ceremony or taking an important client to dinner. The manager also may have to play the role of *liaison* by serving as a go-between for two different groups. As a liaison, a manager might represent his or her firm at meetings of an industry-wide trade organization. Finally, the manager often has to serve as a *leader.* Playing the role of leader includes being an example for others in the organization as well as developing the skills, abilities, and motivation of employees.

informational role a role in which the manager either gathers or provides information

Informational Roles An **informational role** is one in which the manager either gathers or provides information. The informational role can be subdivided as follows: In the role of *monitor,* the manager actively seeks information that may be of value to the organization. For example, a manager who hears about a good business opportunity is engaging in the role of monitor. The second informational role is that of *disseminator.* In this role, the manager transmits key information to those who can use it. As a disseminator, the manager who heard about a good business opportunity would tell the appropriate marketing manager about it. The third informational role is that of *spokesperson.* In this role, the manager provides information to people outside the organization, such as the press, television reporters, and the public.

leadership the ability to influence others

Leadership

5
Learning Objective: Explain the different types of leadership.

Leadership has been defined broadly as the ability to influence others. A leader has power and can use it to affect the behavior of others. Leadership is different from management in that a leader strives for voluntary cooperation, whereas a manager may have to depend on coercion to change employee behavior.

Formal and Informal Leadership

Some experts make distinctions between formal leadership and informal leadership. Formal leaders have legitimate power of position. They have *authority* within an organization to influence others to work for the organization's objectives. Informal leaders usually have no such authority and may or may not exert their influence in support of the organization. Both formal and informal leaders make use of several kinds of power, including the ability to grant rewards or impose punishments, the possession of expert knowledge, and personal attraction or charisma. Informal leaders who identify with the organization's goals are a valuable asset to any organization. However, a business can be brought to its knees by informal leaders who turn work groups against management.

Styles of Leadership

For many years, leadership was viewed as a combination of personality traits, such as self-confidence, concern for people, intelligence, and dependability. Achieving a consensus on which traits were most important was difficult, however, and attention turned to styles of leadership behavior. In the last few decades, several styles of leadership have been identified: authoritarian, laissez-faire, and democratic. The **authoritarian leader** holds all authority and responsibility, with communication usually moving from top to bottom. This leader assigns workers to specific tasks and expects orderly, precise results. The leaders at UPS employ authoritarian leadership. At the other extreme is the **laissez-faire leader**, who gives authority to employees. With the laissez-faire style, subordinates are allowed to work as they choose with a minimum of interference. Communication flows horizontally among group members. Leaders at Apple Computer employ a laissez-faire leadership style to give employees as much freedom as possible to develop new products. The **democratic leader** holds final responsibility but also delegates authority to others, who determine work assignments. In this leadership style, communication is active upward and downward. Employee commitment is high because of participation in the decision-making process. Managers for both Wal-Mart and Saturn have used democratic leadership to encourage employees to become more than just rank-and-file workers.

Leadership style. *Apple CEO, Steve Jobs, has a leadership style that helps to create an environment that nurtures and enhances the creation of technology-based products, many of which become highly successful.*

AP Photo/Herbert Knosowski

authoritarian leader one who holds all authority and responsibility, with communication usually moving from top to bottom

laissez-faire leader one who gives authority to employees and allows subordinates to work as they choose with a minimum of interference; communication flows horizontally among group members

democratic leader one who holds final responsibility but also delegates authority to others, who help to determine work assignments; communication is active upward and downward

decision making the act of choosing one alternative from a set of alternatives

Which Managerial Leadership Style Is Best?

Today, most management experts agree that no "best" managerial leadership style exists. Each of the styles described—authoritarian, laissez-faire, and democratic—has advantages and disadvantages. Democratic leadership can motivate employees to work effectively because they are implementing *their own* decisions. However, the decision making process in democratic leadership takes time that subordinates could be devoting to the work itself.

Although hundreds of research studies have been conducted to prove which leadership style is best, there are no definite conclusions. The "best" leadership seems to occur when the leader's style matches the situation. Each of the leadership styles can be effective in the right situation. The *most* effective style depends on interaction among employees, characteristics of the work situation, and the manager's personality.

Managerial Decision Making

Learning Objective: Discuss the steps in the managerial decision-making process.

Decision making is the act of choosing one alternative from a set of alternatives.[12] In ordinary situations, decisions are made casually and informally. We encounter a problem, mull it over, settle on a solution, and go on. Managers, however, require

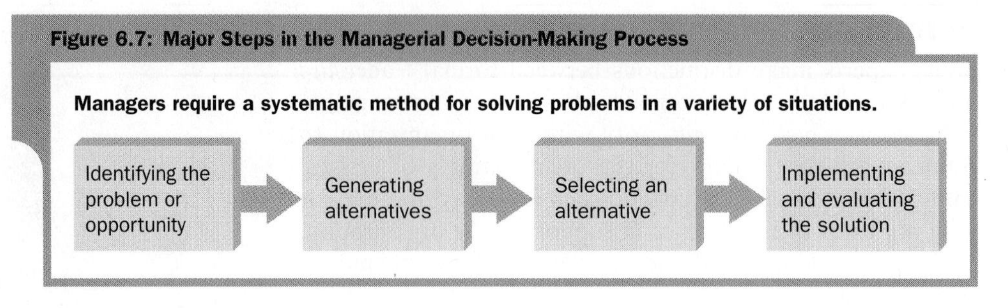

Figure 6.7: Major Steps in the Managerial Decision-Making Process

a more systematic method for solving complex problems. As shown in Figure 6.7, managerial decision making involves four steps: (1) identifying the problem or opportunity, (2) generating alternatives, (3) selecting an alternative, and (4) implementing and evaluating the solution.

Identifying the Problem or Opportunity

problem the discrepancy between an actual condition and a desired condition

A **problem** is the discrepancy between an actual condition and a desired condition—the difference between what is occurring and what one wishes would occur. For example, a marketing manager at Campbell Soup Company has a problem if sales revenues for Campbell's Hungry Man frozen dinners are declining (the actual condition). To solve this problem, the marketing manager must take steps to increase sales revenues (desired condition). Most people consider a problem to be "negative;" however, a problem also can be "positive." A positive problem should be viewed as an "opportunity."

Although accurate identification of a problem is essential before it can be solved or turned into an opportunity, this stage of decision making creates many difficulties for managers. Sometimes managers' preconceptions of the problem prevent them from seeing the actual situation. They produce an answer before the proper question has been asked. In other cases, managers overlook truly significant issues by focusing on unimportant matters. Also, managers may mistakenly analyze problems in terms of symptoms rather than underlying causes.

Effective managers learn to look ahead so that they are prepared when decisions must be made. They clarify situations and examine the causes of problems, asking whether the presence or absence of certain variables alters a situation. Finally, they consider how individual behaviors and values affect the way problems or opportunities are defined.

Generating Alternatives

After a problem has been defined, the next task is to generate alternatives. The more important the decision, the more attention is devoted to this stage. Managers should be open to fresh, innovative ideas as well as obvious answers.

Certain techniques can aid in the generation of creative alternatives. Brainstorming, commonly used in group discussions, encourages participants to produce many new ideas. Other group members are not permitted to criticize or ridicule. Another approach, developed by the U.S. Navy, is called "Blast! Then Refine." Group members tackle a recurring problem by erasing all previous solutions and procedures. The group then re-evaluates its original objectives, modifies them if necessary, and devises new solutions. Other techniques—including trial and error—are also useful in this stage of decision making.

Selecting an Alternative

Final decisions are influenced by a number of considerations, including financial constraints, human and informational resources, time limits, legal obstacles, and political factors. Managers must select the alternative that will be most effective and practical. Risky sub prime loans delivered a huge blow to the financial services giant—Citigroup. The mortgage meltdown forced the company to post $10 billion in losses, which was the worst loss that Citigroup had ever seen. The company also had to write down $18.1 billion on mortgage-backed securities and cut its dividend by 41%. After considering several alternatives that could improve its balance sheet,

Citigroup decided to raise about $20 billion from investors in Abu Dhabi, Singapore, and elsewhere.[13]

At times, two or more alternatives or some combination of alternatives will be equally appropriate. Managers may choose solutions to problems on several levels. The coined word "satisfice" describes solutions that are only adequate and not ideal. When lacking time or information, managers often make decisions that "satisfice." Whenever possible, managers should try to investigate alternatives carefully and select the ideal solution.

Sustaining the Planet

Check the Small Business Administration's Green Business Guide website for a wealth of ideas about starting, managing, and growing a green business. In addition to information about complying with environmental regulations, the site provides tips for improving energy efficiency, developing earth-friendly products, marketing a green business, and more.
www.business.gov/guides/environment

Implementing and Evaluating the Solution

Implementation of a decision requires time, planning, preparation of personnel, and evaluation of results. Managers usually deal with unforeseen consequences even when they have carefully considered the alternatives.

The final step in managerial decision making entails evaluating the effectiveness of a decision. If the alternative that was chosen removes the difference between the actual condition and the desired condition, the decision is judged effective. If the problem still exists, managers may select one of the following choices:

- Decide to give the chosen alternative more time to work.
- Adopt a different alternative.
- Start the problem identification process all over again.

Failure to evaluate decisions adequately may have negative consequences. Hewlett-Packard's former CEO, Carly Fiorina, suffered negative consequences after the controversial merger with Compaq Computer did not help the company's earnings performance. Because Hewlett-Packard's hardware units still were not highly competitive against the market leaders, Fiorina was replaced.[14]

Managing Total Quality

7 **Learning Objective: Describe how organizations benefit from total quality management.**

The management of quality is a high priority in some organizations today. Major reasons for a greater focus on quality include foreign competition, more demanding customers, and poor financial performance resulting from reduced market shares and higher costs. Over the last few years, several U.S. firms have lost the dominant competitive positions they had held for decades.

Total quality management is a much broader concept than just controlling the quality of the product itself (which is discussed in Chapter 9). **Total quality management (TQM)** is the coordination of efforts directed at improving customer satisfaction, increasing employee participation, strengthening supplier partnerships, and facilitating an organizational atmosphere of continuous quality improvement. For TQM programs to be effective, management must address each of the following components:

total quality management (TQM) the coordination of efforts directed at improving customer satisfaction, increasing employee participation, strengthening supplier partnerships, and facilitating an organizational atmosphere of continuous quality improvement

- *Customer satisfaction.* Ways to improve include producing higher-quality products, providing better customer service, and showing customers that the company cares.
- *Employee participation.* This can be increased by allowing employees to contribute to decisions, develop self-managed work teams, and assume responsibility for improving the quality of their work.
- *Strengthening supplier partnerships.* Developing good working relationships with suppliers can ensure that the right supplies and materials will be delivered on time at lower costs.
- *Continuous quality improvement.* This should not be viewed as achievable through one single program that has a target objective. A program based on continuous improvement has proven to be the most effective long-term approach.

Total quality management. *The CEO of Starbucks is presenting information to Starbucks managers regarding the importance and methods associated with total quality management at Starbucks.*

Although many factors influence the effectiveness of a TQM program, two issues are crucial. First, top management must make a strong commitment to a TQM program by treating quality improvement as a top priority and giving it frequent attention. Firms that establish a TQM program but then focus on other priorities will find that their quality-improvement initiatives will fail. Second, management must coordinate the specific elements of a TQM program so that they work in harmony with each other.

Although not all U.S. companies have TQM programs, these programs provide many benefits. Overall financial benefits include lower operating costs, higher return on sales and on investments, and an improved ability to use premium pricing rather than competitive pricing.

What It Takes to Become a Successful Manager Today

8

Learning Objective: Summarize what it takes to become a successful manager today.

Everyone hears stories about the corporate elite who make salaries in excess of $1 million a year, travel to and from work in chauffeur-driven limousines, and enjoy lucrative pension plans that provide for a luxurious lifestyle after they retire. Although management obviously can be a rewarding career, what is not so obvious is the amount of time and hard work needed to achieve the impressive salaries and perks.

A Day in the Life of a Manager

Organizations pay managers for performance. As already pointed out, managers coordinate an organization's resources. They also perform the four basic management functions: planning, organizing, leading and motivating, and controlling. And managers make decisions and then implement and evaluate those decisions. This heavy workload requires that managers work long hours, and most do not get paid overtime. Typically, the number of hours increases as a manager advances.

Today's managers have demanding jobs. Managers spend a great deal of time talking with people on an individual basis. The purpose of these conversations is

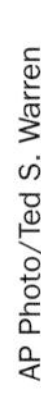
AP Photo/Ted S. Warren

usually to obtain information or to resolve problems. In addition, a manager often spends time in meetings with other managers and employees. In most cases, the purpose of the meetings—some brief and some lengthy—is to resolve problems. And if the work is not completed by the end of the day, the manager usually packs his or her unfinished tasks in a briefcase.

Skills Required for Success

To be successful in today's competitive business environment, you must possess a number of skills. Some of these skills—technical, conceptual, and interpersonal skills—were discussed earlier in this chapter. However, you also need "personal" skills. Oral and written communication skills, computer skills, and critical-thinking skills may give you the edge in getting an entry-level management position.

- *Oral communication skills.* Because a large part of a manager's day is spent conversing with others, the ability to speak *and* listen is critical. Oral communication skills are used when a manager makes sales presentations, conducts interviews, and holds press conferences.
- *Written communication skills.* A manager's ability to prepare letters, e-mails, memos, sales reports, and other written documents may spell the difference between success and failure.
- *Computer skills.* Most employers do not expect you to be an expert computer programmer, but they do expect that you should know how to use a computer to prepare written and statistical reports and to communicate with other managers and employees.
- *Critical-thinking skills.* Employers expect managers to use the steps for effective managerial decision making. They also expect managers to use critical-thinking

Entrepreneurial Challenge

Managing 24/7

In today's 24/7 global economy, time management is a vital skill for every entrepreneur. Here are two tips for making every second count as the boss of your own business:

- *Focus on your goals.* Profit is paramount for most small businesses, so spend your time doing things that are "closest to the money line," advises time-management expert Christi Youd. When unexpected problems pop up, let your goals guide you in deciding what must be done right away and what can wait.
- *Use technology wisely.* Cell phones, e-mail, and Internet technology can help you use your time more productively. The owner of Fritch Custom Log Homes in Oregon saves hours of travel time by holding online meetings with far-flung business contacts. However, avoid the technology trap of checking for messages every minute. And keep things simple: "If you really want to get in touch with me, give me a call," says Internet entrepreneur Jason Calacanis.

Sources: Matthew Bandyk, "Can't Get to a Meeting? Make It Virtual," *U.S. News & World Report,* June 17, 2008; Monica Hesse, "An Unmanageable Circle of Friends," *Washington Post,* August 26, 2007, p. M10; "Five Tips to Boost Productivity," *Wall Street Journal,* November 29, 2007, **www.wsj.com.**

Managerial skills. *An effective manager must be able to integrate and simultaneously employ several skills in order to be successful.*

RF PhotoDisc/Getty Images

skills to identify problems correctly, generate reasonable alternatives, and select the "best" alternatives to solve problems.

The Importance of Education and Experience

Although most experts agree that management skills must be learned on the job, the concepts that you learn in business courses lay the foundation for a successful career. In addition, successful completion of college courses or obtaining a degree can open doors to job interviews and career advancement.

There are methods you can use to "beef up" your résumé and to capitalize on your work experience. First, obtain summer jobs that provide opportunities to learn about the field that interests you. Chosen carefully, part-time jobs can provide work experience that other job applicants may not have. Some colleges and universities sponsor cooperative work/school programs that give students college credit for job experience. Even with solid academics and work experience, many would-be managers find it difficult to land the "right" job. Often they start in an entry-level position to gain more experience.

In the next chapter we examine the organizing function of managers in some detail. We look specifically at various organizational forms that today's successful businesses use. As with many factors in management, how a business is organized depends on its goals, strategies, and personnel.

return to inside business

Google

Decisions at Google are guided by the company's ambitious mission: To organize the world's information and make it universally accessible and useful. Everyone who makes decisions at Google must also follow the company's rule of making money "without doing evil."

Because both technology and the business environment are evolving so quickly, Google's managers know that their decisions must be speedy as well as smart. Sometimes they decide to test a new feature on the Google site, monitor user reaction, and fine-tune it accordingly. Even when the investment is very high—such as when the G1 cell phone was launched—Google's managers recognize that postponing decisions until tomorrow will only postpone the company's future success.

Questions

1. Why would Google want its employees and managers to feel free to participate in so many decisions? Do you agree with this policy? Explain your answer.
2. Of the three broad categories of managerial roles, which is likely to be the most important at Google? Why?

CHAPTER REVIEW

Summary

Define what management is.

Management is the process of coordinating people and other resources to achieve the goals of an organization. Managers are concerned with four types of resources—material, human, financial, and informational.

Describe the four basic management functions: planning, organizing, leading and motivating, and controlling.

Managers perform four basic functions. Management functions do not occur according to some rigid, preset timetable, though. At any time, managers may engage in a number of functions simultaneously. However, each function tends to lead naturally to others. First, managers engage in planning—determining where the firm should be going and how best to get there. Three types of plans, from the broadest to the most specific, are strategic plans, tactical plans, and operational plans. Managers also organize resources and activities to accomplish results in an efficient and effective manner, and they lead and motivate others to work in the best interests of the organization. In addition, managers control ongoing activities to keep the organization on course. There are three steps in the control function: setting standards, measuring actual performance, and taking corrective action.

Distinguish among the various kinds of managers in terms of both level and area of management.

Managers—or management positions—may be classified from two different perspectives. From the perspective of level within the organization, there are top managers, who control the fortunes of the organization; middle managers, who implement strategies and major policies; and first-line managers, who supervise the activities of operating employees. From the viewpoint of area of management, managers most often deal with the areas of finance, operations, marketing, human resources, and administration.

Identify the key management skills and the managerial roles.

Effective managers tend to possess a specific set of skills and to fill three basic managerial roles. Technical, conceptual, and interpersonal skills are all important, although the relative importance of each varies with the level of management within the organization. The primary managerial roles can be classified as decisional, interpersonal, or informational.

Explain the different types of leadership.

Managers' effectiveness often depends on their styles of leadership—that is, their ability to influence others, either formally or informally. Leadership styles include the authoritarian "do-it-my-way" style, the laissez-faire "do-it-your-way" style, and the democratic "let's-do-it-together" style.

Discuss the steps in the managerial decision-making process.

Decision making, an integral part of a manager's work, is the process of developing a set of possible alternative solutions to a problem and choosing one alternative from among the set. Managerial decision making involves four steps: Managers must accurately identify problems, generate several possible solutions, choose the solution that will be most effective under the circumstances, and implement and evaluate the chosen course of action.

Describe how organizations benefit from total quality management.

Total quality management (TQM) is the coordination of efforts directed at improving customer satisfaction, increasing employee participation, strengthening supplier partnerships, and facilitating an organizational atmosphere of continuous quality improvement. To have an effective TQM program, top management must make a strong, sustained commitment to the effort and must be able to coordinate all the program's elements so that they work in harmony. Overall financial benefits of TQM include lower operating costs, higher return on sales and on investment, and an improved ability to use premium pricing rather than competitive pricing.

Summarize what it takes to become a successful manager today.

Organizations pay managers for their performance. Managers coordinate resources. They also plan, organize, lead, motivate, and control. They make decisions that can spell the difference between an organization's success and failure. To complete their tasks, managers work long hours at a hectic pace. To be successful, they need personal skills (oral and written communication skills, computer skills, and critical-thinking skills), an academic background that provides a foundation for a management career, and practical work experience.

Key Terms

You should now be able to define and give an example relevant to each of the following terms:

Review Questions

1. Define the term *manager* without using the word *management* in your definition.
2. What is the mission of a neighborhood restaurant? Of the Salvation Army? What might be reasonable objectives for these organizations?
3. What does the term *optimization* mean?
4. How do a strategic plan, a tactical plan, and an operational plan differ? What do they all have in common?
5. What exactly does a manager organize, and for what reason?
6. Why are leadership and motivation necessary in a business in which people are paid for their work?
7. Explain the steps involved in the control function.
8. How are the two perspectives on kinds of managers—that is, level and area—different from each other?
9. In what ways are management skills related to the roles managers play? Provide a specific example to support your answer.
10. Compare and contrast the major styles of leadership.
11. Discuss what happens during each of the four steps of the managerial decision-making process.
12. What are the major benefits of a total quality management program?
13. What personal skills should a manager possess in order to be successful?

Discussion Questions

1. Does a healthy firm (one that is doing well) have to worry about effective management? Explain.
2. Which of the management functions, skills, and roles do not apply to the owner-operator of a sole proprietorship?
3. Which leadership style might be best suited to each of the three general levels of management within an organization?
4. According to this chapter, the leadership style that is *most* effective depends on interaction among the employees, characteristics of the work situation, and the manager's personality. Do you agree or disagree? Explain your answer.
5. Do you think that people are really as important to an organization as this chapter seems to indicate?
6. As you learned in this chapter, managers often work long hours at a hectic pace. Would this type of career appeal to you? Explain your answer.

Video Case 6.1

Student Advantage Helps College Students Stay Organized

Student Advantage is a Boston Company that is a leader in specialty debit cards. The company provides college students with credit cards that give them discounts on national brands as well as thousands of local shops and restaurants nationwide. Examples of the company's national brand partners include Alamo Rental Cars, AT&T, Amtrak, Barnes & Noble, Dick's Sporting Goods, Foot Locker, Toshiba, Greyhound, Target Stores, and Verizon Wireless, to mention a few. Their credit cards are distributed to student members on over a thousand university campuses in the United States.

Student Advantage started as a small entrepreneurial company that experienced explosive growth. The challenge for Ray Sozzi, the company's founder and CEO, was how to keep the spirit and culture that made the company an initial success while bringing in new processes (and the resultant bureaucracies that come with them) that companies need as they become larger enterprises. His overarching approach was to tie empowerment to accountability. Said simply, he makes sure that his managers take ownership for their decisions. He does not create plans and direct the organization to execute them. Rather, he lets the organization develop their plans and then gives them the empowerment necessary to execute them. He believes that one of the most powerful management strategies is to let people tell him what they want to do and then let them do it. He also believes that if his managers mess up either side of that equation, they're going to fail.

Another way in which he empowers his managers is by giving them a different perspective to what they want to do. Middle managers often have so many day-to-day tasks to confront and people reporting to them that they don't have the time to step back and look at the bigger picture. That's where Ray Sozzi plays an important role as a sounding board or devil's advocate. He believes he plays an important role in helping his managers to firm up the position they're taking or step back and rethink it. Also as CEO, he has a different perspective than his managers since he is more aware of what is happening externally from a competitive standpoint, is exposed to the needs and preferences of the company's shareholders, and understands the balance between investing in the company and providing shareholder value.

Responsibility, delegation, and accountability are central to the company's management style, and these principles are even more important as Student Advantage has grown to over 400 employees. The company is organized into a number of teams: Business Development, Marketing, Finance, Human Resources, etc. It is each team manager's responsibility to make that team's plans work. Communication is key in delegation. All team members need to understand what the team wants to accomplish and what each person's role is to make it happen. It's hard sometimes for a manager to give up control. It requires a certain amount of trust to give other people responsibility for what you're not touching; however, it's critical for an effective running organization. As one Student Advantage manger put it, "if you don't delegate, you die!"

The chain of command from CEO to COO to Department Head to Assistant Manager is pretty clear, but how does an effective organization work laterally, as opposed to vertically? As an example, in Student Advantage's marketing department, the marketing project manager is responsible for acquisition of new members (i.e., students) and member communications. This person works with the account manager who supports the partners, which are the companies who pay for the discounts to the members. Each of these employee's roles is not rigidly defined, but rather they help each other serve their respective members and partners. They help each other brainstorm and use the resources needed to accomplish the department's common goals. The lines between the various job functions in marketing (as well as the other teams) are very soft. Decisions are never made by just one department within marketing. Everyone has to discuss everything with everyone else. It allows each person to get different experiences beyond their job title and responsibility.

Student Advantage is still a relatively small company (albeit, it continues to be on a strong growth path), so their employees wear many different hats. Organizationally, the company is a well balanced organization. They stress a chain of command of flexible job descriptions, teamwork, and staff empowerment. The firm appears to be well organized and managed for continued growth in a very challenging marketplace.[15]

Questions

1. How would you describe Ray Sozzi's leadership style?
2. Based on the Management Process (shown in Figure 6.2), how does Ray Sozzi control the planning function?
3. What are some advantages and disadvantages of management practices that are employed at Student Advantage?

Case 6.2

Decision Making at DocuSign, Inc.

DocuSign, Inc., is the leading provider of fully automated electronic signature services, offering several different software products that allow companies to transmit documents online for e-signature in a fast, secure, and cost-saving way. DocuSign numbers companies in the financial services, e-commerce, mortgage, real estate, travel, and insurance industries among its customers. Founded in 2003 in Seattle, Washington, the firm recently passed the 14-million mark in terms of the number of electronic signatures it has executed.

Not long ago, however, DocuSign's executives faced a big problem. Many of its major customers at that time were mortgage lenders and college loan companies, which relied heavily on its e-signature services to speed the loan-approval process for their customers. But poor economic conditions and increased regulation threatened to slow or even shut down these companies' spending, imperiling DocuSign's revenue stream. "We were faced with large market shifts in two of our top segments," said CEO Matthew Schiltz, "both out of our control, and both within a 60-day period."

Instead of closeting themselves in a conference room to work out a solution to the crisis, Schiltz and his top managers called a town-hall style meeting of the entire company, gathering their 40 employees together to explain the situation. They described the new market conditions they faced, outlined what it meant for DocuSign, and asked everyone for input to help come up with a strategy to solve the problem. "We went straight to the people that deal with these customers on a daily basis, and that's our employees," said Schiltz.

Schiltz's dramatic approach to decision making in the company's moment of crisis worked. The firm began holding monthly company-wide meetings in which employees brainstormed new ways to measure the effect of changing market conditions. Schiltz also created subcommittees, smaller groups of employees charged with coming up with specific solutions like new products. "Dramatic positive change" happened in less than a year as employees rose to the challenge. New clients like lender Wells Fargo Funding and the online travel firm Expedia were signed. A new marketing program was developed to focus potential clients' attention on the environmental benefits of saving large amounts of paper each year, as well as the high costs of overnight shipping of documents, with digital transactions and e-signatures. The company came out of the crisis with a secure enough financial future to obtain more than $12 million in new venture capital to enable it to continue its growth.

Schiltz is happy with the more active role his employees now have in formulating DocuSign's business strategy. "You empower these people by telling them the truth and being open and honest with them," he said, but on the other hand, "we don't always want to get into a situation where our employees think that our senior management team doesn't have any input or doesn't have options. There's a balance there." For more information about the company, go to **www.docusign.com**.[16]

Questions

1. How closely did DocuSign's top managers follow the stages of management decision making as outlined in the chapter? Explain your answer.
2. Do you think Schiltz's move to share top management's decisional role with employees was an effective solution for his firm? Why or why not? Do you think it will be a good choice for the company's future?
3. Have you ever participated in a group decision-making situation, whether at work or in any organization to which you've belonged? Did it follow the stages of decision making outlined in the chapter, and how effective was it in solving a problem or resolving a crisis? What would you do differently, having read the chapter?

Building Skills for Career Success

1. JOURNALING FOR SUCCESS

Discovery statement: This chapter discussed the critical management function of leading and motivating others to work in the best interests of an organization. Think about your current job or a job that you had previously.

1. Who is the most outstanding leader with whom you have worked?
2. What was his or her position and in what capacity did you work with the person?
3. What are this person's outstanding leadership qualities?

4. Select the most outstanding leadership quality above and provide an example that demonstrates this quality.
5. Do most of your coworkers view this person as being an outstanding leader, too? Explain.

2. EXPLORING THE INTERNET

Most large companies call on a management consulting firm for a variety of services, including employee training, help in the selection of an expensive purchase such as a computer system, recruitment of employees, and direction in reorganization and strategic planning.

Large consulting firms generally operate globally and provide information to companies considering entry into foreign countries or business alliances with foreign firms. They use their websites, along with magazine-style articles, to celebrate achievements and present their credentials to clients. Business students can acquire an enormous amount of up-to-date information in the field of management by perusing these sites.

Assignment

1. Explore each of the following websites:
   Accenture: **www.accenture.com**
   BearingPoint (formerly KPMG Consulting): **www.bearingpoint.com**
   Cap Gemini Ernst & Young: **www.capgemini.com**
   Visit the text website for updates to this exercise.
2. Judging from the articles and notices posted, what are the current areas of activities of one of these firms?
3. Explore one of these areas in more detail by comparing postings from each firm's site. For instance, if "global business opportunities" appears to be a popular area of management consulting, how has each firm distinguished itself in this area? Who would you call first for advice?
4. Given that consulting firms are always trying to fill positions for their clients and to meet their own recruitment needs, it is little wonder that employment postings are a popular area on their sites. Examine these in detail. Based on your examination of the site and the registration format, what sort of recruit are they interested in?

3. DEVELOPING CRITICAL-THINKING SKILLS

As defined in the chapter, an organization's mission is a statement of the basic purpose that makes the organization different from others. Clearly, a mission statement, by indicating the purpose of a business, directly affects the company's employees, customers, and stockholders.

Assignment

1. Find the mission statements of three large corporations in different industries. The Internet is one source of mission statements. For example, you might search these sites:
   www.kodak.com
   www.benjerry.com
   www.usaa.com
2. Compare the mission statements on the basis of what each reflects about the philosophy of the company and its concern for employees, customers, and stockholders.
3. Which company would you like to work for and why?
4. Prepare a report on your findings.

4. BUILDING TEAM SKILLS

Over the past few years, an increasing number of employees, stockholders, and customers have been demanding to know what their companies are about. As a result, more companies have been taking the time to analyze their operations and to prepare mission statements that focus on the purpose of the company. The mission statement is becoming a critical planning tool for successful companies. To make effective decisions, employees must understand the purpose of their company.

Assignment

1. Divide into teams and write a mission statement for one of the following types of businesses:
   Food service, restaurant
   Banking
   Airline
   Auto repair
   Cabinet manufacturing
2. Discuss your mission statement with other teams. How did the other teams interpret the purpose of your company? What is the mission statement saying about the company?
3. Write a one-page report on what you learned about developing mission statements.

5. RESEARCHING DIFFERENT CAREERS

A successful career requires planning. Without a plan, or roadmap, you will find it very difficult, if not impossible, to reach your desired career destination. The first step in planning is to establish what your career goal is. You then must set objectives and develop plans for accomplishing those objectives. This kind of planning takes time, but it will pay off later.

Assignment

Complete the following statements:

1. My career goal is to

   ____

   ____

   This statement should encapsulate what you want to accomplish over the long run. It may include the type of job you want and the type of business or industry you want to work in. Examples include the following:
   - My career goal is to work as a top manager in the food industry.
   - My career goal is to supervise aircraft mechanics.
   - My career goal is to win the top achievement award in the advertising industry.
2. My career objectives are to

   ____

   ____

   Objectives are benchmarks along the route to a career destination. They are more specific than a career goal. A statement about a career objective should specify what you want to accomplish, when you will complete it, and any other details that will serve as criteria against which you can measure your progress. Examples include the following:
   - My objective is to be promoted to supervisor by January 1, 20xx.
   - My objective is to enroll in a management course at Main College in the spring semester 20xx.
   - My objective is to earn an A in the management course at Main College in the spring semester 20xx.
   - My objective is to prepare a status report by September 30 covering the last quarter's activities by asking Charlie in Quality Control to teach me the procedures.
3. Exchange your goal and objectives statements with another class member. Can your partner interpret your objectives correctly? Are the objectives concise and complete? Do they include criteria against which you can measure your progress? If not, discuss the problem and rewrite the objective.

7 Creating a Flexible Organization

LEARNING OBJECTIVES

What you will be able to do once you complete this chapter:

1. Understand what an organization is and identify its characteristics.
2. Explain why job specialization is important.
3. Identify the various bases for departmentalization.
4. Explain how decentralization follows from delegation.
5. Understand how the span of management describes an organization.
6. Understand how the chain of command is established by using line and staff management.
7. Describe the four basic forms of organizational structure: bureaucratic, matrix, cluster, and network.
8. Summarize the use of corporate culture, intrapreneurship, committees, coordination techniques, informal groups, and the grapevine.

inside business

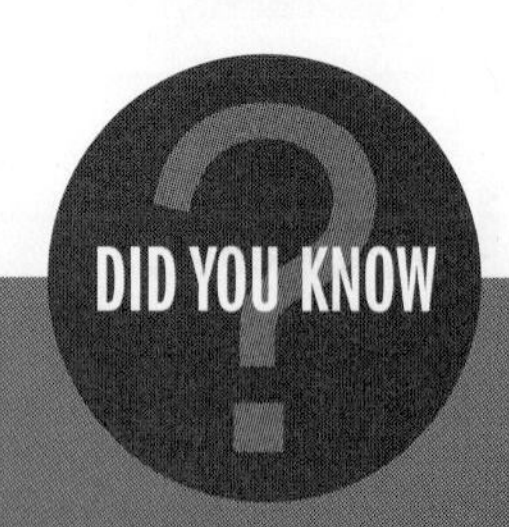

Disney recruits service-minded employees, provides extensive training, and allows new hires 90 days to settle into the organization, even if this means trying them in two or three different jobs.

Walt Disney Rocks by Making Dreams Come True

The Walt Disney Company's organizational world spans the world of entertainment from animated movies to online media, theme parks to consumer products. Founded as a California movie studio in 1923, Disney has expanded from its show-business roots to become a global empire with $35 billion in annual revenue.

Walt Disney Studios, the company's original business, shot to fame in the 1920s with its Mickey Mouse cartoons and the full-length animated film *Snow White and the Seven Dwarfs*. Disney got started in movie merchandising in 1929, when a local firm asked permission to put Mickey Mouse on the cover of a children's notebook. In the 1950s, Disney morphed into an entertainment company by opening the Disneyland theme park in Anaheim, California.

In the 1980s, it created the Disney Channel cable network, founded Touchstone Television to produce programs like *Golden Girls*, and opened the first Disney Store. In the 1990s, it bought ABC and ESPN, expanded online with websites for children and adults, and took Broadway by storm with its staging of *Beauty and the Beast*. Disney also owned (and later sold) the Mighty Ducks hockey team and the Anaheim Angels baseball team.

Over the years, Disney has prospered—even during the recent economic crisis—because of its can-do corporate culture, which focuses on "making dreams come true" customer service. Disney recruits service-minded employees, provides extensive training, and allows new hires 90 days to settle into the organization, even if this means trying them in two or three different jobs. Fitting the right person to the right job is important because "we transfer decision-making authority down to the lowest level possible," says a Disney manager.

In fact, Disney's reputation for top-quality service has led to yet another profitable business opportunity. The Disney Institute, staffed by experienced Disney trainers, charges other companies to take managers behind the scenes at Disney facilities and show them how to make customers' dreams come true through exceptional service.[1]

To survive and to grow, companies such as Disney must constantly look for ways to improve their methods of doing business. Managers at Global Hyatt, like those at many other organizations, deliberately reorganized the company to achieve its goals and to create satisfying products that foster long-term customer relationships.

When firms are organized, or reorganized, the focus is sometimes on achieving low operating costs. Other firms, such as Nike, emphasize providing high-quality products to ensure customer satisfaction. A firm's organization influences its performance. Thus, the issue of organization is important.

We begin this chapter by examining the business organization—what it is and how it functions in today's business environment. Next, we focus one by one on five characteristics that shape an organization's structure. We discuss job specialization within a company, the grouping of jobs into manageable units or departments, the delegation of power from management to workers, the span of management, and establishment of a chain of command. Then we step back for an overall view of four approaches to organizational structure: the bureaucratic structure, the matrix structure, the cluster structure, and the network structure. Finally, we look at the network of social interactions—the informal organization—that operates within the formal business structure.

What Is an Organization?

1

Learning Objective: Understand what an organization is and identify its characteristics.

We used the term *organization* throughout Chapter 6 without really defining it mainly because its everyday meaning is close to its business meaning. Here, however, let us agree that an **organization** is a group of two or more people working together to achieve a common set of goals. A neighborhood dry cleaner owned and operated by a husband-and-wife team is an organization. IBM and Home Depot, which employ thousands of workers worldwide, are also organizations in the same sense. Although each corporation's organizational structure is more complex than the dry-cleaning establishment, all must be organized to achieve their goals.

organization a group of two or more people working together to achieve a common set of goals

An inventor who goes into business to produce and market a new invention hires people, decides what each will do, determines who will report to whom, and so on. These activities are the essence of organizing, or creating, the organization. One way to create this "picture" is to create an organization chart.

Developing Organization Charts

An **organization chart** is a diagram that represents the positions and relationships within an organization. An example of an organization chart is shown in Figure 7.1. Each rectangle represents a particular position or person in the organization. At the top is the president; at the next level are the vice presidents. The solid vertical lines connecting the vice presidents to the president indicate that the vice presidents are in the chain of command. The **chain of command** is the line of authority that extends from the highest to the lowest levels of the organization. Moreover, each vice president reports directly to the president. Similarly, the plant managers, regional sales managers, and accounting department manager report to the vice presidents. The chain of command can be short or long. For example, at Royer's Roundtop Café, an independent restaurant in Roundtop, Texas, the chain of command is very short. Bud Royer, the owner, is responsible only to himself and can alter his hours or change his menu quickly. On the other hand, the chain of command at McDonald's is long. Before making certain types of changes, a McDonald's franchisee seeks permission from regional management, which, in turn, seeks approval from corporate headquarters.

organization chart a diagram that represents the positions and relationships within an organization

chain of command the line of authority that extends from the highest to the lowest levels of an organization

ImagineChina via AP Images

Job specialization. *These workers have jobs with a considerable amount of specialization. In this factory, umbrellas will be completed after more than 80 different processes.*

In the chart, the connections to the directors of legal services, public affairs, and human resources are shown as broken lines; these people are not part of the direct chain of command. Instead, they hold *advisory,* or *staff,* positions. This difference will be examined later in this chapter when we discuss line and staff positions.

Most smaller organizations find organization charts useful. They clarify positions and reporting relationships for everyone in the organization, and they help managers to track growth and change in the organizational structure. For two reasons, however, many large organizations, such as ExxonMobil, Kellogg's, and Procter & Gamble, do not maintain complete, detailed charts. First, it is difficult to chart even a few dozen positions accurately, much less the thousands that characterize larger firms. And second, larger organizations are almost always changing parts of their structure. An organization chart would be outdated before it was completed. However, organization must exist even without a chart in order for a business to be successful. Technology is helping large companies implement up-to-date organization charts. Workstream, Inc., is a provider of enterprise workforce management software and has signed big-name clients. Carol Caruso, an organizational design specialist at Mercedes-Benz USA, reported that the software saves time and effort in communicating organizational structure. Aside from providing organization charts, the software also will support human resources processes such as workflow approval and succession planning.[2]

Five Steps for Organizing a Business

When a firm is started, management must decide how to organize the firm. These decisions are all part of five major steps that sum up the organizing process. The five steps are as follows:

Figure 7.1: A Typical Corporate Organization Chart

A company's organization chart represents the positions and relationships within the organization and shows the managerial chains of command.

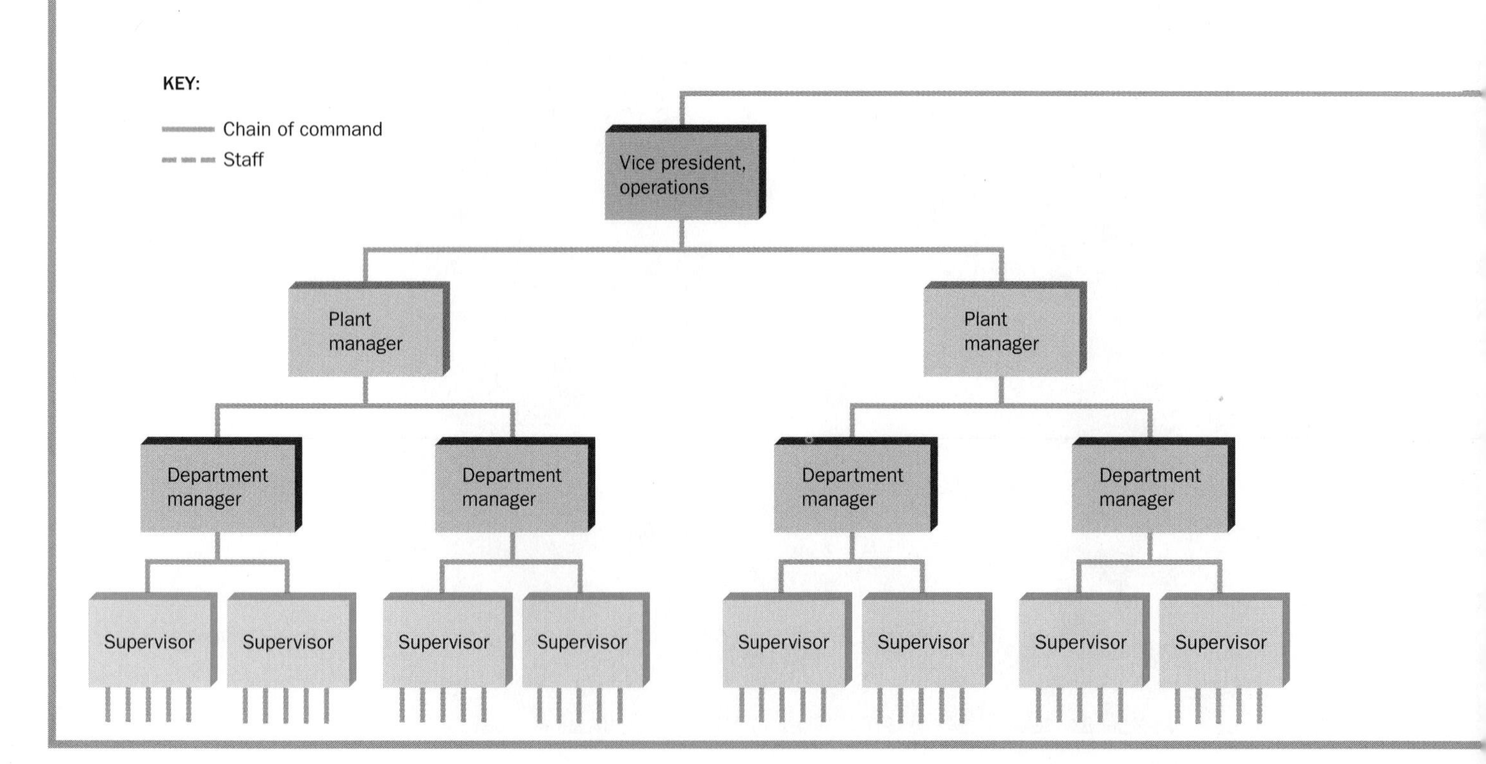

1. *Job design.* Divide the work that is to be done by the entire organization into separate parts, and assign those parts to positions within the organization.
2. *Departmentalization.* Group the various positions into manageable units or departments.
3. *Delegation.* Distribute responsibility and authority within the organization.
4. *Span of management.* Determine the number of subordinates who will report to each manager.
5. *Chain of command.* Establish the organization's chain of command by designating the positions with direct authority and those that are support positions.

Sustaining the Planet

To bring sustainability into every aspect of their business, some corporations are expanding the organization chart to include the job of chief sustainability officer (CSO). At Georgia-Pacific, which makes building products, packaging, and paper, the CSO is responsible for helping each business unit develop sustainability goals, strategies, measurement, and reporting. **www.gp.com**

In the next several sections, we discuss major issues associated with these steps.

Job Design

2 Learning Objective: Explain why job specialization is important.

In Chapter 1, we defined *specialization* as the separation of a manufacturing process into distinct tasks and the assignment of different tasks to different people. Here we are extending that concept to *all* the activities performed within an organization.

Job Specialization

job specialization the separation of all organizational activities into distinct tasks and the assignment of different tasks to different people

Job specialization is the separation of all organizational activities into distinct tasks and the assignment of different tasks to different people. Adam Smith, the

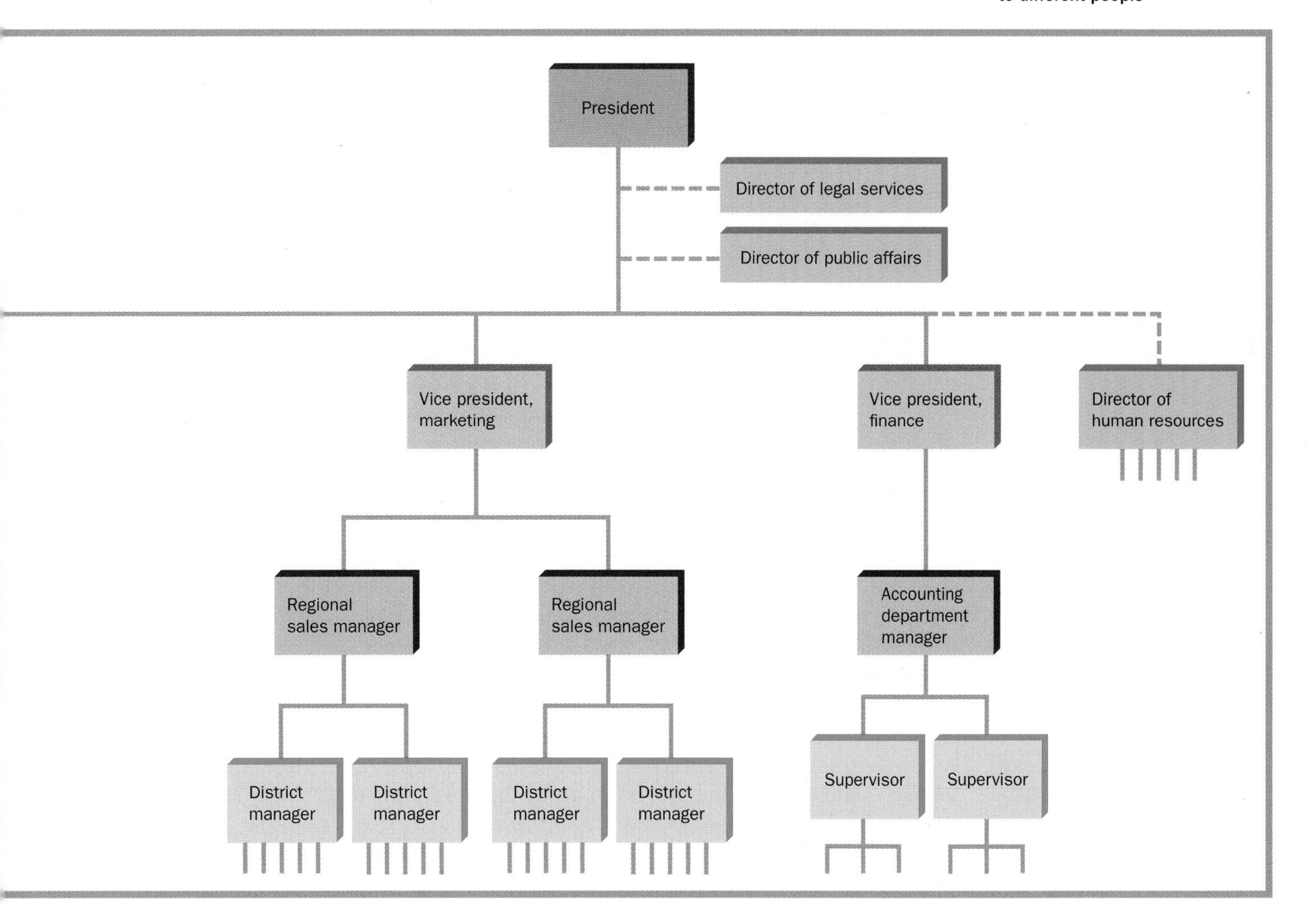

Ethics Matters

Just a Number?

With 385,000 employees worldwide and $99 billion in annual revenue, IBM is always looking for better ways to organize and manage its workforce. It's not surprising that IBM would use its technical expertise to be sure the right people are doing the right things. But is IBM taking job specialization too far by reducing employees' knowledge, skills, activities, and internal connections to numbers that can be mathematically manipulated for maximum efficiency?

The company already collects and analyzes lots of employee information. Although confidential files are excluded, IBM tracks nearly everything else about its technical consultants. It examines their work experience, educational background, and compensation level. It looks at their computerized calendars to see where they are, who they meet, and what they do, hour by hour. And it monitors their online activities, cell-phone usage, and e-mail patterns.

IBM's goal is to use the data to improve the way it defines organizational tasks and relationships. Through sophisticated computer modeling, the company will soon be able to determine the exact role a specific employee might play in a project and calculate the financial impact of having a different employee in that role. Despite the bottom-line possibilities, should IBM pay more attention to human elements rather than approaching job specialization in terms of numbers?

Sources: Eddie Evans, "Mathematicians Are New Masters of the Universe," *Reuters*, September 12, 2008, **www.reuters.com**; Stephen Baker, "Management by the Numbers," *BusinessWeek*, September 8, 2008, pp. 32–38.

eighteenth-century economist whose theories gave rise to capitalism, was the first to emphasize the power of specialization in his book, *The Wealth of Nations*. According to Smith, the various tasks in a particular pin factory were arranged so that one worker drew the wire for the pins, another straightened the wire, a third cut it, a fourth ground the point, and a fifth attached the head. Smith claimed that ten men were able to produce 48,000 pins per day. Before specialization, they could produce only 200 pins per day because each worker had to perform all five tasks!

The Rationale for Specialization

For a number of reasons, some job specialization is necessary in every organization because the "job" of most organizations is too large for one person to handle. In a firm such as DaimlerChrysler, thousands of people are needed to manufacture automobiles. Others are needed to sell the cars, control the firm's finances, and so on.

Second, when a worker has to learn one specific, highly specialized task, that individual should be able to learn it very efficiently. Third, a worker repeating the same job does not lose time changing from operations, as the pin workers did when producing complete pins. Fourth, the more specialized the job, the easier it is to design specialized equipment. And finally, the more specialized the job, the easier is the job training.

Alternatives to Job Specialization

Unfortunately, specialization can have negative consequences as well. The most significant drawback is the boredom and dissatisfaction employees may feel when repeating the same job. Bored employees may be absent from work frequently, may not put much effort into their work, and may even sabotage the company's efforts to produce quality products.

To combat these problems, managers often turn to job rotation. **Job rotation** is the systematic shifting of employees from one job to another. For example, a worker may be assigned a different job every week for a four-week period and then return to the first job in the fifth week. Job rotation provides a variety of tasks so that workers are less likely to become bored and dissatisfied.

job rotation the systematic shifting of employees from one job to another

Two other approaches—job enlargement and job enrichment—also can provide solutions to the problems caused by job specialization. These topics, along with other methods used to motivate employees, are discussed in Chapter 11.

Departmentalization

3

Learning Objective: Identify the various bases for departmentalization.

After jobs are designed, they must be grouped together into "working units," or departments. This process is called *departmentalization*. More specifically, **departmentalization** is the process of grouping jobs into manageable units. Several departmentalization bases are used commonly. In fact, most firms use more than one. Today, the most common bases for organizing a business into effective departments are by function, by product, by location, and by customer.

departmentalization the process of grouping jobs into manageable units

RF Getty

By Function

Departmentalization by function groups jobs that relate to the same organizational activity. Under this scheme, all marketing personnel are grouped together in the marketing department, all production personnel in the production department, and so on.

departmentalization by function grouping jobs that relate to the same organizational activity

Most smaller and newer organizations departmentalize by function. Supervision is simplified because everyone is involved in the same activities, and coordination is easy. The disadvantages of this method of grouping jobs are that it can lead to slow decision making and that it tends to emphasize the department over the whole organization.

By Product

Departmentalization by product groups activities related to a particular good or service. This approach is used often by older and larger firms that produce and sell a variety of products. Each department handles its own marketing, production, financial management, and human resources activities.

departmentalization by product grouping activities related to a particular product or service

Departmentalization by product makes decision making easier and provides for the integration of all activities associated with each product. However, it causes some duplication of specialized activities—such as finance—from department to department. And the emphasis is placed on the product rather than on the whole organization.

By Location

Departmentalization by location groups activities according to the defined geographic area in which they are performed. Departmental areas may range from whole countries (for international firms) to regions within countries (for national firms) to areas of several city blocks (for police departments organized into precincts). Departmentalization by location allows the organization to respond readily to the unique demands or requirements of different locations. Nevertheless, a large administrative staff and an elaborate control system may be needed to coordinate operations in many locations.

departmentalization by location grouping activities according to the defined geographic area in which they are performed

By Customer

Departmentalization by customer groups activities according to the needs of various customer populations. A local Chevrolet dealership, for example, may have one sales staff to deal with individual consumers and a different sales staff to work with corporate fleet buyers. The obvious advantage of this approach is that it allows the firm to deal efficiently with unique customers or customer groups. The biggest drawback is that a larger-than-usual administrative staff is needed.

departmentalization by customer grouping activities according to the needs of various customer populations

Combinations of Bases

Many organizations use more than one of these departmentalization bases.

Take a moment to examine Figure 7.2. Notice that departmentalization by customer is used to organize New-Wave Fashions, Inc., into three major divisions: men's, women's, and children's clothing. Then functional departmentalization is used to distinguish the firm's production and marketing activities. Finally, location is used to organize the firm's marketing efforts.

Delegation, Decentralization, and Centralization

4

Learning Objective: Explain how decentralization follows from delegation.

The third major step in the organizing process is to distribute power in the organization. **Delegation** assigns part of a manager's work and power to other workers. The degree of centralization or decentralization of authority is determined by the overall pattern of delegation within the organization.

Delegation of Authority

delegation assigning part of a manager's work and power to other workers

Because no manager can do everything, delegation is vital to completion of a manager's work. Delegation is also important in developing the skills and abilities of

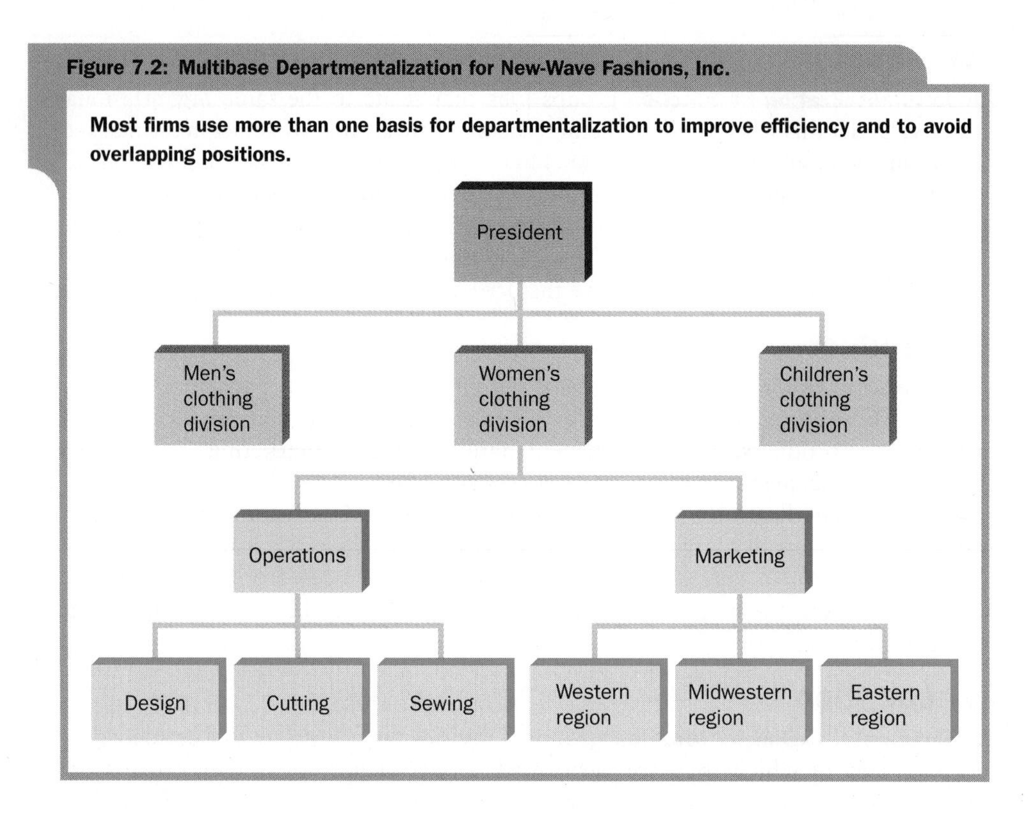

Figure 7.2: Multibase Departmentalization for New-Wave Fashions, Inc.

Most firms use more than one basis for departmentalization to improve efficiency and to avoid overlapping positions.

subordinates. It allows those who are being groomed for higher-level positions to play increasingly important roles in decision making.

responsibility the duty to do a job or perform a task

authority the power, within an organization, to accomplish an assigned job or task

accountability the obligation of a worker to accomplish an assigned job or task

Steps in Delegation The delegation process generally involves three steps (see Figure 7.3). First, the manager must *assign responsibility*. **Responsibility** is the duty to do a job or perform a task. In most job settings, a manager simply gives the worker a job to do. Typical job assignments might range from having a worker prepare a report on the status of a new quality control program to placing the person in charge of a task force. Second, the manager must *grant authority*. **Authority** is the power, within the organization, to accomplish an assigned job or task. This might include the power to obtain specific information, order supplies, authorize relevant expenditures, or make certain decisions. Finally, the manager must *create accountability*. **Accountability** is the obligation of a worker to accomplish an assigned job or task.

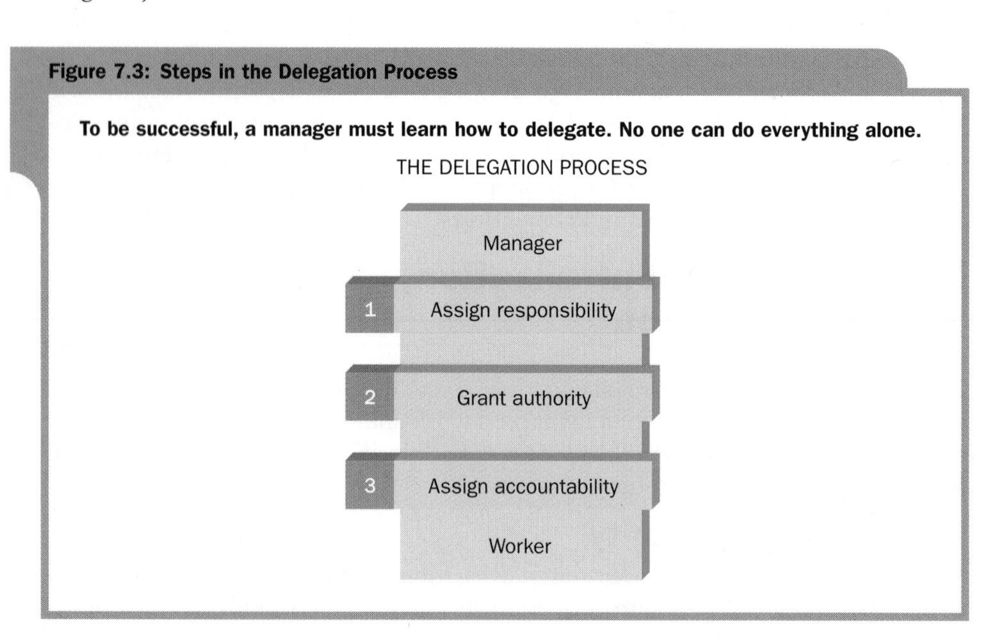

Figure 7.3: Steps in the Delegation Process

To be successful, a manager must learn how to delegate. No one can do everything alone.

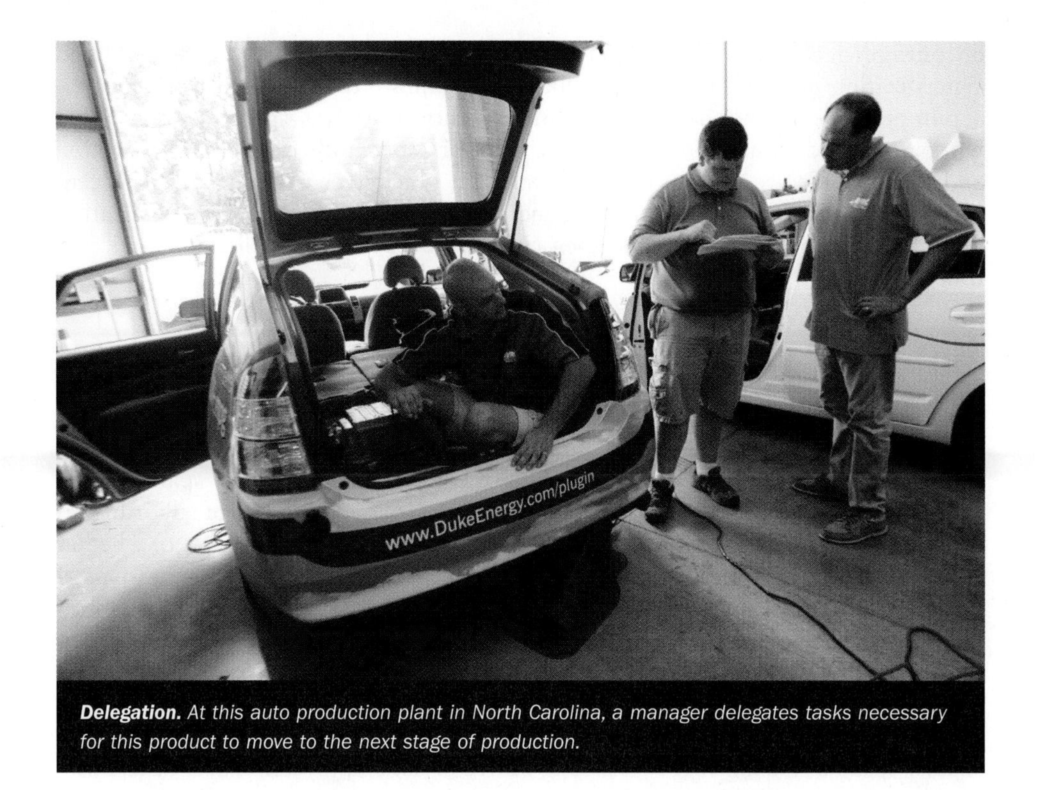

Delegation. *At this auto production plant in North Carolina, a manager delegates tasks necessary for this product to move to the next stage of production.*

Note that accountability is created, but it cannot be delegated. Suppose that you are an operations manager for Target and are responsible for performing a specific task. You, in turn, delegate this task to someone else. You nonetheless remain accountable to your immediate supervisor for getting the task done properly. If the other person fails to complete the assignment, you—not the person to whom you delegated the task—will be held accountable.

Barriers to Delegation For several reasons, managers may be unwilling to delegate work. Many managers are reluctant to delegate because they want to be sure that the work gets done. Another reason for reluctance stems from the opposite situation. The manager fears that the worker will do the work well and attract the approving notice of higher-level managers. Finally, some managers do not delegate because they are so disorganized that they simply are not able to plan and assign work effectively.

Decentralization of Authority

The pattern of delegation throughout an organization determines the extent to which that organization is decentralized or centralized. In a **decentralized organization**, management consciously attempts to spread authority widely across various organization levels. A **centralized organization**, on the other hand, systematically works to concentrate authority at the upper levels. For example, many publishers of college-level textbooks are centralized organizations, with authority concentrated at the top. Large organizations may have characteristics of both decentralized and centralized organizations.

decentralized organization an organization in which management consciously attempts to spread authority widely in the lower levels of the organization

centralized organization an organization that systematically works to concentrate authority at the upper levels of the organization

A number of factors can influence the extent to which a firm is decentralized. One is the external environment in which the firm operates. The more complex and unpredictable this environment, the more likely it is that top management will let lower-level managers make important decisions. After all, lower-level managers are closer to the problems. Another factor is the nature of the decision itself. The riskier or more important the decision, the greater is the tendency to centralize decision making. A third factor is the abilities of lower-level managers. If these managers do not have strong decision-making skills, top managers will be reluctant to decentralize. And, in contrast, strong lower-level decision-making skills

encourage decentralization. Finally, a firm that traditionally has practiced centralization or decentralization is likely to maintain that posture in the future.

In principle, neither decentralization nor centralization is right or wrong. What works for one organization may or may not work for another. Kmart Corporation and McDonald's are very successful—and both practice centralization. But decentralization has worked very well for General Electric and Sears. Every organization must assess its own situation and then choose the level of centralization or decentralization that will work best.

The Span of Management

5

Learning Objective: Understand how the span of management describes an organization.

span of management (or span of control) the number of workers who report directly to one manager

The fourth major step in organizing a business is establishing the **span of management** (or **span of control**), which is the number of workers who report directly to one manager. For hundreds of years, theorists have searched for an ideal span of management. When it became apparent that there is no perfect number of subordinates for a manager to supervise, they turned their attention to the general issue of whether the span should be wide or narrow. This issue is complicated because the span of management may change by department within the same organization. For example, the span of management at FedEx varies within the company. Departments in which workers do the same tasks on a regular basis—customer service agents, handlers and sorters, couriers—usually have a span of management of fifteen to twenty employees per manager. Groups performing multiple and different tasks are more likely to have smaller spans of management consisting of five or six employees.[3] Thus, FedEx uses a wide span of control in some departments and a narrower one in others.

Wide and Narrow Spans of Control

A *wide* span of management exists when a manager has a larger number of subordinates. A *narrow* span exists when the manager has only a few subordinates. Several factors determine the span that is better for a particular manager (see Figure 7.4). Generally, the span of control may be wide when (1) the manager and the subordinates are very competent, (2) the organization has a well-established set

Figure 7.4: The Span of Management

Several criteria determine whether a firm uses a wide span of management, in which a number of workers report to one manager, or a narrow span, in which a manager supervises only a few workers.

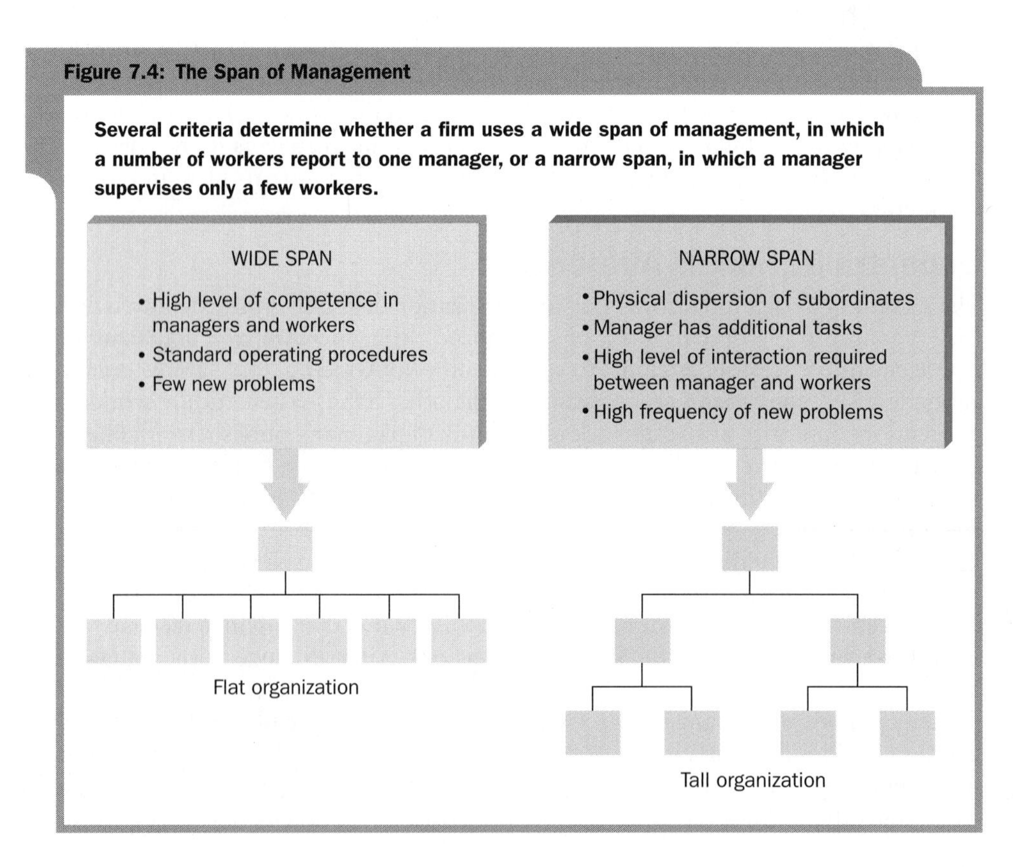

of standard operating procedures, and (3) few new problems are expected to arise. The span should be narrow when (1) workers are physically located far from one another, (2) the manager has much work to do in addition to supervising workers, (3) a great deal of interaction is required between supervisor and workers, and (4) new problems arise frequently.

Organizational Height

The span of management has an obvious impact on relations between managers and workers. It has a more subtle but equally important impact on the height of the organization. **Organizational height** is the number of layers, or levels, of management in a firm. The span of management plays a direct role in determining the height of the organization, as shown in Figure 7.4. If spans of management are wider, fewer levels are needed, and the organization is *flat*. If spans of management generally are narrow, more levels are needed, and the resulting organization is *tall*.

organizational height the number of layers, or levels, of management in a firm

In a taller organization, administrative costs are higher because more managers are needed. Communication among levels may become distorted because information has to pass up and down through more people. When companies are cutting costs, one option is to decrease organizational height in order to reduce related administrative expenses. When a high-tech defense contractor needed to reduce its enormous cost structure, top management decided to eliminate an entire layer of management, resulting in a flatter organization.[4] Although flat organizations avoid these problems, their managers may perform more administrative duties simply because there are fewer managers. Wide spans of management also may require managers to spend considerably more time supervising and working with subordinates.

line management position a part of the chain of command; it is a position in which a person makes decisions and gives orders to subordinates to achieve the goals of the organization

Chain of Command: Line and Staff Management

6

Learning Objective: Understand how the chain of command is established by using line and staff management.

Establishing the chain of command is another step in organizing a business. It reaches from the highest to the lowest levels of management. A **line management position** is part of the chain of command; it is a position in which a person makes decisions and gives orders to subordinates to achieve the goals of the organization. A **staff management position**, by contrast, is a position created to provide support, advice, and expertise to someone in the chain of command. Staff managers are not part of the chain of command but do have authority over their assistants (see Figure 7.5).

staff management position a position created to provide support, advice, and expertise within an organization

Line and Staff Positions Compared

Both line and staff managers are needed for effective management, but the two positions differ in important ways. The basic difference is in terms of authority. Line managers have *line authority*, which means that they can make decisions and issue directives relating to the organization's goals.

Staff managers seldom have this kind of authority. Instead, they usually have either advisory authority or functional authority. *Advisory authority* is the expectation that line managers will consult the appropriate staff manager when making decisions. Functional authority is stronger. *Functional authority* is the authority of staff managers to make decisions and issue directives about their areas of expertise. For example, a legal adviser for Nike can decide whether to retain a particular clause in a contract but not product pricing.

Line-Staff Conflict

For a variety of reasons, conflict between line managers and staff managers is fairly common in businesses. Staff managers often have more formal education and sometimes are younger (and perhaps more ambitious) than line managers. Line managers may perceive staff managers as a threat to their own authority and thus may resent them. For their part,

Line and staff positions. *Ronald McDonald occupies a staff position and does not have direct authority over other employees at McDonald's. The other individuals shown here occupy line positions and do have direct authority over some of the other McDonald's employees.*

Feature Photo Service/McDonald's

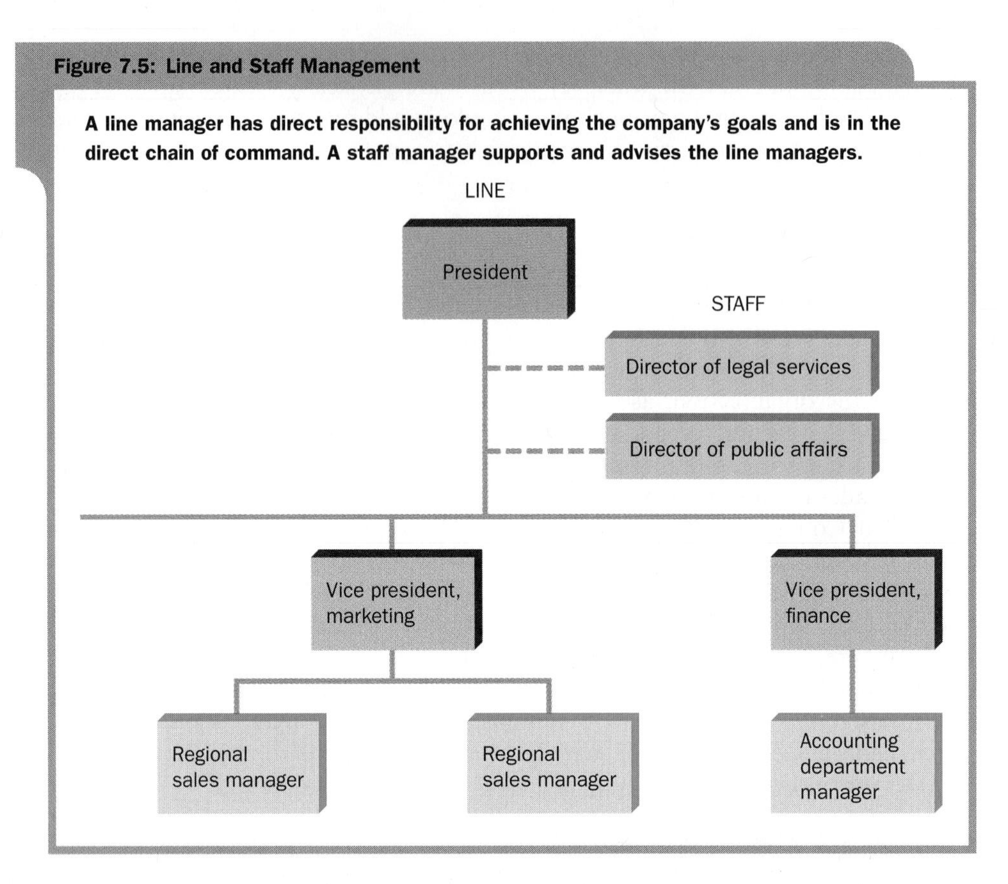

Figure 7.5: Line and Staff Management

A line manager has direct responsibility for achieving the company's goals and is in the direct chain of command. A staff manager supports and advises the line managers.

staff managers may become annoyed or angry if their expert recommendations—in public relations or human resources management, for example—are not adopted by line management.

Fortunately, there are several ways to minimize the likelihood of such conflict. One way is to integrate line and staff managers into one team. Another is to ensure that the areas of responsibility of line and staff managers are clearly defined. Finally, line and staff managers both can be held accountable for the results of their activities.

Before studying the next topic—forms of organizational structure—you may want to review the five organization-shaping characteristics that we have just discussed. See Table 7.1 for a summary.

Table 7.1: Five Characteristics of Organizational Structure

Dimension	Purpose
Job design	To divide the work performed by an organization into parts and assign each part a position within the organization.
Departmentalization	To group various positions in an organization into manageable units. Departmentalization may be based on function, product, location, customer, or a combination of these bases.
Delegation	To distribute part of a manager's work and power to other workers. A deliberate concentration of authority at the upper levels of the organization creates a centralized structure. A wide distribution of authority into the lower levels of the organization creates a decentralized structure.
Span of management	To set the number of workers who report directly to one manager. A narrow span has only a few workers reporting to one manager. A wide span has a large number of workers reporting to one manager.
Line and staff management	To distinguish between those positions that are part of the chain of command and those that provide support, advice, or expertise to those in the chain of command.

Forms of Organizational Structure

7

Learning Objective: Describe the four basic forms of organizational structure: bureaucratic, matrix, cluster, and network.

Up to this point, we have focused our attention on the major characteristics of organizational structure. In many ways, this is like discussing the parts of a jigsaw puzzle one by one. It is time to put the puzzle together. In particular, we discuss four basic forms of organizational structure: bureaucratic, matrix, cluster, and network.

The Bureaucratic Structure

The term *bureaucracy* is used often in an unfavorable context to suggest rigidity and red tape. This image may be negative, but it does capture some of the essence of the bureaucratic structure.

A **bureaucratic structure** is a management system based on a formal framework of authority that is outlined carefully and followed precisely. A bureaucracy is likely to have the following characteristics:

bureaucratic structure a management system based on a formal framework of authority that is outlined carefully and followed precisely

1. A high level of job specialization
2. Departmentalization by function
3. Formal patterns of delegation
4. A high degree of centralization
5. Narrow spans of management, resulting in a tall organization
6. Clearly defined line and staff positions with formal relationships between the two

Perhaps the best examples of contemporary bureaucracies are government agencies, colleges, and universities. Consider the very rigid college entrance and registration procedures. The reason for such procedures is to ensure that the organization is able to deal with large numbers of people in an equitable and fair manner. We may not enjoy them, but regulations and standard operating procedures guarantee uniform treatment.

Another example of a bureaucratic structure is the U.S. Postal Service. Like colleges and universities, the Postal Service relies on procedures and rules to accomplish the organization's goals. However, the Postal Service has streamlined some of its procedures and initiated new services in order to compete with FedEx, UPS, and other delivery services. As a result, customer satisfaction has begun to improve.

AP Photo/Ben Margot

Bureaucratic structure. *The U.S. Postal Service is a bureaucracy with numerous rules, requirements, and specified procedures.*

The biggest drawback to the bureaucratic structure is lack of flexibility. A bureaucracy has trouble adjusting to change and coping with the unexpected. Because today's business environment is dynamic and complex, many firms have found that the bureaucratic structure is not an appropriate organizational structure.

The Matrix Structure

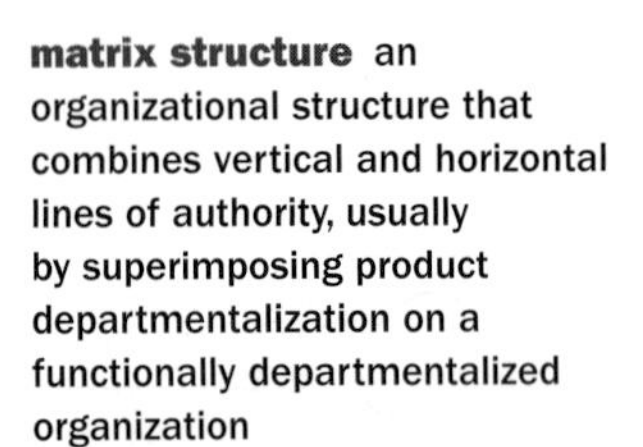

matrix structure an organizational structure that combines vertical and horizontal lines of authority, usually by superimposing product departmentalization on a functionally departmentalized organization

cross-functional team a team of individuals with varying specialties, expertise, and skills that are brought together to achieve a common task

When the matrix structure is used, individuals report to more than one superior at the same time. The **matrix structure** combines vertical and horizontal lines of authority. The matrix structure occurs when product departmentalization is superimposed on a functionally departmentalized organization. In a matrix organization, authority flows both down and across.

To understand the structure of a matrix organization, consider the usual functional arrangement, with people working in departments such as engineering, finance, and marketing. Now suppose that we assign people from these departments to a special group that is working on a new project as a team—a cross-functional team. A **cross-functional team** consists of individuals with varying specialties, expertise, and skills that are brought together to achieve a common task. Frequently, cross-functional teams are charged with the responsibility of developing new products. For example, Ford Motor Company assembled a special project team to design and manufacture its global cars. The manager in charge of a team is usually called a *project manager.* Any individual who is working with the team reports to *both* the project manager and the individual's superior in the functional department (see Figure 7.6).

Cross-functional team projects may be temporary, in which case the team is disbanded once the mission is accomplished, or they may be permanent. These teams often are empowered to make major decisions. When a cross-functional team is employed, prospective team members may receive special training because effective teamwork can require different skills. For cross-functional teams to be successful, team members must be given specific information on the job each performs. The

Figure 7.6: A Matrix Structure

A matrix is usually the result of combining product departmentalization with function departmentalization. It is a complex structure in which employees have more than one supervisor.

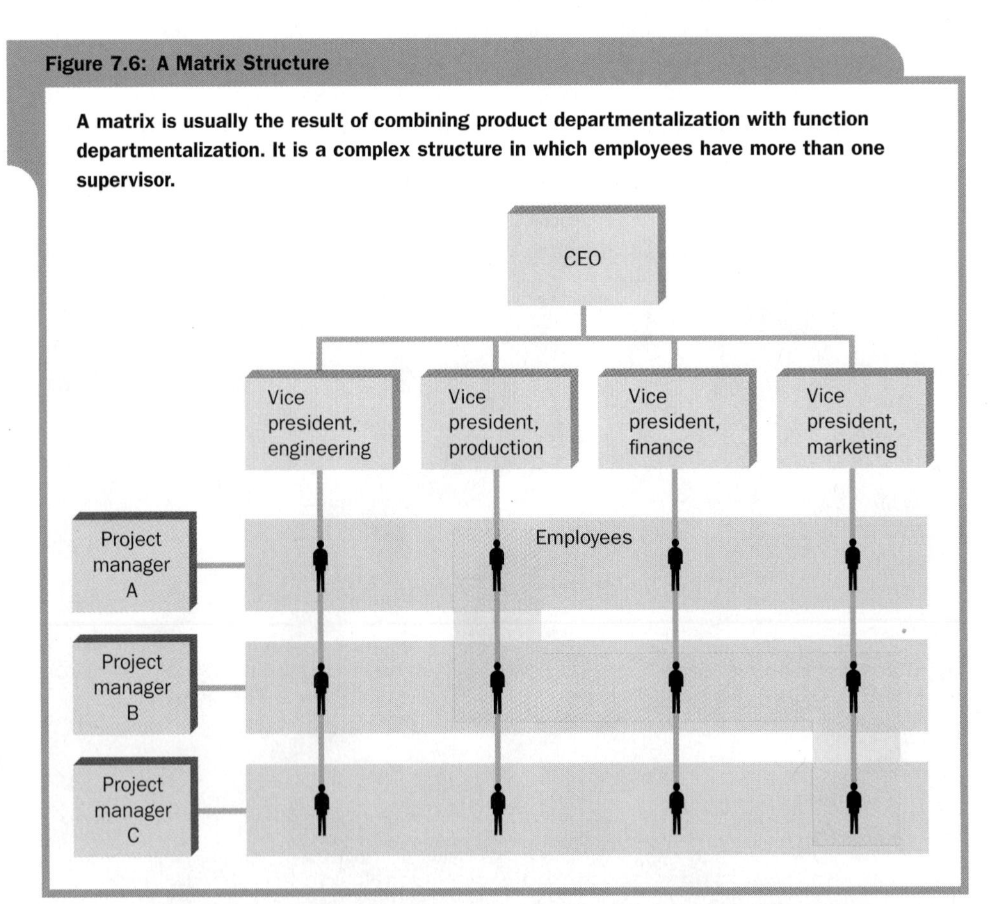

Source: Ricky W. Griffin, *Management,* 9th ed. Copyright © 2008 by Houghton Mifflin Company. Adapted with permission.

team also must develop a sense of cohesiveness and maintain good communications among its members.

Matrix structures offer advantages over other organizational forms. Added flexibility is probably the most obvious advantage. The matrix structure also can increase productivity, raise morale, and nurture creativity and innovation. In addition, employees experience personal development through doing a variety of jobs.

The matrix structure also has disadvantages. Having employees report to more than one supervisor can cause confusion about who is in charge. Like committees, teams may take longer to resolve problems and issues than individuals working alone. Other difficulties include personality clashes, poor communication, undefined individual roles, unclear responsibilities, and finding ways to reward individual and team performance simultaneously. Because more managers and support staff may be needed, a matrix structure may be more expensive to maintain.

The Cluster Structure

A **cluster structure** is a type of business that consists primarily of teams with no or very few underlying departments. This type of structure is also called *team* or *collaborative*. In this type of organization, team members work together on a project until it is finished, and then the team may remain intact and be assigned another project, or team members may be reassigned to different teams, depending on their skills and the needs of the organization. In a cluster organization, the operating unit is the team, and it remains relatively small. If a team becomes too large, it can be split into multiple teams, or individuals can be assigned to other existing teams.

cluster structure an organization that consists primarily of teams with no or very few underlying departments

The cluster organizational structure has both strengths and weaknesses. Keeping the teams small provides the organization with the flexibility necessary to change directions quickly, to try new techniques, and to explore new ideas. Some employees in these types of organizations express concerns regarding job security and the increased amount of stress that arises owing to the fact that changes occur rapidly.[5]

AP Photo/Keith Srakocic

Corporate culture—let the good times roll (and fly)! *Southwest Airlines employees celebrate a new Southwest Airlines route. Southwest Airlines' corporate culture values altruism, humor, hard work, and fun.*

SPOTLIGHT

If You Have Two Equal Job Offers and One Company Is "Green," Would That Affect Your Decision?

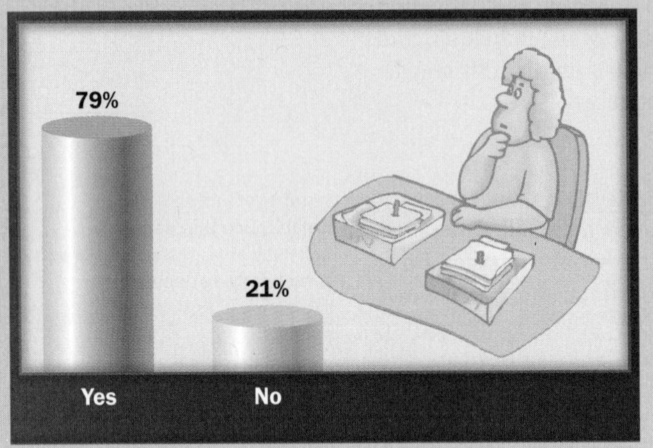

Source: www.experience.com, accessed November 25, 2008.

The Network Structure

In a **network structure** (sometimes called a *virtual organization*), administration is the primary function performed, and other functions such as engineering, production, marketing, and finance are contracted out to other organizations. Frequently, a network organization does not manufacture the products it sells. This type of organization has a few permanent employees consisting of top management and hourly clerical workers. Leased facilities and equipment, as well as temporary workers, are increased or decreased as the needs of the organization change. Thus, there is rather limited formal structure associated with a network organization.

An obvious strength of a network structure is flexibility that allows the organization to adjust quickly to changes. Some of the challenges faced by managers in network-structured organizations include controlling the quality of work performed by other organizations, low morale and high turnover among hourly workers, and the vulnerability associated with relying on outside contractors.

Additional Factors That Influence an Organization

8

Learning Objective: Summarize the use of corporate culture, intrapreneurship, committees, coordination techniques, informal groups, and the grapevine.

network structure an organization in which administration is the primary function, and most other functions are contracted out to other firms

corporate culture the inner rites, rituals, heroes, and values of a firm

As you might expect, other factors in addition to those already covered in this chapter affect the way a large corporation operates on a day-to-day basis. To get a "true picture" of the organizational structure of a huge corporation such as Marriott, for example, which employs over 151,000 people,[6] you need to consider the topics discussed in this section.

Corporate Culture

Most managers function within a corporate culture. A **corporate culture** is generally defined as the inner rites, rituals, heroes, and values of a firm. An organization's culture has a powerful influence on how employees think and act. It also can determine public perception of the organization.

Corporate culture generally is thought to have a very strong influence on a firm's performance over time. Hence, it is useful to be able to assess a firm's corporate culture. Common indicators include the physical setting (building, office layouts), what the company says about its corporate culture (in advertising and news releases), how the company greets guests (does it have formal or informal reception areas?), and how employees spend their time (working alone in an office or working with others).

Goffee and Jones have identified four distinct types of corporate cultures (see Figure 7.7). One is called the *networked culture,* characterized by a base of trust and friendship among employees, a strong commitment to the organization, and an informal environment. The *mercenary culture* embodies the feelings of passion, energy, sense of purpose, and excitement for one's work. The term *mercenary* does not imply that employees are motivated to work only for the money, but this is part of it. In this culture, employees are very intense, focused, and determined to win. In the *fragmented culture,* employees do not become friends, and they work "at" the organization, not "for" it. Employees have a high degree of autonomy, flexibility, and equality. The *communal culture* combines the positive traits of the networked

Going Global

Keeping the Culture from Country to Country

A strong corporate culture can bring a global workforce together even when employees work thousands of miles apart. For example, HSBC Group's corporate culture is shared and shaped by 312,000 bank employees in 85 countries. Although the culture emphasizes bottom-line concepts such as outstanding customer service and profitable performance, it also sends a powerful message about getting involved in social issues. Over the years, HSBC has donated more than $100 million to combat climate change, and employees who help local environmental projects know they'll draw their regular pay while they volunteer.

Some companies go so far as to share their corporate culture with certain partners. The office furniture firm Herman Miller, which is getting ready for a major international expansion, recently outsourced its recruitment function to Spherion. It provided Spherion employees with corporate culture training and had them visit Herman Miller factories to get a first-hand feel for how the culture works. Because of their immersion in Herman Miller's corporate culture, Spherion's employees can do a better job of recruiting candidates for both domestic and international positions.

Sources: Emily Stone, "Bank Sends Workers into the Woods," *Crain's Chicago Business*, August 25, 2008, p. 30; Michelle V. Rafter, "The Culture Connection," *Workforce Management*, July 14, 2008, p. 39.

culture and the mercenary culture—those of friendship, commitment, high focus on performance, and high energy. People's lives revolve around the product in this culture, and success by anyone in the organization is celebrated by all.[7]

Some experts believe that cultural change is needed when a company's environment changes, when the industry becomes more competitive, the company's performance is mediocre, and when the company is growing or is about to become a truly large organization. For example, top executives at Dell Computer allocated considerable time and resources to develop a strong, positive corporate culture aimed at increasing employee loyalty and the success of the company. Organizations in the future will look quite different. Experts predict that tomorrow's businesses will be comprised of small, task-oriented work groups, each with control over its own activities. These small groups will be coordinated through an elaborate computer network and held together by a strong corporate culture. Businesses operating in fast-changing industries will require leadership that supports trust and risk taking. Creating a culture of trust in an organization can lead to increases in growth, profit, productivity, and job satisfaction. A culture of trust can retain the best people, inspire customer loyalty, develop new markets, and increase creativity.

Figure 7.7: Types of Corporate Cultures

Which corporate culture would you choose?

Networked Culture	**Communal Culture**
• Extrovert energized by relationships • Tolerant of ambiguities and have low needs for structure • Can spot politics and act to stop "negative" politics • Consider yourself easygoing, affable, and loyal to others	• You consider yourself passionate • Strong need to identify with something bigger than yourself • You enjoy being in teams • Prepared to make sacrifices for the greater good
Fragmented Culture	**Mercenary Culture**
• Are a reflective and self-contained introvert • Have a high autonomy drive and strong desire to work independently • Have a strong sense of self	• Goal-oriented and have an obsessive desire to complete tasks • Thrive on competitive energy • Keep "relationships" out of work—develop them

Source: "Types of Corporate Culture," in Rob Goffee and Gareth Jones, *The Character of a Corporation* (New York: HarperCollins, 1998). Copyright © 1998 by Rob Goffee and Gareth Jones. Permission granted by Rob Goffee and Gareth Jones by arrangement with The Helen Rees Literary Agency.

Jump-Starting Your Career

Unleash Your Inner Intrapreneur

Do you have what it takes to be an intrapreneur? For a start, you'll need:

- *Ideas.* You don't have to be a top-level executive to have good ideas. "Creative ideas can come from anywhere," says the CEO of software giant Adobe, which actively solicits employees' ideas for new products and projects.
- *Perspective.* Put your idea into perspective. What will it do for customers and the company? "There is no more powerful way to communicate why your idea is an improvement than to use the words of a customer or employee who is clamoring for it," notes Alicia Ledlie, a store manager who was on the team that launched Wal-Mart into the business of in-store health clinics.
- *Persistence.* "Pursuing innovation at today's companies is like running a marathon at a sprint—it's incredibly hard work that seems to go on forever," says Kathy Hollenhorst of Caribou Coffee. She spent more than a year researching and fine-tuning her idea to test a customer loyalty reward program. Hollenhorst's persistence paid off: The test went so well that her program has now been implemented throughout the company.

Sources: Shreya Biswas, "India Inc Bets on 'Intrapreneurs,'" *The Economic Times,* September 10, 2008, **www.economictimes.indiatimes.com**; Georgia Flight, "How They Did It: Seven Intrapreneur Success Stories," *BNet Business Network,* n,d., **www.bnet.com/2403-13070_23-196890.html**; Georgia Flight, "Rules of Innovation from a Wal-Mart Pro," *BNet Business Network,* n.d., **www.bnet.com/2403-13070_23-196887.html.**

intrapreneur an employee who pushes an innovative idea, product, or process through an organization

ad hoc committee a committee created for a specific short-term purpose

standing committee a relatively permanent committee charged with performing some recurring task

Another area where corporate culture plays a vital role is the integration of two or more companies. Business leaders often cite the role of corporate cultures in the integration process as one of the primary factors affecting the success of a merger or acquisition. Experts note that corporate culture is a way of conducting business both within the company and externally. If two merging companies do not address differences in corporate culture, they are setting themselves up for missed expectations and possibly failure.[8]

Improving coordination. *Technologically advanced communication products allow managers to coordinate the activities of workers.*

Intrapreneurship

Since innovations and new-product development are important to companies, and since entrepreneurs are innovative people, it seems almost natural that an entrepreneurial character would surface prominently in many of today's larger organizations. An **intrapreneur** is an employee who takes responsibility for pushing an innovative idea, product, or process through an organization.[9] An intrapreneur possesses the confidence and drive of an entrepreneur but is allowed to use organizational resources for idea development. For example, Art Fry, inventor of the colorful Post-it Notes that Americans can't live without, is a devoted advocate of intrapreneurship. Nurturing his notepad idea at Minnesota Mining and Manufacturing (3M) for years, Fry speaks highly of the intrapreneurial commitment at 3M. Fry indicates that an *intrapreneur* is an individual who does not have all the skills to get the job done and thus has to work within an organization, making use of its skills and attributes.

Committees

Today, business firms use several types of committees that affect organizational structure. An **ad hoc committee** is created for a specific short-term purpose, such as reviewing the firm's employee benefits plan. Once its work is finished, the ad hoc committee disbands. A **standing committee** is a relatively permanent committee charged with performing a recurring task. A firm might establish a budget review committee, for example, to review departmental budget requests on an ongoing basis. Finally, a **task force** is a committee established to investigate a major problem or pending decision. A firm contemplating a merger with another company might form a task force to assess the pros and cons of the merger.

task force a committee established to investigate a major problem or pending decision

Committees offer some advantages over individual action. Their several members are able to bring information and knowledge to the task at hand. Furthermore, committees tend to make more accurate decisions and to transmit their results through the organization more effectively. However, committee deliberations take longer than individual actions. In addition, unnecessary compromise may take place within the committee. Or the opposite may occur, as one person dominates (and thus negates) the committee process.

Coordination Techniques

A large organization is forced to coordinate organizational resources to minimize duplication and to maximize effectiveness. One technique is simply to make use of the **managerial hierarchy**, which is the arrangement that provides increasing authority at higher levels of management. One manager is placed in charge of all the resources being coordinated. That person is able to coordinate them by virtue of the authority accompanying his or her position.

managerial hierarchy the arrangement that provides increasing authority at higher levels of management

Resources also can be coordinated through rules and procedures. For example, a rule can govern how a firm's travel budget is allocated. This particular resource, then, would be coordinated in terms of that rule.

In complex situations, more sophisticated coordination techniques may be called for. One approach is to establish a liaison. A *liaison* is a go-between—a person who coordinates the activities of two groups. Suppose that General Motors is negotiating a complicated contract with a supplier of steering wheels. The supplier might appoint a liaison whose primary responsibility is to coordinate the contract negotiations. Finally, for *very* complex coordination needs, a committee could be established. Suppose that General Motors is in the process of purchasing the steering wheel supplier. In this case, a committee might be appointed to integrate the new firm into General Motors' larger organizational structure.

informal organization the pattern of behavior and interaction that stems from personal rather than official relationships

informal group a group created by the members themselves to accomplish goals that may or may not be relevant to an organization

The Informal Organization

So far, we have discussed the organization as a formal structure consisting of interrelated positions. This is the organization that is shown on an organization chart. There is another kind of organization, however, that does not show up on any chart. We define this **informal organization** as the pattern of behavior and interaction that stems from personal rather than official relationships. Firmly embedded within every informal organization are informal groups and the notorious grapevine.

grapevine the informal communications network within an organization

Informal Groups An **informal group** is created by the group members themselves to accomplish goals that may or may not be relevant to the organization. Workers may create an informal group to go bowling, form a union, get a particular manager fired or transferred, or for lunch. The group may last for several years or a few hours.

Informal groups can be powerful forces in organizations. They can restrict output, or they can help managers through tight spots. They can cause disagreement and conflict, or they can help to boost morale and job satisfaction. They can show new people how to contribute to the organization, or they can help people to get away with substandard performance. Clearly, managers should be aware of these informal groups. Those who make the mistake of fighting the informal organization have a major obstacle to overcome.

Informal groups. *Informal groups, such as these employees at Midway Home Entertainment, can be a source of information and camaraderie for participants. Although informal groups can sometimes create problems for an organization, they can also provide significant benefits.*

The Grapevine The **grapevine** is the informal communications network within an organization. It is completely separate from—and sometimes much faster than—the organization's formal channels of communication. Formal

SPOTLIGHT

Is One or More of Your Coworkers Annoying?

Source: hotjobs.yahoo.com, accessed November 25, 2008.

communications usually follow a path that parallels the organizational chain of command. Information can be transmitted through the grapevine in any direction—up, down, diagonally, or horizontally across the organizational structure. Subordinates may pass information to their bosses, an executive may relay something to a maintenance worker, or there may be an exchange of information between people who work in totally unrelated departments. Grapevine information may be concerned with topics ranging from the latest management decisions to gossip.

How should managers treat the grapevine? Certainly, it would be a mistake to try to eliminate it. People working together, day in and day out, are going to communicate. A more rational approach is to recognize its existence. For example, managers should respond promptly and aggressively to inaccurate grapevine information to minimize the damage that such misinformation might do. Moreover, the grapevine can come in handy when managers are on the receiving end of important communications from the informal organization.

In the next chapter, we apply these and other management concepts to an extremely important business function: the production of goods and services.

return to inside business

Walt Disney

Disney's diverse entertainment businesses—including movie and television studios and channels, theme parks, vacation resorts, cruise ships, movie merchandise, Broadway shows, and online interactive sites, and video games—bring in profits from Florida to France and beyond. The company departmentalizes jobs according to product (in this case, by entertainment unit) and function (such as theme park "cast member").

In addition, Disney hires people who enjoy working with customers, standardizes procedures for consistent service quality, and decentralizes authority so customer-contact managers and employees have the power to make on-the-spot decisions. Finally, Disney recognizes that to deliver great customer service, it must set the stage by delivering a great employee experience throughout the organization.

Questions

1. Do you agree with Disney's policy of trying new hires in different jobs during their first 90 days to find the best fit within the organization? Explain your answer.
2. Given what you know about Disney, would you expect it to have a wide or a narrow span of control? Why?

CHAPTER REVIEW

Summary

Understand what an organization is and identify its characteristics.

An organization is a group of two or more people working together to achieve a common set of goals. The relationships among positions within an organization can be illustrated by means of an organization chart. Five specific characteristics—job design, departmentalization, delegation, span of management, and chain of command—help to determine what an organization chart and the organization itself look like.

Explain why job specialization is important.

Job specialization is the separation of all the activities within an organization into smaller components and the assignment of those different components to different people. Several factors combine to make specialization a useful technique for designing jobs, but high levels of specialization may cause employee dissatisfaction and boredom. One technique for overcoming these problems is job rotation.

3 Identify the various bases for departmentalization.

Departmentalization is the grouping of jobs into manageable units. Typical bases for departmentalization are by function, product, location, or customer. Because each of these bases provides particular advantages, most firms—especially larger ones—use a combination of different bases in different organizational situations.

4 Explain how decentralization follows from delegation.

Delegation is the assigning of part of a manager's work to other workers. It involves the following three steps: (a) assigning responsibility, (b) granting authority, and (c) creating accountability. A decentralized firm is one that delegates as much power as possible to people in the lower management levels. In a centralized firm, on the other hand, power is systematically retained at the upper levels.

5 Understand how the span of management describes an organization.

The span of management is the number of workers who report directly to a manager. Spans generally are characterized as wide (many workers per manager) or narrow (few workers per manager). Wide spans generally result in flat organizations (few layers of management); narrow spans generally result in tall organizations (many layers of management).

6 Understand how the chain of command is established by using line and staff management.

A line position is one that is in the organization's chain of command or line of authority. A manager in a line position makes decisions and gives orders to workers to achieve the goals of the organization. On the other hand, a manager in a staff position provides support, advice, and expertise to someone in the chain of command. Staff positions may carry some authority, but it usually applies only within staff areas of expertise.

7 Describe the four basic forms of organizational structure: bureaucratic, matrix, cluster, and network.

There are four basic forms of organizational structure. The bureaucratic structure is characterized by formality and rigidity. With the bureaucratic structure, rules and procedures are used to ensure uniformity. The matrix structure may be visualized as product departmentalization superimposed on functional departmentalization. With the matrix structure, an employee on a cross-functional team reports to both the project manager and the individual's supervisor in a functional department. A cluster structure is an organization that consists primarily of teams with very few underlying functional departments. In an organization with a network structure, the primary function performed internally is administration, and other functions are contracted out to other firms.

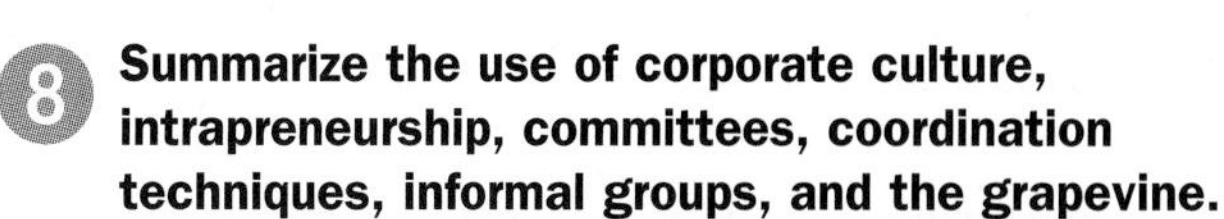

8 Summarize the use of corporate culture, intrapreneurship, committees, coordination techniques, informal groups, and the grapevine.

Corporate culture—the inner rites, rituals, heroes, and values of a firm—is thought to have a very strong influence on a firm's performance over time. An intrapreneur is an employee in an organizational environment who takes responsibility for pushing an innovative idea, product, or process through the organization. Additional elements that influence an organization include the use of committees and the development of techniques for achieving coordination among various groups within the organization. Finally, both informal groups created by group members and an informal communication network called the grapevine may affect an organization and its performance.

Key Terms

You should now be able to define and give an example relevant to each of the following terms:

organization (191)
organization chart (191)
chain of command (191)
job specialization (193)
job rotation (194)
departmentalization (194)
departmentalization by function (195)
departmentalization by product (195)
departmentalization by location (195)
departmentalization by customer (195)
delegation (195)
responsibility (196)
authority (196)
accountability (196)
decentralized organization (197)
centralized organization (197)
span of management (or span of control) (198)
organizational height (199)
line management position (199)
staff management position (199)
bureaucratic structure (201)
matrix structure (202)
cross-functional team (202)
cluster structure (203)
network structure (204)
corporate culture (204)
intrapreneur (206)
ad hoc committee (206)
standing committee (206)
task force (207)
managerial hierarchy (207)
informal organization (207)
informal group (207)
grapevine (207)

Review Questions

1. In what way do organization charts create a picture of an organization?
2. What is the chain of command in an organization?
3. What determines the degree of specialization within an organization?
4. Describe how job rotation can be used to combat the problems caused by job specialization.
5. What are the major differences among the four departmentalization bases?
6. Why do most firms employ a combination of departmentalization bases?
7. What three steps are involved in delegation? Explain each.
8. How does a firm's top management influence its degree of centralization?
9. How is organizational height related to the span of management?
10. What are the key differences between line and staff positions?
11. Contrast the bureaucratic and matrix forms of organizational structure.
12. What are the differences between the cluster structure and the network structure?
13. What is corporate culture? Describe the major types.
14. Which form of organizational structure probably would lead to the strongest informal organization? Why?
15. How may the managerial hierarchy be used to coordinate the organization's resources?

Discussion Questions

1. Explain how the five steps of the organizing process determine the characteristics of the resulting organization. Which steps are most important?
2. Which kinds of firms probably would operate most effectively as centralized firms? As decentralized firms?
3. How do decisions concerning span of management, the use of committees, and coordination techniques affect organizational structure?
4. How might a manager go about formalizing the informal organization?

Video Case 7.1

Organizing for Success at Green Mountain Coffee Roasters

Even with a workforce of 600, Green Mountain Coffee Roasters, based in Waterbury, Vermont, stays as entrepreneurial as when Bob Stiller founded the company in 1981 with one coffee shop and a handful of employees. The original plan was to open a series of coffee shops throughout New England. By the time Green Mountain Coffee had grown to twelve shops, profitability was struggling, so Stiller switched to importing, roasting, and wholesaling high-quality coffee beans to stores, food-service professionals, and restaurants around the country. Today, his company brews up profits from $137 million in annual sales to Aramark Food Service, McDonald's New England outlets, Wild Oats Market groceries, Publix supermarkets, and 7,000 other businesses.

Jobs at Green Mountain Coffee are departmentalized into six functions: sales and marketing, operations, human resources, finance, information systems, and social responsibility. The organization chart shows how specialized jobs are linked by a distinct chain of command leading to CEO Bob Stiller at the top. What the chart doesn't show, however, is how collaboration and communication among all levels—rather than strict hierarchy—gives the company a decision-making edge.

This is a flat organization, with only four levels between a corporate salesperson and the CEO. In line with the company's collaborative culture, decisions are made by inviting employees from different functions and different levels to offer their input. Decisions may take a little more time under this system, but they're more informed and usually yield a better solution to the problem than if handled by a single manager or a tiny group.

For a particularly challenging decision, Green Mountain Coffee relies on a "constellation" of communication to collect ideas from around the organization. Managers frequently post decision data on the corporate computer system and ask coworkers for comments. They also exchange a blizzard of e-mail messages and call cross-functional meetings, when necessary, to share information and opinions. Ultimately, the manager closest to the situation is responsible for evaluating all the data and making the decision, guided by the company's values.

Green Mountain Coffee's values are revealed in its mission statement: "We create the ultimate coffee experience in every life we touch from tree to cup—transforming the way the world understands business." Because the company buys from hundreds of coffee growers and sells to thousands of businesses as well as thousands of consumers who order by mail or online, it touches a lot of lives. Social responsibility ranks high on Green Mountain Coffee's corporate agenda. It is known for donating considerable cash, coffee, and volunteer time to the communities it serves in the United States and in coffee-producing nations.

Every year the company flies dozens of employees to Central America to see how coffee beans are grown, meet the growers, and learn about the farming communities. "The effect is profound," says Stephen Sabol, vice president of development. "The knowledge of the care that goes into the coffee is important, but when [employees] see the social part of it, and how dependent these growers are on us being a quality partner, it hits right home—the obligation we have to do well." After one of these "Coffee Source Trips," employees come back to work with renewed energy and dedication.

Green Mountain Coffee Roasters not only has been cited as one of the fastest-growing companies in the United States, but it also has been named among the most socially responsible. The CEO recognizes that his company must do well in order to do good. "To help the world, we have to be successful," Stiller says. "If we help the world and go out of business, we're not going to help anybody."[10]

For more information about this company, visit its Web site at **www.greenmountaincoffee.com.**

Questions

1. How is Green Mountain Coffee's "constellation" of communication likely to affect the informal organization?
2. Does Green Mountain Coffee appear to have a networked, communal, mercenary, or fragmented culture? Support your answer.
3. Is Green Mountain Coffee a centralized or decentralized organization? How do you know?

Case 7.2

Saturn: Still a Different Kind of Company?

Saturn was only an idea in 1983—General Motors' new idea about how to organize a car company. The idea was to give the company and its employees a lot more autonomy instead of imposing the rigid rules and conventions under which auto factories normally operated. Yet, since 1990, when the Saturn plant opened in Spring Hill, Tennessee, GM has changed the organization little by little. Is today's Saturn still a different kind of car company?

The Saturn project went into high gear after GM and the United Auto Workers came to agreement about having plant employees take a more active role. Instead of operating under an inflexible system of narrow job specialization, the plan was for Saturn's employees to work in teams and handle a variety of tasks as needed. The new company was to be managed as a separate entity and therefore hired its own engineers, developed its own vehicles, and purchased its own supplies and raw materials. GM also built Saturn a new state-of-the-art plant at a cost of $3.5 billion. And to reinforce Saturn's independence from the GM hierarchy, its top manager was designated its CEO.

By the time the first sedans started rolling off the assembly line, Saturn had established itself as a different kind of car company. Customers welcomed the "no haggle, no hassle" pricing policy as a change from the back-and-forth price negotiation they usually had to endure when buying a car. Just as important, Saturn's dealers put extra emphasis on service and satisfaction, making customers feel especially appreciated.

Such a mystique surrounded Saturn that happy customers began dropping by the factory to thank the employees. Saturn soon channeled their enthusiasm into a "homecoming" festival at Spring Hill that drew more than 40,000 customers from all over the United States. The CEO even gave the bride away when the employees of two competing Saturn dealers decided to hold their wedding at Spring Hill. Sales soared, and the plant strained to keep up with demand. For a time, Saturn was more than just a car company—it was a national phenomenon.

By end of the 1990s, however, Saturn had lost its novelty. While GM's officials debated whether to invest in new models, tastes were changing. Competitors' sport-utility vehicles (SUVs) and light pickup trucks had captured the public's imagination and gained market share at Saturn's expense. Eventually, Saturn did introduce the Vue SUV, but it was unable to generate the same kind of magic as the company's original sedan.

Meanwhile, GM was under great pressure to improve its financial performance, and top management was determined to cut costs worldwide. In the past, the president of each region (North America, Europe, Latin America, and Asia-Pacific) was responsible for that region's product development and other key functions. As a result, corporate officials could request but not order changes that would lower costs, such as following one set of engineering standards. By centralizing engineering, purchasing, and product development, the corporate office gained direct control to squeeze out redundancies.

This move toward specialization touched Saturn as well. The Spring Hill plant was efficient but costly to maintain. So GM merged Saturn's engineers with its corporate design staff and began managing the brand like all other brands in the corporate lineup. Spring Hill may manufacture Chevrolets in the future, with Ohio or Mexico producing Saturns. Already the Saturn minivan is being made in Georgia, and some auto industry observers believe GM's award-winning European-designed model, the Opel Insignia, will become the next Saturn Aura model in the United States. With all these changes, is Saturn still a new kind of car company?[11]

For more information about this company, go to **www.saturn.com** and **www.gm.com.**

Questions

1. In a factory such as Saturn's, where certain tasks must be completed in exactly the same way to produce each car, why would the company *not* push for job specialization?
2. Does GM appear to be organized by function, product, location, customer, or more than one of these departmentalization bases?
3. How does eliminating the CEO position at Saturn affect the chain of command at GM?

Building Skills for Career Success

1. JOURNALING FOR SUCCESS

Discovery statement: This chapter described the powerful influence that a corporate culture has on an organization.

Assume that after leaving school, you are hired by your "dream company."

Assignment

1. What are the major corporate culture dimensions of your dream company?
2. Before accepting a job at your "dream company," how will you find out about the company's corporate culture?
3. From Figure 7.7, identify the type of corporate culture that you prefer and explain why?
4. Thinking back to previous jobs that you have had, describe the worst corporate culture you have ever experienced.

2. EXPLORING THE INTERNET

After studying the various organizational structures described in this chapter and the reasons for employing them, you may be interested in learning about the organizational structures in place at large firms. As noted in the chapter, departmentalization typically is based on function, product, location, and customer. Many large firms use a combination of these organizational structures successfully. You can gain a good sense of which organizational theme prevails in an industry by looking at several corporate sites.

Assignment

1. Explore the website of any large firm that you believe is representative of its industry, and find its organization chart or a description of its organization. Create a brief organization chart from the information you have found.
2. Describe the bases on which this firm is departmentalized.

3. DEVELOPING CRITICAL-THINKING SKILLS

A firm's culture is a reflection of its most basic beliefs, values, customs, and rituals. Because it can have a powerful influence on how employees think and act, this culture also can have a powerful influence on a firm's performance. The influence may be for the better, of course, as in the case of Southwest Airlines, or it may be for the worse, as in the case of a bureaucratic organization whose employees feel hopelessly mired in red tape. When a company is concerned about mediocre performance and declining sales figures, its managers would do well to examine the cultural environment to see what might be in need of change.

Assignment

1. Analyze the cultural environment in which you work. (If you have no job, consider your school as your workplace and your instructor as your supervisor.) Ask yourself and your coworkers (or classmates) the following questions and record the answers:
   a. Do you feel that your supervisors welcome your ideas and respect them even when they may disagree with them? Do you take pride in your work? Do you feel that your work is appreciated? Do you think that the amount of work assigned to you is reasonable? Are you compensated adequately for your work?
   b. Are you proud to be associated with the company? Do you believe what the company says about itself in its advertisements? Are there any company policies or rules, written or unwritten, that you feel are unfair? Do you think that there is an opportunity for you to advance in this environment?
   c. How much independence do you have in carrying out your assignments? Are you ever allowed to act on your own, or do you feel that you have to consult with your supervisor on every detail?
   d. Do you enjoy the atmosphere in which you work? Is the physical setting pleasant? How often do you laugh in an average workday? How well do you get along with your supervisor and coworkers?
   e. Do you feel that the company cares about you? Will your supervisor give you time off when you have some pressing personal need? If the company had to downsize, how do you think you would be treated?
2. Using the responses to these questions, write a two-page paper describing how the culture of your workplace affects your performance and the overall performance of the firm. Point out the cultural factors that have the most beneficial and negative effects. Include your thoughts on how negative effects could be reversed.

4. BUILDING TEAM SKILLS

An organization chart is a diagram showing how employees and tasks are grouped and how the lines of communication and authority flow within an organization. These charts can look very different depending on a number of factors, including the nature and size of the business, the way it is departmentalized, its patterns of delegating authority, and its span of management.

Assignment

1. Working in a team, use the following information to draw an organization chart: The KDS Design Center works closely with two home-construction companies, Amex and Highmass. KDS's role is to help customers select materials for their new homes and to ensure that their selections are communicated accurately to the builders. The company is also a retailer of wallpaper, blinds, and drapery. The retail department, the Amex accounts, and the Highmass accounts make up KDS's three departments. The company has the following positions:
   President
   Executive vice president
   Managers, 2
   Appointment coordinators, 2
   Amex coordinators, 2
   Highmass coordinators, 2
   Consultants/designers for the Amex and Highmass accounts, 15
   Retail positions, 4
   Payroll and billing personnel, 1
2. After your team has drawn the organization chart, discuss the following:
   a. What type of organizational structure does your chart depict? Is it a bureaucratic, matrix, cluster, or network structure? Why?
   b. How does KDS use departmentalization?
   c. To what extent is authority in the company centralized or decentralized?
   d. What is the span of management within KDS?
   e. Which positions are line positions and which are staff? Why?
3. Prepare a three-page report summarizing what the chart revealed about relationships and tasks at the KDS Design Center and what your team learned about the value of organization charts. Include your chart in your report.

5. RESEARCHING DIFFERENT CAREERS

In the past, company loyalty and ability to assume increasing job responsibility usually ensured advancement within an organization. While the reasons for seeking advancement (the desire for a better-paying position, more prestige, and job satisfaction) have not changed, the qualifications for career advancement have. In today's business environment, climbing the corporate ladder requires packaging and marketing yourself. To be promoted within your company or to be considered for employment with another company, it is wise to improve your skills continually. By taking workshops and seminars or enrolling in community college courses, you can keep up with the changing technology in your industry. Networking with people in your business or community can help you to find a new job. Most jobs are filled through personal contacts. Who you know can be important.

A list of your accomplishments on the job can reveal your strengths and weaknesses. Setting goals for improvement helps to increase your self-confidence.

Be sure to recognize the signs of job dissatisfaction. It may be time to move to another position or company.

Assignment

Are you prepared to climb the corporate ladder? Do a self-assessment by analyzing the following areas, and summarize the results in a two-page report.

1. Skills
   - What are your most valuable skills?
   - What skills do you lack?
   - Describe your plan for acquiring new skills and improving your skills.
2. Networking
   - How effective are you at using a mentor?
   - Are you a member of a professional organization?
   - In which community, civic, or church groups are you participating?
   - Whom have you added to your contact list in the last six weeks?
3. Accomplishments
   - What achievements have you reached in your job?
   - What would you like to accomplish? What will it take for you to reach your goal?
4. Promotion or new job
   - What is your likelihood for getting a promotion?
   - Are you ready for a change? What are you doing or willing to do to find another job?

8 Producing Quality Goods and Services

LEARNING OBJECTIVES

What you will be able to do once you complete this chapter:

1. Explain the nature of production.
2. Outline how the conversion process transforms raw materials, labor, and other resources into finished products or services.
3. Describe how research and development lead to new products and services.
4. Discuss the components involved in planning the production process.
5. Explain how purchasing, inventory control, scheduling, and quality control affect production.
6. Summarize how productivity and technology are related.

Adrian Bradshaw/Corbis

inside business

Blendtec CEO Tom Dickson routinely tests product quality by crunching blocks of wood in Blendtec blenders.

Quality Powers Blendtec's Blenders

"Will it blend?" Millions of people have watched Blendtec's online videos to find out whether the firm's home blenders can reduce the unlikeliest of objects—an iPhone, a dozen glow sticks, or a *Guitar Hero* videogame—to dust. Based in Orem, Utah, Blendtec originally sold high-powered blenders to restaurants, bars, and other food businesses that need to combine ingredients into sauces, soups, smoothies, and other menu items. When it decided to expand by making high-end blenders for home use, however, it faced two challenges.

First, business buyers knew Blendtec's reputation for quality, but few consumers had ever heard of the company, let alone its top-quality products. Second, Blendtec had almost no budget for reaching out to consumers. Then the marketing director learned that CEO Tom Dickson routinely tested product quality by crunching blocks of wood in Blendtec blenders. He spent $50 on marbles and other odd items and trained his video camera on a Blendtec home blender. Dickson, wearing a laboratory coat and safety goggles, dropped the marbles into the blender, looked into the camera, and asked: "Will it blend?" He paused and started the blender. The marbles were pulverized on camera.

Blendtec posted the videos online, where they were picked up by a number of popular web sites. Within a week, 6 million people had watched Blendtec products chew up everything that Dickson tried to blend. Every few weeks, the company uploaded a new "Will it blend?" video segment, each drawing thousands more viewers and sparking greater interest in its blenders.

By the end of the year, Blendtec's home-blender sales had risen by 43 percent, and commercial sales were soaring as well. Today, although commercial blenders remain the mainstay of Blendtec's business, millions of consumers now know the Blendtec name and the level of quality it represents.[1]

Why purchase a Blendtec blender? Good question! Now for some answers. The goal of the company's Fine Living Products line of home appliances is to provide the world's best food processing solutions through excellence in quality, customer satisfaction, and innovation.[2] As a result of Blendtec's desire to be the best, customers love the products because its blenders and mixers have powerful motors, electronic controls, and programmable blend cycles. And its line of home appliances was created with special attention to appearance and home-use function. The fact is that the Blendtec company is an excellent example of what this chapter's content—the production of quality goods and services—is all about. Today, the people who purchase Blendtec products expect more from the company's products—and they get more.

We begin this chapter with an overview of operations management—the activities required to produce goods and services that meet the needs of customers. In this section, we also discuss competition in the global marketplace and careers in operations management. Next, we describe the conversion process that makes production possible and also note the growing role of services in our economy. Then we examine more closely three important aspects of operations management: developing ideas for new products, planning for production, and effectively controlling operations after production has begun. We close the chapter with a look at productivity trends and ways that productivity can be improved through the use of technology.

What Is Production?

1

Learning Objective: Explain the nature of production.

Have you ever wondered where a new pair of Levi jeans comes from? Or a new Mitsubishi flat panel television, Izod pullover sweater, or Uniroyal tire for your car? Even factory service on a Hewlett-Packard notebook computer or a Maytag clothes dryer would be impossible if it weren't for the activities described in this chapter. In fact, these products and services and millions of others like them would not exist if it weren't for production activities.

Let's begin this chapter by reviewing what an operating manager does. In Chapter 6, we described an *operations manager* as a person who manages the systems that convert resources into goods and services. This area of management is usually referred to as **operations management**, which consists of all the activities managers engage in to produce goods and services.

operations management all activities managers engage in to produce goods and services

To produce a product or service successfully, a business must perform a number of specific activities. For example, suppose that an organization such as Chevrolet has an idea for a new aerodynamic, sporty passenger automobile called the Volt that will cost approximately $30,000 and feature a new gas/electric engine. Marketing research must determine not only if customers are willing to pay the price for this product but also what special features they want. Then Chevrolet's operations managers must turn the concept into reality.

Chevrolet's managers cannot just push the "start button" and immediately begin producing the new automobile. Production must be planned. As you will see, planning takes place both *before* anything is produced and *during* the production process.

Managers also must concern themselves with the control of operations to ensure that the organization's goals are achieved. For a product such as Chevrolet's Volt, control of operations involves a number of important issues, including product quality, performance standards, the amount of inventory of both raw materials and finished products, and production costs.

We discuss each of the major activities of operations management later in this chapter. First, however, let's take a closer look at American manufacturers and how they compete in the global marketplace.

Competition in the Global Marketplace

After World War II, the United States became the most productive country in the world. For almost thirty years, until the late 1970s, its leadership was never threatened. By then, however, manufacturers in Japan, Germany, Great Britain, Taiwan, Korea, Sweden, and other industrialized nations were offering U.S. firms increasing competition. And now the Chinese are manufacturing everything from sophisticated electronic equipment and automobiles to less expensive everyday items—often for lower cost than the same goods can be manufactured in other countries. As a result, the goods Americans purchase may have been manufactured in the United States *or* in other countries around the globe and shipped to the United States. Competition has never been fiercer, and in some ways the world has never been smaller.

In an attempt to regain a competitive edge on foreign manufacturers, U.S. firms have taken another look at the importance of improving quality and meeting the needs of their customers. The most successful U.S. firms also have focused on the following:

1. Motivating employees to cooperate with management and improve productivity
2. Reducing costs by selecting suppliers that offer higher-quality raw materials and components at reasonable prices
3. Replacing outdated equipment with state-of-the-art manufacturing equipment
4. Using computer-aided and flexible manufacturing systems that allow a higher degree of customization
5. Improving control procedures to help ensure lower manufacturing costs
6. Building new manufacturing facilities in foreign countries where labor costs are lower

SPOTLIGHT
Manufacturing Jobs?

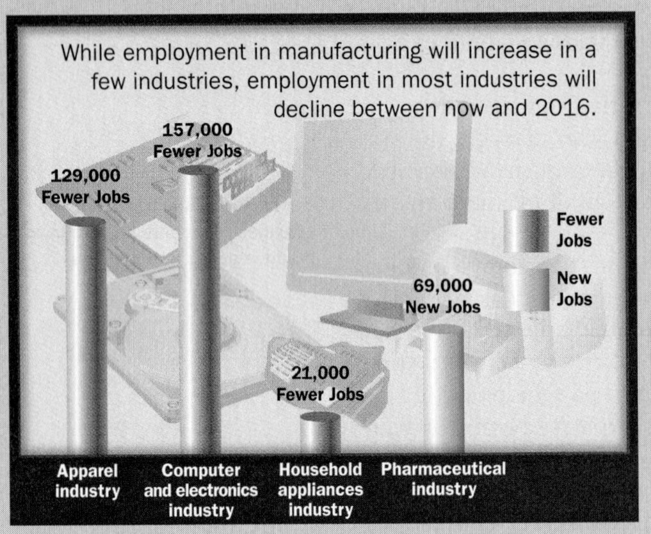

Source: "Tomorrow's Jobs," *The Occupational Outlook Handbook*, The Bureau of Labor Statistics website at www.bls.gov, accessed September 20, 2008.

Although competing in the global economy is a major challenge, it is a worthwhile pursuit. For most firms, competing in the global marketplace is not only profitable, but it is also an essential activity that requires the cooperation of everyone within the organization.

Careers in Operations Management

Although it is hard to provide information about specific career opportunities in operations management, some generalizations do apply to this management area. First, you must appreciate the manufacturing process and the steps required to produce a product or service. A basic understanding of mass production and the difference between an analytical process and a synthetic process is essential. **Mass production** is a manufacturing process that lowers the cost required to produce a large number of identical or similar products over a long period of time. An **analytical process** breaks raw materials into different component parts. For example, a barrel of crude oil refined by Marathon Oil Corporation—a Texas-based oil and chemical refiner—can be broken down into gasoline, oil and lubricants, and many other petroleum by-products. A **synthetic process** is just the opposite of the analytical one; it combines raw materials or components to create a finished product. Black & Decker uses a synthetic process when it combines plastic, steel, rechargeable batteries, and other components to produce a cordless drill.

mass production a manufacturing process that lowers the cost required to produce a large number of identical or similar products over a long period of time

analytical process a process in operations management in which raw materials are broken into different component parts

synthetic process a process in operations management in which raw materials or components are combined to create a finished product

utility the ability of a good or service to satisfy a human need

form utility utility created by people converting raw materials, finances, and information into finished products

Once you understand that operations managers are responsible for producing tangible products or services that customers want, you must determine how you fit into the production process. Today's successful operations managers must

1. be able to motivate and lead people.
2. understand how technology can make a manufacturer more productive and efficient.
3. appreciate the control processes that help lower production costs and improve product quality.
4. understand the relationship between the customer, the marketing of a product, and the production of a product.

If operations management seems like an area you might be interested in, why not do more career exploration? You could take an operations management course if your college or university offers one, or you could obtain a part-time job during the school year or a summer job in a manufacturing company.

The Conversion Process

2

Learning Objective: Outline how the conversion process transforms raw materials, labor, and other resources into finished products or services.

To have something to sell, a business must convert ideas and resources into goods and services. The resources are materials, finances, people, and information—the same resources discussed in Chapters 1 and 6. The goods and services are varied, ranging from consumer products to heavy manufacturing equipment to fast food. The purpose of this conversion of resources into goods and services is to provide utility to customers. **Utility** is the ability of a good or service to satisfy a human need. Although there are four types of utility—form, place, time, and possession—operations management focuses primarily on form utility. **Form utility** is created by people converting raw materials, finances, and information into finished products. The other types of utility—place, time, and possession—are discussed in Chapter 12.

But how does the conversion take place? How does Kellogg's convert grain, sugar, salt, and other ingredients; money from previous sales and stockholders' investments; production workers and managers; and economic and marketing forecasts into Frosted Flakes cereal products? How does New York Life Insurance convert office buildings, insurance premiums, actuaries, and mortality tables into life insurance policies? They do so through the use of a conversion process like the one illustrated in Figure 8.1. As indicated by our New York Life Insurance example, the conversion process is not limited to manufacturing products. The conversion process also can be used to produce services.

Sustaining the Planet

The U.S. Environmental Protection Agency is showing businesses how to protect the environment and operate more efficiently by adopting lean manufacturing techniques. The idea is to cut costly waste and harmful pollution, streamline and modernize production methods, and partner with environmentally-conscious suppliers. The result: Leaner, greener manufacturing and greener, high-quality products. **www.epa.gov/lean**

Manufacturing Using a Conversion Process

The conversion of resources into products and services can be described in several ways. We limit our discussion here to three: the focus or major resource used in the conversion process, its magnitude of change, and the number of production processes employed.

Figure 8.1: The Conversion Process

The conversion process converts ideas and resources such as materials, finances, and information into useful goods and services. The ability to produce products, services, and ideas is a crucial step in the economic development of any nation.

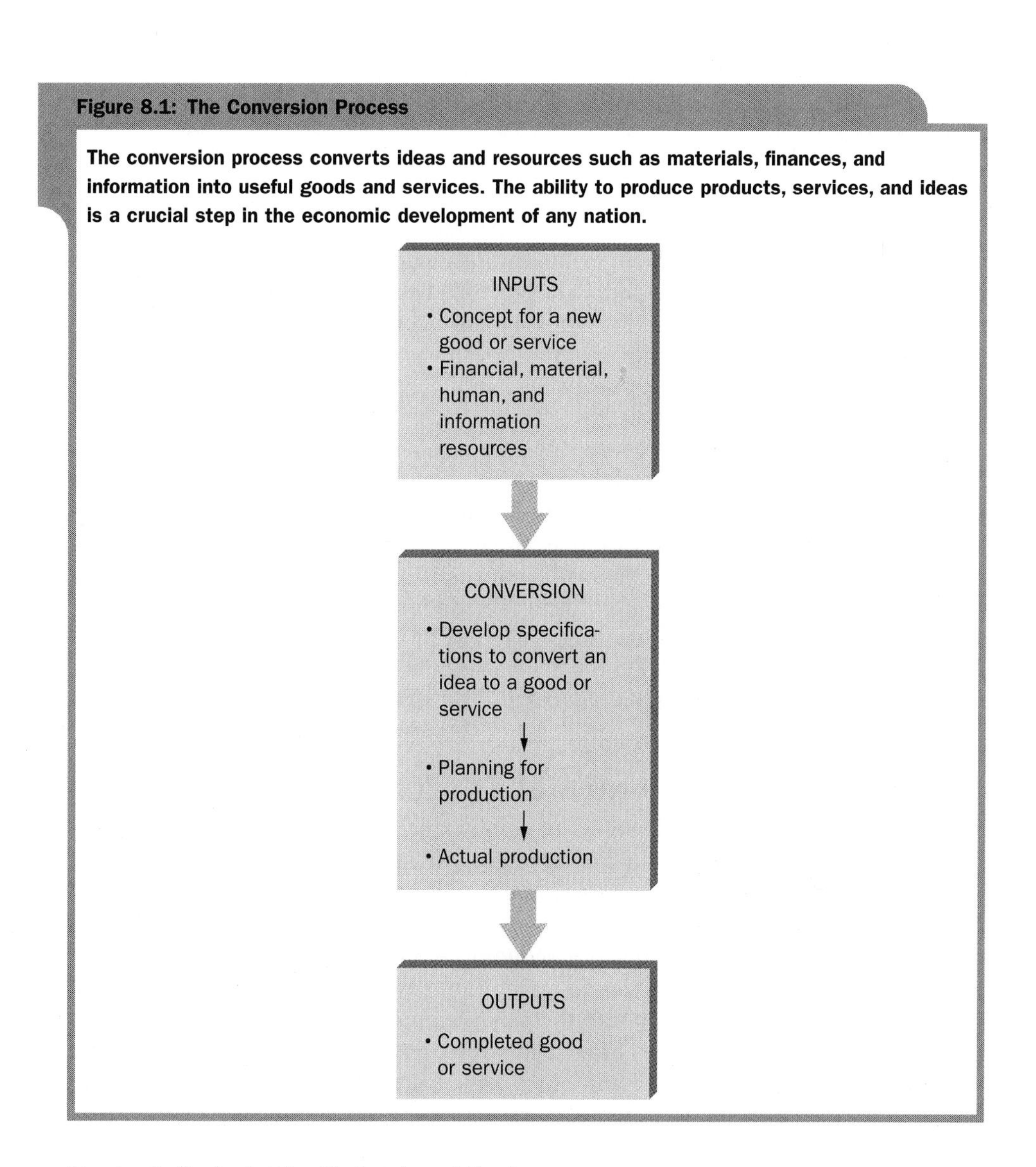

That's a lot of automobiles! *While many people think that Honda automobiles are a "foreign import," the truth is that over 1,000,000 have been built in Honda's Alabama manufacturing facility.*

PRNewsFoto/Honda Manufacturing of Alabama

Focus By the *focus* of a conversion process, we mean the resource or resources that make up the major or most important *input*. For a bank such as Citibank, financial resources are the major resource. A chemical and energy company such as Chevron concentrates on material resources. Your college or university is concerned primarily with information. And temporary employment services focus on the use of human resources.

Magnitude of Change The *magnitude* of a conversion process is the degree to which the resources are physically changed. At one extreme lie such processes as the one by which the Glad Products Company produces Glad Cling Wrap. Various chemicals in liquid or powder form are combined to produce long, thin sheets of plastic Glad Cling Wrap. Here, the original resources are totally unrecognizable in the finished product. At the other extreme, Southwest Airlines produces *no* physical change in its original resources. The airline simply provides a service and transports people from one place to another.

Number of Production Processes A single firm may employ one production process or many. In general, larger firms that make a variety of products use multiple production processes. For example, General Electric manufactures some of its own products, buys other merchandise from suppliers, and operates multiple divisions including a credit division, an insurance division, an entertainment division, and a medical equipment division. Smaller firms, by contrast, may use one production process. For example, Texas-based Advanced Cast Stone, Inc., manufactures one basic product: building materials made from concrete.

The Increasing Importance of Services

The application of the basic principles of operations management to the production of services has coincided with a dramatic growth in the number and diversity of service businesses. In 1900, only 28 percent of American workers were employed in service firms. By 1950, this figure had grown to 40 percent, and by 2008, it had risen to 84 percent.[3] In fact, the American economy is now characterized as a **service economy** (see Figure 8.2). A service economy is one in which more effort is devoted to the production of services than to the production of goods.

service economy an economy in which more effort is devoted to the production of services than to the production of goods

Today, the managers of restaurants, laundries, real estate agencies, banks, movie theaters, airlines, travel bureaus, and other service firms have realized that they can benefit from the experience of manufacturers. And yet the production of services is

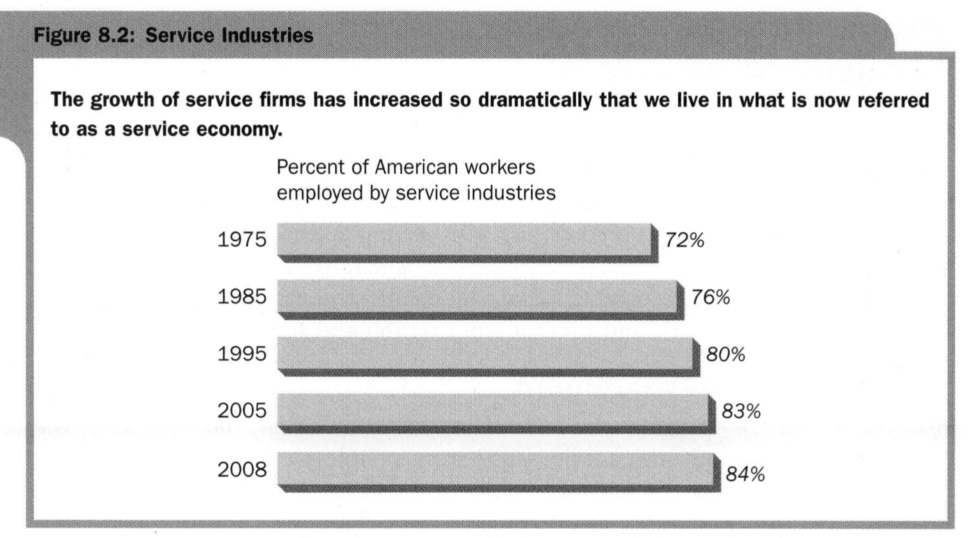

Figure 8.2: Service Industries

The growth of service firms has increased so dramatically that we live in what is now referred to as a service economy.

Source: U.S. Bureau of Labor Statistics website, **www.bls.gov**, accessed September 20, 2008.

very different from the production of manufactured goods in the following four ways:

1. Services are consumed immediately and, unlike manufactured goods, cannot be stored. For example, a hair stylist cannot store completed haircuts.
2. Services are provided when and where the customer desires the service. In many cases, customers will not travel as far to obtain a service.
3. Services are usually labor-intensive because the human resource is often the most important resource used in the production of services.
4. Services are intangible, and it is therefore more difficult to evaluate customer satisfaction.[4]

Although it is often more difficult to measure customer satisfaction, today's successful service firms work hard at providing the services customers want. Compared with manufacturers, service firms often listen more carefully to customers and respond more quickly to the market's changing needs.

In an effort to meet increased demands for customer service, businesses ranging from small mom-and-pop firms to large *Fortune* 500 companies are developing new ways to provide services and meet customer needs. For example, Dell is a well-known manufacturer of computer equipment. In order to be successful, it must gather as much information as possible about the customer in order to meet the needs of each individual customer. Want to buy a new Dell Inspiron computer? All you have to do is to go to the Dell website and work through a series of steps designed to determine the components you need. Still have questions? By clicking on a website tab, you can contact a customer service representative who will help you to make a decision. Service after the sale is also important because Dell maintains an ongoing dialogue with its customers to understand customer concerns and problems and to identify customers who are ready to buy more of the firm's products.[5]

Now that we understand something about the production process that is used to transform resources into goods and services, we can consider three major activities involved in operations management. These are product development, planning for production, and operations control.

Disney's magical express! *Like magic, guests and their baggage are whisked from the Orlando International Airport to the Walt Disney World Resort. Complementary round-trip shuttle service to one of 22 hotels in the Orlando, Florida, area is just one of the many services Disney provides to make a guest's stay more enjoyable.*

PRNewsFoto/Walt Disney World Resort

Where Do New Products and Services Come From?

3

Learning Objective: Describe how research and development lead to new products and services.

No firm can produce a product or service until it has an idea. In other words, someone first must come up with a new way to satisfy a need—a new product or an improvement in an existing product. Apple's iPod and San Disk's Flash Drive began as an idea. While no one can predict with 100 percent accuracy what types of products will be available in the next five years, it is safe to say that companies will continue to introduce new products that will change the way we take care of ourselves, interact with others, and find the information and services we need.

Research and Development

How did we get laptop computers and HD televisions? We got them the same way we got light bulbs and automobile tires—from people working with new ideas. Thomas Edison created the first light bulb, and Charles Goodyear discovered the vulcanization process that led to tires. In the same way, scientists and researchers working in businesses and universities have produced many of the newer products we already take for granted.

These activities generally are referred to as *research and development*. For our purposes, **research and development (R&D)** are a set of activities intended to identify new ideas that have the potential to result in new goods and services.

research and development (R&D) a set of activities intended to identify new ideas that have the potential to result in new goods and services

Today, business firms use three general types of R&D activities. *Basic research* consists of activities aimed at uncovering new knowledge. The goal of basic research is scientific advancement, without regard for its potential use in the development of goods and services. *Applied research,* in contrast, consists of activities geared toward discovering new knowledge with some potential use. *Development and implementation* are research activities undertaken specifically to put new or existing knowledge to use in producing goods and services. The 3M Company has always been known for its development and implementation research activities. As a result of its R&D efforts, the company has developed more than 55,000 products designed to make people's lives easier. Does a company like 3M quit innovating because it has developed successful

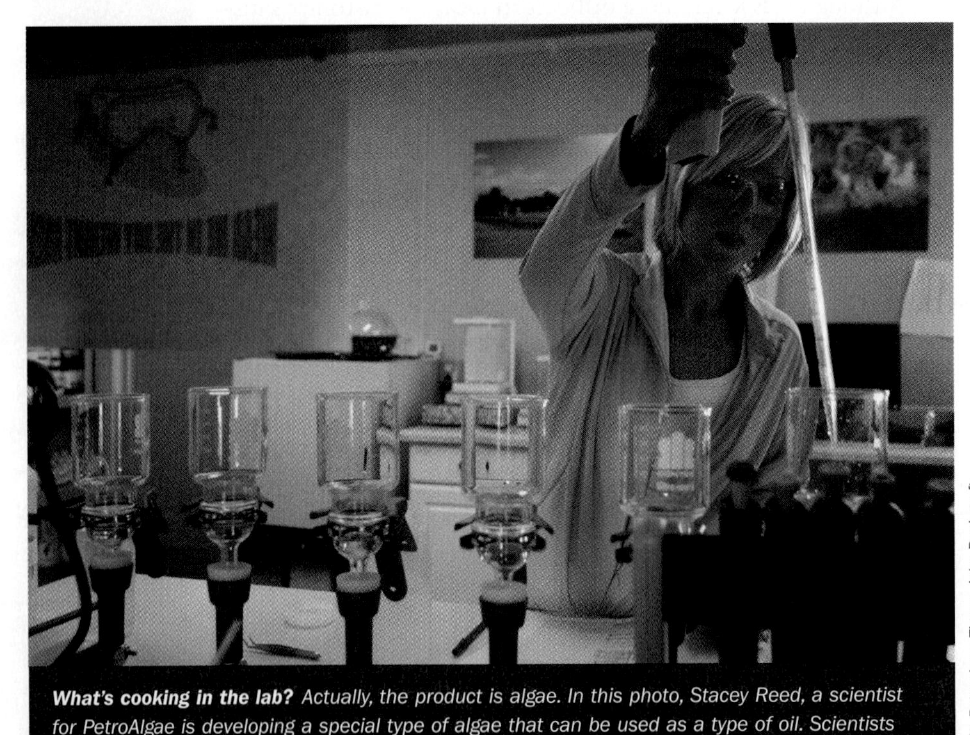

What's cooking in the lab? *Actually, the product is algae. In this photo, Stacey Reed, a scientist for PetroAlgae is developing a special type of algae that can be used as a type of oil. Scientists at PetroAlgae hope their research and development process will create a sustainable, renewable, cost-effective substitute for petroleum oil.*

AP Photo/St. Petersburg Times, John Penlygraft

The Business of Green

Peterbilt Puts Greener Trucks on the Road

Peterbilt trucks are getting greener, thanks to parent company PACCAR's multimillion-dollar investments in research and development. Based in Bellevue, Washington, PACCAR has developed a number of new truck motors and braking systems that reduce engine emissions and increase fuel efficiency. One fuel-saving innovation is the ability to store up energy when the truck brakes and then release it to power acceleration. In addition, these new Peterbilt trucks are quieter and can go longer between service visits.

Courtesy Peterbilt

Greener truck technology takes shape at PACCAR's leading-edge manufacturing center in Mississippi, where engineers and designers collaborate on research and development. After testing prototypes under laboratory conditions, the company creates road-ready versions for extensive field testing. For example, the company is currently testing new trucks that run on diesel-electric hybrid engines and new tractors that run on liquid natural gas.

The Peterbilt production facilities are also going green. Both the Texas and Tennessee plants have received ISO 14001 environmental certification and have programs in high gear to cut waste and conserve natural resources. In today's high-pressure economy, such conservation efforts are a good way to save the planet and save money at the same time.

Sources: Seth Skydel, "Developing Technologies: Pete Hybrids," *Fleet Equipment*, February 2008, p. 6; "Future Focus," *Fleet Owner*, May 1, 2008, n.p.; "PACCAR Breaks Ground for Engine Plant," *Mississippi Business Journal*, July 30, 2007, p. 15; **www.peterbilt.com.**

products? No, not at all! Currently, the company employs more than 7,000 researchers worldwide and has invested more than $6.6 billion over the last five years to develop new products designed to make peope's lives easier and safer. Just recently, the 3M Company used development and implementation to create a new, state-of-the-art passport scanner that can be used to facilitate the check-in process for frequent travelers.[6]

Product Extension and Refinement

When a brand-new product is first marketed, its sales are zero and slowly increase from that point. If the product is successful, annual sales increase more and more rapidly until they reach some peak. Then, as time passes, annual sales begin to decline, and they continue to decline until it is no longer profitable to manufacture the product. (This rise-and-decline pattern, called the *product life cycle*, is discussed in more detail in Chapter 13.)

If a firm sells only one product, when that product reaches the end of its life cycle, the firm will die, too. To stay in business, the firm must, at the very least, find ways to refine or extend the want-satisfying capability of its product. Consider television sets. Since they were introduced in the late 1930s, television sets have been constantly *refined* so that they now provide clearer, sharper pictures with less dial adjusting. During the same time, television sets also were *extended*. There are color sets, television-only sets, and others that include VCR and DVD players. There are even television sets that allow their owners to access the Internet. And the latest development—high-definition (HD) television—has already become the standard for television receivers. Although initial prices were high, prices now have dropped and are more affordable.

Each refinement or extension results in an essentially "new" product whose sales make up for the declining sales of a product that was introduced earlier. When consumers discovered that the original five varieties of Campbell's Soup were of the highest quality, as well as inexpensive, the soups were an instant success. Although one of the most successful companies at the beginning of the 1900s, Campbell's had to continue to innovate, refine, and extend its product line. For example, many consumers in the United States live in what is called an on-the-go society. To meet this need, Campbell's Soup has developed ready-to-serve products that can be popped into a microwave at work or school. In other countries, customer feedback is also

AP Photo/Chiaki Tsukumo

McDonald's has gone fishing. *For McDonald's Holding Company, the Japanese subsidiary of U.S.-based McDonald's Corporation, Fish McDippers are a logical product extension of McDonald's popular fish sandwiches. Similar to the fast-food giant's Chicken McNuggets, McDonald's Japanese unit added more fish items to its menus in order to combat consumer concerns about mad cow disease and the spread of bird flu in Japan.*

used to adapt products to meet the needs of local customers. For example, Liebig Pur, a thick vegetable soup, is sold in cartons with a long shelf life in France.[7]

For most firms, extension and refinement are expected results of their development and implementation effort. Most often, they result from the application of new knowledge to existing products. For instance, improved technology affects the content companies can distribute on the Internet. The Disney Corporation currently has a clear advantage over competitors because much of its content is animation. Animation is the easiest content to transfer to the Internet.

Planning for Production

4

Learning Objective: Discuss the components involved in planning the production process.

Only a few of the many ideas for new products, refinements, and extensions ever reach the production stage. For those ideas that do, however, the next step is planning for production. Once a new product idea has been identified, planning for production involves three major phases: design planning, facilities planning and site selection, and operational planning (see Figure 8.3).

Design Planning

When the R&D staff at Hewlett-Packard recommended to top management that the firm produce and market an affordable notebook computer, the company could not simply swing into production the next day. Instead, a great deal of time and energy had to be invested in determining what the new computer would look like, where and how it would be produced, and what options would be included. These decisions are a part of design planning. **Design planning** is the development of a plan for converting a product idea into an actual product or service. The major decisions involved in design planning deal with product line, required capacity, and use of technology.

design planning the development of a plan for converting a product idea into an actual product or service

product line a group of similar products that differ only in relatively minor characteristics

Product Line A **product line** is a group of similar products that differ only in relatively minor characteristics. During the design-planning stage, a computer manufacturer such as Hewlett-Packard needs to determine how many different models to produce and what major options to offer. A restaurant chain such as Pizza Hut must decide how many menu items to offer.

An important issue in deciding on the product line is to balance customer preferences and production requirements. For this reason, marketing managers play an important role in making product-line decisions. Typically, marketing personnel want a "long" product line that offers customers many options. Because a long product line

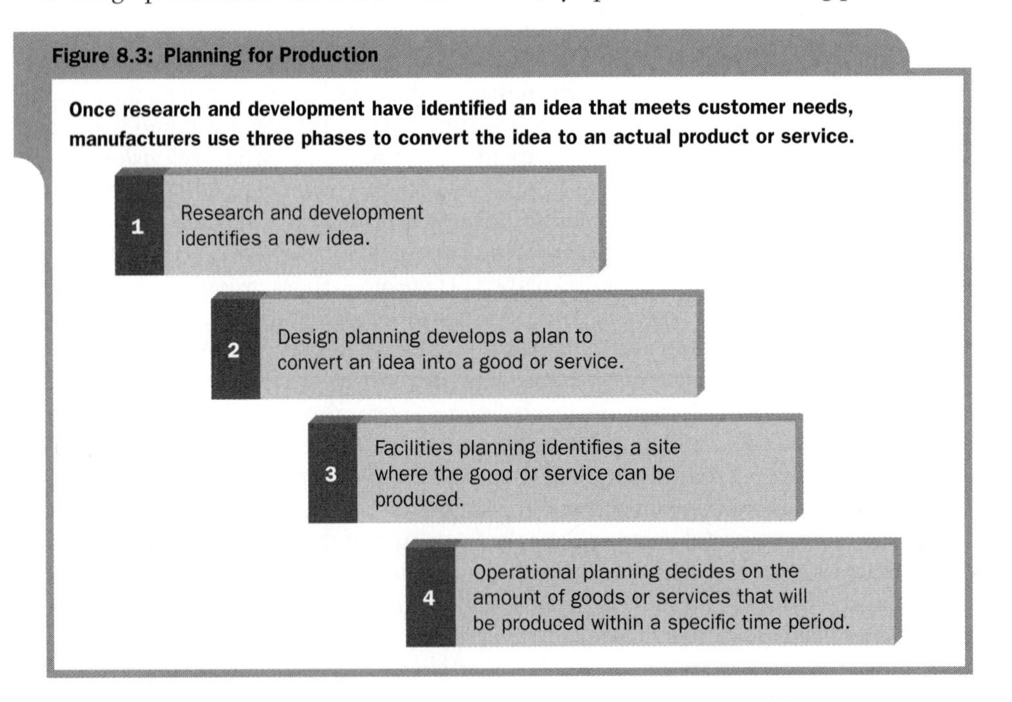

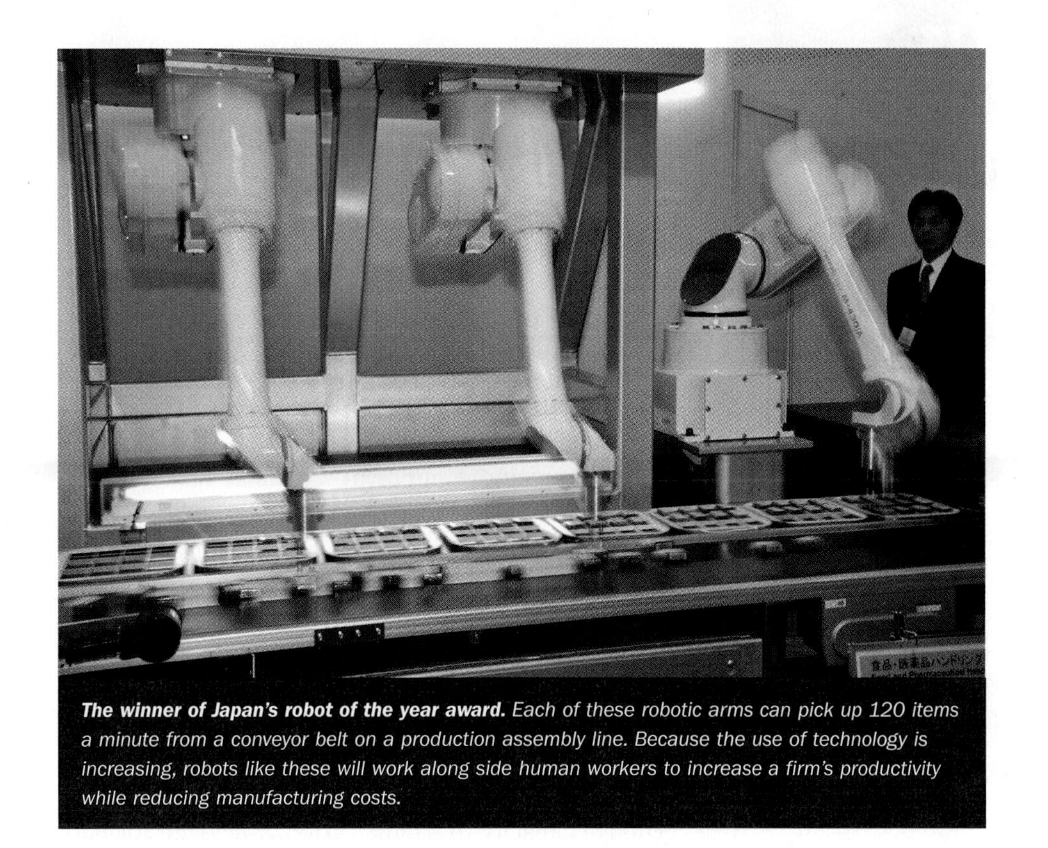

The winner of Japan's robot of the year award. *Each of these robotic arms can pick up 120 items a minute from a conveyor belt on a production assembly line. Because the use of technology is increasing, robots like these will work along side human workers to increase a firm's productivity while reducing manufacturing costs.*

with more options gives customers greater choice, it is easier to sell products that meet the needs of individual customers. On the other hand, production personnel generally want a "short" product line because products are easier to produce. With a short product line, the production process is less complex because there are fewer options, and most products are produced using the same basic steps. In many cases, the actual choice between a long and short product line involves balancing customer preferences with the cost and problems associated with a more complex production process.

Once the product line has been determined, each distinct product within the product line must be designed. **Product design** is the process of creating a set of specifications from which a product can be produced. When designing a new product, specifications are extremely important. For example, product engineers for Whirlpool Corporation must make sure that a new frost-free refrigerator keeps food frozen in the freezer compartment. At the same time, they must make sure that lettuce and tomatoes do not freeze in the crisper section of the refrigerator. The need for a complete product design is fairly obvious; products that work cannot be manufactured without it. But services should be designed carefully as well—and *for the same reason.*

product design the process of creating a set of specifications from which a product can be produced

Required Production Capacity **Capacity** is the amount of products or services that an organization can produce in a given period of time. (For example, the capacity of a Saab automobile assembly plant might be 150,000 cars per year.) Operations managers—again working with the firm's marketing managers—must determine the required capacity. This, in turn, determines the size of the production facility. If the facility is built with too much capacity, valuable resources (plant, equipment, and money) will lie idle. If the facility offers insufficient capacity, additional capacity may have to be added later when it is much more expensive than in the initial building stage.

capacity the amount of products or services that an organization can produce in a given time

Capacity means about the same thing to service businesses. For example, the capacity of a restaurant such as the Hard Rock Cafe in Nashville, Tennessee, is the number of customers it can serve at one time. As with the manufacturing facility described earlier, if the restaurant is built with too much capacity—too many tables and chairs—valuable resources will be wasted. If the restaurant is too small, customers may have to wait for service; if the wait is too long, they may leave and choose another restaurant.

SPOTLIGHT
Production Salaries

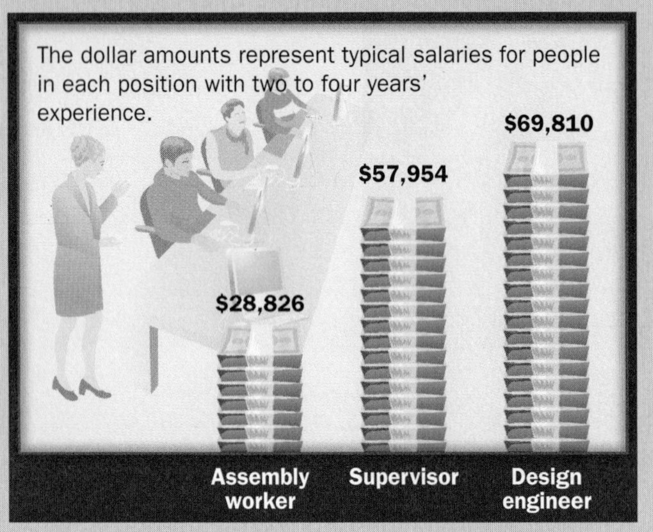

Source: The Monster website, **www.monster.com**, accessed September 21, 2008.

Use of Technology During the design-planning stage, management must determine the degree to which *automation* will be used to produce a product or service. Here, there is a tradeoff between high initial costs and low operating costs (for automation) and low initial costs and high operating costs (for human labor). Ultimately, management must choose between a labor-intensive technology and a capital-intensive technology. A **labor-intensive technology** is a process in which people must do most of the work. Housecleaning services and the New York Yankees baseball team, for example, are labor intensive. A **capital-intensive technology** is a process in which machines and equipment do most of the work. A Motorola automated assembly plant is capital intensive.

labor-intensive technology a process in which people must do most of the work

capital-intensive technology a process in which machines and equipment do most of the work

Facilities Planning and Site Selection

Once initial decisions have been made about a new product line, required capacity, and the use of technology, it is time to determine where the products or services are going to be produced. Generally, a business will choose to produce a new product in an existing factory as long as (1) the existing factory has enough capacity to handle customer demand for both the new product and established products and (2) the cost of refurbishing an existing factory is less than the cost of building a new one.

After exploring the capacity of existing factories, management may decide to build a new production facility. Once again, a number of decisions must be made. Should all the organization's production capacity be placed in one or two large facilities? Or should it be divided among several smaller facilities? In general, firms that market a wide variety of products find it more economical to have a number of smaller facilities. Firms that produce only a small number of products tend to have fewer but larger facilities.

In determining where to locate production facilities, management must consider a number of variables, including the following:

- Locations of major customers and transportation costs to deliver finished products
- Geographic locations of suppliers of parts and raw materials
- Availability and cost of skilled and unskilled labor
- Quality of life for employees and management in the proposed location
- The cost of both land and construction required to build a new production facility
- Local and state taxes, environmental regulations, and zoning laws
- The amount of financial support, if any, offered by local and state governments
- Special requirements, such as great amounts of energy or water used in the production process

The choice of a location often involves balancing the most important variables for each production facility. Before making a final decision about where a proposed plant will be located and how it will be organized, two other factors—human resources and plant layout—should be examined.

Human Resources Several issues involved in facilities planning and site selection fall within the province of the human resources manager. Thus, at this stage, human resources and operations managers work closely together. For example,

The final product: An airliner. *Instead of moving the product along an assembly line, it's easier to move people, machinery, and parts to where they are needed to assemble a large Boeing jetliner. In situations like these, a manufacturer like Boeing will use a fixed-position layout.*

AP Photo/Elaine Thompson

suppose that a U.S. firm such as Reebok International wants to lower labor costs by constructing a sophisticated production plant in China. The human resources manager will have to recruit managers and employees with the appropriate skills who are willing to relocate to a foreign country or develop training programs for local Chinese workers or both.

Plant Layout **Plant layout** is the arrangement of machinery, equipment, and personnel within a production facility. Three general types of plant layout are used (see Figure 8.4).

plant layout the arrangement of machinery, equipment, and personnel within a production facility

The *process layout* is used when different operations are required for creating small batches of different products or working on different parts of a product. The plant is arranged so that each operation is performed in its own particular area. An auto repair facility at a local automobile dealership provides an example of a process layout. The various operations may be engine repair, body work, wheel alignment, and safety inspection. Each operation is performed in a different area. If you take your Lincoln Navigator for a wheel alignment, your car "visits" only the area where alignments are performed.

A *product layout* (sometimes referred to as an *assembly line*) is used when all products undergo the same operations in the same sequence. Workstations are arranged to match the sequence of operations, and work flows from station to station. An assembly line is the best example of a product layout. For example, California-based Maxim Integrated Products, Inc., uses a product layout to manufacture components for consumer and business electronic products.

A *fixed-position layout* is used when a very large product is produced. Aircraft manufacturers and shipbuilders apply this method because of the difficulty of moving a large product such as an airliner or a ship. The product remains stationary, and people and machines are moved as needed to assemble the product. Boeing, for example, uses the fixed-position layout to build 787 Dreamliner jet aircraft at its Everett, Washington, manufacturing facility.

Operational Planning

Once the product has been designed and a decision has been made to use an existing production facility or build a new one, operational plans must be developed. The objective of operational planning is to decide on the amount of products or services each facility will produce during a specific period of time. Four steps are required.

Figure 8.4: Facilities Planning

The process layout is used when small batches of different products are created or when working on different parts of a product. The product layout (assembly line) is used when all products undergo the same operations in the same sequence. The fixed-position layout is used in producing a product too large to move.

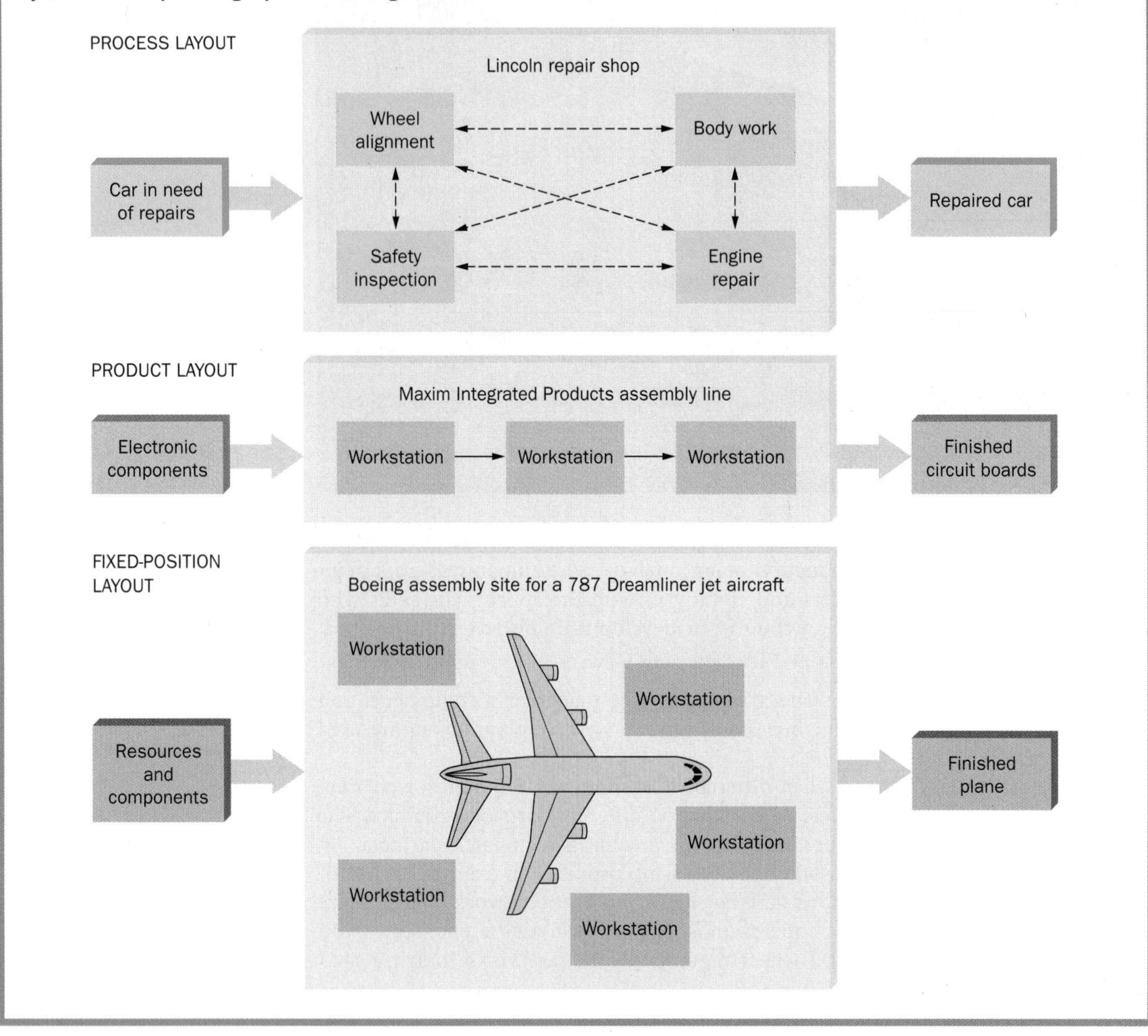

planning horizon the period during which an operational plan will be in effect

Step 1: Selecting a Planning Horizon A **planning horizon** is simply the time period during which an operational plan will be in effect. A common planning horizon for production plans is one year. Then, before each year is up, management must plan for the next.

A planning horizon of one year generally is long enough to average out seasonal increases and decreases in sales. At the same time, it is short enough for planners to adjust production to accommodate long-range sales trends. Firms that operate in a rapidly changing business environment with many competitors may find it best to select a shorter planning horizon to keep their production planning current.

Step 2: Estimating Market Demand The *market demand* for a product is the quantity that customers will purchase at the going price. This quantity must be estimated for the time period covered by the planning horizon. Sales projections developed by marketing managers are the basis for market-demand estimates.

Step 3: Comparing Market Demand with Capacity The third step in operational planning is to compare the estimated market demand with the facility's capacity to satisfy that demand. (Remember that capacity is the amount of products or services that an organization can produce in a given time period.) One of three outcomes may result: Demand may exceed capacity, capacity may exceed demand, or capacity and demand may be equal. If they are equal, the facility should be operated at full capacity. However, if market demand and capacity are not equal, adjustments may be necessary.

Step 4: Adjusting Products or Services to Meet Demand The biggest reason for changes to a firm's production schedule is changes in the amount of products or services that a company sells to its customers. For example, Indiana-based Berry Plastics uses an injection-molded manufacturing process to produce all kinds of plastic products. One particularly successful product line for Berry Plastics is drink cups that can be screen-printed to promote a company or the company's products or services.[8] If Berry Plastics obtains a large contract to provide promotional mugs to a large fast-food chain such as Whataburger or McDonald's, the company may need to work three shifts a day, seven days a week until the contract is fulfilled. Unfortunately, the reverse is also true. If the company's sales force does not generate new sales, there may be only enough work for the employees on one shift.

When market demand exceeds capacity, several options are available to a firm. Production of products or services may be increased by operating the facility overtime with existing personnel or by starting a second or third work shift. For manufacturers, another response is to subcontract or outsource a portion of the work to other manufacturers. If the excess demand is likely to be permanent, the firm may expand the current facility or build another facility.

What happens when capacity exceeds market demand? Again, there are several options. To reduce output temporarily, workers may be laid off and part of the facility shut down. Or the facility may be operated on a shorter-than-normal work week for as long as the excess capacity persists. To adjust to a permanently decreased demand, management may shift the excess capacity of a manufacturing facility to the production of other goods or services. The most radical adjustment is to eliminate the excess capacity by selling unused manufacturing facilities.

Operations Control

5

Learning Objective: Explain how purchasing, inventory control, scheduling, and quality control affect production.

We have discussed the development of an idea for a product or service and the planning that translates that idea into the reality. Now we are ready to push the "start button" to begin the production process. In this section, we examine four important areas of operations control: purchasing, inventory control, scheduling, and quality control (see Figure 8.5).

Purchasing

purchasing all the activities involved in obtaining required materials, supplies, components, and parts from other firms

Purchasing consists of all the activities involved in obtaining required materials, supplies, components (or subassemblies), and parts from other firms. Levi Strauss must purchase denim cloth, thread, and zippers before it can produce a single pair of jeans. Similarly, Nike, Inc., must purchase leather, rubber, cloth for linings, and laces before

Figure 8.5: Four Aspects of Operations Control

Implementing the operations control system in any business requires the effective use of purchasing, inventory control, scheduling, and quality control.

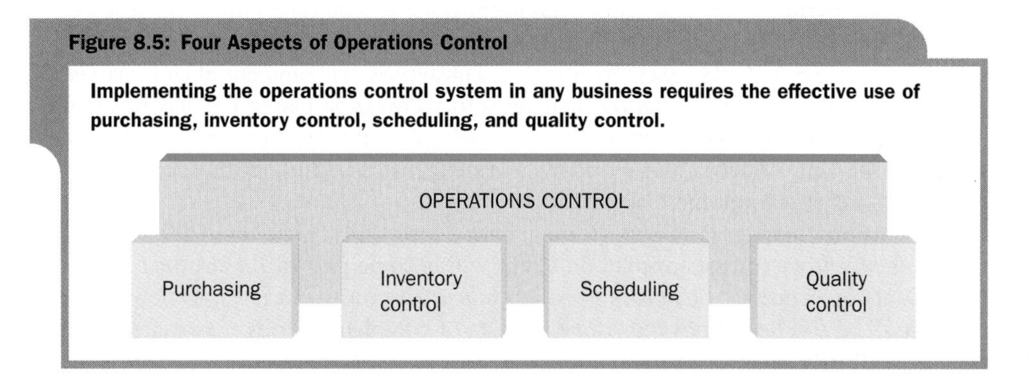

manufacturing a pair of athletic shoes. For all firms, the purchasing function is far from routine, and its importance should not be underestimated. For some products, purchased materials make up more than 50 percent of their wholesale costs. To improve their purchasing systems, aerospace giants Boeing, BAE Systems, Lockheed Martin, and Raytheon jointly developed an online exchange that links more than 37,000 suppliers, hundreds of airlines, and national governments into a single Web-based marketplace for parts. These four firms have used the Internet trading exchange to purchase parts and supplies valued at approximately $70 billion each year since 2000. According to Boeing, "By using a single e-marketplace, all of us—manufacturers, suppliers, airline and government customers, and service providers—can significantly lower transaction costs and deliver more value."[9]

The objective of purchasing is to ensure that required materials are available when they are needed, in the proper amounts, and at minimum cost. Generally, the company with purchasing needs and suppliers must develop a working relationship built on trust. In addition to a working relationship built on trust, many companies believe that purchasing is one area where they can promote diversity. For example, AT&T has developed a Supplier Diversity Program that includes minorities, women, and disabled veteran business enterprises. Goals for the AT&T program include purchasing a total of 21.5 percent of all products and services from these three groups. As a result of its Supplier Diversity Program, the company is now recognized as one of the nation's leading companies in supplier diversity.[10]

Purchasing personnel should be on the lookout constantly for new or backup suppliers, even when their needs are being met by their present suppliers, because problems such as strikes and equipment breakdowns can cut off the flow of purchased materials from a primary supplier at any time.

The choice of suppliers should result from careful analysis of a number of factors. The following are especially critical:

- *Price.* Comparing prices offered by different suppliers is always an essential part of selecting a supplier. Even tiny differences in price add up to enormous sums when large quantities are purchased.
- *Quality.* Purchasing specialists always try to buy materials at a level of quality in keeping with the type of product being manufactured. The minimum acceptable quality is usually specified by product designers.
- *Reliability.* An agreement to purchase high-quality materials at a low price is the purchaser's dream. But the dream becomes a nightmare if the supplier does not deliver.
- *Credit terms.* Purchasing specialists should determine if the supplier demands immediate payment or will extend credit. Also, does the supplier offer a cash discount or reduction in price for prompt payment?
- *Shipping costs.* Low prices and favorable credit terms offered by a supplier can be wiped out when the buyer must pay the shipping costs. Above all, the question of who pays the shipping costs should be answered before any supplier is chosen.

Inventory Control

Can you imagine what would happen if a Coca-Cola manufacturing plant ran out of the company's familiar red and white aluminum cans? It would be impossible to complete the manufacturing process and ship the cases of Coke to retailers. Management would be forced to shut the assembly line down until the next shipment of cans arrived from a supplier. In reality, operations managers for Coca-Cola realize the disasters that a shortage of needed materials can cause and will avoid this type of problem if at all possible. The simple fact is that shutdowns are expensive because costs such as rent, wages, and insurance still must be paid.

Operations managers are concerned with three types of inventories. A *raw-materials inventory* consists of materials that will become part of the product during the production process. The *work-in-process inventory* consists of partially completed products. The *finished-goods inventory* consists of completed goods. Associated with each type of inventory are a *holding cost,* or storage cost, and a *stock-out cost,* the cost of running out of inventory. **Inventory control** is the process of managing inventories in such a way as to minimize inventory costs, including both holding costs and potential stock-out costs.

Today, computer systems are being used to keep track of inventories, provide periodic inventory reports, and alert managers to impending stock-outs. One of the most sophisticated methods of inventory control used today is materials requirements planning. **Materials requirements planning (MRP)** is a computerized system that integrates production planning and inventory control. One of the great advantages of an MRP system is its ability to juggle delivery schedules and lead times effectively. For a complex product such as an automobile or airplane, it is virtually impossible for individual managers to oversee the hundreds of parts that go into the finished product. However, a manager using an MRP system can arrange both order and delivery schedules so that materials, parts, and supplies arrive when they are needed.

Two extensions of MRP are used by manufacturing firms today. The first is known as *manufacturing resource planning,* or simply *MRP II.* The primary difference between the two systems is that MRP involves just production and inventory personnel, whereas MRP II involves the entire organization. Thus MRP II provides a single common set of facts that can be used by all the organization's managers to make effective decisions. The second extension of MRP is known as *enterprise resource planning* (ERP). The primary difference between ERP and the preceding methods is that ERP software is more sophisticated and can monitor not only inventory and production processes but also quality, sales, and even such variables as inventory at a supplier's location.

Ethics Matters

No-Influence Buying

If you were a professional buyer, would a free lunch or T-shirt influence you to choose one supplier over another? Companies worry that purchasing personnel, who have the power to make or break deals, may be swayed if a supplier offers them something for free. In fact, two buyers who used to work for Home Depot recently pleaded guilty to taking money from suppliers in exchange for preferential treatment.

To keep employees out of ethically questionable situations, many firms spell out exactly what buyers can and cannot accept. For example, Wal-Mart's code of ethics states that purchasing personnel are not allowed to receive any type of free goods, services, or entertainment from current or would-be suppliers. Buyers are advised to avoid "even the appearance of a conflict between personal interests and professional responsibility." Both buyers and suppliers know that the retailer will not hesitate to back up its words with action.

Intel's code of ethics is just as specific about buyer-supplier relationships: "We do not seek favors directly or indirectly, such as gifts, entertainment, sponsorships, or contributions from organizations doing business or seeking to do business with Intel." The high-tech firm even provides supplier ethics training (in several languages) so everybody knows the rules.

Sources: David Armstrong, "At CVS Golf Gala, Suppliers Pay for Access to Executives," *Wall Street Journal,* September 24, 2008, **www.wsj.com**; James Bandler and Gary McWilliams, "Wal-Mart Chief Bought Ring from Firm's Vendor," *Wall Street Journal,* May 30, 2007, p. A4; **www.walmart.com**; **www.intel.com**.

Because large firms can incur huge inventory costs, much attention has been devoted to inventory control. The just-in-time system being used by some businesses is one result of all this attention. A **just-in-time inventory system** is designed to ensure that materials or supplies arrive at a facility just when they are needed so that storage and holding costs are minimized. The customer must specify what will be needed, when, and in what amounts. The supplier must be sure that the right supplies arrive at the agreed-on time and location. For example, managers using a just-in-time inventory system at a Toyota assembly plant determine the number of automobiles that will be assembled in a specified time period. Then Toyota purchasing personnel order *just* the parts needed to produce those automobiles. In turn, suppliers deliver the parts *in time* or when they are needed on the assembly line.

Without proper inventory control, it is impossible for operations managers to schedule the work required to produce goods that can be sold to customers.

inventory control the process of managing inventories in such a way as to minimize inventory costs, including both holding costs and potential stock-out costs

materials requirements planning (MRP) a computerized system that integrates production planning and inventory control

just-in-time inventory system a system designed to ensure that materials or supplies arrive at a facility just when they are needed so that storage and holding costs are minimized

Scheduling

Scheduling is the process of ensuring that materials and other resources are at the right place at the right time. The materials and resources may be moved from a warehouse to the workstations, they may move from station to station along an assembly line, or they may arrive at workstations "just in time" to be made part of the work in process there.

As our definition implies, both place and time are important to scheduling. (This is no different from, say, the scheduling of classes. You cannot attend your

scheduling the process of ensuring that materials and other resources are at the right place at the right time

Which type of inventory is this? *Most manufacturers have three types of inventory: Raw-materials inventory, work-in-process inventory, and finished-goods inventory. To keep track of each type of inventory and reduce inventory holding costs, most firms use computers and software to make sure they have just the right amount of inventory.*

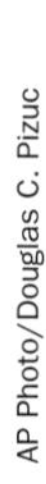

classes unless you know *both* where and when they are held.) The *routing* of materials is the sequence of workstations that the materials will follow. Assume that Drexel-Heritage—one of America's largest and oldest furniture manufacturers—is scheduling production of an oval coffee table made from cherry wood. Operations managers would route the needed materials (wood, screws, packaging materials, and so on) through a series of individual workstations along an assembly line. At each workstation, a specific task would be performed, and then the partially finished coffee table would move to the next workstation. When routing materials, operations managers are especially concerned with the sequence of each step of the production process. For the coffee table, the top and legs must be cut to specifications before the wood is finished. (If the wood were finished before being cut, the finish would be ruined, and the coffee table would have to be stained again.)

When scheduling production, managers also are concerned with timing. The *timing* function specifies when the materials will arrive at each station and how long they will remain there. For the cherry coffee table, it may take workers thirty minutes to cut the table top and legs and another thirty minutes to drill the holes and assemble the table. Before packaging the coffee table for shipment, it must be finished with cherry stain and allowed to dry. This last step may take as long as three days depending on weather conditions and humidity.

Whether or not the finished product requires a simple or complex production process, operations managers are responsible for monitoring schedules—called *follow-up*—to ensure that the work flows according to a timetable. For complex products, many operations managers prefer to use Gantt charts or the PERT technique.

Gantt chart a graphic scheduling device that displays the tasks to be performed on the vertical axis and the time required for each task on the horizontal axis

Scheduling Through Gantt Charts Developed by Henry L. Gantt, a **Gantt chart** is a graphic scheduling device that displays the tasks to be performed on the vertical axis and the time required for each task on the horizontal axis. Gantt charts

- allow you to determine how long a project should take.
- lay out the order in which tasks need to be completed.
- determine the resources needed.
- monitor progress of different activities required to complete the project.

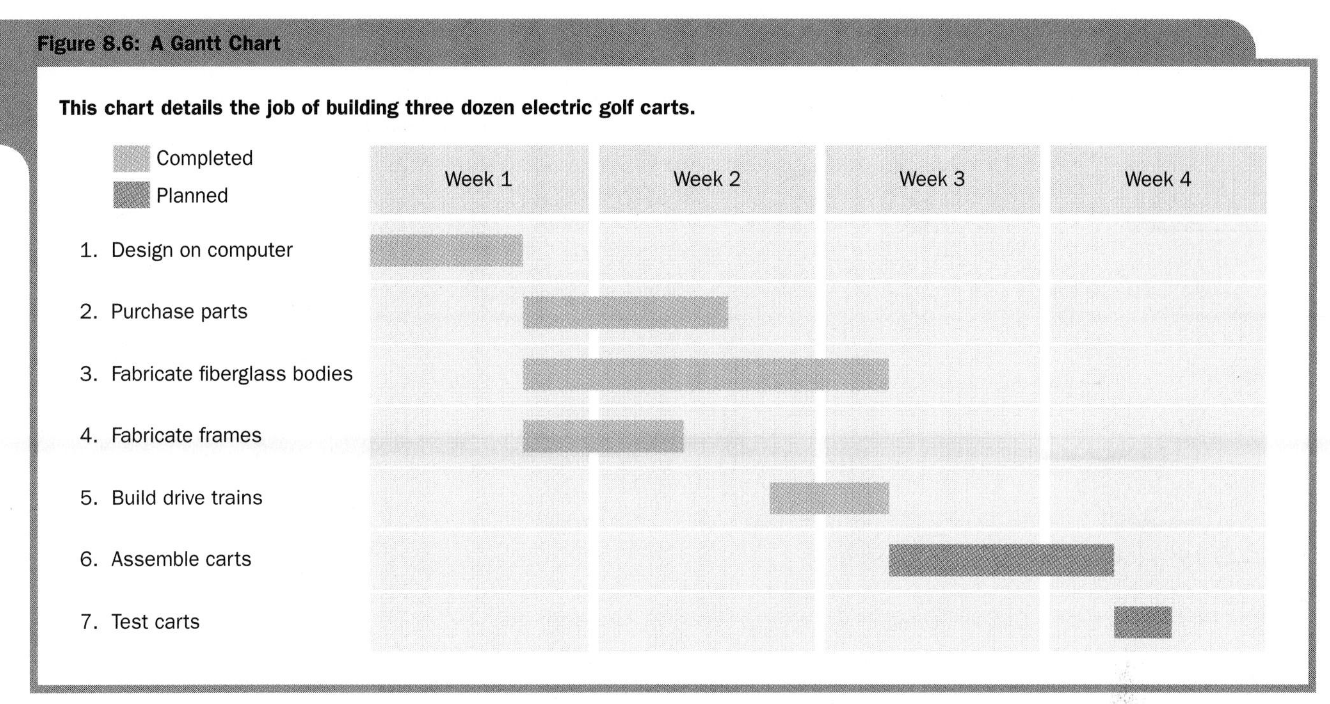

Figure 8.6: A Gantt Chart

Source: Robert Kreitner, *Management,* 10th ed. Copyright © 2007 by Houghton Mifflin Company. Reprinted with permission.

A Gantt chart that describes the activities required to build three dozen golf carts is illustrated in Figure 8.6. Gantt charts usually are not suitable for scheduling extremely complex situations. Nevertheless, using them forces a manager to plan the steps required to get a job done and to specify time requirements for each part of the job.

Scheduling via PERT Another technique for scheduling a complex process or project and maintaining control of the schedule is **PERT (Program Evaluation and Review Technique)**. To use PERT, we begin by identifying all the major *activities* involved in the project. For example, the activities involved in producing your textbook are illustrated in Figure 8.7.

PERT (Program Evaluation and Review Technique) a scheduling technique that identifies the major activities necessary to complete a project and sequences them based on the time required to perform each one

All events are arranged in a sequence. In doing so, we must be sure that an event that must occur before another event in the actual process also occurs before that event on the PERT chart. For example, the manuscript must be edited before the type is set. Next, we use arrows to connect events that must occur in sequence. We then estimate the time required for each activity and mark it near the corresponding arrow. The sequence of production activities that take the longest time from start to finish is called the **critical path**. The activities on this path determine the minimum time in which the process can be completed. These activities are the ones that must be scheduled and controlled carefully. A delay in any one of them will cause a delay in completion of the project as a whole.

critical path the sequence of production activities that takes the longest time from start to finish

The critical path runs from event 1 to event 4 to event 5. It then runs through events 6, 8, and 9 to the finished book at event 10. *Any* delay in an activity on the critical path will hold up publication. Thus, if necessary, resources could be diverted from cover preparation to, say, making up of pages or preparing pages for printing.

Quality Control

As mentioned earlier in this chapter, American business firms that compete in the very competitive global marketplace have taken another look at the importance of improving quality. Today, there is even a national quality award. The **Malcolm Baldrige National Quality Award** is given by the President of the United States to organizations that apply and are judged to be outstanding in specific managerial tasks that lead to improved quality for both products and services. Winners include

Malcolm Baldrige National Quality Award an award given by the President of the United States to organizations that apply and are judged to be outstanding in specific managerial tasks that lead to improved quality for both products and services

Figure 8.7: Simplified PERT Diagram for Producing This Book

A PERT diagram identifies the activities necessary to complete a given project and arranges the activities based on the total time required for each to become an event. The activities on the critical path determine the minimum time required.

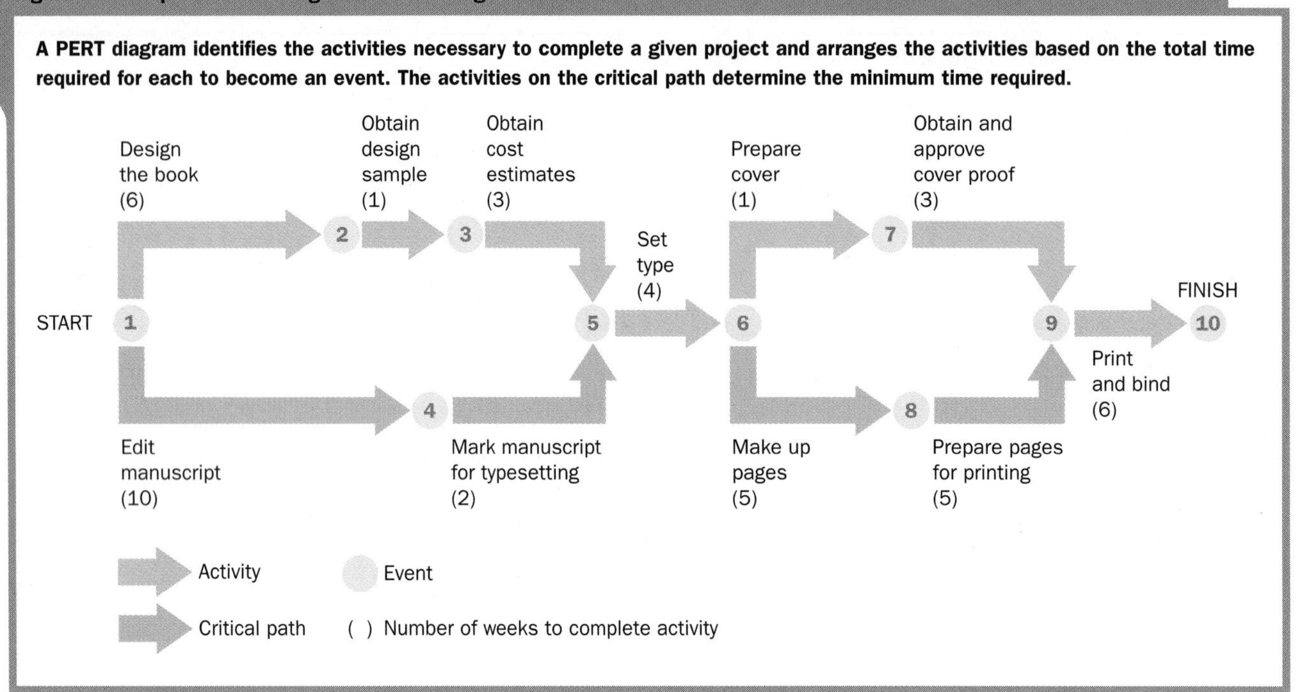

Ritz-Carlton Hotels, Boeing, Motorola, 3M Dental Products Division, Richland Communtiy College (part of the Dallas Community College District), and many others. For many organizations, using the Baldrige criteria results in

- better employee relations,
- higher productivity,
- greater customer satisfaction,
- increased market share, and
- improved profitability.[11]

While winning the "Baldrige" can mean prestige and lots of free media coverage, the winners all have one factor in common: They use quality control to improve their firm's products or services.

quality control the process of ensuring that goods and services are produced in accordance with design specifications

statistical process control (SPC) a system that uses sampling to obtain data that are plotted on control charts and graphs to see if the production process is operating as it should and to pinpoint problem areas

statistical quality control (SQC) a set of specific statistical techniques used to monitor all aspects of the production process to ensure that both work in progress and finished products meet the firm's quality standards

inspection the examination of the quality of work in process

Quality control is the process of ensuring that goods and services are produced in accordance with design specifications. The major objective of quality control is to see that the organization lives up to the standards it has set for itself on quality. Some firms, such as Mercedes-Benz and Neiman Marcus, have built their reputations on quality. Customers pay more for their products in return for assurances of high quality. Other firms adopt a strategy of emphasizing lower prices along with reasonable (but not particularly high) quality.

Many U.S. firms use two systems to gather statistical information about the quality of their products and study the way they operate. **Statistical process control (SPC)** is a system that uses sampling to obtain data that are plotted on control charts and graphs to see if the production process is operating as it should and to pinpoint problem areas. **Statistical quality control (SQC)**, a similar technique, is a set of specific statistical techniques used to monitor all aspects of the production process to ensure that both work in progress and finished products meet the firm's quality standards. A firm can use the information provided by both these to correct problems in the production process and to improve the quality of its products.

Increased effort is also being devoted to **inspection**, which is the examination of the quality of work in process. Inspections are performed at various times during production. Purchased materials may be inspected when they arrive at the production facility. Subassemblies and manufactured parts may be inspected before they become part of a finished product. And finished goods may be inspected before they are shipped to customers. Items that are within design specifications continue on their way. Those that are not within design specifications are removed from production.

Entrepreneurial Challenge

Only the Best

Many small businesses seek a competitive advantage by specializing in top quality and even customizing products to each buyer's needs and specifications. Here's how two entrepreneurs are doing just that.

- *Marlin Steel Wire Products.* Ten years ago, this manufacturer of wire baskets for industrial use was nearly driven out of business by cheap imports. Today, its revenues top $3 million, it employs 27 people, and it has a reputation for fabricating quality products to each customer's exacting requirements. Buyers like General Electric have deadlines of their own to meet, and they "care about quality," Marlin's owner says. "They can't wait eight weeks for an overseas guy to deliver it cheaper—and then find it might not fit."
- *YouBars.com.* The mother-and-son team of Ava Bise and Anthony Flynn are so proud of their high-quality nutrition snacks that they guarantee customer satisfaction. The two had baked nutrition bars with organic ingredients for years before starting their company. Then Flynn set up a website where customers can order bars tailored to their individual tastes, complete with personalized labels. The bars were a big hit: In the first year alone, sales doubled month after month.

Sources: Timothy Aeppel, "Exports Prop up Local Economies," *Wall Street Journal*, September 11, 2008, p. A1; Phaedra Hise, "Five American Manufacturers Doing It Right: Made in the USA," *Popular Mechanics*, March 2008, **www.popularmechanics.com**; Margaret Webb Pressler, "Making It: Not Made in China," *Washington Post*, August 19, 2007, p. W14; Lisa Napoli, "With These Nutrition Bars, Every Order Is Special," *New York Times*, February 20, 2008, p. H4.

Improving Quality Through Employee Participation Historically, efforts to ensure quality increased the costs associated with making that good or service. For this reason, quality and productivity were viewed as conflicting: One was increased at the other's expense. Over the years, more and more managers have realized that quality is an essential "ingredient" of the good or service being provided. This view of quality provides several benefits. The number of defects decreases, which causes profits to increase. Making products right the first time reduces many of the rejects and much of the rework. And making employees responsible for quality often eliminates the need for inspection. An employee is encouraged to accept full responsibility for the quality of his or her work.

Because of increased global competition, many American manufacturers have adopted a goal that calls for better quality in their products. As noted in Chapter 6, a *total quality management* (TQM) program coordinates the efforts directed at improving customer satisfaction, increasing employee participation, strengthening supplier partnerships, and facilitating an organizational atmosphere of continuous quality improvement. Firms such as American Express, AT&T, Motorola, and Hewlett Packard all have used TQM to improve product quality and, ultimately, customer satisfaction.

Another technique that businesses may use to improve not only quality but also overall performance is Six Sigma. **Six Sigma** is a disciplined approach that relies on statistical data and improved methods to eliminate defects for a firm's products and services. While many experts agree that Six Sigma is similar to TQM, Six Sigma often has more top-level support, much more teamwork, and a new corporate attitude or culture. The companies that developed, refined, and have the most experience with Six Sigma are Motorola, General Electric, Allied Signal, and Honeywell. While each of these companies is a corporate giant, the underlying principles of Six Sigma can be used by all firms regardless of size. For more information about Six Sigma, go to **www.isixsigma.com.**[12]

Six Sigma a disciplined approach that relies on statistical data and improved methods to eliminate defects for a firm's products and services

The use of a **quality circle**, a team of employees who meet on company time to solve problems of product quality, is another way manufacturers are achieving better quality at the operations level. Quality circles have been used successfully in such companies as IBM, Northrop Grumman Corporation, and Compaq Computers.

quality circle a team of employees who meet on company time to solve problems of product quality

World Quality Standards: ISO 9000 and ISO 14000 Different companies have different perceptions of quality. Without a common standard of quality, however, customers may be at the mercy of manufacturers and vendors. As the number of companies competing in the world marketplace has increased, so has the seriousness of this problem. To deal with it, the **International Organization for Standardization** (a nongovernmental organization in Geneva, Switzerland, with a membership of 157 countries) brought together a panel of quality experts to define what methods a company must use to produce a quality product.

International Organization for Standardization a nongovernmental organization in Geneva, Switzerland, with a membership of 157 countries that develops standards for products to facilitate trade across national borders

It's a real plus to have help when solving problems. *At Google's European headquarters in Dublin, Ireland, employee participation helps to improve the quality of the services that the world's number one search engine provides to Internet users around the globe.*

In 1987, the panel published ISO 9000 (*iso* is Greek for "equal"), which sets the guidelines for quality management procedures that businesses must use to receive certification. Certification by independent auditors serves as evidence that a company meets the standards for quality control procedures in design, production processes, and product testing.

Although certification is not a legal requirement to do business globally, the organization's 157 member countries have approved the ISO standards. In fact, ISO 9000 is so prevalent in the European Community that many customers refuse to do business with noncertified companies. As an added bonus, companies completing the certification process often discover new, cost-efficient ways to improve their existing quality control programs.

As a continuation of this standardization process, the International Organization for Standardization has developed ISO 14000. ISO 14000 is a family of international standards for incorporating environmental concerns into operations and product standards. As with ISO 9000 certification, ISO 14000 requires that a company's procedures be documented by independent auditors. It also requires that a company develop an environmental management system that will help it to achieve environmental goals, objectives, and targets. Both the ISO 9000 and ISO 14000 family of standards are updated periodically. For example, ISO 9001:2000 reflects new standards for quality when compared with the original ISO standards.

Management of Productivity and Technology

6

Learning Objective: Summarize how productivity and technology are related.

productivity the average level of output per worker per hour

No coverage of production and operations management would be complete without a discussion of productivity. Productivity concerns all managers, but it is especially important to operations managers, the people who must oversee the creation of a firm's goods or services. We define **productivity** as the average level of output per worker per hour. Hence, if each worker at plant A produces seventy-five units per day and each worker at plant B produces only seventy units per day, the workers at plant A are more productive. If one bank teller serves twenty-five customers per hour and another serves twenty-eight per hour, the second teller is more productive.

Productivity Trends

Overall productivity growth for the business sector averaged 3.9 percent for the period 1979–2006.[13] More specifically, manufacturing productivity in 2007 increased 1.6 percent.[14] (*Note:* At the time of publication, 2007 was the last year that complete statistics were available.) Using comparable data for the latest year available, our productivity growth rate ranked twelfth among the 16 countries that the U.S. Bureau of Labor tracks. Our productivity growth is lagging behind the productivity growth rates of such countries as Korea, Taiwan, and most of the European countries.[15]

Several factors have been cited as possible causes of the reduction in America's productivity growth rate. First, the roller coaster economy that accompanied the downturn in the home construction industry and the crisis in banking and finance have caused many businesses to reduce the rate of investment in new equipment and technology. As workers have had to use increasingly outdated equipment, their ability to increase productivity has declined.

Another important factor that has hurt the U.S. productivity growth rate is the tremendous growth of the service sector in the United States. While this sector grew in the number of employees and economic importance, its productivity levels did not grow. Today, many economic experts agree that improving service-sector productivity is the next major hurdle facing U.S. business.

Finally, increased government regulation is frequently cited as a factor affecting productivity. Federal agencies such as the Occupational Safety and Health Administration (OSHA) and the Food and Drug Administration (FDA) are increasingly regulating business practices. Often, the time employees spend complying with government reporting requirements can reduce productivity growth rates.

Improving Productivity Growth Rates

Several techniques and strategies have been suggested to improve current productivity growth rates. For example:

- Government policies that may be hindering productivity growth could be eliminated or at least modified.
- Increased cooperation between labor and management could be fostered to improve productivity.
- Increased employee motivation and participation can enhance productivity.
- Changing the incentives for work and altering the reward system so that people are paid for what they contribute rather than for the time they put in may motivate employees to produce at higher levels.
- Investing more money in facilities, equipment, automation, and employee training could improve productivity.

The Impact of Computers and Robotics on Production

Automation, a development that has been revolutionizing the workplace, is the total or near-total use of machines to do work. The rapid increase in automated procedures has been made possible by the microprocessor, a silicon chip that led to the production of desktop computers for businesses, homes, and schools. In factories, microprocessors are used in robotics and in computer manufacturing systems.

automation the total or near-total use of machines to do work

Robotics

Robotics is the use of programmable machines to perform a variety of tasks by manipulating materials and tools. Robots work quickly, accurately, and steadily. For example, Illumina, Inc., a San Diego company, uses robots to screen blood samples and identify DNA quirks that cause diseases. The information then is sold to some of the world's largest pharmaceutical companies, where it is used to alter existing prescription drugs, develop new drug therapies, and customize diagnoses and treatments for all kinds of serious diseases. As an added bonus, Illumina's robots can work 24 hours a day at much lower costs than if human lab workers performed the same tests.[16]

robotics the use of programmable machines to perform a variety of tasks by manipulating materials and tools

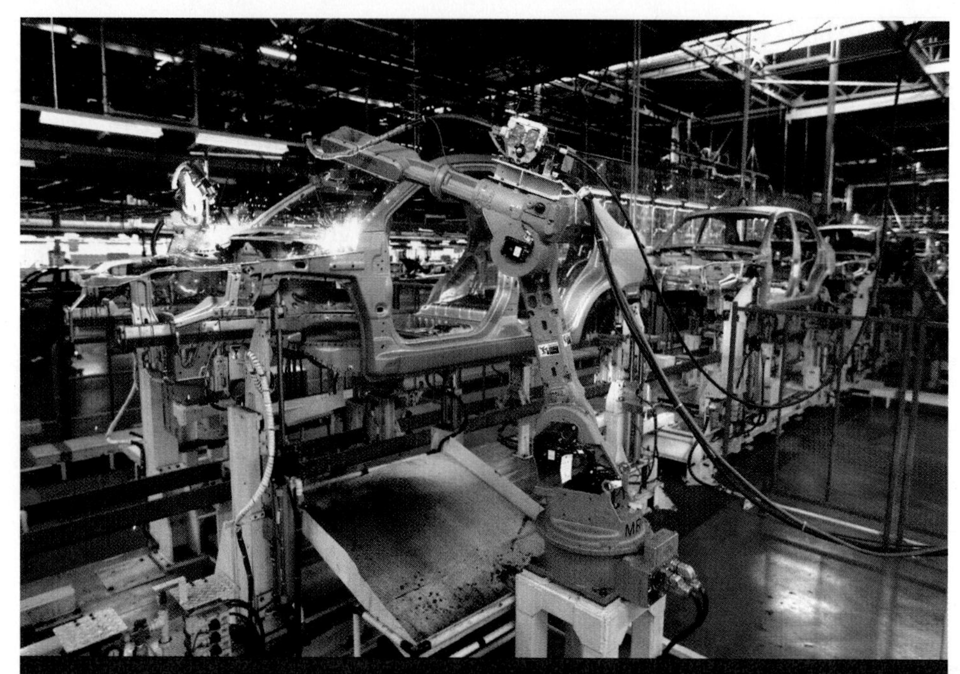

Behold today's automated assembly line. *For years, automobile manufacturers have used robotics, computer-aided design, and automation to improve productivity and reduce costs. Now, other manufacturers are using the same technology to produce their products, reduce manufacturing costs, and improve their bottom-line profits. In this photo, a robot helps assemble a Proton Saga automobile in Shah Alam, Malaysia.*

AP Photo/Vincent Thian

Robots are especially effective in tedious, repetitive assembly-line jobs, as well as in handling hazardous materials. They are also useful as artificial "eyes" that can check the quality of products as they are being processed on the assembly lines. To date, the automotive industry has made the most extensive use of robotics, but robots also have been used to mine coal, inspect the inner surfaces of pipes, assemble computer components, provide certain kinds of patient care in hospitals, and clean and guard buildings at night.

Computer Manufacturing Systems People are quick to point out how computers have changed their everyday lives, but most people do not realize the impact computers have had on manufacturing. In simple terms, the factory of the future has already arrived. For most manufacturers, the changeover began with the use of computer-aided design and computer-aided manufacturing. **Computer-aided design (CAD)** is the use of computers to aid in the development of products. Using CAD, Ford speeds up car design, Canon designs new photocopiers, and American Greetings creates new birthday cards. **Computer-aided manufacturing (CAM)** is the use of computers to plan and control manufacturing processes. A well-designed CAM system allows manufacturers to become much more productive. Not only are a greater number of products produced, but speed and quality also increase. Toyota, Hasbro, Oneida, and Apple Computer all have used CAM to increase productivity.

computer-aided design (CAD) the use of computers to aid in the development of products

computer-aided manufacturing (CAM) the use of computers to plan and control manufacturing processes

If you are thinking that the next logical step is to combine the CAD and CAM computer systems, you are right. Today, the most successful manufacturers use CAD and CAM together to form a computer-integrated manufacturing system. Specifically, **computer-integrated manufacturing (CIM)** is a computer system that not only helps to design products but also controls the machinery needed to produce the finished product. For example, Liz Claiborne, Inc., uses CIM to design clothing, to establish patterns for new fashions, and then to cut

computer-integrated manufacturing (CIM) a computer system that not only helps to design products but also controls the machinery needed to produce the finished product

the cloth needed to produce the finished product. Other advantages of using CIM include improved flexibility, more efficient scheduling, and higher product quality—all factors that make a production facility more competitive in today's global economy.

Flexible Manufacturing Systems Manufacturers have known for a number of years that the old-style, traditional assembly lines used to manufacture products present a number of problems. For example, although traditional assembly lines turn out extremely large numbers of identical products economically, the system requires expensive, time-consuming retooling of equipment whenever a new product is to be manufactured. This type of manufacturing is often referred to as a continuous process. **Continuous process** is a manufacturing process in which a firm produces the same product(s) over a long period of time. Now it is possible to use flexible manufacturing systems to solve such problems. A **flexible manufacturing system (FMS)** combines robotics and computer-integrated manufacturing in a single production system. Instead of having to spend vast amounts of time and effort to retool the traditional mechanical equipment on an assembly line for each new product, an FMS is rearranged simply by reprogramming electronic machines. Because FMSs require less time and expense to reprogram, manufacturers can produce smaller batches of a variety of products without raising the production cost. Flexible manufacturing is sometimes referred to as an intermittent process. An **intermittent process** is a manufacturing process in which a firm's manufacturing machines and equipment are changed to produce different products. When compared with the continuous process (longer production runs), an intermittent process has a shorter production run.

continuous process a manufacturing process in which a firm produces the same product(s) over a long period of time

flexible manufacturing system (FMS) a single production system that combines robotics and computer-integrated manufacturing

intermittent process a manufacturing process in which a firm's manufacturing machines and equipment are changed to produce different products

For most manufacturers, the driving force behind flexible manufacturing systems is the customer. In fact, the term *customer-driven production* is often used by operations managers to describe a manufacturing system that is driven by customer needs and what customers want to buy. For example, advanced software and a flexible manufacturing system have enabled Dell Computer to change to a more customer-driven manufacturing process. The process starts when a customer phones a sales representative on a toll-free line or accesses Dell's website. Then the representative or the customer enters the specifications for the new product directly into a computer. The order then is sent to a nearby plant. Once the order is received, a team of employees with the help of a reprogrammable assembly line can build the product just the way the customer wants it. Products include desktop computers, notebook computers, and other Dell equipment.[17] Although the costs of designing and installing an FMS such as this are high, the electronic equipment is used more frequently and efficiently than the machinery on a traditional assembly line.

Technological Displacement Automation is increasing productivity by cutting manufacturing time, reducing error, and simplifying retooling procedures. Many of the robots being developed for use in manufacturing will not replace human employees. Rather, these robots will work with employees in making their jobs easier and help to prevent accidents. No one knows, however, what the effect will be on the workforce. Some experts estimate that automation will bring new changes to more than half of all jobs within the next ten years. Total unemployment may not increase, but many workers will be faced with the choice of retraining for new jobs or seeking jobs in other sectors of the economy. Government, business, and education will have to cooperate to prepare workers for new roles in an automated workplace.

The next chapter discusses many of the issues caused by technological displacement. In addition, a number of major components of human resources management are described, and we see how managers use various reward systems to boost motivation, productivity, and morale.

return to inside business

BlendTec

To date, Blendtec has produced more than 50 "Will it blend?" videos demonstrating the quality and power of its home and commercial blenders. Although its products will not crush a crowbar, they have been proven to pulverize just about anything else that fits in a blender jar. CEO Tom Dickson has blended iPods, Wii remotes, Transformer toys, video cameras, and even pork and beans—can and all.

The company's website also includes videos of blending experiments that consumers can try at home. Some suggestions are serious (such as grinding fresh coffee beans and blending fruit smoothies) and others are not (such as keeping debt in check by grinding credit cards to dust). Viewers may laugh, but they don't forget Blendtec's mighty blenders.

Questions

1. How do you think Blendtec's video segments affect the company's operational planning?
2. Would you recommend that Blendtec seek certification for meeting ISO quality standards? Explain your answer.

CHAPTER REVIEW

Summary

1 Explain the nature of production.

Operations management consists of all the activities that managers engage in to create goods and services. Operations are as relevant to service organizations as to manufacturing firms. Generally, three major activities are involved in producing goods or services: product development, planning for production, and operations control. Today, U.S. manufacturers are forced to compete in an ever-smaller world to meet the needs of more demanding customers. In an attempt to regain a competitive edge, they have taken another look at the importance of improving quality and meeting the needs of their customers. They also have used new techniques to motivate employees, reduced costs, replaced outdated equipment, used computer-aided and flexible manufacturing systems, improved control procedures, and built new manufacturing facilities in foreign countries where labor costs are lower. Competing in the global economy is not only profitable, but it is also an essential activity that requires the cooperation of everyone within an organization.

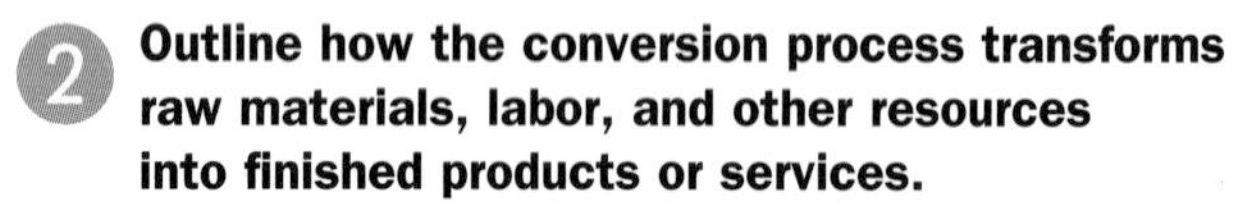

2 Outline how the conversion process transforms raw materials, labor, and other resources into finished products or services.

A business transforms resources into goods and services in order to provide utility to customers. Utility is the ability of a good or service to satisfy a human need. Form utility is created by people converting raw materials, finances, and information into finished products. Conversion processes vary in terms of the major resources used to produce goods and services (focus), the degree to which resources are changed (magnitude of change), and the number of production processes that a business uses. The application of the basic principles of operations management to the production of services has coincided with the growth and importance of service businesses in the United States.

3 Describe how research and development lead to new products and services.

Operations management often begins with product research and development (R&D). The results of R&D may be entirely new products or extensions and refinements of existing products. R&D activities are classified as basic research (aimed at uncovering new knowledge), applied research (discovering new knowledge with some potential use), and development and implementation (using new or existing knowledge to produce goods and services). If a firm sells only one product, when that product reaches the end of its life cycle, the firm will die, too. To stay in business, the firm must, at the very least, find ways to refine or extend the want-satisfying capability of its product.

4 Discuss the components involved in planning the production process.

Planning for production involves three major phases: design planning, facilities planning and site selection, and operational planning. First, design planning is undertaken to address questions related to the product line, required production capacity, and the use of technology. Production facilities, site selection, human resources, and plant layout, then must be considered. Operational planning focuses on the use of production facilities and resources. The steps for operational planning include (a) selecting a planning horizon, (b) estimating market demand, (c) comparing market demand with capacity, and (d) adjusting production of products or services to meet demand.

5 Explain how purchasing, inventory control, scheduling, and quality control affect production.

The major areas of operations control are purchasing, inventory control, scheduling, and quality control. Purchasing involves selecting suppliers. The choice of suppliers should result from careful analysis of a number of factors, including price, quality, reliability, credit terms, and shipping costs. Inventory control is the management of stocks of raw materials, work in process, and finished goods to minimize the total inventory cost. Today, most firms use a computerized system to maintain inventory records. In addition, many firms use a just-in-time inventory system, in which materials or supplies arrive at a facility just when they are needed so that storage and holding costs are minimized. Scheduling ensures that materials and other resources are at the right place at the right time. Both Gantt charts and PERT can be used to improve a firm's ability to schedule the production of products. Quality control guarantees that products meet the design specifications for those products. The major objective of quality control is to see that the organization lives up to the standards it has set for itself on quality.

Summarize how productivity and technology are related.

The productivity growth rate in the United States has fallen behind the pace of growth in some of the other industrialized nations in recent years. Several factors have been cited as possible causes for this disturbing trend, and managers have begun to explore solutions for overcoming them. Possible solutions include less government regulation, increased cooperation between management and labor, increased employee motivation and participation, new incentives for work, and additional investment by business to fund new or renovated facilities, equipment, employee training, and the use of technology.

Automation, the total or near-total use of machines to do work, has for some years been changing the way work is done in factories. A growing number of industries are using programmable machines called robots to perform tasks that are tedious or hazardous to human beings. Computer-aided design, computer-aided manufacturing, and computer-integrated manufacturing use computers to help design and manufacture products. The flexible manufacturing system combines robotics and computer-integrated manufacturing to produce smaller batches of products more efficiently than on the traditional assembly line. Instead of having to spend vast amounts of time and effort to retool the traditional mechanical equipment on an assembly line for each new product, an FMS is rearranged simply by reprogramming electronic machines.

Key Terms

You should now be able to define and give an example relevant to each of the following terms:

operations management (217)
mass production (218)
analytical process (218)
synthetic process (218)
utility (218)
form utility (218)
service economy (220)
research and development (R&D) (222)
design planning (224)
product line (224)
product design (225)
capacity (225)
labor-intensive technology (226)
capital-intensive technology (226)
plant layout (227)
planning horizon (228)
purchasing (229)
inventory control (231)
materials requirements planning (MRP) (231)
just-in-time inventory system (231)
scheduling (231)
Gantt chart (232)
PERT (Program Evaluation and Review Technique) (233)
critical path (233)
Malcolm Baldrige National Quality Award (233)
quality control (234)
statistical process control (SPC) (234)
statistical quality control (SQC) (234)
inspection (234)
Six Sigma (235)
quality circle (235)
International Organization for Standardization (235)
productivity (236)
automation (237)
robotics (237)
computer-aided design (CAD) (238)
computer-aided manufacturing (CAM) (238)
computer-integrated manufacturing (CIM) (238)
continuous process (239)
flexible manufacturing system (FMS) (239)
intermittent process (239)

Review Questions

1. List all the activities involved in operations management.
2. What is the difference between an analytical and a synthetic manufacturing process? Give an example of each type of process.
3. In terms of focus, magnitude, and number, characterize the production processes used by a local pizza parlor, a dry-cleaning establishment, and an auto repair shop.
4. Describe how research and development lead to new products.
5. Explain why product extension and refinement are important.
6. What are the major elements of design planning?
7. What factors should be considered when selecting a site for a new manufacturing facility?
8. What is the objective of operational planning? What four steps are used to accomplish this objective?
9. If you were an operations manager, what would you do if market demand exceeded the production capacity of your manufacturing facility? What action would you take if the production capacity of your manufacturing facility exceeded market demand?
10. Why is selecting a supplier so important?

11. What costs must be balanced and minimized through inventory control?
12. How can materials requirements planning (MRP), manufacturing resource planning (MRP II), and enterprise resource planning (ERP) help to control inventory and a company's production processes?
13. How does the just-in-time-inventory system help to reduce inventory costs?
14. Explain in what sense scheduling is a *control* function of operations managers.
15. How can management and employees use statistical process control, statistical quality control, inspection, and quality circles to improve a firm's products?
16. How might productivity be measured in a restaurant? In a department store? In a public school system?
17. How can CIM and FMS help a manufacturer to produce products?

Discussion Questions

1. Why would Rubbermaid—a successful U.S. company—need to expand and sell its products to customers in foreign countries?
2. Do certain kinds of firms need to stress particular areas of operations management? Explain.
3. Is it really necessary for service firms to engage in research and development? In planning for production and operations control?
4. How are the four areas of operations control interrelated?
5. In what ways can employees help to improve the quality of a firm's products?
6. Is operations management relevant to nonbusiness organizations such as colleges and hospitals? Why or why not?

Video Case 8.1

Washburn Guitars: Signature Model Quality

Washburn Guitars produces a wide variety of acoustic and electric guitars with annual sales of 50,000 guitars totaling $40 million in revenues. Washburn is a Chicago-based company that has been in business for over 123 years. Its workforce consists of craftsmen who love music, play music, and value the craft and design of each guitar.

The tone of a guitar comes from the porosity of its wood. Guitar bodies are made from mahogany, alder, poplar, and swamp ash. The necks are made of mahogany and maple. It takes five board feet to make a body and three board feet to make a neck.

The production process at Washburn starts when an idea for a new product is given to its Auto CAD engineer. He uses computer-aided-drafting (CAD) software and designs a mock-up of the new product. The drawing allows the production people to look at certain aspects of the guitar and make sure that things like string alignment and string angle are properly positioned. Once the drawing is approved, the wood is selected, cut, and reduced to the desired size and thickness. The wood is then sent to CNC machines, a computer-assisted manufacturing device, which cut out the various parts of the guitar to the specifications provided by the CAD software. Anything that the auto CAD draws can be automatically cut by these machines.

Once the CNC machine cuts the guitar parts, the parts are moved to various departments for body sanding, neck assembly, and painting. After being painted, the guitar is then sent to the dry room for two weeks, after which it is leveled and then buffed. It then goes to a subassembly bench where the strings are put on, the instrument is tuned up, and the finished guitar is ultimately played to make sure that it is within Washburn's quality standards. After being played and tune tested, the guitar gets a quality tag that is signed by all the department heads. The keys to quality for a guitar are form, fit, and function. You can have the best-looking guitar on the market, but if it doesn't play and sound good, guitar enthusiasts will not be interested in purchasing it and this news will travel throughout the music industry very quickly.

Two major changes improved Washburn guitar quality substantially in recent years. First, it hired Gil Vasquez as production manager. He had been manufacturing low-volume, high-end guitars for big stars at Baker Guitars on the West Coast. The second change came when Washburn acquired Parker Guitar, a company founded by an aviation engineer that also caters to high-end customers. Parker's production approach injected some quality influences into Washburn's processes, and Washburn's production approach added some volume efficiencies to Parker's processes. Thus, the acquisition improved both companies. Washburn knew when it acquired Parker that it would have to uphold Parker's outstanding quality controls and it did. Gil Vasquez was a major contributor in improving production quality through his relentless pursuit of quality improvements.

Washburn also has a custom shop where it makes more expensive specialty guitars primarily for high-profile musicians and performers. Customers can request specific colors, special woods, unique components, and the highest-grade accessories. A production model guitar, on the other hand, has no variations. If twelve pieces are made in a run, all the guitars are going to be the same. They're all going to come from the same run of wood, be the same color, and have the same features. The custom shop has grown from eight to sixty-five people in just two years. Production of custom guitars has gone from sixty to three hundred guitars during this period.

Signature models are used to increase the appeal of a guitar among aficionados. It makes a statement about the guitar's quality, and it strengthens Washburn's relationship with rock stars such as Dan Donegan (the lead guitarist for the Disturbed rock band) and his millions of fans. Such stars want an instrument that is unique to them and doesn't look like every other guitar that can be found in music stores around the country. In fact, Dan Donegan helped with the design of the Maya Pro DD75, which includes a range of features and high-end components that fit his specific needs. This signature model requires additional hand crafting and care, which can be challenging to a high through-put production facility like Washburn's.

Once the design of a signature model is finalized, the production process is comparable to the process described earlier except that Washburn's craftsmen are especially motivated to do their best for a high-profile guitarist like Donegan. Washburn knows that to be considered a quality producer, it has to be associated with quality users of its products.[18]

For more information about this company, go to **www.washburn.com.**

Questions

1. Using the concepts of focus, magnitude of change, and number of production processes, discuss Washburn's manufacturing conversion process.
2. How would you describe Dan Donegan's role in the production process that produced his signature guitar?
3. What form of plant layout does Washburn employ in the manufacture of its guitars?

Case 8.2 Restoring Quality at Toyota

Toyota Motor Corp. has grown tremendously in the last 10 years and currently boasts about $183 billion in annual sales. With relentless attention to quality, embodied in a global program called the Toyota Way, it has reached the very top ranks of automakers around the world. But after a recent series of embarrassing product recalls and the loss of its automatic "recommended" rating from *Consumer Reports,* Toyota is playing catch-up in the very area in which it has long prided itself—product quality.

During two recent years, the company was forced to recall almost 4 million vehicles in the United States and Japan, prompting its president, Katsuaki Watanabe, to announce a "back to basics" approach for restoring Toyota's once-enviable reputation. The tools to turn things around are already in place and have served the company well in the past. Most observers believe the company can retrieve its lock on quality by taking the right steps now.

Watanabe created a new senior-level position for quality control and set up a Customer First Activities Program Committee. He has also asked employees to look to their own actions on the job, not to rely on quality control processes to catch errors after the fact. "I told them to reaffirm once again whether they did the proper job," he said at a news conference. Nor did he "regard the problem as something that [parts] suppliers are responsible for." One problem, Watanabe believes, is Toyota's rapid growth; the firm challenges General Motors in the race to be the world's biggest car maker. "When Toyota was a small company," he said, "we could expressly communicate" about quality problems and solutions. "But now that Toyota is so big, we've realized that we have not adequately communicated."

One way in which the company communicates about quality is through charts showing the work goals of individual employees and their progress in meeting them. These are not stored out of sight in employees' files; rather, they are posted on office and factory walls for all to see. "It can be a shock to the system to be actually expected to make problems visible," said Latondra Newton, general manager of Toyota's North American manufacturing subsidiary. "Other corporate environments tend to hide problems from bosses."

Another method is the Toyota Institute, a closely guarded center for training upcoming leaders in the Toyota Way so they can carry the quality message to employees around the world. "We must prevent the Toyota Way from getting more and more diluted as Toyota grows overseas," said the institute's head. "Before, when everyone [in the company] was Japanese, we didn't have to make these things explicit. Now we have to set the Toyota Way down on paper and teach it."

Three of the tenets of the Toyota Way are mutual ownership of problems, which employee teams called "quality circles" are dedicated to solving; the need to solve problems at their source, which gives factory employees the right to stop the production line to correct a problem; and an urgent and constant drive to improve work processes, fueled by the company's active employee suggestion program.

Said Ms. Newton about the Toyota Way, "When I saw the folks in high ranks, like Mr. Watanabe, and how consistent and dedicated they were, I knew they were true believers. Now, I'm a true believer too."[19]

For more information about this company, go to **www.toyota.com**.

Questions

1. Do you think Toyota is on the right track to restoring its reputation for quality? Why or why not?
2. What can you say about Toyota's efforts to communicate about quality? Do you think it has been effective?
3. Which of Watanabe's initiatives do you think will do more to restore quality throughout the firm—the naming of a new quality manager and establishment of a "Customer First" committee, or his "back to basics" plea to employees to focus them on their individual responsibilities for maintaining quality? Explain your answer.

Building Skills for Career Success

1. JOURNALING FOR SUCCESS

Today, people purchase all kinds of products ranging from inexpensive items used everyday to expensive, sophisticated products including electronics, automobiles, and even housing. In each case, customers like to think they are "getting their money's worth" when they purchase a product or service.

Assignment

1. Describe a recent purchase that you made. Be sure to include the cost and why you made the purchase.
2. Given the cost of the product or service, were you satisfied? Why?
3. Do you think that the quality of this product or service was acceptable or unacceptable?
4. How could the manufacturer or provider of the service improve the quality of the product or service?

2. EXPLORING THE INTERNET

Improvements in the quality of products and services is an ever-popular theme in business management. Besides the obvious increase to profitability to be gained by such improvements, a company's demonstration of its continuous search for ways to improve operations can be a powerful statement to customers, suppliers, and investors. Two of the larger schools of thought in this field are Six Sigma and the European-based International Organization for Standardization. Visit the text website for updates to this exercise.

Assignment

1. Use Internet search engines to find more information about each of these topics.
2. From the information on the Internet, can you tell whether there is any real difference between these two approaches?
3. Describe one success story of a firm that realized improvement by adopting either approach.

3. DEVELOPING CRITICAL-THINKING SKILLS

Plant layout—the arrangement of machinery, equipment, and personnel within a production facility—is a critical ingredient in a company's success. If the layout is inefficient, productivity and, ultimately, profits will suffer. The purpose of the business dictates the type of layout that will be most efficient. There are three general types: process layout, product layout, and fixed-position layout.

Assignment

1. For each of the following businesses, identify the best type of layout:
   One-hour dry cleaner
   Health club
   Auto repair shop
   Fast-food restaurant
   Shipyard that builds supertankers
   Automobile assembly plant
2. Prepare a two-page report explaining why you chose these layouts and why proper plant layout is important.

4. BUILDING TEAM SKILLS

Suppose that you are planning to build a house in the country. It will be a brick, one-story structure of approximately 2,000 square feet, centrally heated and cooled. It will have three bedrooms, two bathrooms, a family room, a dining room, a kitchen with a breakfast nook, a study, a utility room, an entry foyer, a two-car garage, a covered patio, and a fireplace. Appliances will operate on electricity and propane fuel. You have received approval and can be connected to the cooperative water system at any time. Public sewerage services are not available; therefore, you must rely on a septic system. You want to know how long it will take to build the house.

Assignment

1. Identify the major activities involved in the project and sequence them in the proper order.
2. Estimate the time required for each activity and establish the critical path.
3. Working in a group, prepare a PERT diagram to show the steps involved in building your house.
4. Present your PERT diagram to the class and ask for comments and suggestions.

5. RESEARCHING DIFFERENT CAREERS

Because service businesses are now such a dominant part of our economy, job seekers sometimes overlook the employment opportunities available in production plants. Two positions often found in these plants are quality control inspector and purchasing agent.

Assignment

1. Using the *Occupational Outlook Handbook* at your local library or on the Internet (**http://stats.bls.gov/oco/home.htm**), find the following information for the jobs of quality control inspector and purchasing agent:
   Nature of work, including main activities and responsibilities
   Job outlook
   Earnings
   Training and qualifications
2. Look for other production jobs that may interest you and compile the same sort of information about them.
3. Summarize in a two-page report the key things you learned about jobs in production plants.

Running a Business Part 3

Finagle A Bagel's Management, Organization, and Production Finesse

"We don't have a traditional corporate organizational chart," states Heather Robertson, Finagle A Bagel's director of marketing, human resources, and research and development. When she hires new employees, Robertson draws the usual type of organization chart showing the copresidents on the top and the store employees on the bottom. Then she turns it upside down, explaining: "The most important people in our stores are the crew members, and the store manager's role is to support those crew members. Middle management's role is to support the store managers. And the copresidents' responsibility is to support us," referring to herself and her middle-management colleagues.

In short, the copresidents and all the people in corporate headquarters work as a team to help the general managers (who run the stores) and their crew members. Every store strives to achieve preset sales goals within budget guidelines. Higher-level managers are available to help any general manager whose store's performance falls outside the expected ranges. Moreover, each general manager is empowered to make decisions that will boost sales and make the most of opportunities to build positive relationships with local businesses and community organizations. "We want our general managers to view the store as their business," co-president Laura Trust emphasizes. "If a general manager wants to do something that will alleviate a store problem or increase sales, we give him [or her] the leeway to do it."

MANY BAGELS, ONE FACTORY

Although the copresidents decentralized authority for many store-level decisions, they achieved more efficiency by centralizing the authority and responsibility for food procurement and preparation. For example, headquarters handles payroll, invoices, and many other time-consuming activities on behalf of all the stores. This reduces the paperwork burden on general managers and frees them to concentrate on managing store-level food service to satisfy customers.

Finagle A Bagel also decided to centralize production and supply functions in its recently opened Newton facility, where the factory has enough capacity to supply up to 100 stores. "We outgrew our old facility, and we wanted to find some place we could expand our operations," copresident Laura Trust explains. Production employees prepare and shape dough for 100,000 bagels and mix 2,000 pounds of flavored cream cheese spreads every day. In addition, they slice 1,500 pounds of fruit every week. Then they gather whatever each store needs—raw dough, salad fixings, packages of condiments, or plastic bowls—and load it on the truck for daily delivery.

BAKING BAGELS AND MORE

Once the raw dough reaches a store, crew members follow the traditional New York–style method of boiling and baking bagels in various varieties, ranging from year-round favorites such as sesame to seasonal offerings such as pumpkin raisin. In line with Finagle A Bagel's fresh-food concept, the stores bake bagels every hour and tumble them into a line of bins near the front counter. Each store has a unique piece of equipment, dubbed the "bagel buzz saw," to slice and move bagels to the sandwich counter after customers have placed their orders. This equipment not only helps to prevent employee accidents and speeds food preparation, but it also entertains customers as they wait for their sandwiches.

Finagle A Bagel is constantly introducing new menu items to bring customers back throughout the day. One item the company has perfected is the bagel pizza. Earlier bagel pizzas turned out soggy, but the newest breakfast pizzas are both crunchy and tasty. The central production facility starts by mixing egg bagel dough, forms it into individual flat breads, grills the rounds, and ships them to the stores. There, a crew member tops each round with the customer's choice of ingredients, heats it, and serves it toasty fresh.

MANAGING A BAGEL RESTAURANT

Finagle A Bagel's general managers stay busy from the early morning, when they open the store and help crew members to get ready for customers, to the time they close the store at night after one last look to see whether everything is in order for the next day. General managers such as Paulo Pereira, who runs the Harvard Square Finagle A Bagel in Cambridge, must have the technical skills required to run a fast-paced food-service operation.

General managers also need good conceptual skills so that they can look beyond each individual employee and task to see how everything should fit together. One way Pereira does this is by putting himself in the customer's shoes. He is constantly evaluating how customers would judge the in-store experience, from courteous, attentive counter service to the availability of fresh foods, clean tables, and well-stocked condiment containers.

Just as important, Pereira—like other Finagle A Bagel general managers—must have excellent interpersonal skills to work effectively with customers, crew members, colleagues, and higher-level managers. Pereira knows that he can't be successful without being able to work well with other people, especially those he supervises. "You need to have a good crew behind you to help you every single hour of the day," he says. "Every employee needs to feel special and appreciated. I try to treat employees as fairly as possible, and I try to accommodate their needs."

Questions

1. What does Finagle A Bagel's upside-down organization chart suggest about the delegation of authority and coordination techniques within the company?
2. Is Finagle A Bagel a tall or flat organization? How do you know?
3. What values seem to permeate Finagle A Bagel's corporate culture?
4. Why would Finagle A Bagel build a dough factory that has more capacity than the company needs to supply its stores and its wholesale customers?

Building a Business Plan Part 3

Now you should be ready to provide evidence that you have a management team with the necessary skills and experience to execute your business plan successfully. Only a competent management team can transform your vision into a successful business. You also should be able to describe your manufacturing and operations plans. The three chapters in Part 3 of your textbook, "Understanding the Management Process," "Creating a Flexible Organization," and "Producing Quality Goods and Services," should help you in answering some of the questions in this part of the business plan.

THE MANAGEMENT TEAM COMPONENT

The management team component should include the answers to at least the following questions:

3.1. How is your team balanced in technical, conceptual, interpersonal, and other special skills needed in your business?

3.2. What will be your style of leadership?

3.3. How will your company be structured? Include a statement of the philosophy of management and company culture.

3.4. What are the key management positions, compensation, and key policies?

3.5. Include a job description for each management position, and specify who will fill that position. *Note:* Prepare an organization chart and provide the résumé of each key manager for the appendix.

3.6. What other professionals, such as a lawyer, an insurance agent, a banker, and a certified public accountant, will you need for assistance?

THE MANUFACTURING AND OPERATIONS PLANS COMPONENT

If you are in a manufacturing business, now is a good time to describe your manufacturing and operations plans, space requirements, equipment, labor force, inventory control, and purchasing requirements. Even if you are in a service-oriented business, many of these questions still may apply.

The manufacturing and operations plan component should include the answers to at least the following questions:

3.7. What are the advantages and disadvantages of your planned location in terms of
- Wage rates
- Unionization
- Labor pool
- Proximity to customers and suppliers
- Types of transportation available
- Tax rates
- Utility costs
- Zoning requirements

3.8. What facilities does your business require? Prepare a floor plan for the appendix. Will you rent, lease, or purchase the facilities?

3.9. Will you make or purchase component parts to be assembled into the finished product? Make sure to justify your "make-or-buy decision."

3.10. Who are your potential subcontractors and suppliers?

3.11. How will you control quality, inventory, and production? How will you measure your progress?

3.12. Is there a sufficient quantity of adequately skilled people in the local labor force to meet your needs?

REVIEW OF BUSINESS PLAN ACTIVITIES

Be sure to go over the information you have gathered. Check for any weaknesses, and resolve them before beginning Part 4. Also review all the answers to the questions in Parts 1, 2, and 3 to be certain that all answers are consistent throughout the entire business plan. Finally, write a brief statement that summarizes all the information for this part of the business plan.

The information contained in "Building a Business Plan" will also assist you in completing the online *Interactive Business Plan.*

PART 4 Human Resources

This part of *Business* is concerned with the most important and least predictable of all resources—people. We begin by examining the human resources efforts that organizations use to hire, develop, and retain their best employees. Then we discuss employee motivation and satisfaction. Finally, we look at organized labor and probe the sometimes controversial relationship between business management and labor unions.

altrendo/Getty Images

Attracting and Retaining the Best Employees

9

LEARNING OBJECTIVES

What you will be able to do once you complete this chapter:

1. Describe the major components of human resources management.
2. Identify the steps in human resources planning.
3. Describe cultural diversity and understand some of the challenges and opportunities associated with it.
4. Explain the objectives and uses of job analysis.
5. Describe the processes of recruiting, employee selection, and orientation.
6. Discuss the primary elements of employee compensation and benefits.
7. Explain the purposes and techniques of employee training, development, and performance appraisal.
8. Outline the major legislation affecting human resources management.

Bambu Productions/Iconica/Getty Images

inside business

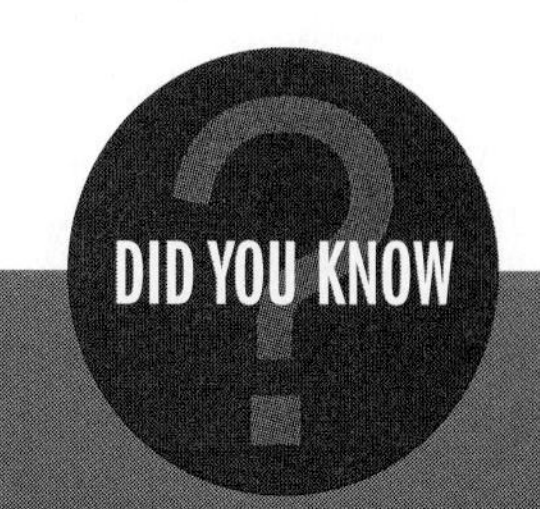

The CEO of the online fashion retailer Zappos.com has devised a simple interview question to gauge the zaniness of prospective employees: "On a scale of 1 to 10, how weird are you?"

Am I Weird Enough?

The CEO of the online fashion retailer Zappos.com has devised a simple interview question to gauge the zaniness of prospective employees: "On a scale of 1 to 10, how weird are you?" Zappos is constantly recruiting because of its spectacular growth. The company, with headquarters near Las Vegas, Nevada, rang up $70 million in annual sales just five years ago.

Today, despite intense competition from online and mall merchants, Zappos rings up $1 billion annually selling stylish shoes as well as an ever-expanding selection of fashion handbags, clothing, sunglasses, and more. Its warehouse in Kentucky operates 24 hours a day, seven days a week, to keep up with the growing flood of customer orders.

Growth is, in fact, one of Zappos' core values. So is "a little weirdness," which is why the company asks job candidates how weird they are. Those who rate themselves as a 1 or 10 on the weirdness scale are not weird enough. Those who say they are a 7 or 8 are a better fit with the hectic Zappos workplace, where weekly costume parties are the norm and outstanding customer service is the top priority.

New employees get a month of training at full pay, learning about the company's strategy, policies, practices, and culture. Before the month is over, Zappos makes this unique offer: "If you quit today, we will pay you for the amount of time you have worked, plus a $2,000 bonus." Why pay people to quit? Zappos wants to quickly weed out employees who come to realize, after a brief trial period, that this is not the job or company for them. Because of the company's thorough and thoughtful recruitment process, however, 97 percent of all new hires refuse the bonus and complete their training. By starting out on the right foot with its employees, Zappos has been able to build a capable workforce fully committed to customer service.[1]

Zappos encourages the hiring and training of employees with diverse ethnic backgrounds. Hiring a diverse mix of employees helps the company to serve a diverse customer base. For many companies, these are important factors to consider when attracting, motivating, and retaining the appropriate mix of human resources.

We begin our study of human resources management (HRM) with an overview of how businesses acquire, maintain, and develop their human resources. After listing the steps by which firms match their human resources needs with the supply available, we explore several dimensions of cultural diversity. Then we examine the concept of job analysis. Next, we focus on a firm's recruiting, selection, and orientation procedures as the means of acquiring employees. We also describe forms of employee compensation that motivate employees to remain with a firm and to work effectively. Then we discuss methods of employee training, management development, and performance appraisal. Finally, we consider legislation that affects HRM practices.

Human Resources Management: An Overview

1

Learning Objective: Describe the major components of human resources management.

human resources management (HRM) all the activities involved in acquiring, maintaining, and developing an organization's human resources

The human resource is not only unique and valuable, but it is also an organization's most important resource. It seems logical that an organization would expend a great deal of effort to acquire and make full use of such a resource. This effort is known as *human resources management* (HRM). It also has been called *staffing* and *personnel management.*

Human resources management (HRM) consists of all the activities involved in acquiring, maintaining, and developing an organization's human resources. As the definition implies, HRM begins with acquisition—getting people to work for the organization. The acquisition process can be quite competitive for certain types of qualified employees. For example, brokerage houses such as JPMorgan, Citigroup, and Merrill Lynch are building their specialized algorithmic-trading teams by recruiting experienced employees from other brokerage firms.[2] Next, steps must be taken to keep these valuable resources. (After all, they are the only business resources that can leave an organization.) Finally, the human resources should be developed to their full capacity.

HRM Activities

Each of the three phases of HRM—acquiring, maintaining, and developing human resources—consists of a number of related activities. Acquisition, for example, includes planning, as well as the various activities that lead to hiring new personnel. Altogether this phase of HRM includes five separate activities. They are as follows:

- *Human resources planning*—determining the firm's future human resources needs
- *Job analysis*—determining the exact nature of the positions
- *Recruiting*—attracting people to apply for positions
- *Selection*—choosing and hiring the most qualified applicants
- *Orientation*—acquainting new employees with the firm

Maintaining human resources consists primarily of encouraging employees to remain with the firm and to work effectively by using a variety of HRM programs, including the following:

- *Employee relations*—increasing employee job satisfaction through satisfaction surveys, employee communication programs, exit interviews, and fair treatment
- *Compensation*—rewarding employee effort through monetary payments
- *Benefits*—providing rewards to ensure employee well-being

The development phase of HRM is concerned with improving employees' skills and expanding their capabilities. The two important activities within this phase are

- *Training and development*—teaching employees new skills, new jobs, and more effective ways of doing their present jobs
- *Performance appraisal*—assessing employees' current and potential performance levels

These activities are discussed in more detail shortly, when we have completed this overview of HRM.

Responsibility for HRM

In general, HRM is a shared responsibility of line managers and staff HRM specialists. In very small organizations, the owner handles all or most HRM activities. As a firm grows in size, a human resources manager is hired to take over staff responsibilities. In firms as large as Disney, HRM activities tend to be very highly specialized. There are separate groups to deal with compensation, benefits, training and development, and other staff activities.

Specific HRM activities are assigned to those who are in the best position to perform them. Human resources planning and job analysis usually are done by staff specialists, with input from line managers. Similarly, recruiting and selection are handled by staff experts, although line managers are involved in hiring decisions. Orientation programs are devised by staff specialists and carried out by both staff specialists and line managers. Compensation systems (including benefits) most often are developed and administered by the HRM staff. However, line managers recommend pay increases and promotions. Training and development activities are the joint responsibility of staff and line managers. Performance appraisal is the job of the line manager, although HRM personnel design the firm's appraisal system in many organizations.

Human Resources Planning

2 **Learning Objective: Identify the steps in human resources planning.**

Human resources planning is the development of strategies to meet a firm's future human resources needs. The starting point is the organization's overall strategic plan. From this, human resources planners can forecast future demand for human resources. Next, the planners must determine whether the needed human resources will be available. Finally, they have to take steps to match supply with demand.

human resources planning the development of strategies to meet a firm's future human resources needs

Forecasting Human Resources Demand

Planners should base forecasts of the demand for human resources on as much relevant information as available. The firm's overall strategic plan will provide information about future business ventures, new products, and projected expansions or contractions of specific product lines. Information on past staffing levels, evolving technologies, industry staffing practices, and projected economic trends also can be helpful.

HRM staff use this information to determine both the number of employees required and their qualifications. Planners use a wide range of methods to forecast specific personnel needs. For example, with one simple method, personnel requirements are projected to increase or decrease in the same proportion as sales revenue. Thus, if a 30 percent increase in sales volume is projected over the next two years, then up to a 30 percent increase in personnel requirements may be expected for the same period. (This method can be applied to specific positions as well as to the workforce in general. It is not, however, a very precise forecasting method.) At the other extreme are elaborate, computer-based personnel planning models used by some large firms such as ExxonMobil Corporation.

AP Photo/The Times and Democrat, Van Hope

Rewarding employees. *Appropriate employee rewards help to attract and retain employees. This employee is receiving an award for having driven a million miles without an accident.*

Forecasting Human Resources Supply

The forecast of the supply of human resources must take into account both the present workforce and any changes that may occur within it. For example, suppose that planners project that in five years a firm that currently employs 100 engineers will need to employ a total of 200 engineers. Planners simply cannot assume that they will have to hire 100 engineers; during that period, some of the firm's present engineers are likely to be promoted, leave the firm, or move to other jobs within the firm. Thus, planners may project the supply of engineers in five years at 87, which means that the firm will have to hire a total of 113 new engineers. When forecasting supply, planners should analyze the organization's existing employees to determine who can be retrained to perform the required tasks.

replacement chart a list of key personnel and their possible replacements within a firm

Two useful techniques for forecasting human resources supply are the replacement chart and the skills inventory. A **replacement chart** is a list of key personnel and their possible replacements within a firm. The chart is maintained to ensure that top-management positions can be filled fairly quickly in the event of an unexpected death, resignation, or retirement. Some firms also provide additional training for employees who might eventually replace top managers.

skills inventory a computerized data bank containing information on the skills and experience of all present employees

A **skills inventory** is a computerized data bank containing information on the skills and experience of all present employees. It is used to search for candidates to fill available positions. For a special project, a manager may be seeking a current employee with specific information technology skills, at least six years of experience, and fluency in French. The skills inventory can quickly identify employees who possess such qualifications. Skill-assessment tests can be administered inside an organization, or they can be provided by outside vendors. For example, SkillView Technologies, Inc., and Bookman Testing Services TeckChek are third-party information technology skill-assessment providers.

Matching Supply with Demand

Once they have forecasted the supply and demand for personnel, planners can devise a course of action for matching the two. When demand is predicted to be greater than supply, plans must be made to recruit new employees. The timing of these actions depends on the types of positions to be filled. Suppose that we expect to open another

Human resources planning. *Human resources planning is initiated by upper-level managers.*

RF Getty Images

plant in five years. Along with other employees, a plant manager and twenty-five maintenance workers will be needed. We probably can wait quite a while before we begin to recruit maintenance personnel. However, because the job of plant manager is so critical, we may start searching for the right person for that position immediately.

When supply is predicted to be greater than demand, the firm must take steps to reduce the size of its workforce. When the oversupply is expected to be temporary, some employees may be *laid off*—dismissed from the workforce until they are needed again.

Perhaps the most humane method for making personnel cutbacks is through attrition. *Attrition* is the normal reduction in the workforce that occurs when employees leave a firm. In the last two years, several thousand of Ford Motor Company's 23,800 white collar workers in North America have left the company through a combination of involuntary layoffs and normal attrition. This helped the company meet its goal of cutting 15 percent of its North American salary costs.[3]

Early retirement is another option. Under early retirement, people who are within a few years of retirement are permitted to retire early with full benefits. Depending on the age makeup of the workforce, this may or may not reduce the staff enough.

As a last resort, unneeded employees are sometimes simply *fired*. However, because of its negative impact, this method generally is used only when absolutely necessary.

Cultural Diversity in Human Resources

3
Learning Objective: Describe cultural diversity and understand some of the challenges and opportunities associated with it.

Today's workforce is made up of many types of people. Firms can no longer assume that every employee has similar beliefs or expectations. Whereas North American white males may believe in challenging authority, Asians tend to respect and defer to it. In Hispanic cultures, people often bring music, food, and family members to work, a custom that U.S. businesses traditionally have not allowed. A job applicant who will not make eye contact during an interview may be rejected for being unapproachable, when, according to his or her culture, he or she was just being polite.

Since a larger number of women, minorities, and immigrants have entered the U.S. workforce, the workplace is more diverse. It is estimated that women make up about 46 percent of the U.S. workforce; African Americans and Hispanics each make up about 13 percent of U.S. workers.[4]

PRNewswire/American Airlines Inc.

The value of cultural diversity. *Organizations that are dedicated to diversity, such as American Airlines, gain significant benefits from their efforts. American Airlines received one of the 40 Best Companies for Diversity awards presented by* Black Enterprise *magazine.*

SPOTLIGHT

When Job Searching Online, How Long Do You Search Daily?

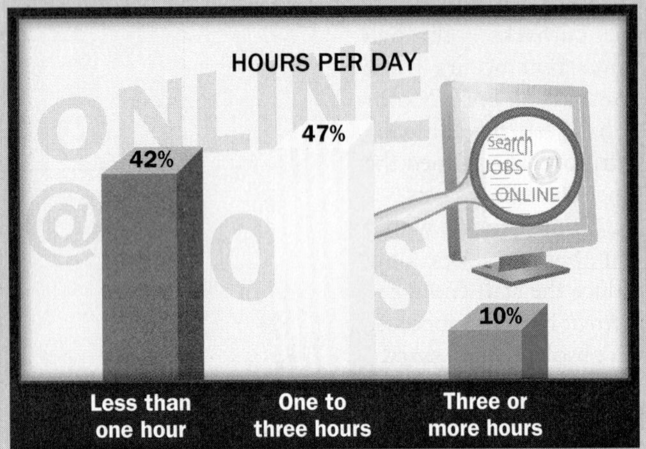

Source: www.risesmart.com, accessed November 28, 2008.

Cultural (or **workplace**) **diversity** refers to the differences among people in a workforce owing to race, ethnicity, and gender. Increasing cultural diversity is forcing managers to learn to supervise and motivate people with a broader range of value systems. The high proportion of women in the work force, combined with a new emphasis on participative parenting by men, has brought many family-related issues to the workplace. Today's more educated employees also want greater independence and flexibility. In return for their efforts, they want both compensation and a better quality of life.

Although cultural diversity presents a challenge, managers should view it as an opportunity rather than a limitation. When managed properly, cultural diversity can provide competitive advantages for an organization. Table 9.1 shows several benefits that creative management of cultural diversity can offer. A firm that manages diversity properly can develop cost advantages over other firms. Moreover, organizations that manage diversity creatively are in a much better position to attract the best personnel. A culturally diverse organization may gain a marketing edge because it understands different cultural groups. Proper guidance and management of diversity in an organization also can improve the level of creativity. Culturally diverse people frequently are more flexible in the types of positions they will accept.

cultural (workplace) diversity differences among people in a workforce owing to race, ethnicity, and gender

Because cultural diversity creates challenges along with advantages, it is important for an organization's employees to understand it. To accomplish this goal, numerous U.S. firms have trained their managers to respect and manage diversity. Diversity training programs may include recruiting minorities, training minorities to be managers, training managers to view diversity positively, teaching English as a second language, and facilitating support groups for immigrants. Many organizations

Table 9.1: Competitive Advantages of Cultural Diversity

Cost	As organizations become more diverse, the cost of doing a poor job of integrating workers will increase. Companies that handle this well thus can create cost advantages over those that do a poor job. In addition, companies also experience cost savings by hiring people with knowledge of various cultures as opposed to having to train Americans, for example, about how German people do business.
Resource acquisition	Companies develop reputations as being favorable or unfavorable prospective employers for women and ethnic minorities. Those with the best reputations for managing diversity will win the competition for the best personnel.
Marketing edge	For multinational organizations, the insight and cultural sensitivity that members with roots in other countries bring to marketing efforts should improve these efforts in important ways. The same rationale applies to marketing subpopulations domestically.
Flexibility	Culturally diverse employees often are open to a wider array of positions within a company and are more likely to move up the corporate ladder more rapidly, given excellent performance.
Creativity	Diversity of perspectives and less emphasis on conformity to norms of the past should improve the level of creativity.
Problem solving	Differences within decision-making and problem-solving groups potentially produce better decisions through a wider range of perspectives and more thorough critical analysis of issues.
Bilingual skills	Cultural diversity in the workplace brings with it bilingual and bicultural skills, which are very advantageous to the ever-growing global marketplace. Employees with knowledge about how other cultures work not only can speak to them in their language but also can prevent their company from making embarrassing moves owing to a lack of cultural sophistication. Thus, companies seek job applicants with perhaps a background in cultures in which the company does business.

Sources: Taylor H. Cox and Stacy Blake, "Managing Cultural Diversity: Implications for Organizational Competitiveness," Academy of Management Executive 5(3):46, 1991; Graciela Kenig, "Yo Soy Ingeniero: The Advantages of Being Bilingual in Technical Professions," *Diversity Monthly,* February 28, 1999, p. 13; and "Dialogue Skills in the Multicultural Workplace," *North American Post,* March 19, 1999, p. 2.

are realizing the necessity of having diversity training. Universities and colleges across the nation have ramped up efforts to increase faculty diversity. These government-funded schools are realizing that a valid education includes cultural diversity.[5] Many companies are realizing the necessity of having diversity training spanning beyond just racial issues. For example, Kroger is among a growing number of companies in Virginia that include diversity training as a regular part of employee training. These companies recognize the need to meld a cohesive workforce from a labor pool that reflects Virginia's rapidly changing demographics.[6]

A diversity program will be successful only if it is systematic, is ongoing, and has a strong, sustained commitment from top leadership. Cultural diversity is here to stay. Its impact on organizations is widespread and will continue to grow within corporations. Management must learn to overcome the obstacles and capitalize on the advantages associated with culturally diverse human resources.

Job Analysis

4

Learning Objective: Explain the objectives and uses of job analysis.

There is no sense in hiring people unless we know what we are hiring them for. In other words, we need to know the nature of a job before we can find the right person to do it.

Job analysis is a systematic procedure for studying jobs to determine their various elements and requirements. Consider the position of clerk, for example. In a large corporation, there may be fifty kinds of clerk positions. They all may be called "clerks," but each position may differ from the others in the activities to be performed, the level of proficiency required for each activity, and the particular set of qualifications that the position demands. These distinctions are the focus of job analysis. Some companies, such as HR.BLR.COM, help employers with preparing the material for job analysis and keeping them updated about state and federal HR employment laws. They provide employers with easy-to-use online service for the resources needed for HR success.[7]

job analysis a systematic procedure for studying jobs to determine their various elements and requirements

The job analysis for a particular position typically consists of two parts—a job description and a job specification. A **job description** is a list of the elements that make up a particular job. It includes the duties to be performed, the working conditions, the responsibilities, and the tools and equipment that must be used on the job (see Figure 9.1).

job description a list of the elements that make up a particular job

A **job specification** is a list of the qualifications required to perform a particular job. Included are the skills, abilities, education, and experience the jobholder must have. When attempting to hire a financial analyst, Bank of America might use the following job specification: "Requires 8–10 years of financial experience, a broad-based financial background, strong customer focus, the ability to work confidently with the client's management team, strong analytical skills. Must have strong Excel and Word skills. Personal characteristics should include strong desire to succeed, impact performer (individually and as a member of a team), positive attitude, high energy level and ability to influence others."

job specification a list of the qualifications required to perform a particular job

The job analysis is not only the basis for recruiting and selecting new employees; it is also used in other areas of HRM, including evaluation and the determination of equitable compensation levels.

Recruiting, Selection, and Orientation

5

Learning Objective: Describe the processes of recruiting, employee selection, and orientation.

In an organization with jobs waiting to be filled, HRM personnel need to (1) find candidates for those jobs and (2) match the right candidate with each job. Three activities are involved: recruiting, selection, and new employee orientation.

Recruiting

Recruiting is the process of attracting qualified job applicants. Because it is a vital link in a costly process (the cost of hiring an employee can be several thousand dollars), recruiting needs to be a systematic process. One goal of recruiters is to attract the "right number" of applicants. The right number is enough to allow a good match between applicants and open positions but not so many that matching them

recruiting the process of attracting qualified job applicants

Figure 9.1: Job Description and Job Specification

This job description explains the job of sales coordinator and lists the responsibilities of the position. The job specification is contained in the last paragraph.

SOUTH-WESTERN
JOB DESCRIPTION

TITLE:	Georgia Sales Coordinator	DATE:	3/25/09
DEPARTMENT:	College, Sales	GRADE:	12
REPORTS TO:	Regional Manager	EXEMPT/NON-EXEMPT:	Exempt

BRIEF SUMMARY:
Supervise one other Georgia-based sales representative to gain supervisory experience. Captain the 4 members of the outside sales rep team that are assigned to territories consisting of colleges and universities in Georgia. Oversee, coordinate, advise, and make decisions regarding Georgia sales activities. Based upon broad contact with customers across the state and communication with administrators of schools, the person will make recommendations regarding issues specific to the needs of higher education in the state of Georgia such as distance learning, conversion to the semester system, potential statewide adoptions, and faculty training.

PRINCIPLE ACCOUNTABILITIES:
1. Supervises/manages/trains one other Atlanta-based sales rep.
2. Advises two other sales reps regarding the Georgia schools in their territories.
3. Increases overall sales in Georgia as well as individual sales territory.
4. Assists regional manager in planning and coordinating regional meetings and Atlanta conferences.
5. Initiates a dialogue with campus administrators, particularly in the areas of the semester conversion, distance learning, and faculty development.

DIMENSIONS:
This position will have one direct report in addition to the leadership role played within the region. Revenue most directly impacted will be within the individually assigned territory, the supervised territory, and the overall sales for the state of Georgia.

KNOWLEDGE AND SKILLS:
Must have displayed a history of consistently outstanding sales in personal territory. Must demonstrate clear teamwork and leadership skills and be willing to extend beyond the individual territory goals. Should have a clear understanding of the company's systems and product offerings in order to train and lead other sales representatives. Must have the communication skills and presence to communicate articulately with higher education administrators and to serve as a bridge between the company and higher education in the state.

requires too much time and effort. For example, if there are five open positions and five applicants, the firm essentially has no choice. It must hire those five applicants (qualified or not), or the positions will remain open. At the other extreme, if several hundred job seekers apply for the five positions, HRM personnel will have to spend weeks processing their applications.

Recruiters may seek applicants outside the firm, within the firm, or both. The source used depends on the nature of the position, the situation within the firm, and sometimes the firm's established or traditional recruitment policies.

external recruiting the attempt to attract job applicants from outside an organization

internal recruiting considering present employees as applicants for available positions

selection the process of gathering information about applicants for a position and then using that information to choose the most appropriate applicant

External Recruiting **External recruiting** is the attempt to attract job applicants from outside an organization. External recruiting may include newspaper advertising, employment agencies, recruiting on college campuses, soliciting recommendations from present employees, conducting "open houses," and online employment organizations. The biggest of the online job-search sites is Monster.com, which has as clients about 490 of the *Fortune* 500 companies.[8] In addition, many people simply apply at a firm's employment office.

Clearly, it is best to match the recruiting means with the kind of applicant being sought. For example, private employment agencies most often handle professional people, whereas public employment agencies (operated by state or local governments) are more concerned with operations personnel. We might approach a private agency when looking for a vice president but contact a public agency to hire a machinist. Procter & Gamble hires graduates directly out of college. It picks the best and brightest—those not "tainted" by another company's culture. It promotes its own "inside" people. This policy makes sure that the company retains the best and brightest and trains new recruits. Procter & Gamble pays competitively and offers positions in many countries. Employee turnover is very low.[9]

The primary advantage of external recruiting is that it brings in people with new perspectives and varied business backgrounds. A disadvantage of external recruiting is that it is often expensive, especially if private employment agencies must be used. External recruiting also may provoke resentment among present employees.

Internal Recruiting **Internal recruiting** means considering present employees as applicants for available positions. Generally, current employees are considered for *promotion* to higher-level positions. However, employees may be considered for *transfer* from one position to another at the same level. Among leading companies, 85 percent of CEOs are promoted from within. In the companies that hire CEOs from outside, 40 percent of the CEOs are gone after eighteen months.[10]

Promoting from within provides strong motivation for current employees and helps the firm to retain quality personnel. General Electric, ExxonMobil, and Eastman Kodak are companies dedicated to promoting from within. The practice of *job posting,* or informing current employees of upcoming openings, may be a company policy or required by union contract. The primary disadvantage of internal recruiting is that promoting a current employee leaves another position to be filled. Not only does the firm still incur recruiting and selection costs, but it also must train two employees instead of one.

In many situations it may be impossible to recruit internally. For example, a new position may be such that no current employee is qualified. Or the firm may be growing so rapidly that there is no time to reassign positions that promotion or transfer requires.

Selection

Selection is the process of gathering information about applicants for a position and then using that information to choose the most appropriate applicant. Note the use of the word *appropriate.* In selection, the idea is not to hire the person with the *most* qualifications but rather the applicant who is *most appropriate.* The selection of an applicant is made by line managers responsible for the position. However, HRM personnel usually help by developing a pool of applicants and by expediting the assessment of these applicants.

Entrepreneurial Challenge

How Small Businesses Attract Top Talent

How can small businesses attract talented employees to keep growing? This is one of the most pressing problems any entrepreneur faces, according to the National Federation of Independent Business. Yet few small businesses have the budget to match the generous compensation and benefits that deep-pocketed corporations can offer.

Even without a big payroll budget, entrepreneurs can play up several important advantages when recruiting job candidates. First, a new hire will have many opportunities to work closely with top management and to get involved in the key decisions that make a real difference in a small business. This is rarely the case in big corporations.

Second, employees often play several roles in a small workplace, which allows them to expand their knowledge, skills, and experience in a short time. In fact, ambitious new hires who learn quickly and prove their value can expect to move up to bigger things in a small business.

Finally, employees who prefer a flexible work environment will probably feel more at home in a small business than in a big one. In their quest for top talent, entrepreneurs are usually very willing to tailor responsibilities, schedules, training, or almost any other aspect of the job for the right candidate.

Sources: Deb Koen, "Promote Strengths to Woo Employees to New, Small Firm," *Rochester Democrat and Chronicle* (Rochester, NY), October 5, 2008, **www.democratandchronicle.com**; "Surveys Agree: It's Still Hard to Find Skills," *WFC Resources Newsbrief*, November 2007, p. 4; Karen E. Klein, "Hiring Advantages for Small Business," *BusinessWeek Online*, July 24, 2007, **www.businessweek.com**.

Recruiting. *This Target ad is a part of this company's recruiting program.*

Courtesy Target

Common means of obtaining information about applicants' qualifications are employment applications, interviews, references, and assessment centers.

Employment Applications An employment application is useful in collecting factual information on a candidate's education, work experience, and personal history (see Figure 9.2). The data obtained from applications usually are used for two purposes: to identify applicants who are worthy of further scrutiny and to familiarize interviewers with their backgrounds.

Many job candidates submit résumés, and some firms require them. A *résumé* is a one- or two-page summary of the candidate's background and qualifications. It may include a description of the type of job the applicant is seeking. A résumé may be sent to a firm to request consideration for available jobs, or it may be submitted along with an employment application.

To improve the usefulness of information, HRM specialists ask current employees about factors in their backgrounds most related to their current jobs. Then these

Figure 9.2: Typical Employment Application

Employers use applications to collect factual information on a candidate's education, work experience, and personal history.

3M Employment Application
Form 14650 - D

3M Staffing Resource Center
3M Center, Building 224-1W-02
P.O. Box 33224
St. Paul, MN 55133-3224

No. 109060

Personal Data (*Print or Type*)

Name — Last — First

Present Address — Street Address — City, State and Zip — Internet e-mail Address

Permanent Address — *Leave blank if same as above* — Street Address — City, State and Zip

Job Interest — Position applied for — Salary desired — Type of position applied for: ☐ Regular ☐ Part-time ☐ Temporary ☐ Summer ☐

Authorization to Work — It is unlawful for 3M to hire individuals that are not authorized to work in the citizens or aliens that are authorized to work in the United States. If you rec offer, before you will be placed on the payroll, you will be required to docum that is authorized to work in the United States.
Are you a United States citizen or a lawful permanent resident? ☐ Yes
If your answer is No, what type of Visa and employment authorization do y

Education History — Schools Attended (Last School First) — Attendance Dates Mo./Yr. From To — Grad. Date
Name of School (City, State)
High School or GED

Additional Education Information (If additional space is needed, attach separate page) — Faculty person who knows you best (name, telephone) — Memberships in professional or honorary societies and any other extracurricular activities — Post graduate research, title and description — Publications/Patents Issued

Please Open Folder and Complete Additional Info

Printed with soy inks on Torchglow Opaque (made of 50% recycled fiber

General Information and Job Requirements — Are you willing to: Work Shifts ☐ Yes ☐ No — Work overtime ☐ Yes ☐ No — Work a schedule other than M/F ☐ Yes ☐ No — Work a rotation work schedule ☐ Yes ☐ No
Travel ☐ Yes ___% ☐ No — List any restrictions regarding relocation — Are you willing to relocate? ☐ Yes ☐ No
If you wish to indicate that you were referred to 3M by any of the following, please check appropriate box and specify
☐ Employment advertisement (Name of publication) ☐ Employment agency (Name of agency) ☐ 3M Employee (Name) ☐ Other
Are you under 18? ☐ Yes ☐ No — Have you ever ☐ been employed by 3M or any 3M Subsidiary ☐ previously applied to 3M or any 3M Subsidiary — If so, please check appropriate box and specify location, date, employee number - (include last two 3M performance reviews if appropriate and available.) — Date/Employee Number

Employment Record — *List most current or recent employer first, include periods of unemployment, include U.S. Military Service (show rank/rate at discharge, but not type of discharge). Include previous 3M experience (summer/part time jobs and Cooperative Education assignments and any volunteer experience which relates to the position you are applying for).*
Employer (company name) — Immediate supervisor's name — Your job title
Street Address — Employment dates (mo. and yr.) From To — Salary Begin End
City, State, Zip Code — Reason for leaving or why do you want to leave?
Company's Product or Service — Summarize your job duties

Additional Information — *(Please include any additional information you think might be helpful to use in considering you for employment, such as additional work experience, activities, accomplishments, etc.)*

Source: Courtesy of 3M.

Recruiting at job fairs. *At job fairs, recruiters and job applicants can meet to discuss job opportunities and applicants' qualifications.*

factors are included on the applications and may be weighted more heavily when evaluating new applicants' qualifications.

Employment Tests Tests administered to job candidates usually focus on aptitudes, skills, abilities, or knowledge relevant to the job. Such tests (basic computer skills tests, for example) indicate how well the applicant will do the job. Occasionally, companies use general intelligence or personality tests, but these are seldom helpful in predicting specific job performance. However, *Fortune* 500 companies, as well as an increasing number of medium- and small-sized companies, are using predictive behavior personality tests as administration costs decrease.

At one time, a number of companies were criticized for using tests that were biased against certain minority groups—in particular, African Americans. The test results were, to a great extent, unrelated to job performance. Today, a firm must be able to prove that a test is not discriminatory by demonstrating that it accurately measures one's ability to perform. Applicants who believe that they have been discriminated against through an invalid test may file a complaint with the Equal Employment Opportunity Commission (EEOC).

Interviews The interview is perhaps the most widely used selection technique. Job candidates are interviewed by at least one member of the HRM staff and by the person for whom they will be working. Candidates for higher-level jobs may meet with a department head or vice president over several interviews.

Interviews provide an opportunity for applicants and the firm to learn more about each other. Interviewers can pose problems to test the candidate's abilities, probe employment history, and learn something about the candidate's attitudes and motivation. The candidate has a chance to find out more about the job and potential coworkers.

Unfortunately, interviewing may be the stage at which discrimination begins. For example, suppose that a female applicant mentions that she is the mother of small children. Her interviewer may assume that she would not be available for job-related travel. In addition, interviewers may be unduly influenced by such factors as appearance. Or they may ask different questions of different applicants so that it becomes impossible to compare candidates' qualifications.

Some of these problems can be solved through better interviewer training and use of structured interviews. In a *structured interview,* the interviewer asks only a prepared set of job-related questions. The firm also may consider using several different interviewers for each applicant, but this is likely to be costly.

References A job candidate generally is asked to furnish the names of references—people who can verify background information and provide personal evaluations. Naturally, applicants tend to list only references who are likely to say good things. Thus, personal evaluations obtained from references may not be of much value. However, references are often contacted to verify such information as previous job responsibilities and the reason an applicant left a former job.

Assessment Centers An assessment center is used primarily to select current employees for promotion to higher-level positions. Typically, a group of employees is sent to the center a few days. While there, they participate in activities designed to simulate the management environment and to predict managerial effectiveness. Trained observers make recommendations regarding promotion possibilities. Although this technique is gaining popularity, the expense involved limits its use.

Orientation

Once all information about job candidates has been collected and analyzed, a job offer is extended. If it is accepted, the candidate becomes an employee.

Soon after a candidate joins a firm, he or she goes through the firm's orientation program. **Orientation** is the process of acquainting new employees with an organization. Orientation topics range from the location of the company cafeteria to career paths within the firm. The orientation itself may consist of a half-hour informal presentation by a human resources manager. Or it may be an elaborate program involving dozens of people and lasting several days or weeks.

orientation the process of acquainting new employees with an organization

Compensation and Benefits

6

Learning Objective: Discuss the primary elements of employee compensation and benefits.

An effective employee reward system must (1) enable employees to satisfy basic needs, (2) provide rewards comparable with those offered by other firms, (3) be distributed fairly within the organization, and (4) recognize that different people have different needs.

A firm's compensation system can be structured to meet the first three of these requirements. The fourth is more difficult because it must account for many variables. Most firms offer a number of benefits that, taken together, generally help to provide for employees' varying needs.

Compensation Decisions

Compensation is the payment employees receive in return for their labor. Its importance to employees is obvious. And because compensation may account for up to 80 percent of a firm's operating costs, it is equally important to management. The firm's **compensation system**, the policies and strategies that determine employee compensation, therefore must be designed carefully to provide for employee needs while keeping labor costs within reasonable limits. For most firms, designing an effective compensation system requires three separate management decisions—wage level, wage structure, and individual wages.

compensation the payment employees receive in return for their labor

compensation system the policies and strategies that determine employee compensation

Wage Level Management first must position the firm's general pay level relative to pay levels of comparable firms. Most firms choose a pay level near the industry average. A firm that is not in good financial shape may pay less than average, and large, prosperous organizations may pay more than average.

To determine what the average is, the firm may use wage surveys. A **wage survey** is a collection of data on prevailing wage rates within an industry or a geographic area. Such surveys are compiled by industry associations, local governments, personnel associations, and (occasionally) individual firms.

wage survey a collection of data on prevailing wage rates within an industry or a geographic area

Wage Structure Next, management must decide on relative pay levels for all the positions within the firm. Will managers be paid more than secretaries? Will secretaries be paid more than custodians? The result of this set of decisions is often called the firm's *wage structure*.

The wage structure almost always is developed on the basis of a job evaluation. **Job evaluation** is the process of determining the relative worth of the various jobs within a firm. Most observers probably would agree that a secretary should make more money than a custodian, but how much more? Job evaluation should provide the answer to this question.

job evaluation the process of determining the relative worth of the various jobs within a firm

A number of techniques may be used to evaluate jobs. The simplest is to rank all the jobs within the firm according to value. A more frequently used method is based on the job analysis. Points are allocated to each job for each of its elements and requirements. For example, "college degree required" might be worth fifty points, whereas the need for a high school education might count for only twenty-five points. The more points a job is allocated, the more important it is presumed to be (and the higher its level in the firm's wage structure).

Individual Wages Finally, the specific payments individual employees will receive must be determined. Consider the case of two secretaries working side by side. Job evaluation has been used to determine the relative level of secretarial pay within the firm's wage structure. However, suppose that one secretary has fifteen years of experience and can type eighty words per minute accurately. The other has two years of experience and can type only fifty-five words per minute. In most firms these two people would not receive the same pay. Instead, a wage range would be established for the secretarial position. In this case, the range might be $7 to $9.50 per hour. The more experienced and proficient secretary then would be paid an amount near the top of the range (say, $8.90 per hour); the less experienced secretary would receive an amount that is lower but still within the range (say, $7.75 per hour).

Two wage decisions come into play here. First, the employee's initial rate must be established. It is based on experience, other qualifications, and expected performance. Later, the employee may be given pay increases based on seniority and performance.

Comparable Worth

One reason women in the workforce are paid less may be that a proportion of women occupy female-dominated jobs—nurses, secretaries, and medical records analysts, for example—that require education, skills, and training equal to higher-paid positions but are undervalued. **Comparable worth** is a concept that seeks equal compensation for jobs that require about the same level of education, training, and skills. Several states have enacted laws requiring equal pay for comparable work in government positions. Critics of comparable worth argue that the market has determined the worth of jobs and laws should not tamper with the pricing mechanism of the market. The Equal Pay Act, discussed later in this chapter, does not address the issue of comparable worth. Critics also argue that artificially inflating salaries for female-dominated occupations encourages women to keep these jobs rather than seek out higher-paying jobs.

comparable worth a concept that seeks equal compensation for jobs requiring about the same level of education, training, and skills

Types of Compensation

Compensation can be paid in a variety of forms. Most forms of compensation fall into the following categories: hourly wage, weekly or monthly salary, commissions, incentive payments, lump-sum salary increases, and profit sharing.

SPOTLIGHT

Do Better Dressed Workers Get Paid More?

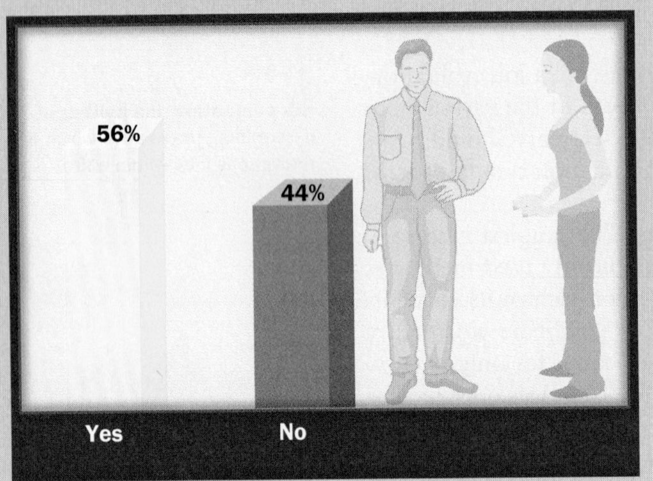

Source: hotjobs.yahoo.com, accessed November 28, 2008.

Hourly Wage An **hourly wage** is a specific amount of money paid for each hour of work. People who earn wages are paid their hourly wage for the first forty hours worked in any week. They are then paid one and one-half times their hourly wage for time worked in excess of forty hours. (That is, they are paid "time and a half" for overtime.) Workers in retailing and fast-food chains, on assembly lines, and in clerical positions usually are paid an hourly wage.

Weekly or Monthly Salary A **salary** is a specific amount of money paid for an employee's work during a set calendar period, regardless of the actual number of hours worked. Salaried employees receive no overtime pay, but they do not lose pay when they are absent from work. Most professional and managerial positions are salaried.

Commissions A **commission** is a payment that is a percentage of sales revenue. Sales representatives and sales managers often are paid entirely through commissions or through a combination of commissions and salary.

Incentive Payments An **incentive payment** is a payment in addition to wages, salary, or commissions. Incentive payments are really extra rewards for outstanding job performance. They may be distributed to all employees or only to certain employees. Some firms distribute incentive payments to all employees annually. The size of the payment depends on the firm's earnings and, at times, on the particular employee's length of service with the firm. Firms sometimes offer incentives to employees who exceed specific sales or production goals, a practice called *gain sharing*.

To avoid yearly across-the-board salary increases, some organizations reward outstanding workers individually through *merit pay*. This pay-for-performance approach allows management to control labor costs while encouraging employees to work more efficiently. An employee's merit pay depends on his or her achievements relative to those of others.

hourly wage a specific amount of money paid for each hour of work

salary a specific amount of money paid for an employee's work during a set calendar period, regardless of the actual number of hours worked

commission a payment that is a percentage of sales revenue

incentive payment a payment in addition to wages, salary, or commissions

Lump-Sum Salary Increases In traditional reward systems, an employee who receives an annual pay increase is given part of the increase in each pay period. For example, suppose that an employee on a monthly salary gets a 10 percent annual pay hike. He or she actually receives 10 percent of the former monthly salary added to each month's paycheck for a year. Companies that offer a **lump-sum salary increase** give the employee the option of taking the entire pay raise in one lump sum. The employee then draws his or her "regular" pay for the rest of the year. The lump-sum payment typically is treated as an interest-free loan that must be repaid if the employee leaves the firm during the year.

lump-sum salary increase an entire pay raise taken in one lump sum

Profit Sharing **Profit sharing** is the distribution of a percentage of a firm's profit among its employees. The idea is to motivate employees to work effectively by giving them a stake in the company's financial success. Some firms—including Sears, Roebuck—have linked their profit-sharing plans to employee retirement programs; that is, employees receive their profit-sharing distributions, with interest, when they retire.

profit sharing the distribution of a percentage of a firm's profit among its employees

Employee Benefits

An **employee benefit** is a reward in addition to regular compensation that is provided indirectly to employees. Employee benefits consist mainly of services (such as insurance) that are paid for partially or totally by employers and employee

employee benefit a reward in addition to regular compensation that is provided indirectly to employees

The National Environmental Education Foundation partners with public and private organizations to educate children, adults, and businesses about environmental issues and responsibility. It also offers training and information resources to help business managers prepare their employees for the green-collar jobs of tomorrow. **www.neefusa.org**

expenses (such as college tuition) that are reimbursed by employers. Currently, the average cost of these benefits is 29.4 percent of an employee's total compensation, which includes wages plus benefits.[11] Thus a person who received total compensation (including benefits) of $50,000 a year earned $35,300 in wages and received an additional $14,700 in benefits.

Types of Benefits Employee benefits take a variety of forms. *Pay for time not worked* covers such absences as vacation time, holidays, and sick leave. *Insurance packages* may include health, life, and dental insurance for employees and their families. Some firms pay the entire cost of the insurance package, and others share the cost with the employee. The costs of *pension and retirement programs* also may be borne entirely by the firm or shared with the employee.

Some benefits are required by law. For example, employers must maintain *workers' compensation insurance,* which pays medical bills for injuries that occur on the job and provides income for employees who are disabled by job-related injuries. Employers also must pay for *unemployment insurance* and contribute to each employee's federal *Social Security* account.

Other benefits provided by employers include tuition-reimbursement plans, credit unions, child care, company cafeterias, exercise rooms, and broad stock-option plans available to all employees. Some companies offer special benefits to U.S. military reservists who are called up for active duty.

Some companies offer unusual benefits in order to attract and retain employees. DaimlerChrysler makes available to every salaried, non–United Auto Workers Union worker a one-time $4,000 work-family account that can be used for child care, adoption costs, elder care, college tuition, or extra retirement funds. Compuware Corporation, a software company, makes cheap meals available to workers to take home after a workout in the company gym. Dayton Hudson not only provides employees with discounts on airfares, rental cars, and hotels for vacations but also allows employees to customize work schedules to fit their personal needs. Google, which is highly ranked in *Fortune* magazine's "Top 100 Companies to Work For," allows its employee to play volleyball on campus. Other fun activities at Google include football, video games, pool, ping pong, and even roller hockey twice a week in the parking lot. Seattle law firm Perkins Coie is known for its unusual perks, like Happiness Committees that consist of teams of employees who roam the offices and drop surprise gifts on the desks of their colleagues. Every quarter, Perkins Coie holds random drawings and gives away six pairs of round-trip airline tickets to lucky winners. This company even has an in-house rock band.[12]

flexible benefit plan compensation plan whereby an employee receives a predetermined amount of benefit dollars to spend on a package of benefits he or she has selected to meet individual needs

AP Photo/Kevin Rivoli

Employee benefits. *This Cornell University employee recently adopted a child from Guatemala. Her employer provides a child adoption benefit that includes $5,000 and up to 16 weeks of partial compensation.*

Flexible Benefit Plans Through a **flexible benefit plan**, an employee receives a predetermined amount of benefit dollars and may allocate those dollars to various categories of benefits in the mix that best fits his or her needs. Some flexible benefit plans offer a broad array of benefit options, including health care, dental care, life insurance, accidental death and dismemberment coverage for both the worker and dependents, long-term disability coverage, vacation benefits, retirement savings, and dependent-care benefits. Other firms offer limited options, primarily in health and life insurance and retirement plans.

Although the cost of administering flexible plans is high, a number of organizations, including Quaker Oats and

Coca-Cola, have implemented this option for several reasons. Because employees' needs are so diverse, flexible plans help firms to offer benefit packages that more specifically meet their employees' needs. Flexible plans can, in the long run, help a company to contain costs because a specified amount is allocated to cover the benefits of each employee. Furthermore, organizations that offer flexible plans with many choices may be perceived as being employee friendly. Thus, they are in a better position to attract and retain qualified employees.

Training and Development

7

Learning Objective: Explain the purposes and techniques of employee training, development, and performance appraisal.

Training and development are extremely important at the Container Store. Because great customer service is so important, every first-year full-time salesperson receives about 185 hours of formal training as opposed to the industry standard, which is approximately seven hours. Training and development continue throughout a person's career. Each store has a full-time trainer called the *super sales trainer* (SST). This trainer provides product training, sales training, and employee development training. A number of top managers believe that the financial and human resources invested in training and development are well worth it.

employee training the process of teaching operations and technical employees how to do their present jobs more effectively and efficiently

management development the process of preparing managers and other professionals to assume increased responsibility in both present and future positions

Both training and development are aimed at improving employees' skills and abilities. However, the two are usually differentiated as either employee training or management development. **Employee training** is the process of teaching operations and technical employees how to do their present jobs more effectively and efficiently. **Management development** is the process of preparing managers and other professionals to assume increased responsibility in both present and future positions. Thus, training and development differ in who is being taught and the purpose of the teaching. Both are necessary for personal and organizational growth. Companies that hope to stay competitive typically make huge commitments to employee training and development. Internet-based e-learning is growing. Driven by cost, travel, and time savings, online learning alone (and in conjunction with face-to-face situations) is a strong alternative strategy. Development of a training program usually has three components: analysis of needs, determination of training and development methods, and creation of an evaluation system to assess the program's effectiveness.

Analysis of Training Needs

When thinking about developing a training program, managers first must determine if training is needed and, if so, what types of training needs exist. At times, what at first appears to be a need for training is actually, on assessment, a need for motivation. Training needs can vary considerably. For example, some employees may need training to improve their technical skills, or they may need training about organizational procedures. Training also may focus on business ethics, product information, or customer service. Because training is expensive, it is critical that the correct training needs be identified.

Training. *Airlines use flight simulators to train pilots.*

PRNewswire/Clay Lacy Aviation

Training and Development Methods

A number of methods are available for employee training and management development. Some of these methods may be more suitable for one or the other, but most can be applied to both training and management development.

- *On-the-job methods.* The trainee learns by doing the work under the supervision of an experienced employee.
- *Simulations.* The work situation is simulated in a separate area so that learning takes place away from the day-to-day pressures of work.

Going Global

Training Across the Miles

Whether their employees work across the continent or around the world, multinational companies are using a variety of high-tech tools for training. For example, Motorola has a "corporate university" with both classroom and online courses to educate its 65,000-employee global workforce about quality control and other key topics.

Quintiles Transnational, which helps pharmaceutical firms develop and introduce new products, also relies on the Internet to train its 21,000 employees on six continents. In addition to offering online courses, it is preparing podcast tutorials for specific job situations so employees can learn even when on the go.

RF Getty Images

Electronic training is a natural fit for Dell's global workforce because of the company's technology expertise. In India, for example, Dell uses software simulations to give managers practice in analyzing specific business problems and trying different solutions.

Rohm and Haas, a manufacturer of chemicals and construction materials, recently set up what it calls a "corporate YouTube" video-training website for its 15,000 employees worldwide. Because the video database is searchable, employees can find exactly what they need for any job or work issue and click to watch right away.

Sources: Heather Havenstein, "Online Video Expands Role in Training, Collaboration," *ComputerWorld*, March 10, 2008, p. 14; Ed Frauenheim, "Your Co-Worker, Your Teacher," *Workforce Management*, January 29, 2007, p. 19; Mahima Puri, "Now, Software-Based Games Enter Training Workshops," *Economic Times*, April 4, 2008, n.p.

- *Classroom teaching and lectures.* You probably already know these methods quite well.
- *Conferences and seminars.* Experts and learners meet to discuss problems and exchange ideas.
- *Role playing.* Participants act out the roles of others in the organization for better understanding of those roles (primarily a management development tool).

Evaluation of Training and Development

Training and development are very expensive. The training itself costs quite a bit, and employees are usually not working—or are working at a reduced load and pace—during training sessions. To ensure that training and development are cost-effective, the managers responsible should evaluate the company's efforts periodically.

The starting point for this evaluation is a set of verifiable objectives that are developed *before* the training is undertaken. Suppose that a training program is expected to improve the skills of machinists. The objective of the program might be stated as follows: "At the end of the training period, each machinist should be able to process thirty parts per hour with no more than one defective part per ninety parts completed." This objective clearly specifies what is expected and how training results may be measured or verified. Evaluation then consists of measuring machinists' output and the ratio of defective parts produced after the training.

The results of training evaluations should be made known to all those involved in the program—including trainees and upper management. For trainees, the results of evaluations can enhance motivation and learning. For upper management, the results may be the basis for making decisions about the training program itself.

Performance Appraisal

performance appraisal the evaluation of employees' current and potential levels of performance to allow managers to make objective human resources decisions

Performance appraisal is the evaluation of employees' current and potential levels of performance to allow managers to make objective human resources decisions. The process has three main objectives. First, managers use performance appraisals to let workers know how well they are doing and how they can do better in the future. Second, a performance appraisal provides an effective basis for distributing

Jump-Starting Your Career

Off to a Fast Start

Congratulations! You've found a new job—now how do you get off to a fast start? Experts offer these tips:

- *Introduce yourself.* Reach out, rather than waiting for colleagues to notice you. "Try to meet at least three new people every single day," advises an Atlanta career coach. "Tell them you recently started, along with your title and department, and ask them what they do."
- *Go for early wins.* Learn your department's goals and find ways to demonstrate your value right away. "Look for small, quick wins that you can accomplish," says a public relations executive.
- *Join the team.* Observe how things get done in your company and make the most of opportunities to get involved. For example, when coworkers or managers need information or assistance with a rush project, offer your help.
- *Ask for early feedback.* Request early feedback on your performance so you can do an even better job as time goes on. "In most circumstances, your boss will agree to meet with you weekly and give you feedback," explains an experienced recruiter.

Sources: Susan Kreimer, "Key Early Days for New Hires," *Washington Post,* August 24, 2008, p. K1; Marshall Goldsmith, "Tough Career Advice for Tough Times," *BusinessWeek Online,* August 13, 2008, **www.businessweek.com**; Guido Sacchi, "Career Advice: Dealing with 'Clueless' New Hires," *ComputerWorld,* October 7, 2008, **www.computerworld.com**.

rewards, such as pay raises and promotions. Third, performance appraisal helps the organization monitor its employee selection, training, and development activities. If large numbers of employees continually perform below expectations, the firm may need to revise its selection process or strengthen its training and development activities.

Common Evaluation Techniques

The various techniques and methods for appraising employee performance are either objective or judgmental in nature.

Objective Methods Objective appraisal methods use some measurable quantity as the basis for assessing performance. Units of output, dollar volume of sales, number of defective products, and number of insurance claims processed are all objective, measurable quantities. Thus, an employee who processes an average of twenty-six insurance claims per week is given a higher evaluation than one whose average is nineteen claims per week.

Such objective measures may require some adjustment for the work environment. Suppose that the first of our insurance-claims processors works in New York City, and the second works in rural Iowa. Both must visit each client because they are processing homeowners' insurance claims. The difference in their average weekly output may be due entirely to the long distances the Iowan must travel to visit clients. In this case, the two workers may very well be equally competent and motivated. Thus, a manager must take into account circumstances that may be hidden by a purely statistical measurement.

Judgmental Methods Judgmental appraisal methods are used much more frequently than objective methods. They require that the manager judge or estimate the employee's performance level. However, judgmental methods are not capricious. These methods are based on employee ranking or rating scales. When ranking is used, the manager ranks subordinates from best to worst. This approach has a number of drawbacks, including the lack of any absolute standard. Rating scales are the most popular judgmental appraisal technique. A *rating scale* consists of a number of statements; each employee is rated on the degree to which the statement applies (see Figure 9.3). For example, one statement might be, "This employee always does high-quality work." The supervisor would give the employee a rating, from 5 down to 1, corresponding to gradations ranging from "strongly agree" to

Figure 9.3: Performance Appraisal

Judgmental appraisal methods are used much more often than objective methods. Using judgmental methods requires the manager to estimate the employee's performance level relative to some standard.

3M Contribution and Development Summary
FORM 37450 - B

Employee Name | Employee Number | Job Title
Department | Location
Coach/Supervisor(s) Name(s) | Review Peri[od] From :

Major Job Responsibilities

Goals/Expectations | Contributions/

Contribution (To be completed by coach/supervisor)
- ☐ Good Level of Contribution for this year
- ☐ Exceptiona[l]
- ☐ Unsatisfactory Level of Contribution for this year

Development Summary
Areas of Strength | Development Priorities

Career Interests
Next job | Longer Range

Current Mobility
- ☐ 0 - Currently Unable to Relocate
- ☐ 1 - Position In Home Country Only (Use if Home Country is Outside U.S.)
- ☐ 2 - Position Within O.U.S. Region (e: Nordic, SEA...)
- ☐ 3 - Position Within O.U.S. Area (ex: Europe, Asia)
- ☐ 4 - Position In U.S.
- ☐ 5 - Position Anywhere In The World

Development
- ☐ W - Well placed. Development plans achievable in current role for at least the next year
- ☐ C - Ready now for a move to a different job for career broadening experience
- ☐ I - Ready now for a move to a different job involving increased responsibility
- ☐ X - Not well placed. Action required to resolve placement issues.

Comments on Development

Employee Comments

Coach/Supervisor Comments | **Other Supervisor (if applicable) and/or Reviewer**

Signatures
Coach/Supervisor Date | Other Coach/Supervisor or Reviewer Date
Employee Date

page 4

Source: Courtesy of 3M.

"strongly disagree." The ratings on all the statements are added to obtain the employee's total evaluation.

Avoiding Appraisal Errors Managers must be cautious if they are to avoid making mistakes when appraising employees. It is common to overuse one portion of an evaluation instrument, thus overemphasizing some issues and underemphasizing others. A manager must guard against allowing an employee's poor performance on one activity to influence his or her judgment of that subordinate's work on other activities. Similarly, putting too much weight on recent performance distorts an employee's evaluation. For example, if the employee is being rated on performance over the last year, a manager should not permit last month's disappointing performance to overshadow the quality of the work done in the first eleven months of the year. Finally, a manager must guard against discrimination on the basis of race, age, gender, religion, national origin, or sexual orientation.

360-Degree evaluation process. *American Eagle stores employ 360-degree evaluations.*

Performance Feedback

No matter which appraisal technique is used, the results should be discussed with the employee soon after the evaluation is completed. The manager should explain the basis for present rewards and should let the employee know what he or she can do to be recognized as a better performer in the future. The information provided to an employee in such discussions is called a *performance feedback,* and the process is known as a *performance feedback interview.*

There are three major approaches to performance feedback interviews: tell and sell, tell and listen, and problem solving. In a *tell-and-sell* feedback interview, the superior tells the employee how good or bad the employee's performance has been and then attempts to persuade the employee to accept this evaluation. Since the employee has no input into the evaluation, the tell-and-sell interview can lead to defensiveness, resentment, and frustration on the part of the subordinate. The employee may not accept the results of the interview and may not be committed to achieving the goals that are set.

With the *tell-and-listen* approach, the supervisor tells the employee what has been right and wrong with the employee's performance and then gives the employee a chance to respond. The subordinate simply may be given an opportunity to react to the supervisor's statements or may be permitted to offer a full self-appraisal, challenging the supervisor's assessment.

In the *problem-solving* approach, employees evaluate their own performance and set their own goals for future performance. The supervisor is more a colleague than a judge and offers comments and advice in a noncritical manner. An active and open dialogue ensues in which goals for improvement are established mutually. The problem-solving interview is more likely to result in the employee's commitment to the established goals.

To avoid some of the problems associated with the tell-and-sell interview, a mixed approach sometimes is used. The mixed interview uses the tell-and-sell approach to communicate administrative decisions and the problem-solving approach to discuss employee-development issues and future performance goals.[13]

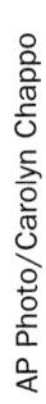
AP Photo/Carolyn Chappo

An appraisal approach that has become popular is called a *360-degree evaluation.* A 360-degree evaluation collects anonymous reviews about an employee from his or her peers, subordinates, and supervisors and then compiles these reviews into a feedback report that is given to the employee. Companies that invest significant resources in employee-development efforts are especially likely to use 360-degree evaluations. An employee should not be given a feedback report without first having a one-on-one meeting with his or her supervisor. The most appropriate way to introduce a 360-degree evaluation system in a company is to begin with upper-level management. Then managers should be trained on how to interpret feedback reports so that they can coach their employees on how to use the feedback to achieve higher-level job-related skills and behaviors.[14]

Finally, we should note that many managers find it difficult to discuss the negative aspects of an appraisal. Unfortunately, they may ignore performance feedback altogether or provide it in a very weak and ineffectual manner. In truth, though, most employees have strengths that can be emphasized to soften the discussion of their weaknesses. An employee may not even be aware of weaknesses and their consequences. If such weaknesses are not pointed out through performance feedback, they cannot possibly be eliminated. Only through tactful, honest communication can the results of an appraisal be fully utilized.

The Legal Environment of HRM

8

Learning Objective: Outline the major legislation affecting human resources management.

Legislation regarding HRM practices has been passed mainly to protect the rights of employees, to promote job safety, and to eliminate discrimination in the workplace. The major federal laws affecting HRM are described in Table 9.2.

National Labor Relations Act and Labor-Management Relations Act

These laws are concerned with dealings between business firms and labor unions. This general area is, in concept, a part of HRM. However, because of its importance, it is often treated as a separate set of activities. We discuss both labor-management relations and these two acts in detail in Chapter 11.

Fair Labor Standards Act

This act, passed in 1938 and amended many times since, applies primarily to wages. It established minimum wages and overtime pay rates. Many managers and other professionals, however, are exempt from this law. Managers, for example, seldom get paid overtime when they work more than forty hours a week.

Equal Pay Act

Passed in 1963, this law overlaps somewhat with Title VII of the Civil Rights Act (see below). The Equal Pay Act specifies that men and women who are doing equal jobs must be paid the same wage. Equal jobs are jobs that demand equal effort, skill, and responsibility and that are performed under the same conditions. Differences in pay are legal if they can be attributed to differences in seniority, qualifications, or performance. However, women cannot be paid less (or more) for the same work solely because they are women.

Civil Rights Acts

Title VII of the Civil Rights Act of 1964 applies directly to selection and promotion. It forbids organizations with fifteen or more employees to discriminate in those areas on the basis of sex, race, color, religion, or national origin. The purpose of Title VII is to ensure that employers make personnel decisions on the basis of employee qualifications only. As a result of this act, discrimination in employment (especially against African Americans) has been reduced in this country.

Table 9.2: Federal Legislation Affecting Human Resources Management

Law	Purpose
National Labor Relations Act (1935)	Established a collective-bargaining process in labor-management relations as well as the National Labor Relations Board (NLRB)
Fair Labor Standards Act (1938)	Established a minimum wage and an overtime pay rate for employees working more than forty hours per week
Labor-Management Relations Act (1947)	Provided a balance between union power and management power; also known as the Taft-Hartley Act
Equal Pay Act (1963)	Specified that men and women who do equal jobs must be paid the same wage
Title VII of the Civil Rights Act (1964)	Outlawed discrimination in employment practices based on sex, race, color, religion, or national origin
Age Discrimination in Employment Act (1967–1986)	Outlawed personnel practices that discriminate against people aged 40 and older; the 1986 amendment eliminated a mandatory retirement age
Occupational Safety and Health Act (1970)	Regulated the degree to which employees can be exposed to hazardous substances and specified the safety equipment that the employer must provide
Employment Retirement Income Security Act (1974)	Regulated company retirement programs and provided a federal insurance program for retirement plans that go bankrupt
Worker Adjustment and Retraining Notification (WARN) Act (1988)	Required employers to give employees sixty days notice regarding plant closure or layoff of fifty or more employees
Americans with Disabilities Act (1990)	Prohibited discrimination against qualified individuals with disabilities in all employment practices, including job-application procedures, hiring, firing, advancement, compensation, training, and other terms, conditions, and privileges of employment
Civil Rights Act (1991)	Facilitated employees' suing employers for sexual discrimination and collecting punitive damages
Family and Medical Leave Act (1993)	Required an organization with fifty or more employees to provide up to twelve weeks of leave without pay on the birth (or adoption) of an employee's child or if an employee or his or her spouse, child, or parent is seriously ill

The Equal Employment Opportunity Commission (EEOC) is charged with enforcing Title VII. A person who believes that he or she has been discriminated against can file a complaint with the EEOC. The EEOC investigates the complaint, and if it finds that the person has, in fact, been the victim of discrimination, the commission can take legal action on his or her behalf.

The Civil Rights Act of 1991 facilitates an employee's suing and collecting punitive damages for sexual discrimination. Discriminatory promotion and termination decisions as well as on-the-job issues, such as sexual harassment, are covered by this act.

Age Discrimination in Employment Act

The general purpose of this act, which was passed in 1967 and amended in 1986, is the same as that of Title VII—to eliminate discrimination. However, as the name implies, the Age Discrimination in Employment Act is concerned only with discrimination based on age. It applies to companies with twenty or more employees. In particular, it outlaws personnel practices that discriminate against people aged 40 or older. (No federal law forbids discrimination against people younger than age 40, but several states have adopted age discrimination laws that apply to a variety of age groups.) Also outlawed are company policies that specify a mandatory retirement age. Employers must base employment decisions on ability and not on a number.

Occupational Safety and Health Act

Passed in 1970, this act is concerned mainly with issues of employee health and safety. For example, the act regulates the degree to which employees can be exposed to hazardous substances. It also specifies the safety equipment that the employer must provide.

The Occupational Safety and Health Administration (OSHA) was created to enforce this act. Inspectors from OSHA investigate employee complaints regarding unsafe working conditions. They also make spot checks on companies operating in particularly hazardous industries, such as chemicals and mining, to ensure compliance with the law. A firm found to be in violation of federal standards can be heavily fined or shut down. Many people feel that issuing OSHA violations is not enough to protect workers from harm.

Employee Retirement Income Security Act

This act was passed in 1974 to protect the retirement benefits of employees. It does not require that firms provide a retirement plan. However, it does specify that *if* a retirement plan is provided, it must be managed in such a way that the interests of employees are protected. It also provides federal insurance for retirement plans that go bankrupt.

Affirmative Action

Affirmative action is not one act but a series of executive orders issued by the President of the United States. These orders established the requirement for affirmative action in personnel practices. This stipulation applies to all employers with fifty or more employees holding federal contracts in excess of $50,000. It prescribes that such employers (1) actively encourage job applications from members of minority groups and (2) hire qualified employees from minority groups not fully represented in their organizations. Many firms that do not hold government contracts voluntarily take part in this affirmative action program.

Americans with Disabilities Act

The Americans with Disabilities Act (ADA) prohibits discrimination against qualified individuals with disabilities in all employment practices—including job-application procedures, hiring, firing, advancement, compensation, training, and other terms and conditions of employment. All private employers and government agencies with fifteen or more employees are covered by the ADA. Defining who is a qualified individual with a disability is, of course, difficult. Depending on how *qualified individual with a disability* is interpreted, up to 43 million Americans can be included under this law. This law also mandates that all businesses that serve the public must make their facilities accessible to people with disabilities.

Not only are individuals with obvious physical disabilities protected under the ADA, but also safeguarded are those with less visible conditions such as heart disease, diabetes, epilepsy, cancer, AIDS, and mental illnesses. Because of this law, many organizations no longer require job applicants to pass physical examinations as a condition of employment.

Employers are required to provide disabled employees with reasonable accommodation. *Reasonable accommodation* is any modification or adjustment to a job or work environment that will enable a qualified employee with a disability to perform a central job function. Examples of reasonable accommodation include

Accommodation of disabled employees. *The Americans with Disabilities Act requires all employers to provide disabled employees with reasonable accommodation. This blind employee at Southern California Edison is permitted to have a guide dog accompany her at her workstation.*

making existing facilities readily accessible to and usable by an individual confined to a wheelchair. Reasonable accommodation also might mean restructuring a job, modifying work schedules, acquiring or modifying equipment, providing qualified readers or interpreters, or changing training programs.

return to inside business

Zappos

Outstanding customer service helps Zappos stand out in the 24/7 world of online retailing. The company always has at least 2 million pairs of shoes in stock, ready to be boxed and shipped at a moment's notice. Customers have a full 365 days in which to return their purchases if they're not satisfied. And unlike some Web retailers, Zappos maintains two toll-free hot lines to help customers with sales or service in English or Spanish at any time, day or night.

None of this would work without the company's responsive, enthusiastic, and dedicated workforce. By recruiting good employees, providing them with thorough training, and empowering them to deliver great service, Zappos is positioning itself for even more growth in the future.

Questions

1. What are the advantages and disadvantages of paying new hires to quit before the end of their training period? Do you agree with what Zappos is doing? Why?
2. If you were a Zappos recruiter, what questions would you ask to determine whether a prospective employee would fit into the company's workforce?

Summary

1 Describe the major components of human resources management.

Human resources management (HRM) is the set of activities involved in acquiring, maintaining, and developing an organization's human resources. Responsibility for HRM is shared by specialized staff and line managers. HRM activities include human resources planning, job analysis, recruiting, selection, orientation, compensation, benefits, training and development, and performance appraisal.

2 Identify the steps in human resources planning.

Human resources planning consists of forecasting the human resources that a firm will need and those that it will have available and then planning a course of action to match supply with demand. Layoffs, attrition, early retirement, and (as a last resort) firing are ways to reduce the size of the workforce. Supply is increased through hiring.

3 Describe cultural diversity and understand some of the challenges and opportunities associated with it.

Cultural diversity refers to the differences among people in a workforce owing to race, ethnicity, and gender. With an increasing number of women, minorities, and immigrants entering the U.S. workforce, management is faced with both challenges and competitive advantages. Some organizations are implementing diversity-related training programs and working to make the most of cultural diversity. With the proper guidance and management, a culturally diverse organization can prove beneficial to all involved.

4 Explain the objectives and uses of job analysis.

Job analysis provides a job description and a job specification for each position within a firm. A job description is a list of the elements that make up a particular job. A job specification is a list of qualifications required to perform a particular job. Job analysis is used in evaluation and in determining compensation levels and serves as the basis for recruiting and selecting new employees.

5 Describe the processes of recruiting, employee selection, and orientation.

Recruiting is the process of attracting qualified job applicants. Candidates for open positions may be recruited from within or outside a firm. In the selection process, information about candidates is obtained from applications, résumés, tests, interviews, references, or assessment centers. This information then is used to select the most appropriate candidate for the job. Newly hired employees then will go through a formal or informal orientation program to acquaint them with the firm.

Discuss the primary elements of employee compensation and benefits.

Compensation is the payment employees receive in return for their labor. In developing a system for paying employees, management must decide on the firm's general wage level (relative to other firms), the wage structure within the firm, and individual wages. Wage surveys and job analyses are useful in making these decisions. Employees may be paid hourly wages, salaries, or commissions. They also may receive incentive payments, lump-sum salary increases, and profit-sharing payments. Employee benefits, which are nonmonetary rewards to employees, add about 28 percent to the cost of compensation.

Explain the purposes and techniques of employee training, development, and performance appraisal.

Employee training and management-development programs enhance the ability of employees to contribute to a firm. When developing a training program, training needs should be analyzed. Then training methods should be selected. Because training is expensive, an organization should evaluate the effectiveness of its training programs periodically.

Performance appraisal, or evaluation, is used to provide employees with performance feedback, to serve as a basis for distributing rewards, and to monitor selection and training activities. Both objective and judgmental appraisal techniques are used. Their results are communicated to employees through three performance feedback approaches: tell and sell, tell and listen, and problem solving.

8 Outline the major legislation affecting human resources management.

A number of laws have been passed that affect HRM practices and that protect the rights and safety of employees. Some of these are the National Labor Relations Act of 1935, the Labor-Management Relations Act of 1947, the Fair Labor Standards Act of 1938, the Equal Pay Act of 1963, Title VII of the Civil Rights Act of 1964, the Age Discrimination in Employment Acts of 1967 and 1986, the Occupational Safety and Health Act of 1970, the Employment Retirement Income Security Act of 1974, the Worker Adjustment and Retraining Notification Act of 1988, the Americans with Disabilities Act of 1990, the Civil Rights Act of 1991, and the Family and Medical Leave Act of 1993.

Key Terms

You should now be able to define and give an example relevant to each of the following terms:

human resources management (HRM) (250)
human resources planning (251)
replacement chart (252)
skills inventory (252)
cultural (workplace) diversity (254)
job analysis (255)
job description (255)
job specification (255)
recruiting (255)
external recruiting (256)
internal recruiting (257)
selection (257)
orientation (260)
compensation (260)
compensation system (260)
wage survey (261)
job evaluation (261)
comparable worth (261)
hourly wage (262)
salary (262)
commission (262)
incentive payment (262)
lump-sum salary increase (262)
profit sharing (262)
employee benefit (262)
flexible benefit plan (263)
employee training (264)
management development (264)
performance appraisal (265)

Review Questions

1. List the three main HRM activities and their objectives.
2. In general, on what basis is responsibility for HRM divided between line and staff managers?
3. How is a forecast of human resources demand related to a firm's organizational planning?
4. How do human resources managers go about matching a firm's supply of workers with its demand for workers?
5. What are the major challenges and benefits associated with a culturally diverse workforce?
6. How are a job analysis, job description, and job specification related?
7. What are the advantages and disadvantages of external recruiting? Of internal recruiting?
8. In your opinion, what are the two best techniques for gathering information about job candidates?
9. Why is orientation an important HRM activity?
10. Explain how the three wage-related decisions result in a compensation system.
11. How is a job analysis used in the process of job evaluation?
12. Suppose that you have just opened a new Ford sales showroom and repair shop. Which of your employees would be paid wages, which would receive salaries, and which would receive commissions?
13. What is the difference between the objective of employee training and the objective of management development?
14. Why is it so important to provide feedback after a performance appraisal?

Discussion Questions

1. How accurately can managers plan for future human resources needs?
2. How might an organization's recruiting and selection practices be affected by the general level of employment?
3. Are employee benefits really necessary? Why?
4. As a manager, what actions would you take if an operations employee with six years of experience on the job refused ongoing training and ignored performance feedback?
5. Why are there so many laws relating to HRM practices? Which are the most important laws, in your opinion?

Video Case 9.1

The New England Aquarium Casts a Wide Recruitment Net

From seals and sea turtles to porpoises and penguins, the nonprofit New England Aquarium houses an incredibly diverse array of the world's sea life. The aquarium's official mission statement is "to present, promote, and protect the world of water." It also wants to appeal to a broad audience and build a work force of paid and unpaid staff that reflects Boston's diversity.

Volunteers are a major resource for the New England Aquarium. Its staff of 1,000 volunteers contributes 100,000 hours of service yearly. Many high school and college students volunteer to try out possible career choices. Adults with and without specialized college degrees (in fields such as marine biology and environmental affairs) volunteer their time as well. And the New England Aquarium's internships offer college students and recent graduates hands-on experience in veterinary services, communications, and other key areas.

The aquarium's director of volunteer programs is a champion for workplace diversity. Most organizations "are good at putting diversity in their mission statements and talking about it, but not actually accomplishing it," she observes. She and her colleagues reach out to recruit volunteers, interns, and employees of different races, ethnicities, socioeconomic levels, physical abilities, and ages. In addition, they welcome people of diverse educational backgrounds, personalities, and viewpoints because of the new ideas these differences can bring to the organization's opportunities and challenges.

One reason the New England Aquarium needs to constantly recruit and train new volunteers (and employees) is that it attracts more visitors every year as it expands exhibit space and educational activities. Also, like most nonprofits, the New England Aquarium has a very limited budget and must manage its payroll carefully. Therefore, the organization is always looking for volunteers to assist paid staff in various departments, including education, administration, and animal rescue.

The New England Aquarium must plan for employees, volunteers, or interns to handle certain tasks whenever the facility is open. For example, it needs cashiers to collect admission fees during daytime, evening, and weekend hours. Volunteers are often available to work during weekend hours, but filling daytime positions can be difficult. This is another reason why aquarium managers attend community meetings and find other ways to encourage volunteerism.

The internet is an important and cost-effective recruiting tool for the aquarium. Prospective volunteers can browse its website to find open positions, read job descriptions and specifications, and download an application form to complete and submit. Aquarium managers read all the applications and ask those who seem the most qualified to come in for a personal interview. Once the final selections are made, volunteers are notified about their assignments and working hours. They receive training in the organization's procedures and learn their specific duties before they start their jobs.

Candidates for internships must send a letter expressing interest in working as an intern and include a résumé plus two academic or professional references. As an option, candidates can send a letter of reference and a college transcript to support the application letter. The New England Aquarium's internship coordinators interview the most promising candidates and make the final selections. Interns, like volunteers, gain valuable experience and can list their positions on their résumés when looking for future employment.

Paid employees receive a full package of valuable benefits, including paid holidays and sick days, insurance, and tuition reimbursement. Just as important, employees gain an opportunity to make a difference. When hired, they become part of an organization that protects the underwater environment, educates the public, and saves the lives of whales and other marine life.[15]

For more information about this organization, go to **www.neaq.org.**

Questions

1. Why would the New England Aquarium require people to apply in writing for unpaid volunteer and internship positions?
2. In addition to using the web and attending community meetings, what other external recruiting techniques would you suggest the aquarium use to attract volunteers? Why?
3. Do you think that the New England Aquarium should evaluate the performance of its volunteers periodically? Support your answer.

Case 9.2

Bucking the High-Turnover Trend at Domino's Pizza

Turnover—the rate at which employees leave their jobs—is notoriously high in the fast-food industry. According to the National Restaurant Association, more than half of all managers in limited-service restaurants change jobs each year, and turnover among lower-level employees is even higher. So it's rare to find a pizza franchise in which employees are so loyal they name their children after the boss. But that's exactly the kind of thing that happens at Dave Melton's Domino's Pizza franchises in New York City.

A newspaper reporter recently found Melton preparing his five Domino's stores for Super Bowl Sunday with his entire staff of about one hundred employees plus twelve former employees who were happy to come back and help on the chain's busiest day of the year. Melton knew business would be "crazy" for the two-and-a-half hours of the game, but he was confident, too. Incredibly, most of his team had been with him long enough to have worked through the Super Bowl together several times already.

All Melton's managers started as minimum-wage delivery workers who worked their way up and have now been with him for at least six years, some for twice as long. They earn as much as $70,000, partly by sharing in the profits of their stores, which each earn about $1 million in annual sales. Regular employees are just as committed to their jobs. Asked why, they respond that Melton treats his workers with dignity and respect. For instance, Melton and his wife encouraged one kitchen worker to take a city food safety course. "I was a little skeptical," she said. "I don't like tests. But I took it and I passed. I did well. I got a raise and I got a bonus for passing the test." And, following one of his basic employment policies, Melton promoted her to assistant manager.

Another employee, an immigrant from Pakistan, started as a delivery worker and now manages one of Melton's stores. Someday he hopes to open his own. "My No. 1 career goal is to be in my own business and bring my family here," he said.

And then there's the employee from Burkina Faso, who has been with Melton for many years and named his son after him.

How does Melton account for his success at retaining people in such a fluid industry? Domino's provides its franchise operators with at least a week of management training and continued support, but Melton's results are special. He admits his first year as a franchise operator was filled with hiring mistakes, often the result of hasty decisions. Some employees were disruptive, argued with customers, had high absentee rates, and even stole from the firm. Melton quickly learned how to do better. "You are on your feet," he says of the jobs in his business. "It is long hours. It takes a certain kind of person to love it"—someone who can work fast and cheerfully. Most of his hires now are referrals from current employees, who come from many countries, and he devotes time to training them, setting goals with them, sharing information about how the stores are faring, and paying bonuses for outstanding work. "My role is being a resource, providing motivation, inspiration, and compensation," he says. "This is one of the places where so many people get their first experience in America. It is fun exposing them to the way capitalism and business in America works."[16]

For more information about this company, go to **www.dominosbiz.com.**

Questions

1. What are some of the strategies Dave Melton uses to retain good employees?
2. What do you think are the advantages of Dave Melton's hiring strategies? Can you think of any disadvantages?
3. What effect do you think Dave Melton's compensation strategies have on his firm's success?

Building Skills for Career Success

1. JOURNALING FOR SUCCESS

Discovery statement: This chapter discussed human resource management from an organizational and business perspective.

Assignment

1. Assuming that you are currently in school and that you plan to begin a new job when you have completed your studies, at what point will you begin looking for a job? Explain why.
2. How will you find out about job openings?
3. What types of information will be important to you when considering whether or not to interview for a specific position?
4. What sources of information will you use to prepare for an interview with a specific organization?

2. EXPLORING THE INTERNET

Although you may believe that your formal learning will end when you graduate and enter the working world, it won't. Companies both large and small spend billions of dollars annually in training employees and updating their knowledge and skills. Besides supporting employees who attend accredited continuing-education programs, companies also may provide more specialized in-house course work on new technologies, products, and markets for strategic planning. The Internet is an excellent search tool to find out about course work offered by private training organizations, as well as by traditional academic institutions. Learning online is a fast-growing alternative, especially for busy employees requiring updates to skills in the information technology (IT) field, where software knowledge must be refreshed continuously. Visit the text website for updates to this exercise.

Assignment

1. Visit the websites of several academic institutions and examine their course work offerings. Also examine the offerings of some of the following private consulting firms:
   Learning Tree International:
   www.learningtree.com
   Accenture: **www.accenture.com**
   KPMG: **www.kpmg.com**
   Ernst & Young: **www.ey.com/global**
2. What professional continuing-education training and services are provided by one of the academic institutions whose site you visited?
3. What sort of training is offered by one of the preceding consulting firms?
4. From the company's point of view, what is the total real cost of a day's worth of employee training? What is the money value of one day of study for a full-time college student? Can you explain why firms are willing to pay higher starting salaries for employees with higher levels of education?
5. The American Society for Training & Development (**www.astd.org/**) and the Society for Human Resource Management (**www.shrm.org/**) are two good sources for information about online training programs. Describe what you found out at these and other sites providing online learning solutions.

3. DEVELOPING CRITICAL-THINKING SKILLS

Suppose that you are the manager of the six supervisors described in the following list. They have all just completed two years of service with you and are eligible for an annual raise. How will you determine who will receive a raise and how much each will receive?

- Joe Garcia has impressed you by his above-average performance on several difficult projects. Some of his subordinates, however, do not like the way he assigns jobs. You are aware that several family crises have left him short of cash.
- Sandy Vance meets her goals, but you feel that she could do better. She is single, likes to socialize, and at times arrives late for work. Several of her subordinates have low skill levels, but Sandy feels that she has explained their duties to them adequately. You believe that Sandy may care more about her friends than about coaching her subordinates. Her workers never complain and appear to be satisfied with their jobs.
- Paul Steiberg is not a good performer, and his work group does not feel that he is an effective leader. You also know that his group is the toughest one to manage. The work is hard and dirty. You realize that it would be very difficult to replace him, and you therefore do not want to lose him.
- Anna Chen runs a tight ship. Her subordinates like her and feel that she is an excellent leader. She listens to them and supports them. Recently, her group won the TOP (The Outstanding Performance) Award. Anna's husband is CEO of a consulting firm, and as far as you know, she is not in financial need.
- Jill Foster has completed every assignment successfully. You are impressed by this, particularly since she has a very difficult job. You recently learned that she spends several hours every week on her own taking classes to improve her skills. Jill seems to be motivated more by recognition than by money.
- Fred Hammer is a jolly person who gets along with everyone. His subordinates like him, but you do not think that he is getting the job done to your expectations. He has missed a critical delivery date twice, and this cost the firm over $5,000 each time. He recently divorced his wife and is having an extremely difficult time meeting his financial obligations.

Assignment

1. You have $25,000 available for raises. As you think about how you will allot the money, consider the following:
   a. What criteria will you use in making a fair distribution?
   b. Will you distribute the entire $25,000? If not, what will you do with the remainder?
2. Prepare a four-column table in the following manner:
   a. In column 1, write the name of the employee.
   b. In column 2, write the amount of the raise.
   c. In column 3, write the percentage of the $25,000 the employee will receive.
   d. In column 4, list the reasons for your decision.

4. BUILDING TEAM SKILLS

The New Therapy Company is soliciting a contract to provide five nursing homes with physical, occupational, speech, and respiratory therapy. The therapists will float among the five nursing homes. The therapists have not yet been hired, but the nursing homes expect them to be fully trained and ready to go to work in three months. The previous therapy company lost its contract because of high staff turnover owing to "burnout" (a common problem in this type of work), high costs, and low-quality care. The nursing homes want a plan specifying how the New Therapy Company will meet staffing needs, keep costs low, and provide high-quality care.

Assignment

1. Working in a group, discuss how the New Therapy Company can meet the three-month deadline and still ensure that the care its therapists provide is of high quality. Also discuss the following:
   a. How many of each type of therapist will the company need?
   b. How will it prevent therapists from "burning out"?
   c. How can it retain experienced staff and still limit costs?
   d. Are promotions available for any of the staff? What is the career ladder?
   e. How will the company manage therapists at five different locations? How will it keep in touch with them (computer, voice mail, monthly meetings)? Would it make more sense to have therapists work permanently at each location rather than rotate among them?
   f. How will the company justify the travel costs? What other expenses might it expect?
2. Prepare a plan for the New Therapy Company to present to the nursing homes.

5. RESEARCHING DIFFERENT CAREERS

A résumé provides a summary of your skills, abilities, and achievements. It also may include a description of the type of job you want. A well-prepared résumé indicates that you know what your career objectives are, shows that you have given serious thought to your career, and tells a potential employer what you are qualified to do. The way a résumé is prepared can make a difference in whether you are considered for a job.

Assignment

1. Prepare a résumé for a job that you want using the information in Appendix A (see text website).
   a. First, determine what your skills are and decide which skills are needed to do this particular job.
   b. Decide which type of format—chronological or functional—would be most effective in presenting your skills and experience.
   c. Keep the résumé to one page, if possible (definitely no more than two pages). (Note that portfolio items may be attached for certain types of jobs, such as artwork.)
2. Have several people review the résumé for accuracy.
3. Ask your instructor to comment on your résumé.

10 Motivating and Satisfying Employees and Teams

LEARNING OBJECTIVES

What you will be able to do once you complete this chapter:

1. Explain what motivation is.
2. Understand some major historical perspectives on motivation.
3. Describe three contemporary views of motivation: equity theory, expectancy theory, and goal-setting theory.
4. Explain several techniques for increasing employee motivation.
5. Understand the types, development, and uses of teams.

LWA/Photographers Choice/Getty Images

inside business

The Container Store's employees are so happy that fewer than 18 percent leave their jobs annually—among the lowest turnover rates in the entire retail industry.

The Container Store Puts Employees First

The Container Store hires only a few hundred new employees in any given year, yet it receives 40,000 applications annually. Why? Here's one hint: For nine consecutive years, The Container Store has ranked near the top of *Fortune* magazine's list of "The 100 Best Companies to Work For." Here's a second hint: Its employees are so happy that fewer than 18 percent leave their jobs annually—among the lowest turnover rates in the entire retail industry.

Based in Dallas, The Container Store has been helping people get organized for more than 30 years. Its 45 stores throughout North America ring up $600 million in annual sales of storage products for home and office. As part of The Container Store's friendly customer service, its 4,000 employees provide free advice on how to organize a roomy closet, a crowded kitchen, a compact home office, or a cramped dorm room.

What motivates The Container Store's employees? Many are customers who apply for an open position because they know and like the company's service and merchandise. "We love to hire customers," says co-founder Kip Tindell. "Who better than your customer to serve other customers?"

Employees—many of them college graduates—receive a generous salary and benefits package that few other retailers can match, plus a big discount on store purchases. They don't work on commission, which means they don't feel pressured to sell certain products or to rush through transaction after transaction. Instead, employees are encouraged to spend as much time as needed to give each customer individual attention. During their first year alone, full-time employees receive 241 hours of training. The focus is on learning all about The Container Store's 10,000 products and working together to solve customers' storage problems.

Still, customers are not The Container Store's top priority. "We actually say that we put the employee first and then the customer," Tindell explains. "If you put the employee first, they'll take care of the customer better than anybody else in the marketplace."[1]

To achieve its goals, any organization—whether it's The Container Store, FedEx, or a local convenience store—must be sure that its employees have more than the right raw materials, adequate facilities, and equipment that works. The organization also must ensure that its employees are *motivated*. To some extent, a high level of employee motivation derives from effective management practices.

In this chapter, after first explaining what motivation is, we present several views of motivation that have influenced management practices over the years: Taylor's ideas of scientific management, Mayo's Hawthorne Studies, Maslow's hierarchy of needs, Herzberg's motivation-hygiene theory, McGregor's Theory X and Theory Y, Ouchi's Theory Z, and reinforcement theory. Then, turning our attention to contemporary ideas, we examine equity theory, expectancy theory, and goal-setting theory. Finally, we discuss specific techniques managers can use to foster employee motivation and satisfaction.

motivation the individual internal process that energizes, directs, and sustains behavior; the personal "force" that causes you or me to behave in a particular way

What Is Motivation?

1

Learning Objective: Explain what motivation is.

A *motive* is something that causes a person to act. A successful athlete is said to be "highly motivated." A student who avoids work is said to be "unmotivated." We define **motivation** as the individual internal process that energizes, directs, and sustains behavior. It is the personal "force" that causes you or me to act in a particular way. For example, job rotation may increase your job satisfaction and your enthusiasm for your work so that you devote more energy to it, but perhaps job rotation would not have the same impact on me.

Morale is an employee's attitude or feelings about the job, about superiors, and about the firm itself. To achieve organizational goals effectively, employees need more than the right raw materials, adequate facilities, and equipment that works. High morale results mainly from the satisfaction of needs on the job or as a result of the job. One need that might be satisfied on the job is the need *to be recognized* as an important contributor to the organization. A need satisfied as a result of the job is the need for *financial security*. High morale, in turn, leads to dedication and loyalty, as well as to the desire to do the job well. Low morale can lead to shoddy work, absenteeism, and high turnover rates as employees leave to seek more satisfying jobs with other firms. A study conducted by the Society for Human Resource Management (SHRM) showed that 75 percent of all employees are actively or passively seeking new employment opportunities. To offset this turnover trend, companies are creating retention plans focused on employee morale. Sometimes creative solutions are needed to motivate people and boost morale. This is especially true where barriers to change are deeply rooted in cultural stereotypes of the job and in the industry.

morale an employee's feelings about his or her job and superiors and about the firm itself

Motivation, morale, and the satisfaction of employees' needs are thus intertwined. Along with productivity, they have been the subject of much study since the end of the nineteenth century. We continue our discussion of motivation by outlining some landmarks of that early research.

Historical Perspectives on Motivation

2

Learning Objective: Understand some major historical perspectives on motivation.

Researchers often begin a study with a fairly narrow goal in mind. After they develop an understanding of their subject, however, they realize that both their goal and their research should be broadened. This is exactly what happened when early research into productivity blossomed into the more modern study of employee motivation.

Photo by Lewis W. Hine/George Eastman House/Hulton Archive/Getty Images

Motivating employees. *Women wrapping purchases in the packing department of a department store. They stood in crowded lines at long tables and worked long hours. Motivation occurred through direct supervision.*

Scientific Management

scientific management the application of scientific principles to management of work and workers

Toward the end of the nineteenth century, Frederick W. Taylor became interested in improving the efficiency of individual workers. This interest stemmed from his own experiences in manufacturing plants. It eventually led to **scientific management**, the application of scientific principles to management of work and workers.

One of Taylor's first jobs was with the Midvale Steel Company in Philadelphia, where he developed a strong distaste for waste and inefficiency. He also observed a practice he called "soldiering." Workers "soldiered," or worked slowly, because they feared that if they worked faster, they would run out of work and lose their jobs. Taylor realized that managers were not aware of this practice because they had no idea what the workers' productivity levels *should* be.

Taylor later left Midvale and spent several years at Bethlehem Steel. It was there that he made his most significant contribution. In particular, he suggested that each job should be broken down into separate tasks. Then management should determine (1) the best way to perform these tasks and (2) the job output to expect when the tasks were performed properly. Next, management should carefully choose the best person for each job and train that person to do the job properly. Finally, management should cooperate with workers to ensure that jobs were performed as planned.

piece-rate system a compensation system under which employees are paid a certain amount for each unit of output they produce

Taylor also developed the idea that most people work only to earn money. He therefore reasoned that pay should be tied directly to output. The more a person produced, the more he or she should be paid. This gave rise to the **piece-rate system**, under which employees are paid a certain amount for each unit of output they produce. Under Taylor's piece-rate system, each employee was assigned an output quota. Those exceeding the quota were paid a higher per-unit rate for *all* units they produced (see Figure 10.1). Today, the piece-rate system is still used by some manufacturers and by farmers who grow crops that are harvested by farm laborers.

When Taylor's system was put into practice at Bethlehem Steel, the results were dramatic. Average earnings per day for steel handlers rose from $1.15 to $1.88. (Don't let the low wages that prevailed at the time obscure the fact that this was an increase of better than 60 percent!) The average amount of steel handled per day increased from sixteen to fifty-seven tons.

Taylor's revolutionary ideas had a profound impact on management practice. However, his view of motivation soon was recognized as overly simplistic and narrow. It is true that most people expect to be paid for their work, but it is also true that people work for a variety of reasons other than pay. Simply increasing a person's pay may not increase that person's motivation or productivity.

Figure 10.1: Taylor's Piece-Rate System

Workers who exceeded their quota were rewarded by being paid at a higher rate per piece for all the pieces they produced.

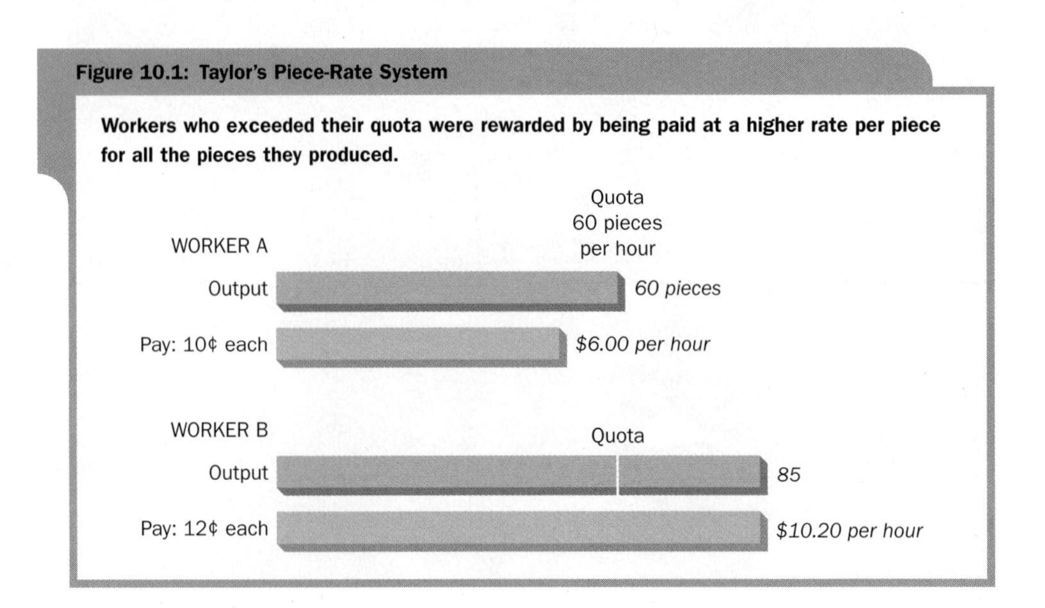

The Hawthorne Studies

Between 1927 and 1932, Elton Mayo conducted two experiments at the Hawthorne plant of the Western Electric Company in Chicago. The original objective of these studies, now referred to as the *Hawthorne Studies,* was to determine the effects of the work environment on employee productivity.

In the first set of experiments, lighting in the workplace was varied for one group of workers but not for a second group. Then the productivity of both groups was measured to determine the effect of the light. To the amazement of the researchers, productivity increased for *both* groups. And for the group whose lighting was varied, productivity remained high until the light was reduced to the level of moonlight!

The second set of experiments focused on the effectiveness of the piece-rate system in increasing the output of *groups* of workers. Researchers expected that output would increase because faster workers would put pressure on slower workers to produce more. Again, the results were not as expected. Output remained constant no matter what "standard" rates management set.

The researchers came to the conclusion that *human factors* were responsible for the results of the two experiments. In the lighting experiments, researchers had given both groups of workers a *sense of involvement* in their jobs merely by asking them to participate in the research. These workers—perhaps for the first time—felt as though they were an important part of the organization. In the piece-rate experiments, each group of workers informally set the acceptable rate of output for the group. To gain or retain the *social acceptance* of the group, each worker had to produce at that rate. Slower or faster workers were pressured to maintain the group's pace.

The Hawthorne Studies showed that such human factors are at least as important to motivation as pay rates. From these and other studies, the *human relations movement* in management was born. Its premise was simple: Employees who are happy and satisfied with their work are motivated to perform better. Hence management would do best to provide a work environment that maximizes employee satisfaction.

Maslow's Hierarchy of Needs

Abraham Maslow, an American psychologist whose best-known works were published in the 1960s and 1970s, developed a theory of motivation based on a hierarchy of needs. A **need** is a personal requirement. Maslow assumed that humans are "wanting" beings who seek to fulfill a variety of needs. He observed that these needs can be arranged according to their importance in a sequence now known as **Maslow's hierarchy of needs** (see Figure 10.2).

need a personal requirement

Maslow's hierarchy of needs a sequence of human needs in the order of their importance

At the most basic level are **physiological needs**, the things we require to survive. They include food and water, clothing, shelter, and sleep. In the employment context, these needs usually are satisfied through adequate wages.

physiological needs the things we require for survival

Figure 10.2: Maslow's Hierarchy of Needs

Maslow believed that people act to fulfill five categories of needs.

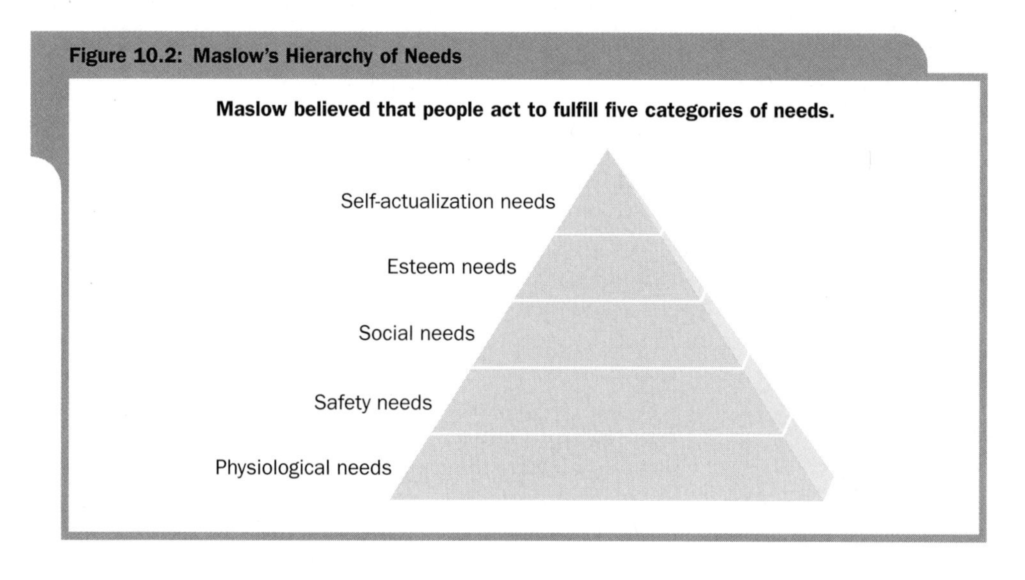

safety needs the things we require for physical and emotional security

At the next level are **safety needs**, the things we require for physical and emotional security. Safety needs may be satisfied through job security, health insurance, pension plans, and safe working conditions. During a time of falling corporate profits, many companies are facing increasing insurance premiums for employee health care. Both General Electric (GE) and Hershey recently endured strikes centered on the issue of increased health care costs. Reduced health care coverage is a threat to employees' need for safety. Some companies are trying to find unique solutions. For example, SAS, a software company, maintains its own health care center that offers free physical examinations, emergency treatment, immunizations, and care for chronic illnesses.[2]

social needs the human requirements for love and affection and a sense of belonging

Next are the **social needs**, the human requirements for love and affection and a sense of belonging. To an extent, these needs can be satisfied through relationships in the work environment and the informal organization. However, social networks beyond the workplace—with family and friends, for example—usually are needed, too. Casino operator Isle of Capri Casinos, Inc., uses unique methods to help employees meet their social needs. The company holds an annual retreat for managers that is fun and exciting. The latest retreat was called "Isle Survive" and featured a *Survivor*-like game where employees were teamed up and given money and other resources and sent on a sort of scavenger hunt. This is just one of the ways Isle of Capri motivates its workers, and the company seems to be successful in meeting its employees' needs, as evidenced by the lowest employee turnover in the industry.

esteem needs our need for respect, recognition, and a sense of our own accomplishment and worth

At the level of **esteem needs**, we require respect and recognition from others and a sense of our own accomplishment and worth (self-esteem). These needs may be satisfied through personal accomplishment, promotion to more responsible jobs, various honors and awards, and other forms of recognition.

self-actualization needs the need to grow and develop and to become all that we are capable of being

At the top of the hierarchy are our **self-actualization needs**, the need to grow, develop, and become all that we are capable of being. These are the most difficult needs to satisfy, and the means of satisfying them tend to vary with the individual. For some people, learning a new skill, starting a new career after retirement, or becoming "the best there is" at some endeavor may be the way to realize self-actualization.

Maslow suggested that people work to satisfy their physiological needs first, then their safety needs, and so on, up the "needs ladder." In general, they are motivated by the needs at the lowest level that remain unsatisfied. However, needs at one level do not have to be satisfied completely before needs at the next-higher level come into play. If the majority of a person's physiological and safety needs are satisfied, that person will be motivated primarily by social needs. But any physiological and safety needs that remain unsatisfied also will be important.

Maslow's hierarchy of needs provides a useful way of viewing employee motivation, as well as a guide for management. By and large, American business has been able to satisfy workers' basic needs, but the higher-order needs present more of a challenge. These needs are not satisfied in a simple manner, and the means of satisfaction vary from one employee to another.

Esteem needs. *Employee recognition helps to satisfy esteem needs. Recognition of this type shows respect for an individual and his or her accomplishments.*

AP/Wide World

Herzberg's Motivation-Hygiene Theory

In the late 1950s, Frederick Herzberg interviewed approximately two hundred accountants and engineers in Pittsburgh. During the interviews, he asked them to think of a time when they had felt especially good about their jobs and their work. Then he asked them to describe the factor or factors that had caused them to feel that way. Next, he did the same regarding a time when they had felt especially bad about their work. He was surprised to find that feeling good and feeling bad resulted from entirely different sets of factors; that is, low pay may have made a particular person feel bad, but it was not high pay that had made that person feel good. Instead, it was some completely different factor.

Satisfaction and Dissatisfaction Before Herzberg's interviews, the general assumption was that employee satisfaction and dissatisfaction lay at opposite ends of the same scale. People felt satisfied, dissatisfied, or somewhere in between. But Herzberg's interviews convinced him that satisfaction and dissatisfaction may be different dimensions altogether. One dimension might range from satisfaction to no satisfaction, and the other might range from dissatisfaction to no dissatisfaction. In other words, the opposite of satisfaction is not dissatisfaction. The idea that satisfaction and dissatisfaction are separate and distinct dimensions is referred to as the **motivation-hygiene theory** (see Figure 10.3).

What motivation factors? *Which motivation factors would be most likely to produce a highly effective racing crew?*

AP/Wide World

The job factors that Herzberg found most frequently associated with satisfaction are achievement, recognition, responsibility, advancement, growth, and the work itself. These factors generally are referred to as **motivation factors** because their presence increases motivation. However, their absence does not necessarily result in feelings of dissatisfaction. When motivation factors are present, they act as *satisfiers*.

Job factors cited as causing dissatisfaction are supervision, working conditions, interpersonal relationships, pay, job security, company policies, and administration. These factors, called **hygiene factors**, reduce dissatisfaction when they are present to an acceptable degree. However, they do not necessarily result in high levels of motivation. When hygiene factors are absent, they act as *dissatisfiers*.

motivation-hygiene theory the idea that satisfaction and dissatisfaction are separate and distinct dimensions

motivation factors job factors that increase motivation but whose absence does not necessarily result in dissatisfaction

hygiene factors job factors that reduce dissatisfaction when present to an acceptable degree but that do not necessarily result in high levels of motivation

Using Herzberg's Motivation-Hygiene Theory Herzberg provides explicit guidelines for using the motivation-hygiene theory of employee motivation. He suggests that the hygiene factors must be present to ensure that a worker can function comfortably. He warns, however, that a state of *no dissatisfaction* never exists. In any situation, people always will be dissatisfied with something.

According to Herzberg, managers should make hygiene as positive as possible but then should expect only short-term, not long-term, improvement in motivation. Managers must focus instead on providing those motivation factors that presumably *will* enhance motivation and long-term effort.

We should note that employee pay has more effect than Herzberg's theory indicates. He suggests that pay provides only short-term change and not true motivation. Yet, in many organizations, pay constitutes a form of recognition and reward for achievement—and recognition and achievement are both motivation factors. The effect of pay may depend on how it is distributed. If a pay increase does not

Figure 10.3: Herzberg's Motivation-Hygiene Theory

Herzberg's theory takes into account that there are different dimensions to job satisfaction and dissatisfaction and that these factors do not overlap.

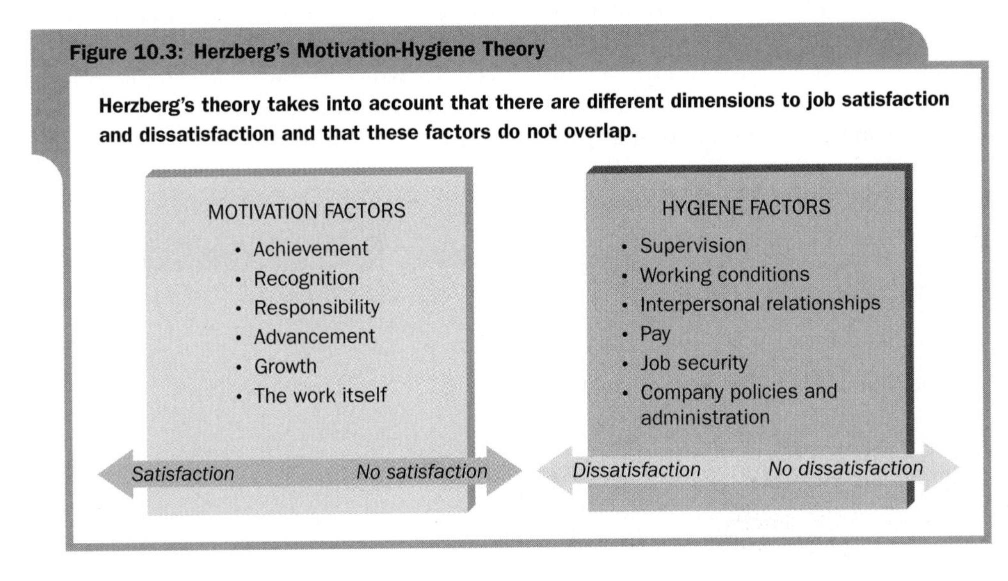

depend on performance (as in across-the-board or cost-of-living raises), it may not motivate people. However, if pay is increased as a form of recognition (as in bonuses or incentives), it may play a powerful role in motivating employees to higher performance.

Theory X and Theory Y

The concepts of Theory X and Theory Y were advanced by Douglas McGregor in his book *The Human Side of Enterprise*. They are, in essence, sets of assumptions that underlie management's attitudes and beliefs regarding worker behavior.[3]

Theory X a concept of employee motivation generally consistent with Taylor's scientific management; assumes that employees dislike work and will function only in a highly controlled work environment

Theory X is a concept of employee motivation generally consistent with Taylor's scientific management. Theory X assumes that employees dislike work and will function effectively only in a highly controlled work environment.

Theory X is based on the following assumptions:

1. People dislike work and try to avoid it.
2. Because people dislike work, managers must coerce, control, and frequently threaten employees to achieve organizational goals.
3. People generally must be led because they have little ambition and will not seek responsibility; they are concerned mainly with security.

The logical outcome of such assumptions will be a highly controlled work environment—one in which managers make all the decisions and employees take all the orders.

Theory Y a concept of employee motivation generally consistent with the ideas of the human relations movement; assumes that employees accept responsibility and work toward organizational goals, if by so doing they also achieve personal rewards

On the other hand, **Theory Y** is a concept of employee motivation generally consistent with the ideas of the human relations movement. Theory Y assumes that employees accept responsibility and work toward organizational goals, and by so doing they also achieve personal rewards. Theory Y is based on the following assumptions:

1. People do not naturally dislike work; in fact, work is an important part of their lives.
2. People will work toward goals to which they are committed.
3. People become committed to goals when it is clear that accomplishing the goals will bring personal rewards.
4. People often seek out and willingly accept responsibility.
5. Employees have the potential to help accomplish organizational goals.
6. Organizations generally do not make full use of their human resources.

Obviously, this view is quite different from—and much more positive than—that of Theory X. McGregor argued that most managers behave in accordance with Theory X. But he maintained that Theory Y is more appropriate and effective as a guide for managerial action (see Table 10.1).

The human relations movement and Theories X and Y increased managers' awareness of the importance of social factors in the workplace. However, human motivation is a complex and dynamic process to which there is no simple key. Neither money nor social factors alone can provide the answer. Rather, a number of factors must be considered in any attempt to increase motivation.

Table 10.1: Theory X and Theory Y Contrasted

Area	Theory X	Theory Y
Attitude toward work	Dislike	Involvement
Control systems	External	Internal
Supervision	Direct	Indirect
Level of commitment	Low	High
Employee potential	Ignored	Identified
Use of human resources	Limited	Not limited

Theory Z

William Ouchi, a management professor at UCLA, studied business practices in American and Japanese firms. He concluded that different types of management systems dominate in these two countries.[4] In Japan, Ouchi found what he calls *type J* firms. They are characterized by lifetime employment for employees, collective (or group) decision making, collective responsibility for the outcomes of decisions, slow evaluation and promotion, implied control mechanisms, nonspecialized career paths, and a holistic concern for employees as people.

American industry is dominated by what Ouchi calls *type A* firms, which follow a different pattern. They emphasize short-term employment, individual decision making, individual responsibility for the outcomes of decisions, rapid evaluation and promotion, explicit control mechanisms, specialized career paths, and a segmented concern for employees only as employees.

A few very successful American firms represent a blend of the type J and type A patterns. These firms, called *type Z* organizations, emphasize long-term employment, collective decision making, individual responsibility for the outcomes of decisions, slow evaluation and promotion, informal control along with some formalized measures, moderately specialized career paths, and a holistic concern for employees.

Ouchi's **Theory Z** is the belief that some middle ground between his type A and type J practices is best for American business (see Figure 10.4). A major part of Theory Z is the emphasis on participative decision making. The focus is on "we" rather than on "us versus them." Theory Z employees and managers view the organization as a family. This participative spirit fosters cooperation and the dissemination of information and organizational values.

Theory Z the belief that some middle ground between his type A and type J practices is best for American business

Reinforcement Theory

Reinforcement theory is based on the premise that behavior that is rewarded is likely to be repeated, whereas behavior that is punished is less likely to recur. A *reinforcement* is an action that follows directly from a particular behavior. It may be a pay raise following a particularly large sale to a new customer or a reprimand for coming to work late.

reinforcement theory a theory of motivation based on the premise that behavior that is rewarded is likely to be repeated, whereas behavior that is punished is less likely to recur

Reinforcements can take a variety of forms and can be used in a number of ways. A *positive reinforcement* is one that strengthens desired behavior by providing a reward. For example, many employees respond well to praise; recognition from their supervisors for a job well done increases (strengthens) their willingness to perform well in the future. A *negative reinforcement* strengthens desired behavior by eliminating an undesirable task or situation. Suppose that a machine shop must be cleaned thoroughly every month—a dirty, miserable task. During one particular

Figure 10.4: The Features of Theory Z

The best aspects of Japanese and American management theories combine to form the nucleus of Theory Z.

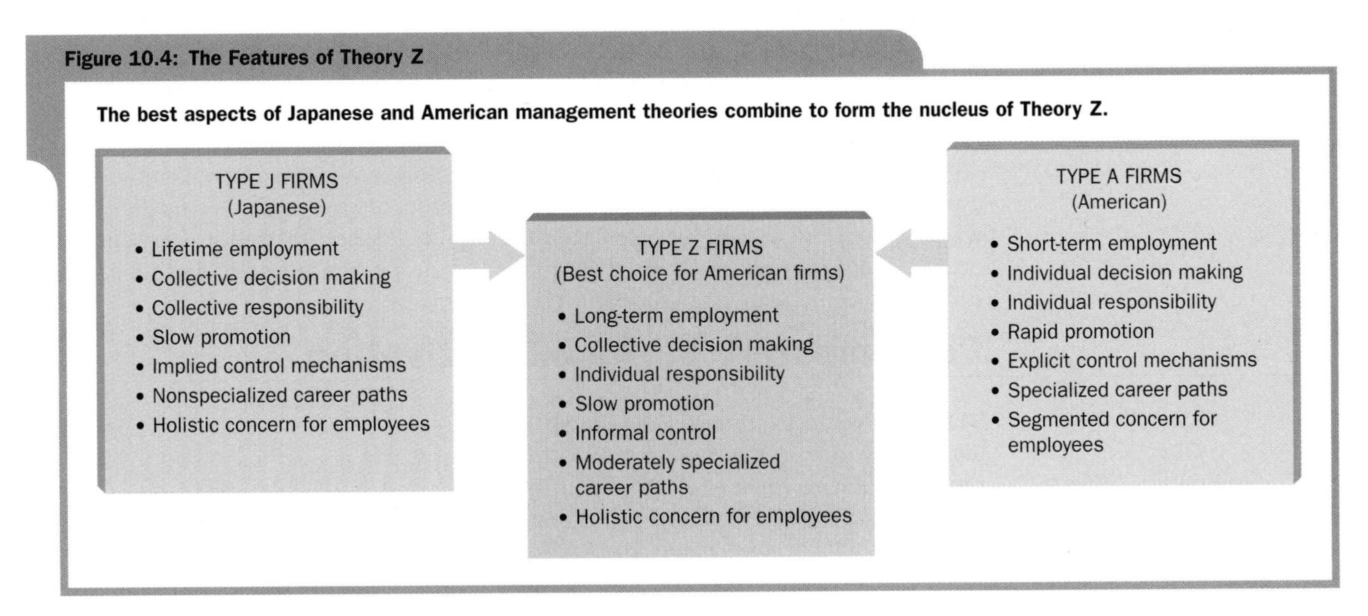

Going Global

A World of Difference in Motivation Worldwide

What motivates employees? The specifics may differ from country to country, but programs that recognize and reward extraordinary performance can translate into motivation anywhere in the world. Here's how three multinationals get the entire workforce involved by asking employees to nominate their peers for special recognition.

- *Fujitsu Services.* Japan-based Fujitsu Services invites employees worldwide to submit the names of colleagues whose hard work has helped the information technology firm achieve its goals or whose performance embodies the company's overall values. Employees who are singled out for recognition can choose their own rewards, such as a weekend trip or an electronic gadget.
- *AstraZeneca.* Headquartered in London, this pharmaceuticals firm has a unique way of honoring outstanding employees who have been nominated for recognition by their managers: It puts their photos on posters displayed around many company locations. "I think it's the type of recognition that people feel good about," says a senior manager.
- *Vodafone.* At Vodafone, a U.K.-based telecommunications company, employees not only nominate coworkers for special achievements, but they also serve on the selection committee. Each year, 100 employees receive companywide recognition and rewards such as luxury getaways. For some recipients, the best part is knowing that colleagues really appreciate their efforts.

David Woolley/Digital Vision/Getty Images

Sources: Paul Gallagher, "Inspiring Employee Engagement," *Human Resource Executive Online,* October 8, 2008, **www.hreonline.com**; "Motivation Case Study: Fujitsu Services," *Employee Benefits,* September 3, 2008, n.p.; "Vodafone UK Puts Shining Behaviour Under Spotlight," *Employee Benefits,* February 8, 2008.

month when the workers do a less-than-satisfactory job at their normal work assignments, the boss requires the workers to clean the factory rather than bringing in the usual private maintenance service. The employees will be motivated to work harder the next month to avoid the unpleasant cleanup duty again.

Punishment is an undesired consequence of undesirable behavior. Common forms of punishment used in organizations include reprimands, reduced pay, disciplinary layoffs, and termination (firing). Punishment often does more harm than good. It tends to create an unpleasant environment, fosters hostility and resentment, and suppresses undesirable behavior only until the supervisor's back is turned.

Managers who rely on *extinction* hope to eliminate undesirable behavior by not responding to it. The idea is that the behavior eventually will become "extinct." Suppose, for example, that an employee has the habit of writing memo after memo to his or her manager about insignificant events. If the manager does not respond to any of these memos, the employee probably will stop writing them, and the behavior will have been squelched.

The effectiveness of reinforcement depends on which type is used and how it is timed. One approach may work best under certain conditions, but some situations lend themselves to the use of more than one approach. Generally, positive reinforcement is considered the most effective, and it is recommended when the manager has a choice.

Continual reinforcement can become tedious for both managers and employees, especially when the same behavior is being reinforced over and over in the same way. At the start, it may be necessary to reinforce a desired behavior every time it occurs. However, once a desired behavior has become more or less established, occasional reinforcement seems to be most effective.

Contemporary Views on Motivation

3

Learning Objective: Describe three contemporary views of motivation: equity theory, expectancy theory, and goal-setting theory.

Maslow's hierarchy of needs and Herzberg's motivation-hygiene theory are popular and widely known theories of motivation. Each is also a significant step up from the relatively narrow views of scientific management and Theories X and Y. But they do have one weakness: Each attempts to specify *what* motivates people, but neither explains *why* or *how* motivation develops or is sustained over time. In recent years, managers have begun to explore three other models that take a more dynamic view of motivation. These are equity theory, expectancy theory, and goal-setting theory.

Equity Theory

The **equity theory** of motivation is based on the premise that people are motivated to obtain and preserve equitable treatment for themselves. As used here, *equity* is the distribution of rewards in direct proportion to the contribution of each employee to the organization. Everyone need not receive the *same* rewards, but the rewards should be in accordance with individual contributions.

equity theory a theory of motivation based on the premise that people are motivated to obtain and preserve equitable treatment for themselves

According to this theory, we tend to implement the idea of equity in the following way: First, we develop our own input-to-outcome ratio. *Inputs* are the time, effort, skills, education, experience, and so on, that we contribute to the organization. *Outcomes* are the rewards we get from the organization, such as pay, benefits, recognition, and promotions. Next, we compare this ratio with what we perceive as the input-to-outcome ratio for some other person. It might be a coworker, a friend who works for another firm, or even an average of all the people in our organization. This person is called the *comparison other*. Note that our perception of this person's input-to-outcome ratio may be absolutely correct or completely wrong. However, we believe that it is correct.

If the two ratios are roughly the same, we feel that the organization is treating us equitably. In this case, we are motivated to leave things as they are. However, if our ratio is the higher of the two, we feel under-rewarded and are motivated to make changes. We may (1) decrease our own inputs by not working so hard, (2) try to increase our total outcome by asking for a raise in pay, (3) try to get the comparison other to increase some inputs or receive decreased outcomes, (4) leave the work situation, or (5) do a new comparison with a different comparison other.

Equity theory is most relevant to pay as an outcome. Because pay is a very real measure of a person's worth to an organization, comparisons involving pay are a natural part of organizational life. Managers can try to avoid problems arising from inequity by making sure that rewards are distributed on the basis of performance and that everyone clearly understands the basis for his or her own pay.

Expectancy Theory

Expectancy theory, developed by Victor Vroom, is a very complex model of motivation based on a deceptively simple assumption. According to expectancy theory, motivation depends on how much we want something and on how likely we think we are to get it (see Figure 10.5). Consider, for example, the case of three sales representatives who are candidates for promotion to one sales manager's job. Bill has had a very good sales year and always gets good performance evaluations. However, he isn't sure that he wants the job because it involves a great deal of travel, long working hours, and much stress and pressure. Paul wants the job badly but doesn't think he has much chance of getting it. He has had a terrible sales year

expectancy theory a model of motivation based on the assumption that motivation depends on how much we want something and on how likely we think we are to get it

Figure 10.5: Expectancy Theory

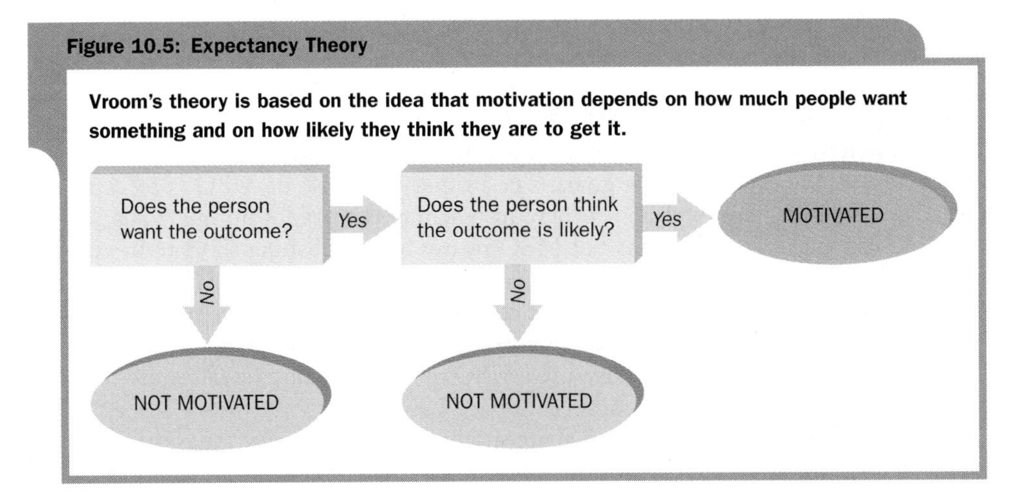

and gets only mediocre performance evaluations from his present boss. Susan wants the job as much as Paul, and she thinks that she has a pretty good shot at it. Her sales have improved significantly this past year, and her evaluations are the best in the company.

Expectancy theory would predict that Bill and Paul are not very motivated to seek the promotion. Bill doesn't really want it, and Paul doesn't think that he has much of a chance of getting it. Susan, however, is very motivated to seek the promotion because she wants it *and* thinks that she can get it.

Expectancy theory is complex because each action we take is likely to lead to several different outcomes; some we may want, and others we may not want. For example, a person who works hard and puts in many extra hours may get a pay raise, be promoted, and gain valuable new job skills. However, that person also may be forced to spend less time with his or her family and be forced to cut back on his or her social life.

For one person, the promotion may be paramount, the pay raise and new skills fairly important, and the loss of family and social life of negligible importance. For someone else, the family and social life may be most important, the pay raise of moderate importance, the new skills unimportant, and the promotion undesirable because of the additional hours it would require. The first person would be motivated to work hard and put in the extra hours, whereas the second person would not be at all motivated to do so. In other words, it is the entire bundle of outcomes—and the individual's evaluation of the importance of each outcome—that determines motivation.

Expectancy theory is difficult to apply, but it does provide several useful guidelines for managers. It suggests that managers must recognize that (1) employees work for a variety of reasons, (2) these reasons, or expected outcomes, may change over time, and (3) it is necessary to clearly show employees how they can attain the outcomes they desire.

Goal-Setting Theory

goal-setting theory a theory of motivation suggesting that employees are motivated to achieve goals that they and their managers establish together

Goal-setting theory suggests that employees are motivated to achieve goals that they and their managers establish together. The goal should be very specific, moderately difficult, and one the employee will be committed to achieve.[5] Rewards should be tied directly to goal achievement. Using goal-setting theory, a manager can design rewards that fit employee needs, clarify expectations, maintain equity, and provide reinforcement. A major benefit of this theory is that it provides a good understanding of the goal the employee is to achieve and the rewards that will accrue to the employee if the goal is accomplished.

Key Motivation Techniques

4

Learning Objective: Explain several techniques for increasing employee motivation.

Today, it takes more than a generous salary to motivate employees. Increasingly, companies are trying to provide motivation by satisfying employees' less tangible needs. In this section, we discuss several specific techniques that help managers to boost employee motivation and job satisfaction.

Management by Objectives

management by objectives (MBO) a motivation technique in which managers and employees collaborate in setting goals

Management by objectives (MBO) is a motivation technique in which managers and employees collaborate in setting goals. The primary purpose of MBO is to clarify the roles employees are expected to play in reaching the organization's goals. For example, Daymark Solutions has put MBO to use by establishing short-term goals for every employee. These quarterly objectives may be achieving a high level of customer satisfaction or receiving specific certifications. These smaller goals directly correlate with the larger company objectives, such as cost containment or revenue goals.[6] A number of companies have used MBO methods, including General Foods, General Motors, and Wells Fargo.[7]

By allowing individuals to participate in goal setting and performance evaluation, MBO increases their motivation. Most MBO programs consist of a series of

Setting and achieving goals. *Abbott provides hybrid cars to its sales force in order to help achieve environmental goals set by this company.*

PRNewsFoto/Abbott

five steps. The first step in setting up an MBO program is to secure the acceptance of top management. It is essential that top managers endorse and participate in the program if others in the firm are to accept it. The commitment of top management also provides a natural starting point for educating employees about the purposes and mechanics of MBO.

Next, preliminary goals must be established. Top management also plays a major role in this activity because the preliminary goals reflect the firm's mission and strategy. The intent of an MBO program is to have these goals filter down through the organization.

The third step, which actually consists of several smaller steps, is the heart of MBO:

1. The manager explains to each employee that he or she has accepted certain goals for the group (the manager as well as the employees) and asks the individual to think about how he or she can help to achieve these goals.
2. The manager later meets with each employee individually. Together they establish goals for the employee. Whenever possible, the goals should be measurable and should specify the time frame for completion (usually one year).
3. The manager and the employee decide what resources the employee will need to accomplish his or her goals.

As the fourth step, the manager and each employee meet periodically to review the employee's progress. They may agree to modify certain goals during these meetings if circumstances have changed. For example, a sales representative may have accepted a goal of increasing sales by 20 percent. However, an aggressive competitor may have entered the marketplace, making this goal unattainable. In light of this circumstance, the goal may be revised downward to 10 or 15 percent.

The fifth step in the MBO process is evaluation. At the end of the designated time period, the manager and each employee meet again to determine which of the individual's goals were met, which were not met, and why. The employee's reward (in the form of a pay raise, praise, or promotion) is based primarily on the degree of goal attainment.

As with every other management method, MBO has advantages and disadvantages. MBO can motivate employees by involving them actively in the life of the

Job enrichment. *Jobs can be enriched by expanding the number of tasks performed and allowing employees to make more decisions that are directly related to performing various tasks.*

AP Photo/Shawano Cleary

firm. The collaboration on goal setting and performance appraisal improves communication and makes employees feel that they are an important part of the organization. Periodic review of progress also enhances control within an organization. A major problem with MBO is that it does not work unless the process begins at the top of an organization. In some cases, MBO results in excessive paperwork. Also, a manager may not like sitting down and working out goals with subordinates and may instead just assign them goals. Finally, MBO programs prove difficult to implement unless goals are quantifiable.

Job Enrichment

job enrichment a motivation technique that provides employees with more variety and responsibility in their jobs

job enlargement expanding a worker's assignments to include additional but similar tasks

Job enrichment is a method of motivating employees by providing them with variety in their tasks while giving them some responsibility for, and control over, their jobs. At the same time, employees gain new skills and acquire a broader perspective about how their individual work contributes to the goals of the organization. Earlier in this chapter, we noted that Herzberg's motivation-hygiene theory is one rationale for the use of job enrichment; that is, the added responsibility and control that job enrichment confers on employees increases their satisfaction and motivation. Employees at 3M get to spend 15 percent of their time at work on whatever projects they choose regardless of the relationship of these "pet projects" to the employees' regular duties. This type of enrichment can motivate employees and create a variety of benefits for the company.[8] At times, **job enlargement**, expanding a worker's assignments to include additional but similar tasks, can lead to job enrichment. Job enlargement might mean that a worker on an assembly line who used to connect three wires to components moving down the line, now connects five wires. Unfortunately, the added tasks often are just as routine as those the worker performed before the change. In such cases, enlargement may not be effective.

Whereas job enlargement does not really change the routine and monotonous nature of jobs, job enrichment does. Job enrichment requires that added tasks give an employee more responsibility for what he or she does. It provides workers with both more tasks to do and more control over how they perform them. In particular, job enrichment removes many controls from jobs, gives workers more authority, and assigns work in complete, natural units. Moreover, employees frequently are given fresh and challenging job assignments. By blending more planning and decision making into jobs, job enrichment gives work more depth and complexity.

Job redesign is a type of job enrichment in which work is restructured in ways that cultivate the worker-job match. Job redesign can be achieved by combining tasks, forming work groups, or establishing closer customer relationships. Employees often are more motivated when jobs are combined because the increased variety of tasks presents more challenge and therefore more reward. Work groups motivate employees by showing them how their jobs fit within the organization as a whole and how they contribute to its success. Establishing client relationships allows employees to interact directly with customers. Not only does this type of redesign add a personal dimension to employment, but it also provides workers with immediate and relevant feedback about how they are doing their jobs.

job redesign a type of job enrichment in which work is restructured to cultivate the worker-job match

Job enrichment works best when employees seek more challenging work. Of course, not all workers respond positively to job-enrichment programs. Employees must desire personal growth and have the skills and knowledge to perform enriched jobs. Lack of self-confidence, fear of failure, or distrust of management's intentions are likely to lead to ineffective performance on enriched jobs. In addition, some workers do not view their jobs as routine and boring, and others even prefer routine jobs because they find them satisfying. Companies that use job enrichment as an alternative to specialization also face extra expenses, such as the cost of retraining. Another motivation for job redesign is to reduce employees' stress at work. A job redesign that carefully matches worker to job can prevent stress-related injuries, which constitute about 60 to 80 percent of all work-related injuries.

Behavior Modification

Behavior modification is a systematic program of reinforcement to encourage desirable behavior. Behavior modification involves both rewards to encourage desirable actions and punishments to discourage undesirable actions. However, studies have shown that rewards, such as compliments and expressions of appreciation, are much more effective behavior modifiers than punishments, such as reprimands and scorn.

behavior modification a systematic program of reinforcement to encourage desirable behavior

When applied to management, behavior modification strives to encourage desirable organizational behavior. Use of this technique begins with identification of a *target behavior*—the behavior that is to be changed. (It might be low production levels or a high rate of absenteeism, for example.) Existing levels of this behavior then are measured. Next, managers provide positive reinforcement in the form of a reward when employees exhibit the *desired behavior* (such as increased production or less absenteeism). The reward might be praise or a more tangible form of recognition, such as a gift, meal, or trip. Apple Company created the Corporate Gifting and Rewards Program in order to give companies the ability to reward their staff with iPods, iPod accessories, and iTunes gift cards.[9] Finally, the levels of the target behavior are measured again to determine whether the desired changes have been achieved. If they have, the reinforcement is maintained. However, if the target behavior has not changed significantly in the desired direction, the reward system must be changed to one that is likely to be more effective. John Kotter, a renowned Harvard Business School professor, states that this is difficult; the kind of emotional persuasion needed for these changes is not taught in business schools and is not often properly considered in many business settings.[10] The key is to devise effective rewards that not only will modify employees' behavior in desired ways but also will motivate them. To this end, experts suggest that management should reward quality, loyalty, and productivity.

Flextime

To most people, a work schedule means the standard nine-to-five, forty-hour work week. In reality, though, many people have work schedules that are quite different from this. S.C. Johnson and Sons' Flexible Work Schedule Program allows employees

Source: www.transitcenter.com/transitresources, accessed November 28, 2008.

to create their own work schedule around their personal lives.[11] Police officers, firefighters, restaurant personnel, airline employees, and medical personnel usually have work schedules that are far from standard. Some manufacturers also rotate personnel from shift to shift. Many professional people—such as managers, artists, and lawyers—need more than forty hours each week to get their work done.

The needs and lifestyles of today's workforce are changing. Dual-income families make up a much larger share of the workforce than ever before, and women are one of its fastest-growing sectors. Additionally, more employees are responsible for the care of elderly relatives. Recognizing that these changes increase the demand for family time, many employers are offering flexible work schedules that not only help employees to manage their time better but also increase employee motivation and job satisfaction.

flextime a system in which employees set their own work hours within employer-determined limits

Flextime is a system in which employees set their own work hours within certain limits determined by employers. Typically, the firm establishes two bands of time: the *core time,* when all employees must be at work, and the *flexible time,* when employees may choose whether to be at work. The only condition is that every employee must work a total of eight hours each day. For example, the hours between 9 and 11 a.m. and 1 and 3 p.m. might be core time, and the hours between 6 and 9 a.m., between 11 a.m. and 1 p.m., and between 3 and 6 p.m. might be flexible time. This would give employees the option of coming in early and getting off early, coming in later and leaving later, or taking an extra long lunch break. But flextime also ensures that everyone is present at certain times, when conferences with supervisors and department meetings can be scheduled. Another type of flextime allows employees to work a forty-hour work week in four days instead of five. Workers who put in ten hours a day instead of eight get an extra day off each week. More than three-quarters of companies currently offer flextime.[12] At times, smaller firms use flextime to attract and retain employees, especially when they cannot match the salaries and benefit package provided by larger companies. For example, independent accounting firm Jefferson Wells uses flexible schedules as an incentive when recruiting high-quality candidates. By offering a customized work schedule and part-time positions with full-time benefits, the firm is able to remain competitive with larger companies.[13]

The sense of independence and autonomy employees gain from having a say in what hours they work can be a motivating factor. In addition, employees who have enough time to deal with nonwork issues often work more productively and with greater satisfaction when they are on the job. Two common problems associated with using flextime are (1) supervisors sometimes find their jobs complicated by having employees who come and go at different times, and (2) employees without flextime sometimes resent coworkers who have it.

Part-Time Work and Job Sharing

part-time work permanent employment in which individuals work less than a standard work week

Part-time work is permanent employment in which individuals work less than a standard work week. The specific number of hours worked varies, but part-time jobs are structured so that all responsibilities can be completed in the number of hours an employee works. Part-time work is of special interest to parents who want more time with their children and people who simply desire more leisure time. One disadvantage of part-time work is that it often does not provide the benefits that come with a full-time position. This is not, however, the case at Starbucks, where approximately 80 percent of its employees work part time. Starbucks does not treat its part-time employees any differently from its full-time employees; all receive the same access to numerous benefits, which even includes a free pound of coffee every week.[14]

Part-time work. At Starbucks, part-time employees receive the same level of benefits as full-time employees.

AP Photo/Henry Ray Abrams

Job sharing (sometimes referred to as *work sharing*) is an arrangement whereby two people share one full-time position. One job sharer may work from 8 a.m. to noon, and the other may work from 1 to 5 p.m., or they may alternate work days. At Verizon Communications, Charlotte Schutzman and Sue Manix share the post of vice president of public affairs and communications. Each of them works two days a week along with alternating Wednesdays. By talking on the phone at least twice a week, they are able to handle a challenging administrative position and still be able to raise their children.[15] Job sharing combines the security of a full-time position with the flexibility of a part-time job. For firms, job sharing provides a unique opportunity to attract highly skilled employees who might not be available on a full-time basis. In addition, companies can save on expenses by reducing the cost of benefits and avoiding the disruptions of employee turnover. For employees, opting for the flexibility of job sharing may mean giving up some of the benefits received for full-time work. In addition, job sharing is difficult if tasks are not easily divisible or if two people do not work or communicate well with one another.

job sharing an arrangement whereby two people share one full-time position

Telecommuting

A growing number of companies allow **telecommuting**, working at home all the time or for a portion of the work week. Personal computers, modems, fax machines, voice mail, cellular phones, and overnight couriers all facilitate the work-at-home trend. Working at home means that individuals can set their own hours and have more time with their families. Even the federal government is recognizing the benefits of telecommuting in that 90 percent of the U.S. Treasury Inspector General for Tax Administration (TIGTA) workers and over 100 lawyers for the U.S. Trademark Office telecommute at least three days a week.[16]

telecommuting working at home all the time or for a portion of the work week

Companies that allow telecommuting experience several benefits, including increased productivity, lower real estate and travel costs, reduced employee absenteeism and turnover, increased work/life balance, improved morale, and access to additional labor pools. Telecommuting also helps improve the community by decreasing air pollutants, reducing traffic congestion, and lowering consumption of fossil fuels, which can give a company a green factor. Also, by having fewer employees commuting to work, the Reason Public Policy Institute estimates that approximately 350 lives are saved per year.[17] Of all the companies that give employees the option

Jump-Starting Your Career

Do You Have What It Takes to Telecommute?

Is telecommuting right for you? Studies show that telecommuters are generally more satisfied and more productive than non-telecommuters. But before you arrange to work from home, ask yourself:

- *Do you have the motivation to work on your own for one or more days every week?* If you can gear up to tackle your tasks without constant supervision, telecommuting may be a good step for you. According to telecommuting expert Toby Johnson, "You have to wear multiple hats and have an entrepreneurial streak."
- *How will you stay in touch with your workplace?* "Communication is critical, and the onus is on you to ensure that out of sight doesn't mean out of mind," Johnson says. Be prepared to stay in contact via phone, fax, e-mail, or whatever methods your company requires or prefers. If you don't like taking the initiative or you don't like technology, you may not like telecommuting.
- *How will you know that you're doing a good job?* Some bosses look only at what telecommuters accomplish; others also expect telecommuters to work a certain number of hours every day. Either way, being a good telecommuter means getting things done on time.

Sources: Marci Alboher, "Your Own Map to Working from Home," *New York Times*, September 14, 2008, p. 12; Ann Meyer, "Telecommuting Is Working for Many," *Chicago Tribune*, September 8, 2008, **www.chicagotribune.com**; D. Schwartz and J. Chamberlin, "Employees Benefit from Flexible Hours, Telecommuting," *Monitor on Psychology*, January 1, 2008, p. 11.

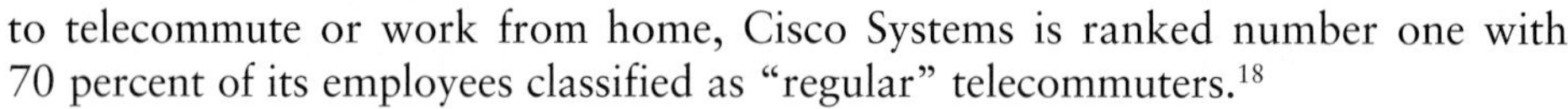

to telecommute or work from home, Cisco Systems is ranked number one with 70 percent of its employees classified as "regular" telecommuters.[18]

Among the disadvantages to telecommuting are feelings of isolation, putting in longer hours, and being distracted by family or household responsibilities. In addition, some supervisors have difficulty monitoring productivity. Although most bosses say that they trust their staff to work from home, many think that home workers are work-shy and less productive than office-based staff. A survey conducted in the United Kingdom found that up to 38 percent of managers surveyed believe that home workers are less productive, and 22 percent think that working from home is an excuse for time off. In addition, some supervisors have difficulty monitoring productivity.[19]

Sun Microsystems, for example, is an industry leader at providing a virtual work environment. Approximately 80 percent of the company's 20,000-member workforce connects to the company remotely. Sun was awarded the Optimas Award for Global Outlook because of its new iWork Program that allows employees to connect to Sun all over the globe. The program has boosted employee satisfaction, reduced turnover, and saved the company $255 million on real estate over the past four years.[20]

Employee Empowerment

empowerment making employees more involved in their jobs by increasing their participation in decision making

Many companies are increasing employee motivation and satisfaction through the use of empowerment. **Empowerment** means making employees more involved in their jobs and in the operations of the organization by increasing their participation in decision making. With empowerment, control no longer flows exclusively from the top levels of the organization downward. Empowered employees have a voice in what they do and how and when they do it. In some organizations, employees' input is restricted to individual choices, such as when to take breaks. In other companies, their responsibilities may encompass more far-reaching issues. For example, at Wegmans grocery stores, employees are empowered to ensure that the store achieves its primary objective: No customer leaves unhappy. Employees are allowed to make any concessions or decisions necessary to provide a good shopping experience. Anything is possible—from baking a family's Thanksgiving turkey in the store's oven to traveling to a customer's home to fix a botched order. Not only are Wegmans employees empowered to make on-the-spot customer-service decisions, but they also receive extensive training in the products they sell so as to guarantee that they can answer customers' questions about recipes, exotic items, and even food preparation.[21]

For empowerment to work effectively, management must be involved. Managers should set expectations, communicate standards, institute periodic evaluations, and guarantee follow-up. Effectively implemented, empowerment can lead to increased job satisfaction, improved job performance, higher self-esteem, and increased organizational commitment. Obstacles to empowerment include resistance on the part of management, distrust of management on the part of workers, insufficient training, and poor communication between management and employees.

Employee Ownership

Some organizations are discovering that a highly effective technique for motivating employees is **employee ownership**—that is, employees own the company they work for by virtue of being stockholders. Employee-owned businesses directly reward employees for success. When the company enjoys increased sales or lower costs, employees benefit directly. The National Center for Employee Ownership, an organization that studies employee-owned American businesses, reports that employee stock ownership plans (ESOPs) provide considerable employee incentive and increase employee involvement and commitment. In the United States today, about 8.5 million employees participate in 11,500 ESOPs and stock bonus plans.[22] As a means to motivate top executives and, frequently, middle-ranking managers who are working long days for what are generally considered poor salaries, some firms provide stock options as part of the employee compensation package. The option is simply the right to buy shares of the firm within a prescribed time at a set price. If the firm does well and its stock price rises past the set price (presumably because of all the work being done by the employee), the employee can exercise the option and immediately sell the stock and cash in on the company's success.

The difficulties of such companies as United Airlines have damaged the idea of employee ownership. United's ESOP has failed to solve problems between employees and management. In addition, Lowe's, the home-improvement retailer, recently stopped its long-running and mostly successful ESOP and transferred remaining money into 401(k) plans.

employee ownership a situation in which employees own the company they work for by virtue of being stockholders

Ethics Matters

The Dark Side of Virtual Teamwork

Virtual teamwork has many benefits—but it can also have a dark side. The entire team's performance and morale can suffer if some members don't get their work done, don't meet deadlines, or don't communicate well with colleagues. There are ethical ways to counteract the dark side of virtual teamwork, however.

Implementing overall team guidelines is a fair and objective way to establish and enforce acceptable norms. For example, to prevent delays and communication gaps, the global energy company BP has companywide rules so virtual team members know how quickly they must reply to e-mails from their colleagues.

Another approach is to have team members collaborate in developing a charter that describes their group goals and the guidelines they commit to following. If possible, members should divide the work in such a way that they can progress at their own pace without holding back the entire team.

Finally, harness members' enthusiasm. Nokia, the international telecommunications firm, encourages employees to volunteer for virtual teams instead of being assigned. Why? When members ask to join a virtual team, they're more likely to be engaged and dedicated—important qualities for members of any type of team.

Sources: Amy Schurr, "Secrets to Virtual Team Success," *NetworkWorld*, October 7, 2008, **www.networkworld.com**; Lynda Gratton, "Working Together . . . When Apart," *Wall Street Journal*, June 16, 2007, p. R4; "Crash Course in . . . Managing a Virtual Team," *Management Today*, September 3, 2007, p. 20.

Teams and Teamwork

5 **Learning Objective: Understand the types, development, and uses of teams.**

The concepts of teams and teamwork may be most commonly associated with sports, but they also are integral parts of business organizations. This organizational structure is popular because it encourages employees to participate more fully in business decisions. The growing number of companies organizing their workforces into teams reflects an effort to increase employee productivity and creativity, because team members are working on specific goals and are given greater autonomy. This leads to greater job satisfaction as employees feel more involved in the management process.[23]

What Is a Team?

In a business organization, a **team** is a group of workers functioning together as a unit to complete a common goal or purpose. A team may be assigned any number of tasks or goals, from development of a new product to selling that product.[24] Jones Walker, a New Orleans–based law firm, assembled a team of business students, alumni, and faculty advisors from Harvard University to assist Mayor C. Ray Nagin's Bring New

team a group of workers functioning together as a unit to complete a common goal or purpose

SPOTLIGHT

My Boss Is My . . .?

Source: Adecco Boss Day survey of 1,070 employees, weighted to represent the actual population.

Orleans Back Commission.[25] While teamwork may seem like a simple concept learned on soccer or football fields, teams function as a microcosm of the larger organization, and it is important to understand the types, development, and general nature of teams.

Types of Teams

There are several types of teams within businesses that function in specific ways to achieve different purposes, including problem-solving teams, self-managed teams, cross-functional teams, and virtual teams.

Problem-Solving Teams The most common type of team in business organizations is the **problem-solving team**. It is generally used temporarily in order to bring knowledgeable employees together to tackle a specific problem. Once the problem is solved, the team typically is disbanded.

In some extraordinary cases, an expert team may be needed to generate ground-breaking ideas. A **virtuoso team** consists of exceptionally highly skilled and talented individuals brought together to produce significant change. As with other kinds of problem-solving teams, virtuoso teams usually are assembled on a temporary basis. Instead of being task oriented, they focus on producing ideas and provoking change that could have an impact on the company and its industry. Because of the high skill level of their members, virtuoso teams can be difficult to manage. And unlike traditional teams, virtuoso teams place an emphasis on individuality over teamwork, which can cause further conflict. However, their conflicts usually are viewed as competitive and therefore productive in generating the most substantial ideas.[26]

problem-solving team a team of knowledgeable employees brought together to tackle a specific problem

virtuoso team a team of exceptionally highly skilled and talented individuals brought together to produce significant change

self-managed teams groups of employees with the authority and skills to manage themselves

Self-Managed Work Teams **Self-managed teams** are groups of employees with the authority and skills to manage themselves. Experts suggest that workers on self-managed teams are more motivated and satisfied because they have more task

What type of team is this? *At Wilson Sporting Goods, this self-managed team makes sure that each football has good seams and laces and weighs the correct amount. These footballs are identical to those used in SuperBowl XLII.*

AP Photo/Skip Peterson

variety and job control. On many work teams, members rotate through all the jobs for which the team is responsible. Some organizations cross-train the entire team so that everyone can perform everyone else's job. In a traditional business structure, management is responsible for hiring and firing employees, establishing budgets, purchasing supplies, conducting performance reviews, and taking corrective action. When self-managed teams are in place, they take over some or all of these management functions. Xerox, Procter & Gamble, Ferrari, as well as numerous other companies, have used self-managed teams successfully. The major advantages and disadvantages of self managed teams are mentioned in Figure 10.6.

Sustaining the Planet

Whether you work in a small business or a big corporation, you can help to sustain the planet by banding together with your coworkers. A good example is General Electric, where employees are motivated to donate time and money to environmental causes through the GE Volunteers Foundation. **www.ge.com/gevolunteersfoundation**

Cross-Functional Teams Traditionally, businesses have organized employees into departments based on a common function or specialty. However, increasingly, business organizations are faced with projects that require a diversity of skills not available within a single department. A **cross-functional team** consists of individuals with varying specialties, expertise, and skills that are brought together to achieve a common task. For example, a purchasing agent might create a cross-functional team with representatives from various departments to gain insight into useful purchases for the company. This structure avoids departmental separation and allows greater efficiency when there is a single goal. Although cross-functional teams aren't necessarily self-managed, most self-managed teams are cross-functional. They also can be cross-divisional, such as at Mercedes Benz, which has begun assembling cross-functional teams to improve quality and cut costs in research and development. Instead of a single team per model, cross-functional teams will be developing standard parts to be used across different types of Mercedes' vehicles.[27] Cross-functional teams also can include a variety of people from outside the company, such as the cross-functional team of ergonomists, users, and university scientists that developed a new natural ergonomic keyboard for Microsoft.[28] Owing to their speed, flexibility, and increased employee satisfaction, it is likely that the use of cross-functional teams will increase.

cross-functional team a team of individuals with varying specialties, expertise, and skills that are brought together to achieve a common task

Virtual Teams With the advent of sophisticated communications technology, it is no longer necessary for teams to be geographically close. A **virtual team** consists of members who are geographically dispersed but communicate electronically. In fact, team members may never meet in person but rely solely on e-mail, teleconferences, faxes, voice mail, and other technologic interactions. In the modern global environment, virtual teams connect employees on a common task across continents, oceans, time zones, and organizations. Oracle recruited former U.S. Army Lieutenant General Keith Kellogg to lead a virtual team to develop technology to address homeland security solutions.[29] In some cases, the physical distances between participants and the lack of face-to-face interaction can be difficult when deadlines approach or communication is not clear.

virtual team a team consisting of members who are geographically dispersed but communicate electronically

Figure 10.6: Advantages and Disadvantages of Self-Managed Teams

While self-managed teams provide benefits, managers must recognize their limitations.

ADVANTAGES	DISADVANTAGES
• Boosts employee morale	• Additional training costs
• Increases productivity	• Teams may be disorganized
• Aids innovation	• Conflicts may arise
• Reduces employee boredom	• Leadership role may be unclear

Figure 10.7: Stages of Team Development

When attempting to develop teams, managers must understand that multiple stages are generally required.

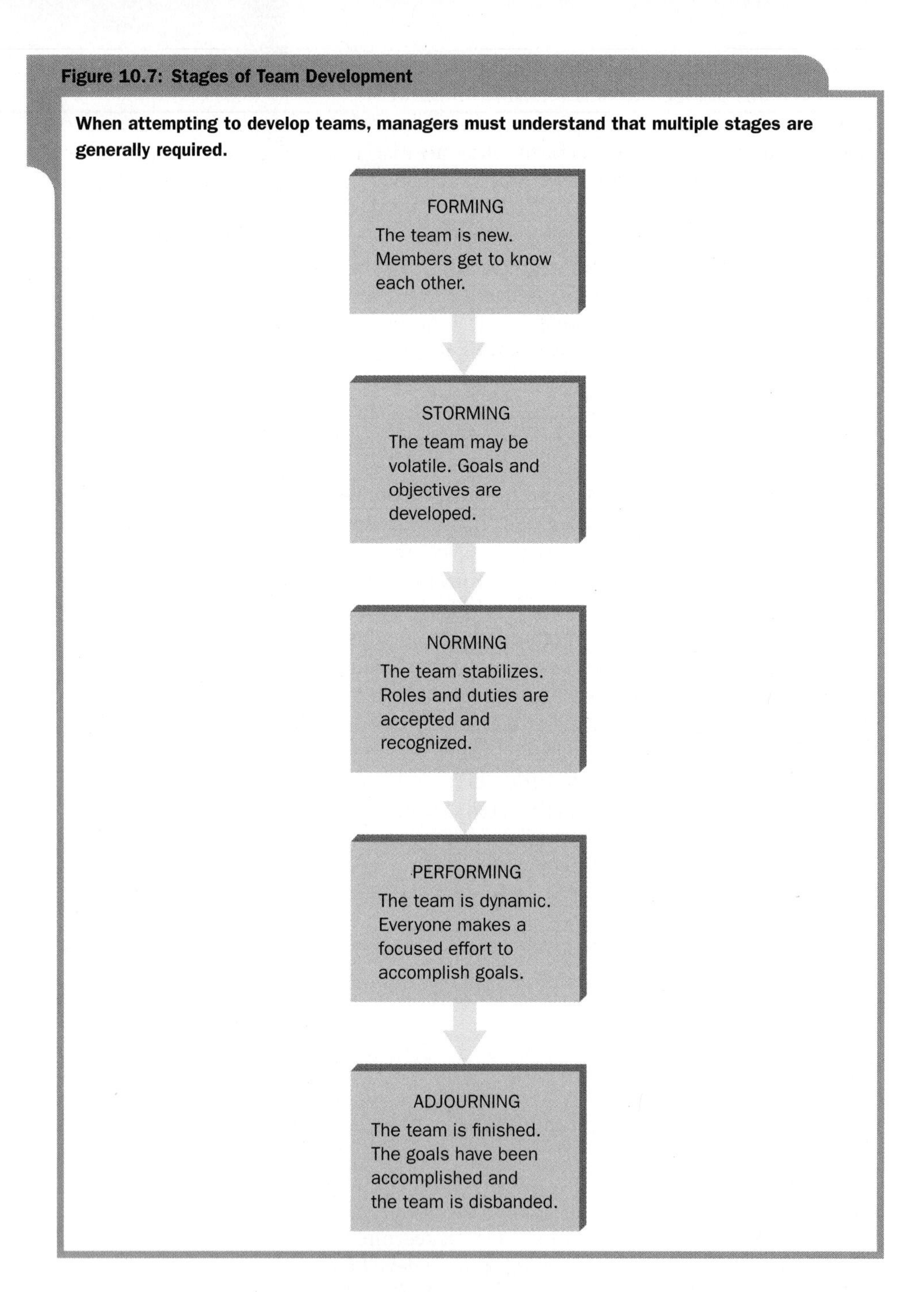

Developing and Using Effective Teams

When a team is first developed, it takes time for the members to establish roles, relationships, delegation of duties, and other attributes of an effective team. As a team matures, it passes through five stages of development, as shown in Figure 10.7.

Forming In the first stage, *forming,* team members are introduced to one another and begin to develop a social dynamic. The members of the team are still unsure how to relate to one another, what behaviors are considered acceptable, and what the ground rules for the team are. Through group member interaction over time, team members become more comfortable, and a group dynamic begins to emerge.

Storming During the *storming* stage, the interaction may be volatile, and the team may lack unity. Because the team is still relatively new, this is the stage at which goals and objectives begin to develop. Team members will brainstorm to develop ideas and plans and establish a broad-ranging agenda. It is important at this stage for team members to grow more comfortable around the others so that they can contribute openly. At this time, the leadership role likely will be formally undefined. A team member may emerge as the informal leader. The success or failure of the ideas in storming determines how long until the team reaches the next stage.

Norming After storming and the first large burst of activity, the team begins to stabilize during the *norming* stage. During this process, each person's role within the group starts to become apparent, and members begin to recognize the roles of others. A sense of unity will become stronger. If it hasn't already occurred, an identified leader will emerge. The group still may be somewhat volatile at this point and may regress back to the second stage if any conflict, especially over the leadership role, occurs.

Performing The fourth stage, *performing,* is when the team achieves its full potential. It is usually slow to develop and occurs when the team begins to focus strongly on the assigned task and away from team-development issues. The members of the team work in harmony under the established roles to accomplish the necessary goals.

Adjourning In the final stage, *adjourning,* the team is disbanded because the project has been completed. Team members may be reassigned to other teams or tasks. This stage does not always occur if the team is placed together for a task with no specific date of completion. For example, a marketing team for Best Buy may continue to develop promotional efforts for a store even after a specific promotional task has been accomplished. This stage is especially common in problem-solving teams that are dismantled after the assigned problem has been resolved.

Roles Within a Team

Within any team, each member has a role to play in helping the team attain its objectives. Each of these roles adds important dimensions to team member interactions. The group member who pushes forward toward goals and places the objective first is playing the *task-specialist role* by concentrating fully on the assigned task. In a cross-functional team, this might be the person with the most expertise relating to the current task. The *socioemotional role* is played by the individual who supports and encourages the emotional needs of the other members. This person places the team members' personal needs over the task of the team. While this may sound unimportant, the socioemotional member's dedication to team cohesiveness will lead to greater unity and higher productivity. The leader of the team, and possibly others as well, will play a *dual role.* This dual role is a combination of both the socioemotional and task-specialist roles because this individual focuses on both the task and the team. The team leader might not always play a dual role, but the team is likely to be most successful when he or she does. Sometimes an individual assumes the *nonparticipant role.* This role behavior is characterized by a person who does not contribute to accomplishing the task and does not provide favorable input with respect to team members' socioemotional needs.

Team Cohesiveness

Developing a unit from a diverse group of personalities, specialties, backgrounds, and work styles can be challenging and complicated. In a cohesive team, the members get along and are able to accomplish their tasks effectively. There are factors that affect cohesiveness within a team. Teams generally are ideal when they contain five to twelve people. Fewer than five people is too few to accomplish tasks and generate a variety of ideas. More than twelve is too large because members do not develop relationships, may feel intimidated to speak, or may disconnect. It also may be beneficial to have team members introduce themselves and describe their past work experiences. This activity will foster familiarity and shared experiences. One of the most reliable ways to build cohesiveness within a team is through competition with other teams. When two teams are competing for a single prize or recognition, they are forced to put aside conflict and accomplish their goal. By adding an incentive

Team-building exercises. *Employees at AT&T participate in team-building exercises that will help them improve their overall abilities to engage in productive teamwork.*

to finishing the task, the team automatically becomes more goal oriented. Also, a favorable appraisal from an outsider may strengthen team cohesiveness. Since the team is being praised as a group, team members recognize their contribution as a unit. Teams are also more successful when goals have become agreed on. A team that is clear about its objective will focus more on accomplishing it. Frequent interaction also builds cohesiveness as relationships strengthen and familiarity increases.

Team Conflict and How to Resolve It

Conflict occurs when a disagreement arises between two or more team members. Conflict traditionally has been viewed as negative, but if handled properly, conflict can work to improve a team. For example, if two team members disagree about a certain decision, both may analyze the situation more closely to determine the best choice. As long as conflict is handled in a respectful and professional manner, it can improve the quality of work produced. If conflict turns hostile and affects the work environment, then steps must be taken to arrive at a suitable compromise. Compromises can be difficult in a business organization because neither party ends up getting everything he or she wants. The best solution is a middle-ground alternative in which each party is satisfied to some degree. It is best to avoid attempting to minimize or ignore conflicts within a group because this may cause the conflict to grow as members concentrate on the problem instead of the task. However the conflict is resolved, it is important to remember that conflict must be acknowledged if it is to be either resolved or serve a constructive purpose.

Benefits and Limitations of Teams

Teamwork within a company has been credited as a key to reducing turnover and costs and increasing production, quality, and customer service. There is also evidence that working in teams leads to higher levels of job satisfaction among employees and a harmonious work environment. Thus, an increasingly large number of companies are considering teams as a viable organizational structure. However, the process of reorganizing into teams can be stressful and time consuming with no guarantee that the team will develop effectively. If a team lacks cohesiveness and is unable to resolve conflict, the company may experience lower productivity.

return to inside business

The Container Store

Managers at The Container Store believe that satisfied employees will be highly motivated to satisfy their customers. The company's enviably low turnover rate is a clear indication of its employees' satisfaction, just as its ability to expand and prosper year after year is a clear indication of its customers' satisfaction.

Teamwork, an essential element in The Container Store's ability to deliver personalized service, is particularly important during the year-end holiday season. Although part-time seasonal employees may be part of a store's team for only a few weeks, they're expected to help each other and work nights and weekends as needed. "We all love our families too, but we have a family here that we need to provide for as well," one store manager tells holiday-season employees.

Questions

1. Is The Container Store motivating its employees according to Theory X or Theory Y? Explain your answer.
2. How is The Container Store using job enrichment to motivate its employees?

Summary

Explain what motivation is.

Motivation is the individual internal process that energizes, directs, and sustains behavior. Motivation is affected by employee morale—that is, the employee's feelings about the job, superiors, and the firm itself. Motivation, morale, and job satisfaction are closely related.

Understand some major historical perspectives on motivation.

One of the first approaches to employee motivation was Frederick Taylor's scientific management, the application of scientific principles to the management of work and workers. Taylor believed that employees work only for money and that they must be closely supervised and managed. This thinking led to the piece-rate system, under which employees are paid a certain amount for each unit they produce. The Hawthorne Studies attempted to determine the effects of the work environment on productivity. Results of these studies indicated that human factors affect productivity more than do physical aspects of the workplace.

Maslow's hierarchy of needs suggests that people are motivated by five sets of needs. In ascending order of importance, these motivators are physiological, safety, social, esteem, and self-actualization needs. People are motivated by the lowest set of needs that remains unfulfilled. As needs at one level are satisfied, people try to satisfy needs at the next level.

Frederick Herzberg found that job satisfaction and dissatisfaction are influenced by two distinct sets of factors. Motivation factors, including recognition and responsibility, affect an employee's degree of satisfaction, but their absence does not necessarily cause dissatisfaction. Hygiene factors, including pay and working conditions, affect an employee's degree of dissatisfaction but do not affect satisfaction.

Theory X is a concept of motivation that assumes that employees dislike work and will function effectively only in a highly controlled work environment. Thus, to achieve an organization's goals, managers must coerce, control, and threaten employees. This theory generally is consistent with Taylor's scientific management. Theory Y is more in keeping with the results of the Hawthorne Studies and the human relations movement. It suggests that employees can be motivated to behave as responsible members of the organization. Theory Z emphasizes long-term employment, collective decision making, individual responsibility for the outcomes of decisions, informal control, and a holistic concern for employees. Reinforcement theory is based on the idea that people will repeat behavior that is rewarded and will avoid behavior that is punished.

Describe three contemporary views of motivation: equity theory, expectancy theory, and goal-setting theory.

Equity theory maintains that people are motivated to obtain and preserve equitable treatment for themselves. Expectancy theory suggests that our motivation depends on how much we want something and how likely we think we are to get it. Goal-setting theory suggests that employees are motivated to achieve a goal that they and their managers establish together.

4 Explain several techniques for increasing employee motivation.

Management by objectives (MBO) is a motivation technique in which managers and employees collaborate in setting goals. MBO motivates employees by getting them more involved in their jobs and in the organization as a whole. Job enrichment seeks to motivate employees by varying their tasks and giving them more responsibility for and control over their jobs. Job enlargement, expanding a worker's assignments to include additional tasks, is one aspect of job enrichment. Job redesign is a type of job enrichment in which work is restructured to improve the worker-job match.

Behavior modification uses reinforcement to encourage desirable behavior. Rewards for productivity, quality, and loyalty change employees' behavior in desired ways and also increase motivation.

Allowing employees to work more flexible hours is another way to build motivation and job satisfaction. Flextime is a system of work scheduling that allows workers to set their own hours as long as they fall within limits established by employers. Part-time work is permanent employment in which individuals work less than a standard work week. Job sharing is an arrangement whereby two people share one full-time position. Telecommuting allows employees to work at home all or part of the work week. All these types of work arrangements give employees more time outside the workplace to deal with family responsibilities or to enjoy free time.

Employee empowerment, self-managed work teams, and employee ownership are also techniques that boost employee motivation. Empowerment increases employees' involvement in their jobs by increasing their decision-making authority. Self-managed work teams are groups of employees with the authority and skills to manage themselves. When employees participate in ownership programs such as employee stock ownership plans (ESOPs), they have more incentive to make the company succeed and therefore work more effectively.

5 Understand the types, development, and uses of teams.

A large number of companies use teams to increase their employees' productivity. In a business organization, a team is a group of workers functioning together as a unit to complete a common goal or purpose.

There are several types of teams within businesses that function in specific ways to achieve different purposes. A problem-solving team is a team of knowledgeable employees brought together to tackle a specific problem. A virtuoso team is a team of highly skilled and talented individuals brought together to produce significant change. A virtual team is a team consisting of members who are geographically dispersed but communicate electronically. A cross-functional team is a team of individuals with varying specialties, expertise, and skills.

The five stages of team development are forming, storming, norming, performing, and adjourning. As a team develops, it should become more productive and unified. The four roles within teams are task specialist, socioemotional, dual, and nonparticipative. Each of these roles plays a specific part in the team's interaction. For a team to be successful, members must learn how to resolve and manage conflict so that the team can work cohesively to accomplish goals.

Key Terms

You should now be able to define and give an example relevant to each of the following terms:

motivation (280)
morale (281)
scientific management (282)
piece-rate system (282)
need (283)
Maslow's hierarchy of needs (283)
physiological needs (283)
safety needs (284)
social needs (284)
esteem needs (284)
self-actualization needs (284)
motivation-hygiene theory (285)
motivation factors (285)
hygiene factors (285)
Theory X (286)
Theory Y (286)
Theory Z (287)
reinforcement theory (287)
equity theory (289)
expectancy theory (289)
goal-setting theory (290)
management by objectives (MBO) (290)
job enrichment (292)
job enlargement (292)
job redesign (293)
behavior modification (293)
flextime (294)
part-time work (294)
job sharing (295)
telecommuting (295)
empowerment (296)
employee ownership (297)
team (297)
problem-solving team (298)
virtuoso team (298)
self-managed teams (298)
cross-functional team (299)
virtual team (299)

Review Questions

1. How do scientific management and Theory X differ from the human relations movement and Theory Y?
2. How did the results of the Hawthorne Studies influence researchers' thinking about employee motivation?
3. What are the five sets of needs in Maslow's hierarchy? How are a person's needs related to motivation?
4. What are the two dimensions in Herzberg's theory? What kinds of elements affect each dimension?

5. What is the fundamental premise of reinforcement theory?
6. According to equity theory, how does an employee determine whether he or she is being treated equitably?
7. According to expectancy theory, what two variables determine motivation?
8. Identify and describe the major techniques for motivating employees.
9. Describe the steps involved in the MBO process.
10. What are the objectives of MBO? What do you think might be its disadvantages?
11. How does employee participation increase motivation?
12. Describe the steps in the process of behavior modification.
13. Identify and describe the major types of teams.
14. What are the major benefits and limitations associated with the use of self-managed teams?
15. Explain the major stages of team development.

Discussion Questions

1. How might managers make use of Maslow's hierarchy of needs in motivating employees? What problems would they encounter?
2. Do the various theories of motivation contradict each other or complement each other? Explain.
3. What combination of motivational techniques do you think would result in the best overall motivation and reward system?
4. Reinforcement theory and behavior modification have been called demeaning because they tend to treat people "like mice in a maze." Do you agree?
5. In what ways are team cohesiveness and team conflict related?

Video Case 10.1

American Flatbread Fires up Employees

George Schenk's passion is making work meaningful, sustainable, and personal. He learned about wood-fired cooking from his grandmother in Vermont and, years later, rekindled his love of cooking with fire when he founded the American Flatbread Company. His company produces frozen wood-fired flatbread pizzas from all-natural, locally grown ingredients, handmade by 100 employees in Waitsfield and Middlebury, Vermont.

On Mondays, Tuesdays, Wednesdays, and Thursdays, two shifts of employees stoke the bakeries' wood-fired ovens to a temperature of 800°F and prepare the flatbreads. After the products are baked, frozen, and wrapped, they are shipped to grocery and specialty stores such as Whole Foods supermarkets. Both bakeries are transformed into casual pizza restaurants on Friday and Saturday nights, where diners sit in view of the gigantic ovens to enjoy salads and flatbreads. Schenk also has licensed American Flatbread's brand and wood-fired cooking methods to bakeries and restaurants in New England and in Los Alamos, California. One-third of American Flatbread's annual revenue comes from the licensing deals and restaurant receipts, whereas the wholesale frozen pizza operation contributes the remaining two-thirds.

Schenk's enthusiasm for wood-fired cooking is matched by his enthusiasm for building a business in which the work has long-term significance to the employees and the community. Among American Flatbread's goals are to "create a pleasant, fulfilling, sustainable, and secure workplace" and "to trust one another and practice respectful relationships with everyone involved in this work."

Another goal mentioned in the mission statement is to be grateful, respectful, and forgiving—and to encourage the same in others. In line with this goal, Schenk has worked hard to avoid what he calls "founder's syndrome," the notion that the founder can do nothing wrong. Because Schenk is quick to admit that he's not perfect, his managers and employees know they can speak up about their mistakes and not lose the opportunity to try new things.

Jennifer Moffroid, the company's director of marketing, stresses that the founder has created an environment in which employees can do work that is in keeping with what they want for their lives. Making the workday fun is one of Schenk's priorities, as is making the workplace an inviting place to be. Moffroid also notes that Schenk not only delegates, but he also "empowers employees and celebrates their work." The company's seven senior managers are involved in decision making, and every suggestion is evaluated on its merit, not on its source. "We're all in this together," Schenk says.

Since the beginning, American Flatbread has supported local food producers and given back to the community in a variety of ways. For example, the restaurants hold "benefit bakes" to raise money for causes such as public health clinics and habitat preservation. In turn, the community has come to the company's aid on more than one occasion. When flood waters inundated American Flatbread's bakery, people came from miles around to clean and rebuild the facility. Thanks to this outpouring of support, the bakery was able to reopen in only seven days. Without the help of the community, Schenk observes, the company might well have failed. Today, the Vermont bakeries turn out 10,000 flatbreads every week; the California bakery produces another 4,000 for distribution in western states. Schenk keeps the company's values in the spotlight by writing a dedication for each week's menu. These dedications focus employees on what's important and provide "food for thought" for restaurant customers. Sharing values, being "a good neighbor," and building trusting, respectful relationships with stakeholders have enabled American Flatbread to keep employees happy and productive, minimize turnover, and strengthen financial performance.[30]

For more information about this company, go to **www.americanflatbread.com.**

Questions

1. Does George Schenk manage American Flatbread as a type A or a type Z firm? Support your answer.
2. Would you recommend that American Flatbread offer bakery and restaurant employees flextime arrangements? Explain.
3. How has George Schenk paved the way for empowerment at his company?

Case 10.2

Google's Great Benefits—Will They Last Forever?

Imagine having a job where you could get generous pay, free lunch and dinner, free snacks, a pet center, free gym membership, a game room, an on-site massage therapist and doctor, hair styling, generous vacation and maternity benefits, parental leave, adoption benefits, paid take-out meals for new parents, stock options, tuition reimbursement, free shuttle to the office, reimbursement toward the purchase of a hybrid or an electric car, telecommuting, on-site oil change and car wash, dry cleaning, fitness classes, bike repair, a sauna, roller hockey, an outdoor volleyball court, and much, much more.

That's life at Google, the Internet's dominant search company and one of the trendiest and fastest-growing businesses in the world. The company, based in Mountain View, California, boasts an informal, dynamic, and collaborative culture "unlike any in corporate America," and with people's pet dogs happily roaming the shared work spaces it's clearly not like most office environments. Google's CEO explains on the company website that "the goal is to strip away everything that gets in our employees' way. . . . Let's face it: programmers want to program, they don't want to do their laundry. So we make it easy for them to do both." Although a few perks are available only at headquarters, employees at all the company's offices can customize their applicable benefits, including traditional health and dental coverage plans, life insurance, and retirement and savings plans, into a package that works for each individual and family.

Those benefits make for 12,000 happy and productive employees, many of whom have become millionaires as the company's stock has appreciated in value. The perks also account in large part for the company's being ranked by *Fortune* magazine as the best place to work in the United States today. Since it must nevertheless compete directly for top-notch talent with other high-tech firms like eBay, Facebook, and Amazon.com, Google is committed to retaining those who fit well with its "Google-y" culture, that is, people who are "fairly flexible, adaptable and not focusing on titles and hierarchy, and just get stuff done," according to the company's chief culture officer. The company even conducts an annual "happiness survey" to find out how committed to Google its employees are, why, and what matters to them and their managers. The results are funneled into the company's continuing focus on career development and growth.

Can a company ever provide too many benefits? Google might be about to find out. It recently announced a major and widely unpopular change in one of its most enviable perks—access to its three-year-old on-site day care facilities. Saying the move was a response to a two-year waiting list for entry into the program, which it called "inequitable," the company sharply raised the fee for using the service to well above the market rate (from $33,000 to $57,000 a year for two children) and also started charging the 700 waiting families several hundred dollars each to stay on the list. The list promptly shrank by more than half. After parents strongly protested the price increase, the company slightly scaled it back but let the basic outline of its decision stand, including changing the company that operates the day care program. Google plans to accommodate those still on the waiting list by opening new facilities within a year.[31]

For more information about this company, go to **www.google.com.**

Questions

1. What does Google gain by offering these generous benefits? Do you think there is any downside to offering so many?
2. Which of Google's benefits appeal to you? Why? Are there any benefits you think the company doesn't need to offer? Why or why not?
3. What do you think will be the long-term effect of Google's changed child-care benefit? Is it a good idea for companies to reduce or withdraw such benefits?

Building Skills for Career Success

1. JOURNALING FOR SUCCESS

Discovery statement: Many managers use special techniques to foster employee motivation and satisfaction.

Assignment

1. Thinking about your current job (or your most recent job), what types of motivation techniques are being used?
2. How well does each technique work on you and on your coworkers?
3. Thinking about the first job that you will take after completing your studies, what types of motivation techniques will be most effective in motivating you to truly excel in your new position? Explain why.
4. Do you expect that most of your coworkers will be motivated by the same techniques that motivate you? Explain.

2. EXPLORING THE INTERNET

There are few employee incentives as motivating as owning "a piece of the action." Either through profit sharing or equity, many firms realize that the opportunity to share in the wealth generated by their effort is a primary force to drive employees toward better performance and a sense of ownership. The Foundation for Enterprise Development (**www.fed.org/**) is a nonprofit organization dedicated to helping entrepreneurs and executives use employee ownership and equity compensation as a fair and effective means of motivating the workforce and improving corporate performance. You can learn more about this approach at the foundation's website. Visit the text website for updates to this exercise.

Assignment

1. Describe the content and services provided by the Foundation for Enterprise Development through its website.
2. Do you agree with this orientation toward motivation of employees/owners, or does it seem contrived to you? Discuss.
3. How else might employees be motivated to improve their performance?

3. DEVELOPING CRITICAL-THINKING SKILLS

This chapter has described several theories managers can use as guidelines in motivating employees to do the best job possible for the company. Among these theories are Maslow's hierarchy of needs, equity theory, expectancy theory, and goal-setting theory. How effective would each of these theories be in motivating you to be a more productive employee?

Assignment

1. Identify five job needs that are important to you.
2. Determine which of the theories mentioned above would work best to satisfy your job needs.
3. Prepare a two-page report explaining how you reached these conclusions.

4. BUILDING TEAM SKILLS

By increasing employees' participation in decision making, empowerment makes workers feel more involved in their jobs and the operations of the organization. While empowerment may seem like a commonsense idea, it is a concept not found universally in the workplace. If you had empowerment in your job, how would you describe it?

Assignment

1. Use brainstorming to explore the concept of empowerment.
   a. Write each letter of the word *empowerment* in a vertical column on a sheet of paper or on the classroom chalkboard.
   b. Think of several words that begin with each letter.
   c. Write the words next to the appropriate letter.
2. Formulate a statement by choosing one word from each letter that best describes what empowerment means to you.
3. Analyze the statement.
   a. How relevant is the statement for you in terms of empowerment? Or empowerment in your workplace?
   b. What changes must occur in your workplace for you to have empowerment?
   c. How would you describe yourself as an empowered employee?
   d. What opportunities would empowerment give to you in your workplace?
4. Prepare a report of your findings.

5. RESEARCHING DIFFERENT CAREERS

Because a manager's job varies from department to department within firms, as well as among firms, it is virtually impossible to write a generic description of a manager's job. If you are contemplating becoming a manager, you may find it very helpful to spend time on the job with several managers learning first hand what they do.

Assignment

1. Make an appointment with managers in three firms, preferably firms of different sizes. When you make the appointments, request a tour of the facilities.
2. Ask the managers the following questions:
   a. What do you do in your job?
   b. What do you like most and least about your job? Why?
   c. What skills do you need in your job?
   d. How much education does your job require?
   e. What advice do you have for someone thinking about pursuing a career in management?
3. Summarize your findings in a two-page report. Include answers to these questions:
   a. Is management a realistic field of study for you? Why?
   b. What might be a better career choice? Why?

11 Enhancing Union-Management Relations

LEARNING OBJECTIVES

What you will be able to do once you complete this chapter:

1. Explain how and why labor unions came into being.
2. Discuss the sources of unions' negotiating power and trends in union membership.
3. Identify the main focus of several major pieces of labor-management legislation.
4. Enumerate the steps involved in forming a union and show how the National Labor Relations Board is involved in the process.
5. Describe the basic elements in the collective-bargaining process.
6. Identify the major issues covered in a union-management contract.
7. Explain the primary bargaining tools available to unions and management.

AP Photo/Paul Sancya

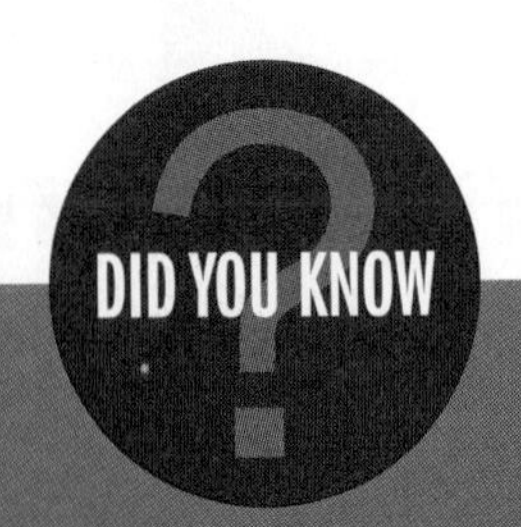

inside business

In the 2008 strike, Boeing had a backlog of 3,600 orders from airlines worldwide, including 900 orders for its new fuel-efficient 787 Dreamliner jets, which sell for about $165 million apiece.

Can Boeing and Its Unions Make Peace?

Is peace ahead for Boeing and the labor unions that represent its employees? Since 1948, the International Association of Machinists and Aerospace Workers has gone on strike against the aircraft manufacturer seven times, clashing with Boeing's management on issues such as pay raises, pensions, and job security. The 1948 strike dragged on for nearly five months; the 1965 strike was settled in less than three weeks.

The most recent strike, which occurred during the economic turmoil of 2008, lasted for some time as 27,000 union members stayed away from Boeing's jet assembly lines in three states. The stakes were high for both sides. Boeing had a backlog of 3,600 orders from airlines worldwide, including 900 orders for its new fuel-efficient 787 Dreamliner jets, which sell for about $165 million apiece. Its customers were not happy about having to wait at least five years for the jets they ordered. Every day the company failed to deliver jets on order, it lost an estimated $100 million in revenue.

The union was seeking higher annual pay increases than Boeing was offering. More important, it wanted Boeing to curtail outsourcing and rehire machinists who had been laid off after the 9/11 terror attacks. At that time, Boeing had cut jobs because airlines had canceled many jet orders. Boeing also got the union to agree that the company could outsource some work to overseas suppliers and have nonunion contractors handle some tasks.

As business improved, outsourcing was supposed to reduce costs and help Boeing launch the 787 on time. Instead, by the time the 2008 strike started, the 787 was a year behind schedule because of delays caused by its overseas suppliers. Before assembling each 787, Boeing's machinists had to rework or add parts to components that came from outsourcers. "If Boeing had let us build that airplane in the first place, it would be in service today," said one union member.

In spite of disputes like this, unions and management have historically come to an agreement that satisfies both parties. Where do you stand on the issues?[1]

labor union an organization of workers acting together to negotiate their wages and working conditions with employers

union-management (labor) relations the dealings between labor unions and business management both in the bargaining process and beyond it

Boeing, like a number of other business organizations, has been unionized for years, and both management and the unions have experienced ups and downs. Many businesses today have highly cooperative relationships with labor unions. A **labor union** is an organization of workers acting together to negotiate their wages and working conditions with employers. In the United States, nonmanagement employees have the legal right to form unions and to bargain, as a group, with management. The result of the bargaining process is a *labor contract,* a written agreement that is in force for a set period of time (usually one to three years). The dealings between labor unions and business management, both in the bargaining process and beyond it, are called **union-management relations** or, more simply, **labor relations.**

Because labor and management have different goals, they tend to be at odds with each other. However, these goals must be attained by the same means—through the production of goods and services. At contract bargaining sessions, the two groups must work together to attain their goals. Perhaps mainly for this reason, antagonism now seems to be giving way to cooperation in union-management relations.

We open this chapter by reviewing the history of labor unions in this country. Then we turn our attention to organized labor today, noting current membership trends and union-management partnerships and summarizing important labor-relations laws. We discuss the unionization process, why employees join unions, how a union is formed, and what the National Labor Relations Board does. Collective-bargaining procedures then are explained. Next, we consider issues in union-management contracts, including employee pay, working hours, security, management rights, and grievance procedures. We close with a discussion of various labor and management negotiating techniques: strikes, slowdowns and boycotts, lockouts, mediation, and arbitration.

The Historical Development of Unions

1

Learning Objective: Explain how and why labor unions came into being.

Until the middle of the nineteenth century, there was very little organization of labor in this country. Groups of workers occasionally did form a **craft union**, an organization of skilled workers in a single craft or trade. These alliances usually were limited to a single city, and they often lasted only a short time. In 1786, the first known strike in the United States involved a group of Philadelphia printers who stopped working over demands for higher wages. When the employers granted the printers a pay increase, the group disbanded.

craft union an organization of skilled workers in a single craft or trade

Early History

In the mid-1800s, improved transportation opened new markets for manufactured goods. Improved manufacturing methods made it possible to supply those markets, and American industry began to grow. The Civil War and the continued growth of the railroads after the war led to further industrial expansion.

Large-scale production required more and more skilled industrial workers. As the skilled labor force grew, craft unions emerged in the more industrialized areas. From these craft unions, three significant labor organizations evolved. (See Figure 11.1 for a historical overview of unions and their patterns of membership.)

Knights of Labor The first significant national labor organization to emerge was the Knights of Labor, which was formed as a secret society in 1869 by Uriah Stephens, a utopian reformer and abolitionist from Philadelphia. Membership reached approximately 700,000 by 1886. One major goal of the Knights was to

Figure 11.1: Historical Overview of Unions

The total number of members for all unions generally rose between 1869, when the first truly national union was organized, and 1980. The dates of major events in the history of labor unions are singled out along the line of membership change.

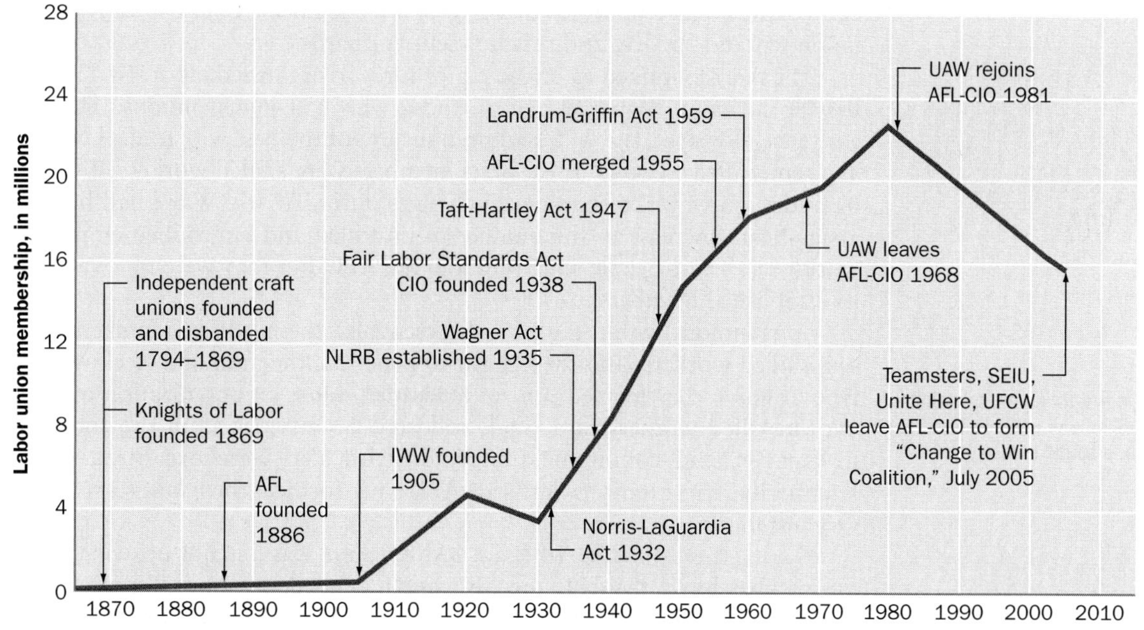

Labor union membership, in millions
28
24
20
16
12
8
4
0
1870 1880 1890 1900 1910 1920 1930 1940 1950 1960 1970 1980 1990 2000 2010
Independent craft unions founded and disbanded 1794–1869
Knights of Labor founded 1869
AFL founded 1886
IWW founded 1905
Norris-LaGuardia Act 1932
Wagner Act NLRB established 1935
Fair Labor Standards Act CIO founded 1938
Taft-Hartley Act 1947
AFL-CIO merged 1955
Landrum-Griffin Act 1959
UAW leaves AFL-CIO 1968
UAW rejoins AFL-CIO 1981
Teamsters, SEIU, Unite Here, UFCW leave AFL-CIO to form "Change to Win Coalition," July 2005

Sources: U.S. Bureau of Labor Statistics, Union Membership, **www.bls.gov**, accessed October 9, 2008.

eliminate the depersonalization of the worker that resulted from mass-production technology. Another was to improve the moral standards of both employees and society. To the detriment of the group, its leaders concentrated so intently on social and economic change that they did not recognize the effects of technological change. Moreover, they assumed that all employees had the same goals as the Knights' leaders—social and moral reform. The major reason for the demise of the Knights was the Haymarket riot of 1886.

At a rally (called to demand a reduction in the length of a work day from ten to eight hours) in Chicago's Haymarket Square, a bomb exploded. Several police officers and civilians were killed or wounded. The Knights were not implicated directly, but they quickly lost public favor.

American Federation of Labor In 1886, several leaders of the Knights of Labor joined with independent craft unions to form the *American Federation of Labor* (AFL). Samuel Gompers, one of the AFL's founders, became its first president. Gompers believed that the goals of the union should be those of its members rather than those of its leaders. The AFL did not seek to change the existing business system, as the Knights of Labor had. Instead, its goal was to improve its members' living standards within that system.

strike a temporary work stoppage by employees, calculated to add force to their demands

Another major difference between the Knights of Labor and the AFL was in their positions regarding strikes. A **strike** is a temporary work stoppage by employees, calculated to add force to their demands. The Knights did not favor the use of strikes, whereas the AFL strongly believed that striking was an effective labor weapon. The AFL also believed that organized labor should play a major role in politics. As we will see, the AFL is still very much a part of the American labor scene.

Industrial Workers of the World The *Industrial Workers of the World* (IWW) was created in 1905 as a radical alternative to the AFL. Among its goals was the overthrow of capitalism. This revolutionary stance prevented the IWW from gaining much of a foothold. Perhaps its major accomplishment was to make the AFL seem, by comparison, less threatening to the general public and to business leaders.

Evolution of Contemporary Labor Organizations

Between 1900 and 1920, both business and government attempted to keep labor unions from growing. This period was plagued by strikes and violent confrontations between management and unions. In steelworks, garment factories, and auto plants, clashes took place in which striking union members fought bitterly against non-union workers, police, and private security guards.

The AFL continued to be the major force in organized labor. By 1920, its membership included 75 percent of all those who had joined unions. Throughout its existence, however, the AFL had been unsure of the best way to deal with unskilled and semiskilled workers. Most of its members were skilled workers in specific crafts or trades. However, technological changes during World War I had brought about a significant increase in the number of unskilled and semiskilled employees in the workforce. These people sought to join the AFL, but they were not well received by its established membership.

industrial union an organization of both skilled and unskilled workers in a single industry

Some unions within the AFL did recognize the need to organize unskilled and semiskilled workers, and they began to penetrate the auto and steel industries. The type of union they formed was an **industrial union**, an organization of both skilled and unskilled workers in a single industry. Soon workers in the rubber, mining, newspaper, and communications industries also were organized into unions. Eventually, these unions left the AFL and formed the *Congress of Industrial Organizations* (CIO).

During this same time (the late 1930s), there was a major upswing in rank-and-file membership in the AFL, the CIO, and independent unions. Strong union leadership, the development of effective negotiating tactics, and favorable legislation combined to increase total union membership to 9 million in 1940. At this point, the CIO began to rival the AFL in size and influence. There was another bitter

Going Global

Multinationals Open Doors to China's Only Union

McDonald's, KFC, Carrefour, Motorola, and Wal-Mart are among the many multinationals that have opened their doors to the only union allowed to represent workers in China. For the last few years, the All China Federation of Trade Unions has been on a drive to build membership among local employees of major multinational corporations. The union, founded in 1925, has more than 150 million members and is active in tens of thousands of businesses with foreign ties.

Even Wal-Mart, which has no significant union representation in its North American stores, has agreed to collective bargaining for all of its 48,000 employees in China. One recent agreement covering Wal-Mart stores in Quanzhou and Shenyang gave employees 8 percent pay raises in two consecutive years. "We support these efforts because of the valuable, mutually beneficial partnership the government-run union offers and because of their commitment to assisting businesses in our growth and development in China," says a Wal-Mart spokesperson.

Sources: David Barboza, "China Tells Businesses to Unionize," *New York Times*, September 12, 2008, p. C1; Peter Ford, "Unions in China Still Feeble, But Gaining Foothold," *Christian Science Monitor*, September 29, 2008, p. 1; Bruce Einhorn, "China Makes Wal-Mart Toe the Labor Line," *BusinessWeek Online*, July 28, 2008, **www.businessweek.com**; "Wal-Mart Strikes Pay Deal With Chinese Union," *Forbes.com*, July 25, 2008, **www.forbes.com**.

rivalry: The AFL and CIO often clashed over which of them had the right to organize and represent particular groups of employees.

Since World War II, the labor scene has gone through a number of changes. For one thing, during and after the war years there was a downturn in public opinion regarding unions. A few isolated but very visible strikes during the war caused public sentiment to shift against unionism. Perhaps the most significant occurrence, however, was the merger of the AFL and the CIO. After years of bickering, the two groups recognized that they were wasting effort and resources by fighting each other and that a merger would greatly increase the strength of both. The merger took place on December 5, 1955. The resulting organization, called the *AFL-CIO*, had a membership of as many as 16 million workers, which made it the largest labor organization of its kind in the world. Its first president was George Meany, who served until 1979.

Unacceptable working conditions. *A crowded tailor's workshop where workers made knee pants and were paid 45 cents per dozen pair.*

Jump-Starting Your Career

A Closer Look at Union Membership

Will you be a union member some time during your career? According to the U.S. Bureau of Labor Statistics, approximately one in eight Americans belongs to a union. Here's a closer look at the demographics of union membership:

- *Gender:* More men than women are union members: 13 percent of all male workers belong to a union, compared with 11 percent of all female workers.
- *Age:* Union membership is lowest (4.8 percent) among workers aged 16–24 and highest (16.1 percent) among workers aged 55–64.
- *Location:* California is home to the highest number of union members (2.5 million); North Carolina and Wyoming have the lowest number (each has about 19,000 union members).
- *Full or part time:* Full-time workers are almost twice as likely as part-time workers to belong to a union.
- *Occupation:* In the public sector, union membership is highest among teachers, police officers, and firefighters. In the private sector, union membership is highest among transportation and utility workers, telecommunications workers, and construction workers.

Source: "Economic News Release: Union Membership 2007," U.S. Department of Labor, Bureau of Labor Statistics, January 25, 2008, **data.bls.gov.**

Organized Labor Today

Learning Objective: Discuss the sources of unions' negotiating power and trends in union membership.

The power of unions to negotiate effectively with management is derived from two sources. The first is their membership. The more workers a union represents within an industry, the greater is its clout in dealing with firms operating in that industry. The second source of union power is the group of laws that guarantee unions the right to negotiate and, at the same time, regulate the negotiating process.

Union Membership

Approximately 12.1 percent of the nation's workers belong to unions.[2] Union membership is concentrated in a few industries and job categories. Within these industries, though, unions wield considerable power.

The AFL-CIO is still the largest union organization in this country, boasting approximately 9 million members. Those represented by the AFL-CIO include actors, barbers, construction workers, carpenters, retail clerks, musicians, teachers, postal workers, painters, steel and iron workers, firefighters, bricklayers, and newspaper reporters.

One of the largest unions not associated directly with the AFL-CIO is the *Teamsters Union.* The Teamsters originally were part of the AFL-CIO, but in 1957 they were expelled for corrupt and illegal practices. The union started out as an organization of professional drivers, but it has begun recently to recruit employees in a wide variety of jobs. Current membership is about 1.4 million workers.

The *United Steelworkers* (USW) and the *United Auto Workers* (UAW) are two of the largest industrial unions. The USW membership has risen to over 850,000 workers. It is known as the dominant union in paper and forestry products, steel, aluminum, tire and rubber, mining, glass, chemicals, petroleum, and other basic resource industries. The UAW represents employees in the automobile industry. The UAW, too, originally was part of the AFL-CIO, but it left the parent union—of its own accord—in 1968. Currently, the UAW has about 640,000 members. For a while, the Teamsters and the UAW formed a semistructured partnership called the *Alliance for Labor Action.* This partnership was dissolved eventually, and the UAW again became part of the AFL-CIO in 1981.

Membership Trends

The proportion of union members relative to the size of the nation's workforce has declined over the last thirty years. Moreover, total union membership has dropped since 1980 despite steadily increasing membership in earlier years (see Figure 11.1).

To a great extent, this decline in membership is caused by changing trends in business, such as the following:

Source: SkillSoft survey of 2,000 employees.

- Heavily unionized industries either have been decreasing in size or have not been growing as fast as nonunionized industries. For example, cutbacks in the steel industry have tended to reduce union membership. At the same time, the growth of high-tech industries has increased the ranks of nonunion workers.
- Many firms have moved from the heavily unionized Northeast and Great Lakes regions to the less unionized Southeast and Southwest—the so-called Sunbelt. At the relocated plants, formerly unionized firms tend to hire nonunion workers.
- The largest growth in employment is occurring in the service industries, and these industries typically are not unionized.
- Some U.S. companies have moved their manufacturing operations to other countries where less unionized labor is employed.
- Management is providing benefits that tend to reduce employees' need for unionization. Increased employee participation and better wages and working conditions are goals of unions. When these benefits are already supplied by management, workers are less likely to join existing unions or start new ones. The number of elections to vote on forming new unions has declined. The unions usually win about half the elections.
- According to Alan Greenspan, former chairman of the Federal Reserve, American labor laws and culture allow for the quicker displacement of unneeded workers and their replacement with those in demand, whereas labor laws in other countries tend to take longer for the change to occur.

It remains to be seen whether unions will be able to regain the prominence and power they enjoyed between the world wars and during the 1950s. There is little doubt, however, that they will remain a powerful force in particular industries.

Union-Management Partnerships

For most of the twentieth century, unions represented workers with respect to wages and working conditions. To obtain rights for workers and recognition for themselves, unions engaged in often-antagonistic collective-bargaining sessions and strikes. At the same time, management traditionally protected its own rights of decision making, workplace organization, and strategic planning. Increasingly, however, management has become aware that this traditionally adversarial relationship does not result in the kind of high-performance workplace and empowered workforce necessary to succeed in today's highly competitive markets. For their part, unions and their members acknowledge that most major strikes result in failures that cost members thousands of jobs and reduce the unions' credibility. Today, instead of maintaining an "us versus them" mentality, many unions are becoming partners with management, cooperating to enhance the workplace, empower workers, increase production, improve quality, and reduce costs. According to the Department of Labor, the number of union-management partnerships in the United States is increasing.

Union-management partnerships can be initiated by union leaders, employees, or management. *Limited partnerships* center on accomplishing one specific task or project, such as the introduction of teams or the design of training programs. For example, Levi Strauss formed a limited partnership with its employees who are members of the Amalgamated Clothing and Textile Workers Union to help the

Union-Management partnerships. *At General Motors' Saturn plant in Spinghill, Tennessee, the UAW and Saturn management have forged a partnership that has resulted in a high level of productivity, and in a comfortable and satisfying work environment for employees.*

company in setting up team operations in its nonunion plants. *Long-range strategic partnerships* focus on sharing decision-making power for a whole range of workplace and business issues. Long-range partnerships sometimes begin as limited ones and develop slowly over time.

Although strategic union-management partnerships vary, most of them have several characteristics in common. First, strategic partnerships focus on developing cooperative relationships between unions and management instead of arguing over contractual rights. Second, partners work toward mutual gain, in which the organization becomes more competitive, employees are better off, and unions are stronger as a result of the partnership. Finally, as already noted, strategic partners engage in joint decision making on a broad array of issues. These issues include performance expectations, organizational structure, strategic alliances, new technology, pay and benefits, employee security and involvement, union-management roles, product development, and education and training.

Good labor-management relations can help everyone to deal with new and difficult labor issues as they develop. For example, many companies hope that their union-management partnerships will be strong enough to deal with the critical issue of rising health care costs. Unions work hard to protect their members from having to pay an increased percentage of health care costs, and they have experienced some success, in that an average union worker pays about 16 percent of his or her health care premiums compared with a nonunion worker's contribution of about 32 percent.[3] Strong union-management partnerships will play a vital role in resolving health care issues.

Union-management partnerships have many potential benefits for management, workers, and unions. For management, partnerships can result in lower costs, increased revenue, improved product quality, and greater customer satisfaction. For workers, benefits may include increased response to their needs, more decision-making opportunities, less supervision, more responsibility, and increased job security. Unions can gain credibility, strength, and increased membership.

The Business of Green

The Blue Green Alliance Goes for a Greener Economy

The Blue Green Alliance—a partnership between unions and environmentalists—is pushing for a greener economy. Started by the United Steel Workers ("blue") and the Sierra Club ("green"), the Blue Green Alliance sees a world of new job opportunities in cleaning up the environment and developing eco-friendly energy systems. In all, the alliance brings together 4 million union members and environmental activists, including members of the "blue" Communication Workers of America and the "green" National Resources Defense Council.

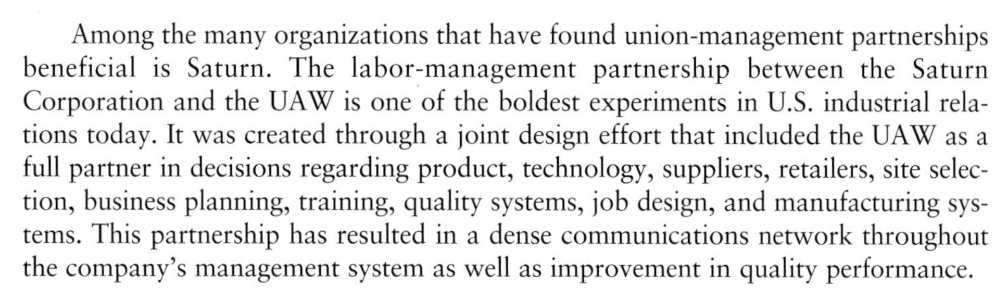

AP Photo/Don Ryan

By educating people about the benefits of green building, the alliance seeks to expand employment in the construction industry, which has been particularly hard hit by recent economic woes. The alliance also supports investments in environmental initiatives that would ultimately create new jobs in manufacturing and installing renewable energy equipment such as wind turbines and solar panels. These initiatives will have a big economic payoff, says the Blue Green Alliance's executive director: "You invest $100 billion over the next two years and what comes out the other end? Two million new jobs."

Sources: Tina Kelley, "In Support of a New (Green) Deal," *New York Times*, September 10, 2008. **www.nytimes.com**; Mark Fischenich, "Solving Problems through Blue Green Alliance," *Mankato Free Press*, September 14, 2008, **www.mankatofreepress.com**; Fred O. Williams, "4,000 Area Jobs Possible in Renewable Energy, Study Says," *Buffalo News*, November 9, 2007, n.p.; **www.bluegreenalliance.org.**

Among the many organizations that have found union-management partnerships beneficial is Saturn. The labor-management partnership between the Saturn Corporation and the UAW is one of the boldest experiments in U.S. industrial relations today. It was created through a joint design effort that included the UAW as a full partner in decisions regarding product, technology, suppliers, retailers, site selection, business planning, training, quality systems, job design, and manufacturing systems. This partnership has resulted in a dense communications network throughout the company's management system as well as improvement in quality performance.

Labor-Management Legislation

3 Learning Objective: Identify the main focus of several major pieces of labor-management legislation.

As we have noted, business opposed early efforts to organize labor. The federal government generally supported anti-union efforts through the court system, and in some cases federal troops were used to end strikes. Gradually, however, the government began to correct this imbalance through the legislative process.

Norris-LaGuardia Act

The first major piece of legislation to secure rights for unions, the *Norris-LaGuardia Act* of 1932, was considered a landmark in labor-management relations. This act made it difficult for businesses to obtain court orders that banned strikes, picketing, or union membership drives. Previously, courts had issued such orders readily as a means of curbing these activities.

National Labor Relations Act

The *National Labor Relations Act,* also known as the *Wagner Act,* was passed by Congress in 1935. It established procedures by which employees decide whether they want to be represented by a union. If workers choose to be represented, the Wagner Act requires management to negotiate with union representatives. Before this law was passed, union efforts sometimes were interpreted as violating the Sherman Act (1890) because they were viewed as attempts to monopolize. The Wagner Act also forbids certain unfair labor practices on the part of management, such as firing or punishing workers because they are pro-union, spying on union meetings, and bribing employees to vote against unionization.

National Labor Relations Board (NLRB) the federal agency that enforces the provisions of the Wagner Act

Finally, the Wagner Act established the **National Labor Relations Board (NLRB)** to enforce the provisions of the law. The NLRB is concerned primarily with (1) overseeing the elections in which employees decide whether they will be represented by a union and (2) investigating complaints lodged by unions or employees. For example, New York University (NYU) graduate teaching and research assistants organized themselves as a union under the UAW. Initially, the NLRB voted to recognize the union, and the students negotiated a 40 percent stipend increase and gained health care benefits. The NLRB later reversed its decision, stating that the graduate students were not employees of the college and should not be recognized as a union. The students went on strike when NYU chose not to renew their union contract and extended offers to students on an individual basis.[4]

Fair Labor Standards Act

In 1938, Congress enacted the *Fair Labor Standards Act.* One major provision of this act permits the federal government to set a minimum wage. The first minimum wage, which was set in the late 1930s and did not include farm workers and retail employees, was $0.25 an hour. Today, the minimum wage is $6.55 (increasing to $7.25 on July 24, 2009) an hour. Some employees, such as farm workers, are still exempt from the minimum-wage provisions. The act also requires that employees be paid overtime rates for work in excess of forty hours a week. Finally, it prohibits the use of child labor.

Labor-Management Relations Act

The legislation of the 1930s sought to discourage unfair practices on the part of employers. Recall from Figure 11.1 that union membership grew from approximately 2 million in 1910 to almost 12 million by 1945. Unions represented over 35 percent of all nonagricultural employees in 1945. As union membership and power grew, however, the federal government began to examine the practices of labor. Several long and bitter strikes, mainly in the coal mining and trucking industries, in the early 1940s led to a demand for legislative restraint on unions. As a result, in 1947 Congress passed the *Labor-Management Relations Act,* also known as the *Taft-Hartley Act,* over President Harry Truman's veto.

The objective of the Taft-Hartley Act is to provide a balance between union power and management authority. It lists unfair labor practices that unions are forbidden to use. These include refusal to bargain with management in good faith, charging excessive membership dues, harassing nonunion workers, and using various means of coercion against employers.

The Taft-Hartley Act also gives management more rights during union organizing campaigns. For example, management may outline for employees the advantages and disadvantages of union membership, as long as the information it presents is accurate. The act gives the President of the United States the power to obtain a temporary injunction to prevent or stop a strike that endangers national health and safety. An **injunction** is a court order requiring a person or group either to perform some act or to refrain from performing some act. Finally, the Taft-Hartley Act authorized states to enact laws to allow employees to work in a unionized firm without joining the union. About twenty states (many in the South) have passed such *right-to-work laws.*

injunction a court order requiring a person or group either to perform some act or to refrain from performing some act

Landrum-Griffin Act

In the 1950s, Senate investigations and hearings exposed racketeering in unions and uncovered cases of bribery, extortion, and embezzlement among union leaders. It was discovered that a few union leaders had taken union funds for personal use and accepted payoffs from employers for union protection. Some were involved in arson, blackmail, and murder. Public pressure for reform resulted in the 1959 *Landrum-Griffin Act.*

This law was designed to regulate the internal functioning of labor unions. Provisions of the law require unions to file annual reports with the U.S. Department of Labor regarding their finances, elections, and various decisions made by union officers. The Landrum-Griffin Act also ensures that each union member has the right to seek, nominate, and vote for each elected position in his or her union. It provides safeguards governing union funds, and it requires management and unions to report the lending of management funds to union officers, union members, or local unions.

The various pieces of legislation we have reviewed here effectively regulate much of the relationship between labor and management after a union has been established. The next section demonstrates that forming a union is also a carefully regulated process.

The Unionization Process

4 **Learning Objective: Enumerate the steps involved in forming a union and show how the National Labor Relations Board is involved in the process.**

For a union to be formed at a particular firm, some employees of the firm first must be interested in being represented by a union. Then they must take a number of steps to formally declare their desire for a union. To ensure fairness, most of the steps in this unionization process are supervised by the NLRB.

Why Some Employees Join Unions

Obviously, employees start or join a union for a variety of reasons. One commonly cited reason is to combat alienation. Some employees—especially those whose jobs are dull and repetitive—may perceive themselves as merely parts of a machine. They may feel that they lose their individual or social identity at work. Union membership is one way to establish contact with others in a firm.

Another common reason for joining a union is the perception that union membership increases job security. No one wants to live in fear of arbitrary or capricious dismissal from a job. Unions actually have only limited ability to guarantee a member's job, but they can help to increase job security by enforcing seniority rules.

Employees also may join a union because of dissatisfaction with one or more elements of their jobs. If they are unhappy with their pay, benefits, or working conditions, they may look to a union to correct the perceived deficiencies.

Some people join unions because of their personal backgrounds. For example, a person whose parents are strong believers in unions might be inclined to feel just as positive about union membership.

In some situations, employees *must* join a union to keep their jobs. Many unions try, through their labor contracts, to require that a firm's new employees join the union after a specified probationary period. Under the Taft-Hartley Act, states may pass right-to-work laws prohibiting this practice.

Steps in Forming a Union

The first step in forming a union is the *organizing campaign* (see Figure 11.2). Its primary objective is to develop widespread employee interest in having a union. To kick off the campaign, a national union may send organizers to the firm to stir this interest. Alternatively, the employees themselves may decide that they want a union. Then they contact the appropriate national union and ask for organizing assistance.

The organizing campaign can be quite emotional, and it may lead to conflict between employees and management. On the one hand, the employees who want the union will be dedicated to its creation. On the other hand, management will be extremely sensitive to what it sees as a potential threat to its power and control.

At some point during the organizing campaign, employees are asked to sign *authorization cards* (see Figure 11.3) to indicate—in writing—their support for the union. Because of various NLRB rules and regulations, both union organizers and company management must be very careful in their behavior

Additional union benefits. *UnionPlus is a program made available to all AFL-CIO members. The program provides additional benefits to union members, including education benefits and benefits associated with special purchases.*

Courtesy unionplus.org

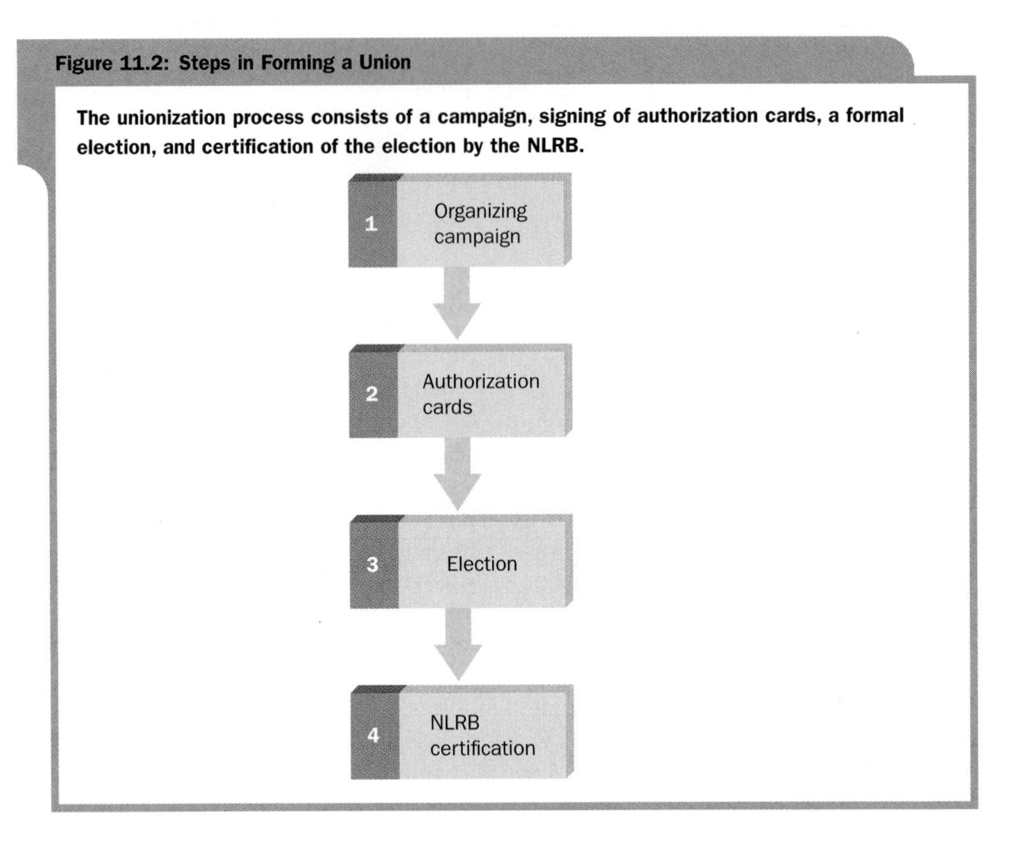

Figure 11.2: Steps in Forming a Union

The unionization process consists of a campaign, signing of authorization cards, a formal election, and certification of the election by the NLRB.

during this authorization drive. For example, employees cannot be asked to sign the cards when they are supposed to be working. And management may not indicate in any way that employees' jobs or job security will be in jeopardy if they *do* sign the cards.

If at least 30 percent of the eligible employees sign authorization cards, the organizers generally request that the firm recognize the union as the employees' bargaining representative. Usually the firm rejects this request, and a *formal election* is held to decide whether to have a union. This election usually involves secret ballots and is conducted by the NLRB. The outcome of the election is determined by a simple majority of eligible employees who choose to vote.

If the union obtains a majority, it becomes the official bargaining agent for its members, and the final step, *NLRB certification,* takes place. The union immediately may begin the process of negotiating a labor contract with management. If the union is voted down, the NLRB will not allow another election for one year.

bargaining unit the specific group of employees represented by a union

Several factors can complicate the unionization process. For example, the **bargaining unit**, which is the specific group of employees that the union is to represent, must be defined. Union organizers may want to represent all hourly employees at a particular site (such as all workers at a manufacturing plant). Or they may wish to represent only a specific group of employees (such as all electricians in a large manufacturing plant).

jurisdiction the right of a particular union to organize particular groups of workers

Another issue that may have to be resolved is that of **jurisdiction**, which is the right of a particular union to organize particular groups of workers (such as nurses). When jurisdictions overlap or are unclear, the employees themselves may decide who will represent them. In some cases, two or more unions may be trying to organize some or all of the employees of a firm. Then the election choices may be union A, union B, or no union at all.

The Role of the NLRB

As we have demonstrated, the NLRB is heavily involved in the unionization process. Generally, the NLRB is responsible for overseeing the organizing campaign, conducting the election (if one is warranted), and certifying the election results.

During the organizing campaign, both employers and union organizers can take steps to educate employees regarding the advantages and disadvantages of having a

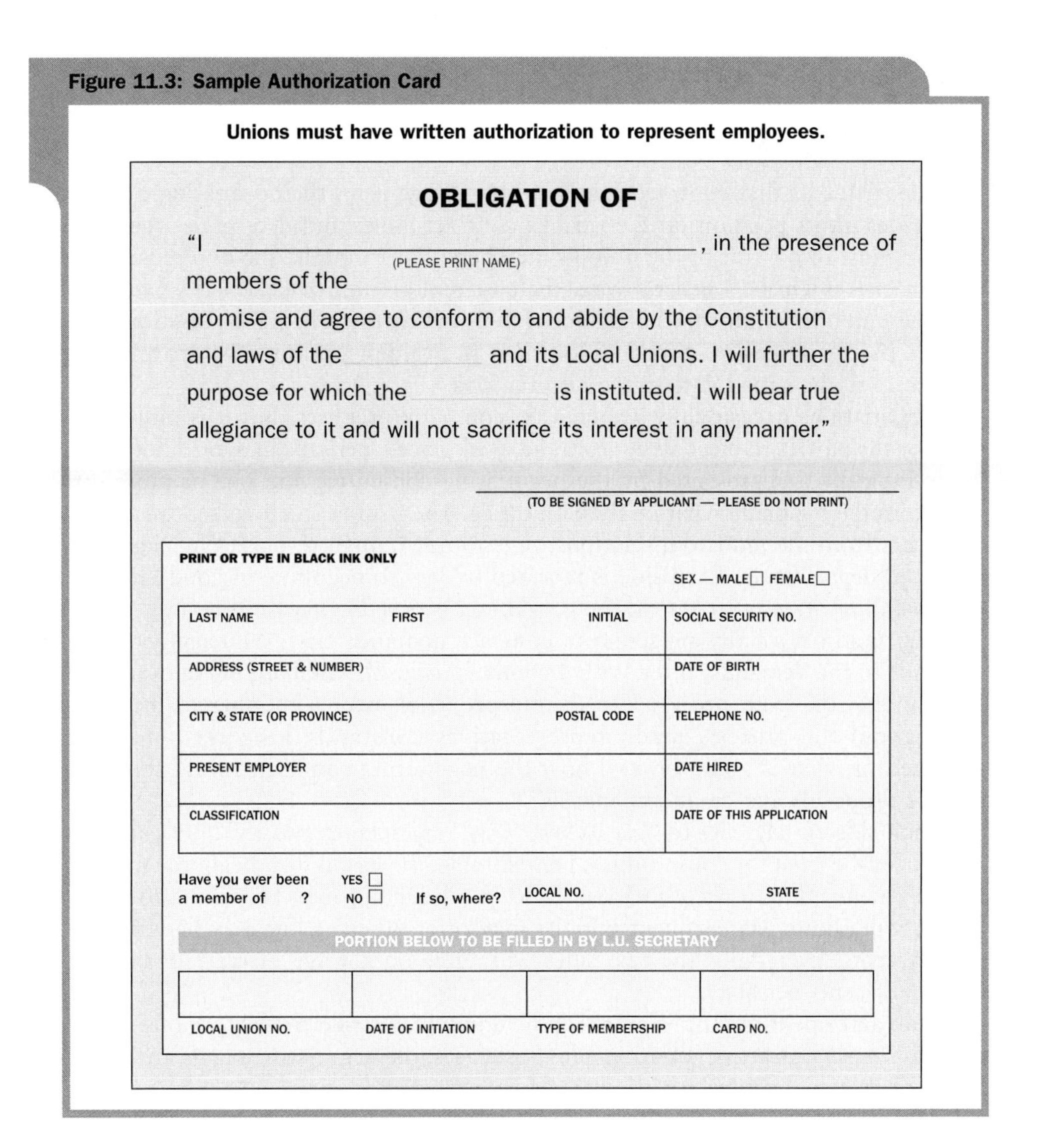
Figure 11.3: Sample Authorization Card

Unions must have written authorization to represent employees.

OBLIGATION OF

"I ______________________, in the presence of
(PLEASE PRINT NAME)
members of the
promise and agree to conform to and abide by the Constitution and laws of the __________ and its Local Unions. I will further the purpose for which the __________ is instituted. I will bear true allegiance to it and will not sacrifice its interest in any manner."

(TO BE SIGNED BY APPLICANT — PLEASE DO NOT PRINT)

PRINT OR TYPE IN BLACK INK ONLY

SEX — MALE☐ FEMALE☐

LAST NAME / FIRST / INITIAL	SOCIAL SECURITY NO.
ADDRESS (STREET & NUMBER)	DATE OF BIRTH
CITY & STATE (OR PROVINCE) / POSTAL CODE	TELEPHONE NO.
PRESENT EMPLOYER	DATE HIRED
CLASSIFICATION	DATE OF THIS APPLICATION

Have you ever been a member of ? YES ☐ NO ☐ If so, where? LOCAL NO. STATE

PORTION BELOW TO BE FILLED IN BY L.U. SECRETARY

LOCAL UNION NO.	DATE OF INITIATION	TYPE OF MEMBERSHIP	CARD NO.

union. However, neither is allowed to use underhanded tactics or to distort the truth. If violations occur, the NLRB can stop the questionable behavior, postpone the election, or set aside the results of an election that has already taken place.

The NLRB usually conducts the election within forty-five days of receiving the required number of signed authorization cards from the organizers. A very high percentage of the eligible voters generally participate in the election, and it is held at the workplace during normal working hours. In certain cases, however, a mail ballot or other form of election may be called for.

Certification of the election involves counting the votes and considering challenges to the election. After the election results are announced, management and the union organizers have five days in which to challenge the election. The basis for a challenge might be improper conduct prior to the election or participation by an ineligible voter. After considering any challenges, the NLRB passes final judgment on the election results.

When union representation is established, union and management get down to the serious business of contract negotiations.

Collective Bargaining

5

Learning Objective: Describe the basic elements in the collective-bargaining process.

Once certified by the NLRB, a new union's first task is to establish its own identity and structure. It immediately signs up as many members as possible. Then, in an internal election, members choose officers and representatives. A negotiating

collective bargaining the process of negotiating a labor contract with management

committee is also chosen to begin **collective bargaining**, the process of negotiating a labor contract with management.

The First Contract

To prepare for its first contract session with management, the negotiating committee decides on its position on the various contract issues and determines the issues that are most important to the union's members. For example, the two most pressing concerns might be a general wage increase and an improved benefits package.

The union then informs management that it is ready to begin negotiations, and the two parties agree on a time and location. Both sides continue to prepare for the session up to the actual date of the negotiations.

Negotiations occasionally are held on company premises, but it is more common for the parties to meet away from the workplace—perhaps in a local hotel. The union typically is represented by the negotiating committee and one or more officials from the regional or national union office. The firm normally is represented by managers from the industrial-relations, operations, human resources management, and legal departments. Each side is required by law to negotiate in good faith and not to stall or attempt to extend the bargaining proceedings unnecessarily.

The union normally presents its contract demands first. Management then responds to the demands, often with a counterproposal. The bargaining may move back and forth, from proposal to counterproposal, over a number of meetings. Throughout the process, union representatives constantly keep their members informed of what is going on and how the negotiating committee feels about the various proposals and counterproposals.

Each side clearly tries to "get its own way" as much as possible, but each also recognizes the need for compromise. For example, the union may begin the negotiations by demanding a wage increase of $1 per hour but may be willing to accept 60 cents per hour. Management initially may offer 40 cents but may be willing to pay 75 cents. Eventually, the two sides will agree on a wage increase of between 60 and 75 cents per hour.

If an agreement cannot be reached, the union may strike. Strikes are rare during a union's first contract negotiations. In most cases, the negotiating teams are able to agree on an initial contract without recourse to a strike.

ratification approval of a labor contract by a vote of the union membership

The final step in collective bargaining is **ratification**, which is approval of the contract by a vote of the union membership. If the membership accepts the terms of the contract, it is signed and becomes a legally binding agreement. If the contract is not ratified, the negotiators must go back and try to iron out a more acceptable agreement.

Later Contracts

A labor contract may cover a period of one to three years or more, but every contract has an expiration date. As that date approaches, both management and the union begin to prepare for new contract negotiations. Now, however, the entire process is likely to be much thornier than the first negotiation.

For one thing, the union and the firm have "lived with each other" for several years, during which some difficulties may have emerged. Each side may see certain issues as being of critical importance—issues that provoke a great deal of emotion at the bargaining table and often are difficult to resolve. Also, each side has learned from the earlier negotiations. Each may take a harder line on certain issues and be less willing to compromise.

The contract deadline itself also produces tension. As the expiration date of the existing contract draws near, each side feels pressure—real or imagined—to reach an agreement. This pressure may nudge the negotiators toward agreement, but it also can have the opposite effect, making an accord more difficult to reach. Moreover, at some point during the negotiations, union leaders are likely to take a *strike vote.* This vote reveals whether union members are willing to strike in the event that a new contract is not negotiated before the old one expires. In almost all cases, this vote supports a strike. Thus, the threat of a strike may add to the pressure mounting on both sides as they go about the business of negotiating.

Union negotiations. *Sometimes negotiations between union members and their employers fail to reach a settlement quickly. These United Mine Workers did not work for several years.*

AP Photo/Jeff Gentner

Union-Management Contract Issues

6
Learning Objective: Identify the major issues covered in a union-management contract.

As you might expect, many diverse issues are negotiated by unions and management and are incorporated into a labor contract. Unions tend to emphasize issues related to members' income, their standard of living, and the strength of the union. Management's primary goals are to retain as much control as possible over the firm's operations and to maximize its strength relative to that of the union. The balance of power between union and management varies from firm to firm.

Employee Pay

An area of bargaining central to union-management relations is employee pay. Three separate issues usually are involved: the forms of pay, the magnitude of pay, and the means by which the magnitude of pay will be determined.

Forms of Pay The primary form of pay is direct compensation—the wage or salary and benefits an employee receives in exchange for his or her contribution to the organization. Because direct compensation is a fairly straightforward issue, negotiators often spend much more of their time developing a benefits package for employees. And as the range of benefits and their costs have escalated over the years, this element of pay has become increasingly important and complex.

We discussed the various employee benefits in Chapter 9. Of these, health, life, disability, and dental insurance are important benefits that unions try to obtain for their members. As the costs of health care continue to increase, insurance benefits are costing employers more, and many are trying to pass a portion of this increased cost on to their employees. Unions do not take these increased burdens lightly, and health care benefits recently led to the first General Electric strike in over thirty years. Many large companies such as General Motors, Ford, Lucent, and Goodyear will face these issues as they negotiate new union contracts in the near future.[5] Deferred compensation, in the form of pension or retirement programs, is also a common focal point. Decisions about deferred compensation can have a long-lasting impact on a company.

Other benefits commonly dealt with in the bargaining process include paid vacation time, holidays, and a policy on paid sick leave. Obviously, unions argue

SPOTLIGHT

Who Works the Most Hours per Year?

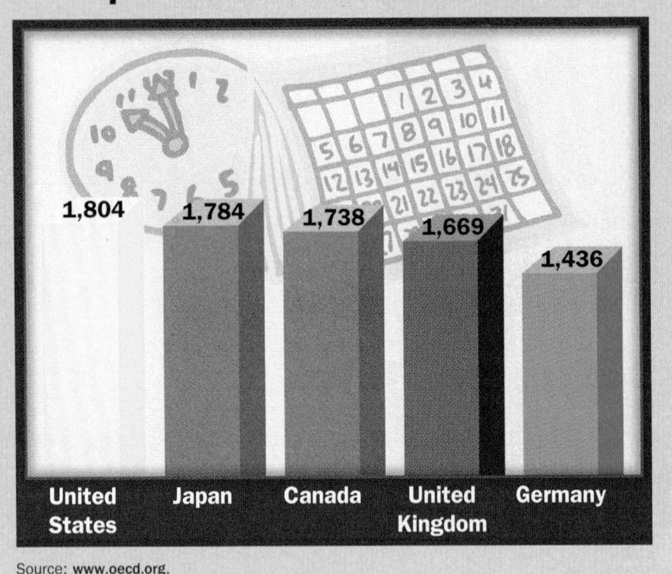

Source: www.oecd.org.

for as much paid vacation and holiday time as possible and for liberal sick-leave policies. Management naturally takes the opposite position.

Magnitude of Pay Of considerable importance is the *magnitude*, or amount, of pay that employees receive as both direct and indirect compensation. The union attempts to ensure that pay is on par with that received by other employees in the same or similar industries, both locally and nationally. The union also attempts to include in the contract clauses that provide pay increases over the life of the agreement. The most common is the *cost-of-living clause,* which ties periodic pay increases to increases in the cost of living, as defined by various economic statistics or indicators.

Of course, the magnitude of pay is also affected by the organization's ability to pay. If the firm has posted large profits recently, the union may expect large pay increases for its members. If the firm has not been very profitable, the union may agree to smaller pay hikes or even to a pay freeze. In an extreme situation (e.g., when the firm is bordering on bankruptcy), the union may agree to pay cuts. Very stringent conditions usually are included in any agreement to a pay cut.

Bargaining with regard to magnitude also revolves around employee benefits. At one extreme, unions seek a wide range of benefits, entirely or largely paid for by the firm. At the other extreme, management may be willing to offer the benefits package but may want its employees to bear most of the cost. Again, factors such as equity (with similar firms and jobs) and ability to pay enter into the final agreement.

Striking for higher pay. *In Los Angeles, Writers Guild of America workers went on strike for greater compensation associated with the sale of DVDs. 12,000 members were affected.*

AP Photo/Ric Francis

The United Nation's International Labour Organization brings together employees, employers, and government groups to promote job creation and decent work opportunities worldwide. In particular, the ILO supports sustainable development initiatives that lead to environmentally friendly jobs and long-term economic improvement. **www.ilo.org**

Pay Determinants Negotiators also address the question of how individual pay will be determined. For management, the ideal arrangement is to tie wages to each employee's productivity. As we saw, this method of payment tends to motivate and reward effort. Unions, on the other hand, feel that this arrangement can create unnecessary competition among employees. They generally argue that employees should be paid—at least in part—according to seniority. **Seniority** is the length of time an employee has worked for an organization.

Determinants regarding benefits also are negotiated. For example, management may want to provide profit-sharing benefits only to employees who have worked for the firm for a specified number of years. The union may want these benefits provided to all employees.

seniority the length of time an employee has worked for an organization

Working Hours

Working hours are another important issue in contract negotiations. The matter of overtime is of special interest. Federal law defines **overtime** as time worked in excess of forty hours in one week. And it specifies that overtime pay must be at least one and one-half times the normal hourly wage. Unions may attempt to negotiate overtime rates for all hours worked beyond eight hours in a single day. Similarly, the union may attempt to obtain higher overtime rates (say, twice the normal hourly wage) for weekend or holiday work. Still another issue is an upper limit to overtime, beyond which employees can refuse to work.

overtime time worked in excess of forty hours in one week (under some union contracts, time worked in excess of eight hours in a single day)

In firms with two or more work shifts, workers on less desirable shifts are paid a premium for their time. Both the amount of the premium and the manner in which workers are chosen for (or choose) particular shifts are negotiable issues. Other issues related to working hours are the work starting times and the length of lunch periods and coffee breaks.

Security

Security actually covers two issues. One is the job security of the individual worker; the other is the security of the union as the bargaining representative of the firm's employees.

Job security is protection against the loss of employment. It is a major concern of individuals. As we noted earlier, the desire for increased job security is a major reason for joining unions in the first place. In the typical labor contract, job security is based on seniority. If employees must be laid off or dismissed, those with the least seniority are the first to go. Some of the more senior employees may have to move to lower-level jobs, but they remain employed.

job security protection against the loss of employment

Union security is protection of the union's position as the employees' bargaining agent. Union security is frequently a more volatile issue than job security. Unions strive for as much security as possible, but management tends to see an increase in union security as an erosion of its control.

Union security arises directly from its membership. The greater the ratio of union employees to nonunion employees, the more secure the union is. In contract negotiations, unions thus attempt to establish various union membership conditions. The most restrictive of these is the **closed shop**, in which workers must join the union before they are hired. This condition was outlawed by the Taft-Hartley Act, but several other arrangements, including the following, are subject to negotiation:

- The **union shop**, in which new employees must join the union after a specified probationary period
- The **agency shop**, in which employees can choose not to join the union but must pay dues to the union anyway (The idea is that nonunion employees benefit from union activities and should help to support them.)
- The **maintenance shop**, in which an employee who joins the union must remain a union member as long as he or she is employed by the firm

union security protection of the union's position as the employees' bargaining agent

closed shop a workplace in which workers must join the union before they are hired; outlawed by the Taft-Hartley Act

union shop a workplace in which new employees must join the union after a specified probationary period

agency shop a workplace in which employees can choose not to join the union but must pay dues to the union anyway

maintenance shop a workplace in which an employee who joins the union must remain a union member as long as he or she is employed by the firm

Management Rights

Of particular interest to the firm are those rights and privileges that are to be retained by management. For example, the firm wants as much control as possible over whom it hires, how work is scheduled, and how discipline is handled. The union, in contrast, would like some control over these and other matters affecting its members. It is interesting that some unions are making progress toward their goal of playing a more direct role in corporate governance. Some union executives have, in fact, been given seats on corporate boards of directors.

Grievance Procedures

grievance procedure a formally established course of action for resolving employee complaints against management

A **grievance procedure** is a formally established course of action for resolving employee complaints against management. Virtually every labor contract contains a grievance procedure. Procedures vary in scope and detail, but they may involve all four steps described below (see Figure 11.4).

Original Grievance The process begins with an employee who believes that he or she has been treated unfairly in violation of the labor contract. For example, an employee may be entitled to a formal performance review after six months on the job. If no such review is conducted, the employee may file a grievance. To do so, the employee explains the grievance to a **shop steward**, an employee elected by union members to serve as their representative. The employee and the steward then discuss the grievance with the employee's immediate supervisor. Both the grievance and the supervisor's response are put in writing.

shop steward an employee elected by union members to serve as their representative

Broader Discussion In most cases the problem is resolved during the initial discussion with the supervisor. If it is not, a second discussion is held. Now the participants include the original parties (employee, supervisor, and steward), a representative from the union's grievance committee, and the firm's industrial-relations representative. Again, a record is kept of the discussion and its results.

Full-Scale Discussion If the grievance is still not resolved, a full-scale discussion is arranged. This discussion includes everyone involved in the broader discussion,

Figure 11.4: Steps in Resolving a Grievance

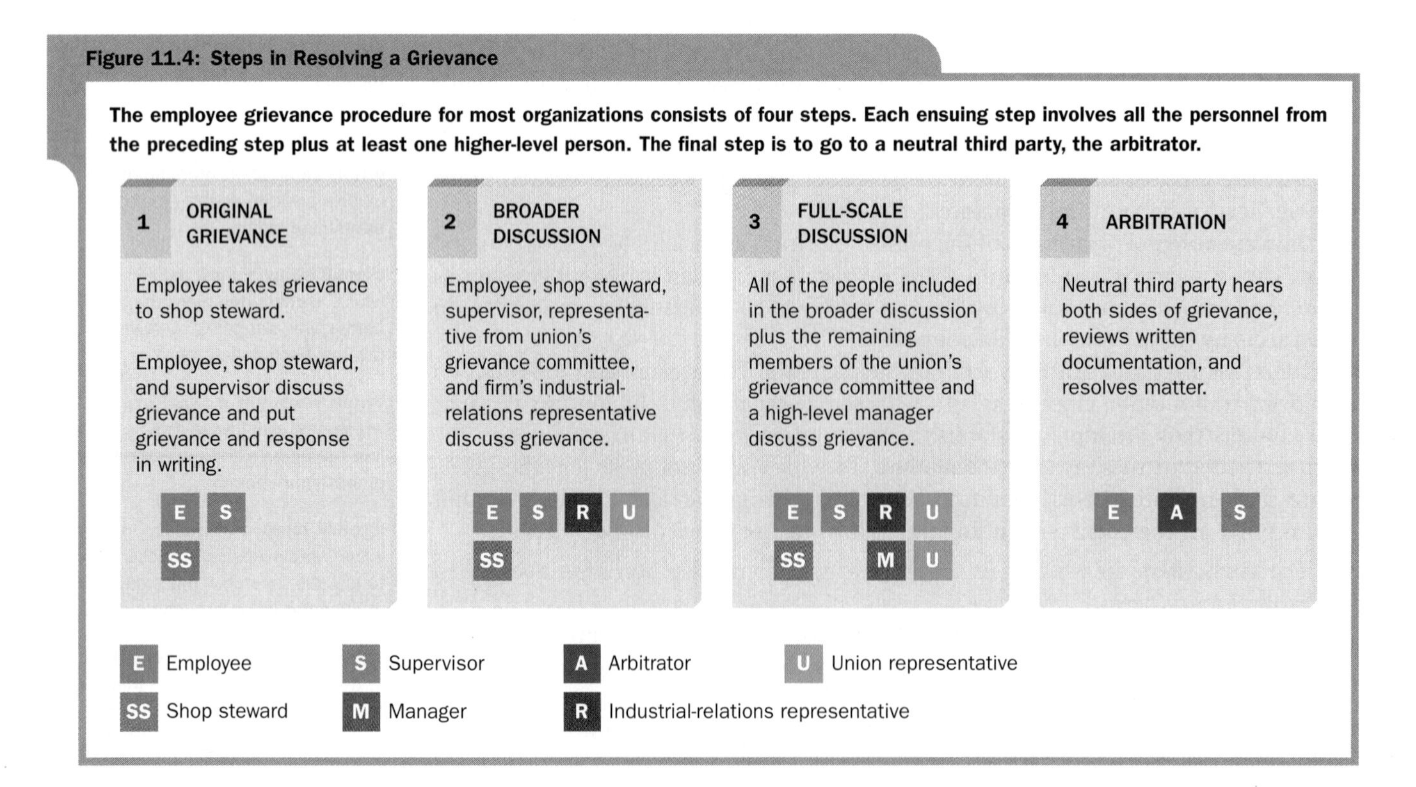

as well as all remaining members of the union's grievance committee and another high-level manager. As usual, all proceedings are put in writing. All participants are careful not to violate the labor contract during this attempt to resolve the complaint.

Arbitration The final step in a grievance procedure is **arbitration**, in which a neutral third party hears the two sides of a dispute and renders a binding decision. As in a court hearing, each side presents its case and has the right to cross-examine witnesses. In addition, the arbitrator reviews the written documentation of all previous steps in the grievance procedure. Both sides may then give summary arguments and/or present briefs. The arbitrator then decides whether a provision of the labor contract has been violated and proposes a remedy. The arbitrator cannot make any decision that would add to, detract from, or modify the terms of the contract. If it can be proved that the arbitrator exceeded the scope of his or her authority, either party may appeal the decision to the courts.

arbitration the step in a grievance procedure in which a neutral third party hears the two sides of a dispute and renders a binding decision

What actually happens when union and management "lock horns" over all the issues we have mentioned? We can answer this question by looking now at the negotiating tools each side can wield.

Union and Management Negotiating Tools

7

Learning Objective: Explain the primary bargaining tools available to unions and management.

Management and unions can draw on certain tools to influence each other during contract negotiations. Both sides may use advertising and publicity to gain support for their respective positions. The most extreme tools are strikes and lockouts, but there are other, milder techniques as well.

Strikes

Unions go out on strike only in a very few instances and almost always only after an existing labor contract has expired. (In 2007, there were only 21 strikes in the United States[6]) Even then, if new contract negotiations seem to be proceeding smoothly, a union does not actually start a strike. The union does take a strike vote, but the vote may be used primarily to show members' commitment to a strike if negotiations fail.

The main objective of a strike is to put financial pressure on the company to encourage management to meet union demands. The recent strike at Boeing Company where 27,000 union members walked off their jobs in a dispute over job security, pay, and benefits cost the company about $100 million a day in lost revenue. Thirty-two days after the strike began, Boeing Company and the Machinists Union agreed to resume negotiations.[7] When union members do go out on strike, it is usually because negotiations seem to be stalled. A strike is simply a work stoppage: The employees do not report for work. In addition, striking workers engage in **picketing**, marching back and forth in front of a place of employment with signs informing the public that a strike is in progress. In doing so, they hope that (1) the public will be sympathetic to the strikers and will not patronize the struck firm, (2) nonstriking employees of the firm will honor the picket line and not report to work either, and (3) members of other unions will not cross the picket line (e.g., to make deliveries) and thus will further restrict the operations of the struck firm. Unions also may engage in informational picketing to let companies know of their dissatisfaction. New York, the city that never sleeps, came to a crashing halt when 33,000 members of the Transport Workers Union went on a three-day strike. The strike shut down the city's 243 bus routes and 26 subway lines, forcing its 7 million daily commuters to rely on taxis, cars, and their own feet. The striking workers were angry over contract negotiations that reduced pensions and raised the price of their health care.[8]

picketing marching back and forth in front of a place of employment with signs informing the public that a strike is in progress

Obviously, strikes are expensive to both the firm and the strikers. The firm loses business and earnings during the strike, and the striking workers lose the wages they would have earned if they had been at their jobs. During a strike, unions try to

Using a strike to negotiate. *A strike can increase public support for a union's position and decrease a firm's ability to operate effectively.*

provide their members with as much support as possible. Larger unions are able to put a portion of their members' dues into a *strike fund*. The fund is used to provide financial support for striking union members. At times, workers may go out on a **wildcat strike**, which is a strike that has not been approved by the union. In this situation, union leaders typically work with management to convince the strikers to return to work.

wildcat strike a strike not approved by the strikers' union

Slowdowns and Boycotts

Almost every labor contract contains a clause that prohibits strikes during the life of the contract. (This is why strikes, if they occur, usually take place after a contract has expired.) However, a union may strike a firm while the contract is in force if members believe that management has violated its terms. Workers also may engage in a **slowdown**, a technique whereby workers report to their jobs but work at a pace that is slower than normal.

slowdown a technique whereby workers report to their jobs but work at a slower pace than normal

boycott a refusal to do business with a particular firm

A **boycott** is a refusal to do business with a particular firm. Unions occasionally bring this strategy to bear by urging members (and sympathizers) not to purchase the products of a firm with which they are having a dispute. Teachers' unions have organized "back to school" boycotts to protest labor practices of retailing giant Wal-Mart. The National Education Association, the largest union in the United States with 2.7 million members, and the 1.3-million-member American Federation of Teachers urged consumers to join the boycott by holding rallies, distributing fliers, and holding news conferences. The boycott was strategically planned during the "back to school" season, the second largest for Wal-Mart aside from the Christmas holiday.[9] A *primary boycott,* aimed at the employer directly involved in the dispute, can be a powerful weapon. A *secondary boycott,* aimed at a firm doing business with the employer, is prohibited by the Taft-Hartley Act. Cesar Chavez, a migrant worker who founded the United Farm Workers Union,

used boycotts to draw attention to the low pay and awful conditions endured by produce pickers.

Lockouts and Strikebreakers

Management's most potent weapon is the lockout. In a **lockout**, the firm refuses to allow employees to enter the workplace. Like strikes, lockouts are expensive for both the firm and its employees. For this reason, they are used rarely and then only in certain circumstances. A firm that produces perishable goods, for example, may use a lockout if management believes that its employees will soon go on strike. The idea is to stop production in time to ensure minimal spoilage of finished goods or work in process.

lockout a firm's refusal to allow employees to enter the workplace

Management also may attempt to hire strikebreakers. A **strikebreaker** is a nonunion employee who performs the job of a striking union member. Hiring strikebreakers can result in violence when picketing employees confront the nonunion workers at the entrance to the struck facility. The firm also faces the problem of finding qualified replacements for the striking workers. Sometimes management personnel take over the jobs of strikers. Managers at telephone companies have handled the switchboards on more than one occasion.

strikebreaker a nonunion employee who performs the job of a striking union member

Mediation and Arbitration

Strikes, strikebreaking, lockouts, and boycotts all pit one side against the other. Ultimately, one side "wins" and the other "loses." Unfortunately, the negative effects of such actions—including resentment, fear, and distrust—may linger for months or years after a dispute has been resolved.

More productive techniques that are being used increasingly are mediation and arbitration. Either one may come into play before a labor contract expires or after some other strategy, such as a strike, has proved ineffective.

Mediation is the use of a neutral third party to assist management and the union during their negotiations. This third party (the mediator) listens to both sides, trying to find common ground for agreement. The mediator also tries to facilitate communication between the two sides, to promote compromise, and generally to keep the negotiations moving. At first the mediator may meet privately with each side. Eventually, however, his or her goal is to get the two to settle their differences. The Federal Mediation and Conciliation Service (FMCS) is an independent government agency that handles mediation for labor disputes. The FMCS resolved a strike led by employees of aircraft maker Hawker Beechcraft by helping the company and the Machinists Union reach a tentative contract deal after several days of negotiations.[10] The agency handles 5,300 collective bargaining negotiations per year, with 85 percent of those mediations reaching an agreement from both parties.[11] The agency reports to have saved businesses and workers approximately $13 billion dollars during 1999–2007, showing the benefits of mediation for both parties.[12]

mediation the use of a neutral third party to assist management and the union during their negotiations

Unlike mediation, the *arbitration* step is a formal hearing. Just as it may be the final step in a grievance procedure, it also may be used in contract negotiations (perhaps after mediation attempts) when the two sides cannot agree on one or more issues. Here, the arbitrator hears the formal positions of both parties on outstanding, unresolved issues. The arbitrator then analyzes these positions and makes a decision on the possible resolution of the issues. If both sides have agreed in advance that the arbitration will be *binding,* they must accept the arbitrator's decision.

If mediation and arbitration are unsuccessful, then, under the provisions of the Taft-Hartley Act, the president of the United States can obtain a temporary injunction to prevent or stop a strike if it would jeopardize national health or security.

This chapter ends our discussion of human resources. Next, we examine the marketing function of business. We begin in Chapter 12 by discussing the meaning of the term *marketing*.

return to **inside business**

Boeing

Over the years, Boeing and its unions have disagreed over key issues such as compensation and job security. When the International Association of Machinists and Aerospace Workers calls a strike, it knows it has a strong position. The company can't easily find trained workers to replace the highly-skilled union machinists, so a strike will stop Boeing's assembly lines and delay jet deliveries.

For its part, Boeing wants to protect its profitability and minimize business disruptions to prevent customers from defecting to Airbus, its European rival. Boeing's chief negotiator says its executives will not "sacrifice our ability to continuously improve productivity and our long-term competitiveness." Both sides are committed to resolving these issues for the benefit of the company and its workforce.

Questions

1. If a union goes out on strike against Boeing for an extended period, should the U.S. government get workers back on the job by seeking an injunction under the Taft-Hartley Act? Why or why not?
2. Do you think that agreeing to unionized employees' demands would constrain Boeing's productivity and competitiveness? Explain your answer.

CHAPTER REVIEW

Summary

Explain how and why labor unions came into being.

A labor union is an organization of workers who act together to negotiate wages and working conditions with their employers. Labor relations are the dealings between labor unions and business management.

The first major union in the United States was the Knights of Labor, formed in 1869 to eliminate the depersonalization of workers. The Knights were followed in 1886 by the American Federation of Labor (AFL). The goal of the AFL was to improve its members' living standards without changing the business system. In 1905 the radical Industrial Workers of the World (IWW) was formed; its goal was the overthrow of capitalism. Of these three, only the AFL remained when the Congress of Industrial Organizations (CIO) was founded as a body of industrial unions between World War I and World War II. After years of competing, the AFL and CIO merged in 1955. The largest union not affiliated with the AFL-CIO is the Teamsters Union.

Discuss the sources of unions' negotiating power and trends in union membership.

The power of unions to negotiate with management comes from two sources. The first is the size of their membership. The second is the groups of laws that guarantee unions the right to negotiate and that regulate the negotiation process. At present, union membership accounts for less than 15 percent of the American workforce, and it seems to be decreasing for various reasons. Nonetheless, unions wield considerable power in many industries—those in which their members comprise a large proportion of the workforce.

Many unions today are entering into partnerships with management rather than maintaining their traditional adversarial position. Unions and management cooperate to increase production, improve quality, lower costs, empower workers, and enhance the workplace. Limited partnerships center on accomplishing one specific task or project. Long-range strategic partnerships focus on sharing decision-making power for a range of workplace and business matters.

Identify the main focus of several major pieces of labor-management legislation.

Important laws that affect union power are the Norris-LaGuardia Act (limits management's ability to obtain injunctions against unions), the Wagner Act (forbids certain unfair labor practices by management), the Fair Labor Standards Act (allows the federal government to set the minimum wage and to mandate overtime rates), the Taft-Hartley Act (forbids certain unfair practices by unions), and the Landrum-Griffin Act (regulates the internal functioning of labor unions). The National Labor Relations Board (NLRB), a federal agency that oversees union-management relations, was created by the Wagner Act.

4 Enumerate the steps involved in forming a union and show how the National Labor Relations Board is involved in the process.

Attempts to form a union within a firm begin with an organizing campaign to develop widespread employee interest in having a union. Next, employees sign authorization cards indicating in writing their support for the union. The third step is to hold a formal election to decide whether to have a union. Finally, if the union obtains a majority, it receives NLRB certification, making it the official bargaining agent for its members. The entire process is supervised by the NLRB, which oversees the organizing campaign, conducts the election, and certifies the election results.

Describe the basic elements in the collective-bargaining process.

Once a union is established, it may negotiate a labor contract with management through the process of collective bargaining. First, the negotiating committee decides on its position on the various contract issues. The union informs management that it is ready to begin negotiations, and a time and place are set. The union is represented by the negotiating committee, and the organization is represented by managers from several departments in the company. Each side is required to negotiate in good faith and not to stall or attempt to extend the bargaining unnecessarily. The final step is ratification, which is approval of the contract by a vote of the union membership.

Identify the major issues covered in a union-management contract.

As the expiration date of an existing contract approaches, management and the union begin to negotiate a new contract. Contract issues include employee pay and benefits, working hours, job and union security, management rights, and grievance procedures.

Explain the primary bargaining tools available to unions and management.

Management and unions can use certain tools to sway one another—and public opinion—during contract negotiations. Advertising and publicity help each side to gain support. When contract negotiations do not run smoothly, unions may apply pressure on management through strikes, slowdowns, or boycotts. Management may counter by imposing lockouts or hiring strikebreakers. Less drastic techniques for breaking contract deadlocks are mediation and arbitration. In both, a neutral third party is involved in the negotiations.

Key Terms

You should now be able to define and give an example relevant to each of the following terms:

labor union (310)
union-management (labor) relations (310)
craft union (311)
strike (312)
industrial union (312)
National Labor Relations Board (NLRB) (318)
injunction (318)
bargaining unit (320)
jurisdiction (320)
collective bargaining (322)
ratification (322)
seniority (325)
overtime (325)
job security (325)
union security (325)
closed shop (325)
union shop (325)
agency shop (325)
maintenance shop (325)
grievance procedure (326)
shop steward (326)
arbitration (327)
picketing (327)
wildcat strike (328)
slowdown (328)
boycott (328)
lockout (329)
strikebreaker (329)
mediation (329)

Review Questions

1. Briefly describe the history of unions in the United States.
2. Describe the three characteristics common to most union-management partnerships. Discuss the benefits of union-management partnerships to management, unions, and workers.
3. How has government regulation of union-management relations evolved during this century?
4. For what reasons do employees start or join unions?
5. Describe the process of forming a union, and explain the role of the National Labor Relations Board (NLRB) in that process.
6. List the major areas that are negotiated in a labor contract.
7. Explain the three issues involved in negotiations concerning employee pay.
8. What is the difference between job security and union security? How do unions attempt to enhance union security?
9. What is a grievance? Describe the typical grievance procedure.
10. What steps are involved in collective bargaining?
11. For what reasons are strikes and lockouts relatively rare nowadays?
12. What are the objectives of picketing?
13. In what ways do the techniques of mediation and arbitration differ?

Discussion Questions

1. Do unions really derive their power mainly from their membership and labor legislation? What are some other sources of union power?
2. Which labor contract issues are likely to be the easiest to resolve? Which are likely to be the most difficult?
3. Discuss the following statement: Union security means job security for union members.
4. How would you prepare for labor contract negotiations as a member of management? As head of the union negotiating committee?
5. Under what circumstances are strikes and lockouts justified in place of mediation or arbitration?

Video Case 11.1

Boston Ballet/Boston Musicians Association

Based on what is reported in newspapers and the electronic media, most people believe that the relationship between companies and unions is always contentious. Salary disputes, disagreements over benefits, demand for more employee productivity, stalled negotiations, and threats of strikes appear to be the only news reported. Fortunately, that is not always the case and certainly not the relationship that exists between the Boston Ballet and the Boston Musicians Association.

According to Barbara Owens, president of the Boston Musicians Union, and Jonathan McPhee, music director for the Boston Ballet, the reason they work well together is because there is an element of trust with both of them knowing that both sides are in this together. They share the same goals: desire for an excellent entertainment product, a healthy organization, and artists that are taken care of and well compensated. Because of these shared goals, when the music director comes up with an idea and needs union support, the union listens to the idea with an open mind. Both organizations may have different responsibilities, but they both want the same result: Success!

The relationship between the union and management wasn't always that way. According to Barbara Owens, her first conversations with Jonathan McPhee were quite adversarial. She concluded that his relationship with previous union officers had been quite contentious. As Barbara recalled: "When we first started working with each other, we weren't working together at all. We were really sparring with each other. It took us awhile to get used to each others' communications style and to realize that we had the same philosophy about the health of the organization and the health of the musicians union. We both wanted a premier ballet company and to keep the musicians working as much as possible."

Jonathan's position is rather unique because he wears two hats. He is fully responsible for the administrative side of music operations for the Boston Ballet. He has to put together a music budget, manage it, and answer to the board for how his budget is managed. He also is a musician and has artistic responsibility for arranging and conducting the music. Jonathan is comfortable wearing two hats. However, it gets difficult when mandates come down from above to cut the budget. This has significant people and union ramifications since 96 percent of his budget is musicians' salaries and benefits.

Such a mandate occurred when the management of the ballet's performance venue chose not to renew the ballet company's contract, citing financial difficulties. Management's decision placed the jobs of the entire orchestra in jeopardy as well. Jonathan fought the decision, arguing that the company just couldn't shut down the Boston Ballet. The dancers would leave the area, and it would be difficult and extremely expensive to ever restart the program. Also, what do you do with your subscribers? These would be lost revenues that would never be replaced. If they were absent from the marketplace, it would open the door for a competitive ballet company to enter the market. After long discussions and looking at a myriad of alternatives, the company made the decision to renew the contract.

Over the last few years, the musicians have become absolutely convinced that Jonathan (who remember is management) is their best friend. He thinks about their interests as well as his own and has proven in this most recent contract crisis that he is their advocate.

When asked about his relationship with the musicians, Jonathan replied that the orchestra was his instrument. He said, "My instrument is made up of 50–90 people who have their own lives, their own problems, and there own instruments. I have the most expensive instrument in classical music. It's one that needs a lot of maintenance too because there are things that constantly change in peoples lives. It is my job to maintain my instrument. Just like you would take your flute to get it overhauled every year, I have to make sure I'm constantly overhauling my instrument to insure that everyone in the orchestra is OK. Their whole life is wrapped up in what they do and frequently they need someone to take care of the surrounding parts of their lives. That's why the musicians union was created to protect them from things they shouldn't have to be dealing with." Now this is a company relationship of which any union would be proud![13]

Questions

1. Describe the three most common characteristics that the Boston Ballet and the Boston Musicians Union employed to maintain their strategic partnership.
2. As described in the case, what were the sources of union power?
3. What is the greatest threat to the Boston Musicians Union in its relationship with the Boston Ballet?

Case 11.2

Can Striking Workers Be Replaced?

Strikes are costly to both the union members walking the picket line and the company whose employees are off the job. Companies may lose business and struggle to get things done properly and on time. Often, they try to minimize the disruption by assigning managers and hiring workers to fill in. Meanwhile, those on strike don't earn what they would if they were at work. But can striking workers be replaced?

In general, U.S. companies can legally replace workers temporarily or permanently during a strike. Consider what happened when the union representing 1,730 nurses at Stanford University Medical Center and Lucile Salter Packard Children's Hospital wanted to get members a raise in the next contract. The union asked for more than 17 percent, but management initially offered 8 percent. The two sides couldn't agree on the size of the raise, so the union notified the hospitals that a strike was imminent.

The hospitals quickly arranged for U.S. Nursing Corp. to fly in hundreds of temporary replacements. "We're not strikebreakers; we're not scab nurses," said Daniel Mordecai, who founded U.S. Nursing. "We're a company that performs an emergency staffing service. If we didn't, the hospital would not be able to care for its patients and the community." The American Nurses Association, an organization of unions representing nurses around the country, countered that the company "undermines the nurses who go out on the picket line, and it encourages lengthy strikes" because the hospitals are less motivated to continue negotiations. In this case, the nurses went back to work after a seven-week strike ended in a new contract with pay raises of up to 12 percent.

Although companies are allowed to hire permanent replacements for employees on strike, few actually do so. Northwest Airlines decided to hire permanent replacements when its mechanics went on strike to protest the financially ailing airline's demand for significant pay cuts. As the dispute dragged on, Northwest intensified its cost-cutting efforts and finally filed for bankruptcy reorganization. The airline kept its jets in the air even as it continued to hire permanent replacements for the striking mechanics.

Opponents say that companies should not be allowed to hire permanent replacements because the practice puts unions at a severe negotiating disadvantage. The unions have far less bargaining power if companies simply can replace workers who strike. Moreover, the striking workers suffer because they lose their jobs—not by being fired but by being replaced. Critics also observe that companies in Canada, Mexico, and many other countries are not legally allowed to hire permanent replacement workers. If so many nations outlaw this practice, should it be legal in the United States?

Until U.S. legislators take action on this issue, unions are looking more closely at other ways of pressuring companies without prolonged strikes. One approach is to hold demonstrations and publicity strikes to call attention to the situation and to try to gain public support. Another approach is to strike intermittently or strike different facilities at different times. Instead of striking, some unions may use slowdowns or file large numbers of grievances to put pressure on management without endangering workers' jobs.

Professor Richard Lippke of James Madison University cites four alternatives to a total ban on permanent replacements. One option is to use permanent replacements only after a strike has lasted for a certain period. A second option is to enact laws discouraging but not forbidding permanent replacements, such as disqualifying companies from receiving government contracts for a specified period. A third option is to ban the practice but permit a company to ask an independent arbitrator to make an exception if warranted. A fourth option is to force both sides to go to arbitration and have both pay penalties for each day they fail to reach an agreement.[14]

For more information about this topic, go to **www.nursingworld.org** and **www.usnursing.com.**

Questions

1. How might management and the public react to a union publicizing a company's use of temporary or permanent replacement workers during a strike?
2. Should U.S. lawmakers forbid all companies from hiring permanent replacements for striking workers? Support your answer.
3. Should U.S. lawmakers forbid all unions from striking unless mediation and arbitration fail to resolve their disputes with management?

Building Skills for Career Success

1. JOURNALING FOR SUCCESS

Discovery statement: This chapter focused on the unionization process and why employees join unions.

Assignment

1. What are the major reasons for joining and being a part of a labor union?
2. Under what conditions would you like to be a union member?
3. Are there any circumstances under which a striking union member should cross a picket line and go back to work? Explain.
4. Will the unions in the United States grow or decline over the next decade? Why?

2. EXPLORING THE INTERNET

Union websites provide a wealth of information about union activities and concerns. Just as a corporate home page gives a firm the opportunity to describe its mission and goals and present its image to the world, so too does a website allow a union to speak to its membership as well as to the public at large. Visit the text website for updates to this exercise.

Assignment

1. Visit the following websites:
   AFL-CIO: **www.aflcio.com**
   United Auto Workers: **www.uaw.org**
2. What are the mission statements of these unions?

3. Briefly describe your impression of the areas of interest to union members.
4. What is your impression of the tone of these websites? Do they differ in any way from a typical business website?

3. DEVELOPING CRITICAL-THINKING SKILLS

Recently, while on its final approach to an airport in Lubbock, Texas, a commercial airliner encountered a flock of ducks. The flight crew believed that one or more of the ducks hit the aircraft and were ingested into the plane's main engine. The aircraft landed safely and taxied to the terminal. The flight crew advised the maintenance and operations crews of the incident. Operations grounded the plane until it could be inspected, but because of the time of day, maintenance personnel available to perform the inspection were in short supply. The airline had to call in two off-duty mechanics. A supervisor, calling from an overtime list, made calls until contacting two available mechanics. They worked on overtime pay to perform the inspection and return the aircraft to a safe flying status. Several days after the inspection, a mechanic on the overtime list who was not home when the supervisor called complained that she had been denied overtime. This union member believed that the company owed her overtime pay for the same number of hours worked by a mechanic who performed the actual inspection. The company disagreed. What options are available to resolve this conflict?

Assignment

1. Using the following questions as guidelines, determine how this dispute can be resolved.
   a. What options are available to the unhappy mechanic? What process must she pursue? How does this process work?
   b. Do you believe that the mechanic should receive pay for time she did not work? Justify your answer.
   c. What do you think was the final outcome of this conflict?
2. Prepare a report describing how you would resolve this situation.

4. BUILDING TEAM SKILLS

For more than a century, American unions have played an important role in the workplace, striving to improve the working conditions and quality of life of employees. Today, federal laws cover many of the workers' rights that unions first championed. For this reason, some people believe that unions are no longer necessary. According to some experts, however, as technology changes the workplace and as cultural diversity and the number of part-time workers increase, unions will increase their memberships and become stronger as we move into the new century. What do you think?

Assignment

1. Form a "pro" group and a "con" group and join one of them.
2. Debate whether unions will be stronger or weaker in the next century.
3. Record the key points for each side.
4. Summarize what you learned about unions and their usefulness in a report, and state your position on the debated issue.

5. RESEARCHING DIFFERENT CAREERS

When applying for a job, whether mailing or faxing in your résumé, you should always include a letter of application, or a cover letter, as it is often called. A well-prepared cover letter should convince the prospective employer to read your résumé and to phone you for an interview. The letter should describe the job you want and your qualifications for the job. It also should let the firm know where you can be reached to set up an appointment for an interview.

Assignment

1. Prepare a letter of application to use with the résumé you prepared in Chapter 9. (An example appears in Appendix A online.)
2. After having several friends review your letter, edit it carefully.
3. Ask your instructor to comment on your letter.

Running a Business Part 4

Inside the People Business at Finagle A Bagel

People are a vital ingredient in Finagle A Bagel's recipe for success. As a quick-serve business, the company strives for high turnover in food, not employees. In fact, careful attention to human resources management has enabled Finagle A Bagel to continue expanding its market share without spending money on advertising. Low workforce turnover means less money and time spent on recruiting and training—an important financial consideration for a fast-growing business. It also means that Finagle A Bagel has the human resources strength to combine super service with fresh food for a distinctive competitive advantage in a crowded marketplace.

THE RIGHT PEOPLE IN THE RIGHT PLACE

"We depend on our crew at the store level—who are interacting with our guests every day—to know their jobs, to understand the company mission, and to communicate with the guests," says Heather Robertson, who directs the company's marketing, human resources, and research and development. "And once we get them on board, people don't leave our company. They just stay. They realize that it can be a career for them."

A sizable number of Finagle A Bagel's managers and employees (including Robertson) were hired years ago and became so excited about the product, the company, and the customers that they simply stayed. Many remain with Finagle A Bagel because they prefer the more personal atmosphere of a 320-employee business over the relatively faceless anonymity of a gigantic corporation. "It's really unusual to have one-on-one interaction on a daily basis with the president of the company or any senior executive member of the company," Robertson states. "Our cashiers, our café attendants, our bakers, and our managers know they can pick up the phone at any point and call anybody here and say, 'Here's my problem. How do I fix it?' or 'I need your help.' The size of our company allows us to do that, and the culture of the company encourages that."

Because bagels are an integral part of every menu item, employees who join Finagle A Bagel must "love" bagels, regardless of any other skills or experiences they bring to their jobs. When Robertson advertises to fill an open position in Finagle A Bagel's headquarters, for example, she always mentions this requirement. As résumés come in, she sorts them according to whether the candidates indicate a fondness for bagels. Those who fail to mention it are automatically disqualified from consideration.

DIFFERENT KINDS OF MANAGERS FOR DIFFERENT LOCATIONS

Alan Litchman, Finagle A Bagel's copresident, says that selecting a candidate to manage one of the Boston stores is easier than selecting one for a suburban store. Given the inner-city location of the company's support center, he or another executive can get to the Boston stores more quickly if a problem arises. Moreover, the city stores compete by providing speedy, accurate service to busy customers who have little time to waste waiting in line. Paulo Pereira, general manager of the Harvard Square store in Cambridge, has become an expert at squeezing inefficiencies from the city stores so that customers are in and out more quickly. By increasing the number of customers served each day and slashing the number of bagels left over at closing, Pereira boosts both sales revenues and profits.

When selecting a manager for a suburban store, Litchman looks for people with an "owner-operator mentality" who have the drive, initiative, and know-how to build business locally. His message to a potential general manager is: "If you want to be a franchisee but don't have the capital, or if you want to own your own business, we're going to put you in business. You don't have to give us any money to do that. And if your store achieves more than a certain level of sales or profits, we'll start splitting the bottom line with you in a bonus program." Consider Nick Cochran, who worked his way up from assistant manager to general manager of the store in Wayland, an affluent Boston suburb. Cochran's enthusiasm for quality and service has drawn a highly loyal customer following and contributed to the Wayland store's success.

HIRING AND MOTIVATING STORE PERSONNEL

General managers such as Cochran and Pereira are responsible for recruiting, interviewing, hiring, training, motivating, and evaluating store-level personnel. They assign job responsibilities according to the skills and strengths of each manager and employee, but they also expect everyone to work as a team during extremely busy periods. In addition to motivating general managers by offering bonuses based on meeting revenue and profit goals, Finagle A Bagel encourages crew members to take advantage of extra training and internal promotions.

"In a company our size," stresses copresident Laura Trust, "there is always opportunity. You just have to find the right fit for the individual." In fact, says her husband, "The best supervisors, coordinators, assistant managers, or managers in any unit—by far—are the ones who have started with us at a lower level and worked their way up."

DIVERSE WORKFORCE, FAMILY BUSINESS

Finagle A Bagel has an extremely diverse workforce made up of people originally from Latin America, Europe, western Africa, and many other areas. Over the years, the company has served as a sponsor for new Americans who need government-issued work permits so that they can legally remain in the United States for work reasons. Despite diversity's many advantages—including creativity, flexibility, and the ability to relate to a broader customer base—it also can create communications challenges when English is not an employee's native language. To avoid confusion, Litchman and Trust insist that employees speak only in English when addressing customers.

As a small, family-run business, Finagle A Bagel sees its workforce as a group of unique individuals, not interchangeable cogs in an impersonal corporate machine. Trust feels strongly that "there's a responsibility that you have to your employees and to your colleagues. These people work for you—they work hard to try and move your company forward—and their efforts need to be recognized." Because the business is still small, she adds, "the people who have become a part of the management team are very much like family to Alan and me. If you run your company that way, then you'll be successful because everybody believes that you care about not only the work they do but everything they do, and every part of their lives affects their job."

Questions

1. What effect has diversity had on Finagle A Bagel?
2. If you were the general manager of a downtown Finagle A Bagel store, what job description and job specification would you prepare for a cashier? Based on these, what kinds of questions would you ask when interviewing candidates for this position?
3. Which of Herzberg's motivation factors are Trust and Litchman emphasizing for general managers?
4. Would it be feasible for Finagle A Bagel to apply the concept of flextime to store employees? To senior managers at the headquarters facility? Explain.

Building a Business Plan Part 4

In this section of your business plan, you will expand on the type and quantity of employees that will be required to operate the business. Your human resources requirements are determined by the type of business and by the size and scale of your operation. From the preceding section, you should have a good idea of how many people you will need. And Part 4 of your textbook, "Human Resources," especially Chapters 9 and 10, should help you in answering some of the questions in this part of the business plan.

THE HUMAN RESOURCES COMPONENT

To ensure successful performance by employees, you must inform workers of their specific job requirements. Employees must know what is expected on the job, and they are entitled to expect regular feedback on their work. It is vital to have a formal job description and job specification for every position in your business. Also, you should establish procedures for evaluating performance.

The labor force component should include the answers to at least the following questions:

4.1. How many employees will you require, and what are their qualifications—including skills, experience, and knowledge? How many jobs will be full time? Part time?
4.2. Will you have written job descriptions for each position?
4.3. Have you prepared a job-application form? Do you know what can legally be included in it?
4.4. What criteria will you use in selecting employees?
4.5. Have you made plans for the orientation process?
4.6. Who will do the training?
4.7. What can you afford to pay in wages and salaries? Is this in line with the going rate in your region and industry?
4.8. Who will evaluate your employees?
4.9. Will you delegate any authority to employees?
4.10. Have you developed a set of disciplinary rules?
4.11. Do you plan to interview employees when they resign?

REVIEW OF BUSINESS PLAN ACTIVITIES

Remember that your employees are the most valuable and important resource. Therefore, make sure that you expend a great deal of effort to acquire and make full use of this resource. Check and resolve any issues in this component of your business plan before beginning Part 5. Again, make sure that your answers to the questions in each part are consistent with the entire business plan. Finally, write a brief statement that summarizes all the information for this part of the business plan.

The information contained in "Building a Business Plan" will also assist you in completing the online *Interactive Business Plan.*

PART 5 Marketing

The business activities that make up a firm's marketing efforts are those most directly concerned with satisfying customers' needs. In this part, we explore these activities in some detail. Initially, we discuss markets, marketing mixes, marketing environment forces, marketing plans, and buying behavior. Then, in turn, we discuss the four elements that together make up a marketing mix: product, price, distribution, and promotion.

Photographers Choice/Getty Images

12 Building Customer Relationships Through Effective Marketing

LEARNING OBJECTIVES

What you will be able to do once you complete this chapter:

1. Understand the meaning of *marketing* and the importance of management of customer relationships.
2. Explain how marketing adds value by creating several forms of utility.
3. Trace the development of the marketing concept and understand how it is implemented.
4. Understand what markets are and how they are classified.
5. Identify the four elements of the marketing mix and be aware of their importance in developing a marketing strategy.
6. Explain how the marketing environment affects strategic market planning.
7. Understand the major components of a marketing plan.
8. Describe how market measurement and sales forecasting are used.
9. Distinguish between a marketing information system and marketing research.
10. Identify the major steps in the consumer buying decision process and the sets of factors that may influence this process.

AP Photo/Charlie Riedel

inside business

DID YOU KNOW

Cirque employs 3,800 people to bring its 17 shows a year, all unique, to fruition.

Cirque du Soleil

Montreal-based Cirque du Soleil, the "circus of the sun," doesn't clown around with marketing. When Guy Laliberté started Cirque in 1984, his goal was to reinvent the circus with the help of a handful of street performers. Now Cirque has grown into a global business with $630 million in annual revenue. It employs 3,800 acrobats, dancers, artists, musicians, singers, choreographers, and other professionals who plan and stage 17 distinctly different shows every year.

Every Cirque show starts with an artistic vision and a specific set of financial objectives. For example, *Zed* is based on Tarot card characters, *Dralion* incorporates Chinese circus tradition, and *Love* revolves around well-known Beatles songs. The company invests as much as $200 million in creating a new production, which is why its marketing experts are always thinking about how to appeal to the audiences they want to attract.

Consider the marketing for *Love*, which is performed at the Mirage Hotel in Las Vegas. "Putting *Lucy in the Sky with Diamonds* together with our acrobats and theater was an industry first," explains Cirque's senior vice president of marketing. "What we also managed to do with marketing was to create enough curiosity that Beatles fans new to the Cirque brand also found us."

Before *Love* opened, Cirque captured media attention by throwing a gala party attended by Sir Paul McCartney, Ringo Starr, and other rock stars of the Beatles era. Cirque also promoted the show to Las Vegas visitors with a heavy schedule of radio, television, and print advertising, plus a colorful banner that remained wrapped around the 30-story Mirage hotel for nearly a year. Finally, Cirque marketers boosted online ticket sales by posting snippets of *Love* footage on the company's website.

Over the years, no two Cirque shows have been marketed in exactly the same way. "Each of our shows is marketed independently, as if they were not part of a bigger partnership," Cirque's top marketer says. "We find it keeps everyone on their toes, to compete to get the most visitors into seats."[1]

Numerous organizations, like Cirque du Soleil, use marketing efforts to provide customer satisfaction and value. Understanding customers' needs, such as "what's cool," is crucial to providing customer satisfaction. Although marketing encompasses a diverse set of decisions and activities performed by individuals and by both business and nonbusiness organizations, marketing always begins and ends with the customer. The American Marketing Association defines **marketing** as "The activity, set of institutions, and processes for creating, communicating, delivering, and exchanging offerings that have value for customers, clients, partners, and society at large."[2] The marketing process involves eight major functions and numerous related activities (see Table 12.1). All these functions are essential if the marketing process is to be effective.

marketing the activity, set of institutions, and processes for creating, communicating, delivering, and exchanging offerings that have value for customers, clients, partners, and society at large

In this chapter, we examine marketing activities that add value to products. We trace the evolution of the marketing concept and describe how organizations practice it. Next, our focus shifts to market classifications and marketing strategy. We analyze the four elements of a marketing mix and also discuss uncontrollable factors in the marketing environment. Then we examine the major components of a marketing plan. We consider tools for strategic market planning, including market

Table 12.1: Major Marketing Functions

Exchange functions: All companies—manufacturers, wholesalers, and retailers—buy and sell to market their merchandise.

1. **Buying** includes obtaining raw materials to make products, knowing how much merchandise to keep on hand, and selecting suppliers.
2. **Selling** creates possession utility by transferring the title of a product from seller to customer.

Physical distribution functions: These functions involve the flow of goods from producers to customers. Transportation and storage provide time utility and place utility and require careful management of inventory.

3. **Transporting** involves selecting a mode of transport that provides an acceptable delivery schedule at an acceptable price.
4. **Storing** goods is often necessary to sell them at the best selling time.

Facilitating functions: These functions help the other functions take place.

5. **Financing** helps at all stages of marketing. To buy raw materials, manufacturers often borrow from banks or receive credit from suppliers. Wholesalers may be financed by manufacturers, and retailers may receive financing from the wholesaler or manufacturer. Finally, retailers often provide financing to customers.
6. **Standardizing** sets uniform specifications for products or services. Grading classifies products by size and quality, usually through a sorting process. Together, standardization and grading facilitate production, transportation, storage, and selling.
7. **Risk taking**—even though competent management and insurance can minimize risks—is a constant reality of marketing because of such losses as bad-debt expense, obsolescence of products, theft by employees, and product-liability lawsuits.
8. **Gathering market information** is necessary for making all marketing decisions.

measurement, sales forecasts, marketing information systems, and marketing research. Last, we look at the forces that influence consumer and organizational buying behavior.

Managing Customer Relationships

1

Learning Objective: Understand the meaning of *marketing* and the importance of management of customer relationships.

Marketing relationships with customers are the lifeblood of all businesses. Maintaining positive relationships with customers is an important goal for marketers. The term **relationship marketing** refers to "marketing decisions and activities focused on achieving long-term, satisfying relationships with customers." Relationship marketing continually deepens the buyer's trust in the company, which, as the customer's loyalty grows, increases a company's understanding of the customer's needs and desires. Successful marketers respond to customer needs and strive to continually increase value to buyers over time. Eventually, this interaction becomes a solid relationship that allows for cooperation and mutual trust. For example, Chico's, a specialty women's retailer, offers a Passport Program that gives members such benefits as monthly coupons, free shipping, and 5 percent off all future purchases. Once a customer has spent over $500 on Chico's merchandise with a Preliminary Passport card, they are eligible to be a member of the Passport Program. Borders likewise offers Borders Rewards, a card-based system that provides incentives for frequent shoppers. Such initiatives give stores the opportunity to build stronger relationships with customers.[3]

relationship marketing establishing long-term, mutually satisfying buyer-seller relationships

To build long-term customer relationships, marketers increasingly are turning to marketing research and information technology. **Customer relationship management (CRM)** focuses on using information about customers to create marketing strategies that develop and sustain desirable customer relationships. By increasing customer value over time, organizations try to retain and increase long-term profitability through customer loyalty.[4]

customer relationship management (CRM) using information about customers to create marketing strategies that develop and sustain desirable customer relationships

Managing customer relationships requires identifying patterns of buying behavior and using that information to focus on the most promising and profitable customers.[5] Companies must be sensitive to customers' requirements and desires and establish communication to build customers' trust and loyalty. In some instances, it may be more profitable for a company to focus on satisfying a valuable existing customer than to attempt to attract a new one who may never develop the same level of loyalty. This involves determining how much the customer will spend over his or her lifetime. The **customer lifetime value** is a combination of purchase frequency, average value of purchases, and brand-switching patterns over the entire

customer lifetime value a combination of purchase frequency, average value of purchases, and brand-switching patterns over the entire span of a customer's relationship with a company

span of a customer's relationship with a company.[6] However, there are also intangible benefits of retaining lifetime-value customers, such as their ability to provide feedback to a company and referring new customers of similar value. The amount of money a company is willing to spend to retain such customers is also a factor. In general, when marketers focus on customers chosen for their lifetime value, they earn higher profits in future periods than when they focus on customers selected for other reasons.[7] Because the loss of a potential lifetime customer can result in lower profits, managing customer relationships has become a major focus of marketers.

utility the ability of a good or service to satisfy a human need

form utility utility created by converting production inputs into finished products

place utility utility created by making a product available at a location where customers wish to purchase it

time utility utility created by making a product available when customers wish to purchase it

Utility: The Value Added by Marketing

2 Learning Objective: Explain how marketing adds value by creating several forms of utility.

possession utility utility created by transferring title (or ownership) of a product to a buyer

As defined in Chapter 8, **utility** is the ability of a good or service to satisfy a human need. A lunch at a Pizza Hut, an overnight stay at a Holiday Inn, and a Mercedes S500L all satisfy human needs. Thus, each possesses utility. There are four kinds of utility.

Form utility is created by converting production inputs into finished products. Marketing efforts may influence form utility indirectly because the data gathered as part of marketing research frequently are used to determine the size, shape, and features of a product.

The three kinds of utility that are created directly by marketing are place, time, and possession utility. **Place utility** is created by making a product available at a location where customers wish to purchase it. A pair of shoes is given place utility when it is shipped from a factory to a department store.

Time utility is created by making a product available when customers wish to purchase it. For example, Halloween costumes may be manufactured in April but not displayed until late September, when consumers start buying them. By storing the costumes until they are wanted, the manufacturer or retailer provides time utility.

Possession utility is created by transferring title (or ownership) of a product to a buyer. For a product as simple as a pair of shoes, ownership usually is transferred by means of a sales slip or receipt. For such products as automobiles and homes, the transfer of title is a more complex process. Along with the title to its products, the seller transfers the right to use that product to satisfy a need (see Figure 12.1).

Place, time, and possession utility have real value in terms of both money and convenience. This value is created and added to goods and services through a wide variety of marketing activities—from research indicating what customers want to product warranties ensuring that customers get what they pay for. Overall, these marketing activities account for about half of every dollar spent by consumers. When they are part of an integrated marketing program that delivers maximum utility to the customer, many would agree that they are worth the cost.

Place, time, and possession utility are only the most fundamental applications of marketing activities. In recent years, marketing activities have been influenced by a broad business philosophy known as the *marketing concept*.

INTRODUCING THE BEST WARRANTY COVERAGE IN THE BUSINESS.

The Chrysler Lifetime Powertrain Limited Warranty is the first to be offered by any automaker. Ever. Because with this warranty, you're covered, and it lasts for as long as you own your vehicle. OUR LIFETIME POWERTRAIN LIMITED WARRANTY IS THE ICING. OUR VEHICLES ARE THE CAKE. The big news is that this powertrain limited warranty applies to the vast majority of our great new Chrysler, Jeep, and Dodge vehicles.* So if you always wanted to leave civilization behind and explore the great outdoors in a Jeep Wrangler or a Patriot, our powertrain warranty goes with you. Or if you ever dreamed about cruising around town in the unmistakable Chrysler 300, relax. You won't be left stranded by a short-term powertrain warranty. Need a tough Dodge Ram truck for your job? You've got the peace of mind of knowing that our powertrain warranty is always there to keep you working. THE NEXT STEP IS SIMPLE. GET TO YOUR CHRYSLER, JEEP, OR DODGE DEALER TODAY. The only difficult decision you have to make is picking which great vehicle you want. For more information, visit your local dealer.

CHRYSLER chrysler.com Jeep jeep.com DODGE dodge.com

Building customer relationships. *Providing warranties that are "best in the business" can help Dodge build long-term customer relationships.*

PRNewsFoto/Chrysler Group

Jump-Starting Your Career

Are You a Future CMO?

The top rung on the marketing career ladder is chief marketing officer (CMO). How can you prepare yourself to move up in marketing?

- *Learn about the bottom line.* CMOs are held accountable for making marketing pay off in bottom-line results for the entire organization. So broaden your thinking beyond the marketing function and look at the big picture in your business.
- *Focus on customers.* Marketing connects the company to its customers. Therefore, a successful career in marketing depends on getting to know your customers and learning how to satisfy their needs. As a CMO, your customer knowledge will be indispensable to shaping and implementing companywide strategies for profitable growth.
- *Be service oriented.* Good service is vital to building long-term customer relationships. The CMO sets the tone, sets the standards, and ensures that everyone in the organization has a service orientation. A good first step, no matter where you are in the marketing hierarchy, is to deliver the very best service that you can.

Some CMOs move up even further, as when Reebok's CMO became its CEO. Where will a career in marketing take you?

Sources: Bill Heath, "Take Command of Service," *Advertising Age*, September 15, 2008, p. 16; Tom Agan and Iain Ellwood, "CMOs Must Be a Part of Cost-Cutting Talks," *Advertising Age*, July 28, 2008, p. 23; Jennifer Rooney, "As If You Didn't Know By Now, It's About the Bottom Line for CMOs," *Advertising Age*, May 5, 2008, p. 3; Eric Newman, "Chief Concern: Why There Are More CMOs," *Brandweek*, May 26, 2008, p. 6; "P&G Taps Exec to Head Marketing," *MMR*, August 11, 2008, p. 45.

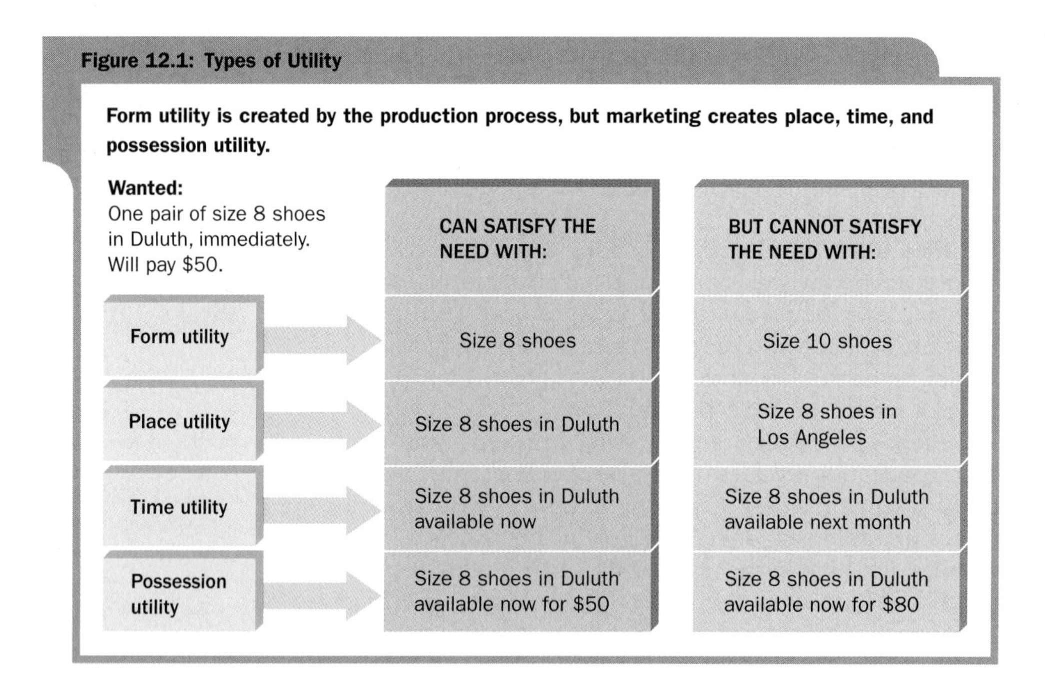

The Marketing Concept

3

Learning Objective: Trace the development of the marketing concept and understand how it is implemented.

marketing concept a business philosophy that a firm should provide goods and services that satisfy customers' needs through a coordinated set of activities that allows the firm to achieve its objectives

The **marketing concept** is a business philosophy that a firm should provide goods and services that satisfy customers' needs through a coordinated set of activities that allows the firm to achieve its objectives. Thus, initially, the firm must communicate with potential customers to assess their product needs. Then the firm must develop a good or service to satisfy those needs. Finally, the firm must continue to seek ways to provide customer satisfaction. This process is an application of the marketing concept, or marketing orientation. Ben & Jerry's, for example, constantly assesses customer demand for ice cream and sorbet. On its website, it maintains a "flavor graveyard" listing combinations that were tried and ultimately failed. It also notes its top ten flavors each month. Thus, the marketing concept emphasizes that marketing begins and ends with customers.

Evolution of the Marketing Concept

From the start of the Industrial Revolution until the early twentieth century, business effort was directed mainly toward the production of goods. Consumer demand for manufactured products was so great that manufacturers could almost bank on selling everything they produced. Business had a strong *production orientation,* in which emphasis was placed on increased output and production efficiency. Marketing was limited to taking orders and distributing finished goods.

In the 1920s, production caught up with and began to exceed demand. Now producers had to direct their efforts toward selling goods rather than just producing goods that consumers readily bought. This new *sales orientation* was characterized by increased advertising, enlarged sales forces, and occasionally, high-pressure selling techniques. Manufacturers produced the goods they expected consumers to want, and marketing consisted primarily of promoting products through personal selling and advertising, taking orders, and delivering goods.

During the 1950s, however, businesspeople started to realize that even enormous advertising expenditures and the most thoroughly proven sales techniques were not enough. Something else was needed if products were to sell as well as expected. It was then that business managers recognized that they were not primarily producers or sellers but rather were in the business of satisfying customers' needs. Marketers realized that the best approach was to adopt a customer orientation—in other words, the organization had to first determine what customers need and then develop goods and services to fill those particular needs (see Table 12.2).

All functional areas—research and development (R&D), production, finance, human resources, and of course, marketing—are viewed as playing a role in providing customer satisfaction.

Source: *BusinessWeek*.

Implementing the Marketing Concept

The marketing concept has been adopted by many of the most successful business firms. Some firms, such as Ford Motor Company and Apple Computer, have gone through minor or major reorganizations in the process. Because the marketing concept is essentially a business philosophy, anyone can say, "I believe in it." To make it work, however, management must fully adopt and then implement it.

To implement the marketing concept, a firm first must obtain information about its present and potential customers. The firm must determine not only what customers' needs are but also how well those needs are being satisfied by products currently on the market—both its own products and those of competitors. It must ascertain how its products might be improved and what opinions customers have about the firm and its marketing efforts.

Table 12.2: Evolution of Customer Orientation

Business managers recognized that they were not primarily producers or sellers but rather were in the business of satisfying customers' wants.

Production Orientation	Sales Orientation	Customer Orientation
Take orders	Increase advertising	Determine customer needs
Distribute goods	Enlarge sales force	Develop products to fill these needs
	Intensify sales techniques	Achieve the organization's goals

What do customers want? *Albertson's conducts customer surveys to help this company find out what customers want.*

The firm then must use this information to pinpoint the specific needs and potential customers toward which it will direct its marketing activities and resources. (Obviously, no firm can expect to satisfy all needs. And not every individual or firm can be considered a potential customer for every product manufactured or sold by a firm.) Next, the firm must mobilize its marketing resources to (1) provide a product that will satisfy its customers, (2) price the product at a level that is acceptable to buyers and that will yield an acceptable profit, (3) promote the product so that potential customers will be aware of its existence and its ability to satisfy their needs, and (4) ensure that the product is distributed so that it is available to customers where and when needed.

Finally, the firm again must obtain marketing information—this time regarding the effectiveness of its efforts. Can the product be improved? Is it being promoted properly? Is it being distributed efficiently? Is the price too high or too low? The firm must be ready to modify any or all of its marketing activities based on information about its customers and competitors. Toyota, for example, has taken the lead in the American automotive industry through its promise of high-quality yet sensible cars. But Toyota isn't satisfied with producing practical cars and is launching a new campaign to make consumers passionate about its product. Toyota is revamping its relationship with customers by forgoing traditional advertising and bringing its cars straight to the consumer. The Toyota Camry, the no. 1 selling car in America, is being redesigned to integrate a flashier grill and a sportier body to add fun to its proven quality. When the hybrid version of the new Camry debuts, Toyota will team up with medical doctors to promote the vehicle as asthma friendly. Toyota will test out its new FJ Cruiser sport-utility vehicle (SUV) at off-road and trail events instead of using more traditional television advertising. As for its truck line, Toyota will focus on fishing and hunting events.[8]

market a group of individuals or organizations, or both, that need products in a given category and that have the ability, willingness, and authority to purchase such products

Markets and Their Classification

4

Learning Objective: Understand what markets are and how they are classified.

A **market** is a group of individuals or organizations, or both, that need products in a given category and that have the ability, willingness, and authority to purchase such products. The people or organizations must want the product. They must be able to purchase the product by exchanging money, goods, or services for it. They must be willing to use their buying power. Finally, they must be socially and legally authorized to purchase the product.

Markets are broadly classified as consumer or business-to-business markets. These classifications are based on the characteristics of the individuals and organizations within each market. Because marketing efforts vary depending on the intended market, marketers should understand the general characteristics of these two groups.

One way to conserve precious natural resources is by signing up to stop unwanted catalogs and promotional mailings. The Direct Marketing Association, Catalog Choice, Green Dimes, and **41pounds.org** can alert marketers to take your name off mailing lists for goods and services that don't interest you. **www.DMAchoice.org, www.catalogchoice.org, www.greendimes.com, www.41pounds.org**

Consumer markets consist of purchasers and/or household members who intend to consume or benefit from the purchased products and who do not buy products to make profits. *Business-to-business markets,* also called *industrial markets,* are grouped broadly into producer, reseller, governmental, and institutional categories. These markets purchase specific kinds of products for use in making other products for resale or for day-to-day operations. *Producer markets* consist of individuals and business organizations that buy certain products to use in the manufacture of other products. *Reseller markets* consist of intermediaries such as wholesalers and retailers that buy finished products and sell them for a profit. *Governmental markets* consist of federal, state, county, and local governments. They buy goods and services to maintain internal operations and to provide citizens with such products as highways, education, water, energy, and national defense. Governmental purchases total billions of dollars each year. *Institutional markets* include churches, not-for-profit private schools and hospitals, civic clubs, fraternities and sororities, charitable organizations, and foundations. Their goals are different from such typical business goals as profit, market share, or return on investment.

marketing strategy a plan that will enable an organization to make the best use of its resources and advantages to meet its objectives

marketing mix a combination of product, price, distribution, and promotion developed to satisfy a particular target market

target market a group of individuals or organizations, or both, for which a firm develops and maintains a marketing mix suitable for the specific needs and preferences of that group

Developing Marketing Strategies

A **marketing strategy** is a plan that will enable an organization to make the best use of its resources and advantages to meet its objectives. A marketing strategy consists of (1) the selection and analysis of a target market and (2) the creation and maintenance of an appropriate **marketing mix**, a combination of product, price, distribution, and promotion developed to satisfy a particular target market.

Target Market Selection and Evaluation

A **target market** is a group of individuals or organizations, or both, for which a firm develops and maintains a marketing mix suitable for the specific needs and preferences of that group. In selecting a target market, marketing managers examine potential markets for their possible effects on the firm's sales, costs, and profits. The managers attempt to determine whether the organization has the resources to produce a marketing mix that meets the needs of a particular target market and whether satisfying those needs is consistent with the firm's overall objectives. They also analyze the strengths and numbers of competitors already marketing to people in this target market. Marketing managers may define a target market as a vast number of people or a relatively small group. Rolls-Royce, for example, targets its automobiles toward a small, very exclusive market: wealthy people who want the ultimate in prestige in an automobile. Other companies target multiple markets with different

Segmentation based on gender. *This product, Dove body wash, is aimed specifically at women.*

Courtesy Unilever United States, Inc.

Undifferentiated Approach. *The producer of Morton Salt uses an undifferentiated approach because people's needs for salt are homogeneous.*

products, prices, distribution systems, and promotion for each one. Nike uses this strategy, marketing different types of shoes to meet specific needs of cross-trainers, rock climbers, basketball players, aerobics enthusiasts, and other athletic-shoe buyers. When selecting a target market, marketing managers generally take either the undifferentiated approach or the market segmentation approach.

Undifferentiated Approach A company that designs a single marketing mix and directs it at the entire market for a particular product is using an **undifferentiated approach** (see Figure 12.2). This approach assumes that individual customers in the target market for a specific kind of product have similar needs and that the organization therefore can satisfy most customers with a single marketing mix. This single marketing mix consists of one type of product with little or no variation, one price, one promotional program aimed at everyone, and one distribution system to reach all customers in the total market. Products that can be marketed successfully with the undifferentiated approach include staple food items, such as sugar and salt, and certain kinds of farm produce. An undifferentiated approach is useful in only a limited number of situations because for most product categories, buyers have different needs. When customers' needs vary, a company should use the market segmentation approach.

undifferentiated approach directing a single marketing mix at the entire market for a particular product

Market Segmentation Approach A firm that is marketing forty-foot yachts would not direct its marketing effort toward every person in the total boat market. Some might want a sailboat or a canoe. Others might want a speedboat or an outboard-powered fishing boat. Still others might be looking for something resembling a small ocean liner. Marketing efforts directed toward such boat buyers would be wasted.

market segment a group of individuals or organizations within a market that shares one or more common characteristics

market segmentation the process of dividing a market into segments and directing a marketing mix at a particular segment or segments rather than at the total market

Instead, the firm would direct its attention toward a particular portion, or *segment,* of the total market for boats. A **market segment** is a group of individuals or organizations within a market that shares one or more common characteristics. The process of dividing a market into segments is called **market segmentation**. As shown in Figure 12.2, there are two types of market-segmentation approaches: concentrated and differentiated. When an organization uses *concentrated* market segmentation, a single marketing mix is directed at a single market segment. If *differentiated* market segmentation is employed, multiple marketing mixes are focused on multiple market segments.

In our boat example, one common characteristic, or *basis,* for segmentation might be "end use of a boat." The firm would be interested primarily in that market segment whose uses for a boat could lead to the purchase of a forty-foot yacht. Another basis for segmentation might be income; still another might be geographic location. Each of these variables can affect the type of boat an individual might purchase. When choosing a basis for segmentation, it is important to select a characteristic that relates to differences in people's needs for a product. The yacht producer, for example, would not use religion to segment the boat market because people's needs for boats do not vary based on religion.

Marketers use a wide variety of segmentation bases. Those bases most commonly applied to consumer markets are shown in Table 12.3. Each may be used as a single basis for market segmentation or in combination with other bases. Best Buy has used multiple bases for market segmentation, catering to customers based on their specific issues. The company classified its most profitable customers into one of

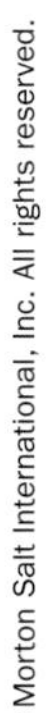

Figure 12.2: General Approaches for Selecting Target Markets

The undifferentiated approach assumes that individual customers have similar needs and that most customers can be satisfied with a single marketing mix. When customers' needs vary, the market segmentation approach—either concentrated or differentiated—should be used.

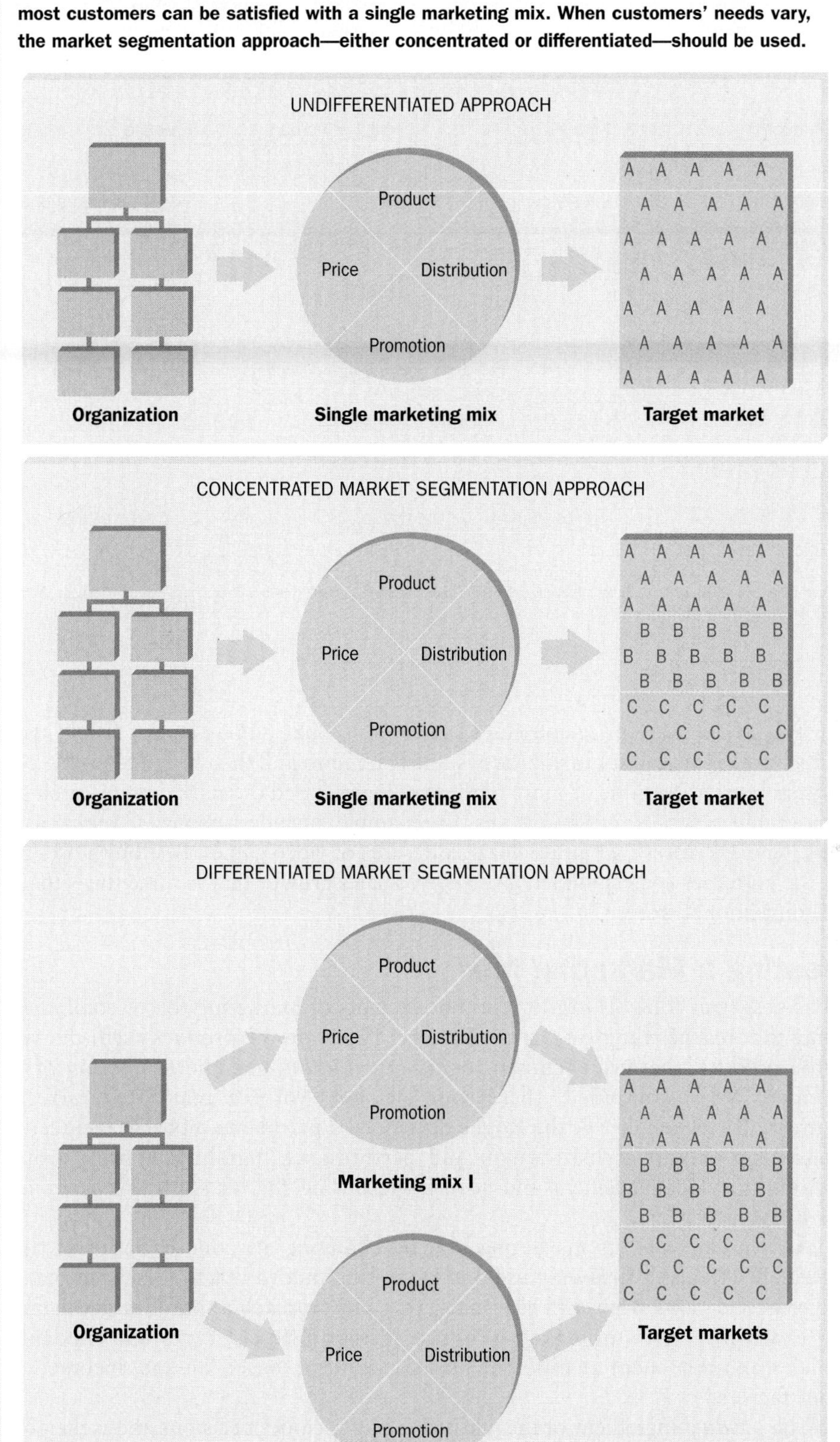

NOTE: The letters in each target market represent potential customers. Customers that have the same letters have similar characteristics and similar product needs.

Source: William M. Pride and O. C. Ferrell, *Marketing: Concepts and Strategies,* 15th ed. (Mason, Ohio: South-Western/Cengage Learning, 2010). Adapted with permission.

Table 12.3: Common Bases of Market Segmentation

Demographic	Psychographic	Geographic	Behavioristic
Age	Personality attributes	Region	Volume usage
Gender	Motives	Urban, suburban, rural	End use
Race	Lifestyles		Benefit expectations
Ethnicity		Market density	Brand loyalty
Income		Climate	Price sensitivity
Education		Terrain	
Occupation		City size	
Family size		County size	
Family life cycle		State size	
Religion			
Social class			

Source: William M. Pride and O. C. Ferrell, *Marketing: Concepts and Strategies,* 15th ed. (Mason, Ohio: South-Western/Cengage Learning, 2010). Adapted with permission.

four typologies: Ray (price-conscious family guy), Buzz (young gadget fiend), Barry (affluent tech enthusiast), or Jill (busy suburban mom) and then began retooling each of its stores to target one or more of the typologies based on marketing research and demographics. Stores that target Jills, for example, include personal shopping assistants, whereas stores that target Buzzes offer lots of video games. Best Buy stores that use the customer-centric model have enjoyed sales growth that is three times that of the conventional stores.[9]

5

Learning Objective: Identify the four elements of the marketing mix and be aware of their importance in developing a marketing strategy.

Creating a Marketing Mix

A business firm controls four important elements of marketing that it combines in a way that reaches the firm's target market. These are the *product* itself, the *price* of the product, the means chosen for its *distribution*, and the *promotion* of the product. When combined, these four elements form a marketing mix (see Figure 12.3). The maker of the Rogue developed a marketing mix that included an economical engine, stylish design, and performance handling; a price around $20,000; product placement and advertising during the hit show *Heroes;* and a five-car giveaway.[10]

A firm can vary its marketing mix by changing any one or more of these ingredients. Thus, a firm may use one marketing mix to reach one target market and a second, somewhat different marketing mix to reach another target market. For example, most automakers produce several different types and models of vehicles and aim them at different market segments based on age, income, and other factors.

The *product* ingredient of the marketing mix includes decisions about the product's design, brand name, packaging, warranties, and the like. When McDonald's decides on brand names, package designs, sizes of orders, flavors of sauces, and recipes, these choices are all part of the product ingredient.

The *pricing* ingredient is concerned with both base prices and discounts of various kinds. Pricing decisions are intended to achieve particular goals, such as to maximize profit or even to make room for new models. The rebates offered by automobile manufacturers are a pricing strategy developed to boost low auto sales. Product and pricing are discussed in detail in Chapter 13.

The *distribution* ingredient involves not only transportation and storage but also the selection of intermediaries. How many levels of intermediaries should be used in the distribution of a particular product? Should the product be distributed as widely as possible? Or should distribution be restricted to a few specialized outlets in each area? These and other questions related to distribution are considered in Chapter 14.

The *promotion* ingredient focuses on providing information to target markets. The major forms of promotion are advertising, personal selling, sales promotion, and public relations. These four forms are discussed in Chapter 15.

These ingredients of the marketing mix are controllable elements. A firm can vary each of them to suit its organizational goals, marketing goals, and target markets. As we extend our discussion of marketing strategy, we will see that the marketing environment includes a number of *uncontrollable* elements.

SPOTLIGHT

Coffee Habit Not Hereditary?

Source: Data from National Coffee Association.

Marketing Strategy and the Marketing Environment

6

Learning Objective: Explain how the marketing environment affects strategic market planning.

The marketing mix consists of elements that a firm controls and uses to reach its target market. In addition, the firm has control over such organizational resources as finances and information. These resources, too, may be used to

Figure 12.3: The Marketing Mix and the Marketing Environment

The marketing mix consists of elements that the firm controls—product, price, distribution, and promotion. The firm generally has no control over forces in the marketing environment.

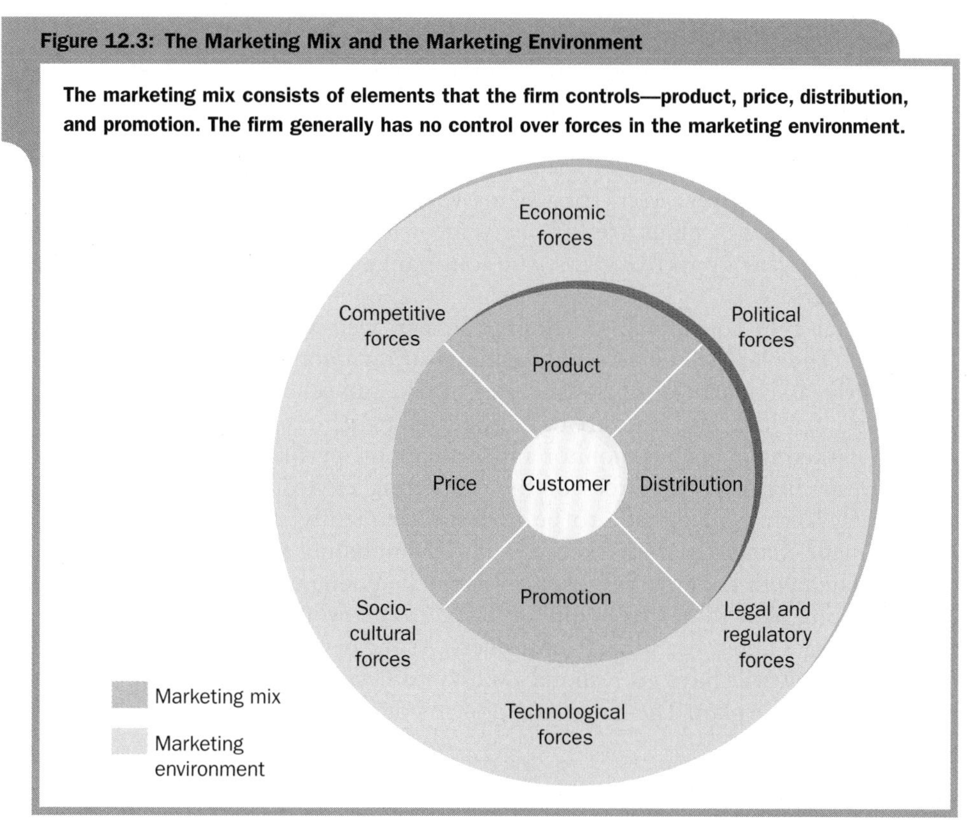

Source: William M. Pride and O. C. Ferrell, *Marketing: Concepts and Strategies*, 15th ed. (Mason Ohio: South-Western/Cengage Learning, 2010). Adapted with permission.

accomplish marketing goals. However, the firm's marketing activities are also affected by a number of external—and generally uncontrollable—forces. As Figure 12.3 illustrates, the forces that make up the external *marketing environment* are

- *Economic forces*—the effects of economic conditions on customers' ability and willingness to buy
- *Sociocultural forces*—influences in a society and its culture that result in changes in attitudes, beliefs, norms, customs, and lifestyles
- *Political forces*—influences that arise through the actions of elected and appointed officials
- *Competitive forces*—the actions of competitors, who are in the process of implementing their own marketing plans
- *Legal and regulatory forces*—laws that protect consumers and competition and government regulations that affect marketing
- *Technological forces*—technological changes that, on the one hand, can create new marketing opportunities or, on the other, can cause products to become obsolete almost overnight

These forces influence decisions about marketing-mix ingredients. Changes in the environment can have a major impact on existing marketing strategies. In addition, changes in environmental forces may lead to abrupt shifts in customers' needs. For example, rising gasoline prices and declining sales of gas-guzzling models have led many automakers, including General Motors, Ford, and Chrysler, to make the improvement of vehicle fuel economy their highest priority. Likewise, Hertz introduced a new service called "Green Collection" that allows customers to rent more fuel-efficient vehicles.[11]

Developing a Marketing Plan

Learning Objective: Understand the major components of a marketing plan.

marketing plan a written document that specifies an organization's resources, objectives, strategy, and implementation and control efforts to be used in marketing a specific product or product group

A **marketing plan** is a written document that specifies an organization's resources, objectives, marketing strategy, and implementation and control efforts to be used in marketing a specific product or product group. The marketing plan describes the firm's current position or situation, establishes marketing objectives for the product, and specifies how the organization will attempt to achieve these objectives. Marketing plans vary with respect to the time period involved. Short-range plans are for one year or less, medium-range plans cover from over one year up to five years, and long-range plans cover periods of more than five years.

Although time-consuming, developing a clear, well-written marketing plan is important. The plan will be used for communication among the firm's employees. It covers the assignment of responsibilities, tasks, and schedules for implementation. It specifies how resources are to be allocated to achieve marketing objectives. It helps marketing managers monitor and evaluate the performance of the marketing strategy. Because the forces of the marketing environment are subject to change, marketing plans have to be updated frequently. Disney, for example, recently made changes to its marketing plans by combining all activities and licensing associated with the Power Rangers, Winnie the Pooh, and Disney Princess into one marketing plan with a $500 million budget. The primary goal is to send consistent messages about branding to customers. As the new marketing plan is implemented, Disney will have to respond quickly to customers' reactions and make adjustments to the plan. The major components of a marketing plan are shown in Table 12.4.

Table 12.4: Components of the Marketing Plan

Plan Component	Component Summary	Highlights
Executive summary	One- to two-page synopsis of the entire marketing plan	
Environmental analysis	Information about the company's current situation with respect to the marketing environment	1. Assessment of marketing environment factors 2. Assessment of target market(s) 3. Assessment of current marketing objectives and performance
SWOT analysis	Assessment of the organization's strengths, weaknesses, opportunities, and threats	1. Strengths 2. Weaknesses 3. Opportunities 4. Threats
Marketing objectives	Specification of the firm's marketing objectives	Qualitative measures of what is to be accomplished
Marketing strategies	Outline of how the firm will achieve its objectives	1. Target market(s) 2. Marketing mix
Marketing implementation	Outline of how the firm will implement its marketing strategies	1. Marketing organization 2. Activities and responsibilities 3. Implementation timetable
Evaluation and control	Explanation of how the firm will measure and evaluate the results of the implemented plan	1. Performance standards 2. Financial controls 3. Monitoring procedures (audits)

Source: William M. Pride and O. C. Ferrell, *Marketing: Concepts and Strategies*, 15th ed. (Mason, Ohio: South-Western/Cengage Learning, 2010). Reprinted with permission.

sales forecast an estimate of the amount of a product that an organization expects to sell during a certain period of time based on a specified level of marketing effort

Market Measurement and Sales Forecasting

8

Learning Objective: Describe how market measurement and sales forecasting are used.

Measuring the sales potential of specific types of market segments helps an organization to make some important decisions. It can evaluate the feasibility of entering new segments. The organization also can decide how best to allocate its marketing resources and activities among market segments in which it is already active. All such estimates should identify the relevant time frame. As with marketing plans, these estimates may be short range, covering periods of less than one year; medium range, covering one to five years; or long range, covering more than five years. The estimates also should define the geographic boundaries of the forecast. For example, sales potential can be estimated for a city, county, state, or group of nations. Finally, analysts should indicate whether their estimates are for a specific product item, a product line, or an entire product category.

A **sales forecast** is an estimate of the amount of a product that an organization expects to sell during a certain period of time based on a specified level of marketing effort. Managers in different divisions of an organization rely on sales forecasts when they purchase raw materials, schedule production, secure financial resources, consider plant or equipment purchases, hire personnel, and plan inventory levels. Because the accuracy of a sales forecast is

Courtesy Irwin Research

Market information provider. *Many organizations, such as Irwin, provide information to help marketers develop, implement, and manage marketing strategies effectively.*

so important, organizations often use several forecasting methods, including executive judgments, surveys of buyers or sales personnel, time-series analyses, correlation analyses, and market tests. The specific methods used depend on the costs involved, type of product, characteristics of the market, time span of the forecast, purposes for which the forecast is used, stability of historical sales data, availability of the required information, and expertise and experience of forecasters.

Marketing Information

9 Learning Objective: Distinguish between a marketing information system and marketing research.

The availability and use of accurate and timely information are critical to making effective marketing decisions. A wealth of marketing information is obtainable. There are two general ways to obtain it: through a marketing information system and through marketing research.

Marketing Information Systems

marketing information system a system for managing marketing information that is gathered continually from internal and external sources

A **marketing information system** is a system for managing marketing information that is gathered continually from internal and external sources. Most of these systems are computer-based because of the amount of data the system must accept, store, sort, and retrieve. *Continual* collection of data is essential if the system is to incorporate the most up-to-date information.

In concept, the operation of a marketing information system is not complex. Data from a variety of sources are fed into the system. Data from *internal* sources include sales figures, product and marketing costs, inventory levels, and activities of the sales force. Data from *external* sources relate to the organization's suppliers, intermediaries, and customers; competitors' marketing activities; and economic conditions. All these data are stored and processed within the marketing information system. Its output is a flow of information in the form that is most useful for making marketing decisions. This information might include daily sales reports by territory and product, forecasts of sales or buying trends, and reports on changes in market share for the major brands in a specific industry. Both the information outputs and their form depend on the requirements of the personnel in the organization.

Marketing Research

marketing research the process of systematically gathering, recording, and analyzing data concerning a particular marketing problem

Marketing research is the process of systematically gathering, recording, and analyzing data concerning a particular marketing problem. Thus, marketing research is used in specific situations to obtain information not otherwise available to decision makers. It is an intermittent, rather than a continual, source of marketing information. JCPenney, for example, conducted extensive research to learn more about a core segment of shoppers who weren't being adequately reached by department stores: middle-income mothers between the ages of 35 and 54. The research involved asking 900 women about their casual clothes preferences. Later, the firm conducted in-depth interviews with 30 women about their clothing needs, feelings about fashion, and shopping experiences. The research helped the company recognize that this "missing middle" segment of shoppers was frustrated with the choices and quality of the clothing available in their price range and stressed out by the experience of shopping for clothes for themselves. Armed with this information, Penney launched two new lines of moderately priced, quality casual women's clothing, including one by designer Nicole Miller.[12] A study by SPSS Inc. found that the most common reasons for conducting marketing research surveys included determining satisfaction (43 percent); product development (29 percent); branding (23 percent); segmentation

(18 percent); awareness, trend tracking, and concept testing (18 percent); and business markets (11 percent).[13]

Table 12.5 outlines a six-step procedure for conducting marketing research. This procedure is particularly well suited to testing new products, determining various characteristics of consumer markets, and evaluating promotional activities. Food-processing companies, such as Kraft Foods and Kellogg's, use a variety of marketing research methods to avoid costly mistakes in introducing the wrong products or products in the wrong way or at the wrong time. They have been particularly interested in using marketing research to learn more about the African-American and Hispanic markets. Understanding of the food preferences, loyalties, and purchase motivators of these groups enables these companies to serve them better.

Using Technology to Gather and Analyze Marketing Information

Technology is making information for marketing decisions increasingly accessible. The ability of firms to track the purchase behaviors of customers electronically and to better determine what they want is changing the nature of marketing. The integration of telecommunications with computing technology provides marketers with access to accurate information not only about customers and competitors but also about industry forecasts and business trends. Among the communication tools that are radically changing the way marketers

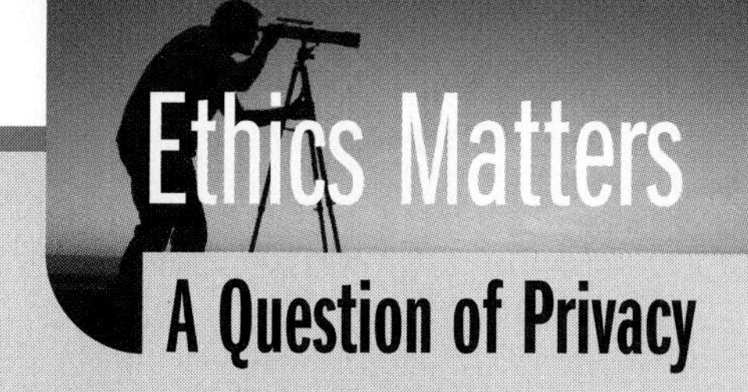

A Question of Privacy

Marketers are always looking for better ways to get the right offer to the right customer at the right time. But do today's highly targeted marketing techniques invade your privacy?

Many marketers use cookies to track where consumers go and what they do on the Internet. This enables marketers to personalize their websites and tailor advertising messages for individual consumers. However, privacy advocates worry about how much information is being collected, how it will be used, and for how long.

With the rise of social networking sites such as Facebook and MySpace, marketers are able to use "a new form of behavioral targeting—a kind of conversational eavesdropping analysis," says the director of the Center for Digital Democracy. Marketers can fine-tune their targeting by analyzing gender, age, and other personal details that participants post. One JCPenney online campaign presented dorm-room products to college students on Facebook.

Targeting is also getting more precise at the store level, now that millions of consumers have joined retailers' loyal shopper programs. Because the stores record what members buy, Nestlé and other marketers can tailor special offers to each customer's purchasing patterns—right at the checkout counter. Should marketers know so much about where you shop and what you buy?

Sources: David Kesmodel, "Personalized Store Ads Take Off," *Wall Street Journal*, October 23, 2008, **www.wsj.com**; Becky Ebenkamp, "Behavioral Targeting: A Tricky Issue for Marketers," *Brandweek*, October 21, 2008, **www.brandweek.com**; Rachel Metz, "MySpace Taps Small Businesses in Ad Money Quest," Associated Press, October 13, 2008, **ap.google.com**.

Table 12.5: The Six Steps of Marketing Research

1. Define the problem	In this step, the problem is stated clearly and accurately to determine what issues are involved in the research, what questions to ask, and what types of solutions are needed. This is a crucial step that should not be rushed.
2. Make a preliminary investigation	The objective of preliminary investigation is to develop both a sharper definition of the problem and a set of tentative answers. The tentative answers are developed by examining internal information and published data and by talking with persons who have some experience with the problem. These answers will be tested by further research.
3. Plan the research	At this stage, researchers know what facts are needed to resolve the identified problem and what facts are available. They make plans on how to gather needed but missing data.
4. Gather factual information	Once the basic research plan has been completed, the needed information can be collected by mail, telephone, or personal interviews; by observation; or from commercial or government data sources. The choice depends on the plan and the available sources of information.
5. Interpret the information	Facts by themselves do not always provide a sound solution to a marketing problem. They must be interpreted and analyzed to determine the choices available to management.
6. Reach a conclusion	Sometimes the conclusion or recommendation becomes obvious when the facts are interpreted. However, in other cases, reaching a conclusion may not be so easy because of gaps in the information or intangible factors that are difficult to evaluate. If and when the evidence is less than complete, it is important to say so.

Marketing research. *Marketing research service companies, such as Market Strategies, provide a variety of marketing research services to organizations that have information needs.*

Courtesy Market Strategies

obtain and use information are databases, online information services, and the Internet.

A *database* is a collection of information arranged for easy access and retrieval. Using databases, marketers tap into internal sales reports, newspaper articles, company news releases, government economic reports, bibliographies, and more. Many marketers use commercial databases, such as LEXIS-NEXIS, to obtain useful information for marketing decisions. Many of these commercial databases are available in printed form (for a fee), online (for a fee), or on purchasable CD-ROMs. Other marketers develop their own databases in-house. Some firms sell their databases to other organizations. *Reader's Digest,* for example, markets a database that provides information on 100 million households. Dunn & Bradstreet markets a database that includes information on the addresses, phone numbers, and contacts of businesses located in specific areas.

Information provided by a single firm on household demographics, purchases, television viewing behavior, and responses to promotions such as coupons and free samples is called *single-source data.* For example, Behavior Scan, offered by Information Resources, Inc., screens about 60,000 households in twenty-six U.S. markets. This single-source information service monitors household televisions and records the programs and commercials viewed. When buyers from these households shop in stores equipped with scanning registers, they present Hotline cards (similar to credit cards) to cashiers. This enables each customer's identification to be coded electronically so that the firm can track each product purchased and store the information in a database.

Online information services offer subscribers access to e-mail, websites, files for downloading (such as with Acrobat Reader), news, databases, and research materials. By subscribing to mailing lists, marketers can receive electronic newsletters and participate in online discussions with other network users. This ability to communicate online with customers, suppliers, and employees improves the capability of a firm's marketing information system and helps the company track its customers' changing desires and buying habits.

Table 12.6: Internet Sources of Marketing Information

Government Sources	Commercial Sources	Periodicals and Books
census.gov	acnielsen.com	adage.com
state.gov	usa.infores.com	salesandmarketing.com
fedworld.gov	gallup.com	Fortune.com
	arbitron.com	inc.com
	chamber-of-commerce.com	businessweek.com
	bloomberg.com	

Source: William M. Pride and O. C. Ferrell, *Marketing: Concepts and Strategies,* 15th ed. (Mason, Ohio: South-Western/Cengage Learning, 2010). Reprinted with permission.

The *Internet* has evolved as a powerful communication medium, linking customers and companies around the world via computer networks with e-mail, forums, Web pages, and more. Growth in Internet use has given rise to an entire industry that makes marketing information easily accessible to both companies and customers. Among the many Web pages useful for marketing research are the home pages of Nielsen marketing research and *Advertising Age.* While most Web pages are open to all Internet users, some companies, such as U.S. West and Turner Broadcasting System, also maintain internal Web pages, called *intranets,* that allow employees to access internal data and facilitate communication among departments.

Table 12.6 lists a number of websites that may serve as valuable resources for marketing research. The Bureau of the Census, for example, uses the Internet to disseminate information that may be useful to marketing researchers, particularly through the *Statistical Abstract of the United States* and data from the most recent Census. The "Census Lookup" option allows marketing researchers to create their own customized information. With this online tool, researchers can select tables by clicking boxes to select a state and then, within the state, the county, place, and urbanized area or metropolitan statistical area to be examined.

Types of Buying Behavior

10

Learning Objective: Identify the major steps in the consumer buying decision process and the sets of factors that may influence this process.

Buying behavior may be defined as the decisions and actions of people involved in buying and using products.[14] **Consumer buying behavior** refers to the purchasing of products for personal or household use, not for business purposes. **Business buying behavior** is the purchasing of products by producers, resellers, governmental units, and institutions. Since a firm's success depends greatly on buyers' reactions to a particular marketing strategy, it is important to understand buying behavior. Marketing managers are better able to predict customer responses to marketing strategies and to develop a satisfying marketing mix if they are aware of the factors that affect buying behavior.

buying behavior the decisions and actions of people involved in buying and using products

consumer buying behavior the purchasing of products for personal or household use, not for business purposes

business buying behavior the purchasing of products by producers, resellers, governmental units, and institutions

Consumer Buying Behavior

Consumers' buying behaviors differ when they buy different types of products. For frequently purchased low-cost items, a consumer employs routine response behavior involving very little search or decision-making effort. The buyer uses limited decision making for purchases made occasionally or when more information is needed about an unknown product in a well-known product category. When buying an unfamiliar, expensive item or one that is seldom purchased, the consumer engages in extensive decision making.

Going Global

Pho 24's Appetite for Global Competition

Even before they opened their first fast-food restaurant in Ho Chi Minh City in 2003, the co-founders of Pho 24 were already thinking about how to stay one step ahead of their future competitors. They recognized that the country's economic growth was bound to attract fast-food chains hungry for profitable new markets. In fact, although McDonald's is not yet represented in Vietnam, KFC now has more than 40 units there and Pizza Hut has three. Jollibee, a highly successful food company headquartered in the Philippines, is also opening hamburger restaurants in Vietnam.

AP Photo/Chitose Suzuki

But Pho 24 will be ready when expansion-minded multinational competitors start to flex their marketing muscles in Vietnam. Its hot noodle dishes are presented the same way in every Pho 24 outlet and are seasoned specifically for local tastes. What's more, its brightly lit restaurants all offer speedy table service, in contrast to the typical self-service model of multinational competitors. By fine-tuning its winning formula as it opens new outlets throughout Vietnam and beyond, Pho 24 will be even better prepared for the global fast-food fight it expects in the coming years.

Sources: James Hookway, "In Vietnam, Fast Food Acts Global, Tastes Local," *Wall Street Journal,* March 12, 2008, p. B1; James Hookway, "Philippines's Jollibee Goes Abroad," *Wall Street Journal,* June 6, 2008, p. B2; Becky Ebenkamp, "Jollibee Is on Fast (Food) Track in Virgin Markets," *Brandweek,* November 12, 2007, p. 14.

A person deciding on a purchase goes through some or all of the steps shown in Figure 12.4. First, the consumer acknowledges that a problem exists. A problem is usually the lack of a product or service that is desired or needed. Then the buyer looks for information, which may include brand names, product characteristics, warranties, and other features. Next, the buyer weighs the various alternatives he or

Figure 12.4: Consumer Buying Decision Process and Possible Influences on the Process

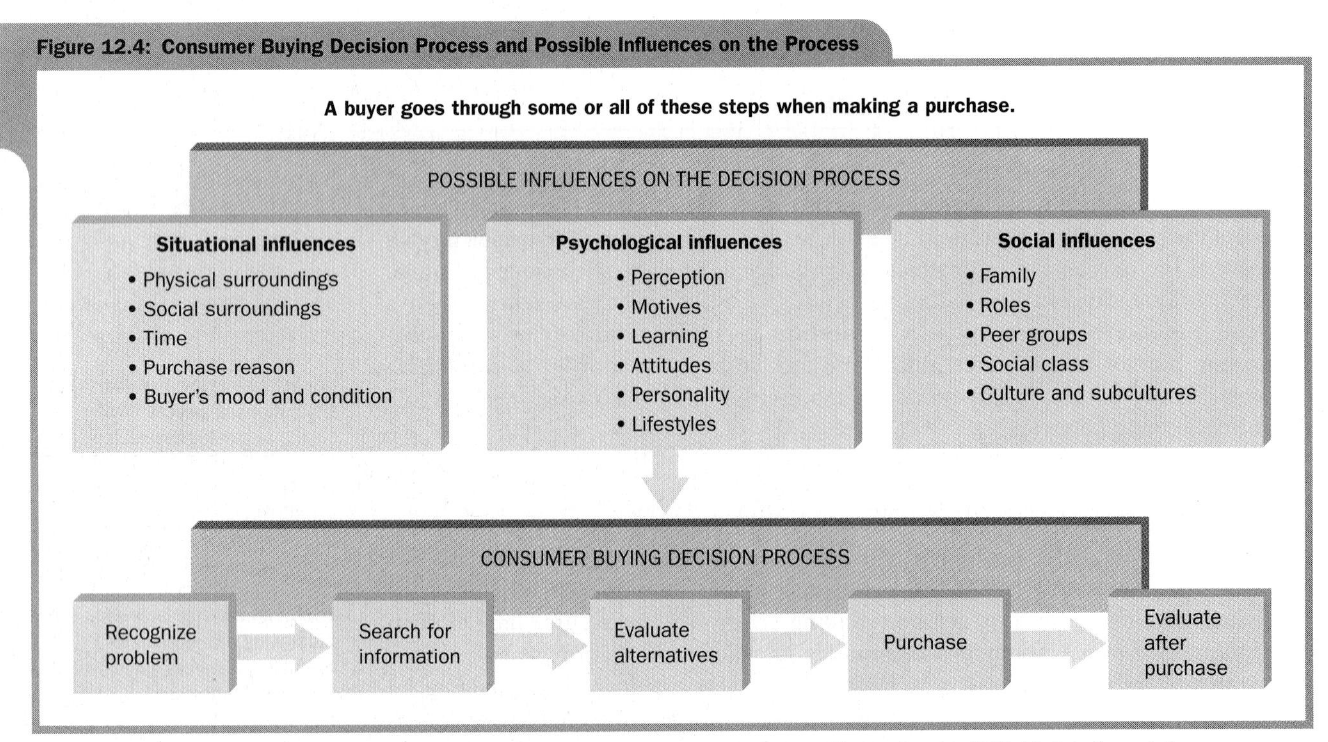

Source: William M. Pride and O. C. Ferrell, *Marketing: Concepts and Strategies,* 15th ed. (Mason, Ohio: South-Western/Cengage Learning, 2010). Adapted with permission.

she has discovered and then finally makes a choice and acquires the item. In the after-purchase stage, the consumer evaluates the suitability of the product. This judgment will affect future purchases. As Figure 12.4 shows, the buying process is influenced by situational factors (physical surroundings, social surroundings, time, purchase reason, and buyer's mood and condition), psychological factors (perception, motives, learning, attitudes, personality, and lifestyle), and social factors (family, roles, reference groups, online social networks, social class, culture, and subculture).

Consumer buying behavior is also affected by ability to buy or buying power, which is largely determined by income. As every taxpayer knows, not all income is available for spending. For this reason, marketers consider income in three different ways. **Personal income** is the income an individual receives from all sources *less* the Social Security taxes the individual must pay. **Disposable income** is personal income *less* all additional personal taxes. These taxes include income, estate, gift, and property taxes levied by local, state, and federal governments. About 3 percent of all disposable income is saved. **Discretionary income** is disposable income *less* savings and expenditures on food, clothing, and housing. Discretionary income is of particular interest to marketers because consumers have the most choice in spending it. Consumers use their discretionary income to purchase items ranging from automobiles and vacations to movies and pet food.

personal income the income an individual receives from all sources *less* the Social Security taxes the individual must pay

disposable income personal income *less* all additional personal taxes

discretionary income disposable income *less* savings and expenditures on food, clothing, and housing

Business Buying Behavior

Business buyers consider a product's quality, its price, and the service provided by suppliers. Business buyers usually are better informed than consumers about products and generally buy in larger quantities. In a business, a committee or group of people, rather than just one person, often decides on purchases. Committee members must consider the organization's objectives, purchasing policies, resources, and personnel. Business buying occurs through description, inspection, sampling, or negotiation. A number of organizations buy a variety of products online.

Recognizing a problem. *Some advertisements, such as this one for Ban deodorant, are aimed at a particular stage of the consumer buying-decision process. This Ban deodorant ad is meant to stimulate the problem-recognition stage of the buying-decision process.*

Courtesy KAO Brands Company

return to inside business

Cirque du Soleil

From *Alegria* to *Zumanity*, Cirque du Soleil's shows have reinvented the circus as multimedia entertainment and captured the imagination of audiences all over the world. Thanks to savvy marketing and positive word of mouth, Cirque shows often sell out quickly and play to packed theaters for years.

Each show's marketing plan calls for repaying its investment within a year or two. After that, the show will earn a profit even if it doesn't sell every ticket for every performance. Soon Cirque will have 23 shows running, each with a unique theme and creative marketing to match. And each new show gives Cirque new opportunities to expand its audience and build long-term profits.

Questions

1. How did Cirque du Soleil apply market segmentation to sell tickets to *Love*? What other bases for segmentation would you suggest for marketing *Love*?
2. What do you see as Cirque du Soleil's strengths, weaknesses, opportunities, and threats? How might this SWOT analysis influence its marketing of new shows?

CHAPTER REVIEW

Summary

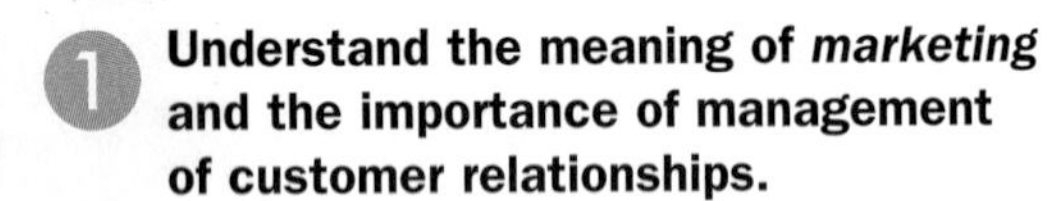

1 Understand the meaning of *marketing* and the importance of management of customer relationships.

Marketing is an organizational function and a set of processes for creating, communicating, and delivering value to customers and for managing customer relationships in ways that benefit the organization and its stakeholders. Maintaining positive relationships with customers is crucial. Relationship marketing is establishing long-term, mutually satisfying buyer-seller relationships. Customer relationship management uses information about customers to create marketing strategies that develop and sustain desirable customer relationships. Managing customer relationships requires identifying patterns of buying behavior and focusing on the most profitable customers. Customer lifetime value is a combination of purchase frequency, average value of purchases, and brand-switching patterns over the entire span of a customer's relationship with the company.

2 Explain how marketing adds value by creating several forms of utility.

Marketing adds value in the form of utility or the power of a product or service to satisfy a need. It creates place utility by making products available where customers want them, time utility by making products available when customers want them, and possession utility by transferring the ownership of products to buyers.

3 Trace the development of the marketing concept and understand how it is implemented.

From the Industrial Revolution until the early twentieth century, businesspeople focused on the production of goods; from the 1920s to the 1950s, the emphasis moved to the selling of goods. During the 1950s, however, businesspeople recognized that their enterprises involved not only producing and selling products but also satisfying customers' needs. They began to implement the marketing concept, a business philosophy that involves the entire organization in the dual processes of meeting the customers' needs and achieving the organization's goals.

Implementation of the marketing concept begins and ends with customers—first to determine what customers' needs are and later to evaluate how well the firm is meeting those needs.

4 Understand what markets are and how they are classified.

A market consists of people with needs, the ability to buy, and the desire and authority to purchase. Markets are classified as consumer and industrial (producer, reseller, governmental, and institutional) markets.

5 Identify the four elements of the marketing mix and be aware of their importance in developing a marketing strategy.

A marketing strategy is a plan for the best use of an organization's resources to meet its objectives. Developing a marketing strategy involves selecting and analyzing a target market and creating and maintaining a marketing mix that will satisfy that target market. A target market is chosen through either the undifferentiated approach or the market-segmentation approach. A market segment is a group of individuals or organizations within a market that have similar characteristics and needs. Businesses that use an undifferentiated approach design a single marketing mix and direct it at the entire market for a particular product. The market-segmentation approach directs a marketing mix at a segment of a market.

The four elements of a firm's marketing mix are product, price, distribution, and promotion. The product ingredient includes decisions about the product's design, brand name, packaging, and warranties. The pricing ingredient is concerned with both base prices and various types of discounts. Distribution involves not only transportation and storage but also the selection of intermediaries. Promotion focuses on providing information to target markets. The elements of the marketing mix can be varied to suit broad organizational goals, marketing objectives, and target markets.

6 Explain how the marketing environment affects strategic market planning.

To achieve a firm's marketing objectives, marketing-mix strategies must begin with an assessment of the marketing environment, which, in turn, will influence decisions about marketing-mix ingredients. Marketing activities are affected by a number of external forces that make up the marketing environment. These forces include economic forces, sociocultural forces, political forces, competitive forces, legal and regulatory forces, and technological forces. Economic forces affect customers' ability and willingness to buy. Sociocultural forces are societal and cultural factors, such as attitudes, beliefs, and lifestyles, that affect customers' buying choices. Political forces and legal and regulatory forces influence marketing planning through laws that protect consumers and regulate competition. Competitive forces are the actions of competitors who are implementing their own marketing plans. Technological forces can create new marketing opportunities or quickly cause a product to become obsolete.

7 Understand the major components of a marketing plan.

A marketing plan is a written document that specifies an organization's resources, objectives, strategy, and implementation and control efforts to be used in marketing a specific product or product group. The marketing plan describes a firm's current position, establishes marketing objectives, and specifies the methods the organization will use to achieve these objectives. Marketing plans can be short range, covering one year or less; medium range, covering two to five years; or long range, covering periods of more than five years.

8 Describe how market measurement and sales forecasting are used.

Market measurement and sales forecasting are used to estimate sales potential and predict product sales in specific market segments.

9 Distinguish between a marketing information system and marketing research.

Strategies are monitored and evaluated through marketing research and the marketing information system that stores and processes internal and external data in a form that aids marketing decision making. A marketing information system is a system for managing marketing information that is gathered continually from internal and external sources. Marketing research is the process of systematically gathering, recording, and analyzing data concerning a particular marketing problem. It is an intermittent rather than a continual source of marketing information. Technology is making information for marketing decisions more accessible. Electronic communication tools can be very useful for accumulating accurate information with minimal customer interaction. Information technologies that are changing the way marketers obtain and use information are databases, online information services, and the Internet.

10 Identify the major steps in the consumer buying decision process and the sets of factors that may influence this process.

Buying behavior consists of the decisions and actions of people involved in buying and using products. Consumer buying behavior refers to the purchase of products for personal or household use. Organizational buying behavior is the purchase of products by producers, resellers, governments, and institutions. Understanding buying behavior helps marketers to predict how buyers will respond to marketing strategies. The consumer buying decision process consists of five steps, including recognizing the problem, searching for information, evaluating alternatives, purchasing, and evaluating after purchase. Factors affecting the consumer buying decision process fall into three categories: situational influences, psychological influences, and social influences.

Key Terms

You should now be able to define and give an example relevant to each of the following terms:

marketing (339)
relationship marketing (340)
customer relationship management (CRM) (340)
customer lifetime value (340)
utility (341)
form utility (341)
place utility (341)
time utility (341)
possession utility (341)
marketing concept (342)
market (344)
marketing strategy (345)
marketing mix (345)
target market (345)
undifferentiated approach (346)
market segment (346)
market segmentation (346)
marketing plan (350)
sales forecast (351)
marketing information system (352)
marketing research (352)
buying behavior (355)
consumer buying behavior (355)
business buying behavior (355)
personal income (357)
disposable income (357)
discretionary income (357)

Review Questions

1. How, specifically, does marketing create place, time, and possession utility?
2. What is relationship marketing?
3. How is a marketing-oriented firm different from a production-oriented firm or a sales-oriented firm?
4. What are the major requirements for a group of individuals and organizations to be a market? How does a consumer market differ from a business-to-business market?
5. What are the major components of a marketing strategy?
6. What is the purpose of market segmentation? What is the relationship between market segmentation and the selection of target markets?
7. What are the four elements of the marketing mix? In what sense are they "controllable"?
8. Describe the forces in the marketing environment that affect an organization's marketing decisions.
9. What is a marketing plan, and what are its major components?
10. What major issues should be specified before conducting a sales forecast?
11. What is the difference between a marketing information system and a marketing research project? How might the two be related?
12. What new information technologies are changing the ways that marketers keep track of business trends and customers?
13. Why do marketers need to understand buying behavior?
14. How are personal income, disposable income, and discretionary income related? Which is the best indicator of consumer purchasing power?

Discussion Questions

1. Are there any problems for a company that focuses mainly on the most profitable customers?
2. In what way is each of the following a marketing activity?
   a. The provision of sufficient parking space for customers at a suburban shopping mall
   b. The purchase by a clothing store of seven dozen sweaters in assorted sizes and colors
   c. The inclusion of a longer and more comprehensive warranty on an automobile
3. How might adoption of the marketing concept benefit a firm? How might it benefit the firm's customers?
4. Is marketing information as important to small firms as it is to larger firms? Explain.
5. How does the marketing environment affect a firm's marketing strategy?

Video Case 12.1

Harley-Davidson: More Than Just a Motorcycle

Harley-Davidson's customers can spot each other instantly by the iconic black, white, and orange logo on their motorcycles, clothing, and saddlebags. More than a century after the first Harley-Davidson motorcycle hit the road, the company's annual worldwide sales have zoomed past $5 billion. Harley-Davidson dominates the U.S. motorcycle market, and sales are also strong in Japan and Europe. Its annual output of 300,000 motorcycles covers 31 models in five product lines (Sportster, Dyna, Softail, VRSA, and Touring).

Although Harley-Davidson teetered on the brink of bankruptcy in the 1980s, it has roared back by limiting production to focus on a consistently high level of quality. Many of its newer products marry the brand's image of freedom and individuality to motorcycles with styling, performance, and features that appeal to younger buyers and women buyers. To attract first-time buyers as well as experienced riders trading up to better bikes, Harley-Davidson prices its motorcycles starting at $6,695 and offers financing and insurance, as well. Each model's price depends on its specific combination of features and styling.

Buyers can also order limited-edition motorcycles custom built with distinctive paint designs and accessories. Customers see their bikes as a way of expressing their individuality. However, Harley-Davidson selects only a small number of orders annually for custom-built bikes. Not surprisingly, these custom products are in high demand.

To encourage the next generation of biking enthusiasts to learn to drive a motorcycle and then buy the Harley-Davidson bike of their dreams, many of the company's dealers offer the Rider's Edge driving course. Since 2000, when the course was first offered, nearly 140,000 people have graduated and earned a motorcycle license. The Rider's Edge also helps experienced riders to hone their driving skills and learn special techniques for riding in groups.

Group riding is such an important part of the overall product experience that the company founded the Harley Owners Group (HOG) to foster a sense of community among its customers. Today, the 1 million HOG members enjoy benefits such as access to dozens of exclusive group rides, a special customer service hotline, and a members-only website. They also receive two magazines: *Hog Tales,* with articles about members and member events, and *Enthusiast,* with articles about Harley-Davidson's goods and services. In addition, customers can use the Harley-Davidson website to plan travel, book hotels, rent bikes, or ship their bikes for their next riding adventure.

Knowing that customers are passionate about motorcycles and about Harley-Davidson in particular, the company arranges tours at four of its factories in Wisconsin, Pennsylvania, and Missouri. It recently opened the Harley-Davidson Museum in Milwaukee, Wisconsin, home of its headquarters, with 130,000 square feet of exhibits. Many of the exhibits feature products from Harley-Davidson's past, including a sample of the bikes, boats, golf carts, and snowmobiles the company once manufactured. Museum-goers can get a taste of the Harley experience by climbing onto one of the company's current bikes for a virtual ride through beautiful country scenery projected on a big screen.

The museum also looks ahead by highlighting Harley-Davidson's latest technology, its newest engines, and the inner workings of its new-product development process. One exhibit shows how a new motorcycle starts life as a sketch, is transformed into a clay model, becomes a testable prototype, and ultimately enters full production. "In creating this museum, we wanted to make sure that it told an evolving story," says the museum director. "We have a rich heritage, but we also have an exciting future."[15]

For more information about this company, go to **www.harley-davidson.com**.

Questions

1. Why would Harley-Davidson put as much emphasis on consistency of quality as it does on level of quality?
2. How does Harley-Davidson use customer services to differentiate its motorcycle products?
3. What role do you think the Harley-Davidson Museum might play in influencing how consumers perceive the company and its products?

Case 12.2

IKEA Targets Do-It Yourselfers

Every day, more than 1 million customers visit IKEA stores worldwide to buy everything from beds and baskets to bookcases and bathmats. The Swedish-based retailer has grown to more than 225 stores worldwide with annual sales of $18 billion by offering 7,000 home furnishings that are well designed, functional, and affordably priced. Its customers like the contemporary look of IKEA's products—and they don't mind assembling their purchases to save money.

IKEA is always driving costs down in manufacturing, marketing, warehousing, and raw materials so that it can pass the savings along to customers. Year after year, the retailer lowers its prices by an average of 2 to 3 percent by buying in bulk, searching for the most efficient suppliers, and sticking to simple, contemporary styles. For a company that buys from 1,700 suppliers, including some that are thousands of miles from company headquarters, even small efficiencies quickly add up to significant savings.

Although IKEA's customers are frugal, they want fashionable furniture that fits their personalities and lifestyles. In fact, the store's appeal cuts across demographic lines. Some customers who can well afford to shop at posh emporiums come to IKEA because they like the combination of chic design, down-to-earth functionality, and speedy assembly. Any item that must be assembled at home is accompanied by clear step-by-step instructions and illustrations, reassuring to even the most inexperienced do-it-yourselfer.

Customers in many countries have responded enthusiastically to IKEA's formula. After expanding beyond Sweden to Norway and Denmark, the company opened stores in Europe, Australia, and North America. More recently, IKEA has come to Russia, Japan, and China. By 2010, fifty IKEA stores will dot the United States from coast to coast.

Product names such as Billy bookcases and Klippan sofas are standard throughout the world and reflect the company's Swedish origins. However, IKEA's designers are careful to modify products for local tastes. "Americans want more comfortable sofas, higher-quality textiles, bigger glasses, more spacious entertainment units," says the head of IKEA North America. Designers and researchers visit customers' homes to observe how they use furniture. As a result, when IKEA makes bedroom furniture for the U.S. market, it adds deeper drawers because "Americans prefer to store most of their clothes folded," notes the product manager. In Europe, product measurements are provided in centimeters, whereas in the United States, measurements are provided in inches.

IKEA translates its catalogs into thirty-six languages and distributes 160 million copies every year. Here again, IKEA looks for ways to minimize expenses. It has all products photographed at a large European studio and transmits the images electronically to printing plants in the different regions where catalogs will be distributed, saving on shipping and mailing costs. Every detail, from paper quality to type size, is scrutinized to identify new cost efficiencies.

IKEA's formula of fashionable, affordable, and functional furniture has won it a loyal following. Customers have been known to line up a week ahead of opening day for a chance to win prizes and fifteen minutes of local fame as the first to see the new store. If customers get hungry while they shop, they can drop into the informal store restaurant for a quick snack or a light meal of Scandinavian delicacies. The most popular dish is Swedish meatballs: Customers devour 150 million of these tiny meatballs every year.

As popular as IKEA has become, CEO Anders Dahlvig sees plenty of room for growth because "awareness of our brand is much bigger than the size of our company." Still, no matter how large and fast IKEA grows, its focus will remain on keeping costs low to satisfy the target market's need for reasonably priced, well-designed assemble-it-yourself home furnishings.[16]

For more information about this company, go to **www.ikea.com**.

Questions

1. Is IKEA's targeting strategy concentrated or undifferentiated? Explain your answer.
2. Which of the variables for segmenting consumer markets is IKEA using, and why are these variables appropriate?
3. What combination of techniques might IKEA apply when preparing sales forecasts for North America?

Building Skills for Career Success

1. JOURNALING FOR SUCCESS

Discovery statement: This chapter emphasized the importance of keeping the customer at the core of every marketing decision.

Assignment

1. Think about the businesses from which you've purchased goods or services. Select the organization that you believe has adopted the marketing concept. Discuss the reasons why you believe that this company has adopted the marketing concept.
2. Describe the marketing mix this company has created for the brand that you purchase from this company.
3. Which two companies are the strongest competitors of this organization? Explain why.

4. Besides competition, which environmental forces have the greatest impact on this company for which you are a customer?
5. Calculate your customer lifetime value to this company. After recording your customer lifetime value, describe how you calculated it.

2. EXPLORING THE INTERNET

Consumer products companies with a variety of famous brand names known around the world are making their presence known on the Internet through websites and online banner advertising. The giants in consumer products include U.S.-based Procter & Gamble (**www.pg.com/**), Swiss-based Nestlé (**www.nestle.com/**), and British-based Unilever (**www.unilever.com/**).

According to a spokesperson for the Unilever Interactive Brand Center in New York, the firm is committed to making the Internet part of its marketing strategy. The center carries out research and development (R&D) and serves as a model for others now in operation in the Netherlands and Singapore. Information is shared with interactive marketers assigned to specific business units. Eventually, centers will be established globally, reflecting the fact that most of Unilever's $52 billion in sales takes place in about 100 countries around the world.

Unilever's view that online consumer product sales are the way of the future was indicated by online alliances established with Microsoft Network, America Online, and NetGrocer.com. Creating an online dialogue with consumers on a global scale is no simple task. Cultural differences often are subtle and difficult to explain but nonetheless are perceived by the viewers interacting with a site. Unilever's website, which is its connection to customers all over the world, has a global feel to it. The question is whether or not it is satisfactory to each target audience. Visit the text website for updates to this exercise.

Assignment

1. Examine the Unilever, Procter & Gamble, and Nestlé sites and describe the features that you think would be most interesting to consumers.
2. Describe those features you do not like and explain why.
3. Do you think that the sites can contribute to better consumer buyer behavior? Explain your thinking.

3. DEVELOPING CRITICAL-THINKING SKILLS

Market segmentation is the process of breaking down a larger target market into smaller segments. One common base of market segmentation is demographics. Demographics for the consumer market, which consists of individuals and household members who buy goods for their own use, include such criteria as age, gender, race, religion, income, family size, occupation, education, social class, and marital status. Liz Claiborne, Inc., retailer of women's apparel, uses demographics to target a market it calls *Liz Lady*. The company knows Liz Lady's age, income range, professional status, and family status, and it uses this profile to make marketing decisions.

Assignment

1. Identify a company that markets to the consumer.
2. Identify the company's major product.
3. Determine the demographics of one of the company's markets.
   a. From the list that follows, choose the demographics that apply to this market. (Remember that the demographics chosen must relate to the interest, need, and ability of the customer to purchase the product.)
   b. Briefly describe each demographic characteristic.

Consumer Market	Description
Age ________	________
Income ________	________
Gender ________	________
Race ________	________
Ethnicity ________	________
Income ________	________
Occupation ________	________
Family size ________	________
Education ________	________
Religion ________	________
Home owner ________	________
Marital status ________	________
Social class ________	________

4. Summarize your findings in a statement that describes the target market for the company's product.

4. BUILDING TEAM SKILLS

Review the text definitions of *market* and *target market*. Markets can be classified as consumer or industrial. Buyer behavior consists of the decisions and actions of those involved in buying and using products or services. By examining aspects of a company's products, you usually can determine the company's target market and the characteristics important to members of that target market.

Assignment

1. Working in teams of three to five, identify a company and its major products.
2. List and discuss characteristics that customers may find important. These factors may include price, quality, brand name, variety of services, salespeople, customer service, special offers, promotional campaign, packaging, convenience of use, convenience of purchase, location, guarantees, store/office decor, and payment terms.
3. Write a description of the company's primary customer (target market).

5. RESEARCHING DIFFERENT CAREERS

Before interviewing for a job, you should learn all you can about the company. With this information, you will be prepared to ask meaningful questions about the firm during the interview, and the interviewer no doubt will be impressed with your knowledge of the business and your interest in it. To find out about a company, you can conduct some market research.

Assignment

1. Choose at least two local companies for which you might like to work.
2. Contact your local Chamber of Commerce. (The Chamber of Commerce collects information about local businesses, and most of its services are free.) Ask for information about the companies.
3. Call the Better Business Bureau in your community and ask if there are any complaints against the companies.
4. Prepare a report summarizing your findings.

13 Creating and Pricing Products that Satisfy Customers

LEARNING OBJECTIVES

What you will be able to do once you complete this chapter:

1. Explain what a product is and how products are classified.
2. Discuss the product life cycle and how it leads to new product development.
3. Define *product line* and *product mix* and distinguish between the two.
4. Identify the methods available for changing a product mix.
5. Explain the uses and importance of branding, packaging, and labeling.
6. Describe the economic basis of pricing and the means by which sellers can control prices and buyers' perceptions of prices.
7. Identify the major pricing objectives used by businesses.
8. Examine the three major pricing methods that firms employ.
9. Explain the different strategies available to companies for setting prices.
10. Describe three major types of pricing associated with business products.

Imagechina via AP Images

inside business

DID YOU KNOW

The Flip offers customers a more permanent, shoot-and-share video camera that is fun, easy to use, and is small and light.

Millions Flip for the Flip

Pure Digital Technologies didn't invent the video camcorder, but it certainly revolutionized the industry when it introduced the Flip. Based in San Francisco, Pure Digital originally made small, one-time-use digital photo and video cameras. Over and over, it heard from customers that they wanted "a more permanent, shoot-and-share video camera that was fun and easy to use," says the company's founder and CEO. Based on this feedback, the founder challenged his product design team to create an inexpensive, small, light, basic camcorder without the fuss and features that can confuse new users.

To ensure that the Flip camcorder is always ready to record, the designers included digital storage for up to 60 minutes of video. Instead of having to insert or change a memory card, users just turn the Flip on and they can see exactly how many minutes of video time they have left to shoot. For point-and-shoot operation, the designers created a big red button to start or stop recording. The Flip includes video editing software plus a convenient flip-out USB connection for uploading videos to a computer. From there, videos can be e-mailed to others or posted on sites such as YouTube and MySpace. Or users can connect the Flip to a television for a quick and easy home-video show.

With 1 million sold in its first year, the Flip was an instant hit and allowed Pure Digital to capture 13 percent of the camcorder market. Despite intense competition from corporate giants such as Sony and Panasonic, Pure Digital has successfully captured more market share by improving on the basics in model after model. The Flip Mino, for example, was smaller and lighter than the first Flip or the second model, the Flip Ultra. Although future Flips will take better-quality videos, they will not have fancy frills or big price tags. "Most companies have a tendency to throw more and more in the product for new versions," says the founder, "and then it gets more complicated. I'm proud of our discipline."[1]

product everything one receives in an exchange, including all tangible and intangible attributes and expected benefits; it may be a good, service, or idea

A **product**, like the Flip camcorder, is everything one receives in an exchange, including all tangible and intangible attributes and expected benefits. An Apple iPod purchase, for example, includes not only the iPod itself but also earphones, instructions, and a warranty. A car includes a warranty, an owner's manual, and perhaps free emergency road service for a year. Some of the intangibles that may go with an automobile include the status associated with ownership and the memories generated from past rides. Developing and managing products effectively are crucial to an organization's ability to maintain successful marketing mixes.

A product may be a good, a service, or an idea. A *good* is a real, physical thing that we can touch, such as a Classic Sport football. A *service* is the result of applying human or mechanical effort to a person or thing. Basically, a *service* is a change we pay others to make for us. A real estate agent's services result in a change in the ownership of real property. A barber's services result in a change in your appearance. An *idea* may take the form of philosophies, lessons, concepts, or advice. Often ideas are included with a good or service. Thus, we might buy a book (a good) that provides ideas on how to lose weight. Or we might join Weight Watchers for ideas on how to lose weight and for help (services) in doing so.

We look first in this chapter at products. We examine product classifications and describe the four stages, or life cycle, through which every product moves. Next, we illustrate how firms manage products effectively by modifying or deleting existing products and by developing new products. We also discuss branding, packaging, and labeling of products. Then our focus shifts to pricing. We explain competitive factors that influence sellers' pricing decisions and also explore buyers' perceptions of prices. After considering organizational objectives that can be accomplished through pricing, we outline several methods for setting prices. Finally, we describe pricing strategies by which sellers can reach target markets successfully.

consumer product a product purchased to satisfy personal and family needs

business product a product bought for resale, for making other products, or for use in a firm's operations

Classification of Products

1

Learning Objective: Explain what a product is and how products are classified.

Different classes of products are directed at particular target markets. A product's classification largely determines what kinds of distribution, promotion, and pricing are appropriate in marketing the product.

Products can be grouped into two general categories: consumer and business (also called *business-to-business* or *industrial products*). A product purchased to satisfy personal and family needs is a **consumer product**. A product bought for resale, for making other products, or for use in a firm's operations is a **business product**. The buyer's use of the product determines the classification of an item. Note that a single item can be both a consumer and a business product. A broom is a consumer product if you use it in your home. However, the same broom is a business product if you use it in the maintenance of your business. After a product is classified as a consumer or business product, it can be categorized further as a particular type of consumer or business product.

convenience product a relatively inexpensive, frequently purchased item for which buyers want to exert only minimal effort

shopping product an item for which buyers are willing to expend considerable effort on planning and making the purchase

specialty product an item that possesses one or more unique characteristics for which a significant group of buyers is willing to expend considerable purchasing effort

Consumer Product Classifications

The traditional and most widely accepted system of classifying consumer products consists of three categories: convenience, shopping, and specialty products. These groupings are based primarily on characteristics of buyers' purchasing behavior.

A **convenience product** is a relatively inexpensive, frequently purchased item for which buyers want to exert only minimal effort. Examples include bread, gasoline, newspapers, soft drinks, and chewing gum. The buyer spends little time in planning the purchase of a convenience item or in comparing available brands or sellers.

A **shopping product** is an item for which buyers are willing to expend considerable effort on planning and making the purchase. Buyers allocate ample time for comparing stores and brands with respect to prices, product features, qualities, services, and perhaps warranties. Appliances, upholstered furniture, men's suits, bicycles, and cellular phones are examples of shopping products. These products are expected to last for a fairly long time and thus are purchased less frequently than convenience items.

A **specialty product** possesses one or more unique characteristics for which a group of buyers is willing to expend considerable purchasing effort. Buyers actually plan the purchase of a specialty product; they know exactly what they want and will not accept a substitute. In searching for specialty products, purchasers do not compare alternatives. Examples include unique sports cars, a specific type of antique dining table, a rare imported beer, or perhaps special handcrafted stereo speakers.

One problem with this approach to classification is that buyers may behave differently when purchasing a specific type of product. Thus, a single product can fit into more than one category. To minimize this problem, marketers think in terms of how buyers are most likely to behave when purchasing a specific item.

***Specialty products.** Most cars are classified as shopping products. However, a few automobiles, such as the Bentley, are extremely expensive, have distinctive styling and amenities, and are distributed exclusively through just a few dealers. These distinctive vehicles are specialty products.*

Courtesy Bentley Motors

Component part. *A computer chip is an example of a component part.*

raw material a basic material that actually becomes part of a physical product; usually comes from mines, forests, oceans, or recycled solid wastes

major equipment large tools and machines used for production purposes

accessory equipment standardized equipment used in a firm's production or office activities

component part an item that becomes part of a physical product and is either a finished item ready for assembly or a product that needs little processing before assembly

Business Product Classifications

Based on their characteristics and intended uses, business products can be classified into the following categories: raw materials, major equipment, accessory equipment, component parts, process materials, supplies, and services.

A **raw material** is a basic material that actually becomes part of a physical product. It usually comes from mines, forests, oceans, or recycled solid wastes. Raw materials usually are bought and sold according to grades and specifications.

Major equipment includes large tools and machines used for production purposes. Examples of major equipment are lathes, cranes, and stamping machines. Some major equipment is custom-made for a particular organization, but other items are standardized products that perform one or several tasks for many types of organizations.

Accessory equipment is standardized equipment used in a firm's production or office activities. Examples include hand tools, fax machines, fractional-horsepower motors, and calculators. Compared with major equipment, accessory items are usually much less expensive and are purchased routinely with less negotiation.

A **component part** becomes part of a physical product and is either a finished item ready for assembly or a product that needs little processing before assembly. Although it becomes part of a larger product, a component part often can be identified easily. Clocks, tires, computer chips, and switches are examples of component parts.

A **process material** is used directly in the production of another product. Unlike a component part, however, a process material is not readily identifiable in the finished product. Like component parts, process materials are purchased according to industry standards or to the specifications of the individual purchaser. Examples include industrial glue and food preservatives.

A **supply** facilitates production and operations but does not become part of a finished product. Paper, pencils, oils, and cleaning agents are examples.

A **business service** is an intangible product that an organization uses in its operations. Examples include financial, legal, online, janitorial, and marketing research services. Purchasers must decide whether to provide their own services internally or to hire them from outside the organization.

The Product Life Cycle

2

Learning Objective: Discuss the product life cycle and how it leads to new product development.

process material a material that is used directly in the production of another product but is not readily identifiable in the finished product

supply an item that facilitates production and operations but does not become part of a finished product

business service an intangible product that an organization uses in its operations

In a way, products are like people. They are born, they live, and they die. Every product progresses through a **product life cycle**, a series of stages in which a product's sales revenue and profit increase, reach a peak, and then decline. A firm must be able to launch, modify, and delete products from its offering of products in response to changes in product life cycles. Otherwise, the firm's profits will disappear, and the firm will fail. Depending on the product, life-cycle stages will vary in length. In this section, we discuss the stages of the life cycle and how marketers can use this information.

Stages of the Product Life Cycle

Generally, the product life cycle is assumed to be composed of four stages—introduction, growth, maturity, and decline—as shown in Figure 13.1. Some products progress through these stages rapidly, in a few weeks or months. Others may take years to go through each stage. The Rubik's Cube had a relatively short life cycle. Parker Brothers' Monopoly game, which was introduced over seventy years ago, is still going strong.

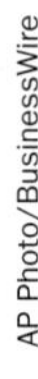
AP Photo/BusinessWire

product life cycle a series of stages in which a product's sales revenue and profit increase, reach a peak, and then decline

Figure 13.1: Product Life Cycle

The graph shows sales volume and profits during the life cycle of a product.

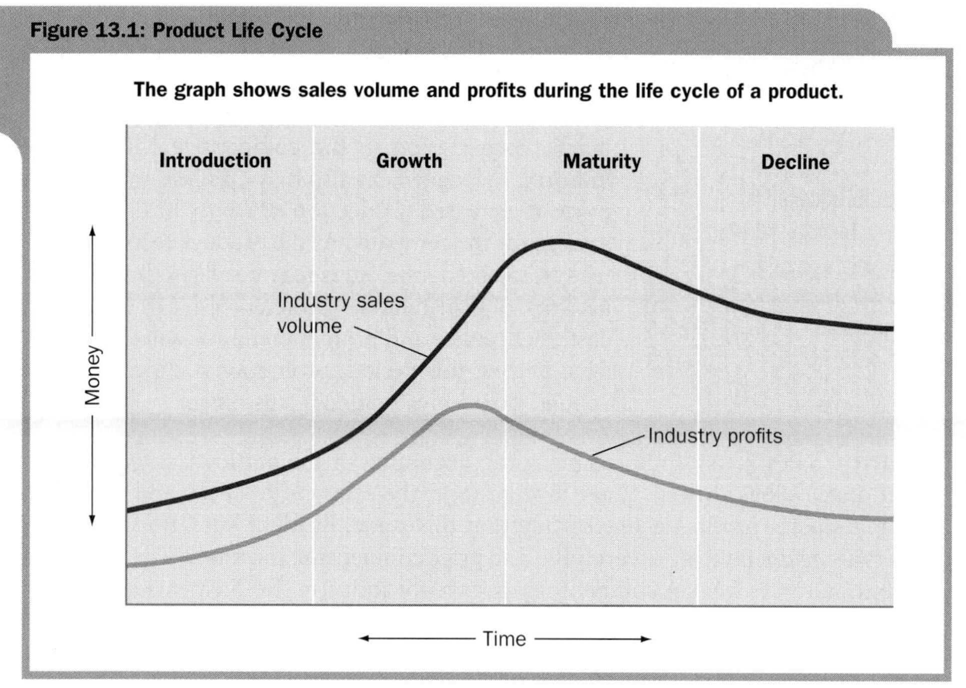

Source: William M. Pride and O. C. Ferrell, *Marketing: Concepts and Strategies,* 15th ed. (Mason, Ohio: South-Western/Cengage Learning, 2010). Adapted with permission.

Introduction In the *introduction stage,* customer awareness and acceptance of the product are low. Sales rise gradually as a result of promotion and distribution activities, but initially, high development and marketing costs result in low profit or even in a loss. There are relatively few competitors. The price is sometimes high, and purchasers are primarily people who want to be "the first" to own the new product. The marketing challenge at this stage is to make potential customers aware of the product's existence and its features, benefits, and uses.

A new product is seldom an immediate success. Marketers must watch early buying patterns carefully and be prepared to modify the new product promptly if necessary. The product should be priced to attract the particular market segment that has the greatest desire and ability to buy the product. Plans for distribution and promotion should suit the targeted market segment. As with the product itself, the initial price, distribution channels, and promotional efforts may need to be adjusted quickly to maintain sales growth during the introduction stage.

Growth In the *growth stage,* sales increase rapidly as the product becomes well known. Other firms probably have begun to market competing products. The competition and lower unit costs (owing to mass production) result in a lower price, which reduces the profit per unit. Note that industry profits reach a peak and begin to decline during this stage. To meet the needs of the growing market, the originating firm offers modified versions of its product and expands its distribution. The 3M Company, the maker of Post-it Notes, has developed a variety of sizes, colors, and designs.

Management's goal in the growth stage is to stabilize and strengthen the product's position by encouraging brand loyalty. To beat the competition, the company may further improve the product or expand the product line to appeal to additional market segments. Apple, for example, has introduced several variations of its wildly popular iPod MP3 player. The iPod Shuffle is the smallest and most affordable version, while the iPod Nano offers song, photo, and video support in a thin, lightweight version. The iPod Classic provides 120 GB of hard drive space, the most of any of the versions. The iPod Touch has a vibrant touch screen display and an additional Wi-Fi connection with a built-in map location-based service. Apple has expanded its iTunes Music Store to include downloadable versions of popular TV shows in high definition that can be purchased per episode or as an entire season, along with exclusive music video

Sustaining the Planet

Outdated, unusable, or unwanted cell phones and wireless devices can be recycled in earth-friendly ways. Recycle Wireless Phones explains step-by-step how to recycle your cell phone safely. Depending on the make, model, and condition, you can either donate or sell your old cell to ReCellular. **www.recyclewirelessphones.com, www.recellular.com**

downloads. Apple greatly expanded its product mix with the release of the iPhone, a combination iPod Touch and cell phone. Continuous product innovation and service expansion have helped to expand Apple's market penetration in the competitive MP3 player industry.[2] Management also may compete by lowering prices if increased production efficiency has resulted in savings for the company. As the product becomes more widely accepted, marketers may be able to broaden the network of distributors. Marketers also can emphasize customer service and prompt credit for defective products. During this period, promotional efforts attempt to build brand loyalty among customers.

Maturity Sales are still increasing at the beginning of the *maturity stage,* but the rate of increase has slowed. Later in this stage, the sales curve peaks and begins to decline. Industry profits decline throughout this stage. Product lines are simplified, markets are segmented more carefully, and price competition increases. The increased competition forces weaker competitors to leave the industry. Refinements and extensions of the original product continue to appear on the market.

During a product's maturity stage, its market share may be strengthened by redesigned packaging or style changes. Also, consumers may be encouraged to use the product more often or in new ways. Pricing strategies are flexible during this stage. Markdowns and price incentives are not uncommon, although price increases may work to offset production and distribution costs. Marketers may offer incentives and assistance of various kinds to dealers to encourage them to support mature products, especially in the face of competition from private-label brands. New promotional efforts and aggressive personal selling may be necessary during this period of intense competition.

Decline During the *decline stage,* sales volume decreases sharply. Profits continue to fall. The number of competing firms declines, and the only survivors in the marketplace are firms that specialize in marketing the product. Production and marketing costs become the most important determinant of profit.

When a product adds to the success of the overall product line, the company may retain it; otherwise, management must determine when to eliminate the product. A product usually declines because of technological advances or environmental factors or because consumers have switched to competing brands. Therefore, few changes are made in the product itself during this stage. Instead, management may raise the price to cover costs, reprice to maintain market share, or lower the price to reduce inventory. Similarly, management will narrow distribution of the declining product to the most profitable existing markets. During this period, the company probably will not spend heavily on promotion, although it may use some advertising and sales incentives to slow the product's decline. The company may choose to eliminate less profitable versions of the product from the product line or may decide to drop the product entirely. For example, although Procter & Gamble's Sure deodorant has been around for nearly three decades, sharply declining sales led the company to delete the product.[3]

Using the Product Life Cycle

Marketers should be aware of the life-cycle stage of each product for which they are responsible. And they should try to estimate how long the product is expected to remain in that stage. Both must be taken into account in making decisions about the marketing strategy for a product. If a product is expected to remain in the maturity stage for a long time, a replacement product might be introduced later in the maturity stage. If the maturity stage is expected to be short, however, a new product should be introduced much earlier. In some cases, a firm may be willing to take the chance of speeding up the decline of existing products. In other situations, a company will attempt to extend a product's life cycle. For example, General Mills has extended the life of Bisquick baking mix (launched in the mid-1930s) by improving the product's formulation significantly and creating and promoting a variety of uses.

Product Line and Product Mix

3

Learning Objective: Define *product line* and *product mix* and distinguish between the two.

A **product line** is a group of similar products that differ only in relatively minor characteristics. Generally, the products within a product line are related to each other in the way they are produced, marketed, or used. Procter & Gamble, for example, manufactures and markets several shampoos, including Prell, Head & Shoulders, and Ivory.

product line a group of similar products that differ only in relatively minor characteristics

Many organizations tend to introduce new products within existing product lines. This permits them to apply the experience and knowledge they have acquired to the production and marketing of new products. Other firms develop entirely new product lines.

product mix all the products a firm offers for sale

An organization's **product mix** consists of all the products the firm offers for sale. For example, Procter & Gamble, which acquired Gillette, has over 100 brands that fall into one of twenty-five product lines ranging from deodorants to paper products.[4] Two "dimensions" are often applied to a firm's product mix. The *width* of the mix is the number of product lines it contains. The *depth* of the mix is the average number of individual products within each line. These are general measures; we speak of a *broad* or a *narrow* mix rather than a mix of exactly three or five product lines. Some organizations provide broad product mixes to be competitive.

Managing the Product Mix

4

Learning Objective: Identify the methods available for changing a product mix.

To provide products that satisfy people in a firm's target market or markets and that also achieve the organization's objectives, a marketer must develop, adjust, and maintain an effective product mix. Seldom can the same product mix be effective for long. Because customers' product preferences and attitudes change, their desire for a product may diminish or grow. In some cases, a firm needs to alter its product mix to adapt to competition. A marketer may have to eliminate a product from the mix because one or more competitors dominate that product's specific market segment. Similarly, an organization may have to introduce a new product or modify an existing one to compete more effectively. A marketer may expand the firm's product mix to take advantage of excess marketing and production capacity. For example, both Coca-Cola and Pepsi have expanded their lines by adding to their existing brands and acquiring new brands as well. In response to the increasing popularity of energy drinks, Coca-Cola has acquired brands including AMP. In an effort to seem more health-conscious, both companies came out with new sugar-free or zero calorie soda products, along with more juice brands. Coca-Cola contains brands such as Minute Maid, Simply Orange, and FUZE, while Pepsi contains Tropicana, Ocean Spray, Dole, and SoBe. For tea and coffee brands, Coca-Cola has Nestea and Georgia coffee, while Pepsi has Lipton and a recent partnership with Starbucks. Both companies are also involved in the fast-growing sports drink category, with Coca-Cola's POWERADE and Pepsi's Gatorade among the top competitors. Coca-Cola even has a brand in the alcohol category: BACARDI Mixers.[5] For whatever reason a product mix is altered, the product mix must be managed to bring about improvements in the mix. There are three major ways to improve a product mix: change an existing product, delete a product, or develop a new product.

Managing Existing Products

A product mix can be changed by deriving additional products from existing ones. This can be accomplished through product modifications and by line extensions.

Multiple uses. *Natural Corn Cobs have multiple uses as litter or bedding for a variety of small animals.*

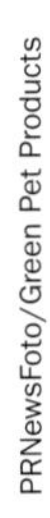

Product Modifications

Product modification refers to changing one or more of a product's characteristics. For this approach to be effective, several conditions must be met. First, the product must be modifiable. Second, existing customers must be able to perceive that a modification has been made, assuming that the modified item is still directed at the same target market. Third, the modification should make the product more consistent with customers' desires so that it provides greater satisfaction. For example, Energizer increased its product's durability by using better materials—a larger cathode and anode interface—that make batteries last longer.

Existing products can be altered in three primary ways: in quality, function, and aesthetics. *Quality modifications* are changes that relate to a product's dependability and durability and usually are achieved by alterations in the materials or production process. *Functional modifications* affect a product's versatility, effectiveness, convenience, or safety; they usually require redesign of the product. Typical product categories that have undergone extensive functional modifications include home appliances, office and farm equipment, and consumer electronics. *Aesthetic modifications* are directed at changing the sensory appeal of a product by altering its taste, texture, sound, smell, or visual characteristics. Because a buyer's purchasing decision is affected by how a product looks, smells, tastes, feels, or sounds, an aesthetic modification may have a definite impact on purchases. Through aesthetic modifications, a firm can differentiate its product from competing brands and perhaps gain a sizable market share if customers find the modified product more appealing.

product modification the process of changing one or more of a product's characteristics

line extension development of a new product that is closely related to one or more products in the existing product line but designed specifically to meet somewhat different customer needs

Line Extensions

A **line extension** is the development of a product closely related to one or more products in the existing product line but designed specifically to meet somewhat different customer needs. For example, Nabisco extended its cookie line to include Reduced Fat Oreos and Double Stuf Oreos.

Many of the so-called new products introduced each year are in fact line extensions. Line extensions are more common than new products because they are a less expensive, lower-risk alternative for increasing sales. A line extension may focus on a different market segment or be an attempt to increase sales within the same market segment by more precisely satisfying the needs of people in that segment. Line extensions are also used to take market share from competitors.

Deleting Products

product deletion the elimination of one or more products from a product line

To maintain an effective product mix, an organization often has to eliminate some products. This is called **product deletion**. A weak product costs a firm time, money, and resources that could be used to modify other products or develop new ones. Also, when a weak product generates an unfavorable image among customers, the negative image may rub off on other products sold by the firm.

Most organizations find it difficult to delete a product. Some firms drop weak products only after they have become severe financial burdens. A better approach is some form of systematic review of the product's impact on the overall effectiveness of a firm's product mix. Such a review should analyze a product's contribution to a company's sales for a given period. It should include estimates of future sales, costs, and profits associated with the product and a consideration of whether changes in the marketing strategy could improve the product's performance.

A product-deletion program definitely can improve a firm's performance. M&M Mars, for example, discontinued all but one variety of its M-Azing candy bar with embedded M&M candies after two years of disappointing performance. However, the company intends to rebrand the remaining M-Azing Crunchy Singles bar.[6]

Developing New Products

Developing and introducing new products is frequently time consuming, expensive, and risky. Thousands of new products are introduced annually. Depending on how we define it, the failure rate for new products ranges between 60 and 75 percent. Although developing new products is risky, failing to introduce new products can be just as hazardous. New products generally are grouped into three categories on the basis of their degree of similarity to existing products. *Imitations* are products designed to be similar to—and to compete with—existing products of other firms. Examples are the various brands of whitening toothpastes that were developed to compete with Rembrandt. *Adaptations* are variations of existing products that are intended for an established market. Product refinements and extensions are the adaptations considered most often, although imitative products also may include some refinement and extension. *Innovations* are entirely new products. They may give rise to a new industry or revolutionize an existing one. The introduction of CDs, for example, has brought major changes to the recording industry. Innovative products take considerable time, effort, and money to develop. They are therefore less common than adaptations and imitations. As shown in Figure 13.2, the process of developing a new product consists of seven phases.

Entrepreneurial Challenge

Big Product Ideas from Small Businesses

Big businesses are on the lookout for big new product ideas from small businesses. Even corporate giants such as Kraft, General Mills, and Procter & Gamble, which have strong track records in product development, are actively inviting the input and innovation of outside entrepreneurs.

Consider the story of Kraft's Bagel-Fuls, a bagel-like roll filled with Philadelphia Cream Cheese (also a Kraft product). Gary Schwartzberg invented an early version of this product but when he had difficulty getting national supermarket distribution, he sent samples to Kraft. Kraft's executives were so impressed that they negotiated an alliance with Schwartzberg's company. Working together, the partners spent two years developing, researching, refining, and test-marketing several flavors of Bagel-Fuls. Today, the product is available under the Kraft brand in supermarkets across the United States and in Canada.

Kraft has also set up an "innovate with Kraft" web site to solicit ideas for new products and new packaging. "We realize there's a very large body of innovators outside of Kraft," says the vice president for open innovation and investment. "The world has gotten much smaller, and innovation is happening at small businesses."

Sources: Simona Covel, "Running the Show: My Brain, Your Brawn," *Wall Street Journal*, October 13, 2008, p. R12; Anjali Cordeiro, "P&G Looks Outside for Ideas," *Wall Street Journal*, April 23, 2008, **www.wsj.com**.

Idea Generation Idea generation involves looking for product ideas that will help a firm to achieve its objectives. Although some organizations get their ideas almost by chance, firms trying to maximize product-mix effectiveness usually develop systematic approaches for generating new product ideas. Ideas may come from managers, researchers, engineers, competitors, advertising agencies, management consultants, private research organizations, customers, salespersons, or top executives. Procter & Gamble gets 35 percent of its ideas from inventors and outside consultants. Consultants are often used as sources for stimulating new-product ideas. For example, Fahrenheit 212 serves as an "idea factory" that provides ready-to-go product ideas, including market potential analysis.[7]

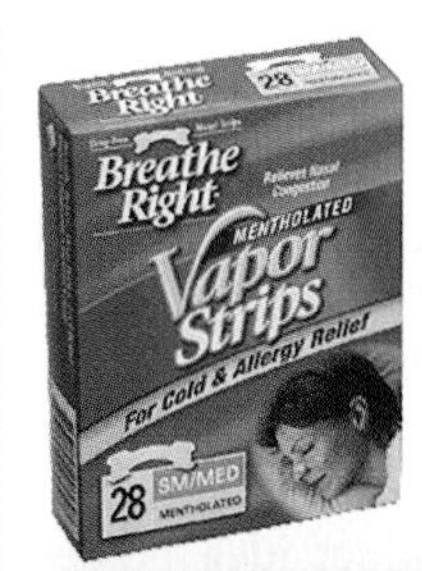

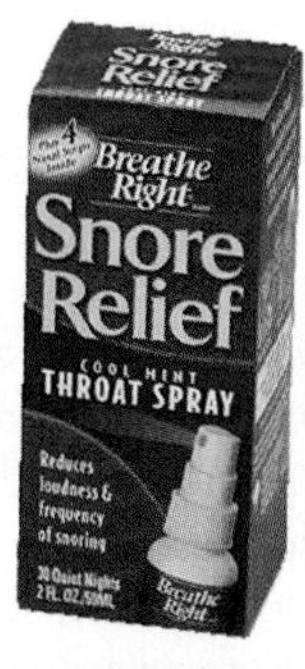

PRNewsFoto/GlaxoSmithKline Consumer Healthcare

Line extensions. *The maker of Breathe Right products has developed several line extensions that include vapor strips, throat spray, throat rinse, and child-size nasal strips.*

Figure 13.2: Phases of New Product Development

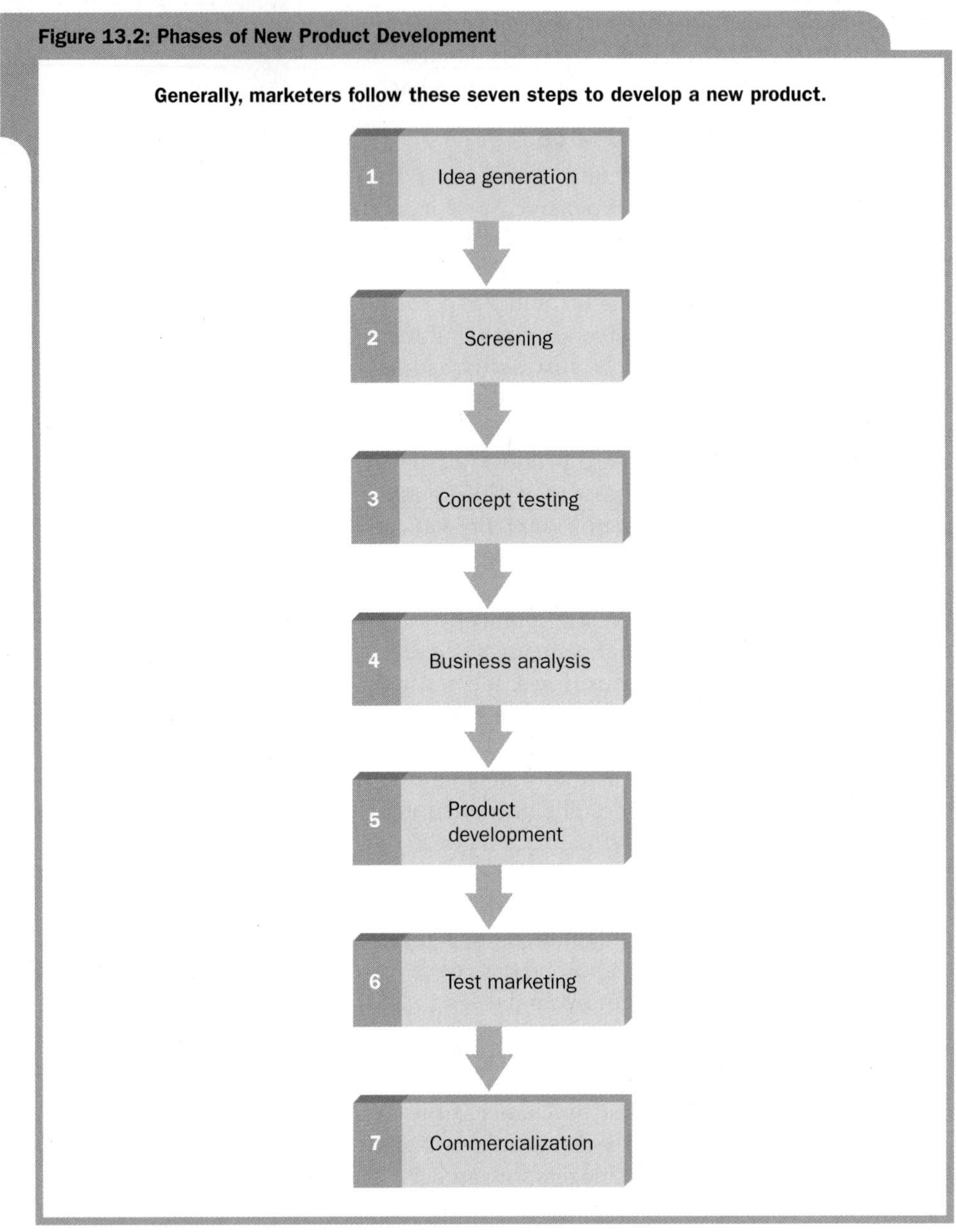

Source: William M. Pride and O. C. Ferrell, *Marketing: Concepts and Strategies,* 15th ed. (Mason, Ohio: South-Western/Cengage Learning, 2010). Adapted with permission.

Screening During screening, ideas that do not match organizational resources and objectives are rejected. In this phase, a firm's managers consider whether the organization has personnel with the expertise to develop and market the proposed product. Management may reject a good idea because the company lacks the necessary skills and abilities. The largest number of product ideas are rejected during the screening phase.

Concept Testing Concept testing is a phase in which a product idea is presented to a small sample of potential buyers through a written or oral description (and perhaps a few drawings) to determine their attitudes and initial buying intentions regarding the product. For a single product idea, an organization can test one or several concepts of the same product. Concept testing is a low-cost means for an organization to determine consumers' initial reactions to a product idea before investing considerable resources in product research and development (R&D). Product development personnel can use the results of concept testing to improve product attributes and product benefits that are most important to potential customers. The types of questions asked vary considerably depending on the type of product idea being tested. The following are typical questions:

- Which benefits of the proposed product are especially attractive to you?
- Which features are of little or no interest to you?
- What are the primary advantages of the proposed product over the one you currently use?
- If this product were available at an appropriate price, how often would you buy it?
- How could this proposed product be improved?

Business Analysis Business analysis provides tentative ideas about a potential product's financial performance, including its probable profitability. During this stage, the firm considers how the new product, if it were introduced, would affect the firm's sales, costs, and profits. Marketing personnel usually work up preliminary sales and cost projections at this point, with the help of R&D and production managers.

Product Development In the product development phase, the company must find out first if it is technically feasible to produce the product and then if the product can be made at costs low enough to justify a reasonable price. If a product idea makes it to this point, it is transformed into a working model, or *prototype*. Honda Motor, for example, developed a prototype minivan that targets Japan's growing population of pet owners with pet-friendly features such as paneled floors and seats that convert to a holding pen. Displayed at the Tokyo Auto Show, the prototype helped Honda assess interest in the concept.[8]

Test Marketing Test marketing is the limited introduction of a product in several towns or cities chosen to be representative of the intended target market. Its aim is to determine buyers' probable reactions. The product is left in the test markets long enough to give buyers a chance to repurchase the product if they are so inclined. Marketers can experiment with advertising, pricing, and packaging in different test areas and can measure the extent of brand awareness, brand switching, and repeat purchases that result from alterations in the marketing mix.

Will this product succeed? *Developing a new product involves considerable risk, because a significant portion of new products fail. However, failure to create new products is also very risky.*

Commercialization During commercialization, plans for full-scale manufacturing and marketing must be refined and completed, and budgets for the project must be prepared. In the early part of the commercialization phase, marketing management analyzes the results of test marketing to find out what changes in the marketing mix are needed before the product is introduced. The results of test marketing may tell the marketers, for example, to change one or more of the product's physical attributes, to modify the distribution plans to include more retail outlets, to alter promotional efforts, or to change the product's price. Products usually are not introduced nationwide overnight. Most new products are marketed in stages, beginning in selected geographic areas and expanding into adjacent areas over a period of time.

Why Do Products Fail? Despite this rigorous process for developing product ideas, most new products end up as failures. In fact, many well-known companies have produced market failures (see Table 13.1).

Why does a new product fail? Mainly because the product and its marketing program are not planned and tested as completely as they should be. For example, to save on development costs, a firm may market-test its product but not its

Table 13.1: Examples of Product Failures

Company	Product
Gillette	For Oily Hair shampoo
3M	Floptical storage disk
IncrEdibles Breakaway Foods	Push n' Eat
General Mills	Betty Crocker MicroRave Singles
Adams (Pfizer)	Body Smarts nutritional bars
General Motors Corp.	Cadillac Allante luxury sedan
Anheuser-Busch Companies	Bud Dry and Michelob Dry beer
Coca-Cola	Surge Citrus drink
Heinz	Ketchup Salsa
Noxema	Noxema Skin Fitness

Sources: **www.newproductworks.com**, accessed January 23, 2006; Robert M. McMath, "Copycat Cupcakes Don't Cut It," *American Demographics*, January 1997, p. 60; Eric Berggren and Thomas Nacher, "Why Good Ideas Go Bust," *Management Review*, February 2000, pp. 32–36.

entire marketing mix. Or a firm may market a new product before all the "bugs" have been worked out. Or, when problems show up in the testing stage, a firm may try to recover its product development costs by pushing ahead with full-scale marketing anyway. Finally, some firms try to market new products with inadequate financing.

Branding, Packaging, and Labeling

5

Learning Objective: Explain the uses and importance of branding, packaging, and labeling.

Three important features of a product (particularly a consumer product) are its brand, package, and label. These features may be used to associate a product with a successful product line or to distinguish it from existing products. They may be designed to attract customers at the point of sale or to provide information to potential purchasers. Because the brand, package, and label are very real parts of the product, they deserve careful attention during product planning.

brand a name, term, symbol, design, or any combination of these that identifies a seller's products as distinct from those of other sellers

brand name the part of a brand that can be spoken

brand mark the part of a brand that is a symbol or distinctive design

trademark a brand name or brand mark that is registered with the U.S. Patent and Trademark Office and thus is legally protected from use by anyone except its owner

trade name the complete and legal name of an organization

manufacturer (or producer) brand a brand that is owned by a manufacturer

store (or private) brand a brand that is owned by an individual wholesaler or retailer

What Is a Brand?

A **brand** is a name, term, symbol, design, or any combination of these that identifies a seller's products and distinguishes it from other sellers' products. A **brand name** is the part of a brand that can be spoken. It may include letters, words, numbers, or pronounceable symbols, such as the ampersand in *Procter & Gamble*. A **brand mark**, on the other hand, is the part of a brand that is a symbol or distinctive design, such as the Nike "swoosh." A **trademark** is a brand name or brand mark that is registered with the U.S. Patent and Trademark Office and thus is legally protected from use by anyone except its owner. A **trade name** is the complete and legal name of an organization, such as Pizza Hut or Cengage Learning (the publisher of this text).

Types of Brands

Brands often are classified according to who owns them: manufacturers or stores. A **manufacturer (or producer) brand**, as the name implies, is a brand that is owned by a manufacturer. Many foods (Frosted Flakes), major appliances (Whirlpool), gasolines (Exxon), automobiles (Honda), and clothing (Levis) are sold as manufacturers' brands. Some consumers prefer manufacturer brands because they usually are nationally known, offer consistent quality, and are widely available.

A **store (or private) brand** is a brand that is owned by an individual wholesaler or retailer. Among the better-known store brands are Kenmore and Craftsman, both owned by Sears, Roebuck. Owners of store brands claim that they can offer lower prices, earn greater profits, and improve customer loyalty with their own brands. Some companies that manufacture private brands also produce their own manufacturer brands. They often find such operations profitable because they can use excess capacity and at the same time avoid most marketing costs. Many private-branded grocery products are produced by companies that specialize in making private-label products. About 20 percent of products sold in supermarkets are private-branded items.[9]

Consumer confidence is the most important element in the success of a branded product, whether the brand is owned by a producer or by a retailer. Because branding identifies each product completely, customers can easily repurchase products that provide satisfaction, performance, and quality. And they can just as easily avoid or ignore products that do not. In supermarkets, the products most likely to keep their shelf space are the brands with large market shares and strong customer loyalty.

A **generic product** (sometimes called a **generic brand**) is a product with no brand at all. Its plain package carries only the name of the product—applesauce, peanut butter, potato chips, or whatever. Generic products, available in supermarkets since 1977, sometimes are made by the major producers that manufacture name brands. Even though generic brands may have accounted for as much as 10 percent of all grocery sales several years ago, they currently represent less than one-half of 1 percent.

generic product (or brand) a product with no brand at all

Benefits of Branding

Both buyers and sellers benefit from branding. Because brands are easily recognizable, they reduce the amount of time buyers must spend shopping; buyers can quickly identify the brands they prefer. Choosing particular brands, such as Tommy Hilfiger, Polo, Nautica, and Nike, can be a way of expressing oneself. When buyers are unable to evaluate a product's characteristics, brands can help them to judge the quality of the product. For example, most buyers are not able to judge the quality of stereo components but may be guided by a well-respected brand name. Brands can symbolize a certain quality level to a customer, allowing that perception of quality to represent the actual quality of the item. Brands thus help to reduce a buyer's perceived risk of purchase. Finally, customers may receive a psychological reward that comes from owning a brand that symbolizes status. The Lexus brand is an example.

Because buyers are already familiar with a firm's existing brands, branding helps a firm to introduce a new product that carries the same brand name. Branding aids sellers in their promotional efforts because promotion of each branded product indirectly promotes other products of the same brand. H.J. Heinz, for example, markets many products with the Heinz brand name, such as ketchup, vinegar, vegetarian beans, gravies, barbecue sauce, and steak sauce. Promotion of one Heinz product indirectly promotes the others.

One chief benefit of branding is the creation of **brand loyalty**, the extent to which a customer is favorable toward buying a specific brand. The stronger the brand loyalty, the greater is the likelihood that buyers will consistently choose the brand. There are three levels of brand loyalty: recognition, preference, and insistence. *Brand recognition* is the level of loyalty at which customers are aware that the brand exists and will purchase it if their preferred brands are unavailable or if they are unfamiliar with available brands. This is the weakest form of brand loyalty. *Brand preference* is the level of brand loyalty at which a customer prefers one brand over competing brands. However, if the preferred brand is unavailable, the customer is willing to substitute another brand. *Brand insistence* is the strongest level of brand loyalty. Brand-insistent customers strongly prefer a specific brand and will not buy substitutes. Brand insistence is the least common type of brand loyalty. Partly owing to marketers' increased dependence on discounted prices, coupons, and other short-term promotions, and partly because of the enormous array of new products with similar characteristics, brand loyalty in general seems to be declining.

brand loyalty extent to which a customer is favorable toward buying a specific brand

Brand equity is the marketing and financial value associated with a brand's strength in a market. Although difficult to measure, brand equity represents the value of a brand to an organization. Some of the world's most valuable brands

brand equity marketing and financial value associated with a brand's strength in a market

include Coca-Cola, IBM, Microsoft, General Electric, and Nokia.[10] The four major factors that contribute to brand equity are brand awareness, brand associations, perceived brand quality, and brand loyalty. Brand awareness leads to brand familiarity, and buyers are more likely to select a familiar brand than an unfamiliar one. The associations linked to a brand can connect a personality type or lifestyle with a particular brand. For example, customers associate Michelin tires with protecting family members; a De Beers diamond with a loving, long-lasting relationship ("A Diamond Is Forever"); and Dr Pepper with a unique taste. When consumers are unable to judge for themselves the quality of a product, they may rely on their perception of the quality of the product's brand. Finally, brand loyalty is a valued element of brand equity because it reduces both a brand's vulnerability to competitors and the need to spend tremendous resources to attract new customers; it also provides brand visibility and encourages retailers to carry the brand. New companies, for example, have much work to do in establishing new brands to compete with well-known brands.

Marketing on the Internet sometimes is best done in collaboration with a better-known Web brand. For instance, Weight Watchers, Tire Rack, wine.com, Office Depot, Toys "R" Us, and Shutterfly all rely on partnerships with Internet retail giant Amazon to increase their sales. Amazon provides special sections on its website to promote its partners and their products. As with its own products, Amazon gives users the ability to post online reviews of its partners' products or to add them to an Amazon "wish list" that can be saved or e-mailed to friends. Amazon even labels its partners as "Amazon Trusted" when customers browse their sites, giving even these well-known real-world companies credibility in the online marketplace.[11]

Choosing and Protecting a Brand

A number of issues should be considered when selecting a brand name. The name should be easy for customers to say, spell, and recall. Short, one-syllable names such as *Tide* often satisfy this requirement. Letters and numbers are used to create such brands as Volvo's S60 sedan or RIM's BlackBerry 8100. Words, numbers, and letters are combined to yield brand names such as Motorola's RAZR V3 phone or BMW's Z4 Roadster. The brand name should suggest, in a positive way, the product's uses, special characteristics, and major benefits and should be distinctive enough to set it apart from competing brands. Choosing the right brand name has become a challenge because many obvious product names already have been used.

It is important that a firm select a brand that can be protected through registration, reserving it for exclusive use by that firm. Some brands, because of their designs, are infringed on more easily than others. Although registration protects trademarks domestically for ten years and can be renewed indefinitely, a firm should develop a system for ensuring that its trademarks will be renewed as needed. To protect its exclusive right to the brand, the company must ensure that the selected brand will not be considered an infringement on any existing brand already registered with the U.S. Patent and Trademark Office. This task may be complicated by the fact that infringement is determined by the courts, which base their decisions on whether a brand causes consumers to be confused, mistaken, or deceived about the source of the product. McDonald's is one company that aggressively protects its trademarks against infringement; it has brought charges against a number of companies with *Mc* names because it fears that the use of the prefix will give consumers the impression that these companies are associated with or owned by McDonald's.

Building brand equity. *Pepsi tries to build brand equity through promotional efforts aimed at brand awareness, perceived brand quality, and the building of brand loyalty.*

A firm must guard against a brand name's becoming a generic term that refers to a general product category. Generic terms cannot be legally protected as exclusive brand names. For example, names such as *yo-yo, aspirin, escalator,* and *thermos*—all exclusively brand names at one time—eventually were declared generic terms that refer to product categories. As such, they could no longer be protected. To ensure that a brand name does not become a generic term, the firm should spell the name with a capital letter and use it as an adjective to modify the name of the general product class, as in Jell-O Brand Gelatin. An organization can deal directly with this problem by advertising that its brand is a trademark and should not be used generically. Firms also can use the registered trademark symbol ® to indicate that the brand is trademarked.

Branding Strategies

The basic branding decision for any firm is whether to brand its products. A producer may market its products under its own brands, private brands, or both. A retail store may carry only producer brands, its own brands, or both. Once either type of firm decides to brand, it chooses one of two branding strategies: individual branding or family branding.

Individual branding is the strategy in which a firm uses a different brand for each of its products. For example, Procter & Gamble uses individual branding for its line of bar soaps, which includes Ivory, Camay, Zest, Safeguard, Coast, and Oil of Olay. Individual branding offers two major advantages. A problem with one product will not affect the good name of the firm's other products, and the different brands can be directed toward different market segments. For example, Marriott's Fairfield Inns are directed toward budget-minded travelers and Marriott Hotels toward upscale customers.

individual branding the strategy in which a firm uses a different brand for each of its products

Family branding is the strategy in which a firm uses the same brand for all or most of its products. Sony, Dell, IBM, and Xerox use family branding for their entire product mixes. A major advantage of family branding is that the promotion of any one item that carries the family brand tends to help all other products with the same brand name. In addition, a new product has a head start when its brand name is already known and accepted by customers.

family branding the strategy in which a firm uses the same brand for all or most of its products

Brand Extensions

A **brand extension** occurs when an organization uses one of its existing brands to brand a new product in a different product category. For example, Procter & Gamble employed a brand extension when it named a new product Ivory Body Wash. A brand extension should not be confused with a line extension. A *line extension* refers to using an existing brand on a new product in the same product category, such as a new flavor or new sizes. For example, when the makers of Tylenol introduced Extra Strength Tylenol PM, the new product was a line extension because it was in the same product category. One thing marketers must be careful of, however, is extending a brand too many times or extending too far outside the original product category, which may weaken the brand.

brand extension using an existing brand to brand a new product in a different product category

Packaging

Packaging consists of all the activities involved in developing and providing a container with graphics for a product. The package is a vital part of the product. It can make the product more versatile, safer, or easier to use. Through its shape, appearance, and printed message, a package can influence purchasing decisions.

packaging all the activities involved in developing and providing a container with graphics for a product

Packaging Functions

Effective packaging means more than simply putting products in containers and covering them with wrappers. The basic function of packaging materials is to protect the product and maintain its functional form. Fluids such as milk, orange juice, and hair spray need packages that preserve and protect them; the packaging should prevent damage that could affect the product's usefulness and increase costs. Since product tampering has become a problem for marketers of many types of goods, several packaging techniques have been developed to counter this danger. Some packages are also designed to foil shoplifting.

The Business of Green

Green Labels for Green Products

More companies are using green labeling to let consumers know that their products are environmentally friendly. Watch for these green designations:

- *Energy Star.* Administered by the U.S. Environmental Protection Agency and the U.S. Department of Energy, the Energy Star label identifies energy-efficient home and office equipment such as dishwashers, washing machines, and laser printers.
- *Green Seal.* This nonprofit organization examines the environmental impact of a product's supplies, production, packaging, consumption, and disposal. Look for the Green Seal logo on paper and other products made from sustainable wood.

- *Forest Stewardship Council.* The Forest Stewardship Council, active in more than 46 nations, labels wood and wood products that originated in forests managed with sustainability in mind.
- *Sustainable Forestry Initiative.* To qualify for this label, all or some of a product's fiber content must come from forests that are managed for sustainability. The label also identifies products that contain recycled materials.
- *Leadership in Energy and Environmental Design (LEED).* LEED certification indicates that a building's design, construction, and operation meet green standards established by the U.S. Green Building Council.

Sources: Adam Aston, "A Tainted Badge of Honor: The Energy Star Logo Implies Efficiency," *BusinessWeek*, October 13, 2008, p. 76; Heather Green and Kerry Capell, "Carbon Confusion," *BusinessWeek*, March 17, 2008, pp. 52–55; Abigail Goldman, "'Green' Labels Come with a Shade of Doubt," *Los Angeles Times*, September 5, 2007, p. C1.

www.energystar.gov

Another function of packaging is to offer consumer convenience. For example, small, aseptic packages—individual-serving boxes or plastic bags that contain liquids and do not require refrigeration—appeal strongly to children and to young adults with active lifestyles. The size or shape of a package may relate to the product's storage, convenience of use, or replacement rate. Small, single-serving cans of vegetables, for instance, may prevent waste and make storage easier. A third function of packaging is to promote a product by communicating its features, uses, benefits, and image. Sometimes a firm develops a reusable package to make its product more desirable. For example, the Cool Whip package doubles as a food-storage container.

Package design. *PBM Products' Parent's Choice Baby Food employs reusable plastic tubs that are designed to be sturdy, spill less, and keep its contents fresh longer.*

PRNewsFoto/PBM Products, LLC

Package Design Considerations Many factors must be weighed when developing packages. Obviously, one major consideration is cost. Although a number of packaging materials, processes, and designs are available, some are rather expensive. While U.S. buyers have shown a willingness to pay more for improved packaging, there are limits.

Marketers also must decide whether to package the product in single or multiple units. Multiple-unit packaging can increase demand by increasing the amount of the product available at the point of consumption (in the home, for example). However, multiple-unit packaging does not work for infrequently used products because buyers do not like to tie up their dollars in an excess supply or to store those products for a long time. However, multiple-unit packaging can make storage and handling easier (as in the case of six-packs used for soft drinks); it also can facilitate special price offers, such as two-for-one sales. In addition, multiple-unit packaging may increase consumer acceptance of a product by encouraging the buyer to try it several times. On the other hand, customers may hesitate to try the product at all if they do not have the option to buy just one.

Marketers should consider how much consistency is desirable among an organization's package designs. To promote an overall company image, a firm may decide that all packages must be similar or include one major element of the design. This approach, called *family packaging,* is sometimes used only for lines of products, as with Campbell's soups, Weight Watchers entrees, and Planters nuts. The best policy is sometimes no consistency, especially if a firm's products are unrelated or aimed at vastly different target markets.

Packages also play an important promotional role. Through verbal and nonverbal symbols, the package can inform potential buyers about the product's content, uses, features, advantages, and hazards. Firms can create desirable images and associations by choosing particular colors, designs, shapes, and textures. Many cosmetics manufacturers, for example, design their packages to create impressions of richness, luxury, and exclusiveness. The package performs another promotional function when it is designed to be safer or more convenient to use if such features help to stimulate demand.

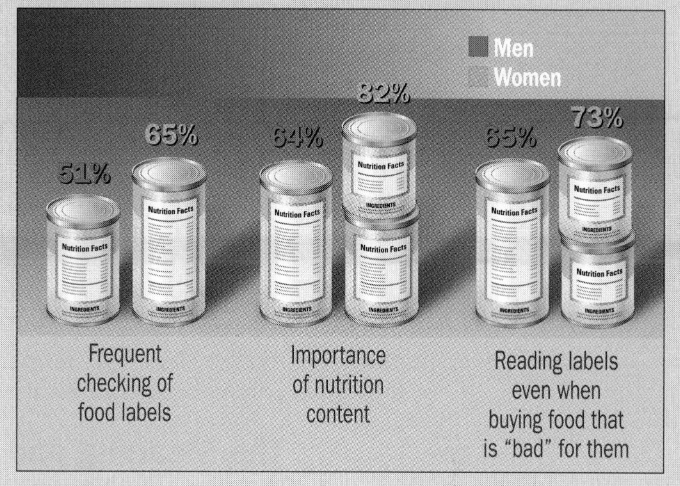

Source: AP-Ipsos.

Packaging also must meet the needs of intermediaries. Wholesalers and retailers consider whether a package facilitates transportation, handling, and storage. Resellers may refuse to carry certain products if their packages are cumbersome.

Finally, firms must consider the issue of environmental responsibility when developing packages. Companies must balance consumers' desires for convenience against the need to preserve the environment. About one-half of all garbage consists of discarded plastic packaging, such as plastic soft drink bottles and carryout bags. Plastic packaging material is not biodegradable, and paper necessitates destruction of valuable forest lands. Consequently, many companies are exploring packaging alternatives and recycling more materials.

Labeling

labeling the presentation of information on a product or its package

Labeling is the presentation of information on a product or its package. The *label* is the part that contains the information. This information may include the brand name and mark, the registered trademark symbol ®, the package size and contents, product claims, directions for use and safety precautions, a list of ingredients, the name and address of the manufacturer, and the Universal Product Code (UPC) symbol, which is used for automated checkout and inventory control.

A number of federal regulations specify information that *must* be included in the labeling for certain products. For example,

- Garments must be labeled with the name of the manufacturer, country of manufacture, fabric content, and cleaning instructions.
- Food labels must contain the most common term for ingredients.
- Any food product for which a nutritional claim is made must have nutrition labeling that follows a standard format.
- Food product labels must state the number of servings per container, the serving size, the number of calories per serving, the number of calories derived from fat, and the amounts of specific nutrients.
- Nonedible items such as shampoos and detergents must carry safety precautions as well as instructions for their use.

Such regulations are aimed at protecting customers from both misleading product claims and the improper (and thus unsafe) use of products.

express warranty a written explanation of the responsibilities of the producer in the event that a product is found to be defective or otherwise unsatisfactory

Labels also may carry the details of written or express warranties. An **express warranty** is a written explanation of the responsibilities of the producer in the event that a product is found to be defective or otherwise unsatisfactory. As a result of consumer discontent (along with some federal legislation), firms have begun to simplify the wording of warranties and to extend their duration. The L.L.Bean warranty states, "Our products are guaranteed to give 100 percent satisfaction in every way. Return anything purchased from us at any time if it proves otherwise. We will replace it, refund your purchase price or credit your credit card, as you wish."

Pricing Products

6

Learning Objective: Describe the economic basis of pricing and the means by which sellers can control prices and buyers' perceptions of prices.

A product is a set of attributes and benefits that has been carefully designed to satisfy its market while earning a profit for its seller. No matter how well a product is designed, however, it cannot help an organization to achieve its goals if it is priced incorrectly. Few people will purchase a product with too high a price, and a product with too low a price will earn little or no profit. Somewhere between too high and too low there is a "proper," effective price for each product. Let's take a closer look at how businesses go about determining a product's right price.

The Meaning and Use of Price

price the amount of money a seller is willing to accept in exchange for a product at a given time and under given circumstances

The **price** of a product is the amount of money a seller is willing to accept in exchange for the product at a given time and under given circumstances. At times, the price results from negotiations between buyer and seller. In many business situations, however, the price is fixed by the seller. Suppose that a seller sets a price of $10 for a particular product. In essence, the seller is saying, "Anyone who wants this product can have it here and now in exchange for $10."

Each interested buyer then makes a personal judgment regarding the utility of the product, often in terms of some dollar value. A particular person who feels that he or she will get at least $10 worth of want satisfaction (or value) from the product is likely to buy it. If that person can get more want satisfaction by spending $10 in some other way, however, he or she will not buy the product.

Price thus serves the function of *allocator*. First, it allocates goods and services among those who are willing and able to buy them. (As we noted in Chapter 1, the answer to the economic question "For whom to produce?" depends primarily on prices.) Second, price allocates financial resources (sales revenue) among producers according to how well they satisfy customers' needs. And third, price helps customers to allocate their own financial resources among various want-satisfying products.

Supply and Demand Affects Prices

supply the quantity of a product that producers are willing to sell at each of various prices

demand the quantity of a product that buyers are willing to purchase at each of various prices

In Chapter 1, we defined the **supply** of a product as the quantity of the product that producers are willing to sell at each of various prices. We can draw a graph of the supply relationship for a particular product, say, jeans (see the left graph in Figure 13.3). Note that the quantity supplied by producers *increases* as the price increases along this *supply curve*.

As defined in Chapter 1, the **demand** for a product is the quantity that buyers are willing to purchase at each of various prices. We also can draw a graph of the demand relationship (see the center graph in Figure 13.3). Note that the quantity demanded by purchasers *increases* as the price decreases along the *demand curve*. The buyers and sellers of a product interact in the marketplace. We can show this interaction by superimposing the supply curve onto the demand curve for our product, as shown in the right graph in Figure 13.3. The two curves intersect at point *E*, which represents a quantity of 15 million pairs of jeans and a price of $30 per pair. Point *E* is on the *supply curve;* thus, producers are willing to supply 15 million pairs at $30 each. Point *E* is also on the demand curve; thus, buyers are willing to purchase 15 million pairs at $30 each. Point *E* represents *equilibrium*. If 15 million pairs are produced and priced at $30, they all will be sold. And everyone who is willing to pay $30 will be able to buy a pair of jeans.

Figure 13.3: Supply and Demand Curves

Supply curve (*left*): The upward slope means that producers will supply more jeans at higher prices. Demand curve (*center*): The downward slope (to the right) means that buyers will purchase fewer jeans at higher prices. Supply and demand curves together (*right*): Point *E* indicates equilibrium in quantity and price for both sellers and buyers.

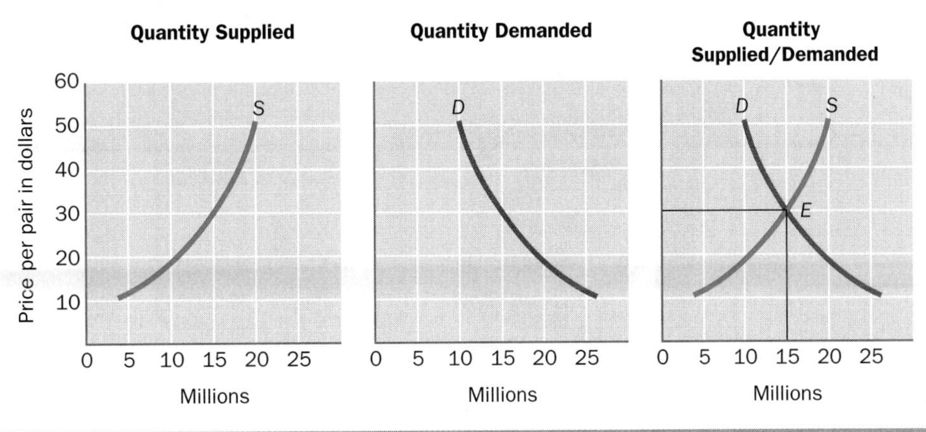

Price and Nonprice Competition

Before the price of a product can be set, an organization must decide on the basis on which it will compete—on the basis of price alone or some combination of factors. The choice influences pricing decisions as well as other marketing-mix variables.

price competition an emphasis on setting a price equal to or lower than competitors' prices to gain sales or market share

Price competition occurs when a seller emphasizes the low price of a product and sets a price that equals or beats competitors' prices. To use this approach most effectively, a seller must have the flexibility to change prices often and must do so rapidly and aggressively whenever competitors change their prices. Price competition allows a marketer to set prices based on demand for the product or in response to changes in the firm's finances. Competitors can do likewise, however, which is a major drawback of price competition. They, too, can quickly match or outdo an organization's price cuts. In addition, if circumstances force a seller to raise prices, competing firms may be able to maintain their lower prices. Consider that when Wal-Mart, Circuit City, and Amazon.com reduced the price of a Toshiba high definition DVD player to $200, consumer interest rose. But when Wal-Mart slashed the price by another $100 for 48 hours, consumers snatched up 90,000 to 100,000 of the players. Best Buy also boosted sales when it dropped the price of a Sony Blue-ray DVD player to $399.[12]

The Internet makes price comparison relatively easy for users. This ease of price comparison helps to drive competition. Examples of websites where customers can compare prices include mysimon.com, pricescan.com, bizrate.com, pricegrabber.com, pricecomparison.com, shopping.yahoo.com, nextag.com, and froogle.google.com.

nonprice competition competition based on factors other than price

Nonprice competition is competition based on factors other than price. It is used most effectively when a seller can make its product stand out from the competition by distinctive product quality, customer service, promotion, packaging, or other features. Buyers must be able to perceive these distinguishing characteristics and consider them desirable. Once customers have chosen a brand for nonprice reasons, they may not be attracted as easily to competing firms and brands. In this way, a seller can build customer loyalty to its brand. A method of nonprice competition is **product differentiation** which is the process of developing and promoting differences between one's product and all similar products. Mars, for example, markets not only Snickers and M&Ms, but also has an upscale candy line called Ethel's Chocolates. Using the tagline, "no mystery middles," Ethel's chocolates bases its competition on taste, appearance, and packaging, so it doesn't need to compete on price.[13]

product differentiation the process of developing and promoting differences between one's product and all similar products

Buyers' Perceptions of Price

In setting prices, managers should consider the price sensitivity of people in the target market. How important is price to them? Is it always "very important"?

Price competition. *Staples engages in price competition for its electronic devices such as digital photo frames and global positioning systems.*

Courtesy Staples

Members of one market segment may be more influenced by price than members of another. For a particular product, the price may be a bigger factor to some buyers than to others. For example, buyers may be more sensitive to price when purchasing gasoline than when purchasing running shoes.

Buyers will accept different ranges of prices for different products; that is, they will tolerate a narrow range for certain items and a wider range for others. Consider the wide range of prices that consumers pay for soft drinks—from 15 cents per ounce at the movies down to 1.5 cents per ounce on sale at the grocery store. Management should be aware of these limits of acceptability and the products to which they apply. The firm also should take note of buyers' perceptions of a given product in relation to competing products. A premium price may be appropriate if a product is considered superior to others in its category or if the product has inspired strong brand loyalty. On the other hand, if buyers have even a hint of a negative view of a product, a lower price may be necessary.

Sometimes buyers relate price to quality. They may consider a higher price to be an indicator of higher quality. Managers involved in pricing decisions should determine whether this outlook is widespread in the target market. If it is, a higher price may improve the image of a product and, in turn, make the product more desirable.

Pricing Objectives

Learning Objective: Identify the major pricing objectives used by businesses.

Before setting prices for a firm's products, management must decide what it expects to accomplish through pricing. That is, management must set pricing objectives that are in line with both organizational and marketing objectives. Of course, one objective of pricing is to make a profit, but this may not be a firm's primary objective. One or more of the following factors may be just as important.

Survival

A firm may have to price its products to survive—either as an organization or as a player in a particular market. This usually means that the firm will cut its price to attract customers, even if it then must operate at a loss. Obviously, such a goal hardly can be pursued on a long-term basis, for consistent losses would cause the business to fail.

Profit Maximization

Many firms may state that their goal is to maximize profit, but this goal is impossible to define (and thus impossible to achieve). What, exactly, is the *maximum* profit? How does a firm know when it has been reached? Firms that wish to set profit goals should express them as either specific dollar amounts or percentage increases over previous profits.

Target Return on Investment

The *return on investment* (ROI) is the amount earned as a result of that investment. Some firms set an annual percentage ROI as their pricing goal. ConAgra, the company that produces Healthy Choice meals and a multitude of other products, has a target after-tax ROI of 20 percent.

SPOTLIGHT
Shopping for iPhones

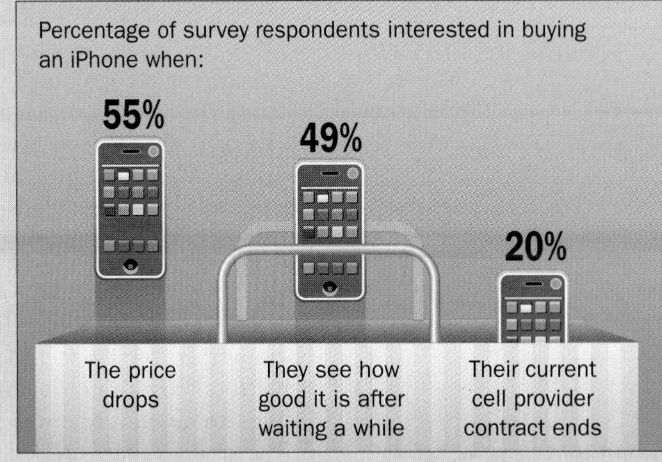

Source: Harris Interactive Survey of 10,410 respondents aged 13 to 64.

Market-Share Goals

A firm's *market share* is its proportion of total industry sales. Some firms attempt, through pricing, to maintain or increase their market shares. To gain market share, both U.S. cola giants try to gain market share through aggressive pricing and other marketing efforts.

Status-Quo Pricing

In pricing their products, some firms are guided by a desire to avoid "making waves," or to maintain the status quo. This is especially true in industries that depend on price stability. If such a firm can maintain its profit or market share

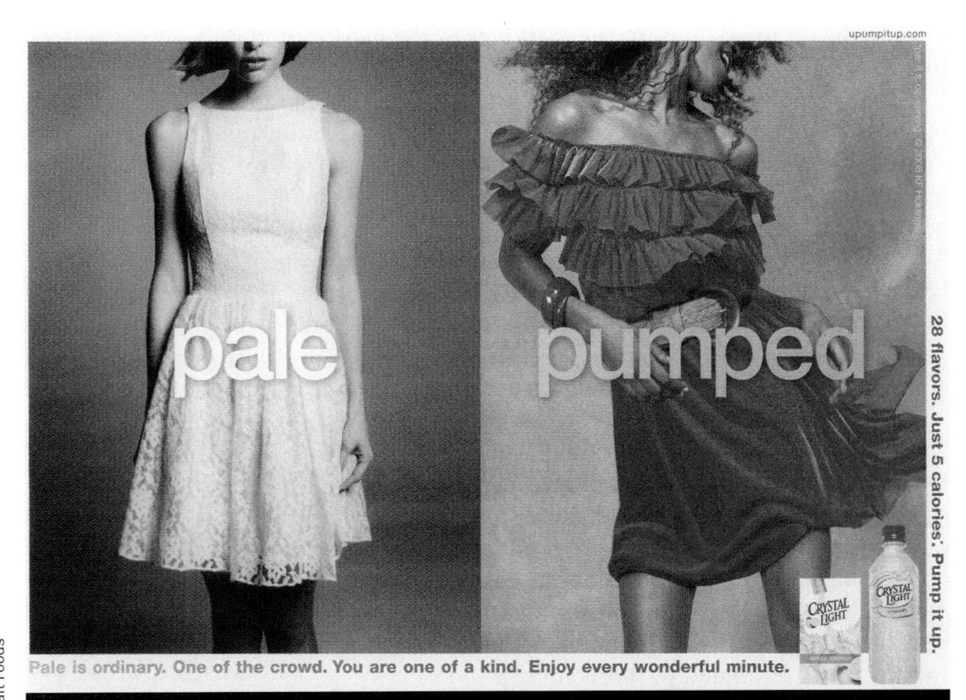

Nonprice competition. *Crystal Light competes with other flavored water mixes on the basis of product attributes. There is no mention of price in this advertisement.*

Courtesy Kraft Foods

simply by meeting the competition—charging about the same price as competitors for similar products—then it will do so.

Pricing Methods

8

Learning Objective: Examine the three major pricing methods that firms employ.

Once a firm has developed its pricing objectives, it must select a pricing method to reach that goal. Two factors are important to every firm engaged in setting prices. The first is recognition that the market, and not the firm's costs, ultimately determines the price at which a product will sell. The second is awareness that costs and expected sales can be used only to establish some sort of *price floor,* the minimum price at which the firm can sell its product without incurring a loss. In this section, we look at three kinds of pricing methods: cost-based, demand-based, and competition-based pricing.

Cost-Based Pricing

Using the simplest method of pricing, *cost-based pricing,* the seller first determines the total cost of producing (or purchasing) one unit of the product. The seller then adds an amount to cover additional costs (such as insurance or interest) and profit. The amount that is added is called the **markup**. The total of the cost plus the markup is the selling price of the product.

markup the amount a seller adds to the cost of a product to determine its basic selling price

A firm's management can calculate markup as a percentage of its total costs. Suppose, for example, that the total cost of manufacturing and marketing 1,000 DVD players is $100,000, or $100 per unit. If the manufacturer wants a markup that is 20 percent above its costs, the selling price will be $100 plus 20 percent of $100, or $120 per unit.

Markup pricing is easy to apply, and it is used by many businesses (mostly retailers and wholesalers). However, it has two major flaws. The first is the difficulty of determining an effective markup percentage. If this percentage is too high, the product may be overpriced for its market; then too few units may be sold to return the total cost of producing and marketing the product. In contrast, if the markup percentage is too low, the seller is "giving away" profit it could have earned simply by assigning a higher price. In other words, the markup percentage needs to be set to account for the workings of the market, and that is very difficult to do.

The second problem with markup pricing is that it separates pricing from other business functions. The product is priced *after* production quantities are determined, *after* costs are incurred, and almost without regard for the market or the marketing mix. To be most effective, the various business functions should be integrated. *Each* should have an impact on all marketing decisions.

breakeven quantity the number of units that must be sold for the total revenue (from all units sold) to equal the total cost (of all units sold)

total revenue the total amount received from sales of a product

Cost-based pricing also can be facilitated through the use of breakeven analysis. For any product, the **breakeven quantity** is the number of units that must be sold for the total revenue (from all units sold) to equal the total cost (of all units sold). **Total revenue** is the total amount received from the sales of a product. We can estimate projected total revenue as the selling price multiplied by the number of units sold.

fixed cost a cost incurred no matter how many units of a product are produced or sold

variable cost a cost that depends on the number of units produced

total cost the sum of the fixed costs and the variable costs attributed to a product

The costs involved in operating a business can be broadly classified as either fixed or variable costs. A **fixed cost** is a cost incurred no matter how many units of a product are produced or sold. Rent, for example, is a fixed cost; it remains the same whether 1 or 1,000 units are produced. A **variable cost** is a cost that depends on the number of units produced. The cost of fabricating parts for a stereo receiver is a variable cost. The more units produced, the higher is the cost of parts. The **total cost** of producing a certain number of units is the sum of the fixed costs and the variable costs attributed to those units.

If we assume a particular selling price, we can find the breakeven quantity either graphically or by using a formula. Figure 13.4 graphs the total revenue earned and the total cost incurred by the sale of various quantities of a

Figure 13.4: Breakeven Analysis

Breakeven analysis answers the question, What is the lowest level of production and sales at which a company can break even on a particular product?

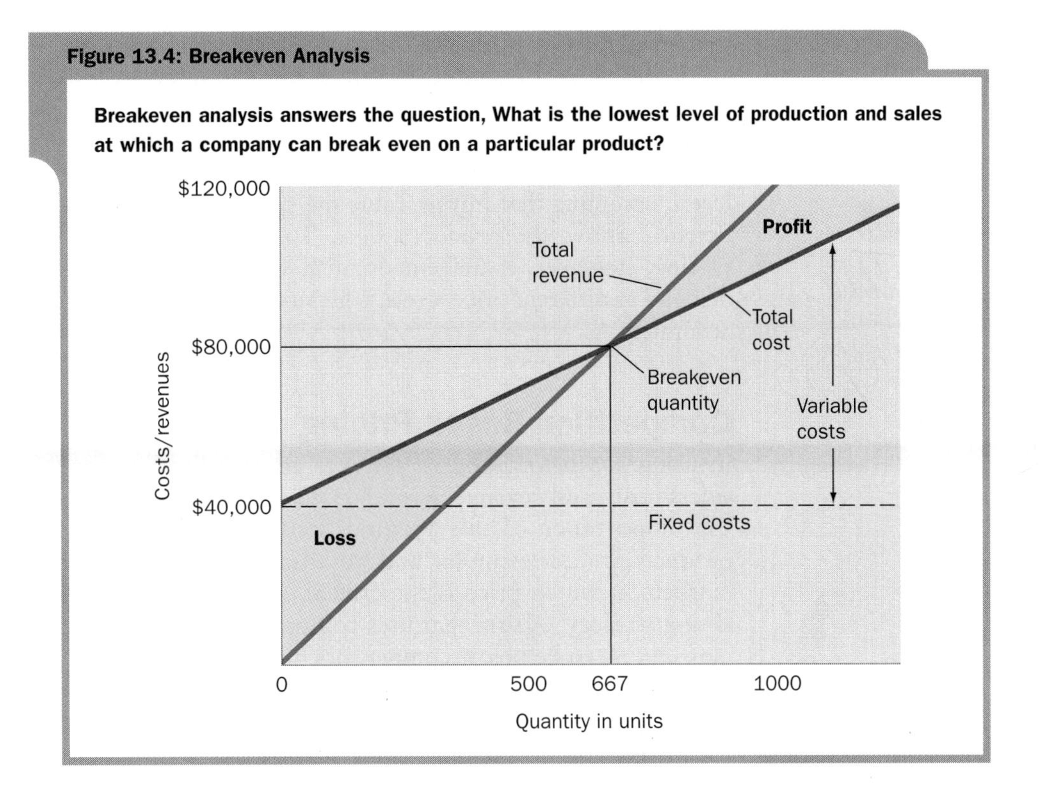

hypothetical product. With fixed costs of $40,000, variable costs of $60 per unit, and a selling price of $120, the breakeven quantity is 667 units. To find the breakeven quantity, first deduct the variable cost from the selling price to determine how much money the sale of one unit contributes to offsetting fixed costs. Then divide that contribution into the total fixed costs to arrive at the breakeven quantity. (The breakeven quantity in Figure 13.4 is the quantity represented by the intersection of the total revenue and total cost axes.) If the firm sells more than 667 units at $120 each, it will earn a profit. If it sells fewer units, it will suffer a loss.

Demand-Based Pricing

Rather than basing the price of a product on its cost, companies sometimes use a pricing method based on the level of demand for the product: *demand-based pricing*. This method results in a high price when product demand is strong and a low price when demand is weak. Some long-distance telephone companies use demand-based pricing. Buyers of new cars that are in high demand, such as Hummer H3, Pontiac Solstice, Dodge Charger, Ford Mustang GT, and Toyota Prius, pay sticker prices plus a premium. To use this method, a marketer estimates the amount of a product that customers will demand at different prices and then chooses the price that generates the highest total revenue. Obviously, the effectiveness of this method depends on the firm's ability to estimate demand accurately.

A firm may favor a demand-based pricing method called *price differentiation* if it wants to use more than one price in the marketing of a specific product. Price differentiation can be based on such considerations as time of the purchase, type of customer, or type of distribution channel. For example, Florida hotel accommodations are more expensive in winter than in summer; a home owner pays more for air-conditioner filters than does an apartment complex owner purchasing the same size filters in greater quantity; and Christmas tree ornaments usually are cheaper on December 26 than on December 16. For price differentiation to work correctly, the company first must be able to segment a market on the basis of different strengths of demand and then must be able to keep the segments separate enough so that segment members who buy at lower prices cannot sell to buyers in segments

Welcome to the Lap of Executive Economy

EXECUTIVE ECONOMY CLASS. NONSTOP TO SINGAPORE.
It's a class of travel all its own. Enjoy the widest seats, 5 inches of extra legroom, 2-3-2 seating, a stand-up passenger lounge, a 9-inch monitor with hundreds of audio-video on-demand entertainment options, World Gourmet Cuisine™ and service even other airlines talk about. Available exclusively on the only nonstop flights to Singapore from Los Angeles and New York. singaporeair.com/usa

SINGAPORE AIRLINES
A great way to fly

Demand-based pricing. *Airlines employ demand-based pricing. When demand for a particular flight is high, prices are elevated. When demand for a particular flight is low, airfare is less expensive. Airlines also employ competition-based pricing, especially on routes on which competing airlines offer very low fares.*

that are charged a higher price. This isolation could be accomplished, for example, by selling to geographically separated segments.

Compared with cost-based pricing, demand-based pricing places a firm in a better position to attain higher profit levels, assuming that buyers value the product at levels sufficiently above the product's cost. To use demand-based pricing, however, management must be able to estimate demand at different price levels, which may be difficult to do accurately.

Competition-Based Pricing

In using *competition-based pricing,* an organization considers costs and revenue secondary to competitors' prices. The importance of this method increases if competing products are quite similar and the organization is serving markets in which price is the crucial variable of the marketing strategy. A firm that uses competition-based pricing may choose to be below competitors' prices, slightly above competitors' prices, or at the same level. The price that your bookstore paid to the publishing company of this text was determined using competition-based pricing. Competition-based pricing can help to attain a pricing objective to increase sales or market share. Competition-based pricing may be combined with other cost approaches to arrive at profitable levels.

Pricing Strategies

9

Learning Objective: Explain the different strategies available to companies for setting prices.

A *pricing strategy* is a course of action designed to achieve pricing objectives. Generally, pricing strategies help marketers to solve the practical problems of setting prices. The extent to which a business uses any of the following strategies depends on its pricing and marketing objectives, the markets for its products, the degree of product differentiation, the life-cycle stage of the product, and other factors. Figure 13.5 contains a list of the major types of pricing strategies. We discuss these strategies in the remainder of this section.

Figure 13.5: Types of Pricing Strategies

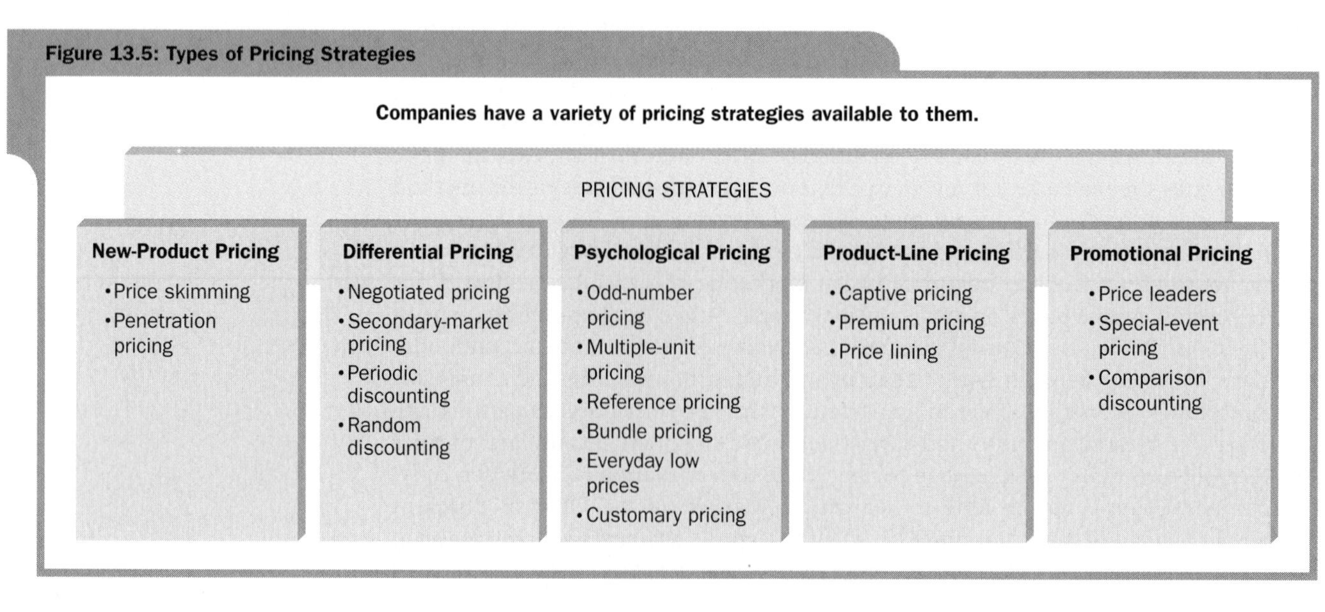

New Product Pricing

The two primary types of new product pricing strategies are price skimming and penetration pricing. An organization can use either one or even both over a period of time.

Price Skimming Some consumers are willing to pay a high price for an innovative product either because of its novelty or because of the prestige or status that ownership confers. **Price skimming** is the strategy of charging the highest possible price for a product during the introduction stage of its life cycle. The seller essentially "skims the cream" off the market, which helps to recover the high costs of R&D more quickly. Also, a skimming policy may hold down demand for the product, which is helpful if the firm's production capacity is limited during the introduction stage. The greatest disadvantage is that a skimming price may make the product appear lucrative to potential competitors, who then may attempt to enter that market.

Penetration Pricing At the opposite extreme, **penetration pricing** is the strategy of setting a low price for a new product. The main purpose of setting a low price is to build market share for the product quickly. The seller hopes that the building of a large market share quickly will discourage competitors from entering the market. If the low price stimulates sales, the firm also may be able to order longer production runs, which result in lower production costs per unit. A disadvantage of penetration pricing is that it places a firm in a less flexible position. It is more difficult to raise prices significantly than it is to lower them.

High Prices for Poor Consumers?

Do rent-to-own companies take advantage of poor consumers by pricing products too high? A $7 billion industry, rent-to-own businesses offer appliances, furniture, musical instruments, and electronics priced to rent by the week or the month. Their customers generally don't have the cash or the credit to buy big-ticket items outright. Although renting is affordable in the short term, it's costly in the long run.

Consider a flat-screen television renting for $86.25 per month at a rent-to-own store. The store informs prospective renters that after 12 monthly payments, they will own the television, at a total cost of $1,035. Yet that same television sells in a nearby electronics store for only $500.

An executive at Rent-A-Center, which operates more than 3,000 rent-to-own stores nationwide, says renting allows consumers to try a product for a short period. If they don't like it or they can't keep up the payments, they can stop renting. "It gives them the flexibility to end it if they want, with no further obligation," he explains. Still, customers who rent by the week or month wind up paying roughly twice as much to own a product as consumers who buy it elsewhere, with cash or credit. Is the price too high?

Sources: Jim Dwyer, "For Just a Few Dollars, A Big TV and Years of Debt," *New York Times*, February 2, 2008, p. B1; Jessica Heffner, "Rent-to-Own Plans Can Cost Cash-Poor Customers in the Long Run," *Middletown (Ohio) Journal*, September 7, 2008, **www.middletown.com**; Marc Heller, "Schumer Targeting Rent-to-Own Stores," *Watertown Daily Times*, June 5, 2008, n.p.

price skimming the strategy of charging the highest possible price for a product during the introduction stage of its life cycle

penetration pricing the strategy of setting a low price for a new product

Differential Pricing

An important issue in pricing decisions is whether to use a single price or different prices for the same product. A single price is easily understood by both employees and customers, and since many salespeople and customers do not like having to negotiate a price, it reduces the chance of a marketer developing an adversarial relationship with a customer.

Differential pricing means charging different prices to different buyers for the same quality and quantity of product. For differential pricing to be effective, the market must consist of multiple segments with different price sensitivities. When this method is employed, caution should be used to avoid confusing or antagonizing customers. Differential pricing can occur in several ways, including negotiated pricing, secondary-market pricing, periodic discounting, and random discounting.

Negotiated Pricing **Negotiated pricing** occurs when the final price is established through bargaining between the seller and the customer. Negotiated pricing occurs in a number of industries and at all levels of distribution. Even when there is a predetermined stated price or a price list, manufacturers, wholesalers, and retailers still may negotiate to establish the final sales price. Consumers commonly negotiate prices for houses, cars, and used equipment.

negotiated pricing establishing a final price through bargaining

Secondary-Market Pricing **Secondary-market pricing** means setting one price for the primary target market and a different price for another market. Often the

secondary-market pricing setting one price for the primary target market and a different price for another market

price charged in the secondary market is lower. However, when the costs of serving a secondary market are higher than normal, secondary-market customers may have to pay a higher price. Examples of secondary markets include a geographically isolated domestic market, a market in a foreign country, and a segment willing to purchase a product during off-peak times (such as "early bird" diners at restaurants and off-peak users of cellular phones).

periodic discounting temporary reduction of prices on a patterned or systematic basis

Periodic Discounting **Periodic discounting** is the temporary reduction of prices on a patterned or systematic basis. For example, many retailers have annual holiday sales, and some women's apparel stores have two seasonal sales each year—a winter sale in the last two weeks of January and a summer sale in the first two weeks of July. From the marketer's point of view, a major problem with periodic discounting is that customers can predict when the reductions will occur and may delay their purchases until they can take advantage of the lower prices.

random discounting temporary reduction of prices on an unsystematic basis

Random Discounting To alleviate the problem of customers' knowing when discounting will occur, some organizations employ **random discounting**. That is, they reduce their prices temporarily on an nonsystematic basis. When price reductions of a product occur randomly, current users of that brand are not likely to be able to predict when the reductions will occur and so will not delay their purchases in anticipation of buying the product at a lower price. Marketers also use random discounting to attract new customers.

Psychological Pricing

Psychological pricing strategies encourage purchases based on emotional responses rather than on economically rational responses. These strategies are used primarily for consumer products rather than business products.

odd-number pricing the strategy of setting prices using odd numbers that are slightly below whole-dollar amounts

Odd-Number Pricing Many retailers believe that consumers respond more positively to odd-number prices such as $4.99 than to whole-dollar prices such as $5. **Odd-number pricing** is the strategy of setting prices using odd numbers that are slightly below whole-dollar amounts. Nine and five are the most popular ending figures for odd-number prices.

Sellers who use this strategy believe that odd-number prices increase sales. The strategy is not limited to low-priced items. Auto manufacturers may set the price of a car at $11,999 rather than $12,000. Odd-number pricing has been the subject of various psychological studies, but the results have been inconclusive.

multiple-unit pricing the strategy of setting a single price for two or more units

Multiple-Unit Pricing Many retailers (and especially supermarkets) practice **multiple-unit pricing**, setting a single price for two or more units, such as two cans for 99 cents rather than 50 cents per can. Especially for frequently purchased products, this strategy can increase sales. Customers who see the single price and who expect eventually to use more than one unit of the product regularly purchase multiple units to save money.

reference pricing pricing a product at a moderate level and positioning it next to a more expensive model or brand

Reference Pricing **Reference pricing** means pricing a product at a moderate level and positioning it next to a more expensive model or brand in the hope that the customer will use the higher price as a reference price (i.e., a comparison price). Because of the comparison, the customer is expected to view the moderate price favorably. When you go to Sears to buy a DVD recorder, a moderately priced DVD recorder may appear especially attractive because it offers most of the important attributes of the more expensive alternatives on display and at a lower price.

bundle pricing packaging together two or more complementary products and selling them for a single price

Bundle Pricing **Bundle pricing** is the packaging together of two or more products, usually of a complementary nature, to be sold for a single price. To be attractive to customers, the single price usually is considerably less than the sum of the prices of the individual products. Being able to buy the bundled combination of products in a single transaction may be of value to the customer as well.

Bundle pricing is used commonly for banking and travel services, computers, and automobiles with option packages. Bundle pricing can help to increase customer satisfaction. Bundling slow-moving products with ones with a higher turnover, an organization can stimulate sales and increase its revenues. Selling products as a package rather than individually also may result in cost savings. As regulations in the telecommunications industry continue to evolve, many experts agree that telecom services will be provided together using bundled pricing in the near future. The new term *all-distance* has emerged, but the bundling of services goes beyond just combined pricing for local and long-distance services. Verizon, for example, is offering the Verizon Triple Freedom plan that gives customers unlimited local, long-distance, wireless, DSL, and DirectTV for a bundled price of about $105 per month.[14]

Everyday Low Prices (EDLPs) To reduce or eliminate the use of frequent short-term price reductions, some organizations use an approach referred to as **everyday low prices (EDLPs)**. When EDLPs are used, a marketer sets a low price for its products on a consistent basis rather than setting higher prices and frequently discounting them. EDLPs, though not deeply discounted, are set far enough below competitors' prices to make customers feel confident that they are receiving a fair price. EDLPs are employed by retailers such as Wal-Mart and by manufacturers such as Procter & Gamble. A company that uses EDLPs benefits from reduced promotional costs, reduced losses from frequent markdowns, and more stability in its sales. A major problem with this approach is that customers have mixed responses to it. In some instances, customers simply do not believe that EDLPs are what they say they are but are instead a marketing gimmick.

everyday low prices (EDLPs) setting a low price for products on a consistent basis

Customary Pricing In **customary pricing**, certain goods are priced primarily on the basis of tradition. Examples of customary, or traditional, prices would be those set for candy bars and chewing gum.

customary pricing pricing on the basis of tradition

Product-Line Pricing

Rather than considering products on an item-by-item basis when determining pricing strategies, some marketers employ product-line pricing. *Product-line pricing* means establishing and adjusting the prices of multiple products within a product line. Product-line pricing can provide marketers with flexibility in price setting. For example, marketers can set prices so that one product is quite profitable, whereas another increases market share by virtue of having a lower price than competing products.

When marketers employ product-line pricing, they have several strategies from which to choose. These include captive pricing, premium pricing, and price lining.

Captive Pricing When **captive pricing** is used, the basic product in a product line is priced low, but the price on the items required to operate or enhance it are set at a higher level. For example, a manufacturer of cameras and film may price a camera at a low level to attract customers but price the film at a relatively high level because customers must continue to purchase film in order to use their cameras.

captive pricing pricing the basic product in a product line low, but pricing related items at a higher level

Premium Pricing **Premium pricing** occurs when the highest-quality product or the most-versatile version of similar products in a product line is given the highest price. Other products in the line are priced to appeal to price-sensitive shoppers or to those who seek product-specific features. Marketers that use premium pricing often realize a significant portion of their profits from premium-priced products. Examples of product categories in which premium pricing is common are small kitchen appliances, beer, ice cream, and television cable service.

premium pricing pricing the highest-quality or most-versatile products higher than other models in the product line

Price Lining **Price lining** is the strategy of selling goods only at certain predetermined prices that reflect definite price breaks. For example, a shop may sell men's ties only at $22 and $37. This strategy is used widely in clothing and accessory

price lining the strategy of selling goods only at certain predetermined prices that reflect definite price breaks

stores. It eliminates minor price differences from the buying decision—both for customers and for managers who buy merchandise to sell in these stores.

Promotional Pricing

Price, as an ingredient in the marketing mix, often is coordinated with promotion. The two variables sometimes are so interrelated that the pricing policy is promotion oriented. Examples of promotional pricing include price leaders, special-event pricing, and comparison discounting.

price leaders products priced below the usual markup, near cost, or below cost

Price Leaders Sometimes a firm prices a few products below the usual markup, near cost, or below cost, which results in prices known as **price leaders**. This type of pricing is used most often in supermarkets and restaurants to attract customers by giving them especially low prices on a few items. Management hopes that sales of regularly priced products will more than offset the reduced revenues from the price leaders.

special-event pricing advertised sales or price cutting linked to a holiday, season, or event

Special-Event Pricing To increase sales volume, many organizations coordinate price with advertising or sales promotions for seasonal or special situations. **Special-event pricing** involves advertised sales or price cutting linked to a holiday, season, or event. If the pricing objective is survival, then special sales events may be designed to generate the necessary operating capital.

comparison discounting setting a price at a specific level and comparing it with a higher price

Comparison Discounting **Comparison discounting** sets the price of a product at a specific level and simultaneously compares it with a higher price. The higher price may be the product's previous price, the price of a competing brand, the product's price at another retail outlet, or a manufacturer's suggested retail price. Customers may find comparative discounting informative, and it can have a significant impact on them. However, because this pricing strategy on occasion has led to deceptive pricing practices, the Federal Trade Commission has established guidelines for comparison discounting. If the higher price against which the comparison is made is the price formerly charged for the product, sellers must have made the previous price available to customers for a reasonable period of time. If sellers present the higher price as the one charged by other retailers in the same trade area, they must be able to demonstrate that this claim is true. When they present the higher price as the manufacturer's suggested retail price, then the higher price must be similar to the price at which a reasonable proportion of the product was sold. Some manufacturers' suggested retail prices are so high that very few products actually are sold at those prices. In such cases, it would be deceptive to use comparison discounting.

Pricing Business Products

10

Learning Objective: Describe three major types of pricing associated with business products.

Many of the pricing issues discussed thus far in this chapter deal with pricing in general. Setting prices for business products can be different from setting prices for consumer products owing to several factors such as size of purchases, transportation considerations, and geographic issues. We examine three types of pricing associated with business products, including geographic pricing, transfer pricing, and discounting.

Geographic Pricing

Geographic pricing strategies deal with delivery costs. The pricing strategy that requires the buyer to pay the delivery costs is called *FOB origin pricing*. It stands for "free on board at the point of origin," which means that the price does not include freight charges, and thus the buyer must pay the transportation costs from the seller's warehouse to the buyer's place of business. *FOB destination* indicates that the price does include freight charges, and thus the seller pays these charges.

Transfer Pricing

When one unit in an organization sells a product to another unit, **transfer pricing** occurs. The price is determined by calculating the cost of the product. A transfer price can vary depending on the types of costs included in the calculations. The choice of the costs to include when calculating the transfer price depends on the company's management strategy and the nature of the units' interaction. An organization also must ensure that transfer pricing is fair to all units involved in the purchases.

transfer pricing prices charged in sales between an organization's units

Discounting

A **discount** is a deduction from the price of an item. Producers and sellers offer a wide variety of discounts to their customers, including the following:

discount a deduction from the price of an item

- *Trade discounts* are discounts from the list prices that are offered to marketing intermediaries, or middlemen. A furniture retailer, for example, may receive a 40 percent discount from the manufacturer. The retailer then would pay $60 for a lamp carrying a list price of $100. Intermediaries, discussed in Chapter 14, perform various marketing activities in return for trade discounts.
- *Quantity discounts* are discounts given to customers who buy in large quantities. The seller's per-unit selling cost is lower for larger purchases. The quantity discount is a way of passing part of these savings on to the buyer.
- *Cash discounts* are discounts offered for prompt payment. A seller may offer a discount of "2/10, net 30," meaning that the buyer may take a 2 percent discount if the bill is paid within ten days and that the bill must be paid in full within thirty days.
- A *seasonal discount* is a price reduction to buyers who purchase out of season. This discount lets the seller maintain steadier production during the year. For example, automobile rental agencies offer seasonal discounts in winter and early spring to encourage firms to use automobiles during the slow months of the automobile rental business.
- An *allowance* is a reduction in price to achieve a desired goal. Trade-in allowances, for example, are price reductions granted for turning in used equipment when purchasing new equipment. This type of discount is popular in the aircraft industry. Another example is a promotional allowance, which is a price reduction granted to dealers for participating in advertising and sales-support programs intended to increase sales of a particular item.

return to inside business

Flip

By the time Pure Digital Technologies introduced its first Flip in 2006, the camcorder was well into its product life cycle. The easy-to-use, pocket-size Flip reinvigorated the product category by attracting first-time buyers and casual users who didn't like the complexity or the cost of traditional camcorders. Pure Digital sold nearly 2 million Flips in its first two years and sparked a new-product frenzy as competitors rushed to bring simple, inexpensive camcorders to market.

With the Flip Mino, Pure Digital has pioneered yet another camcorder innovation. Buyers can log onto the Flip website and order a personalized camcorder by choosing from hundreds of case designs or uploading their own designs. More Flip models are on the way as the company continues its innovative ways.

Questions

1. What are the advantages and disadvantages of the Flip brand name? Do you agree with the company's decision *not* to use Pure Digital Technologies as the camcorder's brand name?
2. Pure Digital Technologies uses premium pricing for products in its Flip line. Is this strategy compatible with the use of penetration pricing for new Flip models? Explain your answer.

Summary

1 Explain what a product is and how products are classified.

A product is everything one receives in an exchange, including all attributes and expected benefits. The product may be a manufactured item, a service, an idea, or some combination of these.

Products are classified according to their ultimate use. Classification affects a product's distribution, promotion, and pricing. Consumer products, which include convenience, shopping, and specialty products, are purchased to satisfy personal and family needs. Business products are purchased for resale, for making other products, or for use in a firm's operations. Business products can be classified as raw materials, major equipment, accessory equipment, component parts, process materials, supplies, and services.

2 Discuss the product life cycle and how it leads to new product development.

Every product moves through a series of four stages—introduction, growth, maturity, and decline—which together form the product life cycle. As the product progresses through these stages, its sales and profitability increase, peak, and then decline. Marketers keep track of the life-cycle stage of products in order to estimate when a new product should be introduced to replace a declining one.

3 Define *product line* and *product mix* and distinguish between the two.

A product line is a group of similar products marketed by a firm. The products in a product line are related to each other in the way they are produced, marketed, and used. The firm's product mix includes all the products it offers for sale. The width of a mix is the number of product lines it contains. The depth of the mix is the average number of individual products within each line.

4 Identify the methods available for changing a product mix.

Customer satisfaction and organizational objectives require marketers to develop, adjust, and maintain an effective product mix. Marketers may improve a product mix by changing existing products, deleting products, and developing new products.

New products are developed through a series of seven steps. The first step, idea generation, involves the accumulation of a pool of possible product ideas. Screening, the second step, removes from consideration those product ideas that do not mesh with organizational goals or resources. Concept testing, the third step, is a phase in which a small sample of potential buyers is exposed to a proposed product through a written or oral description in order to determine their initial reaction and buying intentions. The fourth step, business analysis, generates information about the potential sales, costs, and profits. During the development step, the product idea is transformed into mock-ups and actual prototypes to determine if the product is technically feasible to build and can be produced at reasonable costs. Test marketing is an actual launch of the product in several selected cities. Finally, during commercialization, plans for full-scale production and marketing are refined and implemented. Most product failures result from inadequate product planning and development.

5 Explain the uses and importance of branding, packaging, and labeling.

A brand is a name, term, symbol, design, or any combination of these that identifies a seller's products as distinct from those of other sellers. Brands can be classified as manufacturer brands, store brands, or generic brands. A firm can choose between two branding strategies—individual branding or family branding. Branding strategies are used to associate (or *not* associate) particular products with existing products, producers, or intermediaries. Packaging protects goods, offers consumer convenience, and enhances marketing efforts by communicating product features, uses, benefits, and image. Labeling provides customers with product information, some of which is required by law.

6 Describe the economic basis of pricing and the means by which sellers can control prices and buyers' perceptions of prices.

Under the ideal conditions of pure competition, an individual seller has no control over the price of its products. Prices are determined by the workings of supply and demand. In our real economy, however, sellers do exert some control, primarily through product differentiation. Product differentiation is the process of developing and promoting differences between one's product and all similar products. Firms also attempt to gain some control over pricing through advertising. A few large sellers have considerable control over prices because each controls a large proportion of the total supply of the product. Firms must consider the relative importance of price to buyers in the target market before setting prices. Buyers' perceptions of prices are affected by the importance of the product to them, the range of prices they consider acceptable, their perceptions of competing products, and their association of quality with price.

7 Identify the major pricing objectives used by businesses.

Objectives of pricing include survival, profit maximization, target return on investment, achieving market goals, and maintaining the status quo. Firms sometimes have to price products to survive, which usually requires cutting prices to attract customers. Return on investment

(ROI) is the amount earned as a result of the investment in developing and marketing the product. The firm sets an annual percentage ROI as the pricing goal. Some firms use pricing to maintain or increase their market share. And in industries in which price stability is important, firms often price their products by charging about the same as competitors.

8 Examine the three major pricing methods that firms employ.

The three major pricing methods are cost-based pricing, demand-based pricing, and competition-based pricing. When cost-based pricing is employed, a proportion of the cost is added to the total cost to determine the selling price. When demand-based pricing is used, the price will be higher when demand is higher, and the price will be lower when demand is lower. A firm that uses competition-based pricing may choose to price below competitors' prices, at the same level as competitors' prices, or slightly above competitors' prices.

Explain the different strategies available to companies for setting prices.

Pricing strategies fall into five categories: new product pricing, differential pricing, psychological pricing, product-line pricing, and promotional pricing. Price skimming and penetration pricing are two strategies used for pricing new products. Differential pricing can be accomplished through negotiated pricing, secondary-market pricing, periodic discounting, and random discounting. The types of psychological pricing strategies are odd-number pricing, multiple-unit pricing, reference pricing, bundle pricing, everyday low prices, and customary pricing. Product-line pricing can be achieved through captive pricing, premium pricing, and price lining. The major types of promotional pricing are price-leader pricing, special-event pricing, and comparison discounting.

Describe three major types of pricing associated with business products.

Setting prices for business products can be different from setting prices for consumer products as a result of several factors, such as size of purchases, transportation considerations, and geographic issues. The three types of pricing associated with the pricing of business products are geographic pricing, transfer pricing, and discounting.

Key Terms

You should now be able to define and give an example relevant to each of the following terms:

product (364)
consumer product (365)
business product (365)
convenience product (365)
shopping product (365)
specialty product (365)
raw material (366)
major equipment (366)
accessory equipment (366)
component part (366)
process material (366)
supply (366)
business service (366)
product life cycle (366)
product line (369)
product mix (369)
product modification (370)
line extension (370)
product deletion (370)
brand (374)
brand name (374)
brand mark (374)
trademark (374)
trade name (374)
manufacturer (or producer) brand (374)
store (or private) brand (374)
generic product (or brand) (375)
brand loyalty (375)
brand equity (375)
individual branding (377)
family branding (377)
brand extension (377)
packaging (377)
labeling (379)
express warranty (380)
price (380)
supply (380)
demand (380)
price competition (381)
nonprice competition (381)
product differentiation (381)
markup (384)
breakeven quantity (384)
total revenue (384)
fixed cost (384)
variable cost (384)
total cost (384)
price skimming (387)
penetration pricing (387)
negotiated pricing (387)
secondary-market pricing (387)
periodic discounting (388)
random discounting (388)
odd-number pricing (388)
multiple-unit pricing (388)
reference pricing (388)
bundle pricing (388)
everyday low prices (EDLPs) (389)
customary pricing (389)
captive pricing (389)
premium pricing (389)
price lining (389)
price leaders (390)
special-event pricing (390)
comparison discounting (390)
transfer pricing (391)
discount (391)

Review Questions

1. What does the purchaser of a product obtain besides the good, service, or idea itself?
2. What are the products of (a) a bank, (b) an insurance company, and (c) a university?
3. What major factor determines whether a product is a consumer or a business product?
4. Describe each of the classifications of business products.
5. What are the four stages of the product life cycle? How can a firm determine which stage a particular product is in?
6. What is the difference between a product line and a product mix? Give an example of each.
7. Under what conditions does product modification work best?

8. Why do products have to be deleted from a product mix?
9. Why must firms introduce new products?
10. Briefly describe the seven new product development stages.
11. What is the difference between manufacturer brands and store brands? Between family branding and individual branding?
12. What is the difference between a line extension and a brand extension?
13. How can packaging be used to enhance marketing activities?
14. For what purposes is labeling used?
15. What is the primary function of prices in our economy?
16. Compare and contrast the characteristics of price and nonprice competition.
17. How might buyers' perceptions of price influence pricing decisions?
18. List and briefly describe the five major pricing objectives.
19. What are the differences among markup pricing, pricing by breakeven analysis, and competition-based pricing?
20. In what way is demand-based pricing more realistic than markup pricing?
21. Why would a firm use competition-based pricing?
22. What are the five major categories of pricing strategies? Give at least two examples of specific strategies that fall into each category.
23. Identify and describe the main types of discounts that are used in the pricing of business products.

Discussion Questions

1. Why is it important to understand how products are classified?
2. What factors might determine how long a product remains in each stage of the product life cycle? What can a firm do to prolong each stage?
3. Some firms do not delete products until they become financially threatening. What problems may result from relying on this practice?
4. Which steps in the evolution of new products are most important? Which are least important? Defend your choices.
5. Do branding, packaging, and labeling really benefit consumers? Explain.
6. To what extent can a firm control its prices in our market economy? What factors limit such control?
7. Under what conditions would a firm be most likely to use nonprice competition?
8. Can a firm have more than one pricing objective? Can it use more than one of the pricing methods discussed in this chapter? Explain.
9. What are the major disadvantages of price skimming?
10. What is an "effective" price?
11. Under what conditions would a business most likely decide to employ one of the differential pricing strategies?
12. For what types of products are psychological pricing strategies most likely to be used?

Video Case 13.1

The Smart Car: Tiny with a Price Tag to Match

Tiny car, tiny price tag, tiny gasoline bill. The Smart Car, made by Daimler's Mercedes Car Group in Hambach, France, first appeared on U.S. roads in 2008, just as prices at the gas pump were hitting record highs week after week. The timing could not have been better. Tired of emptying their wallets every time they filled their gas tanks, many U.S. drivers were thinking about downsizing from a big sport-utility vehicle or pickup truck to a smaller vehicle. But were they ready for a 106-inch-long car that seats only two people? Daimler was ready to find out.

The Smart Car had a good track record in other parts of the world. From 1998 to 2008, Daimler sold more than 900,000 Smart Cars in Europe, the Middle East, Asia, Australia, Mexico, and Canada. The car was cute, nimble, and unconventional—a good size for getting through crowded, narrow city streets and fitting into any tight parking spot. Not only was the purchase price highly affordable, but the excellent fuel efficiency made the car especially popular in countries where gas prices were generally high.

To bring the Smart Car to the United States, Daimler redesigned the body and engineering to meet U.S. safety standards. It added six inches to the car's length and included four air bags, an antilock braking system, a collapsing steering column, and other safety features. It also installed a fuel-saving 71-horsepower engine so that the Smart Car would go about 40 highway miles on a gallon of gasoline.

Daimler set the list price of the Smart Fortwo Pure model—the basic version of the two-seater—at $11,590. The list price of the Smart Fortwo Passion Coupe, equipped with more features, was $13,590. The list price of the Smart Fortwo Passion Cabriolet, a convertible with leather seats and additional features, was $16,590. Buyers had the option of ordering extras, such as a metallic-paint finish or an alarm system, for an additional fee. Keeping the list price as tiny as the car allowed Daimler to build market share quickly.

Rather than selling Smart Cars through its regular dealer network, Daimler contracted with the Penske Automotive Group to handle distribution and sales. In another unusual move, Daimler set up a website to let buyers reserve the model of their choice and choose from six interior colors and six exterior colors on the car body's removable panels. Three of the exterior colors were offered as part of the purchase price, while the three metallic exterior colors were offered at an extra cost. The $99 reservation fee was applied to the buyer's purchase price once the ordered model became available. By the time Smart Cars arrived in U.S. showrooms, 30,000 people had paid for reservations.

To build customer interest prior to the introduction, Daimler sent a number of Smart Cars on a 50-city U.S. tour. Nearly 50,000 members of the media and prospective car buyers took test drives. Although many reporters couldn't resist poking fun at the tiny car (*USA Today* called it a "breadbox on wheels"), they all noted its high fuel efficiency and low purchase price.

Soon, demand became so strong that even buyers who had reserved their cars well in advance had to wait months for delivery. A few U.S. customers who didn't want to wait paid as much as

$39,000 for European Smart Cars adapted to meet U.S. safety and emissions standards. Down the road, as more auto manufacturers gear up to bring gas-sipping cars to U.S. markets, will the Smart Car maintain its popularity?[15]

For more information about this company, go to **www.daimler.com**.

Questions

1. Why is bundle pricing appropriate for the various models of Smart Cars?
2. How is demand likely to affect dealers' willingness to negotiate prices with Smart Car buyers?
3. Imagine that Daimler is considering whether to sell unpainted Smart Cars and reduce the list price by $1,500. The Smart Car exterior consists of ten removable panels that can be easily painted. Buyers could paint their own panels, leave the panels unpainted, or pay the dealer an additional fee to personalize their cars by having the panels custom finished in almost any color or design. What are the advantages and disadvantages of this pricing idea?

Case 13.2 Apple Changes iPhone Pricing

Days before the first Apple iPhones went on sale, thousands of buyers lined up outside Apple stores, eager to try the new cell phone's large, user-friendly touch screen and multimedia capabilities. Like Apple's iconic iPod media player, instantly identifiable because of its sleek case and white ear buds, the stylish iPhone became a must-have status symbol for tech-savvy consumers across the United States. However, despite a major promotional campaign, widespread media coverage, many rave reviews, and a fast-growing customer base, the iPhone became the focus of criticism and controversy within two months of its release.

Apple has traditionally set high prices for its new products. One purpose of pricing in this way is to reinforce the brand's high-end positioning and special cachet. Another is to start recouping development costs and build profits from the very start of each product's life. This pricing strategy has worked with the company's Macintosh computers and its iPods, allowing Apple to increase both revenues and profits year after year.

The iPhone was initially priced at $599, not including the cost of monthly phone service through an exclusive deal with AT&T. Two months later, in a break from its usual pattern, Apple abruptly slashed the iPhone's price by $200. Although electronic products often drop in price over time, they rarely sell for so much less so soon after introduction. This time, Apple had its eye on the year-end holidays, believing that setting a more affordable price during the fall would put the iPhone within reach of a larger number of gift-giving buyers. The company also saw an opportunity to close in on its goal of selling 10 million iPhones worldwide within eighteen months of the product's launch.

Apple's pricing decision provoked angry protests from customers who protested that they had overpaid for a cutting-edge product that was going mainstream more quickly than expected. With Apple on the spot, CEO Steve Jobs quickly conceded that customers had a point. "Our early customers trusted us, and we must live up to that trust with our actions in moments like these," he said in a statement posted on Apple's website. To avoid alienating early buyers, the company offered a $100 Apple store credit to each customer who had purchased an iPhone before the price cut. While this policy also drew criticism—because the credit had no value except toward the purchase of something from Apple—the pricing controversy lost steam after a few weeks.

Apple soon launched a series of new iPhone models with more features, more power, and a lower price than when the product was originally introduced. The iPhone has gone on to become an enormous success around the world, sparking excitement and prompting long lines at Apple stores in the United Kingdom, France, and other countries. Just as the iPod attracted many first-time Apple buyers, the iPhone's unique appeal has brought in new customers and given loyal customers another reason to buy from Apple.

The buzz from the iPhone and other new products has also boosted demand for Apple's line of Macintosh computers. In fact, the company gained enough market share to become the third-largest U.S. computer marketer, trailing only market leader Dell and Hewlett-Packard. Higher sales of Apple's entire product mix have resulted in record-setting company profits. Just as important, all these innovations have polished the Apple brand and added to its trend-setting image—which, in turn, allows the company to charge premium prices for its coveted products.[16]

For more information about this company, go to **www.apple.com**.

Questions

1. What was Apple's primary pricing objective when it introduced the iPhone? What was its primary objective in cutting the product's price just two months after introduction?
2. How much weight does Apple appear to have given to its evaluation of competitive pricing?
3. Do you agree with Apple's decision to switch away from price skimming after the iPhone's introduction? Defend your answer.

Building Skills for Career Success

1. JOURNALING FOR SUCCESS

Discovery statement: This chapter explained the importance of product branding.

Assignment

1. Thinking about the brands of products that you use, to which brand are you the most loyal? Explain the functional benefits of this brand.
2. Beyond the functional benefits, what does this brand mean to you?
3. Under what set of circumstances would you be willing to change to another competing brand?
4. Discuss how you first began to use this brand.

2. EXPLORING THE INTERNET

The Internet has quickly taken comparison shopping to a new level. Several websites such as **bizrate.com**, **pricescan.com**, and

mysimon.com have emerged boasting that they can find the consumer the best deal on any product. From computers to watches, these sites offer unbiased price and product information to compare virtually any product. Users may read reviews about products as well as provide their own input from personal experience. Some of these sites also offer special promotions and incentives in exchange for user information. Visit the text website for updates to this exercise.

Assignment

1. Search all three of the websites listed above for the same product.
2. Did you notice any significant differences between the sites and the information they provide?
3. What percentage of searches do you think lead to purchases as opposed to browsing? Explain your answer.
4. Which site are you most likely to use on a regular basis? Why?
5. In what ways do these websites contribute to price competition?

3. DEVELOPING CRITICAL-THINKING SKILLS

A feature is a characteristic of a product or service that enables it to perform its function. Benefits are the results a person receives from using a product or service. For example, a toothpaste's stain-removing formula is a feature; the benefit to the user is whiter teeth. While features are valuable and enhance a product, benefits motivate people to buy. The customer is more interested in how the product can help (the benefits) than in the details of the product (the features).

Assignment

1. Choose a product and identify its features and benefits.
2. Divide a sheet of paper into two columns. In one column, list the features of the product. In the other column, list the benefits each feature yields to the buyer.
3. Prepare a statement that would motivate you to buy this product.

4. BUILDING TEAM SKILLS

In his book, *The Post-Industrial Society,* Peter Drucker wrote:

> Society, community, and family are all conserving institutions. They try to maintain stability and to prevent, or at least slow down, change. But the organization of the post-capitalist society of organizations is a destabilizer. Because its function is to put knowledge to work—on tools, processes, and products; on work; on knowledge itself—it must be organized for constant change. It must be organized for innovation.

New product development is important in this process of systematically abandoning the past and building a future. Current customers can be sources of ideas for new products and services and ways of improving existing ones.

Assignment

1. Working in teams of five to seven, brainstorm ideas for new products or services for your college.
2. Construct questions to ask currently enrolled students (your customers). Sample questions might include:
   a. Why did you choose this college?
   b. How can this college be improved?
   c. What products or services do you wish were available?
3. Conduct the survey and review the results.
4. Prepare a list of improvements and/or new products or services for your college.

5. RESEARCHING DIFFERENT CAREERS

Standard & Poor's Industry Surveys, designed for investors, provides insight into various industries and the companies that compete within those industries. The "Basic Analysis" section gives overviews of industry trends and issues. The other sections define some basic industry terms, report the latest revenues and earnings of more than 1,000 companies, and occasionally list major reference books and trade associations.

Assignment

1. Identify an industry in which you might like to work.
2. Find the industry in *Standard & Poor's.* (*Note: Standard & Poor's* uses broad categories of industry. For example, an apparel or home-furnishings store would be included under "Retail" or "Textiles.")
3. Identify the following:
   a. Trends and issues in the industry
   b. Opportunities and/or problems that might arise in the industry in the next five years
   c. Major competitors within the industry (These companies are your potential employers.)
4. Prepare a report of your findings.

14

Wholesaling, Retailing, and Physical Distribution

LEARNING OBJECTIVES

What you will be able to do once you complete this chapter:

1. Identify the various channels of distribution that are used for consumer and industrial products.
2. Explain the concept of market coverage.
3. Understand how supply-chain management facilitates partnering among channel members.
4. Describe what a vertical marketing system is and identify the types of vertical marketing systems.
5. Discuss the need for wholesalers and describe the services they provide to retailers and manufacturers.
6. Identify and describe the major types of wholesalers.
7. Distinguish among the major types of retailers.
8. Identify the categories of shopping centers and the factors that determine how shopping centers are classified.
9. Explain the five most important physical distribution activities.

AP Photo/Vincent Yu

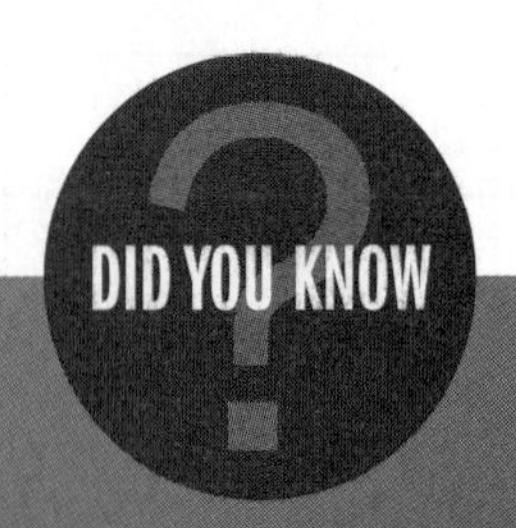

inside business

Target's eye-catching red-and-white bull's-eye logo has come to stand for "cheap chic."

Target Aims for Retailing Bullseye

A new era of retailing began in 1962, when Target, Wal-Mart, and Kmart all opened as discount stores. Target grew so quickly that by 1975, it was bringing in more sales revenue than its parent company's department stores. Discount retailing continued to gain momentum all over the United States, and in 2000, the parent company renamed itself Target.

Rather than trying to be all things to all shoppers, Target has differentiated itself on the basis of good design at discount prices. Designers Mossimo Giannulli and Isaac Mizrahi have created popularly priced fashion clothing for Target. Architect Michael Graves has developed stylish housewares and home décor products for Target. Even the ClearRx bottles in which Target sells prescription drugs have an entirely new look that enhances their functionality. In short, the retailer's eye-catching red-and-white bull's-eye logo has come to stand for "cheap chic."

Target also uses limited-time "pop-up" shops to promote certain product categories or specific designers. In business for a few days or as long as a few weeks, these temporary stand-alone shops give Target a brief but high-profile presence to attract targeted customer segments. Not long ago, Target opened four Bullseye Bodegas in New York City to preview new clothing and accessories by twenty-two designers. By opening during the city's Fashion Week, when couture designs debut, Target brought in crowds eager to see its latest styles. After four days, Target closed the pop-ups and began selling the new fashions throughout its 1,650 stores in forty-seven states.

Despite Target's long record of hitting the retailing bull's eye, economic turmoil and a decline in consumer spending have cut into both sales and profits. In response, the company has slowed the pace of new-store openings and, to compete more effectively with Wal-Mart, intensified its marketing focus on low prices. Will Target's trendy merchandise continue to be a defining feature in the future?[1]

Some companies, like Target, use a particular approach to distribution and marketing channels that gives them a sustainable competitive advantage. More than 2 million firms in the United States help to move products from producers to consumers. Store chains such as Dollar General Stores, Starbucks, Sears, and Wal-Mart operate retail outlets where consumers make purchases. Some retailers, such as Avon Products and Amway, send their salespeople to the homes of customers. Other retailers, such as Lands' End and L.L.Bean, sell through catalogs or through both catalogs and online. Still others, such as Amazon, sell online to customers.

In addition, there are more than half a million wholesalers that sell merchandise to other firms. Most consumers know little about these firms, which work "behind the scenes" and rarely sell directly to consumers. These and other intermediaries are concerned with the transfer of both products and ownership. They thus help to create the time, place, and possession utilities that are critical to marketing. As we will see, they also perform a number of services for their suppliers and their customers.

In this chapter, we initially examine various channels of distribution that products follow as they move from producer to ultimate user. Then we discuss wholesalers and retailers within these channels. Next, we examine the types of shopping centers. Finally, we explore the physical distribution function and the major modes of transportation that are used to move goods.

Channels of Distribution

A **channel of distribution**, or **marketing channel**, is a sequence of marketing organizations that directs a product from the producer to the ultimate user. Every marketing channel begins with the producer and ends with either the consumer or the business user.

A marketing organization that links a producer and user within a marketing channel is called a **middleman**, or **marketing intermediary**. For the most part, middlemen are concerned with the transfer of *ownership* of products. A **merchant middleman** (or, more simply, a *merchant*) is a middleman that actually takes title to products by buying them. A **functional middleman** on the other hand, helps in the transfer of ownership of products but does not take title to the products.

1

Learning Objective: Identify the various channels of distribution that are used for consumer and industrial products.

channel of distribution (or marketing channel) a sequence of marketing organizations that directs a product from the producer to the ultimate user

middleman (or marketing intermediary) a marketing organization that links a producer and user within a marketing channel

merchant middleman a middleman that actually takes title to products by buying them

functional middleman a middleman that helps in the transfer of ownership of products but does not take title to the products

retailer a middleman that buys from producers or other middlemen and sells to consumers

Channels for Consumer Products

Different channels of distribution generally are used to move consumer and business products. The four most commonly used channels for consumer products are illustrated in Figure 14.1.

Producer to Consumer This channel, often called the *direct channel,* includes no marketing intermediaries. Practically all services and a few consumer goods are distributed through a direct channel. Examples of marketers that sell goods directly to consumers include Dell Computer, Mary Kay Cosmetics, and Avon Products.

Producers sell directly to consumers for several reasons. They can better control the quality and price of their products. They do not have to pay (through discounts) for the services of intermediaries. And they can maintain closer ties with customers.

Producer to Retailer to Consumer A **retailer** is a middleman that buys from producers or other middlemen and sells to consumers. Producers sell directly to retailers when retailers (such as Wal-Mart) can buy in large quantities. This channel is used

Figure 14.1: Distribution Channels

Producers use various channels to distribute their products.

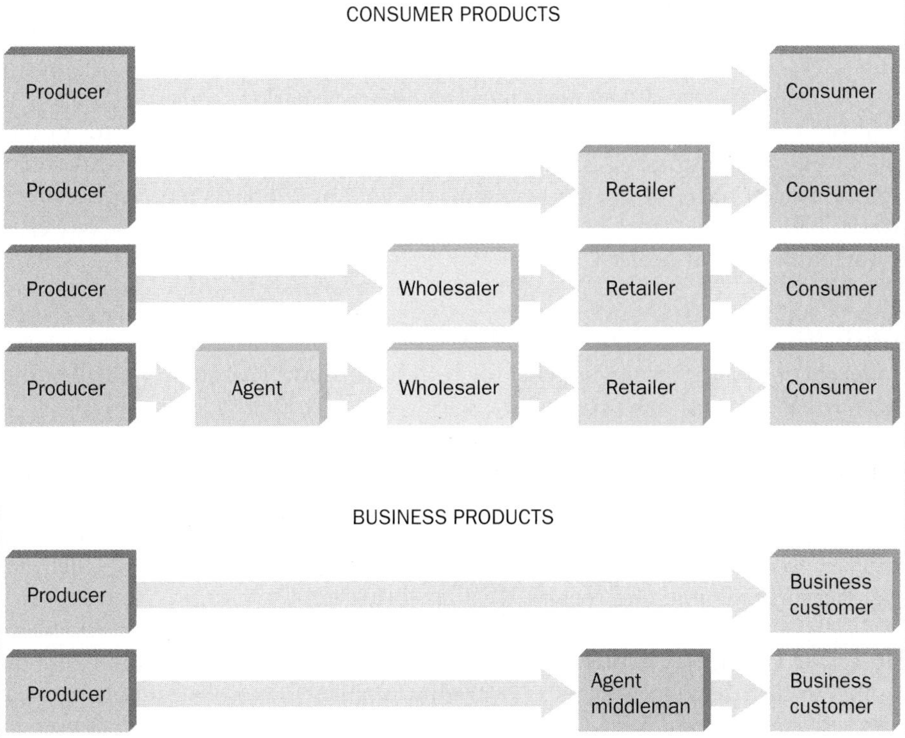

CONSUMER PRODUCTS

Producer → Consumer

Producer → Retailer → Consumer

Producer → Wholesaler → Retailer → Consumer

Producer → Agent → Wholesaler → Retailer → Consumer

BUSINESS PRODUCTS

Producer → Business customer

Producer → Agent middleman → Business customer

Entrepreneurial Challenge

Do You Have What It Takes to Own a Store?

You need more than the right location, the right merchandise, creative ideas, and hard work to succeed as an independent retailer. Before you open a store, ask yourself:

- *Do you have competitive spirit?* Every small store has competition. Karl Benson, who owns two kitchen and gourmet stores in Minnesota, faced a challenge when a national chain opened an outlet nearby. Benson fought back by expanding his line of imported foods and rewarding customer loyalty with special events and discounts.
- *Do you like people?* Personalized service can be a big advantage for a small store. Greg Larson, the owner of Larson's Toys and Games in Arlington, Ohio, enjoys helping customers select age-appropriate toys and offers free gift-wrapping. Dean Holborn, who owns two small stores in Great Britain, is on a first-name basis with customers and will order what they suggest.
- *Do you understand business?* Be ready to balance customer needs with business realities. When Holborn bought his first store, he didn't continue the previous owner's informal practice of letting customers sign for purchases and pay later, because he was concerned about being able to collect. Despite this change, most customers remained loyal because they liked Holborn's personal service.

Sources: Dick Youngblood, "Small Business: Cooks of Crocus Hill Finds New Recipes for Success," *Star Tribune (Minneapolis)*, July 23, 2008, p. 1D; Stefan Chomka, "Store Visit: Holborn's," *Grocer*, April 19, 2008, pp. 34+; Anne Field, "Small Shops See Smallness As Their Big Selling Point," *New York Times*, December 15, 2007, p. C1.

most often for products that are bulky, such as furniture and automobiles, for which additional handling would increase selling costs. It is also the usual channel for perishable products, such as fruits and vegetables, and for high-fashion products that must reach the consumer in the shortest possible time.

Producer to Wholesaler to Retailer to Consumer This channel is known as the *traditional channel* because many consumer goods (especially convenience goods) pass through wholesalers to retailers. A **wholesaler** is a middleman that sells products to other firms. These firms may be retailers, industrial users, or other wholesalers. A producer uses wholesalers when its products are carried by so many retailers that the producer cannot deal with all of them. For example, the maker of Wrigley's gum uses this type of channel.

Producer to Agent to Wholesaler to Retailer to Consumer Producers may use agents to reach wholesalers. Agents are functional middlemen that do not take title to products and that are compensated by commissions paid by producers. Often these products are inexpensive, frequently purchased items. For example, to reach a large number of potential customers, a small manufacturer of gas-powered lawn edgers might choose to use agents to market its product to wholesalers, which, in turn, sell the lawn edgers to a large number of retailers. This channel is also used for highly seasonal products (such as Christmas tree ornaments) and by producers that do not have their own sales forces.

Multiple Channels for Consumer Products Often, a manufacturer uses different distribution channels to reach different market segments. A manufacturer uses multiple channels, for example, when the same product is sold to consumers and business customers. Multiple channels are also used to increase sales or to capture a larger share of the market. With the goal of selling as much merchandise as possible, Firestone markets its tires through its own retail outlets as well as through independent dealers.

wholesaler a middleman that sells products to other firms

intensive distribution the use of all available outlets for a product

selective distribution the use of only a portion of the available outlets for a product in each geographic area

exclusive distribution the use of only a single retail outlet for a product in a large geographic area

Channels for Business Products

Producers of business products generally tend to use short channels. We will outline the two that are used most commonly, which are illustrated in Figure 14.1.

Producer to Business User In this direct channel, the manufacturer's own sales force sells directly to business users. Heavy machinery, airplanes, and major equipment usually are distributed in this way. The very short channel allows the producer to provide customers with expert and timely services, such as delivery, machinery installation, and repairs.

Producer to Agent Middleman to Business User Manufacturers use this channel to distribute such items as operating supplies, accessory equipment, small tools, and standardized parts. The agent is an independent intermediary between the producer and the user. Generally, agents represent sellers.

Going Global

Fashion Firms Get Physical

Fashion firms are profiting in style by streamlining physical distribution. For example, the global retailer Zara, owned by Spain's Inditex, can rush a new design from sketch to finished product and into stores within two weeks. To start, Zara's store managers track sales of every item, ask customers what they like, and report the latest trends to Inditex.

Based on these details, company designers quickly create new styles, have them manufactured in Inditex's European factories, and warehouse everything in Spain. Small batches of each style can be trucked to Zara's European stores within a day and sent by air cargo to Zara stores outside Europe within two days. The result: Zara's stores have a steady stream of new fashions to bring customers back again and again.

Valentino Fashion Group, owner of the Valentino, Hugo Boss, and M Missoni brands, has also revamped physical distribution to get the right fashions to the right stores at the right time. With its inventory management system connected to the sales systems of the department stores it supplies, Valentino can see immediately what's hot and what's not. This helps management decide which merchandise to send where—and when.

Sources: Kerry Capell, "Zara Thrives by Breaking All the Rules," *BusinessWeek*, October 20, 2008, p. 66; Christina Passariello, "Logistics Are in Vogue with Designers," *Wall Street Journal*, June 27, 2008, p. B1.

Market Coverage

2 Learning Objective: Explain the concept of market coverage.

How does a producer decide which distribution channels (and which particular intermediaries) to use? As with every other marketing decision, this one should be based on all relevant factors. These include the firm's production capabilities and marketing resources, the target market and buying patterns of potential customers, and the product itself. After evaluating these factors, the producer can choose a particular *intensity of market coverage*. Then the producer selects channels and intermediaries to implement that coverage.

Intensive distribution is the use of all available outlets for a product. The producer that wants to give its product the widest possible exposure in the marketplace chooses intensive distribution. The manufacturer saturates the market by selling to any intermediary of good financial standing that is willing to stock and sell the product. For the consumer, intensive distribution means being able to shop at a convenient store and spend minimum time buying the product. Many convenience goods, including candy, gum, and soft drinks, are distributed intensively. Companies such as Procter & Gamble that produce consumer packaged items rely on intensive distribution for many of their products because consumers want ready availability.

Selective distribution is the use of only a portion of the available outlets for a product in each geographic area. Manufacturers of goods such as furniture, major home appliances, and clothing typically prefer selective distribution. For example, Apple distributes its iPhone through Best Buy, AT&T, and Apple retail stores in the United States.

Exclusive distribution is the use of only a single retail outlet for a product in a large geographic area. Exclusive distribution usually is limited to very prestigious products. It is appropriate, for instance, for specialty goods such as upscale pianos, fine china, and expensive jewelry. The producer usually places many requirements (such as inventory levels, sales training, service quality, and warranty procedures) on exclusive dealers. For example, Patek Philippe watches, which may sell for $10,000 or more, are available in only a few select locations.

Marketing channels for consumer products. *Clothing often is distributed through the producer-to-retailer-to-consumer marketing channel.*

PRNewsFoto/Levi Strauss & Co.

Selective distribution. *Home appliances are usually distributed through selective distribution.*

Partnering Through Supply-Chain Management

3
Learning Objective: Understand how supply-chain management facilitates partnering among channel members.

supply-chain management long-term partnership among channel members working together to create a distribution system that reduces inefficiencies, costs, and redundancies while creating a competitive advantage and satisfying customers

Supply-chain management is a long-term partnership among channel members working together to create a distribution system that reduces inefficiencies, costs, and redundancies while creating a competitive advantage and satisfying customers. Supply-chain management requires cooperation throughout the entire marketing channel, including manufacturing, research, sales, advertising, and shipping. Supply chains focus not only on producers, wholesalers, retailers, and customers but also on component-parts suppliers, shipping companies, communication companies, and other organizations that participate in product distribution. Suppliers are having a greater impact on determining what items retail stores carry. This phenomenon, called *category management,* is becoming common for mass merchandisers, supermarkets, and convenience stores. Through category management, the retailer asks a supplier in a particular category how to stock the shelves. Many retailers and suppliers claim this process delivers maximum efficiency.

Traditionally, buyers and sellers have been adversarial when negotiating purchases. Supply-chain management, however, encourages cooperation in reducing the costs of inventory, transportation, administration, and handling; in speeding order-cycle times; and in increasing profits for all channel members. When buyers, sellers, marketing intermediaries, and facilitating agencies work together, customers' needs regarding delivery, scheduling, packaging, and other requirements are better met. Home Depot, North America's largest home-improvement retailer, is working to help its suppliers improve productivity and thereby supply Home Depot with better-quality products at lower costs. The company has even suggested a cooperative partnership with its competitors so that regional trucking companies making deliveries to all these organizations can provide faster, more efficient delivery.

Technology has enhanced the implementation of supply-chain management significantly. Through computerized integrated information sharing, channel members reduce costs and improve customer service. At Wal-Mart, for example, supply-chain management has almost eliminated the occurrence of out-of-stock items. Using barcode and electronic data interchange (EDI) technology, stores, warehouses, and suppliers communicate quickly and easily to keep Wal-Mart's shelves stocked with items customers want. Furthermore, there are currently about four hundred electronic trading communities made up of businesses selling to other businesses,

including auctions, exchanges, e-procurement hubs, and multisupplier online catalogs. As many major industries transform their processes over the next five to ten years, the end result will be increased productivity by reducing inventory, shortening cycle time, and removing wasted human effort.

Vertical Marketing Systems

Learning Objective: Describe what a vertical marketing system is and identify the types of vertical marketing systems.

Vertical channel integration occurs when two or more stages of a distribution channel are combined and managed by one firm. A **vertical marketing system (VMS)** is a centrally managed distribution channel resulting from vertical channel integration. This merging eliminates the need for certain intermediaries. One member of a marketing channel may assume the responsibilities of another member, or it actually may purchase the operations of that member. For example, a large-volume discount retailer that ships and warehouses its own stock directly from manufacturers does not need a wholesaler. Total vertical integration occurs when a single management controls all operations from production to final sale. Oil companies that own wells, transportation facilities, refineries, terminals, and service stations exemplify total vertical integration.

vertical channel integration the combining of two or more stages of a distribution channel under a single firm's management

vertical marketing system (VMS) a centrally managed distribution channel resulting from vertical channel integration

There are three types of VMSs: administered, contractual, and corporate. In an *administered VMS,* one of the channel members dominates the other members, perhaps because of its large size. Under its influence, the channel members collaborate on production and distribution. A powerful manufacturer, such as Procter & Gamble, receives a great deal of cooperation from intermediaries that carry its brands. Although the goals of the entire system are considered when decisions are made, control rests with individual channel members, as in conventional marketing channels. Under a *contractual VMS,* cooperative arrangements and the rights and obligations of channel members are defined by contracts or other legal measures. In a *corporate VMS,* actual ownership is the vehicle by which production and distribution are joined. For example, The Limited established a corporate VMS that operates corporate-owned production facilities and retail stores. Most vertical marketing systems are organized to improve distribution by combining individual operations.

Marketing Intermediaries: Wholesalers

Learning Objective: Discuss the need for wholesalers and describe the services they provide to retailers and manufacturers.

Wholesalers may be the most misunderstood of marketing intermediaries. Producers sometimes try to eliminate them from distribution channels by dealing directly with retailers or consumers. Yet wholesalers provide a variety of essential marketing services. Although wholesalers can be eliminated, their functions cannot be eliminated. These functions *must* be performed by other channel members or by consumers. Eliminating a wholesaler may or may not cut distribution costs.

Justifications for Marketing Intermediaries

The press, consumers, public officials, and other marketers often charge wholesalers, at least in principle, with inefficiency and parasitism. Consumers in particular feel strongly that the distribution channel should be made as short as possible. They assume that the fewer the intermediaries in a distribution channel, the lower the price of the product will be.

Those who believe that the elimination of wholesalers would bring about lower prices, however, do not recognize that the services wholesalers perform still would be needed. Those services simply would be provided by other means, and consumers would still bear the costs. Moreover, all manufacturers would have to keep extensive records and employ enough personnel to deal with a multitude of retailers individually. Even with direct distribution, products might be considerably more expensive because prices would reflect the costs of producers' inefficiencies. Figure 14.2 shows that sixteen contacts could result from the efforts of four buyers purchasing the products of four producers. With the assistance of an intermediary, only eight contacts would be necessary.

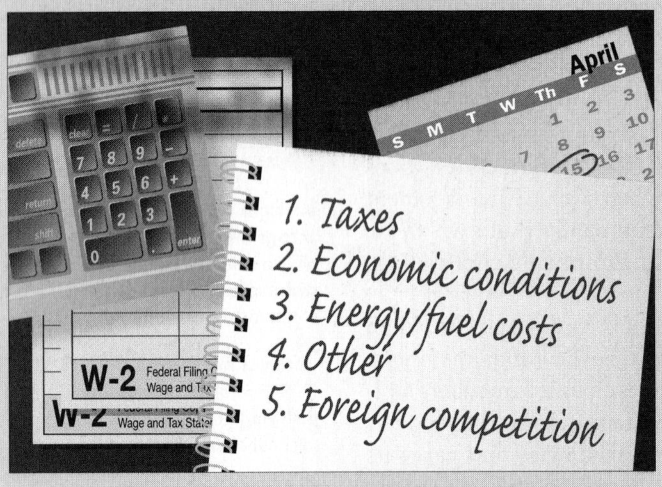

Source: Small Business Research Board Study, in "Top 5 Business Concerns," *Inbound Logistics*, September 2007, p. 20.

To illustrate further the useful role of wholesalers in the marketing system, assume that all wholesalers in the candy industry were abolished. With thousands of candy retailers to contact, candy manufacturers would be making an extremely large number of sales calls just to maintain the present level of product visibility. Hershey Foods, for example, would have to set up warehouses all over the country, organize a fleet of trucks, purchase and maintain thousands of vending machines, and deliver all its own candy. Sales and distribution costs for candy would soar. Candy producers would be contacting and shipping products to thousands of small businesses instead of to a limited number of large wholesalers and retailers. The outrageous costs of this inefficiency would be passed on to consumers. Candy bars would be more expensive and likely available through fewer retailers.

Wholesalers often are more efficient and economical not only for manufacturers, but also for consumers. Because pressure to eliminate them comes from both ends of the marketing channel, wholesalers should perform only those functions that are genuinely in demand. To stay in business, wholesalers also should take care to be efficient and productive and to provide high-quality services to other channel members.

Wholesalers' Services to Retailers

Wholesalers help retailers by buying in large quantities and then selling to retailers in smaller quantities and by delivering goods to retailers. They also stock—in one place—the variety of goods that retailers otherwise would have to buy from many producers. And wholesalers provide assistance in three other vital areas: promotion, market information, and financial aid.

Promotion Some wholesalers help to promote the products they sell to retailers. These services are usually either free or performed at cost. Wholesalers, for example,

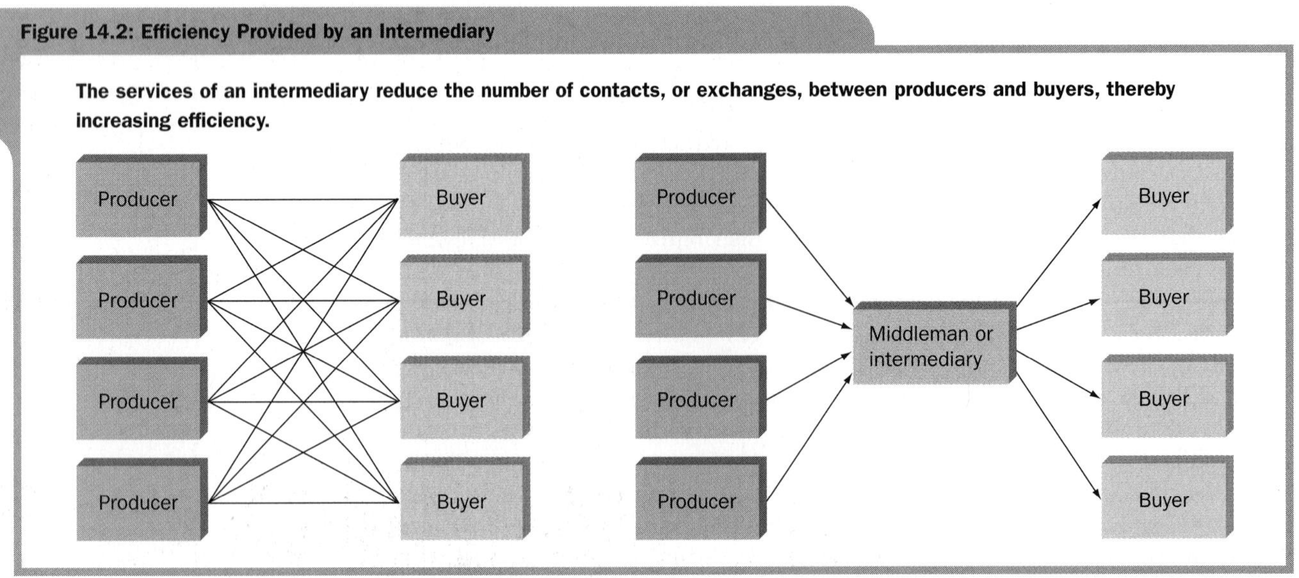

Figure 14.2: Efficiency Provided by an Intermediary

The services of an intermediary reduce the number of contacts, or exchanges, between producers and buyers, thereby increasing efficiency.

Source: William M. Pride and O. C. Ferrell, *Marketing: Concepts and Strategies,* 15th ed. (Mason, Ohio: South-Western/Cengage Learning, 2010). Adapted with permission.

are major sources of display materials designed to stimulate impulse buying. They also may help retailers to build effective window, counter, and shelf displays; they even may assign their own employees to work on the retail sales floor during special promotions.

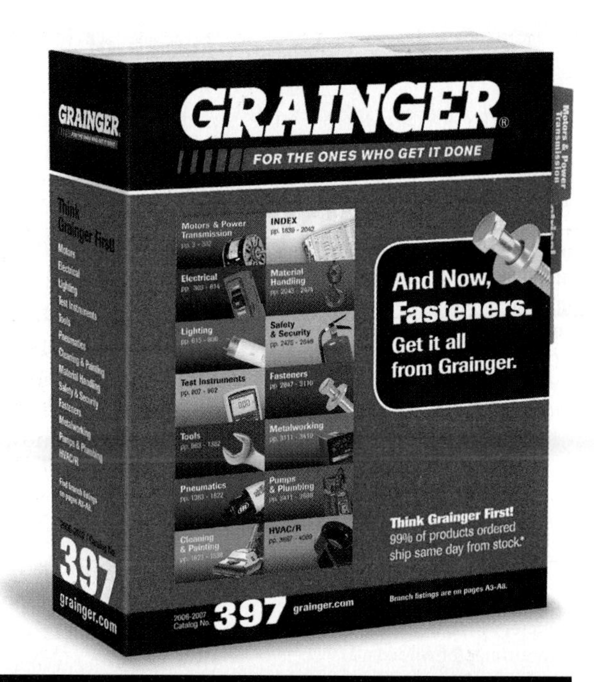

Wholesalers. *Grainger, a facilities maintenance products provider, is an example of a wholesaler.*

PRNewsFoto/W. W. Grainger, Inc.

Market Information Wholesalers are a constant source of market information. Wholesalers have numerous contacts with local businesses and distant suppliers. In the course of these dealings, they accumulate information about consumer demand, prices, supply conditions, new developments within the trade, and even industry personnel. This information may be relayed to retailers informally through the wholesaler's sales force. Some wholesalers also provide information to their customers through websites.

Information regarding industry sales and competitive prices is especially important to all firms. Dealing with a number of suppliers and many retailers, a wholesaler is a natural clearinghouse for such information. And most wholesalers are willing to pass information on to their customers.

Financial Aid Most wholesalers provide a type of financial aid that retailers often take for granted. By making prompt and frequent deliveries, wholesalers enable retailers to keep their own inventory investments small in relation to sales. Such indirect financial aid reduces the amount of operating capital that retailers need.

Wholesalers' Services to Manufacturers

Some of the services that wholesalers perform for producers are similar to those they provide to retailers. Others are quite different.

Providing an Instant Sales Force A wholesaler provides its producers with an instant sales force so that producers' sales representatives need not call on retailers. This can result in enormous savings for producers. For example, Lever Brothers and General Foods would have to spend millions of dollars each year to field a sales force large enough to call on all the retailers that sell their numerous products. Instead, these producers rely on wholesalers to sell and distribute their products to many retailers. These producers do have sales forces, though, that call on wholesalers and large retailers.

Reducing Inventory Costs Wholesalers purchase goods in sizable quantities from manufacturers and store these goods for resale. By doing so, they reduce the amount of finished-goods inventory that producers must hold and thereby reduce the cost of carrying inventories.

Assuming Credit Risks When producers sell through wholesalers, it is the wholesalers who extend credit to retailers, make collections from retailers, and assume the risks of nonpayment. These services reduce the producers' cost of extending credit to customers and the resulting bad-debt expense.

Furnishing Market Information Just as they do for retailers, wholesalers supply market information to the producers they serve. Valuable information accumulated by wholesalers may concern consumer demand, the producers' competition, and buying trends.

Types of Wholesalers

6

Learning Objective: Identify and describe the major types of wholesalers.

Wholesalers generally fall into three categories: merchant wholesalers; commission merchants, agents, and brokers; and manufacturers' sales branches and sales offices. Of these, merchant wholesalers constitute the largest portion. They account for about four-fifths of all wholesale establishments and employees.

merchant wholesaler a middleman that purchases goods in large quantities and then sells them to other wholesalers or retailers and to institutional, farm, government, professional, or industrial users

Merchant Wholesalers

A **merchant wholesaler** is a middleman that purchases goods in large quantities and then sells them to other wholesalers or retailers and to institutional, farm, government, professional, or industrial users. Merchant wholesalers usually operate one or more warehouses at which they receive, take title to, and store goods. These wholesalers are sometimes called *distributors* or *jobbers*.

Most merchant wholesalers are businesses composed of salespeople, order takers, receiving and shipping clerks, inventory managers, and office personnel. The successful merchant wholesaler must analyze available products and market needs. It must be able to adapt the type, variety, and quality of its products to changing market conditions.

full-service wholesaler a middleman that performs the entire range of wholesaler functions

Merchant wholesalers may be classified as full-service or limited-service wholesalers depending on the number of services they provide. A **full-service wholesaler** performs the entire range of wholesaler functions described earlier in this section. These functions include delivering goods, supplying warehousing, arranging for credit, supporting promotional activities, and providing general customer assistance.

general-merchandise wholesaler a middleman that deals in a wide variety of products

limited-line wholesaler a middleman that stocks only a few product lines but carries numerous product items within each line

specialty-line wholesaler a middleman that carries a select group of products within a single line

Under this broad heading are the general-merchandise wholesaler, limited-line wholesaler, and specialty-line wholesaler. A **general-merchandise wholesaler** deals in a wide variety of products, such as drugs, hardware, nonperishable foods, cosmetics, detergents, and tobacco. A **limited-line wholesaler** stocks only a few product lines but carries numerous product items within each line. A **specialty-line wholesaler** carries a select group of products within a single line. Food delicacies such as shellfish represent the kind of product handled by this type of wholesaler.

limited-service wholesaler a middleman that assumes responsibility for a few wholesale services only

In contrast to a full-service wholesaler, a **limited-service wholesaler** assumes responsibility for a few wholesale services only. Other marketing tasks are left to other channel members or consumers. This category includes cash-and-carry wholesalers, truck wholesalers, drop shippers, and mail-order wholesalers.

Commission Merchants, Agents, and Brokers

Commission merchants, agents, and brokers are functional middlemen. Functional middlemen do not take title to products. They perform a small number of marketing activities and are paid a commission that is a percentage of the sales price.

commission merchant a middleman that carries merchandise and negotiates sales for manufacturers

A **commission merchant** usually carries merchandise and negotiates sales for manufacturers. In most cases, commission merchants have the power to set the prices and terms of sales. After a sale is made, they either arrange for delivery or provide transportation services.

agent a middleman that expedites exchanges, represents a buyer or a seller, and often is hired permanently on a commission basis

An **agent** is a middleman that expedites exchanges, represents a buyer or a seller, and often is hired permanently on a commission basis. When agents represent producers, they are known as *sales agents* or *manufacturer's agents*. As long as the products represented do not compete, a sales agent may represent one or several manufacturers on a commission basis. The agent solicits orders for the manufacturers within a specific territory. As a rule, the manufacturers ship the merchandise and bill the customers directly. The manufacturers also set the prices and other conditions of the sales. What do the manufacturers gain by using a sales agent? The sales agent provides immediate entry into a territory, regular calls on customers, selling experience, and a known, predetermined selling expense (a commission that is a percentage of sales revenue).

broker a middleman that specializes in a particular commodity, represents either a buyer or a seller, and is likely to be hired on a temporary basis

A **broker** is a middleman that specializes in a particular commodity, represents either a buyer or a seller, and is likely to be hired on a temporary basis. However, food brokers, which sell grocery products to resellers, generally have long-term relationships with their clients. Brokers may perform only the selling function, or both buying and selling, using established contacts or special knowledge of their fields.

Manufacturers' Sales Branches and Sales Offices A **manufacturer's sales branch** is, in essence, a merchant wholesaler that is owned by a manufacturer. Sales branches carry inventory, extend credit, deliver goods, and offer help in promoting products. Their customers are retailers, other wholesalers, and industrial purchasers.

Because sales branches are owned by producers, they stock primarily the goods manufactured by their own firms. Selling policies and terms usually are established centrally and then transmitted to branch managers for implementation.

A **manufacturer's sales office** is essentially a sales agent owned by a manufacturer. Sales offices may sell goods manufactured by their own firms as well as certain products of other manufacturers that complement their own product lines. For example, Hiram Walker & Sons imports wine from Spain to increase the number of products its sales offices can offer to customers.

SPOTLIGHT
Importance of Retailing in the U.S. Economy

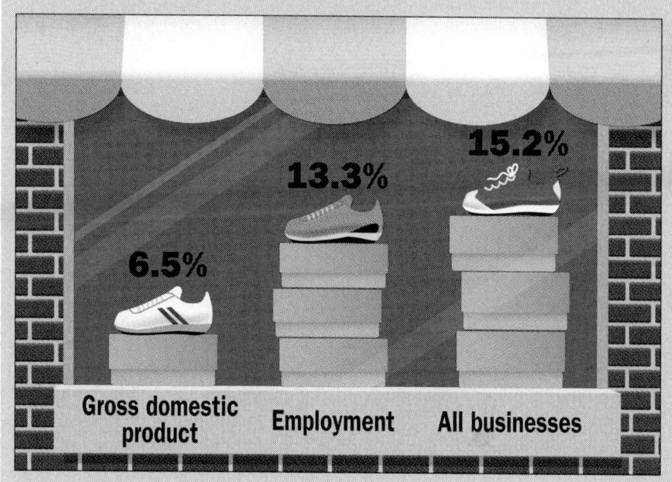

Source: U.S. Bureau of the Census, *Statistical Abstract of the United States,* 2008 (Washington, D.C.: U.S. Government Printing Office, 2007), pp. 431, 496, 647, 650.

Marketing Intermediaries: Retailers

7 **Learning Objective: Distinguish among the major types of retailers.**

Retailers are the final link between producers and consumers. Retailers may buy from either wholesalers or producers. They sell not only goods but also such services as auto repairs, haircuts, and dry cleaning. Some retailers sell both. Sears, Roebuck and Company sells consumer goods, financial services, and repair services for home appliances bought at Sears.

Of approximately 2.6 million retail firms in the United States, about 90 percent have annual sales of less than $1 million. On the other hand, some large retail organizations realize well over $1 million in sales revenue per day. Table 14.1 lists the twenty largest retail organizations and their approximate sales revenues and yearly profits.

manufacturer's sales branch essentially a merchant wholesaler that is owned by a manufacturer

manufacturer's sales office essentially a sales agent owned by a manufacturer

Classes of In-Store Retailers

One way to classify retailers is by the number of stores owned and operated by the firm. An **independent retailer** is a firm that operates only one retail outlet. Approximately three-fourths of retailers are independent. One-store operators, like all small businesses, generally provide personal service and a convenient location.

A **chain retailer** is a company that operates more than one retail outlet. By adding outlets, chain retailers attempt to reach new geographic markets. As sales increase, chains usually buy merchandise in larger quantities and thus take advantage of quantity discounts. They also wield more power in their dealings with suppliers. About one-fourth of retail organizations operate chains.

independent retailer a firm that operates only one retail outlet

chain retailer a company that operates more than one retail outlet

Another way to classify in-store retailers is by store size and the kind and number of products carried. Let's take a closer look at store types based on these dimensions.

Department Stores These large retail establishments consist of several sections, or departments, that sell a wide assortment of products. According to the U.S. Bureau of the Census, a **department store** is a retail store that (1) employs twenty-five or more persons and (2) sells at least home furnishings, appliances, family apparel, and

department store a retail store that (1) employs twenty-five or more persons and (2) sells at least home furnishings, appliances, family apparel, and household linens and dry goods, each in a different part of the store

Table 14.1: Twenty Largest U.S. Retailers

Rank	Company	2007 Revenues (000)	2007 Earnings (000)	No. of Stores
1	Wal-Mart	$378,799,000	$12,731,000	7,262
2	Home Depot	$77,349,000	$4,395,000	2,234
3	CVS Caremark	$76,329,500	$2,622,800	6,301
4	Kroger	$70,235,000	$1,180,500	3,662
5	Costco	$64,400,155	$1,082,772	520
6	Target	$63,367,000	$2,849,000	1,591
7	Walgreen	$53,762,000	$2,041,300	5,997
8	Sears Holdings	$50,703,000	$826,000	3,800
9	Lowe's	$48,283,000	$2,809,000	1,525
10	SUPERVALU	$44,048,000	$593,000	2,474
11	Safeway	$42,286,000	$888,400	1,743
12	Best Buy	$40,023,000	$1,407,000	1,314
13	Macy's	$26,313,000	$893,000	853
14	Rite Aid	$24,326,846	$(1,078,990)	5,029
15	Publix	$23,000,000	$1,200,000	928
16	McDonald's	$22,786,600	$2,395,100	31,377
17	Ahold USA	$21,000,000	N.A.	830
18	JC Penney	$19,860,000	$1,111,000	1,067
19	Staples	$19,372,682	$995,670	2,000
20	TJX	$18,647,126	$771,750	2,563

Source: "2008 Top 100 Retailers," *Stores*, July 2008, p. T5, **www.stores.org/pdf/08TOP100.pdf**. Reprinted with permission from Wrights Reprints.

household linens and dry goods, each in a different part of the store. Marshall Field's in Chicago (and several other cities), Harrods in London, and Au Printemps in Paris are examples of large department stores. Sears, Roebuck and JC Penney are also department stores. Traditionally, department stores have been service oriented. Along with the goods they sell, these retailers provide credit, delivery, personal assistance, liberal return policies, and pleasant shopping atmospheres.

discount store a self-service general-merchandise outlet that sells products at lower-than-usual prices

Discount Stores A **discount store** is a self-service general-merchandise outlet that sells products at lower-than-usual prices. These stores can offer lower prices by operating on smaller markups, by locating large retail showrooms in low-rent areas, and by offering minimal customer services. To keep prices low, discount stores operate on the basic principle of high turnover of such items as appliances, toys, clothing, automotive products, and sports equipment. To attract customers, many discount stores also offer some food and household items at low prices. Popular discount stores include K Mart, Wal-Mart, Dollar General, and Target.

As competition among discount stores has increased, some discounters have improved their services, store environments, and locations. As a consequence, many of the better-known discount stores have assumed the characteristics of department stores. This upgrading has boosted their prices and blurred the distinction between some discount stores and department stores.[2]

catalog showroom a retail outlet that displays well-known brands and sells them at discount prices through catalogs within the store

Catalog and Warehouse Showrooms A **catalog showroom** is a retail outlet that displays well-known brands and sells them at discount prices through catalogs

Department store. *Macy's is an example of a department store.*

within the store. Colorful catalogs are available in the showroom (and sometimes by mail). The customer selects the merchandise, either from the catalog or from the showroom display. The customer fills out an order form provided by the store and hands the form to a clerk. The clerk retrieves the merchandise from a warehouse room that is adjacent to the selling area. Service Merchandise is a catalog showroom.

A **warehouse showroom** is a retail facility with five basic characteristics: (1) a large, low-cost building, (2) warehouse materials-handling technology, (3) vertical merchandise displays, (4) a large on-premises inventory, and (5) minimal service. Some of the best-known showrooms are operated by big furniture retailers. These operations employ few personnel and offer few services. Most customers carry away purchases in the manufacturer's carton, although some warehouse showrooms will deliver for a fee.

warehouse showroom a retail facility in a large, low-cost building with a large on-premises inventory and minimal service

Convenience Stores A **convenience store** is a small food store that sells a limited variety of products but remains open well beyond normal business hours. Almost 70 percent of convenience store customers live within a mile of the store. White Hen Pantry, 7-Eleven, Circle K, and Open Pantry stores, for example, are found in some areas, as are independent convenience stores. There are over 138,205 convenience stores in the United States, and two-thirds of Americans visit at least one of these locations every month. Convenience stores are the fastest-growing category of retailer, with a 9.6 percent growth in sales over the past year compared with an 8 percent decline in overall retail sales.[3] Their limited product mixes and higher prices keep convenience stores from becoming a major threat to other grocery retailers.

convenience store a small food store that sells a limited variety of products but remains open well beyond normal business hours

Supermarkets A **supermarket** is a large self-service store that sells primarily food and household products. It stocks canned, fresh, frozen, and processed foods; paper products; and cleaning supplies. Supermarkets also may sell such items as

supermarket a large self-service store that sells primarily food and household products

AP Photo/Paul Sakuma

The Business of Green

In the Bag: Goodbye Plastic, Hello Green

Many retailers are helping to preserve the planet by encouraging customers to choose reusable shopping bags instead of use-once plastic bags. Although shoppers carry home purchases in 100 billion plastic bags every year, they recycle fewer than 1 billion bags. And because most plastic bags are not biodegradable, the discards remain in landfills forever. That's why a few cities and countries no longer allow large retailers to offer free plastic bags. Ireland, for example, taxes every plastic bag, a strategy so successful that other nations are considering similar measures.

Meanwhile, major retailers are saying goodbye to plastic. IKEA, based in Sweden, has eliminated plastic bags throughout its retail network. Customers can bring their own bags, take purchases home without bags, or buy IKEA's reusable bags for 59 cents each. Any customer who insists on plastic must pay 5 cents per bag, which IKEA donates to a nonprofit forest restoration group.

Wal-Mart, the world's largest retailer, has cut back on plastic bags and sells reusable bags for 50 cents each, moves that will keep 9 billion bags out of landfills. Finally, every Earth Day, a growing number of retailers—including Wal-Mart and Home Depot—give away thousands of reusable bags to encourage customers to go green.

AP Photo/Damian Dovarganes

Sources: "Wal-Mart Sets Goal to Reduce Its Global Plastic Shopping Bag Waste by One-Third," *Biotech Week*, October 8, 2008, p. 3951; "IKEA Bags Use of Plastic Bags," *Atlanta Business Chronicle*, October 1, 2008, **atlanta.bizjournals.com**; Ellen Gamerman, "An Inconvenient Bag," *Wall Street Journal*, September 26, 2008, **www.wsj.com**; Elisabeth Rosenthal, "With Irish Tax, Plastic Bags Go the Way of Snakes," *New York Times*, February 2, 2008, p. A3.

housewares, toiletries, toys and games, drugs, stationery, books and magazines, plants and flowers, and a few clothing items.

Supermarkets are large-scale operations that emphasize low prices and one-stop shopping for household needs. A supermarket has annual sales of at least $2 million. Current top-ranking supermarkets include Kroger, Albertson's, Safeway, Winn-Dixie, and A&P. Many of these supermarket chains are finding it difficult to compete with superstores such as Wal-Mart Supercenters and are experiencing minuscule profit margins. Wal-Mart, for example, expects to generate in its "supermarket-type" stores more revenue than the top three U.S. supermarket chains—Kroger, Albertson's, and Safeway—combined. To attract more customers, Albertson's plans to make grocery shopping quick and easy with new technology that will eliminate checkout lines.[4]

superstore a large retail store that carries not only food and nonfood products ordinarily found in supermarkets but also additional product lines

Superstores A **superstore** is a large retail store that carries not only food and nonfood products ordinarily found in supermarkets but also additional product lines—housewares, hardware, small appliances, clothing, personal-care products, garden products, and automotive merchandise. Superstores also provide a number of services to entice customers. Typically, these include automotive repair, snack bars and restaurants, film developing, and banking.

warehouse club a large-scale members-only establishment that combines features of cash-and-carry wholesaling with discount retailing

Warehouse Clubs The **warehouse club** is a large-scale members-only establishment that combines features of cash-and-carry wholesaling with discount retailing. For a nominal annual fee (about $25), small retailers may purchase products at wholesale prices for business use or for resale. Warehouse clubs also sell to ultimate consumers. Instead of paying a membership fee, individual consumers pay about 5 percent more on each item than do small-business owners. Individual purchasers usually can choose to pay yearly dues for membership cards that allow them to avoid the 5 percent additional charge.

Warehouse clubs offer the same types of products offered by discount stores but in a limited range of sizes and styles. Because their product lines are shallow and sales volumes are high, warehouse clubs can offer a broad range of merchandise, including perishable and nonperishable foods, beverages, books, appliances, housewares, automotive parts, hardware, furniture, and sundries. The sales volume of most warehouse clubs is four to five times that of a typical department store. With stock turning over at an average rate of eighteen times each year, warehouse clubs sell their goods before manufacturers' payment periods are up, thus reducing their need for capital.

To keep their prices 20 to 40 percent lower than those of supermarkets and discount stores, warehouse clubs provide few services. They generally advertise only through direct mail. Their facilities often have concrete floors and aisles wide enough for forklifts. Merchandise is stacked on pallets or displayed on pipe racks. Usually customers must transport purchases themselves. Although at one time there were about twenty competing warehouse clubs, only two major competitors remain: Sam's Club and Costco. Sam's Club stores stock about 4,000 items, with 1,400 available most of the time and the rest being one-time buys. Costco leads the warehouse club industry with sales of $64.4 billion. Sam's Club is second with nearly $40 billion in store sales.[5]

Traditional Specialty Stores A **traditional specialty store** carries a narrow product mix with deep product lines. Traditional specialty stores are sometimes called *limited-line retailers*. If they carry depth in one particular product category, they may be called *single-line retailers*. Specialty stores usually sell such products as clothing, jewelry, sporting goods, fabrics, computers, flowers, baked goods, books, and pet supplies. Examples of specialty stores include Gap Inc., Radio Shack, Bath and Body Works, and Foot Locker.

traditional specialty store a store that carries a narrow product mix with deep product lines

Specialty stores usually offer deeper product mixes than department stores. They attract customers by emphasizing service, atmosphere, and location. Consumers who are dissatisfied with the impersonal atmosphere of large retailers often find the attention offered by small specialty stores appealing.

Off-Price Retailers An **off-price retailer** is a store that buys manufacturers' seconds, overruns, returns, and off-season merchandise at below-wholesale prices and

off-price retailer a store that buys manufacturers' seconds, overruns, returns, and off-season merchandise for resale to consumers at deep discounts

AP Photo/Paul Sakuma

Traditional specialty stores. *Zales is an example of a traditional specialty store.*

sells them to consumers at deep discounts. Off-price retailers sell limited lines of national-brand and designer merchandise, usually clothing, shoes, or housewares. Examples of off-price retailers include T.J. Maxx, Burlington Coat Factory, and Marshalls. Off-price stores charge up to 50 percent less than department stores do for comparable merchandise but offer few customer services. They often include community dressing rooms and central checkout counters, and some off-price retailers have a no-returns, no-exchanges policy.

category killer a very large specialty store that concentrates on a single product line and competes on the basis of low prices and product availability

Category Killers A **category killer** is a very large specialty store that concentrates on a single product line and competes by offering low prices and an enormous number of products. These stores are called *category killers* because they take business away from smaller, high-cost retail stores. Examples of category killers include Home Depot (building materials), Office Depot (office supplies and equipment), and Best Buy (electronics), all of which are leaders in their niche. Toys "R" Us, one of the original category killers, has a bleak future; the inability to maintain high sales year round with a market that focuses on the holidays has had its effect on the toy retailer. Some experts are predicting a decrease in the number of large-scale category killers in the not so distant future owing to other stores focusing on even smaller niches.[6]

Kinds of Nonstore Retailing

nonstore retailing a type of retailing whereby consumers purchase products without visiting a store

Nonstore retailing is selling that does not take place in conventional store facilities; consumers purchase products without visiting a store. This form of retailing accounts for an increasing percentage of total retail sales. Nonstore retailers use direct selling, direct marketing, and vending machines.

direct selling the marketing of products to customers through face-to-face sales presentations at home or in the workplace

Direct Selling **Direct selling** is the marketing of products to customers through face-to-face sales presentations at home or in the workplace. Traditionally called *door-to-door selling,* direct selling in the United States began with peddlers more than a century ago and has since grown into a sizable industry that generates about $30 billion in U.S. sales annually.[7] Instead of the door-to-door approach, many companies today—such as Mary Kay, Kirby, Amway, and Avon—use other approaches. They identify customers by mail, telephone, the Internet, or at shopping malls and then set up appointments. Direct selling sometimes involves the "party plan," which can occur in the customer's home or workplace. One customer will act as a host and invite friends and coworkers to view merchandise in a group setting where the salesperson demonstrates the products. Direct selling through the party plan requires effective salespeople who can identify potential hosts and provide encouragement and incentives for them to organize a gathering of friends and associates. Companies that commonly use the party plan are Tupperware, Stanley Home Products, Pampered Chef, and Sarah Coventry. Mary Kay also uses the party plan by holding group pajama parties, makeovers, and girls' nights out.

Direct selling has both benefits and limitations. It gives the marketer an opportunity to demonstrate the product in an environment—usually customers' homes—where it most likely would be used. Some companies, such as Kirby Vacuums, will even clean the carpet in your home while they demonstrate their product. The direct seller can give the customer personal attention, and the product can be presented to the customer at a convenient time and location. Personal attention to the customer is the foundation on which some direct sellers have built their businesses. For example, your Mary Kay salesperson can recommend beauty and skin products tailored to your special needs. Because commissions are so high, ranging from

Category killers. *Lowe's is a category killer for home improvement products.*

Courtesy Lowe's

30 to 50 percent of the sales price, and great effort is required to isolate promising prospects, overall costs of direct selling make it a very expensive form of retailing. Furthermore, some customers view direct selling negatively owing to unscrupulous and fraudulent practices used by some direct sellers in the past. Some communities even have local ordinances that control or, in some cases, prohibit door-to-door selling.

Direct Marketing **Direct marketing** is the use of the telephone, Internet, and nonpersonal media to communicate product and organizational information to customers, who then can purchase products via mail, telephone, or the Internet. Direct marketing is one type of nonstore retailing. Direct marketing can occur through catalog marketing, direct-response marketing, telemarketing, television home shopping, and online marketing.

direct marketing the use of the telephone, Internet, and nonpersonal media to introduce products to customers, who then can purchase them via mail, telephone, or the Internet

catalog marketing a type of marketing in which an organization provides a catalog from which customers make selections and place orders by mail, telephone, or the Internet

direct-response marketing a type of marketing in which a retailer advertises a product and makes it available through mail, telephone, or online orders

telemarketing the performance of marketing-related activities by telephone

In **catalog marketing**, an organization provides a catalog from which customers make selections and place orders by mail, telephone, or the Internet. Catalog marketing began in 1872, when Montgomery Ward issued its first catalog to rural families. Today, there are more than 7,000 catalog marketing companies in the United States, as well as a number of retail stores, such as JC Penney, that engage in catalog marketing. Some organizations, including Spiegel and JC Penney, offer a broad array of products spread over multiple product lines. Catalog companies such as Lands' End, Pottery Barn, and J. Crew offer considerable depth in one major line of products. Still other catalog companies specialize in only a few products within a single line. The advantages of catalog marketing include efficiency and convenience for customers. The retailer benefits by being able to locate in remote, low-cost areas, save on expensive store fixtures, and reduce both personal selling and store operating expenses. On the other hand, catalog marketing is inflexible, provides limited service, and is most effective for only a selected set of products.

Even though the cost of mailing catalogs continues to rise, catalog sales are growing at double the rate of in-store retailing. Williams-Sonoma, for example, sells kitchenware and home and garden products through five catalogs, including Pottery Barn and Gardeners' Eden. Catalog sales have been increasing owing to the convenience of catalog shopping. Product quality is often high, and because consumers can call toll free 24 hours a day or order online, charge purchases to a credit card, and have the merchandise delivered to their door in one to two days, such shopping is much easier than going to a store.

Direct-response marketing occurs when a retailer advertises a product and makes it available through mail, telephone, or online orders. Examples of direct-response marketing include a television commercial offering a recording artist's musical collection, a newspaper or magazine advertisement for a series of children's books, and even a billboard promoting floral services available by calling 1-800-Flowers. Direct-response marketing is also conducted by sending letters, samples, brochures, or booklets to prospects on a mailing list and asking that they order the advertised products by mail, telephone, or online.

Telemarketing is the performance of marketing-related activities by telephone. Some organizations use a prescreened list of prospective clients. Telemarketing can help generate sales leads, improve customer service, speed up payments on past-due accounts, raise funds for nonprofit organizations, and gather marketing data.

Currently, the laws and regulations regarding telemarketing, while in a state of flux, are becoming more restrictive. Several states have established do-not-call lists of customers who do not want to receive telemarketing calls

Direct marketing. *Although Crate & Barrel has about 160 stores, this company also engages in direct marketing through the use of catalogs.*

from companies. On October 1, 2003, the U.S. Congress implemented the national do-not-call registry for consumers who do not want to receive telemarketing calls. By 2008, the do-not-call registry listed over 157 million phone numbers. Regulations associated with the national do-not-call registry are enforced by the Federal Trade Commission (FTC). Companies are subject to fines of up to $12,000 for each call made to consumers listed on the national do-not-call registry. In February 2008, The Do-Not-Call Fee Extension Act of 2007 came into effect, settling the annual fees telemarketers must pay to access the registry at $54 for each area code of data accessed or $14,850 for access to every area code in the registry, whichever is less.[8] Certain exceptions apply to no-call lists. A company still can use telemarketing to communicate with existing customers. In addition, charitable, political, and telephone survey organizations are not restricted by the national registry.

television home shopping a form of selling in which products are presented to television viewers, who can buy them by calling a toll-free number and paying with a credit card

Television home shopping presents products to television viewers, encouraging them to order through toll-free numbers and pay with credit cards. Home Shopping Network (HSN) originated and popularized this format. The most popular products sold through television home shopping are jewelry (40 percent of total sales), clothing, housewares, and electronics. Home shopping channels have grown so rapidly in recent years that more than 60 percent of U.S. households have access to home shopping programs. HSN and QVC are two of the largest home shopping networks. With the growing popularity of this medium, new channels are being added, even ones that specialize on one specific product category, such as Jewelry Television. Approximately 60 percent of home shopping sales revenues come from repeat purchasers.

The television home shopping format offers several benefits. Products can be demonstrated easily, and an adequate amount of time can be spent showing the product so as to make viewers well informed. The length of time a product is shown depends not only on the time required for doing the demonstration but also on whether the product is selling. Once the calls peak and begin to decline, a new product is shown. Another benefit is that customers can shop at their convenience from the comfort of their homes. HSN recently redesigned its website using green screen technology to make its show's hosts and celebrity guests "virtual video guides." Each product category of the site is hosted by a famous expert who gives the shopper new product information, trend news, and tips. For example, a couple of the cooking section's experts are chefs Wolfgang Puck and Emeril Lagasse.[9]

online retailing retailing that makes products available to buyers through computer connections

Online retailing makes products available to buyers through computer connections. Most brick-and-mortar retailers have websites to sell products, provide information about their company, or distribute coupons. Consumers also can bid on anything from concert tickets, automobiles, or even a wedge of cheese shaped like Elvis on eBay. Netflix has changed the video rental industry by offering its completely online movie rental service. Customers pay a monthly fee for unlimited rentals and browse the Netflix site to compose a list of videos they want to rent. Selections are mailed to their home, and customers are free to keep the rental as long as they want without the late fees typically charged by traditional stores.[10] Brokerage firms have established websites to give their customers direct access to manage their accounts and enable them to trade online. With advances in computer technology continuing and consumers ever more pressed for time, online retailing will continue to escalate. Although online retailing represents a major retailing venue, security remains an issue. In a recent survey conducted by the Business Software Alliance, some Internet users still expressed concerns about shopping online. The major issues are identity theft and credit card theft.

automatic vending the use of machines to dispense products

Automatic Vending

Automatic vending is the use of machines to dispense products. It accounts for less than 2 percent of all retail sales. Video game machines provide an entertainment service, and many banks offer automatic teller machines (ATMs), which dispense cash and perform other services.

Automatic vending is one of the most impersonal forms of retailing. Small, standardized, routinely purchased products (e.g., chewing gum, candy, newspapers, cigarettes, soft drinks, and coffee) can be sold in machines because consumers usually buy them at the nearest available location. Machines in areas of heavy traffic provide efficient and continuous service to consumers. Such high-volume areas may have more diverse product availability—for example, hot and cold sandwiches, DVD rentals, or even iPods (yes, $200 iPods are available in machines with coin slots). San Francisco–based company Zoom Systems has expanded its vending machine offerings from snacks to digital cameras. But its number one seller is the iPod vending machine that offers Apple's popular MP3 players as well as accessories such as headphones, speakers, and battery chargers.[11]

Since vending machines need only a small amount of space and no sales personnel, this retailing method has some advantages over stores. These advantages are partly offset, however, by the high costs of equipment and frequent servicing and repairs.

Sustaining the Planet

The International Council of Shopping Centers has started the Sustainable Energy & Environmental Design (SEED) website to help shopping centers and retailers learn about going green for long-term sustainability. SEED includes links to the latest news and developments in environmentally-sound mall and store construction and operations. **www.icscseed.org**

Planned Shopping Centers

8 Learning Objective: Identify the categories of shopping centers and the factors that determine how shopping centers are classified.

The planned shopping center is a self-contained retail facility constructed by independent owners and consisting of various stores. Shopping centers are designed and promoted to serve diverse groups of customers with widely differing needs. The management of a shopping center strives for a coordinated mix of stores, a comfortable atmosphere, adequate parking, pleasant landscaping, and special events to attract customers. The convenience of shopping for most family and household needs in a single location is an important part of shopping-center appeal.

A planned shopping center is one of four types: lifestyle, neighborhood, community, or regional. Although shopping centers vary, each offers a complementary mix of stores for the purpose of generating consumer traffic.

Lifestyle Shopping Centers

A **lifestyle shopping center** is a shopping center that has an open-air configuration and is occupied by upscale national chain specialty stores. The lifestyle center is more convenient than a traditional enclosed mall and offers the same quality of

lifestyle shopping center an open-air-environment shopping center with upscale chain specialty stores

Lifestyle shopping centers. *The Village of Rochester Hills shopping center is one example of a lifestyle shopping center.*

AP/Wide World/Jerry S. Mendoza

upscale retail, department stores, movie theaters, and dining. A strong emphasis is placed on the architecture of the center and creating a pleasant and "hip" shopping environment. Most lifestyle centers are found in affluent neighborhoods.[12]

Neighborhood Shopping Centers

neighborhood shopping center a planned shopping center consisting of several small convenience and specialty stores

A **neighborhood shopping center** typically consists of several small convenience and specialty stores. Businesses in neighborhood shopping centers might include small grocery stores, drugstores, gas stations, and fast-food restaurants. These retailers serve consumers who live less than ten minutes away, usually within a two- to three-mile radius of the stores. Because most purchases in the neighborhood shopping center are based on convenience or personal contact, these retailers generally make only limited efforts to coordinate promotional activities among stores in the shopping center.

Community Shopping Centers

community shopping center a planned shopping center that includes one or two department stores and some specialty stores, along with convenience stores

A **community shopping center** includes one or two department stores and some specialty stores, along with convenience stores. It attracts consumers from a wider geographic area who will drive longer distances to find products and specialty items unavailable in neighborhood shopping centers. Community shopping centers, which are carefully planned and coordinated, generate traffic with special events such as art exhibits, automobile shows, and sidewalk sales. The management of a community shopping center maintains a balance of tenants so that the center can offer wide product mixes and deep product lines.

Regional Shopping Centers

regional shopping center a planned shopping center containing large department stores, numerous specialty stores, restaurants, movie theaters, and sometimes even hotels

A **regional shopping center** usually has large department stores, numerous specialty stores, restaurants, movie theaters, and sometimes even hotels. It carries most of the merchandise offered by a downtown shopping district. Downtown merchants, in fact, often have renovated their stores and enlarged their parking facilities to meet the competition of successful regional shopping centers. Urban expressways and improved public transportation also have helped many downtown shopping areas to remain vigorous.

Regional shopping centers carefully coordinate management and marketing activities to reach the 150,000 or more customers in their target market. These large centers usually advertise, hold special events, and provide transportation to certain groups of customers. They also maintain a suitable mix of stores. National chain stores can gain leases in regional shopping centers more easily than small independent stores because they are better able to meet the centers' financial requirements.

Physical Distribution

9

Learning Objective: Explain the five most important physical distribution activities.

physical distribution all those activities concerned with the efficient movement of products from the producer to the ultimate user

Physical distribution is all those activities concerned with the efficient movement of products from the producer to the ultimate user. Physical distribution therefore is the movement of the products themselves—both goods and services—through their channels of distribution. It is a combination of several interrelated business functions. The most important of these are inventory management, order processing, warehousing, materials handling, and transportation.

Not too long ago each of these functions was considered distinct from all the others. In a fairly large firm, one group or department would handle each function. Each of these groups would work to minimize its own costs and to maximize its own effectiveness, but the result was usually high physical distribution costs.

Various studies of the problem emphasized both the interrelationships among the physical distribution functions and the relationships between physical distribution and other marketing functions. Long production runs may reduce per-unit product costs, but they can cause inventory-control and warehousing costs to skyrocket. A new automated warehouse may reduce materials-handling costs, but if the warehouse is not located properly, transportation time and costs may increase substantially.

Because of such interrelationships, marketers now view physical distribution as an integrated effort that provides important marketing functions: getting the right product to the right place at the right time and at minimal overall cost.

Inventory Management

In Chapter 8 we discussed inventory management from the standpoint of operations. We defined **inventory management** as the process of managing inventories in such a way as to minimize inventory costs, including both holding costs and potential stock-out costs. Both the definition and the objective of inventory control apply here as well.

Holding costs are the costs of storing products until they are purchased or shipped to customers. *Stock-out costs* are the costs of sales lost when items are not in inventory. Of course, holding costs can be reduced by minimizing inventories, but then stock-out costs could be financially threatening to the organization. And stock-out costs can be minimized by carrying very large inventories, but then holding costs would be enormous.

Inventory management therefore is a sort of balancing act between stock-out costs and holding costs. The latter include the cost of money invested in inventory, the cost of storage space, insurance costs, and inventory taxes. Often, even a relatively small reduction in inventory investment can provide a relatively large increase in working capital. And sometimes this reduction can best be accomplished through a willingness to incur a reasonable level of stock-out costs.

Inventory management technology. *This handheld inventory management device allows employees to have an instant overview of every item—and its price—in the warehouse at any given time.*

AP Wide World/Kevin Rivoli

Companies frequently rely on technology and software to help manage inventory. Efficient inventory management with accurate reorder points is crucial for firms that use a just-in-time (JIT) approach, in which supplies arrive just as they are needed for use in production or for resale. When using JIT, companies maintain low inventory levels and purchase products and materials in small quantities whenever they need them. Usually, there is no safety stock, and suppliers are expected to provide consistently high-quality products. JIT inventory management requires a high level of coordination between producers and suppliers, but it eliminates waste and reduces inventory costs significantly. This approach has been used successfully by many well-known firms, including Chrysler, Harley-Davidson, and Dell Computer, to reduce costs and boost customer satisfaction. When a JIT approach is used in a supply chain, suppliers often move close to their customers.

inventory management the process of managing inventories in such a way as to minimize inventory costs, including both holding costs and potential stock-out costs

Order Processing

Order processing consists of activities involved in receiving and filling customers' purchase orders. It may include not only the means by which customers order products but also procedures for billing and for granting credit.

Fast, efficient order processing is an important marketing service—one that can provide a dramatic competitive edge. The people who purchase goods for intermediaries are especially concerned with their suppliers' promptness and reliability in order processing. To them, promptness and reliability mean minimal inventory costs as well as the ability to order goods when they are needed rather than weeks in advance. The Internet is providing new opportunities for improving services associated with order processing.

order processing activities involved in receiving and filling customers' purchase orders

Warehousing

Warehousing is the set of activities involved in receiving and storing goods and preparing them for reshipment. Goods are stored to create time utility; that is, they are

warehousing the set of activities involved in receiving and storing goods and preparing them for reshipment

held until they are needed for use or sale. Warehousing includes the following activities:

- *Receiving goods*—The warehouse accepts delivered goods and assumes responsibility for them.
- *Identifying goods*—Records are made of the quantity of each item received. Items may be marked, coded, or tagged for identification.
- *Sorting goods*—Delivered goods may have to be sorted before being stored.
- *Dispatching goods to storage*—Items must be moved to specific storage areas, where they can be found later.
- *Holding goods*—The goods are kept in storage under proper protection until needed.
- *Recalling, picking, and assembling goods*—Items that are to leave the warehouse must be selected from storage and assembled efficiently.
- *Dispatching shipments*—Each shipment is packaged suitably and directed to the proper transport vehicle. Shipping and accounting documents are prepared.

A firm may use its own warehouses or rent space in public warehouses. A *private warehouse,* owned and operated by a particular firm, can be designed to serve the firm's specific needs. However, the organization must take on the task of financing the facility, determining the best location for it, and ensuring that it is used fully. Generally, only companies that deal in large quantities of goods can justify private warehouses. With a total of almost 96 million square feet in warehouse space, United Parcel Service (UPS) owns the largest amount of private warehouse space in the world. Wal-Mart is second with 80 million, and Sears is third with 40 million.[13]

Public warehouses offer their services to all individuals and firms. Most are huge one-story structures on the outskirts of cities, where rail and truck transportation are easily available. They provide storage facilities, areas for sorting and assembling shipments, and office and display spaces for wholesalers and retailers. Public warehouses also will hold—and issue receipts for—goods used as collateral for borrowed funds.

Many organizations locate and design their warehouses not only to be cost-efficient but also to provide excellent customer service.

Materials Handling

materials handling the actual physical handling of goods, in warehouses as well as during transportation

Materials handling is the actual physical handling of goods—in warehouses as well as during transportation. Proper materials-handling procedures and techniques can increase the usable capacity of a warehouse or that of any means of transportation. Proper handling can reduce breakage and spoilage as well.

Modern materials handling attempts to reduce the number of times a product is handled. One method is called *unit loading.* Several smaller cartons, barrels, or boxes are combined into a single standard-size load that can be handled efficiently by forklift, conveyer, or truck.

Transportation

transportation the shipment of products to customers

carrier a firm that offers transportation services

As a part of physical distribution, **transportation** is simply the shipment of products to customers. The greater the distance between seller and purchaser, the more important is the choice of the means of transportation and the particular carrier.

A firm that offers transportation services is called a **carrier**. A *common carrier* is a transportation firm whose services are available to all shippers. Railroads, airlines, and most long-distance trucking firms are common carriers. A *contract carrier* is available for hire by one or several shippers. Contract carriers do not serve the general public. Moreover, the number of firms they can handle at any one time is limited by law. A *private carrier* is owned and operated by the shipper.

In addition, a shipper can hire agents called *freight forwarders* to handle its transportation. Freight forwarders pick up shipments from the shipper, ensure that the goods are loaded on selected carriers, and assume responsibility for safe delivery

Waterways. *Waterway transportation is used to move heavy, nonperishable products, such as large equipment, grain, motor vehicles, and chemicals.*

of the shipments to their destinations. Freight forwarders often can group a number of small shipments into one large load (which is carried at a lower rate). This, of course, saves money for shippers.

The U.S. Postal Service offers *parcel post* delivery, which is used widely by mail-order houses. The Postal Service provides complete geographic coverage at the lowest rates, but it limits the size and weight of the shipments it will accept. UPS, a privately owned firm, also provides small-parcel services for shippers. Other privately owned carriers, such as Federal Express, DHL, and Airborne, offer fast—often overnight—parcel delivery both within and outside the United States. There are also many local parcel carriers, including specialized delivery services for various time-sensitive industries, such as publishing.

The six major criteria used for selecting transportation modes are compared in Table 14.2. Obviously, the *cost* of a transportation mode is important to marketers. At times, marketers choose higher-cost modes of transportation because of the benefits they provide. *Speed* is measured by the total time that a carrier possesses the products, including time required for pickup and delivery, handling, and movement between point of origin and destination. Usually, there is a direct relationship between cost and speed; that is, faster modes of transportation are more expensive. A transportation mode's *dependability* is determined by the consistency of service provided by that mode. *Load flexibility* is the degree to which a transportation mode can provide appropriate equipment and conditions for moving specific kinds of products and can be adapted for moving other kinds of products. For example, certain types of products may need controlled temperatures or humidity levels. *Accessibility* refers to a transportation mode's ability to move goods over a specific route or network. *Frequency* refers to how often a marketer can ship products by a specific transportation mode. Whereas pipelines provide continuous shipments, railroads and waterways follow specific schedules for moving products from one location to another. In Table 14.2, each transportation mode is rated on a relative basis for these six selection criteria. Figure 14.3 shows recent trends and a breakdown by use of the five different modes of transportation.

Railroads In terms of total freight carried, railroads are America's most important mode of transportation. They are also the least expensive for many products.

Table 14.2: Relative Ratings of Transportation Modes by Selection Criteria

	Selection Criteria					
Mode	**Cost**	**Speed**	**Dependability**	**Load Flexibility**	**Accessibility**	**Frequency**
Railroads	Moderate	Average	Average	High	High	Low
Trucks	High	Fast	High	Average	Very high	High
Airplanes	Very high	Very fast	High	Low	Average	Average
Waterways	Very low	Very slow	Average	Very high	Limited	Very low
Pipelines	Low	Slow	High	Very low	Very limited	Very high

Almost all railroads are common carriers, although a few coal-mining companies operate their own lines.

Many commodities carried by railroads could not be transported easily by any other means. They include a wide range of foodstuffs, raw materials, and manufactured goods. Coal ranks first by a considerable margin. Other major commodities

Figure 14.3: Changes in Ton-Miles for Various Transportation Modes

Between 1980 and 2005, ton-miles for airplanes, railroads, and trucks increased significantly, whereas pipeline and waterway usage remained steady. Examples of typical products carried by the various modes are shown here.

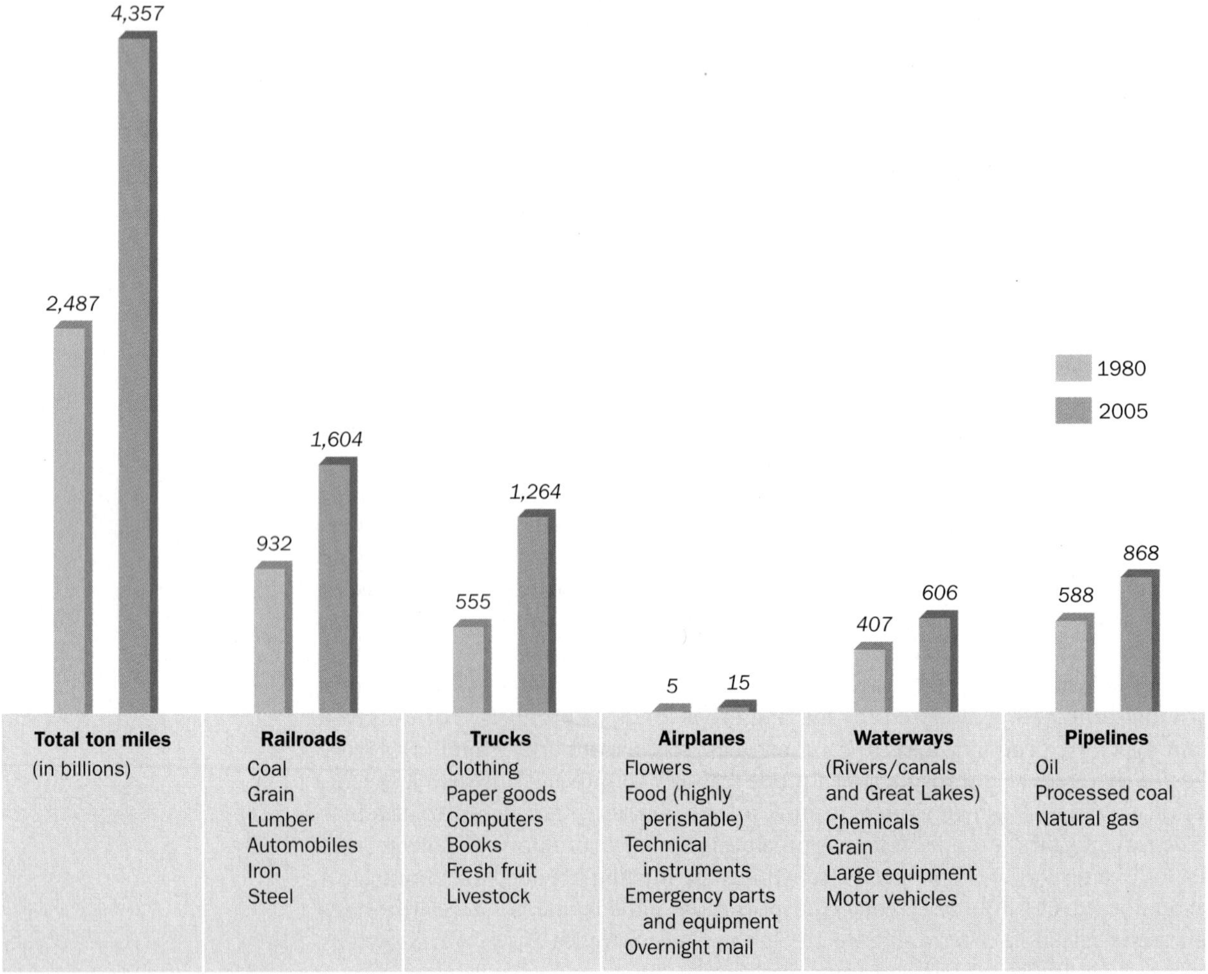

1980
2005

2,487 4,357
Total ton miles
(in billions)

932 1,604
Railroads
Coal
Grain
Lumber
Automobiles
Iron
Steel

555 1,264
Trucks
Clothing
Paper goods
Computers
Books
Fresh fruit
Livestock

5 15
Airplanes
Flowers
Food (highly perishable)
Technical instruments
Emergency parts and equipment
Overnight mail

407 606
Waterways
(Rivers/canals and Great Lakes)
Chemicals
Grain
Large equipment
Motor vehicles

588 868
Pipelines
Oil
Processed coal
Natural gas

Source: U.S. Bureau of Transportation Statistics, *National Transportation Statistics 2005*, **www.bts.gov**, accessed January 30, 2006.

carried by railroads include grain, paper and pulp products, liquids in tank-car loads, heavy equipment, and lumber.

Trucks The trucking industry consists of common, contract, and private carriers. It has undergone tremendous expansion since the creation of a national highway system in the 1920s. Trucks can move goods to suburban and rural areas not served by railroads. They can handle freight quickly and economically, and they carry a wide range of shipments. Many shippers favor this mode of transportation because it offers door-to-door service, less stringent packaging requirements than ships and airplanes, and flexible delivery schedules.

Railroad and truck carriers have teamed up to provide a form of transportation called *piggyback*. Truck trailers are carried from city to city on specially equipped railroad flatcars. Within each city, the trailers are then pulled in the usual way by truck tractors.

Airplanes Air transport is the fastest but most expensive means of transportation. All certified airlines are common carriers. Supplemental or charter lines are contract carriers.

Because of the high cost, lack of airport facilities in many areas, and reliance on weather conditions, airlines carry less than 1 percent of all intercity freight. Only high-value or perishable items, such as flowers, aircraft parts, and pharmaceuticals or goods that are needed immediately, usually are shipped by air.

Waterways Cargo ships and barges offer the least expensive, but slowest, form of transportation. They are used mainly for bulky nonperishable goods such as chemicals, grain, motor vehicles, and large equipment. Of course, shipment by water is limited to cities located on navigable waterways. But ships and barges account for about 14 percent of all intercity freight hauling.

Pipelines Pipelines are a highly specialized mode of transportation. They are used primarily to carry petroleum and natural gas. Pipelines have become more important as the nation's need for petroleum products has increased. Such products as semiliquid coal and wood chips also can be shipped through pipelines continuously, reliably, and with minimal handling.

In the next chapter, we discuss the fourth element of the marketing mix—promotion.

return to inside business

Target

During the recent economic downturn, Target felt the financial pinch as customers pinched pennies. "The customer is very cash-strapped right now and in some ways, our greatest strength has become something of a challenge," said Target's president. "During these tough times, some of our consumers don't want to be tempted as much as they have in the past." Low prices became Target's main message.

The retailer faced another difficult challenge when Isaac Mizrahi, who designed many successful Target clothing lines, switched companies. To fill the sales void, Target started showcasing new designers and offering a wider range of stylish private-label apparel to appeal to shoppers interested in good design at a discount.

Questions

1. Is the distribution channel for Target's private-label clothing and exclusive designs likely to be short or long? What does this mean for Target's costs and pricing?
2. Compared with Target, Wal-Mart has many more stores and much higher sales volume. How would you suggest that Target compete with its rival's low-price positioning?

Summary

1 Identify the various channels of distribution that are used for consumer and industrial products.

A marketing channel is a sequence of marketing organizations that directs a product from producer to ultimate user. The marketing channel for a particular product is concerned with the transfer of ownership of that product. Merchant middlemen (merchants) actually take title to products, whereas functional middlemen simply aid in the transfer of title.

The channels used for consumer products include the direct channel from producer to consumer; the channel from producer to retailer to consumer; the channel from producer to wholesaler to retailer to consumer; and the channel from producer to agent to wholesaler to retailer to consumer. There are two major channels of industrial products: (1) producer to user and (2) producer to agent middleman to user.

2 Explain the concept of market coverage.

Channels and intermediaries are chosen to implement a given level of market coverage. Intensive distribution is the use of all available outlets for a product, providing the widest market coverage. Selective distribution uses only a portion of the available outlets in an area. Exclusive distribution uses only a single retail outlet for a product in a large geographic area.

3 Understand how supply-chain management facilitates partnering among channel members.

Supply-chain management is a long-term partnership among channel members working together to create a distribution system that reduces inefficiencies, costs, and redundancies while creating a competitive advantage and satisfying customers. Cooperation is required among all channel members, including manufacturing, research, sales, advertising, and shipping. When all channel partners work together, delivery, scheduling, packaging, and other customer requirements are better met. Technology, such as bar coding and electronic data exchange (EDI), makes supply-chain management easier to implement.

4 Describe what a vertical marketing system is and identify the types of vertical marketing systems.

A vertical marketing system (VMS) is a centrally managed system. It results when two or more channel members from different levels combine under one management. Administered, contractual, and corporate systems represent the three major types of VMSs.

5 Discuss the need for wholesalers and describe the services they provide to retailers and manufacturers.

Wholesalers are intermediaries that purchase from producers or other intermediaries and sell to industrial users, retailers, or other wholesalers. Wholesalers perform many functions in a distribution channel. If they are eliminated, other channel members—such as the producer or retailers—must perform these functions. Wholesalers provide retailers with help in promoting products, collecting information, and financing. They provide manufacturers with sales help, reduce their inventory costs, furnish market information, and extend credit to retailers.

6 Identify and describe the major types of wholesalers.

Merchant wholesalers buy and then sell products. Commission merchants and brokers are essentially agents and do not take title to the goods they distribute. Sales branches and offices are owned by the manufacturers they represent and resemble merchant wholesalers and agents, respectively.

7 Distinguish among the major types of retailers.

Retailers are intermediaries that buy from producers or wholesalers and sell to consumers. In-store retailers include department stores, discount stores, catalog and warehouse showrooms, convenience stores, supermarkets, superstores, warehouse clubs, traditional specialty stores, off-price retailers, and category killers. Nonstore retailers do not sell in conventional store facilities. Instead, they use direct selling, direct marketing, and automatic vending. Types of direct marketing include catalog marketing, direct-response marketing, telemarketing, television home shopping, and online retailing.

8 Identify the categories of shopping centers and the factors that determine how shopping centers are classified.

There are three major types of shopping centers: neighborhood, community, and regional. A center fits one of these categories based on its mix of stores and the size of the geographic area it serves.

9 Explain the five most important physical distribution activities.

Physical distribution consists of activities designed to move products from producers to ultimate users. Its five major functions are inventory management, order processing, warehousing, materials handling, and transportation. These interrelated functions are integrated into the marketing effort.

Key Terms

You should now be able to define and give an example relevant to each of the following terms:

channel of distribution (or marketing channel) (399)
middleman (or marketing intermediary) (399)
merchant middleman (399)
functional middleman (399)
retailer (399)
wholesaler (400)
intensive distribution (401)
selective distribution (401)
exclusive distribution (401)
supply-chain management (402)
vertical channel integration (403)
vertical marketing system (VMS) (403)
merchant wholesaler (406)
full-service wholesaler (406)
general-merchandise wholesaler (406)
limited-line wholesaler (406)
specialty-line wholesaler (406)
limited-service wholesaler (406)
commission merchant (406)
agent (406)
broker (406)
manufacturer's sales branch (407)
manufacturer's sales office (407)
independent retailer (407)
chain retailer (407)
department store (407)
discount store (408)
catalog showroom (408)
warehouse showroom (409)
convenience store (409)
supermarket (409)
superstore (410)
warehouse club (410)
traditional specialty store (411)
off-price retailer (411)
category killer (412)
nonstore retailing (412)
direct selling (412)
direct marketing (413)
catalog marketing (413)
direct-response marketing (413)
telemarketing (413)
television home shopping (414)
online retailing (414)
automatic vending (414)
lifestyle shopping center (415)
neighborhood shopping center (416)
community shopping center (416)
regional shopping center (416)
physical distribution (416)
inventory management (417)
order processing (417)
warehousing (417)
materials handling (418)
transportation (418)
carrier (418)

Review Questions

1. In what ways is a channel of distribution different from the path taken by a product during physical distribution?
2. What are the most common marketing channels for consumer products? For industrial products?
3. What are the three general approaches to market coverage? What types of products is each used for?
4. What is a vertical marketing system? Identify examples of the three types of VMSs.
5. List the services performed by wholesalers. For whom is each service performed?
6. What is the basic difference between a merchant wholesaler and an agent?
7. Identify three kinds of full-service wholesalers. What factors are used to classify wholesalers into one of these categories?
8. Distinguish between (a) commission merchants and agents and (b) manufacturers' sales branches and manufacturers' sales offices.
9. What is the basic difference between wholesalers and retailers?
10. What is the difference between a department store and a discount store with regard to selling orientation and philosophy?
11. How do (a) convenience stores, (b) traditional specialty stores, and (c) category killers compete with other retail outlets?
12. What can nonstore retailers offer their customers that in-store retailers cannot?
13. Compare and contrast community shopping centers and regional shopping centers.
14. What is physical distribution? Which major functions does it include?
15. What activities besides storage are included in warehousing?
16. List the primary modes of transportation and cite at least one advantage of each.

Discussion Questions

1. Which distribution channels would producers of services be most likely to use? Why?
2. Many producers sell to consumers both directly and through middlemen. How can such a producer justify competing with its own middlemen?
3. In what situations might a producer use agents or commission merchants rather than its own sales offices or branches?
4. If a middleman is eliminated from a marketing channel, under what conditions will costs decrease? Under what conditions will costs increase? Will the middleman's functions be eliminated? Explain.
5. Which types of retail outlets are best suited to intensive distribution? To selective distribution? To exclusive distribution? Explain your answer in each case.
6. How are the various physical distribution functions related to each other? To the other elements of the marketing mix?

Video Case 14.1

Netflix Uses Distribution to Compete

Netflix was launched about twelve years ago. Netflix was originally nothing more than an online version of a traditional video rental store. Customers could visit the Netflix website and choose which items they wished to rent. Each rental cost $4, along with a $2 shipping fee, plus late fees, if applicable. This model was not very price competitive or efficient compared to brick-and-mortar video rental retailers. To gain a competitive advantage, the company slowly transformed itself. Two years later, Netflix evolved into its current form. It has focused on technological advances and improved product offering to be competitive. Today, Netflix has over 8.6 million subscribers.

As with other rental companies, Netflix is membership based. What differs is that members subscribe to various packages based on the number of movies they want to rent per month. Packages vary from two movies per month to four-at-a-time unlimited rentals. Members create a list of movies they would like to see in order of preference, and Netflix delivers them. Customers can keep the movie as long as they like with no late fees, but they are not sent a new one until the old one has been received at their local Netflix distribution center.

As the company became more popular, Netflix expanded its film and television show collection to include Blu-Ray disks. In order to stay ahead of the competition, Netflix added a Play Instantly feature, which allows subscribers to download movies from the Netflix website and watch them on their computer. This service gives people instant access to a wide selection of films. The additional benefit to the company is that it saves on shipping fees. However, many people have opted not to utilize this service, given low computer resolution or problems with the speed of Internet access.

Recently, Netflix started offering a direct-to-television streaming box rental option. To gain access to more than 12,000 movies and television shows from the Netflix library, customers must purchase a box that hooks up to a television set. The box costs around $100 and streams video directly to television via high-speed Internet. Customers must sign up for a plan, but rather than wait for DVDs in the mail, they can watch them instantly on their televisions. Apple and Vudu offer similar products, but their boxes cost two to three times Netflix's price. Also, Netflix recently formed a partnership with Microsoft to stream movies through Xbox systems to the television.

Most recently, Netflix partnered with TiVo to provide movies straight through the Internet. Netflix subscribers that also subscribe to TiVo (and have a Series 3 or HD DVR connected to broadband) can use this service.

Netflix has a number of competitive advantages over companies such as Movielink, Blockbuster, and Wal-Mart. First and foremost, Netflix offers more selections, including more independent and foreign films, documentaries, and television shows, than anyone else. Wal-Mart attempted to compete with Netflix starting in 2002, but admitted that Netflix had won and bowed out of the race less than three years later.

Blockbuster, a company that lost market share as some customers moved away from traditional brick-and-mortar video stores, continues to be Netflix's strongest competitor. The company, which remains the largest in-store movie rental chain in the world, entered the online rental competition about five years ago. Although Blockbuster originally tried to compete with Netflix on price, the two companies eventually settled on similar prices. Their competitive battle also went to court when Netflix sued Blockbuster for infringing on two of its patents. The suit was settled a year later. Competition between these two organizations remains fierce.[14]

For more information about this company, go to **www.netflix.com**.

Questions

1. What type of retailer is Netflix?
2. To compete more efficiently with Blockbuster, should Netflix open brick-and-mortar retail stores? Why or why not?
3. Are there other forms of nonstore retailing that Netflix should consider using along with its current distribution activities?

Case 14.2

Good Customer Values and Many Surprises at Costco

More than 20 years after Costco opened its first warehouse club store in Seattle, Washington, the company's philosophy can still be summed up as "pile 'em high, price 'em low." Costco stores are anything but fancy; in fact, the first store was located inside a warehouse. Yet nearly 50 million consumers and small-business owners pay $50 (fee may vary) annually so they can save on everything from mayonnaise, wine, and prescription medicines to handheld computers, truck-size snow tires, and fine art. In fact, customers never really know what products they will find each time they visit one of the 529 Costco warehouse stores around the world. Surprises are all part of the shopping experience at Costco. "The art form of our business is intuition," says CEO James D. Sinegal. His buyers must choose carefully, because the typical Costco carries less than 10 percent of the number of products displayed in a Wal-Mart store. Moreover, Costco aims for a profit margin of no more than 14 percent, which means inventory must sell quickly. If products sell slowly, they will tie up precious cash that could be better spent on newer or more popular merchandise. Therefore, Costco's buyers watch for particularly hot products and product categories. When the chief electronics buyer noticed the cost of plasma-screen televisions dropping, for example, he took what he calls "an educated gamble" and placed a sizable order. The gamble paid off: the televisions, priced below $5,000, sold out quickly even before the year-end holiday shopping season. Costco carries a broad and varied merchandise assortment, all priced low to move quickly. It sells 55,000 rotisserie chickens every day and $600 million worth of fine wines every year. It also sells 45 million hot dogs and 60,000 carats of diamonds annually. The hot dogs retail for $1.50 each, while a single piece of jewelry can retail for as much as $100,000. Well-known manufacturers' brands share shelf space with Kirkland Signature, Costco's private brand. Members may walk past stacks of best-selling books on the right and color printers on the left as they push their shopping carts down the aisle. This variety enhances the store's appeal, says the CEO: "Our customers do not drive 15 miles to save on a jar of peanut butter. They come for the treasure hunt." Among the treasures they might find: an $8,000 Suzuki grand piano, a $6,000 100-CD Wurlitzer jukebox, and a seven-carat diamond ring for $125,000. Such items now comprise 5 to 10 percent of Costco's sales. Despite the low prices, Costco offers a generous return policy. Customers can return anything at any time. If dissatisfied with their membership, they can even get a full refund on that. The sole exception is computers, which cannot be brought back after six months. No receipt? No problem at Costco. Customers have ample opportunity to exchange or return items because they visit the stores frequently. Research shows that, on average, members visit Costco stores more than 11 times a year and spend $94 on each visit. Costco's main competitor is Sam's Club, owned by Wal-Mart. Given Wal-Mart's buying power and channel leadership, Sam's Club can buy products at very low prices and get them to stores with unusual efficiency. Nonetheless, Costco tops Sam's Club in a number of ways. Each U.S. Costco store rings up, on average, $112 million worth of merchandise annually. By comparison, the average yearly sales of each U.S. Sam's Club store are $63 million. While the average sales per square foot at Sam's Club is $497, Costco's equivalent figure is a whopping $797 per square foot. Although Sam's Club charges a lower membership fee, Costco's members are quite loyal, with a renewal rate of 86 percent. And they have a median income of $72,000, compared to Sam's customers, with a median income of $50,000. In recent years, Costco has expanded by offering new services at low prices. For example, members can log on to the retailer's website (**www.costco.com**) and sign up for long-distance telephone service, apply for a mortgage, buy life insurance, or price a vacation trip. The company has also started a new chain of stores, Costco Home, which specializes in home furnishings. In warehouse retailing, however, Sam's Club remains the competitor to beat. Before Sam's Club opened stores in Canada, Costco prepared for the increased competition by remodeling some of its stores. And price wars sometimes break out when the two competitors battle for customers. The parent company of Sam's Club is by far the largest company in the world, but Costco is so adept at warehouse retailing that it continues to hold its own.[15]

Questions

1. How would you classify Costco as an in-store retailer? Why?
2. How is Costco's strategy different from that of Sam's Club?
3. Evaluate Costco's objective of achieving a 14 percent profit. Justify your answer.

Building Skills for Career Success

1. JOURNALING FOR SUCCESS

Discovery statement: In this chapter you learned that retailers are marketing intermediaries and part of the distribution channel.

Assignment

1. Thinking about brick-and-mortar retail stores, in which store have you had your most enjoyable shopping experience? Describe this retail store.
2. Discuss this shopping experience and why it was such a great shopping experience.
3. At what brick-and-mortar store did you have your worst experience? Describe this store.
4. Discuss this worst shopping experience and be sure to mention the reasons why this shopping experience was the worst one for you.

2. EXPLORING THE INTERNET

One reason the Internet has generated so much excitement and interest among both buyers and distributors of products is that it is a highly effective method of direct marketing. Already a multibillion-dollar industry, e-commerce is growing as more businesses recognize the power of the Internet to reach customers twenty-four hours a day anywhere in the world. In addition to using the Internet to provide product information to potential customers, businesses can use it to process orders and accept payment from customers. Quick delivery from warehouses or stores by couriers such as UPS and FedEx adds to the convenience of Internet shopping.

Businesses whose products traditionally have sold well through catalogs are clear leaders in the electronic marketplace. Books, CDs, clothing, and other frequently purchased, relatively low-cost items sell well through both the Internet and catalogs. As a result, many successful catalog companies are including the Internet as a means of communicating about products. And many of their customers are finding that they prefer the more dynamic online versions of the catalogs.

Assignment

1. Explore the websites listed below, or just enter "shopping" on one of the Web search engines—then stand back! Also visit the text website for updates to this exercise.
   www.llbean.com
   www.jcpenney.com
   www.sears.com
   www.landsend.com
   www.barnesandnoble.com
   www.amazon.com
2. Which website does the best job of marketing merchandise? Explain your answer.
3. Find a product that you would be willing to buy over the Internet and explain why you would buy it. Name the website and describe the product.
4. Find a product that you would be unwilling to buy over the Internet and, again, explain your reasoning. Name the website and describe the product.

3. DEVELOPING CRITICAL-THINKING SKILLS

According to the wheel of retailing hypothesis, retail businesses begin as low-margin, low-priced, low-status operations. As they successfully challenge established retailers for market share, they upgrade their facilities and offer more services. This raises their costs and forces them to increase their prices so that eventually they become like the conventional retailers they replaced. As they move up from the low end of the wheel, new firms with lower costs and prices move in to take their place. For example, Kmart started as a low-priced operation that competed with department stores. Over time, it upgraded its facilities and products; big Kmart stores now offer such exclusive merchandise as Martha Stewart's bed-and-bath collection, full-service pharmacies, café areas, and "pantry" areas stocked with frequently bought grocery items, including milk, eggs, and bread. In consequence, Kmart has become a higher-cost, higher-priced operation and, as such, is vulnerable to lower-priced firms entering at the low end of the wheel.

Assignment

1. Investigate the operations of a local retailer.
2. Explain how this retailer is evolving on the wheel of retailing.
3. Prepare a report on your findings.

4. BUILDING TEAM SKILLS

Surveys are a commonly used tool in marketing research. The information they provide can reduce business risk and facilitate decision making. Retail outlets often survey their customers' wants and needs by distributing comment cards or questionnaires.

The customer survey below is an example of a survey that a local photography shop might distribute to its customers.

Assignment

1. Working in teams of three to five, choose a local retailer.
2. Classify the retailer according to the major types of retailers.
3. Design a survey to help the retailer to improve customer service. (You may find it beneficial to work with the retailer and actually administer the survey to the retailer's customers. Prepare a report of the survey results for the retailer.)
4. Present your findings to the class.

5. RESEARCHING DIFFERENT CAREERS

When you are looking for a job, the people closest to you can be extremely helpful. Family members and friends may be able to answer your questions directly or put you in touch with someone else who can. This type of "networking" can lead to an "informational interview," in which you can meet with someone who will answer your questions about a career or a company and who also can provide inside information on related fields and other helpful hints.

Assignment

1. Choose a retailer or wholesaler and a position within the company that interests you.
2. Call the company and ask to speak to the person in that particular position. Explain that you are a college student interested in the position, and ask to set up an "informational interview."
3. Prepare a list of questions to ask in the interview. The questions should focus on:
   a. The type of training recommended for the position
   b. How the person entered the position and advanced in it
   c. What he or she likes and dislikes about the work
4. Present your findings to the class.

Customer Survey

To help us to serve you better, please take a few minutes while your photographs are being developed to answer the following questions. Your opinions are important to us.

1. Do you live/work in the area? (Circle one or both if they apply.)

2. Why did you choose us? (Circle all that apply.)

Close to home
Close to work
Convenience
Good service
Quality
Full-service photography shop
Other

3. How did you learn about us? (Circle one.)

Newspaper
Flyer/coupon
Passing by
Recommended by someone
Other

4. How frequently do you have film developed? (Please estimate.)

______ Times per month
______ Times per year

5. Which aspects of our photography shop do you think need improvement?

6. Our operating hours are from 8:00 A.M. to 7:00 P.M. weekdays and Saturdays from 9:30 A.M. to 6:00 P.M. We are closed on Sundays and legal holidays. If changes in our operating hours would serve you better, please specify how you would like them changed.

7. Age (Circle one.)

Under 25
26–39
40–59
Over 60

Comments:

---

15 Developing Integrated Marketing Communications

LEARNING OBJECTIVES

What you will be able to do once you complete this chapter:

1. Describe integrated marketing communications.
2. Understand the role of promotion.
3. Explain the purposes of the three types of advertising.
4. Describe the advantages and disadvantages of the major advertising media.
5. Identify the major steps in developing an advertising campaign.
6. Recognize the various kinds of salespersons, the steps in the personal-selling process, and the major sales management tasks.
7. Describe sales promotion objectives and methods.
8. Understand the types and uses of public relations.
9. Identify the factors that influence the selection of promotion-mix ingredients.

AFP/Getty Images

inside business

Lights, camera, action—the homemade commercial is one of the newest trends in advertising.

Consumers Behind the Camera

Lights, camera, action—the homemade commercial is one of the newest trends in advertising. Contests sponsored by PepsiCo's Frito-Lay division, H.J. Heinz, Best Western hotels, Klondike, and other companies have prompted thousands of consumers to write, film, edit, and submit their own commercials for a chance to win prizes and 30 seconds of fame on television, online, and beyond.

Not a replacement for professionally created marketing messages, consumer-generated commercials are intended to show off the creativity of brand fans and offer a fresh take on the advertised product. Make-your-own-commercial contests often attract considerable media coverage. Just as important, they get consumers excited about participating, whether they actually submit entries or simply click to watch and vote for the ads they like.

When PepsiCo's Frito-Lay held a contest inviting consumers to make their own Doritos commercials to air during the Super Bowl in 2007, it received more than 1,000 entries promoting the tortilla chip. The company selected five finalists and then invited the public to view and vote for their favorite ads online. Two commercials received so many votes that both were shown during the Super Bowl. Over the next few weeks, all five finalist commercials aired nationally as part of a new Doritos ad campaign. While the commercials' creators enjoyed their thirty seconds of fame, Doritos received an estimated $36 million in free publicity.

H.J. Heinz has run two contests inviting consumers to submit homemade commercials, as a way to build extra buzz. In both, consumers were asked to upload their ketchup commercials to YouTube and then register on Heinz's **TopThisTV.com** site. Company marketers chose ten semi-finalists from more than 4,000 entries and asked YouTube visitors to vote for the winner. The top prize for the best commercial: $57,000, a spot on national television, and an everlasting presence on YouTube. The top prize for Heinz: Millions of dollars worth of free media attention and a starring role for its famous ketchup in thousands of consumer-generated commercials.[1]

Marketers employ multiple promotional methods to create very favorable company and product images in the minds of customers. Skillful use of promotion is of great benefit to many companies like Frito-Lay, H. J. Heinz, Best Western, and Klondike.

promotion communication about an organization and its products that is intended to inform, persuade, or remind target-market members

Promotion is communication about an organization and its products that is intended to inform, persuade, or remind target-market members. The promotion with which we are most familiar—advertising—is intended to inform, persuade, or remind us to buy particular products. But there is more to promotion than advertising, and it is used for other purposes as well. Charities use promotion to inform us of their need for donations, to persuade us to give, and to remind us to do so in case we have forgotten. Even the Internal Revenue Service uses promotion (in the form of publicity) to remind us of its April 15 deadline for filing tax returns.

promotion mix the particular combination of promotion methods a firm uses to reach a target market

A **promotion mix** (sometimes called a *marketing-communications mix*) is the particular combination of promotional methods a firm uses to reach a target market. The makeup of a mix depends on many factors, including the firm's promotional resources and objectives, the nature of the target market, the product characteristics, and the feasibility of various promotional methods.

In this chapter, we introduce four promotional methods and describe how they are used in an organization's marketing plans. First, we examine the role of advertising in the promotion mix. We discuss different types of advertising, the process of developing an advertising campaign, and social and legal concerns in advertising.

Next, we consider several categories of personal selling, noting the importance of effective sales management. We also look at sales promotion—why firms use it and which sales promotion techniques are most effective. Then we explain how public relations can be used to promote an organization and its products. Finally, we illustrate how these four promotional methods are combined in an effective promotion mix.

What Is Integrated Marketing Communications?

1
Learning Objective: Describe integrated marketing communications.

Integrated marketing communications is the coordination of promotion efforts to ensure maximal informational and persuasive impact on customers. A major goal of integrated marketing communications is to send a consistent message to customers. Integrated marketing communications provides an organization with a way to coordinate and manage its promotional efforts to ensure that customers do receive consistent messages. This approach fosters not only long-term customer relationships but also the efficient use of promotional resources.

integrated marketing communications coordination of promotion efforts to ensure maximal informational and persuasive impact on customers

The concept of integrated marketing communications has been increasingly accepted for several reasons. Mass-media advertising, a very popular promotional method in the past, is used less today because of its high costs and less predictable audience sizes. Marketers now can take advantage of more precisely targeted promotional tools, such as cable TV, direct mail, DVDs, the Internet, special-interest magazines, and podcasts. Database marketing is also allowing marketers to be more precise in targeting individual customers. Until recently, suppliers of marketing communications were specialists. Advertising agencies provided advertising campaigns, sales promotion companies provided sales promotion activities and materials, and public-relations organizations engaged in public-relations efforts. Today, a number of promotion-related companies provide one-stop shopping to the client seeking advertising, sales promotion, and public relations, thus reducing coordination problems for the sponsoring company. Because the overall costs of marketing communications are significant, management demands systematic evaluations of communications efforts to ensure that promotional resources are being used efficiently. Although the fundamental role of promotion is not changing, the specific communication vehicles employed and the precision with which they are used are changing.

The Role of Promotion

2
Learning Objective: Understand the role of promotion.

Promotion is commonly the object of two misconceptions. Often, people take note of highly visible promotional activities, such as advertising and personal selling, and conclude that these make up the entire field of marketing. People also sometimes consider promotional activities to be unnecessary, expensive, and the cause of higher prices. Neither view is accurate.

The role of promotion is to facilitate exchanges directly or indirectly by informing individuals, groups, or organizations and influencing them to accept a firm's products or to have more positive feelings about the firm. To expedite changes directly, marketers convey information about a firm's goods, services, and ideas to particular market segments. To bring about exchanges indirectly, marketers address interest groups (such as environmental and consumer groups), regulatory agencies, investors, and the general public concerning a company and its products. The broader role of promotion, therefore, is to maintain positive relationships between a company and various groups in the marketing environment.

Marketers frequently design promotional communications, such as advertisements, for specific groups, although some may be directed at wider audiences. Several different messages may be communicated simultaneously to different market segments. For example, ExxonMobil Corporation may address customers about a new motor oil, inform investors about the firm's financial performance, and update the general public on the firm's environmental efforts.

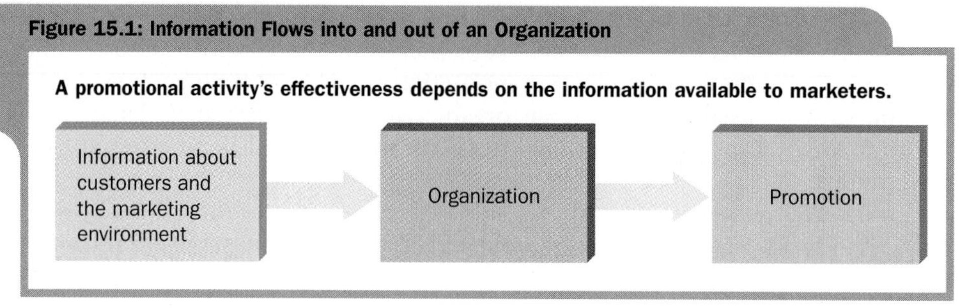

Source: William M. Pride and O. C. Ferrell, *Marketing: Concepts and Strategies,* 15th ed. (Mason, Ohio: South-Western/Cengage Learning, 2010). Adapted with permission.

Marketers must plan, implement, and coordinate promotional communications carefully to make the best use of them. The effectiveness of promotional activities depends greatly on the quality and quantity of information available to marketers about the organization's marketing environment (see Figure 15.1). If a marketer wants to influence customers to buy a certain product, for example, the firm must know who these customers are and how they make purchase decisions for that type of product. Marketers must gather and use information about particular audiences to communicate successfully with them. At times, two or more firms partner in joint promotional efforts. For example, Kraft Foods has teamed up with popular cable channel Nickelodeon to market healthy foods to kids. With consumer advocacy groups complaining about the skyrocketing levels of childhood obesity, Kraft is introducing a whole-grain version of its famous macaroni and cheese, called SuperMac. SuperMac will feature popular Nickelodeon characters SpongeBob SquarePants and The Fairly OddParents both on the box and as noodle shapes. SuperMac also will be reinforced with calcium and several vitamins.[2]

The Promotion Mix: An Overview

Marketers can use several promotional methods to communicate with individuals, groups, and organizations. The methods that are combined to promote a particular product make up the promotion mix for that item.

Advertising, personal selling, sales promotion, and public relations are the four major elements in an organization's promotion mix (see Figure 15.2).

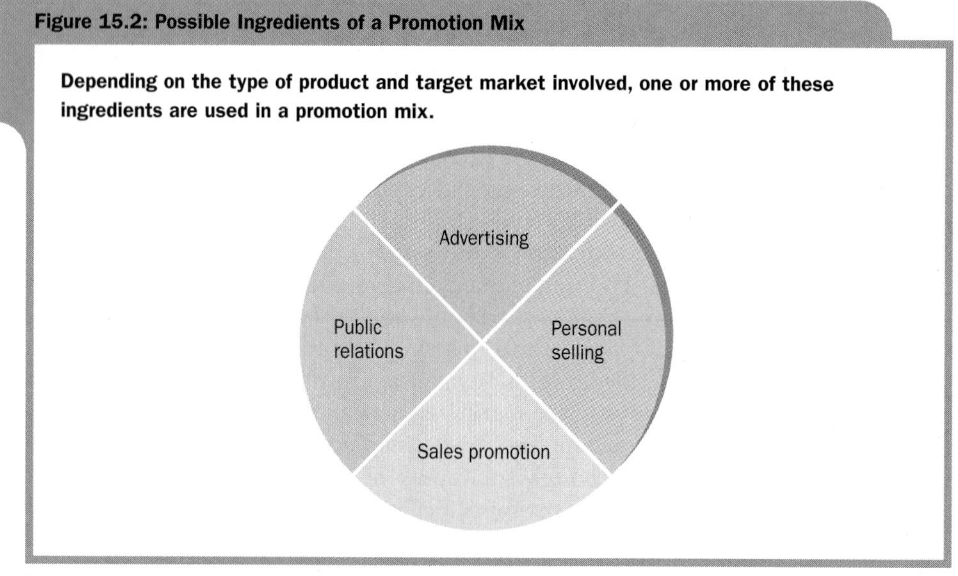

Source: William M. Pride and O. C. Ferrell, *Marketing: Concepts and Strategies,* 15th ed. (Mason, Ohio: South-Western/Cengage Learning, 2010). Adapted with permission.

While it is possible that one ingredient may be used, it is likely that two, three, or four of these ingredients will be used in a promotion mix, depending on the type of product and target market involved.

Advertising is a paid nonpersonal message communicated to a select audience through a mass medium. Advertising is flexible enough that it can reach a very large target group or a small, carefully chosen one. **Personal selling** is personal communication aimed at informing customers and persuading them to buy a firm's products. It is more expensive to reach a consumer through personal selling than through advertising, but this method provides immediate feedback and often is more persuasive than advertising. **Sales promotion** is the use of activities or materials as direct inducements to customers or salespersons. It adds extra value to the product or increases the customer's incentive to buy the product. **Public relations** is a broad set of communication activities used to create and maintain favorable relationships between an organization and various public groups, both internal and external. There are a variety of public relations activites that can be very effective.

SPOTLIGHT

Online Product Reviews

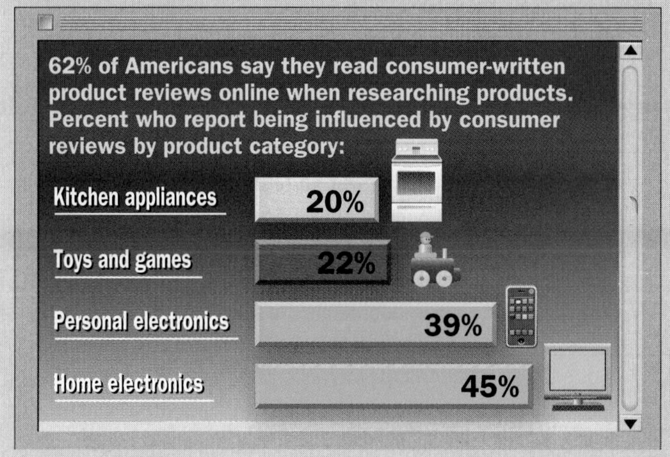

Source: Deloitte & Touche, Margin of error +/– 3%. As seen in *USA Today Snapshot* on November 7, 2007, p. B1.

Advertising

3 Learning Objective: Explain the purposes of the three types of advertising.

In 2008, organizations spent $285 billion on advertising in the United States.[3] Figure 15.3 shows how advertising expenditures are distributed across major media categories.

Types of Advertising by Purpose

Depending on its purpose and message, advertising may be classified into one of three groups: primary demand, selective demand, or institutional.

advertising a paid nonpersonal message communicated to a select audience through a mass medium

personal selling personal communication aimed at informing customers and persuading them to buy a firm's products

sales promotion the use of activities or materials as direct inducements to customers or salespersons

public relations communication activities used to create and maintain favorable relations between an organization and various public groups, both internal and external

Figure 15.3: Percent of Ad Dollars Spent on Selected Media

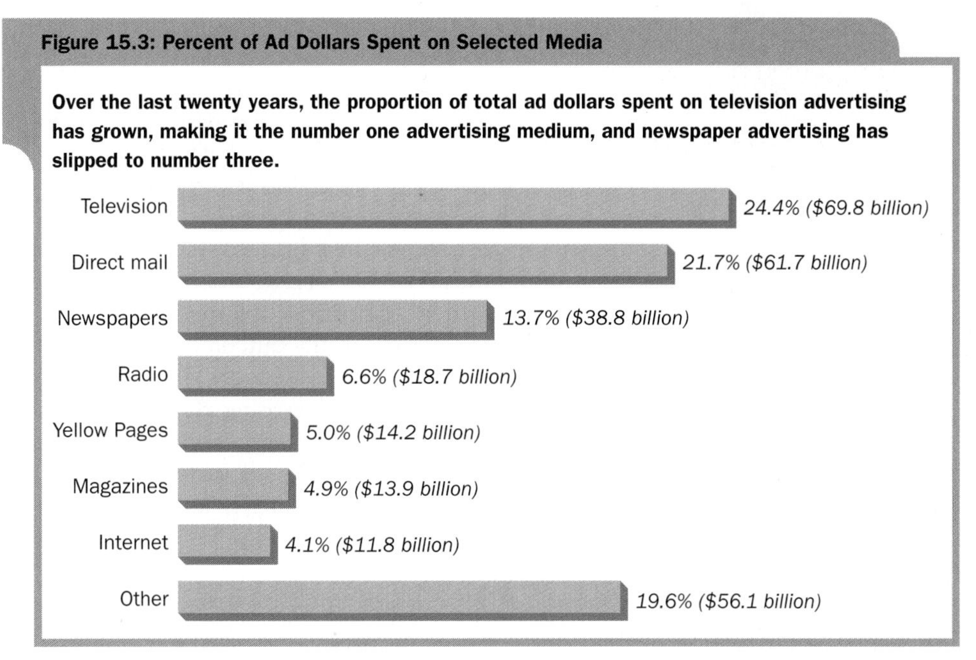

Source: Robert Coen, "Insider's Report," July 2008, p. 4.

Jump-Starting Your Career

Your Place in an Ad, Ad, Ad, Ad World

What can you do to prepare for a career in advertising? Whether you want to work in an ad agency, in a company's advertising department, or in media, you'll need:

- *Creative communication.* Not surprisingly, your communication skills (verbal and nonverbal) will have to be top-notch. But you should also be ready to draw on your full range of talents and your experiences as a consumer to bring fresh insights and unique approaches to advertising challenges. "Advertising people always think outside the box in terms of creative solutions for their clients," notes one advertising expert.
- *Digital intelligence.* Every advertiser must have an Internet presence these days. You don't need a technical background to know your way around the Web, try out the latest online communication tools, and think about how new and traditional types of messages and media can be used, separately and together.
- *Broad perspective.* Can you see the big picture as well as the small details? A broad perspective will help you identify emerging consumer needs, track trends in the business environment, analyze competitive moves, and put your advertising ideas into a bottom-line context.

Sources: Claire Atkinson, "Ad Shops Shift Hiring Tactics," September 22, 2008, p. C9; Rupal Parekh, "Reading, 'Riting, and Reality," *Advertising Age,* September 22, 2008, p. C8; Patricia Moore, "Tinker, Tailor, Adman," *AdMedia,* August 2008, p. 43.

primary-demand advertising advertising whose purpose is to increase the demand for all brands of a product within a specific industry

Primary-Demand Advertising **Primary-demand advertising** is advertising aimed at increasing the demand for *all* brands of a product within a specific industry. Trade and industry associations, such as the California Milk Processor Board ("Got Milk?"), are the major users of primary-demand advertising. Their advertisements promote broad product categories, such as beef, milk, pork, potatoes, and prunes, without mentioning specific brands.

Generating primary demand. *Several milk industry associations promote milk in order to stimulate primary demand. Rather than promote a specific brand, the familiar "got milk?" ad campaigns are meant to increase demand for milk in general.*

PRNewswire/Milk Processor Education Program

Selective-Demand Advertising **Selective-demand** (or **brand**) **advertising** is advertising that is used to sell a particular brand of product. It is by far the most common type of advertising, and it accounts for the lion's share of advertising expenditures. Producers use brand-oriented advertising to convince us to buy everything from BUBBLE YUM to Buicks.

Selective advertising that aims at persuading consumers to make purchases within a short time is called *immediate-response advertising.* Most local advertising is of this type. Often local advertisers promote products with immediate appeal. Selective advertising aimed at keeping a firm's name or product before the public is called *reminder advertising.*

Comparative advertising, which has become more popular over the last three decades, compares specific characteristics of two or more identified brands. Of course, the comparison shows the advertiser's brand to be as good as or better than the other identified competing brands. Comparisons often are based on the outcome of surveys or research studies. Although competing firms act as effective watchdogs against each other's advertising claims, consumers themselves sometimes become rather guarded concerning claims based on "scientific studies" and various statistical manipulations. Comparative advertising is unacceptable or illegal in a number of other countries.

Institutional Advertising **Institutional advertising** is advertising designed to enhance a firm's image or reputation. Many public utilities and larger firms, such as AT&T

and the major oil companies, use part of their advertising dollars to build goodwill rather than to stimulate sales directly. A positive public image helps an organization to attract not only customers but also employees and investors.

selective-demand (or brand) advertising advertising that is used to sell a particular brand of product

Advertising Media

Learning Objective: Describe the advantages and disadvantages of the major advertising media.

The **advertising media** are the various forms of communication through which advertising reaches its audience. The major media are newspapers, magazines, direct mail, Yellow Pages, out-of-home, television, radio, and the Internet. Figure 15.3 shows how organizations allocate advertising dollars among the various media. Note that more money is spent on Yellow Pages than on magazines.

institutional advertising advertising designed to enhance a firm's image or reputation

advertising media the various forms of communication through which advertising reaches its audience

Newspapers Newspaper advertising accounts for about 13.7 percent of all advertising expenditures. Approximately 85 percent is purchased by local retailers. Retailers use newspaper advertising extensively because it is relatively inexpensive compared with other media. Moreover, since most newspapers provide local coverage, advertising dollars are not wasted in reaching people outside the organization's market area. It is also timely. Ads usually can be placed just a few days before they are to appear.

There are some drawbacks, however, to newspaper advertising. It has a short life span; newspapers generally are read through once and then discarded. Color reproduction in newspapers is usually not high quality; thus, most ads are run in black and white. Finally, marketers cannot target specific demographic groups through newspaper ads because newspapers are read by such a broad spectrum of people.

Magazines The advertising revenues of magazines have been almost flat over the last few years. In 2008, they were projected to reach $13.9 billion, or about 4.9 percent of all advertising expenditures.

Advertisers can reach very specific market segments through ads in special-interest magazines. A boat manufacturer has a ready-made consumer audience in subscribers to *Yachting* or *Sail*. Producers of photographic equipment advertise in *Travel & Leisure* or *Popular Photography*. A number of magazines such as *Time* and *Cosmopolitan* publish regional editions, which provide advertisers with geographic flexibility as well.

Magazine advertising is more prestigious than newspaper advertising, and it allows for high-quality color reproduction. In addition, magazine advertisements have a longer life span than those in other media. Issues of *National Geographic*, for example, may be kept for months or years, and the ads they contain may be viewed repeatedly.

The major disadvantages of magazine advertising are high cost and lack of timeliness. Because magazine ads normally must be prepared two to three months in advance, they cannot be adjusted to reflect the latest market conditions. Magazine ads—especially full-color ads—are also expensive. Although the cost of reaching a thousand people may compare favorably with that of other media, the cost of a full-page four-color ad can be very high—$255,840 in *Time*.[4]

Direct Mail **Direct-mail advertising** is promotional material mailed directly to individuals. Direct mail is the most selective medium; mailing lists are available (or can be compiled) to reach almost any target audience, from airplane enthusiasts to zoologists. The effectiveness of direct-mail advertising can be measured because the advertiser has a record of who received the advertisements and can track who responds to the ads.

direct-mail advertising promotional material mailed directly to individuals

Some organizations are using direct e-mail. To avoid customers receiving unwanted e-mail, a firm should ask customers to complete a request form in order to receive promotional e-mail from the company.

The success of direct-mail advertising depends to some extent on appropriate and current mailing lists. A direct-mail campaign may fail if the mailing list is outdated and the mailing does not reach the right people. In addition, this medium is

Ethics Matters

The Ethics of Product Placement

From cars to coffee, cell phones to shredders, branded goods and services seem to be popping up in every type of entertainment—in most cases, not by accident. The goal is to capture viewers' attention while they're caught up in the fun or drama of a movie, television program, or video game. But should marketers be required to disclose when they've paid for product placement?

AP Photo/Richard Lewis

Proponents say that consumers are sophisticated enough not to be misled and realize that marketers often pay to have their brands featured. Critics say that paid product placement should be identified as such. One way to avoid any misunderstanding is to run a notice at the bottom of the screen when the product appears. Another idea is to insert a brief announcement at the beginning or end of the entertainment, the way television shows are required to disclose product plugs.

Product placement is even more controversial when news programs are involved. Not long ago, McDonald's paid to put iced coffee drinks on anchors' desks during television newscasts in Las Vegas. Although the European Union doesn't allow product placement within news shows, the United States has no such ban. What do you think about product placement?

Sources: John Eggerton, "Group to FCC: Lay Off Product Plugs," *Broadcasting & Cable*, October 13, 2008, p. 10; Brian Steinberg, "Pay-for-Play Wends Its Way into TV News," *Advertising Age*, July 28, 2008, p. 4; Stephanie Clifford, "Product Placements Acquire a Life of Their Own on Shows," *New York Times*, July 14, 2008, p. C1; "Should Product Placement Be Allowed in UK News Programmes?" *Marketing*, August 6, 2008, p. 22.

relatively costly. Direct-mail advertising expenditures in 2008 were estimated to be about $61.7 billion, almost 21.7 percent of the total.

Yellow Pages Advertising **Yellow Pages advertising** appearing in print and online telephone directories is presented under specific product categories and may appear as simple listings or as display advertisements. In 2008, advertisers spent an estimated $14.2 billion on Yellow Pages advertising, which represented approximately 5.0 percent of total advertising expenditures. Yellow Pages advertising appears in over 6,000 editions of telephone directories that are distributed to millions of customers annually. Approximately 85 percent of Yellow Pages advertising is used by local advertisers as opposed to national advertisers.

Customers use Yellow Pages advertising to save time in finding products, to find information quickly, and to learn about products and marketers. It is estimated that approximately 60 percent of adults read Yellow Pages advertising at least once a week. Unlike other types of advertising media, Yellow Pages advertisements are purchased for one year and cannot be changed. Advertisers often pay for their Yellow Pages advertisements through monthly charges on their telephone statements.

Out-of-Home Advertising **Out-of-home advertising** consists of short promotional messages on billboards, posters, signs, and transportation vehicles. Advertisers spent $6.2 billion, or 2.2 percent of total advertising expenditures, on out-of-home advertising.

Sign and billboard advertising allows the marketer to focus on a particular geographic area; it is also fairly inexpensive. However, because most outdoor promotion is directed toward a mobile audience, the message must be limited to a few words. The medium is especially suitable for products that lend themselves to pictorial display.

Yellow Pages advertising simple listings or display advertisements presented under specific product categories appearing in print and online telephone directories

out-of-home advertising short promotional messages on billboards, posters, signs, and transportation vehicles

Television Television ranks number one in total advertising revenue. In 2008, almost one-fourth of all advertising expenditures, about $70 billion, went to television. Approximately 99 percent of American homes have at least one television set that is watched an average of seven hours and forty minutes each day. The average U.S. household can receive twenty-eight TV channels, including cable and pay stations, and about 80 percent of households receive basic cable/satellite television. Television obviously provides advertisers with considerable access to consumers.

Television advertising is the primary medium for larger firms whose objective is to reach national or regional markets. A national advertiser may buy *network time*, which means that its message usually will be broadcast by hundreds of local stations affiliated with the network. However, the opportunity to reach extremely large television audiences has been reduced by the increased availability and popularity of cable channels and home videos. Both national and local firms may buy *local time* on a single station that covers a particular geographic area.

Out-of-home advertising. *This train wrap featuring several famous icons from downtown Detroit promotes the Detroit People Mover's "ReDiscover Downtown Detroit" 20th Anniversary.*

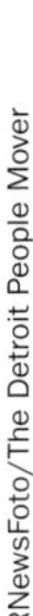

Advertisers may *sponsor* an entire show, participate with other sponsors of a show, or buy *spot time* for a single 10-, 20-, 30-, or 60-second commercial during or between programs. To an extent, they may select their audience by choosing the day of the week and the approximate time of day their ads will be shown. Anheuser-Busch advertises Budweiser Beer during TV football games because the majority of viewers are men, who are likely to buy beer.

Marketers also can employ *product placement,* which is paying a fee to have a product appear in a television program or movie. The product might appear on a table or counter, or one or more of the actors might be using it. Through channel switching and personal video recorders such as TiVo, television viewers can avoid watching regular television commercials. By placing the product directly into the program, viewers are likely to be exposed to the product. The hit NBC show *The Office,* for example, has integrated products from Hewlett-Packard and Staples within storylines. Such product placement has become more important due to the increasing fragmentation of television viewers who have ever-expanding viewing options and technology that can delete advertisements. Research indicates that 60 to 80 percent of digital video recorder users skip over the commercials when they replay programs.[5]

Another option available to television advertisers is the infomercial. An **infomercial** is a program-length televised commercial message resembling an entertainment or consumer affairs program. Infomercials for products such as exercise equipment tell customers why they need the product, what benefits it provides, in what ways it outperforms its competitors, and how much it costs. Although infomercials initially were aired primarily over cable television, today they are becoming more common on other types of television. Currently, infomercials are responsible for marketing over $1 billion worth of products annually. Even some *Fortune* 500 companies are now using them.

infomercial a program-length televised commercial message resembling an entertainment or consumer affairs program

Television advertising rates are based on the number of people expected to be watching when the commercial is aired. In 2008, the cost of a 30-second Super Bowl commercial was $2.7 million. Advertisers spend over $500,000 for a 30-second television commercial during a top-rated prime-time program.[6]

Radio Advertisers spent an estimated $18.7 billion, or 6.6 percent of total expenditures, on radio advertising in 2008. Like magazine advertising, radio advertising offers selectivity. Radio stations develop programming for—and are tuned in by—specific groups of listeners. There are almost half a billion radios in the United States (about six per household), which makes radio the most accessible medium.

Radio advertising can be less expensive than in other media. Actual rates depend on geographic coverage, the number of commercials contracted for, the time period specified, and whether the station broadcasts on AM, FM, or both. Even small retailers are able to afford radio advertising. A radio advertiser can schedule and change ads on short notice. The disadvantages of using radio are the absence of visual images and (because there are so many stations) the small audience size.

Internet Spending on Internet advertising has increased significantly. In 2008, U.S. advertisers spent $11.8 billion on Internet advertising compared with $7.8 billion three years earlier. Internet advertising accounts for 4.1 percent of the total advertising expenditures. Internet advertising can take a variety of forms. The *banner ad* is a rectangular graphic that appears at the top of a website. A lot of websites are able to offer free services because they are supported by banner advertisements. Advertisers can use animation and interactive capabilities to draw more attention to their ads. Yahoo! even invites its users to participate in surveys evaluating the banner ads on its home page. Another type is *sponsorship* (or *cobranded* ads). These ads integrate a company's brand with editorial content. The goal of this type of ad is to get users to strongly identify the advertiser with the site's mission. For example, many food brands such as Kraft advertise on **Allrecipes.com**. This site allows users to share and browse thousands of recipes. Kraft offers its own recipes on the site, and they all include its products. There are also banner ads for Kraft on other recipes, reminding the user of Kraft cheese while they read a recipe for cheese dip. Many Internet advertisers choose to purchase keywords on popular search engines such as Google, Yahoo!, and MSN. For example, Kellogg purchased the word *cereal* on Google so that every time someone conducts a search using that word, a link to Kellogg's website appears. *Interstitial* ads pop up to display a product. For example, users can gain access to online magazine **Salon.com** by watching a commercial that will grant them a twenty-four-hour pass to all of Salon's content, or they can bypass the ad altogether by paying a monthly subscription fee for an ad-free version.

Major Steps in Developing an Advertising Campaign

Learning Objective: Identify the major steps in developing an advertising campaign.

An advertising campaign is developed in several stages. These stages may vary in number and the order in which they are implemented depending on the company's resources, products, and audiences. The development of a campaign in any organization, however, will include the following steps in some form:

1. Identify and Analyze the Target Audience The target audience is the group of people toward which a firm's advertisements are directed. To pinpoint the organization's target audience and develop an effective campaign, marketers must analyze such information as the geographic distribution of potential customers; their age, sex, race, income, and education; and their attitudes toward both the advertiser's product and competing products. How marketers use this information will be influenced by the features of the product to be advertised and the nature of the competition. Precise identification of the target audience is crucial to the proper development of subsequent stages and, ultimately, to the success of the campaign itself. For example, American Airlines identified an Hispanic target audience and focused a multimedia Spanish language advertising campaign with the theme "*No importa cual sea tu destino, nosotros te llevamos*" ("It doesn't matter what your destiny is, we will take you there"). The campaign features vignettes that show Latinos reconnecting with the people and the places they want to see.[7]

2. Define the Advertising Objectives The goals of an advertising campaign should be stated precisely and in measurable terms. The objectives should include the current position of the firm, indicate how far and in what direction from that original reference point the company wishes to move, and specify a definite period of time for the achievement of the goals. Advertising objectives that focus on sales will stress increasing sales by a certain percentage or dollar amount or expanding the firm's market share. Communication objectives will emphasize increasing product or brand awareness, improving consumer attitudes, or conveying product information.

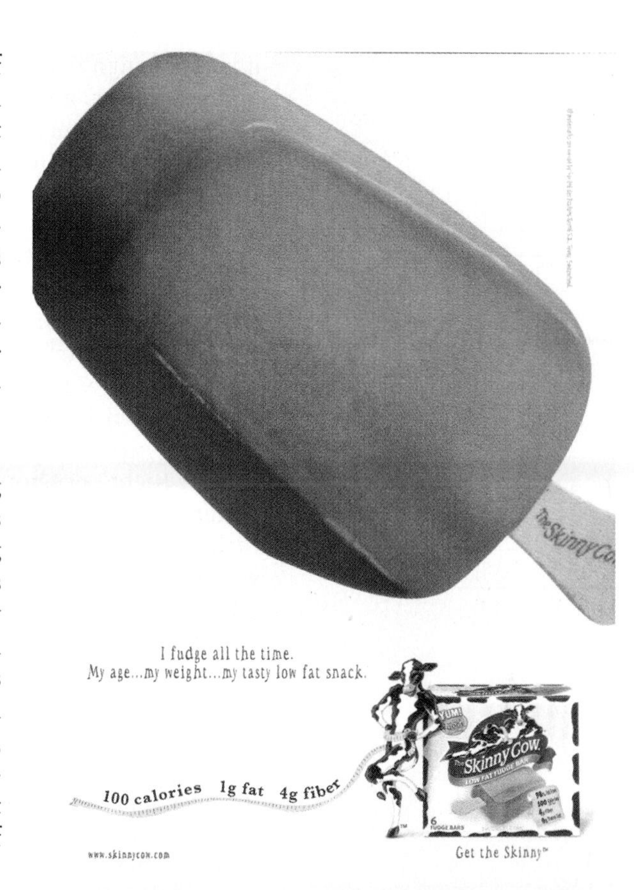

Target audience—Is this ad aimed at everyone? Most advertisements are not aimed at everyone. This Skinny Cow ad tells women 35 and over, "I fudge all the time. My age ... my weight ... my tasty low fat snack."

3. Create the Advertising Platform An advertising platform includes the important selling points or features that an advertiser wishes to incorporate into the advertising campaign. These features should be important to customers in their selection and use of a product, and if possible, they should be features that competing products lack. Although research into what consumers view as important issues is expensive, it is the most productive way to determine which issues to include in an advertising platform. New Balance, for example, launched a campaign that pokes fun at professional athletes while reminding its 25- to 49-year-old target audience about the joys of competing for fun and the love of sports.[8]

4. Determine the Advertising Appropriation The advertising appropriation is the total amount of money designated for advertising in a given period. This stage is critical to the success of the campaign because advertising efforts based on an inadequate budget will understimulate customer demand, and a budget too large will waste a company's resources. Advertising appropriations may be based on last year's (or next year's forecasted) sales, on what competitors spend on advertising, or on executive judgment.

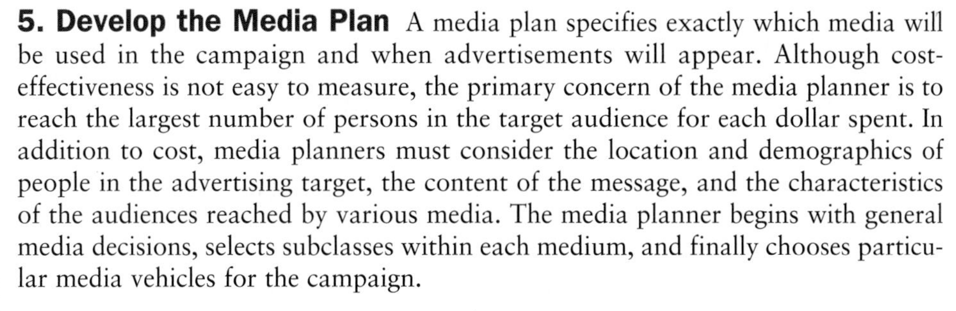

5. Develop the Media Plan A media plan specifies exactly which media will be used in the campaign and when advertisements will appear. Although cost-effectiveness is not easy to measure, the primary concern of the media planner is to reach the largest number of persons in the target audience for each dollar spent. In addition to cost, media planners must consider the location and demographics of people in the advertising target, the content of the message, and the characteristics of the audiences reached by various media. The media planner begins with general media decisions, selects subclasses within each medium, and finally chooses particular media vehicles for the campaign.

6. Create the Advertising Message The content and form of a message are influenced by the product's features, the characteristics of people in the target audience, the objectives of the campaign, and the choice of media. An advertiser must consider these factors to choose words and illustrations that will be meaningful and appealing to persons in the advertising target. The copy, or words, of an advertisement will vary depending on the media choice but should attempt to move the audience through attention, interest, desire, and action. Artwork and visuals should complement copy by attracting the audience's attention and communicating an idea quickly. Creating a cohesive advertising message is especially difficult for a company such as eBay that offers such a broad mix of products. eBay developed a "whatever it is" campaign that features a variety of consumers of every age using a variety of products (a car, a television, a dress, and a laptop) all shaped like the letters "it." The tagline, "Whatever *it* is, you can get it on eBay," emphasizes the massive range of products available from the site and showcases the service that the company provides effectively.

7. Execute the Campaign Execution of an advertising campaign requires extensive planning, scheduling, and coordinating because many tasks must be completed on time. The efforts of many people and firms are involved. Production companies, research organizations, media firms, printers, photoengravers, and commercial artists are just a few of the people and firms that may contribute to a campaign. Advertising managers constantly must assess the quality of the work and take corrective action when necessary. Wendy's, for example, pulled the plug on its "That's Right" promotion campaign after it failed to generate sales. The short-lived campaign, which featured characters wearing pig-tailed red-haired wigs, like the chain's mascot, who declared, "I deserve a hot juicy burger," attracted attention as well as controversy. The company quickly launched a more positive food-focused campaign with an animated Wendy's character and the tag line "Waaaay Better than Fast Food. It's Wendy's."[9]

8. Evaluate Advertising Effectiveness A campaign's success should be measured in terms of its original objectives before, during, and/or after the campaign. An advertiser should at least be able to estimate whether sales or market share went up because of the campaign or whether any change occurred in customer attitudes or brand awareness. Data from past and current sales and responses to coupon offers and customer surveys administered by research organizations are some of the ways in which advertising effectiveness can be evaluated.

Advertising Agencies

advertising agency an independent firm that plans, produces, and places advertising for its clients

Advertisers can plan and produce their own advertising with help from media personnel, or they can hire advertising agencies. An **advertising agency** is an independent firm that plans, produces, and places advertising for its clients. Many large ad agencies offer help with sales promotion and public relations as well. The media usually pay a commission of 15 percent to advertising agencies. Thus, the cost to the agency's client can be quite moderate. The client may be asked to pay for selected services that the agency performs. Other methods for compensating agencies are also used.

Firms that do a lot of advertising may use both an in-house advertising department and an independent agency. This approach gives the firm the advantage of being able to call on the agency's expertise in particular areas of advertising. An agency also can bring a fresh viewpoint to a firm's products and advertising plans.

Table 15.1 lists the nation's twenty leading advertisers in all media. Most recently, the number one advertising spender is Procter & Gamble.

Social and Legal Considerations in Advertising

Critics of U.S. advertising have two main complaints—that it is wasteful and that it can be deceptive. Although advertising (like any other activity) can be performed inefficiently, it is far from wasteful. Let's look at the evidence:

- Advertising is the most effective and least expensive means of communicating product information to a large number of individuals and organizations.
- Advertising encourages competition and is, in fact, a means of competition. It thus leads to the development of new and improved products, wider product choices, and lower prices.
- Advertising revenues support our mass-communications media—newspapers, magazines, radio, and television. This means that advertising pays for much of our news coverage and entertainment programming.
- Advertising provides job opportunities in fields ranging from sales to film production.

Table 15.1: Advertising Expenditures and Sales Volume for the Top Twenty National Advertisers

Rank	Company	Advertising Expenditures (in millions)	Sales (in millions)	Advertising Expenditures as Percentage of Sales
1	Procter & Gamble	$5,230	$ 31,946	16.4
2	AT&T	3,207	118,928	2.7
3	Verizon Communications	3,016	89,504	3.4
4	General Motors	3,010	100,545	3.0
5	Time Warner	2,962	38,256	7.7
6	Ford Motor Co.	2,525	80,874	3.1
7	GlaxoSmithKline	2,457	18,563	13.2
8	Johnson & Johnson	2,409	32,444	7.4
9	Walt Disney Co.	2,293	27,286	8.4
10	Unilever	2,246	18,372	12.2
11	Sprint Nextel Corp.	1,903	40,146	4.7
12	General Electric Co.	1,791	86,200	2.1
13	Toyota Motor Corp.	1,758	79,909	2.2
14	Chrysler	1,739	NA	NA
15	Sony Corp.	1,737	18,841	9.2
16	L'Oreal	1,632	6,049	27.0
17	Sears Holding Corp.	1,628	45,101	3.6
18	Kraft Foods	1,508	21,543	7.0
19	Bank of America Corp.	1,491	59,731	2.5
20	Nissan Motor Corp.	1,423	34,752	4.1

Source: Reprinted with permission from the June 23, 2008 issue of Advertising Age. Copyright, Craine Communications Inc. 2008.

A number of government and private agencies scrutinize advertising for false or misleading claims or offers. At the national level, the Federal Trade Commission (FTC), the Food and Drug Administration (FDA), and the Federal Communications Commission (FCC) oversee advertising practices. Advertising also may be monitored by state and local agencies, Better Business Bureaus, and industry associations.

Personal Selling

6

Learning Objective: Recognize the various kinds of salespersons, the steps in the personal-selling process, and the major sales management tasks.

Personal selling is the most adaptable of all promotional methods because the person who is presenting the message can modify it to suit the individual buyer. However, personal selling is also the most expensive method of promotion.

Most successful salespeople are able to communicate with others on a one-to-one basis and are strongly motivated. They strive to have a thorough knowledge of the products they offer for sale. And they are willing and able to deal with the details involved in handling and processing orders. Sales managers tend to emphasize these qualities when recruiting and hiring.

Many selling situations demand the face-to-face contact and adaptability of personal selling. This is especially true of industrial sales, in which a single purchase may amount to millions of dollars. Obviously, sales of that size must be based on carefully planned sales presentations, personal contact with customers, and thorough negotiations.

Personal selling. *As a major promotion mix ingredient, personal selling is very flexible, can occur in stores, factories, offices, homes, or on the phone, and can be expensive.*

Kinds of Salespersons

Because most businesses employ different salespersons to perform different functions, marketing managers must select the kinds of sales personnel that will be most effective in selling the firm's products. Salespersons may be identified as order getters, order takers, and support personnel. A single individual can, and often does, perform all three functions.

order getter a salesperson who is responsible for selling a firm's products to new customers and increasing sales to present customers

creative selling selling products to new customers and increasing sales to present customers

Order Getters An **order getter** is responsible for what is sometimes called **creative selling**—selling a firm's products to new customers and increasing sales to current customers. An order getter must perceive buyers' needs, supply customers with information about the firm's product, and persuade them to buy the product. Order-getting activities may be separated into two groups. In current-customer sales, salespeople concentrate on obtaining additional sales or leads for prospective sales from customers who have purchased the firm's products at least once. In new-business sales, sales personnel seek out new prospects and convince them to make an initial purchase of the firm's product. The real estate, insurance, appliance, heavy industrial machinery, and automobile industries in particular depend on new-business sales.

order taker a salesperson who handles repeat sales in ways that maintain positive relationships with customers

Order Takers An **order taker** handles repeat sales in ways that maintain positive relationships with customers. An order taker sees that customers have products when and where they are needed and in the proper amounts. *Inside order takers* receive incoming mail and telephone orders in some businesses; salespersons in retail stores are also inside order takers. *Outside* (or *field*) *order takers* travel to customers. Often, the buyer and the field salesperson develop a mutually beneficial relationship of placing, receiving, and delivering orders. Both inside and outside order takers are active salespersons and often produce most of their companies' sales.

Support Personnel **Sales support personnel** aid in selling but are more involved in locating *prospects* (likely first-time customers), educating customers, building goodwill for the firm, and providing follow-up service. The most common categories of support personnel are missionary, trade, and technical salespersons.

sales support personnel employees who aid in selling but are more involved in locating prospects, educating customers, building goodwill for the firm, and providing follow-up service

A **missionary salesperson**, who usually works for a manufacturer, visits retailers to persuade them to buy the manufacturer's products. If the retailers agree, they buy the products from wholesalers, who are the manufacturer's actual customers. Missionary salespersons often are employed by producers of medical supplies and pharmaceuticals to promote these products to retail druggists, physicians, and hospitals.

missionary salesperson a salesperson—generally employed by a manufacturer—who visits retailers to persuade them to buy the manufacturer's products

A **trade salesperson**, who generally works for a food producer or processor, assists customers in promoting products, especially in retail stores. A trade salesperson may obtain additional shelf space for the products, restock shelves, set up displays, and distribute samples. Because trade salespersons usually are order takers as well, they are not strictly support personnel.

trade salesperson a salesperson—generally employed by a food producer or processor—who assists customers in promoting products, especially in retail stores

A **technical salesperson** assists a company's current customers in technical matters. He or she may explain how to use a product, how it is made, how to install it, or how a system is designed. A technical salesperson should be formally educated in science or engineering. Computers, steel, and chemicals are some of the products handled by technical salespeople.

technical salesperson a salesperson who assists a company's current customers in technical matters

Marketers usually need sales personnel from several of these categories. Factors that affect hiring and other personnel decisions include the number of customers and their characteristics; the product's attributes, complexity, and price; the distribution channels used by the company; and the company's approach to advertising.

The Personal-Selling Process

No two selling situations are exactly alike, and no two salespeople perform their jobs in exactly the same way. Most salespeople, however, follow the six-step procedure illustrated in Figure 15.4.

Prospecting The first step in personal selling is to research potential buyers and choose the most likely customers, or prospects. Sources of prospects include business associates and customers, public records, telephone and trade-association directories, and company files. The salesperson concentrates on those prospects who have the financial resources, willingness, and authority to buy the product.

Approaching the Prospect First impressions are often lasting impressions. Thus the salesperson's first contact with the prospect is crucial to successful selling. The best approach is one based on knowledge of the product, of the prospect's needs, and of how the product can meet those needs. Salespeople who understand each customer's particular situation are likely to make a good first impression—and to make a sale.

Making the Presentation The next step is actual delivery of the sales presentation. In many cases, this includes demonstrating the product. The salesperson points out the product's features, its benefits, and how it is superior to competitors' merchandise. If the product has been used successfully by other firms, the salesperson may mention this as part of the presentation.

During a demonstration, the salesperson may suggest that the prospect try out the product personally. The demonstration and product trial should underscore specific points made during the presentation.

Answering Objections The prospect is likely to raise objections or ask questions at any time. This gives the salesperson a chance to eliminate objections that might prevent a sale, to point out additional features, or to mention special services the company offers.

Closing the Sale To close the sale, the salesperson asks the prospect to buy the product. This is considered the critical point in the selling process. Many experienced salespeople make use of a *trial closing*, in which they ask questions based on the

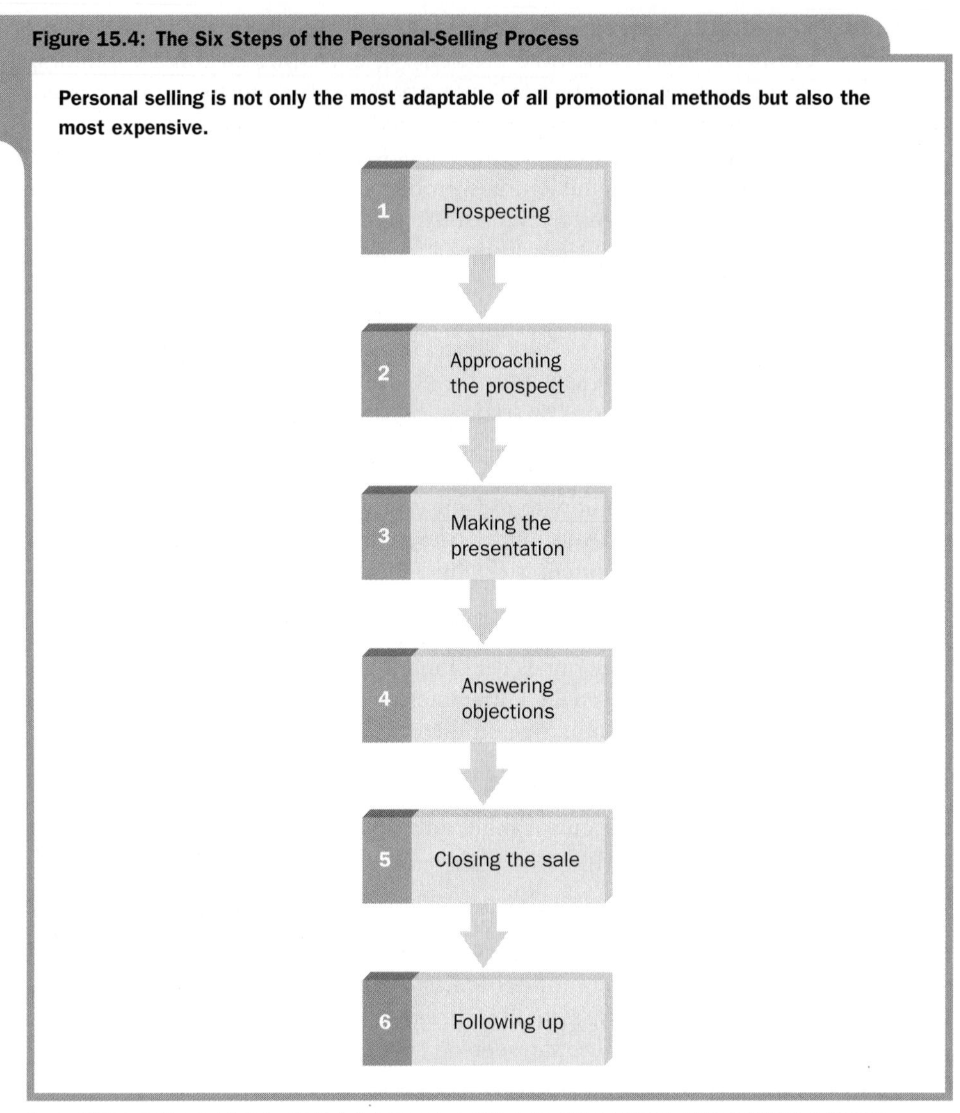

Source: William M. Pride and O. C. Ferrell, *Marketing: Concepts and Strategies,* 15th ed. (Mason, Ohio: South-Western/Cengage Learning, 2010). Adapted with permission.

assumption that the customer is going to buy the product. The questions "When would you want delivery?" and "Do you want the standard model or the one with the special options package?" are typical of trial closings. They allow the reluctant prospect to make a purchase without having to say, "I'll take it."

Following Up The salesperson must follow up after the sale to ensure that the product is delivered on time, in the right quantity, and in proper operating condition. During follow-up, the salesperson also makes it clear that he or she is available in case problems develop. Follow-up leaves a good impression and eases the way toward future sales. Hence, it is essential to the selling process. The salesperson's job does not end with a sale. It continues as long as the seller and the customer maintain a working relationship.

Managing Personal Selling

A firm's success often hinges on the competent management of its sales force. Although some companies operate efficiently without a sales force, most firms rely on a strong sales force—and the sales revenue it brings in—for their success.

Sales managers have responsibilities in a number of areas. They must set sales objectives in concrete, quantifiable terms and specify a certain period of time and a certain geographic area. They must adjust the size of the sales force to meet changes in the firm's marketing plan and the marketing environment. Sales managers must attract and hire effective salespersons. Sales managers must develop a training program and decide where, when, how, and for whom to conduct the training. They must formulate a fair and adequate compensation plan to keep qualified employees. They must motivate salespersons to boost their productivity. They must define sales territories and determine scheduling and routing of the sales force. Finally, sales managers must evaluate the operation as a whole through sales reports, communications with customers, and invoices.

Sales Promotion

7

Learning Objective: Describe sales promotion objectives and methods.

Sales promotion consists of activities or materials that are direct inducements to customers or salespersons. Are you a member of an airline frequent-flyer program? Did you recently receive a free sample in the mail or at a supermarket? Have you recently received a rebate from a manufacturer? Do you use coupons? All these are examples of sales promotion efforts. Sales promotion techniques often are used to enhance and supplement other promotional methods. They can have a significant impact on sales.

The dramatic increase in spending for sales promotion shows that marketers have recognized the potential of this promotional method. Many firms now include numerous sales promotion efforts as part of their overall promotion mix.

Sales Promotion Objectives

Sales promotion activities may be used singly or in combination, both offensively and defensively, to achieve one goal or a set of goals. Marketers use sales promotion activities and materials for a number of purposes, including

1. To attract new customers
2. To encourage trial of a new product
3. To invigorate the sales of a mature brand
4. To boost sales to current customers
5. To reinforce advertising
6. To increase traffic in retail stores
7. To steady irregular sales patterns
8. To build up reseller inventories
9. To neutralize competitive promotional efforts
10. To improve shelf space and displays[10]

Any sales promotion objectives should be consistent with the organization's general goals and with its marketing and promotional objectives.

Sales Promotion Methods

Most sales promotion methods can be classified as promotional techniques for either consumer sales or trade sales. A **consumer sales promotion method** attracts consumers to particular retail stores and motivates them to purchase certain new or established products. A **trade sales promotion method** encourages wholesalers and retailers to stock and actively promote a manufacturer's product. Incentives such as money, merchandise, marketing assistance, and gifts are commonly awarded to resellers who buy products or respond positively in other ways. Of the combined dollars spent on sales promotion and advertising last year, about one-half was spent on trade promotions, one-fourth on consumer promotions, and one-fourth on advertising.

consumer sales promotion method a sales promotion method designed to attract consumers to particular retail stores and to motivate them to purchase certain new or established products

trade sales promotion method a sales promotion method designed to encourage wholesalers and retailers to stock and actively promote a manufacturer's product

A number of factors enter into marketing decisions about which and how many sales promotion methods to use. Of greatest importance are the objectives of the promotional effort. Product characteristics—size, weight, cost, durability, uses, features, and hazards—and target market profiles—age, gender, income, location, density, usage rate, and buying patterns—likewise must be considered. Distribution channels and availability of appropriate resellers also influence the choice of sales promotion methods, as do the competitive and regulatory forces in the environment. Let's now discuss a few important sales promotion methods.

Source: "All About Coupons," Promotion Marketing Association, **www.couponmonth.com/pages/allabout.htm**, accessed February 20, 2008.

Rebates A **rebate** is a return of part of the purchase price of a product. Usually, the refund is offered by the producer to consumers who send in a coupon along with a specific proof of purchase. Rebating is a relatively low-cost promotional method. Once used mainly to help launch new product items, it is now applied to a wide variety of products. Some automakers offer rebates on their vehicles because they have found that many car customers are more likely to purchase a car with a rebate than the same car with a lower price and no rebate. One problem with rebates is that many people perceive the redemption process as too complicated. Only about half of individuals who purchase rebated products actually apply for the rebates.

rebate a return of part of the purchase price of a product

coupon reduces the retail price of a particular item by a stated amount at the time of purchase

Coupons A **coupon** reduces the retail price of a particular item by a stated amount at the time of purchase. Coupons may be worth anywhere from a few cents to a few dollars. They are made available to customers through newspapers, magazines, direct mail, online, and shelf dispensers in stores. Some coupons are precisely targeted at customers. For example, All Online Coupons is an Internet site that provides visitors with links to all online coupons currently being offered. Customers can find coupons by category or store name. Other companies, such as Old Navy and Gap Inc., offer coupons on their websites that can be used online or in stores. Billions of coupons are distributed annually. Of these, less than 2 percent are redeemed by consumers. The average house receives 55 coupons per week, or over 2,800 per year.[11] The largest number of coupons distributed are for household cleaners, condiments, frozen foods, medications and health aids, and paper products. Stores in some areas even deduct double or triple the value of manufacturers' coupons from the purchase price as a sales promotion technique of their own. Coupons also may offer free merchandise, either with or without an additional purchase of a product.

Handing out samples. *In this photo, Joy Behar, co-host of The View, hands out free samples of Kraft Bagel-fuls during the product's launch.*

PRNewsFoto/Kraft Foods, Stuart Ramson

Samples A **sample** is a free product given to customers to encourage trial and purchase. Marketers use free samples to stimulate trial of a product, increase sales volume in the early stages of a product's life cycle, and obtain desirable distribution. Samples may be offered via online coupons, direct mail, or in stores. Many customers prefer to receive their samples by mail. It is the most expensive sales promotion technique, and while it is used often to promote new products, it can be used to promote established brands, too, such as cosmetics companies that use samples to attract customers. In designing a free sample, organizations must consider such factors as seasonal demand for the product, market characteristics, and prior advertising.

Distribution of free samples through websites such as **StartSampling.com** is growing. Consumers choose the free samples they would like to receive and request delivery. The online company manages the packaging and distribution of the samples.

sample a free product given to customers to encourage trial and purchase

Premiums A **premium** is a gift that a producer offers a customer in return for buying its product. They are used to attract competitors' customers, introduce different sizes of established products, add variety to other promotional efforts, and stimulate consumer loyalty. Creativity is essential when using premiums; to stand out and achieve a significant number of redemptions, the premium must match both the target audience and the brand's image. Premiums also must be easily recognizable and desirable. Premiums are placed on or inside packages and also can be distributed through retailers or through the mail.

premium a gift that a producer offers a customer in return for buying its product

frequent-user incentive a program developed to reward customers who engage in repeat (frequent) purchases

point-of-purchase display promotional material placed within a retail store

trade show an industry-wide exhibit at which many sellers display their products

Frequent-User Incentives A **frequent-user incentive** is a program developed to reward customers who engage in repeat (frequent) purchases. Such programs are used commonly by service businesses such as airlines, hotels, and auto rental agencies. Frequent-user incentives foster customer loyalty to a specific company or group of cooperating companies because the customer is given an additional reason to continue patronizing the business. For example, most major airlines offer frequent flier programs that reward customers who have flown a specified number of miles with free tickets for additional travel. There is significant evidence that airline miles are highly valued by customers. Now, more frequent flier miles are awarded to customers of nonairline companies than to airline customers to stimulate customer loyalty. Research shows that 93 percent of people with household incomes above $100,000 participate in frequent-user programs, whereas only 58 percent of people with incomes below $50,000 participate.[12]

Point-of-Purchase Displays A **point-of-purchase display** is promotional material placed within a retail store. The display is usually located near the product being promoted. It actually may hold merchandise (as do L'eggs hosiery displays) or inform customers about what the product offers and encourage them to buy it. Most point-of-purchase displays are prepared and set up by manufacturers and wholesalers.

Trade Shows A **trade show** is an industry-wide exhibit at which many sellers display their products. Some trade shows are organized exclusively for dealers—to permit manufacturers and wholesalers to show their latest lines to retailers. Others are promotions designed to stimulate consumer awareness and interest. Among the latter are boat shows, home shows, and flower shows put on each year in large cities.

AP Photo/Jae C. Hong

Trade show. *Trade show participants look at Hitachi's 1.5-inch thick LCD television display at the Consumer Electronics trade show held annually in Las Vegas.*

buying allowance a temporary price reduction to resellers for purchasing specified quantities of a product

cooperative advertising an arrangement whereby a manufacturer agrees to pay a certain amount of a retailer's media cost for advertising the manufacturer's product

publicity communication in news-story form about an organization, its products, or both

Buying Allowances A **buying allowance** is a temporary price reduction to resellers for purchasing specified quantities of a product. For example, a laundry detergent manufacturer might give retailers $1 for each case of detergent purchased. A buying allowance may serve as an incentive to resellers to handle new products and may stimulate purchase of items in large quantities. While the buying allowance is simple, straightforward, and easily administered, competitors can respond quickly by offering a better buying allowance.

Cooperative Advertising **Cooperative advertising** is an arrangement whereby a manufacturer agrees to pay a certain amount of a retailer's media cost for advertising the manufacturer's products. To be reimbursed, a retailer must show proof that the advertisements actually did appear. A large percentage of all cooperative advertising dollars is spent on newspaper advertisements. Not all retailers take advantage of available cooperative advertising offers because they cannot afford to advertise or do not choose to do so.

Public Relations

8

Learning Objective: Understand the types and uses of public relations.

As noted earlier, public relations is a broad set of communication activities used to create and maintain favorable relationships between an organization and various public groups, both internal and external. These groups can include customers, employees, stockholders, suppliers, educators, the media, government officials, and society in general.

Event sponsorship. *Target dog, Bullseye, at the start of the 36th Annual Iditarod Trail Sled Dog Race, one of Alaska's most favored sports events. Target is currently opening stores in Alaska. (Sarah Palin or Tina Fey?)*

AP Photo/Rob Stapleton

Types of Public-Relations Tools

Organizations use a variety of public-relations tools to convey messages and to create images. Public-relations professionals prepare written materials such as brochures, newsletters, company magazines, annual reports, and news releases. They also create corporate-identity materials such as logos, business cards, signs, and stationery. Speeches are another public-relations tool. Speeches can affect an organization's image and therefore must convey the desired message clearly.

Another public-relations tool is event sponsorship, in which a company pays for all or part of a special event such as a concert, sports competition, festival, or play. Sponsoring special events is an effective way for organizations to increase brand recognition and receive media coverage with comparatively little investment. Nintendo, for example, is targeting older game players by hosting Super Bowl parties with men's magazines *Maxim* and *FHM*, as well as Spring Break parties and music tours, and it sponsored the Burton snowboarding championships.[13]

Some public-relations tools traditionally have been associated specifically with publicity, which is a part of public relations. **Publicity** is communication in news-story form about an organization, its products, or both. Publicity is transmitted through a mass medium, such as newspapers or radio, at no charge. Organizations use publicity to provide information about products; to announce new product launches, expansions, or research; and to strengthen the company's image. Public-relations personnel sometimes organize events, such as grand openings with prizes and celebrities, to create news stories about a company.

Going Global

Corporate Blog, Personal Touch

Corporate blogs are bringing a personal touch to marketing communications. A *blog* (short for *Web log*) is an Internet site where people post thoughts and images, then invite visitors to comment. By blogging and responding to what readers say, executives and employees help create a personal connection with customers and colleagues around the world.

For example, Bill Marriott, CEO of Marriott International, posts audio messages as well as written ideas, photos, and videos on his "Marriott on the Move" blog. Of the blog's 6,000 weekly visitors, 20 percent are employees in Marriott's global network of hotels who want to see what their CEO is doing. Marriott says blogging is a good way to show that he's "human just like everybody else." The blog is a marketing success, as well: Visitors who clicked from the blog to the reservations page have booked $5 million worth of hotel stays.

Toyota's Open Road Blog wraps a car community around the corporate blog. Its management bloggers discuss concept cars, green engine technology, brand rumors, and more. They also react to comments from consumers who join the conversation. Toyota started its blog because "the need to be more innovatively communicative, transparent, and engaged with consumers has never been greater," says the head of corporate communications, a frequent blogger.

Sources: Sarah Halzack, "Marketing Moves to the Blogosphere," *Washington Post*, August 25, 2008, p. D1; "Corporate Blogging: Conversation Starter," *New Media Age*, July 17, 2008, p. 19; Beth Snyder Bulik, "Does Your Company Need a Chief Blogger?" *Advertising Age*, April 14, 2008, p. 24; "A Peek into Corporate Blogging," *Advertising Age*, April 15, 2008, p. 24.

The most widely used type of publicity is the **news release**. It is generally one typed page of about 300 words provided by an organization to the media as a form of publicity. The release includes the firm's name, address, phone number, and contact person. Table 15.2 lists some of the issues news releases can address. There are also several other kinds of publicity-based public-relations tools. A **feature article**, which may run as long as 3,000 words, is usually written for inclusion in a particular publication. For example, a software firm might send an article about its new product to a computer magazine. A **captioned photograph**, a picture accompanied by a brief explanation, is an effective way to illustrate a new or improved product. A **press conference** allows invited media personnel to hear important news

news release a typed page of about 300 words provided by an organization to the media as a form of publicity

feature article a piece (of up to 3,000 words) prepared by an organization for inclusion in a particular publication

captioned photograph a picture accompanied by a brief explanation

press conference a meeting at which invited media personnel hear important news announcements and receive supplementary textual materials and photographs

Table 15.2: Possible Issues for News Releases

Use of new information technology	Packaging changes
Support of a social cause	New products
Improved warranties	Creation of new software
Reports on industry conditions	Research developments
New uses for established products	Company's history and development
Product endorsements	Launching of new website
Winning of quality awards	Award of contracts
Company name changes	Opening of new markets
Interviews with company officials	Improvements in financial position
Improved distribution policies	Opening of an exhibit
Global business initiatives	History of a brand
Sponsorship of events	Winners of company contests
Visits by celebrities	Logo changes
Reports of new discoveries	Speeches of top management
Innovative marketing activities	Merit awards to the organization
Economic forecasts	Anniversaries of inventions

Sustaining the Planet

The first Earth Day, on April 22, 1970, marked a day of environmental awareness across the United States. Today, Earth Day is celebrated worldwide, promoting a variety of sustainability efforts, encouraging environmental education, and getting both children and adults involved in protecting the planet. **www.epa.gov/earthday**

announcements and to receive supplementary textual materials and photographs. Finally, letters to the editor, special newspaper or magazine editorials, films, and tapes may be prepared and distributed to appropriate media for possible use.

The Uses of Public Relations

Public relations can be used to promote people, places, activities, ideas, and even countries. Public relations focuses on enhancing the reputation of the total organization by making people aware of a company's products, brands, or activities and by creating specific company images such as that of innovativeness or dependability. Meyers, a Swiss watch company, which has loaned watches to celebrities like Paris Hilton at the Sundance Film Festival and later auctioned off the returned timepieces for charity, says any resulting publicity from the effort can be worth as much as $750,000.[14]

Promotion Planning

9

Learning Objective: Identify the factors that influence the selection of promotion-mix ingredients.

promotional campaign a plan for combining and using the four promotional methods—advertising, personal selling, sales promotion, and publicity—in a particular promotion mix to achieve one or more marketing goals

A **promotional campaign** is a plan for combining and using the four promotional methods—advertising, personal selling, sales promotion, and public relations—in a particular promotion mix to achieve one or more marketing goals. When selecting promotional methods to include in promotion mixes, it is important to coordinate promotional elements to maximize total informational and promotional impact on customers. Integrated marketing communication requires a marketer to look at the broad perspective when planning promotional programs and coordinating the total set of communication functions.

In planning a promotional campaign, marketers must answer these two questions:

- What will be the role of promotion in the overall marketing mix?
- To what extent will each promotional method be used in the promotion mix?

The answer to the first question depends on the firm's marketing objectives because the role of each element of the marketing mix—product, price, distribution, and promotion—depends on these detailed versions of the firm's marketing goals. The answer to the second question depends on the answer to the first, as well as on the target market.

Promotion and Marketing Objectives

Promotion naturally is better suited to certain marketing objectives than to others. For example, promotion can do little to further a marketing objective such as "reduce delivery time by one-third." It can, however, be used to inform customers that delivery is faster. Let's consider some objectives that *would* require the use of promotion as a primary ingredient of the marketing mix.

Providing Information This is, of course, the main function of promotion. It may be used to communicate to target markets the availability of new products or product features. It may alert them to special offers or give the locations of retailers that carry a firm's products. In other words, promotion can be used to enhance the effectiveness of each of the other ingredients of the marketing mix.

Increasing Market Share Promotion can be used to convince new customers to try a product while maintaining the product loyalty of established customers. Comparative advertising, for example, is directed mainly at those who might—but presently do not—use a particular product. Advertising that emphasizes the product's features also assures those who *do* use the product that they have made a smart choice.

Positioning the Product The sales of a product depend, to a great extent, on its competition. The stronger the competition, the more difficult it is to maintain or increase sales. For this reason, many firms go to great lengths to position their products in the marketplace. **Positioning** is the development of a product image in buyers' minds relative to the images they have of competing products.

Promotion is the prime positioning tool. A marketer can use promotion to position a brand away from competitors to avoid competition. Promotion also may be used to position one product directly against another product. For example, Coca-Cola and Pepsi position their products to compete head to head against each other.

Stabilizing Sales Special promotional efforts can be used to increase sales during slack periods, such as the "off season" for certain sports equipment. By stabilizing sales in this way, a firm can use its production facilities more effectively and reduce both capital costs and inventory costs. Promotion is also used frequently to increase the sales of products that are in the declining stage of their life cycle. The objective is to keep them going for a little while longer.

Product positioning. *Honda positions its products as being fuel efficient.*

Courtesy Honda of America

Developing the Promotion Mix

Once the role of promotion is established, the various methods of promotion may be combined in a promotional campaign. As in so many other areas of business, promotion planning begins with a set of specific objectives. The promotion mix then is designed to accomplish these objectives.

positioning the development of a product image in buyers' minds relative to the images they have of competing products

Marketers often use several promotion mixes simultaneously if a firm sells multiple products. The selection of promotion-mix ingredients and the degree to which they are used depend on the organization's resources and objectives, the nature of the target market, the characteristics of the product, and the feasibility of various promotional methods.

The amount of promotional resources available in an organization influences the number and intensity of promotional methods that marketers can use. A firm with a limited budget for promotion probably will rely on personal selling because the effectiveness of personal selling can be measured more easily than that of advertising. An organization's objectives also have an effect on its promotional activities. A company wishing to make a wide audience familiar with a new convenience item probably will depend heavily on advertising and sales promotion. If a company's objective is to communicate information to consumers—on the features of countertop appliances, for example—then the company may develop a promotion mix that includes some advertising, some sales promotion to attract consumers to stores, and much personal selling.

The size, geographic distribution, and socioeconomic characteristics of the target market play a part in the composition of a product's promotion mix. If the market is small, personal selling probably will be the most important element in the promotion mix. This is true of organizations that sell to small industrial markets and businesses that use only a few wholesalers to market their products. Companies that need to contact millions of potential customers, however, will emphasize sales promotion and advertising because these methods are relatively inexpensive. The age, income, and education of the target market also will influence the choice of promotion techniques. For example, with less-educated consumers, personal selling may be more effective than ads in newspapers or magazines.

In general, industrial products require a considerable amount of personal selling, whereas consumer goods depend on advertising. This is not true in every case, however. The price of the product also influences the composition of the promotion mix. Because consumers often want the advice of a salesperson on an expensive product, high-priced consumer goods may call for more personal selling. Similarly, advertising and sales promotion may be more crucial to marketers of seasonal items because having a year-round sales force is not always appropriate.

The cost and availability of promotional methods are important factors in the development of a promotion mix. Although national advertising and sales promotion activities are expensive, the cost per customer may be quite small if the campaign succeeds in reaching large numbers of people. In addition, local advertising outlets—newspapers, magazines, radio and television stations, and outdoor displays—may not be that costly for a small local business. In some situations, a firm may find that no available advertising medium reaches the target market effectively.

return to inside business

Consumers Behind the Camera

Despite high-profile contests run by Heinz, PepsiCo, and dozens of other companies, consumer-generated commercials are still a novelty. When a marketer invites consumers to send in homemade ads, the entries may be fun, entertaining, unusual, or even heart-warming—but a few may be bizarre, mocking, or even offensive.

In short, when consumers are behind the camera, the results can be downright unpredictable. That's the real reason YouTube visitors tune in, reporters pay attention, and companies think twice before including such promotions in their marketing mix. Nonetheless, PepsiCo has had so much success that it offered $1 million to anyone whose homemade Doritos commercial topped the viewer ratings as the best commercial shown during the Super Bowl in 2009. Will the next rising stars in advertising be consumers behind the camera?

Questions

1. In terms of the four main objectives of promotion in the marketing mix, explain what Heinz wanted to accomplish by inviting consumers to create their own commercials.
2. What are the advantages and disadvantages of PepsiCo running an annual contest for consumer-generated Super Bowl commercials? Would you recommend that PepsiCo do this? Why or why not?

CHAPTER REVIEW

Summary

1 Describe integrated marketing communications.

Integrated marketing communications is the coordination of promotion efforts to achieve maximum informational and persuasive impact on customers.

2 Understand the role of promotion.

Promotion is communication about an organization and its products that is intended to inform, persuade, or remind target-market members. The major ingredients of a promotion mix are advertising, personal selling, sales promotion, and public relations. The role of promotion is to facilitate exchanges directly or indirectly and to help an organization maintain favorable relationships with groups in the marketing environment.

3 Explain the purposes of the three types of advertising.

Advertising is a paid nonpersonal message communicated to a specific audience through a mass medium. Primary-demand advertising promotes the products of an entire industry rather than just a single brand. Selective-demand advertising promotes a particular brand of product. Institutional advertising is image-building advertising for a firm.

4 Describe the advantages and disadvantages of the major advertising media.

The major advertising media are newspapers, magazines, direct mail, outdoor displays, television, radio, and the Internet. Television accounts for the largest share of advertising expenditures. Newspapers are relatively inexpensive compared with other media, reach only people in the market area, and are timely. Disadvantages include a short life span, poor color reproduction, and an inability to target specific demographic groups. Magazine advertising can be quite prestigious. In addition, it can reach very specific market segments, can provide high-quality color reproduction, and has a relatively long life span. Major disadvantages are high cost and lack of timeliness. Direct mail is the most selective medium, and its effectiveness is measured easily. The disadvantage of direct mail is that if the mailing list is outdated and the advertisement does not reach the right people, then the campaign cannot be successful. An advantage of Yellow Pages advertising is that customers use it to save time in finding products, to find information quickly, and to learn about products and marketers. Unlike other types of advertising media, Yellow Pages advertisements are purchased for one year and cannot be changed. Out-of-home advertising allows marketers to focus on a particular geographic area and is relatively inexpensive. Messages, though, must be limited to a few words because the audience is usually moving. Television offers marketers the opportunity to broadcast a firm's message nationwide. However, television advertising can be very expensive and has a short life span, and the advent of cable channels and home videos has reduced the likelihood of reaching extremely large audiences. Radio advertising offers selectivity, can be less expensive than other media, and is flexible for scheduling purposes. Radio's limitations include no visual presentation and fragmented, small audiences. Benefits of using the Internet as an advertising medium include the growing number of people using the Internet, which means a growing audience, and the ability to precisely target specific customers. Disadvantages include the relatively simplistic nature of the ads that can be produced, especially in comparison with television, and the lack of evidence that net browsers actually pay attention to the ads.

5 Identify the major steps in developing an advertising campaign.

An advertising campaign is developed in several stages. A firm's first task is to identify and analyze its advertising target. The goals of the campaign also must be clearly defined. Then the firm must develop the advertising platform, or statement of important selling points, and determine the size of the advertising budget. The next steps are to develop a media plan, to create the advertising message, and to execute the campaign. Finally, promotion managers must evaluate the effectiveness of the advertising efforts before, during, and/or after the campaign.

6 Recognize the various kinds of salespersons, the steps in the personal-selling process, and the major sales management tasks.

Personal selling is personal communication aimed at informing customers and persuading them to buy a firm's products. It is the most adaptable promotional method because the salesperson can modify the message to fit each buyer. Three major kinds of salespersons are order getters, order takers, and support personnel. The six steps in the personal-selling process are prospecting, approaching the prospect, making the presentation, answering objections, closing the sale, and following up. Sales managers are involved directly in setting sales force objectives; recruiting, selecting, and training salespersons; compensating and motivating sales personnel; creating sales territories; and evaluating sales performance.

7 Describe sales promotion objectives and methods.

Sales promotion is the use of activities and materials as direct inducements to customers and salespersons. The primary objective of sales promotion methods is to enhance and supplement other promotional methods. Methods of sales promotion include rebates, coupons, samples, premiums, frequent-user incentives, point-of-purchase displays, trade shows, buying allowances, and cooperative advertising.

8 Understand the types and uses of public relations.

Public relations is a broad set of communication activities used to create and maintain favorable relationships between an organization and various public groups, both internal and external. Organizations use a variety of public-relations tools to convey messages and create images. Brochures, newsletters, company magazines, and annual reports are written public-relations tools. Speeches, event sponsorship, and publicity are other public-relations tools. Publicity is communication in news-story form about an organization, its products, or both. Types of publicity include news releases, feature articles, captioned photographs, and press conferences. Public relations can be used to promote people, places, activities, ideas, and even countries. It can be used to enhance the reputation of an organization and also to reduce the unfavorable effects of negative events.

9 Identify the factors that influence the selection of promotion-mix ingredients.

A promotional campaign is a plan for combining and using advertising, personal selling, sales promotion, and publicity to achieve one or more marketing goals. Campaign objectives are developed from marketing objectives. Then the promotion mix is developed based on the organization's promotional resources and objectives, the nature of the target market, the product characteristics, and the feasibility of various promotional methods.

Key Terms

You should now be able to define and give an example relevant to each of the following terms:

promotion (428)
promotion mix (428)
integrated marketing communications (429)
advertising (431)
personal selling (431)
sales promotion (431)
public relations (431)
primary-demand advertising (432)
selective-demand (or brand) advertising (432)
institutional advertising (432)
advertising media (433)
direct-mail advertising (433)
Yellow Pages advertising (434)
out-of-home advertising (434)
infomercial (435)
advertising agency (438)
order getter (440)
creative selling (440)
order taker (440)
sales support personnel (441)
missionary salesperson (441)
trade salesperson (441)
technical salesperson (441)
consumer sales promotion method (443)
trade sales promotion method (443)
rebate (444)
coupon (444)
sample (445)
premium (445)
frequent-user incentive (445)
point-of-purchase display (445)
trade show (445)
buying allowance (446)
cooperative advertising (446)
publicity (446)
news release (447)
feature article (447)
captioned photograph (447)
press conference (447)
promotional campaign (448)
positioning (449)

Review Questions

1. What is integrated marketing communications, and why is it becoming increasingly accepted?
2. Identify and describe the major ingredients of a promotion mix.
3. What is the major role of promotion?
4. How are selective-demand, institutional, and primary-demand advertising different from one another? Give an example of each.
5. List the four major print media, and give an advantage and a disadvantage of each.
6. Which types of firms use radio, television, and the Internet?
7. Outline the main steps involved in developing an advertising campaign.
8. Why would a firm with its own advertising department use an ad agency?
9. Identify and give examples of the three major types of salespersons.
10. Explain how each step in the personal-selling process leads to the next step.
11. What are the major tasks involved in managing a sales force?
12. What are the major differences between consumer and trade sales promotion methods? Give examples of each.
13. What is cooperative advertising? What sorts of firms use it?
14. What is the difference between publicity and public relations? What is the purpose of each?
15. Why is promotion particularly effective in positioning a product? In stabilizing or increasing sales?
16. What factors determine the specific promotion mix that a firm should use?

Discussion Questions

1. Discuss the pros and cons of comparative advertising from the viewpoint of (a) the advertiser, (b) the advertiser's competitors, and (c) the target market.
2. Which kinds of advertising—in which media—influence you most? Why?
3. Which kinds of retail outlets or products require mainly order taking by salespeople?
4. A number of companies have shifted a portion of their promotion dollars from advertising to trade sales promotion methods? Why?
5. Why would a producer offer refunds or cents-off coupons rather than simply lowering the price of its products?
6. How can public-relations efforts aimed at the general public help an organization?
7. Why do firms use event sponsorship?
8. What kind of promotion mix might be used to extend the life of a product that has entered the declining stage of its product life cycle?

Video Case 15.1

Wholly Toledo, Mud Hens Continue to Connect with Customers and the Community

Since their dismal beginnings in 1896 when they played near a swamp (earning the name Mud Hens in honor of the coots inhabiting the marshy land), the Triple-A Toledo Mud Hens have become one of the most successful minor league baseball teams in the country, and their games some of the best attended. How did they leverage their climb from such a murky start? In a word: marketing. With their two slogans, "Toledo's Family Fun Park" and "Experience the Joy of Mudville," the Mud Hens harness the twin themes of family and history. These days, the Mud Hens are the Triple-A affiliate of the major league team the Detroit Tigers. Because the Tigers do all of the hiring and firing of players, trainers, and medical staff, the Mud Hens' home office can focus all of its energy on improving the image and profitability of the Mud Hens enterprise.

The Mud Hens do not have the star power of the major league teams (aside from their popular bird mascots, Muddy and Muddonna), so marketers must seek another way to promote the games. The games are advertised as wholesome, affordable family fun—an alternative to bowling or going to the movies. People of all ages can come to the games and socialize while watching potential up-and-coming baseball stars develop into mature athletes. Because there is no star paraphernalia to sell, most of the marketing attention is paid to promoting Mud Hens merchandise, like T-shirts and hats, along with food and beverage sales. In fact, the team has been the league leader in ballpark merchandise sales since 2000 and ranks second in the minor league for overall merchandise sales. The on-premise Swampshop offers fifty styles of T-shirts and sixty styles of baseball caps in all sizes. Truly avid fans can shop online from anywhere in the world as well.

The league's continued sales and revenue growth stand in contrast to an overall downturn in attendance and purchases at minor league baseball games. This statistic attests to the strength of the Mud Hens' marketing strategy. They promote directly to advance ticket buyers in order to target those people who are apt to buy tickets early, buy in quantity, and spend cash at the games. Other marketing channels are the more traditional radio, television, and print media. The Mud Hens enjoy an especially close relationship with local newspapers, where a prominent story about the team is almost guaranteed whenever the Mud Hens have a home game.

When the team decided to build the new Fifth Third Field in downtown Toledo, they knew that the move would generate additional excitement about the team. To accommodate and encourage increased spending at games, planners mapped out a huge 3,000-square-foot Swampshop to comfortably accommodate all consumers. The move to the downtown area has dramatically increased overall attendance rates, which have doubled. All of these strategic maneuvers are part of integrated marketing communications, which entails coordinating promotional and marketing efforts so as to have maximum impact on customers.

Clearly, the Toledo Mud Hens know their market, because they are consistently one of the high-revenue generators in the minor leagues. Because the Tigers take care of most of the administrative tasks, the Mud Hens' staff can focus nearly all of their efforts on successfully using the promotion mix (advertising, personal selling, public relations, and promotion) and buzz to get people flocking to the park. The promise of affordable, wholesome family fun has clearly struck a chord with people in this working-class section of Ohio. Games have also been a big hit with corporate season ticket holders as a way to reward employees or to provide a congenial atmosphere for meeting with clients.

The Toledo Mud Hens value their role as a community partner. They have made significant impact in the Toledo-area community. Other than making community appearances, the players have also participated in the "Drug Prevention Program." This program was done in association with the city of Toledo Police Department, Lucas County prosecutors, and the Ohio State Highway Patrol. Representatives from these organizations as well as Mud Hens players talked with kids about the harmful effects of drugs, alcohol, and tobacco.

In honor of former Mud Hens General Manager Gene Cook, who passed away in 2002, the Mud Hens organized the 3rd Annual Baseball Camp for kids who normally would not have had the financial resources to attend such a camp. The Hens also raised around $30,000 for local charities by conducting four jersey auctions and one memorabilia auction during their "Fandemonium" event in January 2008. Other than this, they have formed the "Muddy's Knothole Club," which provides game tickets and meals to underprivileged children in the community. In fact, over the past four years, more than 15,000 underprivileged children have been able to attend a Mud Hens game. The Mud Hens have also worked with organizations like Family and Child Abuse Prevention Center, American Heart Association, and many more in order to raise awareness about important community issues. The Mud Hens also recognize people within their team who make an effort to contribute to the community. They most recently gave the Helping Hen award to the Mud Hens Pitcher Ian Oastlund for his work in the Toledo-area community.[15]

For more information about this team, go to **www.mudhens.com.**

Questions

1. What are the promotion ingredients that the Mud Hens include in the team's promotion mix?
2. In what ways does the Mud Hens' support of the community help to promote the team?
3. What are some additional ways that the Mud Hens could use to promote the team?

Case 15.2

One Tough Mama at Columbia Sportswear

Eighty-four-year-old Gert Boyle is "one tough mother." Not only is she the chairperson of the board for Columbia Sportswear, but she is also its spokeswoman. Gert assumed control of Columbia Sportswear 35 years ago after her husband Neil passed away. Gert reported for duty a mere four days after Neil's death to take the reins of the growing company—a company that has flourished under her tough leadership. Founded by Paul and Marie Lamfrom (Gert Boyle's parents) in 1938, Columbia Sportswear Company is a global leader in the design, sourcing, marketing, and distribution of active outdoor apparel and footwear. The $1.36 billion company employs more than 2,700 people and distributes and sells products in 80 countries to more than 13,000 retailers internationally. As one of the largest outerwear brands in the world and the leading seller of skiwear in the United States, the company has developed an international reputation for quality, performance, functionality, and value. Columbia Sportswear has worked hard over the years to develop its image of offering high-quality products. It promotes itself and its products through event sponsorships, print and television advertising, and a strong public relations program. It is actively involved in event marketing. For example, the company signed up to be the official apparel sponsor of Jeep's "King of the Mountain" series, proclaimed as the richest and most prestigious professional snow racing series in the world. For its involvement, Columbia Sportswear outfitted the event staff and volunteers, as well as VIPs attending the event. Other sponsorships include events such as the Mt. Baker Banked Slalom snowboarding competition, which draws world-class snowboarders; the annual World Superpipe Championships; and the Ski Mountaineering Competition in Korea. The company has used many approaches to promote the quality of its products. Their greatest success however, is a campaign featuring Gert and her son, Tim Boyle. This positioning is an outgrowth of the relationship that has existed between Gert and Tim since they began running the company together. According to people who know them, Tim and his mother have argued from the beginning about how to run Columbia Sportswear. A director of the company says, "Tim and Gert are a lot like the Jack Lemmon and Walter Matthau characters in *The Odd Couple*. They complain all the time, and yet they cherish each other." Over 20 years ago, Borders, Perrin & Norrander, the company's former advertising agency, came up with an idea to use the well-known relationship between Gert and her son to develop an identity for the company—an identity beyond technical claims about product quality. They developed an ad campaign that portrays Gert as "one tough mother," who uses her son to demonstrate that Columbia Sportswear clothes will protect whoever wears them under any weather conditions. In the many spots, Gert appears as a hard-driving mother who refuses to accept anything but the highest quality of products, for both her son and her company. The ads were so successful at positioning and promoting Columbia Sportswear's products that Gert and Tim became the company's ad staples. Showing Gert put her son through a series of catastrophic tests to demonstrate the durability of the company's products did not only communicate product quality, but it also established an identity in the customers' minds. In one commercial, Gert drives an SUV with Tim strapped on top through a series of severe weather situations to show that his clothing is protecting him. The ending scene is a close-up of the jacket he is wearing with the tagline "Tested Tough." This theme is continued throughout a series of commercials that depict Tim in a number of cold-weather survival situations, such as being dropped on the top of a snow-covered mountain by a helicopter piloted by Gert, being under the ice in a hockey arena (staying alive with a breathing tube), and being covered by snow with Gert driving the snowplow. In all cases, Tim is unharmed and Gert is unconcerned—all because he is wearing Columbia outerwear. Columbia Sportswear's signature spot shows Gert in a biker bar. The audio track says, "In a world of rugged individuals, only one is the toughest mother of them all. Mother Gert Boyle—maker of tough mother jeans." There is a close-up of Gert with a tattoo on her bicep that reads "Born to Nag," and the spot ends with a product shot of Columbia jeans. These irreverent and memorable ads appear to be working. Since their inception, Columbia Sportswear has carved out a 50 percent market share in its category. Now that's one tough mother![16]

Questions

1. What are the characteristics of Columbia's target market?
2. What are the major objectives of Columbia Sportswear's promotion program?
3. What recommendations would you make to strengthen Columbia's promotional activities?

Building Skills for Career Success

1. JOURNALING FOR SUCCESS

Discovery statement: As this chapter showed, advertising is an important part of an organization's promotional mix.

Assignment

1. During the last year, you have been exposed to a number of television advertisements. Identify and describe what you believe to be the best TV commercial that you have experienced over the last year.
2. Why did you feel that this ad is the very best?
3. Describe the content of this advertisement in as much detail as possible, and explain what you can recall about this television advertisement.

2. EXPLORING THE INTERNET

As a promotional tool, the Internet stands alone among all media for cost-effectiveness and variety. A well-designed company website can enhance most of the promotional strategies discussed in this chapter. It can provide consumers with advertising copy and sales representatives with personal-selling support services and information any time on demand. In addition, many companies use the Internet for sales promotion. For instance, most newspapers and magazines provide sample articles in the hope that interested readers eventually will become subscribers. And virtually all software companies present demonstration editions of their products for potential customers to explore and test.

Assignment

1. Visit two of the following websites and examine the promotional activities taking place there. Note the sort of promotion being used and its location within the site. Also visit the text website for updates to this exercise.
   www.wsj.com
   www.businessweek.com
   www.forbes.com
2. Describe the promotional tools exhibited on one of these sites.
3. What would you recommend the company do to improve the site?

3. DEVELOPING CRITICAL-THINKING SKILLS

Obviously, salespeople must know the products they are selling, but to give successful sales presentations, they also must know their competition. Armed with information about competing products, they are better able to field prospective customers' questions and objections regarding their own products.

Assignment

1. Choose a product or service offered by one company and gather samples of the competitors' sales literature.
2. After examining the competitors' sales literature, answer the following questions:
   a. What type of literature do the competitors use to advertise their product or service? Do they use full-color brochures?
   b. Do they use videotapes?
   c. Do they offer giveaways or special discounts?
3. Compare the product or service you chose with what the competition is selling.
4. Compile a list of all the strengths and weaknesses you have discovered.

4. BUILDING TEAM SKILLS

The cost of promotional methods is an important factor in a promotional campaign. Representatives who sell advertising space for magazines, newspapers, radio stations, and television stations can quote the price of the medium to the advertiser. The advertiser then can use cost per thousand persons reached (CPM) to compare the cost efficiency of vehicles in the same medium.

Assignment

1. Working in teams of five to seven, choose one of these media: local television stations, newspapers, or radio stations. You can choose magazines if your library has a copy of *Standard Rate and Data Service.*
2. Using the following equation, compare the CPM of advertising in whatever local medium you chose:

$$\text{CPM} = \frac{\text{price of the medium to the advertiser} \times 1{,}000}{\text{circulation}}$$

3. Report your team's findings to the class.

5. RESEARCHING DIFFERENT CAREERS

Most public libraries maintain relatively up-to-date collections of occupational or career materials. Begin your library search by looking at the computer listings under "vocations" or "careers" and then under specific fields. Check the library's periodicals section, where you will find trade and professional magazines and journals about specific occupations and industries. (*Business Periodicals Index,* published by H. W. Wilson, is an index to articles in major business publications. Arranged alphabetically, it is easy to use.) Familiarize yourself with the concerns and activities of potential employers by skimming their annual reports and other information they distribute to the public. You also can find occupational information on videocassettes, in kits, and through computerized information systems.

Assignment

1. Choose a specific occupation.
2. Conduct a library search of the occupation.
3. Prepare an annotated bibliography for the occupation.

Running a Business Part 5

Finagle A Bagel's Approach to Marketing

Round, flat, seeded, plain, crowned with cheese, or cut into croutons, bagels form the basis of every menu item at Finagle A Bagel. "So many other shops will just grab onto whatever is hot, whatever is trendy, in a 'metoo' strategy," observes Heather Robertson, the director of marketing, human resources, and research and development. In contrast, she says, "We do bagels—that's what we do best. And any menu item in our stores really needs to reaffirm that as our core concept." That's the first of Finagle A Bagel's marketing rules.

In addition to its retailing activities, the company wholesales its bagels in bulk to hospitals, schools, and other organizations. It also wholesales a line of Finagle A Bagel–branded bagels for resale in Shaw's Market stores. Whether selling wholesale or retail, the company is always hunting for new product ideas involving bagels.

PRODUCT DEVELOPMENT: MIX, BAKE, BITE, AND TRY AGAIN

To identify a new product idea, Robertson and her colleagues conduct informal research by talking with both customers and employees. They also browse food magazines and cookbooks for ideas about out-of-the-ordinary flavors, taste combinations, and preparation methods. When developing a new bagel variety, for example, Robertson says that she looks for ideas that are uncommon and innovative yet appealing: "If someone else has a sun-dried tomato bagel, that's all the more reason for me not to do it. People look at Finagle A Bagel as kind of the trendsetter."

Once the marketing staff comes up with a promising idea, the next step is to write up a formula or recipe, walk downstairs to the dough factory, and mix up a test batch. Through trial and error, they refine the idea until they like the way the bagel or sandwich looks and tastes. Occasionally, Finagle A Bagel has to put an idea on hold until it can find just the right ingredients.

For example, when Robertson was working on a new bagel with jalapeno peppers and cheddar cheese, she had difficulty finding a cheese that would melt during baking but not dissolve and disappear into the batter. Ultimately, she found a supplier willing to cook up cheese formulas especially for Finagle A Bagel. The supplier would send a batch of cheese overnight for Robertson to incorporate into the next day's test batch of bagels. After baking, Robertson would send some of the bagels overnight to the supplier so that the two of them could discuss the flavor, consistency, and other details.

The cheeses and bagels flew back and forth for eight months until Finagle A Bagel hit on a recipe that worked well. "When we finally got it done," Robertson says, "we shipped test batches to our stores, three stores at a time. And we just gave the product away. We'd make several batches during the week, and guess who would come back wanting to buy dozens of these bagels?" That's when she knew the new product was going to be a hit. Not every new flavor becomes popular, however. Dark chocolate bagels with white chocolate chips sold poorly, as did pineapple-mango-coconut bagels. Today, plain bagels remain the best-selling flavor, followed by sesame.

SAMPLES AND COUPONS SPARK WORD-OF-MOUTH COMMUNICATION

The story of the jalapeno-and-cheese bagel illustrates another of Finagle A Bagel's marketing rules: Spend nothing on advertising. Many quick-serve food companies use television and radio commercials, newspaper advertisements, and other mass-media messages to build brand awareness, promote products, and attract customers. However, Robertson and her colleagues believe that the best way to build the Finagle A Bagel brand and whet customers' appetites for a new menu item is to give them a free taste.

Consider what happened when Finagle A Bagel used samples and coupons to build lunchtime sales by promoting bagel sandwiches in one of the suburban stores. Instead of placing an ad in the local newspaper, Robertson and her staff went to the store and prepared 100 bagel sandwiches. They cut each in half and wrapped the halves individually. Then they set up 200 Finagle A Bagel bags, put a half-sandwich into each, and added a coupon for a free bagel sandwich without any risk. They piled all the bags into a big basket, attached a sign reading, "Free Bagel Sandwiches," and headed to a large intersection just a block from the store.

"Every time the light turned red, we would run out into the middle of the street and throw a bag through someone's car window," Robertson recalls. "We got a lot of strange looks. A few people would roll up their car windows . . . but a lot of people just thought it was hysterically funny. They would be motioning, waving us over, saying, 'What have you got?' And then they'd go back to their office and tell their coworkers, 'Hey, you know what happened to me today? Some crazy lady threw a bagel through my car window, and it was great. You should check it out.'" The entire effort cost $100—and convinced a large number of customers to look around the store, try a sandwich risk-free, and talk up the experience to colleagues, friends, and family.

The popular Finagle A Bagel headquarters tour has become an effective public-relations tool. Community groups, students, and bagel lovers of all ages can visit the "World Headquarters" building and walk through exhibits representing the company's successes and mistakes. In the factory area, visitors watch through a huge window as hundreds of pounds of dough are mixed, cut, and shaped into bagels. The window is set low so even the youngest visitors can get a great view of the process.

BUY A BRANDED BAGEL—AGAIN AND AGAIN

Although some restaurant companies want each unit to look distinctly different, Finagle A Bagel uses consistency to reinforce the brand image—another of its marketing rules. "We believe the stores should have a very similar look and feel so that you can walk into any Finagle A Bagel and know what to expect," says copresident Alan Litchman. For example, every Finagle A Bagel store sports an eye-catching burgundy-and-yellow sign featuring an oversized bagel with a few bites taken out. This bagel icon is repeated on posters highlighting menu items as well as on other store decorations.

Still, the suburban stores are not exactly like the downtown stores. Many of the suburban stores have children's furniture and cushiony chairs so that families can sit and relax. Free weekly concerts by the "Music Man"—a local musician—make these stores decidedly family friendly. The city stores have no children's furniture because they cater to busy working people who want to be in and out in a hurry. The Harvard Square store is unique: It has a liquor license and attracts a large student crowd, which means it is busier on weekends than on weekdays.

One of the most effective sales promotion techniques the company uses is the Frequent Finagler loyalty card, which rewards customers for making repeat purchases. For every dollar customers spend on bagels or other menu items, they receive Frequent Finagler points that can be redeemed for free coffee, free sandwiches, and so on. Customers are pleased because they receive extra value for the money they spend—and Finagle A Bagel is pleased because its average sale to loyal customers is higher.

PRICING A BAGEL

Pricing is an important consideration in the competitive world of quick-serve food. This is where another of Finagle A Bagel's marketing rules comes in. Regardless of cost, the company will not compromise quality. Therefore, the first step in pricing a new product is to find the best possible ingredients and then examine the costs and calculate an approximate retail price. After thinking about what a customer might expect to pay for such a menu item, shopping the competition, and talking with some customers, the company settles on a price that represents "a great product for a fair value," says Robertson.

Although Finagle A Bagel's rental costs vary, the copresidents price menu items the same in higher-rent stores as in lower-rent stores. "We have considered adjusting prices based upon the location of the store, but we haven't done it because it can backfire in a very significant way," copresident Laura Trust explains. "People expect to be treated fairly, regardless of where they live."

Questions

1. Does Finagle A Bagel apply all seven phases of the new product development process when working on a new menu item such as the jalapeno-and-cheese bagel? Explain.
2. Do you agree with Laura Trust's assessment that adjusting prices based on store location can backfire? What arguments can you offer for and against Finagle A Bagel raising prices in higher-rent stores?
3. Finagle A Bagel is both a wholesaler and a retailer. Which of these two marketing intermediary roles do you think the company should develop more aggressively in the next few years? Why?
4. Should Finagle A Bagel continue to spend nothing on media advertising and rely instead primarily on sales promotion techniques such as samples and coupons?

Building a Business Plan Part 5

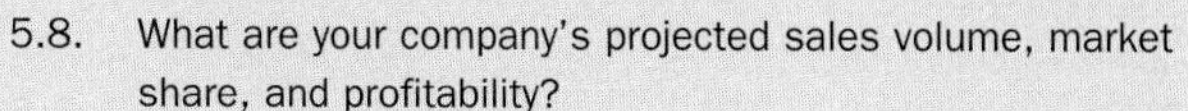

This part is one of the most important components of your business plan. In this part, you will present the facts that you have gathered on the size and nature of your market(s). State market size in dollars and units. How many units and what is the dollar value of the products you expect to sell in a given time period? Indicate your primary and secondary sources of data and the methods you used to estimate total market size and your market share. Part 5 of your textbook covers all marketing-related topics. These chapters should help you to answer the questions in this part of the business plan.

THE MARKETING PLAN COMPONENT

The marketing plan component is and should be unique to your business. Many assumptions or projections used in the analysis may turn out differently; therefore, this component should be flexible enough to be adjusted as needed. The marketing plan should include answers to at least the following questions:

5.1. What are your target markets, and what common identifiable need(s) can you satisfy?

5.2. What are the competitive, legal, political, economic, technological, and sociocultural factors affecting your marketing efforts?

5.3. What are the current needs of each target market? Describe the target market in terms of demographic, geographic, psychographic, and product-usage characteristics. What changes in the target market are anticipated?

5.4. What advantages and disadvantages do you have in meeting the target market's needs?

5.5. How will your product distribution, promotion, and price satisfy customer needs?

5.6. How effectively will your products meet these needs?

5.7. What are the relevant aspects of consumer behavior and product use?

5.8. What are your company's projected sales volume, market share, and profitability?

5.9. What are your marketing objectives? Include the following in your marketing objectives:
- Product introduction, improvement, or innovation
- Sales or market share
- Profitability
- Pricing
- Distribution
- Advertising (Prepare advertising samples for the appendix.)

Make sure that your marketing objectives are clearly written, measurable, and consistent with your overall marketing strategy.

5.10. How will the results of your marketing plan be measured and evaluated?

REVIEW OF BUSINESS PLAN ACTIVITIES

Remember that even though it will be time consuming, developing a clear, well-written marketing plan is important. Therefore, make sure that you have checked the plan for any weaknesses or problems before proceeding to Part 6. Also, make certain that all your answers to the questions in this and other parts are consistent throughout the business plan. Finally, write a brief statement that summarizes all the information for this part of the business plan.

The information contained in this section will also assist you in completing the online *Interactive Business Plan*.

PART 6 Information for Business Strategy and Decision Making

In this part of the book we focus on information, one of the four essential resources on which all businesses rely. First, we discuss the information necessary for effective decision making, where it can be found, how it is organized, and how it can be used throughout an organization by those who need it. We also investigate the world of e-business in Chapter 16. In Chapter 17, we then examine the role of accounting and how financial information is collected, stored, processed, presented, and used to better control managerial decision making.

Tetra Images/Getty Images

16 Understanding Information and e-Business

LEARNING OBJECTIVES

What you will be able to do once you complete this chapter:

1. Examine how information can reduce risk when making a decision.
2. Discuss management's information requirements.
3. Outline the five functions of an information system.
4. Describe how the Internet helps in decision making, communications, sales, and recruiting and training.
5. Analyze how computers and technology change the way information is acquired, organized, and used.
6. Explain the meaning of e-business.
7. Describe the fundamental models of e-business.
8. Explore the factors that will affect the future of e-business.

Lynsey Addario/Corbis

inside business

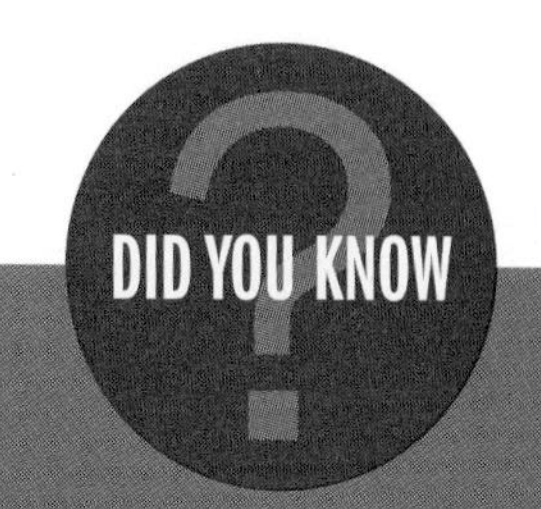

Blue Nile, an e-business, has grown in less than ten years into the world's largest online retailer of diamonds and jewelry, with more than $300 million in annual sales.

Blue Nile Sells Diamonds with a Click

Blue Nile is a gem of an e-business. It was founded in 1999, at the height of the dot-com boom, when Internet experts believed that consumers would buy books or music online but not expensive jewelry. Blue Nile quickly proved the experts wrong. In less than ten years, it has grown into the world's largest online retailer of diamonds and jewelry, with more than $300 million in annual sales.

Blue Nile started life as Internet Diamonds, a website operated by a small jewelry store near the Seattle airport. Mark Vadon, a business consultant, was researching an engagement ring purchase when he happened on the site and read the owner's tips on how to buy a diamond. Having shopped around in big jewelry stores, Vadon liked the low prices and the detailed information he found on Internet Diamonds. He clicked to buy a ring and, after stopping in to see the owner a few weeks later, he made a deal to buy the entire e-business.

Vadon renamed the site Blue Nile **(www.bluenile.com)**, jazzed it up, added a toll-free phone number for questions and orders, and beefed up the material on how to judge diamond quality. He also created a virtual design area where visitors can mix and match thousands of diamonds and settings to create the ring, earrings, or pendant of their dreams (and budget). One thing Vadon didn't change, however, was the discount prices, which are well below what traditional jewelry stores charge.

These days, Blue Nile doesn't actually own all the jewelry available on its website. In some cases, it receives a percentage of the retail price in exchange for serving as an online showroom where suppliers can display their products. It also invites suppliers to tap its sales database so they can see exactly which stones and styles are selling and plan their production accordingly. Despite its track record of success through dot-com boom and bust periods, will Blue Nile continue to prosper during unusually tough economic times?[1]

While some believe that we may be reaching an information saturation point, managers at Blue Nile know how important information is. Blue Nile, the online retailer profiled in the Inside Business opening case, operates with just one goal: Offer high-quality diamonds and fine jewelry at outstanding prices. To help accomplish this goal, employees and managers need information to meet the needs of their customers *and* operate a profitable business. Managers and employees can obtain information about sales and expenses and track customer orders by accessing the firm's management information system. Information is also provided to customers before and after they make their purchases. For example, when customers visit the Blue Nile website, easy-to-understand information helps them find just the right type of jewelry for all occasions. Simply put, information has helped Blue Nile become the largest online retailer of diamonds and jewelry in the world.[2]

To improve the decision-making process, the information used by both individuals and business firms must be relevant or useful to meet a specific need. Using relevant information results in better decisions.

Relevant information → Better intelligence and knowledge → Better decisions

For businesses, better intelligence and knowledge that lead to better decisions are especially important because they can provide a *competitive edge* over competitors and improve a firm's *profits*. We begin this chapter by describing why employees need information.

The first three major sections in this chapter answer the following questions:

- How can information reduce risk when making a decision?
- What is a management information system?
- How do employees use an information system?

Next, we discuss how computers, the Internet, and software—all topics covered in this chapter—are used to obtain the information needed to make decisions on a daily basis. In the last part of this chapter, we take a close look at how firms conduct business on the Internet and what growth opportunities may be available to both new and existing firms.

How Can Information Reduce Risk When Making a Decision?

1

Learning Objective: Examine how information can reduce risk when making a decision.

As we noted in Chapter 1, information is one of the four major resources (along with material, human, and financial resources) managers must have to operate a business. While a successful business uses all four resources efficiently, it is information that helps managers reduce risk when making a decision.

Information and Risk

Theoretically, with accurate and complete information, there is no risk whatsoever. On the other hand, a decision made without any information is a gamble. These two extreme situations are rare in business. For the most part, business decision makers see themselves located someplace between either extreme. As illustrated in Figure 16.1, when the amount of available information is high, there is less risk; when the amount of available information is low, there is more risk.

Suppose that a marketing manager for Procter & Gamble (P&G) responsible for the promotion of a well-known shampoo such as Pantene Pro-V has called a meeting of her department team to consider the selection of a new magazine advertisement. The company's advertising agency has submitted two new advertisements in sealed envelopes. Neither the manager nor any of her team has seen them before. Only one selection will be made for the new advertising campaign. Which advertisement should be chosen?

Without any further information, the team might as well make the decision by flipping a coin. If, however, team members were allowed to open the envelopes and examine the advertisements, they would have more information. If, in addition to allowing them to examine the advertisements, the marketing manager circulated a report containing the reactions of a group of target consumers to each of the two advertisements, the team would have even more information with which to work. Thus, information, when understood properly, produces knowledge and empowers managers and employees to make better decisions.

Information Rules

Marketing research continues to show that discounts influence almost all car buyers. Simply put, if dealers lower their prices, they will sell more cars. This relationship between buyer behavior and price can be thought of as an information rule that usually will guide the marketing manager correctly. An information rule emerges when research confirms the same results each time that it studies the same or a similar set of circumstances.

Figure 16.1: The Relationship Between Information and Risk

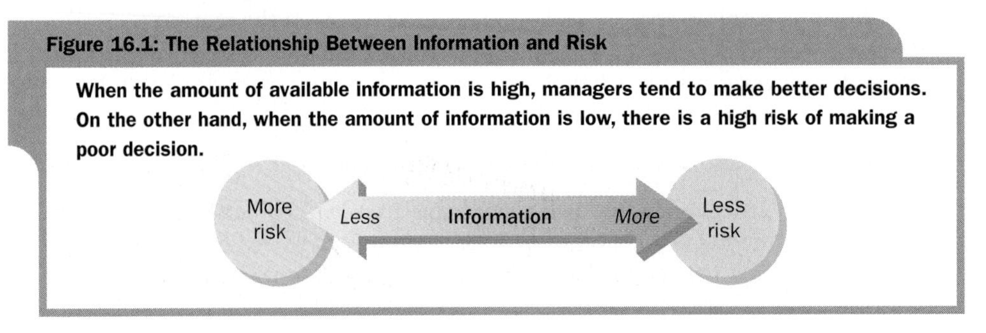

Because of the volume of information they receive each day and their need to make decisions on a daily basis, businesspeople try to accumulate information rules to shorten the time they spend analyzing choices. Information rules are the "great simplifiers" for all decision makers. Business research is continuously looking for new rules that can be put to good use and looking to discredit old ones that are no longer valid. This ongoing process is necessary because business conditions rarely stay the same for very long.

The Difference Between Data and Information

Many people use the terms *data* and *information* interchangeably, but the two differ in important ways. **Data** are numerical or verbal descriptions that usually result from some sort of measurement. (The word *data* is plural; the singular form is datum.) Your current wage level, the amount of last year's after-tax profit for Motorola, and the current retail prices of Honda automobiles are all data. Most people think of data as being numerical only, but they can be nonnumerical as well. A description of an individual as a "tall, athletic person with short, dark hair" certainly would qualify as data.

data numerical or verbal descriptions that usually result from some sort of measurement

Information is data presented in a form that is useful for a specific purpose. Suppose that a human resources manager wants to compare the wages paid to male and female employees over a period of five years. The manager might begin with a stack of computer printouts listing every person employed by the firm, along with each employee's current and past wages. The manager would be hard pressed to make any sense of all the names and numbers. Such printouts consist of data rather than information.

information data presented in a form that is useful for a specific purpose

Now suppose that the manager uses a computer to graph the average wages paid to men and to women in each of the five years. The result is information because the manager can use it for the purpose at hand—to compare wages paid to men with those paid to women over the five-year period. When summarized in the graph, the wage data from the printouts become information. For a manager, information presented in a practical, useful form such as a graph simplifies the decision-making process.

How do you create a database? *Cisco Systems, a company recognized as a technology giant, can provide the computer hardware and software that firms need to not only create and update an information database but also to provide people with the technological tools needed to access information.*

Imaginechina via AP Images

The average company maintains a great deal of data that can be transformed into information. Typical data include records pertaining to personnel, inventory, sales, and accounting. Often each type of data is stored in individual departments within an organization. However, the data can be used more effectively when they are organized into a database. A **database** is a single collection of data stored in one place that can be used by people throughout an organization to make decisions. Today, most companies have several different types of databases. While databases are important, the way the data and information are used is even more important—and more valuable to the firm. As a result, management information experts now use the term **knowledge management (KM)** to describe a firm's procedures for generating, using, and sharing the data and information contained in the firm's databases. Typically, data, information, databases, and knowledge management all become important parts of a firm's management information system.

database a single collection of data stored in one place that can be used by people throughout an organization to make decisions

knowledge management (KM) a firm's procedures for generating, using, and sharing the data and information contained in the firm's databases

What Is a Management Information System?

2

Learning Objective: Discuss management's information requirements.

A **management information system (MIS)** is a system that provides managers and employees with the information they need to perform their jobs as effectively as possible (see Figure 16.2).

management information system (MIS) a system that provides managers and employees with the information they need to perform their jobs as effectively as possible

The purpose of an MIS (sometimes referred to as an information technology system or simply IT system) is to distribute timely and useful information from both internal and external sources to the managers and employees who need it. Today, most medium-sized to large business firms have an information technology (IT) officer. An **information technology (IT) officer** is a manager at the executive level who is responsible for ensuring that a firm has the equipment necessary to provide the information the firm's employees and managers need to make effective decisions.

information technology (IT) officer a manager at the executive level who is responsible for ensuring that a firm has the equipment necessary to provide the information the firm's employees and managers need to make effective decisions

Today's typical MIS is built around a computerized system of record-keeping and communications software so that it can provide information based on a wide variety of data. After all, the goal is to provide needed information to all managers and employees.

Managers' Information Requirements

Managers have to plan for the future, implement their plans in the present, and evaluate results against what has been accomplished in the past. Of course, the specific types of information they need depend on their area of management and on their level within the firm.

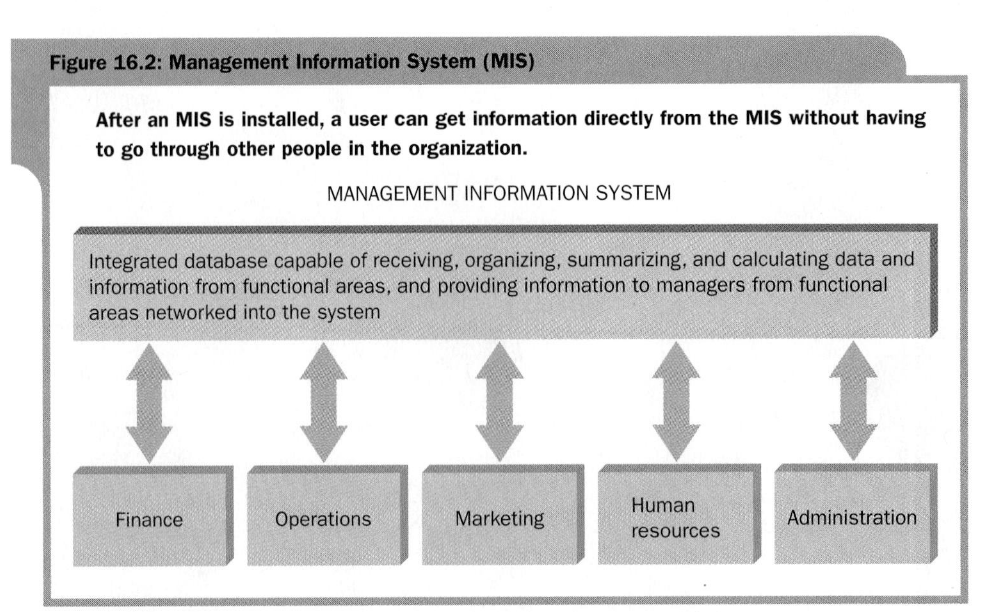

Source: Ricky W. Griffin, *MANAGEMENT*, 9/e (Boston: Houghton Mifflin Company, 2008). Reprinted by permission.

Today, many firms are organized into five areas of management: *finance, operations, marketing, human resources,* and *administration*. Managers in each of these areas need specific information in order to make decisions.

- *Financial managers* obviously are most concerned with their firm's finances. They study its debts and receivables, cash flow, future capitalization needs, financial statements, and other accounting information. Of equal importance to financial managers is information about the present state of the economy, interest rates, and predictions of business conditions in the future.
- *Operations managers* are concerned with present and future sales levels, current inventory levels of work in process and finished goods, and the availability and cost of the resources required to produce products and services. They also must keep abreast of any innovative production technology that might be useful to the firm.
- *Marketing managers* need to have detailed information about their firm's products and the products offered by competitors. Such information includes pricing strategies, new promotional campaigns, and products that competitors are test marketing. Information concerning the firm's customers, current and projected market share, and new and pending product legislation is also important to marketing managers.
- *Human resources managers* must be aware of anything that pertains to the firm's employees. Key examples include current wage levels and benefits packages both within the firm and in firms that compete for valuable employees, current legislation and court decisions that affect employment practices, union activities, and the firm's plans for growth, expansion, or mergers.
- *Administrative managers* are responsible for the overall management of the organization. Thus, they are concerned with the coordination of information—just as they are concerned with the coordination of material, human, and financial resources. First, administrators must ensure that all employees have access to the information they need to do their jobs. Administrative managers must also ensure that the information is used in a consistent manner throughout the firm. Suppose, for example, that General Electric (GE) is designing a new plant that will open in five years and be devoted to manufacturing consumer electronic products. GE's management will want answers to many questions: Is the capacity of the plant consistent with marketing plans based on sales projections? Will human resources managers be able to staff the plant on the basis of employment forecasts? And do sales projections indicate enough income to cover the expected cost of the plant?

  Finally, administrative managers must make sure that all managers and employees are able to use the information technology that is available. Certainly, this requires that all employees receive the skills training required to use the firm's MIS. Finally, administrative managers must commit to the costs of updating the firm's MIS and providing additional training when necessary.

Building employee diversification at Home Depot. *Barbara Serret, a human resources manager at Home Depot, knows the value of bilingual employees for Home Depot—the world's largest home improvement chain. Like many retailers, Home Depot is recruiting Hispanic employees who can provide information to Hispanic customers.*

AP Photo/Luis M. Alvarez

Size and Complexity of the System

An MIS must be tailored to the needs of the organization it serves. In some firms, a tendency to save on initial costs may result in a system that is too small or overly simple. Such a system generally ends up serving only one or two management levels or a single department. Managers in other departments "give up" on the system as soon as they find that it cannot process their data. Often, they look elsewhere for information, process their own data, or simply do without.

The Business of Green

The Paperless Office—At Last?

Is the paperless office finally at hand? Since the dawn of the information age, people have talked about doing away with printed documents to save trees and spare landfills. However, as businesses computerized their operations, they actually printed and filed, faxed, or mailed more and more documents. In 1975, before the personal computer was invented, U.S. offices used an average of 62 pounds of paper per worker per year. By 1999, with a PC on nearly every business desk, annual paper usage per office worker had soared to 143 pounds.

Today, that trend has turned around: Office workers now use about 127 pounds of paper per year. Yes, U.S. firms still print 1.5 trillion pages every year, but paper use is definitely decreasing as companies learn to digitally manage documents.

Businesses of all sizes are going as paperless as possible by scanning documents for electronic storage and retrieval and using Web-based applications to invoice customers and pay employees and suppliers. Increasingly, they're exchanging information through e-mail, text messaging, instant messaging, file sharing, and other electronic methods. And to save paper and cut waste, many offices print on both sides of the page and squeeze more onto a single sheet.

Sources: Stephen H. Wildstrom, "The Paperless Office—Really," *BusinessWeek*, October 29, 2008, **www.businessweek.com;** "On Its Way, At Last: The Paperless Office," *The Economist*, October 11, 2008, p. 79; Arik Hesseldahl, "The New Push to Get Rid of Paper," *BusinessWeek Online*, May 28, 2008, **www.businessweek.com**.

Commercial Eye/Iconica/Getty Images

Almost as bad is an MIS that is too large or too complex for the organization. Unused capacity and complexity do nothing but increase the cost of owning and operating the system. In addition, a system that is difficult to use probably will not be used at all. Obviously, much is expected of an effective MIS system. Let's examine the functions an MIS system must perform to provide the information managers need.

How Do Employees Use an Information System?

3

Learning Objective: Outline the five functions of an information system.

To provide information, an MIS must perform five specific functions. It must collect data, store the data, update the data, process the data into information, and present information to users (See Figure 16.3).

Collecting Data

A firm's employees, with the help of an MIS system, must gather the data needed to establish the firm's *data bank*. The data bank should include all past and current data that may be useful in managing the firm. Clearly, the data entered into the system must be *relevant* to the needs of the firm's managers. And perhaps most important, the data must be *accurate*. Irrelevant data are simply useless; inaccurate data can be disastrous. There are two data sources: *internal* and *external*.

Internal Sources of Data Typically, most of the data gathered for an MIS come from internal sources. The most common internal sources of information are managers and employees, company records and reports, and minutes of meetings.

Past and present accounting data also can provide information about the firm's transactions with customers, creditors, and suppliers. Sales reports are a source of data on sales, pricing strategies, and the effectiveness of promotional campaigns.

Human resources records are useful as a source of data on wage and benefits levels, hiring patterns, employee turnover, and other personnel variables.

Present and past production forecasts also should be included in the firm's data bank, along with data indicating how well these forecasts predicted actual events. And specific plans and management decisions—regarding capital expansion and new product development, for example—should be incorporated into the MIS system.

External Sources of Data External sources of data include customers, suppliers, bankers, trade and financial publications, industry conferences, online computer services, government sources, and firms that specialize in gathering data for organizations. For example, a marketing research company may acquire forecasts pertaining to product demand, consumer tastes, and other marketing variables. Suppliers are also an excellent source of information about the future availability and costs of raw materials and component parts. Bankers often can provide valuable economic insights and projections. And the information furnished by trade publications and industry conferences usually is concerned as much with future projections as with present

To Collect Information, Consumers Often Use the Internet

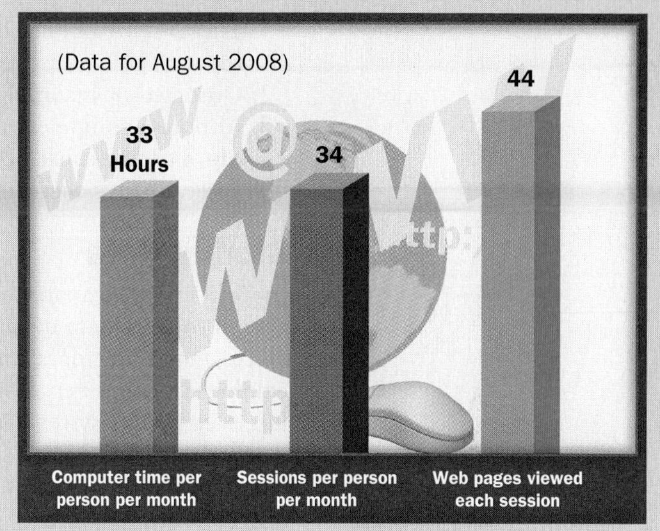

Source: The Nielsen/NetRatings website, **www.netratings.com**, accessed October 12, 2008.

Figure 16.3: Five Management Information System Functions

Every MIS must be tailored to the organization it serves and must perform five functions.

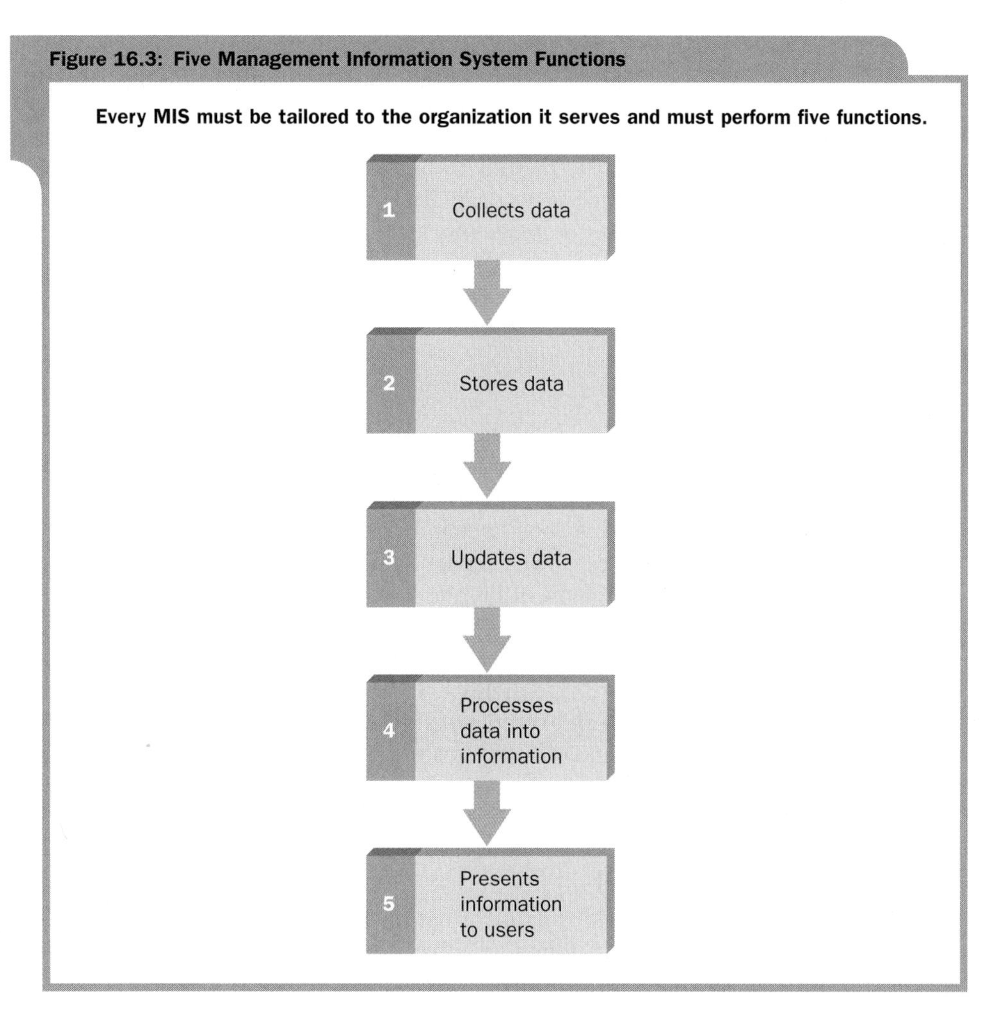

conditions. Legal issues and court decisions that may affect a firm are discussed occasionally in local newspapers and, more often, in specialized publications such as the *Wall Street Journal, Fortune, and BusinessWeek*. Government publications such as the *Monthly Labor Review* and the *Federal Reserve Bulletin* also are quite useful as sources of external data, as are a number of online computer services.

Whether the source of the data is internal or external, always remember the following three cautions:

1. The cost of obtaining data from some external sources, such as marketing research firms, can be quite high.
2. Outdated or incomplete data usually yield inaccurate information.
3. Although computers generally do not make mistakes, the people who use them can make or cause errors. When data (or information) and your judgment disagree, always check the data.

Storing Data

An MIS must be capable of storing data until they are needed. Typically, the method chosen to store data depends on the size and needs of the organization. Small businesses may enter data and then store them directly on the hard drive inside an employee's computer. Generally, medium-sized to large businesses store data in a larger computer system and provide access to employees through a computer network. Today, networks take on many configurations and are designed by specialists who work with a firm's IT personnel to decide on what's best for the company.

Updating Data

Today, an MIS must be able to update stored data regularly to ensure that the information presented to managers and employees is accurate, complete, and up to date. The frequency with which data are updated depends on how fast they change and how often they are used. When it is vital to have current data, updating may occur as soon as the new data are available. For example, Giant Food, a grocery store chain operating in the eastern part of the United States, has cash registers that automatically transmit data on each item sold to a central computer. The computer adjusts the store's inventory records accordingly. In some systems, the computer even may be programmed to reorder items whose inventories fall below some specified level. Data and information also may be updated according to a predetermined time schedule. Data and information, for instance, may be entered into a firm's data bank at certain intervals—every twenty-four hours, weekly, or monthly.

Processing Data

data processing the transformation of data into a form that is useful for a specific purpose

statistic a measure that summarizes a particular characteristic of an entire group of numbers

Some data are used in the form in which they are stored, whereas other data require processing to extract, highlight, or summarize the information they contain. **Data processing** is the transformation of data into a form that is useful for a specific purpose.

For verbal data, this processing consists mainly of extracting the pertinent material from storage and combining it into a report. Most business data, however, are in the form of numbers—large groups of numbers, such as daily sales totals or production costs for a specific product. Such groups of numbers are difficult to handle and to comprehend, but their contents can be summarized through the use of statistics. A **statistic** is a measure that summarizes a particular characteristic of an entire group of numbers. Figure 16.4 is an example of statistics in use. This figure contains only eleven items of data, but most business situations involve hundreds or even thousands of items. Fortunately, computers can be programmed to process such large volumes of numbers quickly.

Presenting Information

An MIS must be capable of presenting information in a usable form. That is, the method of presentation—reports, tables, graphs, or charts, for example—must be appropriate for the information itself and for the uses to which it will be put.

Figure 16.4: Statistics

Managers often examine statistics that describe trends in employee compensation.

Sky Cloud Manufacturing

Employee Salaries for April 2008

Employee	Monthly Salary
Thomas P. Ouimet	$ 3,500
Marina Ruiz	3,500
Ronald F. Washington	3,000
Sarah H. Abrams	3,000
Kathleen L. Norton	3,000
Martin C. Hess	2,800
Jane Chang	2,500
Margaret S. Fernandez	2,400
John F. O'Malley	2,000
Robert Miller	2,000
William G. Dorfmann	1,800
Total	$29,500

Verbal information may be presented in list or paragraph form. Employees often are asked to prepare formal business reports. A typical business report includes (1) an introduction, (2) the body of the report, (3) the conclusions, and (4) the recommendations.

The *introduction*, which sets the stage for the remainder of the report, describes the problem to be studied in the report, identifies the research techniques that were used, and previews the material that will be presented in the report. The *body of the report* should objectively describe the facts that were discovered in the process of completing the report. The body also should provide a foundation for the conclusions and the recommendations. The *conclusions* are statements of fact that describe the finding contained in the report. They should be specific, practical, and based on the evidence contained in the report. The *recommendations* section presents suggestions on how the problem might be solved. Like the conclusions, the recommendations should be specific, practical, and based on the evidence.

A *visual display* can also be used to present information and may be a diagram that represents several items of information in a manner that makes comparison easier. Figure 16.5 illustrates examples of visual displays generated by a computer. Typical visual displays include:

- Graphs
- Bar charts
- Pie charts

Tabular Displays A tabular display is used to present verbal or numerical information in columns and rows. It is most useful in presenting information about two or more related variables. A table, for example, can be used to illustrate the number of salespeople in each region of the country, sales for different types of products, and total sales for all products (see Table 16.1). And information that is to be manipulated—for example, to calculate loan payments—is usually displayed in tabular form.

Tabular displays generally have less impact than visual displays. However, displaying the information that could be contained in a multicolumn table such as Table 16.1 would require several bar or pie charts.

Figure 16.5: Typical Visual Displays Used in Business Presentations

Visual displays help businesspeople to present information in a form that can be understood easily.

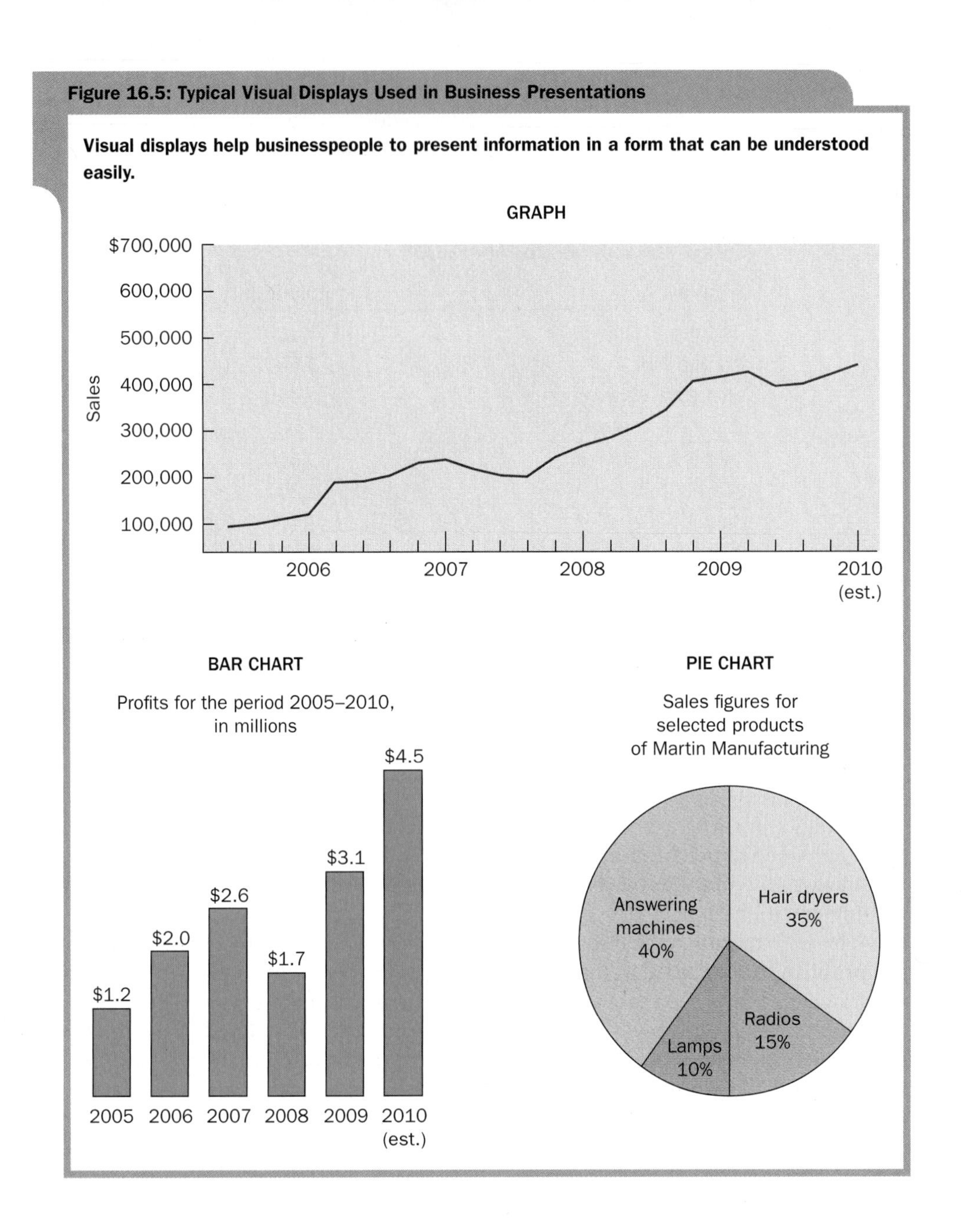

Table 16.1: Typical Three-Column Table Used in Business Presentations

Tables are most useful for displaying information about two or more variables.

All-Star Technology Projected Sales

Section of the Country	Number of Salespeople	Consumer Products	Industrial Products
Eastern territory	15	$1,500,000	$3,500,000
Midwestern territory	20	$2,000,000	$5,000,000
Western territory	10	$1,000,000	$4,000,000
TOTAL	45	$4,500,000	$12,500,000

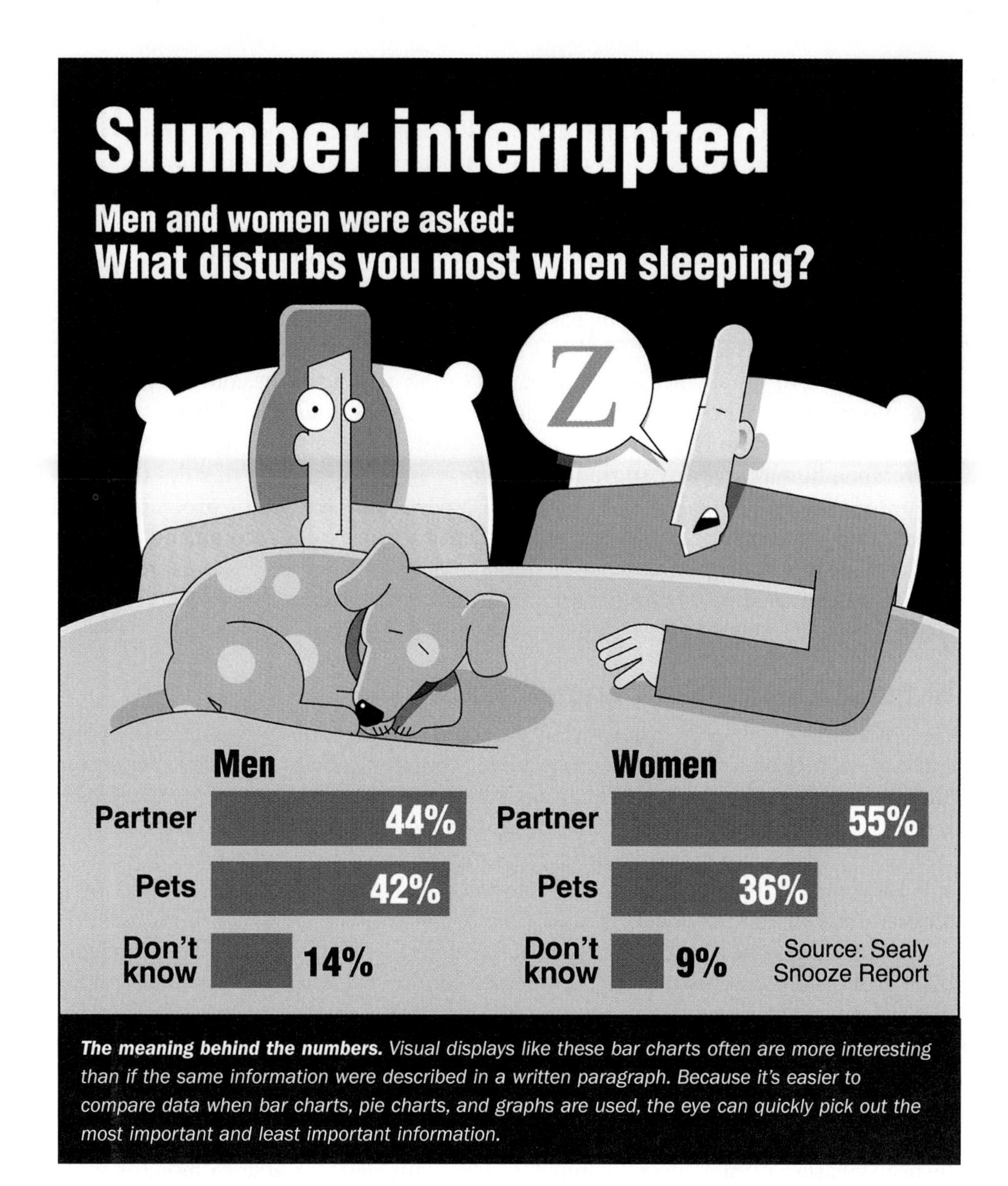

The meaning behind the numbers. *Visual displays like these bar charts often are more interesting than if the same information were described in a written paragraph. Because it's easier to compare data when bar charts, pie charts, and graphs are used, the eye can quickly pick out the most important and least important information.*

PRNewswire/Sealy Inc.

Improving Productivity with the Help of Computers and Technology

4 Learning Objective: Describe how the Internet helps in decision making, communications, sales, and recruiting and training.

In this section, we examine several solutions to challenges created when a firm or its employees use computers and the Internet. In each case, a solution is always evaluated in terms of its costs and compared with the benefits a firm receives, generally referred to as a *cost/benefit analysis*. Typical areas of concern for a business include decision making, communications, sales, recruiting and training employees, and business software applications.

Making Smart Decisions

How do managers and employees sort out relevant and useful information from the spam, junk mail, and useless data? Three different applications actually can help to improve and speed the decision-making process for people at different levels within an organization. First, a **decision-support system (DSS)** is a type of computer program that provides relevant data and information to help a firm's employees make decisions. It also can be used to determine the effect of changing different variables and answer "what if " type questions. For example, a manager at California-based

decision-support system (DSS) a type of computer program that provides relevant data and information to help a firm's employees make decisions

KB Homes may use a DSS to determine prices for new homes built in an upscale, luxury subdivision. By entering the number of homes that will be built along with different costs associated with land, labor, materials, building permits, promotional costs, and all other costs, a DSS can help to determine a base price for each new home. It is also possible to increase or decrease the building costs and determine new home prices for each set of assumptions with a DSS.

executive information system (EIS) a computer-based system that facilitates and supports the decision-making needs of top managers and senior executives by providing easy access to both internal and external information

Although similar to a DSS, an **executive information system (EIS)** is a computer-based system that facilitates and supports the decision-making needs of top managers and senior executives by providing easy access to both internal and external information. With an EIS, executives can obtain information by touching a computer screen, using a mouse, or using voice recognition and simply talking to the computer. Needed data and information can be displayed in graphs, charts, and spreadsheets.

expert system a type of computer program that uses artificial intelligence to imitate a human's ability to think

An **expert system** is a type of computer program that uses artificial intelligence to imitate a human's ability to think. An expert system uses a set of rules that analyze information supplied by the user about a particular activity or problem. Based on the information supplied, the expert system then provides recommendations or suggests specific actions in order to help make decisions. Expert systems, for example, have been used to schedule manufacturing tasks, diagnose illnesses, determine credit limits for credit-card customers, and develop electronic games.

Helping Employees Communicate

One of the first business applications of computer technology was e-mail. Once software was chosen and employees trained, communications could be carried out globally within and outside a firm at any time, twenty-four hours a day, seven days a week. Today, e-mail is also being used as a direct link between businesses and customers. For example, many brokerage and financial firms like Charles Schwab and Fidelity Investments use e-mail to stay in contact with customers and promote different investment products.

groupware one of the latest types of software that facilitates the management of large projects among geographically dispersed employees as well as such group activities as problem solving and brainstorming

Groupware is one of the latest types of software that facilitates the management of large projects among geographically dispersed employees, as well as such group activities as problem solving and brainstorming. Suppose that the home office of a software development firm in a major city has been hired to prepare customized software for a client in another city. The project team leader uses groupware to establish guidelines for the project, check availability of employees around the world, give individuals specific work assignments, and set up a schedule for work completion, testing, and final installation on the client's computer. The team leader is able to monitor work progress and may intervene if asked or if problems develop. When needed, people from various locations, possessing an array of knowledge and skills, can be called to the "workspace" created on the computer system for their contribution. When the work is finally completed, it can be forwarded to the client's computer and installed.

collaborative learning system a work environment that allows problem-solving participation by all team members

Besides being useful in project management, groupware provides an opportunity to establish a collaborative learning system to help solve a specific problem. A **collaborative learning system** is a work environment that allows problem-solving participation by all team members. By posting a question or problem on the groupware site, the team leader invites members, who may be located anywhere in the world, to submit messages that can help to move the group toward a solution.

Assisting the Firm's Sales Force

Internet-based software application programs sometimes referred to as *customer relationship management* (CRM) programs focus on the special informational needs of sales personnel. For example, sales force automation programs support sales representatives with organized databases of information such as names of clients, status of pending orders, and sales leads and opportunities, as well as any related advice or recommendations from other company personnel. Consider what happens when a sales representative for the pharmaceutical division of a company such as Johnson & Johnson is planning to visit doctors, health care providers, and hospitals in the Chicago area. A sales force automation software program can provide information

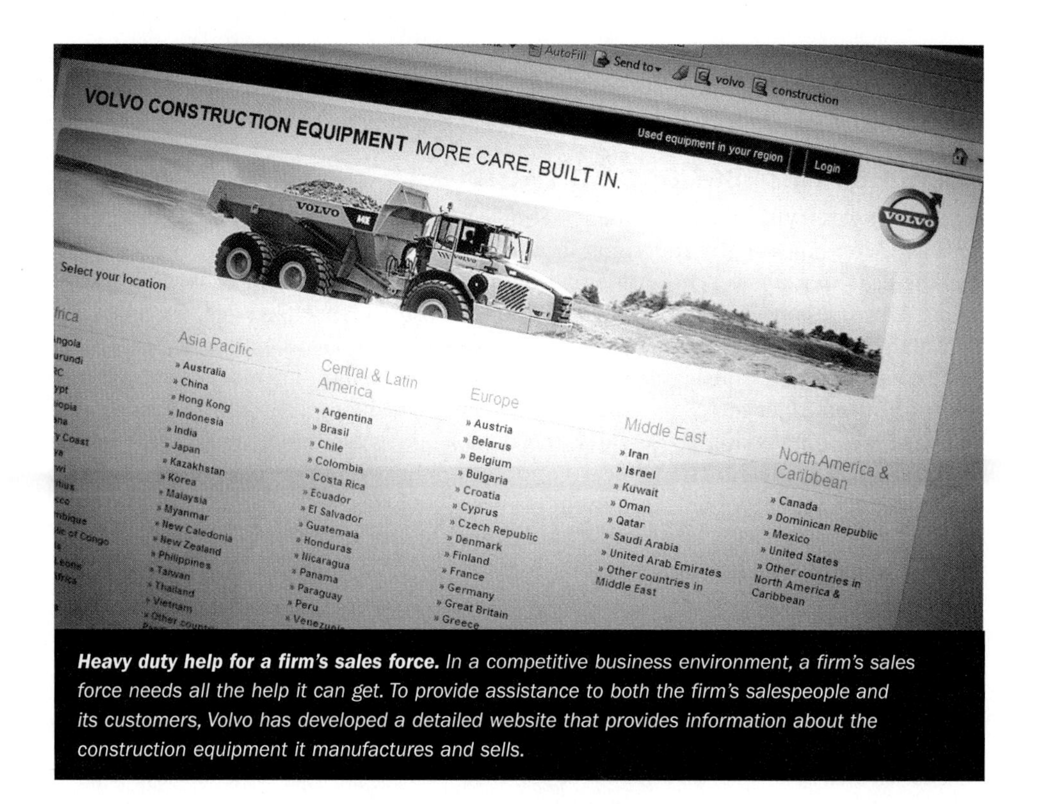

Heavy duty help for a firm's sales force. *In a competitive business environment, a firm's sales force needs all the help it can get. To provide assistance to both the firm's salespeople and its customers, Volvo has developed a detailed website that provides information about the construction equipment it manufactures and sells.*

Courtesy Volvo Construction Equipment

about what the results were of the last contacts, who else in the pharmaceutical firm has interacted with the client, and previous purchases the client has made. For instance, a sales representative might learn from an individual within the client's organization that another department is seeking information about a product that could provide a sales opportunity. Although the sales representative may not be involved directly in that field, the information can be entered into the firm's database of information. At the same time, a message can be sent to the sales representative in the appropriate department that a new opportunity has been identified. Then a sales representative in the appropriate department can provide information to the potential customer and ultimately increase sales of the firm's products or services.

As sales representatives complete their visits, information about what was learned should be entered into the sales force automation system as soon as possible so that everyone can use the latest information.

Recruiting and Training Employees

A common icon on most corporate websites is a link to "Careers" or "Employment Opportunities." Firms looking for people with specialized skills can post their employee needs on their websites and reach potential candidates from around the globe. This is an extremely important method of recruiting employees for positions where labor shortages are common and individuals with the *right* skills are in high demand.

Furthermore, software programs can help large firms such as General Electric, ExxonMobil, and Citigroup to establish a database of potential employees. This is an especially important function for a firm that receives thousands of unsolicited employment applications from people all over the world. The cost of organizing and processing this information is high, but software can reduce this expense when compared with a paper-based system.

Large and midsize companies also spend a great deal of money on educational and training programs for employees. By distributing information about the firm, products and services, new procedures, and general information to employees through the Internet for reading and study at convenient times and places, firms can reduce training costs dramatically. In addition, information on a wide range of topics ranging from ethical behavior to sexual harassment to discrimination also can be distributed to a firm's employees. Often, these sites may be needed only on rare occasions;

however, it is important that employees know that the information exists and where it is. Furthermore, revision and distribution of changes to this type of information are much easier if the information is provided on the company's website.

Business Applications Software

Early software typically performed a single function. Today, however, *integrated software* combines many functions in a single package. Integrated packages allow for the easy *linking* of text, numerical data, graphs, photos, and even audiovisual clips. A business report prepared using the Microsoft Office package, for instance, can include all these components.

Integration offers at least two other benefits. Once data have been entered into an application in an integrated package, the data can be used in another integrated package without having to re-enter the data again. Also, once a user learns one application, it is much easier to learn another application in an integrated package. From a career standpoint, you should realize that firms will assume that you possess, or will possess after training, a high degree of working comfort with several of the software applications described in Table 16.2.

Table 16.2: Current Business Application Software Used to Improve Productivity

Word processing	Users can prepare and edit written documents and store them in the computer or on a memory device.
Desktop publishing	Users can combine text and graphics in reports, newsletters, and pamphlets in professional reports.
Accounting	Users can record routine financial transactions and prepare financial reports at the end of the accounting period.
Database management	Users can electronically store large amounts of data and transform the data into information.
Graphics	Users can display and print pictures, drawings, charts, and diagrams.
Spreadsheets	Users can organize numerical data into a grid of rows and columns.

Using Computers and the Internet to Obtain Information

5

Learning Objective: Analyze how computers and technology change the way information is acquired, organized, and used.

information society a society in which large groups of employees generate or depend on information to perform their jobs

Internet a worldwide network of computers linked through telecommunications

World Wide Web (the Web) the Internet's multimedia environment of audio, visual, and text data

Internet service providers (ISPs) provide customers with a connection to the Internet through various phone plugs and cables

We live in a rapidly changing **information society**—that is, a society in which large groups of employees generate or depend on information to perform their jobs. The need for more and better information will only continue to grow. Today, businesses are using the Internet to find and distribute information to global users. The Internet is also used for communicating between the firm's employees and its customers. Finally, businesses use the Internet to gather information about competitors' products, prices, and other business strategies. Clearly, the Internet is here to stay.

The Internet, the Intranet, and Networks

The **Internet** is a worldwide network of computers linked through telecommunications. Enabling users around the world to communicate with each other electronically, the Internet provides access to a huge array of information sources. The Internet's most commonly used network for finding information is the World Wide Web. The **World Wide Web** (or more simply, **the Web**) is the Internet's multimedia environment of audio, visual, and text data. To get on the Internet, you need a computer, a modem, and an **Internet service provider (ISP)**, such as AT&T, America Online, Verizon, Comcast, or other companies that provide a connection to the Web. Internet service providers (ISPs) provide customers with a connection to the Internet through various phone plugs and cables. Today, connections to the Internet include simple telephone lines or faster digital subscriber lines (DSLs) and cabled broadband

Jump-Starting Your Career

Protect Your Digital Rep

What do you want future bosses to find when they search for you online? Think about that as you post messages, photos, or videos on a blog, on Facebook or MySpace, or on any publicly available Web page. Employers often use search engines to check on candidates before making a job offer. A good online impression can give your career a boost; a revealing YouTube video or a post describing questionable activities might stall your career even before it begins.

To protect your digital reputation:

- *Search yourself.* See what others see when they do a Web search for your name. Do the results confirm or contradict what's on your résumé? Are there any posts or images you should remove?
- *Preserve your privacy.* Be sure your MySpace or Facebook profile is private and avoid disclosing personal details, especially on public sites. Check those photo tags, too.
- *Pause before you post.* Information has a long life online—and nearly anything can be forwarded to a huge audience with just a click or two. So think ahead: Will what you post today be an embarrassment tomorrow?

Sources: Lisa Bolivar, "Can Facebook Ruin You?" *Miami Herald*, November 9, 2008, **www.miamiherald.com**; Liz Wolgemuth, "Using Facebook to Fire up Your Career," *U.S. News & World Report,* August 6, 2008, n.p.; Andy Simmons, "How to Click and Clean," *Reader's Digest,* April 2008, pp. 155–159.

that carry larger amounts of data at quicker transfer speeds. **Broadband technology** is a general term referring to higher speed Internet connections that deliver data, voice, and video material. And with new wireless technology, it is possible to access the Internet by using your laptop computer, cellular phone, and other wireless communications devices. (Wireless technology is especially attractive for many people because not only does it enable them to access the Internet, but it also enables computers and other electronic components to communicate with each other without the multitude of cables and wires common in many offices and homes.)

broadband technology a general term referring to higher-speed Internet connections that deliver data, voice, and video material

In addition to business sites, the World Wide Web has a wide array of government and institutional sites that provide information to a firm's employees and the general public. There are also online sites available for most of the popular business periodicals.

An **intranet** is a smaller version of the Internet for use within a firm. Using a series of customized Web pages, employees can quickly find information about their firm as well as connect to external sources. For instance, an employee might use the intranet to access the firm's policy documents on customer warranties or even take a company-designed course on new products and how to introduce them to customers. Generally, intranet sites are protected, and users must supply both a user name and a password to gain access to a company's intranet site.

intranet a smaller version of the Internet for use within a firm's computer network

Both the Internet and intranets are examples of a computer network. A **computer network** is a group of two or more computers linked together that allows users to share data and information. Today, two basic types of networks affect the way employees and the general public obtain data and information. A **wide-area network (WAN)** is a network that connects computers over a large geographic area, such as a city, a state, or even the world. The world's most popular WAN is the Internet.[3] In addition to the Internet, other WANs include private corporate networks (sometimes referred to as virtual private networks, or VPNs) and research networks. A **local-area network (LAN)** is a network that connects computers that are in close proximity to each other, such as an office building or a college campus. LANs allow users to share files, printers, games, or other applications.[4] Typically, LANs also will allow users to connect to the Internet.

computer network a group of two or more computers linked together that allows users to share data and information

wide-area network (WAN) a network that connects computers over a large geographic area, such as a city, a state, or even the world

local-area network (LAN) a network that connects computers that are in close proximity to each other, such as an office building or a college campus

Accessing the Internet

In order to access the Internet or an intranet, computers and software must be standardized. Establishing standards is vital to ensuring that a Hewlett-Packard computer in McPherson, Kansas, can "talk" with a Dell computer in San Francisco, California. It is just as important for software to be standardized if businesses and individuals are going to use computers to communicate and conduct business activities through the Internet.

SPOTLIGHT

Most Popular Resources on the Internet

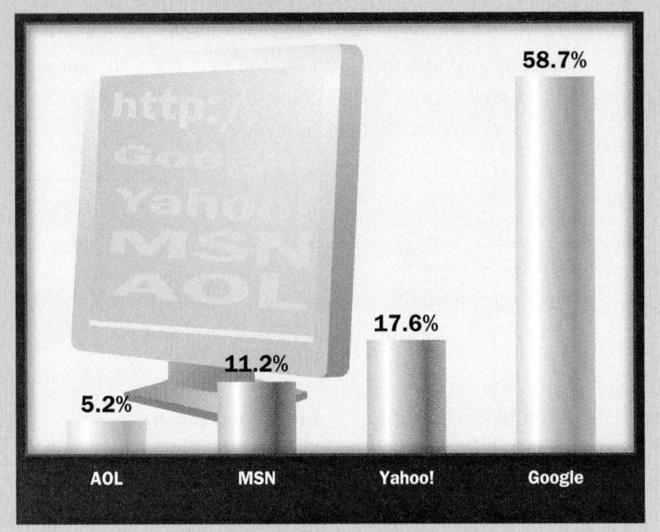

Source: The Nielsen/NetRatings website, **www.netratings.com**, accessed October 11, 2008.

The search for available information often begins with a specific website address or a search engine. Every website on the Internet is identified by its *Uniform Resource Locator* (URL), which acts as its address. To connect to a site, you enter its URL in your Web browser. A Web browser such as Windows Internet Explorer or Mozilla Firefox is software that helps users to navigate around the Internet and connect to different websites. The URLs of most corporate sites are similar to the organizations' real names. For instance, you can reach IBM by entering **http://www.ibm.com.** The first part of the entry, *http*, sets the software protocols for proper transfer of information between your computer and the one at the site to which you are connecting. *Http* stands for *HyperText Transfer Protocol* and frequently is omitted from a URL because your computer adds it automatically when you enter the rest of the address. *HyperText* refers to words or phrases highlighted or underlined on a Web page; when you select these, they link you to other websites.

To find a particular website, you can take advantage of several free search programs available on the Web, such as Google, Yahoo!, and AltaVista. To locate a search engine, enter its URL in your browser. Some URLs for popular search engines are **www.altavista.com, www.google.com,** and **www.yahoo.com.**

The home page for many search engines provides a short list of primary topic divisions, such as *careers, news, shopping, yellow pages,* and *weather,* as well as a search window where you can enter the particular topic you are looking for.

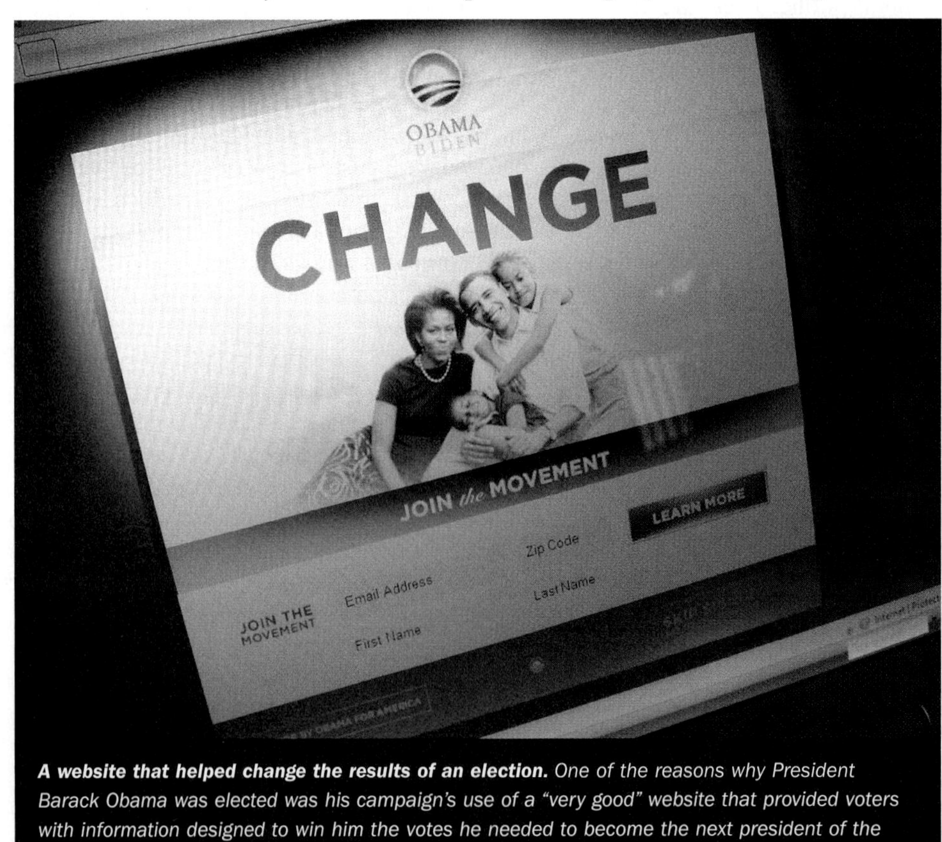

A website that helped change the results of an election. *One of the reasons why President Barack Obama was elected was his campaign's use of a "very good" website that provided voters with information designed to win him the votes he needed to become the next president of the United States.*

Courtesy Obama for America

Creating Web Pages

Looking for an ecologically responsible way to get rid of an unneeded personal computer, laptop, or printer? You can help the planet and help a school or charity at the same time by donating your unneeded equipment to a nonprofit organization such as the National Cristina Foundation. **www.cristina.org**

Today, employees and the general public connect to the Internet, enter a Web address, or use a Web search engine to access information. That information is presented on a website created and maintained by business firms; agencies of federal, state, or local governments; or educational or similar organizations. Because a website should provide accurate information, great care is required when creating a website. Generally, once a *template* or structure for the Web page has been created, content such as text or images can be inserted or changed readily, allowing the site to remain current.

What the website says about a company is important and should be developed carefully to portray the "right" image. Therefore, it is understandable that a firm without the internal human resources to design and launch its website will turn to the talents of creative experts available through Web consulting firms. Regardless of whether the website is developed by the firm's employees or outside consultants, the suggestions listed in Table 16.3 should be considered when creating materials for a firm's website.

Once a website is established, most companies prefer to manage their sites on their own computers. An alternative approach is to pay a hosting service that often will provide guaranteed user accessibility, e-business shopping software, site-updating services, and other specialized services.

Defining e-Business

6

Learning Objective: Explain the meaning of e-business.

e-business (electronic business) the organized effort of individuals to produce and sell, for a profit, the products and services that satisfy society's needs through the facilities available on the Internet

In Chapter 1, we defined *business* as the organized effort of individuals to produce and sell, for a profit, the products and services that satisfy society's needs. In a simple sense, then, **e-business**, or **electronic business**, can be defined as the organized

Table 16.3: Tips for Website Development

Whether you build your site from scratch, use a Web design software program, or hire outside professionals, make sure that your website conveys not only the "right" image but also useful information about your company or organization.

Tip	Description
1. Develop a theme.	A website is like a book and needs a theme to tie ideas together and tell an interesting story.
2. Determine how much information to include on your site.	Get a handle on the type and amount of information that will be contained on your site. Although it is tempting to include "everything," you must be selective.
3. Plan the layout of your site.	Think about how you want your site to look. Websites that combine color, art, and links to narrative material are the most useful.
4. Add graphics.	Obtain graphics that illustrate the types of data and information contained on your site. Choose colors and photos carefully to make sure that they add rather than detract from the site.
5. Outline the material for each page.	Generally, the opening, or home, page contains basic information with links to additional pages that provide more detailed information.
6. Develop plans to update the site.	It is important to develop a plan to update your site on a regular basis. Too often, sites are "forgotten" and contain dated or inaccurate material.
7. Make sure that your site is easy to use.	Stand back and take a look at your site. Is your site confusing, or does it provide a road map to get from point A to point B? If you have trouble getting information, others will too.

Going Global

E-Businesses Tap Cloud Computing

What is cloud computing, and why are e-businesses using it? In cloud computing, a third party makes processing power, applications, databases, and storage available for use on demand from anywhere, via the Internet (aka "the cloud"). Instead of running software and storing data on their employer's network or its individual PCs, the e-business's employees log onto the third party's system and use only the applications and data storage they actually need.

e-businesses, especially startups, see big savings in cloud computing. Should demand spike, they don't have to buy additional hardware, software, or storage capacity to handle the extra load. Their employees can simply process and park huge quantities of data in the cloud during the peak period. And the e-business doesn't have to worry about upgrading applications or maintaining storage, which the cloud-computing company handles.

Consider the experience of Animoto, a young e-business with an automated process for creating videos from uploaded digital photos and music. During a week when more than 700,000 people signed up to try Animoto, the e-business signed up for Amazon.com's cloud-computing services. When demand slowed, Animoto was able to cut back on its use of Amazon's services and save money on its cloud-computing bill, too.

Sources: Serdar Yegulalp, "Cloud Computing Tools for Managing Amazon, Google Services," *InformationWeek*, November 5, 2008, **www.informationweek.com**; John Brandon, "Living in the Cloud," *PC Magazine*, July 2008, pp. 19–20; Michael Fitzgerald, "Cloud Computing: So You Don't Have to Stand Still," *New York Times*, May 25, 2008, p. BU-4.

effort of individuals to produce and sell, for a profit, the products and services that satisfy society's needs *through the facilities available on the Internet.* As you will see in the remainder of this chapter, e-business is transforming key business activities.

Organizing e-Business Resources

As noted in Chapter 1, to be organized, a business must combine *human, material, informational,* and *financial resources*. This is true of e-business, too (see Figure 16.6), but in this case, the resources may be more specialized than in a typical business. For example, people who can design, create, and maintain websites are only a fraction of the specialized human resources required by e-businesses. Material resources must include specialized computers, sophisticated equipment and software, and high-speed Internet connections. Computer programs that track the number of customers to view a firm's website are generally among the specialized

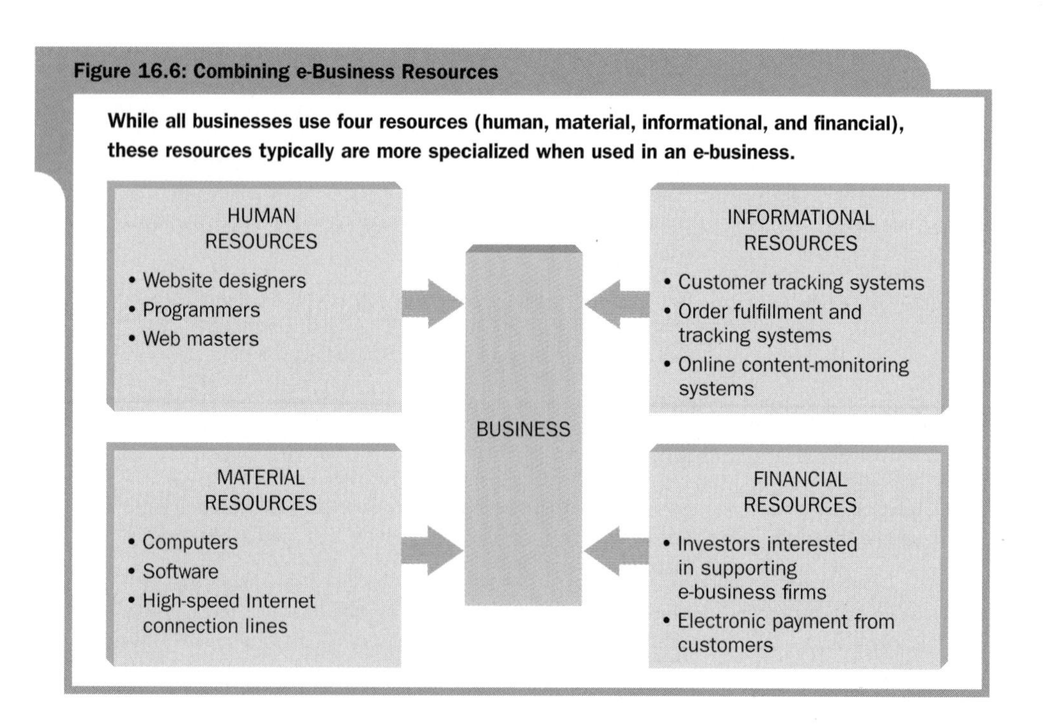

Vietnam captures the attention of some of the largest players in the information technology industry. *Vietnam's young, educated, and affordable programmers are creating an international niche as a software outsourcing base for American, European, and Japanese high-tech firms.*

AP Photo/Richard Vogel

informational resources required. Financial resources, the money required to start and maintain the firm and allow it to grow, usually reflect greater participation by individual entrepreneurs and investors willing to invest in a high-tech firm instead of conventional financial sources such as banks.

In an effort to reduce the cost of specialized resources that are used in e-business, many firms have turned to outsourcing. **Outsourcing** is the process of finding outside vendors and suppliers that provide professional help, parts, or materials at a lower cost. For example, a firm that needs specialized software to complete a project may turn to an outside firm located in another part of the United States, India, or some Eastern European country.

outsourcing the process of finding outside vendors and suppliers that provide professional help, parts, or materials at a lower cost

Satisfying Needs Online

Think for a moment, why do people use the Internet? For most people, the Internet can be used to purchase products or services and as a source of information and interaction with other people. Today, more people use the Internet to satisfy these needs than ever before, and the number of people who use the Internet will continue to grow in the years to come. Because of the explosive growth of the Internet, let's start with two basic assumptions.

- The Internet has created some new customer needs that did not exist before creation of the Internet.
- e-businesses can satisfy those needs, as well as more traditional ones.

Restoration Hardware (**www.restorationhardware.com**), for instance, gives customers anywhere in the world access to the same virtual store of hardware and decorative items. And at eBay's global auction site, customers can, for a small fee, buy and sell almost anything. In each of these examples, customers can use the Internet to purchase a product or service.

In addition to purchasing products, the Internet can be used by both individuals and business firms to obtain information. For example,

- Internet users also can access newspapers and magazines and radio and television programming at a time and place convenient to them.

How one firm satisfies needs online. *Launching its website (www.landsend.com) in 1995, Lands' End was an "early adopter" of the Internet. Today, Lands' End uses its website to match consumer needs with a vast array of clothing items that it sells online. By using technology and the Internet, this highly successful company has created a new revenue stream and reduced expenses.*

- The Internet provides the opportunity for two-way interaction between the online program and the viewer. CNN.com and other news-content sites encourage dialogue among viewers in chat rooms and exchanges with the writers of articles posted to the site.
- Customers can respond to Internet programming by requesting more information about a product or posing specific questions, which may lead to purchasing a product or service.
- Finally, the Internet allows customers to choose the content they are offered. For example, individuals can custom design daily online newspapers and magazines with articles that are of interest to them. Knowing what is of interest to a customer allows an Internet firm to direct appropriate, smart advertising to a specific customer. For example, someone wanting to read articles about the New York Yankees might be a potential customer for products and services related to baseball. For the advertiser, knowing that its advertisements are being directed to the most likely customers represents a better way to spend advertising dollars.

Creating e-Business Profit

Business firms can increase profits either by increasing sales revenue or by reducing expenses through a variety of e-business activities.

revenue stream a source of revenue flowing into a firm

Increasing Sales Revenue Each source of sales revenue flowing into a firm is referred to as a **revenue stream**. One way to increase revenues is to sell merchandise on the Internet. Online merchants can reach a global customer base twenty-four hours a day, seven days a week because the opportunity to shop on the Internet is virtually unrestricted. And yet shifting revenues earned from customers inside a real store to revenues earned from *those same customers online* does not create any real new revenue for a firm. The goal is to find *new customers* and generate *new sales* so that *total revenues are increased.*

Intelligent informational systems also can help to generate sales revenue for Internet firms such as Amazon.com. Such systems store information about each customer's purchases, along with a variety of other information about the buyer's preferences. Using this information, the system can assist the customer the next time he or she visits the website. For example, if the customer has bought a Taylor Hicks or Carrie Underwood CD in the past, the system might suggest CDs by similar artists who have appeared on the popular televised talent-search program *American Idol.*

While some customers in certain situations may not make a purchase online, the existence of the firm's website and the services and information it provides may lead to increased sales in the firm's physical stores. For example, Toyota.com can provide basic comparative information for shoppers so that they are better prepared for their visit to an automobile showroom.

In addition to selling products or services online, e-business revenue streams are created by advertising placed on Web pages and by subscription fees charged for access to online services and content. For example, Hoover's Online (**www.hoovers.com**), a comprehensive source for company and industry information, makes some of its online content free for anyone who visits the site, but more detailed data are available only by paid subscription. In addition, it receives revenue from companies that are called sponsors, who advertise their products and services on Hoover's website.

Many Internet firms that distribute news, magazine and newspaper articles, and similar content generate revenue from commissions earned from sellers of products linked to the site. Online shopping malls, for example, now provide groups of related vendors of electronic equipment and computer hardware and software with a new method of selling their products and services. In many cases, the vendors share online sales revenues with the site owners.

Reducing Expenses Reducing expenses is the second major way in which e-business can help to increase profitability. Providing online access to information customers want can reduce the cost of dealing with customers. Sprint Nextel (**www.sprint.com**), for instance, is just one company that maintains an extensive website where potential customers can learn more about cell phone products and services and current customers can access personal account information, send e-mail questions to customer service, and purchase additional products or services. With such extensive online services, Sprint Nextel does not have to maintain as many physical store locations as it would without these online services. We examine more examples of how e-business contributes to profitability throughout this chapter, especially as we focus on some of the business models for activity on the Internet.

Fundamental Models of e-Business

7

Learning Objective: Describe the fundamental models of e-business.

One way to get a better sense of how businesses are adapting to the opportunities available on the Internet is to identify e-business models. A **business model** represents a group of common characteristics and methods of doing business to generate sales revenues and reduce expenses. Each of the models discussed below represents a primary e-business model. Regardless of the type of business model, planning often depends on if the e-business is a new firm or an existing firm adding an online presence—see Figure 16.7.

business model represents a group of common characteristics and methods of doing business to generate sales revenues and reduce expenses

Business-to-Business (B2B) Model

Many e-businesses can be distinguished from others simply by their customer focus. For instance, some firms use the Internet mainly to conduct business with other businesses. These firms generally are referred to as having a **business-to-business** (or **B2B**) **model.**

business-to-business (or B2B) model a model used by firms that conduct business with other businesses

When examining B2B business firms, two clear types emerge. In the first type, the focus is simply on facilitating sales transactions between businesses. For example, Dell manufactures computers to specifications that customers enter on the Dell website. A large portion of Dell's online orders are from corporate clients who are well informed about the products they need and are looking for fairly priced,

Figure 16.7: Planning for a New Internet Business or Building an Online Presence for an Existing Business

The approach taken to creating an e-business plan will depend on whether you are establishing a new Internet business or adding an online component to an existing business.

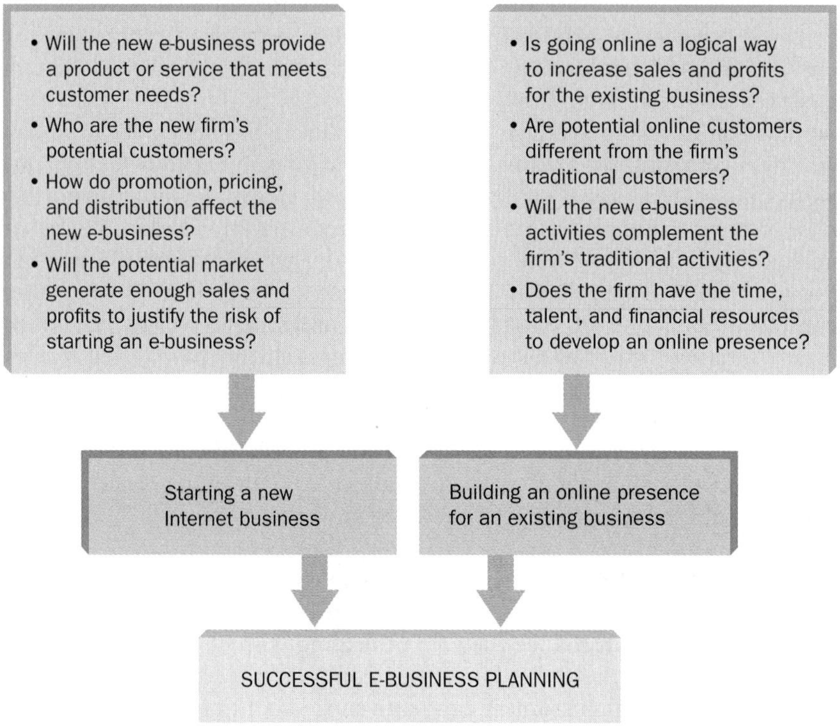

high-quality computer products that will be delivered quickly. Basically, by building only what is ordered, Dell reduces storage and carrying costs and rarely is stuck with unsold inventory. By dealing directly with Dell, customers eliminate costs associated with wholesalers and retailers, thereby helping to reduce the price they pay for equipment.

A second, more complex type of B2B model involves a company and its suppliers. Today, suppliers use the Internet to bid on products and services they wish to sell to a customer and learn about the customer's rules and procedures that must be followed. For example, both General Motors and Ford have developed B2B models to link thousands of suppliers that sell the automobile makers parts worth billions of dollars each year. While the B2B sites are expensive to start and maintain, there are significant savings for General Motors and Ford. Given the potential savings, it is no wonder that many other manufacturers and their suppliers are beginning to use the same kind of B2B systems that are used by the automakers. In fact, suppliers know that to be a "preferred" supplier for a large firm that may purchase large quantities of parts, supplies, or raw materials, they must be tied into the purchaser's B2B system. For example, Ford recently announced that it would reduce the number of suppliers that provide the firm with $70 billion of car parts and $20 billion of other supplies needed each year and increase the volume of purchases with those that remain connected to its system.[5]

Business-to-Consumer (B2C) Model

In contrast to the B2B model, firms such as **Barnesandnoble.com** and **Landsend.com** clearly are focused on individual consumers and so are referred to as having a

The magic of Microsoft. *Microsoft uses a business-to-business (B2B) approach to reach potential business customers. One of its newest software applications is called "virtual product placement" and allows advertisers to place a photo of a product or advertising image into an existing video or movie—such as the Coca-Cola image shown in this photo.*

AP Photo/Ted S. Warren

business-to-consumer (or **B2C**) **model**. In a B2C situation, understanding how consumers behave online is critical to a firm's success. Typically, a business firm that uses a B2C model must answer the following questions:

business-to-consumer (or B2C) model a model used by firms that focus on conducting business with individual consumers

- Will consumers use websites merely to simplify and speed up comparison shopping?
- Will consumers purchase services and products online or end up buying at a traditional retail store?
- What sorts of products and services are best suited for online consumer shopping?
- Which products and services are simply not good choices at this stage of online development?

In addition to providing round-the-clock global access to all kinds of products and services, B2C firms often attempt to build long-term relationships with their customers. Often, firms will make a special effort to make sure that the customer is satisfied and that problems, if any, are solved quickly. Specialized software also can help build good customer relationships. Tracking the decisions and buying preferences as customers navigate a website, for instance, helps management to make well-informed decisions about how best to serve such customers. In essence, this is Barnes and Noble's online selling approach. By tracking and analyzing customer data, Barnes and Noble can provide individualized service to its customers. While a "little special attention" may increase the cost of doing business for a B2C firm, the customer's repeated purchases will repay the investment many times over.

Today, B2B and B2C models are the most popular business models for e-business. And yet, there are other business models that perform specialized e-business activities to generate revenues. Most of the business models described in Table 16.4 are modified versions of the B2B and B2C models.

Table 16.4: Other Business Models That Perform Specialized e-Business Activities

Although modified versions of B2B or B2C, these business models perform specialized e-business activities to generate revenues.

Advertising e-business model	Advertisements that are displayed on a firm's website in return for a fee. Examples include pop-up and banner advertisements on search engines and other popular Internet sites.
Brokerage e-business model	Online marketplaces where buyers and sellers are brought together to facilitate exchange of goods and services. Examples include eBay (**www.ebay.com**), which provides a site for buying and selling virtually anything.
Consumer-to-consumer model	Peer-to-peer software that allows individuals to share information over the Internet. Examples include LimeWire (**www.limewire.com**), which allows users to exchange audio and music files.
Subscription and pay-per-view e-business models	Content that is available only to users who pay a fee to gain access to a website. Examples include investment information provided by Standard & Poor's (**www2.standardandpoors.com**) and business research provided by Forrester Research, Inc. (**www.forrester.com**).

The Future of e-Business: Growth, Opportunities, and Challenges

8

Learning Objective: Explore the factors that will affect the future of e-business.

Since the beginning of commercial activity on the Internet, developments in e-business have been rapid and formidable with spectacular successes such as Google, eBay, and Yahoo!. However, the slowdown in e-business activity that began in 2000 caused a shakeout of excessive optimism in this new-business environment. Today, most firms involved in e-business use a more intelligent approach to development. The long-term view held by the vast majority of analysts is that the Internet will continue to expand along with related technologies. For example, according to

More information equals less risk. *In this photo, CEO and founder Mark Zuckerberg describes Facebook's new initiative that allows advertisers to target potential customers based on what people buy and do on the popular Facebook website. This new approach promises to generate new revenues for Facebook. This approach also helps advertisers to target specific customers that might buy their products or services.*

AP Photo/Craig Ruttle

Forrester Research, Inc., the popularity and growth of consumer broadband access to the Internet have pushed marketers to allocate more money to advertising online in order to reach customers who are moving to the Web and away from traditional media such as television and radio. As a result, Forrester predicts that by 2010, more than $26 billion, or about 8 percent of all advertising spending, will be online.[6]

Internet Growth Potential

To date, only a small percentage of the global population uses the Internet. Current estimates suggest that about 1.2 billion of the nearly 7 billion people in the world use the Web. Clearly, there is much more growth opportunity. Americans comprise 17 percent of all users—the largest group online.[7] Of the 300 million people making up the American population, 210 million use the Internet. With approximately 70 percent of the American population already being Internet users, potential growth in the United States is limited. On the other hand, the number of Internet users in the world's developing countries is expected to increase dramatically. There will also be additional growth as more people begin to use Smartphones and mobile devices. Because of worldwide growth and an increase in wireless computing devices, Computer Industry Almanac projects that worldwide users will exceed 2 billion by 2011 or 2012.[8]

Firms that adapt existing business models to an online environment will continue to dominate development. For example, books, CDs, clothing, hotel accommodations, car rentals, and travel reservations are products and services well suited to online buying and selling. These products or services will continue to be sold in the traditional way, as well as in a more cost-effective and efficient fashion over the Internet.

Environmental Forces Affecting e-Business

Although the environmental forces at work are complex, it is useful to think of them as either *internal* or *external* forces that affect an e-business. Internal environmental forces are those that are closely associated with the actions and decisions taking place within a firm. As shown in Figure 16.8, typical internal forces include a firm's planning

Figure 16.8: Internal and External Forces That Affect an e-Business

Today, managers and employees of an e-business must respond to internal forces within the organization and external forces outside the organization.

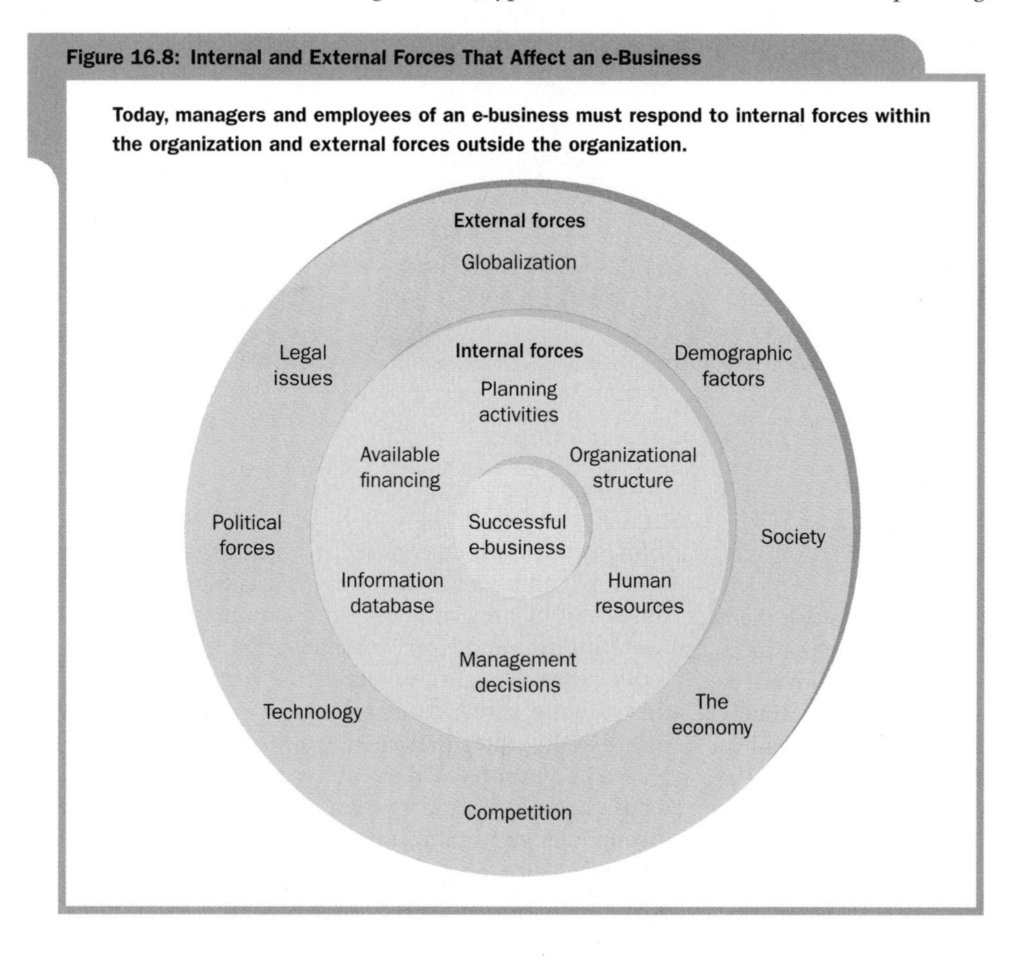

activities, organization structure, human resources, management decisions, information database, and available financing. A shortage of skilled employees needed for a specialized project, for instance, can undermine a firm's ability to sell its services to clients. Unlike the external environmental forces affecting the firm, internal forces such as this one are more likely to be under the direct control of management. In this case, management can either hire the needed staff or choose to pass over a prospective project.

In contrast, external environmental forces are factors affecting e-business planning that originate from outside the organization. These forces are unlikely to be controllable by an e-business firm. Instead, managers and employees of an e-business firm generally will react to these forces, attempting to shield the organization from any undue negative effects and finding ways to take advantage of opportunities in the ever-changing e-business environment. The primary external environmental forces affecting e-business planning include globalization, demographic, societal, economic, competitive, technological, and political and legal forces.

In this chapter, we have explored a business firm's need for information and how a computer, the Internet, and technology can help people to obtain the information they need. We also examined how e-business is changing the way that firms do business. In Chapter 17, we examine the accounting process, which is a major source of information for business.

return to inside business

Blue Nile

As an e-business, Blue Nile doesn't need a prestigious address or fancy décor to succeed. It does need a user-friendly Web site that educates buyers about the fine points of buying fine jewelry and reassures them about making such a big purchase with just a few clicks. That's why every purchase is covered by a money-back guarantee and includes free shipping. Jewelry items that sell for more than $50,000—like the 12.5 carat diamond that sold not long ago—are delivered by armored truck.

Although diamond engagement rings make up more than two-thirds of Blue Nile's business, the company has expanded into colored gemstones and pearls. It is also an increasingly global e-business, now serving customers in twenty-five countries. Can Blue Nile keep building on its e-business expertise to grow in the coming years?

Questions

1. Of the environmental forces affecting e-business, which seem to have had the most influence on Blue Nile's successful growth, and why?
2. Do you agree with Mark Vadon's decision to change the company's name from Internet Diamonds to Blue Nile? Explain your answer.

CHAPTER REVIEW

Summary

Examine how information can reduce risk when making a decision.

The more information a manager has, the less risk there is that a decision will be incorrect. Information produces knowledge and empowers managers and employees to make better decisions. Without accurate and timely information, individual performance will be undermined, and consequently, so will the performance of the entire organization. Because of the volume of information they receive each day and their need to make decisions on a daily basis, businesspeople use information rules to shorten the time spent analyzing choices. Information rules emerge when business research confirms the same results each time it studies the same or a similar set of circumstances. Although many people use the terms *data* and *information* interchangeably, there is a difference. Data are numerical or verbal descriptions that usually result from some sort of measurement. Information is data presented in a form that is useful for a specific purpose. A database is a single collection of data stored in one place that can be used by people throughout an organization to make decisions. While databases are important, the way the data and information are used is even more important. As a result, management information experts now use the term knowledge management (KM) to incorporate a firm's procedures for generating, using, and sharing the data and information contained in the firm's databases.

2 Discuss management's information requirements.

A management information system (MIS) is a means of providing managers with the information they need to perform their jobs as effectively as possible. The purpose of an MIS, (sometimes referred to as an information technology system or simply IT system) is to distribute timely and useful information from both internal and external sources to the decision makers who need it. The specific types of information managers need depend on their area of management and level within the firm. The size and complexity of an MIS must be tailored to the information needs of the organization it serves.

Outline the five functions of an information system.

The five functions performed by an MIS system are collecting data, storing data, updating data, processing data into information, and presenting information. Data may be collected from such internal sources as company records, reports, and minutes of meetings, as well as from the firm's managers. External sources include customers, suppliers, bankers, trade and financial publications, industry conferences, online computer services, and information-gathering organizations. An MIS must be able to store data until they are needed and to update them regularly to ensure that the information presented to managers is accurate, complete, and timely. Data processing is the MIS function that transforms stored data into a form useful for a specific purpose. Large groups of numerical data usually are processed into summary numbers called statistics. Finally, the processed data (which now can be called information) must be presented for use. Verbal information generally is presented in the form of a report. Numerical information most often is displayed in graphs, charts, or tables.

Describe how the Internet helps in decision making, communications, sales, and recruiting and training.

Today, many employees use computers and the Internet to improve productivity and performance and communicate with other employees while at the office or away from the office. Three different applications—decision-support systems, executive information systems, and expert systems—can help managers and employees to speed and improve the decision-making process. Another application in the workplace is electronic mail, or simply e-mail, which provides for communication within and outside the firm at any time, twenty-four hours a day, seven days a week. An extension of e-mail is groupware, which is software that facilitates the management of large projects among geographically dispersed employees as well as such group activities as problem solving and brainstorming. The Internet and a sales force automation software program can provide a database of information that can be used to assist a sales representative. The Internet also can be used to improve employee training and recruitment while lowering costs. A number of software applications—word processing, desktop publishing, accounting, database management, graphics, and spreadsheets—can all help employees improve productivity.

5 Analyze how computers and technology change the way information is acquired, organized, and used.

We live in an information society—one in which large groups of employees generate or depend on information to perform their jobs. To find needed information, many businesses and individuals use the Internet. The Internet is a worldwide network of computers linked through telecommunications. Firms also can use an intranet to distribute information within the firm. Both the Internet and intranets are examples of a computer network. A computer network is a group of two or more computers linked together to allow users to share data and information. Today, two basic types—local-area networks (LANs) and wide-area networks (WANs)—affect the way employees and the general public obtain data and information. Today, employees and the general public connect to the Internet, enter a Web address, or use a Web search engine to access information. That information is presented on a website created and maintained by business firms; agencies of federal, state, and local governments; or educational or similar organizations. Because a website should provide accurate information, great care is required when creating a website.

6 Explain the meaning of e-business.

e-business, or electronic business, can be defined as the organized effort of individuals to produce and sell, for a profit, the goods and services that satisfy society's needs *through the facilities available on the Internet.* The term e-business refers to all business activities and practices conducted on the Internet by an individual firm or the general concept of e-business. The human, material, information, and financial resources that any business requires are highly specialized for e-business. In an effort to reduce the cost of e-business resources, many firms have turned to outsourcing.

Using e-business activities, it is possible to satisfy new customer needs created by the Internet as well as traditional ones in unique ways. Meeting customer needs is especially important when an e-business is trying to earn profits by increasing sales and reducing expenses. Each source of revenue flowing into the firm is referred to as a revenue stream.

7 Describe the fundamental models of e-business.

e-business models focus attention on the identity of a firm's customers. Firms that use the Internet mainly to conduct business with other businesses generally are referred to as having a business-to-business, or B2B, model. When examining B2B business firms, two clear types emerge. In the first type of B2B, the focus is simply on facilitating sales transactions between businesses. A second, more complex type of the B2B model involves a company and its suppliers. In contrast to the focus of the B2B model, firms such as Amazon or eBay clearly are focused on individual buyers and so are referred to as having a business-to-consumer, or B2C, model. In a B2C situation, understanding how consumers behave online is critical to the firm's success. And successful B2C firms often make a special effort to build long-term relationships with their customers. While B2B and B2C models are the most popular e-business models, there are other models that perform specialized e-business activities to generate revenues (see Table 16.4).

8 Explore the factors that will affect the future of e-business.

Since the advent of commercial activity on the Internet, developments in e-business have been rapid and formidable. Clearly, the slowdown in e-business activity that began in 2000 caused a shakeout of excessive optimism in this new business environment. Today, most firms involved in e-business use a more intelligent approach to development. The long-term view held by the vast majority of analysts is that the Internet will continue to expand along with related technologies. While approximately 70 percent of Americans now have access to the Internet, it is expected that worldwide users will exceed 2 billion by 2011 or 2012. Although the environmental forces at work are complex, it is useful to think of them as either internal or external forces that affect an e-business. Internal environmental forces are those that are closely associated with the actions and decisions taking place within a firm. In contrast, external environmental forces are those factors affecting an e-business originating outside an organization.

Key Terms

You should now be able to define and give an example relevant to each of the following terms:

data (463)
information (463)
database (464)
knowledge management (KM) (464)
management information system (MIS) (464)
information technology (IT) officer (464)
data processing (468)
statistic (468)
decision-support system (DSS) (471)
executive information system (EIS) (472)
expert system (472)
groupware (472)
collaborative learning system (472)
information society (474)
Internet (474)
World Wide Web (the Web) (474)
Internet service providers (ISPs) (474)
broadband technology (475)
intranet (475)
computer network (475)
wide-area network (WAN) (475)
local-area network (LAN) (475)
e-business (electronic business) (477)
outsourcing (479)
revenue stream (480)
business model (481)
business-to-business (B2B) model (481)
business-to-consumer (B2C) model (483)

Review Questions

1. In your own words, describe how information reduces risk when you make a personal or work-related decision.
2. What are information rules? How do they simplify the process of making decisions?
3. What is the difference between data and information? Give one example of accounting data and one example of accounting information.
4. List the five functions of an MIS.
5. What are the components of a typical business report?
6. Describe the three types of computer applications that help employees, managers, and executives make smart decisions.
7. How can computers and software help the firm's employees communicate, increase sales, and recruit and train employees?
8. Explain the differences between the Internet and an intranet. What types of information does each of these networks provide?
9. What is the difference between a wide-area network (WAN) and a local-area network (LAN)?
10. What factors should be considered when a firm is developing a Web page?
11. What are the four major factors contained in the definition of e-business?
12. How do e-businesses generate revenue streams?
13. What are the two fundamental e-business models?
14. What is the difference between internal and external forces that affect an e-business? How do they change the way an e-business operates?

Discussion Questions

1. Do managers really need all the kinds of information discussed in this chapter? If not, which kinds can they do without?
2. How can confidential data and information (such as the wages of individual employees) be kept confidential and yet still be available to managers who need them?
3. Why are computers so well suited to management information systems (MISs)? What are some things computers *cannot* do in dealing with data and information?
4. How could the Internet help you to find information about employment opportunities at Coca-Cola, Johnson & Johnson, or Microsoft? Describe the process you would use to access this information.
5. Can advertising provide enough revenue for an e-business to succeed in the long run?
6. Is outsourcing good for an e-business firm? The firm's employees? Explain your answer.
7. What distinguishes a B2B from a B2C e-business model?

Video Case 16.1

Travelocity Takes e-Business a Long Way

One of the original online travel agency sites, Travelocity, has been bookmarked by millions of people seeking low prices on airline tickets, hotel rooms, cruises, and rental cars. The site books $10 billion worth of travel annually to destinations near and far. Customers can search for flights on six major carriers, read descriptions before reserving at one of 20,000 participating hotels, compare car-rental prices, and click to browse and buy specially priced travel packages.

Travelocity began its e-business life as a site for finding the lowest airfares. However, its chief marketing officer notes that the company actually makes its money on hotel rooms and travel packages, not on airline tickets. This is why the site goes beyond emphasizing price to feature vacation packages and hotel choices more prominently—a change that has increased sales of these lucrative offerings dramatically.

Intense competition from Expedia and other online rivals has prompted Travelocity to find new ways of differentiating itself and keeping customers loyal. According to the CEO, the company is particularly interested in creating "an emotional connection with customers, one that builds more trust and bookings." Instead of focusing solely on low prices, Travelocity has invested $80 million in its "Roaming Gnome" ad campaign. The colorful garden gnome attracts attention and brings both personality and humor to the message that Travelocity stands for the whole travel experience, not just low prices.

In addition, the site has posted a "Customer Bill of Rights" guaranteeing customers that "everything about your booking will be right, or we'll work with our partners to make it right and right away." Although many e-businesses offer customer service by live chat, e-mail, and FAQ (frequently asked questions) pages, Travelocity encourages customers to call if something goes wrong with their travel arrangements so that company representatives can fix the problem. The CEO observes that customers whose problems are resolved satisfactorily have a 90 percent return rate, compared with an 80 percent rate for customers who have a good experience.

Not long ago, Travelocity had the opportunity to put the spotlight on its guarantee when it posted a super-low airfare for flights to Fiji. The rock-bottom price was supposed to apply to companion tickets only, but because the fare was posted in error, travelers were unsure initially whether Travelocity really would issue the tickets. The company decided to honor the fare, despite the mistake, to prove its commitment to taking care of customers. This brought a lot of positive media coverage, further enhancing Travelocity's reputation.

The company recently redesigned its website so that customers can find exactly what they want and have more tools for planning all aspects of a trip. For example, customers can buy tickets to city tours, price travel insurance, buy gift certificates, check flight status, read about different destinations, and read what travelers have to say about the hotels.

Before making major changes to the site, Travelocity conducts usability testing to see how customers react to new features and to uncover problems customers might encounter when trying to buy. For example, the company learned that many people forgot their passwords and clicked away at the last minute because they needed the password to complete a purchase. To solve this problem, Travelocity removed the requirement and allowed customers to buy without inputting a password. Sales soared by 10 percent almost overnight, increasing revenue by millions of dollars.

Travelocity operates a number of other travel sites, including **lastminute.com.** The company has been branching out into corporate travel services and specialized travel sites for international markets. It also provides travel services for the members of retirement and community organizations. Where in the world will Travelocity's Roaming Gnome turn up next?[9]

For more information about this company, go to **www.travelocity.com.**

Questions

1. Each year, Travelocity helps millions of customers find low prices on airline tickets, hotel rooms, cruises, and rental cars by providing a website that is easy to use. What type of business model is Travelocity using? Support your answer.
2. Today, competition between Internet travel firms such as Travelocity, Expedia, and other online travel agencies has never been greater. What steps has Travelocity taken to retain its market share and increase revenues and profits?
3. Why would Travelocity publicize the availability of telephone customer service when higher call volume raises the company's costs?

Case 16.2 eBags Does It All

More than 500 luggage stores in the United States closed in the travel slump that began September 11, 2001. eBags, the online luggage and handbag retailer, was just a few years old at the time, and a few thousand dollars away from turning its first profit. But like many other firms, it immediately set up a way for customers to donate money in the wake of the terrorist attacks, collecting almost a quarter of a million dollars.

"We were about four days into it," however, says cofounder and current CEO Jon Nordmark, "when we realized 'Oh my God, we're not getting any orders,'" As fellow cofounder and senior vice president Peter Cobb describes the situation, the fall-off in travel, and therefore in luggage sales, combined with the recent dot-com bust to spell bad news for the firm. "We were really just in a foxhole waiting for nuclear winter to end."

The company moved fast, however, expanding its product offerings to "day" bags—briefcases, backpacks, purses, laptop bags, and so on—and relying on its policy of drop shipping (ordering from suppliers only when customers ordered from eBags, and letting suppliers ship to customers) to avoid holding a big inventory of unsold products. Thanks to quick action and good business planning, eBags did turn a profit that year and never looked back.

Today, it is a $100 million company with about 200 employees and has sold over 7 million bags since its founding. As the biggest online retailer of luggage and bags of all kinds and a leader in the use of Internet technology, it offers about 36,000 different products from 520 brands. Inspired by its fund-raising success after 9/11, the company also continues its commitment to the community, giving more than $500,000 to breast cancer research and donating thousands of bags and packs to foster children around the United States.

Hallmarks of eBags' award-winning website are multiple photos of each product, full-color images in every available color instead of mere swatches, and homemade videos starring employees who seek out and interview up-and-coming New York and Los Angeles designers to showcase their products on the site. Google Maps help shoppers locate other new designers around the country. Specialized search tools locate specific products, like airline-approved carry-ons. Unlimited customer reviews—as many as 4,000 for one popular product and more than 1.5 million overall—encourage customers to rate products and read others' comments. Visitors can even post their own videos. "What we're really saying is, 'It's your whiteboard,'" says Cobb.

The company developed most of these interactive software applications in-house. They're costly to maintain, requiring a staff of forty people and a budget of about $10 million. But eBags believes they contribute directly to sales, which doubled in one recent year and continue to grow. "It is important for us to have unlimited customer reviews, so we do it ourselves," says Cobb. "An outside vendor might limit you to 100 customer reviews. . . . [W]hen you go outside, you tend to be forced to cut corners on innovation—you have to dilute the customer experience to be like everyone else."[10]

For more information about this company, go to **www.ebags.com.**

Questions

1. What are some of the reasons eBags has grown to be so successful?
2. What information do you think a company like eBags collects from its website, and how does it use these data?
3. eBags was one of the first online stores to allow customer reviews on its website, and it recently announced plans to sell the technology it developed to selected other retailers like Case Logic, which makes camera and laptop bags. How else do you think a firm like eBags can continue to grow online in the future?

Building Skills for Career Success

1. JOURNALING FOR SUCCESS

Today, more and more people use the Internet to purchase products or services. And yet, many people are reluctant to make online purchases because of identity and privacy issues. Still others are "afraid" of the technology.

Assignment

1. Have you ever used the Internet to purchase a product or service? If you answered yes, why did you purchase online as compared with purchasing the same product or service in a traditional retail store?
2. In your own words, describe whether the online shopping experience was a pleasant one. What factors contributed to your level of satisfaction or dissatisfaction?
3. If you answered no, describe why you prefer to shop in a traditional retail store as compared with shopping on the Web.

2. EXPLORING THE INTERNET

Computer technology is a fast-paced, highly competitive industry in which product life cycles sometimes are measured in months or even weeks. To keep up with changes and trends in hardware and software, MIS managers routinely must scan computer publications and websites that discuss new products.

A major topic of interest among MIS managers is groupware, software that facilitates the management of large projects among geographically dispersed employees, as well as group activities such as problem solving and brainstorming.

Assignment

1. Use a search engine and enter the keyword "groupware" to locate companies that provide this type of software. Try the demonstration edition of the groupware if it is available.
2. Based on your research of this business application, why do you think groupware is growing in popularity?
3. Describe the structure of one of the groupware programs you examined as well as your impressions of its value to users.

3. DEVELOPING CRITICAL-THINKING SKILLS

To stay competitive in the marketplace, businesses must process data into information and make sure that information is readily available to decision makers. For this, many businesses rely on a management information system (MIS). The purpose of an MIS is to provide managers with accurate, complete, and timely information so that they can perform their jobs as effectively as possible. Because an MIS must fit the needs of the firm it serves, these systems vary in the way they collect, store, update, and process data and present information to users.

Assignment

1. Select a local company large enough to have an MIS. Set up an interview with the person responsible for managing the flow of information within the company.
2. Prepare a list of questions you will ask during the interview. Structure the questions around the five basic functions of an MIS. Some sample questions follow:
    a. *Collecting data*. What types of data are needed? How often are data collected? What sources produce the data? How do you ensure that the data are accurate?
    b. *Storing data*. How are data stored?
    c. *Updating data*. What is the process for updating?
    d. *Processing data*. Can you show me some examples of the types of data that will be processed into information? How is the processing done?
    e. *Presenting information*. Would you show me some examples (reports, tables, graphs, charts) of how the information is presented to various decision makers and tell me why that particular format is used?
3. At the end of the interview, ask the interviewee to predict how the system will change in the next three years.
4. In a report, describe what you believe the strengths and weaknesses of this firm's MIS are. Also describe the most important thing you learned from the interview.

4. BUILDING TEAM SKILLS

An interesting approach taken by Yahoo.com and several other websites is to provide viewers with the tools needed to create a personal Web page or community. Yahoo's GeoCities site (**http://geocities.yahoo.com**) provides simple instructions for creating a site and posting your own content, such as articles and photographs.

Assignment

1. Working in a group, examine some of the GeoCities communities and personal Web pages. Discuss which sites you think work well and which do not. Explain your reasoning.
2. Develop an idea for your own website. Draw a sketch of how you would like the site to appear on the Internet. You may use ideas that look good on other personal pages.
3. Who is your target audience, and why do you think they will want to visit the site?

5. RESEARCHING DIFFERENT CAREERS

Firms today expect employees to be proficient in using computers and computer software. Typical business applications include e-mail, word processing, spreadsheets, and graphics. By improving your skills in these areas, you can increase your chances not only of being employed but also of being promoted once you are employed.

Assignment

1. Assess your computer skills by placing a check in the appropriate column in the following table:

	Skill Level			
Software	**None**	**Low**	**Average**	**High**
e-mail				
Word processing				
Desktop publishing				
Accounting				
Database management				
Graphics				
Spreadsheet				
Groupware				

2. Describe your self-assessment in a written report. Specify the software programs in which you need to become more proficient, and outline a plan for doing this.

17 Using Accounting Information

LEARNING OBJECTIVES

What you will be able to do once you complete this chapter:

1. Explain why accurate accounting information and audited financial statements are important.
2. Identify the people who use accounting information and possible careers in the accounting industry.
3. Discuss the accounting process.
4. Read and interpret a balance sheet.
5. Read and interpret an income statement.
6. Describe business activities that affect a firm's cash flow.
7. Summarize how managers evaluate the financial health of a business.

Photographers Choice/Getty Images RF

inside business

"Without confidence in financial statements, there is little investment, and without investment, there is no growth."

What the Big Accounting Firms Count

Peek behind the scenes at the Oscar, Grammy, and Emmy awards, and you'll see three of the "Big Four" U.S. accounting firms at work, keeping track of ballots and keeping the results confidential until the awards are presented. PricewaterhouseCoopers handles Oscar voting for the Academy of Motion Picture Arts and Sciences. Ernst & Young tallies Emmy votes for the Academy of Television Arts and Sciences. And Deloitte Touche Tohmatsu counts Grammy votes for the Recording Academy. KPMG is the fourth of the "Big Four;" the next-largest accounting firms are Grant Thornton and BDO Seidman.

Although counting and safeguarding ballots puts these firms in the spotlight—sometimes literally, during a televised awards ceremony—it's only a sideline for these giants of the accounting industry. Their main business is providing a wide range of accounting and tax services for many of America's businesses. Public companies need outside experts to double-check their internal accounting procedures, review financial records, prepare tax filings, and sign off on annual reports.

The big accounting firms also help companies dig deeper into financial opportunities and threats. If an acquisition is in the works, the acquirer can ask its accounting firm for a helping hand in evaluating the financial situation of the company to be acquired. Global companies seek advice from the big accounting firms on how to comply with regulatory guidelines, both domestic and international. And if executives suspect theft or fraud, they can hire accounting professionals to investigate, pinpoint any problems, and suggest stronger controls and reporting to avoid future trouble.

In addition, the major accounting firms offer consulting services to help companies make the most of their resources. From personnel planning to technical training, strategic solutions to operational options, the firms have specialists on staff to counsel corporate management on decisions large and small. Especially in troubled economic times, companies appreciate being able to count on their accounting firms.[1]

"Without confidence in financial statements, there is little investment, and without investment, there is no growth."[2] The above statement was made by James Turley, the chairman and CEO of Ernst & Young—one of the four largest accounting firms in the world. His statement says a lot about the importance of accounting information. Without accounting information, managers can't make decisions, investors can't evaluate potential investments, and lenders and suppliers can't extend credit to a business firm. Simply put, without accounting information a business firm cannot operate in a very competitive world. And while accurate accounting information has always been important, it is even more important now in the wake of the recent accounting scandals and the financial crisis in the banking and financial industries.

We begin this chapter by looking at why accounting information is important, the recent problems in the accounting industry, and attempts to improve financial reporting. Then we look at how managers, employees, individuals, and groups outside a firm use accounting information. We also identify different types of accountants and career opportunities in the accounting industry. Next, we focus on the accounting process and the basics of an accounting system. We also examine the three most important financial statements: the balance sheet, the income statement, and the statement of cash flows. Finally, we show how ratios are used to measure specific aspects of a firm's financial health.

Why Accounting Information Is Important

1

Learning Objective: Explain why accurate accounting information and audited financial statements are important.

accounting the process of systematically collecting, analyzing, and reporting financial information

Accounting is the process of systematically collecting, analyzing, and reporting financial information. Today, it is impossible to manage a business without accurate and up-to-date information supplied by the firm's accountants. Just for a moment, think about the following three questions:

1. How much profit did a business earn last year?
2. How much tax does a business owe the Internal Revenue Service?
3. How much cash does a business have on hand?

In each case, the firm's accountants and its accounting system provide the answers to these questions and many others. And while accounting information can be used to answer questions about what has happened in the past, it also can be used to help make decisions about the future. For these reasons, accounting is one of the most important areas within a business organization.

Because the information provided by a firm's accountants and its accounting system is so important, managers and other groups interested in a business firm's financial records must be able to "trust the numbers." Unfortunately, a large number of accounting scandals have caused people to doubt not only the numbers but also the accounting industry.

Recent Accounting Problems for Corporations and Their Auditors

Which of the following firms has been convicted or accused of accounting fraud?

a. Enron
b. WorldCom
c. Fannie Mae
d. Freddie Mac
e. All of the above

Unfortunately, the answer to the question is e—all of the above. While you may not recognize all of the companies included in the above question, each company is a major U.S. business that has been plagued by accounting problems. These problems led to Enron's bankruptcy, prison time for Bernard Ebbers, the CEO of WorldCom, and a massive federal bailout for mortgage giants Fannie Mae and Freddie Mac. The accounting problems at these companies—and similar problems at even more companies—have forced many investors, lenders and suppliers, and government regulators to question the motives behind fraudulent and unethical accounting practices.

Today, much of the pressure on corporate executives to "cook" the books is driven by the desire to look good to Wall Street analysts and investors. Every three months companies report their revenues, expenses, profits, and projections for the future. If a company meets or exceeds "the street's" expectations, everything is usually fine. However, if a company reports financial numbers that are lower than expected, the company's stock value can drop dramatically. An earnings report that is lower by even a few pennies per share than what is expected can cause a company's stock value to drop immediately by as much as 30 to 40 percent or more. Greed—especially when salary and bonuses are tied to a company's stock value—is another factor that can lead some corporate executives to use questionable accounting methods to inflate a firm's financial performance.

In a perfect world, the accountants who inspect the corporate books would catch mistakes and disclose questionable accounting practices. Unfortunately, we do not live in a perfect world. Consider the part that auditors for the accounting firm Arthur Andersen played in the Enron meltdown. When the Securities and Exchange Commission (SEC) launched its inquiry into Enron's financial affairs, Andersen employees shredded the documents related to the audit. As a result, both the SEC and the Department of Justice began to investigate Andersen's role in the failure of

Meet Luis Garcia—a victim of predatory lending. *Some companies use questionable, high-pressure techniques to increase both sales revenues and profits. According to the California attorney general, home lender, Lifetime Financial, pushed Mr. Garcia, a 75-year-old disabled senior citizen from Peru, into an illegal and unconscionable loan.*

AP Photo/Damian Dovarganes

Enron. Eventually, Andersen was convicted of obstruction of justice and was forced to cease auditing public companies. Simply put, Andersen—the once-proud accounting firm—was found guilty.[3] Note: On May 31, 2005, the U.S. Supreme Court overturned the Andersen conviction. In theory, Andersen could resume its accounting and audit operations. However, as of 2008, Arthur Andersen had not returned as a viable business even on a limited scale.[4] It seems that no company wanted the Andersen name on its audit work because of the accounting firm's tarnished reputation. The consequences for Enron were just as devastating. Less than a month after admitting accounting errors that inflated earnings by almost $600 million since 1994, Enron filed for bankruptcy.[5]

Unfortunately, the ones hurt when companies (and their accountants) report inaccurate or misleading accounting information often are not always the high-paid corporate executives. In many cases, it's the employees who lose their jobs and often the money they invested in the company's retirement program and investors, lenders, and suppliers who relied on fraudulent accounting information in order to make a decision to invest in or lend money to the company.

In an indirect way, the recent accounting scandals underscore how important accurate accounting information is for a corporation. To see how the auditing process can improve accounting information, read the next section.

Why Audited Financial Statements Are Important

Assume that you are a bank officer responsible for evaluating loan applications. How do you make a decision to approve or reject a loan request? In this situation, most bank officers rely on the information contained in the firm's balance sheet, income statement, and statement of cash flows, along with other information provided by the prospective borrower. In fact, most lenders insist that these financial statements be audited by a certified public accountant (CPA). An **audit** is an examination of a company's financial statements and the accounting practices that produced them. The purpose of an audit is to make sure that a firm's financial statements have been prepared in accordance with generally accepted accounting

audit an examination of a company's financial statements and the accounting practices that produced them

principles. Today, **generally accepted accounting principles (GAAPs)** have been developed to provide an accepted set of guidelines and practices for companies reporting financial information and the accounting profession. Today, three organizations—the Financial Accounting Standards Board (FASB), the American Institute of Certified Public Accountants (AICPA), and the International Accounting Standards Board (IASB)—have greatly influenced the methods used by the accounting profession.

generally accepted accounting principles (GAAPs) an accepted set of guidelines and practices for companies reporting financial information and for the accounting profession

If an accountant determines that a firm's financial statements present financial information fairly and conform to GAAPs, then he or she will issue the following statement:

> *In our opinion, the financial statements . . . present fairly, in all material respects . . . in conformity with generally accepted accounting principles.*

While an audit and the resulting report do not *guarantee* that a company has not "cooked" the books, it does imply that, on the whole, the company has followed GAAPs. Bankers, creditors, investors, and government agencies are willing to rely on an auditor's opinion because of the historically ethical reputation and independence of auditors and accounting firms. Even with the recent scandals involving corporations and their accountants that falsified or misled the general public, most of the nation's accountants still abide by the rules. And while it is easy to indict an entire profession because of the actions of a few, there are many more accountants who adhere to the rules and are honest, hard-working professionals. Finally, it should be noted that without the audit function and GAAPs, there would be very little oversight or supervision. The validity of a firm's financial statements and its accounting records would drop quickly, and firms would find it difficult to obtain debt financing, acquire goods and services from suppliers, find investor financing, or prepare documents requested by government agencies.

Reform: The Sarbanes-Oxley Act of 2002

According to John Bogle, founder of Vanguard Mutual Funds, "Investing is an act of faith. Without that faith—that reported numbers reflect reality, that companies are being run honestly, that Wall Street is playing it straight, and that investors aren't being hoodwinked—our capital markets simply can't function."[6] In reality, what Mr. Bogle says is true. To help ensure that corporate financial information is accurate and in response to the many accounting scandals that surfaced in the last part of the 1990s and the first part of the twenty-first century, Congress enacted the Sarbanes-Oxley Act. Key components include the following:

- The SEC is required to establish a full-time five-member federal oversight board that will police the accounting industry.
- Chief executive and financial officers are required to certify periodic financial reports and are subject to criminal penalties for violations of securities reporting requirements.
- Accounting firms are prohibited from providing many types of nonaudit and consulting services to the companies they audit.
- Auditors must maintain financial documents and audit work papers for five years.
- Auditors, accountants, and employees can be imprisoned for up to twenty years for destroying financial documents and willful violations of the securities laws.
- A public corporation must change its lead auditing firm every five years.
- There is added protection for whistle-blowers who report violations of the Sarbanes-Oxley Act.

While most people welcome the Sarbanes-Oxley Act, complex rules make compliance more expensive and time consuming for corporate management and more difficult for accounting firms. And yet, most people agree that the cost of compliance is justified. As you read the next section, you will see just how important accurate accounting information is.

Who Uses Accounting Information

2

Learning Objective: Identify people who use accounting information and possible careers in the accounting industry.

Managers and employees, lenders, suppliers, stockholders, and government agencies all rely on the information contained in three financial statements, each no more than one page in length. These three reports—the balance sheet, the income statement, and the statement of cash flows—are concise summaries of a firm's activities during a specific time period. Together they represent the results of perhaps tens of thousands of transactions that have occurred during the accounting period. Moreover, the form of the financial statements is pretty much the same for all businesses, from a neighborhood video store or small dry cleaner to giant conglomerates such as Home Depot, Boeing, and Bank of America. This information has a variety of uses both within the firm and outside it. However, first and foremost, accounting information is management information.

The People Who Use Accounting Information

The primary users of accounting information are *managers*. The firm's accounting system provides information that can be compiled for the entire firm—for each product; for each sales territory, store, or salesperson; for each division or department; and generally in any way that will help those who manage the organization. At a company such as Kraft Foods, for example, financial information is gathered for all its hundreds of food products: Maxwell House Coffee, A1 Steak Sauce, Chips Ahoy Cookies, Jell-O Desserts, Kool Aid, and so on. The president of the company would be interested in total sales for all these products. The vice president for marketing would be interested in national sales for Maxwell House Coffee and Jell-O Desserts. The northeastern sales manager might want to look at sales figures for Kool Aid in New England. For a large, complex organization like Kraft, the accounting system must enable managers to get the information they need.

Does this man have enough money to buy Girl Scout cookies? *You bet! Although there are many reasons why Warren Buffett, chairman of the board of Berkshire Hathaway, has become one of the richest people in the world, his ability to understand accounting information has enabled him to identify investments that are extremely profitable.*

AP Photo/Nati Harnik

Much of this accounting information is *proprietary;* it is not divulged to anyone outside the firm. This type of information is used by a firm's managers and employees to plan and set goals, organize, lead, motivate, and control—all the management functions that were described in Chapter 6.

To see how important accounting is, just think about what happens when an employee or a manager asks a supervisor for a new piece of equipment or a salary increase. Immediately, everyone involved in the decision begins discussing how much it will cost and what effect it will have on the firm's profits, sales, and expenses. It is the firm's accounting system that provides the answers to these important questions. In addition to proprietary information used inside the firm, certain financial information must be supplied to individuals and organizations outside the firm (see Table 17.1).

- *Lenders* require information contained in the firm's financial statements before they will commit themselves to either short- or long-term loans. *Suppliers* who provide the raw materials, component parts, or finished goods a firm needs also generally ask for financial information before they will extend credit to a firm.
- *Stockholders and potential investors* are concerned not only about a company's current financial health but also about the financial risk associated with an investment in its stock.
- *Government agencies* require a variety of information about the firm's tax liabilities, payroll deductions for employees, and new issues of stocks and bonds.

An important function of accountants is to ensure that such information is accurate and thorough enough to satisfy these outside groups.

Different Types of Accounting

While many people think that all accountants do the same tasks, there are special areas of expertise within the accounting industry. In fact, accounting usually is broken down into two broad categories: managerial and financial.

Managerial accounting provides managers and employees with the information needed to make decisions about a firm's financing, investing, and operating activities. By using managerial accounting information, both managers and employees can evaluate how well they have done in the past and what they can expect in the future. **Financial accounting**, on the other hand, generates financial statements and reports for interested people outside of an organization. Typically, stockholders, financial analysts, bankers, lenders, suppliers, government agencies, and other interested groups use the information provided by financial accounting to determine how well a business firm has achieved its goals. In addition to managerial and financial accounting, additional special areas of accounting include the following:

- *Cost accounting*—determining the cost of producing specific products or services.
- *Tax accounting*—planning tax strategy and preparing tax returns for firms or individuals.
- *Government accounting*—providing basic accounting services to ensure that tax revenues are collected and used to meet the goals of state, local, and federal agencies.
- *Not-for-profit accounting*—helping not-for-profit organizations to account for all donations and expenditures.

Ethics Matters

Investigating Forensic Accounting

Here's a clue: If forensic accounting sounds like something out of an episode of *CSI*, that's because it's all about collecting accounting evidence that can be used in court. Forensic accountants are trained to detect signs of theft and fraud, trace missing money, and reconstruct accounting details that have been changed or erased. When they investigate, some bring gloves and tweezers to handle documents, a camera to record the crime scene, and evidence tape to secure what they find. If cases go to trial, forensic accountants may testify as expert witnesses.

One reason to call in a forensic accountant is when a company suspects embezzlement. For example, an accountant auditing a Connecticut firm noticed a $1,169 payment for kitchen supplies. Examining the check, he realized that the original amount was $69—two digits had been added to raise the amount. A forensic accountant determined that the bookkeeper had embezzled $250,000 by adding digits to dozens of checks over the years. The company's owner fired the bookkeeper but, fearing bad publicity, didn't press charges.

Some companies hire forensic accountants to help with insurance claims by projecting revenues and profits lost due to fire or natural disaster. Harrah's Entertainment did this in the aftermath of Hurricane Katrina, for instance. And in good times, forensic accountants can recommend strict accounting controls and procedures to prevent fraud and other problems.

Sources: Gina Bliss, "Forensic Accounting Is a Useful But Varied Field," *Daily Record (Rochester, NY)*, September 26, 2008, n.p.; Judy Greenwald, "Forensic Accountants Mind the Knowledge Gap," *Business Insurance*, August 4, 2008, p. 9; Bernadette Starzee, "How to . . . Choose a Forensic Accounting Firm," *Long Island Business News*, February 8, 2008, n.p.; Janice Podsada, "The CPA Goes CSI," *Hartford Courant*, October 7, 2007, p. D1.

managerial accounting provides managers and employees with the information needed to make decisions about a firm's financing, investing, and operating activities

financial accounting generates financial statements and reports for interested people outside an organization

Careers in Accounting

Wanted: An individual with at least two years of college accounting courses. Must be honest, dependable, and willing to complete all routine accounting activities for a manufacturing business. Salary dependent on experience.

Want a job? Positions such as the one described in this newspaper advertisement increasingly are becoming available to those with the required training.

Table 17.1: Users of Accounting Information

The primary users of accounting information are a company's managers, but individuals and organizations outside the company also require information on its finances.

Management	Lenders and Suppliers	Stockholders and Potential Investors	Government Agencies
Plan and set goals Organize Lead and motivate Control	Evaluate credit risks before committing to short- or long-term financing	Evaluate the financial health of the firm before purchasing stocks or bonds	Confirm tax liabilities Confirm payroll deductions Approve new issues of stocks and bonds

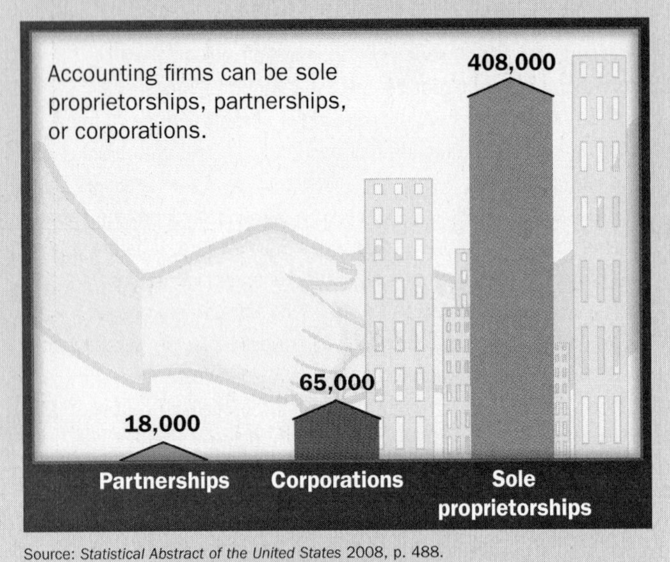

Source: *Statistical Abstract of the United States* 2008, p. 488.

According to the *Occupational Outlook Handbook,* published by the Department of Labor, job opportunities for accountants and auditors in the accounting area are expected to experience strong growth between now and the year 2016.[7]

Many people have the idea that accountants spend their day working with endless columns of numbers in a small office locked away from other people. In fact, accountants do spend a lot of time at their desks, but their job entails far more than just adding or subtracting numbers. Accountants are expected to share their ideas and the information they possess with people who need the information. Accounting can be an exciting and rewarding career—one that offers higher-than-average starting salaries. To be successful in the accounting industry, employees must

- Be responsible, honest, and ethical.
- Have a strong background in financial management.
- Know how to use a computer and software to process data into accounting information.
- Be able to communicate with people who need accounting information.

Today, accountants generally are classified as either private accountants or public accountants. A *private accountant* is employed by a specific organization. A medium-sized or large firm may employ one or more private accountants to design its accounting information system, manage its accounting department, and provide managers with advice and assistance.

Individuals, self-employed business owners, and smaller firms that do not require their own full-time accountants can hire the services of public accountants. A *public accountant* works on a fee basis for clients and may be self-employed or be the employee of an accounting firm. Accounting firms range in size from one-person operations to huge international firms with hundreds of accounting partners and thousands of employees. Today, the largest accounting firms, sometimes referred to as the "Big Four," are PricewaterhouseCoopers, Ernst & Young, KPMG, and Deloitte Touche Tohmatsu.

certified public accountant (CPA) an individual who has met state requirements for accounting education and experience and has passed a rigorous accounting examination prepared by the AICPA

Typically, public accounting firms include on their staffs at least one **certified public accountant (CPA)**, an individual who has met state requirements for accounting education and experience and has passed a rigorous accounting examination prepared by the AICPA. The AICPA uniform CPA examination covers four areas: (1) regulation, taxation, business law, and professional responsibilities, (2) auditing, (3) business environment and concepts, and (4) financial accounting and reporting. More information about general requirements and the CPA profession can be obtained by contacting the AICPA at **www.aicpa.org.**[8] State requirements usually include a college degree or a specified number of hours of college coursework and generally from one to three years of on-the-job experience. Details regarding specific state requirements for practice as a CPA can be obtained by contacting the state's board of accountancy.

Once an individual becomes a CPA, he or she must participate in continuing-education programs to maintain state certification. These specialized programs are designed to provide the current training needed in today's changing business environment.

Certification as a CPA brings both status and responsibility. Only an independent CPA can audit the financial statements contained in a corporation's annual report and express an opinion—as required by law—regarding the acceptability of the corporation's accounting practices. In addition to auditing a corporation's financial statements, typical services performed by CPAs include planning and preparing tax returns, determining the true cost of producing and marketing a firm's goods or services, and compiling the financial information needed to make major management decisions. Fees for the services provided by CPAs generally range from $50 to $300 an hour.

In addition to certified public accountants, there are also certified management accountants. A **certified management accountant (CMA)** is an accountant who has met the requirements for education and experience, passed a rigorous exam, and is certified by the Institute of Management Accountants. The CMA exam is designed to develop and measure not only accounting skills but also decision-making and critical-thinking skills. For more information about the CMA exam, visit the Institute of Management Accountants website at **www.imanet.org.** While both CPAs and CMAs can work for the public, a CMA is more likely to work within a large organization. Also, both types of accountants are excellent career choices.

certified management accountant (CMA) an accountant who has met the requirements for education and experience, passed a rigorous exam, and is certified by the Institute of Management Accountants

assets the resources that a business owns

liabilities a firm's debts and obligations

owners' equity the difference between a firm's assets and its liabilities

The Accounting Process

3

Learning Objective: Discuss the accounting process.

In Chapter 16, *information* was defined as data presented in a form that is useful for a specific purpose. In this section, we examine accounting as the system for transforming raw financial *data* into useful financial *information*. Then, in the next sections we describe the three most important financial statements provided by the accounting process.

accounting equation the basis for the accounting process: *assets = liabilities + owners' equity*

double-entry bookkeeping system a system in which each financial transaction is recorded as two separate accounting entries to maintain the balance shown in the accounting equation

The Accounting Equation

The accounting equation is a simple statement that forms the basis for the accounting process. This important equation shows the relationship between a firm's assets, liabilities, and owners' equity.

- **Assets** are the resources a business owns—cash, inventory, equipment, and real estate.
- **Liabilities** are the firm's debts—what it owes to others.
- **Owners' equity** is the difference between total assets and total liabilities—what would be left for the owners if the firm's assets were sold and the money used to pay off its liabilities.

The relationship between assets, liabilities, and owners' equity is shown by the following **accounting equation**:

Assets = liabilities + owners' equity

Whether a business is a small corner grocery store or a giant corporation such as General Mills, its assets must equal the sum of its liabilities and owners' equity. To use this equation, a firm's accountants must record raw data—that is, the firm's day-to-day financial transactions—using the double-entry system of bookkeeping. The **double-entry bookkeeping system** is a system in which each financial transaction is recorded as two separate accounting entries to maintain the balance shown in the accounting equation. With the double-entry system, an accountant can use the steps in the accounting cycle to generate accounting information and financial statements.

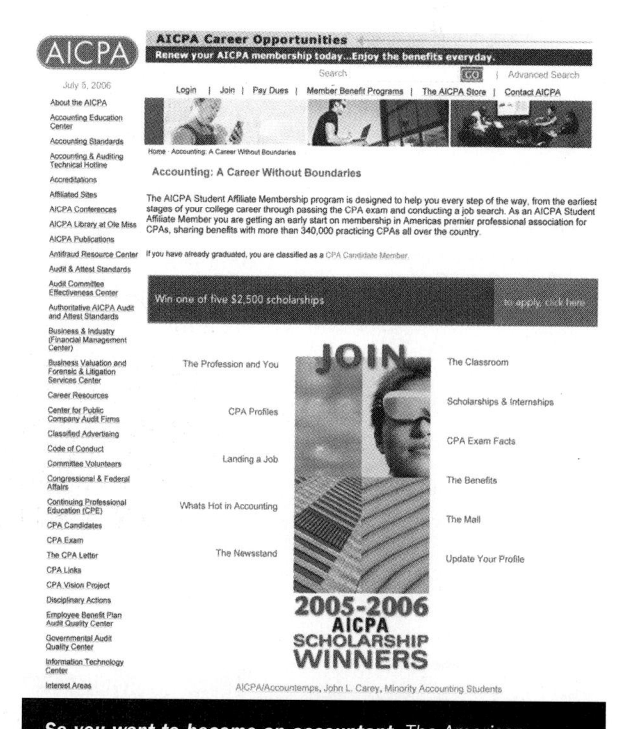

So you want to become an accountant. *The American Institute of Certified Public Accountants (AICPA) provides valuable career information about the accounting profession as well as information about the AICPA certified public accountant exam on its website at www.aicpa.org.*

Courtesy AICPA

The Accounting Cycle

In the typical accounting system, raw data are transformed into financial statements in five steps. The first three—analyzing, recording, and posting—are performed on a regular basis throughout the accounting period. The last two—preparation of the trial balance and preparation of the financial statements and closing the books—are performed at the end of the accounting period.

Analyzing Source Documents Basic accounting data are contained in *source documents,* the receipts, invoices, sales slips, and other documents that show the dollar amounts of day-to-day business transactions. The accounting cycle begins with the analysis of each of these documents. The purpose of the analysis is to determine which accounts are affected by the documents and how they are affected.

Recording Transactions Every financial transaction then is recorded in a journal—a process called *journalizing*. Transactions must be recorded in the firm's general journal or in specialized journals. The *general journal* is a book of original entry in which typical transactions are recorded in order of their occurrence. An accounting system also may include *specialized journals* for specific types of transactions that occur frequently. Thus, a retail store might have journals for cash receipts, cash disbursements, purchases, and sales in addition to its general journal.

Posting Transactions After the information is recorded in the general journal and specialized journals, it is transferred to the general ledger. The *general ledger* is a book of accounts containing a separate sheet or section for each account. Today, most businesses use a computer and software to record accounting entries in the general journal or specialized journals and then to post journal entries to the general ledger.

trial balance a summary of the balances of all general ledger accounts at the end of the accounting period

Preparing the Trial Balance A **trial balance** is a summary of the balances of all general ledger accounts at the end of the accounting period. To prepare a trial balance, the accountant determines and lists the balances for all ledger accounts. If the trial balance totals are correct and the accounting equation is still in balance, the accountant can prepare the financial statements. If not, a mistake has occurred somewhere, and the accountant must find it and correct it before proceeding.

annual report a report distributed to stockholders and other interested parties that describes a firm's operating activities and its financial condition

Preparing Financial Statements and Closing the Books The firm's financial statements are prepared from the information contained in the trial balance. This information is presented in a standardized format to make the statements as accessible as possible to the various people who may be interested in the firm's financial affairs—managers, employees, lenders, suppliers, stockholders, potential investors, and government agencies. A firm's financial statements are prepared at least once a year and included in the firm's annual report. An **annual report** is a report distributed to stockholders and other interested parties that describes a firm's operating activities and its financial condition. Most firms also have financial statements prepared semiannually, quarterly, or monthly.

Once these statements have been prepared and checked, the firm's books are "closed" for the accounting period, and a *postclosing* trial balance is prepared. Although, like the trial balance just described, the postclosing trial balance generally is prepared after *all* accounting work is completed for one accounting period. If the postclosing trial balance totals agree, the accounting equation is still in balance at the end of the cycle. Only then can a new accounting cycle begin for the next accounting period.

With this brief information about the steps of the accounting cycle in mind, let's now examine the three most important financial statements generated by the accounting process: the balance sheet, the income statement, and the statement of cash flows.

The Balance Sheet

4 **Learning Objective:** Read and interpret a balance sheet.

Question: *Where could you find the total amount of assets, liabilities, and owners' equity for Hershey Foods Corporation?*

Answer: The firm's balance sheet.

A **balance sheet** (sometimes referred to as a **statement of financial position**) is a summary of the dollar amounts of a firm's assets, liabilities, and owners' equity accounts at the end of a specific accounting period. The balance sheet must demonstrate that assets are equal to liabilities plus owners' equity. Most people think of a balance sheet as a statement that reports the financial condition of a business firm such as Hershey Foods Corporation, but balance sheets apply to individuals, too. For example, Marty Campbell graduated from college three years ago and obtained a position as a sales representative for an office supply firm. After going to work, he established a checking and savings account and purchased an automobile, stereo, television, and a few pieces of furniture. Marty paid cash for some purchases, but he had to borrow money to pay for the larger ones. Figure 17.1 shows Marty's current personal balance sheet.

balance sheet (or statement of financial position) a summary of the dollar amounts of a firm's assets, liabilities, and owners' equity accounts at the end of a specific accounting period

Marty Campbell's assets total $26,500, and his liabilities amount to $10,000. While the difference between total assets and total liabilities is referred to as *owners' equity* or *stockholders' equity* for a business, it is normally called *net worth* for an individual. As reported on Marty's personal balance sheet, net worth is $16,500. The total assets ($26,500) and the total liabilities *plus* net worth ($26,500) are equal.

Figure 17.2 shows the balance sheet for Northeast Art Supply, a small corporation that sells picture frames, paints, canvases, and other artists' supplies to retailers in New England. Note that assets are reported at the top of the statement, followed by liabilities and stockholders' equity. Let's work through the different accounts in Figure 17.2 from top to bottom.

Assets

On a balance sheet, assets are listed in order from the *most liquid* to the *least liquid.* The **liquidity** of an asset is the ease with which it can be converted into cash.

liquidity the ease with which an asset can be converted into cash

current assets assets that can be converted quickly into cash or that will be used in one year or less

Current Assets

Current assets are assets that can be converted quickly into cash or that will be used in one year or less. Because cash is the most liquid asset, it

Figure 17.1: Personal Balance Sheet

Often individuals determine their net worth, or owner's equity, by subtracting the value of their debts from the value of their assets.

Marty Campbell
Personal Balance Sheet
December 31, 20XX

ASSETS		
Cash	$ 2,500	
Savings account	5,000	
Automobile	15,000	
Stereo	1,000	
Television	500	
Furniture	2,500	
TOTAL ASSETS		$26,500
LIABILITIES		
Automobile loan	$ 9,500	
Credit card balance	500	
TOTAL LIABILITIES		$10,000
NET WORTH (Owner's Equity)		16,500
TOTAL LIABILITIES AND NET WORTH		$26,500

Figure 17.2: Business Balance Sheet

A balance sheet (sometimes referred to as a statement of financial position) summarizes a firm's accounts at the end of an accounting period, showing the various dollar amounts that enter into the accounting equation. Note that assets ($340,000) equal liabilities plus owners' equity ($340,000).

NORTHEAST ART SUPPLY, INC.

Balance Sheet
December 31, 20XX

ASSETS			
Current assets			
Cash		$ 59,000	
Marketable securities		10,000	
Accounts receivable	$ 40,000		
Less allowance for doubtful accounts	2,000	38,000	
Notes receivable		32,000	
Merchandise inventory		41,000	
Prepaid expenses		2,000	
Total current assets			$182,000
Fixed assets			
Delivery equipment	$110,000		
Less accumulated depreciation	20,000	$ 90,000	
Furniture and store equipment	$62,000		
Less accumulated depreciation	15,000	47,000	
Total fixed assets			137,000
Intangible assets			
Patents		$ 6,000	
Goodwill		15,000	
Total intangible assets			21,000
TOTAL ASSETS			$340,000
LIABILITIES AND STOCKHOLDERS' EQUITY			
Current liabilities			
Accounts payable	$ 35,000		
Notes payable	25,675		
Salaries payable	4,000		
Taxes payable	5,325		
Total current liabilities		$ 70,000	
Long-term liabilities			
Mortgage payable on store equipment	$ 40,000		
Total long-term liabilities		$ 40,000	
TOTAL LIABILITIES			$110,000
Stockholders' equity			
Common stock		$150,000	
Retained earnings		80,000	
TOTAL OWNERS' EQUITY			230,000
TOTAL LIABILITIES AND OWNERS' EQUITY			$340,000

is listed first. Next are *marketable securities*—stocks, bonds, and other investments—that can be converted into cash in a matter of days.

Next are the firm's receivables. Its *accounts receivable*, which result from allowing customers to make credit purchases, generally are paid within thirty to sixty days. However, the firm expects that some of these debts will not be collected. Thus, it has reduced its accounts receivables by a 5 percent *allowance for doubtful accounts*. The firm's *notes receivable* are receivables for which customers have signed promissory notes. They generally are repaid over a longer period of time than the firm's accounts receivable.

Northeast's *merchandise inventory* represents the value of goods on hand for sale to customers. Since Northeast Art Supply is a wholesale operation, the inventory listed in Figure 17.2 represents finished goods ready for sale to retailers. For a manufacturing firm, merchandise inventory also may represent raw materials that will become part of a finished product or work that has been partially completed but requires further processing.

Northeast's last current asset is *prepaid expenses*, which are assets that have been paid for in advance but have not yet been used. An example is insurance premiums. They are usually paid at the beginning of the policy year. The unused portion (say, for the last four months of the time period covered by the policy) is a prepaid expense. For Northeast Art, all current assets total $182,000.

Sometimes inventory is pretty. *For a product like poinsettias, the right amount of inventory is very important. The goal for North Carolina-based Metrolina Greenhouses is to make sure that the flowers that arrive at retailer locations across the nation are not only beautiful and healthy, but also just in time for the holiday season.*

Fixed Assets **Fixed assets** are assets that will be held or used for a period longer than one year. They generally include land, buildings, and equipment used in the continuing operation of the business. Although Northeast owns no land or buildings, it does own *delivery equipment* that originally cost $110,000. It also owns *furniture and store equipment* that originally cost $62,000.

Note that the values of both fixed assets are decreased by their *accumulated depreciation*. **Depreciation** is the process of apportioning the cost of a fixed asset over the period during which it will be used, that is, its useful life. The depreciation amount allotted to each year is an expense for that year, and the value of the asset must be reduced by the amount of depreciation expense. Although the actual methods used to calculate the dollar amounts for depreciation expense reported on a firm's financial statements are beyond the scope of this text, you should know that there are a number of different methods that can be used. In the case of Northeast's delivery equipment, $20,000 of its value has been depreciated (or used up) since it was purchased. Its value at this time is thus $110,000 less $20,000, or $90,000. In a similar fashion, the original value of furniture and store equipment ($62,000) has been reduced by depreciation totaling $15,000. Furniture and store equipment now has a reported value of $47,000. For Northeast Art, all fixed assets total $137,000.

fixed assets assets that will be held or used for a period longer than one year

depreciation the process of apportioning the cost of a fixed asset over the period during which it will be used

Intangible Assets **Intangible assets** are assets that do not exist physically but that have a value based on the rights or privileges they confer on a firm. They include patents, copyrights, trademarks, franchises, and goodwill. By their nature, intangible assets are long-term assets—they are of value to the firm for a number of years.

intangible assets assets that do not exist physically but that have a value based on the rights or privileges they confer on a firm

Northeast Art Supply lists two intangible assets. The first is a *patent* for a special oil paint that the company purchased from the inventor. The firm's accountants estimate that the patent has a current market value of $6,000. The second intangible asset, *goodwill*, is the value of a firm's reputation, location, earning capacity, and other intangibles that make the business a profitable concern. Goodwill normally is not listed on a balance sheet unless the firm has been purchased from previous owners. In such a case, the new owners actually have paid an additional amount over and above the fair market value of the firm's assets for goodwill. Goodwill exists because most businesses are worth more as going concerns than as a collection of assets. Northeast Art's accountants included a $15,000 amount for goodwill. The firm's intangible assets total $21,000. Now it is possible to total all three types of assets for Northeast Art. As calculated in Figure 17.2, total assets are $340,000.

Entrepreneurial Challenge

Starting a Business? Start with a CPA

Before you start a new business—even before you put the finishing touches on your business plan—find a good CPA. An experienced accountant can help you develop realistic projections of revenues, profits, costs, and taxes for the best of times and the worst of times. This is especially critical for a business facing an uncertain economy. "If you plan for survival only in the most likely case, that can be disastrous for your business," says CPA Geoff Harlow of Deerfield, Illinois.

Accountants understand the financial demands on new businesses and can suggest ways of squeezing the most out of every start-up dollar. They know what local banks generally ask prospective business borrowers and which documents loan officers expect to see. They can explain the tax deductions available to entrepreneurs and tell you how and when business taxes must be paid. And a CPA with experience in your industry can advise you about growth prospects and introduce you to possible suppliers.

To find a good accountant, ask successful entrepreneurs or your banker for recommendations. Arrange a personal meeting to discuss your business goals, ask specific questions, and find out more about the accountant's expertise and fees. Have your CPA on board before you launch your business, and be ready to face your financials from day one.

Sources: Diana Ransom, "Starting Up: How Much Money Do I Need?" *Wall Street Journal*, February 6, 2008, **www.wsj.com**; Christina Le Beau, "The Quick and the Dead: Get Your Business in Order Before Things Turn Ugly," *Crain's Chicago Business*, April 14, 2008, p. 22; Jeffrey Moses, "How to Find the Accountant Who's Right for You," *National Foundation of Independent Business*, January 3, 2007, **www.nfib.org**; Samantha Stainburn, "It's a Numbers Game," *Crain's Chicago Business*, December 10, 2007, p. 28.

Stockbyte/Getty Images

Liabilities and Owners' Equity

The liabilities and the owners' equity accounts complete the balance sheet. The firm's liabilities are separated into two categories—current and long term.

Current Liabilities A firm's **current liabilities** are debts that will be repaid in one year or less. Northeast Art Supply purchased merchandise from its suppliers on credit. Thus, its balance sheet includes an entry for accounts payable. *Accounts payable* are short-term obligations that arise as a result of a firm making credit purchases.

Notes payable are obligations that have been secured with promissory notes. They are usually short-term obligations, but they may extend beyond one year. Only those that must be paid within the year are listed under current liabilities.

Northeast also lists *salaries payable* and *taxes payable* as current liabilities. These are both expenses that have been incurred during the current accounting period but will be paid in the next accounting period. For Northeast Art, current liabilities total $70,000.

Long-Term Liabilities **Long-term liabilities** are debts that need not be repaid for at least one year. Northeast lists only one long-term liability—a $40,000 *mortgage payable* for store equipment. Bonds and other long-term loans would be included here as well, if they existed. As you can see in Figure 17.2, Northeast's current and long-term liabilities total $110,000.

Owners' or Stockholders' Equity For a sole proprietorship or partnership, the owners' equity is shown as the difference between assets and liabilities. In a partnership, each partner's share of the ownership is reported separately in each owner's name. For a corporation, the owners' equity usually is referred to as *stockholders' equity*. The dollar amount reported on the balance sheet is the total value of stock plus retained earnings that have accumulated to date. **Retained earnings** are the portion of a business's profits not distributed to stockholders.

The original investment by the owners of Northeast Art Supply was $150,000. In addition, $80,000 of Northeast's earnings have been reinvested in the business since it was founded. Thus, owners' equity totals $230,000.

As the two grand totals in Figure 17.2 show, Northeast's assets and the sum of its liabilities and owners' equity are equal—at $340,000. The accounting equation (assets = liabilities + owners' equity) is still in balance.

current liabilities debts that will be repaid in one year or less

long-term liabilities debts that need not be repaid for at least one year

retained earnings the portion of a business's profits not distributed to stockholders

The Income Statement

5

Learning Objective: Read and interpret an income statement.

Question: *Where can you find the profit or loss amount for Gap Inc.?*

Answer: The firm's income statement.

An **income statement** is a summary of a firm's revenues and expenses during a specified accounting period—one month, three months, six months, or a year. The income statement is sometimes called the *earnings statement* or *the statement of income and expenses*. Let's begin our discussion by constructing a personal income statement for Marty Campbell. Having worked as a sales representative for an office supply firm for the past three years, Marty now earns $33,600 a year, or $2,800 a month. After deductions, his take-home pay is $1,900 a month. As illustrated in Figure 17.3, Marty's typical monthly expenses include payments for an automobile loan, credit card purchases, apartment rent, utilities, food, clothing, and recreation and entertainment.

income statement a summary of a firm's revenues and expenses during a specified accounting period

While the difference between income and expenses is referred to as *profit* or *loss* for a business, it is normally referred to as a *cash surplus* or *cash deficit* for an individual. Fortunately for Marty, he has a surplus of $250 at the end of each month. He can use this surplus for savings, investing, or paying off debts.

Figure 17.4 shows the income statement for Northeast Art Supply. Generally, revenues *less* cost of goods sold *less* operating expenses equals net income.

Revenues

Revenues are the dollar amounts earned by a firm from selling goods, providing services, or performing business activities. Like most businesses, Northeast Art obtains its revenues solely from the sale of its products or services. The revenues section of its income statement begins with gross sales. **Gross sales** are the total

revenues the dollar amounts earned by a firm from selling goods, providing services, or performing business activities

gross sales the total dollar amount of all goods and services sold during the accounting period

Figure 17.3: Personal Income Statement

By subtracting expenses from income, anyone can construct a personal income statement and determine if they have a surplus or deficit at the end of each month.

Marty Campbell
Personal Income Statement
For the month ended December 31, 20XX

INCOME (Take-home pay)		$1,900
LESS MONTHLY EXPENSES		
Automobile loan	$ 250	
Credit card payment	100	
Apartment rent	500	
Utilities	200	
Food	250	
Clothing	100	
Recreation & entertainment	250	
TOTAL MONTHLY EXPENSES		1,650
CASH SURPLUS (or profit)		$ 250

Figure 17.4: Business Income Statement

An income statement summarizes a firm's revenues and expenses during a specified accounting period. For Northeast Art, net income after taxes is $30,175.

NORTHEAST ART SUPPLY, INC.

Income Statement
For the Year Ended
December 31, 20XX

Revenues			
Gross sales		$465,000	
Less sales returns and allowances	$ 9,500		
Less sales discounts	4,500	14,000	
Net sales			$451,000
Cost of goods sold			
Beginning inventory, January 1, 20XX		$ 40,000	
Purchases	$346,000		
Less purchase discounts	11,000		
Net purchases		335,000	
Cost of goods available for sale		$375,000	
Less ending inventory December 31, 20XX		41,000	
Cost of goods sold			334,000
Gross profit			$117,000
Operating expenses			
Selling expenses			
Sales salaries	$ 22,000		
Advertising	4,000		
Sales promotion	2,500		
Depreciation—store equipment	3,000		
Depreciation—delivery equipment	4,000		
Miscellaneous selling expenses	1,500		
Total selling expenses		$ 37,000	
General expenses			
Office salaries	$ 28,500		
Rent	8,500		
Depreciation—office furniture	1,500		
Utilities expense	2,500		
Insurance expense	1,000		
Miscellaneous expense	500		
Total general expense		42,500	
Total operating expenses			79,500
Net income from operations			$ 37,500
Less interest expense			2,000
NET INCOME BEFORE TAXES			$ 35,500
Less federal income taxes			5,325
NET INCOME AFTER TAXES			$ 30,175

net sales the actual dollar amounts received by a firm for the goods and services it has sold after adjustment for returns, allowances, and discounts

cost of goods sold the dollar amount equal to beginning inventory *plus* net purchases *less* ending inventory

gross profit a firm's net sales *less* the cost of goods sold

operating expenses all business costs other than the cost of goods sold

net income occurs when revenues exceed expenses

net loss occurs when expenses exceed revenues

dollar amount of all goods and services sold during the accounting period. From this amount are deducted the dollar amounts of

- *Sales returns*—merchandise returned to the firm by its customers
- *Sales allowances*—price reductions offered to customers who accept slightly damaged or soiled merchandise
- *Sales discounts*—price reductions offered to customers who pay their bills promptly

The remainder is the firm's net sales. **Net sales** are the actual dollar amounts received by the firm for the goods and services it has sold after adjustment for returns, allowances, and discounts. For Northeast Art, net sales are $451,000.

Cost of Goods Sold

The standard method of determining the **cost of goods sold** by a retailing or wholesaling firm can be summarized as follows:

Cost of goods sold = beginning inventory + net purchases − ending inventory

A manufacturer must include raw materials inventories, work in progress, finished goods inventory, and direct manufacturing costs in this computation.

According to Figure 17.4, Northeast began its accounting period on January 1 with a merchandise inventory that cost $40,000. During the next twelve months, the firm purchased merchandise valued at $346,000. After taking advantage of *purchase discounts,* however, it paid only $335,000 for this merchandise. Thus, during the year, Northeast had total *goods available for sale* valued at $40,000 plus $335,000, or $375,000.

Twelve months later, at the end of the accounting period on December 31, Northeast had sold all but $41,000 worth of the available goods. The cost of goods sold by Northeast was therefore $375,000 less ending inventory of $41,000, or $334,000. It is now possible to calculate gross profit. A firm's **gross profit** is its net sales *less* the cost of goods sold. For Northeast, gross profit was $117,000.

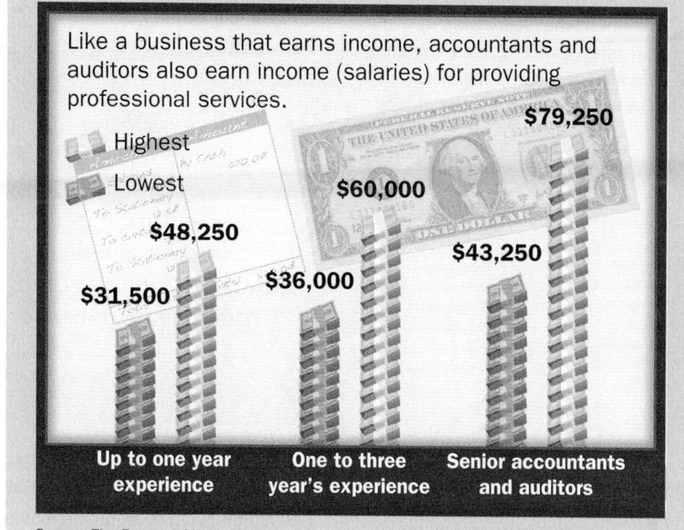

Source: The Bureau of Labor Statistics website at www.bls.gov, September 24, 2008.

Operating Expenses

A firm's **operating expenses** are all business costs other than the cost of goods sold. Total operating expenses generally are divided into two categories: selling expenses or general expenses.

Selling expenses are costs related to the firm's marketing activities. For Northeast Art, selling expenses total $37,000. *General expenses* are costs incurred in managing a business. For Northeast Art, general expenses total $42,500. Now it is possible to total both selling and general expenses. As Figure 17.4 shows, total operating expenses for the accounting period are $79,500.

Net Income

When revenues exceed expenses, the difference is called **net income**. When expenses exceed revenues, the difference is called **net loss**. As Figure 17.4 shows, Northeast Art's *net income from operations* is computed as gross profit ($117,000) less total operating expenses ($79,500). For Northeast Art, net income from operations is $37,500. From this amount, *interest expense* of $2,000 is deducted to obtain a *net income before taxes* of $35,500. The interest expense is deducted in this section of the income statement because it is not an operating expense. Rather, it is an expense that results from financing the business.

Northeast's *federal income taxes* are $5,325. Although these taxes may or may not be payable immediately, they are definitely an expense that must be deducted from income. This leaves Northeast Art with a *net income after taxes* of $30,175. This amount may be used to pay a dividend to stockholders, it may be retained or reinvested in the firm, it may be used to reduce the firm's debts, or all three.

Sometimes a firm must spend money to make money. *The cost of this advertisement for eebee's Adventures—a series of DVDs to help infants learn—is reported on the firm's income statement as a marketing expense. Marketing expenses—along with all other expenses—are deducted from sales revenue to determine if a firm earns a profit.*

PRNewsFoto/Sony Wonder

The Statement of Cash Flows

6

Learning Objective: Describe business activities that affect a firm's cash flow.

statement of cash flows a statement that illustrates how the operating, investing, and financing activities of a company affect cash during an accounting period

Cash is the lifeblood of any business. In 1987, the SEC and the Financial Accounting Standards Board required all publicly traded companies to include a statement of cash flows, along with their balance sheet and income statement, in their annual report. The **statement of cash flows** illustrates how the operating, investing, and financing activities of a company affect cash during an accounting period. A statement of cash flows for Northeast Art Supply is illustrated in Figure 17.5. It provides information concerning the company's cash receipts and cash payments and is organized around three different activities: operations, investing, and financing.

- *Cash flows from operating activities.* This is the first section of a statement of cash flows. It addresses the firm's primary revenue source—providing goods and services. The amounts paid to suppliers, employees, interest, taxes, and other expenses are deducted from the amount received from customers. Finally, the interest and dividends received by the firm are added to determine the total. After all adjustments are made, the total represents a true picture of cash flows from operating activities.

Figure 17.5: Statement of Cash Flows

A statement of cash flows summarizes how a firm's operating, investing, and financing activities affect its cash during a specified period—one month, three months, six months, or a year. For Northeast Art, the amount of cash at the end of the year reported on the statement of cash flows is $59,000—the same amount reported for the cash account on the firm's balance sheet.

NORTHEAST ART SUPPLY, INC.

Statement of Cash Flows
For the Year Ended
December 31, 20XX

Cash flows from operating activities		
Cash received from customers	$ 451,000	
Cash paid to suppliers and employees	(385,500)	
Interest paid	(2,000)	
Income taxes paid	(5,325)	
Net cash provided by operating activities		$ 58,175
Cash flows from investing activities		
Purchase of equipment	$ (2,000)	
Purchase of investments	(10,000)	
Sale of investments	10,000	
Net cash provided by investing activities		(2,000)
Cash flows from financing activities		
Payment of short-term debt	$ (9,000)	
Payment of long-term debt	(17,000)	
Payment of dividends	(15,000)	
Net cash provided by financing activities		(41,000)
NET INCREASE (DECREASE) IN CASH		$ 15,175
Cash at beginning of year		43,825
CASH AT END OF YEAR		$ 59,000

Annual Reports Go Green

It's not easy being green when investors are accustomed to printed annual reports. Although public corporations must post certain investor materials online, many are making their annual reports more eco-friendly by:

- *Offering electronic options.* Interactive online annual reports help investors find the exact information they want. Kellogg's, known for its breakfast cereals, invites the public to click through its interactive online report. It also allows investors to download and read an electronic version of the printed annual report or click to order a printed copy. Wal-Mart's printed annual report is as slim as possible, and the company encourages investors to view more details online.
- *Using earth-friendly paper, inks, and energy.* Itron, which makes water and energy metering systems, prints its annual report with vegetable-based inks on recycled paper and produces it using wind-generated power. The paper choice alone saves 23 trees and 10,000 gallons of waste water.

Can annual reports be even greener? Although hospitals are not required to issue annual reports, Akron General Medical Center traditionally mailed a 30-page report to thousands of community members. Now it mails a postcard showing where to find the report on the Web and offering a DVD version for people who lack Internet access.

Sources: Cheryl Powell, "Akron General Saves by Putting Annual Report Online Only," *Akron Beacon Journal*, April 4, 2008, n.p.; **www.itron.com**; **www.walmart.com**; **www.kellogg.com**.

- *Cash flows from investing activities.* The second section of the statement is concerned with cash flow from investments. This includes the purchase and sale of land, equipment, and other assets and investments.
- *Cash flows from financing activities.* The third and final section deals with the cash flow from all financing activities. It reports changes in debt obligation and owners' equity accounts. This includes loans and repayments, the sale and repurchase of the company's own stock, and cash dividends.

The totals of all three activities are added to the beginning cash balance to determine the ending cash balance. For Northeast Art Supply, the ending cash balance is $59,000. Note that this is the same amount reported for the cash account on the firm's balance sheet. Together, the cash flow statement, balance sheet, and income statement illustrate the results of past business decisions and reflect the firm's ability to pay debts and dividends and to finance new growth.

Evaluating Financial Statements

7

Learning Objective: Summarize how managers evaluate the financial health of a business.

All three financial statements—the balance sheet, the income statement, and the statement of cash flows—can provide answers to a variety of questions about a firm's ability to do business and stay in business, its profitability, its value as an investment, and its ability to repay its debts. Even more information can be obtained by comparing present financial statements with those prepared for past accounting periods.

Using Annual Reports to Compare Data for Different Accounting Periods

Typically, an annual report contains a great deal of information about the company, its operations, current financial statements, and its past and current financial health. The following five suggestions can help you get to the "bottom line" of a corporation's annual report.

1. Look at the firm's income statement to determine whether the company is profitable or not.
2. Read the letters from the chairman of the board and chief executive officer (CEO) that describe the corporation's operations, prospects for the future, new products or services, financial strengths, *and* any potential problems.
3. Compare the corporation's current income statement and balance sheet with previous financial statements. Look at trends for sales, expenses, profits or losses, assets, liabilities, and owners' equity.

Sustaining the Planet

Just as corporations explain key financial trends in their annual reports, the U.S. Environmental Protection Agency explains key environmental trends in its annual Report on the Environment. You can download the entire electronic version or click through the interactive version and drill down into the details as you choose. **www.epa.gov/roe**

4. Examine the footnotes closely, and look for red flags that may be in the fine print. Often, the footnotes contain (and sometimes hide) important information about the company and its finances.
5. Learn how to calculate financial ratios. Some of the most important financial ratios are discussed in the last part of this section.

Most corporations include in their annual reports comparisons of the important elements of their financial statements for recent years. Figure 17.6 shows such comparisons—of revenue, research and development (R&D), operating income, and sales and marketing expenses—for Microsoft Corporation, a world leader in the computer software industry. By examining these data, an operating manager can tell whether R&D expenditures are increasing or decreasing over the past three years. The vice president of marketing can determine if the total amount of sales and marketing expenses is changing. Stockholders and potential investors, on the other hand, may be more concerned with increases or decreases in Microsoft's revenues and operating income over the same time period.

Comparing Data with Other Firms' Data

Many firms also compare their financial results with those of competing firms and with industry averages. Comparisons are possible as long as accountants follow generally accepted accounting principles.

Figure 17.6: Comparisons of Present and Past Financial Statements for Microsoft Corporation

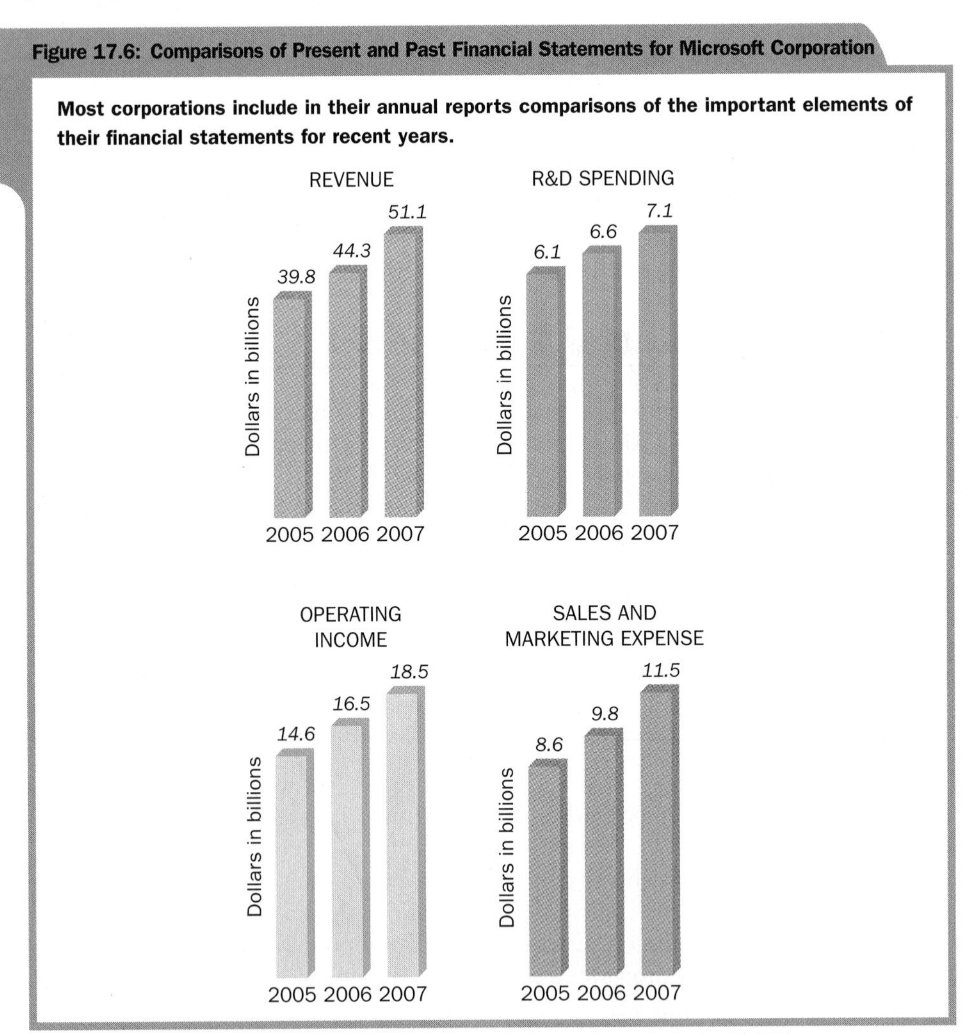

Source: Adapted from the Microsoft Corporation 2007 Annual Report, **www.microsoft.com**, September 25, 2008.

Except for minor differences in format and terms, the balance sheet and income statement of Procter & Gamble, for example, will be similar to those of other large corporations, such as Alberto-Culver, Clorox, Colgate-Palmolive, and Unilever, in the consumer goods industry. Comparisons among firms give managers a general idea of a firm's relative effectiveness and its standing within the industry. Competitors' financial statements can be obtained from their annual reports—if they are public corporations. Industry averages are published by reporting services such as D&B (formerly Dun & Bradstreet) and Standard & Poor's, as well as by some industry trade associations.

Still another type of analysis of a firm's financial health involves computation of financial ratios. A **financial ratio** is a number that shows the relationship between two elements of a firm's financial statements. Among the most useful ratios are profitability ratios, short-term financial ratios, activity ratios, and the debt-to-owners'-equity ratio. Like the individual elements in financial statements, these ratios can be compared with the firm's past ratios, with those of competitors, and with industry averages. The information required to form these ratios is found in a firm's balance sheet and income statement (in our examples for Northeast Art Supply, Figures 17.2 and 17.4).

financial ratio a number that shows the relationship between two elements of a firm's financial statements

Profitability Ratios

A firm's net income after taxes indicates whether the firm is profitable. It does not, however, indicate how effectively the firm's resources are being used. For this latter purpose, three ratios can be computed.

Return on Sales

Return on sales, sometimes called *profit margin,* is a financial ratio calculated by dividing net income after taxes by net sales. For Northeast Art Supply,

return on sales (or profit margin) a financial ratio calculated by dividing net income after taxes by net sales

$$\text{Return on sales} = \frac{\text{net income after taxes}}{\text{net sales}} = \frac{\$30,175}{\$451,000}$$
$$= 0.067, \text{ or } 6.7 \text{ percent}$$

The return on sales indicates how effectively the firm is transforming sales into profits. A higher return on sales is better than a low one. Today, the average return on sales for all business firms is between 4 and 5 percent. With a return on sales of 6.7 percent, Northeast Art Supply is above average. A low return on sales can be increased by reducing expenses, increasing sales, or both.

Return on Owners' Equity

Return on owners' equity is a financial ratio calculated by dividing net income after taxes by owners' equity. For Northeast Art Supply,

return on owners' equity a financial ratio calculated by dividing net income after taxes by owners' equity

$$\text{Return on owners' equity} = \frac{\text{net income after taxes}}{\text{owners' equity}} = \frac{\$30,175}{\$230,000}$$
$$= 0.13, \text{ or } 13 \text{ percent}$$

Return on owners' equity indicates how much income is generated by each dollar of equity. Northeast is providing income of 13 cents per dollar invested in the business. The average for all businesses is between 12 and 15 cents. A higher return on owners' equity is better than a low one, and the only practical ways to increase return on owners' equity is to reduce expenses, increase sales, or both.

Earnings per Share

From the point of view of stockholders, **earnings per share** is one of the best indicators of a corporation's success. It is calculated by dividing net income after taxes by the number of shares of common stock outstanding. If we assume that Northeast Art Supply has issued 25,000 shares of stock, then its earnings per share are

earnings per share a financial ratio calculated by dividing net income after taxes by the number of shares of common stock outstanding

$$\text{Earnings per share} = \frac{\text{net income after taxes}}{\text{common stock shares outstanding}} = \frac{\$30,175}{25,000}$$
$$= \$1.21 \text{ per share}$$

There is no meaningful average for this ratio mainly because the number of outstanding shares of a firm's stock is subject to change as a result of stock splits and stock dividends. Also, some corporations choose to issue more stock than others. As a general rule, however, an increase in earnings per share is a healthy sign for any corporation.

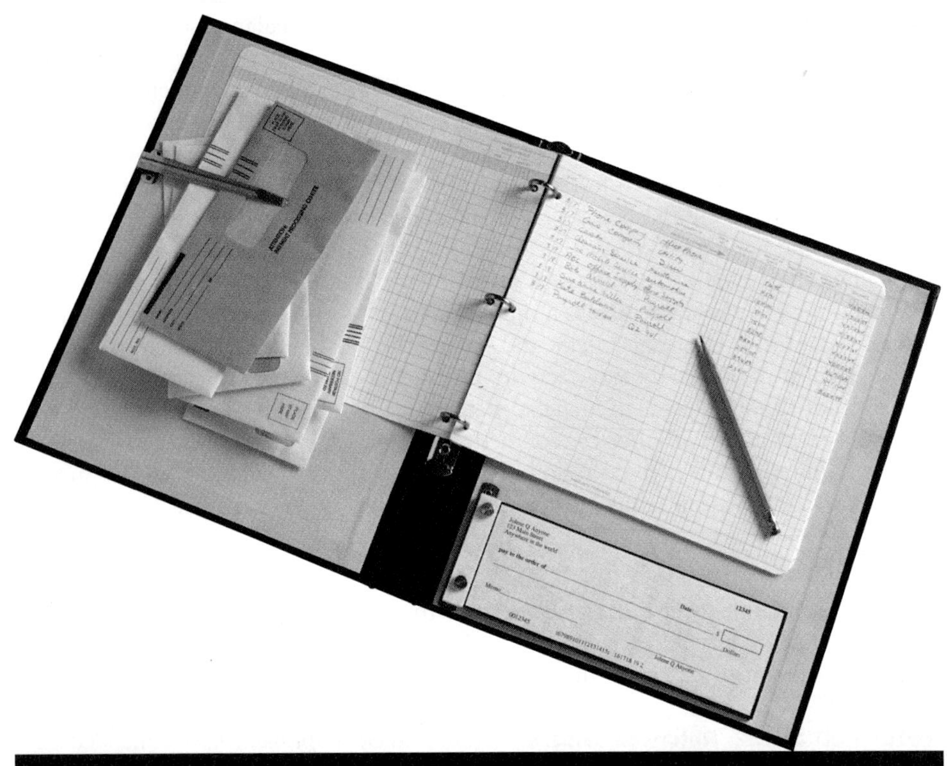

Bouncing checks is not a good idea! *As part of the accounting process, a firm must evaluate the information on its financial statements to establish its ability to pay everyday expenses. To make sure it has enough available cash to "pay the bills," accountants track the amount of working capital a firm has and often calculate a current ratio and an acid-test ratio.*

PhotoDisc/Getty Images

Short-Term Financial Ratios

Two short-term financial ratios permit managers (and lenders) to evaluate the ability of a firm to pay its current liabilities. Before we discuss these ratios, we should examine one other easily determined measure: working capital.

working capital the difference between current assets and current liabilities

Working Capital **Working capital** is the difference between current assets and current liabilities. For Northeast Art,

Current assets	\$182,000
Less current liabilities	70,000
Equals working capital	\$112,000

Working capital indicates how much would remain if a firm paid off all current liabilities with cash and other current assets. The "proper" amount of working capital depends on the type of firm, its past experience, and its particular industry. A firm with too little working capital may have to borrow money to finance its operations.

current ratio a financial ratio computed by dividing current assets by current liabilities

Current Ratio A firm's **current ratio** is computed by dividing current assets by current liabilities. For Northeast Art Supply,

$$\text{Current ratio} = \frac{\text{current assets}}{\text{current liabilities}} = \frac{\$182{,}000}{\$70{,}000} = 2.6$$

This means that Northeast Art Supply has \$2.60 of current assets for every \$1 of current liabilities. The average current ratio for all industries is 2.0, but it varies greatly from industry to industry. A high current ratio indicates that a firm can pay its current liabilities. A low current ratio can be improved by repaying current liabilities, by reducing dividend payments to stockholders to increase the firm's cash balance, or by obtaining additional cash from investors.

Acid-Test Ratio This ratio, sometimes called the *quick ratio,* is a measure of the firm's ability to pay current liabilities *quickly*—with its cash, marketable securities, and receivables. The **acid-test ratio** is calculated by adding cash, marketable securities, and receivables and dividing the total by current liabilities. The value of inventory and other current assets is "removed" from current assets because these assets are not converted into cash as easily as cash, marketable securities, and receivables. For Northeast Art Supply,

acid-test ratio a financial ratio calculated by adding cash, marketable securities and receivables and dividing the total by current liabilities

$$\text{Acid-test ratio} = \frac{\text{cash + marketable securities + receivables}}{\text{current liabilities}} = \frac{\$139{,}000}{\$70{,}000}$$
$$= 1.99$$

For all businesses, the desired acid-test ratio is 1.0. Northeast Art Supply is above average with a ratio of 1.99, and the firm should be well able to pay its current liabilities. To increase a low acid-test ratio, a firm would have to repay current liabilities, reduce dividend payments to stockholders to increase the firm's cash balance, or obtain additional cash from investors.

Activity Ratios

Two activity ratios permit managers to measure how many times each year a company collects its accounts receivables or sells its inventory.

Accounts Receivable Turnover A firm's **accounts receivable turnover** is the number of times the firm collects its accounts receivable in one year. If the data are available, this ratio should be calculated using a firm's net credit sales. Since data for Northeast Art Supply's credit sales are unavailable, this ratio can be calculated by dividing net sales by accounts receivable. For Northeast Art,

accounts receivable turnover a financial ratio calculated by dividing net sales by accounts receivable

$$\text{Accounts receivable turnover} = \frac{\text{net sales}}{\text{accounts receivable}} = \frac{\$451{,}000}{\$38{,}000}$$
$$= 11.9 \text{ times per year}$$

Northeast Art Supply collects its accounts receivables 11.9 times each year, or about every thirty days. If a firm's credit terms require customers to pay in twenty-five days, a collection period of thirty days is considered acceptable. There is no meaningful average for this measure mainly because credit terms differ among companies. A high accounts receivable turnover is better than a low one. As a general rule, a low accounts receivable turnover ratio can be improved by pressing for payment of past-due accounts and by tightening requirements for prospective credit customers.

Inventory Turnover A firm's **inventory turnover** is the number of times the firm sells its merchandise inventory in one year. It is approximated by dividing the cost of goods sold in one year by the average value of the inventory.

inventory turnover a financial ratio calculated by dividing the cost of goods sold in one year by the average value of the inventory

The average value of the inventory can be found by adding the beginning inventory value and the ending inventory value (given on the income statement) and dividing the sum by 2. For Northeast Art Supply, average inventory is \$40,500. Thus

$$\text{Inventory turnover} = \frac{\text{cost of goods sold}}{\text{average inventory}} = \frac{\$334{,}000}{\$40{,}500}$$
$$= 8.2 \text{ times per year}$$

Northeast Art Supply sells its merchandise inventory 8.2 times each year, or about once every forty-five days. The average inventory turnover for all firms is about 9 times per year, but turnover rates vary widely from industry to industry. For example, supermarkets may have inventory turnover rates of 20 or higher, whereas inventory turnover rates for furniture stores are generally well below the national average. The quickest way to improve inventory turnover is to order merchandise in smaller quantities at more frequent intervals.

Debt-to-Owners'-Equity Ratio

debt-to-owners'-equity ratio a financial ratio calculated by dividing total liabilities by owners' equity

Our final category of financial ratios indicates the degree to which a firm's operations are financed through borrowing. Although other ratios can be calculated, the debt-to-owners'-equity ratio is used often to determine whether a firm has too much debt. The **debt-to-owners'-equity ratio** is calculated by dividing total liabilities by owners' equity. For Northeast Art Supply,

$$\text{Debt-to-owners'-equity ratio} = \frac{\text{total liabilities}}{\text{owner's equity}} = \frac{\$110{,}000}{\$230{,}000}$$
$$= 0.48\text{, or } 48 \text{ percent}$$

A debt-to-owners'-equity ratio of 48 percent means that creditors have provided about 48 cents of financing for every dollar provided by the owners. The higher this ratio, the riskier the situation is for lenders. A high debt-to-owners'-equity ratio may make borrowing additional money from lenders difficult. It can be reduced by paying off debts or by increasing the owners' investment in the firm.

Northeast's Financial Ratios: A Summary

Table 17.2 compares the financial ratios of Northeast Art Supply with the average financial ratios for all businesses. It also lists the formulas we used to calculate Northeast's ratios. Northeast seems to be in good financial shape. Its return on sales, current ratio, and acid-test ratio are all above average. Its other ratios are about average, although its inventory turnover and debt-to-equity ratio could be improved.

This chapter ends our discussion of accounting information. In Chapter 18, we begin our examination of business finances by discussing money, banking, and credit.

Table 17.2: Financial Ratios of Northeast Art Supply Compared with Average Ratios for all Businesses

Ratio	Formula	Northeast Ratio	Average Business Ratio	Direction for Improvement
Profitability Ratios				
Return on sales	net income after taxes / net sales	6.7%	4%–5%	Higher
Return on owners' equity	net income after taxes / owners' equity	13%	12%–15%	Higher
Earnings per share	net income after taxes / common stock shares outstanding	$1.21 per share	—	Higher
Short-Term Financial Ratios				
Working capital	current assets – current liabilities	$112,000	—	Higher
Current ratio	current assets / current liabilities	2.6	2.0	Higher
Acid-test ratio	cash + marketable securites + receivables / current liabilities	1.99	1.0	Higher
Activity Ratios				
Accounts receivable turnover	net sales / accounts receivable	11.9	—	Higher
Inventory turnover	cost of goods sold / average inventory	8.2	9	Higher
Debt-to-owners'-equity ratio	total liabilities / owners' equity	48 percent	—	Lower

return to inside business

What the Big Accounting Firms Count

Day in and day out, the big accounting firms and their smaller counterparts help companies, government agencies, and nonprofit organizations such as charities and museums organize, report, and interpret their financial data. When the U.S. Treasury Department set aside $700 billion to bolster the financial sector during recent economic turmoil, it hired two of the Big Four firms to audit the program and provide accounting assistance.

Of course, few assignments are as glamorous as being involved in the Oscar, Grammy, or Emmy awards. Every year, after counting thousands of Emmy ballots, two Ernst & Young accountants are escorted to the awards ceremony with the results locked in silver briefcases handcuffed to their wrists. Until the presenters open the envelopes and announce the winners, only these accountants know the results—and they're sworn to secrecy.

Questions

1. When an accounting firm has been hired to sign off on a public corporation's annual report, should it limit its consulting work for that client to avoid being influenced by financial ties to the corporation? Explain your answer.
2. Why would the Recording Academy, the Academy of Motion Picture Arts and Sciences, and the Academy of Television Arts and Sciences hire major accounting firms instead of using their own employees to count ballots?

Summary

1 Explain why accurate accounting information and audited financial statements are important.

Accounting is the process of systematically collecting, analyzing, and reporting financial information. It can be used to answer questions about what has happened in the past; it also can be used to help make decisions about the future. In fact, it's the firm's accountants and its accounting system that often translate goals, objectives, and plans into dollars and cents to help determine if a decision or plan of action makes "financial sense." Unfortunately, a large number of accounting scandals have caused people to doubt not only the financial information reported by a corporation but also the accounting industry. In a perfect world, accountants and auditors would catch mistakes and disclose questionable accounting practices in a firm's audit. The purpose of an audit is to make sure that a firm's financial statements have been prepared in accordance with generally accepted accounting principles (GAAPs). To help ensure that corporate financial information is accurate and in response to the many accounting scandals that surfaced in the last part of the 1990s and the first part of the twenty-first century, the Sarbanes-Oxley Act was signed into law. This law contains a number of provisions designed to restore public confidence in the accounting industry.

2 Identify the people who use accounting information and possible careers in the accounting industry.

To be successful in the accounting industry, employees must be responsible, honest, and ethical; have a strong background in financial management; know how to use a computer and software to process data into accounting information; and be able to communicate with people who need accounting information. Primarily, management uses accounting information, but it is also demanded by lenders, suppliers, stockholders, potential investors, and government agencies. While many people think that all accountants do the same tasks, there are special areas of expertise within the accounting industry. Typical areas of expertise include managerial, financial, cost, tax, government, and not-for-profit accounting. A private accountant is employed by a specific organization to operate its accounting system. A public accountant performs these functions for various individuals or firms on a fee basis. Most accounting firms include on their staffs at least one certified public accountant (CPA). In addition to CPAs, there are also certified management accountants (CMAs). While both CPAs and CMAs can work for the public, a CMA is more likely to work within a large organization. Also, both types of accountants are excellent career choices.

3 Discuss the accounting process.

The accounting process is based on the accounting equation: Assets = liabilities + owners' equity. Double-entry bookkeeping ensures that the balance shown by the accounting equation is maintained. The accounting process involves five steps: (1) source documents are analyzed, (2) each transaction is recorded in a journal, (3) each journal entry is posted in the appropriate general ledger accounts, (4) at the end of each accounting period, a trial balance is prepared to make sure that the accounting equation is in balance, and (5) financial statements are prepared from the trial balance. A firm's financial statements are included in its annual report. An annual report is a report distributed to stockholders and other interested parties that describes a firm's operating activities and its financial condition. Once statements are prepared, the books are closed. A new accounting cycle then is begun for the next accounting period.

4 Read and interpret a balance sheet.

A balance sheet (sometimes referred to as a statement of financial position) is a summary of a firm's assets, liabilities, and owners' equity accounts at the end of an accounting period. This statement must demonstrate that the accounting equation is in balance. On the balance sheet, assets are categorized as current, fixed, or intangible. Similarly, liabilities can be divided into current liabilities and long-term ones. For a sole proprietorship or partnership, owners' equity is shown as the difference between assets and liabilities. For corporations, the owners' equity section reports the values of stock and retained earnings.

5 Read and interpret an income statement.

An income statement is a summary of a firm's financial operations during the specified accounting period. On the income statement, the company's gross profit is computed by subtracting the cost of goods sold from net sales. Operating expenses and interest expense then are deducted to compute net income before taxes. Finally, income taxes are deducted to obtain the firm's net income after taxes.

6 Describe business activities that affect a firm's cash flow.

Since 1987, the Securities and Exchange Commission (SEC) and the Financial Accounting Standards Board (FASB) have required all publicly traded companies to include a statement of cash flows in their annual reports. This statement illustrates how the operating, investing, and financing activities of a company affect cash during an accounting period. Together, the cash flow statement, balance sheet, and income statement illustrate the results of past decisions and the business's ability to pay debts and dividends and to finance new growth.

7 Summarize how managers evaluate the financial health of a business.

The firm's financial statements and its accounting information become more meaningful when compared with corresponding information for previous years, for competitors, and for the industry in which the firm operates. Such comparisons permit managers and other interested people to pick out trends in growth, borrowing, income, and other business variables and to determine whether the firm is on the way to accomplishing its long-term goals. A number of financial ratios can be computed from the information in a firm's financial statements. These ratios provide a picture of the firm's profitability, its short-term financial position, its activity in the area of accounts receivable and inventory, and its debt financing. Like the information on the firm's financial statements, these ratios can and should be compared with those of past accounting periods, those of competitors, and those representing the average of the industry as a whole.

Key Terms

You should now be able to define and give an example relevant to each of the following terms:

accounting (495)
audit (496)
generally accepted accounting principles (GAAPs) (497)
managerial accounting (499)
financial accounting (499)
certified public accountant (CPA) (500)
certified management accountant (CMA) (501)
assets (501)
liabilities (501)
owners' equity (501)
accounting equation (501)
double-entry bookkeeping system (501)
trial balance (502)
annual report (502)
balance sheet (or statement of financial position) (503)
liquidity (503)
current assets (503)
fixed assets (505)
depreciation (505)
intangible assets (505)
current liabilities (506)
long-term liabilities (506)
retained earnings (506)
income statement (507)
revenues (507)
gross sales (507)
net sales (508)
cost of goods sold (509)
gross profit (509)
operating expenses (509)
net income (509)
net loss (509)
statement of cash flows (510)
financial ratio (513)
return on sales (or profit margin) (513)
return on owners' equity (513)
earnings per share (513)
working capital (514)
current ratio (514)
acid-test ratio (515)
accounts receivable turnover (515)
inventory turnover (515)
debt-to-owners'-equity ratio (516)

Review Questions

1. What purpose do audits and generally accepted accounting principles (GAAPs) serve in today's business world?
2. How do the major provisions of the Sarbanes-Oxley Act affect a public company's audit procedures?
3. List four groups that use accounting information, and briefly explain why each group has an interest in this information.
4. What is the difference between a private accountant and a public accountant? What are certified public accountants and certified management accountants?
5. State the accounting equation, and list two specific examples of each term in the equation.
6. How is double-entry bookkeeping related to the accounting equation?
7. Briefly describe the five steps of the accounting cycle in order.
8. What is the principal difference between a balance sheet and an income statement?
9. How are current assets distinguished from fixed assets? Why are fixed assets depreciated on a balance sheet?
10. Explain how a retailing firm would determine the cost of goods sold during an accounting period.
11. How does a firm determine its net income after taxes?
12. What is the purpose of a statement of cash flows?
13. For each of the accounts listed below, indicate if the account should be included on a firm's balance sheet, income statement, or statement of cash flows.

Type of Account	Statement Where Reported
Assets	______________
Income	______________
Expenses	______________
Operating activities	______________
Liabilities	______________
Investing activities	______________
Owners' equity	______________

14. What type of information is contained in an annual report? How does the information help to identify financial trends?
15. Explain the calculation procedure for and significance of each of the following:
    a. One of the profitability ratios
    b. A short-term financial ratio
    c. An activity ratio
    d. Debt-to-owners'-equity ratio

Discussion Questions

1. Why do you think there have been so many accounting scandals involving public companies in recent years?
2. Bankers usually insist that prospective borrowers submit audited financial statements along with a loan application. Why should financial statements be audited by a CPA?
3. What can be said about a firm whose owners' equity is a negative amount? How could such a situation come about?
4. Do the balance sheet, income statement, and statement of cash flows contain all the information you might want as a potential lender or stockholder? What other information would you like to examine?
5. Why is it so important to compare a firm's current financial statements with those of previous years, those of competitors, and the average of all firms in the industry in which the firm operates?
6. Which do you think are the two or three most important financial ratios? Why?

Video Case 17.1

The Ethics of "Making the Numbers"

Will sales and profits meet the expectations of investors and Wall Street analysts? Managers at public corporations must answer this vitally important question quarter after quarter, year after year. In an ideal world—one in which the economy never contracts, expenses never go up, and customers never buy competing products—the corporation's share price would soar, and investors would cheer as every financial report showed ever-higher sales revenues, profit margins, and earnings.

In the real world, however, many uncontrollable and unpredictable factors can affect a corporation's performance. Customers may buy fewer units or postpone purchases, competitors may introduce superior products, energy costs and other expenses may rise, interest rates may climb, and buying power may plummet. Faced with the prospect of releasing financial results that fall short of Wall Street's expectations, managers may feel intense pressure to "make the numbers" using a variety of accounting techniques.

For example, some executives at WorldCom made earnings look better by booking billions of dollars in ordinary expenses as capital investments. The company was forced into bankruptcy a few weeks after the accounting scam was exposed. As another example, top managers at the drug retailer Rite Aid posted transactions improperly to inflate corporate earnings. Ultimately, Rite Aid had to lower its earnings figures by $1.6 billion, and investors fled, driving the share price down.

Under the Sarbanes-Oxley Act, the CEO and CFO now must certify the corporation's financial reports. This has led hundreds of companies to restate their earnings in recent years, a sign that stricter controls on accounting practices are having the intended effect. "I don't mean to sugarcoat the figure on restatements," says Steve Odland, CEO of Office Depot, "but I think it is positive—it shows a healthy system." Yet not all earnings restatements are due to accounting irregularities. "The general impression of the public is that accounting rules are black and white," Odland adds. "They are often anything but that, and in many instances the changes in earnings came after new interpretations by the chief accountant of the SEC."

Because accounting rules are open to interpretation, managers sometimes find themselves facing ethical dilemmas when a corporation feels pressure to live up to Wall Street's expectations. Consider the hypothetical situation at Commodore Appliances, a fictional company that sells to Home Depot, Lowe's, and other major retail chains. Margaret, the vice president of sales, has told Rob, a district manager, that the company's sales are down 10 percent in the current quarter. She points out that sales in Rob's district are down 20 percent and states that higher-level managers want him to improve this month's figures using "book and hold," which means recording future sales transactions in the current period.

Rob hesitates, saying that the company is gaining market share and that he needs more time to get sales momentum going. He thinks "book and hold" is not good business practice, even if it is legal. Margaret hints that Rob will lose his job if his sales figures don't look better and stresses that he will need the book-and-hold approach for one month only. Rob realizes that if he doesn't go along, he won't be working at Commodore for very much longer.

Meeting with Kevin, one of Commodore's auditors, Rob learns that book and hold meets generally accepted accounting principles. Kevin emphasizes that customers must be willing to take title to the goods before they're delivered or billed. Any book-and-hold sales must be real, backed by documentation such as e-mails to and from buyers, and the transactions must be completed in the near future.

Rob is at a crossroads: His sales figures must be higher if Commodore is to achieve its performance targets, yet he doesn't know exactly when (or if) he actually would complete any book-and-hold sales he might report this month. He doesn't want to mislead anyone, but he also doesn't want to lose his job or put other people's jobs in jeopardy by refusing to do what he is being asked to do. Rob is confident that he can improve his district's sales over the long term. On the other hand, Commodore's executives can't wait—they are pressuring Rob to make the sales figures look better right now. What should he do?[9]

For more information about the Sarbanes-Oxley Act, go to **www.aicpa.org.** (This is the website for the American Institute of Certified Public Accountants and is a good source of information about the act.)

Questions

1. What are the ethical and legal implications of using accounting practices such as the book-and-hold technique to inflate corporate earnings?
2. Why would Commodore's auditor insist that Rob document any sales booked under the book-and-hold technique?
3. If you were in Rob's situation, would you agree to use the book-and-hold technique this month? Justify your decision.
4. Imagine that Commodore has taken out a multimillion-dollar loan that must be repaid next year. How might the lender react if it learned that Commodore was using the book-and-hold method to make revenues look higher than they really are?

Case 17.2

Software Stands Guard over Accounting at Kimberly-Clark

Kimberly-Clark, famous for making Kleenex and Scott paper products, has automated its accounting controls playbook for compliance with the Sarbanes-Oxley Act. This multinational manufacturer generates annual revenues of more than $15 billion and employs 60,000 people in 200 facilities spread across fifty countries. Enforcing strict, consistent controls on accounting information in all locations has long been a top priority for Kimberly-Clark's finance department. Nonetheless, testing and documenting internal controls to bring the company into complete compliance with Sarbanes-Oxley were a major challenge because of the "different languages, cultures, time zones, and systems," remembers Jerry Rehfuss, the finance director who spearheaded the compliance effort. This is why the company decided to have software stand guard over accounting.

The basis of Kimberly-Clark's compliance initiative was its five-book set of corporate financial instructions, a detailed playbook for avoiding fraud and manipulation in accounting procedures. "From location to location, country to country, the actual controls might vary," says Rehfuss. "But the basic principles—say, for each transaction, one person needs to prepare it, and another person needs to authorize it—have been in place for each process."

Next, Rehfuss hired an outside accounting firm to specify the individual accounting processes and controls that could have the greatest impact on accuracy in Kimberly-Clark's financial statements. He also had internal experts review this list with an eye toward adding new controls where needed. The completed list was sent to coordinators in the company's 200 facilities, who, in turn, identified the employees responsible for applying these processes and controls. The objective was to determine the number and type of accounting elements that would have to be tested and documented in each location to comply with Sarbanes-Oxley. In the end, the company tested approximately 4,000 controls worldwide and assembled the information into a "control map" indicating what guidelines were being used in which locations.

To automate these controls, Rehfuss turned to software that allowed or restricted access to accounting systems based on the playbook's rules. The software also alerted employees electronically when it was time to document their processes and controls for legal purposes. Outside auditors used the software on a "read-only" basis to check that problems actually were resolved but not to make changes to the system. Kimberly-Clark managers used the software to obtain problem reports, learn what auditors were testing, and track test results. The company found no fraud, although Rehfuss says that it uncovered some mistakes caused by "human error," such as when a new employee was unaware of certain control details. Finally, special software was installed to prevent employees from handling more aspects of an accounting transaction than the playbook allowed.

Using software to automate the playbook and document controls for compliance is especially important because Kimberly-Clark has thousands of employees tapping into local or corporate systems to post transactions, prepare financial statements, and handle other accounting tasks. Rehfuss says that this "could create the potential for widespread errors and, in the worst case, intentional fraud [without proper control over access] because so much of our business and transactions are run by computers."

Electronically restricting access to authorized personnel only, electronically enforcing the playbook's controls, and electronically reviewing documentation are cost-effective ways for Kimberly-Clark to stand guard over accounting information. In one year, the company was able to slash more than $2 million (25 percent) off the annual cost of complying with the Sarbanes-Oxley Act. The technology also saves the company about forty hours per audit per location while strengthening its protection against accounting fraud.[10]

For more information about this company, go to **www.kimberly-clark.com.**

Questions

1. According to Jerry Rehfuss, Kimberly-Clark uses a basic accounting principle of having more than one person involved in accounting processes to uncover mistakes or fraud. How can getting more people involved in the accounting process act as a safeguard against fraud and mistakes?
2. It would seem that one important goal for a good accounting system would be to provide financial information to any of Kimberly-Clark's 60,000 employees. And yet Kimberly-Clark has restricted access to its accounting system so that only a limited number of people can access certain information. Why is restricted access important?
3. Do you think Kimberly-Clark's outside auditors should be allowed to make changes to the company's accounting software if they discover a serious problem? Why or why not?
4. Today, most large corporations such as Kimberly-Clark spend millions of dollars to ensure that their accounting information is accurate and complies with the Sarbanes-Oxley Act. Is the expense worth it? Why or why not?

Building Skills for Career Success

1. JOURNALING FOR SUCCESS

Today, more and more people are using computers and personal finance and accounting software to manage their finances. To complete this journal entry, use the Internet to research the Quicken and Microsoft Money software packages. Then answer the questions below.

Assignment

1. Both Quicken and Microsoft Money are popular software packages used by millions of people. Based on your initial research, which software package do you prefer? Explain your answer.
2. After examining both packages, do you think that either software package could help you to manage your finances? Why?

2. EXPLORING THE INTERNET

At the time of this text's publication, the U.S. economy was experiencing a financial crisis. Obtaining business loans, home and automobile loans, and consumer credit was more difficult because of tightening of credit policies by major lenders. Stock prices were declining and people were worried. At the heart of the problem were two large home mortgage lenders—Fannie Mae and Freddie Mac—that provide funds to home mortgage lenders by either purchasing mortgage assets or issuing home mortgage loan guarantees that facilitate the flow of funds into the home mortgage market in the United States. Both firms have also been accused of doctoring earnings and questionable accounting practices.

Assignment

1. Using an Internet search engine such as Google or Yahoo!, locate two or three sites providing information about the recent accounting scandals at these two firms.
2. After examining these sites and reading journal articles, report information about the accounting scandals for each firm. What type of questionable accounting practices occurred in these firms?
3. Based on your assessment of the information you have read, what were the consequences of the questionable accounting practices that occurred?
4. In a two-page report, summarize the questionable accounting practices and what the consequences were for each firm and the executives involved in the scandal.

3. DEVELOPING CRITICAL-THINKING SKILLS

According to the experts, you must evaluate your existing financial condition before establishing an investment plan. As pointed out in this chapter, a personal balance sheet provides a picture of your assets, liabilities, and net worth. A personal income statement will tell you whether you have a cash surplus or cash deficit at the end of a specific time period.

Assignment

1. Using your own financial information from last month, construct a personal balance sheet and personal income statement.
2. Based on the information contained in your personal financial statements, answer the following:
   a. What is your current net worth?
   b. Do you have a cash surplus or a cash deficit at the end of the month?
   c. What specific steps can you take to improve your financial condition?
3. Based on your findings, prepare a plan for improving your financial condition over the next six months.

4. BUILDING TEAM SKILLS

This has been a bad year for Miami-based Park Avenue Furniture. The firm increased sales revenues to $1,400,000, but total expenses ballooned to $1,750,000. Although management realized that some of the firm's expenses were out of control, including cost of goods sold ($700,000), salaries ($450,000), and advertising costs ($140,000), it could not contain expenses. As a result, the furniture retailer lost $350,000. To make matters worse, the retailer applied for a $350,000 loan at Fidelity National Bank and was turned down. The bank officer, Mike Nettles, said that the firm already had too much debt. At that time, liabilities totaled $420,000; owners' equity was $600,000.

Assignment

1. In groups of three or four, analyze the financial condition of Park Avenue Furniture.
2. Discuss why you think the bank officer turned down Park Avenue's loan request.
3. Prepare a detailed plan of action to improve the financial health of Park Avenue Furniture over the next twelve months.

5. RESEARCHING DIFFERENT CAREERS

As pointed out in this chapter, job opportunities for accountants and auditors in the accounting area are expected to experience strong growth between now and the year 2016. Employment opportunities range from entry-level positions for clerical workers and technicians to professional positions that require a college degree in accounting, management consulting, or computer technology. Typical job titles in the accounting field include bookkeeper, corporate accountant, public accountant, auditor, managerial accountant, and controller.

Assignment

1. Answer the following questions based on information obtained from interviews with people employed in accounting, from research in the library or by using the Internet, or from information gained from your college's career center.
   a. What types of activities would a person employed in one of the accounting positions listed above perform on a daily basis?
   b. Would you choose this career? Why or why not?
2. Summarize your findings in a report.

Running a Business Part 6

Information Systems and Accounting at Finagle A Bagel

Like the hole in a bagel, any hole in Finagle A Bagel's information and accounting systems means less dough for the company. Copresidents Alan Litchman and Laura Trust and their management team could not make timely, informed decisions to build the business profitably without reliable systems for collecting data, processing them, and presenting the results in a meaningful way.

PUTTING TECHNOLOGY TO WORK

Regina Jerome is Finagle A Bagel's director of information systems. She and her assistant are responsible for running the computerized accounting system in the company support center, as well as the management information and marketing information systems. As a small business, Finagle A Bagel can't afford to spend money for the sake of having the fastest computer equipment or the flashiest software. Having a limited budget means that "it's absolutely imperative that every piece of technology that we invest in directly supports our business," she says.

One of Jerome's biggest challenges has been implementing a point-of-sale system that supports the information needs of the stores as well as of the senior managers. Unlike restaurant chains that sell standard menu items, Finagle A Bagel customizes everything to the individual customer's taste. Thus, store employees must be able to record, prepare, and serve complicated orders. "We designed our point-of-sale system so that when a customer orders, the system follows our menu and enables our cashiers to deliver exactly what the customer ordered," Jerome says. "At the same time, the system collects all the pertinent financial information. Every transaction is recorded and can be retrieved by minute, by day, by store, by cashier, and by terminal." With information from the point-of-sale system, general managers can analyze detailed sales patterns before making decisions about store staffing levels, food orders, and other day-to-day operational issues.

TRACKING CASH, CALCULATING PROFITS

The copresidents use the financial data drawn from every cash register connected to this point-of-sale system to reconcile daily store sales with daily bank deposits. As a result, copresident Litchman knows by 7:30 each morning how much money was deposited on the previous day and the total amount the company has to cover payroll, food purchases, and other expenses. He also knows if a store's reported sales match its bank deposit. If not, a senior manager immediately looks into the discrepancy, which usually turns out to be some kind of error. Once in a while, however, the discrepancy is a sign of store-level theft that requires further investigation and—when warranted—legal action.

Finagle A Bagel's managers use the company's accounting system to make other important decisions. For every dollar of sales, a food service business makes only a few cents in profit. Finagle A Bagel makes about 8 cents in profit from every sales dollar, but Litchman is aiming to make a profit of 10 cents per dollar. He and his team need timely reports showing retailing and wholesaling revenues, the cost of goods sold, and operating expenses to calculate the company's pretax profit and measure progress toward this profit goal. Food and labor costs constitute more than two-thirds of Finagle A Bagel's costs—so the faster managers can see these numbers, the faster they can act if expenses are higher than expected.

TECHNOLOGY DRIVES THE FREQUENT FINAGLER CARD

Thanks to new software running on the point-of-sale system, Finagle A Bagel has been able to introduce a new and improved Frequent Finagler customer loyalty card. Customers pay $1 to buy this card, which is activated immediately at the store. From that point on, the cardholder receives one point for every dollar spent in any Finagle A Bagel store. Points can be redeemed for free food, such as a cup of coffee, a bagel sandwich, or a bottle of fruit juice.

The Frequent Finagler card is an excellent way for the company to learn more about the buying habits of its most valuable customers. Managers can see which menu items loyal customers buy, in which store, and at what time of day. Going a step further, Finagle A Bagel is using the card to start a dialogue with loyal customers. The company's website (**www.finagleabagel.com**) plays a key role in this initiative. When cardholders log on and register personal data such as address, phone number, and e-mail address, they receive five points on their new Frequent Finagler card. Finagle A Bagel receives a wealth of customer data to analyze and use in targeting its marketing efforts more precisely.

ADD A PRODUCT, DROP A PRODUCT

The technologies driving the Frequent Finagler card and the point-of-sale system help Finagle A Bagel to gather sufficient data to support decisions about changing the product line. "We add products to categories that are doing well, we eliminate things that are not selling, and we bring back products that have done well," says Trust. "Being able to know that a product isn't selling so we can get it off the menu and try something new is a vital piece of information."

For example, says Trust, "We just introduced a new sausage bagel pizza based on the fact that our pepperoni pizza sells very well—better than our veggie pizza." When sales data confirmed the popularity of sausage, Finagle A Bagel began introducing it in a breakfast bagel sandwich. Now the company is looking at incorporating sausage into other menu items to delight customers' taste buds and boost sales. However, Trust and her management team won't make any product decisions without first consulting reports based on data collected by the Frequent Finagler card and the point-of-sale system.

Questions

1. Is Finagle A Bagel collecting data from internal sources, external sources, or both? What cautions apply to the sources of its data?
2. Finagle A Bagel uses information to track cash, sales revenues, and expenses on a daily basis. How does this type of accounting system encourage effective decision making and discourage store-level theft?
3. As a small business, which of the financial ratios might Finagle A Bagel want to track especially closely? Why?
4. Do you think the Frequent Finagler card has any effect on Finagle A Bagel's customer loyalty? For the firm, what are the benefits of the loyalty program?

Building a Business Plan Part 6

Now that you have a marketing plan, the next big and important step is to prepare a financial plan. One of the biggest mistakes an entrepreneur makes when faced with a need for financing is not being prepared. Completing this section will show you that if you are prepared and you are creditworthy, the task may be easier than you think. Remember, most lenders and investors insist that you submit current financial statements that have been prepared by an independent certified public accountant (CPA). Chapter 17, "Using Accounting Information," should help you to answer the questions in this part of the business plan.

THE FINANCIAL PLAN COMPONENT

Your financial plan should answer at least the following questions about the investment needed, sales and cash-flow forecasts, breakeven analysis, and sources of funding.

6.1. What is the actual amount of money you need to open your business (start-up budget) and the amount needed to keep it open (operating budget)? Prepare a realistic budget.

6.2. How much money do you have, and how much money will you need to start your business and stay in business?

6.3. Prepare a projected income statement by month for the first year of operation and by quarter for the second and third years.

6.4. Prepare projected balance sheets for each of the first three years of operation.

6.5. Prepare a breakeven analysis. How many units of your products or service will have to be sold to cover your costs?

6.6. Reinforce your final projections by comparing them with industry averages for your chosen industry.

REVIEW OF BUSINESS PLAN ACTIVITIES

Throughout this project, you have been investigating what it takes to open and run a business, and now you are finally at the bottom line: What is it going to cost to open your business, and how much money will you need to keep it running for a year? Before tackling the last part of the business plan, review your answers to the questions in each part to make sure that all your answers are consistent throughout the entire business plan. Then write a brief statement that summarizes all the information for this part of the business plan.

The information contained in this section will also assist you in completing the online *Interactive Business Plan*.

PART 7

Finance and Investment

In this part, we look at another business resource—money. First, we discuss the functions of money and the financial institutions that are part of our banking system. Then we examine the concept of financial management and investing for both firms and individuals.

Getty Images

18 Understanding Money, Banking, and Credit

LEARNING OBJECTIVES
What you will be able to do once you complete this chapter:

1. Identify the functions and characteristics of money.
2. Summarize how the Federal Reserve System regulates the money supply.
3. Describe the organizations involved in the banking industry.
4. Identify the services provided by financial institutions.
5. Understand how financial institutions are changing to meet the needs of domestic and international customers.
6. Explain how deposit insurance protects customers.
7. Discuss the importance of credit and credit management.

AP Photo/Richard Drew

inside business

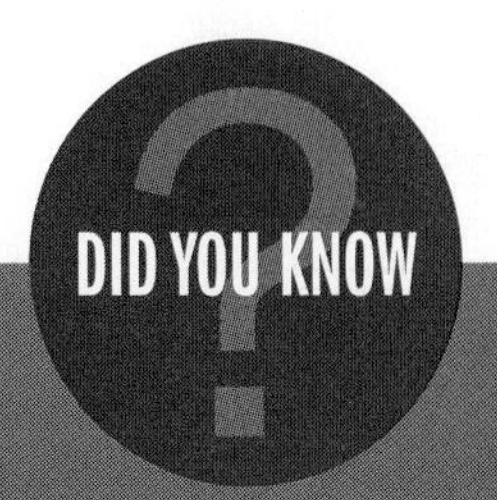

JPMorgan Chase Banks on Wall Street and Main Street

When Aaron Burr founded the Bank of the Manhattan Company in 1799 to finance waterworks for New York City, he could not have foreseen how large and powerful his fledgling bank would become. Over the next 200 years, the bank was renamed numerous times as it merged with or acquired hundreds of financial institutions in New York and beyond, widening its scope and expanding its reach worldwide. It has been associated with some of the most famous names in finance, including David Rockefeller and J. Pierpont Morgan. Some of the banks in its past helped fund the Erie Canal and the Brooklyn Bridge, among many other major projects.

The bank that Burr founded has changed dramatically since the 1990s, when it absorbed two big rivals, Chemical Bank and Manufacturers Hanover Bank, in its quest for growth. In 2000, it joined with the global investment bank JP Morgan to form JPMorgan Chase. By merging with Bank One in 2004, the bank expanded its branch system nationwide and brought millions of additional bank and credit accounts under its corporate umbrella.

The economic turmoil of 2008 led to new opportunities—and new risks. Bear Stearns, then one of the nation's leading investment banks, faced a credit crunch so severe that it was on the verge of collapse. With the blessing of the Federal Reserve Bank, JPMorgan Chase quickly stepped in to buy the company at a steep discount. This move not only reassured the financial markets, but it also added to JPMorgan Chase's strength on Wall Street.

Months later, the U.S. government asked JPMorgan Chase to make another last-minute acquisition. This time, it took over Washington Mutual Savings and Loan (WaMu), which had failed under the weight of bad mortgage loans. JPMorgan Chase had thought about buying WaMu for some time but now it was able to complete the deal at a bargain price, gain entrance to new markets, and introduce itself to millions of new customers.[1]

JPMorgan Chase's purchase of WaMu during the 2008 economic turmoil enabled it to make the deal at a bargain price, gain entrance to new markets, and introduce itself to millions of new customers.

The Banking Crisis! Those three words say a lot about the recent downturn in the nation's economy. Those same three words also don't tell the entire story because the banking crisis caused a ripple effect through the entire economy. In fact, the economic problems caused by the banking crisis affected everyone in the United States in some way. For example,

- Many individuals lost their homes because they obtained loans they couldn't afford.
- The nation experienced record numbers of unemployed workers.
- Many people watched helplessly as their retirement accounts and investments decreased in value.

In reality, most Americans were frightened by an economic crisis that some experts described as the worst the nation had seen since the Great Depression.

To help solve the problems, the Federal Reserve Bank became heavily involved in an effort to inject cash into the nation's banking system. The government also protected bank customers by merging "troubled" banks with financially stable banks. The merger between JPMorgan Chase and Washington Mutual (WaMu) described in this chapter's Inside Business opening case is one example of the government's efforts to protect bank customers. While Washington Mutual had been struggling with bad mortgage debt and nonperforming loans and for a time looked like

It's all money! Regardless of what their money looks like, people around the world know that their currency serves as a medium of exchange, a measure of value, and a store of value. In this photo, a bank clerk exchanges Chinese yuan for U.S. dollars.

it might fail, no depositors lost money because their money was protected by the Federal Deposit Insurance Corporation—the government agency often referred to as the FDIC.

At the time of publication, Congress had just passed and the president had just signed a financial rescue plan designed to restore confidence in the banking industry. After the rescue plan was enacted, two facts became obvious. First, it will take time for the U.S. economy to recover from what some experts describe as a financial meltdown. Second, healthy banks are necessary for both individuals and businesses to function in today's economic world.

Most people regard a bank, savings and loan association, or similar financial institution as a place to deposit or borrow money. When you deposit money, you *receive* interest. When you borrow money, you must *pay* interest. You may borrow to buy a home, a car, or some other high-cost item. In this case, the resource that will be transformed into money to repay the loan is the salary you receive for your labor.

Businesses also transform resources into money. A business firm (even a new one) may have a valuable asset in the form of an idea for a product or service. If the firm (or its founder) has a good credit history and the idea is a good one, a bank or other lender may lend it the money to develop, produce, and market the product or service. The loan—with interest—will be repaid out of future sales revenue. In this way, both the firm and the lender will earn a reasonable profit.

In each of these situations, the borrower needs the money now and will have the ability to repay it later. But also in each situation, the borrowed money will be repaid through the use of *resources*. And while the decision to borrow money from a bank or other financial institution always should be made after careful deliberation, the fact is that responsible borrowing enables both individuals and business firms to meet specific needs.

In this chapter we begin by outlining the functions and characteristics of money that make it an acceptable means of payment for products, services, and resources. Then we consider the role of the Federal Reserve System in maintaining a healthy economy. Next, we describe the banking industry—commercial banks, savings and loan associations, credit unions, and other institutions that offer banking services. Then we turn our attention to how banking practices meet the needs of customers. We also describe the safeguards established by the federal government to protect depositors against losses. In closing, we examine credit transactions, sources of credit information, and effective collection procedures.

What Is Money?

1

Learning Objective: Identify the functions and characteristics of money.

barter system a system of exchange in which goods or services are traded directly for other goods or services

money anything a society uses to purchase products, services, or resources

The members of some societies still exchange goods and services through barter, without using money. A **barter system** is a system of exchange in which goods or services are traded directly for other goods or services. One family may raise vegetables and herbs, and another may weave cloth. To obtain food, the family of weavers trades cloth for vegetables, provided that the farming family is in need of cloth.

The trouble with the barter system is that the two parties in an exchange must need each other's products at the same time, and the two products must be roughly equal in value. Thus, even very isolated societies soon develop some sort of money to eliminate the inconvenience of trading by barter.

Money is anything a society uses to purchase products, services, or resources. Historically, different groups of people have used all sorts of objects as money—whales' teeth, stones, beads, copper crosses, clamshells, and gold and silver, for example. Today, the most commonly used objects are metal coins and paper bills, which together are called *currency*.

The Functions of Money

Money aids in the exchange of goods, services, and resources. However, this is a rather general (and somewhat theoretical) way of stating money's function. Let's look instead at three *specific* functions money serves in any society.

Money as a Medium of Exchange

A **medium of exchange** is anything accepted as payment for products, services, and resources. This definition looks very much like the definition of money. It is meant to because the primary function of money is to serve as a medium of exchange. The key word here is *accepted*. As long as the owners of products, services, and resources *accept* money in an exchange, it is performing this function. For example, if you want to purchase a Hewlett-Packard Photosmart printer that is priced at $149 in a Circuit City store, you must give the store the correct amount of money. In return, the store gives you the product.

medium of exchange anything accepted as payment for products, services, and resources

Money as a Measure of Value

A **measure of value** is a single standard or "yardstick" used to assign values to and compare the values of products, services, and resources. Money serves as a measure of value because the prices of all products, services, and resources are stated in terms of money. It is thus the "common denominator" we use to compare products and decide which we will buy.

measure of value a single standard or "yardstick" used to assign values to and compare the values of products, services, and resources

Money as a Store of Value

Money received by an individual or firm need not be used immediately. It may be held and spent later. Hence, money serves as a **store of value**, or a means of retaining and accumulating wealth. This function of money comes into play whenever we hold onto money—in a pocket, a cookie jar, a savings account, or whatever.

store of value a means of retaining and accumulating wealth

Value that is stored as money is affected by *inflation*. Remember from Chapter 1 that *inflation* is a general rise in the level of prices. As prices go up in an inflationary period, money loses purchasing power. Suppose that you can buy a Bose home theater system for $1,000. Your $1,000 has a value equal to the value of that home theater system. But suppose that you wait and do not buy the home theater system immediately. If the price goes up to $1,050 in the meantime because of inflation, you can no longer buy the home theater system with your $1,000. Your money has *lost* purchasing power because it is now worth less than the home theater system. To determine the effect of inflation on the purchasing power of a dollar, economists often refer to a consumer price index such as the one illustrated in Figure 18.1. The consumer price index measures the changes in prices of a fixed basket of goods purchased by a typical consumer, including food, transportation, housing, clothing, medical care, recreation, education, communication, and other goods and services. The base amount for the consumer price index is 100 and was established by averaging the cost of the items included in the consumer price index over a 36-month period from 1982 to 1984. In June 2008, it took approximately $214 to purchase the same goods that could have been purchased for $100 in the base period 1982–1984.

Important Characteristics of Money

Money must be easy to use, trusted, and capable of performing the three functions just mentioned. To meet these requirements, money must possess the following five characteristics.

Divisibility

The standard unit of money must be divisible into smaller units to accommodate small purchases as well as large ones. In the United States, our standard is the dollar, and it is divided into pennies, nickels, dimes, quarters, and half-dollars. These coins allow us to make purchases of less than a dollar and of odd amounts greater than a dollar. Other nations have their own divisible currencies: the euro in European nations, the rupee in India, and the yen in Japan, to mention a few.

Figure 18.1: The Consumer Price Index and the Purchasing Power of the Consumer Dollar (Base Period 1982–1984 = 100)

Inflation causes a loss of money's stored value. As the consumer price index goes up, the purchasing power of the consumer's dollar goes down.

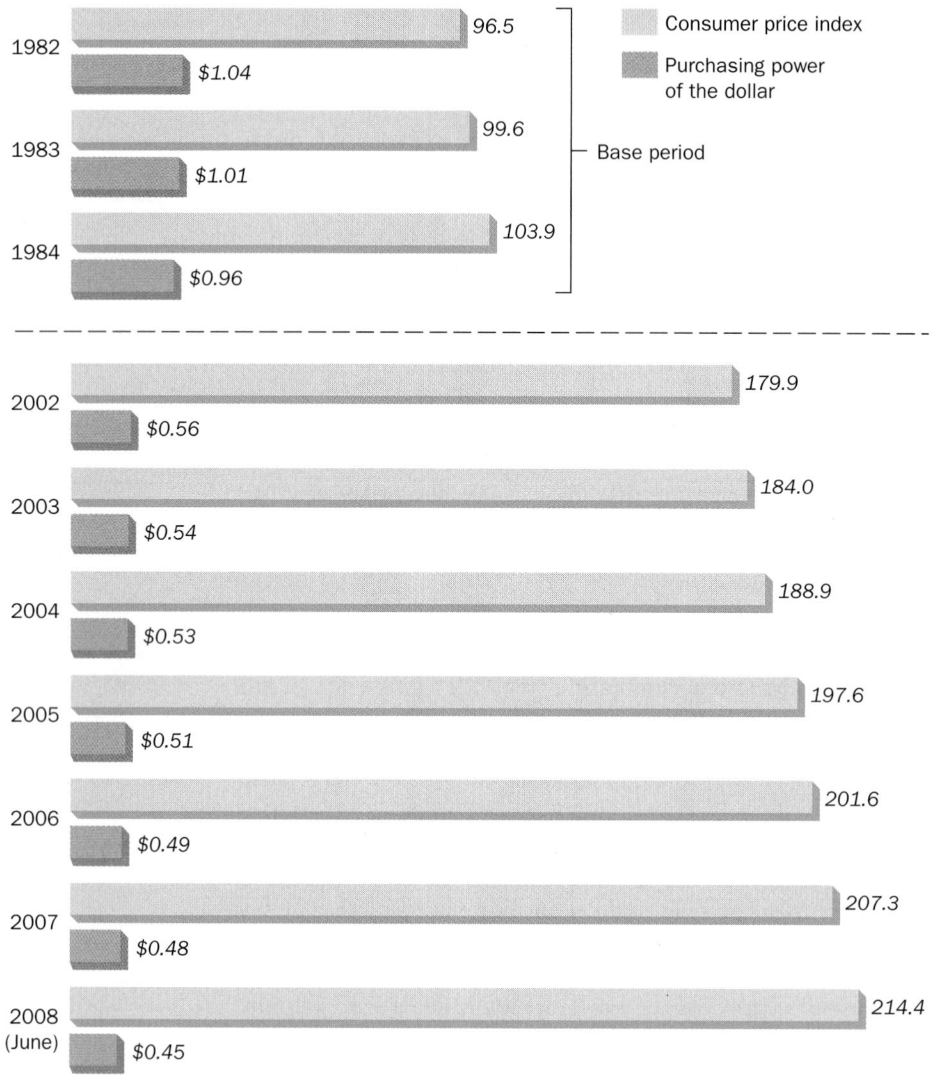

Consumer price index
Purchasing power of the dollar
Base period

1982 96.5 $1.04
1983 99.6 $1.01
1984 103.9 $0.96
2002 179.9 $0.56
2003 184.0 $0.54
2004 188.9 $0.53
2005 197.6 $0.51
2006 201.6 $0.49
2007 207.3 $0.48
2008 (June) 214.4 $0.45

Source: The U.S. Bureau of Labor Statistics website, **www.bls.gov**, September 30, 2008.

Portability Money must be small enough and light enough to be carried easily. For this reason, paper currency is issued in larger *denominations*—multiples of the standard dollar unit. Five-, ten-, twenty-, fifty-, and hundred-dollar bills make our money convenient for almost any purchase.

Stability Money should retain its value over time. When it does not, people tend to lose faith in their money. When money becomes extremely unstable, people may turn to other means of storing value, such as gold and jewels, works of art, and real estate. They even may use such items as a medium of exchange in a barter system. During upheavals in Eastern Europe including Russia in the 1990s, farmers traded farm products for cigarettes because the value of cigarettes was more stable than each nation's money.

Durability The objects that serve as money should be strong enough to last through reasonable usage. No one would appreciate (or use) dollar bills that disintegrated as they were handled or coins that melted in the sun. To increase the life expectancy of paper currency, most nations use special paper with a high fiber content.

Difficulty of Counterfeiting If a nation's currency were easy to counterfeit—that is, to imitate or fake—its citizens would be uneasy about accepting it as payment. Thus, countries do their best to ensure that it is very hard to reproduce their currency. In an attempt to make paper currency more difficult to counterfeit, the U.S. government periodically redesigns its paper currency. Typically, countries use special paper and watermarks and print intricate designs on their currency to discourage counterfeiting.

The Supply of Money: M_1 and M_2

How much money is there in the United States? Before we can answer this question, we need to define a couple of concepts. A **demand deposit** is an amount on deposit in a checking account. It is called a *demand* deposit because it can be claimed immediately—on demand—by presenting a properly made out check, withdrawing cash from an automated teller machine (ATM), or transferring money between accounts.

demand deposit an amount on deposit in a checking account

A **time deposit** is an amount on deposit in an interest-bearing savings account. Financial institutions generally permit immediate withdrawal of money from savings accounts. However, they can require advance written notice prior to withdrawal. The time between notice and withdrawal is what leads to the name *time* deposit. For this reason, they are called *near-monies*. Other near-monies include short-term government securities, money-market mutual fund shares, and the cash surrender values of insurance policies.

time deposit an amount on deposit in an interest-bearing savings account

Now we can discuss the question of how much money there is in the United States. There are two main measures of the supply of money: M_1 and M_2.

The M_1 *supply of money* is a narrow definition and consists only of currency, demand and other checkable deposits, and traveler's checks. By law, currency must be accepted as payment for products, services, and resources. Checks (demand deposits) are accepted as payment because they are convenient, convertible to cash, and generally safe.

The M_2 *supply of money* consists of M_1 (currency and demand deposits) plus savings accounts, certain money-market securities, and small-denomination time deposits or certificates of deposit (CDs) of less than $100,000. The M_2 definition of money is based on the assumption that time deposits can be converted to cash for spending. Figure 18.2 shows the elements of the M_1 and M_2 supply of money.

Figure 18.2: The Supply of Money

Two measures of the money supply are M_1, which includes currency and demand deposits and M_2, which includes M_1 plus certain securities and small-denomination time deposits.

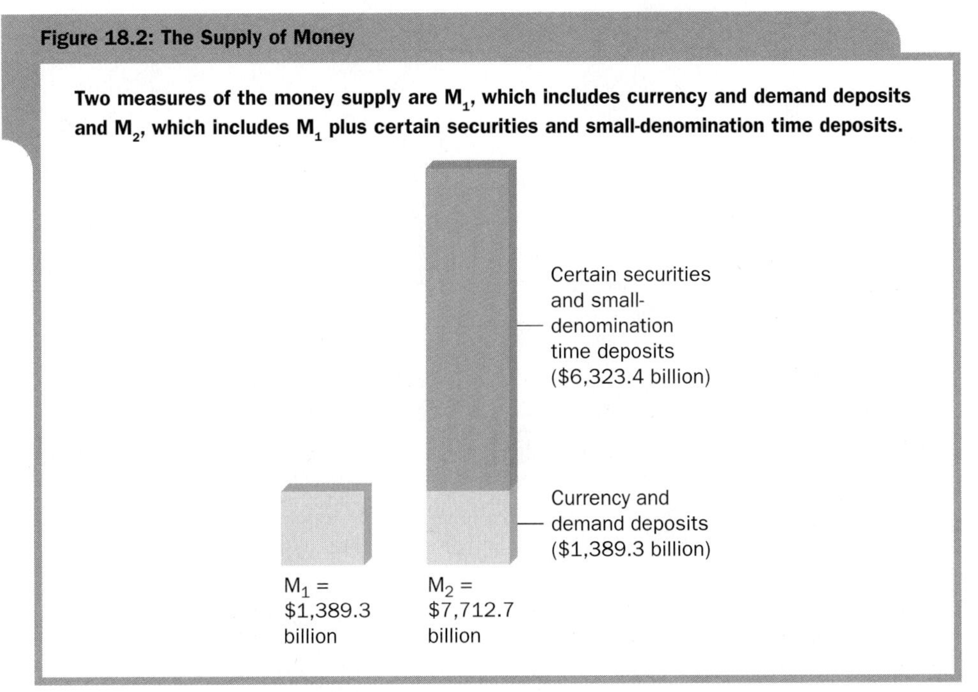

Source: The Federal Reserve website, **www.federalreserve.gov**, accessed September 30, 2008.

We have, then, at least two measures of the supply of money. (Actually, there are other measures as well, which may be broader or narrower than M_1 and M_2.) Therefore, the answer to our original question is that the amount of money in the United States depends very much on how we measure it. Generally, economists, politicians, and bankers tend to focus on M_1 or some variation of M_1.

The Federal Reserve System

2

Learning Objective: Summarize how the Federal Reserve System regulates the money supply.

How do Federal Reserve actions affect me? What is the Federal Reserve System? These are both good questions, and now for some answers. Lately, it seems like the Federal Reserve Board, often referred to as the *Fed*, has been in the news more than usual. Part of the reason is that the Fed is responsible for not only regulating the nation's banking system, but also maintaining a healthy economy. To maintain a healthy economy during the recent banking crisis, the Fed allowed banks in need of cash to borrow money from the Federal Reserve System. Without the ability to borrow needed funds from the Fed, some banks were in danger of failing. The Fed's lending activity also helped encourage other banks to continue loaning money to their customers. If they could not have borrowed money from the Fed, banks would have tightened lending requirements or stopped funding loans to both individuals and business. As a result, the Fed's actions helped to restore confidence in the financial system, to encourage continued lending, to stabilize an unstable economy, and to provide additional time to create the financial rescue plan that was enacted on October 3, 2008.

While many people became aware of the Federal Reserve's actions during the crisis, the Fed's lending programs have been used since the early 1900s to maintain a healthy economy. Here's how it works. The Fed lowers the interest rates that banks pay to borrow money from the Fed in an effort to shore up a sagging economy. When the Fed lowers rates, banks pay less to borrow money from the Fed. In turn, they often lower the interest rates they charge for business loans, home mortgages, car loans, and even credit cards. Lower rates often provide an incentive for both business firms and individuals to buy goods and services, which, in turn, helps to

The nation's two money men. *As chairman of the Federal Reserve Board, Ben Bernanke (right) worked very closely with U.S. Treasury Secretary Henry Paulson (left) to craft a $700 billion bailout plan to stabilize the U.S. economy during the recent financial crisis.*

AP Photo/Manuel Balce Ceneta

Going Global
Coins Instead of Currency?

Should the United States eliminate $1 bills in favor of $1 coins? Dollar bills are as popular as ever, even though the U.S. Mint has launched three types of dollar coins since 1979: The Susan B. Anthony, the Sacagawea, and the Presidential Dollar. Yet Canada was able to take all dollar bills out of circulation after introducing a one-dollar coin in 1987 and a two-dollar coin in 1996. Similarly, the United Kingdom introduced a one-pound coin in 1983, followed by a two-pound coin in 1998, and then eliminated all one-pound bills.

Here's a quick look at coins versus currency:

- *Coins.* A coin can last as long as 40 years, whereas bills can wear out in less than two years. Properly designed dollar coins are easily distinguishable from other change; Canadian dollars are yellow and thicker than other coins, for instance. However, coins are far heavier and bulkier than currency.
- *Currency.* Bills are light, foldable, and convenient to carry and store. Imagine your wallet stuffed with bills—now think of your pockets filled with the same amount in dollar coins. On the other hand, counterfeiting is more of a problem with bills than with coins.

Switching to $1 dollar coins would save $500 million in annual currency printing costs. What about it: Coins or currency?

Sources: Bryce Hoekenga, "Infusion of Dollar Coins Will Make Pockets Jingle More," *Kalamazoo Gazette*, October 30, 2008, **www.mlive.com/news**; Robert J. Samuelson, "A Quiet Revolution in Money," *Washington Post*, June 21, 2007, p. A23; Joel Garreau, "A Flip of the Coin," *Washington Post*, March 21, 2007, p. C1; **www.royalmint.com; www.mint.ca.**

restore the economic health of the nation. On the other hand, rate increases are designed to sustain economic growth while controlling inflation. When the Fed raises rates, banks must pay more to borrow money from the Fed. And the banks, in turn, charge higher rates for both consumer and business loans.

Now let's answer the second question. The **Federal Reserve System** is the central bank of the United States and is responsible for regulating the banking industry. Created by Congress on December 23, 1913, its mission is to maintain an economically healthy and financially sound business environment in which banks can operate.

Federal Reserve System the central bank of the United States responsible for regulating the banking industry

The Federal Reserve System is controlled by its seven-member board of governors, who meet in Washington, D.C. Each governor is appointed by the president and confirmed by the Senate for a fourteen-year term. The president also selects the chairman and vice chairman of the board from among the board members for four-year terms.

The Federal Reserve System consists of twelve district banks located in major cities throughout the United States, as well as twenty-five branch banks (see Figure 18.3). All national (federally chartered) banks must be members of the Fed. State banks may join if they choose to and if they meet membership requirements. For more information about the Federal Reserve System, visit its website at **www.federalreserve.gov.**

The most important function of the Fed is to use monetary policy to regulate the nation's supply of money in such a way as to maintain a healthy economy. In Chapter 1, monetary policy was defined as the Federal Reserve's decisions that determine the size of the supply of money in the nation and the level of interest rates. The goals of monetary policy are continued economic growth, full employment, and stable prices. Three methods—controlling bank reserve requirements, regulating the discount rate, and running open-market operations—are used to implement the Fed's monetary policy.

Regulation of Reserve Requirements

When money is deposited in a bank, the bank must retain a portion of it to satisfy customers who may want to withdraw money from their accounts. The remainder is available to fund loans. By law, the Federal Reserve sets the reserve requirement for financial institutions, whether or not they are members of the Federal Reserve System. The **reserve requirement** is the percentage of its deposits a bank *must* retain, either in its own vault or on deposit with its Federal Reserve district bank. For example, if a bank has deposits of $20 million and the reserve requirement is

reserve requirement the percentage of its deposits a bank *must* retain, either in its own vault or on deposit with its Federal Reserve district bank

Figure 18.3: Federal Reserve System

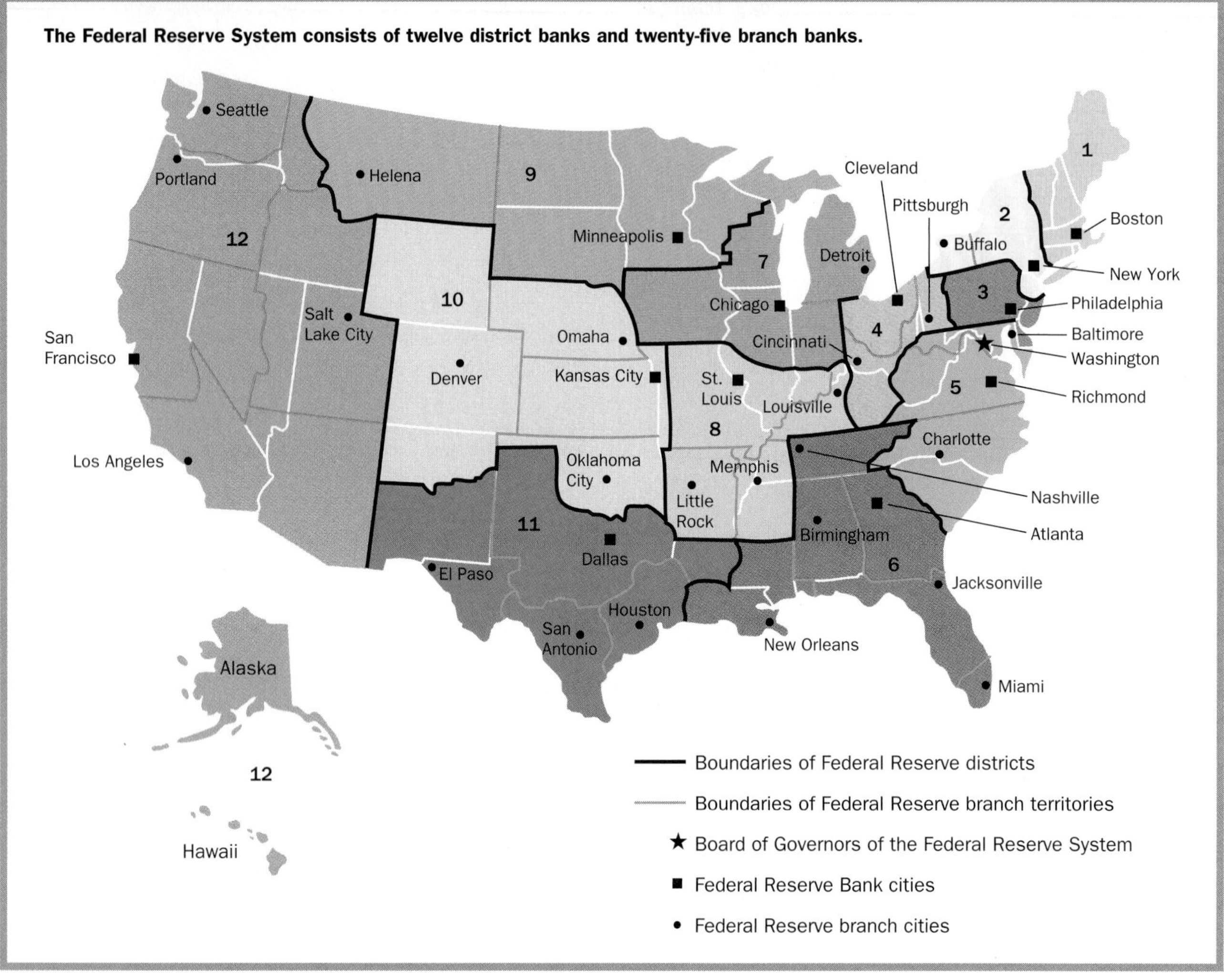

Source: "91st Annual Report, 2004," The Federal Reserve Board website, **www.federalreserve.gov**, accessed October 4, 2008.

10 percent, the bank must retain $2 million. The present reserve requirements range from 0 to 10 percent depending on such factors as the total amount individual banks have on deposit, average daily deposits, and the location of the particular member bank.[2]

Once reserve requirements are met, banks can use remaining funds to create more money and make more loans through a process called *deposit expansion*. In the preceding example, the bank must retain $2 million in a reserve account. It can use the remaining $18 million to fund consumer and business loans. Assume that the bank lends all $18 million to different borrowers. Also assume that before using any of the borrowed funds, all borrowers deposit the $18 million in their bank accounts at the lending institution. Now the bank's deposits have increased by an additional $18 million. Since these deposits are subject to the same reserve requirement described earlier, the bank must maintain $1.8 million in a reserve account, and the bank can lend the additional $16.2 million to other bank customers. Of course, the bank's lending potential becomes steadily smaller and smaller as it makes more loans. And we should point out that since bankers usually are very conservative by nature, they will not use deposit expansion to maximize their lending activities; they will take a more middle-of-the-road approach.

The Fed's board of governors sets the reserve requirement. *When it increases the requirement, banks have less money available for lending.* Fewer loans are made, and the economy tends to slow. *On the other hand, by decreasing the reserve requirement, the Fed can make additional money available for lending to stimulate a slow economy.*

Because this means of controlling the money supply is so very potent and has such far-reaching effects on both consumers and financial institutions, the Fed seldom changes the reserve requirement.

Sustaining the Planet

As part of the PayItGreen Alliance, the Federal Reserve Bank and a group of U.S. banks are encouraging consumers and businesses to protect the environment by switching from paper-based banking to electronic invoices, deposits, payments, and statements. If 20 percent of U.S. households do this, they would save 150 million pounds of paper a year. **www.payitgreen.org**

Regulation of the Discount Rate

Member banks may borrow money from the Fed to satisfy the reserve requirement. The interest rate the Federal Reserve charges for loans to member banks is called the **discount rate**. It is set by the board of directors of each Federal Reserve District bank. For the period from January 2003 to December 2007, the discount rate has been as low as 2 percent and as high as 6.25 percent.[3] Then in January 2008 in an attempt to stabilize the economy and encourage lending, the Federal Reserve began lowering the discount rate. By September 2008, the discount rate was 2.25 percent and remained low throughout the remainder of the year.[4]

discount rate the interest rate the Federal Reserve System charges for loans to member banks

When the Fed *lowers* the discount rate, it is easier and cheaper for banks to obtain money. Member banks feel free to make more loans and to charge lower interest rates. This action generally stimulates the nation's economy. When the Fed *raises* the discount rate, banks begin to restrict loans. They increase the interest rates they charge and tighten their own loan requirements. The overall effect is to slow the economy. Although the discount rate has decreased to 2.25 percent, you should remember that the Fed can increase rates in an effort to maintain a healthy economy.

Open-Market Operations

The federal government finances its activities partly by buying and selling government securities issued by the U.S. Treasury (Treasury bills, notes, and bonds) and federal agency securities. These securities, which pay interest, may be purchased by any individual, firm, or organization—including the Fed. **Open-market operations** are the buying and selling of U.S. government securities by the Federal Reserve System for the purpose of controlling the supply of money.

open-market operations the buying and selling of U.S. government securities by the Federal Reserve System for the purpose of controlling the supply of money

The Federal Open Market Committee (FOMC) is charged with carrying out the Federal Reserve's open-market operations by buying and selling government securities—usually U.S. Treasury bills—through the trading desk of the Federal Reserve Bank of New York. To reduce the nation's money supply, the FOMC simply *sells* government securities on the open market. The money it receives from purchasers is taken out of circulation. Thus, less money is available for investment, purchases, or lending. To increase the money supply, the FOMC *buys* government securities. The money the FOMC pays for securities goes back into circulation, making more money available to individuals and firms.

Because the major purchasers of government securities are banking and financial institutions, open-market operations tend to have an immediate effect on lending and investment.

Of the three tools used to influence monetary policy, the use of open-market operations is the most important. When the Federal Reserve buys and sells securities, the goal is to affect the federal funds rate. The **federal funds rate** is the interest rate at which a bank lends immediately available funds on deposit at the Fed to another bank overnight in order to meet the borrowing bank's reserve requirements. While the FOMC sets a target for the federal funds rate, it does not actually set the rate because it is determined by the open market.[5] (*Note:* There is a difference between the federal funds rate and the discount rate discussed earlier in this section. The *federal funds rate* is the interest rate paid by a bank to borrow funds from other banks. The *discount rate* is the interest rate paid by a bank to borrow funds from the Federal Reserve.) Table 18.1 summarizes the effects of open-market operations and the other tools used by the Fed to regulate the money supply and control the economy.

federal funds rate the interest rate at which a bank lends immediately available funds to another bank overnight in order to meet the borrowing bank's reserve requirements

Table 18.1: Methods Used by the Federal Reserve System to Control the Money Supply and the Economy

Method Used	Immediate Result	End Result
Regulating Reserve Requirement		
1. Fed *increases* reserve requirement	Less money for banks to lend to customers—reduction in overall money supply	Economic slowdown
2. *Fed decreases* reserve requirement	More money for banks to lend to customers—increase in overall money supply	Increased economic activity
Regulating the Discount Rate		
1. Fed *increases* the discount rate	Less money for banks to lend to customers—reduction to overall money supply	Economic slowdown
2. Fed *decreases* the discount rate	More money for banks to lend to customers—increase in overall money supply	Increased economic activity
Open-Market Operations		
1. Fed *sells* government securities	Reduction in overall money supply	Economic slowdown
2. Fed *buys* government securities	Increase in overall money supply	Increased economic activity

Other Fed Responsibilities

In addition to its regulation of the money supply, the Fed is also responsible for serving as the government's bank, clearing checks and electronic transfers, inspecting currency, and applying selective credit controls.

Serving as Government Bank The Federal Reserve is the bank for the U.S. government. As the government's bank, it processes a variety of financial transactions involving trillions of dollars each year. For example, the Federal Reserve provides financial services for the U.S. Treasury, including accounts through which incoming tax deposits and outgoing government payments are handled.

Clearing Checks and Electronic Transfers Today, many people use checks to pay for nearly everything they buy. A check written by a customer of one bank and presented for payment to another bank in the same town may be processed through a local clearinghouse. The procedure becomes more complicated, however, when the banks are not in the same town. This is where the Federal Reserve System comes in. The Fed is responsible for the prompt and accurate collection of over 42.5 billion checks each year.[6] Banks that use the Fed to clear checks are charged a fee for this service. Through the use of electronic equipment, most checks can be cleared within two or three days.

Inspection of Currency As paper currency is handled, it becomes worn or dirty. The typical $1 bill has a life expectancy of less than two years. Most $50 and $100 bills usually last longer because they are handled less. When member banks deposit their surplus cash in a Federal Reserve Bank, the currency is inspected. Bills unfit for further use are separated and destroyed.

Selective Credit Controls The Federal Reserve System has the responsibility for enforcing the Truth-in-Lending Act, which Congress passed in 1968. This act requires lenders to state clearly the annual percentage rate and total finance charge

Smiles during troubled financial times. *Traders on the New York Stock Exchange watch a television monitor as a massive bailout plan is passed by the U.S. Congress. Seven hundred billion dollars (that's right, $700 BILLION) of taxpayer money will be used to stabilize the financial markets and the banking industry.*

for a consumer loan. The Federal Reserve System is also responsible for setting the margin requirements for stock transactions. The *margin* is the minimum amount (expressed as a percentage) of the purchase price that must be paid in cash or eligible securities. (The investor may borrow the remainder.) The current margin requirement is 50 percent. Thus, if an investor purchases $4,000 worth of stock, he or she must pay at least $2,000 in cash or its equivalent in securities. The remaining $2,000 may be borrowed from the brokerage firm. Although the minimum margin requirements are regulated by the Federal Reserve, margin requirements and the interest charged on the loans used to fund margin transactions may vary among brokerage firms and different security exchanges. For example, although an initial investment of at least $2,000 is required to open a margin account, some brokerage firms require more than $2,000.

The American Banking Industry

3 Learning Objective: Describe the organizations involved in the banking industry.

Any banker you ask will tell you that for the American banking industry, the last few years have been frustrating to say the least. And it's not just bankers. Most everyone has been affected in one way or another by the nation's economic problems. The problems became so severe that the nation experienced a financial crisis in late 2008. In fact, problems in the housing, banking, and financial industries were so bad that Congress passed and President Bush signed a comprehensive financial rescue bill on October 3, 2008. While the politicians, the president, economists, business leaders, and the general public still debate the merits of a federal rescue plan, one factor became very apparent: The economy was in trouble. Something had to be done to correct the problems that were causing what some experts described as the nation's worst economic problems since the Great Depression.

Banks, savings and loan associations, credit unions, and other financial institution were at the center of the nation's economic problems. Aggressive lending practices

AP Photo/Richard Drew

that led to record numbers of home foreclosures and nonperforming loans caused a financial meltdown. As the economic problems within the banking industry became larger, the ability to borrow money became more difficult for both individuals and business firms—a very serious problem for both borrowers and lenders. On one side, individuals worried about losing their jobs and businesses with reduced sales revenues and lower profits or losses were reluctant or unable to borrow more money. On the other side, lenders tightened requirements for borrowers. While bankers are in business to make loans, they also want to make sure that the loans will be repaid.

In addition to the nation's economic problems, competition among banks, savings and loan associations, credit unions, and other business firms that want to perform banking activities has never been greater. And banks from Japan, Canada, France, and other foreign nations have thrown their hat into U.S. banking circles. As a result, major banks such as Citibank, Bank of America, Chase, and Wells Fargo have begun to provide innovative services for their customers, including electronic and online banking. Even smaller banks have adopted the full-service banking philosophy and compete aggressively for customers, who expect more services than ever before. Let's begin this section with some information about one of the major players in the banking industry—the commercial bank.

commercial bank a profit-making organization that accepts deposits, makes loans, and provides related services to its customers

national bank a commercial bank chartered by the U.S. Comptroller of the Currency

state bank a commercial bank chartered by the banking authorities in the state in which it operates

savings and loan association (S&L) a financial institution that offers checking and savings accounts and CDs and that invests most of its assets in home mortgage loans and other consumer loans

Commercial Banks

A **commercial bank** is a profit-making organization that accepts deposits, makes loans, and provides related services to its customers. Like other businesses, the bank's primary goal—its mission—is to meet the needs of its customers while earning a profit. In a nutshell, here is how a bank earns its profit: It accepts money in the form of deposits, for which it pays interest. Once money is deposited in the bank, the bank lends it to qualified individuals and businesses that pay interest for the use of borrowed money. If the bank is successful, its income is greater than its expenses, and it will show a profit.

Because they deal with money belonging to individuals and other business firms, banks are carefully regulated. They also must meet certain requirements before they receive a charter, or permission to operate, from either federal or state banking authorities. A **national bank** is a commercial bank chartered by the U.S. Comptroller of the Currency. There are approximately 2,000 national banks.[7] These banks must conform to federal banking regulations and are subject to unannounced inspections by federal auditors.

A **state bank** is a commercial bank chartered by the banking authorities in the state in which it operates. State banks outnumber national banks by about three to one, but they tend to be smaller than national banks. They are subject to unannounced inspections by both state and federal auditors.

Table 18.2 lists the seven largest banks in the United States. All are classified as national banks.

How do entrepreneurs get financing? *Often, entrepreneurs like the lady in this photo have trouble getting the finances they need to start a business. To help solve this problem, many banks and financial institutions are now offering small loans known as "microloans." To date, more than 50 million would-be entrepreneurs worldwide have received microloans to turn their small-business dreams into reality.*

AP/Wide World

Other Financial Institutions

In addition to commercial banks, at least eight other types of financial institutions perform either full or limited banking services for their customers.

Savings and Loan Associations

A **savings and loan association (S&L)** is a financial institution that offers checking and savings accounts and CDs and that invests most of its assets in home mortgage loans and other consumer loans. Originally, S&Ls were permitted to offer their depositors *only* savings accounts. However, since Congress passed the Depository Institutions Deregulation and Monetary Control Act in 1980, they have been able to offer other services to attract depositors.

Table 18.2: The Seven Largest U.S. Banks, Ranked by Total Revenues

Rank	Company	Revenues ($ millions)	Profits ($ millions)	Number of Employees
1	Citigroup	$159,229.0	$ 3,617.0	380,500
2	Bank of America Corp.	119,190.0	14,982.0	209,718
3	JPMorgan Chase & Co.	116,353.0	15,365.0	180,667
4	Wachovia Corp.	55,528.0	6,312.0	121,890
5	Wells Fargo	53,593.0	8,057.0	159,800
6	U.S. Bancorp	20,308.0	4,324.0	52,277
7	Capital One Financial	18,965.5	1,570.3	27,000

Source: The Fortune website, **www.fortune.com**, accessed September 30, 2008.

Today, there are approximately 1,250 S&Ls in the United States.[8] Federal associations are chartered under provisions of the Home Owners' Loan Act of 1933 and are supervised by the Office of Thrift Supervision, a branch of the U.S. Treasury. S&Ls also can be chartered by state banking authorities in the state in which they operate. State-chartered S&Ls are subject to unannounced audits by state authorities.

Credit Unions The United States currently has an estimated 8,400 credit unions.[9] A **credit union** is a financial institution that accepts deposits from and lends money to only those people who are its members. Usually, the membership consists of employees of a particular firm, people in a particular profession, or those who live in a community served by a local credit union. Credit unions may pay higher interest on deposits than commercial banks and S&Ls, and they may provide loans at lower cost. The National Credit Union Administration regulates federally chartered credit unions and many state credit unions. State authorities also may regulate credit unions with state charters.

credit union a financial institution that accepts deposits from and lends money to only those people who are its members

Organizations That Perform Banking Functions Six other types of financial institutions are involved in banking activities. Although not actually full-service banks, they offer customers some banking services.

- *Mutual savings banks* are financial institutions that are owned by their depositors and offer many of the same services offered by banks, S&Ls, and credit unions, including checking accounts, savings accounts, and CDs. Like other financial institutions, they also fund home mortgages, commercial loans, and consumer loans. Unlike other types of financial institutions, mutual savings banks are owned by their depositors. And the profits of a mutual savings bank go to the depositors, usually in the form of dividends or slightly higher interest rates on savings. Today, there are approximately 450 savings banks in operation, primarily in the Northeast.
- *Insurance companies* provide long-term financing for office buildings, shopping centers, and other commercial real estate projects throughout the United States. The funds used for this type of financing are obtained from policyholders' insurance premiums.
- *Pension funds* are established by employers to guarantee their employees a regular monthly income on retirement. Contributions to the fund may come from the employer, the employee, or both. Pension funds earn additional income through generally conservative investments in corporate stocks, corporate bonds, and government securities, as well as through financing real estate developments.
- *Brokerage firms* offer combination savings and checking accounts that pay higher-than-usual interest rates (so-called money-market rates). Many people

have switched to these accounts because they are convenient and to get the higher rates, but banks have instituted similar types of accounts, hoping to lure their depositors back.

- *Finance companies* provide financing to individuals and business firms that may not be able to get financing from banks, S&Ls, or credit unions. Firms such as Ford Motor Credit, GE Capital, and General Motors Acceptance Corporation provide loans to both individuals and business firms. Lenders such as Household Finance Corporation (HFC) and Ace Cash Express, Inc., provide short-term loans to individuals. The interest rates charged by these lenders may be higher than the interest rates charged by other financial institutions.
- *Investment banking firms* are organizations that assist corporations in raising funds, usually by helping sell new issues of stocks, bonds, or other financial securities. Although these firms do not accept deposits or make loans like traditional banking firms, they do help companies raise millions of dollars. More information about investment banking firms and the role they play in American business is provided in Chapters 19 and 20.

Careers in the Banking Industry

Take a second look at Table 18.2. The seven largest banks in the United States employ approximately 1,132,000 people. If you add to this amount the people employed by smaller banks not listed in Table 18.2 and those employed by S&Ls, credit unions, and other financial institutions, the number of employees grows dramatically. But be warned: According to the *Career Guide to Industries,* published by the U.S. Department of Labor, banking employment is projected to grow more slowly than jobs in the economy between now and the year 2016. Even though employment within the industry is expected to increase more slowly when compared with other industries, there will be job growth for customer service representatives, financial services sales representatives, financial analysts, personal bankers, and computer specialists. Also, job opportunities should be favorable for tellers and other administrative support workers because workers often leave these positions for other jobs that offer higher pay or greater responsibilities.[10]

For Union Bank of California, the most important word in its advertisement is "YOU." *Banks operate in a very competitive business environment. One way to rise above the competing banks is to provide excellent customer service to both individuals and businesses.*

Courtesy Union Bank of California

To be successful in the banking industry, you need a number of different skills. For starters, employees for a bank, S&L, credit union, or other financial institution must possess the following traits:

1. *You must be honest.* Because you are handling other people's money, many financial institutions go to great lengths to discover dishonest employees.
2. *You must be able to interact with people.* A number of positions in the banking industry require that you possess the interpersonal skills needed to interact not only with other employees but also with customers.
3. *You need a strong background in accounting.* Many of the routine tasks performed by employees in the banking industry are basic accounting functions. For example, a teller must post deposits or withdrawals to a customer's account and then balance out at the end of the day to ensure accuracy.
4. *You need to appreciate the relationship between banking and finance.* Bank officers must interview loan applicants and determine if their request for money is based on sound financial principles. Above all, loan officers must be able to evaluate applicants and their loan requests to determine if the borrower will be able to repay a loan.
5. *You should possess basic computer skills.* Almost all employees in the banking industry use a computer for some aspect of their work on a daily basis.

Depending on qualifications, work experience, and education, starting salaries generally are between $15,000 and $30,000 a year, but it is not uncommon for college graduates to earn $35,000 a year or more.

If banking seems like an area you might be interested in, why not do more career exploration? You could take a banking course if your college or university offers one, or you could obtain a part-time job during the school year or a summer job in a bank, S&L, or credit union.

Traditional Services Provided by Financial Institutions

4

Learning Objective: Identify the services provided by financial institutions.

To determine how important banking services are to you, ask yourself the following questions:

- How many checks did you write last month?
- Do you have a major credit card? If so, how often do you use it?
- Do you have a savings account or a CD?
- Have you ever financed the purchase of a new or used automobile?
- How many times did you visit an ATM last month?

If you are like most people and business firms, you would find it hard to live a normal life without the services provided by banks and other financial institutions. Typical services provided by a bank or other financial institution are illustrated in Figure 18.4.

The most important traditional banking services for both individuals and businesses are described in this section. Online banking, electronic transfer of funds, and other significant and future developments are discussed in the next section.

Checking Accounts

Imagine what it would be like living in today's world without a checking account. Although a few people do not have one, most of us like the convenience a checking account offers. Firms and individuals deposit money in checking accounts (demand deposits) so that they can write checks to pay for purchases. A **check** is a written order for a bank or other financial institution to pay a stated dollar amount to the business or person indicated on the face of the check. In order to attract new customers, many financial institutions offer free checking; others charge activity fees (or service charges) for checking accounts. Fees and charges generally range between $5 and $20 per month for individuals. For businesses, monthly charges are based on the average daily balance in the checking account and/or the number of checks written. Charges for business checking accounts are often higher than those for individual accounts.

check a written order for a bank or other financial institution to pay a stated dollar amount to the business or person indicated on the face of the check

Figure 18.4: Typical Services Provided by Banks and Other Financial Institutions

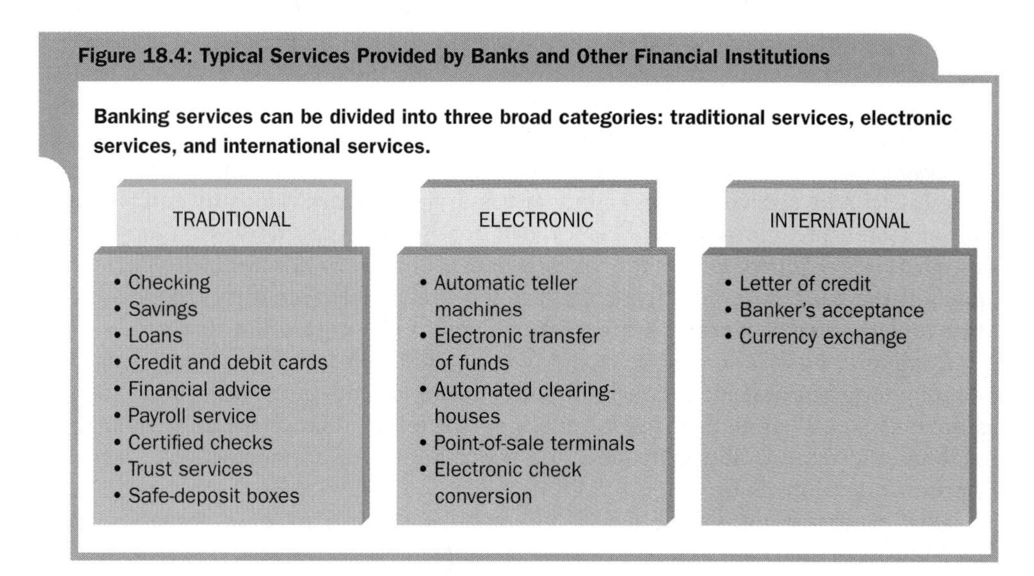

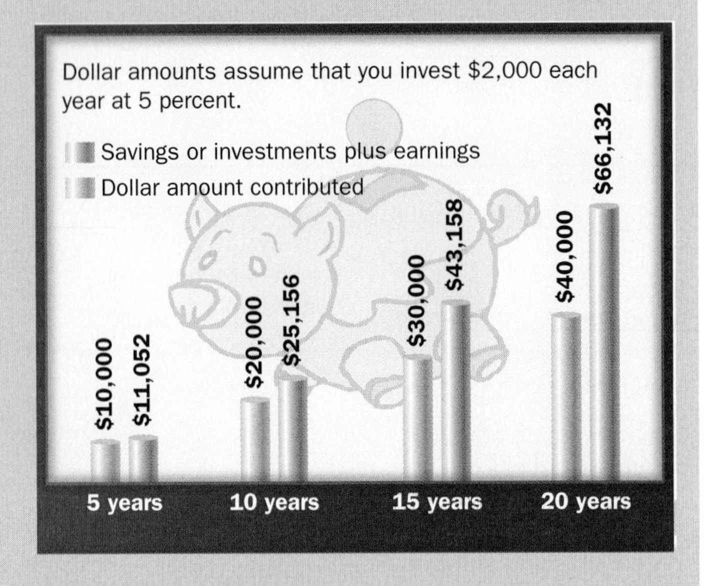

Most financial institutions offer interest-paying checking accounts, often called *NOW accounts*. A **NOW account** is an interest-bearing checking account. (*NOW* stands for *negotiable order of withdrawal*.) For these accounts, the usual interest rate is between 0.25 and 1 percent. Typically, online Internet banks pay slightly higher interest rates. However, individual banks may impose certain restrictions on their NOW accounts, including the following:

- A minimum balance before any interest is paid
- Monthly fees for accounts whose balances fall below a set minimum amount
- Restrictions on the number of checks that may be written each month

Although banks and other financial institutions may pay low interest rates on checking accounts, even small earnings are better than no earnings. In addition to interest rates, be sure to compare monthly fees before opening a checking account.

Savings Accounts

Savings accounts (time deposits) provide a safe place to store money and a very conservative means of investing. The usual *passbook savings account* earns between 0.25 and 2 percent in commercial banks and S&Ls and slightly more in credit unions or online Internet banks.

NOW account an interest-bearing checking account; *NOW* stands for *negotiable order of withdrawal*

certificate of deposit (CD) a document stating that the bank will pay the depositor a guaranteed interest rate on money left on deposit for a specified period of time

A depositor who is willing to leave money on deposit with a bank for a set period of time can earn a higher rate of interest. To do so, the depositor buys a certificate of deposit. A **certificate of deposit (CD)** is a document stating that the bank will pay the depositor a guaranteed interest rate on money left on deposit for a specified period of time. The interest rates paid on CDs change weekly; they once briefly exceeded 11 percent in 1980. Recently, interest rates have ranged from 2 to 5 percent. The rate always depends on how much is invested and for how long. Generally, the rule is: The longer the period of time until maturity, the higher is the rate. Depositors are penalized for early withdrawal of funds invested in CDs.

Short- and Long-Term Loans

Banks, S&Ls, credit unions, and other financial institutions provide short- and long-term loans to both individuals and businesses. *Short-term business loans* must be repaid within one year or less. Typical uses for the money obtained through short-term loans include solving cash-flow problems, purchasing inventory, financing promotional needs, and meeting unexpected emergencies.

line of credit a loan that is approved before the money is actually needed

revolving credit agreement a guaranteed line of credit

collateral real estate or property pledged as security for a loan

To help ensure that short-term money will be available when needed, many firms establish a line of credit. A **line of credit** is a loan that is approved before the money is actually needed. Because all the necessary paperwork is already completed and the loan is preapproved, the business can obtain the money later without delay, as soon as it is required. Even with a line of credit, a firm may not be able to borrow money if the bank does not have sufficient funds available. For this reason, some firms prefer a **revolving credit agreement**, which is a guaranteed line of credit.

Long-term business loans are repaid over a period of years. The average length of a long-term business loan is generally three to seven years but sometimes as long as fifteen years. Long-term loans are used most often to finance the expansion of buildings and retail facilities, mergers and acquisitions, replacement of equipment, or product development.

Most lenders require some type of collateral for long-term loans. **Collateral** is real estate or property (stocks, bonds, equipment, or any other asset of value) pledged as security for a loan. For example, when an individual obtains a loan to pay for a new Chevrolet Malibu, the automobile is the collateral for the loan. If the borrower fails to repay the loan according to the terms specified in the loan agreement, the lender can repossess the car.

Repayment terms and interest rates for both short- and long-term loans are arranged between the lender and the borrower. For businesses, repayment terms may include monthly, quarterly, semiannual, or annual payments. Repayment terms (and interest rates) for personal loans vary depending on how the money will be used and what type of collateral, if any, is pledged. However, individuals typically make monthly payments to repay personal loans. Borrowers always should "shop" for a loan, comparing the repayment terms and interest rates offered by competing financial institutions.

Credit-Card and Debit-Card Transactions

By 2010, 176 million Americans will use credit cards to pay for everything from tickets on American Airlines to Zebco fishing gear.[11] Today, the number of cardholders increases every month. In fact, most Americans receive at least two or three credit-card applications in the mail every month. Why have credit cards become so popular?

For a merchant, the answer is obvious. By depositing charge slips in a bank or other financial institution, the merchant can convert credit-card sales into cash. In return for processing the merchant's credit-card transactions, the financial institution charges a fee that generally ranges between 1.5 and 5 percent. Typically, small, independent businesses pay more than larger stores or chain stores. Let's assume that you use a Visa credit card to purchase a microwave oven for $300 from Gold Star Appliance, a retailer in Richardson, Texas. At the end of the day, the retailer deposits your charge slip, along with other charge slips, checks, and currency collected during the day, at its bank. If the bank charges Gold Star Appliance 5 percent to process each credit-card transaction, the bank deducts a processing fee of $15 ($300 × 0.05 = $15) for your credit-card transaction and immediately deposits the remainder ($285) in Gold Star Appliance's account. The number of credit-card

AP Photo/Journal & Courier/John Terhune

How do you pay for lunch or dinner? *More and more people are using credit or debit cards to pay for their purchases. For the customer, credit cards are easy and convenient. A very real disadvantage is that people often spend more money than they can afford when they use credit cards on a regular basis.*

transactions, the total dollar amount of credit sales, and how well the merchant can negotiate the fees the bank charges determine actual fees.

For the consumer, credit cards permit the purchase of goods and services even when funds are low. Most major credit cards are issued by banks or other financial institutions in cooperation with Visa International or MasterCard International. The unique feature of bank credit cards is that they extend a line of credit to the cardholder, much as a bank's consumer loan department does. Thus credit cards provide immediate access to short-term credit for the cardholder. Of course, the ability to obtain merchandise immediately and pay for it later can lead to credit-card misuse. The average American has a credit-card balance of approximately $9,205.[12] With typical finance charges ranging from 1 to 1.5 percent a month (that's 12 to 18 percent a year), you can end up paying large finance charges. And the monthly finance charges continue until you manage to pay off your credit-card debt. If you find yourself getting deeper into debt, the first step is to *stop shopping!* Next, contact your creditors and discuss options for reducing your finance charges and repaying your debts with lower monthly payments. If you do need assistance, organizations such as a local chapter of Consumer Credit Counseling Services (**www.cccsintl.org**) or Myvesta (**www.myvesta.org**) or a local support group such as Debtors Anonymous (**www.debtorsanonymous.org**) are there to help you.

debit card a card that electronically subtracts the amount of your purchase from your bank account at the moment the purchase is made

Do not confuse debit cards with credit cards. Although they may look alike, there are important differences. A **debit card** electronically subtracts the amount of your purchase from your bank account at the moment the purchase is made. (By contrast, when you use your credit card, the credit-card company extends short-term financing, and you do not make payment until you receive your next statement.) Debit cards are used most commonly to obtain cash at ATMs and to purchase products and services from retailers. The use of debit cards is expected to increase because many people feel that they are more convenient than writing checks.

Innovative Banking Services

Learning Objective: Understand how financial institutions are changing to meet the needs of domestic and international customers.

Samantha Wood used an ATM three times this week. Why? She needed cash and did not have time to make a trip to the bank and wait in line. When Bart Jones, owner of Aquatic Pools, needed a short-term $50,000 loan to solve some of his firm's cash-flow problems, he turned to LendingTree.com (**www.lendingtree.com**), an online loan-matching service. He answered some questions, and within an hour, three financial institutions had bid on his loan. He got approval (and the money he needed) without leaving his office. Like Samantha Wood and Bart Jones, many individuals, financial managers, and business owners are finding it convenient to do their banking electronically. Let's begin by looking at how banking has changed over the last ten years. Then we will discuss how those changes may provide a foundation for change in the future.

Recent Changes in the Banking Industry

In 1999, Congress enacted the Financial Services Modernization Banking Act. This act allowed banks to establish one-stop financial supermarkets where customers can bank, buy and sell securities, and purchase insurance coverage. Now, as a result of this legislation and the increasing use of technology in the banking industry, even the experts are asking the question: How will banking change in the next five to ten years?

While the experts may not be able to predict with 100 percent accuracy the changes that will affect banking, they all agree that banking *will* change. The most obvious changes the experts do agree on are:

- More emphasis on evaluating the creditworthiness of loan applicants as a result of the recent financial crisis.
- An increase in government regulation of the banking industry.
- A reduction in the number of banks, S&Ls, credit unions, and financial institutions because of consolidation and mergers
- Globalization of the banking industry

The Business of Green

Make the Call: Buy or Bank by Mobile Phone

Mobile payments and mobile banking—using cell phones to make purchases and handle banking transactions—are on the move. They're commonplace in Japan and South Korea, where many people make small purchases and pay for commuter cards via cell phone, and they're starting to catch on in Brazil and Canada. Within two years, the number of people using mobile payments could top 100 million worldwide.

However, despite the environmental benefits and the convenience, few U.S. cell-phone users have tried mobile buying or banking. In fact, most of the people questioned in a recent survey didn't even know whether their banks allowed mobile transactions. Now Visa and MasterCard are pushing ahead with pilot programs just as Nokia and other manufacturers are introducing cell phones equipped with sophisticated features for mobile buying and banking.

The goal is to get you to wave your phone near a special reader at the checkout counter and put your purchase on your cell-phone bill or your credit card. Some banks already invite customers to text for their account balances and payment due dates. Are mobile banking and buying in your future?

Sources: Gillian Shaw, "Flash Your Cellphone, Pay by Visa," *Vancouver Sun*, November 1, 2008, **www.canada.com**; Marin Perez, "U.S. Mobile Banking Has Yet to Take Off," *Information Week*, October 7, 2008, **www.informationweek.com**; "News: Trends in Mobile Payment," *Computer Weekly*, April 29, 2008, n.p.; Rebecca Buckman, "Just Charge It—to Your Cellphone," *Wall Street Journal*, June 21, 2007, p. B3.

- The importance of customer service as a way to keep customers from switching to competitors
- Increased use of credit and debit cards and a decrease in the number of written checks
- Increased competition from nonbank competitors that provide many of the same services as banks, S&Ls, credit unions, and other financial institutions
- Continued growth in online banking

Online Banking and International Banking

Online banking allows you to access your bank's computer system from home, the office, or even while you are traveling. For the customer, online banking offers a number of advantages, including the following:

- The ability to obtain current account balances
- The convenience of transferring funds from one account to another
- The ability to pay bills
- The convenience of seeing which checks have cleared
- Easy access to current interest rates
- Simplified loan application procedures

Banks such as Chase (**www.chase.com**), Citibank (**www.citibank.com**), and Commerce Bank (**www.commercebank.com**) are a few good examples for insight into this sector.

For people who bank online, the largest disadvantage is not being able to discuss financial matters with their "personal banker." To overcome this problem, many larger banks are investing huge amounts on electronic customer relationship management systems that will provide the type of service and financial advice that customers used to get when they walked through the doors of their financial institution.

Online banking provides a number of advantages for the financial institution. Probably the most important advantage is the lower cost of processing large numbers of transactions. As you learned in Chapter 17, lower costs often lead to larger profits. In addition to lower costs and increased profits, financial institutions believe that online banking offers increased security because fewer people handle fewer paper documents.

Electronic Funds Transfer (EFT) Although electronic funds transfer systems have been used for years, their use will increase dramatically as we continue through

electronic funds transfer (EFT) system a means of performing financial transactions through a computer terminal or telephone hookup

the twenty-first century. An **electronic funds transfer (EFT) system** is a means of performing financial transactions through a computer terminal or telephone hookup. The following three EFT applications are changing how banks do business:

1. *Automatic teller machines (ATMs).* An ATM is an electronic bank teller—a machine that provides almost any service a human teller can provide. Once the customer is properly identified, the machine dispenses cash from the customer's checking or savings account or makes a cash advance charged to a credit card. ATMs are located in bank parking lots, supermarkets, drugstores, and even gas stations. Customers have access to them at all times of the day or night. There may be a fee for each transaction.
2. *Automated clearinghouses (ACHs).* Designed to reduce the number of paper checks, automated clearinghouses process checks, recurring bill payments, Social Security benefits, and employee salaries. For example, large companies use ACHs to transfer wages and salaries directly into their employees' bank accounts, thus eliminating the need to make out individual paychecks. The ACH system saves time and effort for both employers and employees and adds a measure of security to the transfer of these payments.
3. *Point-of-sale (POS) terminals.* A POS terminal is a computerized cash register located in a retail store and connected to a bank's computer. At the cash register, you pull your credit or debit card through a magnetic card reader. A central processing center notifies a computer at your bank that you want to make a purchase. The bank's computer immediately adds the amount to your account for a credit-card transaction. In a similar process, the bank's computer deducts the amount of the purchase from your bank account if you use a debit card. Finally, the amount of your purchase is added to the store's account. The store then is notified that the transaction is complete, and the cash register prints out your receipt.

electronic check conversion (ECC) a process used to convert information from a paper check into an electronic payment for merchandise, services, or bills

A similar process occurs when a store uses electronic check conversion to process a paper check. **Electronic check conversion (ECC)** is a process used to convert information from a paper check into an electronic payment for merchandise, services, or bills. Here's how ECC works. When you give your completed check to a store cashier, the check is processed through an electronic system that captures your banking information and the dollar amount of the check. Once the check is processed, you are asked to sign a receipt, and you get a voided (canceled) check back for your records. Finally, the funds to pay for your transaction are transferred from your account into the business firm's account. ECC also can be used for checks you mail to pay for a purchase or to pay on an account. *Be warned*: Because the check is processed electronically, money is withdrawn immediately from your account. There is no "float time" for your check. This means that if you write a check, you need to have funds in your account to cover it. If you don't, your check may bounce, and you may be charged a fee by the merchant, your financial institution, or both.

Bankers and business owners generally are pleased with online banking and EFT systems. Both online banking and EFT are fast, and they eliminate the costly processing of checks. However, many customers are reluctant to use online banking or EFT systems. Some simply do not like "the technology," whereas others fear that the computer will garble their accounts. Early on, in 1978, Congress responded to such fears by passing the Electronic Funds Transfer Act, which protects the customer in case the bank makes an error or the customer's EFT (debit) card or personal identification number is stolen.

letter of credit a legal document issued by a bank or other financial institution guaranteeing to pay a seller a stated amount for a specified period of time

International Banking Services For international businesses, banking services are extremely important. Depending on the needs of an international firm, a bank can help by providing a letter of credit or a banker's acceptance.

A **letter of credit** is a legal document issued by a bank or other financial institution guaranteeing to pay a seller a stated amount for a specified period of time—usually thirty to sixty days. (With a letter of credit, certain conditions, such as delivery of the merchandise, may be specified before payment is made.)

A **banker's acceptance** is a written order for a bank to pay a third party a stated amount of money on a specific date. (With a banker's acceptance, no conditions are specified. It is simply an order to pay without any strings attached.)

banker's acceptance a written order for a bank to pay a third party a stated amount of money on a specific date

Both a letter of credit and a banker's acceptance are popular methods of paying for import and export transactions. For example, imagine that you are a business owner in the United States who wants to purchase some leather products from a small business in Florence, Italy. You offer to pay for the merchandise with your company's check drawn on an American bank, but the Italian business owner is worried about payment. To solve the problem, your bank can issue either a letter of credit or a banker's acceptance to guarantee that payment will be made. In addition to a letter of credit and a banker's acceptance, banks also can use EFT technology to speed international banking transactions.

One other international banking service should be noted. Banks and other financial institutions provide for currency exchange. If you place an order for merchandise from a company in Japan valued at $50,000, how do you pay for the order? Do you use U.S. dollars or Japanese yen? To solve this problem, you can use a bank's currency-exchange service. To make payment, you can use either currency, and if necessary, the bank will exchange one currency for the other to complete your transaction.

The FDIC and NCUA

6 **Learning Objective: Explain how deposit insurance protects customers.**

During the Depression, which began in 1929, a number of banks failed, and their depositors lost all their savings. To make sure that such a disaster does not happen again and to restore public confidence in the banking industry, Congress enacted legislation that created the *Federal Deposit Insurance Corporation (FDIC)* in 1933. The primary purpose of the FDIC is to insure deposits against bank failures.

Today, the FDIC provides basic deposit insurance of $100,000 for nonretirement accounts. *Note:* As part of the Emergency Economic Stabilization Act of 2008 (commonly referred to as the banking rescue bill), FDIC coverage was temporarily increased from $100,000 to $250,000 per depositor through December 31, 2009.[13] Regardless of the amount of deposit insurance provided by the FDIC, deposits maintained in different categories of legal ownership are insured separately. Thus, you can have coverage for different categories of ownership in a single institution. The most common categories of ownership are single (or individual) ownership and joint ownership. Deposit insurance is also available for funds held for retirement purposes in self-directed individual retirement accounts (up to $250,000) and certain employee benefit plans and pension plans that are not self-directed. A depositor also may obtain additional coverage by opening separate accounts in different financial institutions. To determine if your deposits are insured or if your bank or S&L is insured, visit the FDIC website at **www.fdic.gov**.

To obtain coverage, banks and S&Ls must pay insurance premiums to the FDIC. The insurance premium each financial institution pays is based on different factors that include the amount of insured deposits as well as the degree of risk the institution poses to the FDIC insurance fund. In a similar manner, the National Credit Union Association (NCUA) insures deposits in member credit unions for up to $100,000 for nonretirement accounts and $250,000 for retirement accounts. As part of the banking rescue plan mentioned above, basic deposit insurance coverage in credit unions was also increased to $250,000 for nonretirement accounts until December 31, 2009.[14] Coverage for retirement accounts ($250,000) remains unchanged.

The FDIC and NCUA have improved banking in the United States. When either of these organizations insures a financial institution's deposits, they reserve the right to examine that institution's operations periodically. If a bank, S&L, savings bank,

A tale of two financial crises. *Although the financial problems in 1929 and the financial crisis of 2008 are similar in many ways, there is one very important difference. Today, the Federal Deposit Insurance Corporation (FDIC) and the National Credit Union Association (NCUA) provide deposit insurance to protect money deposited by both individuals and businesses up to a specified amount.*

AP Photo; AP Photo/Richard Drew

or credit union is found to be poorly managed, it is reported to the proper banking authority.

Lending to individuals and firms is a vital function of banks. And deciding wisely to whom it will extend credit is one of the most important activities of any financial institution or business. The material in the next section explains the different factors used to evaluate credit applicants.

Effective Credit Management

7

Learning Objective: Discuss the importance of credit and credit management.

credit immediate purchasing power that is exchanged for a promise to repay borrowed money, with or without interest, at a later date

Credit is immediate purchasing power that is exchanged for a promise to repay borrowed money, with or without interest, at a later date. A credit transaction is a two-sided business activity that involves both a borrower and a lender. The borrower is most often a person or business that wishes to make a purchase. The lender may be a bank, some other lending institution, or a business firm selling merchandise or services on credit.

For example, suppose that you obtain a bank loan to buy a $100,000 home. You, as the borrower, obtain immediate purchasing power. In return, you agree to certain terms imposed by the bank, S&L, or home mortgage company. The lender requires that you make a down payment, make monthly payments, pay interest, and purchase insurance to protect your home until the loan is paid in full.

Banks and other financial institutions lend money because they are in business for that purpose. The interest they charge is what provides their profit. Other businesses extend credit to their customers for at least three reasons. First, some customers simply cannot afford to pay the entire amount of their purchase immediately, but they *can* repay credit in a number of smaller payments stretched out over some period of time. Second, some firms are forced to sell goods or services on credit to compete effectively when other firms offer credit to their customers. Finally, firms can realize a profit from interest charges that a borrower pays on some credit arrangements.

Getting Money from a Bank or Lender After a Credit Crisis

Many individuals and business owners are nervous when applying for a loan. They are not sure what information they need. And what happens if they are turned down? Let's begin with the basics. While lenders need interest from loans to help pay their business expenses and earn a profit, they also want to make sure that the

PRNewsFoto/Seattle Metropolitan Credit Union

This banker wants to help. *Bob Harvey, president and CEO of Seattle Metropolitan Credit Union, likes to help people and business owners achieve their financial goals. Still, like most bankers, Harvey is concerned with two questions: What will the loan money be used for, and can the applicant repay the loan as scheduled? The answers to these questions often determine if a loan will be approved.*

Entrepreneurial Challenge

Watching the National Debt Clock

As long as America is running in the red, the National Debt Clock in New York City's Times Square will digitally tick off the dollars, one by one. Real estate entrepreneur Seymour Durst paid $120,000 to create and install the National Debt Clock on a billboard in 1989. His purpose was to call attention to what was then a $2.7 trillion national debt. "It'll be up as long as the debt or the city lasts," he told reporters. "If it bothers people, then it's working."

OUR NATIONAL DEBT:
10 149 644 933 872
YOUR *Family share* $86 017
THE NATIONAL DEBT CLOCK

His company, the Durst Organization, has been in charge of the clock ever since. In 1991, America's national debt was piling up so quickly—at $13,000 per second—that they had to overhaul the clock so it could keep pace. They turned the clock off in 2000 when the country had a surplus, then turned it on again in 2002 as debt began to mount. After the national debt reached $10 trillion in 2008, Durst's company had to install a new clock to accommodate the extra digits. If necessary, this clock can show up to a quadrillion dollars in debt.

AP Photo/Kathy Willens

Sources: M. J. Stephey, "The Times Square Debt Clock," *Time,* October 14, 2008, **www.time.com**; Larry McShane, "Times Square National Debt Clock Runs Out of Digits Amid Wall St. Meltdown," *New York Daily News,* October 9, 2008, **www.nydailynews.com**; Carl Bailik, "The Numbers Guy: Countdown Clocks Offer a Lot of Drama but Little Information," *Wall Street Journal,* June 29, 2007, p. B1.

loans they make will be repaid. Your job is to convince the lender that you are able and willing to repay the loan. And your job is more difficult than it has ever been because of the recent crisis in the banking and financial industries. Today, bankers, lenders and suppliers, and credit-card companies are much more careful when evaluating credit applications. A request to obtain a business or personal loan, to purchase supplies and materials on credit, or even to obtain a credit card will be carefully evaluated. The reasons are simple: Many lenders already have a large number of "bad" or nonperforming loans and they want to make sure all borrowers are qualified and will be able to repay borrowed money.

For individuals, the following suggestions may be helpful when applying for a loan:

- Although it may pay to shop around for lower interest rates, you usually have a better chance of obtaining a loan at a bank, S&L, or credit union where you already have an account.
- Obtain a loan application and complete it at home. At home, you have the information needed to answer *all* the questions on the loan application.
- Be prepared to describe how you will use the money and how the loan will be repaid.
- For most loans, an interview with a loan officer is required. Here again, preparation is the key. Think about how you would respond to questions a loan officer might ask.
- If your loan request is rejected, try to analyze what went wrong. Ask the loan officer why you were rejected. If the rejection is based on incorrect information, supply the correct information and reapply.

Business owners in need of financing may find the following additional tips helpful:

- It is usually best to develop a relationship with your banker before you need financing. Help the banker understand what your business is and how you may need future financing for expansion, cash-flow problems, or unexpected emergencies.
- Apply for a preapproved line of credit or revolving credit agreement even if you do not need the money. View the application as another way to showcase your company and its products or services.
- In addition to the application, supply certified public accountant (CPA)–prepared financial statements and business tax returns for the last three years and your own personal financial statements and tax returns for the same period.
- Update your business plan in case the lender wants to review your plan. Be sure the sales estimates and other projections are realistic.
- Write a cover letter describing how much experience you have, whether you are operating in an expanding market, or any other information that would help convince the banker to provide financing.

From the lender's viewpoint, the major pitfall in granting credit is the possibility of nonpayment. However, if a lender follows the five C's of credit management, it can minimize this possibility.

The Five C's of Credit Management

When a business extends credit to its customers, it must face the fact that some customers will be unable or unwilling to pay for their credit purchases. With this in mind, lenders must establish policies for determining who will receive credit and who will not. Most lenders build their credit policies around the five C's of credit.

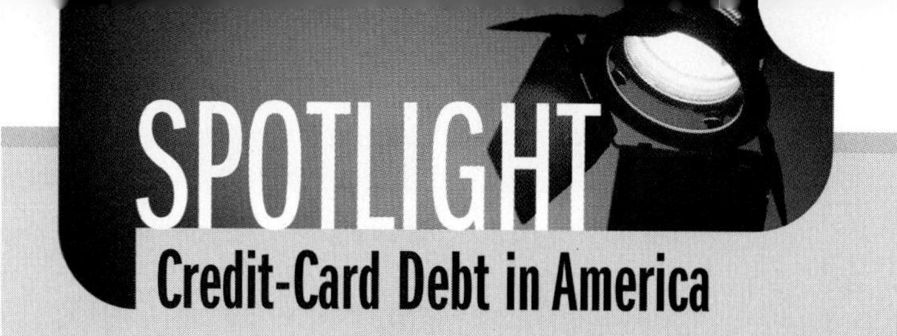

Credit-Card Debt in America

Although Americans love credit cards, the statistics below paint a troubling picture.

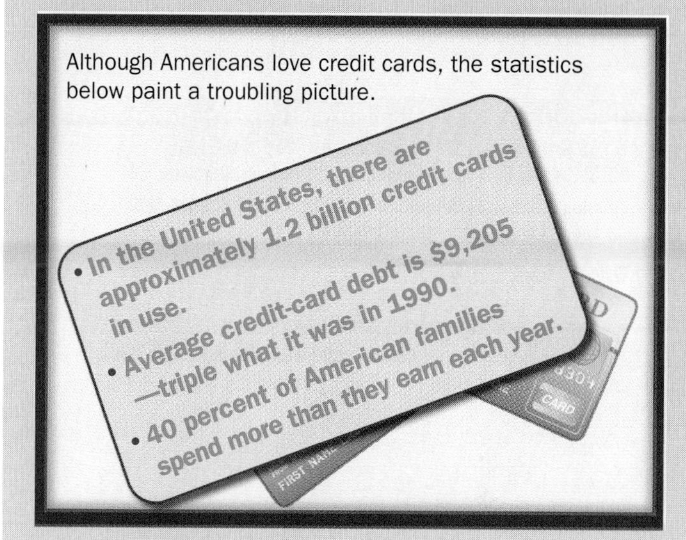

Source: The Bankrate.com website, **www.bankrate.com**, September 30, 2008.

Character *Character* means the borrower's attitude toward credit obligations. Experienced lenders often see this as the most important factor in predicting whether a borrower will make regular payments and ultimately repay a credit obligation. Typical questions to consider in judging a borrower's character include the following:

1. Is the borrower prompt in paying bills?
2. Have other lenders had to dun the borrower with overdue notices before receiving payment?
3. Have lenders been forced to take the borrower to court to obtain payment?
4. Has the customer ever filed for bankruptcy? If so, did the customer make an attempt to repay debts voluntarily?

Although it is illegal to discriminate, personal factors such as drinking or gambling habits may affect a lender's decision to loan money or extend credit to an individual.

Capacity *Capacity* means the borrower's financial ability to meet credit obligations—that is, to make regular loan payments as scheduled in the credit or loan agreement. If the customer is a business, the lender looks at the firm's income statement. For individuals, the lender checks salary statements and other sources of income, such as dividends and interest. The borrower's other financial obligations and monthly expenses are also taken into consideration before credit is approved.

Capital The term *capital* as used here refers to the borrower's assets or net worth. In general, the greater the capital, the greater is the borrower's ability to repay a loan. The capital position of a business can be determined by examining its balance sheet. For individuals, information on net worth can be obtained by requiring that the borrower complete a credit application such as the one illustrated in Figure 18.5. The borrower also must authorize employers and financial institutions to release information to confirm the claims made in the credit application.

Collateral For large amounts of credit—and especially for long-term loans—the lender may require some type of collateral. As mentioned earlier, collateral is real estate or property (stocks, bonds, equipment, or any other asset of value) pledged as security for a loan. If the borrower fails to live up to the terms of the credit agreement, the lender can repossess the collateral and then sell it to satisfy the debt.

Conditions *Conditions* refers to the general economic conditions that can affect a borrower's ability to repay a loan or other credit obligation. How well a business firm can withstand an economic storm may depend on the particular industry the firm is in, its relative strength within that industry, the type of products it sells, its earnings history, and its earnings potential. For individuals, the basic question focuses on security—of both the applicant's job and the firm for which he or she

Figure 18.5: Credit Application Form

Lenders use the information on credit application forms to help determine which customers should be granted credit.

Apply today! Just complete this application or call 1-800-438-9222.

Citizens Bank Customer Credit Card Application

Branch # ________

This offer is for existing Citizens Bank Customers applying for a new credit card account

Existing Citizens Bank cardholders should call 1-800-438-9222 for special cardholder rate information.

Citizens Bank VISA® (Code: BVCFNU)

Please tell us about yourself

First Name Middle Initial Last Name

Address (street)

(City, state, zip)

Date of Birth Social Security Number

❑ Own ❑ Rent ❑ Live with Parents

Years/Months at Present Address

$ ( )

Monthly Housing Payment Home Telephone

Previous Address Years/Months There
(if less than 2 years at present address)

Mother's Maiden Name

Citizens Bank Account Information

❑ Checking ❑ Savings ❑ Loan ❑ Citizens Circle[SM] Checking

account # ________

Please tell us about your employment

Present Employer Position

( )

Years/Months Employed There Business Telephone

Previous Employer Years/Months There
(if less than 2 years at present employer)

$ $

Gross Monthly Household Income Other Monthly Income*

*Alimony, child support, or separate maintenance income need not be revealed if you do not wish it to be considered as a basis for repaying this obligation.

24-hour banking convenience

Your card(s) can be encoded with a four-digit personal identification number (PIN) to obtain cash advances at automated teller machines. This four-digit PIN will be known only to you. So that we may properly encode your card(s), please select the four digits of your choice and enter them in the spaces below:

____ ____ ____ ____

Please send a second card at no cost for

First Name Middle Initial Last Name

Please read and sign

Your Signature Date

All information on this application is true and complete, and Citizens Bank of Rhode Island, the card issuer, is authorized to obtain further credit and employment information from any source. I understand that you will retain this application whether or not it is approved. You may share with others, only for valid business reasons, any information relating to me, this application, and any of my banking relationships with you. I request issuance of a Citizens credit card and agree to be bound by the terms and conditions of the Agreement received with the card(s). I understand that Citizens Bank of Rhode Island will assign a credit line based on information provided and information obtained from any other source; and the issuance of a Gold card is subject to a minimum annual income of $35,000 and qualification for a minimum $5,000 credit line.

Transfer balances and save

Citizens will transfer your high interest rate balances to your new Citizens Bank VISA Card at no extra charge. Use the form below to indicate the amount(s) to be transferred in order of priority. (Citizens Bank will not transfer balances from existing Citizens Bank accounts.) (see reverse side for balance transfer disclosure)

Creditor Name	Account Number	$ Amount
Creditor Name	Account Number	$ Amount
Creditor Name	Account Number	$ Amount

Bank Use Only Bank Code: ❑ CBMA ❑ CBRI ❑ CBCT Sales ID# ________ Application code: 1122

Source: Courtesy of Citizens Financial Group, Inc., Providence, Rhode Island.

works. For example, if the economy takes a downturn, some employees may lose their jobs. Even though these former employees lost their jobs, they still have mortgage payments, car payments, and credit-card payments that must be paid.

Checking Credit Information

The five Cs of credit are concerned mainly with information supplied by the applicant. But how can a lender determine whether this information is accurate? This depends on whether the potential borrower is a business or an individual consumer.

Credit information concerning businesses can be obtained from the following four sources:

- *Global credit-reporting agencies.* D&B (formerly Dun & Bradstreet) is the most widely used credit-reporting agency in the world. D&B reports present detailed credit information about specific companies. For more information on D&B services, visit the company's website at **www.dnb.com.**
- *Local credit-reporting agencies,* which may require a monthly or yearly fee for providing information on a continual basis.
- *Industry associations,* which may charge a service fee.
- *Other firms* that have given the applicant credit.

Various credit bureaus provide credit information concerning individuals. The following are the three major consumer credit bureaus:

- Experian—at **www.experian.com** or toll free at 888–397–3742
- TransUnion—at **www.transunion.com** or toll free at 800–888–4213
- Equifax Credit Information Services—at **www.equifax.com** or toll free at 800–685–1111

Note: With the recent rise in identity theft, experts recommend that you check your credit report at least once a year or more often if you suspect suspicious activity.

Consumer credit bureaus are subject to the provisions of the Fair Credit Reporting Act. This act safeguards consumers' rights in two ways. First, every consumer has the right to know what information is contained in his or her credit bureau file. In addition to the provisions contained in the federal Fair Credit Reporting Act, the Fair and Accurate Credit Transaction Act requires each of the nationwide credit reporting companies—Equifax, Experian, and TransUnion—to provide you with a free copy of your credit report, at your request, once every 12 months. To obtain your free credit report, go to **www.annualcreditreport.com.** (*Note*: Beware of other sites that may look and sound similar to this site.[15]) In other situations, the consumer may obtain the information for a fee that is usually about $8 to $15 per request. It is also possible to obtain credit reports on a monthly or quarterly basis by subscribing to a credit-reporting service, which usually charges higher fees.

Second, a consumer who feels that some information in the file is inaccurate, misleading, or vague has the right to request that the credit bureau verify it. If the disputed information is found to be correct, the consumer can provide a brief explanation, giving his or her side of the dispute. This explanation must become part of the consumer's credit file. If the disputed information is found to be inaccurate, it must be deleted or corrected. Furthermore, you may request that any lender that has been supplied an inaccurate credit report in the last six months be sent a corrected credit report.

Sound Collection Procedures

The vast majority of borrowers follow the lender's repayment terms exactly. However, some accounts inevitably become overdue for a variety of reasons. Experience shows that such accounts should receive immediate attention.

Some firms handle their own delinquent accounts; others prefer to use a professional collection agency. (Charges for a collection agency's services are usually ıp to half the amount collected.) Both tend to use the following techniques, ly in the order in which they are listed:

- btle reminders, such as duplicate statements marked "Past Due"
- lephone calls to urge prompt payment
- ːrsonal visits to business customers to stress the necessity of paying overdue nounts immediately
- egal action, although the time, expense, and uncertain outcome of a lawsuit nake this action a last resort

Good collection procedures should be firm, but they also should allow for compro-. Harassment is both illegal and bad business. Ideally, the customer will be con-ed to make up missed payments, and the firm will retain the customer's goodwill.

In the next chapter, you will see why firms need financing, how they obtain the ney they need, and how they ensure that funds are used efficiently, in keeping w..h their organizational objectives.

return to inside business

JPMorgan Chase

Serving both Wall Street and Main Street, JPMorgan Chase provides all the traditional services that companies and consumers have come to expect from a financial institution. Its history and innovations reflect the many changes that have swept the banking industry over the years. For example, one of the banks it acquired was an ATM pioneer; another was an early proponent of electronic banking.

Today the New York-based bank is one of the world's largest, with a whopping $2.3 trillion in assets, 24 million checking accounts, 180,000 employees, 5,000 branches, and 14,000 ATMs. Looking ahead, the unpredictable global economy will certainly bring new opportunities and new risks as JPMorgan Chase continues to press for growth.

Questions

1. Imagine that you had a checking account at Washington Mutual at the time it failed and was acquired by JPMorgan Chase. What questions would you have asked when you went into your local branch—and why?
2. Would you like to work for a global banking giant such as JPMorgan Chase? Explain your answer.

CHAPTER REVIEW

Summary

1 Identity the functions and characteristics of money.

Money is anything a society uses to purchase products, services, or resources. Money must serve as a medium of exchange, a measure of value, and a store of value. To perform its functions effectively, money must be divisible into units of convenient size, light and sturdy enough to be carried and used on a daily basis, stable in value, and difficult to counterfeit. The M_1 supply of money is made up of coins and bills (currency) and deposits in checking accounts (demand deposits). The M_2 supply includes M_1 plus savings accounts, certain money-market securities, and small-denomination time deposits.

2 Summarize how the Federal Reserve System regulates the money supply.

The Federal Reserve System is responsible for regulating the U.S. banking industry and maintaining a sound economic environment. Banks with federal charters (national banks) must be members of the Fed. State banks may join if they choose to and if they can meet the requirements for membership. Twelve district banks and twenty-five branch banks compose the Federal Reserve System, whose seven-member board of governors is headquartered in Washington, D.C.

To control the supply of money, the Federal Reserve System regulates the reserve requirement, or the percentage of deposits a bank must keep on hand. It also regulates the discount rate, or the interest rate the Fed charges member banks for loans from the Federal Reserve. And it engages in open-market operations, in which it buys and sells government securities. Of the three tools used to influence monetary policy, the use of open-market operations is the most important. When the Federal Reserve buys and sells securities, the goal is to increase or decrease the federal funds rate. The federal

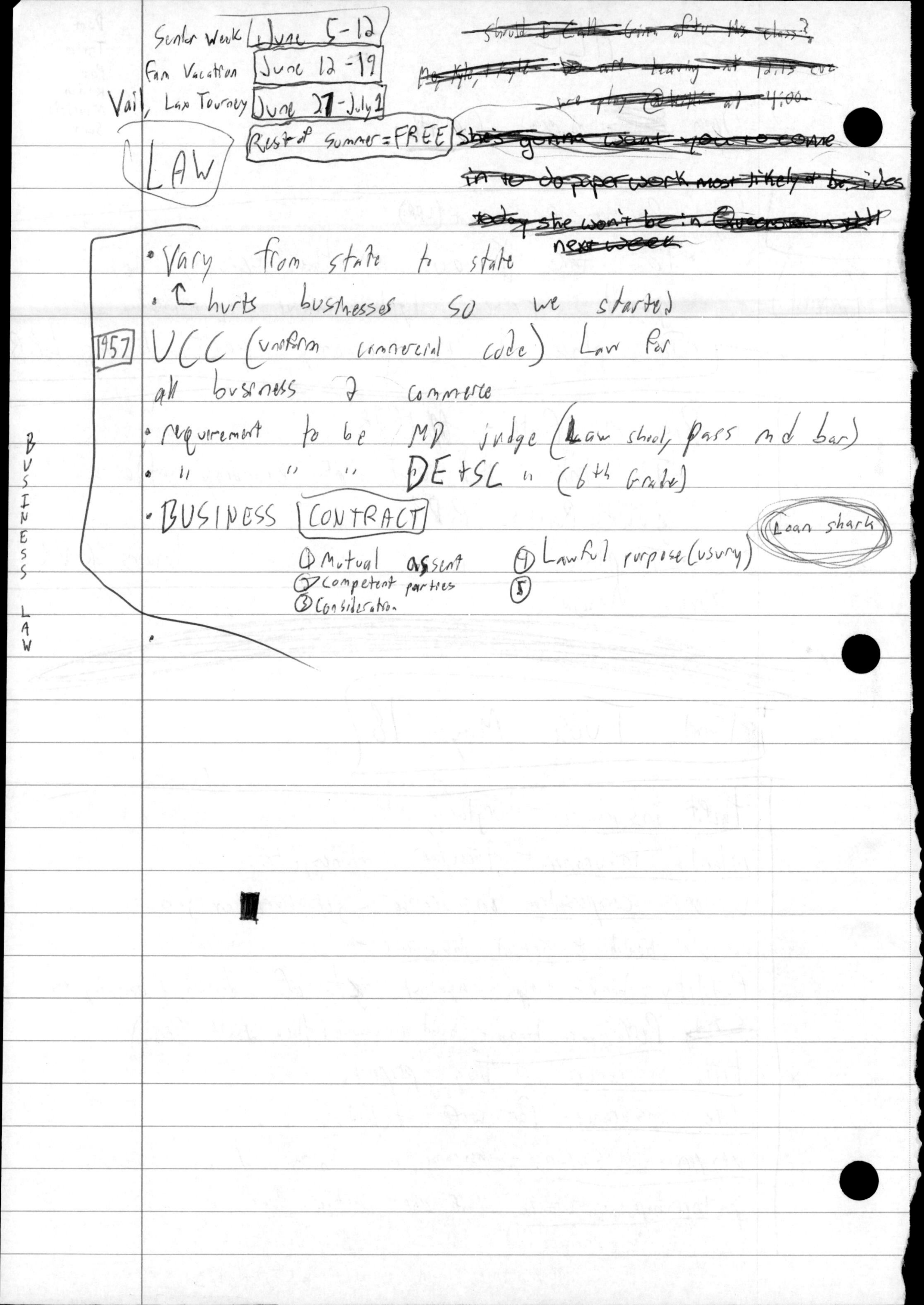

Senior Week | June 5-12

Fam Vacation | June 12-19

Vail, Lax Tourney | June 27-July 1

Rest of Summer = FREE

~~Should I call Gina after the class?~~

~~Me, Kyle, + Kyle are all leaving at 12:15 cuz we play @ \#\#\# at 4:00~~

~~She's gonna want you to come in to do paper work most likely & besides today she won't be in Queenstown \#\# next week~~

LAW

BUSINESS LAW

- Vary from state to state
- ↑ hurts businesses so we started

1957 UCC (uniform commercial code) Law for all business & commerce

- requirement to be MD judge (Law school, pass md bar)
- " " " DE + SC " (6th Grade)
- BUSINESS CONTRACT
  1. Mutual assent
  2. Competent parties
  3. Consideration
  4. Lawful purpose (usury) — Loan shark
  5.
-

ALC

Dom
Tgerm
Poz
Kenan
Mauricio
Sean

Open Market Operation

Legal Reserve Requirement (LRR)

(interest)

- To take $ out of the economy the gov't raises legal reserve requirement
- To place $ in economy gov't lowers LRR

ReDiscount Rate - (RDR)

- To take $$ out of economy the gov't Raises RDR
- To place " in " " " " lowers RDR

Buying Margin

Final, Tues May 18

theft insurance - burglary, etc.
inland insurance - tractor combines, etc.
workers compensation insurance - get hurt on job
accidental health + medical insurance -
fidelity bond - helps against acts of dishonest employees
Performance bond - build a house (they don't finish)
* title insurance - if buy property
life insurance - for wife + kids
key person insurance - insurance on chairman of an industry
partnership insurance - if one partner dies...
serial bonds - bonds of a single issue that mature on different dates

funds rate is the interest rate at which a bank lends immediately available funds on deposit at the Fed to another bank overnight in order to meet the borrowing bank's reserve requirements. The Fed serves as the government's bank and is also responsible for clearing checks and electronic transfers, inspecting currency, enforcing the Truth-in-Lending Act, and setting margin requirements for stock transactions.

3 Describe the organizations involved in the banking industry.

A commercial bank is a profit-making organization that accepts deposits, makes loans, and provides related services to customers. Commercial banks are chartered by the federal government or state governments. Savings and loan associations and credit unions offer the same basic services that commercial banks provide. Mutual savings banks, insurance companies, pension funds, brokerage firms, finance companies, and investment banking firms provide some limited banking services. A large number of people work in the banking industry because of the number of banks and other financial institutions. To be successful in the banking industry, you must be honest, be able to interact with people, have a strong background in accounting, appreciate the relationship between banking and finance, and possess basic computer skills.

4 Identify the services provided by financial institutions.

Banks and other financial institutions offer today's customers a tempting array of services. Among the most important and attractive banking services for both individuals and businesses are checking accounts, savings accounts, short- and long-term loans, and credit-card and debit-card transactions. Other traditional services include financial advice, payroll services, certified checks, trust services, and safe-deposit boxes.

5 Understand how financial institutions are changing to meet the needs of domestic and international customers.

Among the laws enacted during the last thirty years to deregulate the banking industry, probably the most important is the Financial Services Modernization Banking Act. This act allowed banks to establish one-stop financial supermarkets where customers can bank, buy and sell securities, and purchase insurance coverage. Because of this act, competition among banks, brokerage firms, and insurance companies has increased. As we enter the twenty-first century, an increasing use of technology and the need for bankers to help American businesses compete in the global marketplace will change the way banks and other financial institutions do business. The use of technology will increase as financial institutions continue to offer online banking. Increased use of electronic funds transfer systems (automated teller machines, automated clearinghouses, point-of-sale terminals, and electronic check conversion) also will change the way people bank. For firms in the global marketplace, a bank can provide letters of credit and banker's acceptances that will reduce the risk of nonpayment for sellers. Banks and financial institutions also can provide currency exchange to reduce payment problems for import or export transactions.

6 Explain how deposit insurance protects customers.

The Federal Deposit Insurance Corporation (FDIC) and the National Credit Union Association (NCUA) insure accounts in member financial institutions for up to $100,000 for nonretirement accounts and $250,000 for some types of retirement accounts. *Note:* The Emergency Economic Stabilization Act of 2008 increased FDIC and NCUA coverage from $100,000 to $250,000 per depositor through December 31, 2009. Deposits maintained in different categories of legal ownership are insured separately. The most common ownership categories are single ownership and joint ownership. It is also possible to obtain additional coverage by opening separate accounts in different banks, S&Ls, or credit unions. The FDIC and NCUA have improved banking in the United States. When either of these organizations insures a financial institution's deposits, they reserve the right to examine that institution's operations periodically. If a bank, S&L, or credit union is found to be poorly managed, it is reported to the proper banking authority.

7 Discuss the importance of credit and credit management.

Credit is immediate purchasing power that is exchanged for a promise to repay borrowed money, with or without interest, at a later date. Banks lend money because they are in business for that purpose. Businesses sell goods and services on credit because some customers cannot afford to pay cash and because they must keep pace with competitors who offer credit. Businesses also may realize a profit from interest charges.

Decisions on whether to grant credit to businesses and individuals usually are based on the five C's of credit: character, capacity, capital, collateral, and conditions. Credit information can be obtained from various credit-reporting agencies, credit bureaus, industry associations, and other firms. The techniques used to collect past-due accounts should be firm enough to prompt payment but flexible enough to maintain the borrower's goodwill.

Key Terms

You should now be able to define and give an example relevant to each of the following terms:

barter system (528)
money (528)
medium of exchange (529)
measure of value (529)
store of value (529)
demand deposit (531)
time deposit (531)
Federal Reserve System (533)
reserve requirement (533)
discount rate (535)
open-market operations (535)
federal funds rate (535)
commercial bank (538)
national bank (538)
state bank (538)
savings and loan association (S&L) (538)
credit union (539)
check (541)
NOW account (542)
certificate of deposit (CD) (542)
line of credit (542)
revolving credit agreement (542)
collateral (542)
debit card (544)
electronic funds transfer (EFT) system (546)
electronic check conversion (ECC) (546)
letter of credit (546)
banker's acceptance (547)
credit (549)

Review Questions

1. How does the use of money solve the problems associated with a barter system of exchange?
2. What are three functions money must perform in a sound monetary system?
3. Explain why money must have each of the following characteristics:
   a. Divisibility
   b. Portability
   c. Stability
   d. Durability
   e. Difficulty of counterfeiting
4. What is included in the definition of the M_1 supply of money? Of the M_2 supply?
5. What is the Federal Reserve System? How is it organized?
6. Explain how the Federal Reserve System uses each of the following to control the money supply:
   a. Reserve requirements
   b. The discount rate
   c. Open-market operations
7. The Federal Reserve is responsible for enforcing the Truth-in-Lending Act. How does this act affect you?
8. What is the difference between a national bank and a state bank? What other financial institutions compete with national and state banks?
9. Describe the major banking services provided by financial institutions today.
10. For consumers, what are the major advantages of online banking? What is its major disadvantage?
11. How do automated teller machines, automated clearinghouses, and point-of-sale terminals affect how you bank?
12. How can a bank or other financial institution help American businesses to compete in the global marketplace?
13. What is the basic function of the FDIC and NCUA? How do they perform this function?
14. List and explain the five C's of credit management.
15. How would you check the information provided by an applicant for credit at a department store? By a business applicant at a heavy-equipment manufacturer's sales office?

Discussion Questions

1. The Emergency Economic Stabilization Act of 2008 (commonly referred to as the banking rescue bill) was enacted in October 2008. Based on what you know at the time you are answering this question, how would you describe the effect of the rescue bill on the banking industry? On the nation's economy?
2. It is said that financial institutions "create" money when they make loans to firms and individuals. Explain what this means.
3. Why does the Fed use indirect means of controlling the money supply instead of simply printing more money or removing money from circulation when necessary?
4. Why would banks pay higher interest on money left on deposit for longer periods of time (e.g., on CDs)?
5. How could an individual get in financial trouble by using a credit card? If you were in trouble because of credit-card debt, what steps could you take to reduce your debts?
6. Lenders generally are reluctant to extend credit to individuals with no previous credit history (and no outstanding debts). Yet they willingly extend credit to individuals who are in the process of repaying debts. Is this reasonable? Is it fair? Explain your answer.
7. Assume that you want to borrow $10,000. What can you do to convince the loan officer that you are a good credit risk?

Video Case 18.1

First Bank Corporation

Today's economic environment is a challenge for U.S. citizens, investors, businesses, and banking institutions. There have been several recent bank failures led by Washington Mutual, and uncertainty as to how many more failures may occur is a growing concern. The banking industry is working hard to insulate itself from this troublesome economy. First Bank Corporation is a case in point! First Bank owns four affiliated community banks with 33 branches operating throughout Michigan. Often referred to as a super community bank holding company, First Bank subsidiaries offer a full range of deposit and loan products designed to meet the needs of its community and local businesses. In recent years, First Bank Corporation has witnessed a growing trend in bank consolidations, both locally and at the national level. Ten years ago, there were approximately 15,000 banks in the United States. There are roughly 9,000 banks today, and in the future this number could consolidate to 5,000 or 6,000 banks.

The recent increase in bank mergers and acquisitions has created opportunities for depository institutions like First Bank. As banks continue to consolidate, First Bank has adopted a strategy of decentralization. One of the major advantages of decentralizing its operations is that First Bank can provide prompt service to customers because the bank's decision makers are local. Its bank/loan officers live in the community so they react to what is happening in the community and consequently can make decisions faster than a larger bank. In some banks, it takes two loan committees and a board meeting to get approval for a commercial loan. First Bank can react with timing that suits its customers, not the bank. In some cases, the necessary bank officers can get together and make loan decisions in a matter of hours.

To better meet its customers' needs, First Bank Corporation has organized its subsidiary banks to operate independently with a great deal of autonomy. Each bank has a local board of directors and local CEO, president, vice president, and staff. Consequently, all of its product and loan decisions are made at the local level. This results in a much more comfortable situation for both the bank and its customers. When talking to a bank or loan officer, customers know that they are talking to the person who will be intimately involved in the assessment, decision, and response to their banking needs.

First Bank believes that the financial services industry is changing. Acquisition of additional banks will play an important role in its future. First Bank plans to remain an independent holding company of community banks and also to provide additional services that customers want such as investment research, investment banking, insurance, and brokerage services.

First Bank's management believes that the company's future depends on financial growth and its ability to increase shareholder wealth. They know that to remain independent, First Bank must be a high-performance organization. The best way to achieve this is to have happy shareholders by generating above-average industry earnings. Over the past five years, First Bank has accomplished this goal and expects to continue this performance over the next five years. While the economic climate is currently uncertain, it appears that First Bank Corporation has a viable strategy to deal with uncertainty in a changing banking industry.[16]

For more information about this bank, go to **www.firstbank-corp.com.**

Questions

1. First Bank Corporation points to its strategy of decentralization as a big factor in its success. What are some possible disadvantages to its strategy of decentralizing its subsidiary banks?
2. What are some business actions that First Bank can take to continue its record of above-average industry earnings?
3. Given the 40 percent consolidation in the number of banks over the past ten years (from approximately 15,000 to 9,000) and the forecasted decline to 5,000–6,000 banks in the future, what can First Bank do to avoid being taken over by a larger competitor?

Case 18.2

Protecting Your Credit Rating

Never mind the national budget deficit: U.S. consumers are $2.56 trillion deep in consumer debt, an increase of 22 percent since 2000. The average household owes over $9,205 on credit cards, and the average college student graduates with $20,000 in tuition loans and other debts to pay off.

Lenders and credit-card companies have grown more aggressive in signing up new customers, soliciting on campus and marketing heavily to make people feel less guilty about debt. Meanwhile, they've raised interest rates even to good customers (to over 19% from 17.7% in 2005) and found new ways to make money with higher fees for late payments and exceeding credit limits. CardWeb, a credit-card information website, says such fees have more than doubled in the last dozen years. This revenue allows credit companies to lend more to people less likely to pay, while profits rise to new heights.

Diane McLeod worked two jobs to pay two mortgages with escalating interest rates, a car loan, and high-interest credit cards. After the twin disasters of medical emergencies and lost employment, her home is being foreclosed and her credit rating is destroyed. McLeod admits creating some of her own problems by overspending and failing to read the fine print in credit agreements. But interest payments on her debts equal almost half her pretax income, and she owes thousands of dollars in fees alone.

Over 75 percent of undergraduates have at least one credit card, and most carry an average balance of about $2,000; one in four use cards to help pay tuition. "Students are using credit cards as a last resort to pick up the slack when they have difficulty getting loans or jobs to cover their expenses," said a consumer finance analyst. "With fewer loans and jobs available, you have the makings of an increase in college student credit card debt on top of existing student loan debt."

How can you protect yourself from debt? First, don't apply for or carry cards you don't need. Next, check your attitude about money. The National Association of Retail Collection Attorneys reports more than 25 percent of students think it's OK to use cards to raise cash and are overoptimistic about paying back debt. Don't be fooled. With fees and interest rates, your outstanding balance can rise even if you stop using your card. A good rule of thumb is not to charge purchases unless you already have cash on hand to pay for them. Create a personal balance sheet and know what you can afford.

If you have cash, pay cash. It carries no interest charges or hidden fees, and any credit-card "rewards" you might earn will be far from free when the bills come due.

If you must use a card, always pay on time, pay as much as you can, and certainly pay more than the minimum to avoid letting your balance climb. Don't take cash advances on your card (why pay 19 percent interest for money?), and don't make impulse purchases.

While consumer advocates and some members of Congress are trying to make it harder for credit-card companies to help consumers get into trouble, remember, your credit health is really up to you.[17]

To find out more about consumer credit, check the sites mentioned in the chapter or go to **http://www.consumerreports.org/cro/money/credit-loan/index.htm**.

Questions

1. If you have one or more credit cards, check your credit history for free at **www.annualcreditreport.com**. What does your history tell you about your spending and borrowing habits? What if anything do you need to change? Why is regularly checking your credit history advisable?
2. What do you think is the real cost of "free" rewards offered on many credit cards? Who pays it? Do you think these rewards are worth the cost? Why or why not?
3. Imagine you've applied to a bank for a home mortgage, car loan, or tuition loan (or perhaps you already have such a loan or loans). Now put yourself in the bank's place for a moment. How do *you* rate on the five C's of credit management? Which of these criteria is most affected by your credit-card history?

Building Skills for Career Success

1. JOURNALING FOR SUCCESS

You could be one in a million—the 1 million Americans who fall victim to the crime of identity theft every year. Crooks who steal your name, birth date, credit-card numbers, bank account numbers, and Social Security number can withdraw money from your bank accounts, charge merchandise in your name, or contract for cell-phone service.

Assignment

1. Use the Internet to obtain information about how to prevent identity theft. Then according to the professionals, describe the steps someone should take to protect their identity.
2. Complete a "security audit" of your personal information and financial records. Based on your audit and the recommendations from professionals, what should you do now to protect your identity?
3. It always helps to have a plan in case your identity is stolen. Based on the information you obtained from your Internet research, what immediate steps should you take if your identity is stolen?

2. EXPLORING THE INTERNET

Internet-based banking is no longer a new concept. For many Americans, technology has changed the way they conduct their banking transactions. For example, most people no longer carry their paychecks to the bank to be deposited; instead, the money is deposited directly into their accounts. And an increasing number of individuals and businesses are using computers and the Internet to handle their finances, apply for loans, and pay their bills. Banking with the help of a home computer is continually being made easier, giving bank customers access to their accounts twenty-four hours a day and seven days a week. As a result, you have more control over your money.

Assignment

1. Examine the websites of several major banks with which you are familiar. Describe their online banking services. Are they worthwhile in your opinion?
2. In the past three years, how has technology changed the way you handle your money and conduct your banking transactions, such as depositing your paychecks, paying your monthly bills, obtaining cash, paying for purchases, and applying for loans?
3. In the next five to ten years, what will the banking industry be like? How will these changes affect you and the way you do your banking? The Internet and the library can help you to learn what is in the forefront of banking technology.
4. Prepare a report explaining your answers to these questions.

3. DEVELOPING CRITICAL-THINKING SKILLS

Every year, your grandmother in Seattle, Washington, sends you a personal check for $100 for your birthday. You live in Monticello, Georgia, seventy-five miles southeast of Atlanta. You either cash the check or deposit it in your savings account at a local bank. Your banker does not return the canceled check directly to your grandmother, but somehow the money is withdrawn from your grandmother's account. How does this happen? *Hint*: For information about the process used to clear checks, go to **http://federalreserve.gov/paymentsystems/checkservices.**

Assignment

1. Research the process that your bank uses to collect a check that is from an individual located in another city and state.
2. Summarize what you learned and how this information might be helpful to you in the future.

4. BUILDING TEAM SKILLS

Three years ago, Ron and Ginger were happy to learn that upon graduation, Ron would be teaching history in a large high school, making $30,000 a year, and Ginger would be working in a public accounting firm, starting at $34,000. They married immediately after graduation and bought a new home for $110,000. Since Ron had no personal savings, Ginger used her savings for the down payment. They soon began furnishing their home, charging their purchases to three separate credit cards, and that is when their debt began to mount. When the three credit cards reached their $10,000 limits, Ron and Ginger signed up for four additional credit cards with $10,000 limits that were offered through the mail, and they started using them. Soon their monthly payments were more than their combined take-home pay. To make their monthly payments, Ron and Ginger began to obtain cash advances on their credit cards. When they reached the credit ceilings on their seven credit cards, they could no longer get the cash advances they needed to cover their monthly bills. Stress began to mount as creditors called and demanded payment. Ron and Ginger began to argue over money and just about everything else. Finally, things got so bad they considered filing for personal bankruptcy, but ironically, they could not afford the legal fees. What options are available to this couple?

Assignment

1. Working in teams of three or four, use your local library, the Internet, and personal interviews to investigate the following:
   a. Filling for personal bankruptcy.
      - What is involved in filing for personal bankruptcy?
      - How much does it cost?
      - How does bankruptcy affect individuals?
   b. The Consumer Credit Counseling Service at **www.cccsintl.org** or Myvesta at **www.myvesta.org**.
      - What services do these organizations provide?
      - How could they help Ron and Ginger?
      - What will it cost?
2. Prepare a specific plan for repaying Ron and Ginger's debt.
3. Outline the advantages and disadvantages of credit cards, and make the appropriate recommendations for Ron and Ginger concerning their future use of credit cards.
4. Summarize what you have learned about credit-card misuse.

5. RESEARCHING DIFFERENT CAREERS

It has long been known that maintaining a good credit record is essential to obtaining loans from financial institutions, but did you know that employers often check credit records before offering an applicant a position? This is especially true of firms that handle financial accounts for others. Information contained in your credit report can tell an employer a lot about how responsible you are with money and how well you manage it. Individuals have the right to know what is in their credit bureau files and to have the credit bureau verify any inaccurate, misleading, or vague information. Before you apply for a job or a loan, you should check with a credit bureau to learn what is in your file.

Assignment

1. Using information in this chapter, use the Internet or call a credit bureau and ask for a copy of your credit report. A small fee may be required depending on the bureau and circumstances.
2. Review the information.
3. Have the bureau verify any information that you feel is inaccurate, misleading, or vague.
4. If the verification shows that the information is correct, prepare a brief statement explaining your side of the dispute, and send it to the bureau.
5. Prepare a statement summarizing what the credit report says about you. Based on your credit report, would a firm hire you as its financial manager?

19 Mastering Financial Management

LEARNING OBJECTIVES

What you will be able to do once you complete this chapter:

1. Explain the need for financial management in business.
2. Summarize the process of planning for financial management.
3. Describe the advantages and disadvantages of different methods of short-term debt financing.
4. Evaluate the advantages and disadvantages of equity financing.
5. Evaluate the advantages and disadvantages of long-term debt financing.

Stockbyte/Getty Images

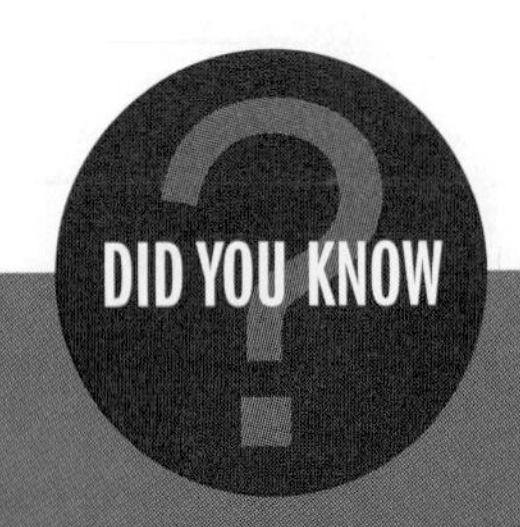

inside business

Raising money through the sale of stock gives Starbucks the funding it needs to open dozens of cafes every year.

Starbucks Brews up Financing for Future Strength

Starbucks, the company that started the country's specialty coffee craze, has brewed up a rich blend of financing sources for today's operations and tomorrow's growth. The company began in 1971 with a single café in Seattle's Pike Place Market. By the time it started selling common stock to investors in 1992, its employees were pulling espresso shots in more than 125 cafés.

Raising money through the sale of stock gave Starbucks the funding it needed to open dozens of cafés every year, develop a wider array of menu items, and open new roasting facilities to accommodate its explosive growth. The company also borrowed more than $160 million to finance national and international expansion. By 2000, Starbucks had 3,500 cafés worldwide. In 2002, a decade after going public under the SBUX stock symbol, the company had grown to 5,800 cafés and introduced such innovations as wireless Internet access. At the end of 2007, Starbucks had more than 10,000 U.S. cafés and was continuing to open dozens of overseas stores every month.

Then deteriorating economic conditions and piping-hot coffee competition cut into the growth momentum. Despite ringing up $10 billion in 2008 global revenues, Starbucks felt the pinch as costs increased, consumers pulled back on spending, and both McDonald's and Dunkin' Donuts picked up competitive steam in coffee sales. In response, Starbucks tightened its belt by closing hundreds of low-performing U.S. locations, slowing the pace of new-store openings, freezing executive salaries, and laying off 1,000 managers and employees. Its share price also slipped as some financial analysts downgraded the stock.

Now Starbucks is putting its money and its marketing muscle behind new products and new programs to reinforce customer loyalty. Thanks to international licensing agreements, new Starbucks cafés will continue to open without burdening the company with hefty initial outlays and ongoing operating expenses. How quickly can Starbucks perk up revenues and get back on its usual fast track to aggressive growth?[1]

In Chapter 1, we defined a *business* as the organized effort of individuals to produce and sell, for a profit, the products and services that satisfy society's needs. Now after reflecting on this definition, imagine that you are a would-be entrepreneur. You have a good idea for a successful business and with hard work, a little luck, *and* some financing you could turn your dream into a reality. That's the situation that many would-be entrepreneurs around the world face when attempting to start a business. For some, like the entrepreneurs that started Starbucks, selling stock and borrowing money provided the financing needed to open more cafes. And yet, just obtaining the money needed to open more cafes is only part of the story. Once the cafes are open, the fact is that all businesses—including Starbucks—need financial management to stay in business and earn a profit.

Regardless of whether the business is a new start-up or an existing business with a track record, they all need money. This continuing need for money became obvious during the 2008 financial crisis. In reality, the crisis was a wake-up call for many corporate executives, managers, and business owners because two factors became obvious. First, the ability to borrow money (debt capital) or obtain money from the owners of a business (equity capital) is necessary for the efficient operation of a business firm *and* our economic system. Second, the factors of supply and demand influence the cost of available financing. As money became "tight," the cost of obtaining needed funds became higher. This in turn increased the cost of operating a business.

Selling stock—along with selling corporate bonds, obtaining short- and long-term loans, and other financing methods—are used on a regular basis to help firms obtain the financing needed to operate in today's competitive business environment. In this chapter we focus on how firms find the financing required to meet two needs of all business organizations: the need for money to start a business and keep it going, and the need to manage that money effectively. We also look at how firms develop financial plans and evaluate financial performance. Then we compare various methods of obtaining short-term financing. We also examine sources of long-term financing.

What Is Financial Management?

1 **Learning Objective: Explain the need for financial management in business.**

Financial management consists of all the activities concerned with obtaining money and using it effectively. Within a business organization, the financial manager not only must determine the best way (or ways) to raise money, but he or she also must ensure that projected uses are in keeping with the organization's goals.

financial management all the activities concerned with obtaining money and using it effectively

The Need for Financing

Money is needed both to start a business and to keep it going. The original investment of the owners, along with money they may have borrowed, should be enough to open the doors. After that, it would seem that sales revenues could be used to pay the firm's expenses and to provide a profit as well.

This is exactly what happens in a successful firm—over the long run. However, income and expenses may vary from month to month or from year to year. Temporary financing may be needed when expenses are high or sales are low. Then, too, situations such as the opportunity to purchase a new facility or expand an existing plant may require more money than is currently available within a firm. In either case, the firm must look for outside sources of financing.

Short-Term Financing **Short-term financing** is money that will be used for one year or less. Many financial managers define short-term financing as money that will be used for one year *or* one operating cycle of the business, whichever is longer. The *operating cycle of a business* may be longer than one year and is the amount of time between the purchase of raw materials and the sale of finished products to wholesalers, retailers, or consumers.

short-term financing money that will be used for one year or less

As illustrated in Table 19.1, there are many short-term financing needs, but two deserve special attention. First, certain business practices may affect a firm's cash flow and create a need for short-term financing. **Cash flow** is the movement of money into and out of an organization. The ideal is to have sufficient money coming into the firm in any period to cover the firm's expenses during that period. The ideal, however, is not always achieved. For example, California-based Callaway Golf offers credit to retailers and wholesalers that carry the firm's golf clubs

cash flow the movement of money into and out of an organization

Table 19.1: Comparison of Short- and Long-Term Financing

Whether a business seeks short- or long-term financing depends on what the money will be used for.

Corporate Cash Needs	
Short-Term Financing Needs	**Long-Term Financing Needs**
Cash-flow problems	Business start-up costs
Current inventory needs	Mergers and acquisitions
Monthly expenses	New product development
Speculative production	Long-term marketing activities
Short-term promotional needs	Replacement of equipment
Unexpected emergencies	Expansion of facilities

Entrepreneurial Challenge

Peer-to-Peer Loans

When the owner of Dessert Noir Café and Bar needed a short-term business loan during the recent economic downturn, she borrowed with her mouse. Banks were reluctant to lend, so the Beaverton, Oregon, entrepreneur clicked to obtain a personal loan for her business through Prosper.com.

Prosper, Lending Circle, and Virgin Money are among the growing numbers of peer-to-peer (P2P) loan sites that connect entrepreneurs and individuals who need short-term financing with people who want to lend money. Most P2P sites check each applicant's credit history and screen out the riskiest would-be borrowers. Next, applicants list how much they would like to borrow and the maximum interest rate they're willing to pay. Would-be lenders browse the loan requests, then click to lend money. For handling the mechanics, the P2P sites receive a percentage of each loan or a flat fee per loan plus, in many cases, a fee for processing payments.

Why go for a P2P loan? "With no hope of new financing in the foreseeable future, I've used Prosper to fill in where the banks refuse to extend credit to me for my business," explains Dessert Noir's owner. "It's worked well for short-term financing that I know I can repay."

Sources: David Migoya, "Help from Friends Boosts Loan-Challenged," *Denver Post*, November 17, 2008, **www.denverpost.com**; Laura Pappano, "Spending It: Loans in the Time of Facebook," *New York Times*, November 2, 2008, **www.nytimes.com**; Michael Sisk, "Peer-to-Peer Lending: The Rise of Lending Communities," *U.S. Banker*, February 2008, p. 18.

and balls. Credit purchases made by Callaway's retailers generally are not paid until thirty to sixty days (or more) after the transaction. Callaway therefore may need short-term financing to pay its bills until its customers have paid theirs.

A second major need for short-term financing is inventory. For most manufacturers, wholesalers, and retailers, inventory requires considerable investment. Moreover, most goods are manufactured four to nine months before they are actually sold to the ultimate customer. This type of manufacturing is often referred to as *speculative production*. **Speculative production** refers to the time lag between the actual production of goods and when the goods are sold. Consider what happens when a firm such as Black & Decker begins to manufacture electric tools and small appliances for sale during the Christmas season. Manufacturing begins in February, March, and April, and Black & Decker negotiates short-term financing to buy materials and supplies, to pay wages and rent, and to cover inventory costs until its products eventually are sold to wholesalers and retailers later in the year. Take a look at Figure 19.1. Although Black & Decker manufactures and sells finished products all during the year, expenses peak during the first part of the year. During this same period, sales revenues are low. Once the firm's finished products are shipped to retailers and wholesalers and payment is received (usually within thirty to sixty days), sales revenues are used to repay short-term financing.

Retailers that range in size from Wal-Mart to the neighborhood drugstore also need short-term financing to build up their inventories before peak selling periods. For example, Dallas-based Bruce Miller Nurseries must increase the number of shrubs, trees, and flowering plants that it makes available for sale during the spring and summer growing seasons. To obtain this merchandise inventory from growers or wholesalers, it uses short-term financing and repays the loans when the merchandise is sold.

speculative production the time lag between the actual production of goods and when the goods are sold

Figure 19.1: Cash Flow for a Manufacturing Business

Manufacturers such as Black & Decker often use short-term financing to pay expenses during the production process. Once goods are shipped to retailers and wholesalers and payment is received, sales revenues are used to repay short-term financing.

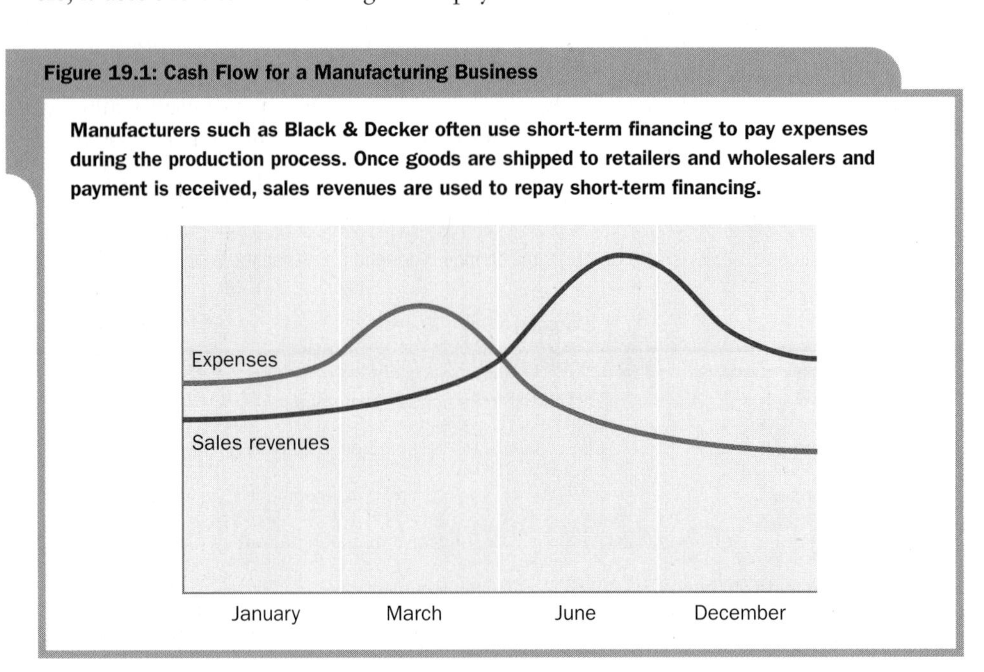

Long-Term Financing **Long-term financing** is money that will be used for longer than one year. Long-term financing obviously is needed to start a new business. As Table 19.1 shows, it is also needed for business mergers and acquisitions, new product development, long-term marketing activities, replacement of equipment that has become obsolete, and expansion of facilities.

The amounts of long-term financing needed by large firms can seem almost unreal. Exxon spends about $10 million to drill an exploratory offshore oil well—without knowing for sure whether oil will be found. And Pfizer invested $8 billion in research and development (R&D) to create new or improved prescription drugs in 2007—the last year that complete dollar amounts were available at the time of this publication.[2]

SPOTLIGHT

Bankruptcies in the United States

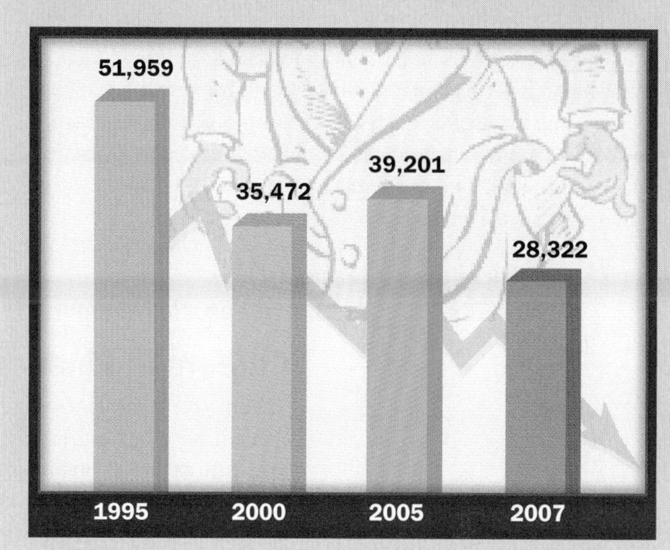

Source: American Bankruptcy Institute website, **www.abiworld.org**, October 17, 2008.

The Need for Financial Management

To some extent, financial management can be viewed as a two-sided problem. On one side, the uses of funds often dictate the type or types of financing needed by a business. On the other side, the activities a business can undertake are determined by the types of financing available. Financial managers must ensure that funds are available when needed, that they are obtained at the lowest possible cost, and that they are used as efficiently as possible. Financial managers also must consider the risk-return ratio when making decisions. The **risk-return ratio** is based on the principle that a high-risk decision should generate higher financial returns for a business. On the other hand, more conservative decisions (with less risk) often generate lesser returns. While financial managers want higher returns, they often must strive for a balance between risk and return. For example, American Electric Power may consider investing millions of dollars to fund research into new solar technology that could enable the company to use the sun to generate electrical power. And yet, financial managers (along with other managers throughout the organization) must determine the potential return before committing to such a costly research project. And finally, financial managers must ensure that funds are available for the repayment of debts in accordance with lenders' financing terms. Prompt repayment is essential to protect the firm's credit rating and its ability to obtain financing in the future.

long-term financing money that will be used for longer than one year

risk-return ratio a ratio based on the principle that a high-risk decision should generate higher financial returns for a business and more conservative decisions often generate lesser returns

Many firms have failed because their managers did not pay enough attention to finances. In fact, poor financial management was one of the major reasons why over 28,000 businesses filed for bankruptcy in 2007—the most recent year for which complete statistics are available.[3] In addition, many fairly successful firms could be highly successful if they managed their finances more carefully. However, many people often take finances for granted. Their first focus may be on production or marketing. As long as there is sufficient financing today, they don't worry about how well it is used or whether it will be there tomorrow. Proper financial management can ensure that:

- Financing priorities are established in line with organizational goals and objectives.
- Spending is planned and controlled.
- Sufficient financing is available when it is needed, both now and in the future.

Inventory management: A complex problem. *For retailers like Best Buy, managing inventory can be a problem, especially before Christmas and other peak selling periods. Although retailers don't want to get stuck with unsold inventory, they must have the right mix and amount of inventory to meet consumer demand. Despite the problems associated with inventory, it's a good feeling to see customers at the cash register purchasing the products they need.*

AP/Wide World

Sustaining the Planet

Funding alternative energy installations can be a major challenge, especially when money is tight. Now groups such as Partnership for Sustainability are easing the financial squeeze by offering loans to individuals, nonprofit groups, and small businesses that install solar energy equipment.
www.partnershipforsustainability.org

- A firm's credit customers pay their bills on time, and the number of past-due or delinquent accounts is reduced.
- Bills are paid promptly to protect the firm's credit rating and its ability to borrow money.
- The funds required for paying the firm's taxes are available when needed to meet tax deadlines.
- Excess cash is invested in certificates of deposit (CDs), government securities, or conservative, marketable securities.

These functions define effective management as applied to a particular resource—money. And like all effective management, financial management begins with people who must set goals and plan for the future.

Careers in Finance

chief financial officer (CFO) a high-level corporate executive who manages a firm's finances and reports directly to the company's chief executive officer or president

When you hear the word *finance,* you may think of highly paid executives who determine what a corporation can afford to do and what it can't. At the executive level, most large business firms have a chief financial officer for financial management. A **chief financial officer (CFO)** is a high-level corporate executive who manages a firm's finances and reports directly to the company's chief executive officer or president. Some firms prefer to use the titles vice president of financial management, treasurer, or controller instead of the CFO title for executive-level positions in the finance area.

While some executives in finance do make $300,000 a year or more, many entry-level and lower-level positions that pay quite a bit less are available. Banks, insurance companies, and investment firms obviously have a need for workers who can manage and analyze financial data. So do businesses involved in manufacturing, services, and marketing. Colleges and universities, not-for-profit organizations, and government entities at all levels also need finance workers.

Would you want his job? *Barney Frank, chairman of the U.S. House of Representatives Financial Services Committee, probably got "on the job financial training" during the recent financial crisis. In fact, his work as chairman of this committee would have been much easier if some executives for large corporations had remembered what it takes to be a successful financial manager.*

AP Photo/Susan Walsh

People in finance must have certain traits and skills. After the scandals that have occurred in the last few years that involve accountants, auditors, and corporate executives, one of the most important priorities for someone interested in a finance career is honesty. Be warned: Investors, lenders, and other corporate executives expect financial managers to be above reproach. And both federal and state government entities have enacted legislation to ensure that corporate financial statements reflect the "real" status of a firm's financial position. In addition to honesty, managers and employees in the finance area must:

1. Have a strong background in accounting or mathematics.
2. Know how to use a computer to analyze data.
3. Be an expert at both written and oral communication.

Typical job titles in finance include bank officer, consumer credit officer, financial analyst, financial planner, loan officer, insurance analyst, and investment account executive. Depending on qualifications, work experience, and education, starting salaries generally begin at $25,000 to $35,000 a year, but it is not uncommon for college graduates to earn higher salaries. In addition to salary, many employees have attractive benefits and other perks that make a career in financial management attractive.

Planning—The Basis of Sound Financial Management

2

Learning Objective: Summarize the process of planning for financial management.

In Chapter 7, we defined a *plan* as an outline of the actions by which an organization intends to accomplish its goals. A **financial plan,** then, is a plan for obtaining and using the money needed to implement an organization's goals.

financial plan a plan for obtaining and using the money needed to implement an organization's goals

Developing the Financial Plan

Financial planning (like all planning) begins with establishing a set of valid goals and objectives. Financial managers next must determine how much money is needed to accomplish each goal and objective. Finally, financial managers must identify available sources of financing and decide which to use. The three steps involved in financial planning are illustrated in Figure 19.2.

Figure 19.2: The Three Steps of Financial Planning

After a financial plan has been developed, it must be monitored continually to ensure that it actually fulfills the firm's goals and objectives.

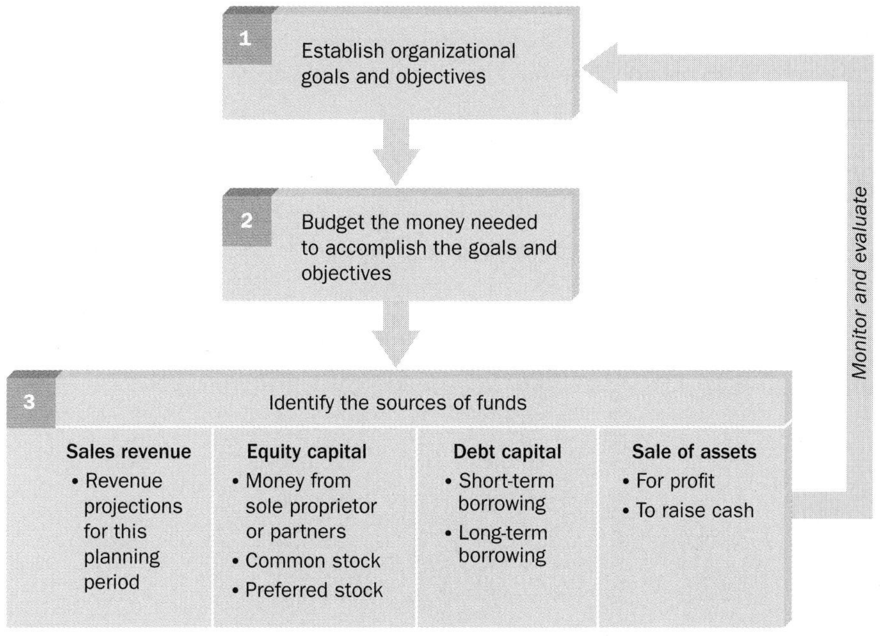

1 Establish organizational goals and objectives

2 Budget the money needed to accomplish the goals and objectives

3 Identify the sources of funds

Sales revenue	Equity capital	Debt capital	Sale of assets
• Revenue projections for this planning period	• Money from sole proprietor or partners • Common stock • Preferred stock	• Short-term borrowing • Long-term borrowing	• For profit • To raise cash

Monitor and evaluate

Establishing Organizational Goals and Objectives As pointed out in Chapter 7, a *goal* is an end result that an organization expects to achieve over a one- to ten-year period. *Objectives* are specific statements detailing what the organization intends to accomplish within a shorter period of time. If goals and objectives are not specific and measurable, they cannot be translated into dollar costs, and financial planning cannot proceed. Goals and objectives also must be realistic. Otherwise, they may be impossible to finance or achieve. For large corporations, goals and objectives can be expensive. For example, when Pepsi wanted to revamp its image in the marketplace, it planned to spend at least $1.2 billion over three years. The goal was to redesign many of Pepsi's packaging graphics for its carbonated soft drink products as well as a redesign of the Pepsi corporate logo.[4]

Budgeting for Financial Needs Once planners know what the firm's goals and objectives are for a specific period—say, the next calendar year—they can budget the costs the firm will incur and the sales revenues it will receive. Specifically, a **budget** is a financial statement that projects income and/or expenditures over a specified future period.

budget a financial statement that projects income and/or expenditures over a specified future period

Usually, the budgeting process begins with the construction of budgets for sales and various types of expenses. (A typical sales budget—for Stars and Stripes Clothing, a California-based retailer—is shown in Figure 19.3.) Financial managers can easily combine each department's budget for sales and expenses into a company-wide cash budget. A **cash budget** estimates cash receipts and cash expenditures over a specified period. Notice in the cash budget for Stars and Stripes Clothing, shown in Figure 19.4, that cash sales and collections are listed at the top for each calendar quarter. Payments for purchases and routine expenses are listed in the middle section. Using this information, it is possible to calculate the anticipated cash gain or loss at the end of each quarter.

cash budget a financial statement that estimates cash receipts and cash expenditures over a specified period

Most firms today use one of two approaches to budgeting. In the *traditional* approach, each new budget is based on the dollar amounts contained in the budget for the preceding year. These amounts are modified to reflect any revised goals and objectives, and managers are required to justify only new expenditures. The problem with this approach is that it leaves room for padding budget items to protect the (sometimes selfish) interests of the manager or his or her department.

This problem is essentially eliminated through zero-base budgeting. **Zero-base budgeting** is a budgeting approach in which every expense in every budget must be justified. It can reduce unnecessary spending dramatically because every budget item must stand on its own merits. However, some managers oppose zero-base budgeting because it requires entirely too much time-consuming paperwork.

zero-base budgeting a budgeting approach in which every expense in every budget must be justified

Figure 19.3: Sales Budget for Stars and Stripes Clothing

Usually, the budgeting process begins with the construction of departmental budgets for sales.

STARS AND STRIPES CLOTHING
Sales Budget
For January 1, 2008 to December 31, 2008

Department	First Quarter	Second Quarter	Third Quarter	Fourth Quarter	Totals
Infants'	$ 50,000	$ 55,000	$ 60,000	$ 70,000	$235,000
Children's	45,000	45,000	40,000	40,000	170,000
Women's	35,000	40,000	35,000	50,000	160,000
Men's	20,000	20,000	15,000	25,000	80,000
Totals	$150,000	$160,000	$150,000	$185,000	$645,000

Figure 19.4: Cash Budget for Stars and Stripes Clothing

A company-wide cash budget projects sales, collections, purchases, and expenses over a specified period to anticipate cash surpluses and deficits.

STARS AND STRIPES CLOTHING
Cash Budget

For January 1, 2008 to December 31, 2008

	First Quarter	Second Quarter	Third Quarter	Fourth Quarter	Totals
Cash sales and collections	$150,000	$160,000	$150,000	$185,000	$645,000
Less payments					
Purchases	$110,000	$ 80,000	$ 90,000	$ 60,000	$340,000
Wages/salaries	25,000	20,000	25,000	30,000	100,000
Rent	10,000	10,000	12,000	12,000	44,000
Other expenses	4,000	4,000	5,000	6,000	19,000
Taxes	8,000	8,000	10,000	10,000	36,000
Total payments	$157,000	$122,000	$142,000	$118,000	$539,000
Cash gain or (loss)	$ (7,000)	$ 38,000	$ 8,000	$ 67,000	$106,000

To develop a plan for long-term financing needs, managers often construct a capital budget. A **capital budget** estimates a firm's expenditures for major assets, including new product development, expansion of facilities, replacement of obsolete equipment, and mergers and acquisitions. For example, Bank of America constructed a capital budget to determine the best way to finance the $50 billion acquisition of Merrill Lynch.[5]

capital budget a financial statement that estimates a firm's expenditures for major assets and its long-term financing needs

Identifying Sources of Funds The four primary sources of funds, listed in Figure 19.2, are sales revenue, equity capital, debt capital, and proceeds from the sale of assets. Future sales revenue generally provides the greatest part of a firm's financing. Figure 19.4 shows that for Stars and Stripes Clothing, sales for the year are expected to cover all expenses and to provide a cash gain of $106,000, or about 16 percent of sales. However, Stars and Stripes has a problem in the first quarter, when sales are expected to fall short of expenses by $7,000. In fact, one of the primary reasons for financial planning is to provide management with adequate lead time to solve this type of cash-flow problem.

A second type of funding is **equity capital**. For a sole proprietorship or partnership, equity capital is provided by the owner or owners of the business. For a corporation, equity capital is money obtained from the sale of shares of ownership in the business. Equity capital is used almost exclusively for long-term financing. Thus, it might be used to start a business and to fund expansions or mergers. It would not be considered for short-term financing needs, such as Stars and Stripes Clothing's first-quarter $7,000 shortfall.

equity capital money received from the owners or from the sale of shares of ownership in a business

A third type of funding is **debt capital**, which is borrowed money. Debt capital may be borrowed for either short- or long-term use—and a short-term loan seems made to order for Stars and Stripes Clothing's shortfall problem. The firm probably would borrow the needed $7,000 (or perhaps a bit more) at some point during the first quarter and repay it from second-quarter sales revenue. Stars and Stripes Clothing already may have established a line of credit at a local bank to cover just such short-term needs. As discussed in Chapter 18, a *line of credit* is a prearranged short-term loan.

debt capital borrowed money obtained through loans of various types

Proceeds from the sale of assets are the fourth type of funding. Selling assets is a drastic step. However, it may be a reasonable last resort when neither equity capital nor debt capital can be found. Assets also may be sold when they are no longer needed or do not "fit" with the company's core business. To concentrate on its core business and

It takes more than a cute advertising gimmick. *Although most people enjoyed seeing the Pets.com sock puppet, they didn't buy the firm's products. Pets.com, a dot-com start-up backed by Amazon, spent millions of dollars on television and other media advertising, but failed to generate enough sales revenue to avoid the cash crisis that eventually led to the company's failure.*

to raise financing, food giant ConAgra sold its commodity trade operations to an affiliate of New York-based Ospraie Management for about $2.1 billion. At the time of the sale, ConAgra's management said it would use the proceeds from the sale to repurchase stock, reduce debt, and to remake itself as a force in consumer packaged goods.[6]

Monitoring and Evaluating Financial Performance

It is important to ensure that financial plans are being implemented properly and to catch potential problems before they become major ones. For example, many Internet-based businesses have reduced various expenses in order to become profitable. Even so, many of these high-tech companies have failed in the past few years. Pets.com is an example of a dot-com start-up that lost control of its finances. Backed by Amazon, the firm spent millions on television and other media advertising to generate awareness and sales. The funny advertisements presented by the famous talking-dog sock puppet could not create the critical mass of buyers quickly enough to offset the advertising and other operational costs. As a result, the firm lost $5 for every dollar of pet supplies revenue received. This quickly created a cash crisis and eventually led to failure. (*Note:* The firm's URL—**www.pets.com**—was purchased by competitor PetSmart.)

To prevent problems such as those just described, financial managers should establish a means of monitoring financial performance. Interim budgets (weekly, monthly, or quarterly) may be prepared for comparison purposes. These comparisons point up areas that require additional or revised planning—or at least areas calling for a more careful investigation. Budget comparisons also can be used to improve the firm's future budgets.

Sources of Short-Term Debt Financing

3

Learning Objective: Describe the advantages and disadvantages of different methods of short-term debt financing.

During the recent financial crisis, many business firms found that it was much more difficult to borrow money for short periods of time. Typically, short-term debt financing is money that will be repaid in one year or less. Needed funds to purchase inventory, buy supplies, pay salaries, and meet everyday expenses was not only more difficult to obtain, but also more expensive because of higher interest rates. To help free up the credit markets, the government passed a $700 billion financial rescue plan in October 2008. While not all the money was used to meet short-term financing needs, the availability of more money did provide funds for businesses that needed short-term financing.

The decision to borrow money does not necessarily mean that a firm is in financial trouble. On the contrary, astute financial management often means regular, responsible borrowing of many different kinds to meet different needs. In this section, we examine the sources of *short-term debt financing* available to businesses. In the next two sections, we look at long-term financing options: equity capital and debt capital.

unsecured financing financing that is not backed by collateral

trade credit a type of short-term financing extended by a seller who does not require immediate payment after delivery of merchandise

Sources of Unsecured Short-Term Financing

Short-term debt financing is usually easier to obtain than long-term debt financing for three reasons:

1. For the lender, the shorter repayment period means less risk of nonpayment.
2. The dollar amounts of short-term loans usually are smaller than those of long-term loans.

Jump-Starting Your Career

Are You a Future CFO?

If your long-term career plan is to become the CFO of a corporation or nonprofit organization, strong accounting and financial skills will not be enough. According to a recent survey of CFOs, you'll need to develop your leadership abilities and your decision-making skills through solid business experience. Another survey finds that CFOs are increasingly focused on profit improvement as well as revenue growth.

Some CFOs learn the business from the ground up by rotating through different parts of one corporation. That's how Jon Moeller, the recently appointed CFO of Procter & Gamble, became familiar with the consumer product giant's inner workings and built a 20-year track record of financial success within the firm. Before being named CFO, Moeller had not only managed accounting and financial departments, but he had also helped acquire a hair-care company and divest a coffee brand.

Other CFOs are brought in from the outside because they can bring a fresh perspective to difficult decisions. When Dell was seeking to revitalize sales and profits during a severe economic downturn, it hired Brian Gladden, formerly of General Electric, to serve as CFO, because of his operational expertise in building businesses. What path will you take to the CFO position?

Sources: Ellen Byron, "P&G Taps Moeller as Finance Chief," *Wall Street Journal,* October 29, 2008, **www.wsj.com**; Jeffrey Marshall and Ellen M. Heffes, "Survey Underscores Changes in Pharmaceutical Firms," *Financial Executive,* June 2008, p. 9; Carolyn Tang, "Are You CFO Material?" *Insight Magazine,* January-February 2008, **www.icpas.org**; Justin Scheck and Joann S. Lublin, "Dell Hires GE Veteran as Finance Chief," *Wall Street Journal,* May 20, 2008, p. B5.

3. A close working relationship normally exists between the short-term borrower and the lender.

Most lenders do not require collateral for short-term financing. When they do, it is usually because they are concerned about the size of a particular loan, the borrowing firm's poor credit rating, or the general prospects of repayment. Remember from Chapter 18 that *collateral* was defined as real estate or property pledged as security for a loan.

Unsecured financing is financing that is not backed by collateral. A company seeking unsecured short-term financing has several options.

Trade Credit Manufacturers and wholesalers often provide financial aid to retailers by allowing them thirty to sixty days (or more) in which to pay for merchandise. This delayed payment, known as **trade credit,** is a type of short-term financing extended by a seller who does not require immediate payment after delivery of merchandise. It is the most popular form of short-term financing, because most manufacturers and wholesalers don't charge interest for trade credit. In fact, from 70 to 90 percent of all transactions between businesses involve some trade credit.

Let's assume that a Barnes & Noble bookstore receives a shipment of books from a publisher. Along with the merchandise, the publisher sends an invoice that states the terms of payment. Barnes & Noble now has two options for payment. First, the book retailer may pay the invoice promptly and take advantage of any cash discount the publisher offers. Cash-discount terms are specified on the invoice. For instance, "2/10, net 30" means that the customer—Barnes & Noble—may take a 2 percent discount if it pays the invoice within ten days of the invoice date. Cash discounts can generate substantial savings and lower the cost of purchasing merchandise for a retailer such as Barnes & Noble. Let's assume that the dollar amount of the invoice is $140,000. In this case, the cash discount is $2,800 ($\$140,000 \times 0.02 = \$2,800$).

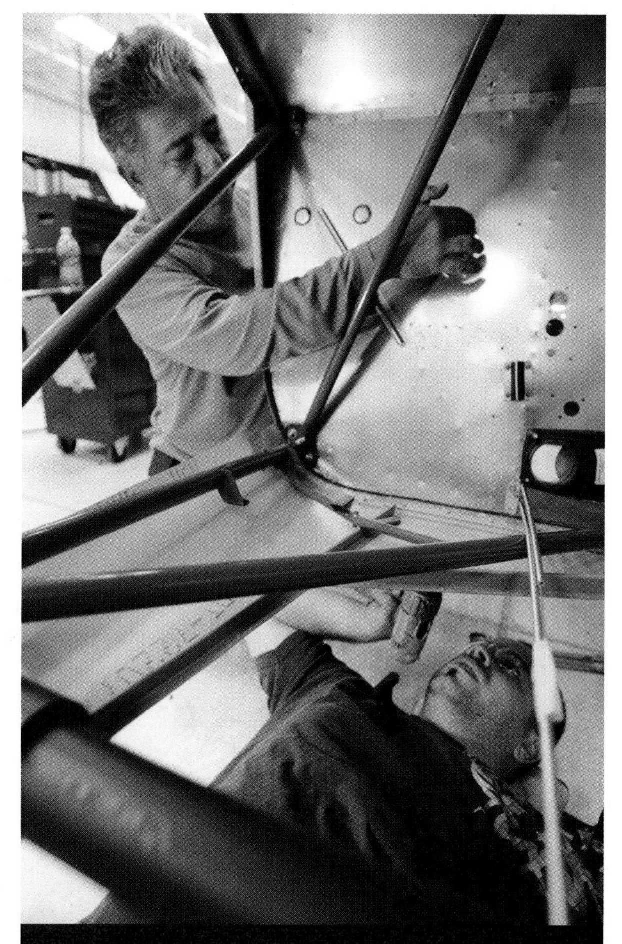

Trade credit helped build this helicopter. *Many companies like California-based Robinson Helicopter use trade credit to purchase the materials they need to manufacture products. When trade credit is used, manufacturers obtain short-term financing and don't have to pay suppliers and vendors for thirty to sixty days or more. As an added bonus, typically there is no finance or interest charge when trade credit is used to purchase materials.*

AP Photo/Reed Saxon

A second option is to wait until the end of the credit period before making payment. If payment is made between eleven and thirty days after the date of the invoice, the customer must pay the entire amount. As long as payment is made before the end of the credit period, the customer maintains the ability to purchase additional merchandise using the trade-credit arrangement.

promissory note a written pledge by a borrower to pay a certain sum of money to a creditor at a specified future date

Promissory Notes Issued to Suppliers A **promissory note** is a written pledge by a borrower to pay a certain sum of money to a creditor at a specified future date. Suppliers uneasy about extending trade credit may be less reluctant to offer credit to customers who sign promissory notes. Unlike trade credit, however, promissory notes usually require the borrower to pay interest. Although repayment periods may extend to one year, most short-term promissory notes are repaid in 60 to 180 days.

A promissory note offers two important advantages to the firm extending the credit. First, a promissory note is a legally binding and enforceable document that has been signed by the individual or business borrowing the money. Second, most promissory notes are negotiable instruments, and the supplier (or company extending credit) may be able to discount, or sell, the note to its own bank. If the note is discounted, the dollar amount the supplier would receive is slightly less than the maturity value because the bank charges a fee for the service. The supplier would recoup most of its money immediately, and the bank would collect the maturity value when the note matured.

prime interest rate the lowest rate charged by a bank for a short-term loan

Unsecured Bank Loans Banks and other financial institutions offer unsecured short-term loans to businesses at interest rates that vary with each borrower's credit rating. The **prime interest rate**, sometimes called the *reference rate*, is the lowest rate charged by a bank for a short-term loan. Figure 19.5 traces the fluctuations in the average prime rate charged by U.S. banks from 1997 to September 2008. This lowest rate generally is reserved for large corporations with excellent credit ratings. Organizations with good to high credit ratings may pay the prime rate plus 2 percent. Firms with questionable credit ratings may have to pay the prime rate plus 4 percent. (The fact that a banker charges a higher interest rate for a higher-risk loan is a practical application of the risk-return ratio discussed earlier in this chapter.) Of course, if the banker believes that loan repayment may be a problem, the borrower's loan application may well be rejected.

Figure 19.5: Average Prime Interest Rate Paid by U.S. Businesses, 1997–2008

The prime rate is the interest rate charged by U.S. banks when businesses with the "best" credit ratings borrow money. All other businesses pay higher interest rates than the prime rate.

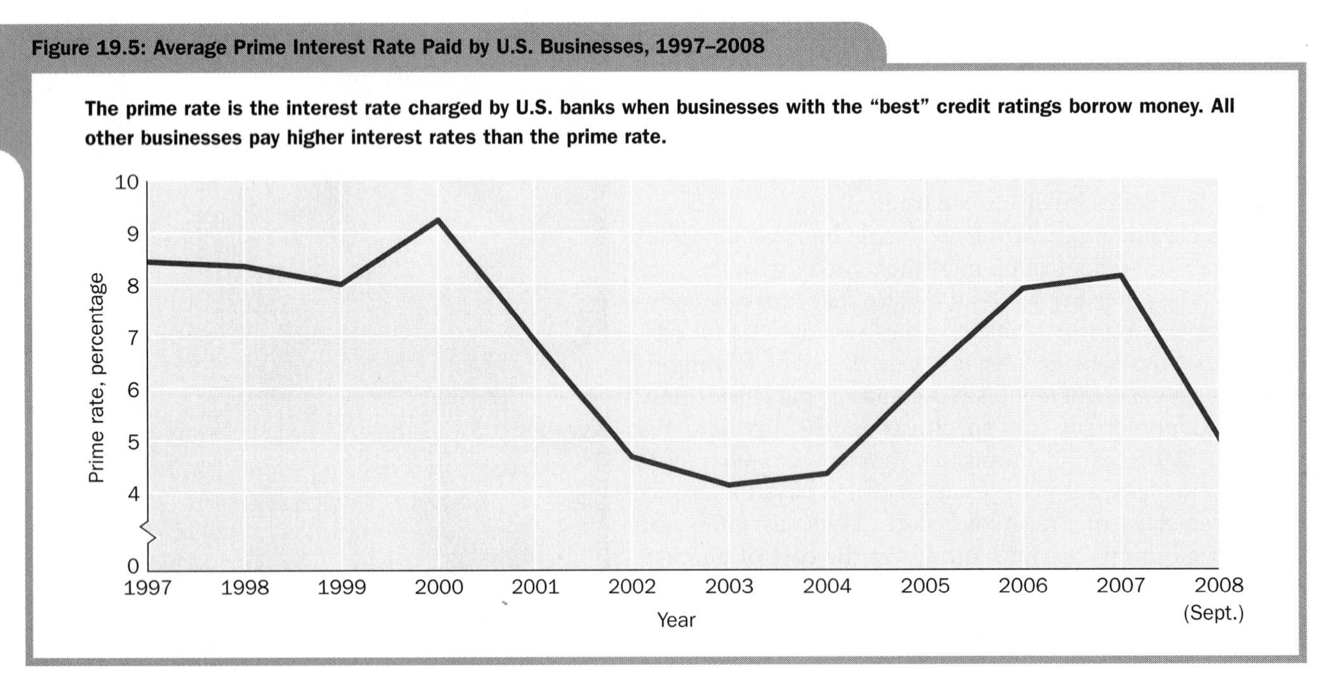

Source: Federal Reserve Bank website, **www.federalreserve.gov**, accessed October 17, 2008.

Banks generally offer unsecured short-term loans through promissory notes, a line of credit, or a revolving credit agreement. A bank promissory note is similar to the promissory note issued to suppliers described in the preceding section. For both types of promissory notes, interest rates and repayment terms may be negotiated between the borrower and a bank or supplier. A bank that offers a promissory note or line of credit may require that a *compensating balance* be kept on deposit at the bank. This balance may be as much as 20 percent of the borrowed funds. Assume that Bank of America requires a 20 percent compensating balance on a short-term promissory note or a line of credit. If you borrow $50,000, at least $10,000 ($50,000 × 0.20 = $10,000) of the loan amount must be kept on deposit at the bank. In this situation, the effective interest rate you must pay on the original $50,000 loan increases because you have the use of only $40,000. The bank also may require that every commercial borrower *clean up* (pay off completely) its short-term promissory note or line of credit at least once each year and not use it again for a period of thirty to sixty days.

Even with a line of credit, a firm may not be able to borrow on short notice if the bank does not have sufficient funds available. For this reason, some firms prefer a *revolving credit agreement,* which is a *guaranteed* line of credit. Under this type of agreement, the bank guarantees that the money will be available when the borrower needs it. In return for the guarantee, the bank charges a commitment fee ranging from 0.25 to 1.0 percent of the *unused* portion of the revolving credit agreement. The usual interest is charged for the portion that *is* borrowed.

Commercial Paper **Commercial paper** is a short-term promissory note issued by a large corporation. Commercial paper is secured only by the reputation of the issuing firm; no collateral is involved. It is usually issued in large denominations, ranging from $5,000 to $100,000. Corporations issuing commercial paper pay interest rates slightly below the interest rates charged by banks for short-term loans. Thus, issuing commercial paper is cheaper than getting short-term financing from a bank. The interest rate a corporation pays when it issues commercial paper is tied to its credit rating and its ability to repay the commercial paper. It is most often used to purchase inventory, pay salaries and other necessary expenses, and solve cash-flow problems.

commercial paper a short-term promissory note issued by a large corporation

Large firms with excellent credit reputations like Microsoft, Procter & Gamble, and Caterpillar can raise large sums of money quickly by issuing commercial paper. However, during the recent financial crisis, even companies that had always been able to sell commercial paper had difficulty finding buyers. For example, both GE and AT&T—two premier names in corporate America—couldn't get the short-term financing they were looking for.[7] To help provide additional short-term financing, the Federal Reserve Bank stepped in and began to purchase the commercial paper from firms in need of financing to pay for day-to-day business operations.[8]

Sources of Secured Short-Term Financing

If a business cannot obtain enough capital through unsecured financing, it must put up collateral to obtain additional short-term financing. Almost any asset can serve as collateral. However, *inventories* and *accounts receivable* are the assets most commonly pledged for short-term financing. Even when it is willing to pledge collateral to back up a loan, a firm that is financially weak may have difficulty obtaining short-term financing.

Loans Secured by Inventory Normally, manufacturers, wholesalers, and retailers have large amounts of money invested in finished goods. In addition, manufacturers carry raw materials and work-in-process inventories. All three types of inventory may be pledged as collateral for short-term loans. However, lenders prefer the much more salable finished merchandise to raw materials or work-in-process inventories.

A lender may insist that inventory used as collateral be stored in a public warehouse. In such a case, the receipt issued by the warehouse is retained by the lender. Without this receipt, the public warehouse will not release the merchandise. The lender releases the warehouse receipt—and the merchandise—to the borrower when the borrowed money is repaid. In addition to paying the interest on the loan, the borrower must pay for storage in the public warehouse. As a result, this type of loan is more expensive than an unsecured short-term loan.

floor planning method of financing in which title to merchandise is given to lenders in return for short-term financing

A special type of financing called *floor planning* is used by automobile, furniture, and appliance dealers. **Floor planning** is a method of financing in which title to merchandise is given to lenders in return for short-term financing. The major difference between floor planning and other types of secured short-term financing is that the borrower maintains control of the inventory. As merchandise is sold, the borrower repays the lender a portion of the loan, and the lender returns the title to the merchandise sold.

Loans Secured by Receivables As defined in Chapter 17, *accounts receivable* are amounts owed to a firm by its customers. They are created when trade credit is given to customers and usually are due within thirty to sixty days. A firm can pledge its accounts receivable as collateral to obtain short-term financing. A lender may advance 70 to 80 percent of the dollar amount of the receivables. First, however, it conducts a thorough investigation to determine the *quality* of the receivables. (The quality of the receivables is the credit standing of the firm's customers, coupled with the customers' ability to repay their credit obligations.) If a favorable determination is made, the loan is approved. When the borrowing firm collects from a customer whose account has been pledged as collateral, it must turn the money over to the lender as partial repayment of the loan. An alternative approach is to notify the borrower's credit customers to make their payments directly to the lender.

Factoring Accounts Receivable

factor a firm that specializes in buying other firms' accounts receivable

Accounts receivable may be used in one other way to help raise short-term financing: They can be sold to a factoring company (or factor). A **factor** is a firm that specializes in buying other firms' accounts receivable. The factor buys the accounts receivable for less than their face value, but it collects the full dollar amount when each account is due. The factor's profit thus is the difference between the face value of the accounts receivable and the amount the factor has paid for them. Generally, the amount of profit the factor receives is based on the risk the factor assumes. Risk, in this case, is the probability that the accounts receivable will not be repaid when they mature.

Even though the firm selling its accounts receivable gets less than face value, it does receive needed cash immediately. Moreover, it has shifted both the task of collecting and the risk of nonpayment to the factor, which now owns the accounts receivable. In many cases, the factor may purchase only selected accounts receivable—usually those with the highest potential of repayment. In other cases, the firm selling its accounts receivable must obtain approval from the factor *before* selling merchandise to a credit customer. Thus, the firm receives instant feedback on whether the factor will purchase the credit customer's account. Generally, customers whose accounts receivable have been factored are given instructions to make their payments directly to the factor.

Cost Comparisons

Table 19.2 compares the various types of short-term financing. As you can see, trade credit is the least expensive. Factoring of accounts receivable is typically the highest-cost method shown.

For many purposes, short-term financing suits a firm's needs perfectly. At other times, however, long-term financing may be more appropriate. In this case, a business may try to raise equity capital or long-term debt capital.

Table 19.2: Comparison of Short-Term Financing Methods

Type of Financing	Cost	Repayment Period	Businesses That May Use It	Comments
Trade credit	Low, if any	30–60 days	All businesses with good credit	Usually no finance charge
Promissory note issued to suppliers	Moderate	1 year or less	All businesses	Usually unsecured but requires legal document
Unsecured bank loan	Moderate	1 year or less	All businesses	Promissory note, a line of credit,or revolving credit agreement generally required
Commercial paper	Moderate	1 year or less	Large corporations with high credit ratings	Available only to large firms
Secured loan	High	1 year or less	Firms with questionable credit ratings	Inventory or accounts receivable often used as collateral
Factoring	High	None	Firms that have large numbers of credit customers	Accounts receivable sold to a factor

Sources of Equity Financing

4

Learning Objective: Evaluate the advantages and disadvantages of equity financing.

Sources of long-term financing vary with the size and type of business. As mentioned earlier, a sole proprietorship or partnership acquires equity capital (sometimes referred to as *owner's equity*) when the owner or owners invest money in the business. For corporations, equity-financing options include the sale of stock and the use of profits not distributed to owners. All three types of businesses also can obtain venture capital and use long-term debt capital (borrowed money) to meet their financial needs. Different types of debt capital are discussed in the next section. Regardless of the type of long-term financing chosen, most financial managers have found that financing is more expensive and harder to obtain since the recent financial crisis. Both investors and lenders are more cautious than they were before the crisis.

Selling Stock

Some equity capital is used to start every business—sole proprietorship, partnership, or corporation. In the case of corporations, stockholders who buy shares in the company provide equity capital.

Initial Public Offerings An **initial public offering (IPO)** occurs when a corporation sells common stock to the general public for the first time. To raise money, the wireless telecommunications firm Metro PCS used an IPO and raised $1.2 billion that it could use to fund expansion and other business activities.[9] Established companies that plan to raise capital by selling subsidiaries to the public also can use IPOs. For example, McDonald's sold shares in its Chipotle casual restaurant subsidiary. The Chipotle IPO raised $133 million to fund new store growth for Chipotle. McDonald's used the money it received from the Chipotle IPO to fund capital expenditures and expansion of its current business activities. Also, selling off Chipotle allowed McDonald's to concentrate on its core fast-food business.[10] Generally, corporations sell off subsidiaries for two reasons. First, the sale of a subsidiary can boost the value of the firm's core business by shedding a unit that is growing more slowly. Second, the sale of a subsidiary also can bolster corporate finances and improve the parent company's balance sheet if the money is used to reduce corporate debt.

initial public offering (IPO) when a corporation sells common stock to the general public for the first time

Ethics Matters

Post-Bailout Controversy at AIG

The U.S. government has loaned insurer American International Group (AIG) many billions of dollars and invested billions more to keep it from failing during the economic crisis. With so much taxpayer money at stake, is it ethical for AIG to keep spending as it always has?

Just days after receiving an $85 billion bailout, AIG paid for a $440,000 weeklong executive meeting in California. Facing public criticism, the CEO agreed to reevaluate such expenditures. "While this sort of gathering has been standard practice in our industry for many years and was planned many months before the Federal Reserve's loan to AIG, we understand that our company is now facing very different challenges," he said. "We owe our employees and the American public new standards and approaches."

Weeks later, AIG held what it called an "essential" training seminar for financial planners at an upscale Arizona hotel. The CEO explained that the participants and some sponsors had paid most of the tab. He also noted that AIG had canceled hundreds of meetings and slashed business travel to save money.

Finally, under government pressure, the company agreed to make changes in top-management compensation by freezing or reducing executive bonuses, salaries, and severance payments. What else should AIG do to live up to the "new standards and approaches" its CEO promised after the bailout?

Sources: Hugh Son, "New York's Cuomo Queries AIG on Bonuses and Raises," *Bloomberg*, November 18, 2008, **www.bloomberg.com**; "Under Fire, AIG Cancels 160 Meetings and Events," *Meeting News*, November 13, 2008, **www.meetingnews.com**; Hugh Son and Erik Holm, "AIG 'Reevaluating' Costs After $440,000 Conference, Liddy Says," *Bloomberg*, October 8, 2008, **www.bloomberg.com**.

AP Photo/Katsumi Kasahara

A corporation selling stock often will use an **investment banking firm**—an organization that assists corporations in raising funds, usually by helping to sell new issues of stocks, bonds, or other financial securities. The investment banking firm generally charges a fee of 2 to 20 percent of the proceeds received by the corporation issuing the securities. The size of the commission depends on the financial health of the corporation issuing the new securities and the size of the new security issue.

Although a corporation can have only one IPO, it can sell additional stock after the IPO, assuming that there is a market for the company's stock. Even though the cost of selling stock (often referred to as *flotation costs*) is high, the *ongoing* costs associated with this type of equity financing are low for two reasons. First, the corporation does not have to repay money obtained from the sale of stock because the corporation is under no legal obligation to do so. If you purchase corporate stock and later decide to sell your stock, you may sell it to another investor—not the corporation.

A second advantage of selling stock is that a corporation is under no legal obligation to pay dividends to stockholders. As noted in Chapter 4, a *dividend* is a distribution of earnings to the stockholders of a corporation. For any reason (if a company has a bad year, for example), the board of directors can vote to omit dividend payments. Earnings then are retained for use in funding business operations. Of course, corporate management may hear from unhappy stockholders if expected dividends are omitted too frequently.

There are two types of stock: common and preferred. Each type has advantages and drawbacks as a means of long-term financing.

Common Stock A share of **common stock** represents the most basic form of corporate ownership. In return for the financing provided by selling common stock, management must make certain concessions to stockholders that may restrict or change corporate policies. By law, every corporation must hold an annual meeting, at which the holders of common stock may vote for the board of directors and approve or disapprove major corporate actions. Among such actions are:

1. Amendments to the corporate charter or corporate by-laws
2. Sale of certain assets
3. Mergers and acquisitions
4. New issues of preferred stock or bonds
5. Changes in the amount of common stock issued

Few investors will buy common stock unless they believe that their investment will increase in value. Information on the reasons why investors purchase stocks and how to evaluate stock investments is provided in Chapter 20.

investment banking firm an organization that assists corporations in raising funds, usually by helping to sell new issues of stocks, bonds, or other financial securities

common stock stock whose owners may vote on corporate matters but whose claims on profits and assets are subordinate to the claims of others

IPOs Can Raise Billions!

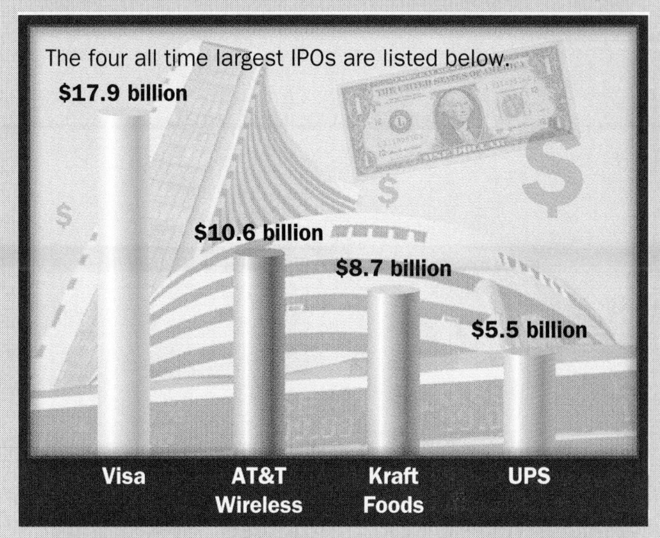

Source: The Renaissance Capital IPO Home website, **www.ipohome.com,** accessed October 19, 2008.

Preferred Stock As noted in Chapter 4, the owners of **preferred stock** must receive their dividends before holders of common stock receive theirs. When compared to common stockholders, preferred stockholders also have first claim (after creditors) on assets if the corporation is dissolved or declares bankruptcy. Even so, as with common stock, the board of directors must approve dividends on preferred stock, and this type of financing does not represent a debt that must be legally repaid. In return for preferential treatment, preferred stockholders generally give up the right to vote at a corporation's annual meeting.

The dividend on a share of preferred stock is stated on the stock certificate either as a percent of the par value of the stock or as a specified dollar amount. The **par value** of a stock is an assigned (and often arbitrary) dollar value printed on the stock certificate. For example, Pitney Bowes—a U.S. manufacturer of office and business equipment—issued 4 percent preferred stock with a par value of $50. The annual dividend amount is $2 per share ($50 par value × 0.04 = $2 annual dividend).

Although a corporation usually issues only one type of common stock, it may issue many types of preferred stock with varying dividends or dividend rates. For example, New York–based Consolidated Edison has one common-stock issue but three preferred-stock issues with different dividend amounts for each type of preferred stock.

When a corporation believes that it can issue new preferred stock at a lower dividend rate (or common stock with no specified dividend), it may decide to "call in,"

preferred stock stock whose owners usually do not have voting rights but whose claims on dividends and assets are paid before those of common-stock owners

par value an assigned (and often arbitrary) dollar value printed on a stock certificate

AP Photo/Richard Drew

Bet you've used the card. *But did you know they just sold stock for the first time? That's right. Visa sold stock for the first time in 2008. Although the company has been issuing credit cards for years, its long-awaited initial public offering (IPO) created quite a stir on Wall Street.*

Buffett to the rescue! *Warren Buffett and his company Berkshire Hathaway invested $5 billion in the Goldman Sachs Group. The deal amounts to a huge vote of confidence for Goldman Sachs—one of Wall Street's largest investment banking and financial firms. The fact that Mr. Buffett is recognized as one of the "best" investors says a lot about Goldman Sach's ability to weather a financial crisis.*

AP Photo/Nati Harnik

or buy back, an earlier stock issue. In this case, management has two options. First, it can buy shares in the market—just like any other investor. Second, it can exercise a call provision because practically all preferred stock is *callable*. When considering the two options, management naturally will purchase the preferred stock in the less costly way.

To make preferred stock more attractive to investors, some corporations include a conversion feature. **Convertible preferred stock** is preferred stock that an owner may exchange for a specified number of shares of common stock. The Textron Corporation—a manufacturer of component parts for the automotive and aerospace industries—has issued convertible preferred stock. Each share of Textron preferred stock is convertible to 8.8 shares of the firm's common stock.[11] This conversion feature provides the investor with the safety of preferred stock and the hope of greater speculative gain through conversion to common stock.

convertible preferred stock preferred stock that an owner may exchange for a specified number of shares of common stock

retained earnings the portion of a corporation's profits not distributed to stockholders

Retained Earnings

Most large corporations distribute only a portion of their after-tax earnings to stockholders. The portion of a corporation's profits *not* distributed to stockholders is called **retained earnings**. Because they are undistributed profits, retained earnings are considered a form of equity financing.

The amount of retained earnings in any year is determined by corporate management and approved by the board of directors. Most small and growing corporations pay no cash dividend—or a very small dividend—to their stockholders. All or most earnings are reinvested in the business for research and development, expansion, or the funding of major projects. Reinvestment tends to increase the value of the firm's stock while it provides essentially cost-free financing for the business. More mature corporations may distribute 40 to 60 percent of their after-tax profits as dividends. Utility companies and other corporations with very stable earnings often pay out as much as 80 to 90 percent of what they earn. For a large corporation, retained earnings can amount to a hefty bit of financing. For example, in 2007, the total amount of retained earnings for General Electric was almost $117 billion.[12]

Venture Capital and Private Placements

To establish a new business or expand an existing one, an entrepreneur may try to obtain venture capital. In Chapter 5, we defined *venture capital* as money invested in small (and sometimes struggling) firms that have the potential to become very successful. Most venture capital firms do not invest in the typical small business—a neighborhood convenience store or a local dry cleaner—but in firms that have the potential to become extremely profitable. And while venture capital firms are willing to take chances, they are also more selective about where they invest their money after the high-tech bust that occurred in the last part of the 1990s and first part of the twenty-first century.

Generally, a venture capital firm consists of a pool of investors, a traditional partnership established by a wealthy family, or a joint venture formed by corporations with money to invest. In return for financing, these investors generally receive an equity position in the business and share in its profits. Venture capital firms vary in size and scope of interest. Some offer financing for start-up businesses, whereas others finance only established businesses.

Another method of raising capital is through a private placement. A **private placement** occurs when stock and other corporate securities are sold directly to insurance companies, pension funds, or large institutional investors. When compared with selling stocks and other corporate securities to the public, there are often fewer government regulations and the cost is generally less when the securities are sold through a private placement. Typically, terms between the buyer and seller are negotiated when a private placement is used to raise capital.

private placement occurs when stock and other corporate securities are sold directly to insurance companies, pension funds, or large institutional investors

Sources of Long-Term Debt Financing

5

Learning Objective: Evaluate the advantages and disadvantages of long-term debt financing.

As we pointed out earlier in this chapter, businesses borrow money on a short-term basis for many valid reasons other than desperation. There are equally valid reasons for long-term borrowing. In addition to using borrowed money to meet the long-term needs listed in Table 19.1, successful businesses often use the financial leverage it creates to improve their financial performance. **Financial leverage** is the use of borrowed funds to increase the return on owners' equity. The principle of financial leverage works as long as a firm's earnings are larger than the interest charged for the borrowed money.

financial leverage the use of borrowed funds to increase the return on owners' equity

To understand how financial leverage can increase a firm's return on owners' equity, study the information for Texas-based Cypress Springs Plastics presented in Table 19.3. Pete Johnston, the owner of the firm, is trying to decide how best to finance a $100,000 purchase of new high-tech manufacturing equipment. He could borrow the money and pay 9 percent annual interest. As a second option, Johnston could invest an additional $100,000 in the firm. Assuming that the firm earns $95,000 a year and that annual interest for this loan totals $9,000 ($100,000 × 0.09 = $9,000), the return on owners' equity for Cypress Springs Plastics would be higher if the firm borrowed the additional financing. Return on owners' equity—a topic covered in Chapter 17—is determined by dividing a firm's net income by the dollar amount of owners' equity. For Cypress Springs Plastics, return on owners' equity equals 17.2 percent ($86,000 ÷ $500,000 = 0.172, or 17.2 percent) if Johnston borrows the additional $100,000. The firm's return on owners' equity would decrease to 15.8 percent ($95,000 ÷ $600,000 = 0.158, or 15.8 percent) if Johnston invests an additional $100,000 in the business.

The most obvious danger when using financial leverage is that the firm's earnings may be less than expected. If this situation occurs, the fixed interest charge actually works to reduce or eliminate the return on owners' equity. Of course, borrowed

Table 19.3: Analysis of the Effect of Additional Capital from Debt or Equity for Cypress Springs Plastics, Inc.

Additional Debt		Additional Equity	
Owners' equity	$ 500,000	Owners' equity	$ 500,000
Additional equity	+0	Additional equity	+100,000
Total equity	$ 500,000	Total equity	$ 600,000
Loan (@ 9 percent)	+100,000	No loan	+0
Total capital	$ 600,000	Total capital	$ 600,000
	Year-End Earnings		
Gross profit	$ 95,000	Gross profit	$ 95,000
Less loan interest	–9,000	No interest	–0
Operating profit	$ 86,000	Operating profit	$ 95,000
Return on owners' equity	17.2%	Return on owners' equity	15.8%
($86,000 ÷ $500,000 = 17.2%)		($95,000 ÷ $600,000 = 15.8%)	

money eventually must be repaid. Finally, because lenders always have the option to turn down a loan request, many managers are reluctant to rely on borrowed money.

lease an agreement by which the right to use real estate, equipment, or other assets is transferred temporarily from the owner to the user

A company that cannot obtain a long-term loan to acquire property, buildings, and equipment may be able to lease these assets. A **lease** is an agreement by which the right to use real estate, equipment, or other assets is transferred temporarily from the owner to the user. The owner of the leased item is called the *lessor*; the user is called the *lessee*. With the typical lease agreement, the lessee makes regular payments on a monthly, quarterly, or yearly basis. Even when a firm is able to obtain long-term debt financing, it may choose to lease assets because, under the right circumstances, a lease can have tax advantages.

For a small business, long-term debt financing generally is limited to loans. Large corporations have the additional option of issuing corporate bonds.

Long-Term Loans

Many businesses finance their long-range activities such as those listed in Table 19.1 with loans from commercial banks, insurance companies, pension funds, and other financial institutions. Manufacturers and suppliers of heavy machinery also may provide long-term debt financing by granting extended credit to their customers.

term-loan agreement a promissory note that requires a borrower to repay a loan in monthly, quarterly, semiannual, or annual installments

Term-Loan Agreements When the loan repayment period is longer than one year, the borrower must sign a term-loan agreement. A **term-loan agreement** is a promissory note that requires a borrower to repay a loan in monthly, quarterly, semiannual, or annual installments. Although repayment may be as long as fifteen to twenty years, long-term business loans normally are repaid in three to seven years.

Assume that Pete Johnston, the owner of Cypress Springs Plastics, decides to borrow $100,000 and take advantage of the principle of financial leverage illustrated in Table 19.3. Although the firm's return on owners' equity does increase, interest must be paid each year, and eventually, the loan must be repaid. To pay off a $100,000 loan over a three-year period with annual payments, Cypress Springs Plastics must pay $33,333 on the loan balance plus $9,000 annual interest, or a total of $42,333 the first year. While the amount of interest decreases each year because of the previous year's payment on the loan balance, annual payments of this amount are still a large commitment for a small firm such as Cypress Springs Plastics.

The interest rate and repayment terms for term loans often are based on such factors as the reasons for borrowing, the borrowing firm's credit rating, and the value of collateral. Although long-term loans occasionally may be unsecured, the lender usually requires some type of collateral. Acceptable collateral includes real estate, machinery, and equipment. Lenders also may require that borrowers maintain a minimum amount of working capital. Finally, lenders may consider the environmental and social impact of the projects they are asked to finance before funding a loan request.

The Basics of Getting a Loan According to many financial experts, preparation is the key when applying for a long-term business loan. In reality, preparation begins before you ever apply for the loan. To begin the process, you should get to know potential lenders before requesting debt financing. While there may be many potential lenders that can provide the money you need, the logical place to borrow money is where your business does its banking. This fact underscores the importance of maintaining adequate balances in the firm's bank accounts. Before applying for a loan, you also may want to check your firm's credit rating with a national credit bureau such as D&B (formerly known as Dun & Bradstreet).

The owners of small- and medium-sized businesses will be asked to fill out a loan application. In addition to the loan application, the lender also will want to see your current business plan. Be sure to explain what your business is, how much funding you require to accomplish your goals and objectives, and how the loan will be repaid. Next, have your certified public accountant (CPA) prepare financial statements. Most lenders insist that you submit current financial statements that have

How do you pay for high-tech research? *While there are many ways to finance Advanced Micro Devices (AMD) research projects, one way is to sell corporate bonds to meet long-term financing needs. Long-term bond financing is especially attractive when developing new products like the AMD Wafer with Quad-Core Microprocessors shown in this photo.*

AP Photo/Paul Sakuma

been prepared by an independent CPA. Then compile a list of references that includes your suppliers, other lenders, or the professionals with whom you are associated. Once you submit your application, business plan, and supporting financial documents, a bank officer or a loan committee will examine the loan application. You also may be asked to discuss the loan request with a loan officer. Hopefully, your loan request will be approved. If not, try to determine why your loan request was rejected. Think back over the loan process and determine what you could do to improve your chances of getting a loan the next time you apply.

Corporate Bonds

In addition to loans, large corporations may choose to issue bonds in denominations of $1,000 to $50,000. Although the usual face value for corporate bonds is $1,000, the total face value of all the bonds in an issue usually amounts to millions of dollars. In fact, one of the reasons why corporations sell bonds is that they can borrow a lot of money from a lot of different bondholders and raise larger amounts of money than could be borrowed from one lender. A **corporate bond** is a corporation's written pledge that it will repay a specified amount of money with interest. Figure 19.6 shows a corporate bond for the American & Foreign Power Company. Note that it includes the interest rate (5 percent) and the maturity date. The **maturity date** is the date on which the corporation is to repay the borrowed money. Today, many corporations do not issue actual bonds like the one illustrated in Figure 19.6. Instead, the bonds are recorded electronically, and the specific details regarding the bond issue, along with the current owner's name and address, are maintained by computer. While some people like to have physical possession of their corporate bonds, computer entries are easier to transfer when a bond is sold. Computer entries also are safer because they cannot be stolen, misplaced, or destroyed—all concerns that you must worry about if you take physical possession of a corporate bond.

corporate bond a corporation's written pledge that it will repay a specified amount of money with interest

maturity date the date on which a corporation is to repay borrowed money

Until a bond's maturity, a corporation pays interest to the bond owner at the stated rate. Owners of the American & Foreign Power Company bond receive 5 percent per year for each bond. Because interest for corporate bonds is usually paid semiannually, bond owners receive a payment every six months for each bond they own.

Figure 19.6: A Corporate Bond

A corporate bond is a corporation's written pledge that it will repay on the date of maturity a specified amount of money with interest.

registered bond a bond registered in the owner's name by the issuing company

debenture bond a bond backed only by the reputation of the issuing corporation

mortgage bond a corporate bond secured by various assets of the issuing firm

convertible bond a bond that can be exchanged, at the owner's option, for a specified number of shares of the corporation's common stock

bond indenture a legal document that details all the conditions relating to a bond issue

Types of Bonds Today, most corporate bonds are registered bonds. A **registered bond**—like the American & Foreign Power Company bond—is a bond registered in the owner's name by the issuing company. Until the maturity date, the registered owner receives periodic interest payments. On the maturity date, the owner receives cash equaling the face value.

Corporate bonds generally are classified as debentures, mortgage bonds, or convertible bonds. Most corporate bonds are debenture bonds. A **debenture bond** is a bond backed only by the reputation of the issuing corporation. To make its bonds more appealing to investors, a corporation may issue mortgage bonds. A **mortgage bond** is a corporate bond secured by various assets of the issuing firm. Typical corporate assets that are used as collateral for a mortgage bond include real estate, machinery, and equipment that is not pledged as collateral for other debt obligations. The corporation also can issue convertible bonds. A **convertible bond** can be exchanged, at the owner's option, for a specified number of shares of the corporation's common stock. An Advanced Micro Devices (AMD) bond that matures in 2015 is convertible: Each bond can be converted to 35.6125 shares of AMD common stock.[13] A corporation can gain in three ways by issuing convertible bonds. First, convertibles usually carry a lower interest rate than nonconvertible bonds. Second, the conversion feature attracts investors who are interested in the speculative gain that conversion to common stock may provide. Third, if the bondholder converts to common stock, the corporation no longer has to redeem the bond at maturity.

Repayment Provisions for Corporate Bonds Maturity dates for bonds generally range from ten to thirty years after the date of issue. If the interest is not paid or the firm becomes insolvent, bond owners' claims on the assets of the corporation take precedence over the claims of both common and preferred stockholders. Some bonds are callable before the maturity date; that is, a corporation can buy back, or redeem, them. For these bonds, the corporation may pay the bond owner a call premium. The amount of the call premium is specified, along with other provisions, in the bond indenture. The **bond indenture** is a legal document that details all the conditions relating to a bond issue.

Before deciding if bonds are the best way to obtain corporate financing, managers must determine if the company can afford to pay the interest on the corporate bonds. It should be obvious that the larger the bond issue, the higher the dollar amount of interest will be. For example, assume that American Express issues bonds with a face value of $100 million. If the interest rate is 4.875 percent, the interest on this bond issue is $4,875,000 ($100 million × 0.04875 = $4,875,000) each year until the bonds are repaid. In addition, corporate bonds must be redeemed for their face value at maturity. If the corporation defaults on (does not pay) either interest payments or repayment of the bond at maturity, owners of bonds can force the firm into bankruptcy.

A corporation may use one of three methods to ensure that it has sufficient funds available to redeem a bond issue. First, it can issue the bonds as **serial bonds**, which are bonds of a single issue that mature on different dates. For example, a company may use a twenty-five-year $50 million bond issue to finance its expansion. None of the bonds mature during the first fifteen years. Thereafter, 10 percent of the bonds mature each year until all the bonds are retired at the end of the twenty-fifth year. Second, the corporation can establish a sinking fund. A **sinking fund** is a sum of money to which deposits are made each year for the purpose of redeeming a bond issue. When Union Pacific Corporation sold a $275 million bond issue, the company agreed to contribute to a sinking fund until the bond's maturity in the year 2025.[14] Third, a corporation can pay off an old bond issue by selling new bonds. Although this may appear to perpetuate the corporation's long-term debt, a number of utility companies and railroads use this repayment method.

serial bonds bonds of a single issue that mature on different dates

sinking fund a sum of money to which deposits are made each year for the purpose of redeeming a bond issue

A corporation that issues bonds also must appoint a **trustee**, an individual or an independent firm that acts as the bond owners' representative. A trustee's duties are handled most often by a commercial bank or other large financial institution. The corporation must report to the trustee periodically regarding its ability to make interest payments and eventually redeem the bonds. In turn, the trustee transmits this information to the bond owners, along with its own evaluation of the corporation's ability to pay.

trustee an individual or an independent firm that acts as a bond owners' representative

Cost Comparisons

Table 19.4 compares some of the methods that can be used to obtain long-term equity *and* debt financing. Although the initial flotation cost of issuing stock is high,

Table 19.4: Comparison of Long-Term Financing Methods

Type of Financing	Repayment	Repayment Period	Cost/Dividends Interest	Businesses That May Use It
Equity				
Common stock	No	None	High initial cost; low ongoing costs because dividends not required	All corporations that sell stock to investors
Preferred stock	No	None	Dividends not required but must be paid before common stockholders receive any dividends	Large corporations that have an established investor base of common stockholders
Debt				
Long-term loan	Yes	Usually 3–7 years	Interest rates between 6 and 13 percent depending on economic conditions and the financial stability of the company requesting the loan	All firms that can meet the lender's repayment and collateral requirements
Corporate bond	Yes	Usually 10–30 years	Interest rates between 5 and 10 percent depending on economic conditions and the financial stability of the company issuing the bonds	Large corporations that are financially healthy

selling common stock generally is the first choice for most financial managers. Once the stock is sold and upfront costs are paid, the *ongoing* costs of using stock to finance a business are low. The type of long-term financing that generally has the highest *ongoing* costs is a long-term loan (debt).

To a great extent, firms are financed through the investments of individuals—money that people have deposited in banks or have used to purchase stocks, mutual funds, and bonds. In Chapter 20, we look at securities markets and how they help people to invest their money in business.

return to inside business

Starbucks

Since going public in 1992, Starbucks has used retained earnings to fuel growth rather than paying dividends to stockholders. The company has also raised capital from a variety of short-term debt financing sources, such as commercial paper, as well as long-term debt financing sources, such as corporate bonds. On the spending side, its executives keep a close eye on costs and are ready to make cuts quickly when sales get sluggish.

Still, Starbucks can't control the global economic climate, which recently dampened consumer demand even for small luxuries such as specialty coffee. That's why the company focuses as much on maintaining its financial strength as it does on offering top-quality menu items and a pleasant café experience.

Questions

1. Although Starbucks doesn't typically pay dividends, McDonald's does. Do you think Starbucks should reconsider its dividend decision? Why or why not?
2. Would you recommend that Starbucks use additional equity or debt financing to step up the pace of growth once economic conditions are more favorable? Explain your answer.

Summary

Explain the need for financial management in business.

Financial management consists of all activities concerned with obtaining money and using it effectively. Short-term financing is money that will be used for one year or less. There are many short-term needs, but cash flow and inventory are two for which financing is often required. Long-term financing is money that will be used for more than one year. Such financing may be required for a business start-up, for a merger or an acquisition, for new product development, for long-term marketing activities, for replacement of equipment, or for expansion of facilities. Financial management can be viewed as a two-sided problem. On one side, the uses of funds often dictate the type or types of financing needed by a business. On the other side, the activities a business can undertake are determined by the types of financing available. Financial managers also must consider the risk-return ratio when making decisions. The risk-return ratio is based on the principle that a high-risk decision should generate higher financial returns for a business. On the other hand, more conservative decisions generate lesser returns. Financial managers must ensure that funds are available when needed, that they are obtained at the lowest possible cost, and that they are available for the repayment of debts.

Summarize the process of planning for financial management.

A financial plan begins with an organization's goals and objectives. Next, these goals and objectives are "translated" into departmental budgets that detail expected income and expenses. From these budgets, which may be combined into an overall cash budget, the financial manager determines what funding will be needed and where it may be obtained. Whereas departmental and cash budgets emphasize short-term financing needs, a capital budget can be used to estimate a firm's expenditures for major assets and its long-term financing needs. The four principal sources of financing are sales revenues, equity capital, debt capital, and proceeds from the sale of assets. Once the needed funds have been obtained, the financial manager is responsible for ensuring that they are used properly. This is accomplished through a system of monitoring and evaluating the firm's financial activities.

3 Describe the advantages and disadvantages of different methods of short-term debt financing.

Most short-term financing is unsecured; that is, no collateral is required. Sources of unsecured short-term financing include trade credit, promissory notes issued to suppliers, unsecured bank loans, and commercial paper. Sources of secured short-term financing include loans secured by inventory and accounts receivable. A firm also may sell its receivables to factors. Trade credit is the least expensive source of short-term financing. The cost of financing through other sources generally depends on the source and on the credit rating of the firm that requires the financing. Factoring generally is the most expensive approach.

4 Evaluate the advantages and disadvantages of equity financing.

A corporation can raise equity capital by selling either common or preferred stock. Common stock is voting stock; holders of common stock elect the corporation's directors and must approve changes to the corporate charter. Holders of preferred stock must be paid dividends before holders of common stock are paid any dividends. Another source of equity funding is retained earnings, which is the portion of a business's profits not distributed to stockholders. Venture capital—money invested in small (and sometimes struggling) firms that have the potential to become very successful—is yet another source of equity funding. Generally, the venture capital is provided by investors, partnerships established by wealthy families, or a joint venture formed by corporations with money to invest. In return, they receive an equity position in the firm and share in the profits of the business. Finally, a private placement can be used to sell stocks and other corporate securities.

5 Evaluate the advantages and disadvantages of long-term debt financing.

For a small business, debt financing generally is limited to loans. Large corporations have the additional option of issuing corporate bonds. Regardless of whether the business is small or large, it can take advantage of financial leverage. Financial leverage is the use of borrowed funds to increase the return on owners' equity. The rate of interest for long-term loans usually depends on the financial status of the borrower, the reason for borrowing, and the kind of collateral pledged to back up the loan. Long-term business loans normally are repaid in three to seven years but can be as long as fifteen to twenty years. Money realized from the sale of corporate bonds must be repaid when the bonds mature. In addition, the corporation must pay interest on that money from the time the bonds are sold until maturity. Maturity dates for bonds generally range from ten to thirty years after the date of issue. Three types of bonds—debentures, mortgage bonds, and convertible bonds—are sold to raise debt capital. When comparing the cost of equity and debt long-term financing, the ongoing costs of using stock (equity) to finance a business are low. The most expensive is a long-term loan (debt).

You should now be able to define and give an example relevant to each of the following terms:

financial management (563)
short-term financing (563)
cash flow (563)
speculative production (564)
long-term financing (565)
risk-return ratio (565)
chief financial officer (CFO) (566)
financial plan (567)
budget (568)
cash budget (568)
zero-base budgeting (568)
capital budget (569)
equity capital (569)
debt capital (569)
unsecured financing (571)
trade credit (571)
promissory note (572)
prime interest rate (572)
commercial paper (573)
floor planning (574)
factor (574)
initial public offering (IPO) (575)
investment banking firm (576)
common stock (576)
preferred stock (577)
par value (577)
convertible preferred stock (578)
retained earnings (578)
private placement (579)
financial leverage (579)
lease (580)
term-loan agreement (580)
corporate bond (581)
maturity date (581)
registered bond (582)
debenture bond (582)
mortgage bond (582)
convertible bond (582)
bond indenture (582)
serial bonds (583)
sinking fund (583)
trustee (583)

Review Questions

1. How does short-term financing differ from long-term financing? Give two business uses for each type of financing.
2. In your own words, describe the risk-return ratio.
3. What is the function of a cash budget? A capital budget?
4. What is zero-base budgeting? How does it differ from the traditional concept of budgeting?
5. What are four general sources of funds?
6. How does a financial manager monitor and evaluate a firm's financing?
7. How important is trade credit as a source of short-term financing?
8. Why would a supplier require a customer to sign a promissory note?
9. What is the prime rate? Who gets the prime rate?
10. What is the difference between a line of credit and a revolving credit agreement?
11. Explain how factoring works. Of what benefit is factoring to a firm that sells its receivables?
12. What are the advantages of financing through the sale of stock?
13. From a corporation's point of view, how does preferred stock differ from common stock?
14. Where do a corporation's retained earnings come from? What are the advantages of this type of financing?
15. What is venture capital?
16. Describe how financial leverage can increase return on owners' equity.
17. For a corporation, what are the advantages of corporate bonds over long-term loans?
18. Describe the three methods used to ensure that funds are available to redeem corporate bonds at maturity.

Discussion Questions

1. During the recent financial crisis, many financial managers and corporate officers have been criticized for (a) poor decisions, (b) lack of ethical behavior, (c) large salaries, (d) lucrative severance packages worth millions of dollars, and (e) extravagant lifestyles. Is this criticism justified? Justify your opinion.
2. What does a financial manager do? How can he or she monitor a firm's financial success?
3. If you were the financial manager of Stars and Stripes Clothing, what would you do with the excess cash that the firm expects in the second and fourth quarters? (See Figure 19.4.)
4. Develop a *personal* cash budget for the next six months. Explain what you would do if there are budget shortfalls or excess cash amounts at the end of any month during the six-month period.
5. Why would a lender offer unsecured loans when it could demand collateral?
6. How can a small-business owner or corporate manager use financial leverage to improve the firm's profits and return on owners' equity?
7. In what circumstances might a large corporation sell stock rather than bonds to obtain long-term financing? In what circumstances would it sell bonds rather than stock?

Video Case 19.1

Pizzeria Uno

How a company manages its financial and operating performance on a daily basis is very important. Margins in the restaurant business average three to five cents out of every dollar of revenue. When managing pennies, how you account for them is very important if you want to end up with the financial performance needed to grow a successful business. Pizzeria Uno is a good example of a company that has learned to manage its financials very effectively and because of that has grown its business dramatically over the years. The Pizzeria Uno Restaurant Corporation started in 1979 and was taken public in 1987. Currently the chain operates in twenty-nine states and four foreign countries with one hundred sixty-five restaurants, both franchised and company owned. Its average restaurant generates $2 million in revenues annually.

Financial management for Uno starts at the store level. The company employs very sophisticated accounting mechanisms in its stores to manage the cost structure of the business. The management team in each restaurant is primarily responsible for collecting data through point-of-sale computers that drive the collection of data. The data from each store are sent nightly from these computers to a corporate database. The type of information they collect includes sales data (what people are buying), what the company needs to buy to replenish inventories (what items have been sold that day), and labor data including hours and wage rates of employees. Uno has developed a theoretical cost control model which tells it what its food and drink costs should be, based on experience and its menu mix. For example, based on its model, Uno's expects each restaurant to sell twenty ounces of Jack Daniels liquor in a particular day. However, if the cost control system shows that one of its restaurants is incurring a cost for twenty-five ounces of Jack Daniels per day (but selling only twenty ounces), the company is paying for five ounces that cannot be accounted for. Either the drink has been given away or the bartenders have been overportioning the beverages. So, if Uno is planning to run the business at 25 percent of the cost of sales, and the data indicate one of the restaurants is actually running at 27 percent of the cost of sales, then corporate will want to know why there is a discrepancy.

The restaurant business is a cash business, and Uno is able to use working capital to its advantage. Because the company is dealing with rapidly consumed products, it has the luxury of using its vendors'/suppliers' money to fund its operations. As an example, if Uno restaurants buy a food product on a thirty-day net pay basis and sell the item within a day, Uno is going to have the use of that money for a period of more than three weeks. Compare that to a manufacturing company. When an auto company builds an automobile, it has to buy the steel to make the car long before it sells the car. Manufacturing companies have to spend working capital to build up their inventory before they can sell that inventory for cash.

Effectively managing its balance sheet is a key component in ensuring that Uno continues to improve shareholder value. Debt is an important tool that it uses to build equity. For example, if Uno can borrow money at 7 percent (approximate short-term interest rate) and put it to use in its restaurants that return 30 percent, it has earned 23 percent on someone else's money—an impressive return on debt.

Building restaurants is very capital intensive. The average Uno restaurant costs $1.6–$1.7 million in upfront capital to build, excluding the land. The company typically buys the land which can be a questionable policy since it does not result in a high return on assets. However, it does allow the company to control its own destiny and future. Also, Uno locks in this large component of its expansion costs forever, plus history shows that land values, more often than not, increase over time. The company uses long-term debt and, in some cases, mortgage debt to finance its land purchases. By using debt, Uno increases its return on equity as long as the company's earnings are larger than the interest charged for the borrowed money. Bottom line, Uno has been able to manage its balance sheet and create situations where it doesn't put the company at risk by overleveraging its debt-equity ratio. Uno uses debt to the benefit of its shareholders to enhance the overall value of the company.

Uno's goal is to operate in the top echelon of restaurant companies. It will periodically use a secondary equity offering to fund its growth strategy. The company believes that it can continue to manage its business to improve profitability, return on sales, and return on capital and to drive net income and earnings per share. Uno's stated goal is to grow its business 20–25 percent annually in earnings per share. It plans to do this by managing the balance sheet, being prudent in investments, and aggressively growing revenues. Pizzeria Uno plans to grow to eight hundred restaurants over the next fifteen years. Based on its track record, this does not appear to be an unrealistic goal.[15]

For more information on this company, go to **www.pizzeria-uno.com.**

Questions

1. What are the primary sources of funds that Pizzeria Uno uses to run its business, and how does it use these funds?
2. How does Uno monitor and evaluate the financial performance of its restaurants?
3. Pizzeria Uno typically buys the land on which it builds new restaurants because "it allows the company to control its own destiny and future." What are some possible disadvantages to this practice?

Case 19.2 The Mountain Thyme Inn Buys the Farm

Mike and Rhonda Hicks dreamed of opening their own bed-and-breakfast business after vacationing in cozy New England inns during one colorful fall season. The would-be entrepreneurs lived in Dallas, where Mike worked in the software industry. Although the two talked and talked about running a bed-and-breakfast, they didn't actually pursue the idea until pushed by Polly Felker, Rhonda's mother.

Felker had retired to Hot Springs, Arkansas, and was working on an herb farm twenty miles out of town in rural Jessieville, at the edge of the Ouachita National Forest. After listening to her daughter and son-in-law kick around the bed-and-breakfast concept any number of times, Felker told them to get down to business. The couple sought permission to buy nine scenic acres from the herb farm. Then they hired an architect to design an attractive country inn with eight spacious guest rooms, an old-fashioned wraparound porch, and private quarters for the owners. The Hickses estimated that purchasing the land, building the inn, buying furniture, and landscaping the property would cost nearly $600,000.

The next step was to get financing for what would be called the Mountain Thyme Bed & Breakfast Inn. The entrepreneurs approached bank after bank, explaining their idea and showing their plans, but could not get their loan application past worried bankers. Was the inn located too far from the well-known spa town of Hot Springs? Would guests find their way through the back roads and down the secluded gravel driveway to the inn? What about the size of the loan? "When you're used to doing simple little home mortgages, funding a project with that kind of price tag was indeed a scary thing," Mike Hicks observes.

After eighteen months of searching, the couple located a financial institution in California that agreed to approve part of the funding as a Small Business Administration loan. The couple also was introduced to the Arkansas Certified Development Corp. (ACDC), part of the nonprofit Arkansas Capital Corporation Group, which specializes in financing small businesses within the state. When an ACDC loan officer drove to Jessieville to see the site of the proposed inn, "he thought it was a little slice of heaven and fell in love with it," Rhonda Hicks remembers. The ACDC allowed the Hickses to borrow the money they needed at a good rate—and construction on the inn finally could begin.

Polly Felker joined her daughter and son-in-law as a partner in the inn. Chef Felker has been cooking up gourmet breakfasts and late-night treats since Mountain Thyme opened in 1998. The inn's comfortable rooms, beautiful surroundings, and delectable food have brought it nationwide acclaim. Moreover, the owners have been listed among the Top 10 Friendliest Innkeepers in the United States.

Now that their dream of operating an inn has come true, the owners host seminars so that others can learn all about the business of inn ownership. They're always improving the inn with new snacks, new services, new gift items, and more. Although the inn isn't always full, its occupancy rate is high enough to make Mountain Thyme a financial success—and to allow the three partners to take a little time off now and then. Despite the years of planning and hard work, Mike Hicks says, "There'd be no bed-and-breakfast" without the funding approved by the ACDC. "But other than the trouble we had finding some money in the beginning, it'd be hard for this to be working out any better."[16]

For more information about this company, go to **www.mountainthyme.com.**

Questions

1. If you were a banker, would you have approved the loan the Hickses needed to build their bed-and-breakfast? Explain your answer.
2. How can establishing realistic goals and objectives, budgeting, and monitoring and evaluating financial performance help the Hickses to manage the Mountain Thyme Inn?
3. Why would the owners need a capital budget for Mountain Thyme years after its opening?
4. Often, small businesses such as this bed-and-breakfast struggle to make ends meet. And yet there is no shortage of people who want to become entrepreneurs. After reading this case and how difficult it was for the Hickses to obtain financing, were the benefits of a small business such as this bed-and-breakfast worth the effort? Justify your answer.

Building Skills for Career Success

1. JOURNALING FOR SUCCESS

Because many people spend more than they make on a regular basis, they often use credit cards to make routine daily purchases. As a result, the amount they owe on credit cards increases each month and there is no money left to begin a savings or investment program. This exercise will help you to understand (1) how you manage your credit cards and (2) what steps you can take to improve your personal finances.

Assignment

1. How many credit cards do you have?
2. Based on the information on your monthly credit-card statements, what types of credit-card purchases do you make?
3. Do you pay your balance in full each month or make minimum payments on your credit cards?
4. Most experts recommend that you have one or two credit cards that you use only if you are in an emergency situation. The experts also recommend that you avoid using credit cards to make inexpensive purchases on a daily basis. Finally, the experts recommend that you pay your credit-card balance in full each month. Based on the preceding information, what steps can you take to better manage your finances?

2. EXPLORING THE INTERNET

Finding capital for new business start-ups is never an easy task. Besides a good business plan, those seeking investor funds must be convincing and clear about how their business activities will provide sufficient revenue to pay back investors who help to get them going in the first place. To find out what others have done, it is useful to read histories of successful start-ups as well as failures in journals that specialize in this area. Visit the text website for updates to this exercise.

Assignment

1. Examine articles that profile at least three successes or failures in the following publications and highlight the main points that led to either result.
   American Venture magazine (**www.americanventuremagazine.com**)
   Business 2.0 (**www.business2.com**)
   Red Herring (**www.redherring.com**)
   Fast Company (**www.fastcompany.com**)
2. What are the shared similarities?
3. What advice would you give to a start-up venture after reading these stories?

3. DEVELOPING CRITICAL-THINKING SKILLS

Financial management involves preparing a plan for obtaining and using the money needed to accomplish a firm's goals and objectives. After a financial plan has been developed, it must be monitored continually to ensure that it actually fulfills these goals and objectives. To accomplish your own goals, you should prepare a *personal* financial plan. Determine what is important in your life and what you want to accomplish, budget the amount of money required to get it, and identify sources for acquiring the funds. You should monitor and evaluate the results regularly and make changes when necessary.

Assignment

1. Using the three steps shown in Figure 19.2, prepare a personal financial plan.
2. Prepare a three-column table to display it.
   a. In column 1, list at least two objectives under each of the following areas:
      Financial (savings, investments, retirement) Education (training, degrees, certificates) Career (position, industry, location) Family (children, home, education, trips, entertainment)
   b. In column 2, list the amount of money it will take to accomplish your objectives.
   c. In column 3, identify the sources of funds for each objective.
3. Describe what you learned from doing this exercise in a comments section at the bottom of the table.

4. BUILDING TEAM SKILLS

Suppose that for the past three years you have been repairing lawn mowers in your garage. Your business has grown steadily, and recently, you hired two part-time workers. Your garage is no longer adequate for your business; it is also in violation of the city code, and you have been fined twice for noncompliance. You have decided that it is time to find another location for your shop and that it also would be a good time to expand your business. If the business continues to grow in the new location, you plan to hire a full-time employee to repair small appliances. You are concerned, however, about how you will get the money to move your shop and get it established in a new location.

Assignment

1. With all class members participating, use brainstorming to identify the following:
   a. The funds you will need to accomplish your business goals
   b. The sources of short-term financing available to you
   c. Problems that might prevent you from getting a short-term loan
   d. How you will repay the money if you get a loan
2. Have a classmate write the ideas on the board.

3. Discuss how you can overcome any problems that might hamper your current chances of getting a loan and how your business can improve its chances of securing short-term loans in the future.
4. Summarize what you learned from participating in this exercise.

5. RESEARCHING DIFFERENT CAREERS

Financial managers are responsible for determining the best way to raise funds, for ensuring that the funds are used to accomplish their firm's goals and objectives, and for developing and implementing their firm's financial plan. Their decisions have a direct impact on the firm's level of success. When managers do not pay enough attention to finances, a firm is likely to fail.

Assignment

1. Investigate the job of financial manager by searching the library or Internet and/or by interviewing a financial manager.
2. Find answers to the following questions:
   a. What skills do financial managers need?
   b. How much education is required?
   c. What is the starting salary? Top salary?
   d. What will the job of financial manager be like in the future?
   e. What opportunities are available?
   f. What types of firms are most likely to hire financial managers? What is the employment potential?
3. Prepare a report on your findings.

20 Understanding Personal Finances and Investments

LEARNING OBJECTIVES
What you will be able to do once you complete this chapter:

1. Explain why you should manage your personal finances and develop a personal investment program.
2. Describe how the factors of safety, risk, income, growth, and liquidity affect your investment program.
3. Understand how securities are bought and sold.
4. Identify the advantages and disadvantages of savings accounts, bonds, stocks, mutual funds, and real estate investments.
5. Describe high-risk investment techniques.
6. Use financial information to evaluate investment alternatives.

Ronnie Kaufman/Iconica/Getty Images

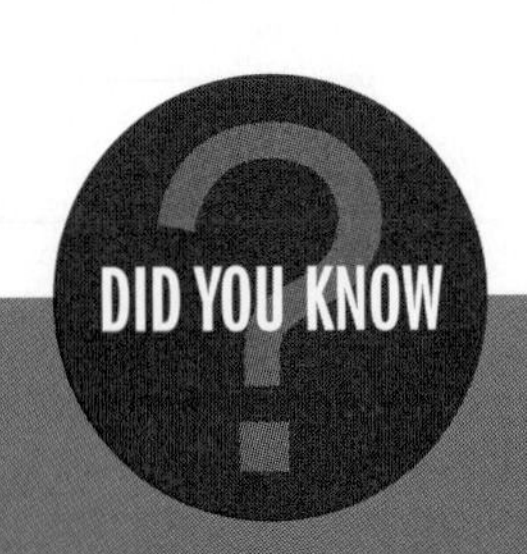

inside business

More than 2 million people visit the Fidelity site daily to access hundreds of articles containing investment tips and strategies.

Fidelity Investments Offers Investments, Tools, and Tips

In more than sixty years of operation, Fidelity Investments has seen its share of Wall Street's ups and downs. The Boston-based company handles more than $1 trillion in investments and offers a wide array of financial services for individuals, entrepreneurs, and employers. Whether customers are saving for vacation or retirement, getting ready to pay for a child's or grandchild's college education, or trying to protect a nest egg during turbulent financial times, Fidelity Investments has investments, tools, and tips to help.

Through the discount brokerage side of the business, Fidelity's customers can buy and sell stocks and bonds, put money into certificates of deposit, and handle many other types of investment transactions. Fidelity also offers hundreds of mutual funds managed by in-house professionals who pool customer money to buy carefully selected investments with specific goals in mind. In addition, Fidelity's specialists will work with individual businesses to design and customize investment and retirement plans for managers and employees.

With so many investment options, how can Fidelity's customers educate themselves and make more informed decisions? For those who prefer to learn about investing online, Fidelity's website **(www.fidelity.com)** features hundreds of articles about the basics and beyond. E-mail newsletters such as *Fidelity Investor's Weekly* and *Active Trader's News* include timely market analysis and tips for tuning up an investment portfolio. Fidelity also provides online calculators for customers to use in estimating how much they need to save for long-term goals such as retirement. In all, more than 2 million people click to the Fidelity site every day.

For more personalized attention and answers to specific questions, customers can contact Fidelity's representatives through instant messaging, e-mail, or a 24/7 toll-free hotline. Or they can sit down with a Fidelity expert at one of the company's 126 Investor Centers nationwide. The stock market may go up and down, but Fidelity knows that its customers are always in the market for sound ideas about how to invest wisely.[1]

As the saying goes, "I've been rich and I've been poor, but believe me, rich is better." And yet, just dreaming of being rich doesn't make it happen. While being rich doesn't guarantee happiness, managing your personal finances and beginning an investment program are both worthy goals. Firms such as Fidelity Investments offer an array of services to help people manage their personal finances, research investments, and buy and sell stocks, bonds, mutual funds, and other securities. Still, you must be willing to invest the time and effort required to become a good money manager and a good investor. And don't underestimate how important you are when it comes to managing your money. No one is going to make you manage your money. No one is going to make you save the money you need to fund an investment program. These are your decisions—important decisions that literally can change your life.

Many people ask the question: Why begin an investment program now? At the time of publication, this is a very important question given the recent financial and banking crisis. While it's true that many investors have lost a great deal of money as a result of the crisis, the experts all agree that the best investment program is one that stresses long-term growth over a twenty- to forty-year period. Although the dollar value of your investments may decrease over a short time period, historically the value of securities has always increased over a long time period. To illustrate this point, it may help to think of the financial markets as a roller coaster ride with ups (periods of increasing values) and downs (periods of declining values). The recent crisis is a very real example of how worldwide economic problems can cause the value of stocks, bonds, mutual funds, real estate, and other investments to decline. Faced with large dollar losses, many investors make a decision to sell their investments at the bottom of the roller coaster ride. Those investors who decide to hold their investments will eventually see their investments recover and increase in value over time. In fact, many experts recommend buying quality stocks, mutual funds, and real estate during an economic downturn. For example, many excellent investments could have been purchased for bargain prices during the fall of 2008 crisis.

A second compelling reason to start an investment program is that the sooner you start an investment program, the more time your investments have to work for you. So why do people wait to begin investing? In most cases, there are two reasons. First, they don't have the money needed to fund an investment program. And yet, once you begin managing your personal finances and get your spending under control, you will be able to save the money needed to fund an investment program. The second reason people don't begin investing is because they don't know anything about investing. Again, this chapter provides the basics to get you started. We begin this chapter by examining everyday money management activities and outlining the reasons for developing a personal investment plan. Next, we examine the process of buying and selling securities. Then we discuss both traditional and high-risk (or speculative) investments. Finally, we explain how to obtain and interpret financial information. It is time! Take the first step, and begin managing your personal finances.

Preparing for an Investment Program

1

Learning Objective: Explain why you should manage your personal finances and develop a personal investment program.

While it would be nice if you could accumulate wealth magically, it's not magic. For most people, the first step is to make sure that their "financial house" is in order. In the next section, we examine several steps for effective money management that will help you to prepare for an investment program.

Managing Your Personal Finances

Many personal finance experts recommend that you begin the process of managing your money by determining your current financial condition. The first step often is to construct a personal balance sheet and a personal income statement. A *personal balance sheet* lists your assets and liabilities on a specific date. By subtracting the total amount of liabilities from the total amount of assets, you can determine your net worth. A *personal income statement* lists your income and your expenses for a specific period of time—usually a month. By subtracting expenses from income, you can determine if you have a surplus or a deficit at the end of the time period. (*Note:* Both personal balance sheets and personal income statements were examined in more detail in Chapter 17.) Based on the information contained in these statements, you can determine your current financial condition and where you spend your money. You also can take the next step: Construct a personal budget.

personal budget a specific plan for spending your income

A **personal budget** is a specific plan for spending your income. You begin by estimating your income for a specific period—for example, next month. For most people, their major source of income is their salary. The second step is to list expenses for the same time period. Typical expenses include savings and investments, housing, food, transportation, entertainment, and so on. For most people, this is the area where you can make choices and increase or decrease the amount spent on different items listed in your budget. For example, you may decide to reduce the dollar amount spent on entertainment in order to increase the amount for savings. Above all, it is important to balance your budget so that your income is equal to the money you spend, save, or invest each month. Unfortunately, many individuals spend more than they make. They purchase items on credit and then must make monthly payments and pay finance charges ranging from 10 to 21 percent. It makes no sense to start an investment program until payments for credit-card and installment purchases, along with the accompanying finance charges, are reduced or eliminated. By reducing or eliminating credit purchases, eventually the amount of cash remaining

Why invest? *Often, beginning investors forget that the driving force behind an investment program should be the goals that they consider important. For some investors, having enough money to retire and sail around the world is a very important goal. For others, financial security and not having to worry about money is a more important goal.*

after the bills are paid will increase and can be used to start a savings program or finance investments.

Investment Goals

personal investment the use of your personal funds to earn a financial return

Personal investment is the use of your personal funds to earn a financial return. Thus, in the most general sense, the goal of investing is to earn money with money. However, such a goal is completely useless for the individual because it is so vague and so easily attained.

In reality, an investment goal must be specific and measurable. It must be tailored to you so that it takes into account your particular financial needs. It also must be oriented toward the future because investing is usually a long-term undertaking. A long-term investment program has a number of advantages. By investing small amounts of money each year over a twenty- to forty-year period, you can accumulate money for emergencies and retirement. Also, if you choose quality investments, the value of your investments will grow over a long period of time. Despite the recent financial and banking crisis, financial experts believe that long-term investors will not only see the value of their investment portfolio recover, but also increase over the next few years. Finally, an investment goal must be realistic in terms of current economic conditions and available investment opportunities.

Some financial planners suggest that investment goals should be stated in terms of money: "By January 1, 2018, I will have total assets of $80,000." Others believe that people are more motivated to work toward goals that are stated in terms of the particular things they desire: "By May 1, 2020, I will have accumulated enough money so that I can take a year off from work to travel around the world." Like the goals themselves, the way they are stated depends on you. The following questions can be helpful in establishing valid investment goals:

1. What financial goals do you want to achieve?
2. How much money will you need, and when?
3. What will you use the money for?
4. Is it reasonable to assume that you can obtain the amount of money you will need to meet your investment goals?

5. Do you expect your personal situation to change in a way that will affect your investment goals?
6. What economic conditions could alter your investment goals?
7. Are you willing to make the necessary sacrifices to ensure that your investment goals are met?
8. What are the consequences of not obtaining your investment goals?

A Personal Investment Program

Once you have formulated specific goals and have some money to invest, investment planning is similar to planning for a business. It begins with the evaluation of different investment opportunities—including the potential return and risk involved in each. At the very least, this process requires some careful study and maybe some expert advice. Investors should beware of people who call themselves "financial planners" but who are in reality nothing more than salespersons for various financial investments, tax shelters, or insurance plans.

A true **financial planner** has had at least two years of training in investments, insurance, taxation, retirement planning, and estate planning and has passed a rigorous examination. As evidence of training and successful completion of the qualifying examination, the Certified Financial Planner Board of Standards (**www.cfp.net**) in Washington, D.C., allows individuals to use the designation Certified Financial Planner (CFP). Similarly, the American College (**www.theamericancollege.edu**) in Bryn Mawr, Pennsylvania, allows individuals who have completed the necessary requirements to use the designation Chartered Financial Consultant (ChFC). Most CFPs and ChFCs do not sell a particular investment product or receive commissions for their investment recommendations. Instead, they charge consulting fees that range from $100 to $250 an hour.

financial planner an individual who has had at least two years of training in investments, insurance, taxation, retirement planning, and estate planning and has passed a rigorous examination

Many financial planners suggest that you accumulate an "emergency fund"—a certain amount of money that can be obtained quickly in case of immediate need—before beginning an investment program. The amount of money that should be salted away in a savings account varies from person to person. However, most financial planners agree that an amount equal to at least three months' living expenses is reasonable.

After the emergency account is established, you may invest additional funds according to your investment program. Some additional funds already may be available, or money for further investing may be saved out of earnings. For suggestions to help you obtain the money needed to fund your investment program, see Table 20.1.

Once your program has been put into operation, you must monitor it and, if necessary, modify it. Your circumstances and economic conditions are both subject to change. Therefore, all investment programs should be re-evaluated regularly.

Table 20.1: Suggestions to Help You Accumulate the Money Needed to Fund an Investment Program

1. *Pay yourself first.* Many financial experts recommend that you (1) pay your monthly bills, (2) save a reasonable amount of money, and (3) use whatever money is left over for personal expenses.
2. *Take advantage of employer-sponsored retirement programs.* Many employers will match part or all of the contributions you make to a 401(k) or 403(b) retirement account.
3. *Participate in an elective savings program.* Elect to have money withheld from your paycheck each payday and automatically deposited in a savings account.
4. *Make a special savings effort one or two months each year.* By cutting back to the basics, you can obtain money for investment purposes.
5. *Take advantage of gifts, inheritances, and windfalls.* During your lifetime, you likely will receive gifts, inheritances, salary increases, year-end bonuses, or federal income tax returns. Instead of spending these windfalls, invest these funds.

Source: Jack R. Kapoor, Les R. Dlabay, and Robert J. Hughes, *Personal Finance*, 9th ed. Copyright © 2009 by The McGraw Hill Companies Inc. Reprinted with permission of The McGraw Hill Companies Inc., p. 415.

Important Factors in Personal Investment

2

Learning Objective: Describe how the factors of safety, risk, income, growth, and liquidity affect your investment program.

How can you (or a financial planner) tell which investments are "right" for your investment program and which are not? One way to start is to match potential investments with your investment goals in terms of safety, risk, income, growth, and liquidity.

blue-chip stock a safe investment that generally attracts conservative investors

Safety and Risk Safety and risk are two sides of the same coin. *Safety* in an investment means minimal risk of loss; *risk* in an investment means a measure of uncertainty about the outcome. If you want a steady increase in value over an extended period of time, choose safe investments, such as certificates of deposit (CDs), highly rated corporate and municipal bonds, and the stocks of highly regarded corporations—sometimes called *blue-chip stocks.* A **blue-chip stock** is a safe investment that generally attracts conservative investors. Blue-chip stocks generally are issued by corporations that often are industry leaders and have provided their stockholders with stable earnings and dividends over a number of years. Selected mutual funds and real estate also may be very safe investments.

If you want higher dollar returns on investments, you generally must give up some safety. In general, *the potential return should be directly related to the assumed risk*. That is, the greater the risk assumed by the investor, the greater the potential monetary reward should be. As you will see shortly, there are a number of risky—and potentially profitable—investments.

rate of return the total dollar amount of return you receive on an investment over a specific period of time divided by the amount invested

Often beginning investors are afraid of the risk associated with many investments. But it helps to remember that without risk, it is impossible to obtain larger returns that really make an investment program grow. In fact, some investors often base their investment decision on projections for rate of return. You also can use the same calculation to determine how much you actually earn on an investment over a specific period of time. To calculate **rate of return**, the total dollar amount of return you receive on an investment over a specific period of time is divided by the amount invested. For example, assume that you invest $5,000 in Home Depot stock. Also assume that you receive $90 in dividends, and the stock is worth $5,400 at the end of one year. Your rate of return is 9.8 percent, as illustrated below.

Step 1: Subtract the investment's initial value from the investment's value at the end of the year.

$$\$5,400 - \$5,000 = \$400$$

Step 2: Add the dividend amount to the amount calculated in step 1.

$$\$90 + \$400 = \$490$$

Step 3: Divide the total dollar amount of return calculated in step 2 by the original investment.

$$\$490 \div \$5,000 = 0.098 = 9.8\%$$

Note: If an investment decreases in value, the steps used to calculate the rate of return are the same, but the answer is a negative number. With this information, it is possible to compare the rate of return for different investment alternatives that offer more or less risk.

Investment Income CDs, corporate and government bonds, and certain stocks pay a predictable amount of interest or dividends each year. Some mutual funds and real estate also may offer steady income potential. Such investments generally are used by conservative investors or retired individuals who need a predictable source of income.

Investors in CDs and bonds know exactly how much income they will receive each year. The dividends paid to stockholders can and do vary, even for the largest and most stable corporations. As with dividends from stock, the income from mutual funds and real estate also may vary from one year to the next.

Investment Growth To investors, *growth* means that their investments will increase in value. For example, growing corporations such as eBay, Bed, Bath, and Beyond, and the Apollo Group usually pay a small cash dividend or no dividend at all. Instead, profits are reinvested in the business (as retained earnings) to finance additional expansion. In this case, the value of their stock increases as the corporation expands.

Other investments that may offer growth potential include selected mutual funds and real estate. For example, many mutual funds are referred to as growth funds or aggressive growth funds because of the growth potential of the individual securities included in the fund.

Investment Liquidity **Liquidity** is the ease with which an investment can be converted into cash. Investments range from cash or cash equivalents (such as investments in government securities or money-market accounts) to the other extreme of frozen investments, which you cannot convert easily into cash.

liquidity the ease with which an investment can be converted into cash

Although you may be able to sell stock, mutual-fund, and corporate-bond investments quickly, you may not regain the amount of money you originally invested because of market conditions, economic conditions, or many other reasons. It also may be difficult to find buyers for real estate. And finding a buyer for investments in certain types of collectibles also may be difficult.

Surviving a Financial Crisis

Although monitoring your investment program and reevaluating your investment choices are always important, the recent financial and banking crisis underscores the importance of managing your personal finances *and* your investment program. Because of the nation's economic problems, many people were caught off guard and had to scramble to find the money to pay their monthly bills. Many of these same individuals had to borrow money or use their credit cards to survive from one payday to the next. And some individuals were forced to sell some or all of their investments at depressed prices just to buy food for the family and pay for everyday necessities.

To survive a financial crisis, many experts recommend that you take action before the crisis to make sure your financial affairs are in order. Seven steps you can take include:

1. *Establish a larger than usual emergency fund.* While under normal circumstances, an emergency fund of three months' living expenses is considered adequate, you may want to increase your fund in anticipation of a crisis.
2. *Know what you owe.* It helps to make a list of all your debts and the amount of the required monthly payments. Then identify the debts that *must* be paid. Typically these include the mortgage or rent, medicine, utilities, food, and transportation costs.
3. *Reduce spending.* Cut back to the basics and reduce the amount of money spent on entertainment, dining at restaurants, and vacations. Although not pleasant, the money saved from reduced spending can be used to increase your emergency fund or pay for everyday necessities.
4. *Pay off credit cards.* Get in the habit of paying your credit-card bill in full each month. If you have credit-card balances, begin by paying off the balance on the credit card with the highest interest rate.
5. *Apply for a line of credit at your bank, credit union, or financial institution.* As defined in Chapter 18, a line of credit is a pre-approved loan and will provide access to cash if needed for future emergencies.
6. *Notify credit-card companies and lenders if you are unable to make payments.* Although not all lenders are willing to help, many will work with you and lower your interest rate, reduce your monthly payment, or extend the time for repayment.
7. *Monitor the value of your investment accounts.* Tracking the value of your stock, mutual-fund, and retirement accounts, for example, will help you decide which investments to sell if you need cash for emergencies. Continued evaluation of your investments can also help you reallocate your investments to reduce investment risk.

Above all, don't panic. While financial problems are stressful, it helps to stay calm and consider all the options. Keep in mind that bankruptcy should be a last resort. The reason is simple: A bankruptcy will remain on your credit report for up to 10 years.

How Securities Are Bought and Sold

3 Learning Objective: Understand how securities are bought and sold.

To purchase a Geoffrey Beene sweater, you simply walk into a store that sells these sweaters, choose one, and pay for it. To purchase stocks, bonds, mutual funds, and many other investments, you often work through a brokerage firm. In turn, an employee of the brokerage firm buys or sells securities for you in either the primary or secondary market.

The Primary Market

primary market a market in which an investor purchases financial securities (via an investment bank) directly from the issuer of those securities

The **primary market** is a market in which an investor purchases financial securities (via an investment bank) directly from the issuer of those securities. As mentioned in Chapter 19, an *investment banking firm* is an organization that assists corporations in raising funds, usually by helping sell new issues of stocks, bonds, or other financial securities. Typically, this type of stock or security offering is referred to as an *initial public offering* (IPO). An example of an IPO sold through the primary market is the stock issue sold by MetroPCS that raised over $1.2 billion.[2] *Caution:* The promise of quick profits often lures investors to purchase an IPO. Investors should be aware, however, that an IPO generally is classified as a **high-risk investment**—one made in the uncertain hope of earning a relatively large profit in a short time. Depending on the corporation selling the new security, IPOs may be too speculative for most people.

high-risk investment an investment made in the uncertain hope of earning a relatively large profit in a short time

The Secondary Market

secondary market a market for existing financial securities that are traded between investors

The **secondary market** is a market for existing financial securities that are traded between investors. Usually, secondary-market transactions are completed through a securities exchange or the over-the-counter market.

Orderly confusion. *What looks like confusion is actually an orderly system that allows investors to buy and sell almost 3,300 different stocks listed on the New York Stock Exchange. Organized under a buttonwood tree in 1792, today the NYSE is one of the largest and best-known security exchanges in the world.*

AP/Wide World

Securities Exchanges A **securities exchange** is a marketplace where member brokers meet to buy and sell securities. Generally, securities issued by larger corporations are traded at the New York Stock Exchange, the American Stock Exchange (now owned by NYSE Euronext), or at *regional exchanges* located in Chicago, Boston (now owned by Nasdaq), and several other cities. The securities of very large corporations may be traded at more than one of these exchanges. Securities of firms also may be listed on foreign securities exchanges—in Tokyo or London, for example.

One of the largest and best-known securities exchanges in the world is the New York Stock Exchange (NYSE) which is now part of the NYSE Euronext holding company. The NYSE lists almost 3,300 different issues.[3] Before a corporation's stock is approved for listing on the NYSE, the firm usually must meet specific criteria. The American Stock Exchange, regional exchanges, and the over-the-counter market have different listing requirements and account for the remainder of securities traded in the United States.

SPOTLIGHT

Age Characteristics of Stock Investors

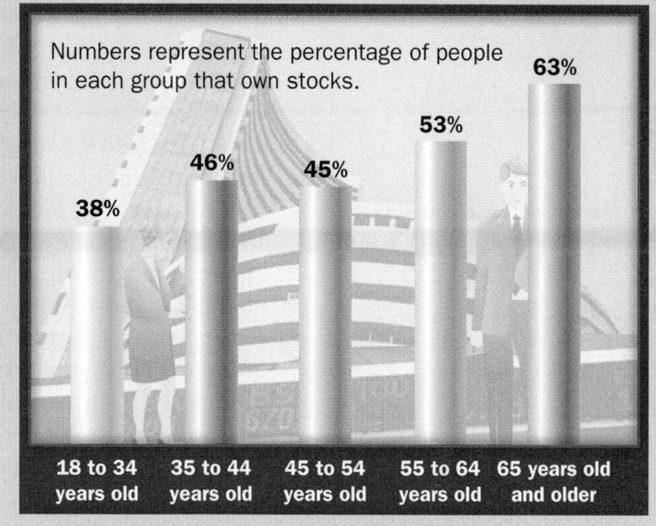

Source: U.S. Census Bureau, *Statistical Abstract of the United States 2008*, p. 744.

The Over-the-Counter Market Stocks issued by several thousand companies are traded in the over-the-counter market. The **over-the-counter (OTC) market** is a network of dealers who buy and sell the stocks of corporations that are not listed on a securities exchange. The term *over-the-counter* was coined more than 100 years ago when securities actually were sold "over the counter" in stores and banks.

securities exchange a marketplace where member brokers meet to buy and sell securities

over-the-counter (OTC) market a network of dealers who buy and sell the stocks of corporations that are not listed on a securities exchange

Nasdaq computerized electronic exchange system through which most OTC securities are traded

Most OTC securities today are traded through an *electronic* exchange called the **Nasdaq** (pronounced "nazzdack"). The Nasdaq quotation system provides price information on approximately 3,200 different stocks.[4] Begun in 1971, the Nasdaq is now one of the largest securities markets in the world. Today, the Nasdaq is known for its forward-looking, innovative, growth companies. Although most companies that trade are small, the stock of some large firms, including Intel, Microsoft, Cisco Systems, and Dell Computer, is traded through the Nasdaq.

When you want to sell shares of a company that trades on the Nasdaq—for example, Apple Computer—your account executive sends your order into the Nasdaq computer system, where it shows up on the screen, together with all the other orders from people who want to buy or sell Apple Computer. A Nasdaq dealer (sometimes referred to as a *marketmaker*) sits at a computer terminal putting together these buy and sell orders for Apple Computer. Once a match is found, your order is completed.

The Role of an Account Executive

An **account executive**—sometimes called a *stockbroker* or *registered representative*—is an individual who buys and sells securities for clients. Choosing an account executive can be difficult for at least two reasons. First, you must exercise a shrewd combination of trust and mistrust when you approach an account executive. Remember that you are interested in the broker's recommendations to increase your wealth, but the account executive is interested in your investment trading as a means to swell commissions.

account executive an individual, sometimes called a *stockbroker* or *registered representative,* who buys and sells securities for clients

Unfortunately, some account executives are guilty of *churning*—a practice that generates commissions by excessive buying and selling of securities.

Second, you must decide whether you need a *full-service* broker or a *discount* broker. A full-service broker usually charges higher commissions but gives you personal investment advice and provides detailed research information. A discount broker simply executes buy and sell orders, usually over the phone or online. Most discount brokers offer no or very little investment advice; you must make your own investment decisions.

Before deciding if you should use a full-service or a discount brokerage firm, you should consider how much help you need when making an investment decision. Many full-service brokerage firms argue that you need a professional to help you make important investment decisions. While this may be true for some investors, most account executives employed by full-service brokerage firms are too busy to spend unlimited time with you on a one-on-one basis, especially if you are investing a small amount. On the other side, many discount brokerage firms argue that you alone are responsible for making your investment decisions. And they argue that discount brokerage firms have both the personnel and research materials to help you to become a better investor.

The Mechanics of a Transaction Once investors have decided on a particular security, most simply telephone their account executive and place a market, limit, or discretionary order. A **market order** is a request that a security be purchased or sold at the current market price. Figure 20.1 illustrates one method of executing a market order to sell a stock listed on the NYSE at its current market value. It is also possible for a brokerage firm to match a buy order for a security for one of its customers with a sell order for the same security from another of its customers. Matched orders are not completed through a security exchange or the OTC market. Regardless of how the security is bought or sold, payment for stocks and many other financial securities generally is required within three business days of the transaction.

market order a request that a security be purchased or sold at the current market price

A **limit order** is a request that a security be bought or sold at a price equal to or better than (lower for buying, higher for selling) some specified price. Suppose that you place a limit order to *sell* Coca-Cola common stock at $41 per share. Your broker's representative sells the stock only if the price is $41 per share or *more.* If you place a limit order to *buy* Coca Cola at $41, the representative buys it only if the price is $41 per share or *less.* Usually, a limit order is good for one day, one week, one month, or good until canceled (GTC).

limit order a request that a security be bought or sold at a price that is equal to or better than some specified price

Investors also can choose to place a discretionary order. A **discretionary order** is an order to buy or sell a security that lets the broker decide when to execute the transaction and at what price. *Caution:* Financial planners advise against using a discretionary order for two reasons. First, a discretionary order gives the account executive a great deal of authority. If the account executive makes a mistake, it is

discretionary order an order to buy or sell a security that lets the broker decide when to execute the transaction and at what price

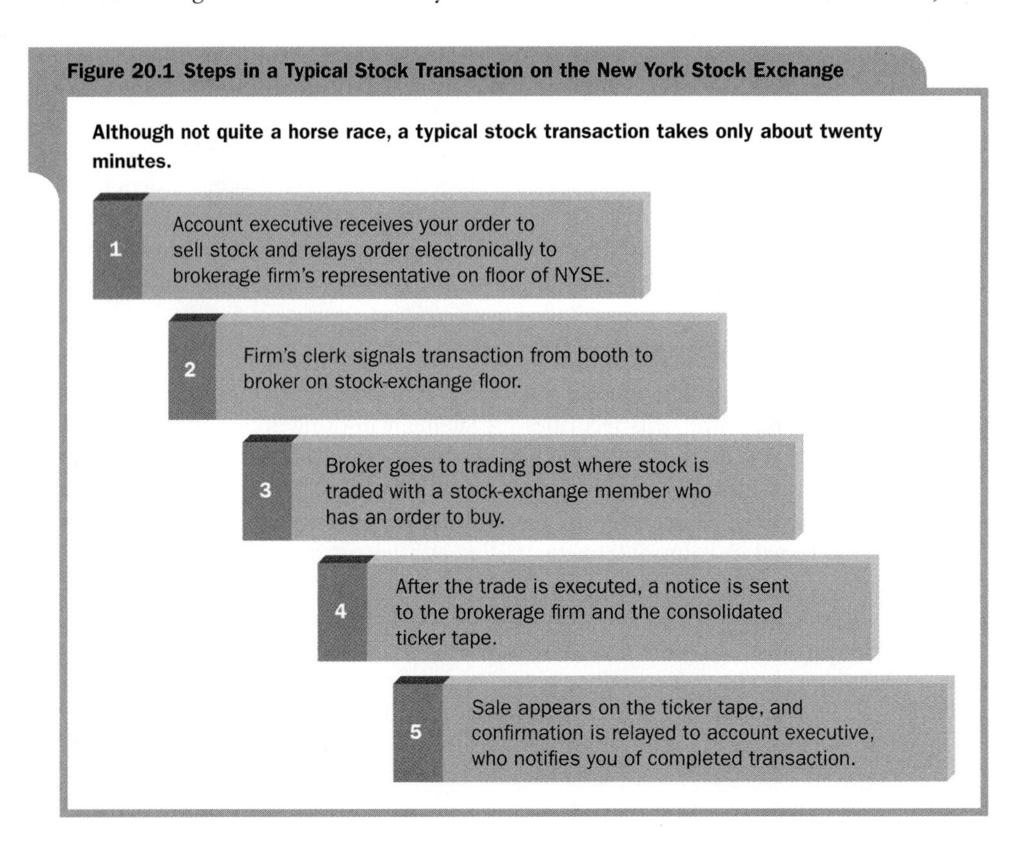

Figure 20.1 Steps in a Typical Stock Transaction on the New York Stock Exchange

Although not quite a horse race, a typical stock transaction takes only about twenty minutes.

the investor who suffers the loss. Second, financial planners argue that only investors (with the help of their account executives) should make investment decisions.

Online Security Transactions A computer and access to the Internet can help you to evaluate potential investments, manage your investments, monitor their value more closely, *and* place buy and sell orders online. As a rule of thumb, the more active an investor is, the more it makes sense to invest online. As you will see in the next section, one very good reason for trading securities online is the lower cost.

Commissions Most full-service brokerage firms have a minimum commission ranging from $25 to $55 for buying and selling stock. Additional commission charges are based on the number of shares and the value of stock bought and sold.

Table 20.2 shows typical commission fees charged by online brokerage firms. Generally, online transactions are less expensive when compared with the costs of trading securities through a full-service brokerage firm. As a rule of thumb, full-service brokerage firms charge as much as 1 1/2 to 2 percent of the transaction amount. Commissions for trading bonds, commodities, and options usually are lower than those for trading stocks.

For example, the charge for buying or selling a $1,000 corporate bond typically is $10 to $20. With the exception of most mutual funds, the investor generally pays a commission when buying *and* selling securities.

It should be apparent that vast sums of money are involved in securities trading. In an effort to protect investors from unfair treatment, both federal and state governments have acted to regulate securities trading.

Ethics Matters

Policing Socially Responsible Investing

Pax World, based in Portsmouth, New Hampshire, is one of the oldest mutual-fund families specializing in socially responsible investments. Yet not long ago, it paid $500,000 to settle SEC charges that some of its funds had, in fact, invested in companies that make weapons and other goods or services considered to not be socially responsible.

How could this happen? A detailed SEC investigation found that some Pax World funds had not followed their own strict investment rules. These funds said they would screen out firms that generate more than 5 percent of their revenues from gambling, alcohol, liquor, or military contracts. Yet two of the funds were found to have bought stocks or bonds from companies that had never been screened or that were already on Pax World's "do not buy" list.

Registered trademark of Pax World Mutual Funds

Pax World has since stepped up its supervision of fund investments and overhauled its stock and bond screening methods. For example, its fund managers now avoid investing in companies that are "significantly involved in the manufacture of weapons or weapons-related products." As interest in socially responsible investing continues to grow, the SEC will be watching to be sure that all mutual-fund families keep their investment promises.

Sources: Ron Lieber, "Socially Responsible, with Egg on Its Face," *New York Times*, August 23, 2008, pp. C1 and 6; John Waggoner, "SEC Fines Funds, Says They Broke Screening Rules," *USA Today*, July 31, 2008, p. 3B; Bob Sanders, "How Pax Came to Alter Its Investment Rules," *New Hampshire Business Review*, August 15, 2008, p. 1.

Regulation of Securities Trading

Government regulation of securities was begun as a response to abusive and fraudulent practices in the sale of stocks, bonds, and other financial securities. Today, with so many news reports of banks with a portfolio of bad loans and of corporations that are in "hot water" over financial reporting problems that range from simple mistakes to out-and-out fraud, the concerns of both government officials and investors have grown over the past few years.

Table 20.2: Typical Commission Costs Charged by Online Brokerage Firms for a Transaction in which 1,000 Shares Are Bought or Sold

	Internet	Interactive Voice-Response Telephone System	Broker-Assisted
TD Ameritrade	$ 9.99	$34.99	$ 44.99
E*Trade	$12.99	$12.99	$ 57.99
Fidelity	$19.95	$67.50	$181.00
Schwab	$12.95	$17.95	$ 37.95

Source: TD Ameritrade website, **www.tdameritrade.com**, accessed October 23, 2008.

Gotcha! *Accused of securities fraud, Matthew Tannin, hedge fund manager for Bear Stearns, is led to jail by federal agents. In order to protect individual investors, a regulatory pyramid consisting of four different levels exists. At the top of the pyramid is the U.S. Congress followed by the Securities and Exchange Commission, and then the individual states. The foundation and most important level is self-regulation by securities firms and brokerage firms.*

full disclosure requirement that investors should have access to all important facts about stocks, bonds, and other securities so that they can make informed decisions

prospectus a detailed, written description of a new security, the issuing corporation, and the corporation's top management

insider trading the practice of board members, corporate managers, and employees buying and selling a corporation's stock

Today, a regulatory pyramid consisting of four different levels exists to make sure that investors are protected. The U.S. Congress is at the top of the pyramid. Early on, Congress passed the Securities Act of 1933 (sometimes referred to as the Truth in Securities Act). This act provides for full disclosure. **Full disclosure** means that investors should have access to all important facts about stocks, bonds, and other securities so that they can make informed decisions. This act also requires that corporations issuing new securities file a registration statement and publish a prospectus. A **prospectus** is a detailed, written description of a new security, the issuing corporation, and the corporation's top management. Since 1933, Congress has passed additional legislation that includes creating the Securities Investor Protection Corporation (SIPC) to protect investors. Congress also has passed legislation to curb insider-trading abuses. **Insider trading** occurs when insiders—board members, corporate managers, and employees—buy and sell a corporation's stock. While insiders can buy and sell a corporation's stock, they must disclose their trading activities to the public. And it is illegal for insiders to trade a corporation's stock based on their knowledge of information that has not been made available to the general public. More recently, Congress passed the Sarbanes-Oxley Act to improve corporate accountability and financial reporting (see Chapter 17).

On the next level of the regulatory pyramid is the Securities and Exchange Commission (SEC). In 1934, Congress passed the Securities Exchange Act of 1934, which created the SEC. The SEC is the agency that enforces federal securities regulations. The SEC also supervises all national exchanges, investment companies, the over-the-counter market, brokerage firms, and just about every other organization involved in trading securities.

On the next level of the regulatory pyramid is individual states. Today, most states require that new security issues be registered with a state agency and that brokers and securities dealers operating within the state be licensed. Most state

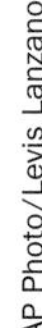

regulations also provide for the prosecution of individuals accused of the fraudulent sale of stocks, bonds, and other securities.

The foundation and most important level of the regulatory pyramid is self-regulation by securities exchanges and brokerage firms. According to the NYSE, self-regulation—the way the securities industry monitors itself to create a fair and orderly trading environment—begins here.[5] To provide guidelines of ethical behavior, the NYSE has published rules, policies, and standards of conduct. These standards are applied to every member in the NYSE's investment community. The NYSE also conducts a thorough examination of each member firm that does business with the public at least once a year.[6] In addition, there are more than 300 brokerage firms that buy and sell securities for their customers. These firms are responsible for ensuring that their employees are highly trained and meet rigorous ethical standards.

Traditional Investment Alternatives

4

Learning Objective: Identify the advantages and disadvantages of savings accounts, bonds, stocks, mutual funds, and real estate investments.

In this section, we look at traditional investments. In the next section, we explore high-risk investments. A number of the investments listed in Table 20.3 have been discussed. Others have only been mentioned and will be examined in more detail. We begin this section with an overview of how portfolio management can reduce investment risk. Then we describe how specific investments can help you to reach your investment goals.

Portfolio Management

"How can I choose the right investment?" Good question! Unfortunately, there are no easy answers because your investment goals, age, tolerance for risk, and financial resources are different from those of the next person. To help you to decide what investment is right for you, consider the following: Since 1926, as measured by the Standard and Poor's 500 stock index, stocks have returned just over 10 percent a year. During the same period, CDs and government bonds have returned about 6 percent.[7] And projections by well-respected Roger Ibbotson, chairman of Ibbotson Associates, an investment consulting, software, and research firm, indicate that these same investments will perform at about the same pace between now and the year 2025.[8] Therefore, why not just invest all your money in stocks or mutual funds that invest in stocks? After all, they offer the largest potential return? In reality, stocks have a place in every investment portfolio, but there is more to investing than just picking a bunch of stocks or stock mutual funds.

Asset Allocation, the Time Factor, and Your Age

Asset allocation is the process of spreading your money among several different types of investments to lessen risk. While the term *asset allocation* is a fancy way of saying it, simply put, it really means that you need to diversify and avoid the pitfall

asset allocation the process of spreading your money among several different types of investments to lessen risk

Table 20.3: Investment Alternatives

Traditional investments involve less risk than high-risk investments.

Traditional	High Risk
Bank accounts	Short transactions
Corporate and government bonds	Margin transactions
Common stock	Stock options
Preferred stock	Commodities
Mutual funds	Precious metals
Real estate	Gemstones
	Coins/antiques/collectibles

Going Global
Mapping International Mutual Funds

You have a world of choices for investing your money in international mutual funds. Consider geography: Do you want to invest in a fund that buys securities within a particular country (such as China) or a wider region (such as Latin America)? Would you prefer a mutual fund that buys only foreign securities (meaning no U.S. securities), or are you interested in a global fund (which can include U.S. securities)?

In addition, you can choose an international mutual fund by industry (such as real estate or technology); level of market development (such as emerging markets); company size (as measured by market capitalization); or security index (such as Japan's Nikkei 225 index or Germany's DAX 30 index).

Before you invest, remember to read the prospectus carefully so you know exactly what the mutual fund invests in, where, and why. For example, a global telecommunications mutual fund might aim for long-term growth by investing at least 80 percent of its assets in foreign telecom firms and no more than 20 percent of its assets in U.S. telecom firms. Where in the world will your investments take you next?

Sources: Andrew Cannarsa, "Investing: T. Rowe Launches Two New Global Mutual Funds," *The Examiner (Baltimore)*, November 23, 2008, **www.baltimoreexaminer.com**; Eleanore K. Szymanski, "Weighing the Benefits of Investing Abroad," *Times of Trenton*, November 16, 2008, **www.nj.com**; "5 Emerging-Market Funds for Better Days," *Smart Money*, November 21, 2008, **www.smartmoney.com**.

of putting all of your eggs in one basket—a common mistake made by investors. Asset allocation often is expressed in percentages. For example, what percentage of my assets do I want to put in stocks and mutual funds? What percentage do I want to put in more conservative investments such as CDs and government bonds? In reality, the answers to these questions are determined by:

- The time your investments have to work for you.
- Your age.
- Investment objectives.
- Ability to tolerate risk.
- How much you can save and invest each year.
- The dollar value of your current investments.
- The economic outlook for the economy.
- And several other factors.

Two factors—the time your investments have to work for you and your age—are so important they deserve special attention. The amount of time you have before you need your investment money is crucial. If you can leave your investments alone and let them work for five to ten years or more, then you can invest in stocks, mutual funds, and real estate. On the other hand, if you need your investment money in two years, you probably should invest in short-term government bonds, highly rated corporate bonds, or CDs. By taking a more conservative approach for short-term investments, you reduce the possibility of having to sell your investments at a loss because of depressed market value or a staggering economy. For example, during the recent banking and financial crisis, many retirees who were forced to sell stocks and mutual funds in order to pay everyday living expenses lost money. On the other hand, many younger investors with long-term investment goals could afford to hold their investments until the price of their securities recovered.

You also should consider your age when developing an investment program. Younger investors tend to invest a large percentage of their nest egg in growth-oriented investments. On the other hand, older investors tend to choose more conservative investments. As a result, a smaller percentage of their nest egg is placed in growth-oriented investments. How much of your portfolio should be in growth-oriented investments? Well-known personal financial expert Suze Orman suggests that you subtract your age from 110, and the difference is the percentage of your assets that should be invested in growth investments. For example, if you are 30 years old, subtract 30 from 110, which gives you 80. Therefore, 80 percent of your assets should be invested in growth-oriented investments, whereas the remaining 20 percent should be kept in safer conservative investments.[9] Now it's time to take a closer look at specific investment alternatives.

Bank Accounts

Bank accounts that pay interest—and therefore are investments—include passbook savings accounts, CDs, and interest-bearing accounts. These were discussed in Chapter 18. The interest paid on bank accounts can be withdrawn to serve as income, or it can be left on deposit and increase the value of the bank account and provide for growth. At the time of this publication, one-year CDs were paying between 3 and 4 percent. While CDs and other bank accounts are risk-free for all practical purposes, many investors often choose other investments because of the potential for larger returns.

Corporate and Government Bonds

In Chapter 19, we discussed the issuing of bonds by corporations to obtain financing. The U.S. government and state and local governments also issue bonds for the same reason. Investors generally choose bonds because they provide a predictable source of income.

Corporate Bonds Because they are a form of long-term debt financing that must be repaid, bonds generally are considered a more conservative investment than either stocks or mutual funds. One of the principal advantages of corporate bonds is that they are primarily long-term, income-producing investments. Between the time of purchase and the maturity date, the bondholder will receive interest payments—usually semiannually, or every six months. For example, assume that you purchase a $1,000 bond issued by the rail-based transportation giant CSX Corporation and that the interest rate for this bond is 6 percent. In this situation, you receive interest of $60 ($1,000 × 0.06 = $60) a year from the corporation. CSX pays the interest every six months in $30 installments.

Most beginning investors think that a $1,000 bond is always worth $1,000. In reality, the price of a bond may fluctuate until its maturity date. Changes in the overall interest rates in the economy are the primary cause of most bond price

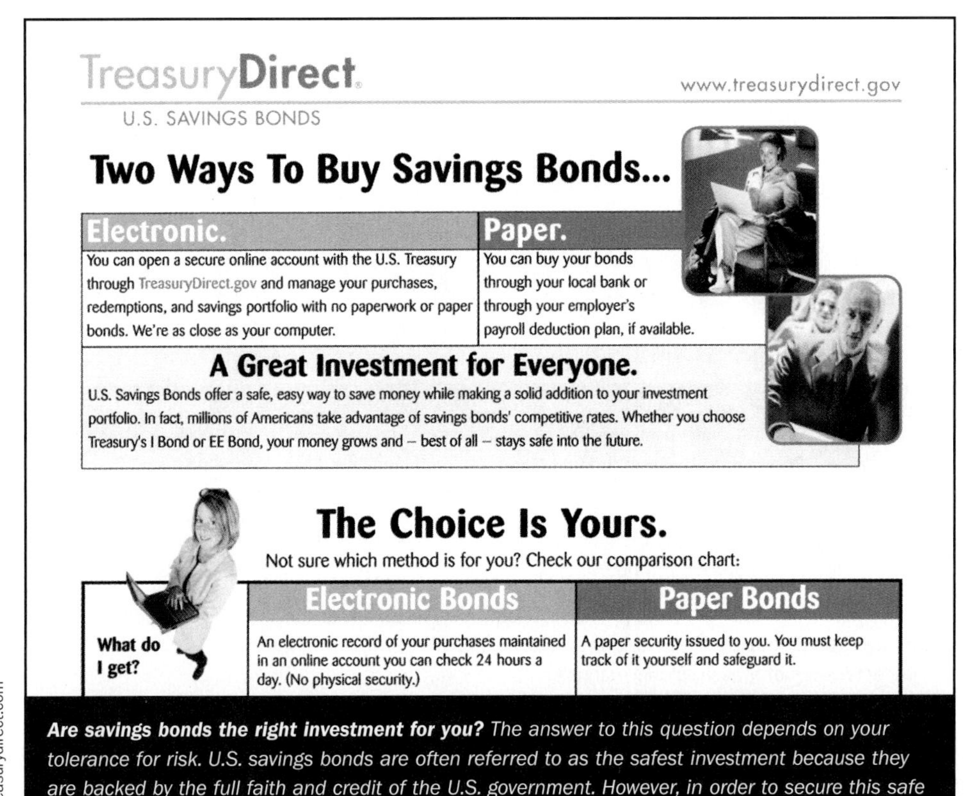

Are savings bonds the right investment for you? *The answer to this question depends on your tolerance for risk. U.S. savings bonds are often referred to as the safest investment because they are backed by the full faith and credit of the U.S. government. However, in order to secure this safe investment, investors must relinquish higher returns. In fact, the search for higher returns is why some investors choose stocks, mutual funds, real estate, and other investment alternatives.*

Courtesy treasurydirect.com

fluctuations. For example, when overall interest rates in the economy are rising, the market value of existing bonds with a fixed interest rate typically declines. They then may be purchased for less than their face value. By holding such bonds until maturity or until overall interest rates decline (causing the bond's market value to increase), bond owners can sell their bonds for more than they paid for them. In this case, the difference between the purchase price and the selling price is profit and is in addition to annual interest income. However, remember that the price of a corporate bond can decrease and that interest payments and eventual repayment may be a problem for a corporation that encounters financial difficulty. To compare potential risk and return on corporate bond issues, many investors rely on the bond ratings provided by Moody's Investors Service, Inc., and Standard & Poor's Corporation. For a summary of corporate bond ratings provided by these two companies, see Table 20.4. Bond ratings also are provided by Fitch Ratings and are similar to those provided by Moody's and Standard & Poor's.

Convertible Bonds Some corporations prefer to issue convertible bonds because they carry a lower interest rate than nonconvertible bonds—by about 1 to 2 percent. In return for accepting a lower interest rate, owners of convertible bonds have the opportunity for increased investment growth. For example, assume that you purchase a Medtronic $1,000 corporate bond that is convertible to 16.18 shares of the company's common stock. This means that you could convert the bond to common stock whenever the price of the company's stock is $61.80 ($1,000 ÷ 16.18 = $61.80) or higher.[10] However, owners may opt not to convert their bonds to common stock even if the market value of the common stock does increase to $61.80 or more. The reason for not exercising the conversion feature is quite simple. As the market value of the common stock increases, the price of the convertible bond also increases. By not converting to common stock, bondholders enjoy interest income from the bond in addition to the increased bond value caused by the price movement of the common stock.

Government Bonds The federal government sells bonds and securities to finance both the national debt and the government's ongoing activities. Generally, investors choose from five different types of U.S. government bonds:

1. *Treasury bills.* Treasury bills, sometimes called *T-bills,* are sold in minimum units of $100, with additional increments of $100 above the minimum. Although the maturities may be as long as one year, the Treasury Department currently only

Table 20.4: Bond Ratings

The following bond ratings are provided by Moody's Investors Service and Standard & Poor's Corporation.

Quality	Moody's	Standard & Poor's
High grade—Bonds in this category are judged to be of high quality by all standards.	Aaa and Aa	AAA and AA
Medium grade—Bonds in this category possess many favorable investment attributes.	A and Baa	A and BBB
Speculative—Bonds in this category are judged to have speculative elements, and they may lack characteristics of a desirable investment.	Ba and B	BB and B
Poor Prospects or Default—Bonds in this category have poor prospects of attaining any real investment standing. The bonds even could be in default and the company in bankruptcy.	Caa, Ca, and C	CCC, CC, C, and D

Source: Moody's Investors Service, **www.moodyseurope.com**, October 27, 2008; Standard & Poor's Corporation, Standard & Poor's Bond Guide, September 2008.

sells T-bills with four-, thirteen-, twenty-six-, and fifty-two-week maturities. T-bills are sold at a discount, and the actual purchase price is less than $1,000. When the T-bill matures, you receive the $1,000 maturity value.

2. *Treasury notes.* Treasury notes are issued in $100 units with a maturity of more than one year but not more than ten years. Typical maturities are two, three, five, and ten years. Treasury notes pay interest every six months until maturity.
3. *Treasury inflation-protected securities (TIPS).* TIPS are sold in $100 units and are sold with five, ten, or twenty-year maturities. The principal of TIPS increases with inflation and decreases with deflation, as measured by the consumer price index. When TIPS mature, you are paid the adjusted principal or original principal, which ever is greater. TIPS also pay interest twice a year, at a fixed rate.
4. *Treasury bonds.* Treasury bonds are issued in minimum units of $100 and have a thirty-year maturity. Like Treasury notes, Treasury bonds pay interest every six months until maturity.
5. *Savings bonds.* Series EE bonds, often called *U.S. savings bonds,* are purchased for one-half their maturity value. Thus, a $100 bond costs $50 when purchased. (*Note:* If the interest derived from savings bonds is used to pay qualified college expenses, it may be exempt from federal taxation.)

The main reason investors choose U.S. government bonds is that they consider them risk-free. The other side of the coin is that these bonds pay lower interest than most other investments. Interest paid on U.S. government securities is taxable for federal income tax purposes, but is exempt from state and local taxation.

Like the federal government, state and local governments sell bonds to obtain financing. A **municipal bond**, sometimes called a *muni,* is a debt security issued by a state or local government. One of the most important features of municipal bonds is that the interest on them may be exempt from federal taxes. Whether or not the interest on municipal bonds is tax exempt often depends on how the funds obtained from their sale are used. *Caution: It is your responsibility, as an investor, to determine whether or not the interest paid by municipal bonds is taxable. It is also your responsibility to evaluate municipal bonds.* Although most municipal bonds are relatively safe, defaults have occurred in recent years.

municipal bond sometimes called a *muni,* a debt security issued by a state or local government

stock dividend a dividend in the form of additional stock

capital gain the difference between a security's purchase price and its selling price

market value the price of one share of a stock at a particular time

Common Stock

As mentioned in Chapter 19, corporations issue common stock to finance their business start-up costs and help pay for expansion and their ongoing business activities. Before investing in stock, keep in mind that corporations don't have to repay the money a stockholder pays for stock. Usually, a stockholder may sell her or his stock to another individual.

How do you make money by buying common stock? Basically, there are three ways: through dividend payments, through an increase in the value of the stock, or through stock splits.

Is this product a good investment? *While everyone in the United States recognizes the familiar Pepsi logo, you have to dig deeper if you want to evaluate the PepsiCo Corporation. Why not use the sources of information described in this chapter—the Internet, newspapers, investor services, research reports, business periodicals, and corporate reports—to determine if PepsiCo is an investment that could help you reach your financial goals.*

PRNewswire/Pepsi-Cola Company

Dividend Payments One of the reasons why many stockholders invest in common stock is *dividend income.* Generally, dividends are paid on a quarterly basis. Although corporations are under no legal obligation to pay dividends, most corporate board members like to keep stockholders happy (and prosperous). A corporation may pay stock dividends in place of—or in addition to—cash dividends. A **stock dividend** is a dividend in the form of additional stock. It is paid to shareholders just as cash dividends are paid—in proportion to the number of shares owned.

Increase in Dollar Value Another way to make money on stock investments is through capital gains. A **capital gain** is the difference between a security's purchase price and its selling price. To earn a capital gain, you must sell when the market value of the stock is higher than the original purchase price. The **market value** is the price of one share of a stock at a particular time. Let's assume that on October 24, 2005, you purchased 100 shares of General Mills at a cost of $48 a share and that you paid $55 in commission charges, for a total investment of $4,855. Let's also assume that you held your 100 shares until October 24, 2008, and then sold the General Mills stock for $64. Your total return on investment is shown in Table 20.5. You realized a profit of $1,930 because you received dividends totaling $4.55 a share during the three-year period and because the stock's market value increased by $16 a share. Of course, if the stock's market value had decreased, or if the firm's board of directors had voted to reduce or omit dividends, your return would have been less than the total dollar return illustrated in Table 20.5.

Stock Splits Directors of many corporations feel that there is an optimal price range within which their firm's stock is most attractive to investors. When the market value increases beyond that range, they may declare a *stock split* to bring the price down. A **stock split** is the division of each outstanding share of a corporation's stock into a greater number of shares.

stock split the division of each outstanding share of a corporation's stock into a greater number of shares

The most common stock splits result in one, two, or three new shares for each original share. For example, in 2008, the board of directors of Cummins, Inc., the manufacturer of diesel and gas engines, approved a two-for-one stock split. After this split, a stockholder who originally owned 100 shares owned 200 shares. The value of an original share was proportionally reduced. In the case of Cummins, Inc., the market value per share was reduced to half the stock's value before the two-for-one stock split. There is no evidence to support that a corporation's long-term performance is improved by a stock split; however, some investors do profit from stock splits on a short-term basis. *BE WARNED: There are no guarantees that the stock will increase in value after a split.* However, the stock may be more attractive to the investing public because of the potential for a rapid increase in dollar value. This attraction is based on the belief that most corporations split their stock only when their financial future is improving and on the upswing.

Preferred Stock

As we noted in Chapter 19, a firm's preferred stockholders must receive their dividends before common stockholders are paid any dividend. Moreover, the preferred-stock dividend amount is specified on the stock certificate. And the owners of preferred stock have first claim, after bond owners and general creditors, on corporate assets if the firm is dissolved or enters bankruptcy. These features make preferred stock a more conservative investment with an added degree

Table 20.5: Sample Common-Stock Transaction for General Mills

Assumptions: 100 shares of common stock purchased on October 24, 2005, for $48 a share; 100 shares sold on October 24, 2008, for $64 a share; dividends for three years total $4.55 a share.

Cost When Purchased		Return When Sold	
100 shares @ $48	$4,800	100 shares @ $64	$6,400
Plus commission	+ 55	Minus commission	- 70
Total investment	$4,855	Total return	$6,330

Transaction Summary	
Total return	$6,330
Minus total investment	–4,855
Profit from stock sale	$1,475
Plus total dividends (3 years)	+ 455
Total return for this transaction	$1,930

Source: Price data and dividend amounts were taken from the Yahoo Finance website, **http://finance.yahoo.com**, accessed October 26, 2008.

of safety and a more predictable source of income when compared with common stock.

In addition, owners of preferred stock may gain through special features offered with certain preferred-stock issues. Owners of *cumulative* preferred stocks are assured that omitted dividends will be paid to them before common stockholders receive any dividends. Owners of *convertible* preferred stock may profit through growth as well as dividends. When the value of a firm's common stock increases, the market value of its *convertible* preferred stock also increases. Convertible preferred stock thus combines the lower risk of preferred stock with the possibility of greater speculative gain through conversion to common stock.

The road to successful investing. *Because of professional management and diversification, investors often choose to invest their money in mutual funds. Mutual-fund families like Franklin Templeton do everything possible to make it easy to obtain research, open an account, and invest and withdraw funds. For more information about Franklin Templeton funds, go to* ***www.franklin-templeton.com.***

Courtesy Franklin Templeton

Mutual Funds

For many investors, mutual funds are the investment of choice. And there are plenty of funds from which to choose. In 1970, there were only about 400 mutual funds. In January 2008, there were just over 10,000 mutual funds.[11]

According to the Mutual Fund Education Alliance (**www.mfea.com**), a **mutual fund** is a company that pools the money of many investors—its shareholders—to invest in a variety of different securities.[12] The major advantages of a mutual fund are its professional management and its diversification, or investment in a wide variety of securities. Diversification spells safety because an occasional loss incurred with one security usually is offset by gains from other investments.

mutual fund a company that pools the money of many investors—its shareholders—to invest in a variety of different securities

Mutual-Fund Basics There are basically three types of mutual funds: (1) closed-end funds, (2) exchange-traded funds, and (3) open-end funds. A *closed-end fund* sells shares in the fund to investors only when the fund is originally organized. Once all the shares are sold, an investor must purchase shares from some other investor who is willing to sell them. The mutual fund itself is under no obligation to buy back shares from investors. An *exchange-traded fund* (ETF) is a fund that invests in the stocks contained in a specific stock index, such as the Standard & Poor's 500 Stock Index, the Dow Jones Industrial Average, or the Nasdaq Composite Index. With both a closed-end fund and an ETF, an investor can purchase as little as one share of a fund because both types are traded on a stock exchange or in the OTC market. The investment company sponsoring an *open-end fund* issues and sells new shares to any investor who requests them. It also buys back shares from investors who wish to sell all or part of their holdings.

The share value for any mutual fund is determined by calculating its net asset value. **Net asset value (NAV)** per share is equal to the current market value of the mutual fund's portfolio minus the mutual fund's liabilities divided by the number of outstanding shares. For most mutual funds, NAV is calculated at least once a day and is reported in newspapers and financial publications and on the Internet.

net asset value (NAV) current market value of a mutual fund's portfolio minus the mutual fund's liabilities divided by the number of outstanding shares

Mutual-Fund Sales Charges and Fees With regard to costs, there are two types of mutual funds: load and no-load funds. An individual who invests in a *load fund* pays a sales charge every time he or she purchases shares. This charge may be as high as 8.5 percent. While many exceptions exist, the average load charge for mutual funds is between 3 and 5 percent. Instead of charging investors a fee when they purchase shares in a mutual fund, some mutual funds charge a *contingent deferred sales fee*. Generally, this fee ranges from 1 to 5 percent of the amount withdrawn during the first five to seven years. Typically, the amount of the

SPOTLIGHT

Characteristics of Mutual-Fund Shareholders

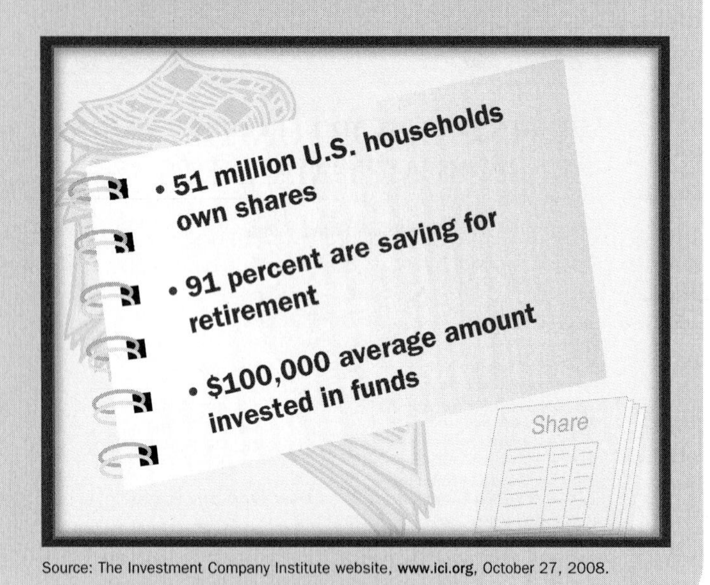

Source: The Investment Company Institute website, www.ici.org, October 27, 2008.

contingent deferred sales fee declines each year that you own the fund until there is no withdrawal fee. The purchaser of shares in a *no-load fund* pays no sales charges at all. Since no-load funds offer the same type of investment opportunities as load funds, you should investigate them further before deciding which type of mutual fund is best for you.

Mutual funds also collect a yearly management fee of about 0.25 to 2 percent of the total dollar amount of assets in the fund. While fees vary considerably, the average management fee is between 0.50 and 1 percent of the fund's assets. Finally, some mutual funds charge a 12b-1 fee (sometimes referred to as a *distribution fee*) to defray the costs of advertising and marketing the mutual fund. Annual 12b-1 fees are calculated on the value of a fund's assets and cannot exceed 1 percent of the fund's assets. Unlike the one-time sales fees that some mutual funds charge to purchase *or* sell mutual-fund shares, the management fee and the 12b-1 fee are ongoing fees charged each year.

Today, mutual funds also can be classified as A, B, or C shares. With A shares, investors pay commissions when they purchase shares in the mutual fund. With B shares, investors pay commissions when money is withdrawn or shares are sold during the first five to seven years. With C shares, investors pay no commissions to buy or sell shares but usually must pay higher ongoing management and 12b-1 fees.

Managed Funds versus Indexed Funds Most mutual funds are managed funds. In other words, there is a professional fund manager (or team of managers) who chooses the securities that are contained in the fund. The fund manager also decides when to buy and sell securities in the fund. Ultimately, the fund manager is responsible for the fund's success.

Instead of investing in a managed fund, some investors choose to invest in an index fund. Why? The answer to this question is simple: Over many years, index funds have outperformed managed funds. The exact statistics vary depending on the year and the specific fund, but a common statistic is that the Standard & Poor's 500 stock index outperforms 80 percent of all managed mutual funds.[13] Simply put: It is hard to beat an index such as the Standard & Poor's 500. If the individual securities included in an index increase in value, the index goes up. Because an index mutual fund is a mirror image of a specific index, the dollar value of a share in an index fund also increases when the index increases. Unfortunately, the reverse is true. A second reason why investors choose index funds is the lower fees charged by these passively managed funds. (*Note:* Various indexes are discussed later in this chapter.)

Types of Mutual-Fund Investments Based on the type of securities they invest in, mutual funds generally fall into three broad categories: stocks, bonds, and other. The majority of mutual funds are *stock funds* that invest in stocks issued by small, medium-size, and large corporations that provide investors with income, growth, or a combination of income and growth. *Bond funds* invest in corporate, government, or municipal bonds that provide investors with interest income. The third category includes funds that stress asset allocation and money-market investments or strive for a balance between stocks and bonds. In most cases, the name of the category gives a pretty good clue to the type of investments included in the fund. Typical fund names include:

- Aggressive growth stock funds
- Global stock funds

- Growth stock funds
- High-yield (junk) bond funds
- Income stock funds
- Index funds
- Lifecycle funds
- Long-term U.S. bond funds
- Regional funds
- Sector stock funds
- Small-cap stock funds

To help investors obtain their investment objectives, most investment companies now allow shareholders to switch from one fund to another fund within the same family of funds. A **family of funds** exists when one investment company manages a group of mutual funds. For example, shareholders, at their option, can change from the AIM Global Equity Fund to the AIM Basic Value Fund. Generally, investors may give instructions to switch from one fund to another fund within the same family either in writing, over the telephone, or via the Internet. Charges for exchanges, if any, are small for each transaction. For funds that do charge, the fee may be as low as $5 per transaction.

family of funds a group of mutual funds managed by one investment company

Real Estate

Real estate ownership represents one of the best hedges against inflation, but it—like all investments—has its risks. A piece of property in a poor location, for example, actually can decrease in value. Table 20.6 lists some of the many factors you should consider before investing in real estate.

There are, of course, disadvantages to any investment, and real estate is no exception. If you want to sell your property, you must find an interested buyer with the ability to obtain enough money to complete the transaction. Finding such a buyer can be difficult if loan money is scarce, the real estate market is in a decline, or you overpaid for a piece of property. For example, many real estate investors were forced to hold some properties longer than they wanted because buyers could not obtain financing during the recent banking and financial crisis. If you are forced to hold your investment longer than you originally planned, taxes, interest, and installment payments can be a heavy burden. As a rule, real estate increases in value and eventually sells at a profit, but there are no guarantees. The degree of your success depends on how well you evaluate different alternatives.

Table 20.6: Real Estate Checklist

Although real estate offers one of the best hedges against inflation, not all property increases in value. Many factors should be considered before investing in real estate.

Evaluation of Property	Inspection of the Surrounding Neighborhood	Other Factors
Is the property priced competitively with similar property?	What are the present zoning requirements?	Why are the present owners selling the property?
What type of financing, if any, is available?	Is the neighborhood's population increasing or decreasing?	How long will you have to hold the property before selling it to someone else?
How much are the taxes?	What is the average income of people in the area?	How much profit can you reasonably expect to obtain?
	What is the state of repair of surrounding property? Do most of the buildings and homes need repair?	Is there a chance that the property value will decrease?

High-Risk Investment Techniques

5

Learning Objective: Describe high-risk investment techniques.

As defined earlier in this chapter, a *high-risk investment* is one made in the uncertain hope of earning a relatively large profit in a short time. (See the high-risk investment category in Table 20.3.) Most high-risk investments become so because of the methods used by investors to earn a quick profit. These methods can lead to large losses as well as to impressive gains. They should not be used by anyone who does not fully understand the risks involved. We begin this section with a discussion of selling short. Then we examine margin transactions and other high-risk investments.

Selling Short

buying long buying stock with the expectation that it will increase in value and then can be sold at a profit

selling short the process of selling stock that an investor does not actually own but has borrowed from a brokerage firm and will repay at a later date

Normally, you buy stocks expecting that they will increase in value and then can be sold at a profit. This procedure is referred to as **buying long**. However, many securities decrease in value for various reasons. Consider what happened to the values of many stocks during the fall of 2008. Because of the nation's depressed economy and the banking and financial crisis, many corporations also experienced a financial downturn. Many of these same corporations experienced lower-than-expected sales revenues and profits. In some cases, corporations actually posted losses during this same time period. For the firms that were able to weather the economic storm, their stock values were quite a bit lower than they were before the economic downturn. When this type of situation occurs, you can use a procedure called *selling short* to make a profit when the price of an individual stock is falling. **Selling short** is the process of selling stock that an investor does not actually own but has borrowed from a brokerage firm and will repay at a later date. The idea is to sell at today's higher price and then buy later at a lower price. To make a profit from a short transaction, you must proceed as follows:

1. Arrange to borrow a certain number of shares of a particular stock from a brokerage firm.

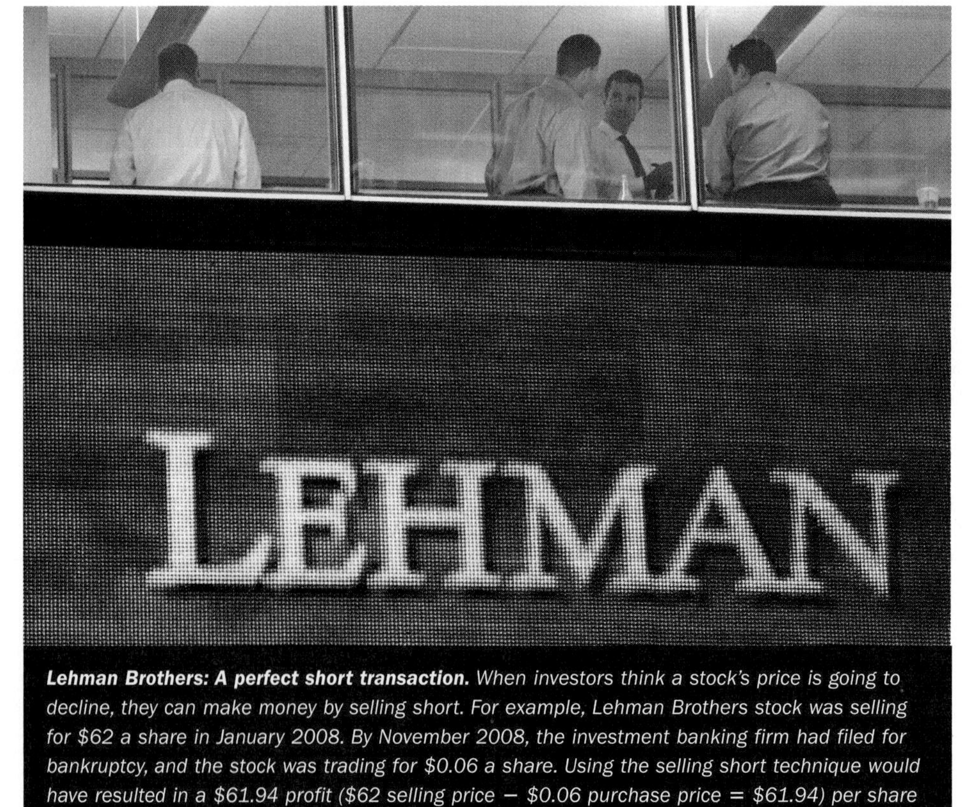

Lehman Brothers: A perfect short transaction. *When investors think a stock's price is going to decline, they can make money by selling short. For example, Lehman Brothers stock was selling for $62 a share in January 2008. By November 2008, the investment banking firm had filed for bankruptcy, and the stock was trading for $0.06 a share. Using the selling short technique would have resulted in a $61.94 profit ($62 selling price − $0.06 purchase price = $61.94) per share sold short.*

AP Photo/Mary Altoffer

2. Sell the borrowed stock immediately, assuming that the price of the stock will drop in a reasonably short time.
3. After the price drops, buy the same number of shares that were sold in step 2.
4. Give the newly purchased stock to the brokerage firm in return for the stock borrowed in step 1.

Your profit is the difference between the amount received when the stock is sold in step 2 and the amount paid for the stock in step 3. For example, assume that you think that General Motors stock is overvalued at $12 a share. You also believe that the stock will decrease in value over the next three to four months. You call your broker and arrange to borrow 100 shares of General Motors stock (step 1). The broker then sells your borrowed General Motors stock for you at the current market price of $12 a share (step 2). Also assume that three months later the General Motors stock has dropped to $5 a share. You instruct your broker to purchase 100 shares of General Motors stock at the current lower price (step 3). The newly purchased General Motors stock is given to the brokerage firm to repay the borrowed stock (step 4). In this example, you made $700 by selling short ($1,200 selling price − $500 purchase price = $700 profit).[14] Naturally, the $700 profit must be reduced by the commissions you paid to the broker for buying and selling the General Motors stock.

People often ask where the broker obtains the stock for a short transaction. The broker probably borrows the stock from other investors who have purchased General Motors stock and left stock certificates on deposit with the brokerage firm. As a result, the person who is selling short must pay any dividends declared on the borrowed stock. The most obvious danger when selling short, of course, is that a loss can result if the stock's value increases instead of decreases.

Buying Stock on Margin

An investor buys stock *on margin* by borrowing part of the purchase price, usually from a stock brokerage firm. The **margin requirement** is the portion of the price of a stock that cannot be borrowed. This requirement is set by the Federal Reserve Board.

margin requirement the portion of the price of a stock that cannot be borrowed

Today, investors can borrow up to 50 percent of the cost of a stock purchase. Some brokerage firms require that you deposit more cash, which reduces the percentage that can be borrowed. But why would investors want to buy stock on margin? Simply because they can buy up to twice as much stock by buying on margin. Suppose that an investor expects the market price of a share of common stock of Duke Energy Corporation—a U.S. energy company—to increase in the next three to four months. Let's say that this investor has enough money to purchase 200 shares of the stock. However, if the investor buys on margin, he or she can purchase an additional 200 shares for a total of 400 shares. If the price of Duke Energy's stock increases by $8 per share, the investor's profit will be $1,600 ($8 × 200 = $1,600) if he or she pays cash. But it will be $3,200 ($8 × 400 = $3,200) if he or she buys on margin. By buying more shares on margin, the investor will earn double the profit (less the interest he or she pays on the borrowed money and customary commission charges).

Financial leverage—a topic covered in Chapter 19—is the use of borrowed funds to increase the return on an investment. When margin is used as leverage, the investor's profit is earned by both the borrowed money and the investor's own money. The investor retains all the profit and pays interest only for the temporary use of the borrowed funds. Note that the stock purchased on margin serves as collateral for the borrowed funds. Before you become a margin investor, you should consider two factors. First, if the market price of the purchased stock does not increase as quickly as expected, interest costs mount and eventually drain your profit. Second, if the price of the margined stock falls, the leverage works against you. That is, because you have purchased twice as much stock, you lose twice as much money.

If the value of a stock you bought on margin decreases to approximately 60 percent of its original price, you may receive a *margin call* from the brokerage firm. You then must provide additional cash or securities to serve as collateral for

The Business of Green

Your Green Portfolio

Thinking about building a green portfolio? You're not alone: Big retirement funds, bank money managers, and corporations with spare cash are putting money into investments that support earth-friendly energy, manufacturing, and business operations.

In addition to using the major Web search engines to locate the latest news about green investment trends, try these online sources of information:

- Social Investment Forum (**www.socialinvest.org**) provides general information about socially responsible investments and user-friendly comparison tools for screening mutual funds based on which support environmental initiatives, among other criteria.
- *GreenMoney Journal* (**www.greenmoneyjournal.com**) covers sustainability issues "from the stock market to the supermarket." Learn more about the big picture of green business before you decide to invest in a particular industry or company.
- *Sustainable Business.com* (**www.sustainablebusiness.com**) tracks the performance of selected earth-friendly stocks and mutual funds, especially young companies that are breaking new ground in environmental technology.

Sources: Elisabeth Rosenthal, "Investment Funds' Dilemma: Environment or Profit," *International Herald Tribune,* November 14, 2008, **www.iht.com**; Barbara Wall, "Handicapping Green Investments Is No Snap," *International Herald Tribune,* March 28, 2008, **www.iht.com**; Anojja Shah, "Green Mutual Funds Ride Wave of Popularity," *Smart Money,* February 13, 2008, **www.smartmoney.com**.

the borrowed money. If you cannot provide additional collateral, the stock is sold, and the proceeds are used to pay off the loan and commissions. Any funds remaining after the loan and commissions are paid off are returned to you.

Other High-Risk Investments

We have already discussed two high-risk investments—selling short and margin transactions. Other high-risk investments include the following:

- Stock options
- Commodities
- Precious metals
- Gemstones
- Coins
- Antiques and collectibles

Without exception, investments of this kind normally are referred to as high-risk investments for one reason or another. For example, the gold market has many unscrupulous dealers who sell worthless gold-plated lead coins to unsuspecting, uninformed investors. It pays to be careful. *Although investments in this category can lead to large dollar gains, they should not be used by anyone who does not fully understand all the potential risks involved.*

Sources of Financial Information

6 **Learning Objective: Use financial information to evaluate investment alternatives.**

A wealth of information is available to investors. Sources include the Internet, newspapers, investors' services, brokerage firm reports, business periodicals, corporate reports, and securities averages.

The Internet

By using the Internet, investors can access a wealth of information on most investment and personal finance topics. For example, you can obtain interest rates for CDs; current price information for stocks, bonds, and mutual funds; and experts' recommendations to buy, hold, or sell an investment. You can even trade securities online.

Because the Internet makes so much information available, you need to use it selectively. One of the Web search engines such as Yahoo! (**www.yahoo.com**), MSN (**www.msn.com**), or Google (**www.google.com**) can help you locate the information you really need. These search engines allow you to do a word search for the personal finance or investment alternative you want to explore. Why not take a look? To access one of the preceding search engines, enter the website address and then type in a key term such as *personal finance* and see the results.

Corporations, investment companies that sponsor mutual funds, and federal, state, and local governments also have home pages where you can obtain valuable investment information. You may want to explore these websites for two reasons. First, they are easily accessible. All you have to do is type in the Web address or use one of the abovementioned search engines to locate the site. Second, the information on these sites may be more up to date than printed material obtained from published sources.

In addition, you can access professional advisory services—a topic discussed later in this section—for information on stocks, bonds, mutual funds, and other investment alternatives. While some of the information provided by these services is free, there is a charge for the more detailed information you may need to evaluate an investment.

Financial Coverage of Securities Transactions

Most local newspapers carry several pages of business news, including reports of securities transactions. The *Wall Street Journal* (published on weekdays) and *Barron's* (published once a week) are devoted almost entirely to financial and economic news. Both include complete coverage of transactions on all major securities exchanges.

Because transactions involving stocks, bonds, and mutual funds are reported differently, we shall examine each type of report separately.

Common and Preferred Stocks Stock transactions are reported in tables that usually look like the top section of Figure 20.2. Stocks are listed alphabetically. Your first task is to move down the table to find the stock you are interested in. To read the *stock quotation,* you read across the table. The highlighted line in Figure 20.2 gives detailed information about common stock issued by global food processor H.J. Heinz Company.

Figure 20.2: Reading Stock Quotations

Reproduced at the top of the figure is a portion of the stock quotations listed in the *Wall Street Journal*. At the bottom is an enlargement of the same information. The numbers above each of the enlarged columns correspond to the numbered entries in the list of explanations that appears in the middle of the figure.

STOCK	(SYM)	CLOSE	NET CHG
Heinz	HNZ	39.45	−0.04
Hellenic	OTE	5.65	−0.34
HelmPayne	HP	25.14	−2.28

1. Name (often abbreviated) of the corporation: Heinz
2. Ticker symbol or letters that identify a stock for trading: HNZ
3. Close is the price paid in the last transaction of the day: $39.45
4. Difference between the price paid for the last share sold today and the price paid for the last share sold on the previous day: –0.04 (in Wall Street terms, Heinz "closed down $0.04" on this day).

1	2	3	4
STOCK	(SYM)	CLOSE	NET CHG
Heinz	HNZ	39.45	−0.04
Hellenic	OTE	5.65	−0.34
HelmPayne	HP	25.14	−2.28

Source: *Wall Street Journal*, October 28, 2008, p. C9.

If a corporation has more than one stock issue, the common stock is listed first. Then the preferred-stock issues are listed and indicated with the letters *pf* behind the firm's name.

Bonds While some newspapers and financial publications provide limited information on some corporate and government bond issues, it is usually easier to obtain more detailed information on more bond issues by accessing the Internet. Regardless of the source, bond prices are quoted as a percentage of the face value, which is usually \$1,000. Thus, to find the current price, you must multiply the face value (\$1,000) by the quotation. For example, a price quoted as 84 translates to a selling price of \$840 (\$1,000 × 0.84 = \$840). Detailed information obtained from the Yahoo! Finance website for a \$1,000 AT&T corporate bond, which pays 5.60 percent interest and matures in 2018, is provided in Figure 20.3.

Mutual Funds Purchases and sales of shares of mutual funds are reported in tables like the one shown in Figure 20.4. As in reading stock quotations, your first task is to move down the table to find the mutual fund you are interested in. Then, to find the mutual-fund price quotation, read across the table. Figure 20.4 gives detailed information for the Dodge & Cox Income mutual fund.

Figure 20.3: Reading Bond Quotations

Reproduced at the top of the figure is bond information obtained from the Yahoo! Finance website. The numbers beside each line correspond to numbered entries in the list of explanations that appears at the bottom of the figure.

AT&T INC	
OVERVIEW	
1. Price	86.57
2. Coupon (%)	5.600
3. Maturity Date	15-Mar-2018
4. Yield to Maturity (%)	7.605
5. Current Yield (%)	6.468
6. Fitch Ratings	A
7. Coupon Payment Frequency	Semi-Annual
8. First Coupon Date	15-Nov-2008
9. Type	Corporate
10. Callable	No

1. Price quoted as a percentage of the face value: \$1,000 × 86.57% = \$865.70
2. Coupon (%) is the rate of interest: 5.600 percent
3. Maturity Date is the date when bondholders will receive repayment: March 15, 2018
4. Yield to Maturity (%) takes into account the relationship among a bond's maturity value, the time to maturity, the current price, and the amount of interest: 7.605 percent
5. Current Yield (%) is determined by dividing the dollar amount of annual interest by the current price of the bond: (\$56 ÷ \$865.70 = 0.06468 = 6.468 percent)
6. Fitch Ratings is used to assess risk associated with this bond: A
7. Coupon Payment Frequency tells bondholders how often they will receive interest payments: Semi-Annual
8. First Coupon Date: November 15, 2008
9. Type: Corporate
10. Callable: No

Source: The Yahoo! Finance bond website at **http://bonds.yahoo.com**, accessed October 28, 2008.

Figure 20.4: Reading Mutual-Fund Quotations

Reproduced at the top of the figure is a portion of the mutual-fund quotations as reported by the *Wall Street Journal*. At the bottom is an enlargement of the same information. The numbers above each of the enlarged columns correspond to numbered entries in the list of explanations that appears in the middle of the figure.

FUND	NAV	NET CHG	YTD %RET
US SmCpVal	13.81	–0.57	–41.6
Dodge & Cox			
Balanced	48.16	–1.11	–38.1
Income	11.22	–0.02	–6.5
Intl Stk	20.97	–1.27	–54.4
Stock	69.65	–2.36	–47.1

1. The name of the mutual fund: Dodge & Cox Income
2. The net asset value (NAV) is the value of one share of the Dodge & Cox Income Fund: $11.22
3. The difference between the net asset value today and the net asset value on the previous trading day: –0.02 (in Wall Street terms, the "Dodge & Cox Income fund closed down $0.02" on this day)
4. The YTD% RET gives the total return for the Dodge and Cox Income fund for the year to date: –6.5%

1 FUND	2 NAV	3 NET CHG	4 YTD %RET
US Sm CpVal	13.81	–0.57	–41.6
Dodge & Cox			
Balanced	48.16	–1.11	–38.1
Income	11.22	–0.02	–6.5
Intl Stk	20.97	–1.27	–54.4
Stock	69.65	–2.36	–47.1

Source: *Wall Street Journal,* October 28, 2008, p. C11.

Other Sources of Financial Information

In addition to the Internet and newspaper coverage, other sources, which include investors' services, brokerage firm reports, business periodicals, and corporate reports, offer detailed and varied information about investment alternatives.

Investors' Services For a fee, various investors' services provide information about investments. Information from investors' services also may be available at university and public libraries.

As illustrated in Table 20.4, Moody's and Standard & Poor's provide information that can be used to determine the quality and risk associated with bond issues. Standard & Poor's, Mergent, Inc., and Value Line also rate the companies that issue common and preferred stock. Each investor service provides detailed financial reports. Take a look at the Mergent's research report for Polo Ralph Lauren illustrated in Figure 20.5. Notice that there are six main sections that provide financial data, summary information about the company's business operations, recent developments, prospects, and other valuable information. Research reports published by Standard & Poor's and Value Line are like Mergent's report and provide similar information.

A number of investors' services provide detailed information on mutual funds. Morningstar, Inc., Standard & Poor's, Lipper Analytical Services, and Value Line are four widely tapped sources of such information. Although some information may be free, a fee generally is charged for more detailed research reports. In addition, various mutual-fund newsletters supply financial information to subscribers for a fee.

Figure 20.5: Mergent's Research Report for Polo Ralph Lauren

A research report from Mergent is divided into six main parts that describe not only the financial condition of a company but also its history and outlook for the future.

POLO RALPH LAUREN CORP.

Exchange	Symbol	Price	52Wk Range	Yield	P/E
NYS	RL	$69.85 (5/30/2008)	102.30-51.33	0.29	17.46

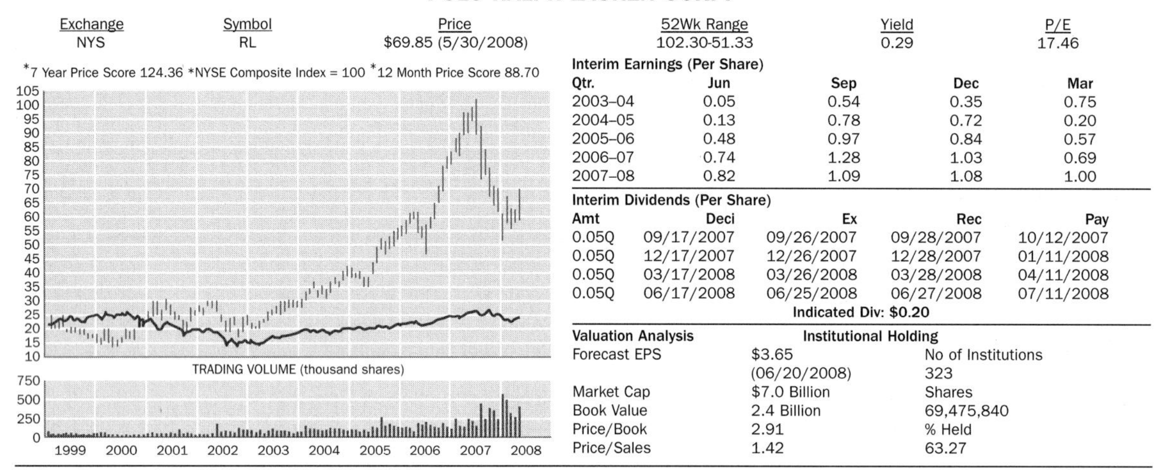

Interim Earnings (Per Share)

Qtr.	Jun	Sep	Dec	Mar
2003–04	0.05	0.54	0.35	0.75
2004–05	0.13	0.78	0.72	0.20
2005–06	0.48	0.97	0.84	0.57
2006–07	0.74	1.28	1.03	0.69
2007–08	0.82	1.09	1.08	1.00

Interim Dividends (Per Share)

Amt	Decl	Ex	Rec	Pay
0.05Q	09/17/2007	09/26/2007	09/28/2007	10/12/2007
0.05Q	12/17/2007	12/26/2007	12/28/2007	01/11/2008
0.05Q	03/17/2008	03/26/2008	03/28/2008	04/11/2008
0.05Q	06/17/2008	06/25/2008	06/27/2008	07/11/2008

Indicated Div: $0.20

Valuation Analysis		**Institutional Holding**	
Forecast EPS	$3.65 (06/20/2008)	No of Institutions	323
Market Cap	$7.0 Billion	Shares	69,475,840
Book Value	2.4 Billion	% Held	63.27
Price/Book	2.91		
Price/Sales	1.42		

Business Summary: Apparel (MIC: SIC: 2329 NAIC: 315211)

Polo Ralph Lauren is engaged in designing, marketing and distribution of lifestyle products, including men's, women's and children's apparel, accessories, fragrances and home furnishings. Co.'s apparel and accessories products include men's, women's and children's clothing, footwear, eyewear, jewelry, hats, belts and leathergoods. Co.'s home furnishing collections include bed and bath linens, china, crystal, silver, decorative accessories, gifts, garden and beach, window hardware, furniture, fabric, trimmings and wallcovering. As of Mar 29 2008, Co. operated 155 full-price retail stores and 158 factory outlet stores worldwide.

Recent Developments: For the year ended Mar 29 2008, net income increased 4.7% to US$419.8 million from US$400.9 million in the prior year. Revenues were US$4.88 billion, up 13.6% from US$4.30 billion the year before. Operating income was US$653.4 million versus US$652.6 million in the prior year, an increase of 0.1%. Direct operating expenses rose 14.4% to US$2.24 billion from US$1.96 billion in the comparable period the year before. Indirect operating expenses increased 17.9% to US$1.98 billion from US$1.68 billion in the equivalent prior-year period.

Prospects: For the fiscal quarter ending June 30 2008, Co. expects consolidated revenues to grow at a low to mid-single digit rate with consolidated operating margin down about 300 to 400 basis points. Meanwhile, for the fiscal year ending Mar 29 2009, Co. continues to expect consolidated revenues to increase by a low-to-mid single digit percentage with diluted earnings of $3.95 to $4.05 per share. Going forward, Co. plans to expand its accessories and other product offerings, grow its specialty retail store base, and expand its presence internationally. Notably, Co. intends to pursue global expansion of its retail presence, including in Paris, France, during fiscal 2009 and beyond.

Financial Data (US$ in Thousands)	**03/29/2008**	**03/31/2007**	**04/01/2006**	**04/02/2005**	**04/03/2004**	**03/29/2003**	**03/30/2002**	**03/31/2001**
Earnings Per Share	3.99	3.73	2.87	1.83	1.69	1.76	1.75	0.61
Cash Flow Per Share	6.82	7.65	4.32	3.77	2.09	2.74	3.02	1.04
Tang Book Value Per Share	10.71	11.99	10.35	10.38	10.56	8.93	7.38	5.76
Dividends Per Share	0.200	0.200	0.200	0.200	0.200	...	...	...
Dividend Payout %	5.01	5.36	6.97	10.93	11.83	...	...	...
Income Statement								
Total Revenue	4,880,100	4,295,400	3,746,300	3,305,415	2,649,654	2,439,340	2,363,707	2,225,774
EBITDA	869,100	783,500	637,800	3,809,390	355,121	366,533	378,951	201,666
Depn & Amortn	201,300	144,700	136,100	3,503,633	83,189	78,645	83,919	78,599
Income Before Taxes	642,100	643,300	502,900	299,366	261,932	274,386	275,999	97,954
Income Taxes	222,300	242,400	194,900	107,336	95,055	100,151	103,499	38,692
Net Income	419,800	400,900	308,000	190,425	170,954	174,235	172,500	59,262
Average Shares	105,200	107,600	107,200	104,010	100,960	99,263	98,522	97,446
Balance Sheet								
Current Assets	1,893,500	1,685,900	1,378,500	1,413,763	1,271,319	1,166,007	1,008,057	901,721
Total Assets	4,365,500	3,758,000	3,088,700	2,726,669	2,270,241	2,038,822	1,749,497	1,626,093
Current Liabilities	908,600	640,300	843,500	622,410	501,130	500,347	391,771	439,577
Long-Term Obligations	546,000	445,900	24,200	290,960	277,345	248,494	285,414	296,988
Total Liabilities	1,975,800	1,423,100	1,039,100	1,050,961	848,168	830,055	751,302	816,784
Stockholders' Equity	2,389,700	2,334,900	2,049,600	1,675,708	1,422,073	1,208,767	998,195	809,309
Shares Outstanding	99,500	104,000	105,400	103,118	100,632	98,722	98,227	97,177
Statistical Record								
Return on Assets %	10.36	11.74	10.62	7.64	7.81	9.22	10.25	3.66
Return on Equity %	17.82	18.34	16.58	12.33	12.79	15.83	19.14	7.51
EBITDA Margin %	17.81	18.24	17.02	115.25	13.40	15.03	16.03	9.06
Net Margin %	8.60	9.33	8.22	5.76	6.45	7.14	7.30	2.66
Asset Turnover	1.20	1.26	1.29	1.33	1.21	1.29	1.40	1.37
Current Ratio	2.08	2.63	1.63	2.27	2.54	2.33	2.57	2.05
Debt to Equity	0.23	0.19	0.01	0.17	0.20	0.21	0.29	0.37
Price Range	102.30-51.33	89.64-46.50	61.47-35.10	42.60-31.04	35.13-22.41	30.64-16.57	30.98-18.41	30.45-13.25
P/E Ratio	25.64-12.86	24.03-12.47	21.42-12.23	23.28-16.96	20.79-13.26	17.41-9.41	17.70-10.52	49.92-21.72
Average Yield %	0.26	0.29	0.40	0.54	0.71	...	...	...

Address: 650 Madison Avenue, New York, NY 10022	Web Site: www.investor.polo.com	Auditors: Ernst & Young LLP
Telephone: 212-318-7000	Officers: Ralph Lauren—Chairman, Chief Executive Officer Roger N. Farah—President, Chief Operating Officer	**Investor Contact:** 212-813-7862
Fax: 212-888-5780		**Transfer Agents:** The Bank of New York, New York, NY

Source: From *Mergent's Handbook of Common Stocks*, Fall 2008 (New York: Mergent, Inc., copyright © 2008). Reprinted by permission of John Wiley & Sons, Inc.

Brokerage Firm Analysts' Reports Brokerage firms employ financial analysts to prepare detailed reports on individual corporations and their securities. Such reports are based on the corporation's sales, profits or losses, management, and planning, plus other information on the company, its industry, demand for its products, its efforts to develop new products, and the current economic environment. The reports, which may include buy or sell recommendations, usually are provided free to the clients of full-service brokerage firms. Firms offering this service include UBS Wealth Management, Smith Barney, Merrill Lynch, and most other full-service brokerage firms. Brokerage firm reports also may be available from discount brokerage firms, but they may charge a fee.

Sustaining the Planet

The Dow Jones Sustainability Indexes, started in 1999, are averages of the current market prices of the top sustainability-driven companies around the world. Different indexes cover the leading global sustainability stocks, leading European sustainability stocks, and leading North American sustainability stocks. **www.sustainability-index.com**

Business Periodicals Business magazines such as *BusinessWeek, Fortune,* and *Forbes* provide not only general economic news but also detailed financial information about individual corporations. Trade or industry publications such as *Advertising Age* and *Business Insurance* include information about firms in a specific industry. News magazines such as *U.S. News & World Report, Time,* and *Newsweek* feature financial news regularly. *Money, Kiplinger's Personal Finance Magazine, Smart Money,* and similar magazines provide information and advice designed to improve your investment skills. These periodicals are available at libraries and are sold at newsstands and by subscription. Many of these same periodicals sponsor an online website that may contain all or selected articles that are contained in the print version. Why not check out the investing information available from *BusinessWeek Online* at **www.businessweek.com** or *Kiplinger's Personal Finance Magazine* at **www.kiplinger.com.**

Corporate Reports Publicly held corporations must publish annual reports which include a description of the company's performance provided by the corporation's top management, information about the firm's products or services, and detailed financial statements that readers can use to evaluate the firm's actual performance. There also should be a letter from the accounting firm that audited the corporation. As mentioned in Chapter 17, an audit does not guarantee that a company hasn't "cooked" the books, but it does imply that the company has followed generally accepted accounting principles to report profits, assets, liabilities, and other financial information.

In addition, a corporation issuing a new security must—by law—prepare a prospectus and ensure that copies are distributed to potential investors. A corporation's prospectus and its annual and quarterly reports are available to the general public.

Security Averages

Investors often gauge the stock market through the security averages reported in newspapers and on television news programs. A **security average** (or **security index**) is an average of the current market prices of selected securities. Over a period of time, these averages indicate price trends, but they do not predict the performance of individual investments. At best, they can give the investor a "feel" for what is happening to investment prices generally.

security average (or security index) an average of the current market prices of selected securities

The *Dow Jones Industrial Average,* established in 1896, is the oldest security index in use today. This average is composed of the prices of the common stocks of thirty leading industrial corporations. In addition, Dow Jones publishes a transportation average, a utility average, and a composite average.

In addition to the Dow Jones' averages, the Standard & Poor's 500 Stock Index, the New York Stock Exchange Composite Index, and the Nasdaq Composite Index include more stocks when compared with the Dow averages. Thus, they tend to reflect the stock market more fully. In addition to stock averages, there are averages for bonds, mutual funds, real estate, commodities, precious metals, fine art, most collectibles, and many other potential investments.

Before they can start investing, most people have to decide on a career and obtain a job that will provide the money needed to finance an investment program. To help you find the right job (and the money needed to fund an investment program), read Appendix A where we provide information that can help you to explore different career options (see text website).

return to inside business

Fidelity Investments

As the U.S. leader in mutual funds, Fidelity's five largest funds hold nearly $300 billion in investor money. On any given day, the company fields 189 million phone calls, letting its automated system handle routine inquiries so its experts can take the time to personally respond to more complex requests.

The financial woes of an economic downturn can hurt Fidelity just as much as any other business. For instance, during the recent market turmoil, Fidelity saved money by cutting overhead expenses and laying off 3,000 employees. Still, whether the stock market is up or down, Fidelity continues to expand its education efforts and give investors access to the tools and tips they need for good investment decisions.

Questions

1. Would you choose a full-service brokerage firm, a discount brokerage firm such as Fidelity, or a deep-discount brokerage firm when investing for a long-term goal such as retirement? Explain your answer.
2. Unlike competitor Charles Schwab, Fidelity is not a public corporation. How do you think this might affect Fidelity's decisions about new investment offerings and customer service support?

CHAPTER REVIEW

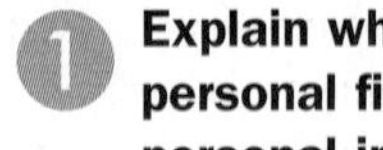

Summary

1 Explain why you should manage your personal finances and develop a personal investment program.

Many personal finance experts recommend that you begin the process of managing your money by determining your current financial condition. The first step often is to construct a personal balance sheet and a personal income statement. You also can construct a personal budget. For most people, the next step is to formulate measurable and realistic investment goals. A personal investment program then is designed to implement those goals. Many financial planners also suggest that the investor should establish an emergency fund equivalent to at least three months' living expenses. Then additional funds may be invested according to the investment program. Finally, all investments should be monitored carefully, and if necessary, the investment program should be modified.

2 Describe how the factors of safety, risk, income, growth, and liquidity affect your investment program.

Depending on their particular investment goals, investors seek varying degrees of safety, risk, income, growth, and liquidity from their investments. Safety is, in essence, freedom from the risk of loss. Generally, the greater the risk, the greater should be the potential return on an investment. To determine how much risk you are willing to assume, many investors calculate the rate of return. It is also possible to compare the rate of return for different investments that offer more or less risk. Income is the periodic return from an investment. Growth is an increase in the value of the investment. Liquidity is the ease with which an asset can be converted to cash.

3 Understand how securities are bought and sold.

Securities may be purchased in either the primary or the secondary market. The primary market is a market in which an investor purchases financial securities (via an investment bank) directly from the issuer of those securities. The secondary market involves transactions for existing securities that are currently traded between investors and usually are bought and sold through a securities exchange or the over-the-counter (OTC) market.

If you invest in securities, chances are that you will use the services of an account executive who works for a brokerage firm. It is also possible to use a discount broker or trade securities online with a computer. Today, a regulatory pyramid consisting of four different levels exists to make sure that investors are protected. The U.S. Congress, the Securities and Exchange Commission (SEC), individual states, and securities exchanges and brokerage firms all are involved in regulating the securities industry.

Identify the advantages and disadvantages of savings accounts, bonds, stocks, mutual funds, and real estate investments.

Asset allocation is the process of spreading your money among several different types of investments to lessen risk. Two other factors—the time your investments have to work for you and your age—also should be considered before deciding where to invest your money. Once the factors of asset allocation, time your investments have to work for you, and your age are considered, it is time to examine different investment alternatives. In this section, we examined traditional investments that include bank accounts, corporate bonds, government bonds, common stock, preferred stock, mutual funds, and real estate. Although bank accounts and bonds can provide investment growth, they generally are purchased by investors who seek a predictable source of income. Both corporate and government bonds are a form of debt financing. As a result, bonds generally are considered a more conservative investment than stocks or most mutual funds. With stock investments, investors can make money through dividend payments, an increase in the value of the stock, or stock splits. The major advantages of mutual-fund investments are professional management and diversification. Today, there are mutual funds to meet just about any conceivable investment objective. The success of real estate investments is often tied to how well each investment alternative is evaluated.

Describe high-risk investment techniques.

High-risk investment techniques can provide greater returns, but they also entail greater risk of loss. You can make money by selling short when the market value of a financial security is decreasing. Selling short is the process of selling stock that an investor does not actually own but has borrowed from a brokerage firm and will repay at a later date. An investor also can buy stock on margin by borrowing part of the purchase price, usually from a stock brokerage firm. Because you can purchase up to twice as much stock by using margin, you can increase your return on investment as long as the stock's market value increases. Other high-risk investments include stock options, commodities, precious metals, gemstones, coins, and antiques and collectibles.

Use financial information to evaluate investment alternatives.

Today, there is a wealth of information on stocks, bonds, and other securities and the firms that issue them. There is also a wealth of investment information on other types of investments, including mutual funds, real estate, and high-risk investment alternatives. Two popular sources—the Internet and newspapers—report daily securities transactions. The Internet also can be used to obtain detailed financial information about different investment alternatives. Often, the most detailed research information about securities—and the most expensive—is obtained from investors' services. In addition, brokerage firm reports, business periodicals, and corporate reports also can be used to evaluate different investment alternatives. Finally, there are a number of security indexes or averages that indicate price trends but reveal nothing about the performance of individual securities.

Key Terms

You should now be able to define and give an example relevant to each of the following terms:

personal budget (593)
personal investment (594)
financial planner (595)
blue-chip stock (596)
rate of return (596)
liquidity (597)
primary market (598)
high-risk investment (598)
secondary market (598)
securities exchange (599)
over-the-counter (OTC) market (599)
Nasdaq (599)
account executive (599)
market order (600)
limit order (600)
discretionary order (600)
full disclosure (602)
prospectus (602)
insider trading (602)
asset allocation (603)
municipal bond (607)
stock dividend (607)
capital gain (607)
market value (607)
stock split (608)
mutual fund (609)
net asset value (NAV) (609)
family of funds (611)
buying long (612)
selling short (612)
margin requirement (613)
security average (or security index) (619)

Review Questions

1. How could developing a personal budget help you obtain the money needed to fund your investment program?
2. What is an "emergency fund," and why is it recommended?
3. What is the tradeoff between safety and risk? How do you calculate rate of return?
4. In general, what kinds of investments provide income? What kinds provide growth?
5. What is the difference between the primary market and the secondary market?
6. When a corporation decides to sell stock, what is the role of an investment banking firm? What is an IPO?
7. What is the difference between a securities exchange and the over-the-counter market?
8. Describe how the securities industry is regulated.
9. How do you think that asset allocation, the time your investments have to work for you, and your age affect the choice of investments for someone who is 25 years old? For someone who is 59 years old?
10. Characterize the purchase of corporate and government bonds as an investment in terms of safety, risk, income, growth, and liquidity.
11. Describe the three methods by which investors can make money with stock investments.
12. An individual may invest in stocks either directly or through a mutual fund. How are the two investment methods different?
13. When would a speculator sell short?
14. What are the risks and rewards of purchasing stocks on margin?
15. How could the Internet help you to research an investment?
16. In what ways are newspaper stock quotations useful to investors? In what ways are security averages useful?
17. In addition to the Internet and newspapers, what other sources of financial information could help you to obtain your investment goals?

Discussion Questions

1. At the time of publication, many investors had lost money on stocks and mutual funds because of an economic downturn caused by the banking and financial crisis. At the same time, many experts argued that this was a "real investing opportunity" because of the depressed prices for many stocks and mutual funds. Based on current economic and investment information available at the time you answer this question, do you think that it is a good time to begin an investment program? Justify your answer.
2. What personal circumstances might lead investors to emphasize income rather than growth in their investment planning? What might lead them to emphasize growth rather than income?
3. In this chapter, it was apparent that stocks have outperformed other investment alternatives over a long period of time. With this fact in mind, why would investors choose to use asset allocation to diversify their investments?
4. What type of individual would invest in government bonds? In global mutual funds? In real estate?
5. Suppose that you have just inherited 500 shares of IBM common stock. What would you do with it, if anything?
6. What kinds of information would you like to have before you invest in a particular common stock or mutual fund? From what sources can you get that information?
7. Take another look at Figure 20.5 (Mergent's research report for Polo Ralph Lauren). Based on the research provided by Mergent's, would you buy stock in Polo Ralph Lauren? Justify your decision by providing specific examples from Figure 20.5.

Video Case 20.1

Is a Bull or Bear Market Ahead for Build-A-Bear Workshop?

Can Build-A-Bear Workshop continue its bear-sized success? Founder Maxine Clark was a retailing executive for twenty-five years before she became an entrepreneur in 1997. Thinking back to her much-loved teddy bear and the magic she remembered in special shopping trips as a child, Clark wanted her new business to combine entertainment and retailing to please children of all ages. The retail company she founded, Build-A-Bear Workshop, Inc., has now blossomed into an international chain of more than 200 stores ringing up $375 million in annual sales.

Master Bear Builders (store employees) help customers choose the types of animals they want. Bears, bunnies, kittens, ponies, and frogs, available in small or large sizes, are just some of the choices. Next, customers select the fake-fur color and the amount of stuffing and then carefully insert the heart. To add a voice, they can insert a prerecorded sound chip or record a personalized sound chip. Then customers help stitch the seams, gently fluff the fur, and name their new friends. If they wish, they can pick out clothing and accessories such as angel wings or miniature cowboy gear. The result is a one-of-a-kind stuffed animal that goes home in a house-shaped package.

As part of the buying procedure, customers enter their animal's names and their own names and addresses, e-mail addresses, gender, and birth dates at computer stations in each store. Build-A-Bear uses this information to generate each toy's birth certificate, signed by Clark as CEB. (By the way, Clark's CEB title stands for Chief

Executive Bear.) Then the information is pooled with sales data and other details, analyzed carefully, and used to plan newsletters and other promotional efforts. In addition, because each animal contains a unique bar-coded tag, the company can return lost toys by consulting the database to determine ownership. So far the company has used the system to reunite fifty lost animals with their owners.

Each Build-A-Bear store rings up $600 per square foot in annual sales, roughly twice the average of a typical mall store. The mix of products is constantly evolving to keep customers coming back again and again. "We add new products monthly to stay in step with the latest fashions and trends," she says. "More than 80 percent of our line changes at least twice a year."

To raise millions of dollars for rapid expansion, Clark and her management team decided to take Build-A-Bear public. After filing the legally required forms for an IPO with the SEC, the company was listed on the NYSE, and shares began trading under the BBW symbol on October 28, 2004. First-day trading was brisk: Nearly 6 million shares changed hands, and the stock closed at $25.05 a share.

Now that Build-A-Bear is a public corporation, its executives present formal financial reports every quarter and every year. They also take questions from brokerage firm analysts during earnings conference calls, industry meetings, and other events. Senior managers have been asked about actual and projected revenue, profit margins, store traffic, new product lines, inventory levels, advertising, new stores, and other issues that shed light on how the business—and, in turn, the stock—is likely to perform in the future. Armed with this information, the analysts then issue recommendations about investing in Build-A-Bear.

Build-A-Bear has been growing by promoting online purchasing, opening stores in sports stadiums, and branching out into doll-making products. New advertising campaigns are attracting new customers and repeat business from customers who want to add to their collection. Its investors are watching the company's financial position closely and weighing how the overall economic climate will affect the retailer's future. Is a bull or bear market ahead for Build-A-Bear?[15]

For more information about this company, go to **www.buildabear.com**.

Questions

1. What are the advantages and disadvantages of a corporation such as Build-A-Bear Workshop going public and selling stock?
2. Now, with new stores funded by the money obtained from selling stock, Build-A-Bear has more than 200 stores that generate annual sales revenues of $375 million. Would you buy stock in this company? Explain your answer.
3. What specific information would you want to have before deciding to buy Build-a-Bear stock, and where would you obtain this information?
4. If you were attending Build-A-Bear's annual meeting, what questions would you ask top management—and why?

Case 20.2

Investing: The Time Is Now

Nearly four in ten people in your age group (18 to 35) have already started investing for their future. Is the time right for you, too?

Despite recent swings in the stock market, most financial experts would say yes. While you may not think you have enough money to invest just now, you can start saving small amounts on a regular basis—weekly or monthly, or each time you get paid—and soon you'll have enough to consider making some long-term investments with it.

Before you decide to put this step off, consider the cost of waiting. If you invest just $150 a month beginning at age 25, you can put away $1,800 a year. If the investments you choose earn 11 percent per year, you'll have $1,047,294 by the time you're 65. If you wait a mere ten years, however, and begin at age 35, you'll have only $358,236. That's a loss of almost $700,000.

Keep in mind that there has never been a twenty-year period over which the stock market has lost money, and shares in most large U.S. companies have averaged gains of 10 percent per year. Those statistics not only attest to the value of investing, but they also emphasize that you'll want to take the long view when you commit your funds. Ironically, the market's recent downturns signal to many experts the opportunity to earn even larger gains by investing now. You've probably heard the advice, "Buy low, sell high"—during an economic slowdown, it's more relevant than ever.

Where should you put your investment? John C. Bogle, founder of the Vanguard Investment Company, is bullish about the stock market and mutual funds invested in it. "The probabilities for stock market investing right now are very compelling," he says, citing share prices that have recently declined around the world, making stocks both cheaper to buy and more likely to yield high returns long term. Bogle counsels choosing a conservative portfolio that's both balanced and diversified. Increase your investment regularly, he says, and ignore day-to-day market fluctuations. Remember, you're in this for the long term.

The late Sir John Templeton, whom *Money* magazine called "arguably the greatest stock picker of the century," founded a fund called Templeton Growth that grew an average of more than 15 percent each year for almost half a century. His maxims for successful investing agree with Bogle's focus on the long term. "Invest," Templeton advised. "Don't trade or speculate." Keep in mind that buying shares in companies that continue to grow, like Procter & Gamble or McDonald's, is investing in their ability to keep earning money in good times and bad. Frantically buying and selling shares at the first sign of a decline is more like gambling than investing.

Of course, before you invest money you plan to park for the next twenty years or so, make sure you've eliminated as much of your current debts as possible, such as credit cards or student loans. Allow yourself enough financial flexibility to start (or continue) contributing to a separate retirement fund, especially if your employer matches your contributions. And protect your liquidity. Set aside cash for emergencies, as well as for near-term purchases like a home or car down payment or graduate school if those are in your five-year plan.

Finally, remember Bogle's observation: "If you were to put your money away and not look at it for many years, until you were ready for retirement, when you finally looked at it, you'd probably faint with amazement at how much money is in there."[16]

To see what he means, check out the interactive growth calculator at **http://www.finance.cch.com/sohoApplets/CompoundSavings.asp.**

Questions

1. Assume you can invest only half the amount suggested above, or about $75 a month. Use the growth calculator link in the case (or another such tool) to calculate how much you can earn at 11 percent interest by age 65, starting at ages 25 and 35. What does the difference between the two results suggest to you about the value of long-term investing?
2. Why do you think experts advise buying low and selling high? Try reading the financial pages of a major newspaper for a few days and paying particular attention to the behavior of buyers and sellers of securities. Do you think they consistently follow this advice? Why or why not? What other ways can investors profit from buying stock shares?
3. Make a list of your financial liabilities. How much debt do you need to pay down before you can begin setting aside money for long-term investing? Don't forget to allow for other kinds of saving, such as for retirement and emergencies.

Building Skills for Career Success

1. JOURNALING FOR SUCCESS

According to many financial experts, the logical place to begin the search for a quality investment is to examine the products and services you use on a regular basis—products and services that provide a high level of consumer satisfaction.

The preceding statement is based on the assumption that if you like the product or service and you feel that you got excellent value for your money, other consumers will too. And while it may be obvious, a satisfied, growing customer base can mean increased sales revenues, profits, and ultimately, higher stock values for the company that manufactured the product or provided the service.

Assignment

1. To begin this journal exercise, think about purchases you made over the last month. Describe one product or service that you feel "was worth the money."
2. For the product or service you chose, describe the attributes or features that impressed you.
3. Determine if the company that made the product or provided the service is a public company that has issued stock.* Then use the Internet or go to the library to research the investment potential for this company. Finally, describe why you feel this would be a good or bad investment at this time.

*If the company that manufactured the product or service you chose is not a public company, choose another product or service.

2. EXPLORING THE INTERNET

For investors seeking information about individual companies and the industry to which they belong, the Internet is an excellent source. If you find the right website, it provides sales and revenue histories, graphs of recent trading activity, and discussions of anticipated changes within a firm or an industry. The interested investor also can look at Internet business reports of stock and bond market activity. Among the many companies that issue these reports are Dow Jones, Standard & Poor's, Moody's, and Value Line—all firms that provide, for a fee, analysis and private research services. Visit the text website for updates to this exercise.

Assignment

1. Suppose that you are interested in investing within a particular industry, such as the semiconductor or computer industry. Explore some of the websites listed below, gathering information about the industry and a few related stocks that are of interest to the "experts."
   BusinessWeek: **www.businessweek.com**
   Fortune: **www.fortune.com**
   Nasdaq: **www.nasdaq.com**
   Standard & Poor's: **www2.standardandpoors.com**
   New York Stock Exchange: **www.nyse.com**
   Wall Street Journal: **www.wsj.com**
2. List the stocks the experts recommend and their current trading value. Also list several stocks the experts do not like and their current selling prices. You can use one of the Web search engines such as Yahoo! Finance (**http://finance.yahoo.com**) to check the price. Then list your own choices of "good" and "bad" stocks.
3. Explain why you and the experts believe that these stocks are good or poor buys today. (You might want to monitor the value of all stocks over the next six months to see how well your stocks are performing.)

3. DEVELOPING CRITICAL-THINKING SKILLS

One way to achieve financial security is to invest a stated amount of money on a systematic basis. This investment strategy is called *dollar-cost averaging.* When the cost is lower, your investment buys more shares. When the cost is higher, your investment buys fewer shares. A good way to begin investing is to select a mutual fund that meets your financial objectives and to invest the same amount each month or each year.

Assignment

1. Select several mutual funds from the financial pages of the *Wall Street Journal* or a personal finance periodical such as *Money, Kiplinger's Personal Finance,* or *SmartMoney* that provides information about mutual funds. Call the toll-free number for each fund and ask about its objectives. Also request that the company send you a prospectus and an annual report.
2. Select one fund that meets your financial objectives.
3. Prepare a table that includes the following data:
   a. An initial investment of $2,000 in the mutual fund you have selected
   b. The NAV (net asset value)
   c. The number of shares purchased
4. Record the investment information on a weekly basis. Look in the *Wall Street Journal* or on the Internet to find the NAV for each week.

5. Determine the value of your investment until the end of the semester.
6. Write a report describing the results. Include a summary of what you learned about investments. Be sure to indicate if you think that dollar-cost averaging (investing another $2,000 next year) would be a good idea.

4. BUILDING TEAM SKILLS

Investing in stocks can be a way to beat inflation and accumulate money. Traditionally, stocks have returned just over 10 percent per year since 1926. Fixed-rate investments, on the other hand, often earn little more than the inflation rate, making it very difficult to accumulate enough money for retirement.

Assignment

1. Form teams of three people. The teams will compete against each other, striving for the largest gain in investments.
2. Assume that you are buying stock in three companies; some should be listed on the NYSE, and some should be traded in the OTC market.
   a. Research different investments, and narrow your choices to three different stocks.
   b. Divide your total investment of $25,000 into three amounts.
   c. Determine the number of shares of stock you can purchase in each company by dividing the budgeted amount by the price of the stock. Allow enough money to pay for the commission. To find the cost of the stock, multiply the number of shares you are going to purchase by the closing price of the stock.
   d. Assume that the commission is 1 percent. Calculate it by multiplying the cost of the stock by 0.01. Add the dollar amount of commission to the cost of the stock to determine the total purchase price.
3. Set up a table to reflect the following information:
   a. Name of the company
   b. Closing price per share
   c. Number of shares purchased
   d. Amount of the commission
   e. Cost of the stock
4. Record the closing price of the stock on a weekly basis. Prepare a chart to use for this step.
5. Before the end of the semester, assume that you sell the stock.
   a. Take the closing price on the day you sell your stocks and multiply it by the number of shares; then calculate the commission at 1 percent.
   b. Deduct the amount of commission from the selling price of the stock. This is the total return on your investment.
6. Calculate your profit or loss. Subtract the total purchase price of the stock from the total return. If the total return is less than the total purchase price, you have a loss.
7. Prepare a report summarizing the results of the project. Include the table and individual stock charts, as well as a statement describing what you learned about investing in stocks.

5. RESEARCHING DIFFERENT CAREERS

Account executives (sometimes referred to as *stockbrokers*) are agents who buy and sell securities for clients. After completing this exercise, you will have a better understanding of what account executives do on a daily basis.

Assignment

1. Look in the telephone directory for the names and numbers of financial companies or securities firms that sell stock.
2. Contact an account executive at one of these firms and explain that you would like to set up an interview so that you can learn firsthand about an account executive's job.
3. Summarize the results of your interview in a report. Include a statement about whether the job of account executive appeals to you, and explain your thoughts.

Running a Business Part 7

FINAGLE A BAGEL

Managing Money at Finagle A Bagel

Like many other entrepreneurs, when Laura Trust and Alan Litchman decided to buy a business, they raised some money from friends and family. Unlike many entrepreneurs, however, they were so adamant about retaining full control of the business they bought—Finagle A Bagel—that they would not even consider venture capital financing or selling stock. Instead, Litchman says, "We made the decision to get banks to finance this company, which is a difficult thing."

BAGELS, BANKING, AND BORROWING

Ideally, banks prefer to make loans secured by assets such as inventory or accounts receivable. However, Finagle A Bagel has no inventory aside from each day's raw ingredients and fresh-baked bagels, which cannot be repossessed and resold if the company is unable to repay a loan. Nor does it have significant accounts receivable because most of its revenues come from cash transactions in the twenty stores. The company has commercial ovens and other equipment in its headquarters production facility, but, says copresident Litchman, banks do not consider such assets sufficient collateral for a secured loan. And not every bank is willing to offer an unsecured line of credit to a small, fast-growing company such as Finagle A Bagel.

Fortunately, the copresidents bought Finagle A Bagel after the previous owner (who stayed on for a time after the purchase) had built the business into a highly successful six-store chain. To a bank, a company with a proven record of success and a detailed, practical business plan for continued growth looks less risky as a borrower than a newly established company without customers, assets, or cash flow. Thus Finagle A Bagel was able to negotiate an unsecured line of credit of nearly $4 million. As long as Trust and Litchman could show that the company was healthy and achieving certain financial ratios, they would be allowed to draw on the credit line to open new stores or for other business purposes.

Initially, the copresidents only paid the interest on borrowed money so that they would have more money available for growth. Within a few years, however, they began repaying the principal as well as the interest. This meant less money to fuel growth, but it also lightened the company's debt load.

TWENTY STORES, THREE BANKS, TWO CHECKING ACCOUNTS

Even though Finagle A Bagel operates twenty stores plus a wholesale division, it needs only two corporate checking accounts. Here's how the system works. For safety reasons, management does not want general managers or their assistants traveling too far to deposit each day's receipts. Yet no single bank has a branch near every Finagle A Bagel store because the stores are spread throughout downtown Boston and the outlying suburbs. Therefore, the company deals with three New England banks that have local branches located near the stores. For each store, Finagle A Bagel opens an account in the closest branch of one of these three banks. After the day's deposits are made, money is transferred using an electronic funds transfer system to the company's main checking account.

Every morning, Litchman looks at the current balance in the main checking account and examines the report showing the previous day's sales and deposits. That tells him how much money he has to cover the bills to be paid that day. Given the slim profit margin in the food-service business—only pennies per sales dollar—Finagle A Bagel uses most of its cash to pay for food and labor. Clearly, cash flow is critical for a small, fast-growing business. Especially on slower sales days, Litchman observes, "You may be one check away from being cash-negative." If its main checking account balance is too low to cover checks that are presented for payment that day, the company may have to draw on its line of credit with the bank. Once this happens, the company must pay interest on any money it borrows, even for just a day.

Finagle A Bagel uses its second checking account only for payroll. This is a zero-balance account containing no money because its sole function is to clear payroll checks. Having two checking accounts allows the company to separate its payroll payments from its payments for supplies, rent, and other business expenses, a convenience for tax and accounting purposes. It also helps the copresidents maintain tight control over corporate finances: No check can be issued without either Litchman's or Trust's signature.

THE FUTURE OF FINAGLE A BAGEL

Looking ahead, the copresidents plan to continue growing the Finagle A Bagel brand and opening new stores. They are also working toward franchising their brand and fresh-food concept. Within a few years, however, the firm's future course could take a very different turn. "The opportunity to be bought by, just for an example, a McDonald's or a Wendy's or one of the larger operators becomes more plausible as you start to prove to people that you can survive as a multiunit chain with twenty or more stores," says Trust. Because big companies are always on the lookout for innovative food-service concepts, Finagle A Bagel's owners might receive an acquisition offer that's too good to pass up.

Even if the big companies have not yet noticed Finagle A Bagel's outstanding bagels and great performance, other people have. A few years ago the company was named Greater Boston's Small Business of the Year, and *Boston* magazine put it on the "Best of Boston" list for two consecutive years. As important and gratifying as such honors may be for a small business, money always must be—literally—the bottom line for Finagle A Bagel. "You have to make money," Trust emphasizes. "If you don't make money, you're not in business."

Questions

1. If the copresidents of Finagle A Bagel had approached venture capitalists for funding, they probably would have been able to open more new stores in less time. Instead, they opted to use bank financing that has to be repaid. Do you agree with their decision? Why?
2. Given their growth plans, why would the copresidents repay principal and interest on borrowed money rather than pay interest only? Which repayment plan would Finagle A Bagel's bank prefer?
3. Assuming that Finagle A Bagel decides to raise money through an IPO, what are the advantages and disadvantages of issuing stock to obtain the money needed to start or expand a business?
4. As an investor, would you be willing to buy shares in Finagle A Bagel? Explain why the company's stock would or would not be a good investment for you.

Building a Business Plan Part 7

BUILDING A BUSINESS PLAN

In this last section, provide some information about your exit strategy, and discuss any potential trends, problems, or risks that you may encounter. These risks and assumptions could relate to your industry, markets, company, or personnel. Make sure to incorporate important information not included in other parts of the business plan in an appendix. Now is also the time to go back and prepare the executive summary, which should be placed at the beginning of the business plan.

THE EXIT STRATEGY COMPONENT

Your exit strategy component should at least include answers to the following questions:

7.1. How do you intend to get yourself (and your money) out of the business?

7.2. Will your children take over the business, or do you intend to sell it later?

7.3. Do you intend to grow the business to the point of an IPO?

7.4. How will investors get their money back?

THE CRITICAL RISKS AND ASSUMPTIONS COMPONENT

Your critical risks and assumptions component should answer at least the following questions:

7.5. What will you do if your market does not develop as quickly as you predicted? What if your market develops too quickly?

7.6. What will you do if your competitors underprice or make your product obsolete?

7.7. What will you do if there is an unfavorable industrywide trend?

7.8. What will happen if trained workers are not available as predicted?

7.9. What will you do if there is an erratic supply of products or raw materials?

THE APPENDIX COMPONENT

Supplemental information and documents often are included in an appendix. Here are a few examples of some documents that can be included:

- Résumés of owners and principal managers
- Advertising samples and brochures
- An organization chart
- Floor plans

REVIEW OF BUSINESS PLAN ACTIVITIES

As you have discovered, writing a business plan involves a long series of interrelated steps. As with any project involving a number of complex steps and calculations, your business plan should be reviewed carefully and revised before you present it to potential investors.

Remember, there is one more component you need to prepare after your business plan is completed: The executive summary should be written last, but because of its importance, it appears after the introduction.

THE EXECUTIVE SUMMARY COMPONENT

In the executive summary, give a one- to two-page overview of your entire business plan. This is the most important part of the business plan and is of special interest to busy bankers, investors, and other interested parties. Remember, this section is a summary; more detailed information is provided in the remainder of your business plan.

Make sure that the executive summary captures the reader's attention instantly in the first sentence by using a key selling point or benefit of the business.

Your executive summary should include answers to at least the following:

7.10. *Company information.* What product or service do you provide? What is your competitive advantage? When will the company be formed? What are your company objectives? What is the background of you and your management team?

7.11. *Market opportunity.* What is the expected size and growth rate of your market, your expected market share, and any relevant market trends?

Once again, review your answers to all the questions in the preceding parts to make sure that they are all consistent throughout the entire business plan.

Although many would-be entrepreneurs are excited about the prospects of opening their own business, remember that it takes a lot of hard work, time, and in most cases a substantial amount of money. While the business plan provides an enormous amount of information about your business, it is only the first step. Once it is completed, it is now your responsibility to implement the plan. Good luck in your business venture.

The information contained in "Building a Business Plan" will also assist you in completing the online *Interactive Business Plan.*

Glossary

A

absolute advantage the ability to produce a specific product more efficiently than any other nation (74)

accessory equipment standardized equipment used in a firm's production or office activities (366)

acid-test ratio a financial ratio calculated by adding cash, marketable securities, and receivables and dividing the total by current liabilities (515)

accountability the obligation of a worker to accomplish an assigned job or task (196)

account executive an individual, sometimes called a stockbroker or registered representative, who buys and sells securities for clients (599)

accounting the process of systematically collecting, analyzing, and reporting financial information (495)

accounting equation the basis for the accounting process: assets = liabilities + owners' equity (501)

accounts receivable turnover a financial ratio calculated by dividing net sales by accounts receivable (515)

ad hoc committee a committee created for a specific short-term purpose (206)

administrative manager a manager who is not associated with any specific functional area but who provides overall administrative guidance and leadership (176)

advertising a paid, nonpersonal message communicated to a select audience through a mass medium (429)

advertising agency an independent firm that plans, produces, and places advertising for its clients (438)

advertising media the various forms of communication through which advertising reaches its audience (433)

affirmative action program a plan designed to increase the number of minority employees at all levels within an organization (57)

agency shop a workplace in which employees can choose not to join the union but must pay dues to the union anyway (325)

agent a middleman that expedites exchanges, represents a buyer or a seller, and often is hired permanently on a commission basis (406)

alien corporation a corporation chartered by a foreign government and conducting business in the United States (117)

analytical process a process in operations management in which raw materials are broken into different component parts (218)

annual report a report distributed to stockholders and other interested parties that describes a firm's operating activities and its financial condition (502)

arbitration the step in a grievance procedure in which a neutral third party hears the two sides of a dispute and renders a binding decision (327)

asset allocation the process of spreading your money among several different types of investments to lessen risk (603)

assets the resources that a business owns (501)

audit an examination of a company's financial statements and the accounting practices that produced them (496)

authoritarian leader one who holds all authority and responsibility, with communication usually moving from top to bottom (179)

authority the power, within an organization, to accomplish an assigned job or task (196)

automatic vending the use of machines to dispense products (414)

automation the total or near-total use of machines to do work (237)

B

balance of payments the total flow of money into a country minus the total flow of money out of that country over some period of time (74)

balance of trade the total value of a nation's exports minus the total value of its imports over some period of time (74)

balance sheet (or statement of financial position) a summary of the dollar amounts of a firm's assets, liabilities, and owners' equity accounts at the end of a specific accounting period (503)

banker's acceptance a written order for a bank to pay a third party a stated amount of money on a specific date (547)

bargaining unit the specific group of employees represented by a union (320)

barter a system of exchange in which goods or services are traded directly for other goods and/or services without using money (23)

barter system a system of exchange in which goods or services are traded directly for other goods or services (528)

behavior modification a systematic program of reinforcement to encourage desirable behavior (293)

bill of lading document issued by a transport carrier to an exporter to prove that merchandise has been shipped (88)

blue-chip stock a safe investment that generally attracts conservative investors (596)

board of directors the top governing body of a corporation, the members of which are elected by the stockholders (118)

bond indenture a legal document that details all the conditions relating to a bond issue (582)

boycott a refusal to do business with a particular firm (328)

brand a name, term, symbol, design, or any combination of these that identifies a seller's products as distinct from those of other sellers (374)

brand equity marketing and financial value associated with a brand's strength in a market (375)

brand extension using an existing brand to brand a new product in a different product category (377)
brand loyalty extent to which a customer is favorable toward buying a specific brand (375)
brand mark the part of a brand that is a symbol or distinctive design (374)
brand name the part of a brand that can be spoken (374)
breakeven quantity the number of units that must be sold for the total revenue (from all units sold) to equal the total cost (of all units sold) (384)
broadband technology a general term referring to higher-speed Internet connections that deliver data, voice, and video material (475)
broker a middleman that specializes in a particular commodity, represents either a buyer or a seller, and is likely to be hired on a temporary basis (406)
budget a financial statement that projects income and/or expenditures over a specified future period (568)
bundle pricing packaging together two or more complementary products and selling them for a single price (388)
bureaucratic structure a management system based on a formal framework of authority that is outlined carefully and followed precisely (201)
business the organized effort of individuals to produce and sell, for a profit, the products and services that satisfy society's needs (9)
business buying behavior the purchasing of products by producers, resellers, governmental units, and institutions (355)
business cycle the recurrence of periods of growth and recession in a nation's economic activity (18)
business ethics the application of moral standards to business situations (37)
business model represents a group of common characteristics and methods of doing business to generate sales revenues and reduce expenses (481)
business plan a carefully constructed guide for the person starting a business (147)
business product a product bought for resale, for making other products, or for use in a firm's operations (365)
business service an intangible product that an organization uses in its operations (366)
business-to-business (B2B) model a model used by firms that conduct business with other businesses (481)
business-to-consumer (B2C) model a model used by firms that focus on conducting business with individual buyers (483)
buying allowance a temporary price reduction to resellers for purchasing specified quantities of a product (446)
buying behavior the decisions and actions of people involved in buying and using products (355)
buying long buying stock with the expectation that it will increase in value and then can be sold at a profit (612)

C

capacity the amount of products or services that an organization can produce in a given time (225)
capital budget a financial statement that estimates a firm's expenditures for major assets and its long-term financing needs (5)
capital gain the difference between a security's purchase price and its selling price (605)
capital-intensive technology a process in which machines and equipment do most of the work (226)
capitalism an economic system in which individuals own and operate the majority of businesses that provide goods and services (12)
captioned photograph a picture accompanied by a brief explanation (447)
captive pricing pricing the basic product in a product line low, but pricing related items at a higher level (389)
carrier a firm that offers transportation services (418)
cash budget a financial statement that estimates cash receipts and cash expenditures over a specified period (568)
cash flow the movement of money into and out of an organization (563)
catalog marketing a type of marketing in which an organization provides a catalog from which customers make selections and place orders by mail, telephone, or the Internet (413)
catalog showroom a retail outlet that displays well-known brands and sells them at discount prices through catalogs within the store (408)
category killer a very large specialty store that concentrates on a single product line and competes on the basis of low prices and product availability (412)
caveat emptor a Latin phrase meaning "let the buyer beware" (50)
centralized organization an organization that systematically works to concentrate authority at the upper levels of the organization (197)
certificate of deposit (CD) a document stating that the bank will pay the depositor a guaranteed interest rate on money left on deposit for a specified period of time (542)
certified management accountant (CMA) an accountant who has met the requirements for education and experience, passed a rigorous exam, and is certified by the Institute of Management Accountants (501)
certified public accountant (CPA) an individual who has met state requirements for accounting education and experience and has passed a rigorous two-day accounting examination prepared by the AICPA (500)
chain of command the line of authority that extends from the highest to the lowest levels of an organization (191)
chain retailer a company that operates more than one retail outlet (407)
channel of distribution (or marketing channel) a sequence of marketing organizations that directs a product from the producer to the ultimate user (399)
check a written order for a bank or other financial institution to pay a stated dollar amount to the business or person indicated on the face of the check (541)
chief financial officer (CFO) a high-level corporate executive who manages a firm's finances and reports directly to the company's chief executive officer or president (566)
closed corporation a corporation whose stock is owned by relatively few people and is not sold to the general public (116)
closed shop a workplace in which workers must join the union before they are hired; outlawed by the Taft-Hartley Act (325)
cluster structure an organization that consists primarily of teams with no or very few underlying departments (203)
code of ethics a guide to acceptable and ethical behavior as defined by the organization (42)
collaborative learning system a work environment that allows problem-solving participation by all team members (472)
collateral real estate or property pledged as security for a loan (542)
collective bargaining the process of negotiating a labor contract with management (322)

command economy an economic system in which the government decides what goods and services will be produced, how they will be produced, for whom available goods and services will be produced, and who owns and controls the major factors of production (15)

commercial bank a profit-making organization that accepts deposits, makes loans, and provides related services to its customers (538)

commercial paper a short-term promissory note issued by a large corporation (573)

commission a payment that is a percentage of sales revenue (262)

commission merchant a middleman that carries merchandise and negotiates sales for manufacturers (406)

common stock stock whose owners may vote on corporate matters but whose claims on profits and assets are subordinate to the claims of others (118)

community shopping center a planned shopping center that includes one or two department stores and some specialty stores, along with convenience stores (416)

comparable worth a concept that seeks equal compensation for jobs requiring about the same level of education, training, and skills (261)

comparative advantage the ability to produce a specific product more efficiently than any other product (74)

comparison discounting setting a price at a specific level and comparing it with a higher price (390)

compensation the payment employees receive in return for their labor (260)

compensation system the policies and strategies that determine employee compensation (260)

competition rivalry among businesses for sales to potential customers (20)

component part an item that becomes part of a physical product and is either a finished item ready for assembly or a product that needs little processing before assembly (366)

computer-aided design (CAD) the use of computers to aid in the development of products (238)

computer-aided manufacturing (CAM) the use of computers to plan and control manufacturing processes (238)

computer-integrated manufacturing (CIM) a computer system that not only helps to design products but also controls the machinery needed to produce the finished product (238)

computer network a group of two or more computers linked together that allows users to share data and information (475)

conceptual skill the ability to think in abstract terms (177)

consumer buying behavior the purchasing of products for personal or household use, not for business purposes (355)

consumer price index (CPI) a monthly index that measures the changes in price of a fixed basket of goods purchased by a typical consumer in an urban area (18)

consumer products goods and services purchased by individuals for personal consumption (14, 365)

consumer sales promotion method a sales promotion method designed to attract consumers to particular retail stores and to motivate them to purchase certain new or established products (443)

consumerism all activities undertaken to protect the rights of consumers (53)

contingency plan a plan that outlines alternative courses of action that may be taken if an organization's other plans are disrupted or become ineffective (171)

continuous process a manufacturing process in which a firm produces the same product(s) over a long period of time (239)

controlling the process of evaluating and regulating ongoing activities to ensure that goals are achieved (172)

convenience product a relatively inexpensive, frequently purchased item for which buyers want to exert only minimal effort (365)

convenience store a small food store that sells a limited variety of products but remains open well beyond normal business hours (409)

convertible bond a bond that can be exchanged, at the owner's option, for a specified number of shares of the corporation's common stock (582)

convertible preferred stock preferred stock that an owner may exchange for a specified number of shares of common stock (576)

cooperative an association of individuals or firms whose purpose is to perform some business function for its members (124)

cooperative advertising an arrangement whereby a manufacturer agrees to pay a certain amount of a retailer's media cost for advertising the manufacturer's product (446)

corporate bond a corporation's written pledge that it will repay a specified amount of money with interest (581)

corporate culture the inner rites, rituals, heroes, and values of a firm (204)

corporate officers the chairman of the board, president, executive vice presidents, corporate secretary, treasurer, and any other top executive appointed by the board of directors (119)

corporation an artificial person created by law with most of the legal rights of a real person, including the rights to start and operate a business, to buy or sell property, to borrow money, to sue or be sued, and to enter into binding contracts (116)

cost of goods sold the dollar amount equal to beginning inventory plus net purchases less ending inventory (509)

countertrade an international barter transaction (91)

coupon reduces the retail price of a particular item by a stated amount at the time of purchase (444)

craft union an organization of skilled workers in a single craft or trade (311)

creative selling selling products to new customers and increasing sales to present customers (440)

credit immediate purchasing power that is exchanged for a promise to repay borrowed money, with or without interest, at a later date (549)

credit union a financial institution that accepts deposits from and lends money to only those people who are its members (539)

critical path the sequence of production activities that takes the longest time from start to finish (233)

cross-functional team a team of individuals with varying specialties, expertise, and skills that are brought together to achieve a common task (202, 299)

cultural (or workplace) diversity differences among people in a workforce owing to race, ethnicity, and gender (6, 254)

currency devaluation the reduction of the value of a nation's currency relative to the currencies of other countries (77)

current assets assets that can be converted quickly into cash or that will be used in one year or less (503)

current liabilities debts that will be repaid in one year or less (506)

current ratio a financial ratio computed by dividing current assets by current liabilities (514)

customary pricing pricing on the basis of tradition (389)

customer lifetime value a combination of purchase frequency, average value of purchases, and brand-switching patterns over the entire span of a customer's relationship with a company (340)

customer relationship management (CRM) using information about customers to create marketing strategies that develop and sustain desirable customer relationships (340)

D

data numerical or verbal descriptions that usually result from some sort of measurement (463)

data processing the transformation of data into a form that is useful for a specific purpose (468)

database a single collection of data stored in one place that can be used by people throughout an organization to make decisions (464)

debenture bond a bond backed only by the reputation of the issuing corporation (582)

debit card a card that electronically subtracts the amount of your purchase from your bank account at the moment the purchase is made (544)

debt capital borrowed money obtained through loans of various types (569)

debt-to-owners'-equity ratio a financial ratio calculated by dividing total liabilities by owners' equity (516)

decentralized organization an organization in which management consciously attempts to spread authority widely in the lower levels of the organization (197)

decision making the act of choosing one alternative from a set of alternatives (179)

decisional role a role that involves various aspects of management decision making (178)

decision-support system (DSS) a type of computer program that provides relevant data and information to help a firm's employees make decisions (471)

deflation a general decrease in the level of prices (17)

delegation assigning part of a manager's work and power to other workers (195)

demand the quantity of a product that buyers are willing to purchase at each of various prices (21, 380)

demand deposit an amount on deposit in a checking account (531)

democratic leader one who holds final responsibility but also delegates authority to others, who help to determine work assignments; communication is active upward and downward (179)

department store a retail store that (1) employs twenty-five or more persons and (2) sells at least home furnishings, appliances, family apparel, and household linens and dry goods, each in a different part of the store (407)

departmentalization the process of grouping jobs into manageable units (194)

departmentalization by customer grouping activities according to the needs of various customer populations (195)

departmentalization by function grouping jobs that relate to the same organizational activity (195)

departmentalization by location grouping activities according to the defined geographic area in which they are performed (195)

departmentalization by product grouping activities related to a particular product or service (195)

depreciation the process of apportioning the cost of a fixed asset over the period during which it will be used (505)

depression a severe recession that lasts longer than a recession (20)

design planning the development of a plan for converting a product idea into an actual product or service (224)

direct marketing the use of the telephone, Internet, and nonpersonal media to introduce products to customers, who then can purchase them via mail, telephone, or the Internet (413)

direct selling the marketing of products to customers through face-to-face sales presentations at home or in the workplace (412)

directing the combined processes of leading and motivating (172)

direct-mail advertising promotional material mailed directly to individuals (433)

direct-response marketing a type of marketing in which a retailer advertises a product and makes it available through mail, telephone, or online orders (413)

discount a deduction from the price of an item (391)

discount rate the interest rate the Federal Reserve System charges for loans to member banks (535)

discount store a self-service general-merchandise outlet that sells products at lower-than-usual prices (408)

discretionary income disposable income less savings and expenditures on food, clothing, and housing (357)

discretionary order an order to buy or sell a security that lets the broker decide when to execute the transaction and at what price (600)

disposable income personal income less all additional personal taxes (357)

dividend a distribution of earnings to the stockholders of a corporation (118)

domestic corporation a corporation in the state in which it is incorporated (117)

domestic system a method of manufacturing in which an entrepreneur distributes raw materials to various homes, where families process them into finished goods to be offered for sale by the merchant entrepreneur (24)

double-entry bookkeeping system a system in which each financial transaction is recorded as two separate accounting entries to maintain the balance shown in the accounting equation (501)

draft issued by the exporter's bank, ordering the importer's bank to pay for the merchandise, thus guaranteeing payment once accepted by the importer's bank (88)

dumping exportation of large quantities of a product at a price lower than that of the same product in the home market (77)

E

earnings per share a financial ratio calculated by dividing net income after taxes by the number of shares of common stock outstanding (513)

e-business (electronic business) the organized effort of individuals to produce and sell, for a profit, the goods and services that satisfy society's needs through the facilities available on the Internet (26, 477)

economic community an organization of nations formed to promote the free movement of resources and products among its members and to create common economic policies (85)

economic model of social responsibility the view that society will benefit most when business is left alone to produce and market profitable products that society needs (51)

Economic Stabilization Act a $700 billion bailout plan created to stabilize the nation's economy and restore confidence in the banking and financial industries (4)

economics the study of how wealth is created and distributed (11)

economy the way in which people deal with the creation and distribution of wealth (11)

electronic check conversion (ECC) a process used to convert information from a paper check into an electronic payment for merchandise, services, or bills (546)

electronic funds transfer (EFT) system a means of performing financial transactions through a computer terminal or telephone hookup (546)

embargo a complete halt to trading with a particular nation or in a particular product (77)

employee benefit a reward in addition to regular compensation that is provided indirectly to employees (262)

employee ownership a situation in which employees own the company they work for by virtue of being stockholders (297)

employee training the process of teaching operations and technical employees how to do their present jobs more effectively and efficiently (264)

empowerment making employees more involved in their jobs by increasing their participation in decision making (296)

entrepreneur a person who risks time, effort, and money to start and operate a business (12)

Equal Employment Opportunity Commission (EEOC) a government agency with power to investigate complaints of employment discrimination and power to sue firms that practice it (58)

equity capital money received from the owners or from the sale of shares of ownership in a business (569)

equity theory a theory of motivation based on the premise that people are motivated to obtain and preserve equitable treatment for themselves (289)

esteem needs our need for respect, recognition, and a sense of our own accomplishment and worth (284)

ethics the study of right and wrong and of the morality of the choices individuals make (37)

everyday low prices (EDLPs) setting a low price for products on a consistent basis (389)

exclusive distribution the use of only a single retail outlet for a product in a large geographic area (401)

executive information system (EIS) a computer-based system that facilitates and supports the decision-making needs of top managers and senior executives by providing easy access to both internal and external information (472)

expectancy theory a model of motivation based on the assumption that motivation depends on how much we want something and on how likely we think we are to get it (289)

expert system a type of computer program that uses artificial intelligence to imitate a human's ability to think (472)

Export-Import Bank of the United States an independent agency of the U.S. government whose function it is to assist in financing the exports of American firms (93)

exporting selling and shipping raw materials or products to other nations (74)

express warranty a written explanation of the responsibilities of the producer in the event that a product is found to be defective or otherwise unsatisfactory (380)

external recruiting the attempt to attract job applicants from outside an organization (256)

F

factor a firm that specializes in buying other firms' accounts receivable (574)

factors of production resources used to produce goods and services (11)

factory system a system of manufacturing in which all the materials, machinery, and workers required to manufacture a product are assembled in one place (25)

family branding the strategy in which a firm uses the same brand for all or most of its products (377)

family of funds a group of mutual funds managed by one investment company (611)

feature article a piece (of up to 3,000 words) prepared by an organization for inclusion in a particular publication (447)

federal deficit a shortfall created when the federal government spends more in a fiscal year than it receives (20)

federal funds rate the interest rate at which a bank lends immediately available funds to another bank overnight in order to meet the borrowing bank's reserve requirements (535)

Federal Reserve System the central bank of the United States responsible for regulating the banking industry (533)

financial accounting generates financial statements and reports for interested people outside an organization (499)

financial leverage the use of borrowed funds to increase the return on owners' equity (579)

financial management all the activities concerned with obtaining money and using it effectively (563)

financial manager a manager who is primarily responsible for an organization's financial resources (175)

financial plan a plan for obtaining and using the money needed to implement an organization's goals (567)

financial planner an individual who has had at least two years of training in investments, insurance, taxation, retirement planning, and estate planning and has passed a rigorous examination (595)

financial ratio a number that shows the relationship between two elements of a firm's financial statements (513)

first-line manager a manager who coordinates and supervises the activities of operating employees (174)

fiscal policy government influence on the amount of savings and expenditures; accomplished by altering the tax structure and by changing the levels of government spending (20)

fixed assets assets that will be held or used for a period longer than one year (505)

fixed cost a cost incurred no matter how many units of a product are produced or sold (384)

flexible benefit plan compensation plan whereby an employee receives a predetermined amount of benefit dollars to spend on a package of benefits he or she has selected to meet individual needs (263)

flexible manufacturing system (FMS) a single production system that combines robotics and computer integrated manufacturing (239)

flextime a system in which employees set their own work hours within employer-determined limits (294)

floor planning method of financing in which title to merchandise is given to lenders in return for short-term financing (574)

foreign corporation a corporation in any state in which it does business except the one in which it is incorporated (117)

foreign-exchange control a restriction on the amount of a particular foreign currency that can be purchased or sold (77)

form utility utility created by converting raw materials, finances, and information into finished products (218, 341)

franchise a license to operate an individually owned business as though it were part of a chain of outlets or stores (152)

franchisee a person or organization purchasing a franchise (152)

franchising the actual granting of a franchise (152)

franchisor an individual or organization granting a franchise (152)

free enterprise the system of business in which individuals are free to decide what to produce, how to produce it, and at what price to sell it (4)

frequent-user incentive a program developed to reward customers who engage in repeat (frequent) purchases (445)

full disclosure requirement that investors should have access to all important facts about stocks, bonds, and other securities so that they can make informed decisions (602)

full-service wholesaler a middleman that performs the entire range of wholesaler functions (406)

functional middleman a middleman that helps in the transfer of ownership of products but does not take title to the products (399)

G

Gantt chart a graphic scheduling device that displays the tasks to be performed on the vertical axis and the time required for each task on the horizontal axis (232)

General Agreement on Tariffs and Trade (GATT) an international organization of 153 nations dedicated to reducing or eliminating tariffs and other barriers to world trade (83)

general partner a person who assumes full or shared responsibility for operating a business (111)

general partnership a business co-owned by two or more general partners who are liable for everything the business does (111)

generally accepted accounting principles (GAAPs) an accepted set of guidelines and practices for companies reporting financial information and for the accounting profession (497)

general-merchandise wholesaler a middleman that deals in a wide variety of products (406)

generic product (or brand) a product with no brand at all (375)

goal an end result that an organization is expected to achieve over a one- to ten-year period (169)

goal-setting theory a theory of motivation suggesting that employees are motivated to achieve goals that they and their managers establish together (290)

government-owned corporation a corporation owned and operated by a local, state, or federal government (123)

grapevine the informal communications network within an organization (207)

grievance procedure a formally established course of action for resolving employee complaints against management (326)

gross domestic product (GDP) the total dollar value of all goods and services produced by all people within the boundaries of a country during a one-year period (17)

gross profit a firm's net sales less the cost of goods sold (509)

gross sales the total dollar amount of all goods and services sold during an accounting period (507)

groupware one of the latest types of software that facilitates the management of large projects among geographically dispersed employees, as well as such group activities as problem solving and brainstorming (472)

H

hard-core unemployed workers with little education or vocational training and a long history of unemployment (58)

high-risk investment an investment made in the uncertain hope of earning a relatively large profit in a short time (598)

hostile takeover a situation in which the management and board of directors of a firm targeted for acquisition disapprove of the merger (126)

hourly wage a specific amount of money paid for each hour of work (262)

human resources management (HRM) all the activities involved in acquiring, maintaining, and developing an organization's human resources (250)

human resources manager a person charged with managing an organization's human resources programs (175)

human resources planning the development of strategies to meet a firm's future human resources needs (251)

hygiene factors job factors that reduce dissatisfaction when present to an acceptable degree but that do not necessarily result in high levels of motivation (285)

I

import duty (tariff) a tax levied on a particular foreign product entering a country (76)

import quota a limit on the amount of a particular good that may be imported into a country during a given period of time (77)

importing purchasing raw materials or products in other nations and bringing them into one's own country (74)

incentive payment a payment in addition to wages, salary, or commissions (262)

income statement a summary of a firm's revenues and expenses during a specified accounting period (507)

independent retailer a firm that operates only one retail outlet (407)

individual branding the strategy in which a firm uses a different brand for each of its products (377)

industrial union an organization of both skilled and unskilled workers in a single industry (312)

inflation a general rise in the level of prices (17)

infomercial a program-length televised commercial message resembling an entertainment or consumer affairs program (435)

informal group a group created by the members themselves to accomplish goals that may or may not be relevant to an organization (207)

informal organization the pattern of behavior and interaction that stems from personal rather than official relationships (207)

information data presented in a form that is useful for a specific purpose (463)

information society a society in which large groups of employees generate or depend on information to perform their jobs (474)

information technology (IT) officer a manager at the executive level who is responsible for ensuring that a firm has the equipment necessary to provide the information the firm's employees and managers need to make effective decisions (462)

informational role a role in which the manager either gathers or provides information (178)

initial public offering (IPO) when a corporation sells common stock to the general public for the first time (575)

injunction a court order requiring a person or group either to perform some act or to refrain from performing some act (318)

insider trading the practice of board members, corporate managers, and employees buying and selling a corporation's stock (600)

inspection an examination of the quality of work in process (234)

institutional advertising advertising designed to enhance a firm's image or reputation (432)

intangible assets assets that do not exist physically but that have a value based on the rights or privileges they confer on a firm (505)

integrated marketing communications coordination of promotion efforts to ensure maximal informational and persuasive impact on customers (429)

intensive distribution the use of all available outlets for a product (401)

intermittent process a manufacturing process in which a firm's manufacturing machines and equipment are changed to produce different products (239)

internal recruiting considering present employees as applicants for available positions (256)

international business all business activities that involve exchanges across national boundaries (73)

International Monetary Fund (IMF) an international bank with 184 member nations that makes short-term loans to developing countries experiencing balance-of-payment deficits (95)

International Organization for Standardization a nongovernmental organization in Geneva, Switzerland, with a membership of 157 countries that develops standards for products in order to facilitate trade across national borders (235)

Internet a worldwide network of computers linked through telecommunications (474)

Internet service providers (ISPs) provide customers with a connection to the Internet through various phone plugs and cables (474)

interpersonal role a role in which the manager deals with people (178)

interpersonal skill the ability to deal effectively with other people (177)

intranet a smaller version of the Internet for use within a firm's computer network (475)

intrapreneur an employee who pushes an innovative idea, product, or process through an organization (206)

inventory control the process of managing inventories in such a way as to minimize inventory costs, including both holding costs and potential stock-out costs (231)

inventory management the process of managing inventories in such a way as to minimize inventory costs, including both holding costs and potential stock-out costs (417)

inventory turnover a financial ratio calculated by dividing the cost of goods sold in one year by the average value of the inventory (515)

investment banking firm an organization that assists corporations in raising funds, usually by helping to sell new issues of stocks, bonds, or other financial securities (576)

invisible hand a term created by Adam Smith to describe how an individual's own personal gain benefits others and a nation's economy (12)

J

job analysis a systematic procedure for studying jobs to determine their various elements and requirements (255)

job description a list of the elements that make up a particular job (255)

job enlargement expanding a worker's assignments to include additional but similar tasks (292)

job enrichment a motivation technique that provides employees with more variety and responsibility in their jobs (292)

job evaluation the process of determining the relative worth of the various jobs within a firm (261)

job redesign a type of job enrichment in which work is restructured to cultivate the worker-job match (293)

job rotation the systematic shifting of employees from one job to another (194)

job security protection against the loss of employment (325)

job sharing an arrangement whereby two people share one full-time position (295)

job specialization the separation of all organizational activities into distinct tasks and the assignment of different tasks to different people (193, 253)

job specification a list of the qualifications required to perform a particular job (255)

joint venture an agreement between two or more groups to form a business entity in order to achieve a specific goal or to operate for a specific period of time (124)

jurisdiction the right of a particular union to organize particular groups of workers (320)

just-in-time inventory system a system designed to ensure that materials or supplies arrive at a facility just when they are needed so that storage and holding costs are minimized (231)

K

knowledge management (KM) a firm's procedures for generating, using, and sharing the data and information contained in the firm's databases (464)

L

labeling the presentation of information on a product or its package (379)

labor-intensive technology a process in which people must do most of the work (226)

labor union an organization of workers acting together to negotiate their wages and working conditions with employers (310)

laissez-faire leader one who gives authority to employees and allows subordinates to work as they choose with a minimum of interference; communication flows horizontally among group members (179)

leadership the ability to influence others (178)

leading the process of influencing people to work toward a common goal (172)

lease an agreement by which the right to use real estate, equipment, or other assets is transferred temporarily from the owner to the user (580)

letter of credit issued by a bank on request of an importer stating that the bank will pay an amount of money to a stated beneficiary (88, 546)

leveraged buyout (LBO) a purchase arrangement that allows a firm's managers and employees or a group of investors to purchase the company (128)

liabilities a firm's debts and obligations (501)

licensing a contractual agreement in which one firm permits another to produce and market its product and use its brand name in return for a royalty or other compensation (87)

lifestyle shopping center an open-air-environment shopping center with upscale chain specialty stores (415)

limit order a request that a security be bought or sold at a price that is equal to or better than some specified price (600)

limited liability a feature of corporate ownership that limits each owner's financial liability to the amount of money that he or she has paid for the corporation's stock (120)

limited partner a person who contributes capital to a business but has no management responsibility or liability for losses beyond the amount he or she invested in the partnership (112)

limited partnership a business co-owned by one or more general partners who manage the business and limited partners who invest money in it (112)

limited-liability company (LLC) a form of business ownership that combines the benefits of a corporation and a partnership while avoiding some of the restrictions and disadvantages of those forms of ownership (122)

limited-line wholesaler a middleman that stocks only a few product lines but carries numerous product items within each line (406)

limited-service wholesaler a middleman that assumes responsibility for a few wholesale services only (406)

line extension development of a new product that is closely related to one or more products in the existing product line but designed specifically to meet different customer needs (370)

line management position a part of the chain of command; a position in which a person makes decisions and gives orders to subordinates to achieve the goals of the organization (199)

line of credit a loan that is approved before the money is actually needed (542)

liquidity the ease with which an asset can be converted into cash (503, 597)

local-area network (LAN) a network that connects computers that are in close proximity to each other, such as in an office building or on a college campus (475)

lockout a firm's refusal to allow employees to enter the workplace (329)

log-file records files that store a record of the websites visited (130)

long-term financing money that will be used for longer than one year (562)

long-term liabilities debts that need not be repaid for at least one year (506)

lump-sum salary increase an entire pay raise taken in one lump sum (262)

M

macroeconomics the study of the national economy and the global economy (11)

maintenance shop a workplace in which an employee who joins the union must remain a union member as long as he or she is employed by the firm (325)

major equipment large tools and machines used for production purposes (366)

Malcolm Baldrige National Quality Award an award given by the President of the United States to organizations that apply and that are judged to be outstanding in specific managerial tasks that lead to improved quality for both products and services (233)

management the process of coordinating people and other resources to achieve the goals of an organization (167)

management by objectives (MBO) a motivation technique in which managers and employees collaborate in setting goals (290)

management development the process of preparing managers and other professionals to assume increased responsibility in both present and future positions (264)

management information system (MIS) a system that provides managers and employees with the information they need to perform their jobs as effectively as possible (464)

managerial accounting provides managers and employees with the information needed to make decisions about a firm's financing, investing, and operating activities (499)

managerial hierarchy the arrangement that provides increasing authority at higher levels of management (207)

manufacturer (or producer) brand a brand that is owned by a manufacturer (374)

manufacturer's sales branch essentially a merchant wholesaler that is owned by a manufacturer (407)

manufacturer's sales office essentially a sales agent owned by a manufacturer (407)

margin requirement the portion of the price of a stock that cannot be borrowed (613)

market a group of individuals or organizations, or both, that need products in a given category and that have the ability, willingness, and authority to purchase such products (344)

market economy an economic system in which businesses and individuals decide what to produce and buy, and the market determines quantities sold and prices (13)

market order a request that a security be purchased or sold at the current market price (600)

market price the price at which the quantity demanded is exactly equal to the quantity supplied (21)

market segment a group of individuals or organizations within a market that shares one or more common characteristics (346)

market segmentation the process of dividing a market into segments and directing a marketing mix at a particular segment or segments rather than at the total market (346)

market value the price of one share of a stock at a particular time (607)

marketing the activity, set of institutions, and processes for creating, communicating, delivering, and exchanging offerings that have value for customers, clients, partners, and society at large (339)

marketing concept a business philosophy that a firm should provide goods and services that satisfy customers' needs through a coordinated set of activities that allows the firm to achieve its objectives (342)

marketing information system a system for managing marketing information that is gathered continually from internal and external sources (352)

marketing manager a manager who is responsible for facilitating the exchange of products between an organization and its customers or clients (175)

marketing mix a combination of product, price, distribution, and promotion developed to satisfy a particular target market (345)

marketing plan a written document that specifies an organization's resources, objectives, strategy, and implementation and control efforts to be used in marketing a specific product or product group (350)

marketing research the process of systematically gathering, recording, and analyzing data concerning a particular marketing problem (352)

marketing strategy a plan that will enable an organization to make the best use of its resources and advantages to meet its objectives (345)

markup the amount a seller adds to the cost of a product to determine its basic selling price (384)

Maslow's hierarchy of needs a sequence of human needs in the order of their importance (283)

mass production a manufacturing process that lowers the cost required to produce a large number of identical or similar products over a long period of time (218)

master limited partnership (MLP) a business partnership that is owned and managed like a corporation but often taxed like a partnership (112)

materials handling the actual physical handling of goods, in warehouses as well as during transportation (418)

materials requirements planning (MRP) a computerized system that integrates production planning and inventory control (231)

matrix structure an organizational structure that combines vertical and horizontal lines of authority, usually by superimposing product departmentalization on a functionally departmentalized organization (202)

maturity date the date on which a corporation is to repay borrowed money (581)

measure of value a single standard, or "yardstick," used to assign values to and compare the values of products, services, and resources (529)

mediation the use of a neutral third party to assist management and the union during their negotiations (329)

medium of exchange anything accepted as payment for products, services, and resources (529)

merchant middleman a middleman that actually takes title to products by buying them (399)

merchant wholesaler a middleman that purchases goods in large quantities and then sells them to other wholesalers or retailers and to institutional, farm, government, professional, or industrial users (406)

merger the purchase of one corporation by another (126)

microeconomics the study of the decisions made by individuals and businesses (11)

middle manager a manager who implements the strategy and major policies developed by top management (174)

middleman (or marketing intermediary) a marketing organization that links a producer and user within a marketing channel (399)

minority a racial, religious, political, national, or other group regarded as different from the larger group of which it is a part and that is often singled out for unfavorable treatment (57)

mission a statement of the basic purpose that makes an organization different from others (169)

missionary salesperson a salesperson—generally employed by a manufacturer—who visits retailers to persuade them to buy the manufacturer's products (441)

mixed economy an economy that exhibits elements of both capitalism and socialism (13)

monetary policies Federal Reserve decisions that determine the size of the supply of money in the nation and the level of interest rates (20)

money anything a society uses to purchase products, services, or resources (528)

monopolistic competition a market situation in which there are many buyers along with a relatively large number of sellers who differentiate their products from the products of competitors (22)

monopoly a market (or industry) with only one seller (23)

morale an employee's feelings about his or her job, superiors, and the firm itself (281)

mortgage bond a corporate bond secured by various assets of the issuing firm (580)

motivating the process of providing reasons for people to work in the best interests of an organization (172)

motivation the individual internal process that energizes, directs, and sustains behavior; the personal "force" that causes you or me to behave in a particular way (280)

motivation factors job factors that increase motivation but whose absence does not necessarily result in dissatisfaction (285)

motivation-hygiene theory the idea that satisfaction and dissatisfaction are separate and distinct dimensions (285)

multilateral development bank (MDB) an internationally supported bank that provides loans to developing countries to help them grow (93)

multinational enterprise a firm that operates on a worldwide scale without ties to any specific nation or region (91)

multiple-unit pricing the strategy of setting a single price for two or more units (388)

municipal bond sometimes called a *muni*—a debt security issued by a state or local government (607)

mutual fund a company that pools the money of many investors—its shareholders—to invest in a variety of different securities (609)

N

Nasdaq computerized electronic exchange system through which most over-the-counter securities are traded (599)

National Alliance of Business (NAB) a joint business government program to train the hard-core unemployed (59)

national bank a commercial bank chartered by the U.S. Comptroller of the Currency (538)

national debt the total of all federal deficits (20)

National Labor Relations Board (NLRB) the federal agency that enforces the provisions of the Wagner Act (318)

natural monopoly an industry requiring huge investments in capital and within which any duplication of facilities would be wasteful and thus not in the public interest (23)

need a personal requirement (283)

negotiated pricing establishing a final price through bargaining (387)

neighborhood shopping center a planned shopping center consisting of several small convenience and specialty stores (416)

net asset value (NAV) current market value of a mutual fund's portfolio minus the mutual fund's liabilities and divided by the number of outstanding shares (609)

net income occurs when revenues exceed expenses (509)

net loss occurs when expenses exceed revenues (509)

net sales the actual dollar amount received by a firm for the goods and services it has sold after adjustment for returns, allowances, and discounts (508)

network structure an organization in which administration is the primary function, and most other functions are contracted out to other firms (204)

news release a typed page of about 300 words provided by an organization to the media as a form of publicity (447)

nonprice competition competition based on factors other than price (381)

nonstore retailing a type of retailing whereby consumers purchase products without visiting a store (412)

nontariff barrier a nontax measure imposed by a government to favor domestic over foreign suppliers (77)

not-for-profit corporation a corporation organized to provide a social, educational, religious, or other service rather than to earn a profit (124)

NOW account an interest-bearing checking account; NOW stands for *negotiable order of withdrawal* (542)

O

objective a specific statement detailing what an organization intends to accomplish over a short period of time (169)

odd-number pricing the strategy of setting prices using odd numbers that are slightly below whole-dollar amounts (388)

off-price retailer a store that buys manufacturers' seconds, overruns, returns, and off-season merchandise for resale to consumers at deep discounts (411)
oligopoly a market (or industry) in which there are few sellers (22)
online retailing retailing that makes products available to buyers through computer connections (414)
open corporation a corporation whose stock can be bought and sold by any individual (116)
open-market operations the buying and selling of U.S. government securities by the Federal Reserve System for the purpose of controlling the supply of money (535)
operating expenses all business costs other than the cost of goods sold (509)
operational plan a type of plan designed to implement tactical plans (171)
operations management all activities managers engage in to produce goods and services (217)
operations manager a manager who manages the systems that convert resources into goods and services (175)
order getter a salesperson who is responsible for selling a firm's products to new customers and increasing sales to present customers (440)
order processing activities involved in receiving and filling customers' purchase orders (417)
order taker a salesperson who handles repeat sales in ways that maintain positive relationships with customers (440)
organization a group of two or more people working together to achieve a common set of goals (191)
organization chart a diagram that represents the positions and relationships within an organization (191)
organizational height the number of layers, or levels, of management in a firm (199)
organizing the grouping of resources and activities to accomplish some end result in an efficient and effective manner (171)
orientation the process of acquainting new employees with an organization (260)
out-of-home advertising short promotional messages on billboards, posters, signs, and transportation vehicles (434)
outsourcing the process of finding outside vendors and suppliers that provide professional help, parts, or materials at a lower cost (479)
over-the-counter (OTC) market a network of dealers who buy and sell the stocks of corporations that are not listed on a securities exchange (599)
overtime time worked in excess of forty hours in one week (under some union contracts, time worked in excess of eight hours in a single day) (325)
owners' equity the difference between a firm's assets and its liabilities (501)

P

packaging all the activities involved in developing and providing a container with graphics for a product (377)
partnership a voluntary association of two or more persons to act as co-owners of a business for profit (111)
part-time work permanent employment in which individuals work less than a standard work week (294)
par value an assigned (and often arbitrary) dollar value printed on a stock certificate (577)
penetration pricing the strategy of setting a low price for a new product (387)
perfect (or pure) competition the market situation in which there are many buyers and sellers of a product, and no single buyer or seller is powerful enough to affect the price of that product (20)
performance appraisal the evaluation of employees' current and potential levels of performance to allow managers to make objective human resources decisions (265)
periodic discounting temporary reduction of prices on a patterned or systematic basis (388)
personal budget a specific plan for spending your income (593)
personal income the income an individual receives from all sources less the Social Security taxes the individual must pay (357)
personal investment the use of personal funds to earn a financial return (594)
personal selling personal communication aimed at informing customers and persuading them to buy a firm's products (431)
PERT (Program Evaluation and Review Technique) a scheduling technique that identifies the major activities necessary to complete a project and sequences them based on the time required to perform each one (233)
physical distribution all those activities concerned with the efficient movement of products from the producer to the ultimate user (416)
physiological needs the things we require for survival (283)
picketing marching back and forth in front of a place of employment with signs informing the public that a strike is in progress (327)
piece-rate system a compensation system under which employees are paid a certain amount for each unit of output they produce (282)
place utility utility created by making a product available at a location where customers wish to purchase it (341)
plan an outline of the actions by which an organization intends to accomplish its goals and objectives (170)
planning establishing organizational goals and deciding how to accomplish them (169)
planning horizon the period during which an operational plan will be in effect (228)
plant layout the arrangement of machinery, equipment, and personnel within a production facility (227)
point-of-purchase display promotional material placed within a retail store (445)
pollution the contamination of water, air, or land through the actions of people in an industrialized society (59)
positioning the development of a product image in buyers' minds relative to the images they have of competing products (449)
possession utility utility created by transferring title (or ownership) of a product to a buyer (341)
preferred stock stock owned by individuals or firms who usually do not have voting rights but whose claims on dividends are paid before those of common-stock owners (118)
premium a gift that a producer offers a customer in return for buying its product (445)
premium pricing pricing the highest-quality or most versatile products higher than other models in the product line (389)
press conference a meeting at which invited media personnel hear important news announcements and receive supplementary textual materials and photographs (447)
price the amount of money a seller is willing to accept in exchange for a product at a given time and under given circumstances (380)
price competition an emphasis on setting a price equal to or lower than competitors' prices to gain sales or market share (381)

price leaders products priced below the usual markup, near cost, or below cost (390)
price lining the strategy of selling goods only at certain predetermined prices that reflect definite price breaks (389)
price skimming the strategy of charging the highest possible price for a product during the introduction stage of its life cycle (387)
primary-demand advertising advertising whose purpose is to increase the demand for all brands of a product within a specific industry (432)
primary market a market in which an investor purchases financial securities (via an investment bank) directly from the issuer of those securities (598)
prime interest rate the lowest rate charged by a bank for a short-term loan (572)
private placement occurs when stock and other corporate securities are sold directly to insurance companies, pension funds, or large institutional investors (579)
problem the discrepancy between an actual condition and a desired condition (180)
problem-solving team a team of knowledgeable employees brought together to tackle a specific problem (298)
process material a material that is used directly in the production of another product but is not readily identifiable in the finished product (366)
producer price index (PPI) an index that measures prices at the wholesale level (18)
product everything one receives in an exchange, including all tangible and intangible attributes and expected benefits; it may be a good, service, or idea (364)
product deletion the elimination of one or more products from a product line (370)
product design the process of creating a set of specifications from which a product can be produced (225)
product differentiation the process of developing and promoting differences between one's products and all similar products (22, 381)
product life cycle a series of stages in which a product's sales revenue and profit increase, reach a peak, and then decline (366)
product line a group of similar products that differ only in relatively minor characteristics (224, 369)
product mix all the products a firm offers for sale (369)
product modification the process of changing one or more of a product's characteristics (370)
productivity the average level of output per worker per hour (16, 236)
profit what remains after all business expenses have been deducted from sales revenue (10)
profit sharing the distribution of a percentage of a firm's profit among its employees (262)
promissory note a written pledge by a borrower to pay a certain sum of money to a creditor at a specified future date (572)
promotion communication about an organization and its products that is intended to inform, persuade, or remind target-market members (428)
promotion mix the particular combination of promotion methods a firm uses to reach a target market (428)
promotional campaign a plan for combining and using the four promotional methods—advertising, personal selling, sales promotion, and publicity—in a particular promotion mix to achieve one or more marketing goals (448)
prospectus a detailed, written description of a new security, the issuing corporation, and the corporation's top management (602)
proxy a legal form listing issues to be decided at a stockholders' meeting and enabling stockholders to transfer their voting rights to some other individual or individuals (118)
proxy fight a technique used to gather enough stockholder votes to control a targeted company (126)
public relations communication activities used to create and maintain favorable relations between an organization and various public groups, both internal and external (431)
publicity communication in news-story form about an organization, its products, or both (446)
purchasing all the activities involved in obtaining required materials, supplies, components, and parts from other firms (229)

Q

quality circle a team of employees who meet on company time to solve problems of product quality (235)
quality control the process of ensuring that goods and services are produced in accordance with design specifications (234)

R

random discounting temporary reduction of prices on an unsystematic basis (388)
rate of return the total dollar amount of return you receive on an investment over a specific period of time divided by the amount invested (596)
ratification approval of a labor contract by a vote of the union membership (322)
raw material a basic material that actually becomes part of a physical product; usually comes from mines, forests, oceans, or recycled solid wastes (366)
rebate a return of part of the purchase price of a product (444)
recession two or more consecutive three-month periods of decline in a country's GDP (19)
recruiting the process of attracting qualified job applicants (255)
reference pricing pricing a product at a moderate level and positioning it next to a more expensive model or brand (388)
regional shopping center a planned shopping center containing large department stores, numerous specialty stores, restaurants, movie theaters, and sometimes even hotels (416)
registered bond a bond registered in the owner's name by the issuing company (582)
reinforcement theory a theory of motivation based on the premise that behavior that is rewarded is likely to be repeated, whereas behavior that is punished is less likely to recur (287)
relationship marketing establishing long-term, mutually satisfying buyer-seller relationships (340)
replacement chart a list of key personnel and their possible replacements within a firm (252)
research and development (R&D) a set of activities intended to identify new ideas that have the potential to result in new goods and services (222)
reserve requirement the percentage of its deposits a bank must retain, either in its own vault or on deposit with its Federal Reserve district bank (533)
responsibility the duty to do a job or perform a task (196)
retailer a middleman that buys from producers or other middlemen and sells to consumers (399)
retained earnings the portion of a business's profits not distributed to stockholders (506, 578)

return on owners' equity a financial ratio calculated by dividing net income after taxes by owners' equity (513)

return on sales (or profit margin) a financial ratio calculated by dividing net income after taxes by net sales (513)

revenue stream a source of revenue flowing into a firm (480)

revenues the dollar amounts earned by a firm from selling goods, providing services, or performing business activities (507)

revolving credit agreement a guaranteed line of credit (542)

risk-return ratio a ratio based on the principle that a high-risk decision should generate higher financial returns for a business, and that more conservative decisions often generate lesser returns (565)

robotics the use of programmable machines to perform a variety of tasks by manipulating materials and tools (237)

S

safety needs the things we require for physical and emotional security (284)

salary a specific amount of money paid for an employee's work during a set calendar period, regardless of the actual number of hours worked (262)

sales forecast an estimate of the amount of a product that an organization expects to sell during a certain period of time based on a specified level of marketing effort (351)

sales promotion the use of activities or materials as direct inducements to customers or salespersons (431)

sales support personnel employees who aid in selling, but who are more involved in locating prospects, educating customers, building goodwill for the firm, and providing follow-up service (441)

sample a free product given to customers to encourage trial and purchase (445)

Sarbanes-Oxley Act of 2002 provides sweeping new legal protection for employees who report corporate misconduct (41)

savings and loan association (S&L) a financial institution that offers checking and savings accounts and CDs, and that invests most of its assets in home mortgage loans and other consumer loans (538)

scheduling the process of ensuring that materials and other resources are at the right place at the right time (231)

scientific management the application of scientific principles to management of work and workers (282)

secondary market a market for existing financial securities that are traded between investors (598)

secondary-market pricing setting one price for the primary target market and a different price for another market (387)

S-corporation a corporation that is taxed as though it were a partnership (122)

securities exchange a marketplace where member brokers meet to buy and sell securities (599)

security average (or security index) an average of the current market prices of selected securities (619)

selection the process of gathering information about applicants for a position and then using that information to choose the most appropriate applicant (256)

selective distribution the use of only a portion of the available outlets for a product in each geographic area (401)

selective-demand (or brand) advertising advertising that is used to sell a particular brand of product (432)

self-actualization needs the need to grow and develop and to become all that we are capable of being (284)

self-managed teams groups of employees with the authority and skills to manage themselves (298)

selling short the process of selling stock that an investor does not actually own but has borrowed from a brokerage firm and will repay at a later date (612)

seniority the length of time an employee has worked for an organization (325)

serial bonds bonds of a single issue that mature on different dates (685)

Service Corps of Retired Executives (SCORE) a group of retired businesspeople who volunteer their services to small businesses through the SBA (149)

service economy an economy in which more effort is devoted to the production of services than to the production of goods (220)

shopping product an item for which buyers are willing to expend considerable effort on planning and making the purchase (365)

shop steward an employee elected by union members to serve as their representative (326)

short-term financing money that will be used for one year or less (563)

sinking fund a sum of money to which deposits are made each year for the purpose of redeeming a bond issue (583)

Six Sigma a disciplined approach that relies on statistical data and improved methods to eliminate defects from a firm's products and services (235)

skills inventory a computerized data bank containing information on the skills and experience of all present employees (252)

slowdown a technique whereby workers report to their jobs but work at a slower pace than normal (328)

small business one that is independently owned and operated for profit and is not dominant in its field (136)

Small Business Administration (SBA) a governmental agency that assists, counsels, and protects the interests of small businesses in the United States (148)

small-business development centers (SBDCs) university-based groups that provide individual counseling and practical training to owners of small businesses (157)

small-business institutes (SBIs) groups of senior and graduate students in business administration who provide management counseling to small businesses (150)

small-business investment companies (SBICs) privately owned firms that provide venture capital to small enterprises that meet their investment standards (152)

social audit a comprehensive report of what an organization has done and is doing with regard to social issues that affect it (64)

social needs the human requirements for love, affection, and a sense of belonging (284)

social responsibility the recognition that business activities have an impact on society and the consideration of that impact in business decision making (44)

socioeconomic model of social responsibility the concept that business should emphasize not only profits but also the impact of its decisions on society (52)

sole proprietorship a business that is owned (and usually operated) by one person (108)

span of management (or span of control) the number of workers who report directly to one manager (198)

special-event pricing advertised sales or price cutting linked to a holiday, season, or event (390)

specialization the separation of a manufacturing process into distinct tasks and the assignment of the different tasks to different individuals (25)

specialty product an item that possesses one or more unique characteristics for which a significant group of buyers is willing to expend considerable purchasing effort (365)

specialty-line wholesaler a middleman that carries a select group of products within a single line (406)

speculative production the time lag between the actual production of goods and when the goods are sold (564)

staff management position a position created to provide support, advice, and expertise within an organization (199)

stakeholders all of the different people or groups of people who are affected by the policies and decisions made by an organization (10)

standard of living a loose, subjective measure of how well off an individual or a society is, mainly in terms of want-satisfaction through goods and services (23)

standing committee a relatively permanent committee charged with performing some recurring task (206)

state bank a commercial bank chartered by the banking authorities in the state in which it operates (538)

statement of cash flows a statement that illustrates how the operating, investing, and financing activities of a company affect cash during an accounting period (510)

statistic a measure that summarizes a particular characteristic of an entire group of numbers (468)

statistical process control (SPC) a system that uses sampling to obtain data that are then plotted on control charts and graphs to see if the production process is operating as it should and to pinpoint problem areas (234)

statistical quality control (SQC) a set of specific statistical techniques used to monitor all aspects of the production process to ensure that both work in progress and finished products meet the firm's quality standards (234)

strategic alliance a partnership formed to create competitive advantage on a worldwide basis (90)

strategic plan an organization's broadest plan, developed as a guide for major policy setting and decision making (170)

strategic planning the process of establishing an organization's major goals and objectives and allocating the resources to achieve them (169)

strike a temporary work stoppage by employees, calculated to add force to their demands (312)

strikebreaker a nonunion employee who performs the job of a striking union member (329)

stock the shares of ownership of a corporation (116)

stock dividend a dividend in the form of additional stock (607)

stock split the division of each outstanding share of a corporation's stock into a greater number of shares (608)

stockholder a person who owns a corporation's stock (116)

store (or private) brand a brand that is owned by an individual wholesaler or retailer (374)

store of value a means of retaining and accumulating wealth (529)

supermarket a large self-service store that sells primarily food and household products (409)

superstore a large retail store that carries not only food and nonfood products ordinarily found in supermarkets but also additional product lines (410)

supply the quantity of a product that producers are willing to sell at each of various prices (21, 380)

supply an item that facilitates production and operations but does not become part of a finished product (366)

supply-chain management long-term partnership among channel members working together to create a distribution system that reduces inefficiencies, costs, and redundancies while creating a competitive advantage and satisfying customers (402)

supply-chain management (SCM) software software solutions that focus on ways to improve communication between the suppliers and users of materials and components (402)

sustainability meeting the needs of the present without compromising the ability of future generations to meet their own needs (27)

syndicate a temporary association of individuals or firms organized to perform a specific task that requires a large amount of capital (125)

synthetic process a process in operations management in which raw materials or components are combined to create a finished product (218)

T

tactical plan a smaller-scale plan developed to implement a strategy (170)

target market a group of individuals or organizations, or both, for which a firm develops and maintains a marketing mix suitable for the specific needs and preferences of that group (345)

task force a committee established to investigate a major problem or pending decision (207)

team a group of workers functioning together as a unit to complete a common goal or purpose (297)

technical salesperson a salesperson who assists a company's current customers in technical matters (441)

technical skill a specific skill needed to accomplish a specialized activity (176)

telecommuting working at home all the time or for a portion of the work week (295)

telemarketing the performance of marketing-related activities by telephone (413)

television home shopping a form of selling in which products are presented to television viewers, who can buy them by calling a toll-free number and paying with a credit card (414)

tender offer an offer to purchase the stock of a firm targeted for acquisition at a price just high enough to tempt stockholders to sell their shares (126)

term-loan agreement a promissory note that requires a borrower to repay a loan in monthly, quarterly, semiannual, or annual installments (580)

Theory X a concept of employee motivation generally consistent with Taylor's scientific management; assumes that employees dislike work and will function only in a highly controlled work environment (286)

Theory Y a concept of employee motivation generally consistent with the ideas of the human relations movement; assumes that employees accept responsibility and work toward organizational goals if by so doing they also achieve personal rewards (286)

Theory Z the belief that some middle ground between Ouchi's type A and type J practices is best for American business (287)

time deposit an amount on deposit in an interest-bearing savings account (531)

time utility utility created by making a product available when customers wish to purchase it (341)

top manager an upper-level executive who guides and controls the overall fortunes of an organization (174)

total cost the sum of the fixed costs and the variable costs attributed to a product (384)

total quality management (TQM) the coordination of efforts directed at improving customer satisfaction, increasing employee participation, strengthening supplier partnerships, and facilitating an organizational atmosphere of continuous quality improvement (181)

total revenue the total amount received from sales of a product (384)

trade credit a type of short-term financing extended by a seller who does not require immediate payment after delivery of merchandise (571)

trade deficit a negative balance of trade (74)

trademark a brand name or brand mark that is registered with the U.S. Patent and Trademark Office and thus is legally protected from use by anyone except its owner (374)

trade name the complete and legal name of an organization (374)

trade salesperson a salesperson—generally employed by a food producer or processor—who assists customers in promoting products, especially in retail stores (441)

trade sales promotion method a sales promotion method designed to encourage wholesalers and retailers to stock and actively promote a manufacturer's product (443)

trade show an industry-wide exhibit at which many sellers display their products (445)

trading company provides a link between buyers and sellers in different countries (90)

traditional specialty store a store that carries a narrow product mix with deep product lines (411)

transfer pricing prices charged in sales between an organization's units (391)

transportation the shipment of products to customers (418)

trial balance a summary of the balances of all general ledger accounts at the end of the accounting period (502)

trustee an individual or an independent firm that acts as a bond owners' representative (583)

U

undifferentiated approach directing a single marketing mix at the entire market for a particular product (346)

union-management (labor) relations the dealings between labor unions and business management both in the bargaining process and beyond it (310)

union security protection of the union's position as the employees' bargaining agent (325)

union shop a workplace in which new employees must join the union after a specified probationary period (325)

unlimited liability a legal concept that holds a business owner personally responsible for all the debts of the business (110)

unsecured financing financing that is not backed by collateral (571)

utility the ability of a good or service to satisfy a human need (218, 341)

V

variable cost a cost that depends on the number of units produced (384)

venture capital money that is invested in small (and sometimes struggling) firms that have the potential to become very successful (151)

vertical channel integration the combining of two or more stages of a distribution channel under a single firm's management (403)

vertical marketing system (VMS) a centrally managed distribution channel resulting from vertical channel integration (403)

virtual team a team consisting of members who are geographically dispersed but communicate electronically (299)

virtuoso team a team of exceptionally highly skilled and talented individuals brought together to produce significant change (298)

W

wage survey a collection of data on prevailing wage rates within an industry or a geographic area (261)

warehouse club a large-scale members-only establishment that combines features of cash-and-carry wholesaling with discount retailing (410)

warehouse showroom a retail facility in a large, low-cost building with a large on-premises inventory and minimal service (409)

warehousing the set of activities involved in receiving and storing goods and preparing them for reshipment (417)

whistle-blowing informing the press or government officials about unethical practices within one's organization (42)

wholesaler a middleman that sells products to other firms (400)

wide-area network (WAN) a network that connects computers over a large geographic area, such as a city, a state, or even the world (475)

wildcat strike a strike not approved by the strikers' union (328)

working capital the difference between current assets and current liabilities (514)

World Trade Organization (WTO) powerful successor to GATT that incorporates trade in goods, services, and ideas (84)

World Wide Web (the Web) the Internet's multimedia environment of audio, visual, and text data (474)

Y

Yellow Pages advertising simple listings or display advertisements presented under specific product categories appearing in print and online telephone directories (434)

Z

zero-base budgeting a budgeting approach in which every expense in every budget must be justified (568)

Notes

Chapter 1

1. Brad Stone, "Apple Shifts Spotlight to iPod and Revamps iTunes Software," *New York Times,* September 10, 2008, p. C3; Matt Vella, "How Great Design Makes People Love Your Company," *BusinessWeek Online,* September 4, 2008, **www.businessweek.com**; Chi-Chu Tschang, "Apple Struggles to Win Fans in China," *BusinessWeek Online,* July 22, 2008, **www.businessweek.com**; Yukari Iwatani Kane and Nick Wingfield, "For Apple iPhone, Japan Could Be the Next Big Test," *Wall Street Journal,* December 19, 2007, p. B1; Nick Wingfield, "Apple Businesses Fuel Each Other," *Wall Street Journal,* October 23, 2007, p. A3.
2. The Dudley Products, Inc., website at **www.dudleyq.com**, September 25, 2005.8, 2008.
3. The Horatio Alger website at **www.horatioalger.com**, September 25, 2005.8, 2008.
4. Alan Goldstein, "Most Dot.Coms Doomed to Fail, Cuban Tells Entrepreneurs," *Dallas Morning News,* April 7, 2000, p. 1D. The Wikipedia web site at **www.wikipedia.org**, September 9, 2008.
5. Idy Fernandez, "Julie Stav," *Hispanic*, June–July 2005, p. 24.
6. The Wal-Mart Stores, Inc. website at **www.walmart.com**, September 25, 2005.10, 2008.
7. The Bureau of Economic Analysis website at **www.bea.gov**, September 12, 2008.
8. The Bureau of Labor Statistics website at **www.bls.gov**, September 12, 2008.
9. "Gains in U.S. Productivity: Stopgap Measures or Lasting Change?" *FRSBSF Economic Letter*, March 11, 2005, p. 1.
10. Bill Weir, "Made in China: Your Job, Your Future, Your Fortune," ABC News website at **www.abcnews.com**, September 20, 2005.
11. The Bureau of Economic Analysis website at **www.bea.gov**, September 14, 2008.
12. The Bureau of Labor Statistics website at **www.bls.gov**, September 14, 2008.
13. The Bureau of Economic Analysis website at **www.bea.gov**, September 14, 2008.
14. The Treasury Direct website at **www.treasurydirect.gov**, September 15, 2008.
15. The Investopedia website at **www.investopedia.com**, September 14, 2008.
16. The Bureau of Labor Statistics website at **www.bls.gov**, September 14, 2008.
17. Bill Weir, "Made in China: Your Job, Your Future, Your Fortune," ABC News website at **www.abcnews.com**, September 20, 2005.
18. The Environmental Protection Agency website at **www.epa.com**, accessed September 13, 2008.
19. Based on information from the video, *Peet's Coffee & Tea: Building a Community.*
20. Based on information from "Wipro to Open First Software Development Centre in Beijing," *Asia Africa Intelligence Wire, September 12, 2005, n.p.; Steve Hamm, "Taking a Page from Toyota's Playbook," BusinessWeek, August 22–29, 2005, pp. 69–72; "Wipro to Invest More in Core Outsourcing," Asia Africa Intelligence Wire, September 7, 2005, n.p.; Wipro Quarterly Profit Rises 41% on Outsourcing," InformationWeek, July 22, 2005, n.p.; "Wipro, Ltd.," Wall Street Journal, July 25, 2005, p. C12; Terry Atlas, "Bangalore's Big Dreams," U.S. News & World Report, May 2, 2005, pp. 50+*; Ashlee Vance, "Wipro's New Strategy: Outsource Locally," **www.nytimes.com**, November 4, 2008.

Chapter 2

1. Doug Tsuruoka, "A Touchy-Feely Style Keeps Bakery Cookin,'" *Investor's Business Daily,* August 29, 2008, **http://www.investors.com/editorial/IBDArticles.asp?artsec=24&issue=20080829**; Patrick McGroarty, "Dancing Deer Has an Expanding Appetite," *Boston Globe,* January 21, 2007, p. 3; Stacy Perman, "Scones and Social Responsibility," *BusinessWeek,* August 21, 2006, p. 38; **www.dancingdeer.com.**
2. Carrie Johnson, "Adelphia, U.S. Settle for $75 Million," *Washington Post,* April 26, 2005, p. E1.
3. Charles Haddad and Amy Barrett, "A Whistle-Blower Rocks an Industry," *BusinessWeek,* June 24, 2002, pp. 126–130.
4. Albert B. Crenshaw, "Tax Shelter Leaders Get Jail Time, Must Pay Restitution," *Washington Post,* April 23, 2005, p. E2.
5. *Frontlines* (Washington: U.S. Agency for International Development), September 2005, p. 16.
6. Deere & Company Corporate Governance—Code of Ethics, **http://www.deere.com/en_US/investinfo/corpgov/ethics.html**, accessed September 8, 2008.
7. Anthony Bianco, William Symonds, and Nanette Byrnes, "The Rise and Fall of Dennis Kozlowski," *BusinessWeek,* December 23, 2002, pp. 64–77.
8. **www.whistleblowers.org/**, accessed September 21, 2005.
9. General Mills Foundation **http://www.generalmills.com/corporate/commitment/foundation.aspx?print=true**, accessed September 8, 2008.
10. Dell Communities Outreach, **http://dell.com/content/topics/global.aspx/corp/diversity/en/outreach?c=us&1=en&s=c**, accessed September 8, 2008.
11. IBM Corporate Citizenship, **http://www.ibm.com/ibm/ibmgives/**, accessed September 8, 2008.
12. GE Annual Report 2007, p. 38.
13. Charles Schwab 2007 Annual Report, p. 22.
14. Verizon Communications 2007 Annual Report, p. 15.
15. ExxonMobil 2007 Summary Annual Report, p. 15.
16. AT&T Inc. 2007 Annual Report, pp. 22–23.
17. Based on information from "New Belgium Brewery: Four Principles of Sustainable Business," Triplepundit.com, June 7, 2008, **http://www.triplepundit.com/pages/new-belgium-bre.php**; "New Belgium Brewing Wins Ethics Award," *Denver Business Journal*, January 2, 2003, **Denver.bizjournals.com/Denver/stories/2002/12/30/daily21.html**; Richard Brandes, "Beer Growth Brands," *Beverage Dynamics*, September–October 2002, pp. 37ff; **www.newbelgium.com**.
18. Based on information from company website **http://www.belu.org/**, accessed September 30, 2008; Schwab Foundation for Social Entrepreneurship, "Reed Paget," **http://schwabfound.weforum.org/sf/SocialEntrepreneurs/Profiles/index.htm?sname=0&sorganization=73206&sarea=0&ssector=0&stype=0**, accessed September 30, 2008; "Case Study: Belu Water," **http://www.thisislondon.co.uk/itsyourbusiness/article-23383046-details/Case+study:+Belu+Water/article.do**, accessed September 30, 2008.

Chapter 3

1. Patricia Jiayi Ho, "GM Pares Outlook for China Sales," *Wall Street Journal,* September 17, 2008, **www.wsj.com;** Lawrence R. Gustin, "GM 100: GM in China," *AutoWeek,* September 11, 2008, **www.autoweek.com;** Peter Hall, "MG TF LE500: The Return of MG," Telegraph (U.K.), September 13, 2008, **www.telegraph.co.uk;** "SAIC Motor Corp.," *Wall Street Journal,* August 30, 2008, p. B6; Tony Lewin, "Summer Restart for Ex-Rover Plant," *Automotive News Europe,* April 28, 2008, p. 3; Anil K. Gputa and Haiyan Wang, "Business Insight: How to Get China and India Right," *Wall Street Journal,* April 28, 2007, p. R4; Dexter Roberts, "China Autos: Chevy Keeps Accelerating," *BusinessWeek Online,* January 7, 2008, **www.businessweek.com.**
2. The White House, Office of the Press Secretary, Press Release, August 6, 2002.
3. U.S. Bureau of Economic Analysis, U.S. Bureau of Commerce, **http://bea.gov/international/bp_web/simple.cfm?anon=78260&table_id=1&area_id=3,** accessed September 26, 2008.

4. This section draws heavily from *The World Economic Outlook Executive Summary,* International Monetary Fund, **www.imf.org/external/pubs/ft/reo/2008/whd/eng/wreo0408.htm,** accessed September 24, 2008.
5. Micheal Chriszt and Elena Whisler, "China's Economic Emergence," *Econ South,* First Reserve Bank of Atlanta, Second Quarter 2005, pp. 4–7.
6. Office of the United States Trade Representative, *NAFTA Facts,* March 2008, p. 1, **www.ustr.gov,** accessed September 23, 2008.
7. Office of the United States Trade Representative, *USTR News,* February 27, 2008, **www.ustr.gov,** accessed September 23, 2008.
8. Office of the United States Trade Representative, *Fact Sheet,* **http://www.ustr.gov/Trade_Agreements/Regional/Enterprice_for_ASEAN_Initiative/,** accessed September 26, 2008.
9. William M. Pride and O. C. Ferrell, *Marketing,* Library Edition, (Boston: Houghton Mifflin, 2006) p. 133.
10. Based on video entitled *Fossil—Keeping Watch on a Global Business* © Cengage Learning.
11. Based on information from "Coca-Cola Beats Profit Forecast," *Reuters,* October 15, 2008, **www.nytimes.com;** Andrew Ross Sorkin, "Coca-Cola's Group in China," *Deal Book,* September 3, 2008, **www.nytimes.com;** Chad Terhune, "Coke's Net Rises; Emerging Markets Bolster Revenue," *Wall Street Journal,* July 22, 2005, p. B2; "Coca-Cola to Stick It Out in Zimbabwe," *Africa News Service,* August 8, 2005, n.p.; "Fizzical Facts: Coke Claims 60% Market Share in India," *Asia Africa Intelligence Wire,* August 6, 2005, n.p.; Matthew Forney, "Who's Getting It Right?" *Time International,* November 1, 2004, p. 44; "Coca-Cola Seeks to Increase Its China Presence," *Asia Africa Intelligence Wire,* December 13, 2004, n.p.; Jonathan Wheatley, "Coke Pops the Top Off an Emerging Market," *BusinessWeek,* May 2, 2005, pp. 31; **www.cocacola.com.**

Chapter 4

1. Bruce Geiselman, "Sustainable SC Johnson," *Waste News,* May 12, 2008, p. 7; William Armbruster, "Don't Blame China for Import Safety," *Journal of Commerce Online,* December 4, 2007; "S.C. Johnson Recognized as Outstanding Employer," *MMR,* October 29, 2007, p. 32; **www.scjohnson.com.**
2. The Ivy Planning Group website at **www.ivygroupllc.com,** accessed September 16, 2008.
3. The National Association of Publicly Traded Partnerships website at **www.naptp.org,** accessed September 16, 2008.
4. The Procter & Gamble website at **www.pg.com,** accessed September 16, 2008.
5. The Yahoo! Small Business website at **http://smallbusines.yahoo.com,** accessed September 17, 2008.
6. The Hispanic PR Wire website at **www.hispanicprwire.com,** accessed September 12, 2008.
7. The Internal Revenue Service website at **www.irs.gov,** accessed September 12, 2008.
8. The Ocean Spray Cranberries website at **www.oceanspray.com,** accessed September 17, 2008.
9. The BusinessWeek website at **www.businessweek.com,** accessed August 7, 2007.
10. The Sony Ericcson website at **www.sonyericsson.com,** accessed September 19, 2008.
11. The Boston.com Business website at **www.boston.com,** accessed May 23, 2006.
12. The Wal-Mart Stores, Inc. website at **www.walmart.com,** accessed September 10, 2008.
13. The Oracle website at **www.oracle.com,** accessed September 17, 2008.
14. The IBM website at **www.ibm.com,** accessed September 18, 2008.
15. Based on information from Keith Reed, "Bowing Out at Jordan's," *Boston Globe,* December 22, 2006, p. C1; David Gianatasio, "Rooms to Grow," *Adweek,* January 14, 2003, p. 3; Jon Chesto, "Buffet Helps Jordan's Flip Switch," *Boston Herald,* August 22, 2002, p. 37; "At the Movies with Buffet," *Financial Express,* October 28, 2002; Barry Tatelman, "You Can't Take That Away from Us," *Operations Management* (n.d.), **www.furninfo.com/operations/jordans0402.html; www.jordansfurniture.com.**
16. Based on information from Lee Brodie, "Can Disney Magic Defeat Recession?" **www.cnbc.com,** November 6, 2008; Brooks Barnes, "Slowdown Begins to Show at Stalwart Disney," **www.nytimes.com,** November 6, 2008; Ronald Grover, "How Eisner Saved the Magic Kingdom," *BusinessWeek Online,* September 30, 2005, **www.businessweek.com;** Ben Fritz, "Mouse Plays Board Games," *Daily Variety,* August 19, 2005, p. 1; Kim Christensen, "Disney Board Gives Shareholders More Clout," *Los Angeles Times,* August 19, 2005, p. C2; Gary Gentile, "Roy Disney, Company Resolve Their Disputes," *Washington Post,* July 9, 2005, p. D1; Merissa Marr, "One Year Later, Disney Attempts Smoother Ride," *Wall Street Journal,* February 7, 2005, p. B1; Joann S. Lublin and Bruce Orwall, "Funds Press Disney for Timeline to Replace Eisner," *Wall Street Journal,* May 21, 2004, p. B2.

Chapter 5

1. Simona Covel, "New York Eatery Looks for the Sweet Spot Overseas," *Wall Street Journal,* September 4, 2008, p. B4; Bradley Hope, "Boutiques Arrive with Tea and Sweets," *The National,* September 21, 2008, **www.thenational.ae;** Diana Kuan, "How the Big Apple Tastes to a Chocolate Lover," *Boston Globe,* July 27, 2008, p. M3.
2. U.S. Small Business Administration, **http://www.sba.gov/services/contractingopportunities/sizestandardstopics/summarywhatis/,** accessed October 3, 2008.
3. Office of Advocacy estimates based on data from the U.S. Department of Commerce, Bureau of the Census, and U.S. Department of Labor, Employment and Training Administration, **http://app1.sba.gov/faqs/faqIndexAll.cfm?areaid=24,** accessed October 3, 2008.
4. Ibid.
5. Small Business Administration, Office of Advocacy, *Quarterly Indicators,* Second Quarter 2008, **www.sba.gov/advo,** accessed October 3, 2008.
6. Thomas A. Garrett, "Entrepreneurs Thrive in America," *Bridges,* Federal Reserve Bank of St. Louis, Spring 2005, p. 2.
7. U.S. Small Business Administration, SBA Press Office, *News Release,* September 10, 2008, and *2007 The Small Business Economy,* a Report to the President, U.S. Small Business Administration, Washington, D.C., December 2007, pp. 67–90.
8. U.S. Small Business Administration News Release Number 05–53, September 13, 2005, **www.sba.gov/teens/brian_hendricks.html.**
9. U.S. Small Business Administration, Office of Advocacy, *Frequently Asked Questions,* September 2008, **http://app1.sba.gov/faqs/faqindex.cfm?arealD=24, pick#6,** accessed October 3, 2008.
10. U.S. Small Business Administration, **www.sba.gov/advo/,** accessed October 5, 2008.
11. U.S. Small Business Administration, Advocacy Small Business Statistics and Research, *Frequently Asked Questions,* **http://app1.sba.gov/faqs/faqIndexAll.cfm?areaid=24,** accessed October 5, 2008.
12. Timothy S. Hatten, *"Small Business Management: Entrepreneurship and Beyond,"* 4th ed., Copyright © 2009 by Houghton Mifflin Company, p. 238. Reprinted with permission.
13. U.S. Small Business Administration, **http://www.sba.gov/aboutsba/sbaprograms/sbdc/aboutus/index.html,** accessed October 2, 2008.
14. SCORE *FY2007 Annual Report,* p. 2, **www.score.org,** accessed October 6, 2008.
15. U.S. Small Business Administration, *2007 The Year in Review,* p. 7, **www.sba.gov,** accessed October 5, 2008.
16. Ibid.
17. SBA Press Release, *Fact Sheet,* September 11, 2008, p. 2.
18. U.S. Small Business Administration, *Small Business Investment Companies,* **http://app1.sba.gov/faqs/faqIndexAll.cfm?areaid=9,** accessed September 29, 2008.
19. Cindy Elmore, "Putting the Power into the Hands of Small Business Owners," *Marketwise,* Federal Reserve Bank of Richmond, Issue II, 2005, p. 13.
20. U.S. Small Business Administration, **www.sba.gov/managing/marketing/intlsales.html,** accessed October 4, 2008.
21. The U.S. Commercial Service, **http://www.trade.gov/promotingtrade/index.asp,** accessed October 6, 2008.
22. Based on information from Krystal Grow, "Newbury Comics Coming Back," *The Norwood Record,* May 8, 2008, **http://norwoodrecord.com/default.asp?sourceid=&smenu=304&twindow=&mad=&sdetail=3571&wpage=1&skeyword=&sidate=&ccat=&ccatm=&restate=&restatus=&reoption=&retype=&repmin=&repmax=&rebed=&rebath=&subname=&pform=&sc=2631&hn=norwoodrecord&he=.com;** Donna Goodison, "Norwood Superstore Sets Newbury Comics Record," *Boston Herald,* August 20, 2008, **http://news.bostonherald.com/business/general/view/2008_08_20_Norwood_superstore_sets_Newbury_Comics_record/srvc=home&position=also;** Ed Christman, "Newbury Comics Cuts Staff," *Billboard,* September 10, 2005, p. 8; Wendy Wilson, "Newbury Comics," *Video Business,* December 20, 2004, p. 18; Ed Christman, "'We Have All Had to Grow Up a Little,'" *Billboard,* September 27, 2003, pp. N3ff; **www.newburycomics.com.**
23. Company website, **http://www.tumbleweedhouses.com,** accessed September 30, 2008; Steven Kurutz, "The Next Little Thing?" *The New York Times,* September 11, 2008, pp. F1 and F8; Carol Lloyd, "Small Houses Challenge Our Notions of Need as Well as Minimum-Size Standards," *SFGate.com,* April 27, 2007, **http://www.sfgate.com;** Bethany Little, "Think Small," *The New York Times,* February 16, 2007,

http://travel.nytimes.com; Hannah Bloch, "Downsizing, Seriously," *The New York Times,* September 10, 2006, http://www.nytimes.com.

Chapter 6

1. Steve Lohr, "Google, Zen Master of the Market," *New York Times,* July 7, 2008, p. C1; "Search Marketing: Google's Legacy for Its Pioneers," *New Media Age,* September 11, 2008, n.p.; Fay Hansen, "Top of the Class," *Workforce Management,* June 23, 2008, pp. 1+; Adam Lashinsky, "Where Does Google Go Next?" *Fortune,* May 26, 2008, pp. 104+; "Google Rebrands Froogle," *InformationWeek,* April 19, 2007, **www.info.com.**
2. **www.ustoday.com.**
3. **www.google.com/corporate/**, accessed September 22, 2008.
4. Lucas Conley, "Climbing Back up the Mountain," *Fast Company,* April 2005, p. 84.
5. **www.cosmeticsdesign.com.**
6. Procter & Gamble.
7. **www.bizjournals.com.**
8. **www.fastcompany.com; www.ge.com.**
9. **Quancost.com/monster**, accessed September 23, 2008.
10. Henry Mintzberg, "The Manager's Job: Folklore and Fact," *Harvard Business Review,* July–August 1975, pp. 49–61.
11. Chana R. Shoenberger, "The Greenhouse Effect," **www.forbes.com/global/2003/0203/0_print.html**, accessed November 25, 2008.
12. Ricky W. Griffin, *Management,* 9th ed. (Boston: Houghton Mifflin, 2008), p. 234.
13. **http://money.cnn.com.**
14. Paul R. LaMonica, "After Carly, Is HP a Bargain?" *Money,* April 2005, p. 108.
15. Company website, **www.docusign.com**, accessed October 7, 2008; "Snapshot: DocuSign, Inc.," BusinessWeek, **http://www.businessweek.com**, accessed October 7, 2008; "DocuSign Names Former Citrix Systems and Compaq Computer Corporation Marketing Executive Doug Wheeler as Vice President of Marketing," press release, **http://news.yahoo.com**, September 11, 2008; Douglas MacMillan, "The Issue: Workers as Crisis Consultants," BusinessWeek, **http://www.businessweek.com**, April 9, 2008.
16. Based on video entitled *Student Advantage Helps College Students Stay Organized* © Cengage Learning.

Chapter 7

1. Peter Sanders, "Headwind Threatens Disney Parks," *Wall Street Journal,* October 1, 2008, p. B2; Margery Weinstein, "Inside the Disney Institute," *Training,* July 28, 2008, n.p.; Margery Weinstein, "Keys to the Kingdom, Part I: Disney Delivers Quality Training," *Training,* July 28, 2008, n.p.; Merissa Marr and Nick Wingfield, "Big Media Companies Want Back in the Game," *Wall Street Journal,* February 19, 2008, p. B1; **http://corporate.disney.go.com.**
2. "Mercedes-Benz USA Selects Workstream," *Business Editors; Automotive Writers,* March 2005.
3. Robert Kreitner, *Student Achievement Series: Foundations of Management: Basics and Best Practices* (Boston: Houghton Mifflin, 2008), pp. 175–176.
4. Paul Kaihla, "Raytheon on Target," *Business 2.0,* **www.business2.com/articles/mag/0,1640,46335,00.html**, February 4, 2003.
5. Kreitner, *Management*, p. 183.
6. **www.Premiumhoovers.com**, accessed September 23, 2008.
7. Rob Goffee and Gareth Jones, "The Character of a Corporation: How Your Company's Culture Can Make or Break Your Business," *Jones Harper Business,* p. 182.
8. "Mergers' Missing Link: Cultural Integration," *PR Newswire,* January 23, 2003.
9. Kreitner, *Management,* p. 47.
10. Based on information from Paul Rolfes, "Green Mountain Coffee Roasters: Grounds for Growth," SmallCapInvestor.com, July 23, 2008, **http://www.smallcapinvestor.com/stockresearch/spotlight/2008-07-23-green_mountain_coffee_roasters_grounds_for_growth**; Tony Baer, "Brewing a New Kind of Connection," *Manufacturing Business Technology,* January 2005, pp. 40–42; Mark Pendergrast, "Green Mountain Coffee Roasters: Doing Well by Doing Good," *Tea & Coffee Trade Journal,* April 20, 2004, pp. 100+; Ellyn Spragins, "The Three-Peat," *Fortune Small Business,* July–August 2003, n.p.; **www.greenmountaincoffee.com.**
11. Based on information from Kevin Miller, "Opel Insignia Wins European Car of the Year," November 17, 2008, **http://www.autosavant.com/**; Lindsay Chappell, "GM Just Didn't Get the Magic of Spring Hill," *Automotive News,* July 25, 2005, pp. 14+; Dave Guilford, "Once Different Saturn Looks More Like GM," *Automotive News,* June 14, 2004, p. 30V; Lindsay Chappell, "GM's Saturn Plant May Lose Its Saturns," *Automotive News,* July 27, 2005, pp. 1+; Lee Hawkins, Jr., and Joann S. Lublin, "Emergency Repairman," *Wall Street Journal,* April 6, 2005, pp. B1+; **www.gm.com.**

Chapter 8

1. Rob Walker, "Mixing It Up," *New York Times Magazine,* August 24, 2008, p. 20; Marianne Kolbasuk McGee, "YouTube Videos Stir Up New Sales For 'Will It Blend' Maker," *Information Week,* September 27, 2007, **www.informationweek.com**; Laura Lorber, "Small Business Link: How Online Marketing Videos Became a Hit in Their Own Right," *Wall Street Journal,* July 2, 2007, p. B4; Samantha Murphy, "Blend-Worth Technology: Companies Take Online Videos to the Next Level," *Chain Store Age,* July 2007, p. 82.
2. The Blendtec website at **www.blendtec.com**, accessed September 20, 2008.
3. The Bureau of Labor Statistics website at **www.bls.gov**, accessed September 20, 2008.
4. Robert Kreitner, *Management*, 9th ed. (Boston: Houghton Mifflin, 2004), pp. 577–578.
5. The Dell website at **www.dell.com**, accessed September 20, 2008.
6. The 3M Corporate website at **www.3m.com**, accessed September 20, 2008.
7. The Campbell Soup Company website at **www.campbellsoupcompany.com**, accessed September 20, 2008.
8. The Berry Plastics website at **www.berryplastics.com**, accessed September 21, 2008.
9. The Boeing website at **www.boeing.com**, accessed September 21, 2008.
10. The AT&T Supplier website at **www.attsuppliers.com**, accessed September 21, 2008.
11. The National Institute for Standards and Technology (NIST) website at **www.nist.gov**, accessed September 21, 2008.
12. The Six Sigma website at **www.isixsigma.com**, accessed September 21, 2008.
13. The Bureau of Labor Statistics website at **www.bls.gov**, accessed September 12, 2008.
14. Ibid., accessed September 20, 2008.
15. Ibid., accessed September 12, 2008.
16. The Illumina, Inc. website at **www.illumina.com**, accessed September 18, 2008.
17. The Dell Corporate website at **www.dell.com**, accessed September 21, 2008.
18. Based on video entitled *Washburn Guitar* © Cengage Learning.
19. Micheline Maynard, "Quality Is Major Concern of Toyota's Visiting Chief," *The New York Times,* **http://www.nytimes.com**, January 15, 2008; Micheline Maynard, "The Dings and Dents of Toyota," *The New York Times,* **http://www.nytimes.com**, November 3, 2007; "Ford Beats Toyota in Quality Ratings," *The Associated Press,* **http://www.msnbc.com**, June 6, 2007; Martin Fackler, "The 'Toyota Way' Is Translated for a New Generation of Foreign Managers," *The New York Times,* **http://www.nytimes.com**, February 13, 2007.

Chapter 9

1. Keith McFarland, "Why Zappos Offers New Hires $2,000 to Quit," *BusinessWeek,* September 16, 2008, **www.businessweek.com**; Christopher Gergen and Gregg Vanourek, "Zappos Culture Sows Spirit," *Washington Times,* July 16, 2008, p. B3; Helen Coster, "A Step Ahead," *Forbes,* June 2, 2008, p. 78; Bill Taylor, "Why Zappos Pays New Employees to Quit—And You Should Too," *Harvard Business Publishing,* May 19, 2008, **discussionleader.hbsp.com**.
2. Ivy Schmerken, "The Hiring Game," *Wall Street & Technology,* Spring 2005, pp. 28+.
3. "Ford Meets Cost Cutting Goal," Associated Press, August 6, 2008, **www.courier-journal.com**
4. U.S. Department of Labor, Bureau of Labor Statistics, **www.bls.gov**, accessed September 30, 2008.
5. Wendy Killeen, "Colleges Press Issue of Cultural Diversity," *Boston Globe,* March 13, 2005, p. 7.
6. "Diversity Training," *Virginia Business,* **VirginiaBusiness.com**, May 2007, **www.virginiabusiness.com/edit/magazine/yr2007/may07/diver3.shtml**
7. **http://hr.blr.com/lps/jobdescriptions.aspx?source=MKD&effort=2038&gclid=CPuFtY23-pUCFRKLxwodZnBrEg.**
8. Linnea Anderson, "Monster Worldwide, Inc.," Hoovers.com, **http://cobrands.hoovers.com/global/cobrands/proquest/factsheet.xhtml?COID=41617.**

9. The Procter & Gamble website at **www.pg.com**, accessed September 29, 2008.
10. Nanette Byrnes, "Start Search," *BusinessWeek,* October 10, 2005, pp. 74–76.
11. U.S. Department of Labor, Bureau of Labor Statistics, News Release, September 10, 2008, **www.bls.gov.**
12. Milton Moskowitz, "100 Top Companies to Work For" *Fortune*, February 4, 2008, **http://money.cnn.com/magazines/fortune/bestcompanies/2008/.**
13. Cynthia D. Fisher, Lyle F. Schoenfeldt, and James B. Shaw, *Human Resource Management* (Boston: Houghton Mifflin, 2006), p. 464.
14. Ibid., pp. 465.
15. Naomi R. Kooker, "Aquarium Chief Doesn't See Economy Tanking," *Boston Business Journal,* January 4, 2008, **boston.bizjournals.com**; Geoff Edgers, "With Eye on Growth, Aquarium Names New Chief," *Boston Globe,* June 15, 2005, **www.bostonglobe.com**; Stephanie Vosk, "It's February, But on Summer Jobs, Hope Springs Eternal," *Boston Globe,* February 20, 2005, p. 3; Jeffrey Krasner, "New England Aquarium Plunges into Financial Turmoil," *Boston Globe,* December 13, 2002, **www.boston.com/global; www.neaq.org.**
16. The Domino's website at **www.dominosbiz.com**, accessed October 14, 2008; Louise Kramer, "For a Franchise, Success Is in the Hiring," *The New York Times*, **http://www.nytimes.com**, January 6, 2008; Mark A. DeSorbo, "65 Percent of Fast Food Restaurants Report Increased Employment in Q4," *QSR Magazine,* **http://www.qsrmagazine.com**, November 2007.

Chapter 10

1. Justin Fox, "How to Succeed? Make Employees Happy," *Time,* June 26, 2008, **www.time.com**; Justin Fox, "The Curious Capitalist: Former Housemates John Mackey and Kip Tindell Talk . . ." *Time blog,* June 26, 2008, **time-blog.com/curious_capitalist**; "100 Best Companies to Work For," *Fortune,* February 4, 2008, **www.fortune.com**; Sheryl Jean, "Container Store's Handy Worker Pool: Customers," *Fort Worth Star-Telegram*, October 5, 2007, n.p.; Jayne O'Donnell, "Stores Shop the Aisles for New Hires," *USA Today,* October 24, 2007, p. 1B; **www.containerstore.com.**
2. Sheree R. Curry, "Retention Getters," *Incentive,* April 2005, pp. 14+, **www.sap.com/usa/about/careers/benefits/index.epx**, accessed October 7, 2008.
3. Douglas McGregor, *The Human Side of Enterprise* (New York: McGraw-Hill, 1960).
4. William Ouchi, *Theory Z* (Reading, MA: Addison-Wesley, 1981).
5. Ricky W. Griffin, *Fundamentals of Management,* 3d ed. (Boston: Houghton Mifflin, 2006), p. 334.
6. Rochelle Garner, "Company Growth and Rankings," *Computer Reseller,* January 31, 2005.
7. **http://www.sbaer.uca.edu/Research/sbida/1992/pdf/04.pdf**, 1992.
8. Alison Overholt, "Power up the People: Economy Stuck in the Doldrums? Morale Stuck There Too? Here Are a Few Things That You Can Do to Jazz Things up in 2003," *Fast Company,* January 2003, p. 50.
9. **http://news.softpedia.com/news/Apple-Offers-Corporate-Gifting-and-Rewards-Program-86164.shtml**, May 21, 2008.
10. Alan Deutschman, "Making Change," *Fast Company,* May 2005, p. 52.
11. **http://www.scjohnson.com/careers/car_aie.asp.**
12. **marketplace.publicradio.org/display/web/2008/05/21/flex_time/.**
13. Nanette Byrnes, "Star Search," *BusinessWeek,* October 10, 2005, p. 78.
14. **www.starbucks.com/aboutus/jobcenter.asp.**
15. Carolyn Hirschman, "Share and Share Alike," *HR Magazine,* September 2005.
16. "Telework Succeeds for U.S. Agencies," *Work & Family Newsbrief,* January 2003, p. 7.
17. **www.judywolf.com/articles_pr/articles_news/convincing_your_boss.html.**
18. **http://money.cnn.com/magazines/fortune/bestcompanies/2008/benefits/telecommuting.html**, February 4, 2008 issue.
19. Arif Mohamed, "Bosses Split Over Productivity of Teleworkers," *Computer Weekly,* March 29, 2005, p. 55.
20. Samuel Greengard, "Sun's Shining Example," *Workforce Management,* March 2005, pp. 48+.
21. Matthew Boyle and Ellen Florian Kratz, "The Wegmans Way," *Fortune,* January 24, 2005, p. 62.
22. "A Short History of ESOP," **www.nceo.org**, January 2006.
23. Ricky W. Griffin, *Fundamentals of Management* (Boston: Houghton Mifflin, 2006), pp. 428–447.
24. Barry L. Reece and Rhonda Brandt, *Effective Human Relations: Personal and Organizational Applications* (Boston: Houghton Mifflin, 2005), pp. 280–285.
25. "Jones Walker Law Firm Taps Harvard for New Orleans Rebuild Advice," *New Orleans CityBusiness,* News Section, January 3, 2006, n.p.
26. Bill Fischer and Andy Boynton, "Virtuoso Teams," *Harvard Business Review,* July–August 2005, pp. 116–123.
27. Jens Meiners, "M-B Changes Product Development," *Automotive News,* September 12, 2005, p. 18.
28. Linda Webb, "Microsoft's New Ergonomic Keyboard More Comfortable," *Cleveland Plain Dealer,* November 7, 2005, p. E4.
29. "Trusted Computer Solutions Names Top Military IT Expert to Advisory Board," *PR Newswire,* October 12, 2004.
30. Based on information from "American Flatbread," **FoodGPS.com**, February 16, 2008, **http://www.foodgps.com/review/american-flatbread-los-alamos-ca-saturday-february-16-2008/**; *Pioneering American Flatbread* video by Houghton Mifflin; Andrew Nemethy, "Waitsfield: American Flatbread," *Vermont,* February 21, 2001, **seevermont.nybor.com/dining/story/20722.html; www.americanflatbread.com.**
31. The Google website at **www.google.com**, accessed October 14, 2008; "'Don't Touch My Perks': Companies that Eliminate Them Risk Employee Backlash," Knowledge@Wharton, **http://knowledge.wharton.upenn.edu**, July 23, 2008; Joe Nocera, "On Day Care, Google Makes a Rare Fumble," *The New York Times*, **http://www.nytimes.com**, July 5, 2008; John Cook, "Perks Make Google Office Hardly Feel Like Work," *Seattle Post-Intelligencer*, **http://seattlepi.nwsource.com**, January 16, 2008; Elinor Mills, "Newsmaker: Meet Google's Culture Czar," *CNet News*, **http://news.cnet.com**, April 27, 2007.

Chapter 11

1. Micheline Maynard, "Boeing Negotiations 'At a Standstill,'" *New York Times,* September 26, 2008, p. C4; Tim Klass, "Unions Show Muscle in Aerospace and Steel," *Houston Chronicle,* September 14, 2008, p. 3; Tim Klass, "Long Strike Could Hurt U.S.," *Los Angeles Times,* September 9, 2008, p. C7; J. Lynn Lunsford, "Outsourcing at Crux of Boeing Strike," *Wall Street Journal,* September 8, 2008, p. B1; Joseph Weber, "The Dreamliner's Cost to Boeing," *BusinessWeek Online,* August 29, 2008, **www.businessweek.com.**
2. U.S. Department of Labor, Bureau of Labor Statistics, News Release, January 25, 2008.
3. U.S. Department of Labor, Bureau of Labor Statistics, Survey of Employer Costs, June 2005.
4. "NYU Will Not Renew Contract with Graduate Students Union," Associated Press, August 6, 2005; "New York University Issues Ultimatum to Striking Graduate Students," Associated Press, November 29, 2005.
5. Christopher Bowe and Andrew Hill, "Workers Feeling Sick over Rising Healthcare Costs," *Financial Times,* January 14, 2003, p. 21.
6. U.S. Department of Labor, Bureau of Labor Statistics, Economic News Release, February 13, 2008.
7. Maynard Micheline, "Boeing Negotiations 'at a standstill,'" *New York Times,* September 26, 2008, p. C4.
8. Pete Donohue and Corky Siemaszko, "What a Relief, Strike Ends, Riders Thaw, Talks to Resume," *New York Daily News,* December 23, 2005, p. 3; Shannon D. Harrington and Soni Sangha, "Back to Normal: Transit Strike Ends in Time for the Morning Commute," *The Record,* December 23, 2005, p. A01; David B. Caruso, "New York Transit Strike Enters Day Two Amid Court Battle," Associated Press State and Local Wire, December 21, 2005.
9. Kim Chapman, "Teachers' Unions Boycott Wal-Mart," *The Houston Chronicle,* August 11, 2005, p. B1.
10. Chris Frank, "Hawker Beechcraft, Machinist Reach Tentative Deal," *KAKE* August 25, 2008, **www.fmcs.gov.**
11. Alvin Hattal, "Organization Case Study: FMCS Boosts Its Reputation through Success," *PR Week,* September 5, 2005.
12. "Study Shows that Federal Mediation Makes Good Business Sense for Labor and Management in Collective Bargaining," *PR Newswire,* November 17, 2005.
13. Based on video entitled *Boston Ballet/Boston Musicians Association* © Cengage Learning.
14. Based on information from Martin J. Moylan, "Northwest Resumes Hiring Replacement Mechanics after Union Refuses Vote," *Saint Paul Pioneer Press,* October 22, 2005, **www.twincities.com**; "Nurses at Stanford Hospitals Approve Contract, End Strike," *Los Angeles Times,* July 29, 2000, p. 20; Barbara Feder, "Replacement Nurses at California Hospitals Draw Strikers' Ire, Healthy Pay," *San Jose Mercury News,* June 20, 2000, **www.sjmercury.com**; Richard L. Lippke, "Government Support of Labor Unions and the Ban on Striker Replacements," *Business and Society Review 109,* Summer 2004, pp. 127–151.

Chapter 12

1. Richard Ouzounian, "Cirque Looks Hot to Globe-Trot," *Variety,* June 30, 2008, p. 51; Kate Fitzgerald, "Mario D'Amico: Senior VP-Marketing, Cirque du Soleil," *Advertising Age,* May 19, 2008, p. S9; Forrest Glenn Spencer, "It's One Big Circus," *Information Outlook,* October 2007, pp. 22–23; Douglas Belkin, "Talent Scouts for Cirque du Soleil Walk a Tightrope," *Wall Street Journal,* September 8, 2007, p. A1; **www.cirquedusoleil.com**.
2. Marketing Power (American Marketing Association), **http://www.marketingpower.com/AboutAMA/Pages/DefinitionofMarketing.aspx** accessed October 13, 2008.
3. Mya Frazier, James Tenser, and Tricia Despres, "Retail Lesson: Small Programs Best," *Advertising Age,* March 20, 2006, p. S-3.
4. Lynette Ryals and Adrian Payne, "Customer Relationship Management in Financial Services: Towards Information-Enabled Relationship Marketing," *Journal of Strategic Marketing,* March 2001, p. 3.
5. Werner J. Reinartz and V. Kumark, "On the Profitability of Long-Life Customers in a Noncontractual Setting: An Empirical Investigation and Implications for Marketing," *Journal of Marketing,* October 2000, pp. 17–35.
6. Roland T. Rust, Katherine N. Lemon, and Valarie A. Zeithaml, "Return on Marketing: Using Customer Equity to Focus Marketing Strategy," *Journal of Marketing 68,* January 2004, pp. 109–127.
7. Rajkumar Venkatesan and V. Kumar, "A Customer Lifetime Value Framework for Customer Selection and Resource Allocation Strategy," *Journal of Marketing 68,* October 2004, pp. 106–125.
8. Gina Chon, "Toyota's Marketers Get Respect—Now They Want Love," *Wall Street Journal,* January 11, 2006, p. B1.
9. Matthew Boyle, "Best Buy's Giant Gamble," *Fortune,* March 29, 2006, **money.cnn.com**.
10. "Launch Week Also Marks Debut of Cross Promo Ads," *USA Today,* September 23, 2007, **www.usatoday.com/**; G. Chambers William III, "2008 Nissan Rogue," *Ft. Worth Star-Telegram,* August 31, 2007, **www.star-telegram.com/chambers_williams/story/219830.html**.
11. Joseph White, "Detroit Finally Learns Tough Lesson," *Wall Street Journal,* September 11, 2006, **online.wsj.com**.
12. Ellen Byron, "New Penney: Chain goes for 'Missing Middle,'" *Wall Street Journal,* February 14, 2005, **online.wsj.com/**.
13. Catherine Arnold, "Self-Examination: Researchers Reveal State of MR in Survey," *Marketing News,* February 1, 2005, pp. 55 and 56.
14. William M. Pride and O. C. Ferrell, *Marketing: Concepts and Strategies*, 15th ed. (Mason, Ohio: South-Western/Cengage Learning, 2010), p. 194.
15. Based on information from Rick Barrett, "A Home for Harley's Heritage," *Milwaukee Journal-Sentinel,* June 29, 2008, **www.journalsentinel.com**; Matthew Goodman, "Harley-Davidson Chief Jim Ziemer Is Not Enjoying an Easy Ride," *The Sunday Times,* June 29, 2008, **business.timesonline.co.uk**; Jacqueline Mitchell, "Ten Auto Gifts for Dad," *Forbes,* June 5, 2008, **forbes.com**; **www.harley-davidson.com**.
16. Based on information from Mike Albo, "A Diverse Brooklyn, with Meatballs," July 3, 2008, **www.nytimes.com**; Kerry Capell, Ariane Sains, and Cristina Lindblad, "IKEA: How the Swedish Retailer Became a Global Cult Brand," *BusinessWeek,* November 14, 2005, p. 96; "IKEA's Growth Limited by Style Issues, Says CEO," *Nordic Business Report,* January 21, 2004, **www.nordicbusinessreport.com**; "IKEA Sets New Heights with Cat," *Printing World,* August 21, 2003, p. 3; **www.ikea-usa.com**.

Chapter 13

1. Jefferson Graham, "Flip Mino Lets You Pick a Look for Your Video Camera," *USA Today,* October 15, 2008, **www.usatoday.com**; Reena Jana, "Pure Digital Flips the Script," *BusinessWeek,* April 28, 2008, pp. 76–78; David Pogue, "Camcorder Brings Zen to the Shoot," *New York Times,* March 20, 2008, p. C1; Jefferson Graham, "Fun Flip Wows Camcorder Crowd with Ease of Use, Low Price," *USA Today,* September 12, 2007, p. 5B.
2. **http://www.apple.com/itunes/marketing/**, accessed October 13, 2008.
3. Dennis K. Berman and Ellen Byron, "P&G Sells Sure Deodorant Label to Private Firm Innovative Brands," *Wall Street Journal,* September 26, 2006, p. B2, **online.wsj.com**.
4. Procter & Gamble, **www.pg.com**, accessed October 14, 2008.
5. **http://www.thecoca-colacompany.com/brands/index.html, http://www.pepsico.com/PEP Company/BrandsCompanies/index.cfm#container5.**
6. Stephanie Thompson, "Mars to Scale Back M-Azing Brand," *Advertising Age,* October 26, 2006, **www.adage.com**.
7. "Inside a White-Hot Idea Factory," *BusinessWeek,* January 15, 2007, pp. 72–73.
8. Jathon Sapsford, "Honda Caters to Japan's Pet Population Boom," *Wall Street Journal,* October 5, 2005, p. B1, **online.wsj.com/public/us**.
9. "Market Update," **www.plma.com**, accessed October 14, 2008.
10. "World's Most Valuable Brands," *Interbrand,* **www.interbrand.com**, July 2005.
11. **www.amazon.com**, accessed November 28, 2008.
12. Yukari Iwatani Kane and Sarah McBride, "Latest Cut in DVD-Player Duel: Prices," *The Wall Street Journal,* November 23, 2007, pp. B1 and B2.
13. Lauren Young, "Candy's Getting Dandy," *BusinessWeek,* February 13, 2006, pp. 88–89.
14. The Verizon website at **www.verizon.com**, accessed October 16, 2008
15. Based on information in Steve Miller, "Vroom for Two," *Brandweek,* June 2, 2008, pp. 20≥; Bill Marsh, "Welcome, Little Smart Car, to the Big American Road," *New York Times,* January 6, 2008, Sec. 4, p. 3; Chris Woodyard, "America Crazy about Breadbox on Wheels Called Smart Car," *USA Today,* November 11, 2007, **www.usatoday.com/money/autos/2007-11-11-smartcar_N.htm**; Royal Ford, "Smallest Car, Biggest Market," *Boston Globe,* December. 6, 2007, p. E1.
16. Alice Z. Cuneo, "iPhone: Steve Jobs," *Advertising Age,* November 12, 2007, p. S13; Katie Hafner and Brad Stone, "iPhone Owners Crying Foul over Price Cut," *The New York Times,* September 7, 2007, pp. C1 and C7; Yukari Iwatani Kane and Nick Wingfield, "For Apple iPhone, Japan Could Be the Next Big Test," *Wall Street Journal,* December 19, 2007, p. B1; Brad Kenney, "Apple's iPhone: IW's IT Product of the Year," *Industry Week,* December 2007, pp. 47+; Josh Krist, "The Painful Cost of First-on-the-Block Bragging Rights," *PC World,* December 2007, pp. 53+; Alex Markels, "Apple's Mac Sales Are Surging," *U.S. News & World Report,* September 26, 2007, n.p.; Jon Swartz, "iPhone Helps Apple Earn Juicy Profit," *USA Today*, October 23, 2007, p. 1B.

Chapter 14

1. "Isaac Mizrahi Quitting as Target Designer," *Dallas Morning News,* October 22, 2008, **www.dallasnews.com**; "Target Will Slow Expansion," *MMR,* September 8, 2008, p. 1; "Target Adds 43 Units to Store Base," *MMR,* August 11, 2008, p. 2; Sharon Edelson, "On and Off the Mark: Wal-Mart Finding Way with Target in Sights," *WWD,* January 31, 2008, pp. 1+; Sharon Clott, "Target to Showcase Diffusion Lines in Manhattan Pop-Up Shops," *New York Magazine,* August 20, 2008, **www.nymag.com**; **target.com**.
2. William M. Pride and O. C. Ferrell, *Marketing: Concepts and Strategies* (Mason, Ohio: South-Western/Cengage Learning, 2010), p. 403.
3. "Industry Report 2005," *Convenience Store News,* April 18, 2005.
4. Stanley Holmes, "The Jack Welch of the Meat Aisle; Former GE Exec Larry Johnson Brings High-Tech to Troubled Albertson's," *BusinessWeek,* January 24, 2005, p. 60.
5. Sam's Club Fact Sheet, Costco Wholesale Corporation Fact Sheet, Hoover's Online, **www.hoovers.com/free**, accessed November 28, 2008.
6. Michael Barbaro, "Readings," *Washington Post,* January 23, 2005, p. F3; David Moin, "Category Killers' Concerns: Overgrowth and Extinction," *WWD,* January 6, 2005, p. 17.
7. **www.dsa.org**, accessed October 16, 2008.
8. **www.donotcall.gov**, accessed October 16, 2008.
9. **http://www.hsni.com/releasedetail.cfm?ReleaseID=326976**, accessed October 16, 2008—article dated August 2007.
10. **www.netflix.com**, accessed January 30, 2006.
11. Robert McMillan, "Got 796 Quarters Handy? Get Yourself an iPod," *PC World,* January 2006, p. 54
12. Sandra O'Loughlin, "Out with the Old: Malls versus Centers," *Brandweek,* May 9, 2005, p. 30.
13. Corinne Kator, "Warehouse Giants," *Modern Materials Handing,* November 2006, **www.Mmh.corarticle/6389111.html**, accessed October 1, 2008.
14. Based on information from David Lieberman, "Netflix, TiVo team up to deliver films on demand via Internet," *USA Today,* October 30, 2008, **usatoday.com/money/media/2008-10-30-netflix-tivo-films–on-demand_N.htm** (accessed November 6, 2008); *Netflix,* **www.netflix.com**, accessed November 5, 2008; Associated Press Staff Writer, "Movie rental giant Netflix rolls out its post-postal plan," *New York Daily News,* May 21, 2008, **www.nydailynews.com/money/2008/05/21/2008-05-21_movie_rental_giant_netflix_rolls_out_its-1.html**, accessed November 5, 2008; Associated Press Staff Writer, "Microsoft's Xbox 360 to stream Netflix movies," *New York Daily News,* July 14, 2008, **www.nydailynews.com/**

money/2008/07/14/2008-07-14_microsofts_xbox_360_to_stream_netflix_mo.html, accessed November 5, 2008.
15. Based on information in "The Costco Way," *Business Week*, Apr. 12, 2004, www.businessweek.com/magazine/content/04_15/b3878084_mz021.htm; Doug Desjardins, "Costco Comps Up 7%, Despite 4Q Lag," *DSN Retailing Today*, Oct. 27, 2003, p. 8; 1053751_EN_E-1-E28.qxd, Nov. 5, 2008, page N-20; Doug Desjardins, "Costco Home to Expand in '04," *DSN Retailing Today*, Dec. 15, 2003, p. 8; John Helyar, "The Only Company Wal-Mart Fears," *Fortune*, Nov. 24, 2003, p. 158; Kris Hudson, "Warehouses Go Luxe," *The Wall Street Journal*, Nov. 11, 2005, p. B1, http://online.wsj.com/public/us; "Investor Relations: Company Profile," Costco, http://phx.corporate-ir.net/phoenix.zhtml?c_83830&p_irol-homeprofile, accessed Jan. 25, 2008.

Chapter 15

1. Based on Stephanie Clifford, "Finding a Gold Mine in Digital Ditties," *New York Times*, October 28, 2008, pp. A1+; Betsy McKay, "PepsiCo Seeks to Raise Stakes on Super Bowl Ads," *Wall Street Journal*, September 24, 2008, p. B5; Teresa F. Lindeman, "Ad Contest Has Heinz Seeking More from Public," *Pittsburgh Post-Gazette*, September 15, 2007, www.post-gazette.com.
2. Stephanie Thompson, "Kraft Gets into the Groove," *Advertising Age*, January 23, 2006, p. 25.
3. Robert Coen, "Insider's Report," July 2008, www.universalmccann.com.
4. "2008 U.S. National Edition Rates," *Time*, www.time.com/time/mediakit/US/timemagazine/rates/nation/index.html, accessed October 21, 1008.
5. Lynna Goch, "The Place to Be," *Best's Review*, February 2005, pp. 64–65.
6. Bruce Horovitz, "Budweiser's Dog and Pony Show Takes Top Ad Meter Spot," *USA Today*, February 6, 2008.
7. Della de Lafuente, "American Takes Latinos Home for the Holidays," *Brandweek*, November 19, 2007, http://www.brandweek.com/bw/news/article_display.jsp?vnu_content_id=1003674048.
8. Joe Pereira, "New Balance Sneaker Ads Jab at Pro Athletes' Pretensions," *Wall Street Journal*, March 10, 2005, p. B1.
9. Eric Newman, "Wendy's Flips Its Wig," *BrandWeek*, January 28, 2008, http://www.brandweek.com/bw/news/article_display.jsp?vnu_content_id=1003702918.
10. Terence Shimp, *Advertising, Promotion, and Supplemental Aspects of Integrated Marketing Communications* (Mason, Ohio: South-Western 2007), p. 527.
11. Allison Bruce, "Throwing Coupons a Lifeline," *Ventura County Star*, http://www.venturacountystar.com/news/2007/sep/23/throwing-coupons-a-life-line-as-fewer-consumers, accessed October 21, 2008.
12. Mya Frazier, James Tenser, and Tricia Despres, "Retail Lesson: Small Programs Best," *Advertising Age*, March 20, 2008, pp. S2–S3.
13. Beth Snyder Bulik, "Nintendo 'Maximi'-izes to Lure Older Generation of Gamers," *Advertising Age*, February 7, 2005, p. 8.
14. Kiri Blakely, "Secrets of Celebrity Swag Season,:" Forbes, February 12, 2008, www.forebes.com/business/2008/02/11/hollywood-celebrity-retailing-bix-media_cz_kb_0212swag.html.
15. Based on information from *The Toledo Mud Hens*, http://www.mudhens.com (accessed November 5, 2008); *The Detroit Tigers*, http://tigers.mlb.com, accessed November 5, 2008.
16. Based on information in "Columbia Sportswear Named Official Apparel Sponsor of Jeep Ski/Snowboard Series," The Auto Channel, Dec. 1, 2005, www.theautochannel.com/news/2005/12/01/153912. html; Erica Iacono, "Corporate Case Study—Columbia Sportswear Speaks to Many with One Voice," *PR Week*, Jan. 16, 2006; George Anders, "Drama's Profitable at Sportswear Maker—Columbia Run by Mother and Son," *The Seattle Times*, Oct. 12, 2005; Columbia Sportswear Press Release, *Columbia Sportswear Company Announces Butler, Shine, Stern & Partners as Advertising Agency of Record*, Apr. 21, 2008, http://columbia.com/who/press_release.aspx?type_c&id_178, accessed May 23, 2008; Columbia Sportswear, www.columbia.com, accessed May 23, 2008.

Chapter 16

1. Information based on "Blue Nile Ratchets up Financing Program," *National Jeweler Network*, November 11, 2008, www.nationaljewelernetwork.com; Jay Greene, "Blue Nile: A Guy's Best Friend," *BusinessWeek*, June 9, 2008, pp. 38–40; "A Boy's Best Friend," *The Economist*, March 22, 2008, p. 76; Gary Rivlin, "When Buying a Diamond Starts with a Mouse," *New York Times*, January 7, 2007, sec. 3, p. 1; www.bluenile.com.
2. The Blue Nile website at www.bluenile.com, accessed October 12, 2008.
3. Bradley Mitchell, "WAN—Wide Area Network," About.com website at www.about.com, accessed October 9, 2008.
4. Bradley Mitchell, "LAN—Local Area Network," About.com website at www.about.com, accessed October 9, 2008.
5. Dee-Ann Durbin, *The Cincinnati Post* website at http://news.cincypost.com, accessed September 30, 2005.
6. Charlene Li and Shar VanBoskirk, "U.S. Online Marketing Forecast: 2005 to 2010," Forrester Research, Inc., website at www.forrester.com, accessed May 5, 2005.
7. The Computer Industry Almanac, Inc. website at www.c-i-a.com, accessed October 12, 2008.
8. Ibid.
9. Based on information in "Travelocity's Holiday Bailout Gives Vacationers a Break on the First Trip of 2009," *Business Wire*, December 4, 2008, http://www.businesswire.com/portal/site/google/?ndmViewId=news_view&newsId=20081204005065&newsLang=en; Dennis Schaal, "Satisfaction 'Guaranteed' by Travelocity," *Travel Weekly*, May 2, 2005, p. 1; Suzanne Marta, "Travelocity Trying to Expand Services beyond Lower Prices," *Dallas Morning News*, March 1, 2005, dallasnews.com; Avery Johnson, "Booking a $51 Flight to Fiji Online," The Flyertalk website: www.flyertalk.com, April 26, 2005; www.travelocity.com
10. Based on information found in www.ebags.com/about, accessed October 21, 2008; "Customer Interaction Is in the Bag at eBags," Internet Retailer, http://www.internetretailer.com, October 8, 2008; Katie Deatsch, "Corralling Content," Internet Retailer, http://www.internetretailer.com, September 2008; Company press release, "eBags.com Wins 2008 Website of the Year," June 3, 2008, http://www.ebags.com; "eBags Broadens Its Horizons as Tech Provider to Retailers," *Internet Retailer*, http://www.internetretailer.com, March 18, 2008; Janet Forgieve, "Refusing to Pack It In," *Rocky Mountain News*, www.rockymountainnews.com, September 9, 2006.

Chapter 17

1. Based on information in "Big 4 Accounting Firms to Manage Bailout," *CBS News*, October 21, 2008, www.cbsnews.com; Alana Semuels, "They're Really Attached to Their Jobs," *Los Angeles Times*, July 29, 2007, p. C2; Paul Grant, "What's It Like to Work in . . . Film and Television," *Accountancy Age Jobs*, March 30, 2007, www.accountancyage.com; "PwC Partners Gear up for Oscar Fever," *Accountancy Age*, February 13, 2007, www.accountancyage.com; "PricewaterhouseCoopers Entrusted with Hollywood's Longest Kept Secret for 74 Years Running," *PriceWaterhouseCoopers News Release*, January 8, 2008, www.pwc.com; "Ernst & Young Achieves 20-Year Milestone for Counting Ballots," *Ernst & Young News Release*, September 17, 2008, www.prnewswire.com.
2. "Ernst & Young Head Stresses Important Role of Accounting Profession," the Ernst & Young website at www.ey.com, May 2, 2006.
3. "Arthur Andersen," the Wikipedia website at www.wikipedia.org, September 28, 2008.
4. Ibid.
5. The American Institute of Certified Public Accountants (AICPA) website at www.aicpa.org, September 28, 2008.
6. "System Failure," *Fortune*, June 24, 2002, p. 64.
7. The Bureau of Labor Statistics website at www.bls.gov, September 23, 2008.
8. The American Institute of Certified Public Accountants website at www.aicpa.org, September 23, 2008.
9. Based on information from Jane Sasseen, "White-Collar Crime: Who Does Time?" *BusinessWeek*, February 6, 2006, www.businessweek.com; Stephen Labaton, "Four Years Later, Enron's Shadow Lingers as Change Comes Slowly," *New York Times*, January 5, 2006, p. C1; *Making the Numbers at Commodore Appliance* (Houghton Mifflin video).
10. Based on information from "Complaint Procedures for Accounting and Auditing Matters," www.kimberly-clark.com, accessed November 29, 2008; R. Dilip Krishna, "Enterprise Risk Management: Illuminate the Unknown," *Intelligent Enterprise*, December 2005, www.intelligententerprise.com/showarticle.jhtml?articleID0174300345; Cathleen Moore, "Compliance Strives for Automation," *InforWorld*, May 23, 2005, p. 15; Anna Maria Virzi, "Kimberly-Clark: Benefiting from SOX," *Baseline*, September 7, 2005, www.baseliniemag.com; Matthew Schwartz, "Q&A: The Future of Security, Control, and SOX Compliance," *Enterprise Systems*, December 13, 2005, www.esj.com.

Chapter 18

1. Based on information in Matthias Rieker, "Update: JP Morgan Chairman: Unemployment Has 'Huge Impact' on Co," *Dow Jones Newswires,* November 12, 2008, **money.conn.com/news**; Robin Sidel and Dan Fitzpatrick, "J.P. Morgan Bets on the Consumer," *Wall Street Journal,* September 27, 2008, p. B1; Roddy Boyd, "The Last Days of Bear Stearns," *Fortune,* March 28, 2008, **www.fortune.com; www.jpmorganchase.com.**
2. The Federal Reserve Board website at **www.federalreserve.gov**, October 2, 2008.
3. Ibid.
4. Ibid.
5. The Investopedia website at **www.investopedia.com**, October 4, 2008.
6. The Federal Reserve Board website at **www.federalreserve.gov**, October 2, 2008.
7. The Office of the Comptroller of the Currency website at **www.occ.treas.gov**, October 4, 2008.
8. The Federal Deposit Insurance Corporation website at **www2.fdic.gov**, October 2, 2008.
9. U.S. Census Bureau, *Statistical Abstract of the United States, 2008* (Washington, D.C.: U.S. Government Printing Office, 2008), p. 734.
10. "Career Guide to Industries," U.S. Department of Labor, Bureau of Labor Statistics website at **www.bls.gov**, October 4, 2008.
11. U.S. Census Bureau, *Statistical Abstract of the United States, 2008* (Washington, D.C.: U.S. Government Printing Office, 2008), p. 734.
12. The Bankrate.com website at **www.bankrate.com**, September 30, 2008.
13. The Federal Deposit Insurance Corporation (FDIC) website at **www2.fdic.gov**, October 2, 2008.
14. The National Credit Union Administration website at **www.ncua.gov**, accessed October 5, 2008.
15. The Federal Trade Commission website: **www.ftc.gov**, accessed October 4, 2008.
16. Based on video entitled *First Bank Corporation,* © Cengage Learning.
17. Based on information in "Credit Scores," Consumer Reports.org, **http://www.consumerreports.org**, accessed October 27, 2008; Ron Lieber, "One Thing You Can Control: Your Credit Score," *The New York Times,* **http://www.nytimes.com**, October 11, 2008; "Kaulkin Ginsberg Report Says Increased College Student Credit Card Debt Causing Financial Straits for Graduating Students," *Business Wire,* **http://www.reuters.com**, September 12, 2008; Gretchen Morgenson, "Given a Shovel, Americans Dig Deeper into Debt," *The New York Times,* **http://www.nytimes.com**, July 20, 2008; Charles De La Fuente, "Pushing Colleges to Limit Credit Offers to Students," *The New York Times,* **http://www.nytimes.com**, October 17, 2007; Rob Walker, "A For-Credit Course," *The New York Times,* **http://www.nytimes.com**, September 30, 2007.

Chapter 19

1. Brad Stone, "Discretionary Tastes Suffer, Making Starbucks Suffer," *New York Times,* November 11, 2008, p. B1; Michael Applebaum, "Coffee Jitters: Shuttering Stores and Scalded by Hot Competition, Starbucks Is Facing the Fight of Its 37-Year Life," *Brandweek,* November 10, 2008, pp. 22+; Robert Passikoff, "Why Starbucks Has Ground to a Halt," *Brandweek,* November 10, 2008, p. 16; Janet Adamy, "Starbucks Curbs Salary Increases for Top Officers," *Wall Street Journal,* August 28, 2008, p. B4; **www.starbucks.com.**
2. The Pfizer corporate website at **www.pfizer.com**, October 19, 2008.
3. The American Bankruptcy Institute website at **www.abiworld.org**, October 17, 2008.
4. Natalie Zmuda, "PepsiCo Lauches Massive Overhaul," the Advertising Age website at **www.adage.com**, October 14, 2008.
5. The Merrill Lynch & Company website at **www.ml.com**, October 18, 2008.
6. Judith Crown, "ConAgra's New Recipe," the BusinessWeek website at **www.businessweek.com**, March 27, 2008.
7. Maria Bartiromo, "BlackRock's Peter Fisher on When the Pain Will End," the BusinessWeek website at **www.businessweek.com**, October 7, 2008.
8. Matthew Boyle, "The Fed's Commercial Paper Chase," the BusinessWeek website at **www.businessweek.com**, October 7, 2008.
9. The Red Herring website at **www.redherring.com**, accessed October 19, 2008.
10. Scott Reeves, "Chipotle's IPO: Mild to Medium," the Forbes website at **www.forbes.com**, accessed October 9, 2008.
11. The Textron corporate website at **www.textron.com**, accessed October 19, 2008.
12. The General Electric website at **www.ge.com**, accessed October 17, 2008.
13. The Advanced Micro Devices website at **www.amd.com**, October 19, 2008.
14. *Mergent Transportation Manual* (New York: Mergent, Inc., 2008), p. 604.
15. Based on video entitled *Pizzeria Uno* © Cengage Learning.
16. Based on information from "Mountain Thyme Bed & Breakfast Inn," **http://www.bedandbreakfast.com/arkansas**, accessed November 29, 2008; Nate Hinkel, "Couple's Bed-and-Breakfast Benefits from SBA Loan," *Arkansas Business,* May 16, 2005, p. 22; Farrah Austin, "Thyme Out in Arkansas," *Southern Living,* April 2003, p. 33; **www.mountainthyme.com.**

Chapter 20

1. Jay Fitzgerald, "Fidelity Investments Pitches Federally Insured CDs," *Boston Herald,* November 25, 2008, **www.bostonherald.com**; Humberto Cruz, "The Savings Game: Many Know Little About the Most Valuable Retirement Asset," *Salt Lake Tribune,* November 21, 2008, **www.sltrib.com**; Sree Vidya Bhaktavatsalam, "Fidelity Will Eliminate 1,700 More Jobs in Early 2009," *Bloomberg,* November 14, 2008, **www.bloomberg.com.**
2. The Red Herring website at **www.redherring.com**, October 18, 2008.
3. New York Stock Exchange website at **www.nyse.com**, October 23, 2008.
4. The Nasdaq website at **www.nasdaq.com**, October 23, 2008.
5. "The Regulatory Pyramid," The New York Stock Exchange website at **http://www.nyse.com/pdfs/ts_reg_pyramid.pdf**, October 26, 2008.
6. Ibid.
7. "Money 101 Lesson 4: Basics of Investing," the CNN/Money website at **http://money.cnn.com/magazines/moneymag/money101/lesson4**, October 26, 2008.
8. Roger G. Ibbotson, "Predictions of the Past and Forecasts for the Future 1976–2025," Ibbotson Associates, **www.ibbotson.com**, April 9, 2005.
9. Suze Orman, *The Road to Wealth* (New York: Riverbend Books, 2001), p. 371.
10. *Mergent Bond Record* (New York: Mergent, Inc., July 2008), p. 177.
11. The Investment Company Institute website at **www.ici.org**, accessed October 27, 2008.
12. The Mutual Fund Education Alliance website at **www.mfea.com**, accessed October 27, 2008.
13. The Investopedia website at **www.investopedia.com**, accessed October 25, 2008.
14. The Yahoo! Finance website at **http://finance.yahoo.com**, accessed October 24, 2008.
15. Based on information from Christopher Tritto, "Build-a-Bear Retools Strategy to Boost Holiday Sales," *St. Louis Business Journal*, November 21, 2008, **http://stlouis.bizjournals.com/stlouis/stories/2008/11/24/story13.html;** Lucas Conley, "Customer-Centered Leader: Maxine Clark," *Fast Company,* October 2005, p. 64; "Q3 2005 Build-A-Bear Workshop, Inc., Earnings Conference Call," *America's Intelligence Wire,* October 2, 2005, n.p.; Mary Jo Feldstein, "St. Louis Toy Retailer Build-A-Bear Claws Its Way to Profitable IPO," *St. Louis Post-Dispatch,* October 29, 2004, **www.stltoday.com**; Alyson Grala, "'Bear'ing It All," *License!,* May 2004, pp. 22–24; Allison Fass, "Bear Market," *Forbes,* March 1, 2004, p. 88; Thomas K. Grose, "Teddy Bear Tussle," *U.S. News & World Report,* November 11, 2002, p. 46.
16. Based on information in Jim Mueller, "3 Lessons from an Investing Master," The Motley Fool.com, **http://www.fool.com**, October 31, 2008; Elizabeth Ody, "Start Investing in 3 Simple Steps," *The Washington Post*, **http://www.washingtonpost.com**, October 30, 2008; David Leonhardt, "Are Stocks the Bargain You Think?" *The New York Times*, **http://www.nytimes.com**, October 29, 2008; Jeff Sommer, "Extolling the Value of the Long View," *The New York Times*, **http://www.nytimes.com**, October 26, 2008.

Name Index

A

B

C

D

E

F

G

H

I

J

K

L

T

U

V

W

X

Y

Z

Subject Index

A

B

C

D

E

F

G

H

I

J

K

L

M

N

O

P

Q

R

S

T

U

V

W

Y

Z

The Sky's the Limit

With ***Business, 10e's*** robust Web site and step-by-step Business Plan Builder, "the sky's the limit" on your success—inside the classroom and inside business. The Business Plan Builder helps you create a solid business plan that you can immediately put into action! In addition, the Web site is packed with tools to help you make the most of your study time for course success!

Business Plan Builder

This powerful, interactive online tool walks you step-by-step through building a business plan—a skill that will benefit you throughout your career. The system provides informational modules about each part of the business plan and then prompts you to fill in the templates with information supporting your own business plan. Step-by-step, the program literally "builds" the business plan from the ground up for future entrepreneurs and business leaders.

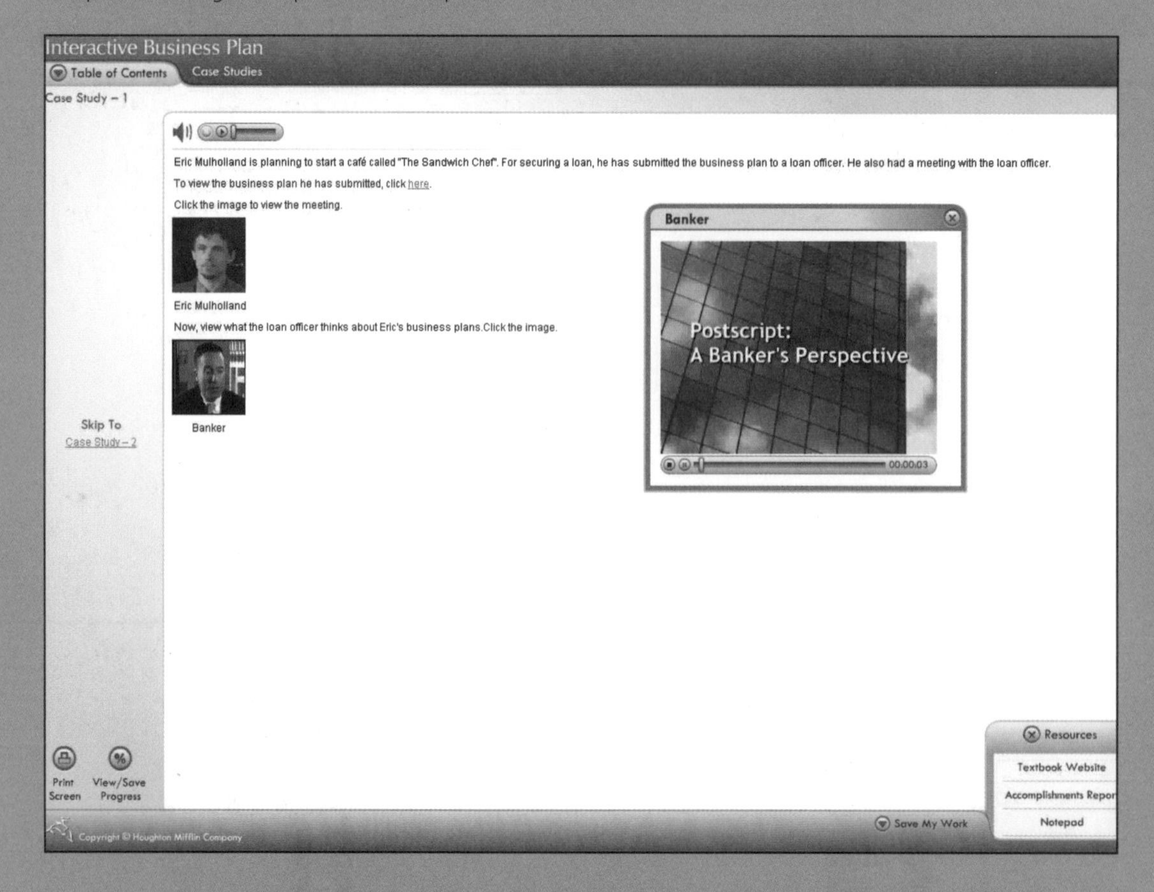